ISBN: 9781313229708

Published by:
HardPress Publishing
8345 NW 66TH ST #2561
MIAMI FL 33166-2626

Email: info@hardpress.net
Web: http://www.hardpress.net

APV

I.

DOGGETT – DAGGETT ARMS.

A HISTORY

OF THE

DOGGETT-DAGGETT FAMILY

BY

SAMUEL BRADLEE DOGGETT

MEMBER OF THE NEW ENGLAND HISTORIC GENEALOGICAL SOCIETY, THE
AMERICAN HISTORICAL ASSOCIATION, AND CORRESPONDING
MEMBER OF THE GEORGIA HISTORICAL SOCIETY

BOSTON
PRESS OF ROCKWELL AND CHURCHILL
1894

Three hundred copies of this volume

make up the edition, of which this is

No. **95**

PREFACE.

A DESIRE to know my own Doggett ancestry led me to begin a search of the records in 1876.

In the search I found branches of my own line who had changed the spelling of the name to Daggett, while other branches had moved to distant parts of the country.

In trying to find these branches I had correspondence and gathered information of families who were descended from different immigrant ancestors.

Wishing to know more of *these* families and *their* ancestry, I began a thorough search of the early records. This search has occupied my spare moments from 1876 to the present time. The records of more than forty Massachusetts towns have been examined ; the county records of Suffolk, Norfolk, Plymouth, Bristol, Barnstable, Dukes, Essex, Worcester, and Middlesex have each added some points to the record, while an examination of more than three hundred and fifty volumes at the State House, in Boston, and many books in public and private libraries, were among the methods used to gather what relates to our family in Massachusetts.

I have also examined county, town, church, or private records in Nova Scotia, New Brunswick, Maine, New Hampshire, Vermont, Rhode Island, Connecticut, New York, Pennsylvania, Maryland, and Virginia; have called on many members of the family in different parts of the country; have corresponded extensively, and have received more than twelve hundred letters in answer to my inquiries.

By the kindness of correspondents and the returns of experts, whom I employed, many facts have been gathered regarding the family in England.

Several rectors of churches in England were interested, and very kind in sending extracts from their records.

Mr. William H. Doggett, of Leighton Buzzard, Beds., and the late Edward G. Doggett, Esq., of Bristol, have added many facts to the family history. My thanks are also due to many in this country who have contributed to the records, but owing to the number, I will not mention them by name, knowing they will feel amply repaid by the knowledge that they have done their parts toward preserving the family records.

Errors and omissions will be found in the compilation, but in many cases it is the fault of those who have made mistakes in their returns or neglected to answer my repeated requests for full particulars.

The amount of material having become so large, and so long a time having been devoted to its collection, I have thought best to now submit the history to my kinsmen, believing the facts thus made known may lead to the correction of errors and aid in bringing to light the points that are wanted to connect the several branches of the family.

SAMUEL B. DOGGETT.

HOLLIS, COR. TREMONT STREET,
    BOSTON, MASS., January, 1894.

CONTENTS.

ILLUSTRATIONS.

Half-tone engravings made and printed by LUX ENGRAVING COMPANY, Boston.

DOGGETT-DAGGETT.

DERIVATION AND ORTHOGRAPHY.

THE name "DOGGETT" seems quite distinct from "Duckett" and "Daggett," although possibly all may be from the same root.

Doggett and Duckett were often applied at different periods to the same individual in early times, and the name "Doggett" has been changed and continued as "Daggett" by people of the present day. The larger part of the family in America, whether Doggett or Daggett, must look for their ancestors to the Doggett family of England.

The name "Doggett" is one of the oldest surnames. It seems to be a surname pure and simple. We do not find "de" prefixed to it from which to conclude it to be a name derived from the name of a place, as is so often the case with other surnames. Sir Walter Scott thought it a fit name for a Saxon, for he makes a Norman noble say: "Here thou Dogget-warder son of a Saxon wolf-hound" [The Betrothed]. Many expressions of opinion have been made as to the derivation of the name.

Lower, in his "Dictionary of Names," London, 1860, says: "Doggett is an old London name probably corrupted from 'Dowgate,' one of the Roman gateways of the city. Ferguson makes it a diminutive of the Icelandic 'Doggr' and the English 'Dog,' but no such diminutive is found."

Robert Ferguson, in his "Teutonic Name System applied to Family Names," London, 1864, under the heading "The Brute and its Attributes," says: "There are few names derived from the dog. Doggett, which I before classed under this head, I must now withdraw, as I think it belongs to the roots of Anglo-Saxon dugan, to be of use or value."

As derived from the "Inner Man" we have from the Anglo-Saxon dugan ; Old High German tugan, to be virtuous, good, honorable; Anglo-Saxon thraw; Old High German dau, morals, behavior, — probably the following:

Simple forms — English, "Tuggy," "Tuck," "Duck," etc.
Diminutives — English, "Duckling."
Compounds — English, "Duckett," "Doggett."
Compounds — French, "Duquet," "Douet," "Tugot," and many others.

Many ancient endings, as "and" or "ead," prosperity, had "war," "bait," "hood," converge in modern names into "et."

Prof. John Marshall Doggett, of Richmond, Va., formerly professor of languages in Vanderbilt University, has made a special study of the subject, and has announced his opinion that the name "Doggett" is derived from the Aryan word "Dok" or "Dog," meaning point or cut.

From this word comes, 1st, the Greek "Δόγ-μα" (dogma, that is a point out "doctrine"); 2d, Doc-eo (originally pronounced hard Dok-eo), that is, point out, show, teach; Doc-umentum; Duc-o dux (leader, guide, shower), from which is derived Doge (possibly Ducquet); 3d, Dig (that is, to cut in), from which comes Duglas, possibly Dagger and Dock (that is, cut, hence Docket), "dock-tailed," possibly Dog; "Docket" Gallicized to Docquet; 4th, Dogger (or sharp cut-nosed fish).

Hence, "'Dogget,'" equal or derived from docket (or dock-hand, that is, Docker)."

Sir George Duckett, Bart., in his "Memoirs of the Family of Duket," called "Duchetiana," published in London, 1874, says: "The family of Ducket derives clearly from that of 'Duchet,' seated at the time of the English Conquest in the Duchy of Burgundy. The surname of Duchet (Duket) is recorded in two of the Battle Abbey Rolls."

The name is also found in the tenth year of the Conquest; again (as Duchet) in the oldest roll now extant next to Domesday, the great Roll of the Exchequer, 60 or 70 years after the Conquest, commonly called the Great Roll, 1131; and it is recorded in a very remarkable manner in the "Chronicles of the Abbey of St. Albans," A.D. 1119.

A copious account of the Norman family of Ducé is to be seen in the "Annales Civiles et Militaires du Pays d'Avranches."

The name "Ducé" is found as witness to two grants to Clerkenwell Nunnery, founded by Henry I., A.D. 1100; but that of Duchet is seen equally early, and the orthography of the name inclines us to accept this as most probably the original name.

If at this early date, however, the Saxon pronunciation had not affected the orthography of the name, as clearly as in after times happened in the instances of Doket, Doget, Douket, Dokkyt, no better proof could be adduced that Duket was not the original name, than, perhaps, the earliest authentic mention we find of it in the person of one Herbert Duchet (or Ducket, as he is styled in the entry). The Herbert in question was living in 1119, and in consequence of the incident recorded in the " Gesta Abbatum S. Albani," he obtained the cognomen of Duket as an alterative of his previous name. From the time of the Conqueror to the reign of Henry VII., and from that again to the reign of Elizabeth, the name is found varied in different ways according as the Saxon pronunciation came in time to prevail over the Norman and to reappear as the common language of the country.

Duchet	Duschet	Dutschet	Tuchet	Tuschet
Ducet	Dechet	Duquet	Duket	Dukett
Dukket	Dughet	Doket	Doget	Doggette
Dokkytt	Docket	Dowket	Doucket	
Duckette	Ducket	Duckett		

Such appear at different epochs, the orthography of the name giving apparently twenty-two variations.

At one period the name appears as " Doget." Under this last mode of spelling the name is found in Lincolnshire, Norfolk, and elsewhere, but (as also in the case of " Tuchet ") only a few and exceptional instances.

Sir D. Hardy, on the orthographical variations of proper names of persons and the arbitrary mode of spelling in ancient times, often regulated by etymology, sound, or abbreviations, remarks that names were Latinized or Gallicized, whenever it was possible to do so, according to the fancy of the scribe, one document frequently exhibiting material variations in the spelling of the same name, and to such a degree that a person would scarcely be able to recognize the modern name. The conclusion, therefore, is that the fault rested with the scribe alone, whether writing from oral instruction or copying from the original writ.

Nichols, in reviewing " Duchetiana," says the name was evidently *personal*, not *local*, and that it is derived from a race named Duchet (French), seated before the Norman Conquest in the Duchy of Burgundy.

Even as lately as 1601 there appears to be some confusion as regards " Dogett " and " Ducket," for in Samuel Toddes' " Pedigrees of English Families " of that date, wherein what are evidently the arms of the early Duckett family, he gives the name of Dogett, and all through the pedigree he continues this style. There is nothing, however, elsewhere to support the idea that any other of the Dogett family bore such arms or married into the families mentioned in the pedigree.   Moreover, Sir George Duckett shows that the arms were borne by the Duckett family, and accounts for Mr. Toddes' reading by the many forms of orthography.

William Daggett, Esq., of Newcastle-on-Tyne, writing of the derivation of the name of Daggett, says, his father "seemed to think it meant ' a little Dagger,' but on the other hand I have been told it is a Scandinavian (Danish) word meaning 'the dawn of day.'   Lower says Dagger is a Scottish surname, and it may be that Daggett is a diminutive derived therefrom.   I cannot, however, trace any part of my family to North Britain."

THE FAMILY COATS OF ARMS.

The system of Heraldry can be traced to the beginning of the thirteenth century.   The first assumer or grantee of a coat of arms took that as his own distinguishing mark.   It became hereditary in his own family, and whoever afterward uses it proclaims himself a lineal descendant from the person who first assumed it.

In the middle of the reign of Queen Elizabeth [1558–1603] the only arms for the family are reported as those used by a family of the name "Dogget" or "Doggett;" also spelled "Dogate" and "Doget."

"It is a maxim with the heralds that the more simple a coat of arms, the more ancient it is," and it is a maxim that eminently applies to the arms of Doggett.

1.   DOGATE — Erm. on a bend sa. — three leopards' heads, argent.

2.   DOGET [Kent] — Erm. — on a bend sa. — three talbots' heads, erased or [another ar.].
     Crest — on a chapeau a bull collared and thereto a bell pendant, proper.

3.   DOGET [John Doget, merchant, London] — Two greyhounds combatant, or, collared ar., bell pendant.
     Crest — Unicorn's head, or.

4.   DOGGET [Honing, Serborne, and Wronger — Co. Norfolk] — Gu — two greyhounds salient, combatant, or — collared sa.
     Crest — a lion's head gorged with a mural coronet, sable.

5.   DOGGETT [Norfolk] — Gules — two greyhounds combatant, argent, collared or.

6.   DOGGETT — Sable — two greyhounds combatant, or.
7.   DOGGETT — Same as Doget, first named.
8.   DAGGETT — Ar. — two greyhounds in full course, gules, collared, or.
9.   DAGGETT — Or — on a chief azure, three crescents of the first. Crest — an eagle displayed charged with a bezant, gules.
10.   DAGGETT [Roxby & Pickhill — Yorkshire] — Or — on a chief azure, three crescents.
11.   DAGGETT [Edinburgh] — Same as last. Crest — a demi-talbot, sable-collared.

The " Duckett " coat of arms and crests are all entirely different from that of Doggett of Norfolk or Kent.

The greyhound which figures so prominently on the arms of " Doggett " is an animal which was not allowed to be possessed by any save the princes and nobles until only within a few years, comparatively speaking. Upon the smooth surface of the monuments that adorn the broad plains of Egypt, erected 1200 B.C., we find chiselled by the side of his royal master the form of the greyhound, which from that time to this the sportsmen of the world have associated with them in the pursuit of game. The term " greyhound " is a corruption of the word " gazehound," signifying that it pursues its game by sight and not by scent. In ancient Greece and Rome he was the companion of the nobles, and no household was considered complete in all its appointments without him.

In such high esteem was this dog held by the nobles that the killing or even maiming of one was felony punishable with death.

The use of the greyhound is coursing. The great event in coursing circles in England is the " Waterloo Cup," valued at £500, which is run for at Altcar, near Liverpool, annually.

Thomas, Duke of Norfolk, in Queen Elizabeth's reign, was the first to compile a set of rules governing coursing, whereby points of merit earned in the race could be properly awarded. Coursing has made the greyhound *the* dog of the " British Isles." The greyhound signifies swiftness, vigilance, fidelity.

A talbot is a kind of hound with a large snout and large, thick, hanging ears.

The crescent is frequently used to distinguish the coat armor of a second brother or junior family from that of the principal branch.

JOHN DOGET, OF LONDON, AND HIS DESCENDANTS.

12. JOHN DOGET,[1] born London(?), England, about 1240; married Agnes.

Issue:

13*. i. THOMAS DOGET,[2] born England, about 1270.

The following item, probably relating to the John Doget above mentioned, is copied from the City Press, London, November 14, 1868, under the heading "Crimes of Old London," signed "Alept:"

"December 6, 1276. Edward I. Dispute between Symon de Winton and his servant called Roger de Westminster was terminated by the latter killing his master. Roger opens the shop as usual until the third day after, when he decamps with plunder.

"The house remains closed until January 1, 1277, when John Doget, a taverner, came to recover a debt due him from Symon, when the murder and robbery is discovered."

13. THOMAS DOGET[2] (*John*[1]), born England, about 1270; buried probably St. Leonard's, Eastcheap, London, as a tomb to Thomas and wife Letitia was once there; married Letice.

Issue:

14. i. WALTER DOGET,[3] born England, about 1310.

14. WALTER DOGET[3] (*Thomas,*[2] *John*[1]), born England, about 1310; died London, England, between July 16 and August 31, 1387; married Alice; living July 16, 1387.

Issue:

15. i. JOHN DOGET,[4] born England, about 1350.

"November 11, 1364. A seller of unsoured wines punished by being made to drink it. John Righwys and John Penrose were attached for trespass because in the tavern of Walter Doget, in the parish of Eastchepe, there they sold red wine to all comers unsoured and unwholesome for man to the grevious damage of the commonalty.

"Acquitting John Righwys they said that John Penrose was guilty and they wished him to be imprisoned for a year and a day," etc "Alept." [City Press, September 5, 1868, Wines of Old London.]

1380 and 1381, Walter Doget was sheriff of London.

---

* A number placed before a name distinguishes that particular person. Anything further relating to that person will be found with the same number.

The will of Walter Doget is in Register Courtney, folio 223, at the Lambeth Library.

" 1387, July 16. ' Ego Waltus Doget, cinis & vinetar london.' To be buried ' in arcu in Cancello ecctie sci Leonardi de Estchepe London iux^u ymagine pdci Leonardi vsus ptem boriatem.'

" For his burial there and that of Alice his wife if she should please to be there buried £20.

" To the rector of that church for tithes, &c. £10.

" To each chaplain to celebrate there and pray for my soul xl^d.

" To six other chaplains celebrating there on the day of my burial xij^d each.

" To the principal clerk ' maiori clico ' of the same church xl^d. To the under clerk xx^d.

" For 1,000 masses for my soul and the souls of Thomas, my father, Letice, my mother, John de Croiden, Christiana, his wife, John Doget, my grandfather, and Agnes, wife of same John Doget, and of all the faithful dead £10. Of which 1,000 masses, the Preaching Friars of London are to celebrate 100 and to have xx^s of the aforesaid £10; the Carmelite Friars of London to celebrate 100 and to have xx^s. The Friars Minors of London to celebrate 100 and to have xx^s. The Augustinian Friars of London to celebrate 100 and to have xx^s. The Friars of the Holy Cross of London to celebrate 100 and to have xx^s. To the hospital of the blessed Mary without Bysshopus-gate, London; to that of S^t. Bartholomew; of the blessed Mary of Elsyng Spitell; of S^t. Giles of Holbourne; of S^t. James without Westminster; and of S^t. Thomas of Suthwerk; namely, to each hospital 20 shillings for 100 masses.

" I bequeath 5 marks to have celebrated for my soul and the souls aforesaid, in the first year after my decease, 10 triginals of masses in the feasts of Pentecost, of the Holy Trinity, of the Assumption of the blessed Mary, of her Nativity, of the Epiphany of the Lord, of the Purification and Annunciation of the blessed Mary, of the Resurrection and Ascension of the Lord, and in the octaves of the same feasts in places where it shall seem best to my executors to arrange.

" For expences at my burial &c. £40. And if there be any surplus it shall be disposed of for the good of my soul and the souls for whom I am bound [to pray] among the poor, the sick in the aforenamed hospitals, and the lepers about the city of London ' in Crastino Mens obit mei.' To each order of Friars, viz. : the said Preachers, Minors, Carmelites, Augustinians and Holy Cross vj^s viij^d.

" To each house of lepers at Lok Hakeney, in S^t. Giles's hospital and in the hospital of S^t. James by Westminster vjs viij^d.

" For the infirm and sick of the house of Bethlehem vjs viij^d.

" To the prisoners of Newgate 100 shillings to be equally divided.

" To Christiana Cokke of Eltham if she shall be living at the time of my death xl^s.

" For mending the common way which leads to the Chantry between the church of S^t. George Southwerk and the Loke 100 shillings.

" To the more needy poor within the isle of Hertye in the county of Lancaster xl^s.

" To John Kirkeby my servant 100 shillings.

" I will that my executors remit to John Shirbourne my servant 50 of those 100 marks, ' inqui bz michi tenet^u p tram suam obligator' provided that the said John shall pay the remaining 50 marks within one year after my death and conducts himself kindly towards Alice my wife.

" To Geoffrey Hakes my servant xl^s.

" To Alice Ful of Mary xx^s.

" To each other of my servants vj^s viij^d.

" All my linen and woollen garments to be parted among my servants except 2 of my better cloaks [clocis].

" Three fit chaplains to celebrate for my soul and the aforenamed souls for 2 years in the aforesaid S^t. Leonard's church and to have £40.

" I bequeath £20 for the painting of the altar in the chapel of the blessed Mary in that church, also for the painting of the image of the blessed Mary in the afores^d chapel &c. And if there be any surplus it is to be applied to the use of the said church for mending the sepulchre of our Lord there.

"To John Doget my son £100 together with £200 received before for his marriage.

"Residue of goods to my wife Alice; she and my son John and Wᵐ Spauldyng 'sassorem' and Sir Ralph Lude my chaplain, to be executors and each to have £10. Overseers to be Henry Vanner and Wᵐ Gresewyk, to each of whom 100 shillings."

Proved 31 August, 1387.

15. John Doget [4] (*Walter,*[3] *Thomas,*[2] *John*[1]), born England, about 1350; died London, before 1456; married, before 1387, Alice. Issue:

16. (Possibly) Walter Doget,[5] who was buried, St. Leonard, Eastcheap, 1480.

"Sᵗ. Leonard's, Eastcheap, Rectory. In this church were monuments of the Doggets, one of which, namely, John Doggett, Vintner, who with Alice, his wife. were about 1456 buried here; he gave lands to this church. The church was burnt down by the Great Fire of London." [Ecclesiastical Parochial History of the Diocese of London, by Richard Newcourt, London, 1708.]

JOHN DOGGETT, OF ST. FAITH, NORFOLK, AND HIS DESCENDANTS.

Arms: Quarterly, 1 and 4 — Gules, 2 dogs salient, combatant, or, collared sa., Doggett.

2 and 3 — Argent, a chevron between 3 seamows, sa., Norman.

Impaling sa., a chevron embattled between 3 cinquefoils, argent. Smalpece.

"In the old hall and other rooms of 'Lewes Priory Manor' are these following arms, painted on glass: Gules, 2 greyhounds combatant, or. — Dogget — impaled argent, a chevron between 3 seamow's heads, sable — Norman — with the quarterings of Sherbourn and others." [Blomefield's Hist., Norfolk.]

17. John Doggett,[1] was of St. Faith, in Co. Norfolk, Gent.; married Joane Risley, daughter of John Risley, of Kimberley, Norfolk, Gent.

Issue:

18. i. William Doggett,[2] born St. Faith, Norfolk.

18. William Doggett [2] (*John*[1]), born St. Faith, Norfolk; married Joane Norman, daughter and heir of John and Emma [Morley]

Norman, of Honingham, Norfolk; buried, Black Friar's Church, Norwich (by St. Barbara's Altar), 1518.

Issue:

19. i. EDMUND DOGGETT,[3] born Honingham, Norfolk.
20. ii. ELIZABETH DOGGETT,[3] married William Hamshill, of London, Gentleman.

Huningham Hall or Curson's Manor belonged to Sir Robert de Tateshale and Mary de Navile in 1279.

It came afterward to the Cursons, in 1345, who held it of the heirs of Robert de Tateshale.

Job Curson died intestate in 1401, and it was held in trust for Katerine, daughter of John Curson, then wife of Nicholas Norman, of London.

In 1442, the said Katerine settled "Cursons" on her son, John Norman.

In 1465, John married Emma, daughter of Robert Morley, Esq., upon whom he settled this Manor. His seal is his Arms, with an annulet, viz.: Argent, a chev. between three martlets, sable. Hers is Morley's arms, but the Lyon hath no crown.

They left one daughter, Jane, who married William Doggett, of St. Faith's, Gentleman.

[Blomesfield's Hist. Co. Norfolk, 1739.]

19. EDMUND DOGGETT[3] (*William*,[2] *John*[1]), born Honingham, Norfolk; married Elizabeth Sherborne, sister to Sir Henry Sherborne and daughter of John Sherborne, who died 1487.

Issue:

21. i. ANTHONY DOGGETT.[4]
22. ii. EDMUMD DOGGETT.[4]
23. iii. JOHN DOGGETT.[4]
24. iv. MARGARET DOGGETT,[4] married Roger Butler, of Weston, Esq.

In 1547, Edmund Doggett and Anthony, his son, sold "Huningham Hall" to Richard Catlyne, Esq.

21. ANTHONY DOGGETT[4] (*Edmund*,[3] *William*,[2] *John*[1]), of Sherborn and Honingham; married Anne (or Agnes) Smalpece, daughter of Humphrey Smalpece, of Hocking, Norfolk, Gentleman.

Issue: son and three daughters; all died young.

25. i. HUGH DOGGETT,[5] died young.

22. EDMUND DOGGETT[4] (*Edmund*,[3] *William*,[2] *John*[1]), was of Wormegay, Norfolk; married Elizabeth Hertley, of Herts.

Issue:

26. i. THOMAS DOGGETT.[5]
27. ii. ANTHONY DOGGETT.[5]
28. iii. EDMUND DOGGETT.[5]
29. iv. BLYTHE DOGGETT.[5]

JOHN DÁGGETT, OF PICKHILL, YORKSHIRE, AND HIS DESCENDANTS.

Arms: Three crescents or, chief azure, field argent.
Crest: An eagle displayed gules, charged with a bezant.
Motto: Nil Desperandum.   [Granted 1730.]

" These arms were granted to our ancestor in the twelfth century. He was in the wars of the Crusades, and in one engagement captured a prince of the Royal House opposed to him.

" This prince was ransomed for money, which is signified by the Eagle being displayed and having the ' bezant' on its heart.   The Eagle is the Royal sign; the bezant on the heart means his life redeemed for gold.   (The bezant was the gold coin of Byzantium, now Constantinople.)

" The three crescents denote three engagements during the wars. These crescents are on a pale blue engrailed ground, the shield is white, the motto ' Nil Desperandum,' or ' Never despair.'   No family in England has a more honorable or ancient origin."   [Letter of William C. Daggett to Thomas Daggett, dated December 8, 1880.]

" From the earliest time to which I have been able to trace them (this branch), they have been a purely Yorkshire Family, and their name has been spelt either Daggett or Dagget, the former almost universally.   I do not think they were akin to the Doggetts of East Anglia."   [William Daggett, Esq., of Newcastle-upon-Tyne.]

30.   JOHN DAGGETT,[1] buried Pickhill, Yorkshire, April 15, 1608; married.

Issue :

31. i. WILLIAM DAGGETT,[2] born Pickhill, Yorkshire, 1557-8 or 9.

A family of " Daggett," apparently small yeomen, were settled for several generations at Pickhill or Pickhall, in the North Riding of York, about six miles from the market town of Thirsk.

The earliest of the family of whom any record has been traced is John Daggett, and the only information is contained in a Deed Roll dated 20 October, 1580 [22 Elizabeth], in which he conveyed certain of his real and personal estate to his eldest son, William.

31.   WILLIAM DAGGETT [2] (*John* [1]), born Pickhill, Yorkshire, 1557–8 or 9, called " senior; " died Pickhill, Yorkshire, December, 1638; married, November 5, 1580, Isabella Kay.

Issue :

32. i. WILLIAM DAGGETT,[3] bapt. Pickhill, Yorkshire, about 1588.

32. WILLIAM DAGGETT [3] (*William,*[2] *John*[1]), bapt. Pickhill, York-shire, about 1588 ; buried Pickhill, Yorkshire, April 15, 1651 ; married, July, 1632, Ann Winde.

Issue :

33. i. WILLIAM DAGGETT,[4] bapt. Pickhill, Yorkshire, March 26, 1636.

William Daggett was nicknamed " Magnus " and " Magog." He left a will by which he desired that his eldest son should not enter upon his lands until he should attain the age of 28. This will was proved in 1651 by his widow before the " Keepers of the liberties of England."

33. WILLIAM DAGGETT [4] (*William,*[3] *William,*[2] *John*[1]), bapt. Pick-hill, Yorkshire, March 26, 1636 ; buried Pickhill, Yorkshire, December 13, 1687 ; married Margaret ; buried Kirkby Wiske, March 24, 1699.

Issue :

34. i. WILLIAM DAGGETT,[5] bapt. Pickhill, Yorkshire, April 8, 1688.

William Daggett, the eldest son of " Magnus," was himself commonly called " Longus."

The full maiden name of his wife has not been ascertained or the date of her marriage.

After the death of her husband she married a second time, one Christopher Dickson.

34. WILLIAM DAGGETT [5] (*William,*[4] *William,*[3] *William,*[2] *John*[1]), bapt. Pickhill, Yorkshire, April 8, 1688 ; buried Pickhill, Yorkshire, October 31, 1749 ; married, in or previous to 1713, Margaret Theakston.

Issue :

35. i. WILLIAM DAGGETT,[6] bapt. Pickhill, Yorkshire, April 7, 1714.

William Daggett was an only son, and was commonly called " William Daggett, of Roxby, senior " (Roxby being a township in the Parish of Pickhill).

He died intestate, and administration of his personal estate was granted in the year 1751 to his eldest son William by the Archdeaconry Court of Richmond.

35. WILLIAM DAGGETT [6] (*William,*[5] *William,*[4] *William,*[3] *William,*[2] *John*[1]), baptized Pickhill, Yorkshire, April 7, 1714 ; buried Pickhill,

Yorkshire, October 18, 1763; married, November 5, 1744, Margaret Daggett, of Kirkby Wiske, born 1718; buried Pickhill, Yorkshire, September 8, 1811.

Issue:

36. i. WILLIAM DAGGETT,[7] bapt. Pickhill, Yorkshire, October 18, 1745.

36.   WILLIAM DAGGETT[7] (*William*,[6] *William*,[5] *William*,[4] *William*,[3] *William*,[2] *John*[1]), bapt. Pickhill, Yorkshire, October 18, 1745; died Pickhill, Yorkshire, May 12, 1781; married, January 10, 1770, Elizabeth Hunton; buried Pickhill, Yorkshire.

Issue: " A large family."

37.   WILLIAM DAGGETT,[8] bapt. Pickhill, Yorkshire, February 3, 1774.

37.   WILLIAM DAGGETT[8] (*William*,[7] *William*,[6] *William*,[5] *William*,[4] *William*,[3] *William*,[2] *John*[1]), bapt. Pickhill, Yorkshire, February 3, 1774; buried Pickhill, Yorkshire, September 21, 1812; married, April 18, 1799, Elizabeth Pybus; born 1778; buried Pickhill, Yorkshire, July 3, 1805.

Issue:

38.   JANE DAGGETT,[9] bapt. Pickhill, Yorkshire, August 18, 1802.

38.   JANE DAGGETT[9] (*William*,[8] *William*,[7] *William*,[6] *William*,[5] *William*,[4] *William*,[3] *William*,[2] *John*[1]), bapt. Pickhill, Yorkshire, August 18, 1802; buried Pickhill, Yorkshire, December 10, 1849; married, January 6, 1824, Henry Ingledew, of Newcastle-upon-Tyne, solicitor; died Newcastle-upon-Tyne, May 24, 1882.

Issue: Eight children.

39. i. ANN P'ANSON INGLEDEW;[10] living [1888]; married, and has a large family.
40. ii. WILLIAM DAGGETT INGLEDEW,[10] bapt. Newcastle-upon-Tyne, February 18, 1826.

40.   WILLIAM DAGGETT INGLEDEW[10] (*Jane Daggett*,[9] *William*,[8] *William*,[7] *William*,[6] *William*,[5] *William*,[4] *William*,[3] *William*,[2] *John*[1]), bapt. Newcastle-upon-Tyne, February 18, 1826.   In 1851 dropped the surname of Ingledew, and since known and called William Daggett, " solicitor; " resides 1 Victoria Square, Newcastle-upon-Tyne, England (1888); married, 1853; wife died Newcastle-upon-Tyne, March 17, 1877.

Issue: Eight children.

41.   WILLIAM DAGGETT,[11] born Newcastle-upon-Tyne, December 20, 1856; " solicitor; " resides Newcastle-upon-Tyne (1888).

CHURCH AT BOXFORD, SUFFOLK, ENGLAND.

Built probably at the end of the 14th century.

JOHN DOGGETT, OF HARLESTON, NORFOLK, AND HIS DESCENDANTS.

42. JOHN DOGGETT,[1] buried Harleston, Norfolk, May 12, 1607; married Joan; buried Harleston, Norfolk, February 28, 1613; administration granted on her estate by Consistory Court of Norwich, 28 February, 1613.

Issue:

43. i. FRANCIS DOGGETT,[2] bapt. Harleston, Norfolk, December 7, 1561.
44. ii. REBECCA DOGGETT,[2] bapt. Harleston, Norfolk, July 25, 1566.
45. iii. GERVIS DOGGETT,[2] bapt. Harleston, Norfolk, December 26, 1570.
46. iv. AMBROSE DOGGETT,[2] bapt. Harleston, Norfolk, March 9, 1571.

46. AMBROSE DOGGETT [2] (*John* [1]), bapt. Harleston, Norfolk, March 9, 1571; married Margaret.

Issue:

47. i. FRANCIS DOGGETT,[3] bapt. Harleston, Norfolk, February 24, 1604.
48. ii. JOHN DOGGETT,[3] bapt. Harleston, Norfolk, November 30, 1606.
49. iii. JOAN DOGGETT,[3] bapt. Harleston, Norfolk, September 21, 1609.
50. iv. RICHARD DOGGETT,[3] bapt. Harleston, Norfolk, August 18, 1611.

WILLIAM DOGGETT, OF BOXFORD, SUFFOLK, AND HIS DESCENDANTS.

51. WILLIAM DOGGETT,[1] born 1557; died October 10, 1610; married Boxford, Suffolk, June 1, 1591, Avis Lappadge, daughter of Thomas Lappadge, of Boxford, Suffolk; living September 23, 1650.

Issue:

52. i. ANNE DOGGETT,[2] bapt. Boxford, Suffolk, May 11, 1592.
53. ii. THOMAS DOGGETT,[2] bapt. Boxford, Suffolk, December 30, 1594.
54. iii. SUSAN DOGGETT,[2] bapt. Boxford, Suffolk, January 25, 1595.
55. iv. AVIS DOGGETT,[2] bapt. Boxford, Suffolk, February 27, 1598; married, Boxford, Suffolk, July 23, 1620, John Bond; buried Boxford, Suffolk, 1625.
56. v. WILLIAM DOGGETT,[2] bapt. Boxford, Suffolk, February 27, 1599; mentioned in will of John Brand, of Sherbourne, Suffolk, dated 31 January, 1641.
57. vi. ALICE DOGGETT,[2] bapt. Boxford, Suffolk, May 14, 1601.
58. vii. JOHN DOGGETT,[2] bapt. Boxford, Suffolk, November 4, 1602; possibly John, of Martha's Vineyard, Mass. (No. 679.)
59. viii. BRIDGET DOGGETT,[2] bapt. Boxford, Suffolk, May 10, 1604.
60. ix. DOROTHY DOGGETT,[2] bapt. Boxford, Suffolk, November 28, 1605; mentioned in will of John Brand, of Sherbourne, Suffolk, dated 31 January, 1641.
61. x. LAPPADGE DOGGETT,[2] bapt. Boxford, Suffolk, February 12, 1606.
62. xi. RICHARD DOGGETT,[2] bapt. Boxford, Suffolk, December 1, 1608; mentioned in will of John Brand, of Sherbourne, Suffolk, dated 31 January, 1641.
63. xii. Son, —— DOGGETT.[2]

One of the daughters married Mr. Rowarth, and had son John, mentioned in will of John Brand, of Sherbourne.

In the will of Alice Edgar, 1595 [p. 341, Ipswich Probate], is mentioned " my cosine Avis Dogett fortye shillgs," etc., also " her husband my cousine William Dogett, one gold ring with a black stone."

The will of Thomas Lappage, of Boxford, Suffolk, dated 29 January, 1611, mentions all goods and chattels in the house of Avis Doggett my daughter and her children, also children of Susan Brand my daughter and my godson John Dogget. [Somerset House Lawes, fo. 34.]

In 1884 a pew was moved in the Boxford Church to find the stone of William Doggett. It was found to be an altar tomb, having the inscription on a handsome black marble slab with four brasses engraved with arms on the four corners. The inscription :

" Here lyeth Willia' Doggett marchant adveterer citizen and mercer of London and free of the East India Company who tooke to wife Avis Lappadge ye daught of Thomas Lappadge of Boxford wᵗʰ whô he lyved 19 yeares and had issue by her 6 sõnes & 6 daughters ye said Will' depted this life ye 10ᵗʰ of Octobʳ 1610 beinge of the age of 53 yeares."

The arms at the four corners are : 1st, City of London ; 2d, Mercers' Company ; 3d, Merchant Adventurers ; 4th, East India Company.

On the Dole Board in the Boxford Church the following words occur without date : " William Doggett gave 4 acres near Slades Green Edwardeston held by Mr John Gosling at 9£ per annum, given away in bread " Boxford Charities " Plumbs & Doggetts Charities rent £16 per annum, to the poor." [Page's Supplement to Davy's Suffolk Collections, Ipswich, 1843.]

53. Thomas Doggett ² (*William* ¹), bapt. Boxford, Suffolk, December 30, 1594 ; married Groton, Suffolk, April 22, 1617, by Mr. Bird, to Margaret Clopton, daughter of William and Margaret (Waldegrave) Clopton, of Castleins.

Issue :

64. i. William Doggett,³ bapt. Groton, Suffolk, January 5, 1618 ; mentioned in will of John Brand, of Sherbourne, Suffolk, dated 31 January, 1641, as his godson.

Thomas Doggett was married to Margaret Clopton, who was of that famous family of Cloptons which Sir Simonds D'Ewes, having married one of them himself, has thus celebrated in his Autobiography : " There is scarce a second private family of nobility or gentry, either in England or in Christendom, that can show so many goodly monuments of itself in any one church, cathedral or parochial, as remains of the Cloptons in that of Melford in Suffolk [1638]."

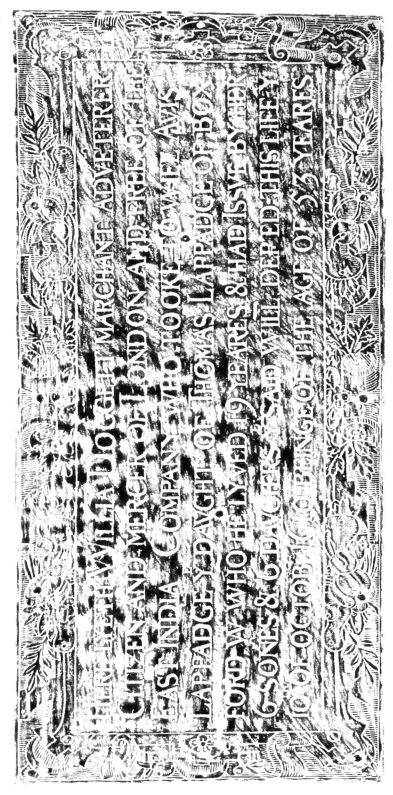

HERE LYETH WILLIAM DOGGETT MERCHANT ADVENTERER
CITIZEN AND MERCER OF LONDON AND FREE OF THE
EAST INDIA COMPANY WHO TOOKE TO WIFE AVIS
LAP[P]ADGE DAVGHT OF THOMAS LAP[P]ADGE OF BOX
BOURD AY WHO HE HAD ISSVE 9 BEARES & HAD ISSVE BY HER
6 SONES & 6 DAVGHTERS AND WILL DEPERED THIS LIFE Y
10 OF OCTOBER BEING OF THE AGE OF 93 YEARES

RUBBING OF INSCRIPTION ON TOMB OF WILLIAM DOGGETT IN BOXFORD CHURCH.

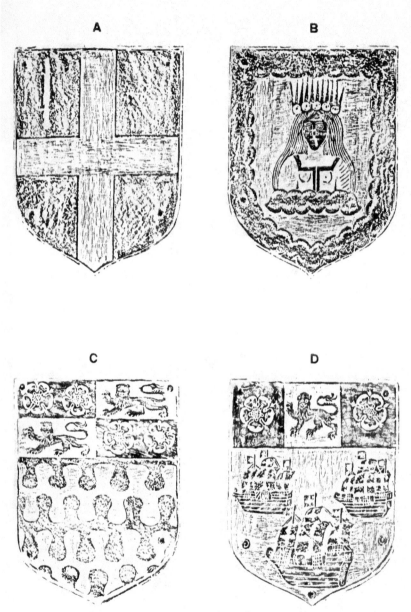

RUBBINGS OF THE FOUR BRASSES.

Tomb of William Doggett in Boxford Church.

In the " Life and Letters of John Winthrop," Boston, 1864, is the
account of the death-bed of Thomasine Clopton, wife of John Winthrop and sister of Margaret Clopton, who married Thomas Doggett.
" It may help to fix in our mind the exact period at which it was
written if we remember that Shakspeare died the same year [1616]
at Stratford-upon-Avon, where he had lived in a house [New Place]
which had been built by Sir Hugh Clopton." In this account, as she
feels she is approaching the end she calls for her sisters : " Then she
called for her sister Margerye whom she exhorted to serve God and
take heede of pride and to have care in hir matchinge that she looked
not at riches and worldly respects but at the feare of God for that
would bringe hir comfort at hir death although she should meet with
many afflictions."

In the Collections of the Mass. Hist. Society, vol. 1, page 179, is a
letter of Thomas Dogett to John Winthrop :

" To the Right Wor[ll] and his very loving brother Mr. John Winthrop, Esq., at
his house in Groton.   dd
" Sr — I humblie thanke you for yo[r] loue towards me in all things, but especially in this, that you desire to helpe me wth a chapman for my house and
land, w[ch] if you shall effecte for me [the case standing wth me as it doth] I shall
be bound to pray for you and shall eu[r] thinke myselfe beholding vnto yo[r] worpp.
I am to goe [God willing] wth my vnckle Brand to London vppon Monday morning, likewise to parley about the sale of it wth one or 2 gent but it is as yet free
for any man and there is no incumbrance uppon it but only a statute w[ch] my
vnckle Brand have, for monyes, w[ch] he hath disbursed for me w[ch] he will very
willingly release vppon the repaying of that mony w[ch] is due to him; my evidence are all at London where I have also a plott of all my lands in pticular and
how many acres euery pticular field and close cōteyne w[ch] you shall there haue
[if you please].
" I have been bidden 1800 [li] for it by 2 or 3, but my vnckle thinks it to be
to littell and therefore he doth [I thanke him] forbeare me the longer that I might
take my best chapman.   I would willingly haue 1900 [li] for it but vse mony and
chardges runn on and therefore rather than faile I will take 1800 [li] for it.
" And thus w[th] my loue remembred to yo[r] worpp wishing all happiness to
yo[r]selfe and youres, I humbly take my leave, resting Eu[r]
" Yo[r] worpp[s] poore neighbor and freind to comand.
                                                    " THOMAS DOGGETT.
" Oct. 6, 1627.
" My price is 1800 [li] if I may have a lease of it agayne at a C [li] p annū ; other-
wise if a gent will buye it to dwell in my prise is twoe thousand pound."

57.   ALICE DOGGETT [2] (*William* [1]), bapt. Boxford, Suffolk, May
14, 1601; married, Boxford, Suffolk, July 14, 1624, Christopher
Scarlet; he died Hayland, Suffolk, 1650.

The will of Christopher Scarlett, of Hayland, Suffolk, dated September 23, 1650, mentions " my mother in law Mrs Avis Doggett."
[Grey, 99, Somerset House.]

JOHN DOGETT, OF GROTON, SUFFOLK, AND HIS DESCENDANTS.

Arms: Two greyhounds combatant, or; collared ar.; bell pendant.
Crest: Unicorn's head, or.

Arms of John Doget, Merchant, London [Groton, Suffolk]. Harleian MSS., British Museum, fo. 216, No. 1086, London Visitation, 1664.

65. JOHN DOGETT,[1] buried Groton, Suffolk, May 29, 1619; married Dorothy; buried Groton, Suffolk, March 4, 1605.

Issue:

66. i.   JOHN DOGETT,[2] bapt. Groton, Suffolk, July 24, 1582.
67. ii.   SUSAN DOGETT,[2] bapt. Groton, Suffolk, May 9, 1585; buried Groton, Suffolk, July 28, 1585.
68. iii. BRIDGET DOGETT,[2] bapt. Groton, Suffolk, August 21, 1586.
69. iv. SUSAN DOGETT,[2] bapt. Groton, Suffolk, September 3, 1588; married Groton, Suffolk, December 10, 1611, Louis Kedbye.
70. v.   ELIZABETH DOGETT,[2] bapt. Groton, Suffolk, November 9, 1589; married Groton, Suffolk, April 7, 1618, George Ward.
71. vi. WILLIAM DOGETT,[2] bapt. Groton, Suffolk, January 17, 1590; buried Groton, Suffolk, January 27, 1590.
72. vii. WILLIAM DOGETT,[2] bapt. Groton, Suffolk, September 20, 1592; buried Groton, Suffolk, October 24, 1592.
73. viii. MARTHA DOGETT,[2] bapt. Groton, Suffolk, October 16, 1593.
74. ix. JOSEPH DOGETT,[2] bapt. Groton, Suffolk, October 20, 1595.
75. x.   ANNE DOGETT,[2] bapt. Groton, Suffolk, June 16, 1597.
76. xi. BENJAMIN DOGETT,[2] bapt. Groton, Suffolk, November 19, 1598.
77. xii. ABRAHAM DOGETT,[2] bapt. Groton, Suffolk, December 8, 1601.
78. xiii. MARY DOGETT,[2] bapt. Groton, Suffolk, February 20, 1602; buried Groton, Suffolk, March 14, 1602.

From the Diary of Adam Winthrop, father of Gov. John Winthrop, is the following regarding John Dogett:

"July 25, 1603 Rob' Surrey was maried to John Dogetts maide Thomasin Hubbard.

"1604 the xij[th] of Aprill Mr Clopton and Mr Dogett made an awarde between me and Adam Wynthrop my nephew.

"1606 The second of March being Sunday about vij of the clocke in the evenynge the goodwyfe Dogett died.

"1609 The first day of Novembre John Rawlinge kept a feast at his new house where Mr Thoms Tilney Mr Dogett and diu[rs] others dined."

That John Doget was a tenant of the Manor of Groton appears in the assignment of the Lordship to John Winthrop by Adam, his father.

GROTON: Memorandum that the 14th daie of November Anno Domini millessimo sex centessimo decimo octavo [1618] et domini Jacobi regis Angliae &c decimo sexto. Johannes Nurton scnr came before John Winthrop Esq lorde

CHURCH AT GROTON, SUFFOLK, ENGLAND.

Built probably early in the 15th century.

of the manor of Groton and out of the Court of the said manor in the presence of Adam Winthrop, gent, John Doget and Steven Gostlin, two customary tenantes of the said manor did surrender into the hands of the said John Winthrop all that his moitie and portion of the customary lands which he holdeth of the said John Winthrop as of the manor aforesaid to the use of the said John Winthrop and his heirs and the said John Winthrop being so seized of the moitie aforesaid did presently in the presence of the said Adam Winthrop John Doget and Steven Goslin deliver out of his hands all that moitie and portion of the said customary lands unto the said John Nutton for the use of the said John Nutton and his heirs and assigns forever under these conditions here expressed that is to say, that if the said John Nutton his heirs or assigns doe not yearly pay or cause to be paid unto Anne Gale the daughter of William Gale or her assigns during her life three pounds four shillings of lawful money of England by sixteen shillings every quarter of the year the first payment thereof to be at the feast of the nativity of our Lord God next coming after the date hereof and so forth every quarter previous or within fourteen days next after every of the said days of payment at or within the church porch of the parish church of Groton aforesaid that then this estate shall be void and that the said John Winthrop or his heirs shall be seized of and in the said moitie and portion of land to the only use and behalfe of the above named Anne Gale her heirs and assigns to be holden of the said John Winthrop his heirs or assigns of the manor aforesaid by the rent customs and services before due and accustomed

By me
JOHN NUTTON

ADAM WINTHROP
JOHN DOGET
STEVEN GOSTLINGE.

The will of John Doggett is of unusual length. It is dated 1619. He remembers six Puritan preachers in his immediate neighborhood.

The testator by his will founded two charities, both of which are still in existence. He makes his son John one of the executors, and goes on: " But because my sonne John his abode is beyond the Sea soe that he cannot suddenly loke to the p'formance of this busynes ; " and goes on to make provision to meet the case until his son could return.

" One of the charities was £10 bequeathed for the poor which was conveyed to Trustees 1st Charles I. [1625]." [Page's Supplement to Davy's Suffolk, vol. 5, page 942, Ipswich, 1843.]

66. JOHN DOGGETT[2] (*John*[1]), bapt. Groton, Suffolk, July 24, 1582; died Hamburg, Germany, between 1632 and 1653; married, England, Elizabeth Bladwell; died Hamburg, Germany, 1653.

Issue :

79. i. JOHN DOGGETT,[3] born Hamburg, Germany.
80. ii. RICHARD DOGGETT.[3]
81. iii. THOMAS DOGGETT.[3]
82. iv. ELIZABETH DOGGETT.[3]
83. v. ANNE DOGGETT.[3]

John Doggett, in 1632, was a merchant at Hamburg, Germany, as appears from the following:

" Will of Thomas Bladwell of London, merchant, dated 29 Nov. 1632, proved 1632, mentions Brother in law John Doggett, merchant,

at present residing at Hambro, beyond the seas, and his wife Elizabeth Doggett and children of said John and Elizabeth, viz: John,
Richard, Thomas, Elizabeth, Anne." [Somerset House, Audley,
53.]

" Will of Elizabeth Doggett widow of the late John Dogett, merchant in Hamburgh. Proved at Westminster 17 Jan. 1654, signed
at Hamburgh 10 October, 1653, mentions therein, John Doggett,
England, her son and sole executor." [Somerset House, Alchin,
320.]

73. MARTHA DOGETT[2] (*John* [1]), bapt. Groton, Suffolk, October
16, 1593; removed to America with Winthrop, 1630, died, Boston (?); married Giles Firmin; died Boston, Mass., September,
1634.

Issue:

84. i. GILES FIRMIN.[3]

Giles Firmin removed from Sudbury, Suffolk, to America in 1630.
He probably came in the fleet with Winthrop, and first settled at
Watertown, from whence he removed in two years to Boston.

Here he was chosen deacon in 1633; was also a selectman. Was
made freeman 4 March, 1634.

79. JOHN DOGGETT[3] (*John,* [2] *John* [1]), born Hamburg, Germany;
died London, England, 1680; married Alice (Smith?); died London,
England, 1703.

Issue:

85. i. JOHN DOGGETT.[4]
86. ii. BENJAMIN DOGGETT.[4]
87. iii. ALICE DOGGETT,[4] married David Debary.
88. iv. ELIZABETH DOGGETT,[4] born about 1651.
89. v. —— DOGGETT.[4]

1652–3. John Dogett, merchant and others.

1665–6. Contract for navy stores. [Calendar of State Papers,
British Museum, Vol. 34, p. 218.]

20 December, 1671, of St. Andrew Undershaft, Esq. [Mar. Hist.
of Dean Ely.]

Abstract of the will of John Dogett:

" I John Dogett of London, Esquire being sane and of sound and disposing
memory, . . . and my body to be buried in a decent manner at the discretion
of my Executrix . . . to my beloved wife Alice Dogett whome I nominate
and appoint to be my sole Executrix . . . To my 3 children unmarried,
Jno and Benjamine Dogett my two children ' each £1000 viz at 24 years
£500 and at 28 years £500 and for my daughter Alice att the age of Twenty
one yeares or day of marriage £1,500 . . . to my daughter Elizabeth Otgher
and to her children . . . and to John Otgher her sonne at 21 years, ' Item
I give to the poore of the church of Christ whereof I am att Present

related as a member thereof £30 'to the Reverend Pastor of the said Church of Christ unto which I stand related £20' to Tenn poor Ministers of the Gospell of Christ £50 viz to each of them £5 . . . to my cozen Thomas Kett (Scott?) £5 and to his daughter Elizabeth daughter to his former wife Francis . . . to my Three neises daughters of my sister Watson deceased vigt Esther now wife of Hugh Norris . . . and to Margaret and Katherine Watson.

"To Christ Hospital £50.

"Item: I give to the Poore orphants house at Hambrowe the place of my nativity, called 'Dat Wesenhus' Fifty Rix Iony 50 Rix doller att Hab^r by the appointment of my executrix in 12 moneths after my decease . . . to my Apprentices that shall be in actuall service att my decease Five pounds . . . I doe hereby desire and request my loveing Brother in Law Mr. John Smith and my loveing sonne in Lawe Justus Otgher to be supervisors and assistants to my wife and Executrix."

Residue to wife . . . dated 26 December, 1679. Signed in the presence of John Panton, Aba Otgher, Thomas Grosvenor.

Proved 6 April, 1680, by Alice Dogett, relict of said deceased and Executrix.

[P.C.C. 46 Bath.]

Probate account book, 6 April, 1680, was proved the will of John Dogett, late of the Parish of St. Laurence Pountney, London, Esqr., deceased, by Alice Dogett, relict and Executrix.

The will of Alice Dogett is recorded P.C.C. 127 Degg. "28 Augt 1699 — 11th W^m 3rd."

"I Alice Doggett widdow late the wife of John Dogett of London, Esqr deceased being at present in good health . . . and my body I comitt to the earth to be decently buryed according to the discreecon of my Executor . . . to my Loveing son in Law Mr Justus Otgher . . . to my daughter Alice Debary . . . unto my sister Mrs Mary Woolsey for mourning Ten Pounds and Five pounds to Mrs Angell and to my son John Dogett and his wife Twenty pounds for mourning and to my son Benjamin Dogett Twenty pounds for mourning . . . I have given my son Justus Otgher towards the advancing of his Daughter Katherine which sume time since marryed unto Mr David Longnemantle and shall pay the residue and Interest and Proffitts thereof and the rest and residue of the said Two Fifths parts to such other Children which he had by my said Daughter Elizabeth . . . my said Daughter Alice the wife of David Debary . . . to my son John Dogett deducting thereout Four hundred and Sixty pounds formerly given him to buy a place and one hundred pounds since lent him for the better carrying on his trade of a Woodmonger and the sume of Threescore Pounds lately paid his Creditors by his direccon . . . to my Son Benjamin Dogett He first deducting thereout Two Hundred pounds which I have formerly given him And one Hundred pounds since Lent him to carry on his Trade of Woodmonger and the sume of Threescore pounds paid to his Creditors by his Order . . . my Loveing Son in Law Justus Otgher to be my Full and Sole Executor . . . Alice Dogett . . . in the presence of Sarah Hawkins, her marke. Anne Day, James Peters."

Proved 5 May, 1703, by Justus Otgher, the executor.

Probate account to above will from the "Probate Act Book," "5 May, 1703, was proved the will of Alice Doggett, late of the Parish of S^t. Andrew, Holbourne, Co. Middx, widow dec'd, by Justus Otgher, Exec."

82. ELIZABETH DOGGETT [3] (*John,*[2] *John*[1]), married Mr. Taylor.
Issue :

90. i. JOHN TAYLOR,[4] not yet 21 in October, 1653.
91. ii. FRANCIS TAYLOR,[4] not yet 21 in October, 1653.

83. ANNE DOGGETT [3] (*John,*[2] *John*[1]), died London (?), Eng.,
before 26 December, 1679 ; married George Watson.
Issue :

92. i. ESTHER WATSON,[4] married Hugh Norris before 26 December, 1679.
93. ii. MARGARET WATSON,[4] not married 1679.
94. iii. KATHERINE WATSON,[4] not married 1679.

84. GILES FIRMIN [3] (*Martha Dogett,*[2] *John*[1]), died Ridgewell,
England, April, 1697 ; married, Massachusetts, Susan Ward, daughter of Rev. Nathaniel Ward.

Giles Firmin settled in Boston previous to his father ; he then
removed to Ipswich, Mass.   Was afterward at Haverhill, Mass.
Made freeman 22 May, 1639.   He was educated at the University of
Cambridge, and in 1644, or soon after, went to England, where he
preached with good effect.   Was settled as rector at Shalford, in
Essex.

In a sermon before Parliament and the Westminster Assembly he
said that " in our country in seven years I never heard one profane
oath, and all that time never did see a man drunk," which is better
proof of his keeping good company than of searching for opportunity.

85. JOHN DOGGETT [4] (*John,*[3] *John,*[2] *John*[1]), wife and children at
Carolina, America (1706).

"John Dogett living and not aged 24 years, 26 December, 1679,
living and married 28 August, 1699, and a ' wood monger ' by trade,
£60 paid his creditors.   [See his mother's will.]   Per will of brother
Benjamin 14 March, 1706, it appears from will of Benjamin that his
brother John ' lodgeth in the Fleet,' and that said John done ' very
ill ' to come from his wife and children at Carolina to serve the
Coll : who is but in bad circumstances himself."

86. BENJAMIN DOGGETT [4] (*John,*[3] *John,*[2] *John*[1]), died Kingston,
Jamaica, between 1703 and 1706.

Benjamin Doggett living and not aged 24, 26 December, 1679,
living 28 August, 1699, and " wood monger " by trade, £60 paid to
his creditors.   [See mother's will.]

His will is really a letter from Benjamin Doggett to his brother
John Doggett, and is dated Kingston, Jamaica, 8 July, 1703, and in
which he mentions sister De Bary.   Brother Otgher (recites a letter
from him (*i.e.,* Otgher), in which it is stated that John Doggett

"lodgeth in the Fleet") mother deceased. "Since we are all mortall and a like I have to expect, I here tell you I make you my sole Executor in case of mortality, designeing to make my will at first and leave you all I have or can lay claime to." Brother Otgher also mentions in *his* letter to Benjamin Doggett, that John Doggett had "done very ill to come from his wife and children at Carolina to serve the Coll: who is but in bad circumstances himself."

Benjamin Doggett's will (*i.e.*, the letter), sworn to by Anthony Grindall, of the Parish of St. Bridgett, also St. Brides, London, Esqr., aged above 30 years, and John Seymour, of the Parish of St. Buttolph, without Aldgate, Co. Middx, distiller, aged 30 years, who deposed they knew Benjamin Dogett, late of London, merchant, "but dyeing, as these deponents believe, at Jamaica."

Called in the sentence "Benjamin Dogett late at Kingston in the Island of Jamaica, Bachelor, deceased." Proved 14 November, 1706, by John Dogett, brother of deceased, and executor. [Commissary Court of London.]

88. ELIZABETH DOGGETT [4] (*John*,[3] *John*,[2] *John* [1]), born about 1651; married, London, Eng., license dated 20 December, 1671, at St. Helen, Bishopgate, or St. James, Duks Place, to Justus Otgher, of St. Mary Hill, London, merchant; born about 1646.

Issue:

95. i. KATHERINE OTGHER,[5] living and married David Longuemantle (1699).
96. ii. JOHN OTGHER,[5] living, under age, 26 December, 1679.

RICHARD DOGGETT AND BROTHERS, OF LEIGHTON BUZZARD, BEDFORDSHIRE, AND THEIR DESCENDANTS.

Issue:

97. i. RICHARD DOGGETT,[1] born Leighton Buzzard, Beds., 1605.
98. ii. RALPH DOGGETT.[1]
99. iii. FRANCIS DOGGETT,[1] married and had daughter Elizabeth Doggett; he died before 1679.
100. iv. LAWRENCE DOGGETT,[1] married and had Edward Doggett, who married and had Richard Doggett.

97. RICHARD DOGGETT,[1] born Leighton Buzzard, Beds., 1605; died Leighton Buzzard, Beds., July 13, 1682; married Elizabeth Turney; born Leighton Buzzard, Beds., 1609; died Leighton Buzzard, Beds., November 12, 1689.

Issue:

101. i. THOMAS DOGGETT.[2]
102. ii. DEBORAH DOGGETT.[2]
103. iii. JUDITH DOGGETT.[2]

Richard Doggett, of Leighton Buzzard, Beds., died 1682, leaving a will dated 1679, in which he makes a bequest to the town of Leighton, and besides the relatives mentioned in the pedigree speaks of cousins Anne Edwards; Elizabeth Shephearth, of Shefford; Thomas Harwood, alias Smith; Sarah Stevens, of Aston; Richard Jenkins; Sarah Brown; Thomas Doggett, of Standbridge, near Leighton; Robert Turney; Robert Parrott.

Speaks of property at Steeple Claydon, Bucks; at Bitton parish, Fowdingbridge; Co. Southton, and at Elnig, Southton, where lived Mr. Pawlett, Senr.

Funeral expenses to be £100; £20 to be paid for a monument over grave. [Somerset House, Cottle, 96.]

The will of Elizabeth Doggett, of Leighton Buzzard, Beds., widow:

"I give to the poor of Leighton the sum of 50 shillings.
"To Matthew Disney of Bradwell, Bucks, clerk William Lea of Lillingston Dayrill, Bucks clerk John Truelove of Leighton Buzzard, all my Estate, Title, & Interest ground &c at Steeple Claydon, Bucks, upon special trust & confidence for my grandchild Martha Pawlett the now wife of William Pawlett of Bitton, Southampton, her heirs failing which, I give the same to Matthew Disney & Sarah his wife.
"To Judith & Rebecca Turney the daughters of my Brother Edward Turney of Hemel Hempstead £20 between them.
"Edward Turney son of Brother Edward.
"Thomas Turney " " " "
"Grandchild Richard Pawlett my house where I now dwell."

Dated 18 May, 1687.
Codicil 20 June, 1688 (no different names). Probate, 1689.
[Somerset House, Ent. 173.]

98. RALPH DOGGETT,[1] died before 1679; married.
Issue:
104. i. RALPH DOGGETT.[2]
105. ii. THOMAS DOGGETT.[2]

102. DEBORAH DOGGETT[2] (*Richard*[1]), married Mr. Pawlett.
Issue:
106. i. WILLIAM PAWLETT,[3] married Martha Fronside (?) before 1687.
107. ii. RICHARD PAWLETT,[3] living May 18, 1687.

103. JUDITH DOGGETT[2] (*Richard*[1]), married Mr. Fronside.
Issue:
108. i. SARAH FRONSIDE,[3] married Mathew Disney(?) before 1687.
109. ii. MARTHA FRONSIDE,[3] married William Pawlett (?) before 1687.

105. THOMAS DOGGETT[2] (*Ralph*[1]), married March 7, 1653; by Samuel Bedford, Esq., to Elizabeth Edwards, of Biggleswade, the daughter of Thomas Edwards, of Langford, Co. Bedford.
Issue: Children mentioned in will of Richard Doggett, 1679.

DOGGETT HOUSE AT LEIGHTON BUZZARD.

The residence of some of the earliest members of the LEIGHTON BUZZARD branch of the family.

Mr. WILLIAM H. DOGGETT of Leighton Buzzard had the above copy made from a painting of the house which has been in his family for many generations.

JOHN DOGGET, OF REIGATE, SURREY.

110. John Dogget,[1] married Alice.

Issue :

111. i.   Alice Dogget,[2] bapt. Reigate, Co. Surrey, June 2, 1644.
112. ii.   John Dogget,[2] bapt. Reigate, Co. Surrey, May 8, 1647.
113. iii. Mary Dogget,[2] bapt. Reigate, Co. Surrey, July 10, 1651.
114. iv.   Anna Dogget,[2] bapt. Reigate, Co. Surrey, August 20, 1655.
115. v.   —— Dogget,[2] buried Reigate, Co. Surrey, July 17, 1657.
116. vi.   John Dogget,[2] born Mitcham, Co. Surrey, August 30, 1660.
117. vii. Benjamin Dogget,[2] died Mitcham, Surrey, May 9, 1661.

WILLIAM DOGGETT, OF LEIGHTON BUZZARD, BEDS., AND HIS DESCENDANTS.

118. William Doggett,[1] born Leighton Buzzard, Beds., 1681; died Leighton Buzzard, Beds., August 12, 1760; married 1st; married 2d, 1722, Anne; born 1698; died Leighton Buzzard, July 19, 1753.

Issue :

119. i.   William Doggett.[2]
120. ii.   John Doggett.[2]
121. iii. Thomas Doggett,[2] born Leighton Buzzard, 1723.
122. iv.   Richard Doggett,[2] born Leighton Buzzard, 1730; died Leighton Buzzard, November 16, 1776.
123. v.   Ann Doggett,[2] born Leighton Buzzard; married 1st, William Gresham, 2d, John Pancross, 3d, John Millard; no issue; she died Leighton Buzzard, December 13, 1795.

121. Thomas Doggett [2] (*William* [1]), born Leighton Buzzard, 1723; died Leighton Buzzard, July 25, 1792; married Elizabeth Bullen; born 1737; died Leighton Buzzard, March 16, 1799.

Issue :

124. i.   William Doggett,[3] born Leighton Buzzard, 1768; died Leighton Buzzard, January 14, 1772.
125. ii.   Ann Doggett,[3] born Leighton Buzzard, December 5, 1769; married Joseph Simons; no issue; died November 28, 1825.
126. iii. Mary Doggett,[3] born Leighton Buzzard, February 11, 1771; died Leighton Buzzard, February 14, 1846.
127. iv.   Thomas Doggett,[3] born Leighton Buzzard, May 5, 1772.
128. v.   Elizabeth Doggett,[3] born Leighton Buzzard, October 20, 1773; died Leighton Buzzard, June 5, 1802.

127. THOMAS DOGGETT [3] (*Thomas*,[2] *William* [1]), born Leighton Buzzard, May 5, 1772; died April 15, 1851; married Caroline Williams; born Brixton(?), August 15, 1780; died Leighton Buzzard, April 12, 1851.

Issue:

129. i.   THOMAS DOGGETT,[4] born Leighton Buzzard, April 9, 1799; died Leighton Buzzard, October 28, 1828.

130. ii.   RICHARD DOGGETT,[4] born Leighton Buzzard, March 31, 1801; married 1st, Elizabeth Wallher; married 2d, Sophia Hayward; no issue; he died Leighton Buzzard, November 15, 1865.

131. iii. FRANCIS DOGGETT,[4] born Leighton Buzzard, October 8, 1802; died Leighton Buzzard, March 22, 1806.

132. iv.   ELIZABETH DOGGETT,[4] born Leighton Buzzard, March 20, 1804; died Leighton Buzzard, October 20, 1807.

133. v.   WILLIAM DOGGETT,[4] born Leighton Buzzard, March 23, 1806.

134. vi.   EDWARD BOWERS DOGGETT,[4] born Leighton Buzzard, January 3, 1808.

135. vii. FRANCIS DOGGETT,[4] born Leighton Buzzard, September 5, 1809; died Leighton Buzzard, November 20, 1828.

136. viii. CHARLES DOGGETT,[4] born Leighton Buzzard, September 27, 1811; died December 14, 1851.

137. ix.   CAROLINE DOGGETT,[4] born Leighton Buzzard, August 18, 1813; married Henry John Robinson.

138. x.   ANNE DOGGETT,[4] born Leighton Buzzard, October 17, 1815; married Thomas Price.

139. xi.   GEORGE HENRY DOGGETT,[4] born Leighton Buzzard, January 18, 1818; died November 19, 1839.

140. xii. MARY DOGGETT,[4] born Leighton Buzzard, January 17, 1820; died May, 1857.

141. xiii. MARTHA DOGGETT,[4] born Leighton Buzzard, April 25, 1821; married Edward D. Lines.

142. xiv. SOPHIA DOGGETT,[4] born Leighton Buzzard, September 3, 1824; married D. J. McLauchlan.

133. WILLIAM DOGGETT [4] (*Thomas*,[3] *Thomas*,[2] *William* [1]), born Leighton Buzzard, March 23, 1806; died October 24, 1873; married Louisa Robinson.

Issue:

143. i.   LOUISA CAROLINE DOGGETT,[5] born Leighton Buzzard, March 18, 1836; married Charles White; resides Leighton Buzzard (1879).

144. ii.   SOPHIA ANNE DOGGETT,[5] born Leighton Buzzard, January 1, 1838; married Charles Claudge; resides Leighton Buzzard (1879).

145. iii. ELIZABETH GEORGIA DOGGETT,[5] born Leighton Buzzard, February 19, 1840; married George Bush.

146. iv.   MARTHA ROBINSON DOGGETT,[5] born Leighton Buzzard, January 31, 1843.

147. v.   WILLIAM HENRY DOGGETT.[5] born Leighton Buzzard, January 22, 1845.

148. vi.   LYDIA FANNY DOGGETT.[5] born Leighton Buzzard, March 1, 1847; married George Saunders.

149. vii. GERTRUDE MARY DOGGETT,[5] born Leighton Buzzard, April 1, 1849; died Leighton Buzzard, April 29, 1852.

134. EDWARD BOWERS DOGGETT [4] (*Thomas*,[3] *Thomas*,[2] *William* [1]), born Leighton Buzzard, January 3, 1808; died July 29, 1854; married Celia.

Issue: Two sons and three daughters. One of the sons died young.

150. i. THOMAS DOGGETT,[5] born 1839; of " H.M. Bengal Service; " died Calcutta, India, March 10, 1883; married and had two daughters.

147. WILLIAM HENRY DOGGETT [5] (*William,*[4] *Thomas,*[3] *Thomas,*[2] *William*[1]), born Leighton Buzzard, January 22, 1845; resides Netherleigh, 28 Osborne Road, Finsbury Park, London, N. (1893); married, Leighton Buzzard, January 5, 1887, by Rev. W. H. Chambers, to Ann Louisa Parsons, daughter of Jonathan Parsons.

Mr. William H. Doggett, of Leighton Buzzard, at present residing in London, has supplied many facts for the family history. He very kindly assisted by searching among the wills at Somerset House, and making extracts at the British Museum.

WILLIAM DOGGETT, OF WALTON, SOMERSET, AND HIS DESCENDANTS.

151. WILLIAM DOGGETT,[1] died 1739; married, Walton, Somerset, April 6, 1703, Mary Stafford.

Issue:

152. i. WILLIAM DOGGETT,[2] bapt. Walton, August 26, 1705.
153. ii. EDWARD DOGGETT,[2] bapt. Walton, October 26, 1707.
154. iii. MARY DOGGETT,[2] bapt. Walton, October 26, 1707.
155. iv. JAMES DOGGETT, bapt. Walton, April 9, 1710.

The registers at Walton do not go back further than 1667, from which date to 1810 search was made for entries relative to the family of Doggett.

155. JAMES DOGGETT [2] (*William*[1]), bapt. Walton, Somerset, April 9, 1710; buried Clevedon, Somerset, October 21, 1746; married Rachel; buried Clevedon, Somerset, November 10, 1776.

Issue:

156. i. WILLIAM DOGGETT,[3] bapt. August 29, 1742.
157. ii. HANNAH DOGGETT,[3] bapt. May 18, 1746.

156. WILLIAM DOGGETT [3] (*James,*[2] *William*[1]), bapt. August 29, 1742; died July 16, 1771.

William Doggett lies buried in the old churchyard at Clevedon, where is the following inscription:

" In memory of William Doggett of Pill, of the Parish of S[t]. George, who died the 16th of July, 1771, aged 28 years."

" Forbear dear wife and child to weep "
Tho' I was swallow'd in the deep.
" Tho' Neptuous waves besett me round
I hope that I have mercy found."

THOMAS DOGGET, OF WALTHAM, HOLY CROSS.

158. THOMAS DOGGET,[1] of Waltham, Holy Cross.

Issue:

159. i.   JOSEPH DOGGET,[2] bapt. Waltham, Holy Cross, September 12, 1711;
          buried, Waltham, Holy Cross, December 5, 1718.
160. ii. LYDIA DOGGET,[2] bapt. Waltham, Holy Cross, November 3, 1713.
161. iii. SARAH DOGGET,[2] bapt. Waltham, Holy Cross, October 3, 1715; buried
          Waltham, Holy Cross, December 14, 1718.
162. iv. ELIZABETH DOGGET,[2] bapt. Waltham, Holy Cross, September 21, 1719;
          buried Waltham, Holy Cross, April 18, 1720.

EDWARD DOGGETT, OF CLEVEDON, SOMERSET, AND HIS DESCENDANTS.

163. EDWARD DOGGETT,[1] born 1713; died Clevedon, Somerset,
Eng., April 12, 1779; married Martha; born 1716; died Clevedon,
Somerset, May 2, 1765.

Issue:

164. i.   EDWARD DOGGETT,[2] bapt. Clevedon, Somerset, July 17, 1737; buried
          March 12, 1737/8.
165. ii. EDWARD DOGGETT,[2] bapt. Clevedon, Somerset, May 1, 1743.
166. iii. CHARLES DOGGETT,[2] bapt. Clevedon, Somerset, March 10, 1744/5; died
          Clevedon, Somerset, May 24, 1762.
167. iv. WILLIAM DOGGETT,[2] died unmarried.
168. v.   HENRY DOGGETT,[2] bapt. Clevedon. Somerset, January 14, 1752/3; died
          Clevedon, Somerset, June 8, 1762.
169. vi. NANCY DOGGETT.[2]

165. EDWARD DOGGETT[2] (*Edward[1]*), bapt. Clevedon, Somerset,
May 1, 1743; died Clevedon, Somerset, November 18, 1811; married 1st; married 2d, 1771, Sarah Greenfield, daughter of Hugh
Greenfield, of Nailsea; born 1749; died Clevedon. Somerset, March
16, 1792.

Issue:

170. i.   MARTHA DOGGETT,[3] married Thomas Hunt.
171. ii. NANCY DOGGETT, married Benjamin Godwin.
172. iii. ELIZABETH DOGGETT,[3] born September 20, 1772; married Clevedon,
          Somerset, April 9, 1796, Richard Hayman; she died Bristol, England,
          January 12, 1847.
173. iv. HESTER DOGGETT,[3] born February 14, 1774; married Clevedon, Somer-
          set, April 18, 1812, Samuel Alvis; issue, one child, who died aged
          10 or 12 years; she was buried Wraxall, Somerset.
174. v.   EDWARD DOGGETT,[3] born August 2, 1775; married a widow, Baker;
          no issue; buried Wraxall.

175. vi.   CHARLES DOGGETT,[3] born May 11, 1777; married Hannah; she born
            1780; died January 12, 1851; he died Clevedon, Somerset, February
            19, 1855.
176. vii. WILLIAM DOGGETT,[3] born Clevedon, Somerset, January 24, 1779;
            married Elizabeth Wedmore, daughter of Thomas Wedmore, of
            Nailsea; died between 1849 and 1852.
177. viii. SARAH DOGGETT,[3] born Clevedon, Somerset, January 25, 1781; mar-
            ried Clevedon, Somerset, November 19, 1810, John Manning, of
            Barrington; died about 1848; buried at Yatton.
178. ix.   HANNAH DOGGETT,[3] born Clevedon, Somerset, May 16, 1783; married
            William Oram; died 1850 or 1851.
179 x.   MARY DOGGETT,[3] born Clevedon, Somerset, March 25, 1785; married
            Richard Bishop; no issue; died Yatton, Somerset, April 1, 1854.
180. xi.   HENRY DOGGETT,[3] born Clevedon, Somerset, July 21, 1787.
181. xii. SOPHIA DOGGETT,[3] born Clevedon, Somerset, August 17, 1789; mar-
            ried Mark May, of Puxton; issue, three sons and five daughters;
            died Puxton, Somerset, July 30, 1869.
182. xiii. HARRIET DOGGETT,[3] born Clevedon, Somerset, February 2, 1792;
            married George Wyatt, of Kingston, Seymour, Somerset; issue,
            four sons and five daughters; died Somerset, January 8, 1854.

Edward Doggett was buried at Clevedon, with the following inscription over his grave:

        " Affliction sore long time he bore,
          Physicians were in vain
          Till . . . . pleased
          To . . . ."

Sarah Doggett was also buried at Clevedon, where on her foot-
stone is the following:

        " My husband kind and children dear
          Grieve not for me in vain
          For here I rest in hopes to raise
          Salvation to obtain."

169. NANCY DOGGETT[2] (*Edward*[1]), married William Frappell.
Issue:

183. i.   WILLIAM FRAPPELL,[3] died Bedminster, leaving issue.
184. ii. HENRY FRAPPELL,[3] died Suttonwick; no issue.
185. iii. PHŒBE FRAPPELL,[3] died young.
186. iv. NANCY FRAPPELL,[3] married William Oldfield, of Bedminster; had 1 son
           and 3 daughters.

180. HENRY DOGGETT[3] (*Edward*,[2] *Edward*[1]), born Clevedon,
Somerset, July 21, 1787; died Nailsea, Somerset, December 13,
1859; married, Nailsea, Somerset, June 7, 1812, Elizabeth Coombs,
daughter of John and Hannah Coombs, of Nailsea; born September
23, 1783; died Nailsea, Somerset, January 25, 1869.
Issue:

187. i.   HENRY DOGGETT,[4] born Somerset, August 2, 1813; died Nailsea, Som-
           erset, June 17, 1841.
188. ii. HANNAH WEDMORE DOGGETT,[4] born Somerset, August 10, 1815; mar-
           ried, Severn, Glostershire, Robert Willcox, of Oldbury; no issue.
189. iii. EDWARD GREENFIELD DOGGETT,[4] born Somerset, May 25, 1817.
190. iv. ESTHER DOGGETT,[4] died Staverton or Darlington, Devon.
191. v.   CHARLES COOMBS DOGGETT,[4] born Devon, January 2, 1822; died
           February 14, 1840.

189. Edward Greenfield Doggett[4] (*Henry,*[3] *Edward,*[2] *Edward*[1]), born Somerset, May 25, 1817; died Clifton, Bristol, February 18, 1887; married 1st, West Hackney, Middlesex, June 22, 1847, Mary Evans Browett, daughter of Thomas and Mary Browett, born Northampton, November 20, 1824; died Somerset, February 21, 1856; married 2d, Maria Robinson, of Coventry; married 3d, Sarah Ann Salmond, of Bristol.

Issue:

192. i. Hugh Greenfield Doggett,[5] born Upper Montpelier, Bristol, August 25, 1853.

Mr. Edward G. Doggett was much interested in the family history, and kindly added to the collection the points he had gathered regarding his own branch and the family in early times.

192. Hugh Greenfield Doggett[5] (*Edward G.,*[4] *Henry,*[3] *Edward,*[2] *Edward*[1]), born Upper Montpelier, Bristol, August 25, 1853, "solicitor," resides 31 Richmond Terrace, Clifton, Bristol (1888); married, Hull, Yorkshire, August 1, 1878, Rachel Sibree Bremner, daughter of James and Sarah Adams (Sibree) Bremner, of Bristol; born Bristol, February 15, 1853.

Issue: 2 daughters (1883).

THOMAS DOGGETT, OF SILOE, BEDFORDSHIRE, AND HIS DESCENDANTS.

193. Thomas Doggett,[1] married.

Issue:

194. i.   George Doggett,[2] born Siloe, Bedfordshire.
195. ii.   John Doggett,[2] died.
196. iii. Elizabeth Doggett,[2] married Richard Welch.
197. iv. Mary Doggett,[2] married 1st, Robert Field; 2d, Mr. Arnold.

194. George Doggett[2] (*Thomas*[1]), born Siloe, Bedfordshire; married.

Issue:

198. i. John Doggett.[3]

198. John Doggett[3] (*George,*[2] *Thomas*[1]), married.

Issue:

199. i.   George Doggett[4] was a commercial traveller for a jewelry firm; married and had 2 sons and 1 daughter; one of the sons moved to America, 1877; a daughter also moved to America, but returned after a time.
200. ii.   Vincent Doggett,[4] born 1810.
201. iii. William Doggett,[4] married and had 3 sons and 3 daughters.
202. iv. John Doggett,[4] Inland Revenue officer; married and had 4 sons and 1 daughter.

Edward G. Doggett

203. v.   Lucy Doggett,[4] married Mr. Ward; has 3 sons, 1 daughter.
204. vi. Mary Doggett,[4] married Mr. Barnard. No issue.
205. vii. Benjamin Doggett,[4] died aged 8 years.
206. viii. Frederick Doggett,[4] "Somerset House officer," married and had 2 sons and 1 daughter.
207. ix. Thomas Doggett,[4] died.

200. Vincent Doggett[4] (*John,*[3] *George,*[2] *Thomas*[1]), born 1810; "market gardener;" resides Clophill, Ampthill, Beds. (1880); married.

Issue : 5 sons, 8 daughters.

208. 5th son Doggett,[5] born 1854, came to America 1870; died Cleveland, O., 1872.

JOHN DOGGETT, OF LONDON, AND HIS DESCENDANTS.

209. John Doggett,[1] born about 1725; died near London, Eng.; married near London, Eng.

Issue :

210. i. Henry Doggett,[2] born London, Eng.

210. Henry Doggett[2] (*John*[1]), born London, Eng.; died London, Eng.; married London, Eng.

Issue :

211. i. Henry Doggett,[3] born London, Eng.

211. Henry Doggett[3] (*Henry,*[2] *John*[1]), born London, Eng.; married Cornwall.

Issue :

212. i. Henry Doggett,[4] born Cornwall.
213. ii. Thomas Doggett.[4]
214. iii. Benjamin Doggett,[4] served on board H.M. ships.

212. Henry Doggett[4] (*Henry,*[3] *Henry,*[2] *John*[1]), born Cornwall; married London, Eng.

Issue :

215. i. Samuel Tonkin Doggett,[5] born London, Eng., May, 1828; office-stool and chair maker, 29 Mansell Street, Aldgate, London, E. (1880).

JOHN DOGGETT, OF LONDON.

216. John Doggett,[1] married Mary.

Issue :

217. i. Ruth Doggett,[2] born and christened St. James, Clerkenwell, London, March 15, 1730.
218. ii. Elizabeth Doggett,[2] born and christened St. James, Clerkenwell, London, February 12, 1732.
219. iii. Mary Doggett,[2] born and christened St. James, Clerkenwell, London, September 9, 1734.
220. iv. Susannah Doggett,[2] born and christened St. James, Clerkenwell, London, October 31, 1735.
221. v. John James Doggett,[2] born and christened St. James, Clerkenwell, London, December 21, 1737.
222. vi. Ann Doggett,[2] born April 15; christened St. James, Clerkenwell, London, April 16, 1741.

DANIEL DOGGETT AND BROTHER, OF WINFARTH-ING, NORFOLK, AND THEIR DESCENDANTS.

223. DOGGETT.[1]

Issue :

224. i.   DANIEL DOGGETT,[2] born Winfarthing, Norfolk, 1756.
225. ii. JEREMIAH DOGGETT,[2] born 1761.

224. DANIEL DOGGETT,[2] born Winfarthing, Norfolk, 1756; buried Winfarthing, Norfolk, December 29, 1840; married Arabella Betts, born 1764; died Bramfield, Suffolk; buried Winfarthing, February 17, 1849.

Issue :

226. i.   SOPHIA DOGGETT,[3] bapt. Winfarthing, Norfolk, May 3, 1789; married Robert Howard, of Bramfield, Suffolk, October 6, 1812.
227. ii.   WILLIAM DOGGETT,[3] bapt. Winfarthing, Norfolk, July 25, 1790.
228. iii. HARRIET DOGGETT,[3] buried Winfarthing, Norfolk, October 5, 1791.
229. iv.   EDWARD DOGGETT,[3] bapt. Winfarthing, Norfolk, 1791; died Shelford, Cambridge; buried Winfarthing, June 16, 1849.
230. v.   CAROLINE DOGGETT,[3] bapt. Winfarthing, Norfolk, April 27, 1794.
231. vi.   GEORGE DOGGETT,[3] bapt. Winfarthing, Norfolk, June 14, 1795.
232. vii. HENRY DOGGETT,[3] bapt. Winfarthing, Norfolk, December 18, 1796.
233. viii. PHILIP DOGGETT,[3] bapt. Winfarthing, Norfolk; buried Winfarthing, Norfolk, August 4, 1799.
234. ix.   HARRIET DOGGETT,[3] bapt. 1801; buried Winfarthing, Norfolk, December 13, 1809.
235. x.   FRANCIS DOGGETT,[3] bapt. Winfarthing, Norfolk, December 2, 1804; removed to United States, 1849; died United States America, 1870.
236. xi.   EMILY DOGGETT,[3] bapt. Winfarthing, Norfolk; married Mr. Cowell, of Ipswich, Suffolk, where she lives (1880).

The Winfarthing oak stands on the estate of the Right Honorable the Earl of Albemarle, in the midst of what was formerly " Winfarthing Great Park," anciently a royal demesne belonging to the adjacent Palace of Kenninghall Place, from which Mary of unhappy memory was called to the throne in 1553. It is conjectured that this tree must have been in existence before the Christian era. The oak in 1820 was seventy feet in circumference at the extremity of the roots. The trunk is completely hollow, and the inside presenting an appearance resembling the rugged masonry befitting a Druidical temple.

Over the doorway entrance is placed by the late Mr. Doggett, many years the respected tenant of the surrounding farm, a brass plate with an inscription soliciting from visitors to the oak donations for the Bible Society :

"Ye who this venerable Oak survey,
    Which still survives through many a stormy day,
Deposit here your mite with willing hands,
To spread in foreign climes, through foreign lands,
The Sacred Volume so divinely given
Whose pages teach the narrow way to Heaven."
                                            DOGGETT.

        " O send out thy light and thy truth."
                                        KING DAVID.

" May every subject in my dominions possess a Bible and be able to read it."
                                        KING GEORGE III.

225. JEREMIAH DOGGETT,[2] abode " Little Park," a " church-warden ; " born Winfarthing, Norfolk, 1761 ; buried Winfarthing, Norfolk, June 16, 1813 ; married, Winfarthing, Norfolk, Mary Crowe; born 1763 ; buried Winfarthing, Norfolk, June 11, 1818.

Issue :

237. i.   DAVEY DOGGETT,[3] bapt. Winfarthing, Norfolk, April 6, 1788 ; buried
            Winfarthing, Norfolk, October 2, 1802.
238. ii.   JOHN DOGGETT,[3] born Winfarthing, Norfolk, February 22, 1789.
239. iii. ANN DOGGETT,[3] bapt. Winfarthing, Norfolk, October 23, 1792 ; buried
            Winfarthing, Norfolk, March 26, 179⅔.
240. iv.   JEREMIAH DOGGETT,[3] bapt. Winfarthing, Norfolk, 1794.
241. v.   RICHARD DOGGETT,[3] bapt. Winfarthing, Norfolk, July 3, 1796.
242. vi.   THOMAS DOGGETT,[3] bapt. Winfarthing, Norfolk, July 20, 1798 ; died
            London ; buried Winfarthing, December 17, 1818.
243, vii. CALVER DOGGETT,[3] bapt. Winfarthing, Norfolk, February 10, 1799 ;
            buried Winfarthing, Norfolk, February 17, 1799.
244. viii. ESTHER DOGGETT,[3] bapt. Winfarthing, Norfolk, September 18, 1803.
245. ix.   ROBERT DANIEL DOGGETT,[3] bapt. Winfarthing, Norfolk, May 13, 1807.

227. WILLIAM DOGGETT [3] (*Daniel* [2]), bapt. Winfarthing, Norfolk, July 25, 1790 ; died Newnham, Herts., August, 1859, where is a stained-glass window to his memory ; married ; she died Newnham, Herts.

Issue :

246. i.   THOMAS WILLIAM DOGGETT.[4]
247. ii.   JOHN DOGGETT.[4]
248. iii. ARTHUR DOGGETT,[4] married 1865 ; resides (1880) Newnham, Herts.

240. JEREMIAH DOGGETT [3] (*Jeremiah* [2]), bapt. Winfarthing, Norfolk, 1794 ; died Thetford, Norfolk, February 25, 1885 ; married.

Issue :

249. i.   RUSSELL DOGGETT,[4] born 1831 ; died Holkham, Norfolk, July 9, 1888.
250. ii.   RICHARD DOGGETT.[4]
251. iii. MARY DOGGETT,[4] died Wells next the Sea, England, April 16, 1888.

241. RICHARD DOGGETT [3] (*Jeremiah* [2]), bapt. Winfarthing, Norfolk, July 3, 1796 ; married Sarah Chapman.

Issue :

252. i.   JAMES RICHARD DOGGETT,[4] bapt. Winfarthing, Norfolk, August 13, 1826.
253. ii.   SARAH DOGGETT,[4] bapt. Winfarthing, Norfolk, May 28, 1828.
254. iii. MARIA DOGGETT,[4] bapt. Winfarthing, Norfolk, August 29, 1829 ; buried
            Winfarthing, Norfolk, 1829.

246. THOMAS WILLIAM DOGGETT [4] (*William,[3] Daniel [2]*), resides Sandon Bury, Royston, Herts. (1880); married 1857.

Issue:

255. i.   WILLIAM HAROLD DOGGETT,[5] born 1859.
256. ii. FRANK FOSTER DOGGETT,[5] born 1863.
257. iii. ARTHUR HENRY DOGGETT,[5] born 1865.
258. iv. FLORENCE EMILY DOGGETT,[5] born 1867.
259. v.   ELLA MARY DOGGETT,[5] born 1872.
260. vi. ROSA ETHEL DOGGETT,[5] born 1878.

247. JOHN DOGGETT [4] (*William,[3] Daniel [2]*), born England; removed to the United States; resides Kansas City, Mo. (1892); married.

Issue:

261. i.   ARTHUR DOGGETT.[5]
262. ii. HERBERT L. DOGGETT.[5]
263. iii. ISABEL DOGGETT.[5]

Mr. Doggett is one of the most prominent men of Kansas City, and is president of the Doggett Dry Goods Company.

263. ISABEL DOGGETT [5] (*John,[4] William,[3] Daniel [2]*), married Kansas City, Mo., June 6, 1888, by Rev. C. L. Thompson, to Arthur Chandler Coates, son of Kersey Coates.

THOMAS DOGGETT, OF STOKE, MIDDLESEX, AND HIS DESCENDANTS.

264. THOMAS DOGGETT,[1] of Stoke Newington, Middlesex, married Elizabeth Bouts.

Issue:

265. i.   JAMES DOGGETT,[2] died single.
266. ii. THOMAS DOGGETT,[2] born July 13, 1770.
267. iii. ELIZABETH DOGGETT,[2] married Edward Woollams.
268. iv. SARAH DOGGETT,[2] died young.
269. v.   FREDERICK DOGGETT,[2] born August 3, 1772.
270. vi. ANN DOGGETT,[2] died single.

266. THOMAS DOGGETT [2] (*Thomas [1]*), born July 13, 1770; married.

Issue:

271. i.   THOMAS DOGGETT,[3] born August 1, 1800; married.
272. ii. MARY DOGGETT,[3] born July 23, 1805; living (1884).
273. iii. JAMES DOGGETT,[3] born May 15, 1806; married and had daughter who married Mr. Ward; she lives (1884) Montreal, Canada.

269. FREDERICK DOGGETT[2] (*Thomas*[1]), born August 3, 1772; died February 10, 1852; married October 28, 1798, Ann Dawborne; born February 28, 1775; died November 29, 1853.

Issue:

274. i.   ELIZABETH BARTON DOGGETT,[3] born August 25, 1799.
275. ii.   SARAH DOGGETT,[3] born May 13, 1801; married November 2, 1824, William Chaldecott; died May 27, 1883.
276. iii. MARY DOGGETT,[3] born March 23, 1803; married December, 1827, Thomas Watts Chaldecott; died December 1, 1880.
277. iv.   CHARLES DOGGETT,[3] born August 16, 1804; died September 25, 1804.
278. v.   CHARLES COOPER DOGGETT,[3] born December 11, 1805; "poet;" died December 10, 1846.
279. vi.   MARTHA DOGGETT,[3] born August 26, 1807; married October, 1828, James Goddard Chaldecott; died October 21, 1874.
280. vii. ANN DOGGETT,[3] born July 30, 1809; married May 25, 1848, Samuel Bouts.
281. viii. JANE BARTON DOGGETT,[3] born March 31, 1811; died July 24, 1871.
282. ix.   FREDERICK WILLIAM DOGGETT,[3] born February 10, 1813.
283. x.   PHEBE DAWBORNE DOGGETT,[3] born March 3, 1815; died July 26, 1882.
284. xi.   CAROLINE BOUTS DOGGETT,[3] born July 9, 1818.

282. FREDERICK WILLIAM DOGGETT[3] (*Frederick*,[2] *Thomas*[1]), born February 10, 1813; died August 16, 1871; married, St. Johns, Hackney, May 16, 1842, Lydia Jane Thompson.

Issue:

285. i.   ADA DOGGETT,[4] born April 12, 1844; died June 21, 1848.
286. ii.   ARTHUR DOGGETT,[4] born October 10, 1845; died October 18, 1845.
287. iii. FREDERICK ERNEST DOGGETT,[4] born October 2, 1846; resides Pockthorp, Norwich (1883).
288. iv.   CHARLES ALFRED DOGGETT,[4] born February 9, 1848; resides 21 Lordship Park, Stoke Newington (1883).
289. v.   FLORENCE MAUD DOGGETT,[4] born April 23, 1849.
290. vi.   WILLIAM LEONARD DOGGETT,[4] born March 25, 1851; resides 42 Kyverdale Road, Stoke Newington (1883).
291. vii. EVELYN LYDIA DOGGETT,[4] born July 7, 1853.
292. viii. HENRY EDGAR DOGGETT,[4] born September 1, 1854; resides Leytonstone, Essex (1883).

284. CAROLINE BOUTS DOGGETT[3] (*Frederick*,[2] *Thomas*[1]), born July 9, 1818; resides "The Cottage," Holmwood, Dorking, Surrey (1883).

Miss Doggett is the author of many instructive tales. She was assisted by her sister, Phebe D. Doggett, who passed away in 1882. Among their works are "Brookleigh Manor," "Seedtime and Harvest," "My Garden Party," "Nellie Graham," "The Light on the Beacon Rock," "Minnie and Mopsey," "The Two Houses, and Lost and Found," "The Autobiography of Trusty."

THOMAS DOGGETT, OF UPWELL, CAMBRIDGE-SHIRE, AND HIS DESCENDANTS.

Arms: Gules, two greyhounds, salient, combatant, argent, collared, sa.

Crest: A lion's head, erased or, gorged with a mural coronet sable.

Motto: "In collo guies."

293. THOMAS DOGGETT,[1] born Huntingdon (?); died (buried Upwell Churchyard) 1793 or 1794; married Miss Phillips.

Issue:

294. i.	WILLIAM DOGGETT,[2] born Upwell, Cambridgeshire, April 23, 1787..
295. ii.	THOMAS DOGGETT,[2] born Upwell. Cambridgeshire, June 17, 1789; died East Indies, August 7, 1812.
296. iii.	JOHN DOGGETT,[2] born Upwell, Cambridgeshire, March 20, 1791.

The Christian name of the first known ancestor of this branch is supposed to be Thomas, although not positively known. He came from Huntingdon in 1760. At one time he enlisted as a soldier, but whether before or after marriage is unknown. He deserted and came to live at Upwell, Cambridgeshire.

His wife, who was Miss Phillips, had a brother who lived in Old Charge City.

Mrs. Doggett married, 2d, Samuel Beckett. by whom she had children Samuel and Ann.

A brother of Thomas was head gardener at one of the colleges at Cambridge University, and had a daughter or daughters who went to St. Ives, Herts.

294. WILLIAM DOGGETT[2] (*Thomas*[1]). born Upwell. Cambridgeshire, April 23, 1787; died May 8, 1833; married March 6, 1810, Ann Biggs.

Issue:

297. i.	MARY ANN DOGGETT,[3] born London, England, November 16, 1811.
298. ii.	THOMAS ISAAC DOGGETT,[3] born September 25. 1813; died May 3, 1817.
299. iii.	SUSAN DOGGETT,[3] born November 6, 1815; died March 27, 1818.
300. iv.	JOHN DOGGETT,[3] born September 3, 1817; died 1820.
301. v.	SARAH DOGGETT,[3] born April 19, 1820; died January 31, 1849.
302. vi.	WILLIAM DOGGETT,[3] born August 13, 1822; died October 1, 1877.
303. vii.	THOMAS DOGGETT,[3] born October 19, 1824; married; several children.
304. viii.	DINAH DOGGETT,[3] born October 23, 1826.
305. ix.	REBECCA DOGGETT,[3] born March 19, 1829.
306. x.	JABEZ DOGGETT,[3] born October 10, 1832.

William Doggett came to London from Cambridgeshire, and was employed by a wholesale tea-dealer as warehouseman.

296. JOHN DOGGETT [2] (*Thomas* [1]), born Upwell, Cambridgeshire, March 20, 1791; died London, 1825; married, 1812, Hannah Prior.
Issue:

307. i. HANNAH DOGGETT,[3] born London, Eng., 1813.
308. ii. WILLIAM DOGGETT,[3] born London, Eng., 1818; died 1819.
309. iii. ELIZA DOGGETT,[3] born London, Eng., 1820; died 1844.
310. iv. JOHN DOGGETT,[3] born London, Eng., 1822.
311. v. MARTHA DOGGETT,[3] born London, Eng., 1824.

John Doggett came to London, and was employed as a warehouseman at a wholesale tea-dealer's.

310. JOHN DOGGETT [3] (*John*,[2] *Thomas* [1]), born London, Eng., 1822; married.
Issue:

312. i. JOHN THOMAS DOGGETT,[4] born London, Eng., 1849; resides 3 Chepstow terrace, Malfort road, Denmark Park, London, S.E. (1880).
313. ii. GEORGE DOGGETT,[4] born 1851; married.
314. iii. EMILY DOGGETT,[4] born 1853; married.
315. iv. JAMES DOGGETT,[4] born 1855; died in infancy.
316. v. ALFRED DOGGETT,[4] born 1856.
317. vi. WILLIAM CHARLES DOGGETT,[4] born 1858.
318. vii. FREDERICK JAMES DOGGETT,[4] born 1861.
319. viii. CLARA ELIZABETH DOGGETT,[4] born 1863.

JOSEPH DOGGETT, OF LONDON, AND HIS DESCENDANTS.

320. JOSEPH DOGGETT [1] was of the firm "Taylor & Doggett," boot and shoe makers to His Royal Highness the Duke of Gloucester, Davies street, Berkeley square, London, Eng.
Issue:

321. i. JOSEPH DOGGETT.[2]
322. ii. WILLIAM DOGGETT,[2] born London, Eng., 1810.
323. iii. MARTIN DOGGETT.[2]
324. iv. JANE DOGGETT.[2]
325. v. EMILY DOGGETT.[2]
326. vi. FANNY DOGGETT.[2]
327. vii. ROSA DOGGETT.[2]

322. WILLIAM DOGGETT [2] (*Joseph* [1]), born London, Eng., 1810; removed to America 1835; killed in a railroad accident July 27, 1879; married New York, 1838, Matilda Davis; born N.S., 1821; died Brooklyn, N.Y., January 24, 1878.
Issue:

328. i. JOSEPH DOGGETT,[3] born New York, January 29, 1839.
329. ii. MARIA DOGGETT,[3] born 1842; married Peter Folk, "sash and blind maker;" issue: Peter Augustus Folk and William Folk; resides Brooklyn, N.Y. (1883).
330. iii. SUSAN DOGGETT,[3] died in infancy.
331. iv. EMILY DOGGETT,[3] died in infancy.
332. v. LUCINDA DOGGETT,[3] married, 1st, Leander Woodhull; married, 2d, Levere Clark; issue: Josie Woodhull.

William Doggett, when a boy, was indentured to a "currier" to learn the trade.

328. JOSEPH DOGGETT [3] (*William,*[2] *Joseph* [1]), born New York, January 29, 1839; resides 181 N. Seventh street, Brooklyn, N.Y. (1883); married August 14, 1864, Sarah Jane DeWolf; born August 16, 1848.

Issue :

333. i. WILLIAM BENJAMIN DOGGETT,[4] born October 22, 1865; resides 741 Dorchester avenue, Boston (1892).
334. ii. JOSEPH DOGGETT,[4] born September 14, 1867; died February 19, 1875.
335. iii. SARAH MARIA DOGGETT,[4] born March 31, 1869; died August 31, 1870.
336. iv. OLIVER HOYT DOGGETT,[4] born December 19, 1870; died December 22, 1871.
337. v. EDGAR DOGGETT,[4] born August 29, 1872; died June 25, 1873.
338. vi. CHARLES HENRY DOGGETT,[4] born February 6, 1875.
339. vii. GEORGE HOLLIS DOGGETT,[4] born August 1, 1879.
340. viii. SEAMAN GARFIELD DOGGETT,[4] born August 15, 1881.
341. ix. MARTHA WASHINGTON DOGGETT,[4] born February 22, 1883; died February 28, 1883.

WILLIAM DOGGETT AND BROTHERS, OF HERT-FORDSHIRE, AND THEIR DESCENDANTS.

Issue :

342. i. WILLIAM DOGGETT,[1] head park ranger to Lord Clarendon, Grove Park, Watford, Herts.; died 1815.
343. ii. DANIEL DOGGETT.[1]
344. iii. RUBEN DOGGETT.[1]
345. iv. JONATHAN DOGGETT.[1]
346. v. JOHN DOGGETT[1] left England for Salt Lake City, U.S. No further reported.
347. vi. THOMAS ABENDIGO DOGGETT,[1] born Penmans Green, Herts., 1795.

347. THOMAS ABENDIGO DOGGETT,[1] born Penmans Green, Herts., 1795; died 1869; married.

Issue : 3 sons, 2 daughters.

348. i. WILLIAM DOGGETT.[2]
349. ii. FREDERICK DOGGETT,[2] manager of the leather manufactory of Mr. Margetson, of Bermondsey.
350. iii. MONTAGUE DOGGETT.[2]
351. iv. —— DOGGETT,[2] born Rickemansworth; one daughter lives there.
352. v. Daughter —— DOGGETT,[2] died.

Thomas A. Doggett was first dog-boy to Lord Essex, Cassiobury Park, Herts., from whence he was employed under his brother William, who was head park ranger to Lord Clarendon, Grove Park, Watford. Here he remained until he was fourteen years old, when he was apprenticed to a carpenter and joiner, with whom he remained six years.

At this time, 1815, he became head park ranger to Lord Clarendon, taking the position made vacant by the death of his elder brother.

On the death of Lord Clarendon he resigned his position, and followed his trade as carpenter to Lord Ebery, Moor Park, Rickemansworth, Herts., in which occupation he remained until his death in 1869.

348. WILLIAM DOGGETT [2] (*Thomas A.* [1]) resides London; married. Issue:

353. i. FREDERICK WILLIAM DOGGETT.[3]
354. ii. GEORGE WOODBRIDGE DOGGETT.[3]
355. iii. WILLIAM HARRY DOGGETT.[3]
356. iv. MONTAGUE DOGGETT.[3]
357. v. Daughter —— DOGGETT.[3]
358. vi. Daughter —— DOGGETT.[3]

William Doggett began his life as dog-boy under his father, and then went into the stables of Mr. Peter Chutterbuck, New House, Herts.

On June 20, 1842, he walked to London and engaged himself as groom to the family of Mrs. Margetson, of Peckham Rye.

From there he soon went into the service of her son, a Bermondsey leather manufacturer, and at his suggestion, in 1850, Mr. Doggett established himself as a leather stripper and manufacturer on Baalzephon, now Weston street.

The great success which has attended his efforts and the respect in which he is held may be seen by an article which appeared in the " Leather Trades Review " regarding the completion of his new warehouse, in 1878.

As an illustration of the manner in which individual energy and enterprise may affect the character and prospects of an entire industry, the business of Mr. Doggett is referred to, as almost wholly monopolizing the business of stripping, which formerly occupied several small establishments. Mr. Doggett is mentioned as one of the best known and respected members of the metropolitan leather trades.

The success achieved by him is the more remarkable and encouraging by reason of the same having been self-acquired. Nothing is impossible to those who possess strong wills.

The building just completed (1878) stands as a monument to his indomitable skill and energy.

JOHN DOGGETT, OF HERTFORDSHIRE, AND HIS DESCENDANTS.

359. JOHN DOGGETT,[1] born (Hertfordshire?); " Builder of St. Albans, Herts. ;" married.

Issue :

360. i. THOMAS DOGGETT.[2]
361. ii. ANN DOGGETT.[2]
362. iii. JOHN DOGGETT.[2]
363. iv. JOSEPH DOGGETT.[2]

360. THOMAS DOGGETT [2] (*John* [1]).

Issue :

364. i. JOSEPH ROBERT DOGGETT,[3] born London, Eng., April, 1817.

364. JOSEPH ROBERT DOGGETT [3] (*Thomas,*[2] *John* [1]), born London, Eng., April, 1817 ; married London, Eng., 1836, Amy Dennett.

Issue :

365. i.   DINAH MARY ANN DOGGETT,[4] born London, Eng., 1836 ; married London, Eng., James Wealleans ; issue, 10 children ; resides New Zealand (1884).
366. ii. ROBERT DOGGETT,[4] born London, Eng., 1838 ; died 1841.
367. iii. YOUNG DOGGETT,[4] born London, Eng., 1840.
368. iv. ELIZABETH CAROLINE DOGGETT,[4] born London, Eng., 1843 ; married London, Henry Cook ; issue, 4 children ; resides Leddescomb, Sussex.
369. v.   THOMAS JAMES DOGGETT,[4] born London, Eng., 1846 ; " Tin Plate Worker," 4 Church lane, Islington, London (1884).
370. vi. ROBERT JOSEPH DOGGETT,[4] born London, Eng., 1848 ; died London, Eng., 1852.
371. vii. HARRY DOGGETT,[4] born London, Eng., 1852.
372. viii. AMY DOGGETT,[4] born London, Eng., 1853.

367. YOUNG DOGGETT [4] (*Joseph Robert,*[3] *Thomas,*[2] *John* [1]), born London, Eng., 1840 ; married London, Eng., Rosa May ; she died before 1884.

Issue :

373. i. AMY DOGGETT.[5]
374. ii. ROSA DOGGETT.[5]

371. HARRY DOGGETT [4] (*Joseph Robert,*[3] *Thomas,*[2] *John* [1]), born London, Eng., 1852 ; married London, Eng., Emily Basset.

Issue :

375. i. THOMAS DOGGETT.[5]
376. ii. EMILY DOGGETT.[5]

372. AMY DOGGETT [4] (*Joseph Robert,*[3] *Thomas,*[2] *John* [1]), born London, Eng., 1853 ; married London, Eng., Edwin Mackenzie.

Issue :

377. i. EDWIN MACKENZIE.[5]

GEORGE DOGGETT AND BROTHER, AND THEIR DESCENDANTS.

Issue:

378. i. GEORGE DOGGETT.[1]
379. ii. EDGAR DOGGETT[1] was librarian and secretary to Lord Holland, Holland House, Kensington, Eng.

378. GEORGE DOGGETT.[1]
Issue:

380. i. FREDERICK E. DOGGETT.[2]

380. FREDERICK E. DOGGETT[2] (*George*[1]), removed to America between 1872 and 1874; resides New York city; married Liverpool, Eng., May 10, 1857, Sarah Ann Hilton; resides 1311 Castle avenue, Philadelphia, Pa. (1887).

Issue:

381. i. FREDERICK WILLIAM ERNEST DOGGETT,[3] born Great Malvern, Worcestershire, Eng., March 11, 1858; of Doggett Bros., New York; resides Brooklyn, N.Y. (1889).
382. ii. MADELINE JANE DOGGETT,[3] born Dublin, Ire., July 22, 1859; resides Philadelphia, Pa. (1889).
383. iii. SIDNEY HERBERT DOGGETT,[3] born St. Pancras, London, Eng., September 20, 1861.
384. iv. AMY ELIZABETH DOGGETT,[3] born Hammersmith, Middlesex, Eng., November 19, 1863.
385. v. HILTON JOHN DOGGETT,[3] born Hammersmith, Middlesex, Eng., December 14, 1865; of Doggett Bros., New York; resides Brooklyn, N.Y. (1889).
386. vi. EVELYN DOGGETT,[3] born Hammersmith, Middlesex, Eng., January 4, 1868.
387. vii. STANLEY DOGGETT,[3] born Hammersmith, Middlesex, Eng., January 24, 1870.
388. viii. GERTRUDE OCTAVIA DOGGETT,[3] born Hammersmith, Middlesex, Eng., April 13, 1872.
389. ix. REGINALD LOUIS SCOTT DOGGETT,[3] born Hoboken, N.J., June 14, 1874.
390. x. GEORGE HENRY DOGGETT,[3] born Brooklyn, N.Y., July 25, 1877.

384. AMY ELIZABETH DOGGETT[3] (*Frederick E.*,[2] *George*[1]), born Hammersmith, Middlesex, Eng., November 19, 1863; resides 1618 So. Carlisle street, Philadelphia, Pa. (1889); married Philadelphia, Pa., September 18, 1888, by Rev. Henry R. Percival, to J. Frank Peterson, son of John Henry and Mary Nixon [Cline] Peterson, born Philadelphia, Pa., June 15, 1866.

WILLIAM DAGGETT, OF MANCHESTER, AND HIS DESCENDANTS.

391. WILLIAM DAGGETT,[1] married in Higtonshire a daughter of Capt. John Cumming, of the Royal Navy.

Issue:

392. i. ROBERT DAGGATT.[2]
393. ii. GEORGE DAGGATT,[2] born 1809; "minister."

William Daggett, who also called his name Daggatt, was a lieutenant in the navy. He was on board the "Royal George," Admiral Kempenfeldt being first cousin to his father, and while he was sent on shore to the library, the ship was lost, and about eight hundred persons drowned. His likeness set in gold is in the possession of his descendants.

On his return from the West Indies he found his effects had been administered upon, as his mother had heard that he had died there of yellow fever.

On his marriage he left the navy, and commenced cotton spinning, at Manchester, in 1810.

He had two half-sisters, one of whom married a Powell. About 1800 this family of Powell took the name of Daggett, and went to America — New York, it is reported.

It is said that William Daggett changed the spelling of his name to Daggatt, because it rhymed:

> "Two A's, two T's, two G's, and a D,
> Put them together and spell them for me."

392. ROBERT DAGGATT[2] (*William*[1]), educated as a minister in the Scottish church; died Hulme, Manchester, Eng.; married.

Issue:

394. i. WILLIAM CUMMING DAGGATT[3] called his name Daggett; married and died before 1885.
395. ii. CHARLES HENRY DOUGLAS DAGGATT,[3] captain and quartermaster Her Majesty's Auxiliary Forces, Old Trafford, Manchester (1885).

—

GEORGE DAGGITT, OF WHITCOMB, YORKSHIRE, AND HIS DESCENDANTS.

396. GEORGE DAGGITT;[1] married.

Issue:

397. i. GEORGE DAGGITT,[2] born Whitcomb, Yorkshire, Eng.
398. ii. JOHN DAGGITT,[2] born Whitcomb, Yorkshire, Eng.

397. GEORGE DAGGITT[2] (*George*[1]), born Whitcomb, Yorkshire, England; came to America 1815; died New York city, 1840; married England, Elizabeth Moody; born Nottingham, Eng.; died New York city, September 19, 1860.

Issue: Seven children.

399. i. SARAH ELIZABETH DAGGITT,[3] married Samuel Burhans, Jr., 37 Maiden lane, N.Y. (1883).
400. ii. Son —— DAGGITT, married and had John Daggitt, who resides Bay Shore, L.I. (1883).

George Daggitt and his wife and brother John Daggitt arrived in America from England in 1815.

The vessel they sailed in, was wrecked in the Bay of Fundy, and they were taken from the wreck and brought to New York city.

398. JOHN DAGGITT[2] (*George*[1]), born Whitcomb, Yorkshire, Eng.; came to America 1815; called his name Daggett; died New Jersey; married.

John Daggett, after residing many years in New York, retired from business and bought a farm in New Jersey.

WILLIAM DOGGETT, OF LONG STANTON, AND HIS DESCENDANTS.

401. WILLIAM DOGGETT,[1] lived in Long Stanton; married.
Issue:

402. i. WILLIAM DOGGETT.[2]
403. ii. JOHN DOGGETT,[2] married and had two sons.

402. WILLIAM DOGGETT[2] (*William*[1]), married.
Issue:

404. i. JOHN W. DOGGETT,[3] born Long Stanton; "farmer," Grange Farm, near Cambridge, also one at Lolworth.
405. ii. Son —— DOGGETT,[3] resides Long Stanton (1880).
406. iii. Daughter —— DOGGETT,[3] died 1880.

DOGGETT-DAGGETT.

GLEANINGS IN ENGLAND.

407. 1076, Raymond Duket.

408. 1119, Herbert Duchet, or Doket, St. Albans Abbey.

409. 1200, The Dogets were vintners down to the early part of the thirteenth century. (City Press, July 11, 1868.) The Doggetts seem to have been opulent vintners in London. (London and London Life, 1276–1419.)

410. 1206, Amecia Ducet.

411. 1219, John Doget, of Hutton. (In the Dodswork MS., 27, the same name appears as Doket, Doget, Duket, Docket. In MS. 112 Dod. (copies of the Testa de Nevil), the same orthography is repeated.

412. 1228, Robert Dogget granted lands by fine to the prior of Westacre in Appleton.

413. 1250, John, son of Reginald de Inglose, quitclaimed land in Lodne, formerly Dogget's, to the Abbot of Langley.

414. 1278, Richard Doget, of Lincolnshire.

415. 1281–1311, Nicholas Duchet, of Hainston, Lincolnshire, under the orthography of Tuchet or Tuschet, was summoned 9 Edwd 1st to answer certain questions.

416. 1283, Simon Doget, also Dokett.

417. 1288, Petr' Doget, de corf pro Priore de Warham Whyte veye terr' &c. 16 Edwd 1st Dorset (Calendarium Inquisition Post Mortem sive Escaetarum, Vol. I., No. 46, page 97).

418. 1291, John Doget, of East Barnet, Herts., an inhabitant with small assessment.

419. 1291, Peter Doget and wife Margery, land in Sussex.

420. 1294, Adam Doget had a house at Winchester.

421. 1295, John Doget.

422. 1296, Rogerus Doget, 24 Edward 1st, Hildresham, maner extent, Cantabri, Boterwyk, maner extent, Lincoln; Estboterwyk, extent terr. and Lincoln. [Cal. Inq., No. 43, page 128.]

423. 1297, ROBERTUS DOGET et Alicia. [Vol. 1, F 18, p. 49, Harleian Charters, MS. B.M.]

424. 1297, ROBERT DOGET, a baker, of Wallingford, assessed to taxes there.

425. 1305, ROBERT DOGETT, and Alice, his wife, held here (Rochford Hundred Essex) 1 messuage and 26 acres of arable land, purchased by (**426**) BEATRIX DOGETT, and 60 acres purchased by John Rocheford. [Hist. and Antiquities of Essex, 1768.]

427. 1305, ROBERTUS DOGET et Alicia, uxor ejus Rocheford unum messuag' & iiij—xx acrterr & 20 terr itm de Reilegh baronia, Essex, 33 Edward 1st. [Cal. Inq., No. 199, page 203.]

428. 1305, DOGGETT or DOCCET is a reputed manor, and was holden by an ancient family of that name in 1305; belonged to the Earl of Warwick in 1619; belongs now to Hon. W. T. S. P. Wellesley. [Hist. Essex, London, 1836, page 593, Vol. II.]

429. 1307, ROBERT DOKET, held land at Ampthill, Beds.

430. 1313,) RICHARD DOGGET, vicar of Hardley, Norfolk. [25
1370,) Edward III.]

431. 1321, WILLIAM DOGET.

432. 1334, ROBERT DAGGET, rector of Gillingham, was presented to the living, by Thomas de Brotherton, Earl of Norfolk.

433. 1340, ADAM DOGET held land in Essex.

434. 1342, WILLIAM DOGET [16 Edward III.].

435. 1346, GALFRUS DOGET [19 Edward III.], Bulenore in Insula Vectis 60 acr'terr, &c., ut de honore castri de Caresbrok, Southton. (Cal. Inq., No. 12, page 122, Vol. II.)

436. 1354, MARGARETA fil et heres GALFRIDI DOGET (**437**) Bolenore 40 acr'terr, &c., ut de honore castri de Caresbrok, Southton. 27 Edward III. [Cal. Inq., No. 42, page 182, Vol. II.]

438. 1357, STEPHANS DOGET [30 Edward III.].

439. 1358, EUDO DOGET, de Cumberworth, 31 Edward III., Cumberworth 3 acr'terr, &c., Lincoln. [Cal. Inq., No. 20, page 202, Vol. II.]

440. 1370, Sir JOHN DOGET changed lands in Morningthorp with John Martyn, for Hoxne.

441. 1371, RICHARD DUKET, of Norfolk.

442. 1372, RICHARD DOGET, late Vicar of Hardale, patron of Yelverton.

443. 1392, JOHN DOGET, on inquisition mentioned as holding land at Herts.

444. 1395, JOHN DOGET, of Dover, grants lands at Hythe to St. Bartholomew Hospital, London.

445. 1399, JOHN DOGET, his heirs and assigns, is granted messauges at Snettesham by Sir William Flete, Knight, on Wednesday after Feast of St. Peter.

446. 1399, WILLIAM DUCKET.

447. 1400, MARMADUKE DUKET.

448. 1400, THOMAS DOGGET, Rector, Lawford Rectory.

449. 1406, RAD DOGET, 7 Henry IV.

450. 1417, RICHARD DUKET.

451. 1417, RICHARD DOKET, Norfolk.

452. 1428, RICHARD DOKET, named in Close Rolls.

453. 1429, RICHARD DOKET.

454. 1430, RICHARD DOGET, 8 Henry VI.

455. 1433, May 9, will of JOHN DOGET, of Coddicott, Herts., wife Joan, son (**456**) JOHN, no probate (Stoneham Arch, St. Albans, 24).

457. 1450, ALICE DOGETT.

458. 1450, February 22, RICHARD DOKET, 28 Henry VI.

459. 1453, RICHARD DOGET, 31 Henry VI.

460. 1459, RICHARD DOKET.

461. 1459, HENRY DUKET.

462. 1464, JOHN DOGGETT, of Ashill.

463. 1467, July 22, ANDREW DOKETT, A.M., collated in Lichfield. 1470, exchanged it for the chancellorship. [Brown Willis, Survey of Cathedrals, 1742, Vol. I., page 457.]

464. 1469, HENRY DOGET. [Harleian Charters, MS. B. M., Vol. III., p. 233.]

465. 1469, JOHN DOCKETT.

466. 1470, ANDREW DOKET or DRICKET, first master of Queen's College, Cambridge; was admitted about 1470; chancellor of Lichfield, and resigned July 6, 1476. [Brown Willis, Survey of Cathedrals, 1742, Vol. I., page 437.]

467. 1488, JOHN DOKETT.

468. 1492, } WILLIAM DOGETT, Mayor of Bristol, Eng. (Entry 1494, } from account book of Co. of Tuckers.)

469. 1496, THOMAS DOGGET, Rector of Burnham, buried in Norwich Cathedral.

470. 1509, JOHN DOGET, Sheriff of London. (Allen's Hist. London, Vol. II., page 265.) Was also alderman of London, and owned a tomb [1509] in the church of St. John the Evangelist.

471. 1511, ⎧ JOHN DOGGETT, Senr.
472. 1515, ⎨ JOHN DOGGETT, Jr. [Somerset House, "Fetiplace."]

473. 1515, MARGERY DOGGET, widow, tombstone in Norwich Cathedral.

474. 1515, John Dogget, buried by St. Barbara's Altar, Norwich Cathedral,

475. 1522, } Joan Doggett. [Somerset House, "Bodfelde."]
1524, }

476. 1521, } Thomas Doggett, vicar, Clacton Magna.
1529, }

477. 1528, Ralph Ducket.

478. 1529, Richard Doggett, East Winch, will [Norwich].

479. 1532, Anthony Dogett, vicar of Totham Magna.

480. 1535, William Duckett.

481. 1545. May 30, Thomas Dyrgatt, buried, St. Dionis Backchurch, London.

482. 1555, Margaret Doggett, Horning, widow, will. [Consistory of Norwich.]

483. 1556, Elizabeth Doggett, Wormegay, widow, will. [Consistory of Norwich.]

484. 1556, Hakewell Docettes, alias Dogettys.

485. 1557, { July 26, Jamys Docket, son of Dr. Peter Docket,

486. { christened at St. Dionis Backchurch.

487. 1558, Robert Doggett, held lands at Albany, Herts.

488. 1559, Edmund Doggett, Wormegay, will. [Consistory of Norfolk.]

489. 1561, Doggett married a Wade, of Bildeston (about then).

490. "   "   Goswold   "

491. "   "   Stubbey   "

492. 1561, Robert Gosnell, of Otley, Esq., married, 2d, Anne Bacon, daughter of Richard Doggett, and had no issue. [Visitation of Suffolk, Harleian Col.]

493. 1561, July 9, William Doggett, of Morningthorpe, adm., granted on his estate to Rose Doggett the relict. [Consis. Court of Norwich.]

494. 1564, Thomas Doggett married Joan Hext, daughter of John and Elizabeth, and heir of P. Colswell, of Exeter. [Visitation of Devonshire, Guildhall Library.]

495. 1572, February 22, John Doggett, son of Thomas, bapt. Harleston, Norfolk.

496. 1573, January 27, John Doggett, of Stratton, Strawless, adm., granted to Alice Doggett, relict. [Consistory of Norwich.]

497. 1574, July 4, Christopher Docket and Esbell Flecher, widow, married Waltham, Holy Cross.

498. 1576, March 17, Thomas Doggett, son of Richard, bapt. Harleston, Norfolk.

499. 1576, September 4, Marie Doget and Edwarde Lewes married at St. Mary's, Aldermay, London. [Harleian Society.]

500. 1576, June 18, ANNA DOGETT married Simond Pollinge, bachelor, Groton, Suffolk.

501. 157⅘, February 19, WILLIAM DOCET, of Crichurch, married Joane Reade, of parish of St. Dionis Backchurch.

502. 1579, June 7, ROBERT DOGGETT, son of Richard, bapt. Harleston, Norfolk.

503. 1583, April 28, FRANCIS DOGGETT, son of Bryan, bapt. Harleston, Norfolk.

504. 1585, January 2, WILLIAM DOGGETT, son of Richard, bapt. Harleston, Norfolk.

505. 1585, October 10, WILLIAM DOGGETT, son of Bryan, bapt. Harleston, Norfolk.

506. 1587, JOHN DUCKET.

507. 1588, JAMES DUCKETT.

508. 1588, February 9, JOHN DOGGETT, son of Bryan, bapt. Harleston, Norfolk.

509. 1590, JOHN DOGGETT, of Albany, Herts., held lands there, next to those of (**510**) WILLIAM DOGGETT.

511. 1600 (about), WILLIAM DOGGETT, of Ipswich, married Anne, daughter of Geoffrey and Anne Langley, of Colchester.

512. 1603, December 15, FRANCIS DOGGETT, buried Harleston, Norfolk.

513. 1604, FRANCIS DOGGETT, Harleston, will. [Consistory of Norwich.]

514. 1613, JOHN DOGGETT, Harleston, will. [Consistory of Norfolk.]

515. 1615, April 24, BRIDGET DOGGETT, of St. Dunstan, West London, daughter of —— Doggett, deceased, and Nathaniel Court, of same, cloth worker, at St. Dunstan, aforesaid. [London Marriage Licenses.]

516. 1617, August 24, WILLIAM DOGGETT, buried Bungay, Suffolk.

517. 1621, ANDREW DOGGETT, East Dereham, will. [Consistory of Norfolk.]

518. 1625, Assessed to the Subsidy in Hadleigh, 22 James I., AVICE DOGETT, for Lands inj¹ xoj, Woodkecke St.

519. 1626, THOMAS DOGGETT, gent., lands Woodkecke St. iij xij. [Davy's Suff. Coll., Vol. 51.]

520. 1631, September 4, RICHARD DOGGETT married Anne Dodsonne, Bungay, Suffolk.

521. 1632, November 11, ANNE DOGGETT, daughter of Richard & Anne, bapt. Bungay, Suffolk.

522. 1638, JOHN DOGGETT, of Herts., deceased, adm. granted to Susanna Doggett, his wife.

523. 1640, August 7, MARIE DOGGETT, daughter of Richard & Anne, bapt. Bungay, Suffolk.

524. 1640, } WILLIAM DOGGETT, of Claptonswick, Somerset, At-
1641, } tachment degree. [Calendar of State Papers B.M.]

525. 1652, December 6, JOSEPH, son of THOMAS DOGGETT, and Anne his wife, christened at St. Michael's, Cornhill, London. [Harleian Society.]

526. 1657, November 10, ANCE DOGED, spinster, of St. Peters, Cornhill, London, married Beiamen Spooner, butcher, of Dedford. [Harleian Society.]

527. 1658, JOHN DOGGETT, Registrar of Sudbury, Suffolk.

528. 1662, August 18, AVIS DOGGETT, spinster, 19, daughter of William Doggett, of St. Mary, Whitechapel, Middlesex, gent., who consents at Stepney, and John Williams of Stepney, Middlesex, bachelor, 22. [London Marriage Licenses, 1521–1869.]

529. 1662, September 24, SUSAN DOGGETT, spinster, 23, daughter of William Doggett, of St. Mary, Whitechapel, gent., who consents at Stepney or Whitechapel, aforesaid, and John Spering, of Stepney, Middlesex, bachelor, 24. [London Marriage Licenses.]

530. 1665, } NATHANIEL DOGGETT, of the Reserve, begs payment
1666, } of freight money. [Calendar of State Papers B.M.]

531. 1666, October 25, ELIZABETH DOGGETT, of St. Giles, Cripplegate, spinster, about 25, her parents dead, and Robert Smith, of Woollidge, Kent., gent, bachelor, about 30 years, at St. Giles, Cripplegate, All Hallows in the wall or St. Clement Danes. [London Marriage Licenses.]

532. 1670, KATHERINE DOGGETT, Redenhall, will. (Consistory of Norwich.)

533. 1672, April 16, RICHARD DOGGETT, bachelor, and Judith Roberts, maiden, marriage license at Worcester, to be married at Upton-on-Severn.

534. 1677, JOHN DOGGETT, merchant of London, Pountney Hill. [1st London Directory of Merchants.]

535. 1679, HESTER DOGGETT, Harleston, will. (Consistory of Norfolk.)

536. 1679, ALICE DOGGETT, Harleston, will. (Consistory of Norfolk.)

537. 1679, November 27, JOSEPH DOGGETT, University College, M.A. [Oxford Graduates.]
Was son of Thomas, of Leighton Buzzard, Beds. Matriculated 5 May, 1673, aged 18. B.A. 15 February, 1676–7. Vicar of Wolverton Berks, 1684.

538. 1679, JOHN DOGATT, of Clapton, will proved at Wells. [Epis. Consistory Court.]

539. 1686, JOHN DOGATT, of Clevedon, will proved at Wells. [Epis. Consistory Court.]

540. 1687, RICHARD DOGGETT, Harleston, will. [Consistory of Norfolk.]

541. 1689, ELIZABETHA DOGGETT, of Bedford. [Drs. Commons, London.]

542. 1695, JOHN DOGGETT, of London. [Adms. Drs. Commons.]

543. 1695, June 12, ROBERT DOGGETT, of Hockliffe, Bedford, bachelor, deceased. [Adms. Drs. Commons.]

544. 1695, June 12, JOHN DOGGETT, of Hockliffe, Bedford, bachelor, deceased, adm. granted to brother (**545**) THOMAS DOGGETT. [Adms. Drs. Commons, London.]

546. 1700, BRIDGETT DOGETT, of Clevedon, will proved at Wells. [Epis. Consistory Court.]

547. 1702, WILLIAM DOGGETT, Sudbury. [Suffolk Poll.]

548. 1710, August 6, ROBERT DOGITT, Hiringham, Suffolk, yeoman and widower, and Elizabeth Nicolls, of Brandish, widow, marriage license to be married at Stradbroke; Robert Norman, bondsman.

549. 1714, May 24, ANNE DOGGETT, buried Bungay, Suffolk.

550. 1716, December 27, MARGARET DOGGETT, of Stoke Ash, single, age 21, and Henry Houchin, yeoman, Gislingham, aged 22, license to be married at Stoke Ash or Gislingham; Benjamin Doggett, of Gislingham, bondsman.

551. 1720, December 30, ANN DOGGETT, of ye towne, spinster, buried Waltham, Holy Cross.

552. 1720, RICHARD DOGGETT, Alburgh, will. [Consistory of Norwich.]

553. 1727, ELIZABETH DAGGET, single, and Edward Dove, bachelor, both of St. Margaret's, Westminster, married. [Harleian Society.]

554. 1730, August 17, ELIZABETH DOGGETT, buried Waltham, Holy Cross.

555. 1731, July 14, LYDIA, daughter of Thomas Doggett, bapt. at Waltham, Holy Cross.

556. 1734, December 19, WILLIAM DOGGET, of Waltham, Holy Cross, buried.

557. 1734, December 22, THOMAS, son of Thomas Dogget, of Waltham, Holy Cross, buried.

558. 1737, July 17, HANNAH DOGGETT buried at Clevedon.

559. 1737, September 23, Mr. DOGGET, Senior, of Waltham Cross, buried.

560. 1740, October 14, HANNAH DOGGETT, of Bedingham, Norfolk, single, married there to Samuel Crisp, of Frossington, Suffolk.

561. 174⅞, February 22, MARY DOGGETT, buried at Clevedon.

562. 1753, THOMAS DOGGETT, Bunwell, will. [Consistory of Norfolk.]

563. 1764, THOMAS DOGGETT, Roydon, will. [Consistory of Norfolk.]

564. 1768, } BENJAMIN DOGGETT, of Battersea. [Poll of the 1776, } livery of the City of London for four citizens to represent the city in Parliament.]

565. 1772, April 10, JAMES DOGGETT and Mary Miriam Dean married at Clevedon.

566. 1775, August 21, ANN DOGGET and Thomas Howcroft. License at St. George, Hanover square, London. [Harleian Society.]

567. 1776, June 19, ELIZABETH DOGGETT, married Winfarthing, Norfolk, to Arch. Rowing, of Tibenham.

568. 1779, October 26, DEBORAH DOGGETT, married Winfarthing, Norfolk, to W. Betts, of Old Buckenham.

569. 1784, JAMES DOGGETT, of Walcot. [Adms. Wells, Epis. Consis. Ct.]

570. 1785, June 3, HANNAH, wife of J. Doggett, buried Winfarthing, Norfolk.

571. 1792, April 25, SARAH DOGGETT, married Winfarthing, Norfolk, to Anthony Freestone of St. Margaret, S. Elmham.

572. 1795, April 10, RICHARD DOGGETT, of Diss, married man, buried Winfarthing, Norfolk.

573. 1798, November 17, ELIZABETH DOGGETT, of Diss, widow, buried Winfarthing, Norfolk.

574. 1802, January 24, MIRIAM DOGGETT, buried at Clevedon.

575. 1803, March 20, THOMAS DAGGETT, of Hunton, died, aged 50 years, buried Pickhill, Yorkshire.

576. 1807, April 28, WILLIAM DOGGETT, buried at Clevedon.

577. 1811, October 24, WILLIAM DOGGETT, from Tickerham, buried at Clevedon.

578. 1819, June 2, JOHN DOGGETT, gent., of Mendham, Suffolk, died. [Davy's Suf. Collections.]

579. 1822, August 27, ELIZABETH DOGGETT, of Winfarthing Park, age 32 years, buried Winfarthing, Norfolk.

580. 1857, June 10, THOMAS DOGGETT, died, aged 69.

581. 1873, May 16, ANN DOGGETT, died. [Buried in Highgate Cem., London, lot of George Hindes Smith, Ave. House, Stamford Hill, London.]

582. The Staffordshire Assize Roll of 56 Henry III. (1272) is headed "Placita de juratis et assisis apud Lichefeld in Comitatu

Stafford in Crastino Sanctae Trinitatis, coram R. de Hengham et sociis suis Justiciariis anno regni Regis Henrici filii Regis Johannis L. Sexto."

The borough of Stafford came by 12 jurymen and stated that: " Respecting prises (de prisis) they say that Roger Doget, the constable of Certesleye (Chartley) took a doleum of wine from Richard Gilbert who was carting wine from the cellars of St. Botolph and forced him to carry it to the castle of Certesleye to his own use and the value of it was 5 mark of which he paid nothing and they say the same Roger takes Prises in the vill of Stafford of bread, meat, fish and other things against the will of those to whom the things belong and pays nothing for them. The sheriff is ordered to produce him before the court." [Coll. for a Hist. of Staffordshire, Eng., by Wm. Salt, 1883.]

583. 1358 [32 Edward 3d] Carta qua Joannes Poulyn de Whyttone, concedit Johanni Doget peciam prati in Whytton. Test Walton Weyland, wid Ringedale, Joh die Halle, et alus. Dat die Merc in festo S. Marci Evangel (seal of wax attached). [Additional Charters, Vol. IV., Ext. No. 100–10 B.M.]

584. JOHN DOGGETT, born at Sherborne, Dorset, 1425; was a nephew of Cardinal Bountner.

Elected from Eaton to King's College, Cambridge, 1451. 1459, September 22, being then M.A. and fellow of King's, ordained acolyte and sub-deacon, by Gray, Bishop of Ely.

1460, priest.

1473, January 22, prebendary of Roxcombe, in church of Sarum.

1476, prebendary of Bitten in church of Sarum.

1479, one of the ambassadors to the Pope.

1480, in commission to king of Denmark.

1483, chaplain to Richard III.

1494, master of Trinity College, Arundel.

1499, provost of King's College, Cambridge.

1501, died; buried in Salisbury Cathedral.

[Cooper's Athenae Cantabrigiensis, Vol. I., 4, 520.]

He was archdeacon of Chester, an author, an early Greek scholar.

1488, February 13, chancellor of Lichfield. John Doggett, LL.D., died about April, 1501, and was buried in Salisbury Cathedral, of which he was canon, as also prebendary of Lincoln, and treasurer of Chichester. [Brown Willis, Survey of Cathedrals, 1742, Vol. I., page 407.]

585. The will of RICHARD DOGETT, of Mendham: To be buried in the cemetery of All Saints church in Mendham; to high altar of same church 6s 8d; to the Prior of Mendham 6s. 8d.; to the Sub Prior of do. 20d; to Dominus John Cryston 20d; to each of the leper houses of Dunwich, 4d; of Beccles 4d; of Norwich 4d; of Eye 4d.; to making new candelabra in Mendham church 40s.; each godchild 12d; Katherine Dogett, wife, Thomas Dogett, son, Robert Dogett, son, executors and residuary legatees. Dated 6 March, 1451. Proved 11 March, 1451. [Norwich Consistory Registry, "Aleyn," fo. 109.]

586. May 24, 1469 [9 Edw. IV.]. Carta qua Reginaldus Grey, Dominus de Wilton super Wyam in com Hereford et Tacina unor sua per consensum Joannis Grey, filue sui, concedunt Rogero Hebbes de Feny Stratford [Bucks]. Joanni Doget de Etone, William Danyelle et Alianore, uxori ejus messuagium et terra in Vill^a de Etone [Co Hereford] reddend, ude annuatine sexdecim sol. Test Edwd Grey, Arm, Rog Etone, Clerico, Will Jakeman et alus (three seals of wax attached). [Additional Charters, Vol. IV., Ext. 8128 B.M.]

587. The will of ROBERT DOGGET, of Beccles: To be buried in church of S^t. Michael the Archangel of Beccles; to high altar there 3s. 4d.; to chapel of S^t. Peter of Beccles 12d; to repair of the great bridge there 3s 4d; to guild of S^t. Michael of Beccles 6s 8d; Agnes Dogget, wife; John Ablerd, Webster, Roger Boton, Beccles, Executors; a trentall of St. Gregory to be sung for his soul; messuage in Northgate mentioned; Guild of S^t. Peter of Beccles; repair of the church at Beccles; to the poor of Beccles; John Dogget, son; messuages in Gelyngham & Whetacreburgh; Emma, servant; Richard Cidemer & Isabel his wife; John Dogget, my brother. Dated 20 Nov., 1473. Proved 9 Dec., 1473. [Consistory Registry, Norwich, "Hubert," 23.]

588. The will of JOHN DOKETT, of Aspall: To be buried in church of Aspall; high altar of Aspall 20d; of Werlynworth 12d; of Abyuton 8d; of Debenham 12d; a torch for Aspall 3s 4d; a trentall to be sung at Aspall church 10s; wife £8 and the tenement that was hers before marriage; my five children 40s each; son Robert; child my wife is with; Chrystyon, daughter; John, the elder, my son; John, the younger, my son; Agnes, daughter; Robert Colman & John, the elder, my son, Executors. Dated 15 Oct., 1492. Proved 1 July, 1493. [Consistory Registry, Norwich, "Woolman," 168.]

589. The will of JOHN DOGGETT, of Beccles: Soul to Almighty God, and our lady Saint Mary, and all the saints of heaven; body to be buried in churchyard of Burgh, in Norfolk, "by syde" Beccles;

to high Alter xii^d; to Repacons of sd church xii^d; I will have Saint Gregory's Trentall sung for me as shortly as may be; to Elyn, my wieffe, my place at Beccles, and my place at Burgh, and all household Stuffe, and she to be Executrix. (No other names mentioned of children or relations.) Dated 10 March, 1499. Proved at Beccles, 22 April, 1501. [Ipswich Probate.]

590. The will of ROBERT DOGET, of Wynfield: To be buried in churchyard of St. Andrew, in Wynfield; to high altar 20d; Robert Clerke, my godson, my tenement, Executor; said Robert to sing two trentalls, in Wynfield church; to the Grey Friars of Donwiche; legacy towards making an image of S^t. Margaret, a yard long. At the south end of St. John's aisle an " yeryn candlestyk; " my yerthday to be kept. Sir Robert Bryche, of Winfield, Lewys Bradley, Sir Richard Fresynfeld, & others, witnesses. Dated January, 1500. Proved 2 March, 1500. [Consistory Registry, Norwich, " Cage," 228.]

591. The will of ROBERT DOKETT, of Warlyngworth (Doggett in Index): Soul to God, &c.; body to be buried in Church of our Lady, at Warlynworth, before the " perclos " of the Trinite; I bequeath my best beeste for my mortuarye; to High Altar of sd church for tythes, forgotten or not trulie payd, iii^s iiij^d; to High Altar of Church of St. Peter, of Alyngton, iii^s iiij^d; to the mother Church of Norwich iii^s iiij^d; to the Guild of the Trinite, in Warlyngworth, v marks; to Repacons of said Church of Warlyngworth vi^s viij^d; to Elizabeth, my oldest daughter, to hir mariage x^{li}; to Anne, my Second daughter, to hir marriage x^{li}; to Margarett, my youngest daughter, to hir mariage x^{li}; to Alys, my wife, her jointure; also, Alyngton Close for her life; Thomas, my eldest son, to have other houses and lands, plows, cart horses, & harness; if Thomas die without issue, all to go to daughters and their heires; Alys, wife, & Thomas, son, Executors. Dated 15 August, 1503. Proved Saxfield, 27 August, 1503. [Ipswich Probate.]

592. The will of ROBERT DOGETT, of Leiston, and late of Theberton: To be buried in the churchyard of Leiston; to high altar there 12d.; to light before our Lady of Pity 12d.; to high altar of Theberton 12d.; to repair of Theberton church, 2 bushels of wheat and 3 of malt; a dirge and mass to be sung for his soul in Leiston church; " a drynkyng " to be kept on his burial at Leiston, to comfort the " poure people as much as may be borne of my goodes; " mentions his father's will; soul of my wife to be sung for. Convent of Austin Friars, in Orford, lands in Theberton and Westilton; Margaret Doget, daughter; my sister Margaret Leeff; Richard Gararde of Theberton & Thos.

Walpole of Yoxforth, Executors. Dated 28 Oct., 1513. Proved 25 Sept., 1526. [Consistory of Norwich, "Grindesburgh," 188.]

593. The will of THOMAS DOGETT, of Stradbroke: Soul to God, &c.; body to be buried in Church yard of Stradbroke; to High Altar for tythes and oblacons negligently forgoten or w'holden xij^d; to Johan, wife, houses & lands for natural life; after her death to Robert, son; to William, son, lands at [Stubaoste?]; Johan all household Stuffe & moveables; she Executrix. Dated 29 Aug., 1517. Proved Stradbroke, 16 Sept., 1517. [Ipswich Probate.]

594. The will of JOHN DOGGETT, of Wingfield, Suffolk: All his property to Mary, his wife, who was sole executrix. Dated 22 June, 1526. Proved 3 July, 1526. [Consistory of Norwich.]

595. The will of ROBERT DOGETT, of Norwich, "tailor": To be buried in churchyard of S^t. Peter, Mancroft, in Alley on North side of the church near the body of Anne, my wife; high altar there 6s. 8d.; to a mass of Jesus to be celebrated and sung 13s. 4d.; to the light in the lamp hanging before the crucifix in the church there 3s. 4d.; to the sepulchre there a taper of wax of 6 lb.; 30s. in charity to be given at my burial; Margaret Dogett, my daughter; Maude, my maid; each godchild, 12s.; Beatrice, my now wife, sole executrix; Thomas Conye of Norwich, grocer, supervisor; witnesses: Thomas Cappe, vicar of S^t. Stephens, William Newman, John Gryme, Clerk, Robert Roberts, Clerk, John Sewall. Dated 10 Nov., 1541. Proved 1543 (no day given). [Consistory of Norwich, "Cooke," 232.]

596. The will of JOHN DOGGETT, of East Winch, Norfolk: John Doggett, son, Executor; William Doggett, son; Robert Doggett, son; left small sums "to repair of church there;" to be buried in churchyard there. Dated 20 Dec., 1545. Proved 20 Dec., 1545. [Norwich Archdeaconry.]

597. Will of ROBERT ASHEFIELD, of Glovalangloste, Suffolk, A.D. 1550, mentions my brother John Dogett, and two sons of said John Dogett which he had by Martha, my sister. [Somerset House, Coode, 12.]

598. The will of JOHN DOGGETT, of Hingham, Norfolk, leaves bequests to the high altar there, the poor there, and to the repair of the church; Thomasine, his wife, Sole Executrix; Dorothy Doggett, alias Adkok; William Doggett, alias Adkok, "my bowe and shafts" when 20 years of age; leaves his wife his house which he bought of Parson Fox. Dated 17 July, 3d year of Edward VI. [1550]. Proved 23 Oct., 1550. [Consistory of Norwich.]

599.   The will of THOMAS DOGGETT, of Worlingworth. Gentleman:
To be buried in the church there; sons: John Doggett, Thomas
Doggett, Robert Doggett; daughters: Elizabeth, Thomasin; John
Harrison, clerk, Elizabeth Burrough, daughter, Thomas Watling,
Executors & residuary Legatees.   Dated 13 Oct., 6th year of Edward
VI. [1553].   Proved 13 April, 1554.   [Consistory of Norwich.]

600.   The will of ROBERT DOGGET, of Stradbroke: Soul to God,
&c.; body to church yard of Stradbroke; to Katheryn, wife, lands,
&c., in Stradbroke for natural life; then to Arthur, son, on condition
that he pays to my other children such sums of money as follows:
to Thomas, son, V£; to Margaret, daughter, 20s.; to Johan, daughter,
20s.; to Dorathye, daughter, 20s.; to Katheryn, daughter, 40s.;
to Agnes, daughter, 20s; after death of wife, daughter Margaret to
have house in which Margery Pecke, widow, now dwells.   Wife and
John Godbold, Executors.   Dated 10 April, 1558.   Proved at Stradbroke 20 March, 1558.   [Ipswich Probate.]

601.   Will of THOMAS MALBY, citizen and alderman of Norwich,
dated 20 Oct., 1558, mentions Margaret, my wife, & Katherine
Dogett, my sister, dwelling in Shathbroke.   [Somerset House,
Welles, 11.]

602.   Will of WILLIAM MORE, of Groton, Suffolk, dated 1 October, 1565. 8th Elizabeth R. mentions Thomas Lappage my son in
law, to whom he gives land at Boxford; Alice my wife; and John
Dogat, Anne Dogat; if the former attains 21 years to have £5, to latter
when she marries 40ˢ.   Bed and Bedding to Wm Dogatte the younger
& £5 if he attains 21 years.   My son in law Thos Lappage after
death of his mother to have the order and execution of last will
and Testament of my brother John Dogete to whom I was executor
and trustee to children of John Dogete. [Somerset House, Stonerd, 9.]

603.   The will of ROBERT DOGGET, of Mendham, butcher: Soul
to God, &c.; body to Church yard at Mendham; to poor of Mendham
20ᵈ; to poor of Harleston 20ᵈ; Johan, wife, tenement lands,
meadows, Pastures &c at Mendham for natural life, after death to
Thomas, son, on condition he gives to Cycelie & Marie, my daughters,
xxˡⁱ apiece; to Robert Doggett, my father, 20ˢ; residue not mentioned
to Johan wife towards bringing up of children; to Stephen Warde my
wife's father my néwe frieze gowne; Johan, wife, & Thomas Doggett,
brother, executors.   Dated 8 Nov., 1580.   Proved at Mendham 23
Dec., 1580.   [Ipswich Probate.]

604. The will of BRYAN DOGGETT, the elder, of Hardwick: Robert, eldest son; Bryan, William, John, my three other sons; Bryan to have all his Carpenters tools; legacies to be paid at the house of his brother in law Nicholas Cooke, who was to be Supervisor; Margaret Doggett his wife Executrix; Thomas Doggett, Butcher, brother; witnesses Richard Person, George Smith. Dated 16 Jan., 1608. Proved 28 May, 1610. [Norfolk Archdeaconry.]

605. Administration was granted on the estate of CHRISTOPHER DOGGETT, of Caister, St. Edmund, 18 Dec., 1608, to Edmund Reimes, grandfather on the mother's side, during minority of Susan, Edmund, Grace, and Magaret Doggett, children of deceased. [Consistory of Norwich.]

606. Will of ALICE WADE, widow, of Bildeston, Suffolk, dated 19 May, 1610: Buried at Bildeston by side of husband. House &c in occupation of son in law Edmonde Doggett, I give to John, Edmund, Nathaniel and Alice Doggett or of them that are 21 years of age at time of my death. Also William, Samuel, Edmonde and Millos Markes children of my late daughter Alice Doggett by her late husband Edmonde Markes. [Somerset House, Weldon, 5.]

607. The will of THOMAS DOGGETT, of Mendham, County Suffolk, made 12 May, 1612 (cordyner): Leaves to Johan his wife all lands and goods in Mendham and makes her sole executrix. She to bring up and educate his children, none of whose names are mentioned. Witnesses of will, John Skillet, Christopher Burly, John Westgate. Proved at Ipswich 10 June, 1612. [Ipswich Probate.]

608. The nuncupative will of JOHN DOGGETT, of Mendham, yeoman: Leaves all he possessed to Susan, his wife; mentions no other relatives; witnessed by John Sowthes, George Smith, Nat. Graygoose. Dated 7 April, 1613. Proved 30 April, 1613. [Consistory of Norwich.] John Doggett was buried Harleston, Norfolk, April 15, 1613.

609. The will of JOHN DOGGETT, of Oxteed (or Orheed), County Surrey, 13 Feb., 1617, proved 1618, wills that he be buried at Oxheed, and mentions brother Nicholas; John, son of Nicholas (above named); sister Johane. also sister of Nicholas; Mary Cooper, daughter of sister Johane; children of brother Thomas; James Doggett my brother to be executor and residuary legatee. [Somerset House, Meade, 32.]

610. Will of THOMAS DOGGET. of Howmonden, Kent, mentions my son Thomas Doggett; Elizabeth Willard my grandchild; Mary

Willard my grandchild; my daughter Mary, not 21 years of age; Isabel, my wife; Wm Willard, my son in law. Dated 2 May, 1621. Proved 1621. [Somerset House, Dale, 64.]

611. Will of Isack Doggatt, of Buthington, County Kent, yeoman, 14 Feb. [1623], twentieth year James I., mentions my brother Thomas Prowde of Nottington Kent and my sister Mary Prowde, his wife; Thomas Prowde, son of my said brother Thomas; John Prowde, son of my said brother Thomas; Isack Prowde, son of my said brother Thomas, and other sons whose names I know not; my sister Francis Doggat. [Somerset House, Swan, 17.]

612. The will of Robert Doggett, of Brokedish (Brockdish), Norfolk: His tenements in Brokedish to William Smart and Joan, wife of said William; William Smart executor. Dated 19 April, 1627. Proved 13 Sept., 1635. [Consistory of Norwich.]

613. The will of Mary Doggett, of Hockering, single woman, is a declaration before Mr. Robert Wickes, Richard Brackenbury, and Mary Lion, that she desired her property to go to Philip Sammon and Elinor Sammon, of Hockering, her "cozens," and to John Scammon, of Hockering, her uncle. Dated 20 July, 1634. Proved 4 Aug., 1634. [Norfolk Archdeaconry.]

614. The will of Thomas Doggett, of Bungay, County Suffolk, made 29 December, 1637 (Butcher): To Margarie his wife all his goods and sole executrix. No other name mentioned in will or whether there were children or not. Witnesses, John Skelton, Richard Doggett. Proved at Bungay 10 Jan., 1637. [Ipswich Probate.]

Thomas Doggett had a daughter, Anne Doggett, buried Bungay, Suffolk, June 20, 1628.

615. Will of Richard Moungngs, of Stoke, next Hayland, Suffolk, date 1638, mentions Susan, my daughter, wife of Benjamin Doggett. Proved 1639. [Somerset House, Harvey, 48.]

616. Will of Elizabeth LeGris, of Weston, Suffolk, dated 17 August, 1642: I give to Sarah my daughter wife of Richard Dogget of Hadleigh Suffolk, my house lands &c. situate at Boxford; three children of Richard and Sarah Dogget viz.: Richard, Anig & Elizabeth not 21 years old; Mary Palmer & Anne Gaunt my daughters: Sarah Dogget Executrix. [Somerset House, Fines, 4.]

617. Will of Francis Doggett, of Eaton, County Bedfordshire, yeoman, dated 22 January, 1653, proved 8 May, 1654: Desires to be buried at Eaton; mentions legacies of £5 each, to brother Thomas Doggett and sister Mary, wife of Richard Beamont, Brother William, of Southmins, Co. Middlesex, Brother John Doggett and sister Elizabeth, wife of William Doggett, of Whipsnade, Co. Beds. Residue to Margaret, my wife, whom he makes sole executrix. [Somerset House, Alchin, 198.]

618. Will of EDMOND DOGGETT, proved 27 June, 1653 (no date or place mentioned) : To my sister Adrey Doggett, the wife of Barnaby Sydey, I give 20 . . . of gold; my plate & compasses and fowe staffe & Quadrante to Arthur Bartlett; one half of Red Cloth to my mate Henry Oake the other half to Mr. Lambert, the surgeon; 10 lbs of East India stuffe in my chest where it once belonged to Mr. Henry Wafdalle; all the other to my sister Adrey; my suit of best clothes to Walter Elton; my West India Hammack to gunner Thomas Clarke. To John Tribbett a pair compasses plans & sea Books. My clothes and all wages due to me to my sister Adrey or if deceased to her son Barnaby Sydey. Adm. granted to Barnaby Sydey, husband of A. Doggett, the nat[l] & lawful daughter of Edmond Doggett deceased. [Somerset House, Brent, 245.]

619. Will of FRANCIS DOGGETT, of Chesham, County Bucks, yeoman, signed 24 December, 1653, proved 1 May, 1654 : Wishes to be buried at Chesham, mentions my wife Mary Doggett, to whom he gives messuage land and tenement in Chesham, wherein William Parratt doth live, also house & premises wherein I now dwell in Chesham, to hold the same until my son Francis Doggett shall reach 21 years, also to my son Francis lands lying at George Doll's close on the Latimer Road. Mary his wife sole executrix & residuary legatee. [Somerset House, Alchin, 397.]

620. The will of JOHN DOGGETT, of Redenhall, butcher : John Doggett, son ; Alice Doggett, wife, sole executrix ; Elizabeth Daughter; Alice Daughter not 21 years old ; Hanna Daughter not 21 years old ; Sarah Daughter not 21 years old ; Esther Daughter not 21 years old. His wife was to enter into a bond to Mr. Robert Bransby, of Redenhall, for the due performance of the will. Witnesses, Henry Tubbye, John Matthewes. Dated 21 May, 1665. Proved 26 May, 1665. [Consistory of Norwich.]

621. 9 November, 1676, adm. to MARY DOGGET, relict of John Dogget, late of Walton, within the Parish of Aylesbury, County Bucks, dec'd. 4 Oct 1683, adm. to Rich[d] Haywood, Thomas Barnaby and William Rice, guardians during the minority of John and Mary Dogget, children of John Dogget, late of Walton in the Parish of

Ailesbury, Co. Bucks. Mary Dogget, widow and relict, having de-
ceased without fully administering. 4 July 1693. Adm. to John
Doggett, son of John Dogget, late of Walton within the Parish of
Aylesbury Co. Bucks, dec'd, Mary Doggett, widow and relict of
said deceased, having died without fully administering. [Adm.
P.C.C.]

622. Will of THOMAS DOGGET. of Hockliffe, in the County of
Bedford, 10 December, 1684. Proved November, 1685:   I bequeath to Joseph Doggett my eldest son £20; to my daughter
Rebecca, the daughter of Mary, my late wife, who was the daughter
of Robert Burthnon of Bathsdon, Co. Bedford. yeoman deceased,
£50; to Thomas Doggett my son by my wife Mary all that my mas-
suage in Hockliffe now in my occupation with all my pastures, grounds
& meadows in Hocklife. All that my halfe acre of arrable land in
Ridgeway furlong in Egginton Fields purchased of Edward Clarke,
also my Rood or more of meadow ground purchased of John Man of
Egginton; to Robert Doggett my son by Mary; Richard Doggett,
my son, Sarah Doggett, my daughter, Rebecca Doggett, my daughter,
sole executors. Thomas Joyce. my brother in law, who married my
wife's sister, and Sarah his wife, I appoint trustees and guardian of
my children. Dated 18 Aug.. 1684.   [Somerset House, Cam, 133.]

623. 18 April, 1696, 8 William III. " I, JOHN DOGGETT Citizen
and Goldsmith of London being at the present time something indis-
posed as to my bodily health but of sound and perfect mind and
memory." To be buried at discretion of executors.   " I give and
devise unto my nephew John Randolph (my sister's sonne). his heirs
and assigns forever." lands. &c.. in the parish of Walton, Co.
Bucks; "unto my brother-in-law, John Randolph and my sister
Mary his wife;" "to Thomas Barnaby, Senr. (my Uncle);" " to
Thomas Barnaby, Junr. (my cousin);" " to my cousin William
Barnaby;" " to my cousin Martha Worcester;" " to the children of
my cozen John Heywood;" "to the children of my cozen Henry
Bell;" " to my cousin Joseph Heywood and to his children;" "to
my cousin Mrs. Moore. my cousins John Fells. John Mills and
Ralph White;" poor of Walton, £10; poor of Aylesbury, Co.
Bucks, £10; residue of estate to sister Mary Randolph and her son,
my nephew John Randolph. and appoints them joint executor and
Executrix. Signed " JNO: DOGGETT." Proved P.C.C. 28 March,
1700, by Mary Randolph. Power reserved to John Randolph.
[Somerset House, 46, Noel.]

624. The will of MARY DOGGETT, of Leighton Buzzard, widdow,
dated 1698. mentions therein. my neice Elizabeth, wife of Thomas

Allin of Buckingham, malster, £20; my neice Frances Wowsley, spinster, daughter of my sister Jane Wowsley, £20; nephew John Stuthbury, son of my brother Andrew Stuthbury, 40s.; Elizabeth Stuthbury, widdow, late wife of my nephew Christopher Stuthbury & children of same mentioned; neice Mary Squire & Joana Sholton, daughters of my brother Andrew Stuthbury; residue to my loving nephew John Wowsley of Winslow, Co. Bucks, & William Sholton of Winslow and Oliver Maine of Winslow and John Wowsley [if he does not marry Rebeca Hunt] my executors. [Somerset House, Noel, 97.]

625. The will of Johannis (John) Doggett: All wages, bounty prize money due to me in His Majestys service and other lands Tenements goods &c. to wife Rebecca Doggett, sole Executrix. Signed 10 March, 170$\frac{0}{1}$, 12 William. Proved 1703. [Somerset House, Degg, 4.]

626. John Doggett of his Ship the Biddiford, Capt. Searls, leaves all to his friend Richard Roberts. Date 2 June, 11 William III., 1701. [Somerset House, Dyer, 137.]

627. The will of Richard Doggett, of Middlesex, schoolmaster: Buried at Parish Church, Hendon, at which place I live now. I give to my Brother Thomas all pieces and parcels of Land at Egginton Leighton Buzzard, known as Ardells; an annuity to my sister Rebekah Palmer. Sister Sarah Babham to have above land in the event of Thomas leaving no heir male, for the term of her life and to her heirs male in default of which it is to go to my sister Rebeckah and after to her heirs male of her body and in want of such heirs to the female heirs of brother Thomas or wanting such to female heirs of Sarah Palmer in want of which I leave to my cousin Thomas Doggett of the parish of Hockly (Hockliffe) Co. Beds. and his heirs forever; Sarah my sister, wife of William Babham of Wendover Bucks.; Thomas Palmer my Godson; residue to my brother Thomas, my sole executor. Dated 19 Jan., 170$\frac{5}{6}$. Proved 1706. [Somerset House, Fedes, 105.]

628. The will of Nathaniel Doggett, now residing at Hampstead, Co. Middlesex, gentleman: I give unto my grandchild Cox Thathe £300; my grandchildren John Thathe & Rachel Thathe £250 each; to my friends Thomas Haynes & Anthony Neale £10 each; all the remainder of my monies, Stocks, Bonds, debts &c to my daughter Lucretia Thathe, now living in Jamaica. Dated 24 May, 1715. Codicil of same date: To my cousin Augustin Bedford 40s.

per annum for 5 years to be paid to widow Thathe with whom my said kinsman lives. Proved June, 1715. [Somerset House, Fagg, 111.]

629. The will of FRANCIS DAGGETT, made July 1, 1715, proved 1718, of the parish of St. Leonards, Shoreditch, London, mentions therein Anne, his late wife; son George; grandson David Daggett, second son of son George; grandson George Daggett, eldest son of George; grandson Ralph Daggett, third son of George; daughter Mary Daggett; daughter Anne Daggett. From codicil: Sarah, wife of son George; Thomas Hardwick, husband of Anne. [Somerset House, Tennison, 57.]

630. Will of GEORGE DAGGETT, of Marylebone, Middlesex, mentions Brother-in-law Thomas Harwood, of Hackney, Middlesex; James Harwood, of St. Leonards, Shoreditch; my daughter Sarah Daggett; sons Ralph & George; my brother in law to be guardian of children until 21 years of age. Dated 31 Oct., 1727. Proved 1727. [Somerset House, Farrant, 292.]

631. The will of ELIZABETH DOGGETT, of College Hill:

I, Elizabeth Dogett of College Hill in the City of London, Spinster . . . and first my will and desire is that my Body be decently Buried at the discretion of my Executor . . . unto my very worthy Friend Alexander Broughton of South Carolina, Esquire, one Gold Ring as a small mite or Humble token of my Good will and gratitude for the favors I have received . . . unto my loving Sister Ann Dogett and Mary Lewin one Gold Ring to each as a token of my love . . . unto my loving Brother Benjamin Dogett of the Parish of Battersea in the County of Surry, Gentleman, All and every of my Estate and Estates Real and Personal, Bonds, Bills, Notes, Securities, Papers, Writings, Goods, Chattels and Effects of any kind, name, nature, or denomination whatsoever whether in Great Britain, Carolina America or in any other part of the World . . . and appoint my said dearly beloved Brother Benjamin Dogett, my Universal Heir and Sole Executor 9 June 1765   E. DOGETT (L.S.)
Witnesses hereunto, Ann Harding, Elizabeth Harding, Elizabeth Brown.

Proved 1st Feb. 1775, by Benjamin Dogett the Brother of the dec'd and sole exec.

Probate Act to above will from the "Probate Act Book," 1775, Feb 1: The will of Elizabeth Dogett formerly of South Carolina in America but late of Battersea Co. Surry, Spinster, dec'd, was proved by Benjamin Dogett the Brother and sole exec. [Somerset House, 46 Alexander.]

632. Great Gaddeston, Herts. Doggatt appears often in early parochial registers.
633. Sarratt Rickmansworth, Herts. Doggett appears often in register.

"Thomas Doggett dancing The "Cheshire Rounds"
From a painting which used to be preserved at the Duke's Head
in Lynn. Regis. Norfolk. (18th Century)

634. St. Michael's, St. Albans, Herts. Dogget frequently mentioned in registers.

635. "Doggett's Path," Leighton Buzzard, Beds.

636. "Doggett's Pightle," Hundred of Hoxne, Suff., mentioned in 1667.

THOMAS DOGGETT, OF DUBLIN, IRELAND.

637. THOMAS DOGGETT, born Dublin, Ireland;[1] died Eltham, Kent, England, September 22, 1721; married, first, before 1682, Mary; she died 1712; married, second, ——.

Thomas Doggett was born in Castle street, Dublin, Ireland, and made his first theatrical attempt on the stage of that metropolis, but does not appear to have achieved any great success there.

He strolled the provinces before his talents procured him a foremost position upon the London stage, where he made his appearance in 1691.

He has been described as a "little lively sprack man" who "dressed neat and something fine, in a plain cloth coat and a brocaded waistcoat."

His name has been traced into the thirteenth century, when one Gilbertus Dogget is mentioned in connection with an unpublished "Pipe Roll" of the year 1261. (Search has been made in London for this roll, but without success.)

Anthony Aston says he "was the most faithful and pleasing actor that ever was," and "the best face-painter and gesticulator."

"He was the most original observer of nature of all his contemporaries," says Cibber.

He could paint his face to represent seventy, eighty, or ninety years of age. Sir Godfrey Kneller told him one day that he excelled him in painting; for that he could only copy nature from the original before him, but that he (Doggett) could vary them at pleasure and yet keep a close likeness.

Aston says: "In behavior he was modest, cheerful, and complaisant; he sang in company very agreeably, and in public very comically, and he danced the Cheshire Round full as well as the fam'd Captain George, but with much more nature and nimbleness."

The same old writer says: "I have had the pleasure of his conversation for one year, when I travelled with him in his strolling company, and found him a man of very good sense, but illiterate;

---

[1] It is reported of one family of the Irish branch of the Doggetts that one brother took the side of Charles I., while another sided with Cromwell.

for he wrote me word thus : ' Sir, I will give you a hole instead of half share.' While I travelled with him each sharer kept his horse and was everywhere respected as a gentleman."

Dogget made his first appearance in London, after his prosperous career as a stroller, in Bartholomew Fair ; and we append a copy of the bill announcing it :

At Parke's and Dogget's Booth,
near Hosier Lane End, during the time of
BARTHOLOMEW FAIR,
Will be presented a new Droll, called
Fryar Bacon : or the Country Justice :
With the Humours of Toll Free, the Miller and his son Ralph
acted by Mr. Dogget.
With variety of Scenes, Machinery, Songs and Dances.

VIVAT REX 1691.

In the year following he made a great hit as Solon in D'Urfey's comedy of the " Marriage Hater Matched." The " Spectator," in a paper which denounces " the intolerable folly and confidence of players " in " putting in words of their own," calls them " savages, who want all manner of regard and deference to the rest of mankind, come only to show themselves, without any other purpose than that of letting us know they despise us," and speaks of the acting of Doggett, who scorned " gagging," in the highest terms, saying : " There is something so miraculously pleasant in Doggett's acting, the awkward triumph and comic sorrow of Hob in different circumstances, that I shall not be able to stay away whenever it is acted."

The writer, Sir Richard Steel, adds his regret that the audience do not recognize the refined subtilty of the actor's execution and conception, but merely the coarse horse-play of his part.

His manner, though borrowed from none, frequently served as model to many ; and he possessed that peculiar art which so very few performers are masters of, namely, the arriving at the perfectly ridiculous without stepping into the least impropriety to attain it.

As a writer Mr. Dogget has left behind him only one comedy, which has not been performed in its original state for many years, entitled " The Country Wake " (1696). It has been altered, however, into a ballad farce, which has frequently made its appearance under the title of " Flora " or " Hob in the Well."

Dogget was joint manager of Drury Lane Theatre, in conjunction with Colley Cibber and Robert Wilks. In 1697 Dogget, having some cause of complaint against the patentee of Drury Lane Theatre, threw up his engagement and went to Norwich.

In those days the power of the Lord Chamberlain over theatres and actors was without limit, as may be gleaned from the following story :

Powell, the actor, being discontented with his position at Drury Lane, accepted an engagement at the Duke's Theatre, in Lincoln's-Inn Fields, where Betterton was one of his lordship's personal friends and favorites. Shortly after, he determined to return to his old post at Drury Lane, and did so, when the Lord Chamberlain sent a "messenger" to seize and convey him to prison; and he was confined for two days in the Porter's Lodge. As with Powell so with Dogget. The patentee complained and a messenger was despatched to Norwich, who there seized Dogget and brought him to London. The actor, proud to suffer in the cause of liberty, was not at all intimidated, but went cheerfully with the officer; and finding his expenses were to be paid took care to live well on the road, calling for the best at every inn they alighted at. Arriving in town he appealed from the Chamberlain to the Lord Chief Justice for his habeas corpus; and, aided by clever legal advice, fought the cause of the players against the Lord Chamberlain with such effect, that he not only secured his own liberty, but brought censure down upon the head of the capricious tyrant by whom both he and Powell were oppressed.

Dogget played Shylock to the great Betterton's Bassanio. He always acted Shylock as a ferociously comic character.

It may be remembered that Dogget was manager when, Colley Cibber having given him offence, he fined him five shillings, and on being informed by the treasurer that Colley was but an apprentice, not yet in receipt of a salary, he replied, "Then put him down for ten shillings a week and forfeit him five," — an arrangement which gave young Colley no small satisfaction and delight.

Congreve discerned Dogget's talents, and wrote for him Fondlewife in the "Old Bachelor," Sir Paul Pliant in the "Double Dealer," and the very different part of Ben in "Love for Love."

He continued a joint manager with Wilks & Cibber of the Drury Lane Theatre until 1712, when he, being disgusted at Mr. Booth's being forced on them as a sharer in the management, threw up his part in the property of the theatre, though it was looked on to have been worth a thousand pounds per annum.

His great passion was stock-jobbing, and no man was better known upon "'Change," for every moment he could spare from his professional duties was passed there. He was obstinate and testy, and impatient of crosses and contradiction.

Dogget succeeded in saving a fortune sufficient to make him in easy circumstances, and after the death of his first wife he married a lady with a well-stocked purse. He then devoted himself to politics, and became a "Whig."

He was a great friend of Steel and of Addison, and frequented the great coffee-houses of that day.

He became a member of the Fishmongers' Company, and in loyalty and gratitude, being a " Whig up to the head and ears," he gave a waterman's coat and silver badge to be rowed for, in honor and commemoration of the accession of King George I. to the throne.

The date of this first contest was 1715.

As a lasting compliment to royalty as exemplified in the Hanoverian succession, he made arrangements in his will for a continuance forever of this annual contest. " Ten pounds to be laid out providing a waterman's coat of cloth (orange color) of the value of eighteen shillings, with a silver badge of the value of five pounds, upon which shall be the impress of a white horse in such manner as was used by Mr. Dogget in his lifetime, round the plate there shall be, in fair letters, these words, ' The gift of Thomas Dogget, the famous comedian.' " The prize was to be contested for by six young watermen, who were not to have exceeded the time of their apprenticeship by twelve months, and the claimants were to start off upon a given signal at the time of the tide, when the current was strongest against them, over a course of about five miles in distance from the Old Swan at London Bridge to the White Swan at Chelsea.

The Fishmonger Company's barge-master, resplendent in a cocked hat and the livery of the company, officiated as umpire, and was shown up in a cutter manned by watermen, the majority of whom were coat-and-badge winners of previous years.

The following is the present [1879] value of the prizes for Doggett's coat and badge :

```
              £   s.  d.
1st man,  6   6   0  with coat and badge.
2d    "   5   5   0
3d    "   3   3   0
4th   "   2   2   0
5th   "   1  11   6
6th   "   1   6   0
```

On a glass window in Lambeth, on August 1, 1736, some one wrote as follows :

" Tom Dogget, the greatest sly drole in his parts
In acting was certain a master of arts,
A monument left — no herald is fuller, —
His praise is sung yearly by many a sculler.
Ten thousand years hence, if the world lasts so long,
Tom Dogget must still be the theme of their song."

Motto for Thomas Dogget dancing the Cheshire rounds :

Ne sutor ultra crepidam.

Charles Dibdin was so amused with the sight of the contest for Dogget's prize that in 1774 he brought out at the Haymarket Theatre a ballad opera entitled " The Waterman; or, The First of August," the hero of which is Tom Tug, who sings the songs commencing, " And did you never hear tell of a jolly young waterman," and " Then farewell, my trim-built wherry."

A waterman who was inclined to be poetical wrote regarding the race :

> " Let your oars like lightning flog it,
> Up the Thames as swiftly jog it,
> An you'd win the prize of Doggett
> The Glory of the river.

> " Bendin! bowing; strainin; rowin;
> Perhaps the wind in fury blowin;
> Or the tide again you flowin;
> The Coat & Badge for ever."

The race, of course, is an historical one, and, to a certain degree, is but second to the Oxford and Cambridge contest for supremacy. The men, we need scarcely add, are socially wide apart.

An interesting reminder of the first wife of the comedian is a very curious quarto book MS. (British Museum. Add MS. 27,466–203–613), the title-page of which is as follows : " Mary Doggett. Her Book of Receits, 1682." The greater part is very beautifully written.

This is the last Will and Testament of me Thomas Doggett of the Parish of St Paul's Covent Garden in the County of Middlesex, Gentleman, made this Tenth day of September Anno Domini One Thousand seven Hundred Twenty and one.

Imprimis. I give and bequeath the Sum of One Thousand pounds unto Twenty poor men (to be chosen by my Executors herein after named) who are ffreemen of and are or have been Shop keepers in the City of London and who were never respectively worth ffifty pounds in the Stock of their severall Trades that is to say to each one of the said twenty poor Men ffifty pounds.

Item. I give unto my Kinsman Captain Jacob Hallister of Bristol the Sume of Two Hundred pounds and my Gold Watch.

Item. I give unto Mrs. Mary Peck of Eltham in Kent Widow the Sume of One Hundred pounds.

Item. In case my Neice Mary Young continues alive and in Ireland at my Death Then I give to her the Sume of Two Hundred pounds.

Item. I give to my Servant Ann Gibbons the Sume of Thirty Pounds per annum during her natural Life to be paid Quarterly at the four usual Quarter days in the year the ffirst payment to be made on such of the said Quarter days as shall happen next after my decease; I further give unto the said Ann Gibbons the Sume of Twenty pounds for Mourning and all my Cloaths and wearing Apparel, Linnen and Wollen and my Household ffurniture.

Item. I give unto Catherine Gibbons Sister of the said Anne the sume of Ten pounds.

Item. I give unto Mrs Mary Reynolds, wife of Thomas Reynolds Esqr one of my Executors herein after appointed my best Diamond Ring.

Item. It is my Will and I do hereby direct that my Executors shall forthwith by and out of my personal Estate purchase ffreehold Lands of Inheritance to the value of Ten pounds per Annum and to cause such Lands when purchased to be conveyed unto Edward Burt of the Admiralty office Esqr his Heirs and assignes subject to and charged and for ever Chargeable with the laying out ffurnishing and procuring yearly on the ffirst day of August for ever the following particulars that is to say, ffive pounds for a Badge of Silver weighing about twelve ounces and representing Liberty to be given to be rowed for by Six young Watermen according to my Custom, Eighteen Shillings for Cloath for a Livery whereon the said Badge is to be put, one pound one shilling for making up the said Livery and Buttons and Appurtenances to it and Thirty Shillings to the Clerk of Watermens Hall All which I would have to be continued for ever yearly in Comemoration of his Majesty King Georges happy Accession to the Brittish Throne. The Remainder of the Rents and profitts of the said Lands when purchased I give and bequeath unto the said Edward Burt his Heirs and Assignes for ever.

And in the meantime until such purchase I direct my Executors to ffurnish the said Badge Livery and other things in manner aforesaid upon every ffirst day of August that shall happen.

I desire that my Body may be decently buried in like manner as my late Wife was, both as to privacy and Expence.

Item. I give devise and bequeath unto my very good ffriends Sir George Markham of the Temple Baronett and Thomas Reynolds of South Mims in the County of Middlesex, Esq[r]. All my South Sea Stock, Subscripeons and Bonds All my Cash, Jewells plate, Goods and Effects whatsoever not hereinbefore disposed of. And all the rest and residue of all my Estate reall and personal of what nature or kind soever and wheresoever to the proper use and benefit of them the said Sir George Markham and Thomas Reynolds Executors of this my Will[1] And I hereby revoke and declare void all former and other Wills or Testaments by me at any time heretofore made And do declare this present Writing to be my last Will and Testament.

In Witness whereof I have hereunto Sett my hand and Seal the Tenth day of September Anno Domini One Thousand Seven hundred Twenty and one above menconed

THO: DOGGETT

Signed sealed published and declared by the before named Thomas Doggett for and as his last Will and Testament in the presence of us who have hereunto Subscribed our names as Witnesses in his presence

JOHN BILTON, fferdn JOHN PARIS.

Proved 2 October, 1721.   [Somerset House, " Buckingham," 177.]

THOMAS DAGGETT, OF IRELAND, AND HIS DESCENDANTS.

638. THOMAS DAGGETT married Elizabeth; she born Ireland, 1799; died Cambridge, Mass., Feb. 27, 1855.

Issue:

639. i. THOMAS DAGGETT,[2] born Ireland, 1830.

639. THOMAS DAGGETT[2] (*Thomas*[1]), born Ireland, 1830; " laborer," " shovel welder," resided Boston, Mass. (1858); married Boston,

---

[1] In the margin opposite to this part the following words are written: " the said S[r] George Markham and Thomas Reynolds their Heirs Executors Administrators and assigns for ever, they first paying all my Debts Legacys and ffuneral Expences, I do hereby constitute and appoint."

Mass., May 2, 1858, by Rev. Thomas McNulty, to Susan Hart, daughter of Daniel and Jane Hart; born Ireland, 1835.

Issue:

640. i. JAMES H. DAGGETT,[3] born Boston, Mass., May 7, 1858; died Boston, Mass., September 11, 1858.
641. ii. THOMAS WILLIAM DAGGETT,[3] born West Bridgewater, Mass., March 6, 1861; died Bridgewater, Mass., June 18, 1862.

CHARLES DOGGETT, OF IRELAND, AND HIS DESCENDANTS.

642. CHARLES DOGGETT,[1] born Ireland; married Catherine.

Issue:

643. i. CATHERINE DOGGETT,[2] born Ireland, 1814; married Boston, Mass., April 4, 1837, by Rev. Michael Healy, to Daniel Slattery; she died Dedham, Mass., October 23, 1849.
644. ii. JOHN DOGGETT,[2] born Ireland, November 27, 1824.

644. JOHN DOGGETT[2] (*Charles*[1]), born Ireland, November 27, 1824; "farmer;" died Dedham, Mass., August 16, 1880; married 1st, Mary Holland, daughter of Patrick and Catharine Holland; born Ireland; died Dedham, Mass., February 24, 1861; married 2d, Roxbury, Mass., November 26, 1861, by Rev. P. O'Beirne, to Mrs. Margaret Typhens, daughter of John and Margaret Lyman; born Ireland, 1833.

Issue:

645. i. JAMES DOGGETT,[3] born Dedham, Mass., 1848.
646. ii. CATHERINE ANN DOGGETT,[3] born Dedham, Mass., February 21, 1850; married Blackstone, Mass., November 27, 1878, William Henry Burlingame.
647. iii. JOHN A. DOGGETT,[3] born Dedham, Mass., September 14, 1851; died Dedham, Mass., November 14, 1855.
648. iv. MARGARET JANE DOGGETT,[3] born Dedham, Mass., January 5, 1852; died Dedham, Mass., April 19, 1857.
649. v. ELLEN M. DOGGETT,[3] born Dedham, Mass., May 3, 1855; died Dedham, Mass., November 15, 1855.
650. vi. MARY E. DOGGETT,[3] born Dedham, Mass., May 3, 1855; died Dedham, Mass., November 28, 1855.
651. vii. MARY J. DOGGETT,[3] born Dedham, Mass., July 5, 1859.
652. viii. JOHN FRANCIS DOGGETT,[3] born Dedham, Mass., February 24, 1861.
653. ix. THOMAS DOGGETT,[3] born Dedham, Mass., September 1, 1862.
654. x. MARGARET M. DOGGETT,[3] born Dedham, Mass., July 3, 1864; died Dedham, Mass., September 13, 1884.
655. xi. WILLIAM H. DOGGETT,[3] born Dedham, Mass., March 10, 1870.

645. JAMES DOGGETT[3] (*John*,[2] *Charles*[1]), born Dedham, Mass., 1848; "shoemaker;" resides Dedham, Mass. (1878); married Boston, Mass., April 28, 1872, by Rev. James A. Healey, to Mrs. Mary

Isabella Rogers, daughter of Patrick and Mary Cohen; born Ireland, 1846.

656. i.   JAMES DOGGETT,[4] born Dedham, Mass., February 5, 1875; died Dedham, Mass., February 6, 1875.
657. ii. JAMES HENRY DOGGETT,[4] born Dedham, Mass., October 19, 1876.
658. iii. KITTIE V. DOGGETT,[4] born Dedham, Mass., December 14, 1878.

651. MARY J. DOGGETT[3] (*John*,[2] *Charles*[1]), born Dedham, Mass., July 5, 1859; married Boston, Mass., March 16, 1883, by Rev. Robert G. Seymour, to George F. Arnold, son of Daniel and Amy [Eldredge] Arnold; "R.R. Engineer;" born Providence, R.I., 1850.

652. JOHN FRANCIS DOGGETT[3] (*John*,[2] *Charles*[1]), born Dedham, Mass., February 24, 1861; "farmer;" resides Canton, Mass. (1885); married Canton, Mass., June 5, 1881, by Rev. M. F. Delaney, to Catherine Sullivan; born Stoughton, Mass., 1857.

Issue:

659. i.   JOHN FRANCIS DOGGETT,[4] born Canton, Mass., August 14, 1881.
660. ii. JAMES H. DOGGETT,[4] born Canton. Mass, June 29, 1883.
661. iii. MARY J. DOGGETT,[4] born Canton, Mass., November 17, 1885.

WILLIAM DOGGETT, OF DUBLIN, IRELAND, AND HIS DESCENDANTS.

662. WILLIAM DOGGETT,[1] born (in or near) Dublin, Ireland, 1806; removed to America 1836; died Salem, Mass., June 10, 1872; married Garristown, County Dublin, Ireland, 1826, Katherine Roony; she resides Salem, Mass. (1884).

Issue:

663. i.   JOHN DOGGETT,[2] born Dublin, Ireland, 1829.
664. ii.   LAWRENCE DOGGETT,[2] born Salem, Mass., 1838.
665. iii. CHRISTOPHER DOGGETT,[2] born Salem, Mass., 1840.
666. iv.   WILLIAM DOGGETT,[2] born Salem, Mass., August 24, 1842; died Salem, Mass., September 8, 1842.
667. v.   JANE DOGGETT,[2] born Salem, Mass., February, 1847.
668. vi.   SUSAN DOGGETT,[2] born Salem, Mass., November, 1847.
669. vii. CATHERINE DOGGETT,[2] born Salem, Mass., October 9, 1849.
670. viii. KATE DOGGETT,[2] born Salem, Mass., 1851.
671. ix.   JAMES DOGGETT,[2] born Salem, Mass., May 5, 1854; died Salem, Mass., August 13, 1885.

663. JOHN DOGGETT[2] (*William*[1]), born Dublin, Ireland, 1829; "spinner;" resided Lawrence, Mass. (1851); married 1st, Lawrence, Mass., November 22, 1851, by Rev. James O'Donnell, to Elizabeth Riley, daughter of Peter and Ann Riley; born Ireland, 1832; married, 2d Lawrence, Mass., May 14, 1866, by Rev. L. M.

Edge, to Elizabeth Rooney, widow, daughter of John and Winnie
Rudden; born 1834.

Issue:

672. i. WILLIAM DOGGETT,[3] born Lawrence, Mass., December 3, 1852.
673. ii. MARY ANN DOGGETT,[3] born Lawrence, Mass., July 11, 1854.
674. iii. JOHN DOGGETT,[3] born Lawrence, Mass., July 11, 1856.
675. iv. MATILDA DOGGETT,[3] born Salem, Mass., 1859.

665. CHRISTOPHER DOGGETT[2] (*William* [1]), born Salem, Mass.,
1840; "currier;" married Hannah Kenney; born Ireland.

Issue:

676. i. MARY J. DOGGETT,[3] born Salem, Mass., March 1, 1871; died Salem,
         Mass., June 16, 1873.
677. ii. JOHN DOGGETT,[3] born Salem, Mass., May 2, 1873.
678. iii. HANNAH DOGGETT,[3] born Salem, Mass., September 1, 1875.

673. MARY ANN DOGGETT[3] (*John,*[2] *William* [1]), born Lawrence,
Mass., July 11, 1854; "operative;" resided Templeton, Mass.
(1874); married Templeton, Mass., July 12, 1874, by Rev. Joseph
Coyne, to Francis Roark, son of Michael and Mary Roark; born
Lowell, Mass., 1844.

675. MATILDA DOGGETT[3] (*John,*[2] *William* [1]), born Salem, Mass.,
1859; married Ware, Mass., June 30, 1879, by Rev. Charles
Boucher, to John McBride, son of Thomas and Catherine McBride;
born Millbury, Mass., 1858.

DOGGETT-DAGGETT FAMILY IN AMERICA.

JOHN DOGGETT, OF MARTHA'S VINEYARD.

FIRST GENERATION.

679. JOHN DOGGETT [1] (sometimes spelled with one "t," also at times one "g"); born England; removed to New England with Governor Winthrop, 1630; died Plymouth, Mass., May (between 17th and 26th), 1673; married 1st (date, place, and to whom not found); married 2d, Plymouth, Mass., August 29, 1667, Bathsheba Pratt, widow.

Issue :

680. i.   JOHN DOGGETT,[2] born England (?), about 1626.
681. ii. THOMAS DOGGETT,[2] born Watertown, Mass. (?), about 1630.
682. iii. JOSEPH DOGGETT,[2] born Watertown, Mass. (?), about 1634.
683. iv. ELIZABETH DOGGETT,[2] born Watertown, Mass. (?) about 1638; married Jeremiah Whitton. Mr. Whitton bought land in Tisbury of Joseph Daggett, Jan. 28, 1701. [Dukes Deeds, 1-193.]
684. v.   HEPZIBAH DOGGETT,[2] born Watertown, Mass. (?), 1643.

Of the parentage and date of birth of John Doggett no positive proof has been found.

The fact that he came to America with Winthrop, and that Doggetts resided at Groton, from whence Winthrop came, would naturally lead us to follow out the history of the family there to see if John Doggett might not be one of them. In this search Martha Doggett (No. 73), of Groton, who married Giles Firmin, is found to have come to America with Winthrop, while in the adjoining parish of Boxford the Doggetts and Winthrops were connected by the marriage of Thomas Doggett and Margaret Clopton.

Of the Groton Doggetts named John, those of suitable age to have come to America in 1630 can all be placed, but not so with the Boxford Doggetts ; for among them we have John, baptized November 4, 1602 (No. 58), of whom the parish records give no further information, and it is possible that he is the one who joined in the "Great Emigration" in 1630. To describe this emigration, it is necessary to have a general idea of the movements which led to the planting of the Colony of Massachusetts Bay, in which John Doggett was one of the pioneers.

In March, 1628, the Plymouth Company sold to a company of six gentlemen in England the territory extending from a line three miles north of Merrimac river to one three miles south of Charles river, and from the Atlantic to the Pacific ocean. These gentlemen, with others who became associated with them, obtained a charter for their company, which was called the "Massachusetts Bay Company," and in June, 1628, sent over a company of emigrants, who landed at Salem, and commenced the settlement of that ancient town.

In July, 1629, it was proposed to transfer the government of the plantation from England to the colony, "to those that shall inhabit there."

On August 29 it was determined by a vote that the "government patent should be settled in New England," and on the 19th of October John Winthrop was chosen governor for New England. John Winthrop was then in his forty-first year, having been born in Edwardston, near Groton, in Suffolk, on the 12th day of January, 158⅞.

The considerations which induced Winthrop and the others to come over to New England were of no mere private or personal character. They had relation to the condition of England at that day, its social, moral, religious, and political condition.

The spreading of the gospel and the conversion of the heathen were foremost in the contemplation of the New England fathers.

Seventeen emigrant ships left England in the year 1630, of which fourteen sailed before the 1st of June. On the 8th of April four ships, the "Arbella," the "Jewell," the "Ambrose," and the "Talbot," sailed from the Isle of Wight, bringing the governor and others who afterward held prominent places in the early history of the colony.

The passengers who arrived in these ships were not satisfied with Salem, and soon after landing went, on the 17th of June, to select a place for settlement. Having selected the peninsula of Charlestown for that purpose, they returned to Salem, and as soon as preparations could be made the fleet proceeded from Salem to Charlestown.

Soon after the removal of the emigrants from Salem to Charlestown, a large portion of them, with Sir Richard Saltonstall as their leader, accompanied by Rev. George Phillips as their pastor, proceeded about four miles up Charles river and commenced a settlement, at first sometimes called Sir Richard Saltonstall's plantation, but soon after by the court named Watertown. The exact date of the settlement of Watertown is not known, but it was probably before the middle of July. 1630.

Bond, in his history of Watertown, says "that it is almost certain that for the first four years Watertown was the most populous town in the colony, and it is not improbable that it continued so for fifteen or twenty years."

As a full list of those who made up the " Great Emigration," or of those who accompanied Sir Richard Saltonstall to Watertown, is not known, we must infer from the records still in existence as to who took part in these movements. From such evidence Savage and other well-known antiquarians all agree that John Doggett came in the same fleet with Winthrop, arriving in Salem sometime between June 12 and July 2, 1630, according to which of the four vessels brought him to New England. He removed with Sir Richard Saltonstall, and was one of the earliest settlers of Watertown.

Watertown was more remote from the bay than either of the other plantations begun that year, and was the first of the inland towns. It was, however, upon the tide-water of Charles river, which was there navigable for only small vessels. As the company of planters who first went there was large, and as they were not compacted into a village or dense population, like other early plantations, they must have been scattered over a very considerable extent of territory.

The homestall of Sir Richard was situated on Charles river, within that strip of territory which was taken from Watertown and annexed to Cambridge in 1754, and was about a mile from the site of Harvard College. Between the homestall of Sir Richard and the New Town (Cambridge) line there was only one intervening lot, which belonged to John Doggett and contained thirteen acres. This lot he sold to Thomas Brigham in 1637, and it may have been his homestall from his settlement there in 1630 to 1637, although I am inclined to think his " homestall " during his residence in Watertown was the fifteen-acre lot bounded north and west by the (Fresh) pond and Nicholas Busby, south by highway, east by W. Paine, and probably embracing the lot of the Fresh Pond Hotel.

The records of Watertown do not show that John Doggett took any prominent part in the affairs of the town during the time he made it his residence, as his name does not occur on the town records which have been preserved.

October 19, 1630, John Doggett applied to be made " freeman," and on May 18, 1631, he took the oath. [Col. Records, Vol. 1, pp. 62–3.]

In order for such admission, it was necessary to be a church member, and for this reason there were some men holding respectable social positions who never were thus admitted, or not until advanced age. It was not necessary, however, to be a church member or a freeman in order to hold office in the town, or appointments from the court. This could be done by taking the oath of fidelity.

The first church of Watertown was organized July 28, 1630, and next after that of Salem is the oldest in the Colony of Massachusetts Bay. Rev. George Phillips was the pastor until his death, which occurred July 1, 1644.

After the small lots, the earliest grants by the freemen, July 25, 1636, were called the Great Dividend, and the fourth Great Dividend began at the small lots and was bounded north by Cambridge line. Of these, No. 12 fell to John Doggett and contained thirty acres, which was afterward bought by Richard Wait.

Another grant made $163\frac{6}{7}$ shows among those who received land in the Further Plain (in later times called Waltham Plain), bounded south by Charles river, north by the Great Dividends, the name John Doggett, six acres, which was afterward bought by R. Wait.

In a volume of the Town Record, containing the schedule of possessions, is a list of grantees of the town plot, of which John Doggett had six acres, recorded in the division dated April 9, 1638. Pequusset Meadow was divided into numerous small lots, of which J. Doggett had two acres, which was afterward bought by John Flemming.

Thus during his residence in Watertown John Doggett gradually increased his landed possessions, and was doubtless busily engaged in agricultural pursuits.

Among his fellow-townsmen with whom he became associated was Mr. Thomas Mayhew, who probably arrived in 1631. For the ensuing thirteen years, it appears by the Colonial Records that few, if any, other persons so often received important appointments from the General Court as Thomas Mayhew.

He built the first bridge over Charles river; was temporarily proprietor of the mill, of the fishing-weirs, of the Oldham farm, and of the Bradstreet farm, in Cambridge Village (now Newton).

October 10, 1641, James Forett, agent of the Earl of Sterling, granted to Thomas Mayhew, of Watertown, merchant, and to Thomas Mayhew, his son, Nantucket and two small islands adjacent; and on the 23d of the same month he granted to them Martha's Vineyard and the Elizabeth Islands.

The Government Mayhew shall set up shall be such as is now established in the Massachusetts, aforesaid and to enjoy as much privilege touching their plantg inhabiting and enjoying of all and every part of the premises, as by the patent to the patentees of Massachusetts.

The Mayhews having received grants of these islands proceeded to arrange for their settlement, by sharing with several others the privileges granted to them. Among their fellow-townsmen of Watertown who became interested in the project was John Doggett, as appears in the following record:

Whereas Thomas Mayhew sen and Thomas Mayhew Jr, have granted to them by James Forett Marthas Vineyard and Elizabeth Isles,

This is to certify, that we, Thomas and Thomas 2nd, do hereby grant unto John Doggett, Daniel Pierce, and Richard Beers and John Smith and Francis Smith, with ourselves, to make choice for the Present of a large Town, upon the same terms with us and equal possession administration of all that shall present themselves to come to live upon any part of the whole grant of all the Islands and we grant also to them and their associates with us, to receive another township for posterity upon the same terms as we have from the Grantees.

Tawanquatick	March 16, 1641	Isaac Robinson
Chappaquiddick		Thomas Trapp
		Nicholas Horton
		John Pease
		Thomas Bayly
		Thomas Burchard
		John Bolles
		Thomas Butler
		Joseph Norton
		Isaac Norton

The Vineyard, called in early records Martin's Vineyard, is nineteen miles long and, upon an average, five miles broad. It is generally level, though in the northern and western parts the land rises into hills of two hundred and fifty feet above the adjacent country. There is a plain in the southern part, upon which Edgartown is situated, eight miles in length and five or six in breadth, and it is the site selected "for the Present of a large Town," to which was given the name of Edgartown. The point of the Vineyard nearest Boston is but little over eighty miles.

Dr. Freeman, when writing of the Vineyard, says that "Not less than three thousand Indians, it has been generally estimated, were on the island when it was entered by Mayhew." "Like the other savages of New England, they were in a low state of civilization; and they had attained few of the arts which contribute to the comfort of human life." They were, however, a hospitable and tractable people, and among them the younger Mr. Mayhew attempted to introduce the gospel. Several English families began a settlement and gathered a church as early as 1641, of which Thomas Mayhew, Jr., was pastor.

"The savages received Mr. Mayhew with kindness, and with readiness listened to his exhortations. The wonderful progress which the Christian religion, through the zeal of this eminent evangelist and his worthy successors, made in Martha's Vineyard surprised and delighted the pious of that age." "The Indians were converted to the Christian faith, and attempts were made to reduce them to a state of civilization."

Thomas Mayhew, Sr., and John Doggett still continued to reside at Watertown, while the younger Mr. Mayhew began his work and the settlement of the island in 1641. The following year (1642) John Doggett takes the next step toward removing to the island, as appears in the following grant:

We do hereby grant, unto JOHN DOGGET of Watertown and to his heirs and assigns forever, twenty acres of land upon the point beginning at the great stone next to my lot and twenty acres of meadow and also Five hundred acres of land for a farm he have liberty to take up, wherever he the said John Dogget wishes only provided he take not up his farm within three miles of the spring that is by the harbor in my lot aforesaid before I, that is Thomas Mayhew, the elder, have made choice of twenty acres of meadow and a farm of Five hundred acres for myself, the which first choice not being made within one year, ensuing the date hereof, then the said John Dogget have liberty to choose for himself.
Witness hereunto our hands

THOMAS MAYHEW
THOMAS MAYHEW
JOHN SMITH.

Dec. 1, 1642

[Dukes Deeds, 1–189.]

It does not appear that John Doggett moved directly to the Vineyard, but instead made his home for a time at the new settlement at Rehoboth.

John Doggett, husbandman, was one of the earliest settlers of Rehoboth, Mass., which comprised in its greatest extent the present town, together with Seekonk, Pawtucket, Attleboro', Cumberland, R.I., and that part of Swansea and Barrington which was called by the Indians Wannamoiset. It does not appear that any general or permanent settlement was made here earlier than about the year 1643; and it was after this that John Doggett joined the settlement, at the time of removal from Watertown, possibly as a step toward his settlement at Martha's Vineyard. The first notice that we find of him in Rehoboth is:

The 8th of the 8th mo. 1646 at a general meeting of the town upon public notice given, it was agreed that John Doget shall have all the lands that were laid out for John Megges and because there was no lot laid out for him upon the great plain, it was agreed upon that he shall have both his allotments according to the estate upon the great plain and to begin upon the south side.

The 9th of the 12th mo., 1646, at a meeting of the townsmen, John Dogget and others were made choice of "to view the fence of the town lots."

The same day it was agreed that Edward Sale, John Dogget, William Sabin, John Peram, and William Thayer shall have leave to set up a "weier" upon the cove before William Devill's house, and one upon Pawtucket river.

It is also of interest to read that by this agreement " they shall sell their alwives at 2s. a thousand, and their other fish at reasonable rates."

The 18th of the 12th mo., 1646, at a meeting of the town, it was agreed to draw lots for the new meadow, and John Dogget drew No. 40.

The 12th of the 2d mo., 1648, at a general meeting of the town, upon public notice given, John Dogget and Robert Titus were chosen deputies for the towne.   [Bliss Hist. Rehoboth.]

The records at Plymouth, dated June 7, 1648, give the committee for the court for Rehoboth as Robert Titus, John Dogged.   [Court Orders, 2–164.]

June 7, 1648, at Plymouth, among the names of those who were propounded for freemen, was John Dogged.   [Court Orders, 2–167.]

The same day his name is recorded among those that were to take the oath.   [Court Orders, 2–166.]

Again, on the same day, he was appointed surveyor of the highways for Rehoboth, and during that year he was also an exciseman.

The same date, it is recorded that:

Whereas it doth apeer, yt ther is a debt of five pound and eight shillings apertaining unto Georg. Wright in the hands of John Dogged of Rehoboth the court have ordered yt the said debt remayne atached in the hands of John Dogged aforesaid for the use of Leiftenant Nash and Sergeant Church in consideration of the damage befaling them by the above said Georg Wright, the breaking of his bonds for the good behavior.

It would seem that leaving his son John at Rehoboth, he removed, about this time, to the Vineyard, where it is possible his son Thomas had already settled.

The early records on the Vineyard are quite imperfect, and, aside from the wills and deeds, those that have been preserved are mostly in the collection of the late Hon. Richard L. Pease, of Edgartown, Mass.

It is probable, after his arrival here, John Doggett was occupied much the same as at Watertown, in agricultural pursuits, and in making his home in the new town, which they laid out and called Edgartown.

March 29, 1651, the town chose him corporal.

1652.   "Ordered that Mr. Mayhew, ye elder, and John Doggett, shall lay out all highways belonging to this town."

October 31, 1654, vote regarding John Doggett's ram.

June 5, 1655, he was chosen assistant for the year.

John Doggett went from Martha's Vineyard to Nantucket in 1659, for the purpose of gunning, where he lived as boarder with Thomas Macy, the first English settler on Nantucket.

March 3, 1660, he buys "Farm Neck" of Wampanog, alias Samuel, Sachem of Sauchacantackett, or Farm Neck. [Dukes Deeds, 2–253.]

Edgartown Town meeting 17 Dec 1660 These are to warne you by ye authority of ye town to levy upon ye estate of John Doggett, ye elder, upon Marthas Vineyard, ye sum of five thousand, upon ye breach of order in purchasing lands. To William Weeks constable. Voted by the town this 17 Dec 1660. This is by ye authority of ye town.

THOMAS MAYHEW.

2 Oct 1662 At this court [Plymouth] John Doged of the Island called Martins Vineyard complained against the towne of the said Vineyard in an action of the case for the title of a certain peell of land granted unto the said John Dogged by Mr. Thomas Mayhew . . . which the said inhabitants doe unjustly and illegally disturbe him in his quiet enjoyment of the same which said case is by joynt consent on both ptyes refered to the determination of the court. The Jury find for the plantiff the full title granted him by Mr Thomas Mayhew, Senr. [Rec. of Mass. Bay in N.E., Vol. VII., p. 104.]

Jan. 29, 1665 There was a purchase of commonage of grass also $\frac{1}{2}$ of the $\frac{1}{5}$ of lot next the sea that faleth to the town upon the Island called Martins Vineyard these several things being purchased by John Doggett the Elder from Towanicut the sachem thereof and delv'd the same over into the hands of the Townsmen. [Dukes Deeds, 1–354.]

These few facts are all that have been found relating to his residence on the Vineyard. It is probable that his wife died and was buried here, but there are no records found of the date or place.

He was married again at Plymouth, Mass., August 29, 1667, and was then called "John Doged of Martins Vineyard."

After his marriage to Bathsheba Pratt, he probably resided most of the time at Plymouth, and the records there under date 1670, May 29, mention him as John Doggett, Senior, of Plymouth, transcribed on the list of "freemen."

In the Dukes County Deeds, 1–321, is "The record of John Dagget sen'r will."

Plymouth May 17, 1673

I John Doggett finding the symptoms of Death upon me do make this my last will and testament hereby Revoking all former wills. I give to my Beloved wife all my househould goods and all my wearing cloaths and all my debts in any part of Plymouth Collonie : also I give her one ox at Sacconesit in the hands of William Week Jr : also I give my said wife that five pounds in goods which I was to receive of John Edy as part of pay for the two oxen of mine he sold for 10 pounds : also I give her the hide and Tallow of an ox that is at the Vineyard to be sent to Boston, and the four quarters of the ox I give equally to my sons and daughters at the Vineyard.

My lands at Marthas Vineyard undivided and their priviledges which are part of the twenty seventh part of that Township called now Edgartown, I give to my two sons John and Joseph to be equally divided betwixt them and to remain to their heirs forever.

My twenty akers of meadow given me upon the same tearm, my farme upon the said Island was granted to me which is not yet laid out to me, I give 10 akers of it to my son Thomas, 5 akers to my son John, 5 akers to my son Joseph.

A small parcell of meadow I have at Chappaquiddick Joining to my son Thomas, his meadow there ; I give it to my son Thomas.

fourty akers of upland and two akers of meadow that ly at one of Elyzabeth Islands namely that Island which Mr Peleg Sanford Bought which upland and meadow I bought of Francis Vssleton who had the said land of aged Mr Mayhew, this said upland and meadow I give to my son Thomas.

My whole farm I have already equally divided betwixt my three sons.

My ten akre lot uppon the line now where John Gee dwelt I give equally to be divided between my two sons John and Joseph.

My land at Aquampache and at Felix neck and at Konomache and a piece of meadow at Sangekantackett and any other portion of land I have not before named I give to be equally divided betwixt my two Daughters Elizabeth and Hephzibah.

All my cattle and horse kind at Marthas Vineyard I give to be equally divided between my two daughters.

My will is that my son John send my wife two payer of shoes and then to discharge him of all further debt.

With Reference to my estate at the Islands above mentioned I desire my loving friends Isaac Robinson and John Edy my son in law to be overseers of this my will and to see that it be performed and concerning my estate in this Collonie, my desire is that Lieutenant Morton and Andrew Ring be overseers of this will and that they take care to se it performed.

The ⎰ Marke of
JOHN ⎱ DAGGETT senr

The said John Doggett senr did attest the above written to be his last will and Testament before us, he being then of sound mind and understanding:

Witnesses

JOHN COTTON.
JOHN ATWOOD.
ANDREW RING.

This will is legally and orderly proved and Recorded at the Court of his majesties holden at Plymouth the 4th of June 1673 as attesteth Nathaniel Morton Secretary to the Court for the Jurisdiction of New Plymouth.

This will is by the court held at Edgartown upon Mart. Vineyard Oct. 1, 1673 accepted and approved as legall with this proviso only, that the farm is to contain 500 akers of upland and 20 akers of meadow and no more and so ordered to be recorded, as attest,

MATT. MAYHEW, Secretary.

Inventory of John Doged of Plymouth on oath of Bathsheba Doged, widow, 26 May 1673, at court 4 June 1673, amts to

	£	s	d	
	16	18	9	
also due		16	4	EPHR. NORTON
due funeral		19	4	ANDREW RINGE

Whereas there hath been some controversie concerning some particulars in the Will and Testament of John Dogget senr on the other side Recorded, it is agreed and concluded as followeth, viz.

That whereas it is said in the said will that land undivided and their privileges are given to his sons John and Joseph: yet notwithstanding in the subsequent of the said will a certain parcell of land called Aquompache undivided is otherwise disposed of viz: to his two daughters: The said John and Joseph do hereby wholly relinquish any right, Tythe, or interest which they might claim by virtue of any clause in the said will unto the said land at Aquompache to be held as in the subsequent part of the will is declared to be given and for confirmation thereof we have desired this our account to be recorded in his Majesties Court of Records at Marthas Vineyard and have hereunto in witness thereof subscribed with our hands in this publique Record, May 29, In the 27th year of his Majesties Reign A.D. 1675.

JOHN DOGGET
JOSEPH DOGGET.

Recorded this 29 May 1675 pr Matt Mayhew Secretary

[Dukes Deeds, 1–322.]

John Edy and Jeremiah Whitton, the husbands of said Elizabeth and Hephziba, relinquish any right which they might claim to land near the Neck, to his son Joseph Dagget, May 29, 1675. [Dukes Deeds, 1–322.]

Whereas there is a certain tract of land in the town of Edgartown commonly called a Dividend near a neck called Felix his neck which belonged to John Dogget sen^r of Marthas Vineyard lately deceased but before his death given to his son Joseph Dagget but not recorded, therefore John Dagget son and heir to John Dagget releases any right he might have May 29, 1675 before Thomas Mayhew, Gov.

signed JOHN DOGGET

[Dukes Deeds, 1–280.]

Sept 15, 1677. Know all men whom it may concern that we whose names are underwritten have agreed to divide the farm our father gave us [then follows division]   signed   JOHN DOGGETT
THOMAS DAGGETT
JOSEPH DOGGETT

Acknowledged before me by the three brethren above written by Thomas Mayhew, Gov.

[Dukes Deeds, 1–15.]

JOHN DOGGETT, OF MARTHA'S VINEYARD.

SECOND GENERATION.

680. JOHN DOGGETT [2] (*John*[1]), born England (?), about 1626; died Rehoboth, Mass., September 9, 1707; married Rehoboth, Mass., 23, 9 mo., 1651, Anne Sutton.

Issue:

685. i. ANNA DOGGETT,[3] born Rehoboth, Mass., middle of August, 1653; married Rehoboth, Mass., March 12, 1684, Joseph, son of Sampson Mason; he born Rehoboth, Mass., March 6, 1663.
686. ii. JOHN DOGGETT,[3] born Rehoboth, Mass., January 8, 1655; died Rehoboth, Mass., last of March, 1662.
687. iii. JOSEPH DOGGETT,[3] born Rehoboth, Mass., middle of November, 1657.
688. iv. NATHANIEL DOGGETT,[3] born Rehoboth, Mass., middle of August, 1661.
689. v. ELIZABETH DOGGETT,[3] born Rehoboth, Mass., October 23, 1666.

John Doggett was one of the early settlers of Rehoboth. The record of his family may still be seen in the town book, and the following is a tracing from the original entry:

1651

1653
1655
1657
1661
1666

‒ ‒ ‒ 1662

1688

John Dogget maried to Anne Sutton ye 23 8b 98 9Xb°

The Childern of John Doghead age
m

Anna Doghead borne aboutt midle of August

John Doghead borne 8 thy January

Joseph Doggett borne ye midle of November

Nathanell Doggett borne midle of August

Elizabeth Dogett borne ye 23 of October

John Dogget Juneor dyed ye last of March .. ‒ ‒ ‒ 1662

Nath Dagget Son of Nathanell Dagget Burn
the ‒ 2ll of August   88

He does not appear, from the records examined, to have taken any part in public affairs until June 1 1658, when he was " on the grand enquest." This year (1658) he took the oath of fidelity in Reheboth.

"June 22, 1658. At a town meeting lawfully warned, lots were drawn for the meadows that lie on the north side of the town (now in Attleboro'), and lot No. 34 fell to John Dogget." [Bliss, Rehoboth.]

"June 1, 1663. John Doged of Rehoboth being by Capt Willett convicted of 2 lyes, is fined 20 shillings." [Court Orders, 4–48.]

In 1666 a purchase of lands in the north side of Rehoboth (became afterward Attleboro') was first called the North Purchase, and of the seventy-nine shares in the land John Doggett had one share.

> Oct 16, 1666. John Doggett, John Woodcock and John Titus were chosen by the town to see what timber trees are fallen on the late purchased lands on the north side of our town and they shall have the forfeiture for their pains and the trees to those that the land shall fall to.

May 26, 1668. John Doggett drew a lot in the meadow lands in the North Purchase.

July 7, 1668. John Doged begins suit against George Robinson, for slander, and George Robinson makes acknowledgment to the court :

> I George Robinson acknowledge I have done John Doged wronge, in speaking words that tend to his defamation, for which I am sorry, and I had not ground so to report him in the case now depending in the court and therefore desire him to passe it by. [Mass. Col. Rec., Vol. VIII., p. 147.]

"March 2, 166$\frac{8}{9}$. Capt Thomas Willet complained against Mr. John Doged and John Miller, in an action of trespas, on the case to the damage of five pounds, for making and carrying away a p'cell of hay from lower Skesett the last hay season without his leave and order." Marked in margin, "This action was withdrawn."

Among the names of those who drew for a division on the North Purchase, March 18, 166$\frac{8}{9}$, was John Doggett. [Daggetts, Attleboro'.]

June 4, 1669. A writing of the lands of John Doged, of Rehoboth. [Court Orders, 3–140.]

January 9, 167$\frac{0}{1}$. John Dogget had liberty granted him to build a warehouse and wharf at the water side.

June 5, 1672. He was surveyor of highways.

June 3, 1674. Was sworn as constable.

During King Philip's war Rehoboth was much disturbed, and many of her residents killed, and their houses burned by the Indians. At one period of the war advances of money were made, and John Dogget contributed £11 1s. 3$\frac{1}{2}$d.

At the death of his father John Dogget came into possession of land on Martha's Vineyard, and the records on the Vineyard speak of him sometimes as Doggett and others as Daggett, the first indications of such change in spelling being found on those records.

May 29, 1675. He sells Joseph Daggett land at Edgartown. [Dukes Deeds, 1–280.]

This tendency on the Vineyard to change in spelling is perhaps better illustrated by an exchange of lands between him and his brother, October 9, 1677, when:

John Dogget of Rehoboth sells land at Rehoboth 22 acres, to his brother Thomas Dogget of Edgartown on Marthas Vineyard, his brother to take choice of one of 3 lots, signed by John and Anne Dogget (Bristol Deeds, 1–22), and Thomas Daggett, of Edgartown, sells land on the Vineyard, late belonging " to my father John Doggett deceased with the bounds as made lately between my brother John myself and my brother Joseph Daggett to my brother John Daggett," Thomas Doggett releasing all rights. Signed Thomas and Hannah Daggett. [Dukes Deeds, 1–323.]

2 June, 1685, John Dogget was surveyor at Rehoboth.

In a list of the inhabitants of Rehoboth, holding land under a certain grant, February 7, 1689, his name is mentioned as John Daggett, and afterward so spelled on the records at Rehoboth. A point of land between Ten-mile river and the Pawtucket, upon the north side of the former, is mentioned by Bliss as the probable location of a point called " Daggett's Point."

August 5, 1692, John Daggett of Rehoboth, in the Province of Mass. Bay in N.E. for 85£ paid by James Allin of the town of Chilmark, on Marthas Vineyard, land in the township of Edgartown 330 acres near farm pond. [Dukes Deeds, 1–151.]

This is probably his portion in his father's estate, together with the portion he bought of his brother, October 9, 1677.

Feb. 1, 170¾. Sells John Dagget of Chilmark on Marthas Vineyard, 25 acres land in Attleboro. [Bristol Deeds, 5–246.]

In the Bristol probate records, October 1, 1707, Nathaniel Daggett, son and executor of John Daggett, late of Rehoboth, deceased. Inventory amounts to £39 12s. 10d.

681. THOMAS DOGGETT[2] (*John*[1]), born Watertown, Mass. (?), about 1630; called his name Daggett; died Edgartown, Mass. (?), between March 18 and September 15, 1691; married, about 1657, Hannah Mayhew, daughter of Gov. Thomas and Jane Mayhew, of Edgartown, Mass.; born Watertown, Mass., 15, 4th mo., 1635; died Edgartown, Mass., 1722.

Issue:

690. i.   THOMAS DOGGETT,[3] born Edgartown, Mass., about 1658.
691. ii. SAMUEL DOGGETT,[3] born Edgartown, Mass., about 1660; died Edgartown, Mass., February 26, 17¼⁷.
692. iii. JOHN DOGGETT,[3] born Edgartown, Mass., 1662.
693. iv. JOSHUA DOGGETT,[3] born Edgartown, Mass., about 1664.
694. v.   ISRAEL DOGGETT,[3] born Edgartown, Mass., about 1672.
695. vi. MERCY DOGGETT,[3] born Edgartown, Mass.

Thomas Doggett married the eldest daughter of Governor Mayhew.

The Mayhew family were prominent in the management of affairs on the island, and most of the early records now existing are in the handwriting of members of that family.

These records are the first showing a tendency to spell the name
"Daggett," but for several years both spellings are used.

Long after the name was spelled Daggett on the Vineyard (in the
Registry of Deeds), the son Thomas was called Doggett in the
Bristol county records, and I should therefore be inclined to
the opinion that the Thomas Doggett who married Hannah Mayhew
may not have himself called his name Daggett until near the close of
his life.

November 11, 1652.   He and William Weeks are voted whale
cutters for the year.

In 1652 he was living in Edgartown, as at that time "Richard
Arey hath given him, a house lott between Mr Burchard and Thomas
Daggett's." [Hon. R. L. Pease.]

August 3, 1670.   Thomas Doged was clarke to the court at the
Vineyard.   [Plymouth Records.]

June 20, 1679, he promises whatever Thomas Mayhew shall give
to his daughter Hannah (his wife), she shall be at liberty to dispose
of as she likes.   [Dukes Deeds, 1–322.]

The Dukes and Bristol county deeds contain many transfers of
land made by both Thomas and Hannah Daggett.

Thomas Daggett is said to have been at one time magistrate of the
island.

March 18, 1691.   Hannah Daggett, wife of Thomas Daggett, of Edgartown.
for 30£, paid by son Thomas Daggett, late of the town of Bristol, in N.E. ¾ of
¼ of all the lands given me by the Worshipfull Thomas Mayhew Esq late of
Marthas Vineyard dec'd.   The whole 1¼ mile by the sea side, and about 2 miles
inland, called Chickomo.   [Dukes Deeds, 5-84.]

Thomas Daggett died between March 18 and September 15, 1691,
probably at Edgartown, but there are no records there to show the
exact date.

Even the probate records do not assist, as they are very imperfect,
and contain no mention of the settlement of his estate.

That he left no will is shown by a record in the Registry of Deeds,
1–221, where his son Thomas gives Israel, his brother, land,
regarding which he says:

Lands which came to me the said Thomas, as heir to said Thomas Daggett,
as well from the knowledge of the intent of my said father, had Providence
allowed him making a will.

Dated September 15, 1691.

Between September 12, 1695, and 1705, Mrs. Daggett married
Capt. Samuel Smith, of Edgartown, and died in Edgartown, 1722.

"The last will and testament of Hannah Smith of ye town of Edgartown in
Dukes County in Province of ye Massachusetts Bay, in New England, being in

sound mind and understanding. doth make this my last will and testament, heretofore by me made, done or supposed to be made," gives natural son, Israel Daggett, land at Edgartown, and Chappaquiddick, until his eldest son Samuel
Daggett be 21 years, then to him and his heirs forever. Her two sons, Joshua
and Israel, land at Edgartown. The same her executors. Dated Aug. 22, 1710.
Proved Feb. 7, 172¾. [Dukes Probate, 1–145.]

682. Joseph Doggett[2] (*John*[1]), born Watertown, Mass. (?),
about 1634 ; called his name Daggett; married an Indian of Martha's
Vineyard.

Issue :

696. i.   Joseph Daggett,[3] born Tisbury, Mass. (?)
697. ii. Ellis (Alice) Daggett,[3] died between March 19 and May 11, 1711.
698. iii. Esther Daggett,[3] married Edward Cottle, and had issue, Esther
          Cottle.[4]

Joseph Doggett probably removed from Watertown to the Vineyard at an early age. The only information regarding him is found
on the records at the Vineyard, and in the majority of cases his name
is spelled Daggett.

One instance, however, in the deeds, 1–322, May 29, 1675, is
marked in the margin in pencil, " apparently original signatures,"
and in that case his name is spelled " Dogget." In all other cases
the name is in the handwriting of the one who made the record, and
is sometimes spelled one way, and at other times the other.

I should be inclined to the opinion that in this case, as with his
brother Thomas, he may not have himself called his name Daggett;
but if so, not until near the close of his life.

The name of his wife does not appear, but the following deed to
his two daughters would indicate that his wife may have been an
Indian :

Know all men by these presents that I, Puttuspagun, of Sanchacantackett, do
freely give unto my cousins Hester and Ellis Daggett, a certain tract of meadow
lying and being on the north side of Ohkeshkepe Neck, lying between Quaniamo
and the western end of Asanostackitt Pond. I say, I do freely and firmly give,
all the meadow with all the nookes and coves lying between the mentioned bounds,
to my abovementioned cousins, their heirs and assigns, to have and to hold, forever free from me, my heirs or assigns, and this I do and have done for the
natural love and affection to them, being of my near kindred, always to be
understood that if they cannot enjoy the said meadow by reason of the English
claim, that then it shall return to me or my heirs. And in witness, and in confirmation of the premises, I have hereunto subscribed with my hand and put to
my seal this five and twentieth day of March and in the year of our Lord, one
thousand six hundred eighty and five.

                                        The mark of Puttuspagun

Witness
Samuel Tilton
Samuel : C :

Acknowledged before Thomas Mayhew, Justice of Peace, and before Matt
Mayhew, Chief Magistrate, by Mr Sam. alias Wabamuck, Sachim of Sanchacantackett, that the above was by his knowledge and free approbation.

Entered April 22, 1685. [Vol. I., p. 251, Land Records.]

May 29, 1675. A tract of land in Edgartown, near a neck called Felix, his neck, which belonged to John Dogget, Senr., of Martha's Vineyard, lately deceased, but before his death given to his son Joseph Daggett, but not recorded, therefor John Dagget, son and heir to John Dagget, releases any right he might have. [Dukes Deeds, 1–280.]

Sept. 15, 1677. The undersigned agree to divide the farm our father gave us. John Dogget, Thomas Daggett, Joseph Doggett. Acknowledged before me by the three brethren above named by Thomas Mayhew Gov. [D.D., 1–15.]

Many transfers of land are recorded in the name of Joseph Daggett, and he is mentioned as wheelwright, yeoman, husbandman, and gentleman.

Judge Sewall, in his Diary, under date of Monday, April 6, 1702, says : " Refresh at Chases, from thence ride to Tisbury, first man I speak with is Joseph Dogget. He tells me Mr. Kithcart keeps an ordinary."

He seems to have lived in Tisbury until sometime between September 11, 1711, and June 24, 1715, when he is called of Edgartown. The last record of him that has been found is March 5, 1720, when he is called one of the proprietors of Tisbury land. [D. D., 5–210.]

684. Hepzibah Doggett² (*John*¹), born Watertown, Mass. (?), 1643 ; died May 3, 1726 ; married John Eddy ; he died Tisbury (?), Mass., previous to December 24, 1717.

Issue :

699. i. Benjamin Eddy (?).

John Eddy was one of the overseers of John Doggett's will, May, 1673. He resided in Tisbury.

JOHN DOGGETT, OF MARTHA'S VINEYARD.

THIRD GENERATION.

687. Dr. Joseph Doggett³ (*John*,² *John*¹), born Rehoboth, Mass., middle of November, 1657 ; called his name Daggett ; died Rehoboth, Mass., January 19, 1727 ; married Rehoboth, Mass., February 14, 168$\frac{8}{9}$, Mary Palmer, daughter of Jonah Palmer, of Rehoboth, Mass. ; born Rehoboth, Mass., February 23, 1663 ; died Rehoboth, Mass., April 15, 1757.

Issue :

700. i. John Daggett,⁴ born Rehoboth, Mass., January 19, 168$\frac{9}{90}$.
701. ii. Mary Daggett,⁴ born Rehoboth, Mass., August 30, 1692.
702. iii. Hannah Daggett,⁴ born Rehoboth, Mass., November 20, 1695 ; died Rehoboth, Mass., January 9, 1715.
703. iv. Joseph Daggett,⁴ born Rehoboth, Mass., June 13, 1699.
704. v. Hepsibah Daggett,⁴ born Rehoboth, Mass., September 29, 1701.
705. vi. Martha Daggett,⁴ born Rehoboth, Mass., September 29, 1701.
706. vii. Israel Daggett,⁴ born Rehoboth, Mass., March 20, 170$\frac{3}{4}$.

Dr. Joseph Doggett resided in Rehoboth, Mass., where he appears to have practised medicine, and also to have been wheelwright and miller.

Among the Rehoboth soldiers who served in King Philip's war was Joseph Doggett, who was engaged in the Narragansett expedition in 1676. [Bliss, Rehoboth.]

Oct. 27, 1686, he buys with his brother Nathaniel, and Thomas Daggett, Esq., of Edgartown, 50 acres of land, on both sides of the Ten Mile river, at the falls, in the North Purchase. [Bristol Deeds, 5–84.]

This was the land immediately around the falls, including the privilege.

" The first mill built at the falls was a corn mill, owned and occupied by Joseph Daggett. This was doubtless the first mill in town." [Daggett's Hist. Attleboro'.]

February 7, 1689. Joseph Daggett is named in a list of inhabitants and proprietors of Rehoboth holding land under a grant from William Bradford. In 1690 he killed a wolf.

Gay Head, on Martha's Vineyard, with its high-colored and variegated earth, suggested at an early day the existence of minerals.

August 17, 1692, Joseph Daggett, of Rehoboth, and Samuel Gaskell, of Boston, buy of Thomas Harlock and Hannah Daggett, the right to search for mines or minerals, precious stones, &c., at Gayhead. [Dukes Deeds, 1–184.]

" March 30, 1703, the town [Attleboro'] voted that Joseph Daggett, of Rehoboth, have the privilege that the stream at the Ten Mile river falls shall go free of all sorts of taxes until a corn mill has the constant custom of threescore families." [Hist. Attleboro.]

The will of Dr. Joseph Daggett, of Rehoboth, is dated December 23, 1726, and was proved March 21, 172$\frac{6}{7}$.

In it he mentions his wife and children, and appoints his wife Mary Daggett executrix. [Bristol Probate.]

688. NATHANIEL DOGGETT [3] (*John*,[2] *John*,[1]), born Rehoboth, Mass., middle of August, 1661; called his name Daggett; died Rehoboth, Mass. (?), 1708; married Rehoboth, Mass., June 24, 1686, Rebecca Miller, daughter of John Miller, of Rehoboth, Mass.; born Rehoboth, Mass., middle of November, 1661; died Rehoboth, Mass., April 9, 1711.

Issue :

707. i.   NATHANIEL DAGGETT,[4] born Rehoboth, Mass., August 11, 1688; died Rehoboth, Mass., August 22, 1688.
708. ii. REBECCA DAGGETT,[4] born Rehoboth, Mass., October 8, 1689.
709. iii. ELIZABETH DAGGETT,[4] born Rehoboth, Mass., November 14, 1691; died Rehoboth, Mass., February 11, 169$\frac{1}{2}$.
710. iv. JEMIMA DAGGETT,[4] born Rehoboth, Mass;, December 12, 1692.

711. v.   NATHANIEL DAGGETT,[4] born Rehoboth, Mass., April 3, 1695.
712. vi. JOHN DAGGETT,[4] born Rehoboth, Mass., March 16, 169⅞.
713. vii. ABIGAIL DAGGETT,[4] born Rehoboth, Mass., March 19, 170⁰.
714. viii. AMOS DAGGETT,[4] born Rehoboth, Mass., January 18, 170⅞.

Nathaniel Doggett, wheelwright and weaver, resided in Rehoboth.

"February 7, 1689, Nathaniel Daggett mentioned in a list of the names of the inhabitants and proprietors of Rehoboth holding land under a grant to William Bradford." [Bliss, Rehoboth.]

In a purchase of land at Rehoboth in 1694, he is called Dogget, while in another purchase in 1695 his name is spelled Daggett.

In the Bristol probate files are several papers relating to the settlement of the estate of Nathaniel Daggett:

His will, dated Feb. 5, 1708, in which his wife is named executrix.
An inventory of the estate of Nathaniel Daggett, left him by his father John Daggett, in reversion, after his mother's decease. Dated Dec. 30, 1708.

Rebecca Daggett, his widow, did not long survive him, and in the Bristol Probate is an

Inventory of the estate of widow Rebecca Daggett, late of Rehoboth, amounting to £121 2s. 15d., and dated April 27, 1711.
An account of George Wood, of Rehoboth, administrator of the estate of Rebecca Daggett, widow, May 12, 1713.

690.   Capt. THOMAS DOGGETT[3] (*Thomas,*[2] *John*[1]), born Edgartown, Mass., about 1658; called his name Daggett; died Edgartown, Mass., August 23, 1726; married, about 1685, Elizabeth Hawes; she died Edgartown, Mass., between December 25, 1732, and February 15, 1733.

Issue:

715. i.   SAMUEL DOGGETT,[4] bapt. Bristol, Mass. (now R.I.), July 22, 1688.
716. ii.   HANNAH DOGGETT,[4] bapt. Bristol, Mass. (now R.I.), July 22, 1688.
717. iii. TIMOTHY DAGGETT,[4] born Edgartown, Mass. (?), 1690.
718. iv.   ELIZABETH DAGGETT,[4] born Edgartown, Mass. (?), about 1690; married Edgartown, Mass., December 16, 1708, by Mr. Donham, to John Butler, Jr.
719. v.   BENJAMIN DAGGETT,[4] born Edgartown, Mass. (?), about 1691.
720. vi.   THOMAS DAGGETT,[4] born Edgartown, Mass. (?), about 1692.
721. vii. THANKFUL DAGGETT,[4] born Edgartown, Mass. (?).
722. viii. MARY DAGGETT,[4] born Edgartown, Mass., August 8, 1698.
723. ix.   JEMIMA DAGGETT,[4] born Edgartown, Mass. (?).
724. x.   DESIRE DAGGETT,[4] born Edgartown, Mass. (?); died between July 8, 1726, and December 25, 1732.

Captain Thomas Daggett, carpenter, gentleman, seems to have been called, like others of his family, both "Doggett" and "Daggett." The existing records at Bristol speak of him as the first, and those at Edgartown always as the last.

The records of the Church of Christ at Bristol, R.I. (formerly Mass.), mention, July 22, 1688, the baptism, by Rev. Samuel Lee, of Samuel and Hannah Doggett, children of Thomas Doggett. [Gen. Register, Vol. 34, p. 132.]

The exact date of his settlement at Bristol has not been found, but is supposed to have been about 1685. Possibly he was previously at Rehoboth, and the Thomas who was constable there, June 3, 1684.

February 11, 168⅗. Among the list of families in New Bristol, copied from original records of the "Church of Christ in Bristol," is Thomas Doggett, his wife, two children, and two servants. [Gen. Register, Vol. 34, p. 405.]

Dec 30, 1689. Thomas Doggett of Bristol, county Bristol, in New England, carpenter, and Elizabeth his now wife, for 16£ paid by Thomas Walker of Bristol, Tanner, land in Bristol at the south end of the town, bounded west by the street, being an estate of inheritance, recorded May 16, 1695. [Bristol Deeds, 2–150.]

He removed from Bristol to Edgartown between December 30, 1689, and March 18, 1691, or just before the death of his father.

March 18, 1691. Samuel Daggett of Marthas Vineyard, for 20£ paid by his brother Thomas Daggett, late of the town of Bristol, in New England, sells all his rights at Chicomo. [Dukes Deeds, 5–84.]
Oct. 29, 1692. Thomas Daget, now or late of Bristol, carpenter, and Elizabeth, his now wife, for 42£ paid by William Stone, of Bristol, mariner, one house lot, and land containing 2 acres, in Bristol, bounded north by Corn Street, east by High St. South by land of Samuel Gallop, west by land of Benj. Ingles, and Jos. Baston, 16 × 20 rods, also $\frac{1}{50}$th part of 600 acres land laid out for common. Recorded Aug 11, 1713. [Bristol Deeds, 7–650.]

Among the many transfers of land in which he was one of the parties he is mentioned as Lieutenant Daggett until 1697, and then as Captain Daggett, beginning with a deed in 1705.

The only information that has been found regarding the life of Captain Daggett is what may be gathered from the deeds, with the single exception of a memorandum of him, which is found in the Diary of Rev. William Homes, of Chilmark: "Aug 28, 1726, On Thursday night last Capt Thomas Daggett of oldtown [Edgartown] departed this life. He had been ill several weeks. He was a peaceable man and well inclined, and of good understanding."

The will of Captain Daggett is dated July 8, 1726, and by it he gives son Samuel's children, he being deceased, ½ the land that was his fathers homestead; son Thomas Daggett the other half of the homestead; son Timothy Daggett land at Edgartown; son Benjamin Daggett land at Edgartown; loving wife Elizabeth; six daughters Hannah, Elizabeth, Thankful, Mary, Jemina, Desire, gives them ½ the stock, cattle, sheep and horses; 3 living sons Executors. Proved Oct. 1726. [Dukes Probate, 1–14, 15.]

Inventory recorded May 12, 1727; real estate valued at £1393.

Elizabeth did not long survive her husband, and at her decease left a will, an extract of which follows:

Dec 25, 1732. Will of Elizabeth Daggett of Edgartown, gentlewoman: loving son Benjamin; daughters, Thankful, Mary Norton, Jemima Butler, Hannah, Elizabeth; daughter in law Mary; sons Timothy, Thomas, Benjamin; grandson Samuel Daggett; grandchildren, Seth, Solomon, Silvanus, Betty alias Elizabeth Daggett; granddaughter Lydia Norton; son Timothy sole executor. Proved Feb 15, 173¾. [Dukes Probate, 1–79.]

692. Deacon JOHN DOGGETT [3] (*Thomas*, [2] *John* [1]), born Edgartown, Mass., 1662; called his name Daggett; died Attleboro', Mass., September 7, 1724; married, about 1685, Sarah ~~Norton~~ (?) *Brot Pease*

Issue:

725. i.   MAYHEW DAGGETT, [4] born about 1686.
726. ii.   EBENEZER DAGGETT, [4] born Martha's Vineyard, August 29, 1690.
727. iii.   THOMAS DAGGETT. [4]
728. iv.   NAPTHALI DAGGETT, [4] died Attleboro', Mass., March 6, 171$\frac{7}{8}$.
729. v.   ABIGAIL DAGGETT, [4] born 1701.
730. vi.   JANE DAGGETT. [4]
731. vii.   ZILPHA DAGGETT. [4]
732. viii.   PATIENCE DAGGETT, [4] born Martha's Vineyard, 1705.
733. ix.   MARY DAGGETT. [4]

Deacon John Daggett, yeoman, tanner, and innholder, was probably born in Edgartown, Mass. He resided there until sometime previous to February 8, 1683, when

"John Daggett late of Edgartown on Marthas Vineyard" sells "10 acres of land which the town of Edgartown gave me," to "my father Thomas Daggett of Edgartown." [Dukes Deeds, 5-72.]

February 20, 169$\frac{1}{2}$. John Daggett releases any claim he might have to estate of his mother, Hannah Daggett, "located near the Gurnet." [Dukes Deeds, 1-104.]

March 17, 1693. John Daggett of Prudence, on Marthas Vineyard, buys 14 acres land on road from Tisbury to Holmes Hole, from his brother Joshua Daggett. [Dukes Deeds, 1-225.]
March 17, 1693. John Daggett of Prudence, on Marthas Vineyard, buys 80 acres land of his brother Joshua Daggett. [Dukes Deeds, 1-315.]

Prudence, which is here named as his residence, was a portion of Tisbury, and the records speak of "the mannour of Tisbury, commonly called Chilmark," so that although each of these places is named at different times as his residence, it is probable that after leaving Edgartown he resided during his residence on the island in what is now called Tisbury.

Sept. 12, 1695. Hannah Daggett, widow of Capt Thomas Daggett, late of Edgartown, on Marthas Vineyard, in consideration of love, and natural affection, for her son John Daggett, of Marthas Vineyard, gives him land at the Vineyard. [Dukes Deeds, 1-389.]

The following deeds are of the first purchases of land made by him in Attleboro':

Nov 12, 1701 Israel Daggett, of Marthas Vineyard, for 40£, paid by John Daggett of Marthas Vineyard, his brother, land in Attleboro, 25 acres at the falls. [Bristol Deeds, 15-505.]
Feb. 1, 170$\frac{3}{4}$. John Daggett, of Rehoboth, sells 25 acres land in Attleboro, to John Daggett, of Chilmark, on Marthas Vineyard. [Bristol Deeds, 5-246.]
July 28, 1704. Thomas Butler, of Chilmark, sells John Daggett of same lands and meadow in Rehoboth, and Attleboro, County Bristol, formerly in tenure

of Thomas Doggett, Esq : late deceased, and Israel Daggett, his son, excepting only those lands and marshes, which were sold by Israel Daggett, or Thomas Butler. [Bristol Deeds, 4–304.]

June 10, 1711. John Daggett, of Chilmark, yeoman, and Mayhew Daggett, of Attleboro, County Bristol, yeoman, bind themselves to John Devotion, of Attleboro, in the sum of 200£.   [Bristol Deeds, 7–267.]

Mayhew Daggett, as seen in above, having preceded his father in the removal to Attleboro', may have been an inducement to hasten the removal of the family there.

The purchase of the farm to which the family removed was on July 10, 1711, " when John Devotion, of Attleboro', for 400£, conveys farm in Attleboro containing 280 acres, bounded by Wrentham line, to John Daggett, of Chilmark, Marthas Vineyard, with 25 acres on 10 mile river, except 2 acres, the barn, and orchard, now in possession of Penticost Blackinton ; also whole share in the undivided lands in Attleboro."   [Bristol Deeds, 7–27.]

John Daggett and family removed from Martha's Vineyard to Attleboro' between October 17, 1711, and December 24, 1712.

After the purchase of the farm at Attleboro' he sells much of his land at the Vineyard.

Having removed to Attleboro', it would seem that he at once became an innkeeper, and soon became interested in town and church affairs. His house is reported as being used as a garrison house.

His lands being located on the road from Boston to Rhode Island, and his tavern a convenient stopping-place en route, he soon became well known, not only to the people of Attleboro', but to all travellers between Boston and Rhode Island.

" In 1720 Deacon John Daggett was representative of the town of Attleboro."   [Hist. Attleboro'.]

April 16, 1722. John Daggett of Attleboro, yeoman. for 550£ sells, Alexander Maxey of Gloucester, County Essex, yeoman. homestead farm in Attleboro, at a place called Ten Mile River, to a place called M[t] Hope hill, 170 acres, excepting a small piece of ground 6 rods square, where the burying place now is, which I, the said Daggett, reserved for my own use and the use of my neighbors. [Bristol Deeds, 15–85.]

April 6, 1724, he sells 103 acres, on Ten Mile river, at the falls, to son Mayhew Daggett. [Bristol Deeds, 15–504.]

Deacon John Daggett died September 7, 1724, leaving a will dated April 13, 1724, in which he leaves his property to his wife and children. This will was proved October 20, 1724.

The inventory, dated September 28, 1724, amounts to £525 4s. 1d., and mentions land at Martha's Vineyard and at Mansfield, Conn. [Bristol Probate.]

In what was, apparently, originally the centre of the old Hatch burying-ground in Attleboro', there stands erect, in a good state of preservation, a stone, with cherub at the top and ornaments at the sides, with the following inscription :

Here lies Interred
Ye Body of Dea-
con John Daggett
Dec^d Septr ye 7th
1724 in ye 63^d
year of his age

Among the family papers of an old Boston family was found the following epitaph, which has been sent the writer, and is supposed to refer to Deacon John Daggett, and shows the retention of the original spelling :

EPITAPH ON LANDLORD DOGGETT
Innholder at Attleborough.

Traveller
If ever dram to thee was dear,
Drop on John Doggett's grave a Tear;
Who when alive so well did tend,
The Rich, the Poor, the Foe, the Friend;
To every knock, and every call,
He said I'm coming unto all;
At length Death knocks! poor Doggett cry'd,
And said " I'm coming Sir! and Dy'd.

After the death of her husband, Mrs. Daggett authorizes her son to sell lands on the Vineyard :

Aug. 27, 1733. widow of John Daggett, of Attleboro, appoints Ebenezer Daggett, her son, of Attleboro, Innkeeper, her agent, to sell all lands on Marthas Vineyard, by her own and her husbands right. [Dukes Deeds, 5-383.]

Sept. 3, 1733. Ebenezer Daggett, of Attleboro, Innholder, by above right, sells 30 acres of land, at Holmes Hole, in Edgartown, being that tract his father, John Daggett, bought of Thomas West, late of Holmes Hole Dec 18, 1699. (Dukes Deeds, 5-385.)

Mrs. Sarah Daggett, widow of Deacon John Daggett, married Banfield Capron, December 16, 1735. She was his third wife. He died August 20, 1752, aged ninety-two years. When she died or where she is buried the descendants cannot tell.

693. JOSHUA DOGGETT[3] (*Thomas,*[2] *John* [1]), born Edgartown, Mass., about 1664, called his name Daggett; died Edgartown, Mass., between September 10, 1737, and February 14, 1738; married, about 1686, Hannah Norton, daughter of Isaac and Ruth (Bayes) Norton.
Issue :

734. i.   BROTHERTON DAGGETT,[4] born Edgartown, Mass., 1687.
735. ii.   MARTHA DAGGETT,[4] born Prudence, Mass., about 1688; married (intention August 4, 1709) Nicholas Norton, son of Benjamin Norton.
736. iii. JACOB DAGGETT,[4] born Prudence, Mass., about 1690.
737. iv.   HEPSIBAH DAGGETT,[4] born Prudence, Mass., about 1692; married Edgartown, Mass., between January and June 10, 1716, by Mr. Samuel Wiswall, to Jabez Trapp.
738. v.   DEBORAH DAGGETT,[4] born Edgartown, Mass., about 1694; married Edgartown, Mass., May 9, 1717, by Enoch Coffin, to John Isham, of Barnstable, Mass.

Joshua Daggett, yeoman, resided at Prudence and Edgartown, Martha's Vineyard.

The records contain many deeds to and from him, and among them one, July 26, 1717, where he sells land in Edgartown to John Isham, late of Barnstable, now of Edgartown, and another in which he conveys to Brotherton Daggett the west part of his house and·land, December 27, 1718.

The will of Joshua Daggett, of Edgartown, yeoman, is dated September 10, 1737, and was proved February 14, 173⅞. In it he mentions: loving wife Hannah Daggett; son Brotherton Daggett; son-in-law John Isham; son Jacob Daggett; daughters Martha, Hepzibah, and Deborah. Wife Hannah and son Brotherton named as executors. [Dukes Probate, 1–86.]

July 29, 1743. Hannah Daggett, widow of Joshua Daggett, sells land in Edgartown, to Jabez Tripp, of Edgartown, and John Isham of Windsor, Conn. [Dukes Deeds, 7–275.]

694. ISRAEL DOGGETT [3] (*Thomas,*[2] *John* [1]), born Edgartown, Mass., about 1672; called his name Daggett; married Edgartown, Mass., January 31, 1701, by Mr. Donham, to Ruth Norton, daughter of Nicholas (?) Norton.

Issue:

739. i. SAMUEL DAGGETT,[4] born Edgartown, Mass., January 7, 1702; died Edgartown, Mass., November 13, 1717.
740. ii. MARY DAGGETT,[4] born Edgartown, Mass., January 29, 1704.
741. iii. SARAH DAGGETT,[4] born Edgartown, Mass., December 2, 1706.
742. iv. JOSHUA DAGGETT,[4] born Edgartown, Mass., August 4, 1709.
743. v. JANE DAGGETT,[4] born Edgartown, Mass., December 22, 1711; married Temple Philip Cooke.

Israel Daggett, husbandman, mason, resided in Edgartown, Mass.

Sept 15, 1691 Thomas Daggett of Edgartown, upon Marthas Vineyard, in the Province of New York, whereas, my father Thomas Daggett, late deceased, dyed seized of lands, lying, situate, and being, in the town of Rehoboth, in the county of New Bristol, in the Colony of New Plymouth, in America, being a house lot, and divers other parcels of land, in said Township, which lands came to me, the said Thomas, as heir to said Thomas Daggett, as well from the knowledge of the intent of my said father, had Providence allowed him making a will, as also in consideration of the love, good will, and natural affection, which I bear to my youngest brother, Israel Daggett . . . gives him the lands, provided he live to 21 years, or commit lawful matrimony, and until he does one, or the other, gives the lands to the care of William Carpenter. [Dukes Deeds, 1–221.]
May, 13, 1701. Indenture between Israel Dogget, of Edgartown, in Dukes County, and Thomas Butler, of the same. For 80£, Israel Dogget, sells land in Rehoboth, being land laid out to Thomas Doggett, Esq., deceased, father of Israel. [Bristol Deeds, 3–255.]

This last deed shows the retention of the original spelling.

He sells many different pieces of land on the Vineyard and at Attleboro'.

One deed, March 6, 173¾, in which he calls himself mason, and sells house and land in Edgartown, near "the Clay Pitts," to Enoch Coffin. [Dukes Deeds, 6–180.]

Israel Daggett was a member of the church in Edgartown.

696. Joseph Daggett [3] (*Joseph,*[2] *John*[1]), born Tisbury, Mass. (?); died Edgartown, Mass. (?), 1718; married Tisbury, Mass. (?), about 1693, Amy Mantor (?).

Issue:

744. i. John Daggett,[4] born about 1694.
745. ii. Amy Daggett,[4] born about 1696.
746. iii. Joseph Daggett,[4] born about 1698; October 21, 1718, has James Allen appointed his guardian.
747. iv. Temperance Daggett,[4] born about 1701; October 21, 1718, has cousin Samuel Mantor appointed her guardian; released July 28, 1719.
748. v. Elizabeth Daggett,[4] born about 1704; August 3, 1719, receives her share in her father's estate.
749. vi. Hepsiba Daggett,[4] born about 1706.

Joseph Daggett, of Tisbury, left a will dated October 11, 1704, and proved August 12, 1718.

He mentions his wife, Amy Daggett, as executrix; son John Daggett, land in Edgartown; son Joseph Daggett, land in Tisbury; mentions daughters Amy, Temperance, and Elizabeth Daggett [Dukes Probate, 1–60.]

JOHN DOGGETT, OF MARTHA'S VINEYARD.

FOURTH GENERATION.

700. Lieut. John Daggett [4] (*Joseph,*[3] *John,*[2] *John*[1]), born Rehoboth, Mass., January 19, 1689–90; died Rehoboth, Mass., January 8, 1772; married Elizabeth Dorman, daughter of Timothy and Elizabeth (Knowlton) Dorman, of Boxford, Mass.; born Boxford, Mass., December 7, 1691; died Rehoboth, Mass., August 7, 1767.

Issue:

750. i. John Daggett,[5] born Rehoboth, Mass., August 2, 1723; died Rehoboth, Mass., August 22, 1723.
751. ii. Mary Daggett,[5] born Rehoboth, Mass., December 21, 1727; died Rehoboth, Mass., August 21, 1741.
752. iii. John Daggett,[5] born Rehoboth, Mass., June 30, 1730; died Rehoboth, Mass., June 30, 1732.
753. iv. John Daggett,[5] born Rehoboth, Mass., April 27, 1732; died Rehoboth, Mass., previous to 1767.

Lieut. John Daggett, housewright, was a resident of Rehoboth, Mass.

Feb. 12, 172⅘, he purchased land adjoining his house. [Bristol Deeds, 19–187.]

Nov. 25, 1728, and Dec. 4, 1730, he made other purchases of land in Rehoboth. [Bristol Deeds, 19–36, and 482.]

The will of John Daggett, of Rehoboth, is dated September 10, 1767, and was proved January 27, 1772.

In it he gives his nephew, William Daggett, son of his brother Israel Daggett, land in Cumberland which belonged to his grandfather, John Daggett, and called "the Mine Lot."

Daniel Daggett, son of his brother Israel Daggett, land in Rehoboth.

Mentions also John, son of abovesaid Daniel Daggett. Daniel Daggett executor. [Bristol Probate.]

701. MARY DAGGETT [4] (*Joseph,*[3] *John,*[2] *John* [1]), born Rehoboth, Mass., August 30, 1692; married, Rehoboth, Mass., December 20, 1716, Timothy Ide, son of Timothy and Elizabeth Ide; born Rehoboth, Mass., October 1, 1688.

Issue:

754. i.   ICHABOD IDE,[5] born Rehoboth, Mass., March 31, 1717.
755. ii. TIMOTHY IDE,[5] born Rehoboth, Mass., March 31, 1719.
756. iii. JOHN IDE,[5] born Rehoboth, Mass., February 27, 1728.
757. iv. PELEG IDE,[5] born Rehoboth, Mass., January 27, 173½.

703. JOSEPH DAGGETT [4] (*Joseph,*[3] *John,*[2] *John* [1]), born Rehoboth, Mass., June 13, 1699; died Attleboro', Mass., February 16, 173⅘; married Rehoboth, Mass., December 29, 172–, by Rev. John Greenwood, to Margaret Pullen, of Bristol, R.I.

Issue:

758. i. SIMEON DAGGETT,[5] born Attleboro', Mass., October 14, 1723; died between 1746 and 1758.
759. ii. HANNAH DAGGETT,[5] born Attleboro', Mass., January 21, 172–.

Joseph Daggett, wheelwright, of Rehoboth, was baptized in 1699, at the Rehoboth church.

Nov 13, 1725 and Feb 23 172⅝ he makes transfers of real estate. [Bristol Deeds, 17–404 and 156.]

An inventory of the estate of Joseph Daggett was taken March 10, 173¾.

Margaret Daggett, widow, was appointed administratrix of the estate of Joseph Daggett, of Attleboro', May 20, 1735.

Account of Margaret Tree, late widow of Joseph Daggett, late of Attleboro'. [Bristol Probate.]

Richard Tree and Margaret Daggett were married in Attleboro'
April 27, 1736, and had:

EUNICE TREE, born Attleboro', January 30, 173⁴⁄₇.
LEVINA TREE, born Attleboro', January 13, 1741; died Attleboro', January
13, 1741.

The records of the Massachusetts House of Representatives,
March, 1745, contain the

Petition of Richard Tree of Rehoboth and others, heirs of Joseph Dogget,
late of Attleboro, deceased, showing that the real estate of said deceased was
distributed to Margaret, Hannah, the petitioners, and Simeon, his only son,
agreeable to Law, that the said Simeon Dagget (being then a minor) had his
uncle Israel Dagget, of Rehoboth, duly appointed his Guardian, who accepted
that trust; that about 5 years since the said Simeon went abroad and has never
been heard of since and is probably dead, yet the guardian so appointed refuses
(though the said Simeon if living is 22 years of age) to deliver up the said
estate, or income thereof, to the petitioners, the true heirs, but converts it to
his own use. They therefore pray that said guardian be ordered to deliver possession.
March 15, 1745. Ordered that the estate be distributed.

This petition and order was evidently premature, as the will of
Simeon Daggett, of Attleboro', dated August 20, 1746, calls himself
"mariner," mentions his sister Hannah and uncle Israel, and this
instrument was proved April 5, 1758, showing that he had returned
after the above order was passed.

The Bristol probate records also disclose the fact that Simeon
Daggett's mother, while a widow, gave him to his uncle John Daggett, of Rehoboth, after which she married Richard Tree, and then
wanted him, to which he objected, August 25, 1736.

704. HEPSIBAH DAGGETT⁴ (*Joseph*,³ *John*,² *John*¹), born Rehoboth, Mass., September 29, 1701; died Rehoboth, Mass., August
12, 1736; married Rehoboth, Mass., December 16, 1725, by Rev.
John Greenwood, to Noah Chaffee, son of Nathaniel and Experience
Chaffee, of Rehoboth; born Rehoboth, Mass., December 17, 1692;
died previous to 1736.
Issue:

760. i. ISAIAH CHAFFEE,⁵ born Rehoboth, Mass., November 4, 1727.
761. ii. SHUBAEL CHAFFEE,⁵ born Rehoboth, Mass., March 23, 172⁹⁄₃₀.
762. iii. CHRISTOPHER CHAFFEE,⁵ born Rehoboth, Mass., August 7, 1731.

705. MARTHA DAGGETT⁴ (*Joseph*,³ *John*,² *John*¹), born Rehoboth, Mass., September 29, 1701; married Rehoboth, Mass., August
23, 1720, Nathaniel Cooper, son of Thomas and Susanna Cooper, of
Rehoboth; born Rehoboth, Mass., January 9, 169½.
Issue:

763. i. JUDITH COOPER,⁵ born Rehoboth, Mass., March 8, 1726.
764. ii. HEPSIBETH COOPER,⁵ born Rehoboth, Mass., April 8, 1729.
765. iii. MARTHA COOPER,⁵ born Rehoboth, Mass., April 8, 1729; died Rehoboth, Mass., December 2, 1729.

706. ISRAEL DAGGETT [4] (*Joseph*,[3] *John*,[2] *John* [1]), born Rehoboth, Mass., March 20, 170¾; died Rehoboth, Mass., 1777; married, 1st, Boxford, Mass., April 15, 1724, Hannah Dorman, daughter of Timothy and Elizabeth (Knowlton) Dorman, of Boxford; born Boxford, Mass., December 22, 1698; married, 2d, Lydia.

Issue:

766. i.   TIMOTHY DAGGETT,[5] born Rehoboth, Mass., June 9, 1725; died Rehoboth, Mass., February 20, 1726.
767. ii. JOSEPH DAGGETT,[5] born Rehoboth, Mass., December 2, 1726; died Rehoboth, Mass., February 24, 1727.
768. iii. HEPSABETH DAGGETT,[5] born Rehoboth, Mass., October 7, 1728; died Rehoboth, Mass., December 27, 1728.
769. iv. WILLIAM DAGGETT,[5] born Rehoboth, Mass., November 1, 1729.
770. v.   DANIEL DAGGETT,[5] born Rehoboth, Mass., November 16, 1731.
771. vi. HANNAH DAGGETT,[5] born Rehoboth, Mass., June 9, 1734.
772. vii. ISRAEL DAGGETT,[5] born Rehoboth, Mass., April 28, 1737.
773. viii. LYDIA DAGGETT,[5] born Rehoboth, Mass., June 15, 1739.
774. ix. SARAH DAGGETT,[5] born Rehoboth, Mass., April 23, 1742.
775. x.   MARTHA DAGGETT,[5] born Rehoboth, Mass., January 31, 174⅝.

Israel Daggett was baptized in the Rehoboth church, April 30, 1704.

A negro, called " Prince," is mentioned as his man servant in 1772.

The will of Israel Daggett, of Rehoboth, is dated January 12, 1767, and was proved June 24, 1777. In it he mentions beloved wife Lydia Daggett; sons William, Israel, and Daniel; daughters Lydia, Sarah, and Martha. [Bristol Probate.]

708. REBECCA DAGGETT [4] (*Nathaniel*,[3] *John*,[2] *John* [1]), born Rehoboth, Mass., October 8, 1689; married Rehoboth, Mass., April 30, 1710, George Wood, son of Thomas and Rebecca Wood, of Swansea, Mass.; born Swansea, Mass., July 30, 1679.

Issue:

776. i.   THANKFUL WOOD,[5] born Swansea, Mass., January 16, 1721.
777. ii. LYDIA WOOD,[5] born Swansea, Mass., May 6, 1726.
778. iii. JAMES WOOD,[5] born Swansea, Mass., May 6, 1729.

711. NATHANIEL DAGGETT [4] (*Nathaniel*,[3] *John*,[2] *John* [1]), born Rehoboth, Mass., April 3, 1695; married Attleboro', Mass., April 30, 1724, Lydia Tiffany.

Issue:

779. i.   LYDIA DAGGETT,[5] born Attleboro', Mass., May 2, 1727; married Attleboro', Mass., August 13, 1748, John Crane, of Raynham, Mass.
780. ii. BETHIAH DAGGETT,[5] born Attleboro', Mass., July 17, 1729.
781. iii. NATHANIEL DAGGETT,[5] born Attleboro', Mass., June 19, 1731.
782. iv. REUBEN DAGGETT,[5] born Attleboro', Mass., August 31, 1733.
783. v.   AMOS DAGGETT,[5] born Attleboro', Mass., September 5, 1735.
784. vi. JOSEPH DAGGETT,[5] born Attleboro', Mass., October 14, 1737.
785. vii. AMY DAGGETT,[5] born Attleboro', Mass., January 14, 1744.
786. viii. NATHANIEL DAGGETT,[5] born Attleboro', Mass., April 29, 1747.

Nathaniel Daggett, " cooper," " husbandman," resided in Rehoboth, and afterward in Attleboro', Mass.

April 11, 1719 he sold land in Rehoboth [Bristol Deeds, 13–187] and May 2, 1719 bought 107½ acres " upland, swamp, and meadow" in Attleboro. [Bristol Deeds, 13–114.]
May 12, 1729 Nathaniel Daggett of Attleboro sells land there to John Titus of Rehoboth. [Bristol Deeds, 19–513.]

Possibly Mrs. Daggett may have married, 2d, at Rehoboth, by Thomas Brown, to John Wood, of Newport.

712. JOHN DAGGETT[4] (*Nathaniel,*[3] *John,*[2] *John*[1]), born Rehoboth, Mass., March 16, 169⅜; died Rehoboth, Mass., July (?), 1738; married Swansea, Mass., June 15, 1721, Hopestill Wood, daughter of John and Bethia (Mason) Wood, of Swansea, Mass.; born Swansea, Mass., February 20, 169⅝.

Issue :

787. i.   REBECCA DAGGETT,[5] born Rehoboth, Mass., May 2, 1722.
788. ii.   JOHN DAGGETT,[5] born Rehoboth, Mass., November 6, 1723.
789. iii.   HOPESTILL DAGGETT,[5] born Rehoboth, Mass., January 9, 1725.
790. iv.   SARAH DAGGETT,[5] born Rehoboth, Mass., January 26, 172⅞; married Mr. Pain.
791. v.   ABIGAIL DAGGETT,[5] born Rehoboth, Mass., January 19, 172 9/0.
792. vi.   JAMES DAGGETT,[5] born Rehoboth, Mass., January 2, 173½.
793. vii.   NATHAN DAGGETT,[5] born Rehoboth, Mass., December 24, 1733.
794. viii.   JOSHUA DAGGETT,[5] born Rehoboth, Mass., December 25, 1735.

The inventory of the estate of John Daggett, of Rehoboth, was taken July 14, 1738, and amounted to £1401 10s. 11d.

Hope Daggett, widow, was appointed administratrix of the estate September 19, 1738:

November 10, 1744, Rebecca Daggett, daughter of John, wishes a division of her father's estate.

Hope Brown, late widow and administratrix of the estate of John Daggett, wishes a division, November 12, 1744.

December 10, 1744. Aaron Wheeler, husband of Hopestill, daughter of John Daggett, wishes a division.

The estate was divided March 18, 174½, among Hope, late widow of deceased, now wife of Joseph Brown; sons John, James, Nathan, and Joshua Daggett; and daughters Rebecca Brown, Hope Wheeler, Sarah Pain, and Abigail Daggett.   [Bristol Probate.]

714. AMOS DAGGETT[4] (*Nathaniel,*[3] *John,*[2] *John*[1]), born Rehoboth, Mass., January 18, 170⅔; died Swansea, Mass., 1771; married, Swansea, Mass., July 3, 1733, Mary Sisson.

Issue :

795. i.   MARY DAGGETT,[5] born Swansea, Mass., April 2, 1734; died Swansea, Mass.
796. ii.   MARY DAGGETT,[5] born Swansea, Mass., April 2, 1735.
797. iii.   ELIZABETH DAGGETT,[5] born Swansea, Mass., April 24, 1740; married Swansea, Mass., March 16, 1769, William Salisbury, of Warren, R.I.
798. iv.   JOB DAGGETT,[5] born Swansea, Mass., March 2, 1746.

Amos Daggett was a " husbandman" of Swansea.

April 6, 1709, Moses Reed was appointed his guardian, and he was called " aged about 6 years, son of Nathaniel Daggett, late of Rehoboth." [Bristol Probate.]

Nov. 13, 1725, he calls himself of Swansea, in a deed of land in Rehoboth. [Bristol Deeds, 17–404.]

The will of Amos Daggett, of Swansea, is dated June 25, 1770, and was proved November 11, 1771.

He gives to his daughters, Mary Daggett and Elizabeth Salisbury, each ten silver dollars.

To his beloved son Job Daggett he gives all the rest of his estate. [Bristol Probate.]

715. SAMUEL DOGGETT [4] (*Thomas*,[3] *Thomas*,[2] *John* [1]), bapt. Bristol, Mass., July 22, 1688; called his name Daggett; died before 1726; married, Edgartown, Mass., July 11, 1705, by Benjamin Skiffe, Esq., to Mary Pease, daughter of Sergeant Thomas and Bathsheba Pease, of Edgartown; born Edgartown, Mass., February 17, 1685.

Issue:

799. i.   SAMUEL DAGGETT,[5] born Edgartown, Mass. (?), about 1706.
800. ii.   SETH DAGGETT,[5] born February 5, 1713.
801. iii. SOLOMON DAGGETT.[5]
802. iv.   SYLVANUS DAGGETT.[5]
803. v.   LOVE DAGGETT,[5] married Rev. John Lischer. Issue: i. Lewis Lischer;[6] ii. William Lischer.[6]
804. vi.   ELIZABETH DAGGETT.[5]

July 22, 1688, Samuel, son of Thomas Doggett, was baptized by Rev. Samuel Lee, pastor of the Church of Christ at Bristol, R.I. (formerly Mass.). This church was organized May 3, 1687.

The name in this baptismal record is spelled with an " o," but as the family soon returned to the Vineyard the only records extant conform to the changed spelling, and we afterward find him referred to as Daggett.

Married when quite young, he doubtless made his home in Tisbury.

717. Capt. TIMOTHY DAGGETT [4] (*Thomas*,[3] *Thomas*,[2] *John* [1]), born Edgartown, Mass. (?), 1690; died Edgartown, Mass., September 17, 1775; married Edgartown, Mass., May 6, 1717, by Enoch Coffin, Esq., to Mary Smith, daughter of Benjamin Smith, of Edgartown; born 1694; died Edgartown, Mass., October 2, 1781.

Capt. Timothy Daggett, gentleman, resided in Edgartown, Mass.

Feb. 2, 172$\frac{2}{3}$, his father gave him 2 acres of land in Edgartown. [Dukes Deeds, 3-528.]

He (with his two brothers) was executor of his father's estate in 1726, and in 1733 the sole executor of his mother's estate.

The will of Benjamin Smith, of Edgartown, 14 February, 1719, mentions his daughter Mary Daggett.

The lands which thus came to them by inheritance were increased between this time and January 23, 1759, by the purchase of six other estates, all located in the town of Edgartown.

His name also occurs in the Dukes Deeds, between January 13, 172$\frac{7}{8}$, and January 13, 1773, as making eighteen different sales of land in Edgartown, at Cape Poeg, at Chappaquiddick, and at Farm Neck.

Sept 26, 1737, Timothy Daggett of Edgartown Gentleman, exchanges lands in Edgartown for others at Chappaquiddick. [Dukes Deeds, 6–304, 6, 10.]

Feb 16, 1710 he is appointed Attorney for Sylvanus Daggett of Providence [Dukes Deeds, 7–130], and in March 1743 is acting as guardian of John Worth.

There are but seventy-three stones remaining in the first burial place in Edgartown, and of this number three are for Daggetts. Of these are:

"Capt. Timothy Daggett died Sept 17, 1775 aged 85 yrs." and " Mary Daggett wife of Capt Timothy died Oct. 2, 1781, aged 87 years."

719.   Deacon BENJAMIN DAGGETT [4] (*Thomas*,[3] *Thomas*,[2] *John* [1]), born Edgartown, Mass. (?), about 1691; died Fox Island, Me., 1783; married, 1734, Margery Homes, daughter of Rev. William and Catherine (Craighead) Homes, of Chilmark; died (buried Edgartown) May 3, 1783.

Issue:

805. i.   ELIZABETH DAGGETT,[5] bapt. Edgartown, Mass., April 20, 1735; married Edgartown, Mass., November 3, 1757, Samuel Whelden.
806. ii.   CATHERINE DAGGETT,[5] bapt. Edgartown, Mass., 1736; unmarried, February 7, 1762.
807. iii.   WILLIAM DAGGETT,[5] born Edgartown, Mass., November 18, 1738; died Edgartown, Mass., September 14, 1740.
808. iv.   TIMOTHY DAGGETT,[5] born Edgartown, Mass., January 31, 174$\frac{0}{41}$; died Edgartown, Mass., February 3, 174$\frac{1}{42}$.
809. v.   BENJAMIN DAGGETT,[5] born Edgartown, Mass., December 1, 1742.
810. vi.   JOHN DAGGETT,[5] bapt. Edgartown, Mass., November 4, 1744.
811. vii.   HANNAH DAGGETT,[5] bapt. Edgartown, Mass., January 28, 1748; married Edgartown, Mass., September 21, 1769, Thomas Stewart.
812. viii.   MARY DAGGETT,[5] bapt. Edgartown, Mass., May 5, 1751.

Deacon Benjamin Daggett, yeoman, seems to have lived in Edgartown, afterward at Chilmark, and toward the close of his life at Tisbury.

He held the office of deacon in the church for forty years. Benjamin Daggett was admitted to the church in Edgartown, April 20, 1735.

Dukes Deeds contain 15 different transfers of real estate in which he was either buying or selling land in Edgartown, at Cape Poeg, at Farm neck and at Chappaquiddick.

720. THOMAS DAGGETT[4] (*Thomas,*[3] *Thomas,*[2] *John*[1]), born Edgartown, Mass. (?), about 1692; married Love Coffin, daughter of Enoch and Beulah (Eddy) Coffin, of Martha's Vineyard; born 1702.

Thomas Daggett, yeoman, gentleman, resided in Edgartown, Mass. He appears from the Registry of Deeds to have bought or sold eight different pieces of land in Edgartown, between 1727 and 1746.

Love Daggett, his wife, owned the covenant, and was baptized in the church in Edgartown, October 10, 1742; admitted to the church, August 3, 1746.

Thomas Daggett was admitted to full communion at the church in Edgartown in 1748.

Between this time and 1769 he makes seven more transfers of real estate, and on the last-named year sells one-half pew in Edgartown. No further records regarding him have been found.

722. MARY DAGGETT[4] (*Thomas,*[3] *Thomas,*[2] *John*[1]), born Edgartown, Mass., August 8, 1698; married, 1722, Matthew Norton, son of Benjamin Norton; born April 12, 1696.

Issue:

813. i. JOHN NORTON,[5] born Edgartown, Mass., July 25, 1723.
814. ii. MATTHEW NORTON,[5] born Edgartown, Mass., August 18, 1725.
815. iii. ELIZABETH NORTON,[5] born Edgartown, Mass., March 23, 172$\frac{2}{7}$.
816. iv. HULDAH NORTON,[5] born Edgartown, Mass., July 10, 1731.
817. v. BERIAH NORTON,[5] born Edgartown, Mass., January 12, 173$\frac{3}{4}$.
818. vi. JERUSHA NORTON,[5] born Edgartown, Mass., July 8, 1736.
819. vii. LOIS NORTON,[5] born Edgartown, Mass., April 20, 1739.

723. JEMIMA DAGGETT[4] (*Thomas,*[3] *Thomas,*[2] *John*[1]), married Thomas Butler, son of John and Mary Butler.

Issue:

820. i. DAVID BUTLER, married December 2, 1725, Anna Hatch, daughter of Samuel and Lydia Hatch, of Chilmark.

725. Capt. MAYHEW DAGGETT[4] (*John,*[3] *Thomas,*[2] *John*[1]), born about 1686; died Attleboro', Mass., March 17, 1752; married Attleboro', Mass., October 11, 1709, Joanna Biven, of Deerfield, Mass.

Issue:

821. i. ELIHU DAGGETT,[5] born Attleboro', Mass., August 6, 1710.
822. ii. SARAH DAGGETT,[5] born Attleboro', Mass., May 17, 1715.
823. iii. BEULAH DAGGETT,[5] born Attleboro', Mass., November 17, 1719.
824. iv. ZILPHA DAGGETT,[5] born Attleboro', Mass., October 23, 172$\frac{2}{3}$.
825. v. ANNA DAGGETT,[5] born Attleboro', Mass., July 18, 1728; married Carrol Marten.

Capt. Mayhew Daggett, also called deacon, was of Attleboro', yeoman, June 10, 1711. [Bristol Deeds, 7–267.]

How long before 1709 (the date of his marriage) he had resided in Attleboro' does not appear.

He bought land there Aug 2, 1715. [B.D., 13–33] July 26, 1722 [B.D., 14–541] Nov 22, 1725 [B.D., 17–157] and Feb 23, 172$\frac{5}{6}$ [B.D., 17–156].

Among several other transactions in real estate was a sale of land in Attleboro', December 19, 1724 [B.D., 17–128], and land at a place between Mt. Hope and the fall on Ten-mile river, November 18, 1725. [B.D., 17–155.]

Capt. Mayhew Daggett appears to have been prominent in the affairs of the town, of which he was the representative, 1736, 1737, 1741, 1742, 1744, and 1746.

Captain Daggett died in 1752, and his estate was settled by his wife, Joanna Daggett.

The probate papers mention the children as Elihu Daggett, Jeduthan Fuller, Sarah Fuller, Abiah Fuller, Beulah Fuller, Zilpha Daggett, Anna Marten, and Carrol Marten. [Bristol Probate.]

√   **726.** EBENEZER DAGGETT[4] (*John*,[3] *Thomas*,[2] *John*[1]), born Martha's Vineyard, August 29, 1690; died Attleboro', Mass., August 30, 1740; married Attleboro', Mass., November 9, 1721, Mary Blackinton, daughter of Penticost Blackinton; born Marblehead, Mass., November 25, 1698; died Attleboro', Mass., December 1, 1772.

Issue:

826. i.   BATHSHEBA DAGGETT,[5] born Attleboro', Mass., August 22, 1722.
827. ii.   JOHN DAGGETT,[5] born Attleboro', Mass., September 2, 1724.
828. iii.   NAPHTALI DAGGETT,[5] born Attleboro'. Mass., September 8, 1727.
829. iv.   SAMUEL DAGGETT,[5] born Attleboro', Mass., January 3, 173⁰.
830. v.   EBENEZER DAGGETT,[5] born Attleboro', Mass., October 15, 1732.
831. vi.   MARY DAGGETT,[5] born Attleboro', Mass., April 21, 1735; married Mr. Johnson.
832. vii.   MICAJAH DAGGETT,[5] born Attleboro', Mass., January 8, 173⅞; November 13, 1752, Mary Daggett appointed his guardian.
833. viii.   PHILIP DAGGETT,[5] born Attleboro', Mass., September 11, 1739.

Ebenezer Daggett, of Attleboro', was " husbandman," " tanner," and " innholder."

Sept 19, 1720 he bought 32 acres of land in Attleboro [B.D., 17–63] and Oct 26, 1723 land on the W side of the E road which goes from Rehoboth to Boston. [B.D., 16–246.]

Jan 10, 1727 [B.D., 19–321] and March 19, 1729 [B.D., 20–273] he buys additional land.

In a purchase made March 31, 1731 [B.D., 20–7], he is called innkeeper, and his occupation the same in succeeding deeds.

He makes further purchases Oct. 13, 1731 [B.D., 21–250] and March 24, 1732. [B.D., 21–503.]

August 27, 1733, he is appointed by his mother as her agent to sell lands on Martha's Vineyard [Dukes Deeds, 5–383], and September 3, 1733, he sells land there. [Dukes Deeds, 5–385.] He died in Attleboro', and a stone in the cemetery there marks his grave.

November 23, 1752, Mary Daggett, widow, is appointed administratrix of the estate of Ebenezer Daggett, deceased; John Daggett,
eldest son. [Bristol Probate.]

727. THOMAS DAGGETT[4] (*John,*[3] *Thomas,*[2] *John*[1]), married 1st,
Attleboro', Mass., March 21, 172$\frac{2}{3}$, Sarah Stanley; died Attleboro',
Mass., August 31, 1728; married 2d, Wrentham, Mass., January
29, 172$\frac{8}{9}$, by Mr. Henry Messinger, to Elizabeth Blake.

Issue:

834. i. NAPHTALI DAGGETT,[5] born Attleboro', Mass., January 6, 172$\frac{3}{4}$; died
        Attleboro', Mass., May 14, 1724.
835. ii. ABIGAIL DAGGETT,[5] born Attleboro', Mass., April 11, 1726.
836. iii. ICHABOD DAGGETT,[5] born Attleboro', Mass., March 22, 172$\frac{5}{8}$; died
        Attleboro', Mass., May, 172$\frac{3}{4}$.
837. iv. SAMUEL DAGGETT,[5] born Attleboro', Mass., July 22, 1728; died Attle-
        boro', Mass., July 25, 1728.
838. v. MAYHEW DAGGETT,[5] born Attleboro', Mass., January 10, 1729.
839. vi. THOMAS DAGGETT,[5] born Providence, R.I., September 25, 1731.
840. vii. CONTENT DAGGETT,[5] born Attleboro', Mass., November 15, 1733; died
        Attleboro', Mass., December 12, 1734.
841. viii. CONTENT DAGGETT,[5] born Attleboro', Mass., November 11, 1735.
842. ix. BROTHERTON DAGGETT,[5] born Attleboro', Mass., October 13, 1737.
843. x. NAOMI DAGGETT,[5] born Attleboro', Mass., June 16, 174$\frac{1}{2}$.

729. ABIGAIL DAGGETT[4] (*John,*[3] *Thomas,*[2] *John*[1]), born 1701;
died Attleboro', Mass., November 20, 1798; married Attleboro',
Mass., October 12, 1714, Ebenezer Guild, son of Samuel and Mary
(Woodcock) Guild, of Dedham, Mass.; born Dedham, Mass., July
23, 1692; died Attleboro', Mass., June 8, 1774.

Issue:

844. i. JOSEPH GUILD,[5] born Attleboro', Mass., June 22, 1716.
845. ii. BENJAMIN GUILD,[5] born Attleboro', Mass., August 28, 1718.
846. iii. NAPHTALI GUILD,[5] born Attleboro', Mass., July 3, 1719.
847. iv. EBENEZER GUILD,[5] born Attleboro', Mass., August 29, 1722.

730. JANE DAGGETT[4] (*John,*[3] *Thomas,*[2] *John*[1]), married Attleboro', Mass., November 9, 1721, Caleb Hall.

Issue:

848. i. CHRISTOPHER HALL,[5] born Attleboro', Mass., April 17, 1723.
849. ii. CALEB HALL,[5] born Attleboro', Mass., May 16, 1724; died Attleboro',
        Mass., April 1, 1740.
850. iii. JOHN HALL,[5] born Attleboro', Mass., April 14, 1726; died Attleboro',
        Mass., December 24, 1726.
851. iv. JOHN HALL,[5] born Attleboro', Mass., November 19, 1727.
852. v. REUBEN HALL,[5] born Attleboro', Mass., March 14, 172$\frac{9}{30}$.
853. vi. EVE HALL,[5] born Attleboro', Mass., March 4, 173$\frac{3}{4}$.
854. vii. LEABEN HALL,[5] born Attleboro', Mass., November 13, 1734; died
        Attleboro', Mass., August 28, 1738.
855. viii. DAN HALL,[5] born Attleboro', Mass., June 6, 1736.
856. ix. ADAM HALL,[5] born Attleboro', Mass., June 25, 1738.
857. x. HANNAH HALL,[5] born Attleboro', Mass., February 20, 174$\frac{0}{1}$.
858. xi. CALEB HALL,[5] born Attleboro', Mass., March 28, 1743.

731. ZILPHA DAGGETT [4] (*John,*[3] *Thomas,*[2] *John* [1]), married Attleboro', Mass., July 18, 1721, Nathaniel Robinson.

Issue:

859. i.   NATHAN ROBINSON,[5] born Attleboro', Mass., April 21, 1722.
860. ii.   NATHANIEL ROBINSON,[5] born Attleboro', Mass., April 4, 1724.
861. iii. GEORGE ROBINSON,[5] born Attleboro', Mass., July 23, 1726.
862. iv.   ZILPHA ROBINSON,[5] born Attleboro', Mass., October 9, 1728.
863. v.   ELIZABETH ROBINSON,[5] born Attleboro', Mass., March 4, 173$\frac{0}{1}$.
864. vi.   ELIHU ROBINSON.[5] born Attleboro', Mass., January 14, 1733.
865. vii. AMOS ROBINSON,[5] born Attleboro', Mass., September 7, 1735.
866. viii. ABIGAIL ROBINSON,[5] born Attleboro', Mass., June 15, 1737.
867. ix.   MARGRET ROBINSON,[5] born Attleboro', Mass., January 8, 173$\frac{9}{40}$.

732. PATIENCE DAGGETT [4] (*John,*[3] *Thomas,*[2] *John* [1]), born Martha's Vineyard, 1705; died Attleboro', Mass., September 27, 1793; married Attleboro', Mass., October 4, 1723, Lieut. Noah Robinson; born 1702; died Attleboro', Mass., December 7, 1788.

Issue:

868. i.   LAPHANIAH ROBINSON,[5] born Attleboro', Mass., September 29, 1723.
869. ii.   MARY ROBINSON,[5] born Attleboro', Mass., December 20, 1725.
870. iii. ELIJAH ROBINSON,[5] born Attleboro', Mass., October 3, 1728.
871. iv.   WILLIAM ROBINSON,[5] born Attleboro', Mass., October 25, 1732.
872. v.   HULDA ROBINSON,[5] born Attleboro', Mass., November 10, 1735; died Attleboro', Mass., December 5, 1735.
873. vi.   ENOCH ROBINSON,[5] born Attleboro', Mass., November 4, 1738.
874. vii. COMFORT ROBINSON,[5] born Attleboro', Mass., June 7, 1740.

733. MARY DAGGETT [4] (*John,*[3] *Thomas,*[2] *John* [1]), married Attleboro', Mass., January 18, 172$\frac{7}{8}$, John Titus.

Issue:

875. i.   LYDIA TITUS,[5] born Attleboro', Mass., November 19, 1728.
876. ii.   ABIGAIL TITUS,[5] born Attleboro', Mass., April 16, 1731.
877. iii. SAMUEL TITUS,[5] born Attleboro', Mass., March 13, 173$\frac{3}{4}$.
878. iv.   JOHN TITUS,[5] born Attleboro', Mass., August 26, 1739.
879. v.   MOLLY TITUS,[5] born Attleboro', Mass., March 11, 1737.
880. vi.   SIMEON TITUS,[5] born Attleboro', Mass., June 26, 1741.
881. vii. RODAN TITUS,[5] born Attleboro', Mass., April 8, 1743.
882. viii. CORNELIUS TITUS,[5] born Attleboro', Mass., March 4, 174$\frac{3}{8}$; died Attleboro', Mass., July 3, 1768.

734. BROTHERTON DAGGETT [4] (*Joshua,*[3] *Thomas,*[2] *John* [1]), born Edgartown, Mass., 1687; died Edgartown, Mass., March 5, 1740; married, about 1724, Thankfull ——, widow.

Issue:

883. i.   BROTHERTON DAGGETT,[5] bapt. Edgartown, Mass., February 7, 1725.
884. ii.   THANKFULL DAGGETT,[5] bapt. Edgartown, Mass., March 12, 1727; married Cornelius Marchant, Jr.
885. iii. THOMAS DAGGETT,[5] bapt. Edgartown, Mass., November 10, 1728.
886. iv.   TIMOTHY DAGGETT,[5] bapt. Edgartown, Mass., February 28, 1731.
887. v.   ELIJAH DAGGETT,[5] bapt. Edgartown, Mass., April 21, 1734.
888. vi.   JETHRO DAGGETT,[5] bapt. Edgartown, Mass., May 23, 1736.
889. vii. EBENEZER DAGGETT,[5] bapt. Edgartown, Mass., August 26, 1739; died Union, Me., April 29, 1816.

Brotherton Daggett, yeoman, husbandman, resided in Edgartown, Mass.

Nov 17, 1712 he bought land in Edgartown, of his parents [Dukes Deeds, 2–347–349] and Dec 27, 1718 he buys of his father, the W part of his fathers house, in Edgartown. [D.D., 3–190.]

Oct. 15, 1720 [D.D., 4–252] Dec 10, 1734 [D.D., 6–104] and Sept 10, 1737 [D.D., 6–209] he buys land in Edgartown and Chappaquiddick.

March 22, 173⅓ he and Nicholas Norton, hire land in Edgartown, on a lease. [D.D., 6–409.]

Brotherton Daggett attended the First Church in Edgartown, and the records of the church contain the following : " Brotherton Daggett, being an adult Person ; was baptised March 12, 1727."

One of the three stones to the memory of the Daggetts which yet remain in the old burial ground in Edgartown is for

Brotherton Daggett died March 5, 1740 aged 53 years.

June 16, 1741. Thankful Daggett was appointed administratrix of Brotherton Daggett, husbandman, deceased.

Inventory taken, July 8, 1741. [Dukes Probate.]

736. JACOB DAGGETT [4] (*Joshua*,[3] *Thomas*,[2] *John*[1]), born Prudence, Mass., about 1690; died Sherborn, Nantucket, March, 1760; married Nantucket, Mass., October 24, 1714, by William Worth, J.P., to Hannah Skiffe, daughter of James and Sarah Skiffe; born 1687 ; living 1773.

Issue :

890. i.   AARON DAGGETT,[5] born Nantucket, Mass., 4, 4 mo., 1715 ; died previous to February 7, 1761.

891. ii.   HEPZIBAH DAGGETT,[5] born Nantucket, Mass., 1717.

892. iii. STEPHEN DAGGETT,[5] born Nantucket, Mass., May 19, 1721 ; died previous to February 7, 1761.

893. iv.   NATHAN DAGGETT,[5] born Nantucket, Mass., December 21, 1723.

894. v.   HULDAH DAGGETT,[5] born Nantucket, Mass., June 12, 1726 ; married Nantucket, Mass., February 1, 1749, by Josiah Coffin, J.P., to Thomas, son of David Gwinn; she died previous to 1761.

895. vi.   JOSEPH DAGGETT,[5] born Nantucket, Mass., September 17, 1728.

896. vii. BENJAMIN DAGGETT,[5] born Nantucket, Mass., April 21, 1731.

Jacob Daggett removed to Sherborn, Nantucket.

Oct. 26, 1730 his father gives him land in Edgartown near Mattakase pond, on account of love he has for him. [Dukes Deeds, 5–38.]

Jacob Daggett of Nantucket sells land, in Edgartown, Oct 28, 1754, Nov 1756 and Nov 3, 1757. [Dukes Deeds, 8–311–401–454.]

Hannah Daggett appointed administratrix of the estate of her husband, Jacob Daggett, late of Sherborn, April 5, 1760. [Nantucket Probate, 2–382.]

The inventory of his estate, May 12, 1760, mentions dwelling-house, £11. His estate was valued, real estate, £84 16s. 0d. ; personal, £34 17s. 23d.

744. John Daggett[4] (*Joseph*,[3] *Joseph*,[2] *John*[1]), born about 1694; died Edgartown, Mass. (?), about 1739; married before September 23, 1720, Sarah ——.

Issue:

897. i. Joseph (?) Daggett,[5] born 1721 (?).
898. ii. Prince (?) Daggett,[5] born 1723; bapt. December 9, 1794, age 71 years; then dangerously sick; died Edgartown, Mass., 1794 (?).
899. iii. Ebenezer (?) Daggett.[5]
900. iv. Amey ?) Daggett.[5]
901. v. John (?) Daggett.[5]

John Daggett, laborer, husbandman, yeoman, resided in Edgartown, Mass.

His father left him land in Edgartown, portions of which he sells from time to time.

Sept 23, 1720 [Dukes Deeds, 4–123] he makes the first sale, and in the following October, buys his sister Elizabeth's portion, in their father's estate. [D.D., 4–184.]
Aug 10, 1725, he sells land, in Edgartown [D.D., 4–103], and July 22, 1726 land at a place commonly called "Daggetts farm." [D.D., 4–186.]
A sale made Oct. 14, 1726 is to Joseph Potompson, an Indian. [D.D., 7–106.]
Other sales are made, Aug 6, 1729, land at "Squash meadow" [D.D., 5–153], June 24, 1734 to John Tolman, Indian husbandman [D.D., 5–405], and Aug 17, 1736. [D.D., 6–267.]

October 1, 1739, Sarah Daggett appointed administratrix of John Daggett, of Edgartown, husbandman. [Dukes Probate.]

745. Amy Daggett[4] (*Joseph*,[3] *Joseph*,[2] *John*[1]), born about 1696; married Edgartown, Mass., December 22, 1715, by Pain Mayhew, Esq., to Thomas Martin.

Thomas and Amy Martin receipt to John Daggett, of Edgartown, for their portion in the estate of "our honored father Joseph Daggett," August 3, 1719. [Dukes Probate.]

Thomas Martin was of Edgartown, "cordwainer," September 23, 1720. [Dukes Deeds, 4–123.]

749. Hepsiba Daggett[4] (*Joseph*,[3] *Joseph*,[2] *John*[1]), born about 1706; married Edgartown, Mass., December 17, 1725, Enoch Norton.

Issue:

902. i. Temperance Norton,[5] born Edgartown, Mass., October 3, 1726.
903. ii. Abigail Norton,[5] born Edgartown, Mass., February 10, 172⅚.
904. iii. Cornelius Norton,[5] born Edgartown, Mass., January 13, 173⅘.
905. iv. Hepsiba Norton,[5] born Edgartown, Mass., November 26, 1734.
906. v. Amy Norton,[5] born Edgartown, Mass., January 7, 173⅞.
907. vi. Elizabeth Norton,[5] born Edgartown, Mass., July 23, 1739.

October 21, 1718, Thomas Martin was appointed guardian of Hepziba Daggett. [Dukes Probate.]

August 3, 1719, Mr. Martin received Hepziba Daggett's share in her father's estate.

JOHN DOGGETT, OF MARTHA'S VINEYARD.

FIFTH GENERATION.

759. HANNAH DAGGETT [5] (*Joseph*,[4] *Joseph*,[3] *John*,[2] *John* [1]), born Attleboro', Mass., Jan. 21, 172–; married Rehoboth, Mass., July 6, 1749, by Rev. John Greenwood, to Simeon Cole, son of John and Mercy Cole, of Rehoboth, Mass.; born Rehoboth, Mass., August 17, 1726.

Issue :

908. i.   KEZIAH COLE,[6] born Rehoboth, Mass., January 9, 174$\frac{9}{50}$.
909. ii.   MARGARET COLE,[6] born Rehoboth, Mass., February 11, 1752.
910. iii. SIMEON COLE,[6] born Rehoboth, Mass., September 19, 1754.
911. iv.   EUNICE COLE,[6] born Rehoboth, Mass., May 22, 1757.
912. v.   CYNTHIA COLE,[6] born Rehoboth, Mass., March 11, 1761.
913. vi.   HANNAH PATIENCE COLE,[6] born Rehoboth, Mass., September 15, 1768; married Frederick Bliss of Calais, Vt., April 27, 1785; died Worcester, Mass., December 3, 1851.

769. WILLIAM DAGGETT [5] (*Israel*,[4] *Joseph*,[3] *John*,[2] *John* [1]), born Rehoboth, Mass., November 1, 1729; died Seekonk, Mass., between August, 1813, and April, 1819; married Rehoboth, Mass., November 4, 1760, by Rev. Robert Rogerson, to Hannah Braily.

Issue :

914. i.   WILLIAM DAGGETT,[6] born Seekonk, Mass.; died No. Providence, R.I., 1838.
915. ii.   JOHN DAGGETT,[6] born Seekonk, Mass.
916. iii. ABEL DAGGETT,[6] born Seekonk, Mass.; died Pawtucket, Mass., 1843.
917. iv.   JESSE DAGGETT,[6] born Seekonk, Mass.
918. v.   SIMEON DAGGETT,[6] born Seekonk, Mass., September 13, 1768; millwright; married; died Seekonk, Mass., December 13, 1850.
919. vi.   ISRAEL DAGGETT,[6] born Seekonk, Mass.
920. vii. LEMUEL DAGGETT,[6] born Seekonk, Mass., November 25, 1775; farmer; married; died Seekonk, Mass., February 25. 1850.
921. viii. AMEY DAGGETT,[6] born Seekonk, Mass.; died Pawtucket, Mass., 1855.

William Daggett received by the will of his uncle, John Daggett, land in Cumberland, called "the Mine lot." The will was dated September 10, 1767, and proved January 27, 1772. [Bristol Probate.]

770. DANIEL DAGGETT [5] (*Israel*,[4] *Joseph*,[3] *John*,[2] *John* [1]), born Rehoboth, Mass., November 16, 1731; died between July 22 and October 24, 1799; married, Providence, R.I., July 10, 1759, by Jabez Bowen, to Bebe Perry, of Attleboro', Mass.

Issue :

922. i.   JOHN DAGGETT,[6] born Rehoboth, Mass., July 4, 1760; died Seekonk, Mass., June 4, 1814.
923. ii.   MARY DAGGETT,[6] born Rehoboth, Mass., April 3, 1762; married, William Daggett. See 986.

924. iii.   JACOB DAGGETT,[6] born Rehoboth, Mass., March 12, 1765.
925. iv.   ELIZABETH DAGGETT,[6] born Rehoboth, Mass., August 11, 1767; married
Robert Daggett. See 974.

The will of Daniel Daggett, of Rehoboth, was dated July 22, 1799, and proved November 5, 1799.   He mentions beloved wife Bebe Daggett; son John Daggett; Nathan Daggett, son of my daughter Mary Daggett; son Jacob Daggett; daughter Elizabeth Daggett; residue to son Jacob, who is also executor.   [Bristol Probate.]

772.   ISRAEL DAGGETT [5]   (*Israel*,[4]   *Joseph*,[3]   *John*,[2]   *John*[1]), born Rehoboth, Mass., April 28, 1737; died between 1769 and 1777; married Rehoboth, Mass., July 15, 1763, by Thomas Bowen, to Frances Bowen, widow.

Issue:

926. i.   JOSEPH DAGGETT,[6] born Rehoboth, Mass., May 4, 1764; June 24, 1777,
William Daggett appointed his guardian.
927. ii.   MARTHA DAGGETT,[6] born Rehoboth, Mass., October 6, 1765; June 24,
1777, Daniel Daggett appointed her guardian.
928. iii.   LYDIA DAGGETT,[6] born Rehoboth, Mass., February 6, 1769; June 24,
1777, William Daggett appointed her guardian.

August, 1784.   Israel Daggett, having deceased, property left him is set off to eldest daughter, Martha Daggett; only son, Joseph Daggett; youngest daughter, Lydia Daggett.   [Bristol Probate.]

782.   REUBEN DAGGETT [5]   (*Nathaniel*,[4]   *Nathaniel*,[3]   *John*,[2]   *John*[1]), born Attleboro', Mass., August 31, 1733; married Rehoboth, Mass., November 21, 1754, by Elder Nathan Pearce, to Isabel Round, of Rehoboth, Mass.

Issue:

929. i.   REUBEN DAGGETT,[6] born Attleboro', Mass., November 11, 1755.
930. ii.   SIMON DAGGETT,[6] born Attleboro', Mass., December 4, 1758; died
possibly, Cattaraugus county, N.Y.
931. iii.   DARIUS DAGGETT,[6] born Attleboro', Mass., July 17, 1760; married
Westmoreland, N.H., by Rev. Eben. Bailey, to Hepsebah Dean,
July 18, 1781; he died Vermont.
932. iv.   DANIEL DAGGETT,[6] born Attleboro', Mass., July 27, 1762.
933. v.   ISABEL DAGGETT,[6] born Attleboro', Mass., May 17, 1764.

April 27, 1778.   Reuben Daggett, of Attleboro', buys land in Marlboro' of Benoni Wilmarth.   [Bristol Deeds, 58–259.]

783.   AMOS DAGGETT [5]   (*Nathaniel*,[4]   *Nathaniel*,[3]   *John*,[2]   *John*[1]), born Attleboro', Mass., September 5, 1735; married Hannah Fisher.

Issue:

934. i.   AMOS DAGGETT,[6] born Attleboro', Mass., April 9, 176-.
935. ii.   SAMUEL DAGGETT,[6] born Attleboro', Mass., June 24, 17-.
936. iii.   JAMES DAGGETT,[6] born Attleboro', Mass., December 2, 17-.
937. iv.   NAOMI DAGGETT,[6] born Attleboro', Mass., February 27, 17-.
938. v.   HANNAH DAGGETT,[6] born Attleboro', Mass., August 21, 1771.
939. vi.   RACHEL DAGGETT,[6] born Attleboro', Mass., August 21, 1773.

786. NATHANIEL DAGGETT [5] (*Nathaniel*,[4] *Nathaniel*,[3] *John*,[2] *John*[1]), born Attleboro', Mass., April 29, 1747; married Beulah Dryer.

Issue:

940. i.   JOHN DAGGETT,[6] born Attleboro', Mass., July 24, 1771.
941. ii. NANCY DAGGETT,[6] born Attleboro', Mass., June 10, 1773.
942. iii. LYDIA DAGGETT,[6] born Attleboro', Mass., January 14, 1775.

787. REBECCA DAGGETT [5] (*John*,[4] *Nathaniel*,[3] *John*,[2] *John*[1]), born Rehoboth, Mass., May 2, 1722; married Rehoboth, Mass., November 22, 1744, by Thomas Bowen, Esq., to Caleb Brown, son of Joseph and Elizabeth Brown, of Rehoboth; born Rehoboth, Mass., June 30, 1720.

Issue:

943. i.   ANN BROWN,[6] born Rehoboth, Mass., September 24, 1745.
944. ii.   AMY BROWN,[6] born Rehoboth, Mass., April 24, 1747.
945. iii. SARAH BROWN,[6] born Rehoboth, Mass., April 20, 1749.
946. iv.   BETHIAH BROWN,[6] born Rehoboth, Mass., January 12, 1752.
947. v.   CALEB BROWN,[6] born Rehoboth, Mass., April 2, 1754.
948. vi.   LEVI BROWN,[6] born Rehoboth, Mass., March 26, 1756.
949. vii. REBECCA BROWN,[6] born Rehoboth, Mass., January 4, 1758.
950. viii. ELIZABETH BROWN,[6] born Rehoboth, Mass., May 13, 1760.
951. ix.   CHLOE BROWN,[6] born Rehoboth, Mass., July 5, 1763.

788. JOHN DAGGETT [5] (*John*,[4] *Nathaniel*,[3] *John*,[2] *John*[1]), born Rehoboth, Mass., November 6, 1723; died between August 7 and September 1, 1789; married Swansea, Mass., April 4, 1752, Penelope Wood, daughter of John and Charity [Millerd (Thurber)] Wood, of Swansea; born Swansea, Mass., May 23, 1722.

Issue:

952. i.   JOHN DAGGETT,[6] born Rehoboth, Mass., September 27, 1754.
953. ii. MARY DAGGETT,[6] born Rehoboth, Mass., March 16, 1755; married Rehoboth, Mass., May 16, 1779, by Wm. Cole, J.P., to Squier Munro.
954. iii. JOSHUA DAGGETT,[6] born Rehoboth, Mass., August 8, 1757.
955. iv. LEVI DAGGETT,[6] born Rehoboth, Mass., April 12, 1761.
956. v.   HOPE DAGGETT,[6] born Rehoboth, Mass., December 16, 1762.

The will of John Daggett, of Rehoboth, dated August 7, 1789, was proved September 1, 1789. Mentions wife Penelope; daughter Molle Monrow, wife of Squier Monrow; daughter Hopestill Davis, wife of John Davis; son Levi Daggett; grandson Joshua Davis; son Levi, executor. [Bristol Probate.]

789. HOPESTILL DAGGETT [5] (*John*,[4] *Nathaniel*,[3] *John*,[2] *John*[1]), born Rehoboth, Mass., January 9, 1725; married Rehoboth, Mass., December 9, 1742, by Thomas Bowen, Esq., to Aaron Wheeler, son of Philip and Martha Wheeler, of Rehoboth; born Rehoboth, Mass., January 17, 1722.

Issue:

957. i. HOPESTILL WHEELER,[6] born Rehoboth, Mass., March 17, 174⁶⁄₇.
958. ii. MOLLY WHEELER,[6] born Rehoboth, Mass., May 5, 1749.

959. iii.   CHLOE WHEELER,[6] born Rehoboth, Mass., September 2, 1750.
960. iv.   AARON WHEELER,[6] born Rehoboth, Mass., July 29, 1752.
961. v.   MEHITABLE WHEELER,[6] born Rehoboth, Mass., March 25, 1754.
962. vi.   NATHAN WHEELER,[6] born Rehoboth, Mass., April 11, 1755.
963. vii.   AMY WHEELER,[6] born Rehoboth, Mass., January 21, 1757.

791.   ABIGAIL DAGGETT [5] (*John*,[4] *Nathaniel*,[3] *John*,[2] *John* [1]), born Rehoboth, Mass., January 19, 172$\frac{9}{30}$; married Rehoboth, Mass., January 1, 1746, by Thomas Bowen, Esq., to Joseph Franklin.

Issue :

964. i.   HOPESTILL FRANKLIN,[6] born Rehoboth, Mass., November 2, 1747.
965. ii.   LYDIA FRANKLIN,[6] born Rehoboth, Mass., December 17, 1749.
966. iii.   WILLSON FRANKLIN,[6] born Rehoboth, Mass., April 10, 1752.
967. iv.   ABEL FRANKLIN,[6] born Rehoboth, Mass., August 15, 1754.
968. v.   JOSEPH FRANKLIN,[6] born Rehoboth, Mass., August 23, 1757.
969. vi.   JOHN FRANKLIN,[6] born Rehoboth, Mass., February 17, 1760.
970. vii.   BENJAMIN FRANKLIN,[6] born Rehoboth, Mass., May 10, 1762.
971. viii. THOMAS FRANKLIN,[6] born Rehoboth, Mass., March 31, 1766.
972. ix.   ESTHER FRANKLIN,[6] born Rehoboth, Mass., January 1, 1768.

792.   JAMES DAGGETT [5] (*John*,[4] *Nathaniel*,[3] *John*,[2] *John* [1]), born Rehoboth, Mass., January 2, 173$\frac{1}{2}$; died Rehoboth, Mass., May 24, 1806 ; married Rebecca ——. She died Seekonk, Mass., about 1827.

Issue :

973. i.   JAMES DAGGETT,[6] born Rehoboth, Mass., June 25, 1761; died Rehoboth, Mass., 1830, before April 5.
974. ii.   ROBERT DAGGETT,[6] born Rehoboth, Mass., May 1, 1763.
975. iii.   GILBERT DAGGETT,[6] born Rehoboth, Mass., February 24, 1765.
976. iv.   BETTE DAGGETT,[6] born Rehoboth, Mass., March 21, 1767; died Rehoboth, Mass., August 29, 1778.
977. v.   SAMUEL DAGGETT,[6] born Rehoboth, Mass., January 27, 1769; married Rehoboth, Mass., November 3, 1805, by J. Hills, to Martha Carpenter.
978. vi.   REBECCA DAGGETT,[6] born Rehoboth, Mass., November 22, 1770; married Rehoboth, Mass., between April, 1795, and April, 1796, by John Ellis, to Dr. Haze Humphrey. She died Rehoboth, Mass., February 10, 1798.
979. vii.   LYDIA DAGGETT,[6] born Rehoboth, Mass., October 14, 1772; married Rehoboth, Mass., September 29, 1791, by J. Ellis, to Ezra Ide.
980. viii. SUSANNA DAGGETT,[6] born Rehoboth, Mass., October 25, 1774; died after 1830.
981. ix.   EUNICE DAGGETT,[6] born Rehoboth, Mass., October 31, 1776; died Rehoboth, Mass., August 26, 1778.
982. x.   TIMOTHY DAGGETT,[6] born Rehoboth, Mass., December 3, 1778; died Rehoboth, Mass., January 6, 1799.
983. xi.   HENRY DAGGETT,[6] born Rehoboth, Mass., April 14, 1781.
984. xii.   EDWARD DAGGETT,[6] born Rehoboth, Mass., April 14, 1781; "a sailor;" died Seekonk, Mass., August 2, 1850.

James Daggett, yeoman, of Rehoboth, also probably innholder, as one James Daggett is licensed, March 23, 1758, to be an innholder there. February 11, 1744, John Wood was appointed his guardian. [Bristol Probate.]

May 20, 1763, he became a member of the First Parish Church in Rehoboth.

James Daggett died intestate in 1806, and July 1, 1806, Robert and Samuel Daggett were appointed administrators of his estate, which amounted to $5,202.75.

A division was made September 6, 1808, between the widow, Rebecca, and children, James, Robert, Samuel, Lydia Ide, Edward, Susanna, and Henry. [Bristol Probate.]

Rebecca Daggett, of Seekonk, where her will was dated October 27, 1818, and proved January 4, 1828.

She mentions sons James, Samuel, Henry, Edward, and Robert, and daughters Lydia Ide, widow of Ezra Ide, and Susanna Daggett. [Bristol Probate.]

793. Major Nathan Daggett [5] (*John,* [4] *Nathaniel,* [3] *John,* [2] *John* [1]), born Rehoboth, Mass., December 24, 1733; died Rehoboth, Mass., April 18, 1778; married 1st, Rehoboth, Mass., November 5, 1755, by Rev. John Greenwood, to Abigail Carpenter, widow; died Rehoboth, Mass., April 29, 1760; married 2d, Rehoboth, Mass., September 25, 1760, by Rev. John Carnes, to Martha Read, of Rehoboth; died after 1813.

Issue :

985. i.   Sarah Daggett,[6] born Rehoboth, Mass., August 27, 1756; married Mr. Brayton.
986. ii.   William Daggett,[6] born Rehoboth, Mass., February 26, 1758.
987. iii. Abigail Daggett,[6] born Rehoboth, Mass., April 16, 1760.
988. iv.   Lucy Daggett,[6] born Rehoboth, Mass., October 4, 1761; married, Rehoboth, Mass., October 12, 1780, by Rev. E. Hyde, to Moses Read, 3d, of Sharon, Mass.
989. v.   George Daggett,[6] born Rehoboth, Mass., October 11, 1763; died Rehoboth, Mass., March 18, 1778.
990. vi.   Nathan Daggett,[6] born Rehoboth, Mass., March 5, 1766; died Rehoboth, Mass., November (?), 1798.
991. vii. Anne Daggett,[6] born Rehoboth, Mass., January 4, 1768; married Mr. Bucklen.
992. viii. Benjamin Daggett,[6] born Rehoboth, Mass., March 15, 1770.
993. ix.   Russell Daggett,[6] born Rehoboth, Mass., April 29, 1772; married, Providence, R.I., July 25, 1799, Polly Ormsbee.
994. x.   John Daggett,[6] born Rehoboth, Mass., May 2, 1774; died Rehoboth, Mass., September 14, 1775.
995. xi.   Martha Daggett,[6] born Rehoboth, Mass., May 28, 1776; died Seekonk, Mass., November 11, 1861.

Major Nathan Daggett was one of the patriots of Rehoboth during the stirring times of the Revolution.

" In 1773 a letter full of fire and patriotism was addressed to the representative of Rehoboth by the Committee of Correspondence, which was composed of six men, of which one was Nathan Daggett.

" Nov. 6, 1775. The town voted to borrow four pieces of cannon of Capt. John Lyon and Maj. Nathan Daggett." [Bliss Hist. of Rehoboth.]

May 20, 1763. Nathan Daggett was a member of the First Parish Church in Rehoboth.

On the decease of Maj. Nathan Daggett, his widow, Martha, was appointed the guardian of Nathan, Lucy, Martha, Anna, Russell, and Benjamin Daggett, August 4, 1778. [Bristol Probate.]

The estate of Maj. Nathan Daggett amounted to £522 10s. 0d., and a division was ordered December 7, 1779, among the widow, Martha, and children, William, Nathan, Benjamin, Russell, Sarah Brayton, Abigail, Lucy, Nancy, and Martha.

Martha Daggett, widow of Maj. Nathan Daggett, married, by Rev. E. Hyde, to Capt. John Bishop, January 25, 1781.

The estate of Maj. Nathan Daggett does not appear to have been divided in the first instance, as under date of Seekonk, December 28, 1813, the estate is mentioned as divided among widow Martha; William, Nathan, Benjamin, and Russell Daggett, the sons; and Sally Brayton, Abigail Read, Lucy Read, Nancy Bucklen, and Martha Daggett, the daughters. [Bristol Probate.]

798. JOB DAGGETT [5] (*Amos*,[4] *Nathaniel*,[3] *John*,[2] *John*[1]), born Swansea, Mass., March 2, 1746; married Swansea, Mass., June 11, 1778, Phœbe Sisson.

Issue:

996. i. CALEB DAGGETT,[6] born Swansea, Mass., March 29, 1779.
997. ii. ABIGAIL DAGGETT,[6] born Swansea, Mass., August 17, 1781.
998. iii. PATIENCE DAGGETT,[6] born Swansea, Mass., June 12, 1784.
999. iv. EZEKIEL DAGGETT,[6] born Swansea, Mass., June 3, 1788.

799. SAMUEL DAGGETT [5] (*Samuel*,[4] *Thomas*,[3] *Thomas*,[2] *John*[1]), born Edgartown, Mass. (?), about 1706; married Tisbury, Mass., November 8, 1733, Sarah Chase, daughter of Thomas and Jane Chase, of Tisbury, Mass.

Issue:

1000. i. TIMOTHY DAGGETT,[6] born Tisbury, Mass., August 16, 1734.
1001. ii. ISAAC DAGGETT,[6] born Tisbury, Mass., November 26, 1737.
1002. iii. JANE DAGGETT,[6] born Tisbury, Mass.; married Jonathan Merry; issue: Sarah Noyes Merry, married December 3, 1770, Jonathan Cottle.

January 13, 172⅞. Samuel Daggett, of Edgartown, "cordwainer," grandson of Capt. Thomas Daggett, sells rights in Cape Poeg. [Dukes Deeds, 4–321.]

Samuel Daggett seems to have removed to Tisbury at the time of his marriage, and November 6, 1735, calls himself of Tisbury, "cordwainer," at which time he and his wife Sarah mention "rights in Holmes Hole neck, which belonged to our father Thomas Chase." [Dukes Deeds, 6–90 and 93.]

Jan. 14, 173⅚. Samuel Daggett, of Holmes hole, in Constablerick of Tisbury, Cordwainer, sells rights to his brother Seth. [Dukes Deeds, 6-105.]
Jan. 14, 1737 Samuel Daggett, of Tisbury, Cordwainer, as Atty to Pasco

Hadlock and Elizabeth his wife, of Lebanon, Conn., sell land at Chappaquiddick. [Dukes Deeds, 6–207.]

Sept. 27, 1737 he and others, sell land in Edgartown, and on Chappaquiddick. [Dukes Deeds, 6–331.]

Jan. 12, 173⅜, Samuel Daggett, cordwainer, of Holmes hole, and his brother Seth, sell land in Edgartown. [Dukes Deeds, 6–431.]

Feb. 15, 1740, he buys land. [Dukes Deeds, 6–388.]

May 28, 1741. Sarah Daggett, sells land at Holmes hole Tisbury, to Abraham Chase. [Dukes Deeds, 6–454.]

800. SETH DAGGETT [5] (*Samuel,*[4] *Thomas,*[3] *Thomas,*[2] *John* [1]), born February 5, 1713; died Tisbury, Mass., April 14, 1779; married Tisbury, Mass., December 23, 1734. Elizabeth West, daughter of Abner and Jean (Cottle) West; born July 18, 1720; died July 18, 1807.

Issue :

1003. i.   WILLIAM DAGGETT.[6]
1004. ii.   PETER DAGGETT,[6] born Tisbury, Mass., May 4, 1738.
1005. iii. SAMUEL P. DAGGETT,[6] born Tisbury, Mass., May 4, 1738.
1006. iv.   SAMUEL DAGGETT,[6] born Tisbury, Mass., May 9, 1745.
1007. v.   NATHAN DAGGETT.[6]
1008. vi.   SETH DAGGETT,[6] born 1755; died 1761.
1009. vii. SILAS DAGGETT,[6] born Tisbury, Mass., May 14, 1757.
1010. viii. MARY DAGGETT,[6] bapt. 1760.
1011. ix.   WEST DAGGETT,[6] bapt. 1764; died " from a fall at sea," 1779.
1012. x.   JANE DAGGETT,[6] bapt. 1765.

Seth Daggett is said to have resided at Tashmoo (Lake?).

Ten transfers of land are made in his name, and in them he is called " carpenter " and " housewright," of Holmes Hole in Tisbury.

" Abner West father of Elizabeth the wife of Seth Daggett was the son of Thomas West and grandson of Francis West who settled in Virginia in 1607. He was Rear Admiral in the British Army under the title of Sir Francis. His son Thomas came to Marthas Vineyard, from Plymouth, in 1675, and settled in Chilmark."

801. SOLOMON DAGGETT [5] (*Samuel,*[4] *Thomas,*[3] *Thomas,*[2] *John* [1]), married Jane Hillman (?).

Solomon Daggett, laborer, of Edgartown, sells land there, and also at Chappaquiddick and Chilmark, between 1737 and 1763.

802. SYLVANUS DAGGETT [5] (*Samuel.*[4] *Thomas,*[3] *Thomas,*[2] *John* [1]), married Tisbury, Mass., May 2, 1756, Alice Stuart.

Issue :

1013. i.   SOLOMON DAGGETT,[6] died in the " Gen. Arnold," December 25, 1798.
1014. ii.   SAMUEL DAGGETT,[6] died at sea.
1015. iii. SYLVANUS DAGGETT,[6] died at sea, December 25, 1798.
1016. iv.   TIMOTHY DAGGETT,[6] died at sea, December 25, 1798.
1017. v.   MICHAEL DAGGETT,[6] born Tisbury, Mass., November 14, 1770.
1018. vi.   FREEMAN DAGGETT,[6] born November, 1772.
1019. vii. HEPZIBAH DAGGETT,[6] married Shubael Butler.

Sylvanus Daggett, mariner, resided in Edgartown, in Newport, and in Providence, as appears from the following deeds:

Sept 26, 1737 Silvanus Daggett, "seafaring man" of Edgartown. [Dukes Deeds, 6–304.]

July 21, 1738 Silvanus Daggett now resident in Newport "Mariner" appoints his brother Samuel as his attorney. [Dukes Deeds, 6–311.]

Feb 14, 1740 Silvanus Daggett of Newport sells land in Edgartown to Thomas Daggett. [Dukes Deeds, 6–437.]

Feb 16, 174⁰ Silvanus Daggett of Rhode Island, Providence Plantation in New England sells rights in undivided lands in Edgartown. [Dukes Deeds, 7–10.]

Feb 16, 174⁰ Silvanus Daggett of Providence R.I. "mariner" appoints his uncle Timothy Daggett of Edgartown, his attorney. [Dukes Deeds, 7–130.]

Nov 12, 1764 he and Alice his wife sell land in Chilmark to Cornelius Bassett. [Dukes Deeds, 9–419.]

804. ELIZABETH DAGGETT [5] (*Samuel,*[4] *Thomas,*[3] *Thomas,*[2] *John*[1]), married Lebanon, Conn., November 1, 1736, Pasco Hadlock.

Issue:

1020. i. JOHN HADLOCK,[6] born Lebanon, Conn., January 24, 1738.
1021. ii. SARAH HADLOCK,[6] born Lebanon, Conn., June 15, 1739.
1022. iii. SAMUEL HADLOCK,[6] born Lebanon, Conn., February 16, 1741.
1023. iv. JONATHAN HADLOCK,[6] born Lebanon, Conn., September 19, 1742.
1024. v. JAMES HADLOCK,[6] born Lebanon, Conn., April 17, 1744.
1025. vi. ELIZABETH HADLOCK,[6] born Lebanon, Conn., October 11, 1747.
1026. vii. SOLOMON HADLOCK,[6] born Lebanon, Conn., May 5, 1748.

809. BENJAMIN DAGGETT [5] (*Benjamin,*[4] *Thomas,*[3] *Thomas,*[2] *John*[1]), born Edgartown, Mass., December 1, 1742; died Dixmont, Maine, 1802; married Dartmouth, Mass. (intention November 6, 1766), Elizabeth Hathaway; born Dartmouth, Mass.

Issue:

1027. i. DESIAH DAGGETT,[6] born Edgartown, Mass., January 29, 1768; married Thomaston or Warren, Me., 1794, Alexander, son of Deacon John and Sarah Crawford; born 1762; issue: one son, three daughters; lived in Northport, Me.

1028. ii. BETSEY DAGGETT,[6] born Edgartown, Mass., October 27, 1769; married Elijah Toothacre; issue: nine children; one son married and died; widow lived in Belfast, Me.

1029. iii. HULDAH DAGGETT,[6] born Edgartown, Mass., February 18, 1771; married William Spring, of Camden, Me.; issue: three sons, three daughters.

1030. iv. THOMAS DAGGETT,[6] born Edgartown, Mass., September 4, 1774.

1031. v. LOVE DAGGETT,[6] born Edgartown, Mass., 1776.

1032. vi. PHŒBE DAGGETT,[6] bapt. Edgartown, Mass., June 7, 1778; married Jeremiah McRusick, of Dixmont, Me.; issue: one son, three daughters.

1033. vii. DIANA DAGGETT,[6] bapt. Edgartown, Mass., December 31, 1780; married Nathaniel Beverage; issue: one son, three daughters.

1034. viii. RICHMOND DAGGETT,[6] bapt. Edgartown, Mass., April 13, 1782.

1035. ix. RICHMOND DAGGETT,[6] born Edgartown, Mass., July 15, 1783.

1036. x. CATHERINE DAGGETT,[6] married 1st, Nathaniel Toothacre; married 2d, Thomas Butler, of Union, Me.; he born Tisbury, Mass., July 15, 1769; issue: three children.

1037. xi. ABIGAIL DAGGETT,[6] born Vinal Haven, Mass., October 24, 1785.

Benjamin Daggett, Jr., and Elizabeth, his wife, were received to full communion, and baptized in the church in Edgartown in August, 1774.

They resided in Edgartown until between 1783 and 1787, when they removed to Fox Island, Maine.

Oct. 24, 1787, Benjamin Daggett, of Fox Island, Maine, sells land in Edgartown, to John Daggett Jr and Ishmael Lobb. [Dukes Deeds, 12–389.]

Nov. 14, 1801, Benjamin Daggett, of New Canaan plantation, for $200, sells 100 acres of land, in New Canaan, to Henry Knox of Thomaston. [Lincoln Deeds, 48–93.]

812. Mary Daggett [5] (*Benjamin,* [4] *Thomas,* [3] *Thomas,* [2] *John* [1]), bapt. Edgartown, Mass., May 5, 1751; married Edgartown, Mass., October 8, 1775, Benjamin Davis, son of Melatiah and Jemima (Dunham) Davis; born 1752; died Edgartown, Mass., July 23, 1838.

Issue:

1038. i.   Henry Davis, [6] born Edgartown, Mass., November 20, 1778; married December 12, 1805, Betsey Athearn, of Tisbury, Mass.
1039. ii.   Zadoc Davis, [6] born Edgartown, Mass.; married Elizabeth Bassett; settled in Cincinnati, Ohio.
1040. iii. Sally Davis, [6] born Edgartown, Mass.; married Argalis Pease.
1041. iv.   Polly D. Davis, [6] born Edgartown, Mass., July 3, 1795; married Charles Smith, of Edgartown.
1042. v.   Benjamin Davis, [6] born Edgartown, Mass., February 2, 1805; married Almira Newcomb, of Edgartown.

Benjamin Davis, farmer, resided in Edgartown. He married 2d, Miriam, daughter of Ephraim Hunt, of Middleboro'.

821. Elder Elihu Daggett [5] (*Mayhew,* [4] *John,* [3] *Thomas,* [2] *John* [1]), born Attleboro', Mass., August 6, 1710; died Attleboro', Mass., August 29, 1769; married Attleboro', Mass., August 6, 1734, Rebecca Stanley, daughter of Jacob and ~~Elizabeth (Guild)~~ Stanley, of Attleboro', Mass.; born Attleboro', Mass., March 28, 1715; died Attleboro', Mass., September 20, 1799.

Issue:

1043. i.   Mayhew Daggett, [6] born Attleboro', Mass., April 28, 1735.
1044. ii.   Ichabod Daggett, [6] born Attleboro', Mass., December 7, 1736.
1045. iii. Daniel Daggett, [6] born Attleboro', Mass., February 1, 1738.
1046. iv.   Henry Daggett, [6] born Attleboro', Mass., April 9, 1741.
1047. v.   Desire Daggett, [6] born Attleboro', Mass., September 3, 1743.
1048. vi.   Elihu Daggett, [6] born Attleboro', Mass., December 4, 1745.
1049. vii. Jacob Daggett, [6] born Attleboro', Mass., May 16, 1748.
1050. viii. Anna Daggett, [6] born Attleboro', Mass., August 2, 1750.
1051. ix.   Enoch Daggett, [6] born Attleboro', Mass., April 18, 1753; died before 1769.
1052. x.   Elijah Daggett, [6] born Attleboro', Mass., April 14, 1754.
1053. xi.   Joseph Daggett, [6] born Attleboro', Mass., February 14, 1758.

Elder Elihu Daggett was elder and first preacher for the South Baptist Society of Attleboro', which was established in 1760. It is believed that he was never regularly settled here. He occasionally preached at the North Baptist Church. His sons, Mayhew and Ichabod, having entered the army, and not being heard from, he became anxious, and shouldering his musket started to seek them.

[handwritten notes] aco ... d ... Daggett ... .
... : Topsfie'd ... tal Records
pages: 98, 157, 188, 60

Reaching the seat of war he found a battle raging and entered the
action.   After the fight was ended, he found his two sons unharmed
on the field.   The powder-horn which the elder wore in this battle is
now (1893) in possession of Miss C. L. R. Daggett, Attleboro'
Falls, Mass.   He had a captain's commission in the provincial army.
He was interred in the North Burying-ground, and on his gravestone is the following inscription:

Sacred to the memory of
ELDER ELIHU DAGGETT,
who died Aug 29, 1769,
in the 60th year of his age.

Sacred to the memory of
MRS REBECCAH DAGGETT,
(his widow) who died Sept 20, 1799
in the 85th year of her age.
What we left behind others possess,
What we gave to the poor, we carried with us.

The will of Elihu Daggett, of Attleboro', was dated January 6,
1769, and proved October 2, 1769.   In it he mentions wife Rebecca,
sons Mayhew, Ichabod, Daniel, Henry, Jacob, Elijah, Elihu, Joseph,
and daughters Desire and Anna.   [Bristol Probate.]

822.   SARAH DAGGETT[5] (*Mayhew*,[4] *John*,[3] *Thomas*,[2] *John*[1]),
born Attleboro', Mass., May 17, 1715; married Attleboro', Mass.,
March 10. 173⁹⁄₇, Jeduthan Fuller.
   Issue:

1054. i.   JOANNA FULLER,[6] born Attleboro', Mass., December 6, 1737.
1055. ii.   AMOS FULLER,[6] born Attleboro', Mass., September 4, 1739.
1056. iii.   SARAH FULLER,[6] born Attleboro', Mass., June 22, 1741; died Attleboro', Mass., February 26, 174½.
1057. iv.   SARAH FULLER,[6] born Attleboro', Mass., February 8, 174⅔.
1058. v.   ZILPHA FULLER,[6] born Attleboro', Mass., May 5, 1745; died Attleboro', Mass., June, 1751.
1059. vi.   ABIALL FULLER,[6] born Attleboro', Mass., June 5, 1747.
1060. vii.   JONATHAN FULLER,[6] born Attleboro', Mass., June, 1749.
1061. viii.   ——IN FULLER,[6] born Attleboro', Mass., September 16, 1751.
1062. ix.   ZILPHA FULLER,[6] born Attleboro', Mass., November 5, 1753; died
Attleboro', Mass., November 12, 1753.
1063. x.   ——LP FULLER,[6] born Attleboro', Mass., October 5, 1755.
1064. xi.   MARGARET FULLER,[6] born Attleboro', Mass., February 8, 1757.

823.   BEULAH DAGGETT[5] (*Mayhew*,[4] *John*,[3] *Thomas*,[2] *John*[1]),
born Attleboro', Mass., November 17, 1719; married Abiall Fuller.
   Issue:

1065. i.   NATHAN FULLER,[6] born Attleboro', Mass., September 1, 1739.
1066. ii.   JABEZ FULLER,[6] born Attleboro', Mass., April 27, 1741.
1067. iii.   ELISHA FULLER,[6] born Attleboro', Mass., November 25, 1743.
1068. iv.   MICAIJAH FULLER,[6] born Attleboro', Mass., February 2, 174⅚.
1069. v.   ISAAC FULLER,[6] born Attleboro', Mass., August 26, 1748.
1070. vi.   SIMON FULLER,[6] born Attleboro', Mass., April 15, 1751.

1071. vii. BEULAH FULLER,[6] born Attleboro', Mass., October 4, 1753.
1072. viii. ZILPHA FULLER,[6] born Attleboro', Mass., January 21, 1755; died
      Attleboro', Mass., January 26, 1755.
1073. ix. ANNA FULLER,[6] born Attleboro', Mass., December 31, 1757.

824. ZILPHA DAGGETT[5] (*Mayhew,*[4] *John,*[3] *Thomas,*[2] *John*[1]),
born Attleboro', Mass., October 23, 172$\frac{6}{7}$; died Attleboro', Mass.,
October 19, 1807; married Attleboro', Mass., October 6, 1752,
William Stanley; born Attleboro', Mass., April 5, 1726; died Attleboro', Mass., January 27, 1806.

Issue:

1074. i. ABIGAIL STANLEY,[6] born Attleboro', Mass., May 28, 1753; died Attle-
      boro', Mass., September 26, 1754.
1075. ii. ABIGAIL STANLEY,[6] born Attleboro', Mass., Nov. 12. 1754.
1076. iii. PHŒBE STANLEY,[6] born Attleboro', Mass., October 20, 1756.
1077. iv. WILLIAM STANLEY,[6] born Attleboro', Mass., May 29, 1759.

826. BATHSHEBA DAGGETT[5] (*Ebenezer,*[4] *John,*[3] *Thomas,*[2] *John*[1]),
born Attleboro', Mass.. August 22, 1722; died Attleboro', Mass.,
December 29, 1808; married Capt. Henry Sweet.

Issue:

1078. i. HENRY SWEET,[6] born Attleboro', Mass., June 26, 1761.
1079. ii. HANNAH SWEET,[6] born Attleboro', Mass., November 14, 1763; died
      Attleboro', Mass., July 31, 1784.
1080. iii. BATHSHEBA SWEET,[6] born Attleboro', Mass., November 21, 1767.

✗ **827.** Col. JOHN DAGGETT[5] (*Ebenezer,*[4] *John,*[3] *Thomas,*[2] *John*[1]),
born Attleboro', Mass., September 2, 1724; died Attleboro', Mass.,
January 20, 1803; married 1st, Wrentham, Mass., November 19, 1751,
by Rev. Jos. Bean, to Mercy Shepard, daughter of John Shepard, of
Wrentham, Mass.; born Wrentham, Mass. (?); died Attleboro',
Mass., February 3, 1783; married 2d, Mass.. August 5, 1784, Mary
Tucker, widow. daughter of Mr. Brintnall; died about 1813.

Issue:

1081. i. JOHN DAGGETT,[6] born Attleboro', Mass., October 1, 1752.
1082. ii. JOAB DAGGETT,[6] born Attleboro', Mass., October 19, 1754.
1083. iii. JESSE DAGGETT,[6] born Attleboro', Mass., March 6, 1757.
1084. iv. BATHSHEBA DAGGETT,[6] born Attleboro', Mass., April 28, 1759; married
      Zenas Cutting.
1085. v. MARCY DAGGETT,[6] born Attleboro', Mass., July 2, 1761.
✗ 1086. vi. EBENEZER DAGGETT,[6] born Attleboro', Mass., April 16, 1763.
1087. vii. LEVI DAGGETT,[6] born Attleboro', Mass., April 4. 1766; died before
      1793.
1088. viii. HANNAH DAGGETT,[6] born Attleboro', Mass., December 19, 1768.
1089. ix. HULDAH DAGGETT,[6] born Attleboro', Mass., January 27, 1771.

Col. John Daggett was one of the principal public characters and
leading men of Attleboro', especially during the trying period of the
Revolution.

He and Colonel May were the two on whom the town placed the
utmost reliance.

December 9, 1763, he was chosen clerk of the Propriety.   He was possessed of a strong and sound mind, and was marked by a resolute and decided character.

He was a Puritan in the plainness and simplicity of his manners, and was a firm friend to the civil institutions and republican customs of New England.

September 12, 1774, he was chosen on the Committee of Safety by the town, and on the 29th of the same month was chosen representative to the General Court at Salem.

December 6, 1774, the town established a Superior and an Inferior Court to hear and determine controversies that have arisen or may arise.   Of the five men who were chosen superior judges, Colonel Daggett was chosen second justice.

He took an early and decided stand in the commencement of those proceedings which produced the Revolution.

One of the incidents in which he figured took place in December, 1774, when the Committee of Safety gave notice that one Aldrich, a Tory, who lived in Franklin, Mass., was selling British goods contrary to the resolutions of the General Court.   Colonel Daggett issued orders to the several companies of the town to furnish a certain number of men, who, being collected, marched on a bitter cold night for the place of Aldrich's residence, to put a stop to the business.   They arrived late at night, and, surrounding his house, ordered him out.   After threatening to fire on each other, Aldrich at last came out, and, after engaging not to vend any more British goods during the controversy, was released.

On the 9th of April, 1775, occurred another expedition, which Colonel Daggett undertook for the purpose of seizing a deposit of arms and ammunition, at Assonett Village (Freetown), which the Committee of Safety understood was collected there for the use of the loyalists.

They discovered forty stands of arms and equipments in possession of the Tories, together with a large quantity of ammunition, the whole of which was taken by the patriots.

January 2, 1775, the town chose Col. John Daggett " to represent us at the Congress to be holden at Cambridge on the 1st of Feb. next and to serve in that capacity until the month of May next or until the time fixed for the dissolution of said Congress."

He was representative, 1768, 1769, 1770, 1771, 1772, 1773, 1774, 1775, 1781.

May 21, 1777, Colonel Daggett was on a committee appointed to make a report relative to the new Constitution of the United States, and on the following day was one of a committee to prepare instructions for the representative.

August 2, 1779, he was one of a committee of three, sent by the town, to attend a convention at Cambridge, on the first of September following, at which time was formed the present Constitution of Massachusetts.

He was generally called to serve on the most important committees which were raised in town meeting, to consider the many difficult subjects which were then brought before the people during and subsequent to the Revolution.

August 18, 1778, General Sullivan, during his expedition to Rhode Island, requested the government of Massachusetts to send him reënforcement.

In compliance with this request, the orders were issued by the council of the State, directing Colonel Daggett, of the Fourth Regiment (including as now Attleboro', Mansfield, Norton, and Easton), to take charge of the detachment. In obedience to these orders, a regiment, consisting of nine hundred men, was formed out of the several regiments, which repaired to Rhode Island and served under the command of Colonel Daggett during the remainder of the campaign. Colonel Daggett also commanded the regiment from Bristol county, in Spencer's expedition. At home he was extensively employed as a surveyor, and was engaged in various other kinds of public business, such as the ordinary transactions of life require between citizens. [Daggett's Hist. Attleboro'.]

The will of John Daggett, of Attleboro', was dated January 7, 1793, and proved February 1, 1803.

Mentions wife Mary; sons John, Joab, and Jesse; daughters Bathsheba Cutting, wife of Zenas Cutting, Mercy Bolcom, wife of Elijah Bolcom, Hannah Ide, wife of Nathaniel Ide, Jr., Huldah Hodges, wife of Elijah Hodges; son Ebenezer, rest of estate; also makes him executor. [Bristol Probate.]

Mary, the widow of John Daggett, Esq., made a will, dated December 3, 1806, and proved 1813.

Mentions her brothers Nathaniel and Job Brintnall, also Lydia Maxcy Daggett, the daughter of Ebenezer Daggett. [Bristol Probate.]

828. Rev. NAPHTALI DAGGETT, D.D.[5] (*Ebenezer,*[4] *John,*[3] *Thomas,*[2] *John*[1]), born Attleboro', Mass., September 8, 1727; died New Haven, Conn., November 25, 1780; married Smithtown, L.I., N.Y., December 19, 1753, by Rev. Ebenezer Prime, to Mrs. Sarah Smith.

Issue:

1090. i. HENRY DAGGETT,[6] born Smithtown, L.I., N.Y., October 14, 1754; died Smithtown, L.I., N.Y., May 8, 1755.
1091. ii. SARAH DAGGETT,[6] born Smithtown, L.I., N.Y., April 17, 1756; married Dr. Solomon Meers; she died St. Marys, Geo., October 3, 1808.

1092. iii. HENRY DAGGETT,[6] born New Haven, Conn., February 27, 1758.
1093. iv. EBENEZER DAGGETT,[6] born New Haven, Conn., December 21, 1760;
            died before April 5, 1785, when bro. Henry appointed adm.
1094. v. JOHN DAGGETT,[6] born New Haven, Conn., March 1, 1763; possibly
            John who died Lewiston, Vt., about 1804.
1095. vi. EZRA DAGGETT,[6] born New Haven, Conn., April 18, 1765.
1096. vii. MARY DAGGETT,[6] born New Haven, Conn., April 16, 1767; married
            Robert Platts, Esq.; she died Plattsburg, N.Y., February 20, 1853.
1097. viii. ELIZABETH DAGGETT,[6] born New Haven, Conn., April 9, 1769.

Rev. Naphtali Daggett, D.D., President of Yale College, was the second son among eight children.

His father dying while he was yet young, he was left under the direction of a mother, who was, however, in every respect peculiarly qualified to discharge the duties which devolved upon her.

He soon after commenced studies preparatory to college. He entered Yale College in 1744, and graduated in 1748, at the age of twenty-one.

He was distinguished during his college life for industry and close application.

He was settled as minister of Smithtown, on Long Island, in 1751. In September, 1755, he was elected the first professor of divinity in Yale College, which appointment he accepted, and removed to New Haven, and was inducted into office on March 4 following. This office he held during his life. After the resignation of Mr. Clap, September 10, 1766, he officiated as president till April 1, 1777, when he resigned the office, but still continued to hold that of professor of divinity. The learned Dr. Stiles was his successor in the presidency.

During the barbarous attack on New Haven by the British army, in July, 1779, he took an active part in the defence of the country, and was distinguished for his resolution and intrepidity.

He made himself obnoxious by his open and active opposition to the British cause.

He had often inculcated upon the students under his charge, in the pulpit and in the lecture-room, the duty of resistance to British oppression. He had, therefore, incurred the special displeasure of the invaders.

He had openly preached and prayed against the success of their cause.

He knew no difference between preaching and practising, and when the crisis came, he carried his own principles into action.

He shouldered his musket and went into the field with the rest, to repel the invaders.

He was taken prisoner by the enemy. They beat and bruised him, and offered him every indignity in their power. His clerical character, in their eyes, was no exemption from the most outrageous abuses.

They demanded of him who he was; he unhesitatingly replied: " My name is Naphtali Daggett.   I am one of the officers of Yale College. I require you to release me."— " But we understand you have been in the habit of praying against our cause." — " Yes, and I never made more sincere prayers in my life."   He was at first left for dead on the ground.   He was saved by the intrepidity of the lady into whose house he had been conveyed.   After the British had retired, an offi- cer and a file of soldiers were sent back to convey him a prisoner on board their transports.   They came to the house and inquired for him, and were answered by the lady, who appeared at the door and resolutely refused to admit them, that he was so badly wounded it would be impossible to convey him on board alive.   " My orders," said the officer, " are positive to take him with me." — " But you would not surely carry away a dying man; he is now in the agonies of death."

After repeated demands and refusals, the officer finally determined to return and report the case to his superior, and ask for further orders, but he never came back after his prisoner.   He was taken prisoner, and came near losing his life.

Dr. Daggett died in consequence of the wounds he had received on that occasion, November 25, 1780, at the age of fifty-three.   He presided over the university about eleven years, and held the office of professor of divinity twenty-five years.

Possessed of a strong, clear, and comprehensive mind, he applied himself with assiduity and success to the various branches of knowl- edge, particularly to the learned languages and divinity.

Dr. Holmes, in his life of President Stiles, says: " He was a good classical scholar, well versed in moral philosophy, and a learned divine."   Clearness of understanding and accuracy of thought were characteristics of his mind.

He received the honorary degree of Doctor in Divinity from Yale College, and also from Princeton.   He published a sermon on the death of President Clap, 1767; another delivered at the ordination of Rev. Ebenezer Baldwin, 1770; and a third delivered at the ordination of Rev. J. Howe, 1773.   [Daggett's Hist. Attleboro'.]

Alden Bradford, in his notices of distinguished men in New Eng- land, says of Dr. Daggett that " he was respectable as a theologian and a general scholar.   While he acted as president of the college, it was in a prosperous state, and several of the alumni, distinguished afterwards in public life, were educated while he was at the head of that seminary.   In his character as a scholar, we find indications and traits rather of solid and useful learning than of brilliancy, or of original genius.   In that generation of men, there was more of a desire to be useful than to excite admiration."

December 25, 1780, administration was granted to Henry Daggett, and Henry Daggett, Jr., on the estate of Dr. Naphtali Daggett. [New Haven Probate, 12–435.]

Feb 7, 1781 Inventory was presented in which moveables amounted to £293 17s 4d. Among the items are: 6 acres land on S.E. side of the road leading into the 2nd quarter; 4 acres land lying in the Commons E. of Carmel road; ½ acre lying in the town plot opposite Prof. of Divinitys House; 10 acres woodland in Westfield; 2 acres in Yorkshire quarter; ½ acre in Yorkshire quarter; ¼ Right of land in Ludlow Vt; 1 Right of land in Wells Vt; 1 Right of land in Windhall Vt. [New Haven Probate, 12–444.]

Nov 26, 1783. A further account of adm. on the Estate shows: moveables £232 14s 5d; lands £204–15–4; to be divided among the 7 children of said deceased. [14–210.]

Dec 15, 1783 The estate was distributed and among the items: Henry Daggett, eldest son had land in Ludlow and Windhall Vt, 1 Pinchbeck watch, a negro woman named Sue. To legal representative of Ebenezer Daggett, Right of land in Wells and Ludlow Vt; to John Daggett, 4 acres land in Commons E. of Carmel Road, 2 acres in Yorkshire quarter, 5 acres in Westfield, and land in Windhall Vt; To Ezra Daggett, ½ acre land in town plot, opposite Professor's House, land in Ludlow Vt; To Sally Meers, Negro girl named Olive, silver porringer, 2 Table Spoons, — 4 tea spoons; To Polly Daggett, 1½ acres land, and land in Windhall Vt; To Betsey Daggett, land in Windhall Vt. [14–224.]

829. SAMUEL DAGGETT[5] (*Ebenezer,*[4] *John,*[3] *Thomas,*[2] *John* [1]), born Attleboro', Mass., January 3, 173$\frac{0}{1}$; died Schuylerville, N.Y., August, 1806; married Needham, Mass., March 6, 174$\frac{9}{50}$, Abial Kingsbury, daughter of Nathaniel (?) Kingsbury.

Issue:

1098. i.   MOSES DAGGETT,[6] born Needham, Mass., May 4, 1750.
1099. ii.   ELIZABETH DAGGETT,[6] born Needham, Mass., September 28, 1752; married Needham, Mass., November 9, 1775, John McIntosh, of Needham.
1100. iii. SAMUEL DAGGETT,[6] born 1754.
1101. iv.   EBENEZER DAGGETT,[6] born Needham, Mass., June 11, 1757; died Needham, Mass., July 21, 1761.
1102. v.   ASA DAGGETT,[6] born Needham, Mass., October 22, 1759; died Needham, Mass., July 16, 1761.
1103. vi.   EBENEZER DAGGETT,[6] born Needham, Mass., May 16, 1762.
1104. vii. POLLY DAGGETT,[6] born Needham, Mass., April 26, 1763.
1105. viii. ASA DAGGETT,[6] born Needham, Mass., December 17, 1765.
1106. ix.   LEVI DAGGETT,[6] born Needham, Mass., March 4, 1768.
1107. x.   JULIET DAGGETT,[6] born Needham, Mass., October 24, 1770; died Belchertown, Mass., January 16, 1850.
1108. xi.   MICAJAH DAGGETT; [6] no further reported.

Samuel Daggett, gentleman, yeoman, settled first in Needham, Mass.

March 13, 1767. Nathaniel Kingsbury sells 40 acres of land to him, near the meeting-house in Needham. [Suffolk Deeds, 110–69.]

Dec. 28, 1787, he deeds land, to his son Moses Daggett. [Suffolk Deeds, 162–142.]

March 5, 1788, he sells land, to Timothy Daniels. [Suffolk Deeds, 162–151.]

Jan. 12, 1789. Sells 50 acres, to Daniel Ware. [Suffolk Deeds, 164–90.]

July 8, 1789, sells land in the West Parish, in Needham. [Suffolk Deeds, 166–162.]

830. Dr. EBENEZER DAGGETT [5] (*Ebenezer*, [4] *John*, [3] *Thomas*, [2] *John* [1]), born Attleboro', Mass., October 15, 1732 ; died Wrentham, Mass., February 26, 1782 ; married Wrentham, Mass., May 25, 1758, Susanna Metcalf, daughter of Timothy and Mary Metcalf, of Wrentham ; born Wrentham, Mass., February 2, 1731 ; died Wrentham, Mass., November 17, 1797.

Issue :

1109. i. SUSANNA DAGGETT, [6] born Walpole, Mass., May 13, 1759.
1110. ii. EUNICE DAGGETT, [6] born Walpole, Mass., December 10, 1760; died Wrentham, Mass., September 18, 1788.
1111. iii. EBENEZER DAGGETT, [6] born Walpole, Mass., September 30, 1762.
1112. iv. OLIVE DAGGETT, [6] born Walpole, Mass., February 10, 1765.
1113. v. HERMAN DAGGETT, [6] born Walpole, Mass., September 11, 1766.
1114. vi. PLINY DAGGETT, [6] born Walpole, Mass., July 5, 1770; " housewright; " died at sea, May, 1797.

Dr. Ebenezer Daggett, physician, settled first in Walpole, Mass., where he purchased, October 14, 1757, a farm with dwelling-house and barn, for which he paid Solomon Bullard £48 13s. 4d. [Suffolk Deeds, 95–214.] He followed this purchase by others, as follows :

Dec. 8, 1759, 3 acres in Walpole. [Suffolk Deeds, 95–215.]
Feb 20, 1762, ½ of a meadow in Dedham. [Suffolk Deeds, 100–196.]
March 1, 1762, 17 acres with house and barn in Walpole near the Neponset River. [Suffolk Deeds, 97–168.]
Sept 13, 1763, dwelling house & land in Stoughton. [Suffolk Deeds, 100–197.]
July 22, 1766, an agreement was made between a number of people, among whom was Ebenezer Daggett, of Walpole, to build a furnace on a parcel of land in Stoughton, to cast hollow ware. [Suffolk Deeds, 109–24.]
May 10, 1771, he sells ½ meadow in Dedham. [Suffolk Deeds, 150–4.] Aug. 2, 1771, sells land in Walpole. [Suffolk Deeds, 119–215.]

Between this time and October 20, 1772, he removed from Walpole to Wrentham, Mass., at which last date he is called of Wrentham, physician, and buys 167 acres of land there for £400. [Suffolk Deeds, 134–217.]

Dr. Daggett was one of those interested in the measures which led to the Revolution, and at the meeting in Franklin, Mass., January 4, 1775, was appointed one of a committee of fifteen inspectors to see to the execution of the advice of the Continental and Provincial Congresses. [Hist. Franklin.]

Dr. Daggett acquired an extensive practice, and was considered an excellent physician.

April 2, 1782. Susanna Daggett, of Wrentham, was appointed administratrix of the estate of her husband, Ebenezer Daggett, late of Wrentham, physician, deceased, intestate. [Suffolk Probate, 81–90.]

An inventory of the estate of Dr. Ebenezer Daggett, late of Wrentham, deceased, taken April 29, 1782 :

	£	s.	d.
Cash on hand	1	19	0
Armor Books and Apparel	21	17	9
Clock, Watch, Silver buckles &c.	19	6	6
Surgeon Instruments & medicinal drugs	9	2	4
6 beds and beding, house linen & cloth	53	15	7
Desk, draws, chests, tables, & chairs	15	0	11
Pewter, glass and Earthen ware	16	15	9
Brass, iron, tin and wooden ware	21	9	0
Chaise, horse, furniture, husbandry tools & Tacklin,	26	0	0
Yarn, flax and sundry indoor moveables	14	0	7
Sundrys of old lumber	0	16	0
Sundrys of Provision	13	10	4
Stock of cattle	49	19	8
Lands & buildings	· 400	0	0
	657	14	11

[Suffolk Probate, 81–220.]

June 5, 1787, Susanna Daggett presented her account of her administration, which includes among the receipts amounts from over one hundred people, residents of the locality where he lived, and probably are in payment for professional services rendered.   [Suffolk Probate, 86–308.]

June 5, 1787, the personal property is distributed among the children [Suffolk Probate, 86–311], and the real estate is ordered to be distributed.   [Suffolk Probate, 86–417.]

August 7, 1787, occurs the division of the real estate between the widow and children, the portion for the children being purchased by the eldest son, Ebenezer Daggett, by paying each of his brothers and sisters £30.   [Suffolk Probate, 86, 417–418.]

Oct 8, 1795 Susanna Daggett, widow, and others, of Wrentham, sell land on Scottows Creek, Boston.   [Suffolk Deeds, 181–269.]

833. PHILIP DAGGETT [5] (*Ebenezer*,[4] *John*,[3] *Thomas*,[2] *John*[1]), born Attleboro', Mass., September 11, 1739; died New Haven, Conn., December 13, 1783; married Bede Mansfield, daughter of Thomas Mansfield; born North Haven, Conn., November 21, 1746; died after November 6, 1810.

Issue:

1115. i. SAMUEL DAGGETT,[6] born 1768; died September 13, 1772.
1116. ii. WILLIAM DAGGETT,[6] married Polly; resided College street, New Haven; will dated November 6, 1810; inventory, $4,663.95.
1117. iii. AMELIA DAGGETT,[6] born New Haven, Conn., 1780.
1118. iv. CHAUNCY DAGGETT,[6] born about 1781; Mr. Cooper, of North Haven, his guardian, appointed October 31, 1796.

November 13, 1752, Mary Daggett was appointed guardian of Philip Daggett, "under fourteen years."   [Bristol Probate.]

Philip Daggett graduated at Yale College, 1762. He settled and died in New Haven, Conn.

February 2, 1784. Administration was granted on the estate of

Philip Daggett to Beede Daggett, widow, on bond of £300. [New Haven Probate, 14–237.]

May 10, 1784. Walter Munson and Beede Daggett, administrators on estate of Philip Daggett, return inventory, of which the movable estate was £47 10s. 7d. [14–283.]

A further account of the settlement mentions youngest child not four years old. [14–315.]

Mrs. Bede Daggett married, October 24, 1785, Ensign Thomas Cooper.

838. MAYHEW DAGGETT[5] (*Thomas,*[4] *John,*[3] *Thomas,*[2] *John*[1]) born Attleboro', Mass., January 10, 1729; died Attleboro', Mass., May 7, 1775; married Martha Newell; she died after 1777.

Issue:

1119. i. NANCY DAGGETT,[6] born Attleboro', Mass., October 28, 1767; died Attleboro', Mass., March 12, 1768.
1120. ii. CHLOE DAGGETT,[6] born Attleboro', Mass., April 15, 1769.
1121. iii PATTE DAGGETT,[6] born Attleboro', Mass., February 2, 1771.
1122. iv. LYDIA DAGGETT,[6] born Attleboro', Mass., April 14, 1773; died Attleboro', Mass., January 31, 1775.
1123. v. DESIRE DAGGETT,[6] born Attleboro', Mass., December 2, 1775.

May 29, 1775, Martha Daggett was appointed administrator of the estate of Mayhew Daggett, of Attleboro'.

839. THOMAS DAGGETT[5] (*Thomas,*[4] *John,*[3] *Thomas,*[2] *John*[1]), born Providence, R.I., September 25, 1731; died Providence, R.I., August 19, 1807; married Attleboro', Mass., November 21, 1754, Sibulah Stanley.

Issue:

1124. i. ABNER DAGGETT,[6] born Attleboro', Mass., August 8, 1755.
1125. ii. NAPHTALI DAGGETT,[6] born Attleboro', Mass., March 18, 1757; died Attleboro', Mass., July 13, 1769.
1126. iii. MELLETIER DAGGETT,[6] born Attleboro', Mass., February 13, 1759.
1127. iv. LUCY DAGGETT,[6] born Attleboro', Mass., November 15. 1760.
1128. v. LEONARD DAGGETT,[6] born Attleboro', Mass., January 13, 1763.
1129. vi. DAVID DAGGETT,[6] born Attleboro', Mass., December 31. 1764.
1130. vii. DEXTER DAGGETT,[6] born Attleboro', Mass., March 15, 1767.
1131. viii. DAUGHTER ——,[6] born Attleboro', Mass., May 10, 1769.
1132. ix. NAPHTALI DAGGETT,[6] born Attleboro', Mass., August 19, 1771.

Thomas Daggett was of Attleboro', "innholder," on May 29, 1777, at which time he made purchase of land and buildings in Attleboro'.

He was interested in several transfers of real estate there during his life.

He was a man of vigorous intellect, strong common sense, and decided and earnest religious character.

His son, Judge David Daggett, speaks of his father's strong sympathy with the friends of the "Great Awakening," which occurred in the earlier part of his manhood, under the preaching of Whitefield,

Edwards, Bellamy, and the Tennents. In the controversy which, in subsequent years, grew out of that awakening, he was earnest on the side of its friends; so much so that he had a partiality for the "Separates" of that day, though he never united himself with them. He was a Baptist in sentiment.

843. NAOMI DAGGETT [5] (*Thomas,*[4] *John,*[3] *Thomas,*[2] *John*[1]), born Attleboro', Mass., June 16, 1744½; died Attleboro', Mass., June 22, 1776; married Ebenezer Sweet.

Issue:

1133. i. CALVIN SWEET,[6] born Attleboro', Mass., March 11, 1765.
1134. ii. ARNOLD SWEET,[6] born Attleboro', Mass., March 3, 1767.
1135. iii. ELIZABETH SWEET,[6] born Attleboro', Mass., October 2, 1768.
1136. iv. ELLIS SWEET,[6] born Attleboro', Mass., November 20, 1770.
1137. v. ABEH SWEET,[6] born Attleboro', Mass., September 20, 1772.
1138. vi. EBENEZER SWEET,[6] born Attleboro', Mass., July 20, 1774; died Attleboro', Mass., January 3, 1785.
1139. vii. NAOMI SWEET,[6] born Attleboro', Mass., June 4, 1776; died Attleboro', Mass., June 5, 1776.

844. JOSEPH GUILD [5] (*Abigail Daggett,*[4] *John,*[3] *Thomas,*[2] *John*[1]), born Attleboro', Mass., June 22, 1716; died Attleboro', Mass., September 18, 1792; married 1st, Attleboro', Mass., November 11, 1741, Hannah White, daughter of Rev. Ebenezer White, of Attleboro'; died Attleboro', Mass., June 16, 1764; married 2d, 1775, Elizabeth Thayer.

Issue:

1140. i. ABIGAIL GUILD,[6] born Attleboro', Mass., 1743; married Daniel Cheever.
1141. ii. HANNAH GUILD,[6] born Attleboro', Mass., September 23, 1747; married Penticost Walcott.
1142. iii. JOSEPH GUILD,[6] born Attleboro', Mass., October 5, 1751; married May 21, 1778, Sarah Woodcock, who died May, 1843; he died 1829.
1143. iv. ELIZABETH GUILD,[6] born Attleboro', Mass., September 23, 1753; married Mr. Pullen, of Maine.
1144. v. SAMUEL GUILD,[6] born Attleboro', Mass., October 22, 1755; married Mittie Parmenter.
1145. vi. LYDIA GUILD,[6] born Attleboro', Mass., October 19, 1777; died in Pennsylvania.
1146. vii. NATHAN GUILD,[6] born Attleboro', Mass., April 22, 1782; died in Gibson, Pa.

845. BENJAMIN GUILD [5] (*Abigail Daggett,*[4] *John,*[3] *Thomas,*[2] *John*[1]), born Attleboro', Mass., August 28, 1718; died November 2, 1802; married Jemima Morse; died May 7, 1782.

Issue:

1147. i. EUNICE GUILD,[6] born ——; married Nathan Mann, of Franklin, Mass.
1148. ii. ELIAS GUILD,[6] born August, 1760; married Mary White.
1149. iii. NAAMAH GUILD,[6] born ——; married James Daniels, of Foxboro'.

Benjamin Guild moved to Wrentham, where he was selectman,

1766–7. In 1778, he was directed to call the first town-meeting of Foxboro'.

846. NAPHTALI GUILD [5] (*Abigail Daggett*,[4] *John*,[3] *Thomas*,[2] *John*[1]), born Attleboro', Mass., July 3, 1719; married Joanna; born 1721; died September 22, 1786.

Issue:

1150. i. NAPHTALI GUILD,[6] born about 1755; married and had three children.
1151. ii. HARRIET GUILD.[6]
1152. iii. JOHN GUILD,[6] born Attleboro', Mass., July 28, 1763; married Margaret Daggett. See No. 1333.
1153. iv. EUNICE GUILD,[6] married 1st, Hidden; 2d, Cooper; died Lansingburg, N.Y.
1154. v. LUCY GUILD,[6] married Wilmarth; died Ira, Vt.
1155. vi. ABIGAIL GUILD,[6] married, 1788, Ira Barrus; eight children.

847. EBENEZER GUILD [5] (*Abigail Daggett*,[4] *John*,[3] *Thomas*,[2] *John*[1]), born Attleboro', Mass., August 29, 1722; died Wrentham, Mass.; married Phebe Day, of Wrentham.

Issue:

1156. i. PHEBE GUILD,[6] born September 24, 1753; married Mr. Cheever, of Wrentham.
1157. ii. MARY GUILD,[6] born June 8, 1755; died February 27, 1760.
1158. iii. EBENEZER GUILD,[6] born March 1, 1759; married Mary Lane.
1159. iv. MARY GUILD,[6] born November 4, 1761; died Wrentham, Mass., December 20, 1832.
1160. v. DAVID GUILD,[6] born September 17, 1764; married 1st, Olive Day; 2d, Phebe Puffer.
1161. vi. JUDITH GUILD,[6] born February 20, 1767; married George Blackinton.
1162. vii. SUSANNA GUILD,[6] born September 21, 1769; married John Wilkinson, of Wrentham; no issue.

883. BROTHERTON DAGGETT [5] (*Brotherton*,[4] *Joshua*,[3] *Thomas*,[2] *John*[1]), baptized Edgartown, Mass., February 7, 1725; married Boston, Mass., November 7, 1751, by Rev. Samuel Cooper, to Mary Tucker; possibly married second, Edgartown, Mass., June 9, 1782, Mrs. Jerusha Bunker.

Issue:

1163. i. BROTHERTON DAGGETT.[6] born Edgartown, Mass., September 16, 1752.
1164. ii. HENRY DAGGETT.[6] born Edgartown, Mass., July 2, 1755.
1165. iii. MOLLY DAGGETT,[6] born Edgartown, Mass., August 8, 1757.
1166. iv. THANKFULL DAGGETT,[6] born Edgartown. Mass., April 16, 1760.
1167. v. JETHRO DAGGETT,[6] born Edgartown, Mass., October 21, 1762.
1168. vi. SARAH DAGGETT,[6] born Edgartown, Mass., October 29, 1764.
1169. vii. SUSA DAGGETT,[6] born Edgartown, Mass., January 23, 1767.
1170. viii. TIMOTHY DAGGETT,[6] born Edgartown, Mass., March 23, 1768.
1171. ix. ISAAC DAGGETT,[6] born Edgartown, Mass., May 26, 1770.

October 9, 1763, Mary, wife of Brotherton Daggett, was admitted to full communion in the church in Edgartown.

885. THOMAS DAGGETT [5] (*Brotherton*,[4] *Joshua*,[3] *Thomas*,[2] *John*[1]), baptized Edgartown, Mass., November 10, 1728; died Union, Me.,

May 15, 1806; married Rebecca Athearn; died Union, Me., August 3, 1805.

Issue:

1172. i.   SAMUEL DAGGETT,[6] born Tisbury, Mass., May 19, 1753.
1173. ii. THOMAS DAGGETT,[6] born Tisbury, Mass., 1755.
1174. iii. HANNAH DAGGETT;[6] married Mr. Norton.
1175. iv. AARON DAGGETT,[6]
1176. v.   REBECCA DAGGETT,[6] born Tisbury, Mass., 1765; married Matthew Daggett. See No. 1182.
1177. vi. ANDREW DAGGETT.[6]

Thomas Daggett probably removed to Tisbury about the time of his marriage.

Dukes Deeds show the following sales of real estate, which he made from time to time, having doubtless in view his removal from the Island:

Feb. 19, 1765 he and wife Rebecca to Lemuel Butler and Hannah his wife land in Chilmark. [Dukes Deeds, 9-444.]
April 5, 1765 land in Tisbury to Robert Manter. [Dukes Deeds, 9-433.]
April 5, 1765 land in Tisbury to Samuel Cobb. [Dukes Deeds, 9-553.]
July 8, 1765 land in Chilmark to Moses Lumbert. [Dukes Deeds, 9-466.]
Oct. 31, 1765 land in Tisbury to Thos. Walrod. [Dukes Deeds, 9-483.]
April 11, 1769 he & others divide land in Tisbury. [Dukes Deeds, 9-648.]
Feb. 12, 1772 land in Tisbury to Lemuel Butler. [Dukes Deeds, 9-818.]

Brotherton Daggett says: "The Daggetts being strongly inclined to move from Martha's Vineyard sent Thomas Daggett, Jr., to Albany and the vicinity in New York to look up a farm. He was not a judge of land, and returned without finding one to suit him.

"Thomas Daggett, Senr., came along the coast, went back from Camden into the woods, and with some others was about to purchase the whole of Appleton Ridge, except the proprietors' reserved lots.

"On going to the rear of the Ridge and seeing the Cedar Swamp, his courage failed him, and he went home without concluding a bargain.

"A year or two afterward Thomas Daggett, Jr., and Aaron Daggett came to Union.

"They purchased the place since owned by Olney Titus, cleared a piece, and sowed rye.

"In the fall they took as a specimen a box of soil from the land now owned by Nahum Thurston, returned to Martha's Vineyard, and spent the winter.

"Their father, Thomas Daggett, Senr., was prevailed on to accompany them to Union in the following May."

He bought May 29, 1789 — 700 acres of land in Union of Mason Wheaton of Thomaston for 245£ and called himself of Tisbury. [Lincoln Deeds, 23-185.]
July 14, 1789 he and his wife Rebecca of Union sell 90 acres land in Union to Samuel Daggett of Tisbury "cordwainer." [Lincoln Deeds, 25-111.]
The same date he of Union, gentleman, sells 100 acres in Union to Aaron Daggett, of Union. [Lincoln Deeds, 26-164.]

Thomas Daggett came with his family to Union between May 29 and July 14, 1789.

" He landed at Warren. Everything seemed different from what it was in May.

" He was a nervous man, and finding himself here for life he exclaimed, ' I am completely undone.' The forests looked formidable. It was too woody for him. The family came to Union from Warren in boats." [Sibley's Hist. of Union, Me.]

April 5, 1790, Thomas Daggett was one of a committee to hire preaching, and served again on a similar committee March 7, 1796.

March 7, 1791, he was on a committee to receive and price lumber for use in building a meeting-house.

May 7, 1792, one of the town's committee to make choice of a spot for a meeting-house.

In 1798 he was " tithingman," and had pew No. 14, for which he paid $20.50.

As regards the habits of the people at the church, Thomas Daggett, Senr., Capt. Nicholson, and Ebenezer Daggett, consulting their own convenience and comfort, were in the habit, even in meeting, of wearing cotton caps which rivalled the snow in whiteness.

March 7, 1803, he with others, including the selectmen, were a committee to confer with Mr. Gushee, respecting his settling there as a minister.

When the Congregational church was organized, March 3, 1803, the articles and covenant were signed by Thomas Daggett, Mrs. Rebecca Daggett, and others.

June 24, 1806, Samuel Daggett was appointed administrator of Thomas Daggett, late of Union, deceased, intestate. [Lincoln Probate, 9–102.]

Inventory amounted to $592.64. [Lincoln Probate, 12–255.]

June 29, 1813, Samuel Daggett renders his account, from which it appears there were five heirs to the estate. [Lincoln Probate, 17–140.]

886. TIMOTHY DAGGETT [5] (*Brotherton*,[4] *Joshua*,[3] *Thomas*,[2] *John* [1]), bapt. Edgartown, Mass., February 28, 1731; married Taunton, Mass. (?). Sibbel Smith, daughter of Ebenezer Smith, of Taunton, Mass.

Issue :

1178. i. SIBELL DAGGETT,[6] born Dighton, Mass., January 30, 1756.
1179. ii. TIMOTHY DAGGETT,[6] born Dighton, Mass., April 8, 1762.

July 13, 1765, Timothy Daggett, of Dighton, and Sybil his wife, sell land in Edgartown to Brotherton Daggett. [Dukes Deeds, 9–532½.]

887. Elijah Daggett[5] (*Brotherton,[4] Joshua,[3] Thomas,[2] John[1]*), bapt. Edgartown, Mass., April 21, 1734; "shipwright;" died Nantucket, Mass., previous to June 7, 1771; married Tisbury, Mass., November 9, 1757, Jedidah Chase, daughter of Thomas and Elizabeth (Athearn) Chase; born Tisbury, Mass., February 14, 1736; died New Vineyard, Me.

Issue:

1180. i. Tristram Daggett,[6] born August 22, 1758.
1181. ii. Elijah Daggett.[6]
1182. iii. Matthew Daggett,[6] born 1764.
1183. iv. Abigail Daggett,[6] born 1766; married Capt. Samuel Daggett. See No. 1006.
1184. v. Mary Daggett,[6] married Mr. Long.
1185. vi. Nathan Daggett,[6] said to have been pilot to the French fleet while in American waters during the Revolution.

Mrs. Daggett married 2d, Mr. Kimblen, and spent the last of her days with her son-in-law Capt. Samuel Daggett.

Nov. 16, 1757 Elijah Daggett, sells land in Tisbury. [Dukes Deeds, 8–650.]
May 8, 1766 Elijah Daggett, of Nantucket, and Jedidah his wife, sell land in Edgartown. [Dukes Deeds, 9–533.]

Christopher Starbuck appointed administrator of the estate of Elijah Daggett, of Sherborn, shipwright, deceased, June 7, 1771. [Nantucket Probate, 3–149.]

Inventory of estate of Elijah, August 3, 1771: Dwelling-house, £360; twelve rods of land, at £10 per rod; whole estate, old tenor, £525 4s. 0d. [N.P., 3–166.]

January 3, 1772. The estate was rendered insolvent.

June 4, 1773. Order of court to set off to Jedidah, widow of Elijah, her dower:

⅓ of Dwelling house to Jedidah, and land it stands on; whole of the kitchen and the whole of the bedroom, in south end of said kitchen, except such part of said kitchen as is included by a line drawn from the outward part of the south jamb in the kitchen, to the bedroom partition which is allowed for a stairway to the other ⅔. 15 June 1773. [N.P., 3–212.]

December 3, 1773. The widow's portion to be divided among the creditors after her decease. [N.P., 3–215.]

888. Jethro Daggett[5] (*Brotherton,[4] Joshua,[3] Thomas,[2] John[1]*), bapt. Edgartown, Mass., May 23, 1736; died Newport, R.I. (?), previous to Nov. 2, 1784; married Hannah (?).

Issue:

1186. i. James Daggett,[6] born Newport, R.I., 1770.

891. Hepzibah Daggett[5] (*Jacob,[4] Joshua,[3] Thomas,[2] John[1]*), born Nantucket, Mass., 1717; married 1st, Nantucket, Mass.,

August 15, 1738, by John Coffin, J.P., to John Jones; he died previous to 1761; married 2d, Mr. Butler.

Issue:

1187. i. HEPZIBAH JONES,[6] born Nantucket, Mass., January 4, 173⅜.
1188. ii. JOHN JONES,[6] born Nantucket, Mass., May 1, 1741.

893. NATHAN DAGGETT[5] (*Jacob*,[4] *Joshua*,[3] *Thomas*,[2] *John*[1]), born Nantucket, Mass., December 21, 1723; died previous to November 12, 1760; married Nantucket, Mass., December 21, 1743, by John Coffin, J.P., to Margaret Gardner, daughter of Ebenezer and Eunice Gardner.

Issue:

1189. i. STEPHEN DAGGETT,[6] born Nantucket, Mass., 1744.
1190. ii. HEPSABETH DAGGETT,[6] born Nantucket, Mass., 1748; married Nantucket, Mass., July 17, 1766, by Eben Calef, J.P., to William Tuckerman. (In New Bedford, 1835.)
1191. iii. TIMOTHY DAGGETT,[6] born Nantucket, Mass., 1751; died single.
1192. iv. LYDIA DAGGETT,[6] born Nantucket, Mass., 9, 1, 1758.

Nathan Daggett, mariner, having deceased, his children appoint their uncle, Uriah Gardner, as their guardian, February 10, 1761.

Mrs. Margaret (Gardner) Daggett married, at Nantucket, Mass., November 12, 1760, by Grafton Gardner, J.P., to Isaac Mayo.

896. BENJAMIN DAGGETT[5] (*Jacob*,[4] *Joshua*,[3] *Thomas*,[2] *John*[1]), born Nantucket, Mass., April 21, 1731; died previous to February 6, 1761; married.

Issue:
1193. i. HULDAH DAGGETT,[6] born Nantucket, Mass., 1751.

899. EBENEZER DAGGETT[5] (*John*,[4] *Joseph*,[3] *Joseph*,[2] *John*[1]) (?), "weaver;" died (probably in New Vineyard, Me.); married Edgartown, Mass., March 6, 1759, Jedidah Vinson, daughter of Nathaniel and Deborah (Stuart) Vinson; died Industry, Me.

Issue:

1194. i. PETER DAGGETT,[6] born Martha's Vineyard, January 17, 1770.
1195. ii. AARON DAGGETT,[6] born Martha's Vineyard.
1196. iii. BETSEY DAGGETT,[6] born Martha's Vineyard. Received by letter from Tisbury Baptist Church at the Industry Baptist Church, October 21, 1810. Probably returned to Martha's Vineyard.
1197. iv. HANNAH DAGGETT,[6] born Martha's Vineyard, September 21, 1776.

Ebenezer Daggett, weaver, of Tisbury, Mass., bought, in company with Peter, lot No. 18, second range of lots in New Vineyard, February 25, 1793. March 11, 1796, he sells his interest to his son Aaron.

Owing to imperfect records, and the frequent repetition of the same name in different families, doubt exists as to the ancestry of Ebenezer Daggett. Mrs. A. C. Pratt, of Chelsea, Mass., who has made a study of Martha's Vineyard families, and who succeeded to the collections of the late Hon. R. L. Pease, of Edgartown, sets up as a hypothetical line the one adopted above. This is adopted, and should be accepted only as a possible solution of the question. The future may prove or disprove it, but at present it seems the most likely of any possible line.

901. JOHN DAGGETT[5] (*John*,[4] *Joseph*,[3] *Joseph*,[2] *John*[1]) (?), died New Vineyard, Me., 1794–5; married 1st, Rachel Coffin; died soon after marriage; married 2d, Edgartown, Mass., June 11, 1761, Thankful Vinson, daughter of Nathaniel and Deborah (Stuart) Vinson; died New Vineyard, Me., at an advanced age.

Issue :

1198. i.   JOHN DAGGETT,[6] born Martha's Vineyard, 1758.
1199. ii. RACHEL DAGGETT,[6] school-teacher on Martha's Vineyard. Died of consumption soon after the family removed to Maine.
1200. iii. THANKFUL DAGGETT,[6] died unmarried, aged 62 years.
1201. iv. DEBORAH DAGGETT,[6] married March 22, 1795, Willard Spaulding; had son, John D. Spaulding.

John Daggett, prior to his removal to Maine, resided in Edgartown. He was a " miller," and tradition says he operated a windmill on the island. He was a soldier in the Revolutionary war. He bought, February 11, 1793, lot No. 2 in the second range of lots in New Vineyard Township, and probably began a clearing the same year. He received injuries while piling his chopping, from which he never recovered, and died soon after his removal from the Vineyard.

Dr. Hatch suggests, in his History of Industry, that John may have been a brother of Ebenezer.

Owing to imperfect records, the placing of this John as the John,[5] son of John,[4] is only hypothetical, and should not be accepted, except as a theory, which may be proved right or wrong in the future.

JOHN DOGGETT, OF MARTHA'S VINEYARD.

SIXTH GENERATION.

915. JOHN DAGGETT[6] (*William*,[5] *Israel*,[4] *Joseph*,[3] *John*,[2] *John*[1]), born Seekonk, Mass.; died Seekonk, Mass., March, 1846; married Hannah Barnes, daughter of Samuel and Hannah Barnes; born Barrington, R.I., 1782; died Seekonk, Mass., December 1, 1858.

Issue :

1202. i. WILLIAM DAGGETT.[7]

919. Israel Daggett [6] (*William*,[5] *Israel*,[4] *Joseph*,[3] *John*,[2] *John* [1]), born Seekonk, Mass. ; died Pawtucket, Mass., March, 1842 ; married Lucy Bicknell.

Issue :

1203. i.   Hannah Dorman Daggett,[7] born Rehoboth, Mass., April 23, 1805; married Jefferson Daggett. See No. 1208.

924. Jacob Daggett [6] (*Daniel*,[5] *Israel*,[4] *Joseph*,[3] *John*,[2] *John* [1]), born Rehoboth, Mass., March 12, 1765 ; died Seekonk, Mass., July 18, 1814 ; married Lydia Slack, daughter of Samuel and Ruth (Stearns) Slack ; born Rehoboth, Mass., April 20, 1771 ; died Rehoboth, Mass., May 6, 1815.

Issue :

1204. i.   John Sterns Daggett,[7] born Rehoboth, Mass., June 26, 1793; " blacksmith;" married; no issue; died Seekonk, Mass., January 1, 1864.
1205. ii.   Mary Daggett,[7] born Rehoboth, Mass., May 26, 1795; died See-konk, Mass., December 6, 1866.
1206. iii. Sidney Daggett,[7] born Rehoboth, Mass., May 3, 1797; " farmer;" died Seekonk, Mass., February 6, 1883.
1207. iv.   Adan Daggett,[7] born Rehoboth, Mass., March 25, 1799; died See-konk, Mass., February 22, 1874.
1208. v.   Jefferson Daggett,[7] born Rehoboth, Mass., November 30, 1800.
1209. vi.   Lydia Daggett,[7] born Rehoboth, Mass., September 10, 1802; resides Seekonk, Mass. (1892).
1210. vii. Cynthia Daggett,[7] born Rehoboth, Mass., February 2, 1806; died Seekonk, Mass., March 4, 1876.
1211. viii. Jacob Daggett,[7] born Seekonk, Mass., December 28, 1807.
1212. ix.   Samuel Slack Daggett,[7] born Seekonk, Mass., July 9, 1809.
1213. x.   Nancy Daggett,[7] born Seekonk, Mass., September 2, 1811; married Bridgman; had son Brainard; resided at Denver, Col., at one time; she died August 25, 1876.
1214. xi.   Emma Daggett,[7] born Seekonk, Mass., August 2, 1813; died See-konk, Mass., September 16, 1846.

The estate of Jacob Daggett, of Seekonk, was administered on by his son John S. Daggett.

929. Reuben Daggett [6] (*Reuben*,[5] *Nathaniel*,[4] *Nathaniel*,[3] *John*,[2] *John* [1]), born Attleboro', Mass., November 11, 1755 ; died Daggett's Mills, Pa., February 8, 1835 ; married 1st, Westmoreland, N.H., December 11, 1777, by Rev. Ebenezer Bailey, to Esther Cobb ; born 1750 ; died Paris, N.Y., December 2, 1798 ; married 2d, near Utica, N.Y., December 9, 1800, Kesiah Darby ; born 1753 ; died Jackson, Pa., March 15, 1827 ; married 3d, Jackson, Pa., May 31, 1827, Abigail Woodward.

Issue :

1215. i.   Reuben Daggett,[7] born Westmoreland, N.H., February 19, 1781.
1216. ii.   Chloe Daggett,[7] born Westmoreland, N.H., July 20, 1783.
1217. iii. Esther Daggett,[7] born Westmoreland, N.H., December 26, 1785.
1218. iv.   Rhoda Daggett,[7] born Westmoreland, N.H., March 8, 1788; married Moses Bennett; died Vermont.
1219. v.   Seth Daggett,[7] born Westmoreland, N.H., July 3, 1790.

1220. vi.   SALOMA DAGGETT,[7] born Westmoreland, N.H., July 3, 1790.
1221. vii.   RUFUS DAGGETT,[7] born Westmoreland, N.H., December 3, 1792.
1222. viii. BELINDA DAGGETT,[7] born Westmoreland, N.H., July 9, 1795; married
             James Cooper; issue: four children; removed to Illinois about
             1825.
1223. ix.   LYDIA DAGGETT,[7] born Westmoreland, N.H., October 16, 1797.

Reuben Daggett served in the Revolutionary war. He resided in Westmoreland, N.H., until 1797, when he removed to Paris Furnace, eight miles from Utica, N.Y., then ten years later to Daggett's Mills, Tioga county, Pa. Daggett's Mills Post-office originated from the building of grist and saw mills in that place by the sons of Reuben Daggett.

They were the first settlers in the locality.

932. DANIEL DAGGETT[6] (*Reuben*,[5] *Nathaniel*,[4] *Nathaniel*,[3] *John*,[2] *John*[1]), born Attleboro', Mass., July 27, 1762; died Glocester, R.I., April 12, 1825; married November 11, 1783, Sarah Ball; born Taunton, Mass., 1763 (living, 1843, age eighty years).

Issue:

1224. i.   DANIEL DAGGETT.[7]
1225. ii.   RUFUS DAGGETT,[7] born 1793.
1226. iii.   REUBEN DAGGETT.[7]
1227. iv.   GEORGE DAGGETT.[7]
1228. v.   JOEL DAGGETT.[7]
1229. vi.   CHARLES DAGGETT.[7]
1230. vii.   NANCY DAGGETT.[7]
1231. viii. REANEY DAGGETT.[7]
1232. ix.   SEREL N. DAGGETT,[7] born Burrillville, R.I., 1812.

Daniel Daggett, a nailer by trade, lived for several years after his marriage in Attleboro', then removed to Rhode Island. He resided in North Providence in 1818, and in 1821 was in Glocester, R.I. In the Revolution, he enlisted in June, 1777, before he was fifteen years old, and served for nearly a year as waiter to Colonel Daggett.

In 1778 he engaged as a private for three years with Captain Cole, in the Massachusetts regiment commanded by Col. Henry Jackson, and was in 1778 in Rhode Island during General Sullivan's campaign.

955. LEVI DAGGETT[6] (*John*,[5] *John*,[4] *Nathaniel*,[3] *John*,[2] *John*[1]), born Rehoboth, Mass., April 12, 1761; died Seekonk, Mass., December, 1823; married Keziah Peck, daughter of Comfort and Keziah (Peck) Peck, of Seekonk, Mass.; born Seekonk, Mass., January 2, 1764; died Seekonk, Mass., April 4, 1836.

Issue:

1233. i.   MARY DAGGETT,[7] born Rehoboth, Mass., July 5, 1788; died E. Providence, R.I., December 19, 1874.
1234. ii.   KEZIAH DAGGETT,[7] born Rehoboth, Mass., November 16, 1790.
1235. iii.   JOHN DAGGETT,[7] born Rehoboth, Mass., April 20, 1792.

1236. iv. LEVI DAGGETT,[7] born Rehoboth, Mass., January 29, 1794; died Seekonk, Mass., March 31, 1855.
1237. v. HANNAH DAGGETT,[7] born Rehoboth, Mass., January 19, 1796.
1238. vi. BETSEY DAGGETT,[7] born Rehoboth, Mass., January 19, 1796; died Seekonk, Mass., March 26, 1824.
1239. vii. FANNY DAGGETT,[7] born Rehoboth, Mass., March 14, 1798; died Seekonk, Mass., March, 1829.
1240. viii. LYDIA DAGGETT,[7] born Rehoboth, Mass., April 10, 1801.

956. HOPE DAGGETT [6] (*John,*[5] *John,*[4] *Nathaniel,*[3] *John,*[2] *John* [1]), born Rehoboth, Mass., December 16, 1762; married Rehoboth, Mass., December 20, 1781, by Rev. E. Hyde, to John Davis.

Issue:

1241. i. JOSHUA DAVIS.[7]

974. ROBERT DAGGETT [6] (*James,*[5] *John,*[4] *Nathaniel,*[3] *John,*[2] *John* [1]), born Rehoboth, Mass., May 1, 1763; died after 1830; married Rehoboth, Mass., September 23, 1784, by Rev. Robert Rogerson, to Elizabeth Daggett, daughter of Daniel and Bebe (Perry) Daggett, (No. 925); born Rehoboth, Mass., August 11, 1767.

Issue:

1242. i. PRESTON DAGGETT,[7] born Rehoboth, Mass., November 27, 1784.
1243. ii. BEBE DAGGETT,[7] born Rehoboth, Mass., November 17, 1786; married Rehoboth, Mass., July 7, 1805, by John Hills, to George Bishop.
1244. iii. BETSEY DAGGETT,[7] born Rehoboth, Mass., January 10, 1788.
1245. iv. GILBERT DAGGETT,[7] born Rehoboth, Mass., March 21, 1791; married Rehoboth, Mass., April 21, 1811, Eliza Pearce; removed to Providence, R.I.
1246. v. ROBERT DAGGETT,[7] born Rehoboth, Mass., September 13, 1793.
1247. vi. REBECCA HUMPHREY DAGGETT,[7] born Rehoboth, Mass., December 31, 1797.
1248. vii. DANIEL DAGGETT,[7] born Rehoboth, Mass., January 10, 1799.
1249. viii. TIMOTHY DAGGETT,[7] born Rehoboth, Mass., February 25, 1800; died March, 1828.
1250. ix. MARY DAGGETT,[7] born Rehoboth, Mass., May 12, 1803.
1251. x. GEORGE HAMMOND DAGGETT,[7] born Rehoboth, Mass., June 27, 1805; married Seekonk, Mass., April 1, 1832, by Rev. James O. Barney, to Mrs. Hannah Mercy.

983. HENRY DAGGETT [6] (*James,*[5] *John,*[4] *Nathaniel,*[3] *John,*[2] *John* [1]), born Rehoboth, Mass., April 14, 1781; died Seekonk, Mass., 1839; married Belinda Webster (?); died Seekonk, Mass., 1853.

Issue:

1252. i. JAMES HENRY DAGGETT,[7] born 1828; died Seekonk, Mass., 1857.
1253. ii. ELLEN V. DAGGETT,[7] born Seekonk, Mass., 1843.

986. WILLIAM DAGGETT [6] (*Nathan,*[5] *John,*[4] *Nathaniel,*[3] *John,*[2] *John* [1]), born Rehoboth, Mass., February 26, 1758; married Rehoboth, Mass., October 22, 1778, by Rev. E. Hyde, to Mary Daggett, daughter of Daniel and Bebe (Perry) Daggett (No. 923); born Rehoboth, Mass., April 3, 1762.

987. ABIGAIL DAGGETT [6] (*Nathan*,[5] *John*,[4] *Nathaniel*,[3] *John*,[2] *John* [1]), born Rehoboth, Mass., April 16, 1760; died Swanzey, N.H., 183$\frac{7}{8}$; married Rehoboth, Mass., August 25, 1781, by Rev. E. Hyde, to David Read, son of Nathan and Dorothy (Titus) Read; born Rehoboth, Mass., June 3, 1756; died Swanzey, N.H., 1819.

Issue:

1254. i. WILLIAM READ,[7] born Rehoboth, Mass., July 31, 1782.
1255. ii. DAVID READ,[7] born Rehoboth, Mass., November 29, 1784.
1256. iii. OBADIAH READ.[7]
1257. iv. AARON READ.[7]
1258. v. LEWIS READ,[7] died January 6, 1823.
1259. vi. NATHAN DAGGETT READ,[7] born October 7, 1800.
1260. vii. ABIGAIL READ.[7]
1261. viii. SALLY READ.[7]
1262. ix. MARY READ.[7]

1001. ISAAC DAGGETT [6] (*Samuel*,[5] *Samuel*,[4] *Thomas*,[3] *Thomas*,[2] *John* [1]), born Tisbury, Mass., November 26, 1737; died Tisbury, Mass., October 26, 1805; married 1st, Tisbury, Mass., January 17, 1759, Abigail West, daughter of Dr. Elisha and Abigail (Gibbs) West; born Tisbury, Mass., June 26, 1742; died Tisbury, Mass., July 22, 1772; married 2d, Falmouth, Mass., August 4, 1772, Mrs. Rebecca Tobey, widow of Samuel Tobey, daughter of Mr. Hatch; died Tisbury, Mass., January 23, 1823.

Issue:

1263. i. ABIGAIL DAGGETT,[7] born Tisbury, Mass., November 4, 1759.
1264. ii. Son —— DAGGETT,[7] born Tisbury, Mass., January 8, 1762; died Tisbury, Mass., January 8, 1762.
1265. iii. Son —— DAGGETT,[7] born Tisbury, Mass., December 7, 1762; died Tisbury, Mass., December 7, 1762.
1266. iv. Son —— DAGGETT,[7] born Tisbury, Mass., June 7, 1764; died Tisbury, Mass., June 7, 1764.
1267. v. Daughter —— DAGGETT,[7] born Tisbury, Mass., August 26, 1765; died Tisbury, Mass., August 26, 1765.
1268. vi. SARAH DAGGETT,[7] born Tisbury, Mass., August 6, 1769; married Tisbury, Mass., May 4, 1788, Peter West, Jr.
1269. vii. REBECCA DAGGETT,[7] born Tisbury, Mass., June 16, 1773; married Samuel Daggett. See No. 1284.
1270. viii. MARY DAGGETT,[7] born Tisbury, Mass., January 30, 1775.
1271. ix. HANNAH DAGGETT,[7] born Tisbury, Mass., June 3, 1777; died Tisbury, Mass., July 13, 1777.
1272. x. JANE DAGGETT,[7] born Tisbury, Mass., June 6, 1778; married William Daggett. See No. 1273.

1003. WILLIAM DAGGETT [6] (*Seth*,[5] *Samuel*,[4] *Thomas*,[3] *Thomas*,[2] *John* [1]), married Mary Stuart.

Issue:

1273. i. WILLIAM DAGGETT,[7] born Tisbury, Mass., August, 1773.
1274. ii. SETH DAGGETT,[7] born Tisbury, Mass., March 7, 1780.
1275. iii. PETER DAGGETT,[7] born Tisbury, Mass., 1780.

1276. iv. MARY DAGGETT,[7] married Tisbury, Mass., March 17, 1795, Capt.
     William Cottle; issue: William Cottle,[8] who married Jane Manter,
     and had issue Mary Cottle.[9]
1277. v. JANE DAGGETT,[7] married 1st, Tisbury, Mass., November 24, 1792,
     Paschal Paoli Bartlett; married 2d, Mr. Arnold.
1278. vi. ABIGAIL DAGGETT.[7]
1279. vii. SYLVANUS DAGGETT.[7]

1004. PETER DAGGETT [6] (*Seth*,[5] *Samuel*,[4] *Thomas*,[3] *Thomas*,[2]
John [1]), born Tisbury, Mass., May 4, 1738; died at sea; married
Harwich, Mass. (intention, Nov. 24, 1756), Deliverance Cahoon.

Issue:

1280. i. BETSEY DAGGETT,[7] born 1758.
1281. ii. NATHAN DAGGETT.[7]
1282. iii. ISAAC DAGGETT.[7]
1283. iv. DILLIE DAGGETT,[7] married a Philadelphia lawyer, and had issue
     Sarah,[8] Eliza.[8]

1006. Capt. SAMUEL DAGGETT [6] (*Seth*,[5] *Samuel*,[4] *Thomas*,[3]
Thomas,[2] *John* [1]), born Tisbury, Mass., May 9, 1745; died New
Vineyard, Me., May 30, 1835; married 1st, Tisbury, Mass., Sarah
Butler, born August 23, 1744; died Boston, Mass., March 27, 1789;
married 2d, Holmes Hole, Mass., Abigail Daggett, daughter of
Elijah and Jedidah (Chase) Daggett (No. 1183); born 1766;
died Farmington, Me., September 30, 1846.

Issue:

1284. i. SAMUEL DAGGETT,[7] born Tisbury, Mass., July 11, 1764.

Capt. Samuel Daggett, accompanied by his son Samuel, moved
from Martha's Vineyard to the district of Maine, then a part of
Massachusetts, in 1794. and settled in what was afterwards New
Vineyard, now a part of Industry. Sarah Butler, the first wife of
Capt. Daggett, died in Boston, Mass., and was buried in the Granary
Burial-ground, where a stone stands to her memory, inscribed as
follows:

> In memory of
> MRS SARAH DAGGETT
> the amiable consort of
> CAPT SAMUEL DAGGETT
> died March 27, 1789
> aged 44 yrs 7 mos & 4 days.
> A kind companion & tender Parent
>
> In life the ways of truth she trod
> And now we trust she lives with God.

Captain Daggett is mentioned as a man of some property, careful
and methodical in business transactions, precise in his use of language,
and a moral, upright man. In 1781 was probably in command of the
ship "Mars," six guns, twenty men.

1007. Nathan Daggett [6] (*Seth*,[5] *Samuel*,[4] *Thomas*,[3] *Thomas*,[2] *John*[1]), died New Vineyard, Me. ; married Tisbury, Mass., May 14, 1773, Ann Wilkins.

Issue :

1285. i. West Daggett.[7]
1286. ii. Betsey Daggett,[7] married Richard Pomeroy; went West.
1287. iii. Catherine Daggett,[7] married John Gray, of Embden.
1288. iv. Nancy Daggett,[7] married Eben Colby, of New Vineyard; went West with Mrs. Pomeroy.
1289. v. Lydia Daggett,[7] married 1st, April 28, 1817, John Elliott, of New Portland; married 2d, Moses Wescott; went West.
1290. vi. Thomas West Daggett,[7] married (published July 20, 1819) Hannah Merrill, of New Portland; lived in Madison; probably died there.
1291. vii. Jesse Daggett,[7] married (published November 15, 1821) Sophia Lovejoy, sister of Thomas and Loyal Lovejoy; went West.
1292. viii. Nathan Daggett,[7] married February 5, 1815, Polly Elliott, of New Portland, sister of John Elliott.

Nathan Daggett removed to Industry about 1793.

1009. Capt. Silas Daggett [6] (*Seth*,[5] *Samuel*,[4] *Thomas*,[3] *Thomas*,[2] *John*[1]), born Tisbury, Mass., May 14, 1757 ; died Farmington, Me., September 12, 1847 ; married December 17, 1778, Deborah Butler, daughter of Elijah and Thankful (Smith) Butler; born Edgartown, Mass., November 13, 1759.

Issue :

1293. i. Mary Daggett,[7] born Tisbury, Mass., August 17, 1778.
1294. ii. West Daggett,[7] born Tisbury, Mass., November 26, 1780.
1295. iii. Silas Daggett,[7] born Tisbury, Mass., February 9, 1782.
1296. iv. Deborah Daggett,[7] born Tisbury, Mass., July 5, 1785.
1297. v. Sarah Daggett,[7] born Tisbury, Mass., December 6, 1787.
1298. vi. Joseph Bassett Daggett,[7] born Tisbury, Mass., December 14, 1790.
1299. vii. Elizabeth West Daggett,[7] born Tisbury, Mass., September 24, 1793; married August 25, 1812, Bartlett Luce, of Farmington, Me., son of Alsbury and Sarah (Burgess) Luce.
1300. viii. Sophronia Daggett,[7] born Tisbury, Mass., July 31, 1796; married 1815, William Donham; she died Tisbury, Mass., August 11, 1871; he died before 1871.

Capt. Silas Daggett settled in Industry, Me., as early as 1806. He was town clerk in Industry, Me., in 1809 ; also town treasurer for the same year.

Concerning the last-mentioned office, William Allen, in his History of Industry, relates the following :

The next year the captain brought in his account entered in a treasury book, and declined a reëlection, because his book would not tell the truth ; that he had charged all bills paid, and entered all the orders he had drawn on collectors to pay bills with; that he had done all the business by orders and bills; had not received or paid a dollar in money on the town's account; but his book showed a considerable balance due to him, which he knew was not the case.

Captain Daggett lived in the town a few years, and then returned to Martha's Vineyard.

He was a sailor, and also a commander of vessels.
Capt. Silas Daggett composed the following:

> Sister Jedidah doth believe,
>   The electing plan she well doth know;
> And out of a thousand more than one
>   To Heaven, she's sure, there cannot go.
> A young man heard her, then with ease
>   (You know him well, 'twas Wm. Downs)
> Said, "Tell, Miss Dida, if you please,
>   Who is to go from these three towns?"
> "La! Mr. Wm., so I can!
>   My good old mother she must go,
> And Ebenezer, that good man,
>   'Twas fore-ordained it must be so.
> And sister Betsy is all devotion,
>   And " — "Stop! stop!" says Bill, "you can't have more,
> Our island has its full proportion."

1010. MARY DAGGETT [6] (*Seth*,[5] *Samuel*,[4] *Thomas*,[3] *Thomas*,[2] *John* [1]), bapt. 1760; married Tisbury, Mass., May 13, 1779, Peleg Hillman.

In "Romance of the Revolution," by Oliver Bruce, is the story of the blowing up of the liberty pole at Vineyard Haven, then Holmes Hole, by three young ladies.

One of the three was Mary Daggett, who afterward married Mr. Hillman. She is said to have been a woman of superior mental ability.

1017. MICHAEL DAGGETT [6] (*Sylvanus*,[5] *Samuel*,[4] *Thomas*,[3] *Thomas*,[2] *John* [1]), born Tisbury, Mass., November 14, 1770; died Tisbury, Mass., September 28, 1852; married 1st, Tisbury, Mass., March 30, 1795, Elizabeth Butler, daughter of Thomas and Abigail (West) Butler; died July 20, 1803; married 2d, March 27, 1804, Remembrance Nye, daughter of John and Tamar Nye, of Chilmark, Mass.; married 3d, Tisbury, Mass., March 28, 1813, Mercy Look, daughter of Samuel and Margaret Look.

Issue:

1301. i. ABIGAIL WEST DAGGETT,[7] born Tisbury, Mass., August 5, 1798; died Tisbury, Mass., February 14, 1878.
1302. ii. PETER BUTLER DAGGETT,[7] born Tisbury, Mass., November 16, 1801.
1303. iii. AUGUSTA NYE DAGGETT,[7] born Tisbury, Mass., March 27, 1806.
1304. iv. TIMOTHY DAGGETT,[7] born Tisbury, Mass., September 5, 1807.
1305. v. CHARLES NYE DAGGETT,[7] born Tisbury, Mass., 1810.

1018. FREEMAN DAGGETT [6] (*Sylvanus*,[5] *Samuel*,[4] *Thomas*,[3] *Thomas*,[2] *John* [1]), born November, 1772; died at sea, November, 1809; married Rhoda Chase; born Tisbury, Mass., 1779; died Tisbury, Mass., September 21, 1850.

Issue:

1306. i. RHODA DAGGETT,[7] married Grafton Luce; resides San Francisco, Cal. (1892).

1307. ii. HEPSIE DAGGETT.[7]
1308. iii. FRANKLIN DAGGETT,[7] born Tisbury, Mass., October 26, 1804.
1309. iv. FREEMAN DAGGETT.[7]

Freeman Daggett was lost at sea while on a pilot trip.

1030. THOMAS DAGGETT [6] (*Benjamin,*[5] *Benjamin,*[4] *Thomas,*[3] *Thomas,*[2] *John* [1]), born Edgartown, Mass., September 4, 1774; died Palmyra, Me., March 26, 1845; married January 1, 1796, Abigail Mills, daughter of Mr. and Mrs. (Loker) Mills; born Tewksbury, Mass., December 8, 1774; died Palmyra, Me., Oct. 19, 1840.

Issue:

1310. i.   BENJAMIN DAGGETT,[7] born Fox Island, Me., October 4, 1796.
1311. ii.   ELIHU DAGGETT,[7] born Northport, Me., July 6, 1798.
1312. iii. DARIUS DAGGETT,[7] born Lincolnville, Me., February 17, 1801.
1313. iv.   JONAS DAGGETT,[7] born Lincolnville, Me., May 16, 1803.
1314. v.   SALLY DAGGETT,[7] born Montville, Me., June 26, 1805.
1315. vi.   ZENAS DAGGETT,[7] born October 13, 1807.
1316. vii. CATHARINE DAGGETT,[7] born Hope, Me., August 3, 1811; died Hope, Me., June 10, 1821.
1317. viii. MOSES L. DAGGETT,[7] born Hope, Me., January 13, 1819.

1031. LOVE DAGGETT [6] (*Benjamin,*[5] *Benjamin,*[4] *Thomas,*[3] *Thomas,*[2] *John* [1]), born Edgartown, Mass., 1776; married Elijah Luce.

Issue: three boys.

1318. i. FREEMAN LUCE,[7] resides Herman, Me. (1892).
1319. ii. OLIVER LUCE,[7] resides Herman, Me. (1892).

1035. RICHMOND DAGGETT [6] (*Benjamin,*[5] *Benjamin,*[4] *Thomas,*[3] *Thomas,*[2] *John* [1]), born Edgartown, Mass., July 15, 1783; died Bangor, Me., December 12, 1833; married November 19, 1806, Kezia Baker.

Issue:

1320. i.   SAMUEL BAKER DAGGETT,[7] born Palmyra, Me., September 6, 1807.
1321. ii. HENRY MARDIN DAGGETT,[7] born Palmyra, Me., January 23, 1809.
1322. iii. MARTHA DAGGETT,[7] born Palmyra, Me., January 10, 1811.
1323. iv. ELIZABETH DAGGETT,[7] born Palmyra, Me., October 23, 1812; married March 29, 1832, John Hellier, of Bangor, Me.
1324. v.   MARY DAGGETT,[7] born Palmyra, Me., November 28, 1817; married April 18, 1837, Rev. Joseph Aspenwall; died February 7, 1839.
1325. vi. CATHARINE DAGGETT,[7] born Palmyra, Me., August 10, 1821; resides Bangor, Me. (1883).

Richmond Daggett moved from Lincolnville to Palmyra, where he lived about eighteen years.

He was agent for the town of Pittsfield, and also a farmer. Moved to Bangor, Me., in 1827, where he kept a hotel. Was the first man in Bangor to pull down the "strong drink" sign and put up a "temperance" sign.

1037. ABIGAIL DAGGETT [6] (*Benjamin,*[5] *Benjamin,*[4] *Thomas,*[3] *Thomas,*[2] *John* [1]), born Vinal Haven, Mass., October 24, 1785; mar-

ried October 1, 1818, Timothy Stewart; born Edgartown, Mass.,
August 27, 1770; died Union, Me., March 29, 1844.

Issue:

1326. i. O. O. Stewart,[7] married Miss Robbins; resides Union, Me. (1892).

1043. Mayhew Daggett [6] (*Elihu*,[5] *Mayhew*,[4] *John*,[3] *Thomas*,[2]
John [1]), born Attleboro', Mass., April 28. 1735; died Pittstown,
N.Y. (?); married 1st (place, date, and to whom not found);
married 2d, Attleboro', Mass., March 5, 1789, Lucy Daggett, widow
of Ichabod Daggett, and daughter of Mr. Hadden; died Attleboro',
Mass., January 21, 1798.

Entered the army, and was with his brother Ichabod under Colonel
Bradstreet when Fort Frontenac was taken.

1044. Ichabod Daggett [6] (*Elihu*,[5] *Mayhew*,[4] *John*,[3] *Thomas*,[2]
John [1]), born Attleboro', Mass., December 7, 1736; died Attleboro',
Mass., September 3, 1781; married Rehoboth, Mass., June 15, 1769,
by Rev. Samuel Peck, to Lucy Hadden, of Rehoboth; died Attleboro',
Mass., January 21, 1798.

Issue:

1327. i. Ichabod Daggett,[7] born Attleboro', Mass., November 20, 1771.
1328. ii. David Daggett,[7] born Attleboro', Mass., November 10, 1773; died
Stockholm, N.Y.
1329. iii. Lucy Daggett,[7] born Attleboro', Mass., October 6. 1775; married
Joab Fuller, and removed to New York or Pennsylvania; issue:
Eunice Fuller,[8] who married Levi P. Daggett (No. 1831).
1330. iv. Henry Daggett,[7] born Attleboro', Mass., September 29, 1778.

Entered the army, and was with Colonel Bradstreet when Fort
Frontenac was taken.

1045. Lieut. Daniel Daggett [6] (*Elihu*,[5] *Mayhew*,[4] *John*,[3]
Thomas,[2] *John* [1]), born Attleboro', Mass., February 1. 1738; died
Attleboro', Mass.. December 3, 1796; married Margaret Woodcock;
born 1742; died Attleboro'. Mass., August 11, 1829.

Issue:

1331. i. Benjamin Daggett,[7] born Attleboro', Mass., November 16, 1763.
1332. ii. Mary Daggett,[7] born Attleboro', Mass., May 21, 1766.
1333. iii. Margaret Daggett,[7] born Attleboro', Mass , July 27, 1768.
1334. iv. Abigail Daggett.[7] born Attleboro', Mass., August 28, 1770.
1335. v. Sarah Daggett,[7] born Attleboro', Mass., November 25, 1772;
married Attleboro', Mass., June 19, 1796, Edward Price.
1336. vi. Daniel Daggett.[7] born Attleboro', Mass., February 11, 1775.
1337. vii. Betsey Daggett.[7] born Attleboro', Mass., September 5, 1777.
1338. viii. Olive Daggett,[7] born Attleboro', Mass., 1785.

Daniel Daggett served as sergeant in Capt. Jabez Ellis's company
of minute-men that were called out January 5, 1776, and marched
thirty-five miles.

HENRY DAGGETT.

ELISABETH [PRESCOTT] DAGGETT.

From August 23 to September 2, 1778, he served as private in Capt. Elisha May's company. March 6 to 14, 1781, was private in Capt. Sam. Robinson's company, in Colonel Deane's regiment, in Rhode Island.

Was lieutenant in Capt. Enoch Robinson's company, July 31 to August 8, 1780. They seem to have marched on the alarm to Tiverton.

Also under Capt. Moses Wilmarth's company from sometime in March to July 31 or August 7, 1781. [Revolutionary Rolls, State House, Boston.]

The will of Lieut. Daniel Daggett, of Attleboro', gentleman, is dated October 17, 1796, and was proved January 17, 1797. [Bristol Probate.]

Lieut. Daniel Daggett and his wife were both buried in the burying-ground at Attleboro' Falls, where are stones erected to their memory.

1046. HENRY DAGGETT[6] (*Elihu*,[5] *Mayhew*,[4] *John*,[3] *Thomas*,[2] *John* [1]), born Attleboro', Mass., April 9, 1741; died New Haven, Conn., September 24, 1830; married 1st, New Haven, Conn., November 26, 1771, Elisabeth Prescott, daughter of Benjamin and Rebecca (Minot) Prescott, of Danvers, Mass.; born Danvers, Mass., December 1, 1752; died New Haven, Conn., May 11, 1813; married 2d, Danbury, Conn., May 24, 1814, Mrs. Elizabeth Taylor, of Danbury, Conn., widow of Col. Timothy Taylor, and daughter of Hon. Joseph Platt and Sophia (Benedict) Cook; born Danbury, Conn., July 23, 1764; died New Haven, Conn., October 20, 1834.

Issue:

1339. i.   ELISABETH DAGGETT,[7] born New Haven, Conn., October 14, 1772; died New Haven, Conn., November 19, 1772.
1340. ii.   REBECCA DAGGETT,[7] born New Haven, Conn., October 30, 1773; died New Haven, Conn., December 16, 1773.
1341. iii.   ELIHU DAGGETT,[7] born New Haven, Conn., May 1, 1775; died New Haven, Conn., May 17, 1775.
1342. iv.   HENRY DAGGETT,[7] born New Haven, Conn., October 19, 1776; died New Haven, Conn., January 21, 1777.
1343. v.   ELISABETH DAGGETT,[7] born New Haven, Conn., March 21, 1778; died New Haven, Conn., June 1, 1778.
1344. vi.   AMELIA MARTHA DAGGETT,[7] born New Haven, Conn., August 25, 1779.
1345. vii.   ELIHU DAGGETT,[7] born New Haven, Conn., September 28, 1781; died New Haven, Conn., September 21, 1813.
1346. viii.   HENRY DAGGETT,[7] born New Haven, Conn., January 10, 1784; died New Haven, Conn., February 3, 1784.
1347. ix.   ELISABETH DAGGETT,[7] born New Haven, Conn., July 5, 1786.
1348. x.   MARY DAGGETT,[7] born New Haven, Conn., December 5, 1792.

Henry Daggett graduated at Yale College 1771. He lived on the corner of High and Chapel streets, New Haven. The estate is now owned by Yale College. He was a merchant, magistrate, and alderman.   The will of Henry Daggett is dated November 30, 1827, and it names Edward Hooker as executor.   The inventory amounted to $17,232.32.

1048.   Adj. ELIHU DAGGETT[6] (*Elihu,*[5] *Mayhew,*[4] *John,*[3] *Thomas,*[2] *John*[1]), born Attleboro', Mass., December 4, 1745; died Attleboro', Mass., June 14, 1833; married Norton, Mass., December 9, 1773, by Rev. Peter Thatcher, to Charity Galieucia, of Norton; born Massachusetts, October 14, 1746; died Attleboro', Mass., April 16, 1823.

Issue:

1349. i.   GEORGE DAGGETT,[7] born Attleboro', Mass., December 29, 1774.
1350. ii.   ROSAMOND DAGGETT,[7] born Attleboro', Mass., January 6, 1777.
1351. iii.   BECCA DAGGETT,[7] born Attleboro', Mass., January 25, 1779; died Attleboro', Mass., May 19, 1860.
1352. iv.   MAYHEW DAGGETT,[7] born Attleboro', Mass., July 24, 1781; lived South; came North in 1810, after which he returned; not since heard from.
1353. v.   ELIHU DAGGETT,[7] born Attleboro', Mass., February 24, 1785.
1354. vi.   JACOB DAGGETT,[7] born Mansfield, Mass., April 20, 1787.
1355. vii.   THIRZA DAGGETT,[7] born Attleboro', Mass., July 11, 1789; died Attleboro', Mass., October 13, 1813.

1049.   JACOB DAGGETT[6] (*Elihu,*[5] *Mayhew,*[4] *John,*[3] *Thomas,*[2] *John*[1]), born Attleboro', Mass., May 16, 1748; died New Haven, Conn., February 6, 1796; married December 26, 1774, Rhoda Humiston, daughter of David and Ruth (Bassett) Humiston, of Plymouth, Conn.; born 1751; died New Haven, Conn., August 31, 1831.

Issue:

1356. i.   SARAH DAGGETT,[7] born January 5, 1776.
1357. ii.   CHAUNCY DAGGETT,[7] born June 7, 1779.
1358. iii.   REBECCA DAGGETT,[7] born December 14, 1781; married Naphtali Daggett; born 1769; died April 4, 1813; she died March 26, 1813.
1359. iv.   NANCY DAGGETT,[7] born May 27, 1784; married 1841, Bennett Bronson; he born Waterbury, Conn., November 14, 1775; she died New Haven, Conn., August 14, 1867.

Henry Daggett, Jr., was appointed administrator of estate of Jacob Daggett, February 26, 1796.

1050.   ANNA DAGGETT[6] (*Elihu,*[5] *Mayhew,*[4] *John,*[3] *Thomas,*[2] *John*[1]), born Attleboro', Mass., August 2, 1750; died Attleboro', Mass., November 11, 1784; married Daniel Stanley, Jr.; born 1748; died Attleboro', Mass., February 9, 1798.

Issue:

1360. i.   CYRIL STANLEY,[7] born Attleboro', Mass., February 11, 1772.
1361. ii.   SYLVESTER STANLEY,[7] born Attleboro', Mass., January 14, 1774.
1362. iii.   DANIEL STANLEY,[7] born Attleboro', Mass., April 4, 1777.
1363. iv.   ESTHER STANLEY,[7] born Attleboro', Mass., August 1, 1779; died Attleboro', Mass., August 12, 1784.

1364. v.   Job Stanley,[7] born Attleboro', Mass., February 22, 1782; died Attleboro', Mass., July 19, 1784.
1365. vi.   Anna Stanley,[7] born Attleboro', Mass., April 12, 1784.
1366. vii. William Stanley,[7] perhaps born 1770, who went to Maine with George Daggett, resided Sidney, Kennebec county, Me.; married Polly Stone, and had three sons and one daughter; one son, William S., married Charity G. Daggett (No. 1889).

1052. Capt. Elijah Daggett[6] (*Elihu*,[5] *Mayhew*,[4] *John*,[3] *Thomas*,[2] *John*[1]), born Attleboro', Mass., April 14, 1754; died Attleboro', Mass., August, 1825; married Esther Orne, daughter of Lieut. James and Esther (Everett) Orne; born North Attleboro', Mass., March 31, 1763; died Attleboro', Mass., August 4, 1818.

Issue:

1367. i.   Gardner Daggett,[7] born Attleboro', Mass., December 20, 1782; graduated Brown University, 1802; lived in Providence; lawyer; died Providence, R.I.; unmarried.
1368. ii.   Clarisa Daggett,[7] born Attleboro', Mass., November 28, 1784; married Attleboro', Mass., November 11, 1810, Bant Brondson, of Boston; she died Attleboro', Mass., June, 1816.
1369. iii. Charlotte Daggett,[7] born Attleboro', Mass., December 31, 1786; died Attleboro', Mass., March 27, 1796.
1370. iv.   Lyman Daggett,[7] born Attleboro', Mass., February 12, 1789; died Attleboro', Mass., January 25, 1808.
1371. v.   James Manning Daggett,[7] born Attleboro', Mass., July 30, 1791; died Attleboro', Mass., October 9, 1791.
1372. vi.   Milton Daggett,[7] born Attleboro', Mass., October 15, 1792.
1373. vii. Marietta Daggett,[7] born Attleboro', Mass., April 4, 1795.
1374. viii. Charlotte Daggett,[7] born Attleboro', Mass., May 25, 1797; died Attleboro', Mass., June, 1816.
1375. ix.   Maria Daggett,[7] born Attleboro', Mass., November 9, 1799.
1376. x.   Manus Daggett,[7] born Attleboro', Mass., December 18, 1801.
1377. xi.   James Henry Daggett,[7] born Attleboro', Mass., November 12, 1804; died Attleboro', Mass., May, 1825.
1378. xii. Charles Foster Daggett,[7] born Attleboro', Mass., —— 5, 1806; died Attleboro', Mass., May 15, 1806.

Captain Daggett is reported as serving in the Revolution.

He was an innkeeper on Dock square, Boston, in 1805, 1806, 1807.

Captain Daggett and wife, with some of their children, are buried in Plainville, Mass. On the stone is this inscription:

"Blessed are the dead that die in the Lord."

On the stone erected to the memory of their son Lyman Daggett is the following:

A nit's a feather and a chief's a rod
An honest man's the noblest work of God.

1053. Joseph Daggett[6] (*Elihu*,[5] *Mayhew*,[4] *John*,[3] *Thomas*,[2] *John*[1]), born Attleboro', Mass., February 14, 1758; died Cattaraugus county, N.Y., 1856; married May 11, 1780, Melitiah Clark; died August 22, 1830.

Issue:

1379. i. FANNY DAGGETT,[7] born Attleboro', Mass., June 26, 1781; married Seth H. Cutler; resided, 1848, Pembroke, N.Y.
1380. ii. NANCY DAGGETT,[7] born Attleboro', Mass., March 18, 1783; died an infant (?).
1381. iii. NANCY DAGGETT,[7] born March 6, 1785; married Abel Goodnow; resided (1848) Leicester, Vt.
1382. iv. CLARK DAGGETT,[7] born October 14, 1787.
1383. v. JOSEPH DAGGETT,[7] born September 19, 1790; not married; resided (1848) Pittsford, Vt.
1384. vi. REBECCA DAGGETT,[7] born February 2, 1793; married Azel Kelley, 1814; resided (1848) Danby, Vt.; removed to Cattaraugus county, N.Y.
1385. vii. CHLOE DAGGETT,[7] born June 12, 1795; not married (1848).
1386. viii. MANNING DAGGETT,[7] born October 10, 1802; married Elizabeth Seelye; resided (1848) Leicester, Vt.

1081. JOHN DAGGETT[6] (*John*,[5] *Ebenezer*,[4] *John*,[3] *Thomas*,[2] *John*[1]), born Attleboro', Mass., October 1, 1752; died Leicester, Vt., December 13, 1781; married Judith Capron, daughter of Joseph and Sarah (Robeson) Capron; born Attleboro', Mass., March 8, 1754; died 1838.

Issue (all probably removed to Malone, N.Y., after 1781):

1387. i. JOHN DAGGETT,[7] born Leicester, Vt.
1388. ii. PLINY DAGGETT.[7]
1389. iii. EBENEZER DAGGETT.[7]
1390. iv. MERCY DAGGETT.[7]

1082. JOAB DAGGETT[6] (*John*,[5] *Ebenezer*,[4] *John*,[3] *Thomas*,[2] *John*[1]), born Attleboro', Mass., October 19, 1754; died Attleboro', Mass., March 7, 1816; married Chloe Blackinton, daughter of John Blackinton; born Attleboro', Mass., October 24, 1764; died Attleboro', Mass., February 16, 1853.

Issue:

1391. i. OTIS DAGGETT,[7] born Attleboro', Mass., Oct. 4, 1785.
1392. ii. IRA DAGGETT,[7] born Attleboro', Mass., August 27, 1787.
1393. iii. LEVI DAGGETT,[7] born Attleboro', Mass., June 12, 1789.
1394. iv. JOAB DAGGETT,[7] born Attleboro', Mass., October 1, 1791; died Attleboro', Mass. (before September 2), 1828.
1395. v. MARCUS DAGGETT,[7] born Attleboro', Mass., July 21, 1793.
1396. vi. LUCAS DAGGETT,[7] born Attleboro', Mass., November 6, 1795.
1397. vii. CHLOE DAGGETT,[7] born Attleboro', Mass., February 28, 1798; died Attleboro', Mass., September 28, 1803.
1398. viii. PLINY DAGGETT,[7] born Attleboro', Mass., May 16, 1800; died Attleboro', Mass., September 21, 1803.
1399. ix. PAUL DAGGETT,[7] born Attleboro', Mass., August 22, 1802; died Attleboro', Mass., September 29, 1803.
1400. x. PLINY DAGGETT,[7] born Attleboro', Mass., December 20, 1804.
1401. xi. CHLOE DAGGETT,[7] born Attleboro', Mass., November 8, 1807; married Mr. Carpenter; living (1853).
1402. xii. NANCY DAGGETT,[7] born Attleboro', Mass., July 26, 1810.

The will of Joab Daggett, of Attleboro', is dated March 6, 1816.

He mentions his wife Chloe; his son Otis; gives Ira and Joab all his lands in Surry, N.H.; his son Levi all his lands in Troy, N.H. Also mentions Marcus, Lucas's family in Wrentham, Pliny, Chloe, and gives Nancy land in Foxboro'. Proved April 2, 1816. [Bristol Probate.]

1083. JESSE DAGGETT[6] (*John*,[5] *Ebenezer*,[4] *John*,[3] *Thomas*,[2]*John*[1]), born Attleboro', Mass., March 6, 1757; died Boston, Mass., September 7, 1831; married Attleboro', Mass., March 6, 1792, Lois Robinson; born 1764; died Boston, Mass., January 13, 1837.

Issue:

1403. i. LOIS DAGGETT,[7] born Attleboro', Mass., November 28, 1797.

The will of Jesse Daggett is recorded in Suffolk Probate, 130[1]–184. It is dated October 19, 1830, and in it he calls himself Jesse Daggett, of Boston, yeoman. He gives to his wife all of his estate that may be required for her support, and the remainder, if any, that may be left at her decease he gives to his daughter Lois Bates.

Ebenezer Daggett, Esq., is named as sole executor. The will was allowed, Feb. 13, 1832.

The inventory, dated May 14, 1832, mentions: " Lot of land containing 10 acres with the old mansion house and outhouses thereon, situate in Attleboro, Bristol Co."

1085. MARCY DAGGETT[6] (*John*,[5] *Ebenezer*,[4] *John*,[3] *Thomas*,[2] *John*[1]), born Attleboro', Mass., July 2, 1761; married Elijah Bolkcom.

Issue:

1404. i. OLIVE BOLKCOM,[7] born Attleboro', Mass., July 29, 1787.
1405. ii. MILLA BOLKCOM,[7] born Attleboro', Mass., October 25, 1788.
1406. iii. EBENEZER BOLKCOM,[7] born Attleboro', Mass., May 29, 1790.
1407. iv. ELIJAH BOLKCOM,[7] born Attleboro', Mass., September 30, 1791.
1408. v. DEXTER BOLKCOM,[7] born Attleboro', Mass., April 27, 1793.
1409. vi. STEPHEN BOLKCOM,[7] born Attleboro', Mass., October 2, 1794.

1086. Hon. EBENEZER DAGGETT[6] (*John*,[5] *Ebenezer*,[4] *John*,[3] *Thomas*,[2] *John*[1]), born Attleboro', Mass., April 16, 1763; died Boston, Mass., March 4, 1832; married Attleboro', Mass., September 3, 1797, Sally Maxcy, daughter of Lieut. Benjamin and Amy (Ide) Maxcy; born Attleboro', Mass., November 20, 1778; died Saundersville, Mass., April 30, 1867.

Issue:

1410. i. JOHN DAGGETT,[7] born Attleboro', Mass., September 9, 1800; died Attleboro', Mass., July 5, 1803.
1411. ii. LYDIA MAXCY DAGGETT,[7] born Attleboro', Mass., October 16, 1802.
1412. iii. JOHN DAGGETT,[7] born Attleboro', Mass., February 10, 1805.
1413. iv. EBENEZER DAGGETT,[7] born Attleboro', Mass., May 14, 1807; died at sea, November 17, 1831.
1414. v. HARVEY MAXCY DAGGETT,[7] born Attleboro', Mass., June 10, 1809.

1415. vi. Ama Ide Daggett,[7] born Attleboro', Mass., November 24, 1811.
1416. vii. Marcy Shepard Daggett,[7] born Attleboro', Mass., Jan. 14, 1814.
1417. viii. ——— Daggett,[7] born Attleboro', Mass., June 5, 1818; died Attleboro', Mass., June 6, 1818.
1418. ix. Handel Naphtali Daggett,[7] born Attleboro', Mass., January 27, 1821.
1419. x. Homer Micajah Daggett,[7] born Attleboro', Mass., January 27, 1821.

Hon. Ebenezer Daggett, of Attleboro', held a commission of Justice of the Peace for nearly thirty years, and honorably discharged its most important duties. He served the town at various times in the capacity of Selectman, and was Town Clerk for upwards of twenty years.

He represented the town several years in the General Court. A large part of the last thirty years of his life was occupied in some public employment. In various ways he rendered himself serviceable to his fellow-citizens.

In the spring of 1831 he was elected a member of the Senate for this district. At the succeeding November election he was rechosen to the same office, and while in the discharge of the honorable and responsible duties of this station he was called by the order of Providence to close his life at Boston, in the sixty-ninth year of his age.

Possessed of natural abilities above mediocrity, which he had improved by self-education, he always directed them to useful purposes. Plain and unassuming in his manners, mild and uniform in his disposition, he had won the confidence of his fellow-citizens, but never sought after the honors which were bestowed upon him.

Guided by fixed and pure principles, he was upright and honorable in all his dealings with his fellow-men, and preserved a character of unsullied integrity through a long and active life. He was regarded by his neighbors as their father and adviser. If they were in difficulty or doubt, they came to him for counsel and assistance, and both were freely offered. So great was their confidence in his integrity and judgment, that he was generally the chosen umpire in cases of controversies between his fellow-citizens.

He was in fine, in the true and enlarged sense of the word, a useful man. His life affords an encouraging example of the truth that respectable talents, united with integrity and industry, will raise a man to honor and usefulness. [Daggett's Hist. Attleboro'.]

John Daggett, of Attleboro', was administrator of his father's estate.

1088. Hannah Daggett[6] (*John*,[5] *Ebenezer*,[4] *John*,[3] *Thomas*,[2] *John*[1]), born Attleboro', Mass., December 19, 1768; married Nathaniel Ide, Jr.

Issue:

1420. i. Lynda Ide,[7] born Attleboro', Mass., February 10, 1793.
1421. ii. Ebenezer Ide,[7] born Attleboro', Mass., April 26, 1795.

1422. iii. MAXCY SHEPARD IDE,[7] born Attleboro', Mass., February 22, 1797.
1423. iv.   HOLMAN IDE,[7] born Attleboro', Mass., August 17, 1800.
1424. v.   HANLINUS IDE,[7] born Attleboro', Mass., June 6, 1801.
1425. vi.   THERON IDE,[7] born Attleboro', Mass., February 26, 1803.
1426. vii. LYDIA EMALINE IDE,[7] born Attleboro', Mass., January 15, 1812.

1089.   HULDAH DAGGETT[6] (*John*,[5] *Ebenezer*,[4] *John*,[3] *Thomas*,[2] *John*[1]), born Attleboro', Mass., January 27, 1771; married (published Attleboro', Mass., March 10, 1788) Elisha Hodges, son of Job and Ruth (Andrews) Hodges, of Norton (now Mansfield); born Norton, Mass.; bapt. October 19, 1760; died Mansfield, Mass., April 10, 1824.

Issue :

1427. i.   MILTON HODGES,[7] resided Mansfield, Mass.
1428. ii.   EBENEZER HODGES.[7]
1429. iii. ELISHA HODGES,[7] resided Mansfield, Mass.
1430. iv.   JESSE HODGES,[7] resided Mansfield, Mass.
1431. v.   NANCY HODGES.[7]
1432. vi.   ALONA HODGES.[7]
1433. vii. RUTH HODGES,[7] married Stephen Smith, and died Mansfield, December 20, 1828.
1434. viii. MERCY HODGES.[7]

1092.   Lieut. HENRY DAGGETT[6] (*Naphtali*,[5] *Ebenezer*,[4] *John*,[3] *Thomas*,[2] *John*[1]), born New Haven, Conn., February 27, 1758; died New Haven, Conn., June 20, 1843; married New Haven, Conn., July 7, 1784, Anna Ball, daughter of Stephen and Abigail (Atwater) Ball; born New Haven, Conn., March 28, 1764; died New Haven, Conn., January 20, 1844.

Issue :

1435. i.   HARRIET DAGGETT,[7] born January 26, 1783; married Frederick Hunt, son of Frederick and Elizabeth Hunt; he died before 1849; she died January 11, 1849.
1436. ii.   EBENEZER DAGGETT,[7] born New Haven, Conn., May 1, 1787; died New Haven, Conn., November 10, 1825.
1437. iii. GRACE ANN DAGGETT,[7] born 1788.
1438. iv.   HENRY DAGGETT,[7] died probably 1831.
1439. v.   STEPHEN DAGGETT,[7] born New Haven, Conn., July 1, 1798.
1440. vi.   MARY DAGGETT.[7]
1441. vii. HORACE DAGGETT,[7] born New Haven, Conn., February 26, 1801.
1442. viii. ELIZA DAGGETT.[7]
1443. ix.   JOHN DAGGETT,[7] died soon after 1844.

Henry Daggett graduated from Yale College, 1776; a merchant and an officer of the army of the Revolution, serving seven years. There were in New Haven three other persons bearing the same name, and for many years he added "Jr." to his name to designate himself from the others.

He enlisted in May, 1777, under Captain Stevens, in Col. Heman Swift's Connecticut regiment. He was an unusually good penman, and was taken into Colonel Swift's family, and was recommended by him to General Huntington for appointment as quartermaster to the regiment, October 31, 1777. He was commissioned as ensign, then as second lieutenant, to rank from April 24, 1778, both signed by John Jay, President of Congress, and as first lieutenant, to rank from April 11, 1780, signed by Samuel Huntington, President of Congress. He was discharged at the close of the war.

1095. Ezra Daggett[6] (*Naphtali,*[5] *Ebenezer.*[4] *John,*[3] *Thomas,*[2] *John*[1]), born New Haven, Conn., April 18, 1765; died New Haven, Conn., March 18, 1844; married 1st, New Haven, Conn., March 20, 1790, Eunice Tuttle, daughter of Ebenezer and Eunice (Moss) Tuttle; born New Haven, Conn., March 12, 1769; died New Haven, Conn., July 24, 1826; married 2d. New Haven. Conn.. October 15, 1826, by Benjamin M. Hill, to Mrs. Desire DeWolfe; born 1777; died New Haven, Conn., March 16, 1846.

Issue :

1444. i. Elizabeth Daggett,[7] born New Haven, Conn., January 26, 1791.
1445. ii. Smith Daggett,[7] born New Haven, Conn., March 13, 1793.
1446. iii. Julia Daggett,[7] born New Haven, Conn., December 27, 1794; died New Haven, Conn., September 22, 1874.
1447. iv. Ezra Daggett,[7] born New Haven, Conn., January 29, 1797; died April 23, 1852.
1448. v. Alfred Daggett,[7] born New Haven, Conn.. September 30, 1799.
1449. vi. William Daggett,[7] born New Haven, Conn., December 12, 1801.
1450. vii. Mary Daggett,[7] born New Haven, Conn., November 29, 1803.
1451. viii. Frederick Daggett,[7] born New Haven. Conn., October 23, 1805; died New Haven, Conn., January 6, 1806.
1452. ix. Sarah Daggett,[7] born New Haven. Conn., October 7, 1807.
1453. x. Frederick Daggett,[7] born New Haven, Conn., November 28, 1809.
1454. xi. Harriet Daggett,[7] born New Haven. Conn., September 15, 1811; died New Haven, Conn., January 3, 1833.

1097. Elizabeth Daggett[6] (*Naphtali,*[5] *Ebenezer,*[4] *John,*[3] *Thomas,*[2] *John*[1]), born New Haven, Conn., April 9, 1769; died New Haven, Conn., May 20, 1790; married New Haven, Conn., February 4, 1789, Jeremiah M. Atwater, son of Jeremiah Atwater; born New Haven, Conn., February 15, 1767; died New Haven, Conn., February 27, 1832.

No issue.

1100. Samuel Daggett[6] (*Samuel,*[5] *Ebenezer,*[4] *John,*[3] *Thomas,*[2] *John*[1]), born 1754; died Newark, N.Y., 1826; married 1st, Needham, Mass., March 2, 1775, Hannah McIntier, of Needham; married 2d, Albany, N.Y., Hannah Murphy; died Newark, N.Y., 1850.

Issue :

1455. i. Silence Daggett,[7] born Needham, Mass., June 9, 1775; died Needham, Mass., June 9, 1775.
1456. ii. Hannah Daggett,[7] born Needham, Mass., April 24, 1778.
1457. iii. Mary Daggett,[7] born Needham, Mass., February 9, 1780; died Needham, Mass., September 15, 1781.
1458. iv. Michael Daggett,[7] born Needham, Mass., August 3, 1781; died Needham, Mass., August 27, 1781.

(over)

1459. v.   LEVI DAGGETT,[7] born Albany, N.Y., April 29, 1788.
1460. vi.   JOHN DAGGETT.[7]
1461. vii.   ELISHA DAGGETT.[7]
1462. viii.   PRISCILLA DAGGETT,[7] born near Albany, N.Y., June, 1790.
1463. ix.   POLLY DAGGETT.[7]
1464. x.   SAMUEL DAGGETT,[7] born May 31, 1797.
1465. xi.   MARGARET DAGGETT,[7] born May 31, 1797.
1466. xii.   SALLY DAGGETT,[7] born near Albany, N.Y., April 4, 1799.
1467. xiii.   BETSEY DAGGETT,[7] married Nathan Strong, of Sodus, N.Y.
1468. xiv.   PHŒBE DAGGETT,[7] married Willis Sage, of Rochester, N.Y.
1469. xv.   LOIS DAGGETT.[7]

Mr. Daggett by his second marriage had eleven children. The family lived then about eight miles from Albany, N.Y., working at the glass-works in the mill, sawing lumber for glass boxes.

Then they were at Guilford, N.Y., afterward at Newark, N.Y.

1103. EBENEZER DAGGETT[6] (*Samuel,*[5] *Ebenezer,*[4] *John,*[3] *Thomas,*[2] *John*[1]), born Needham, Mass., May 16, 1762; " blacksmith; " died Jordan, N.Y., 1845; married Jennett Patterson, daughter of David and Lydia (Brattan) Patterson; born Enfield, Mass., April 24, 1767; died Jordan, N.Y., May 13, 1848.

Issue :

1470. i.   HERMAN DAGGETT,[7] born Enfield, Mass., September 30, 1790.
1471. ii.   MOSES DAGGETT,[7] born Enfield, Mass., April 7, 1796.
1472. iii.   EBENEZER DAGGETT,[7] born Enfield, Mass., June 16, 1798.
1473. iv.   LYDIA DAGGETT,[7] born 1800.
1474. v.   JENNETTE DAGGETT,[7] married Mr. Case; died Jordan, N.Y.
1475. vi.   PRISCILLA DAGGETT,[7] born 1803.
1476. vii.   MARY DAGGETT,[7] born Enfield, Mass.; died Springfield, Mass.

1104. POLLY DAGGETT[6] (*Samuel,*[5] *Ebenezer,*[4] *John,*[3] *Thomas,*[2] *John*[1]), born Needham, Mass., April 26, 1763; married Needham, Mass., February 28, 1787, Elisha Hunttington; resided western New York.

Issue :

1477. i.   POLLY HUNTTINGTON,[7] married Mr. Rich, of Batavia, N.Y.

1105. ASA DAGGETT[6] (*Samuel,*[5] *Ebenezer,*[4] *John,*[3] *Thomas,*[2] *John*[1]), born Needham, Mass., December 17, 1765; died Needham, Mass., October 28, 1806; married Needham, Mass., November 12, 1787, Lydia Kingsbury.

Issue :

1478. i.   JABEZ DAGGETT,[7] bapt. First Church, Needham, September 12, 1790.
1479. ii.   MARY DAGGETT,[7] bapt. as above; married Needham, Mass., November 11, 1810, by Rev. Stephen Palmer, to Asa Reed, of Boston.

1106. LEVI DAGGETT[6] (*Samuel,*[5] *Ebenezer,*[4] *John,*[3] *Thomas,*[2] *John*[1]), born Needham, Mass., March 4, 1768; died Palmyra, N.Y., May 12, 1835; married October 17, 1795, Lydia Patterson, daughter

of David and Lydia (Brattan) Patterson; born March 4, 1773; died
Aurora, N.Y., January 29, 1853.

Issue:

1480. i.   Levi Daggett,[7] born Schuylerville, N.Y., November 23, 1796.
1481. ii.   David Patterson Daggett,[7] born Schuylerville, N.Y., July 3, 1799.
1482. iii. Sarah Daggett,[7] born May 18, 1803.
1483. iv.   Lydia Daggett,[7] born September 21, 1805.
1484. v.   Augustus K. Daggett,[7] born March 26, 1808.
1485. vi.   Julia Jeannette Daggett,[7] born May 14, 1810.
1486. vii. Elizabeth Daggett,[7] born May 5, 1811.
1487. viii. Terressa Daggett,[7] born Saratoga, N.Y., September 9, 1812.
1488. ix.   Mary Daggett,[7] born Brutus, N.Y., April 23, 1816.

Levi Daggett was born in Massachusetts. He moved to Saratoga,
N.Y., thence to Palmyra, N.Y. He was a manufacturer and machinist.

1109. Susanna Daggett[6] (*Ebenezer,*[5] *Ebenezer,*[4] *John,*[3] *Thomas,*[2]
John[1]), born Walpole, Mass., May 13, 1759; died Walpole, Mass.,
April 13, 1788; married Dedham, Mass., May 30, 1782, by Rev.
Mr. Chickering, to Ichabod Clap, of Walpole, son of Thomas and
Susanna Clap; born Walpole, Mass., February 21, 1750; died
Walpole, Mass., January 5, 1832.

Issue:

1489. i.   Nancy Clap,[7] born March 13, 1783; died January 23, 1867.
1490. ii. Metcalf Clap,[7] born March 4, 1786; married and had issue: Ebenezer
           D. Clap,[8] born March 11, 1813. Metcalf Clap died July 28, 1828.

1111. Ebenezer Daggett[6] (*Ebenezer,*[5] *Ebenezer,*[4] *John,*[3]
Thomas,[2] *John*[1]), born Walpole, Mass., September 30, 1762; died
Dorchester, Mass., September 11, 1812; married Dedham, Mass.,
March 6, 1793, by Rev. Jason Haven, to Alice Draper, daughter
of Abijah and Alice (Eaton?) Draper; born April 13, 1771; died
New Boston, N.H., June 27, 1852.

Issue:

1491. i.   Carlos Daggett,[7] born Wrentham, Mass., December 2, 1793.
1492. ii. Sarah Daggett,[7] born Wrentham, Mass., May 8, 1797; died Wren-
           tham, Mass., January 11, 1800.
1493. iii. Herman Daggett,[7] born Wrentham, Mass., March 27, 1800.
1494. iv. Albert Pliny Daggett,[7] born Dorchester, Mass., October 13, 1805;
           died at sea, October 15, 1827.
1495. v.   Susannah Alice Daggett,[7] born Dorchester, Mass., February 16,
           1809; died November 17, 1825.

Ebenezer Daggett, of Dorchester, "gentleman," did not leave a
will. Application for administration was made October 6, 1812.
[Norfolk Probate.]

Alice Daggett, widow, was made guardian of the minor children,
February 6, 1816.

1112. Olive Daggett[6] (*Ebenezer,*[5] *Ebenezer,*[4] *John,*[3] *Thomas,*[2]
John[1]), born Walpole, Mass., February 10, 1765; died Franklin,

Mass., July 21, 1788; married Wrentham, Mass., July 5, 1786, by
Rev. David Avery, to Ward Adams, of Franklin, son of Peter
Adams; born Franklin, Mass., November 28, 1762; died Franklin,
Mass., October 25, 1792.

Issue:

1496. i. EBENEZER WARD ADAMS,[7] born Franklin, Mass., July 23, 1787; married Minna Adams, daughter of Joel Adams; born June 22, 1791;
removed to Union, Me.

1113. Rev. HERMAN DAGGETT [6] (*Ebenezer,*[5] *Ebenezer,*[4] *John,*[3]
Thomas,[2] *John* [1]), born Walpole, Mass., September 11, 1766; died
May 19, 1832; married Providence, R.I., September 3, 1792, Sarah
Matthewson, daughter of Col. John Matthewson, of Providence;
born Glocester, R.I. (?), May 24, 1762; died November 20, 1843.

No issue.

Rev. Herman Daggett was at his father's decease between fifteen
and sixteen years of age.   Quickened in his efforts by his zeal for
knowledge he passed rapidly and successfully through his course preparatory to college, and became a member of Brown University in
1784.   His standing there as a scholar was highly respectable, and
he graduated in 1788.   In the second year of his college course his
mind, which had before been seriously directed by the influence of a
Christian education, became deeply impressed with the subject of
religion as a practical concern, and it was to this period that he referred the commencement of his religious life.   His ardor in literary
pursuits seems not to have been at all repressed by the change in his
moral feelings, though all his faculties and attainments were from
this time evidently consecrated to the glory of God and the benefit of
his fellow-creatures.

After graduation he placed himself as a theological student under
Dr. Emmons.   After spending a year in his preparatory studies, he
was licensed to preach by the association holding its session at North-
bridge, October, 1789.

Within a short time after he was licensed, he visited Long Island
with a view of being engaged as a preacher, thinking that the climate
would prove more congenial to his health than that of New England.
For a year he supplied the Presbyterian congregation at Southold,
and though they gave him a unanimous call, yet, being unwilling
to practise on the "Half-way Covenant," he felt constrained to
decline it.   Thence he was called to preach at Southampton, where
also he was unanimously invited to the pastorship.   He was set apart,
by the Presbytery, to the pastoral office, April 12, 1792.   Almost
immediately after his settlement, a difficulty arose on the subject of
the "Half-way Covenant," and throughout the whole controversy
which followed he behaved with great moderation and dignity, and

his character for discretion was never impugned.   This controversy
was the principal, if not the entire, cause of his resigning his charge.
It was sufficient evidence that he came out of this controversy
unscathed, that almost immediately after he was at liberty he was
called to the pastoral care of the church at West Hampton, a village
in the immediate neighborhood of the one he had left.   Here he continued greatly beloved and respected by his people from September,
1797, to September, 1801.

In October, 1801, he was installed pastor of the church at Fire
Place and Middle Island, in the town of Brookhaven, and preached
alternately to the two congregations till April, 1807, when his health
had become so far reduced that he resigned his charge.

He was greatly esteemed, especially by his brethren in the ministry,
for the wisdom of his counsels, not less than for the consistency of
his general deportment.

After leaving Long Island his health improved, and for a year
he preached and taught school at Cairo, N.Y.   For some time he
preached also at Patterson, Putnam county, and for two years he
preached and taught an academy at North Salem ; thence he went to
New Canaan, Conn., where he took charge of an academy.   When
the Foreign Mission School was established by the American Board
at Cornwall, Conn., Mr. Daggett was placed at the head of it, May
6, 1818.   Here he labored with success for nearly six years, until
1824, when he retired.   [Early History of Southampton, L.I., 1866.]

1117.   AMELIA DAGGETT [6] (*Philip,*[5] *Ebenezer,*[4] *John,*[3] *Thomas,*[2]
John[1]), born New Haven, Conn., 1780; died New Haven, Conn.,
June 1, 1869; married New Haven, Conn., November 21, 1805,
Joshua Barnes, son of Joshua and Mercy (Tuttle) Barnes ; born New
Haven, Conn., December 27, 1781; died New Haven, Conn., No-
vember 25, 1847.

Issue :

1497. i.   CHAUNCEY M. BARNES,[7] went to California, 1849; died there.
1498. ii.   CAROLINE BARNES,[7] married Beri Todd.
1499. iii. AMELIA BARNES,[7] married Sidney Boardman, of Dalton, Mass.
1500. iv.   JEANNETTE BARNES,[7] died aged eighteen years.
1501. v.   JULIA ANN BARNES,[7] born New Haven, Conn., May, 1816; married
            Jared Chidsey, of Branford, Ct.; resides New Haven (1883).
1502. vi.   WILLIAM JOSHUA BARNES,[7] married Mary Page.
1503. vii. DAGGETT BARNES.[7]

1120.   CHLOE DAGGETT [6] (*Mayhew,*[5] *Thomas,*[4] *John,*[3] *Thomas,*[2]
John[1]), born Attleboro', Mass., April 15, 1769; died Union, Me.,
May 13, 1793; married Attleboro', Mass., July 5, 1789, Josiah
Maxcy, son of Lieut. Benjamin and Sarah (Fuller) Maxcy; born
July 25, 1766.

HON. DAVID DAGGETT, L. L.D.

1124. ABNER DAGGETT[6] (*Thomas,*[5] *Thomas,*[4] *John,*[3] *Thomas,*[2] *John* [1]), born Attleboro', Mass., August 8, 1755; died Providence, R.I., August 25, 1832; married Attleboro', Mass., April 20, 1779, by Rev. Habijah Weld, to Mary Holmes; born Attleboro', Mass., July 6, 1757; died Providence, R.I., October 2, 1842.

Issue:

1504. i. ANN DAGGETT,[7] born Attleboro', Mass., April 24, 1780; died Boston, Mass., October 26, 1876.
1505. ii. LEWIS DAGGETT,[7] born Attleboro', Mass., January 14, 1782; died Attleboro', Mass., October 16, 1791.
1506. iii. CHARLOTTE DAGGETT,[7] born Walpole, Mass., May 14, 1784; died Providence, R.I. (?), April 13, 1799.
1507. iv. MARY DAGGETT.[7] born Walpole, Mass., March 23, 1786.
1508. v. HARRIET LEWIS DAGGETT,[7] born Providence, R.I. (?), April 23, 1797; died Providence, R.I., February 12, 1863.

Abner Daggett enlisted at Attleboro', Mass., in April, 1773, under Capt. Caleb Fish, in the regiment commanded by Col. Timothy Walker, and marched to participate in the siege of Boston.

At different periods during the Revolution he was stationed at Roxbury, Dorchester, and as guard at Preston's Point in the harbor, opposite the castle, until December, 1775, when he was discharged. About January 1, 1776, he again enlisted in the same company and regiment, as a bombadier, commanded by Colonel Crane of the artillery, for one year, and was in the battle of Long Island, August 27, 1776, and witnessed the capture of Lord Sterling, of New Jersey. After the evacuation of New York city, September 15, 1776, he followed the army on its retreat to White Plains, his route being a fatiguing march through swamps and marshes.

A few years after he left the army he lived in Walpole, Mass., and about 1798 he settled in Providence, R.I.

John Howland, of Providence, in August, 1838, said that "Abner Daggett was a person of great respectability, and for several years was a member of the town council, before Providence was incorporated as a city, and died after a long illness."

His will, dated January 4, 1816, was proved September 18, 1832. He calls himself "Merchant," and mentions, besides his children, his "dutiful grandson, George Edwin Monson."

1129. Hon. DAVID DAGGETT, LL.D.[6] (*Thomas,*[5] *Thomas,*[4] *John,*[3] *Thomas,*[2] *John* [1]), born Attleboro', Mass., December 31, 1764; died New Haven, Conn., April 12, 1851; married 1st, New Haven, Conn., September 10, 1786, by Rev. Chauncey Whittlesey, to Wealthy Ann Munson, daughter of Dr. Eneas Munson, of New Haven, Conn.; born New Haven, Conn., March 3, 1767; died New Haven, Conn., July 9, 1839; married second, New Haven, Conn., May 4, 1840, by Rev. S. W. S. Dutton, to Mary Lines, daughter of Major and Susanna

(Mansfield) Lines, of New Haven; born New Haven, Conn., March 31, 1788; died New Haven, Conn., December 26, 1854.

Issue:

1509. i.   MARIA DAGGETT,[7] born New Haven, Conn., June 13, 1787; died New Haven, Conn., June 13, 1787.
1510. ii.   SUSAN EDWARDS DAGGETT,[7] born New Haven, Conn., June 30, 1788.
1511. iii. LEONARD AUGUSTUS DAGGETT,[7] born New Haven, Conn., April 30, 1790.
1512. iv.   DAVID LEWIS DAGGETT,[7] born New Haven, Conn., February 8, 1792; died New Haven, Conn., October 2, 1810.
1513. v.   ENEAS MUNSON DAGGETT,[7] born New Haven, Conn., February 10, 1795; died New Haven, Conn., July 29, 1803.
1514. vi.   WEALTHY ANN DAGGETT,[7] born New Haven Conn., November 29, 1796.
1515. vii. GEORGE WASHINGTON DAGGETT,[7] born New Haven, Conn., February 11, 1800; died New Haven, Conn., August 12, 1803.
1516. viii. FRANCES DAGGETT,[7] born New Haven, Conn., November 5, 1801; died New Haven, Conn., November 6, 1801.
1517. ix.   JANE DAGGETT,[7] born New Haven, Conn., October 27, 1802; died New Haven, Conn., October 28, 1802.
1518. x.   JANE CLARINDA DAGGETT,[7] born New Haven, Conn., November 3, 1803; died New Haven, Conn., August 28, 1804.
1519. xi.   FRANCES DAGGETT,[7] born New Haven, Conn., May 19, 1805; died New Haven, Conn., June 8, 1805.
1520. xii. EDWARD DAGGETT,[7] born New Haven, Conn., May 19, 1806; died New Haven, Conn., June 3, 1806.
1521. xiii. OLIVER ELLSWORTH DAGGETT,[7] born New Haven, Conn., January 14, 1810.
1522. xiv. MARY WOOSTER DAGGETT,[7] born New Haven, Conn., November 4, 1811; died New Haven, Conn., August 14, 1815.

Five children died at birth; not named.

Hon. David Daggett resided in his native town until the fall of 1779. In 1781 he went to New Haven and entered the junior class in Yale College two years in advance. He graduated in 1783 with high honor. When he took his second or master's degree, he spoke an oration of such marked excellence that it received the honor, quite unusual in that day, of publication.

Having a strong preference for the profession of the law, he commenced, soon after leaving college, the study preparatory to that profession, with Charles Chauncey, Esq., of New Haven, and continued till January, 1786, when he was admitted to the bar of New Haven county, at the age of twenty-one, and immediately entered upon practice in the town. While pursuing his legal studies under Judge Chauncey, he supported himself by performing the duties of butler in college, and of preceptor in the Hopkins Grammar School.

A few months after he was admitted to the bar, he was chosen to the office of tutor in Yale College, which he declined, being eager to pursue the practice of the profession which he had chosen.

Mr. Daggett was early called into political service.

In 1791 he was chosen to represent the town of New Haven in the General Assembly, and was annually reëlected for six years till 1797, when he was chosen a member of the Council, or Upper House. Though one of the youngest members of the House of Representatives, he soon became one of the most influential, and in 1794 he was chosen to preside over it as its speaker, at the early age of twenty-nine.

To this office he was elected year after year until he was chosen to the Council.

Mr. Daggett retained his seat in the Council for seven years, until he resigned in 1804.

In 1805 he was again a member of the House of Representatives. In 1809 he was again chosen a member of the Upper House, and continued to hold a place in that body till May, 1813, when he was chosen a senator in the Congress of the United States for six years from the preceding fourth of March. In 1811 (June) he was appointed State's attorney for the county of New Haven, and continued in that office till he resigned it when chosen senator in 1813.

At the close of his senatorial term in 1819, he returned to his extensive practice of law, which conduced much more to his private interest than had the public service of the State.

In November, 1824, he became an associate instructor of the Law School in New Haven, and in 1826 he was appointed Kent professor of law in Yale College.

In these positions he continued until, at a very advanced age, his infirmities induced him to resign them. In the autumn of 1826 he received from the corporation of Yale College the honorary degree of LL.D. In May, 1826, he was chosen an associate judge of the Superior Court of the State of Connecticut. To this office he was appointed by a Legislature in which a decided majority were opposed to him in political principles and preferences. This fact is worthy of remark on account of its strong testimony to his preëminent fitness, at that time, for that high office, and also on account of the honorable testimony which it gives respecting his political opponents, — whom he never courted, and in political conflict never spared, — that in the election to an office so responsible, so remote from political interests and strifes as that of a judge of the Supreme Court, they were willing to lay aside partisan partialities, and to be controlled by a regard to superior intellectual, legal, and moral qualifications. During the years 1828 and 1829 he was mayor of the city of New Haven.

In May, 1832, he was made chief justice of the Supreme Court. Here, again, was singular testimony to his preëminently judicial qualifications; for, contrary to the usual custom, he was appointed to that chief place notwithstanding the fact that he was not the senior in office among the judges on the bench.

Judge Daggett continued to perform the duties of that station until

December 31, 1834, when he reached seventy years of age, the limit
which the Connecticut State Constitution assigns to the judicial
office.

The eminence of Judge Daggett in his profession, and among the
public men of the State, is sufficiently attested by the many positions
of high responsibility and trust in which he was placed by the
guardians of Yale College, and by the people of New Haven and
the State; especially when we remember that the political party to
which he belonged, which was dominant in the State till he was past
middle life, and gave him the most of his honors, embraced, con-
fessedly, many of the most powerful and brilliant minds of the State;
and if we remember also that some of the highest of these trusts were
devolved upon him when his political opponents had come into power
and his own party had passed into a minority.

The features of Judge Daggett's intellectual character, his quick
and thorough insight, his well-balanced judgment and strong common
sense, his quick and ready perception of fitness, his wit and humor,
his power of varied and felicitous illustration, his ready memory, his
energy of feeling, his concentration, his clear and nervous language,
his practical knowledge of law, — these, joined to his qualities of
person and manner, his tall and commanding form, always dressed
carefully, richly, and in perfect taste, rising and dilating as he
warmed with his subject, his large and piercing eye, his expressive
brow, his strong-featured Roman face, his powerful voice ranging
through the whole scale, from a subdued yet distinct whisper till it
sounded like a trumpet call, his utterance varying from solemn delib-
eration to the vehemence of a torrent, — these qualities of mind,
person, and manner made him an advocate who, in his best days,
had, on the whole, no superior, if he had an equal, at the bar of
Connecticut.

He was a true and accomplished gentleman. He was in a very
extraordinary degree polished in his manners, gracefully and
scrupulously observant of all civilities. His courtesy was remarkable.

The religious life of Judge Daggett began with the thorough training which he received in his childhood and youth. This "nurture
and admonition of the Lord," under the parental roof, and the
memories and records of his pious ancestry, had a strong influence
upon him. He commenced his active life with great respect for religion and its ordinances. [Extract, Address Rev. S. W. S. Dutton,
New Haven, 1851.]

1130. DEXTER DAGGETT [6] (*Thomas,*[5] *Thomas,*[4] *John,*[3] *Thomas,*[2]
John [1]), born Attleboro', Mass., March 15, 1767; died Providence,

R.I. [Inventory, April 20, 1808]; married February 20, 1795, Hannah Richards; born November 29, 1767; died September 20, 1822.

Issue :

1523. i.   Thomas R. Daggett,[7] born July 2, 1798; died young.
1524. ii. Eliza Daggett,[7] born April 27, 1800; died young.
1525. iii. George W. Daggett,[7] born August 14, 1803; died young.
1526. iv. Julia A. Daggett,[7] born November 28, 1805.

1167.   Capt. Jethro Daggett [6] (*Brotherton,*[5] *Brotherton,*[4] *Joshua,*[3] *Thomas,*[2] *John* [1]), born Edgartown, Mass., October 21, 1762; married Tisbury, Mass., November 8, 1796, Hannah Cottle.

Issue :

1527. i. Susan Daggett, bapt. Edgartown, Mass., September 27, 1829.

1170.   Hon. Timothy Daggett [6] (*Brotherton,*[5] *Brotherton,*[4] *Joshua,*[3] *Thomas,*[2] *John* [1]), born Edgartown, Mass., March 23, 1768; " mariner; " died Edgartown, Mass., April 26, 1847; married Edgartown, Mass., February 9, 1797, Sally Jernigan.

Issue :

1528. i.   Isaac Daggett,[7] born Edgartown, Mass., June 25, 1798.
1529. ii. Lloyd Daggett,[7] born Edgartown, Mass., July 14, 1801; "black smith; " married; died Edgartown, Mass., November 17, 1869.
1530. iii. Charles Daggett,[7] bapt. Edgartown, Mass., September 25, 1805.
1531. iv. William Franklin Daggett,[7] bapt. Edgartown, Mass., July 10, 1808

1172.   Samuel Daggett [6] (*Thomas,*[5] *Brotherton,*[4] *Joshua,*[3] *Thomas,*[2] *John* [1]), born Tisbury, Mass., May 19, 1753; died Union Me., October 2, 1835; married Tisbury, Mass., March 13, 1777 Jedidah Butler; died Union, Me., February 21, 1830.

Issue :

1532. i.   Brotherton Daggett,[7] born Tisbury, Mass., January 4, 1778.
1533. ii.   James Daggett,[7] born Tisbury, Mass., September 9, 1779.
1534. iii. Polly Daggett,[7] born Tisbury, Mass., May 12, 1781; married Union Me., September 5, 1799, Thomas Mitchell; she died Union, Me. 1835.
1535. iv.   Jonathan Daggett,[7] born Tisbury, Mass., May 20, 1783.
1536. v.   William Daggett,[7] born Tisbury, Mass., April 9, 1785.
1537. vi.   Samuel Daggett,[7] born Union, Me., October 15, 1792.
1538. vii. Ebenezer Daggett,[7] born Union, Me., August 2, 1797.
1539. viii. Daniel Weston Daggett,[7] born Union, Me., May 19, 1800.

Samuel Daggett was selectman of the town of Union, Me., in 1791 1803, 1804, 1805, 1807. He was tithingman in 1808.

April 2, 1792, he was one of a committee to make choice of a spo for a meeting-house; April 2, 1801, one of a ministerial committee and April 1, 1805, on a committee to hire a candidate to preach May 7, 1821, the selectmen were authorized to purchase a piece o land of Samuel Daggett, provided they could obtain a sufficien quantity for a burying-ground for twenty-five dollars.

During the Revolutionary war Samuel Daggett was captured or

board a privateer and confined four months in the Jersey prison-ship
at New York. Of ninety who went on board with him, all died but
himself and eight more. November 8, 1790, he was on a committee
to look after the collection of taxes. In 1798 he was on the school
committee.

1173. THOMAS DAGGETT [6] (*Thomas,*[5] *Brotherton,*[4] *Joshua,*[3]
Thomas,[2] *John*[1]), born Tisbury, Mass., 1755; died Union, Me.,
January 13, 1822; married Tisbury, Mass., October 31, 1782,
Rebecca Luce; died Union, Me., February 6, 1832.

Issue:

1540. i. HANNAH DAGGETT,[7] born Tisbury, Mass. (?), April 14, 1783; died
Union, Me., April 23, 1826.
1541. ii. BERINTHA DAGGETT,[7] born September 11, 1786; married Union, Me.,
April 23, 1809, John Chapman Robbins; she died Union, Me.,
July 5, 1839.
1542. iii. THOMAS DAGGETT,[7] born June 4, 1788.
1543. iv. SALLY DAGGETT,[7] born Union, Me., May 6, 1790; married Union,
Me., September 20, 1818, Samuel Goodwin, of Searsmont, Me.
1544. v. EDMUND DAGGETT,[7] born Union, Me., August 23, 1792.
1545. vi. HENRY DAGGETT,[7] born Union, Me., August 3, 1794; married September 26, 1816, Meribah Jackson, of Belmont; moved to Wisconsin.
1546. vii. MATTHEW DAGGETT,[7] born Union, Me., October 1, 1798; died Union,
Me., December 10, 1798.

Thomas Daggett, of Union, Me., was made deacon of the Baptist
church in Warren, April 30, 1808. His will, dated December 20,
1821, was proved May 13, 1822.

1175. AARON DAGGETT [6] (*Thomas,*[5] *Brotherton*[4], *Joshua,*[3]
Thomas,[2] *John*[1]), "mariner;" died probably 1813, as his wife
applied for administration June 29, 1813; married Rebecca Peabody,
daughter of Stephen Peabody, of Warren, Me.

Issue:

1547. i. RUTH DAGGETT,[7] born Union, Me., January 1, 1792.
1548. ii. OLIVE DAGGETT,[7] born Union, Me., February 2, 1794.
1549. iii. MARGARET DAGGETT,[7] born Union, Me., July 17, 1796.
1550. iv. POLLY DAGGETT,[7] born Union, Me., February 23, 1798; died Union,
Me., 1802.
1551. v. AARON DAGGETT,[7] born Union, Me., April 7, 1800; died Union, Me.,
1801.
1552. vi. LUCY DAGGETT,[7] born Union, Me., November 10, 1802.
1553. vii. ELIJAH A. DAGGETT,[7] born Union, Me., March 2, 1806.
1554. viii. AARON ATHEARN DAGGETT,[7] born Union, Me., December 17, 1808.

1179. TIMOTHY DAGGETT [6] (*Timothy,*[5] *Brotherton,*[4] *Joshua,*[3]
Thomas,[2] *John*[1]), born Dighton, Mass., April 8, 1762; married
Sybil.

Issue:

1555. i. JAMES GODFREY DAGGETT,[7] born Dighton, Mass., March 13, 1800;
"carpenter;" died Providence, R.I., August 19, 1866.

1180. Tristram Daggett [6] (*Elijah,*[5] *Brotherton,*[4] *Joshua,*[3] *Thomas,*[2] *John*[1]), born August 22, 1758; died Parkman, Me., 1848; married 1st, Tisbury, Mass., September 11, 1785, Jane Merry; born November. 1761; married 2d, Industry, Me. (published October 23, 1830), Nancy Norton, widow of Sprowell Norton, and daughter of James and Betsey (Williams) Eveleth; born Salem, Mass.. January 14, 1783; died Industry, Me., April 18, 1846.

Issue :

1556. i.   Elijah Daggett,[7] born June, 1786; died young.
1557. ii.   Henry Daggett,[7] born Industry, Me., May 27, 1789.
1558. iii. Susan Daggett,[7] born Industry, Me., May 25, 1791; died Industry,
            Me., August 1808.
1559. iv.   Abigail Daggett,[7] born Industry, Me., July 22, 1793.
1560. v.   Jane Daggett,[7] born Industry, Me., March 12, 1796; died Industry,
            Me., April 27, 1861.
1561. vi.   Mathew Daggett,[7] born Industry, Me., May 9, 1797; married a
            Cleveland; he and his wife died fall of 1835.
1562. vii. Tristram Daggett,[7] born Industry, Me., June 8, 1799.
1563. viii. Timothy Daggett,[7] born Industry, Me., May 26, 1802.
1564. ix.   Isaac Daggett,[7] born Industry, Me., August 13, 1805; died Industry,
            Me., September, 1808.

Tristram Daggett, in early life, was a sailor.

He was a Revolutionary soldier under Washington. He endured much suffering, and received an honorable discharge as follows :

By his Excellency George Washington Esq General and Commander in Chief of the forces of the United States of America.

These certify that the bearer hereof Tristram Daggett soldier in the Seventh Massachusetts Regiment having faithfully served the United States and being enlisted for the war only is hereby discharged from the American Army.

Given at Head Quarters the eighth day of June 1783.

G. Washington.

By his Excellencys Command, J. Trumbull, Jr.

Registered in the Books of the Regiment. The above Tristram Daggett, soldier has been honored with a badge of merit for 5 yrs. faithful service.

J. Brooks, L⁺ Col. Com. 7ᵗʰ Mass. Regt.

Mr. Daggett was one of the original purchasers of the township of New Vineyard, Me., and drew his one hundred acres east of the New Vineyard mountains, in the first range adjoining the Lowell strip, and was the first to commence operations for a settlement in that quarter.

In June, 1791, he procured a back-load of provisions at the settlement at the river, now Farmington, and went to the gore by the path, where he got Mr. Collins to pilot him up the mountain to the town line, which had then been newly marked by spotted trees, with the corners of the lots marked, and numbered on the line.

Thence he proceeded afoot and alone, with his pack on his back and his axe in his hand, noticing the numbers of the lots until he came to his lot, where he made a temporary camp near a spring, and commenced cutting down the trees to make a farm. He often said he never enjoyed himself better in his life than when thus employed. Mr. Daggett built a log house, into which he moved the next year, and remained there three years, when he sold his new farm to Charles Luce, and moved on the Lowell strip, now Industry, Me.

He was an honest, well-meaning man, and worked hard as long as he was able.

He sold the farm which he made on the Lowell strip to David Luce, settled on a lot near by, and then on a small lot near West's Mills. In his old age, he moved to the town of Parkman, where he died.

1181. Elijah Daggett[6] (*Elijah,[5] Brotherton,[4] Joshua,[3] Thomas,[2] John[1]*), "mariner;" died either at sea or Martha's Vineyard; married Tisbury, Mass., April 4, 1787, Peggy Smith, daughter of Captain Smith; died about August 1, 1812.

Issue:

1565. i.   Love Daggett,[7] born Martha's Vineyard, Mass.; married May 14, 1812, Samuel C. Leeman, son of Jacob and Keziah (Chapman) Leeman, of Stark, Me.
1566. ii.   Lucinda Daggett,[7] born Martha's Vineyard, Mass.
1567. iii. Elijah Daggett,[7] born Martha's Vineyard, Mass.; married and resided New York city; mariner on packet between New York and Liverpool.
1568. iv.   Sarah Daggett,[7] born Martha's Vineyard, Mass., December 7, 1792.
1569. v.   Matthew Daggett,[7] enlisted in 1813 for remainder of war; died unmarried, Lake Ontario, about 1814.
1570. vi.   Margaret Daggett,[7] born Martha's Vineyard; married Mr. Tucker from Virginia; resided Falmouth, Mass.; died young; one child.
1571. vii. Samuel S. Daggett,[7] born Tisbury, Mass., 1799.

Mrs. Daggett married, April 16, 1812, Deacon Levi Greenleaf, of Industry.

1182. Capt. Matthew Daggett[6] (*Elijah,[5] Brotherton,[4] Joshua,[3] Thomas,[2] John[1]*), born Tisbury, Mass., 1764; died Warren, Me., October 15, 1831; married Tisbury, Mass., March 28, 1788, Rebecca Daggett, daughter of Thomas and Rebecca (Athearn) Daggett (No. 1176); born Tisbury, Mass., 1765; died Warren, Me., October 16, 1848.

Issue:

1572. i.   Matthew Daggett,[7] born December 16, 1789.
1573. ii.   Thomas Daggett,[7] born June, 1791.
1574. iii. Sebastian C. Daggett,[7] born December, 1792.
1575. iv.   Frederick Daggett,[7] born Warren, Me., December 21, 1794; died at sea; "unmarried."
1576. v.   Nancy Athearn Daggett,[7] born Warren, Me., December 1, 1799.

Captain Daggett went to Warren, Me., about 1798, and purchased an estate. He was employed as master of various vessels in the coasting and foreign trade till his death in 1831.

1186. JAMES DAGGETT [6] (*Jethro,*[5] *Brotherton,*[4] *Joshua,*[3] *Thomas,*[2] *John*[1]), born Newport, R.I., 1770; married Dighton, Mass., June 21, 1792, by Ezra Richmond, J.P., to Sibble Babcock; born Swansea, Mass.

Issue:

1577. i. TIMOTHY DAGGETT,[7] born Dighton, Mass., March 31, 1793.
1578. ii. THOMAS GILBERT DAGGETT,[7] born Dighton, Mass., March 2, 1795.
1579. iii. EBENEZER DAGGETT,[7] born Dighton, Mass., November 11, 1798; died Rehoboth, Mass., May 6, 1877.
1580. iv. JETHRO DAVIS DAGGETT,[7] born Rehoboth, Mass., August 27, 1802.

November 2, 1784, John Whitmarsh appointed guardian of James Daggett, son of Jethro Daggett, late of Newport, R.I. [Bristol Probate.]

April 17, 1792, Timothy Daggett, for James Daggett, requests the judge of probate to allow the account of John Whitmarsh, of Dighton. [Bristol Probate.]

1192. LYDIA DAGGETT [6] (*Nathan,*[5] *Jacob,*[4] *Joshua,*[3] *Thomas,*[2] *John*[1]), born Nantucket, Mass., 9–1–1758; married Nantucket, Mass., July 8, 1773, by Rev. B. Shaw, to John House, from Newfoundland; born 8–6–1747; died Nantucket, Mass., 5–30–1816.

Issue:

1581. i. WILLIAM DAGGETT HOUSE,[7] born Nantucket, Mass., 2–28–1779; married Janet Coleman, daughter of Solomon and Mehitable Coleman.
1582. ii. BETSEY HOUSE,[7] born Nantucket, Mass., 12–24–1785; married 1st, Gotham Alley; 2d, William Archer; 3d, George Manter.
1583. iii. TIMOTHY DAGGETT HOUSE,[7] born Nantucket, Mass., 9–28–1788.
1584. iv. LYDIA HOUSE,[7] born Nantucket, Mass., 3–12–1792; married David Ellis, son of Simeon and Charity Ellis.
1585. v. POLLY HOUSE,[7] born Nantucket, Mass., 7–12–1794; married Shubael Swain, son of Joshua Swain.
1586. vi. SALLY HOUSE,[7] born Nantucket, Mass., 12–3–1798; married Stephen Rice, son of Stephen Rice.
1587. vii. PEGGY HOUSE.[7]
1588. viii. HEPSABETH HOUSE.[7]

1194. PETER DAGGETT [6] (*Ebenezer,*[5] [*John,*[4] *Joseph,*[3] *Joseph,*[2] *John*[1]](?)), born Martha's Vineyard, January 17, 1770; died Industry, Me., November 5, 1833; married 1st, Tisbury, Mass., December 1, 1791, Damaris Luce, daughter of Jonathan and Urana (Luce) Luce; born Martha's Vineyard, October 30, 1764; died Industry, Me., August 3, 1810; married 2d (published February 27, 1811), Hannah Snow, widow of Ezekiel Snow, and daughter of Paul and Jael (Bennett) Pratt; born 1775; died New Vineyard, Me., December 14, 1862.

Issue:

1589. i. WILLIAM DAGGETT,[7] born Tisbury, Mass., August 8, 1792.
1590. ii. PLAMENTIN DAGGETT,[7] born Industry, Me., May 5, 1795.

1591. iii.   JONATHAN LUCE DAGGETT,[7] born Industry, Me., October 11, 1797.
1592. iv.   LEANDER DAGGETT,[7] born Industry, Me., May 15, 1799.
1593. v.   ALBERT DAGGETT,[7] born Industry, Me., July 8, 1801.
1594. vi.   BETSEY DAGGETT,[7] born Industry, Me., February 7, 1804; married
             1st, April 13, 1826, Samuel Green, of Wilton; married 2d, Mr.
             Gower; issue: Augustus Green;[8] resides Elkader, Kansas (1893).
1595. vii.   PETER DAGGETT,[7] born Industry, Me., 1807; died Industry, Me.,
             November 23, 1810.
1596. viii. LAVINA DAGGETT,[7] born Industry, Me., March 23, 1812.

Mr. Daggett came from New Vineyard to Industry about 1798, and
settled on the "Lowell Strip." He was a member of the Methodist
church, and the leader of the class in his neighborhood for many
years. He built on his lot the first frame house erected in Industry
Plantation, and became in time a well-to-do farmer.

1195. AARON DAGGETT[6] (*Ebenezer,*[5] [*John,*[4] *Joseph,*[3] *Joseph,*[2]
John[1]](?)), settled in Hallowell, Me.; married March 2, 1796,
Susanna Hillman, of New Vineyard.

Mr. Daggett was in trade in Industry, 1810–12.

1197. HANNAH DAGGETT[6] (*Ebenezer,*[5] [*John,*[4] *Joseph,*[3] *Joseph,*[2]
John[1]](?)), born Martha's Vineyard, September 21, 1776; died
Industry, Me., May 4, 1807; married Farmington, Me., June 21,
1796, Rowland Luce, son of Daniel and Elizabeth (Merry) Luce,
"farmer;" born Sharon, Conn., March 13, 1776; died Industry,
Me., December 22, 1862.

Issue:

1597. i.   JONATHAN LUCE,[7] born Industry, Me., December 12, 1797.
1598. ii.   LEONARD LUCE,[7] born Industry, Me., November 17, 1799.
1599. iii. ELIZA LUCE,[7] born Industry, Me., November 30, 1801.
1600. iv.   HANNAH LUCE,[7] born Industry, Me., July 22, 1804.

1198. JOHN DAGGETT[6] (*John,*[5] [*John,*[4] *Joseph,*[3] *Joseph,*[2]
John[1]](?)), born Martha's Vineyard, 1758; died New Vineyard,
Me., October 26, 1840; married (published October 25, 1814) Love
Benson, widow of Charles Benson and daughter of Samuel and
Sarah (Chesley) Pinkham.

Issue:

1601. i.   JOHN DAGGETT,[7] born New Vineyard, Me.; died in infancy.
1602. ii.   SARAH DAGGETT,[7] born New Vineyard, Me., January 5, 1816.
1603. iii. JOHN ATWELL DAGGETT,[7] born New Vineyard, Me., August 24, 1819.
1604. iv.   DEBORAH DAGGETT,[7] born New Vineyard, Me., April 29, 1822; mar-
            ried April 9, 1844, Josiah Tinkham, son of Ariel and Susan (Bray)
            Tinkham, of Anson. Mr. Tinkham is a farmer, and resides Anson,
            Me. (1892).
1605. v.   LOVE DAGGETT[7]; married Capt. Chas. H. Beck, of Augusta, Me.
1606. vi.   WILLIAM RILEY DAGGETT,[7] born New Vineyard, Me.
1607. vii. WARREN DAGGETT,[7] born New Vineyard, Me., May 1, 1829.
1608. viii. ANN CORDELIA DAGGETT,[7] born New Vineyard, Me., March 6, 1838.

John Daggett was a sailor prior to his marriage; afterward a farmer.

JOHN DOGGETT, OF MARTHA'S VINEYARD.

SEVENTH GENERATION.

1208. JEFFERSON DAGGETT[7] (*Jacob,*[6] *Daniel,*[5] *Israel,*[4] *Joseph,*[3] *John,*[2] *John*[1]), born Rehoboth, Mass., November 30, 1800; "farmer;" died Pawtucket, R.I., January, 1870; married Seekonk, Mass., March 14, 1827, by Rev. B. Pearse, to Hannah Dorman Daggett, daughter of Israel and Lucy (Bicknell) Daggett (No. 1203); born Rehoboth, Mass., April 23, 1805; died Pawtucket, R.I., April 2, 1892.

Issue :

1609. i. ELISABETH FRANCES DAGGETT,[8] born Seekonk, Mass., January 9, 1828; resides Pawtucket, R.I. (1892).

1610. ii. EDWIN OSCAR DAGGETT,[8] born Seekonk, Mass., March 5, 1829.

1611. iii. ANNA JUDSON DAGGETT,[8] born Seekonk, Mass., March 12, 1830.

1612. iv. LUCY BICKNELL DAGGETT,[8] born Pawtucket, R.I., August 4, 1831; died Pawtucket, R.I., October 9, 1831.

1613. v. ALBERT AUGUSTUS DAGGETT,[8] born Pawtucket, R.I., December 27, 1832; died Pawtucket, R.I., September 12, 1833.

1614. vi. ISRAEL ALBERT DAGGETT,[8] born Pawtucket, R.I., February 5, 1834; died Pawtucket, R.I., June 20, 1837.

1615. vii. MARY KNOWLTON DAGGETT,[8] born Pawtucket, R.I., April 29, 1837.

1616. viii. ISRAEL R. DAGGETT,[8] born Pawtucket, R.I., June 24, 1838; died Pawtucket, R.I., October 8, 1838.

Mr. Daggett was well known in Pawtucket. For years he lived on what is known as the "Daggett farm," near the Ten-mile river, and his widow had resided there since his death.

She was wont to say that she had "lived in three towns and two States, and not moved from the house."

The farm was originally in Rehoboth, Mass., but when that town was divided, this portion of the town became Seekonk. Later Seekonk was divided, and this portion became the old town of Pawtucket, in Massachusetts. In 1863, when the boundary line between Rhode Island and Massachusetts was adjusted, Pawtucket was set off to Rhode Island, and thus she moved into another State. Since then she had seen the old town of Pawtucket annexed to a portion of North Providence, and became the new town of Pawtucket, and then the town made a city. Mrs. Daggett was a life-long member of the Pawtucket Congregational church.

1211. JACOB DAGGETT[7] (*Jacob,*[6] *Daniel,*[5] *Israel,*[4] *Joseph,*[3] *John,*[2] *John*[1]), born Seekonk, Mass., December 28, 1807; "house carpenter;" died Seekonk, Mass., August 29, 1890; married Pawtucket, R.I., February 2, 1834, Juliana Ide, daughter of Edward

and Betsy (Carpenter) Ide; born Seekonk, Mass., August 13, 1809;
died Seekonk, Mass., May 12, 1892.

Issue:

1617. i.   JACOB THEODORE DAGGETT,[8] born Pawtucket, R.I., April 6, 1837;
            died Pawtucket, R.I., October 19, 1838.
1618. ii.   ELLEN ELIZABETH DAGGETT,[8] born Pawtucket, R.I., July 5, 1839;
            died Pawtucket, R.I., August 3, 1839.
1519. iii. ALBERT BRIDGMAN DAGGETT,[8] born Pawtucket, R.I., June 13, 1842;
            ided Pawtucket, R.I., July 23, 1843.
1620. iv.   JOSEPHINE DAGGETT,[8] born Pawtucket, R.I., December 14, 1844;
            resides Pawtucket, R.I. (1892).
1621. v.   ANN ELIZABETH DAGGETT,[8] born Pawtucket, R.I., October 2, 1846.
1622. vi.   HERBERT SIDNEY DAGGETT,[8] born Pawtucket, R.I., July 3, 1849.
1623. vii. ADAH DAGGETT,[8] born Pawtucket, R.I., March 16, 1856; died See-
            konk, Mass., November 7, 1881.

1212.   SAMUEL SLACK DAGGETT [7] (*Jacob*,[6] *Daniel*,[5] *Israel*,[4] *Joseph*,[3]
John,[2] *John* [1]), born Seekonk, Mass., July 9, 1809; died Pawtucket,
R.I., April 29, 1887; married East Greenwich, R.I., June 8, 1845,
by Rev. John H. Baker, to Matilda Cochie Sheldon, daughter of
William James and Sarah (Tillinghast) Sheldon; born West Green-
wich, R.I., September 2, 1817.

Issue:

1624. i.   SAMUEL SHELDON DAGGETT,[8] born Pawtucket, R.I., May 23, 1848.
1625. ii.   WILLIAM JAMES DAGGETT,[8] born Pawtucket, R.I., January 9, 1851.
1626. iii. SARAH MATILDA DAGGETT,[8] born Pawtucket, R.I., August 25, 1853.

1215.   REUBEN DAGGETT [7] (*Reuben*,[6] *Reuben*,[5] *Nathaniel*,[4] *Nathaniel*.[3] *John*,[2] *John* [1]), born Westmoreland, N.H., February 19,
1781; removed to Cattaraugus county, N.Y.; married Westmoreland,
N.H., March 3, 1800, by Rev. Allen Pratt, to Jennie Briggs.

Issue:

1627. i.   LOREN DAGGETT,[8] lived in Cattaraugus county, N.Y.
1628. ii.   NELSON DAGGETT.[8]
1629. iii. REUBEN DAGGETT.[8]

1216.   CHLOE DAGGETT [7] (*Reuben*,[6] *Reuben*,[5] *Nathaniel*,[4] *Nathaniel*,[3] *John*,[2] *John* [1]), born Westmoreland, N.H., July 20, 1783;
died June, 1842; married Miller Vaughn; died June, 1842.

Issue: five children.

1630. i.   MARY VAUGHN,[8] married Mr. Gifford; resides Wellsboro', Pa. (1892).

1217.   ESTHER DAGGETT [7] (*Reuben*,[6] *Reuben*,[5] *Nathaniel*,[4] *Nathaniel*,[3] *John*,[2] *John* [1]), born Westmoreland, N.H., December 26,
1785; died Cooper's Plains, N.Y., about 1852; married John
Franklin.

Issue:

1631. i.   RUFUS FRANKLIN,[8] resides Cooper's Plains, N.Y. (1892).
1632. ii.   KESIAH FRANKLIN,[8] married Mr. Bidler; resides Caton, Steuben county,
            N.Y. (1892).

1219. Seth Daggett [7] (*Reuben,* [6] *Reuben,* [5] *Nathaniel,* [4] *Nathaniel,* [3] *John,* [2] *John* [1]), born Westmoreland, N.H., July 3, 1790; died Tioga, Tioga county, Pa., January 2, 1874; married near Utica, N.Y., October 10, 1810, Eunice Allen, daughter of Joseph and Eunice (Kingsley) Allen; born Barnstable, Mass., March 15, 1790; died Tioga, Pa., March 22, 1864.

Issue:

1633. i.   Allen Daggett,[8] born Jackson, Tioga county, Pa., October 6, 1811.
1634. ii. George Daggett,[8] born Jackson, Pa., July 30, 1813.
1635. iii. Lewis Daggett,[8] born Jackson, Pa., May 5, 1816.
1636. iv. Clymena E. Daggett,[8] born Jackson, Pa., March 16, 1818.
1637. v.   Minerva Daggett,[8] born Jackson, Pa., May 19, 1822.
1638. vi. Rowena Daggett,[8] born Jackson, Pa., March 2, 1824.
1639. vii. Richard Daggett,[8] born Jackson, Pa., June 28, 1827; died Tioga, Pa., February 11, 1846.
1640. viii. Mary Ann Daggett,[8] born Tioga, Pa., September 11, 1829.
1641. ix. Charlotte Daggett,[8] born Jackson, Pa., July 8, 1831; died Tioga, Pa., December 10, 1849.

Major Seth Daggett married Eunice Allen, a niece of Samuel Allen, who was defeated on the Democratic ticket for governor of Massachusetts. Soon after their marriage they removed to Tioga county, where Major Daggett became widely known and much respected.

He was made major of militia, and served one or two terms as sheriff of the county.

He engaged extensively in lumbering, and at one time owned large tracts of land.

The family lived in Jackson township, Tioga county, Daggett's Mills Post-office.

1220. Saloma Daggett [7] (*Reuben,* [6] *Reuben,* [5] *Nathaniel,* [4] *Nathaniel,* [3] *John,* [2] *John* [1]), born Westmoreland, N.H., July 3, 1790; died Rutland, Pa., spring of 1855; married 1st, near Elmira, N.Y., 1809, William Keyes, son of Peabody and Persis (Brook) Keyes; born Princeton, Mass.; died Wells, Pa., June, 1813; married 2d, Jackson, Pa., 1815, Alexander Harris, and moved to Vermont.

Issue:

1642. i.   Seth Q. Keyes,[8] born Jackson, Pa., July 3, 1810.
1643. ii. William B. Keyes,[8] born Jackson, Pa., March 16, 1812.
1644. iii. Abel Harris,[8] resides Plainfield, Wis. (1892).
1645. iv. Diadaura Harris,[8] married Mr. Soper; resides Rutland, Pa. (1892).
1646. v.   Polly Harris,[8] married Mr. Baker; resides Jackson, Pa. (1892).
1647. vi. Saloma Harris,[8] married Mr. Rosell.

And three other children.

1221. Rufus Daggett [7] (*Reuben,* [6] *Reuben,* [5] *Nathaniel,* [4] *Nathaniel,* [3] *John,* [2] *John* [1]), born Westmoreland, N.H., December 3,

1792; died January 31, 1835; married January 8, 1817, Hannah
Sharp; born 1796; died Daggett's Mills, Pa., February 26, 1883.

Issue:

1648. i.   WILLIAM DAGGETT,[8] born Pennsylvania, December 26, 1817.
1649. ii.   RUFUS DAGGETT,[8] born Pennsylvania, February 25, 1819.
1650. iii. HANNAH DAGGETT,[8] born Pennsylvania, November 21, 1821; married
            March 18, 1841, Runalds Sixbee.
1651. iv.   LUCINDA DAGGETT,[8] born Pennsylvania, December 28, 1823; married
            September 10, 1840, Charles Lefler.
1652. v.   CRONELUS C. DAGGETT,[8] born Pennsylvania, August 5, 1825.
1653. vi.   SALLY DAGGETT,[8] born Pennsylvania, April 25, 1827; married No-
            vember, 1849, Samuel Crip.
1654. vii. LANEY DAGGETT,[8] born Pennsylvania, November 30, 1828; married
            September 18, 1850, Lyman Burton.
1655. viii. MARANDA DAGGETT,[8] born Pennsylvania, November 18, 1833; married
            February 12, 1854, Furnam Lucas.

1223. LYDIA DAGGETT[7] (*Reuben*,[6] *Reuben*,[5] *Nathaniel*,[4] *Nathaniel*,[3] *John*,[2] *John*[1]), born Westmoreland, N.H., October 16,
1797; died Jackson, Pa., November 20, 1843; married Jackson,
Pa., 1817, John Conable, son of John and Lydia (Stebbins) Conable; born Leyden, Mass., April 19, 1797; died Jackson, Pa.,
August 5, 1839.

Issue:

1656. i.   EMILY BELINDA CONABLE,[8] born Jackson, Pa., January 24, 1818.
1657. ii.   SQUIRE MAXWELL CONABLE,[8] born Litchfield, N.Y., February 24,
            1820; married 1st, Sarah Sophronia Stowell; married 2d, Sabina
            Ann Crippen; resides Pike, Pa. (1892).
1658. iii. LYDIA SOPHRONIA CONABLE,[8] born Jackson, Pa., July 29, 1822; mar-
            ried John W. Joslin, M.D.
1659. iv.   CLARINDA CONABLE,[8] born Friendship, N.Y., July 5, 1824; married
            Jackson, Pa., December 25, 1842, Daniel Cornwell; he resides
            Plainfield, Wis. (1886); she died Pine Grove, Wis., May 15, 1860.
1660. v.   ELMIRA MATILDA CONABLE,[8] born Fredonia, N.Y., September 14,
            1826; "teacher;" died Jackson, Pa., November 11, 1852.
1661. vi.   JULIA CONABLE,[8] born Jackson, Pa., August 10, 1828; "teacher;"
            died Jackson, Pa., December 14, 1851.
1662. vii. SETH CONABLE,[8] born Jackson, Pa., September 21, 1835; married
            Sarah Ann Burrows.

Mr. Conable removed with his parents, when he was about thirteen years old, to Litchfield, Herkimer county, N.Y. He enlisted in
the war of 1812, at or near Litchfield, about October 1, 1814, under
Captain Bellinger, in Colonel Myers's regiment of New York militia,
and was discharged at Sackett's Harbor, N.Y., in the following
December.

1225. RUFUS DAGGETT[7] (*Daniel*,[6] *Reuben*,[5] *Nathaniel*,[4] *Nathaniel*,[3] *John*,[2] *John*[1]), born 1793; died New York, 1842; married
Esther Dexter; born 1796.

Issue:

1663. i.   GEORGE DAGGETT.[8]
1664. ii.   CYRUS DAGGETT.[8]

1665. iii. Rufus Daggett.[8]
1666. iv. Susan Daggett,[8] married Mr. Perkins; resides Unadilla Forks, N.Y.

1232. Serel N. Daggett [7] (*Daniel,[6] Reuben,[5] Nathaniel,[4] Nathaniel,[3] John,[2] John [1]*), born Burrillville, R.I., 1812; "laborer;" resided Glocester, R.I. (1839); married Glocester, R.I., October 2, 1831, by Elder Andrew Stone, to Susan Logee, daughter of Elisha and Jerusha Logee, of Burrillville, R.I.; born Burrillville, R.I., December 4, 1814.
Issue:
1667. i. Thomas W. Dorr Daggett,[8] born Seekonk, Mass., January 5, 1849.

1234. Keziah Daggett [7] (*Levi,[6] John,[5] John,[4] Nathaniel,[3] John,[2] John [1]*), born Rehoboth, Mass., November 16, 1790; married Seekonk, Mass., March 1, 1818, by Rev. John Pitman, to Alfred Barnes, of Barrington, son of Samuel and Hannah (Peck) Barnes; born Barrington, R.I.; died Barrington, R.I.
Issue:
1668. i. Thomas Barnes,[8] resides California (1892).

1235. John Daggett [7] (*Levi,[6] John,[5] John,[4] Nathaniel,[3] John,[2] John [1]*), born Rehoboth, Mass., April 20, 1792; "farmer;" died Seekonk, Mass., December 11, 1857; married 1st, Seekonk, Mass., September 3, 1823, by Bartlett Pearse, to Amey Cole, daughter of Joseph and Rachel (Braley) Cole; born Rehoboth, Mass., March 16, 1792; died Seekonk, Mass., August 3, 1826; married 2d, Barrington, R.I., September 3, 1827, Hannah Barnes, daughter of Samuel and Hannah (Peck) Barnes; born Barrington, R.I., March 22, 1782; died Seekonk, Mass., December 1, 1860.
Issue:
1669. i. William Daggett,[8] born Seekonk, Mass., June 19, 1824.

1237. Hannah Daggett [7] (*Levi,[6] John,[5] John,[4] Nathaniel,[3] John,[2] John [1]*), born Rehoboth, Mass., January 19, 1796; died Providence, R.I., 1871; married 1st, Joseph Cole, son of Joseph and Rachel (Braley) Cole; born Rehoboth, Mass.; died Seekonk, Mass.; married 2d, Thomas Cole, son of Joseph and Rachel (Braley) Cole; born Rehoboth, Mass.; died Seekonk, Mass.
Issue:
1670. i. Thomas Cole.[8]
1671. ii. Rachel Cole,[9] born March, 1819; married Whiting Baker; resides West Dedham, Mass. (1892); has son Edwin W. Baker.[9]
1672. iii. Allen Cole.[8]
1673. iv. Joseph Cole.[8]
1674. v. —— Cole.[8]
1675. vi. Levi Cole.[8]
1676. vii. Betsey Cole.[8]

1677. viii. AMEY COLE.[8]
1678. ix.   BENJAMIN COLE.[8]
1679. x.   FRANCIS COLE,[8] living (1892).
1680. xi.   —— COLE,[8] died in infancy.
1681. xii.   —— COLE,[8] died in infancy.

1240.   LYDIA DAGGETT[7] (*Levi,[6] John,[5] John,[4] Nathaniel,[3] John,[2] John[1]*), born Rehoboth, Mass., April 10, 1801; died Barrington, R.I., 1874; married Alfred Barnes, of Barrington, son of Samuel and Hannah (Peck) Barnes; born Barrington, R.I.; died Barrington, R.I.

Issue:

1682. i.   JOHN BARNES,[8] born Barrington, R.I.; resides there (1892).
1683. ii.   KEZIAH BARNES,[8] born Barrington. R.I.
1684. iii.   LYDIA BARNES,[8] born Barrington, R.I.
1685. iv.   SAMUEL BARNES,[8] born Barrington, R.I.
1686. v.   ALFRED BARNES,[8] born Barrington, R.I.
1687. vi.   HANNAH BARNES,[8] born Barrington, R.I.
1688. vii.   LEVI D. BARNES,[8] born Barrington, R.I.; resides Providence, R.I. (1892).
1689. viii.   MILLIE BARNES,[8] born Barrington, R.I.

1242.   PRESTON DAGGETT[7] (*Robert,[6] James,[5] John,[4] Nathaniel,[3] John,[2] John[1]*), born Rehoboth, Mass., November 27, 1784; married Rehoboth, Mass., February 23, 1806, by J. Hills, to Nancy Read.

Issue:

1690. i.   PRESTON DAGGETT,[8] born 1807; "carpenter;" died Providence, R.I., 1876.

1246.   ROBERT DAGGETT[7] (*Robert,[6] James,[5] John,[4] Nathaniel,[3] John,[2] John[1]*), born Rehoboth, Mass., September 13, 1793; died Seekonk, Mass., March, 1831; married Seekonk, Mass., February 17, 1814, by Rev. John Mills, to Mary Botton; born Connecticut, December 8, 1791; died Seekonk, Mass., February 8, 1850.

Issue:

1691. i.   FANNY MARIA DAGGETT,[8] married Seekonk, Mass., April 15, 1858, James Bicknell, son of Joshua Bicknell.
1692. ii.   DAVID ALDRICH DAGGETT,[8] possibly died before 1831.
1693. iii.   LOUISA DAGGETT.[8]
1694. iv.   ABBY DAGGETT.[8]
1695. v.   PHILA ALDRICH DAGGETT.[8]
1696. vi.   CAROLINE AMELIA DAGGETT,[8] born Seekonk, Mass., 1826; married Seekonk, Mass., September 14, 1848, by Rev. James A. Barney, to John A. Woodworth, of Fall River, "laborer."

1253.   ELLEN V. DAGGETT[7] (*Henry,[6] James,[5] John,[4] Nathaniel,[3] John,[2] John[1]*), born Seekonk, Mass., 1843; resides Rehoboth, Mass. (1876); married 2d, Rehoboth, Mass., November 16, 1876, by Samuel Farley, to Thomas Parker, son of Adam and Lydia Parker; "farmer;" born North Providence, R.I., 1841.

Issue:

1697. i.   DAUGHTER ——, born Berkley, Mass., December 2, 1869.

1273.   Capt. William Daggett[7] (*William*,[6] *Seth*,[5] *Samuel*,[4] *Thomas*,[3] *Thomas*,[2] *John*[1]), born Tisbury, Mass., August, 1773; "mariner;" died Tisbury, Mass., June 17, 1858; married Tisbury, Mass., February 11, 1796, Jane Daggett, daughter of Isaac and Rebecca (Tobey) Daggett (No. 1272); born Tisbury, Mass., June 6, 1778.

Issue :

1698. i.   William Daggett,[8] born Tisbury, Mass., February 20, 1797.
1699. ii.   Jane Daggett,[8] born Tisbury, Mass., February 12, 1799.
1700. iii. Isaac Daggett,[8] born Tisbury, Mass., March 7, 1801; "farmer;" married Abigail Robinson; no issue; died Tisbury, Mass., March 10, 1876.
1701. iv.   Dolly Bacon Daggett,[8] born Tisbury, Mass., January 12, 1803.
1702. v.   Henry Bacon Daggett,[8] born Tisbury, Mass., January 22, 1807; died Tisbury, Mass., March 30, 1807.
1703. vi.   Abigail Daggett,[8] born Tisbury, Mass., March 30, 1808.
1704. vii. Henry Daggett,[8] born Tisbury, Mass., February 8, 1811.
1705. viii. Ariadne Daggett.[8]
1706. ix.   Edward Daggett.[8]
1707. x.   Emily Brush Daggett.[8]

1274.   Capt. Seth Daggett[7] (*William*,[6] *Seth*,[5] *Samuel*,[4] *Thomas*,[3] *Thomas*,[2] *John*[1]), born Tisbury, Mass., March 7, 1780; "pilot;" died Tisbury, Mass., October 7, 1867; married Tisbury, Mass., February 28, 1799, Mary Dunham, daughter of David and Content (Luce) Dunham; died before 1867.

Issue :

1708. i.   Leander Daggett,[8] born Tisbury, Mass., January 8, 1800; "captain;" married 1821 (intention September 9), Almira Luce, of New Sharon, Me.
1709. ii.   Edwin Daggett,[8] born Tisbury, Mass., July 3, 1802; died 1821.
1710. iii. Augustus Frederick Daggett,[8] born 1804.
1711. iv.   Augustus Chandler Ludlow Daggett,[8] born 1806.
1712. v.   Mary Daggett,[8] born Tisbury, Mass., May 8, 1808; married December 10, 1827, Edward Hatch.
1713. vi.   Alonzo Daggett,[8] born Tisbury, Mass., November 19, 1810.
1714. vii. Alphonso Seth Daggett.[8]
1715. viii. Alphonso Seth Daggett.[8]
1716. ix.   Oscar Daggett,[8] born Tisbury, Mass., October, 1815.
1717. x.   Caroline West Daggett,[8] born December 15, 1818.
1718. xi.   Georgiana Daggett,[8] born Tisbury, Mass., December 7, 1827.

1275.   Peter Daggett[7] (*William*,[6] *Seth*,[5] *Samuel*,[4] *Thomas*,[3] *Thomas*,[2] *John*[1]), born Tisbury, Mass., 1780; "pilot;" died Tisbury, Mass., May 4, 1854; married Tisbury, Mass., February 18, 1803, Martha Luce, daughter of Timothy Luce.

Issue :

1719. i.   Mary Daggett,[8] married Thomas Dunham.
1720. ii.   Elenora Daggett,[8] married James S. West.
1721. iii. Patty Daggett.[8]
1722. iv.   Albima Daggett,[8] married Joseph C. Fish.
1723. v.   Martha Daggett,[8] born Tisbury, Mass., 1825; married William Sprague; she died Tisbury, Mass., September 21, 1870.
1724. vi.   Philander Daggett,[8] married Sophia Jane Cook.
1725. vii. Harmonia Daggett,[8] married Robert Lewin.

1279. Sylvanus Daggett [7] (*William*,[6] *Seth*,[5] *Samuel*,[4] *Thomas*,[3] *Thomas*,[2] *John* [1]), married Mary Luce, daughter of Abijah Luce.

Issue :

1726. i. John Luce Daggett,[8] born Holmes Hole, Mass., April 27, 1809 ; died Boston, Mass., May 8, 1871.

1280. Betsey Daggett [7] (*Peter*,[6] *Seth*,[5] *Samuel*,[4] *Thomas*,[3] *Thomas*,[2] *John* [1]), born 1758 ; died Harwich, Mass., May 19, 1833 ; married Harwich, Mass., April 8, 1775, William Eldridge, Esq., of Harwich.

Issue :

1727. i. Peter Daggett Eldridge.[8]
1728. ii. Daughter —— Eldridge,[8] born 1788.

1282. Isaac Daggett [7] (*Peter*,[6] *Seth*,[5] *Samuel*,[4] *Thomas*,[3] *Thomas*,[2] *John* [1]), married Jane West.

Issue : five sons, three daughters.

Isaac Daggett is said to have been quite original, and his branch have quoted for the writer some of his impromptu verse, of which is the following :

> Amidst the wood bold Isaac stood,
>   And gave his axe a wheel ;
> The boughs did bend, and the trees did rend,
>   And off the bark would peel ;
> The messmates gone, and the wheel went round,
>   And you are left to keep the ground,
> And those lofty hills which we do spy.
> Are made to please the Almighty's eye :
> On us for sin to cast a stain,
> Go up the hill against the grain.
>   Get up old Hoss.

> Jane West my true and loving wife,
> The joy and comfort of my life ;
> I have by you and you by me,
> Five pretty sons and daughters three ;
> Likewise in wealth we have our share,
> As well in health as others are ;
> Beef, Pork, and Mutton is our meat,
> Sometimes roast turkeys we can eat,
> Pumpkin for sauce, and if that won't do,
> Use Turnips and Potatoes too.

1284. Capt. Samuel Daggett [7] (*Samuel*,[6] *Seth*,[5] *Samuel*,[4] *Thomas*,[3] *Thomas*,[2] *John* [1]), born Tisbury, Mass., July 11, 1764 ; died Tisbury, Mass., September 23, 1860 ; married Tisbury, Mass., October 3, 1790, Rebecca Daggett, daughter of Isaac and Rebecca (Tobey) Daggett (No. 1269) ; born Tisbury, Mass., June 16, 1773 ; died Holmes Hole, Mass., September 23, 1832.

Issue :

1729. i.   Sarah Daggett,[8] born Vineyard Haven, Mass., December 29, 1791.
1730. ii.   Isaac Daggett,[8] born New Vineyard, Me., August 5, 1794.

1731. iii. REBECCA DAGGETT,[8] born New Vineyard, Me., November 25, 1796; married William Daggett (see No. 1698).
1732. iv. SAMUEL DAGGETT,[8] born New Vineyard, Me., December 24, 1798.
1733. v. ABIGAIL DAGGETT,[8] born New Vineyard, Me., May 25, 1800; died New Vineyard, Me., November, 1800.
1734. vi. ABIGAIL DAGGETT,[8] born New Vineyard, Me., November 16, 1802; died Vineyard Haven, Mass., October 27, 1827.
1735. vii. MARY MERRY DAGGETT,[8] born New Vineyard, Me., May 7, 1805; died Vineyard Haven, Mass., January 28, 1821.
1736. viii. JOHN TOBEY DAGGETT,[8] born New Vineyard, Me., September 29, 1807.
1737. ix. BRADFORD BRUSH DAGGETT,[8] born Vineyard Haven, Mass., April 15, 1812; "whaleman;" sailed from New York, October 3, 1846; not since heard from.
1738. x. AMANDA MALVINA DAGGETT,[8] born Vineyard Haven, Mass., August 4, 1815.

Captain Samuel Daggett went to New Vineyard, now a part of Industry, Me., in 1794, and settled there with his father. Fourteen years afterward he returned to Martha's Vineyard, and resumed his former occupation, a pilot, at Holmes Hole. He was a Revolutionary pensioner. Was chairman of the Board of Selectmen in New Vineyard in 1803.

Capt. Samuel Daggett, in his ninety-sixth year, composed the following:

UNIVERSALIST CREED.

Upright in heart, in all our dealings just,
In God's free grace we put our only trust;
And in his boundless, universal love,
We place our hope of Heaven and bliss above;
And when life's scene is drawing to a close,
Calmly we sink into our last repose;
And as in Adam death o'er all doth reign,
Even so in Christ shall all be raised again.

1285. WEST DAGGETT [7] (*Nathan,*[6] *Seth,*[5] *Samuel,*[4] *Thomas,*[3] *Thomas,*[2] *John* [1]), died in a Western State; married Farmington, Me., Betsey Talcott, widow of William Talcott, and daughter of Ezra and Elizabeth (Benson) Thomas, of Farmington, Me.; born New Bedford, Mass., September 28, 1789; died Anson, Me., December 24, 1878.

Issue:

1739. i. NATHAN DAGGETT,[8] died in the Civil War.
1740. ii. WEST DAGGETT,[8] died in the Civil War.

1295. SILAS DAGGETT [7] (*Silas,*[6] *Seth,*[5] *Samuel,*[4] *Thomas,*[3] *Thomas,*[2] *John* [1]), born Tisbury, Mass., February 9, 1782; died at sea; married Tisbury, Mass., August 2, 1802, Margaret Cleveland, daughter of Zebdial and Abigail (Luce) Cleveland; born Tisbury, Mass., September 13, 1781; died Tisbury, Mass., December 28, 1871.

Issue:

1741. i. LENDAL DAGGETT,[8] born Tisbury, Mass., October 14, 1804.
1742. ii. ABIGAIL CLEVELAND DAGGETT,[8] born Industry, Me., May 16, 1807.

1743. iii. WEST DAGGETT,[8] born Maine, 1808; married (published June .7, 1837), Ann Ricker, of New Vineyard, Me.; resided Solon, Me., then went to Iowa; seven sons.
1744. iv. HIRAM DAGGETT.[8]
1745. v. JOSEPH DAGGETT,[8] born Farmington, Me., May 15, 1814.
1746. vi. ISAAC CHACE DAGGETT,[8] born New Vineyard, Me., February 6, 1816.
1747. vii. DEBORAH DAGGETT,[8] born Tisbury, Mass., July, 1818.
1748. viii. MARY DAGGETT,[8] born Maine.
1749. ix. SILAS DAGGETT,[8] born Vineyard Haven, Mass.; removed to Maine; unmarried.

Silas Daggett removed from Tisbury to Industry, Me., and afterwards went back to Tisbury with his family, excepting his oldest son, who remained in Industry; was "farmer" and "mariner."

1297. SARAH DAGGETT [7] (*Silas,*[6] *Seth,*[5] *Samuel,*[4] *Thomas,*[3] *Thomas,*[2] *John*[1]), born Tisbury, Mass., December 6, 1787; died November 17, 1869; married (published May 31, 1809) Joseph Johnson, son of Thomas and Thankful (Smith) Johnson; born Edgartown, Mass., March 31, 1786; died Reedsburg, Wis., March 18, 1867.

Issue:

1750. i. MARY WEST JOHNSON,[8] born Farmington, Me., December 11, 1809.
1751. ii. JOSEPH SMITH JOHNSON,[8] born Farmington, Me., June 15, 1811; resides Minneapolis, Minn. (1885).
1752. iii. CHARLES EDWIN JOHNSON,[8] born Farmington, Me., July 25, 1814.
1753. iv. ABIGAIL DAGGETT JOHNSON,[8] born Farmington, Me., February 10, 1817.
1754. v. SILAS DAGGETT JOHNSON,[8] born Farmington, Me., July, 1821; resides Reedsburg Wis., (1885).
1755. vi. CHARLOTTE JOHNSON,[8] born Farmington, Me., December 21, 1823.
1756. vii. AUGUSTUS JOHNSON,[8] born Farmington, Me., May 22, 1828; resides Pittsburgh, Pa. (1885).

Mr. Johnson first settled in Industry, Me., but soon moved to Farmington, Me., where he became one of the leading business men: drover, merchant, lumberman, and innholder in the old Backus House in Farmington Centre village; postmaster, sheriff, representative State Legislature, member Governor's Council, etc.

1303. AUGUSTA NYE DAGGETT [7] (*Michael,*[6] *Sylvanus,*[5] *Samuel,*[4] *Thomas,*[3] *Thomas,*[2] *John*[1]), born Tisbury, Mass., March 27, 1806; died December 15, 1890; married March 14, 1828, Joseph Claghorn.

Issue:

1757. i. SARAH JANE CLAGHORN,[8] born March 13, 1829; married Mr. Lewis; died.
1758. ii. PETER DAGGETT CLAGHORN,[8] born January 2, 1832.
1759. iii. MERCY ANN CLAGHORN,[8] born July 16, 1833; died November 4, 1847.
1760. iv. HANNAH WILSON CLAGHORN,[8] born February 10, 1837; died June, 1837.
1761. v. ETHELINDA THAXTER CLAGHORN,[8] born December 20, 1839.
1762. vi. JAMES PAXTON CLAGHORN,[8] born September 2, 1844; died April 6, 1847.
1763. vii. JAMES PAXTON CLAGHORN,[8] born April 6, 1847.

1304. TIMOTHY DAGGETT [7] (*Michael,*[6] *Sylvanus,*[5] *Samuel,*[4] *Thomas,*[3] *Thomas,*[2] *John*[1]), born Tisbury, Mass., September 5, 1807; "pilot;" died Tisbury, Mass., August 19, 1874; married Billingsgate Island, October 20, 1833, Tabitha Mayo Gill, daughter of Abijah and Tabitha (Mayo) Gill; born Eastham, December 19, 1814.

Issue:

1764. i. SILVANUS DAGGETT,[8] born Tisbury, Mass., February 7, 1836; died August 14, 1855.
1765. ii. ELIZABETH BUTLER DAGGETT,[8] born Tisbury, Mass., May 10, 1837; resides Vineyard Haven, Mass. (1892).
1766. iii. AUGUSTA NYE DAGGETT,[8] born Tisbury, Mass., May 11, 1843; died Tisbury, Mass., September 24, 1847.
1767. iv. HENRY WALKER DAGGETT,[8] born Tisbury, Mass., April 14, 1853.

1305. CHARLES NYE DAGGETT [7] (*Michael,*[6] *Sylvanus,*[5] *Samuel,*[4] *Thomas,*[3] *Thomas,*[2] *John*[1]), born Tisbury, Mass., 1810; "mariner;" died Tisbury, Mass., November 20, 1857; married Betsey ——.

Issue:

1768. i. CHARLES NYE DAGGETT,[8] born Edgartown, Mass., December 24, 1843.
1769. ii. Daughter —— DAGGETT,[8] born Tisbury, Mass., November 8, 1847.

1307. HEPSIE DAGGETT [7] (*Freeman,*[6] *Sylvanus,*[5] *Samuel,*[4] *Thomas,*[3] *Thomas,*[2] *John*[1]), resides San Francisco, Cal. (1892); married 1st, William Andrews; married 2d, Providence, R.I., February 27, 1850, by Rev. J. P. Cleveland, to Franklin D. Cottle, son of James and Jane (Daggett) Cottle.

1308. FRANKLIN DAGGETT [7] (*Freeman,*[6] *Sylvanus,*[5] *Samuel,*[4] *Thomas,*[3] *Thomas,*[2] *John*[1]), born Tisbury, Mass., October 26, 1804; "mariner;" died Tisbury, Mass., October 15, 1854; married Tisbury, Mass., October 7, 1830, Serena Manter, daughter of Thomas and Hannah (Luce) Manter; born Tisbury, Mass., August 15, 1808; resides Vineyard Haven, Mass. (1892).

Issue:

1770. i. CHARLES DIAS DAGGETT,[8] born Tisbury, Mass., 1840; died at sea, February 14, 1861.
1771. ii. JOHN DAGGETT,[8] born Tisbury, Mass., July 1, 1843; died Tisbury, Mass., October 13, 1843.
1772. iii. Son —— DAGGETT,[8] born Tisbury, Mass., September 2, 1844; died an infant.
1773. iv. Daughter —— DAGGETT,[8] born Tisbury, Mass., September 2, 1844; died Tisbury, Mass., September 9, 1845.
1774. v. Son —— DAGGETT,[8] born Tisbury, Mass., July 5, 1846; died Tisbury, Mass., July, 1846.
1775. vi. FREEMAN DAGGETT,[8] born Tisbury, Mass., January 14, 1848; died Tisbury, Mass., May 2, 1848.
1776. vii. Son —— DAGGETT,[8] born Tisbury, Mass., November 13, 1849; died Tisbury, Mass., December 13, 1849.
1777. viii. SERENA DAGGETT,[8] born Tisbury, Mass., November 13, 1849.

1778. ix.   LOVETA LAMBERT DAGGETT,[8] born Tisbury, Mass., October 18, 1852; resides Vineyard Haven, Mass. (1892).

1779. x.   FRANKLIN DAGGETT,[8] married; issue: Leander Bradley Daggett,[9] born San Francisco, Cal., July 27, 1874.

1309.   FREEMAN DAGGETT [7] (*Freeman,*[6] *Sylvanus,*[5] *Samuel,*[4] *Thomas,*[3] *Thomas,*[2] *John*[1]), died at sea, 1843; married February 26, 1828, Mary Ferguson, daughter of William and Mary (Luce) Ferguson; born Chilmark, Mass., April 3, 1804; died Tisbury, Mass., February 12, 1876.

Issue :

1780. i.   GRAFTON LUCE DAGGETT,[8] born Tisbury, Mass., November 24, 1829.

1781. ii.   MARTHA FERGUSON DAGGETT,[8] born Tisbury, Mass., December 22, 1837.

1782. iii.   CAROLINE FRANCES DAGGETT,[8] born Tisbury, Mass., October 24, 1840; died Tisbury, Mass., November 6, 1862.

Freeman Daggett was first officer of the ship "Addison" at the time of his death.

1310.   BENJAMIN DAGGETT [7] (*Thomas,*[6] *Benjamin,*[5] *Benjamin,*[4] *Thomas,*[3] *Thomas,*[2] *John*[1]), born Fox Island, Me., October 4, 1796; died St. Albans, Me., December 27, 1888; married Lincolnville, Me., December 25, 1820, Mehetable Neal: died Palmyra, Me., September 17, 1851.

Issue :

1783. i.   KESIAH DAGGETT,[8] born Palmyra, Me., February 20, 1822; died Palmyra, Me., March 15, 1881.

1784. ii.   BETSEY JANE DAGGETT,[8] born Palmyra, Me., February 26, 1827.

1785. iii.   HENRIETTA DAGGETT,[8] born Palmyra, Me., January 19, 1829.

1786. iv.   MARY LAURETTA DAGGETT,[8] born Palmyra, Me., October 30, 1830; married Palmyra, Me., July 4, 1876, William Benjamin Cookson; divorced: no issue; address M. L. Daggett, Bangor House, Bangor, Me. (1892).

1787. v.   ADAM CLARK DAGGETT,[8] born Palmyra, Me., May 8, 1834; died Palmyra, Me., November 7, 1858.

1788. vi.   CAROLINE DAGGETT,[8] born Palmyra, Me., December 30, 1839.

1311.   ELIHU DAGGETT [7] (*Thomas,*[6] *Benjamin,*[5] *Benjamin,*[4] *Thomas,*[3] *Thomas,*[2] *John*[1]), born Northport, Me., July 6, 1798; died Searsmont, Me., November 17, 1872; married 1st, Warren, Me., April 4, 1722, Catherine Mathews, daughter of Deacon James and Mary (Elwell) Mathews; died Hope, Me., June, 1834; married 2d, Esther Sweatland; died Searsmont, Me.

Issue :

1789. i.   CATHERINE DAGGETT,[8] married Artist Pease; resides Appleton, Me.

1790. ii.   JAMES DAGGETT,[8] married; moved to Aroostook, Me., where he died.

1791. iii.   SILAS DAGGETT,[8] married 1st, a sister of James's wife; married 2d, ——; resides Lincolnville or Searsmont, Me. (1892).

1312.   DARIUS DAGGETT [7] (*Thomas,*[6] *Benjamin,*[5] *Benjamin,*[4] *Thomas,*[3] *Thomas,*[2] *John*[1]), born Lincolnville, Me., February 17,

1801 ; died Madison, Wis., September 8, 1892 ; married Searsmont, Me., October 1, 1826, Mary Hemenway, daughter of Joshua and Polly (Blake) Hemenway ; born Union, Me., August 15, 1806 ; died Madison, Wis., December 30, 1883.

Issue :

1792. i.   ABIGAIL DAGGETT,[8] born Searsmont, Me., January 30, 1829.
1793. ii. HARRIET LOUISA DAGGETT,[8] born Vassalboro', Me., February 8, 1834.
1794. iii. GEORGE ANSON DAGGETT,[8] born St. Stephens, N.B., July 3, 1839 ; died Bangor, Me., January 15, 1847.

Darius Daggett was at one time county treasurer for Aroostook county, Me.

1313. JONAS DAGGETT [7] (*Thomas*,[6] *Benjamin*,[5] *Benjamin*,[4] *Thomas*,[3] *Thomas*,[2] *John* [1]), born Lincolnville, Me., May 16, 1803 ; died Illinois, January 14, 1850 ; married ——.

Issue :

1795. i. MOSES DAGGETT,[8] married ——; died about 1883.
1796. ii. ABBY DAGGETT,[8] married Mr. Thayer (?).

Mrs. Jonas Daggett married 2d, Mr. St. Clair ; resides Alton, Ill. (1892).

1314. SALLY DAGGETT [7] (*Thomas*,[6] *Benjamin*,[5] *Benjamin*,[4] *Thomas*,[3] *Thomas*,[2] *John* [1]), born Montville, Me., June 26, 1805 ; died Clarion, Iowa, November 8, 1891 ; married November 9, 1826, Joseph Pitcher ; married 2d, Palmyra, Me., December 17, 1831, Paschal Peela Nichols ; born February 2, 1801 ; died April 12, 1849 ; married 3d, Moses Jenkins ; married 4th, David Jewett.

Issue :

1797. i.   JOSEPHINE PITCHER,[8] born August 24, 1829.
1798. ii. FRANCES A. NICHOLS,[8] born August 4, 1835.
1799. iii. EDWIN R. NICHOLS,[8] born January 5, 1837.
1800. iv. THOMAS OWEN NICHOLS,[8] born Detroit, Mich., June 14, 1845 ; resides Clarion, Iowa (1892).

1315. ZENAS DAGGETT [7] (*Thomas*,[6] *Benjamin*,[5] *Benjamin*,[4] *Thomas*,[3] *Thomas*,[2] *John* [1]), born October 13, 1807 ; died Placerville, Cal., 1878 ; married.

Issue : three children.

1801. i. FRANK DAGGETT,[8] resided in Stockton, Me., a few years ago (1892).

1317. MOSES L. DAGGETT [7] (*Thomas*,[6] *Benjamin*,[5] *Benjamin*,[4] *Thomas*,[3] *Thomas*,[2] *John* [1]), born Hope, Me., January 13, 1819 ; died Madison, Wis., March 24, 1881 ; married Palmyra, Me., April 29, 1841, Tamson Hutchinson ; born August 11, 1821.

Issue :

1802. i. ZEBULAN MANTER DAGGETT,[8] born Palmyra, Me., November 14, 1842 ; " a soldier ; " died Reaves Station, Mo., April 25, 1862.

1803. ii.   ASBURY MOSES DAGGETT,[8] born Palmyra, Me., December 1, 1846.
1804. iii. FLORENCE AUGUSTA DAGGETT,[8] born Madison, Wis., May 19, 1859;
            died Madison, Wis., October 25, 1875.

1320.   SAMUEL BAKER DAGGETT [7] (*Richmond,[6] Benjamin,[5] Benjamin,[4] Thomas,[3] Thomas,[2] John [1]*), born Palmyra, Me., September 6, 1807; died Shasta, Cal., August 10, 1852; married Holden, Me., February 5, 1835, Almira Jones, daughter of Luther and Lucy (Nye) Jones; born Holden, Me., October 26, 1813; died Bangor, Me., April 12, 1880.

Issue:

1805. i.   ALBERT WESLEY DAGGETT,[8] born Bangor, Me.. May 10, 1836; died
            Bangor, Me., July 30, 1837.
1806. ii.   ALMIRA JANE DAGGETT,[8] born Bangor, Me.. June 6, 1839.
1807. iii. SAMUEL WESLEY DAGGETT,[8] born Bangor, Me., December 1, 1840.
1808. iv.   SUSAN DAGGETT,[8] born Bangor, Me., July 30, 1842.
1809. v.   ELLEN DAGGETT,[8] born Bangor, Me., May 30, 1844; resides Bangor,
            Me. (1892).
1810. vi.   LUCY MARIA DAGGETT,[8] born Bangor, Me., March 12, 1846.
1811. vii. ALBERT HENRY DAGGETT,[8] born Bangor, Me., September 17, 1849;
            died Bangor, Me., September 17, 1850.

Samuel B. Daggett went to California in 1850, and opened a hotel in Shasta — the only temperance hotel at that time in the town.

1321.   HENRY MARTIN DAGGETT [7] (*Richmond,[6] Benjamin,[5] Benjamin,[4] Thomas,[3] Thomas,[2] John [1]*), born Palmyra, Me., January 23, 1809; died Bangor, Me., May 15, 1850; married Skowhegan, Me., March 13, 1833, Catharine Robinson Malbon, daughter of Nathaniel and Mary (Robinson) Malbon; born Cornville, Me.; died Bangor, Me., January 23, 1871.

Issue:

1812. i.   HENRY RICHMOND DAGGETT,[8] born Bangor, Me., October 17, 1835;
            married; resides Petoskey, Mich. (1892).
1813. ii.   HARRIET ANN DAGGETT,[8] born Bangor, Me., May 5, 1836; died
            Bangor, Me., October 14, 1852.
1814. iii. JAMES MILTON DAGGETT,[8] born Bangor, Me., February 7, 1840.
1815. iv.   AUGUSTUS MORRILL DAGGETT,[8] born Bangor, Me., June 1, 1842; re-
            sides Petoskey, Mich. (1892).
1816. v.   CHARLES HAYWARD DAGGETT,[8] born Bangor, Me., May 1, 1847; died
            Washington, D.C., June 30, 1863.

1322.   MARTHA DAGGETT [7] (*Richmond,[6] Benjamin,[5] Benjamin,[4] Thomas,[3] Thomas,[2] John [1]*), born Palmyra, Me., January 10, 1811; died Saco, Me., October 31, 1891; married Bangor, Me., November 11, 1832, Calvin Osgood.

Issue:

1817. i.   CALVIN RICHMOND OSGOOD,[8] born Bangor, Me.
1818. ii.   MARTHA FRANCIS OSGOOD,[8] born Bangor, Me.
1819. iii. WESLEY ALMOND OSGOOD,[8] born Bangor, Me. (?).
1820. iv.   HENRY AUGUSTUS OSGOOD,[8] born Garland, Me.
1821. v.   SAMUEL DAGGETT OSGOOD,[8] born Garland, Me.

1822. vi.   BENJAMIN FRANKLIN OSGOOD,[8] born Garland, Me.; resides 39 Acorn street, Malden, Mass. (1892).
1823. vii.   CHARLES FREDERIC OSGOOD,[8] born Garland, Me.; resides Everett, Mass. (1892).
1824. viii.   ANNA AUGUSTA OSGOOD,[8] born Garland, Me.; resides Saco, Me. (1892).
1825. ix.   GEORGE WASHINGTON OSGOOD,[8] born Garland, Me.

Mr. and Mrs. Osgood removed from Bangor to Garland, Me., in 1836.

1327.   ICHABOD DAGGETT [7] (*Ichabod,*[6] *Elihu,*[5] *Mayhew,*[4] *John,*[3] *Thomas,*[2] *John* [1]), born Attleboro', Mass., November 20, 1771; died Thetford, Vt.; married Attleboro', Mass., February 4, 1796, Hannah Whiting, daughter of David and Hannah (Walcott) Whiting; born Attleboro', Mass., May 14, 1772.

Issue :

1826. i.   MANNING DAGGETT,[8] resides Whiting, Vt. (1883).

1330.   HENRY DAGGETT [7] (*Ichabod,*[6] *Elihu,*[5] *Mayhew,*[4] *John,*[3] *Thomas,*[2] *John* [1]), born Attleboro', Mass., September 29, 1778; died Parishville, N.Y., July 7, 1862; married July 2, 1800, Pamelia Tamebling; born January 19, 1781; died Stockholm, N.Y., August 6, 1850.

Issue :

1827. i.   POLLY DAGGETT,[8] born Cornwall, Vt., April 15, 1802.
1828. ii.   STEPHEN ABBOT DAGGETT,[8] born Cornwall, Vt., June 19, 1804.
1829. iii.   EMILA DAGGETT,[8] born Cornwall, Vt., March 2, 1806; died Parishville, N.Y., October 31, 1882.
1830. iv.   DAVID DAGGETT,[8] born Cornwall, Vt., August 9, 1809.
1831. v.   LEVI PARSONS DAGGETT,[8] born Cornwall, Vt., July 5, 1811.
1832. vi.   ORPHA MANELLA DAGGETT,[8] born Cornwall, Vt., May 23, 1816.
1833. vii.   LUCY ELMIRA DAGGETT,[8] born Stockholm, N.Y., August 26, 1818.

Henry Daggett went to Cornwall, Vt., and in 1817 removed to Stockholm, N.Y.

1331.   BENJAMIN DAGGETT [7] (*Daniel,*[6] *Elihu,*[5] *Mayhew,*[4] *John,*[3] *Thomas,*[2] *John* [1]), born Attleboro', Mass., November 16, 1763; died Attleboro', Mass., September 11, 1807; married Wrentham, Mass., October 2, 1792, by Rev. David Avery, to Polly Guild; born 1764; died Attleboro', Mass., March 10, 1820.

Issue :

1834. i.   JOHN DICKINSON DAGGETT,[8] born Attleboro', Mass., October 4, 1793; removed to Missouri.
1835. ii.   MARIA DAGGETT,[8] born Attleboro', Mass., August 16, 1795; died Attleboro', Mass., August 25, 1800.
1836. iii.   DANIEL GUILD DAGGETT,[8] born Attleboro', Mass., August 1, 1798.
1837. iv.   JAMES HERVY DAGGETT,[8] born Attleboro', Mass., November 27, 1800.
1838. v.   ELIZA MARIA DAGGETT,[8] born Attleboro', Mass., February 3, 1804.

Benjamin Daggett, trader, of Attleboro'; his wife appointed administrator of his estate, October 6, 1807. [Bristol Probate.]

1332. MARY DAGGETT [7] (*Daniel,*[6] *Elihu,*[5] *Mayhew,*[4] *John,*[3] *Thomas,*[2] *John* [1]), born Attleboro', Mass., May 21, 1766; died Attleboro', Mass., June 28, 1829; married 1st, Oliver Blackinton, son of Oliver and Mary Blackinton; born 1760; died Attleboro', Mass., April 3, 1810; married 2d, Josiah Draper.

Issue:

1839. i.   CATHERINE BLACKINTON,[8] born Attleboro', Mass., January 22, 1785.
1840. ii.   LEVI BLAKINTON,[8] born Attleboro', Mass., August 2, 1788.
1841. iii.   NANCY BLACKINTON,[8] born Attleboro', Mass., December 23, 1790.
1842. iv.   MARY BLAKINTON,[8] born Attleboro', Mass., June 26, 1793.
1843. v.   OLIVE D. BLACKINTON,[8] born Attleboro', Mass., September 7, 1795.
1844. vi.   AZUBA BLACKINTON,[8] born Attleboro', Mass., December 15, 1797.
1845. vii.   OLIVER BLACKINTON,[8] born Attleboro', Mass., August 6, 1800.
1846. viii.   AARON BLACKINTON,[8] born Attleboro', Mass., April 8, 1803.
1847. ix.   CHLOE BLACKINTON,[8] born Attleboro', Mass., July 13, 1805.

1333. MARGARET DAGGETT [7] (*Daniel,*[6] *Elihu,*[5] *Mayhew,*[4] *John,*[3] *Thomas,*[2] *John* [1]), born Attleboro', Mass., July 27, 1768; died Pawlet, Vt., August 8, 1830; married Attleboro', Mass., May 5, 1788, John Guild, son of Naphtali and Joanna Guild (see No. 1152); born Attleboro', Mass., July 28, 1763; died Pawlet, Vt., September 20, 1850.

Issue:

1848. i.   CHAUNCY GUILD,[8] born Attleboro', Mass., July 3, 1789; married Celinda Bourn.
1849. ii.   PLYNE GUILD,[8] born Attleboro', Mass., June 19, 1792; died July 19, 1836.
1850. iii.   MILTON GUILD,[8] born Attleboro', Mass., January 1, 1795; married at an advanced age; no issue.
1851. iv.   EUNICE GUILD,[8] born Attleboro', Mass., October 24, 1799; married April 19, 1818, Milton Brown.
1852. v.   LUCY GUILD,[8] born Pawlet, Vt., March 7, 1804; married May, 1829, Charles Wilgus, of West Troy; three children.
1853. vi.   ABIGAIL GUILD,[8] born Pawlet, Vt., December 12, 1806; married December 8, 1833, Dr. David R. Barrus; she died December 16, 1884.

John Guild moved to Pawlet, Vt., in 1802; erected the first cotton factory in that State, and had the management of it for several years. He was a Revolutionary soldier. He married 2d, November 16, 1831, Martha Cook.

1334. ABIGAIL DAGGETT [7] (*Daniel,*[6] *Elihu,*[5] *Mayhew,*[4] *John,*[3] *Thomas,*[2] *John* [1]), born Attleboro', Mass., August 28, 1770; married Attleboro', Mass., January 22, 1793, James Hodges, Jr., of Norton, son of James and Mary (Briggs) Hodges; born Norton, Mass., August 23, 1767; perished at sea; date unknown.

Issue:

1854. i.   HARLAND HODGES,[8] married February 1, 1818, at Norton, to Polly Bates, of Norton.

1336. DANIEL DAGGETT [7] (*Daniel,*[6] *Elihu,*[5] *Mayhew,*[4] *John,*[3] *Thomas,*[2] *John* [1]), born Attleboro', Mass., February 11, 1775; died

Attleboro', Mass., August 19, 1838; married 1st, Attleboro', Mass., November 20, 1794, Hannah Everet; born 1774; died Attleboro', Mass., October 11, 1800; married 2d, Attleboro', Mass., March 20, 1803, Margaret Briggs, daughter of Rufus and Margaret Briggs; born 1775; died Attleboro', Mass., March 5, 1828.

Issue:

1855. i.   ABIGAIL DAGGETT,[8] born Attleboro', Mass., March 8, 1795.
1856. ii. RHODA DAGGETT,[8] born Attleboro', Mass., November 25, 1797.
1857. iii. DANIEL DAGGETT,[8] born Attleboro', Mass., October 31, 1804.
1858. iv. MARGARET DAGGETT,[8] born Attleboro', Mass., March 16, 1806; died Attleboro' Falls, Mass., December 14, 1886.
1859. v.   HANNAH DAGGETT,[8] born Attleboro', Mass., March 1, 1810.
1860. vi. SAMUEL SLATER DAGGETT,[8] born Attleboro', Mass., April 19, 1812.
1861. vii. MINERVA DAGGETT,[8] born Attleboro', Mass., April 3, 1814; died Attleboro', Mass., September 1, 1850.
1862. viii. MINA BRIGGS DAGGETT,[8] born Attleboro', Mass., April 7, 1817.

1337. BETSEY DAGGETT [7] (*Daniel*,[6] *Elihu*,[5] *Mayhew*,[4] *John*,[3] *Thomas*,[2] *John* [1]), born Attleboro', Mass., September 5, 1777; died Attleboro' Falls, Mass., May 22, 1859; married Attleboro', Mass., November 24, 179–, Artemas Stanley, son of Deacon Jonathan and Martha (Pond) Stanley; born 1775; died November 7, 1856.

Issue:

1863. i.   FANNY STANLEY,[8] born Attleboro', Mass., February 13, 1797; married Silas Tyler; issue: (1) Silas,[9] married Maria Tifft; (2) Artemas,[9] resides Lowell, Mass. (1893).
1864. ii. SYLVAN STANLEY,[8] born Attleboro', Mass., April 7, 1798.
1865. iii. OLIVIA STANLEY,[8] born Attleboro', Mass., June 8, 1800; died Attleboro', Mass., November 10, 1861.
1866. iv. VERNAL STANLEY,[8] born Attleboro', Mass., May 30, 1802.
1867. v.   CHLOE READ STANLEY,[8] born Attleboro', Mass., February 25, 1805.
1868. vi. OTIS STANLEY,[8] born Attleboro', Mass., March 9, 1807.
1869. vii. BETSEY SHEPARD STANLEY,[8] born Attleboro', Mass., November 24, 1808.
1870. viii. MILTON STANLEY,[8] born Attleboro', Mass., July 15, 1810.
1871. ix. JONATHAN HARVEY STANLEY,[8] born Attleboro', Mass., July 6, 1812.
1872. x.   HARRIET EMILY STANLEY,[8] born Dracut, Mass., May 17, 1815.

1338. OLIVE DAGGETT [7] (*Daniel*,[6] *Elihu*,[5] *Mayhew*,[4] *John*,[3] *Thomas*,[2] *John* [1]), born Attleboro', Mass., 1785; died Pawtucket, R.I.; married 1st, Mr. Thatcher; married 2d, Attleboro', Mass., July 14, 1816, Charles O. Cheney; died Attleboro', Mass.

Issue:

1873. i.   ADALINE THATCHER,[8] born Attleboro', Mass., September 12, 1805; died North Attleboro', Mass.
1874. ii. HARRIETTE CHENEY,[8] married James Davis; issue, two daughters; died Pawtucket, R.I.

1344. AMELIA MARTHA DAGGETT [7] (*Henry*,[6] *Elihu*,[5] *Mayhew*,[4] *John*,[3] *Thomas*,[2] *John* [1]), born New Haven, Conn., August 25, 1779; died New Haven, Conn., September 24, 1807; married New Haven, Conn., June 13, 1802, Captain John Bulkley, son of John and Sarah

(Wright) Bulkley; born Wethersfield, Conn., 1777; died New York city, October, 1852.

Issue:

1875. i. HENRY DAGGETT BULKLEY,⁸ born New Haven, Conn., April 20, 1803.
1876. ii. AMELIA MARTHA BULKLEY,⁸ born New Haven, Conn., March 13, 1806.

Capt. John Bulkley was a merchant in New York and descended from Rev. Peter Bulkley, one of the earliest immigrants, and one of the founders of Concord, Mass. After the death of Amelia Martha Bulkley, he married 2d, 1808, Mrs. Priscilla Sturges, daughter of Mr. Burr, of Fairfield, Conn.

1347. ELISABETH DAGGETT⁷ (*Henry*,⁶ *Elihu*,⁵ *Mayhew*,⁴ *John*,³ *Thomas*,² *John*¹), born New Haven, Conn., July 5, 1786; died Hartford, Conn., August 2, 1869; married New Haven, Conn., May 24, 1812, Edward Hooker, Esq., son of Col. Noadiah and Rebekah (Griswold) Hooker, of Farmington, Conn.; born Farmington, Conn., April 27, 1785; died Farmington, Conn., May 5, 1846.

Issue:

1877. i. ELISABETH DAGGETT HOOKER,⁸ born Farmington, Conn., May 1, 1813.
1878. ii. JOHN HOOKER,⁸ born Farmington, Conn., April 19, 1816.
1879. iii. EDWARD HOOKER,⁸ born Farmington, Conn., December 30, 1819; died Farmington, Conn., May 20, 1821.
1880. iv. EDWARD HOOKER,⁸ born Farmington, Conn., December 25, 1822.
1881. v. MARY HOOKER,⁸ born Farmington, Conn., May 3, 1825; died Farmington, Conn., October 1, 1826.

1348. MARY DAGGETT⁷ (*Henry*,⁶ *Elihu*,⁵ *Mayhew*,⁴ *John*,³ *Thomas*,² *John*¹), born New Haven, Conn., December 5, 1792; died New Haven, Conn., August 14, 1875; married New Haven, Conn., June 5, 1821, Rev. Samuel Rogers Andrew, son of Samuel and Charlotte (Rogers) Andrew, of Milford, Conn.; born Milford, Conn., May 6, 1787; died New Haven, Conn., May 26, 1858.

Issue:

1882. i. SAMUEL WORCESTER ANDREW,⁸ born Woodbury, Conn., June 8, 1822.
1883. ii. HENRY DAGGETT ANDREW,⁸ born Woodbury, Conn., April 24, 1824; died New York city, April 19, 1890.
1884. iii. MARY ELIZABETH ANDREW,⁸ born Woodbury, Conn., November 13, 1825; married April 2, 1851, Rev. William Atchison; she died Fitchville, Conn., January 12, 1853.
1885. iv. CHARLOTTE ROGERS ANDREW,⁸ born Woodbury, Conn., October 26, 1828; married Rev. James Gallup; resides Madison, Conn.
1886. v. EDWARD HOOKER ANDREW,⁸ born Woodbury, Conn., October 14, 1841; married 1st, October 14, 1858, Amelia Hubbell, of New Haven; she died November 17, 1859; married 2d, December 25, 1867, Mrs. Louisa Crane, of New York: no issue; he died New York city, January 5, 1876.

Rev. Samuel R. Andrew descended from Rev. Samuel Andrew, Harvard College, 1656. He was settled at Woodbury, Conn., where he continued until 1846, when he was dismissed at his own request on account of failing health, and removed to New Haven. The last years of his life he was trustee of Yale College and secretary of the Board.

1349. George Daggett [7] (*Elihu,*[6] *Elihu,*[5] *Mayhew,*[4] *John,*[3] *Thomas,*[2] *John* [1]), born Attleboro', Mass., December 29, 1774; died Atkinson, Me., November 18, 1845; married Dresden, Me., November, 1797, by Rev. Mephibosheth Cain, to Mary Bodfish, daughter of Nimphus and Mercy (Goodwin) Bodfish; born Dresden, Me., September 3, 1782; died Atkinson, Me., March 25, 1873.
Issue:

1887. i.   Daughter —— Daggett,[8] born Fairfield, Me., August or September, 1798; died soon after birth.
1888. ii. Daughter —— Daggett,[8] born Fairfield, Me, August or September, 1798; died soon after birth.
1889. iii. Charity Galieucia Daggett,[8] born Fairfield, Me., September 16, 1800.
1890. iv. Lydia Tuycross Daggett,[8] born Fairfield, Me., January 8, 1805.
1891. v.   Emily Appleton Daggett,[8] born Fairfield, Me., March 22, 1807.
1892. vi. George Randolph Daggett,[8] born Fairfield, Me., November 18, 1809.
1893. vii. Mary Ann Daggett,[8] born Fairfield, Me., October 7, 1811.
1894. viii. Earl Percy Daggett,[8] born Fairfield, Me., May 30, 1820.
1895. ix. Albion K. Paris Daggett,[8] born Fairfield, Me., February 20, 1822.

George Daggett was a school teacher and farmer. He belonged to a company of militia during the war of 1812, and was clerk of the company. They were called out and stationed to guard some property, for which service his widow received a land warrant for one hundred and sixty acres of land, about 1853.

Mr. Daggett was a man of the highest moral character; a man who read, and was gifted in conversation and writing. He was something of a poet, but none of his compositions are known to be preserved.

He moved from Fairfield to Atkinson, Me., about 1831.

1350. Rosamond Daggett [7] (*Elihu,*[6] *Elihu,*[5] *Mayhew,*[4] *John,*[3] *Thomas,*[2] *John* [1]), born Attleboro', Mass., January 6, 1777; died Attleboro', Mass., September 28, 1851; married Attleboro', Mass., January 3, 1818, Thomas Cobb Martin; born Attleboro', Mass., August 6, 1776; died Attleboro', Mass., January 28, 1857.
No issue:

1353. Capt. Elihu Daggett [7] (*Elihu,*[6] *Elihu,*[5] *Mayhew,*[4] *John,*[3] *Thomas,*[2] *John* [1]), born Attleboro', Mass., February 24, 1785; died Attleboro', Mass., January 25, 1871; married Pembroke, Mass., November 28, 1810, Lucinda White, daughter of Capt. William and

Hannah [Stetson (Cushing)] White; born Pembroke, Mass., September 22, 1788; died Attleboro', Mass., October 1, 1847.

Issue:

1896. i. LYMAN WHITE DAGGETT,[8] born Attleboro', Mass., July 28, 1812.
1897. ii. ANN JANETTE STANLEY DAGGETT,[8] born Attleboro', Mass., October 13, 1814; died Attleboro', Mass., August 20, 1838.
1898. iii. CORISSANDE LA ROCHE DAGGETT,[8] born Attleboro', Mass., February 7, 1819; died Attleboro', Mass., January 16, 1837.
1899. iv. STATIRA ARCHADEMIA DAGGETT,[8] born Attleboro', Mass., September 15, 1821; died Attleboro', Mass., September 28, 1821.

1354. JACOB DAGGETT[7] (*Elihu*,[6] *Elihu*,[5] *Mayhew*,[4] *John*,[3] *Thomas*,[2] *John*[1]), born Mansfield, Mass., April 20, 1787; died Attleboro', Mass., March 2, 1869; married Mansfield, Mass., November, 1808, Nancy Fisher, daughter of Samuel Fisher; born Mansfield, Mass., May 12, 1786; died Wrentham, Mass., May 12, 1854.

Issue:

1900. i. JAMES MADISON DAGGETT,[8] born Attleboro', Mass., May 10, 1809.
1901. ii. HENRY LEFRELET DAGGETT,[8] born Attleboro', Mass., August 10, 1812.
1902. iii. MAYHEW FISHER DAGGETT,[8] born Attleboro', Mass., December 4, 1814.
1903. iv. THIRZA ANN DAGGETT,[8] born Attleboro', Mass., July 8, 1816; married William Clark; resides Troy, N.Y. (1892).
1904. v. WILLARD ELIHU DAGGETT,[8] born Attleboro', Mass., February 8, 1818.

Jacob Daggett was a jeweller, and resided in Wrentham, Mass.

1356. SARAH DAGGETT[7] (*Jacob*,[6] *Elihu*,[5] *Mayhew*,[4] *John*,[3] *Thomas*,[2] *John*[1]), born January 5, 1776; died Milford, Conn. (?), November 9, 1852; married Rev. Sherman Johnson, of Milford, Conn.; died 1806.

Issue:

1905. i. ROGER SHERMAN JOHNSON,[8] born 1805; died January, 1849; married Catherine Woodman; issue: (1) Sherman Johnson;[9] (2) Sarah C. Johnson;[9] married Stuart Barnes.

Rev. Sherman Johnson graduated from Yale in 1802. He was the fourth pastor of the Second Congregational Church in Milford, Conn.

1357. CHAUNCY DAGGETT[7] (*Jacob*,[6] *Elihu*,[5] *Mayhew*,[4] *John*,[3] *Thomas*,[2] *John*[1]), born June 7, 1779; married Mehitable Mulford, daughter of Barnabas and Mehitable (Gorham) Mulford; born New Haven, Conn., January 25, 1780; died New Haven, Conn., September 8, 1854.

Issue:

1906. i. BARNABAS M. DAGGETT,[9] married, November 30, 1830, Charity, widow of Leonard Tift, of Attleboro', and daughter of Gardner and Jemima (Rice) Wright, of Sutton; she born June 3, 1804; died February 21, 1841; he died November 10, 1839.

1372. Milton Daggett [7] (*Elijah,[6] Elihu,[5] Mayhew,[4] John,[3] Thomas,[2] John [1]*), born Attleboro', Mass., October 15, 1792; died Charlestown, Mass., May 25, 1872; married (intention March 5, 1816) Nancy Smith, daughter of Jacob Smith, of Worcester; born Worcester, Mass., March 20, 1794; died Boston, Mass., October 7, 1869.

Issue:

1907. i.   Milton Orne Daggett,[8] died young.
1908. ii. Caroline P. Daggett,[8] born Lincoln, Mass., 1820.
1909. iii. Lyman Daggett,[8] born Lincoln, Mass., January 16, 1821.

1373. Marietta Daggett [7] (*Elijah,[6] Elihu,[5] Mayhew,[4] John,[3] Thomas,[2] John [1]*), born Attleboro', Mass., April 4, 1795; died North Attleboro', Mass., December 31, 1846; married Attleboro', Mass., May 19, 1814, by Rev. Mr. Read, to Abraham Hayward, son of Abraham and Sarah [Brewer (Lowd)] Hayward; born Boston, Mass., May 10, 1790; died North Attleboro', Mass., August 11, 1872.

Issue :

1910. i.   Ann Maria Hayward,[8] born North Attleboro', Mass., March 22, 1815; married Mr. Chapin; living (1892).
1911. ii. Marietta Hayward,[8] born North Attleboro', Mass., March 31, 1817; died North Attleboro', Mass., June 28, 1849,
1912. iii. Gardner Daggett Hayward,[8] born North Attleboro', Mass., June 30, 1820; living (1892).
1913. iv. William Abraham Hayward,[8] born North Attleboro', Mass., April 29, 1822; died December 23, 1870.
1914. v.   Charles Edward Hayward,[8] born North Attleboro', Mass., August 28, 1824; died May 4, 1886.
1915. vi. Sarah E. Hayward,[8] born North Attleboro', Mass., April 21, 1827; married Jonathan A. Briggs; died March 14, 1852.
1916. vii. Henry Lincoln Hayward,[8] born North Attleboro', Mass., November 18, 1832; resides there (1892); has son, Walter E. Hayward,[9] of Hayward & Sweet, jewelry.

1375. Maria Daggett [7] (*Elijah,[6] Elihu,[5] Mayhew,[4] John,[3] Thomas,[2] John [1]*), born Attleboro', Mass., November 9, 1799; died Attleboro', Mass., January 17, 1890; married Attleboro', Mass., between June and November 12, 1825, William Earl.

Issue :

1917. i. Thomas Earl,[8] resides Springfield, Mass. (1892).
1918. ii. William D. Earl.[8]

1382. Clark Daggett [7] (*Joseph,[6] Elihu,[5] Mayhew,[4] John,[3] Thomas,[2] John [1]*), born October 14, 1787; died Trumansburg, N.Y., June, 1875; married, Vermont, Anna Perrigo; died 1875.

Issue :

1919. i. Truman G. Daggett,[8] resides Trumansburg, Tompkins county, N.Y. (1882).

1920. ii.   Lucius T. Daggett,[8] resides Dodge City, Minn. (1882).
1921. iii. D. Daggett,[8] born 1830; resides Oswego, N.Y. (1882); married and
            has C. L. Daggett.[9]

1391.   Otis Daggett [7] (*Joab,[6] John,[5] Ebenezer,[4] John,[3] Thomas,[2] John* [1]), born Attleboro', Mass., October 4, 1785; died Surry, N.H.; married 1st, Cumberland, R.I., November 12, 1809, by Elder Stephen Place, to Content Smith, daughter of Aria Smith; married 2d, Surry, N.H., October 2, 1828, by Erastus Otis, Esq., to Lydia Sargeant, of Rindge, N.H., daughter of Samuel and Mary (Darling) Sargeant; born February 11, 1794.

Issue:

1922. i.   Susan Content Daggett,[8] born Cumberland, R.I., March 7, 1810;
            married Harvey M. Daggett (see No. 1414).
1923. ii.   George Washington Daggett,[8] born Surry, N.H., May 1, 1812;
            married Westport, Mo.; died Westport, Mo.; issue: one daughter.
1924. iii. Mary Ann Daggett,[8] born Surry, N.H., September 18, 1813.
1925. iv.   John Gilman Daggett,[8] born Surry, N.H., June 21, 1816.
1926. v.   Angelina Daggett,[8] born Surry, N.H., May 30, 1819; married
            Homer M. Daggett (see No. 1419).
1927. vi.   Otis Smith Daggett,[8] born Surry, N.H., March 23, 1821; "chair
            manufacturer:" died Attleboro', Mass., October 9, 1852.
1928. vii. Nancy Maria Daggett,[8] born Surry, N.H., April 4, 1823; died
            Concord, N.H., May, 1875.
1929. viii. Amelia Sophia Daggett,[8] born Surry, N.H., July 11, 1829; died
            Surry, N.H., in childhood.
1930. ix.   Lydia Eliza Daggett,[8] born Surry, N.H., July 22, 1832; died
            Attleboro', Mass.
1931. x.   Martha Jane Daggett,[8] born Surry, N.H., February 1, 1836.

Mrs. Lydia (Sargeant) Daggett married 2d, Isaiah Wilder.

1393.   Levi Daggett [7] (*Joab,[6] John,[5] Ebenezer,[4] John,[3] Thomas,[2] John* [1]), born Attleboro', Mass., June 12, 1789; died Rindge, N.H., September 20, 1860; married Troy, N.H., April 15, 1818, Abigail Butler, daughter of Joseph and Parnae (Temple) Butler; born Bolton, Mass., June 3, 1798; died Richland Centre, Wis., March 27, 1870.

Issue:

1932. i.   Abigail Daggett,[8] born Troy, N.H., February 11, 1819.
1933. ii.   Levi Daggett,[8] born Troy, N.H., July 3, 1820.
1934. iii. Joab Daggett,[8] born Troy, N.H., August 7, 1822.
1935. iv.   Emeline Daggett,[8] born Marlborough, N.H., September 23, 1824;
            died Richland Centre, Wis., January 6, 1879.
1936. v.   Cordelia Daggett,[8] born Attleboro', Mass., May 15, 1830; died
            Richland Centre, Wis., October 31, 1876.
1937. vi.   Caroline Daggett,[8] born Attleboro', Mass., November 2, 1832;
            married Jaffrey, N.H., August 17, 1853, Henry John Blodgett; she
            died Gardner, Mass., May 18, 1868; he resided Chelsea, Mass.
            (1888).
1938. vii. Harrison Daggett,[8] born Attleboro', Mass., July 4, 1840; died Attle-
            boro', Mass., August 10, 1843.

1395.   Marcus Daggett [7] (*Joab,[6] John,[5] Ebenezer,[4] John,[3] Thomas,[2] John* [1]), born Attleboro', Mass., July 21, 1793; resides

Fisherville, N.H. (1881) ; married Attleboro', Mass., November 15,
1817, Martha Nye, of Falmouth, Mass.; died March 21, 1861.

Issue :

1939. i.   MARTHA ANN DAGGETT,[8] born Marlborough, N.H., November 29,
           1818; married David A. Brown.
1940. ii. MARCUS LAFAYETTE DAGGETT,[8] born Marlborough, N.H., June 15,
           1820.
1941. iii. FANNY B. DAGGETT,[8] born Marlborough, N.H., June 2, 1822; resides
           Fisherville, N.H. (1881).
1942. iv. ELIZA M. DAGGETT,[8] born Marlborough, N.H., January 14, 1825; re-
           sides Attleboro', Mass. (1881).
1943. v.   JOSEPH M. DAGGETT,[8] born November 14, 1828; resides California
           (1881).
1944. vi. EBENEZER DAGGETT,[8] born Attleboro', Mass., June 14, 1832; died
           1863.
1945. vii. ELLEN A. DAGGETT,[8] born Attleboro', Mass., May 1, 1835; resided
           Boston, Mass. (1881).

Marcus Daggett went to Marlborough, N.H., in 1818, and located
on the farm since owned by Noah Porter.   After residing here eight
years, he removed to Rindge, N.H., where he remained one year, and
then returned to his native town.

1396. LUCAS DAGGETT[7] (*Joab*,[6] *John*,[5] *Ebenezer*,[4] *John*,[3]
Thomas,[2] *John*[1]), born Attleboro', Mass., November 6, 1795; died
Attleboro', Mass., February 18, 1864; married Attleboro', Mass.,
February 23, 1824, Nancy Capron, daughter of Otis and Rachel
(Sweet) Capron; born Attleboro', Mass., August 29, 1796.

1400. PLINY DAGGETT[7] (*Joab*,[6] *John*,[5] *Ebenezer*,[4] *John*,[3] *Thomas*,[2]
John[1]), born Attleboro', Mass., December 20, 1804; "farmer;"
died Attleboro', Mass., March 8, 1865; married Troy, N.H., March
22, 1825, Anne Lawrence, daughter of John and Irene (Newell)
Lawrence, of Troy, N.H.; born Troy, N.H., November 24, 1809;
died Berlin, Wis., March 14, 1880.

Issue :

1946. i.   ELIZABETH ANN DAGGETT,[8] born Troy, N.H., March 21, 1826.
1947. ii.   ALONZO DAGGETT,[8] born Troy, N.H., April 20, 1828.
1948. iii. LORENZO DAGGETT,[8] born Troy, N.H., February 14, 1830; sailed
            from New Bedford, Mass., October 3, 1849, on whale-ship "Her-
            cules;" put ashore sick at Valparaiso, Chili, from where he wrote,
            1850, that he was about to embark on an Austrian bark; not since
            heard from.
1949. iv.   MARY JANE DAGGETT,[8] born Troy, N.H., February 7, 1832.
1950. v.   NANCY MARIA DAGGETT,[8] born Troy, N.H., March 19, 1834; died
            Attleboro', Mass., September 10, 1836.
1951. vi.   FERDINAND DAGGETT,[8] born Attleboro', Mass., May 26, 1836.
1952. vii. PLINY AUGUSTUS DAGGETT,[8] born Attleboro', Mass., January 29,
            1838.
1953. viii. HOMER DAGGETT,[8] born Attleboro', Mass., August 2, 1840; died
            Attleboro', Mass., September 6, 1841.
1954. ix.   EUGENE CLARENCE DAGGETT,[8] born Attleboro', Mass., October 23,
            1842; died Attleboro', Mass., January 14, 1844.

1955. x.   ELLA JOSEPHINE DAGGETT,[8] born Attleboro', Mass., April 29, 1845;
            died Attleboro', Mass., August 18, 1845.
1956. xi.   EUGENE HERBERT DAGGETT,[8] born Attleboro', Mass., September 12,
            1848; died Attleboro', Mass., October 7, 1848.
1957. xii. CLARA LOUISE DAGGETT,[8] born Attleboro', Mass., January 8, 1852.

1402. NANCY DAGGETT [7] (*Joab,*[6] *John,*[5] *Ebenezer,*[4] *John,*[3]
Thomas,[2] *John*[1]), born Attleboro', Mass., July 26, 1810; married
1st, Mr. Mason; married 2d, Mr. Capron.

Issue :

1958. i.   JOSEPH MASON,[8] born Attleboro', Mass.; died Fortress Monroe, Va.

1403. LOIS DAGGETT [7] (*Jesse,*[6] *John,*[5] *Ebenezer,*[4] *John,*[3] *Thomas,*[2]
John[1]), born Attleboro', Mass., November 28, 1797 ; resided Attle-
boro', Mass. (1853) ; married Attleboro', Mass., December 6, 1821,
Ezekiel Bates, of Boston, " housewright," son of Gamaliel and Mary
(Carver) Bates ; born November 5, 1795.

Issue :

1959. i.   JESSE D. BATES,[8] born July 31, 1823; married Mary E. Fowle, July
            9, 1845; had Lois D. Bates;[9] born September 1, 1850.
1960. ii.   JOHN T. BATES,[8] born November 25, 1831.
1961. iii. MARY A. BATES,[8] born September 3, 1836.

1411. LYDIA MAXCY DAGGETT [7] (*Ebenezer,*[6] *John,*[5] *Ebenezer,*[4]
John,[3] *Thomas,*[2] *John*[1]), born Attleboro', Mass., October 16, 1802;
died Attleboro', Mass., February 2, 1882; married Attleboro', Mass.,
June 21, 1824, by Hon. Ebenezer Daggett, to Capron Peck, son of
Jonathan and Sabra (Capron) Peck ; born Attleboro', Mass., Feb-
ruary 4, 1797; died Attleboro', Mass., September 7, 1874.

Issue :

1962. i.   SABRA PECK,[8] born Attleboro', Mass., April 4, 1825; resides there
            (1892).
1963. ii.   SALLY MAXCY PECK,[8] born Attleboro', Mass., October 12, 1826;
            resides there (1892).
1964. iii. JOSEPH CAPRON PECK,[8] born Attleboro', Mass., April 12, 1828; died
            Attleboro', Mass., February 3, 1829.
1965. iv.   JONATHAN MAXCY PECK,[8] born Attleboro', Mass., November 25,
            1829.
1966. v.   LYDIA DAGGETT PECK,[8] born Attleboro', Mass., February 2, 1833;
            died Attleboro', Mass., February 23, 1834.
1967. vi.   Son —— PECK,[8] born Attleboro', Mass., February 17, 1834; died
            Attleboro', Mass., February 17, 1834.
1968. vii. EBENEZER DAGGETT PECK,[8] born Attleboro', Mass., May 22, 1835;
            died Attleboro', Mass., December 26, 1841.
1969. viii. JOHN McCLELLAN PECK,[8] born Attleboro', Mass., May 28, 1837; died
            Attleboro', Mass., August 14, 1838.
1970. ix.   JOHN DAGGETT PECK,[8] born Attleboro', Mass., July 12, 1838; died
            Attleboro', Mass., September 2, 1839.
1971. x.   GEORGE CAPRON PECK,[8] born Attleboro', Mass., October 21, 1840;
            died Attleboro', Mass., February 21, 1841.
1972. xi.   MARY ISADORA PECK,[8] born Attleboro', Mass., April 15, 1842; died
            Attleboro', Mass., May 10, 1852.
1973. xii. LYDIA DAGGETT PECK,[9] born Attleboro', Mass., February 3, 1844;
            resides there (1892).

✝ **1412.** Hon. JOHN DAGGETT [7] (*Ebenezer*,[6] *John*,[5] *Ebenezer*,[4] *John*,[3] *Thomas*,[2] *John* [1]), born Attleboro', Mass., February 10, 1805; died Attleboro', Mass., December 13, 1885; married Sutton, Mass., June 18, 1840, by Rev. Job B. Boomer, to Nancy McClellan Boomer, daughter of Rev. Job Borden and Nancy (McClellan) Boomer, of Sutton, Mass.; born Sutton, Mass., September 29, 1819; died Attleboro', Mass., June 22, 1886.

Issue :

1974. i. MARY BOOMER DAGGETT,[8] born Attleboro', Mass., June 17, 1842; died Attleboro', Mass.. September 9, 1842.
1975. ii. MARCIA McCLELLAN DAGGETT,[8] born Attleboro', Mass., December 26, 1843; died Attleboro', Mass., August 19, 1854.
1976. iii. JOHN MAYHEW DAGGETT,[8] born Attleboro', Mass., November 16, 1845.
1977. iv. CHARLES SHEPARD DAGGETT,[8] born Attleboro', Mass., June 5, 1848; died Attleboro', Mass., June 27, 1855.
✕1978. v. AMELIA MAXCY DAGGETT,[8] born Attleboro', Mass., October 23, 1850.
1979. vi. HENRY HERMAN DAGGETT,[8] born Attleboro', Mass.. September 10, 1852; died Attleboro', Mass., August 13, 1854.
1980. vii. HERMAN SHEPARD DAGGETT,[8] born Attleboro', Mass., September 6, 1855; died Attleboro', Mass., March 9, 1858.

Hon. John Daggett was fitted for college at Wrentham Academy and entered Brown University in 1822, graduating in course in 1826. His law studies occupied three years : one year with Joseph L. Tillinghast, of Providence ; one year with J. J. Fiske, of Wrentham ; and one with Judge Theron Metcalf, of Dedham. He was admitted to the bar in Dedham in December, 1829, and immediately commenced the practice of law in Attleboro', where he remained till his death. Without abandoning his profession, he filled various offices during his long life. For two years, 1833 and 1834, he was editor of the " Dedham Patriot." Mr. Daggett was a member of the Massachusetts House of Representatives for four years, 1836–1839 inclusive, and was again a member in 1866. He was a member of the Senate in 1850. He filled the office of register of probate of the county of Bristol eleven years, from 1850 to 1862, and he was also for many years chairman of the School Committee in Attleboro'. He also found time for literary and historical studies. He published a little book called " Parris's Remains," which contained a memoir, together with selections from the writings. of Samuel Parris, M.D. [B.U., 1821].

Mr. Daggett was one of the constituent members of the Old Colony Historical Society, and for many years was its president. He was also a member of the New England Genealogical Society. His interest in inquiries and studies pertaining to the objects of these societies induced him to write and publish the history of his native town, " Attleboro'," a task which he so worthily discharged as to win for him, with the respect and love of his townsmen, the name and influence of an authority in all that pertained to the annals of their town. It is a fact worthy of record and remembrance that from the year he entered college to the year of his death he was present at every commencement, attending thus sixty-three successive commencements. The "Bristol County Republican," under date of December 18, 1885, says of him:

On the 10th of February last, there was a large gathering of relatives and friends to greet him on the advent of his octogenarian birthday, a day of congratulation to him and his esteemed wife. His gentle kindliness, courtesy, and integrity of character as a counsellor and friend — always to say a kind word, never a hard one — secured for him the title of honest John Daggett, which he wore with his modest grace and merit from his college days, during these sixty years, to the time when death claimed him as a shining mark. He has passed away, but his life-long deeds of kindness will live after him, and his memory as the Christian gentleman will ever be cherished.

Mr. Daggett was much interested in the Doggett-Daggett genealogy, and during his life made several collections of material to aid in such a work, and, together with Mr. Wm. R. Deane, tried to solve some of the obscure points in the early history of the family.

1414. HARVEY MAXCY DAGGETT [7] (*Ebenezer*,[6] *John*,[5] *Ebenezer*,[4] *John*,[3] *Thomas*,[2] *John* [1]), born Attleboro', Mass., June 10, 1809; died Attleboro', Mass., September 28, 1886; married 1st, Attleboro', Mass., June 28, 1836, Susan Content Daggett, daughter of Otis and Content (Smith) Daggett (No. 1922); born Cumberland, R.I., March 7, 1810; died Attleboro', Mass., November 29, 1846; married 2d, Attleboro', Mass., March 14, 1850, by Rev. N. G. Lovell, to Nancy Jane Bates, daughter of Dexter and Bethiah (Wilmarth) Bates; born Attleboro', Mass., January 24, 1817; resides North Attleboro', Mass. (1892), " on the old homestead."

Issue :

1981. i. SARAH MAXCY DAGGETT,[8] born Attleboro', Mass., April 29, 1837; died Attleboro', Mass., March 26, 1850.
1982. ii. EBENEZER DAGGETT,[8] born Attleboro', Mass., August 5, 1839; died Attleboro', Mass., January 13, 1842.
1983. iii. HARVEY BATES DAGGETT,[8] born Attleboro', Mass., October 16, 1851; died Attleboro', Mass., June 11, 1882.
1984. iv. NANCY ELLA DAGGETT,[8] born Attleboro', Mass., March 8, 1853.

Harvey Maxey Daggett was a farmer on the old homestead.

1415. AMA IDE DAGGETT [7] (*Ebenezer*,[6] *John*,[5] *Ebenezer*,[4] *John*,[3] *Thomas*,[2] *John*[1]), born Attleboro', Mass., November 24, 1811; resides 22 Harrington avenue, Worcester, Mass. (1892); married Attleboro', Mass., October 14, 1834, by Rev. Jonathan E. Forbush, to John

McClellan, of Sutton, Mass., son of James and Beulah (Bacon) McClellan; born Sutton, Mass., December 13, 1806; died Grafton, Mass., March 21, 1886.

Issue:

1985. i.   JAMES E. McCLELLAN,[8] born Sutton, Mass., June 16, 1838.
1986. ii.   EMMA C. McCLELLAN,[8] born Sutton, Mass., January 21, 1841; resides 22 Harrington avenue, Worcester, Mass. (1892).
1987. iii. SARAH J. McCLELLAN,[8] born Sutton, Mass., April 14, 1843; resides Worcester, Mass. (1892).
1988. iv. MARCY T. McCLELLAN,[8] born Sutton, Mass., July 22, 1845; died Sutton, Mass., August 27, 1848.
1989. v.   JOHN E. McCLELLAN,[8] born Sutton, Mass., September 5, 1847.
1990. vi. ARTHUR D. McCLELLAN,[8] born Sutton, Mass., May 21, 1850; married New York city, October 9, 1882, Mrs. Mary A. Hartwell; address, 82 Devonshire street, Boston, Mass. (1892).
1991. vii. LEILA A. McCLELLAN,[8] born Sutton, Mass., February 23, 1852; died Grafton, Mass., July 29, 1875.
1992. viii. FRANCIS A. McCLELLAN,[8] born Sutton, Mass., December 24, 1854; married New York city, October 9, 1888, Ella A. Armsby; she resides Worcester, Mass. (1892); he died Boston, Mass., January 18, 1889.
1993. ix. JENNIE I. McCLELLAN,[8] born Grafton, Mass., July 7, 1857; resides Worcester, Mass. (1892).

John McClellan, when a young man, was major of the State militia, and was called by this title to some extent through his life. While still young, he was made deacon of the Baptist church in Grafton, and served in that capacity until his death.

He filled the various offices of trust and honor which could be bestowed by his townsmen, being especially active during the civil war. He represented his district in the State Legislature in 1867.

1416. MARCY SHEPARD DAGGETT[7] (*Ebenezer,[6] John,[5] Ebenezer,[4] John,[3] Thomas,[2] John[1]*), born Attleboro', Mass., January 14, 1814; died Boston, Mass., November 23, 1843; married Attleboro', Mass., December 3, 1835, by Rev. Jonathan E. Forbush, to Erastus David Everett, of Boston, son of Deacon Silas and Tryphena (Shepard) Everett; born Attleboro', Mass., September 23, 1810; died Falls Church, Va., February 28, 1881.

Issue:

1994. i.   ELLEN LOUISA EVERETT,[8] born August 31, 1836; resides Attleboro', Mass. (1892).
1995. ii.   EDWARD MAXCY EVERETT,[8] born August 4, 1838; died September 3, 1845.
1996. iii. CHARLES EBENEZER EVERETT,[8] born July 27, 1840; died September 20, 1840.
1997. iv. SHEPARD SILAS EVERETT,[8] born Boston, Mass., October 27, 1841.

1418. HANDEL NAPHTALI DAGGETT[7] (*Ebenezer,[6] John,[5] Ebenezer,[4] John,[3] Thomas,[2] John[1]*), born Attleboro', Mass., January 27, 1821; resides Attleboro' Falls, Mass. (1892); married 1st, Wrentham, Mass., June 20, 1844, by Rev. Reuben Morey, to Eunice

Whipple Shephard, daughter of Jonathan and Jemima Shephard, of Wrentham; born Wrentham, Mass., April 29, 1823; died Attleboro', Mass., January 22, 1848; married 2d, Livonia, N.Y., December 20, 1848, by Rev. Mr. Riley, to Jane Amelia Adams, of Livonia, N.Y., daughter of Ephraim and Lavinia (Morey) Adams; born Richmond, N.Y., December 22, 1825; died Attleboro', Mass., March 4, 1854; married 3d, Livonia, N.Y., June 19, 1855, by Rev. Mr. Fowler, to Lucy Frost Adams, daughter of Ephraim and Lavinia (Morey) Adams; born Richmond, N.Y., March 13, 1828; died Attleboro', Mass., May 23, 1870; married 4th, Boston, Mass., November 10, 1875, by Rev. W. Burnet Wright, to Mrs. Annie Parsons Furbish, of Boston, whose maiden name was Annie Merritt Parsons, daughter of Fidelio and Rachel Anne (Bowker) Parsons; born Bangor, Me., August 31, 1842.

Issue:

1998. i. JOSEPHINE SHEPHARD DAGGETT,[8] born Attleboro', Mass., June 21, 1845.

1999. ii. FRANCIS WHIPPLE DAGGETT,[8] born Attleboro', Mass., December 30, 1847; died Livonia, N.Y., August 19, 1854.

2000. iii. EUNICE EUDORA DAGGETT,[8] born Attleboro', Mass., May 21, 1851; died Attleboro', Mass., September 16, 1852.

2001. iv. FLORA EUGENIA DAGGETT,[8] born Attleboro', Mass., September 21, 1853; died Attleboro', Mass., March 4, 1857.

2002. v. Daughter —— DAGGETT,[8] born Attleboro', Mass., February 11, 1856; died Attleboro', Mass., February 11, 1856.

2003. vi. FLORENCE JANE DAGGETT,[8] born Attleboro', Mass., November 25, 1857.

2004. vii. FRANCES ADAMS DAGGETT,[8] born Attleboro', Mass., January 16, 1860.

2005. viii. BLANCHE DAGGETT,[8] born Attleboro', Mass., March 8, 1879.

Handel Naphtali Daggett is a manufacturer. Has been selectman and representative.

His home is an elegant estate at Attleboro' Falls, which was formerly the homestead of Deacon Mayhew, the three Elihus, and Rev. Lyman W. Daggett.

1419. Hon. HOMER MICAJAH DAGGETT [7] (*Ebenezer,*[6] *John,*[5] *Ebenezer,*[4] *John,*[3] *Thomas,*[2] *John*[1]), born Attleboro', Mass., January 27, 1821; resides Attleboro', Mass. (1892); married Attleboro', Mass., May 28, 1843, by Rev. Reuben Morey, to Angelina Daggett, of Surry, N.H., daughter of Otis and Content (Smith) Daggett (No. 1926); born Surry, N.H., May 30, 1819; died Attleboro', Mass., October 9, 1885.

Issue:

2006. i. ALICE ANGELINA DAGGETT,[8] born Attleboro', Mass., July 10, 1846; resides there (1892).

2007. ii. HOMER MICAJAH DAGGETT,[8] born Attleboro', Mass., May 22, 1848.

2008. iii. JESSE TAYLOR DAGGETT,[8] born Attleboro', Mass., January 8, 1850; died Attleboro', Mass., June 3, 1853.

2009. iv. SANFORD DAGGETT,[8] born Attleboro', Mass., October 14, 1852.
2010. v.   JENNY DAGGETT,[8] born Attleboro', Mass., September 1, 1854; died
           Attleboro', Mass., October 5, 1854.
2011. vi. Son —— DAGGETT,[8] born Attleboro', Mass., February 3, 1858; died
           Attleboro', Mass., February 3, 1858.
2012. vii. FREDERIC EUGENE DAGGETT,[8] born Attleboro', Mass., December 3,
           1860; died Attleboro', Mass., August 9, 1864.

Hon. Homer Micajah Daggett is a banker; was senator from his
district.

1437. GRACE ANN DAGGETT [7] (*Henry*,[6] *Naphtali*,[5] *Ebenezer*,[4]
John,[3] *Thomas*,[2] *John* [1]), born 1788; died New Haven, Conn.,
November 15, 1880.

Grace Ann Daggett was a communicant of the Centre Church,
New Haven, for sixty-nine years.

On the evening of July 4, 1879, she was serenaded by the " Howe
Band," in commemoration of the prominent part taken by her grandfather, Rev. Naphtali Daggett, in defence of New Haven a century
before.

1439. STEPHEN DAGGETT [7] (*Henry*,[6] *Naphtali*,[5] *Ebenezer*,[4] *John*,[3]
Thomas,[2] *John* [1]), born New Haven, Conn., July 1, 1798; died Pon-
totoc, Miss., September 15, 1880; married Cotton Gin, Miss.,
February 28, 1828, by Thomas C. Stewart, to Sarah Walton, daugh-
ter of Jesse and Joanna (Walton) Walton; born Richmond, Va.,
July 2, 1808; died Pontotoc, Miss., May 18, 1889.

Issue :

2013. i.   GRACE ANN DAGGETT,[8] born Pontotoc, Miss., September 28, 1842.
2014. ii. HARRIET HUNT DAGGETT,[8] born Pontotoc, Miss., August 15, 1844.
2015. iii. JULIA DRIVER DAGGETT,[8] born Pontotoc, Miss., January 30, 1847.
2016. iv. MARY WALTON DAGGETT,[8] born Pontotoc, Miss., June 3, 1850; died
           in infancy.
2017. v.   SARAH HOPKINS DAGGETT,[8] born Pontotoc, Miss., March 13, 1853.
2018. vi. CHARLES WALTON DAGGETT,[8] born Pontotoc, Miss., September 9,
           1856.

Stephen Daggett was a " civil engineer." He was sent by government to make survey of the land purchased from the Chickasaw
Indians. He was afterward appointed land agent, and had charge
of the government land-office at Pontotoc.

1441. HORACE DAGGETT [7] (*Henry*,[6] *Naphtali*,[5] *Ebenezer*,[4] *John*,[3]
Thomas,[2] *John* [1]), born New Haven, Conn., February 26, 1801;
" merchant; " died Pontotoc, Miss., June 23, 1867; married 1st,
October 22, 1832, Jane Hawley; born Plattsburg, N.Y.; died Cotton
Gin, Miss., September 10, 1836; married 2d, York, Ohio, July 26,
1840, by Rev. Mr. Grawville, to Lydia Beckwith Root, widow of
Samuel M. Root, and daughter of Reynold and Martha (Butler)

Beckwith; born Pittsfield, Mass., January 20, 1813; died near Oakland. Miss., June 26, 1872.

Issue :

2019. i.   HENRY DAGGETT,[8] born Mobile, Ala., April 11, 1842; died Iuka, Miss. (U.S. Hospital), June 23, 1862.
2020. ii. FRED HUNT DAGGETT,[8] born New Haven, Conn., April 2, 1844.
2021. iii. JANE HAWLEY DAGGETT,[8] born Mobile, Ala., September 22, 1846.
2022. iv. MARTHA MOSELEY DAGGETT,[8] born Pontotoc. Miss., December 4, 1850; died Pontotoc, Miss., January 10, 1851.
2023. v.   IDA HUNTINGTON DAGGETT,[8] born Pontotoc, Miss., October 15, 1854.

1442. ELIZA DAGGETT [7] (*Henry,*[6] *Naphtali,*[5] *Ebenezer,*[4] *John,*[3] *Thomas,*[2] *John* [1]). lived in Waterville, Lucas Co.. Ohio; married Mr. Isham.

Issue :

2024. i.   ALFRED ISHAM.[8]
2025. ii. WILLIAM F. ISHAM.[8]
2026. iii. HENRY S. ISHAM.[8]
2027. iv. SARAH ISHAM.[8]
2028. v.   CAROLINE E. ISHAM.[8]

1444. ELIZABETH DAGGETT [7] (*Ezra,*[6] *Naphtali,*[5] *Ebenezer,*[4] *John,*[3] *Thomas,*[2] *John* [1]), born New Haven, Conn., January 26, 1791; died July, 1876; married May 9, 1813. Thomas Kensett; born Hampton Court, Middlesex. Eng.. August 6, 1786; died June 16, 1829.

Issue :

2029. i.   THOMAS KENSETT,[8] born February 12. 1814; married 1st, Eliza Wheeler; married 2d, Eliza Ann Wheeler; married 3d, Gertrude W. Brown; was a dealer in canned goods, Baltimore. Md.; died August 5, 1877.
2030. ii. JOHN FREDERICK KENSETT,[8] born Cheshire, Conn., March 22, 1816.
2031. iii. ELIZABETH DAGGETT KENSETT,[8] born August 11, 1817.
2032. iv. FREDERICK NEWBURY KENSETT,[8] born December 27, 1819; died Brooklyn, N.Y., August 27, 1881.
2033. v.   EZRA DAGGETT KENSETT,[8] born August 19, 1821; died July 26, 1822.
2034. vi. SARAH MARSHALL KENSETT,[8] born December 2. 1822; married Noah J. Kellogg: resides 668 Nostrand avenue, Brooklyn, N.Y. (1892).

Thomas Kensett was an engraver, and published. about 1806, the map of New Haven, drawn by General Wadsworth in 1748. This was the first map of New Haven published, although an earlier one was drawn in 1724, by Joseph Brown.

1445. SMITH DAGGETT [7] (*Ezra,*[6] *Naphtali,*[5] *Ebenezer,*[4] *John,*[3] *Thomas,*[2] *John* [1]). born New Haven, Conn., March 13, 1793; died March 13, 1840; married, April 12. 1818. Sarah Godfrey; born 1800; died November 6, 1840.

Issue :

2035. i.   ELIZA DAGGETT,[8] born January 28, 1821; died October 2, 1821.
2036. ii. ELIZA DAGGETT,[8] born January 24, 1824; married John Y. Isham; she died January 27, 1848.

2037. iii.   ALFRED DAGGETT,[8] born March 13, 1826.
2038. iv.   HARRIET DAGGETT,[8] born November 17, 1828; died October 12, 1832.
2039. v.   WILLIAM FRED DAGGETT,[8] born May 24, 1830; married Alvira Scribner.
2040. vi.   HENRY S. DAGGETT,[8] born February 20, 1832; resides Lafayette, Ind.
2041. vii.   GEORGE W. DAGGETT,[8] born March 12, 1834; died September 10, 1834.
2042. viii.   SARAH F. DAGGETT,[8] born January 11, 1836; resides Lake Odessa, Mich. (1892).
2043. ix.   CAROLINE E. DAGGETT,[8] born March 4, 1840; married Henry Short.

1448. ALFRED DAGGETT[7] (*Ezra*,[6] *Naphtali*,[5] *Ebenezer*,[4] *John*,[3] *Thomas*,[2] *John*[1]), born New Haven, Conn., September 30, 1799; died New Haven, Conn., January 27, 1872; married New Haven, Conn., November 26, 1829, by Rev. James Young, to Laura Gilbert, daughter of Elias and Phebe (Benedict) Gilbert, of New Haven; born Torringford, Conn., June 2, 1812; resides San Diego, Cal. (1892).

Issue:

2044. i.   PHEBE ANNE DAGGETT,[8] born New Haven, Conn., March 5, 1831; died New Haven, Conn., January 31, 1832.
2045. ii.   CORNELIA GILBERT DAGGETT,[8] born New Haven, Conn., November 26, 1832; died New Haven, Conn., May 4, 1852.
2046. iii.   VIRGINIA BENEDICT DAGGETT,[8] born New Haven, Conn., March 29, 1835; died New Haven, Conn., February 5, 1848.
2047. iv.   ALFRED DAGGETT,[8] born New Haven, Conn., August 23, 1837.
2048. v.   LAURA DAGGETT,[8] born New Haven, Conn., October 8, 1839.
2049. vi.   HENRY DAGGETT,[8] born New Haven, Conn., July 12, 1841.
2050. vii.   CHARLES DAGGETT,[8] born New Haven, Conn., January 22, 1845; died New Haven, Conn., April 25, 1849.

Alfred Daggett was a bank-note engraver, and taught the art to his nephew, John F. Kensett. He was first selectman for the town of New Haven for several years.

He was, about 1846–7, chief engineer of the New Haven Fire Department, and was afterward an officer of the Customs.

1449. WILLIAM DAGGETT[7] (*Ezra*,[6] *Naphtali*,[5] *Ebenezer*,[4] *John*,[3] *Thomas*,[2] *John*[1]), born New Haven, Conn., December 12, 1801; died New Haven, Conn., December 3, 1884; married St. Albans, Vt., November 26, 1828, Ursula Hunt, daughter of Elijah and Abigail (Gibbs) Hunt, of St. Albans, Vt.; born St. Albans, Vt., April 23, 1809; died New Haven, Conn., December 30, 1878.

Issue:

2051. i.   ELIZA HUNT DAGGETT,[8] born New Haven, Conn., December 30, 1829; resides 1172 Chapel street, New Haven, Conn. (1892).
2052. ii.   WILLIAM DAGGETT,[8] born New Haven, Conn., December 3, 1831.
2053. iii.   SARAH CORNELIA DAGGETT,[8] born New Haven, Conn., October 12, 1834; resides 1172 Chapel street, New Haven, Conn. (1892).
2054. iv.   ROBERT PLATT DAGGETT,[8] born New Haven, Conn., January 13, 1847.

1450. MARY DAGGETT[7] (*Ezra*,[6] *Naphtali*,[5] *Ebenezer*,[4] *John*,[3] *Thomas*,[2] *John*[1]), born New Haven, Conn., November 29, 1803;

died March 15, 1850; married May 7, 1831, Amos Bradley; born August 21, 1799; died September 4, 1860.

Issue:

2055. i.   SILAS AMOS BRADLEY,[8] born March 9, 1832; died 1892.
2056. ii. FREDERICK DAGGETT BRADLEY,[8] born November 22, 1833.
2057. iii. JOHN THOMAS BRADLEY,[8] born August 31, 1835.
2058. iv. HARRIET ELIZABETH BRADLEY,[8] born August 22, 1838.
2059. v.   JULIA ANN BRADLEY,[8] born January 23, 1841; died August 29, 1841.
2060. vi. MARY JANE BRADLEY,[8] born July 24, 1846; died August 14, 1846.

1452. SARAH DAGGETT[7] (*Ezra,[6] Naphtali,[5] Ebenezer,[4] John,[3] Thomas,[2] John[1]*), born New Haven, Conn., October 7, 1807; married April 25, 1832, John C. Mersick.

Issue:

2061. i. EDWIN FRANCIS MERSICK,[8] born January 8, 1838.
2062. ii. CHARLES SMITH MERSICK,[8] born December 13, 1840; married October 10, 1865, Ellen Louisa English; issue: May English Mersick,[9] born May 6, 1868.

1453. FREDERICK DAGGETT[7] (*Ezra,[6] Naphtali,[5] Ebenezer,[4] John,[3] Thomas,[2] John[1]*), born New Haven, Conn., November 28, 1809; "cabinet-maker;" died New Haven, Conn., April 23, 1854; married 1st, 1836, Susan A. Hall; born Hamden, Conn., 1818; died New Haven, Conn., October 23, 1851; married 2d, New Haven, Conn., April 9, 1854, by Rev. John S. Mitchell, to Mrs. Frances J. Bailey; born Canandaigua, N.Y., 1818.

Issue:

2063. i.   NELSON DAGGETT,[8] born New Haven, Conn., September 7, 1837; died New Haven, Conn., March 15, 1861.
2064. ii. FREDERICK DAGGETT,[8] born May 24, 1841; died March, 1879.
2065. iii. DWIGHT E. DAGGETT,[8] born May 18, 1845; died New Haven, Conn., July 29, 1864.
2066. iv. EZRA DAGGETT,[8] born New Haven, Conn., November 9, 1847.
2067. v.   MARY A. DAGGETT,[8] born New Haven, Conn., December 23, 1850.

1459. LEVI DAGGETT[7] (*Samuel,[6] Samuel,[5] Ebenezer,[4] John,[3] Thomas,[2] John[1]*), born Albany, N.Y., April 29, 1788; died Penfield, N.Y., June 4, 1865; married Bainbridge, N.Y., March 20, 1819, Fannie Larribee; born Brattleboro', Vt., December 10, 1795; died Penfield, N.Y., January 21, 1872.

Issue:

2068. i.   CATHERINE DAGGETT,[8] born Bainbridge, N.Y., May 22, 1820.
2069. ii.   GEORGE DAGGETT,[8] born Arcada, N.Y., June 27, 1821.
2070. iii. CAROLINE DAGGETT,[8] born Bainbridge, N.Y., April 13, 1824.
2071. iv.   HANNAH DAGGETT,[8] born Campbelltown, N.Y., September 7, 1826.
2072. v.   BETSY DAGGETT,[8] born Campbelltown, N.Y., April 12, 1828; died April 20, 1832.
2073. vi.   SALLY DAGGETT,[8] born Campbelltown, N.Y., May 18, 1830; died May 16, 1831.
2074. vii. MARY DAGGETT,[8] born Bath, N.Y., May 12, 1832; died November 25, 1853.

2075. viii. JOHN DAGGETT,[8] born Addison, N.Y., May 2, 1834; "soldier;" died Salsbury Prison, February 14, 1865.
2076. ix. MARTIN VAN BUREN DAGGETT,[8] born Caneadea, N.Y., August 30, 1838.
2077. x. HORACE DAGGETT,[8] born Caneadea, N.Y., March 10, 1841; 2d lieut. 8th N.Y. Cavalry; died in battle, April 10, 1865.

1460. JOHN DAGGETT[7] (*Samuel,*[6] *Samuel,*[5] *Ebenezer,*[4] *John,*[3] *Thomas,*[2] *John* [1]), born Flatbush, N.Y.; married Eliza Cooper; lived in Newark, N.Y.

Issue:

2078. i. DAVID DAGGETT.[8]
2079. ii. SAMUEL DAGGETT.[8]
2080. iii. JOHN DAGGETT,[8] born Newark, N.Y., May 9, 1833.
2081. iv. WILLIAM DAGGETT.[8]
2082. v. BENJAMIN DAGGETT.[8]
2083. vi. LUCINDA DAGGETT.[8]
2084. vii. OPHELIA DAGGETT.[8]
2085. viii. EMILY DAGGETT.[8]
2086. ix. SUSAN DAGGETT [8]
2087. x. ELIZA DAGGETT.[8]
2088. xi. MARY DAGGETT.[8]
2089. xii. ALICE DAGGETT.[8]
2090. xiii. HATTIE DAGGETT.[8]
2091. xiv. LIBBIE DAGGETT.[8]
2092. xv. KATIE DAGGETT.[8]

John Daggett moved first to Bainbridge, N.Y., and about 1824 to Newark, N.Y.

Here he was proprietor of an extensive manufactory of woollen machinery.

1461. ELISHA DAGGETT [7] (*Samuel,*[6] *Samuel,*[5] *Ebenezer,*[4] *John,*[3] *Thomas,*[2] *John* [1]), lived and died Colesville, N.Y.; married Tabitha Loomis.

Issue:

2093. i. LAFAYETTE DAGGETT.[8]
2094. ii. EVERETT DAGGETT.[8]
2095. iii. ELLIOT DAGGETT.[8]
2096. iv. ANTOINETTE DAGGETT.[8]
2097. v. HENRIETTA DAGGETT.[8]

1462. PRISCILLA DAGGETT [7] (*Samuel,*[6] *Samuel,*[5] *Ebenezer,*[4] *John,*[3] *Thomas,*[2] *John* [1]), born near Albany, N.Y., June, 1790; died Lowell, Mich., August 8, 1864; married Newark, N.Y., by Rev. Peter Sabins, to Roswell Jennings; born 1778; "farmer;" lived and died Walworth, N.Y., March 3, 1847.

Issue:

2098. i. ELISHA JENNINGS,[8] born Walworth, N.Y., July 31, 1825.
2099. ii. SARAH JENNINGS,[8] born Walworth, N.Y., June 24, 1827; unmarried; resides Lowell, Mich. (1884).

1463. POLLY DAGGETT [7] (*Samuel,*[6] *Samuel,*[5] *Ebenezer,*[4] *John,*[3] *Thomas,*[2] *John*[1]), married Jacob Force; resided Newark, N.Y.

Issue:

2100. i. JOHN FORCE.[8]
2101. ii. LEVI FORCE.[8]
2102. iii. ORSON FORCE,[8] died about 1849.
2103. iv. AUGUSTUS FORCE.[8]
2104. v. HENRY FORCE.[8]
105. vi. MARY JANE FORCE.[8]

Several others died young of small-pox.

1464. SAMUEL DAGGETT [7] (*Samuel,*[6] *Samuel,*[5] *Ebenezer,*[4] *John,*[3] *Thomas,*[2] *John*[1]), born May 31, 1797; died April 3, 1871; married September 5, 1833, Lydia Willett; born May 6, 1811; lived in Newark, N.Y.; died December 30, 1871.

Issue:

2106. i. HANNAH DAGGETT,[8] born August 20, 1834; died June 6, 1847.
2107. ii. STEPHEN DAGGETT,[8] born February 22, 1836; married December 5, 1863, Mary Lyons; he died January 22, 1865.
2108. iii. JOHN DAGGETT,[8] born March 26, 1838; died April 12, 1862.
2109. iv. LUCINDA DAGGETT,[8] born March 28, 1841; died June 6, 1847.
2110. v. AMELIA DAGGETT,[8] born November 8, 1843; married January 1, 1863, Henry Buennemann.
2111. vi. JULIA A. DAGGETT,[8] born October 22, 1846; married March 22, 1873, John Coy; resides Yankee Springs, Mich. (1884).
2112. vii. JOSEPHINE P. DAGGETT,[8] born March 10, 1850; married Mr. Valentine; resides Yankee Springs, Mich. (1884).
2113. viii. ROYAL A. DAGGETT,[8] born May 26, 1853; resides Yankee Springs, Mich. (1884).
2114. ix. ELIZA DAGGETT,[8] born March 1, 1855; died October 16, 1856.

1465. MARGARET DAGGETT [7] (*Samuel,*[6] *Samuel,*[5] *Ebenezer,*[4] *John,*[3] *Thomas,*[2] *John*[1]), born May 31, 1797; married Constant Weaver; resided Newark, N.Y.

Issue:

2115. i. HESTER ANN WEAVER,[8] married David Jennings, son of Roswell and —— (Aldrich) Jennings; address, Palo, Mich., box 140.

1466. SALLY DAGGETT [7] (*Samuel,*[6] *Samuel,*[5] *Ebenezer,*[4] *John,*[3] *Thomas,*[2] *John*[1]), born near Albany, N.Y., April 4, 1799; died, Walworth, N.Y., August 31, 1874; married 1st, Newark, N.Y., Michael Lusk, son of Jeremiah and Elizabeth Lusk; "farmer;" born near Newark, N.Y., July 8, 1796; died Walworth, N.Y., April 4, 1835; married 2d, Newark, N.Y., James Whittleton, son of Edmund Whittleton; "farmer;" born England, April 6, 1802; died Walworth, N.Y., September 11, 1883.

Issue:

2116. i. ELIZABETH LUSK,[8] born Walworth, N.Y., July 26, 1831; married Walworth, N.Y., spring of 1871, William Hall; she died November 6, 1872.
2117. ii. JEREMIAH LUSK,[8] born Walworth, N.Y., January 2, 1834.

1469. Lois Daggett [7] (*Samuel,*[6] *Samuel,*[5] *Ebenezer,*[4] *John,*[3] *Thomas,*[2] *John* [1]), resides Oaks Corners, Ontario county, N.Y. (1885) ; married Heman Bostwick, of Newark, N.Y.

Issue :

2118. i.   George W. Bostwick,[8] resides Geneva, N.Y. (1885).
2119. ii. I. Benson Bostwick,[8] resides Rochester, N.Y. (1885).
2120. iii. Nellie Bostwick,[8] married Mr. Henderson; resides Tiffin, Ohio (1884).

1470. Herman Daggett [7] (*Ebenezer,*[6] *Samuel,*[5] *Ebenezer,*[4] *John,*[3] *Thomas,*[2] *John* [1]), born Enfield, Mass., September 30, 1790; " hotel-keeper; " died Jordan, N.Y., February 27, 1832; married Brutus, N.Y.

Issue :

2121. i. Robert P. Daggett,[8] born 1820; resides Jordan, N.Y. (1892).
2122. ii. Burton Daggett,[8] born 1844.

1471. Moses Daggett [7] (*Ebenezer,*[6] *Samuel,*[5] *Ebenezer,*[4] *John,*[3] *Thomas,*[2] *John* [1]), born Enfield, Mass., April 7, 1796; " blacksmith; " died Springfield, Mass., April 18, 1876; married 1st, Lovica Pinney, daughter of Joel Pinney; born Somers, Conn., 1800; died Springfield, Mass., March 6, 1857; married 2d, Springfield, Mass., November 30, 1859, by Rev. Geo. DeF. Folsom, to Miranda Burnham, daughter of Eleazer and Wealthy Ann Burnham; born Rockville, Conn., 1816; died Springfield, Mass., January 21, 1876.

Issue :

2123. i.   Mariette Daggett,[8] born Springfield, Mass., June 30, 1827; died Springfield, Mass., August 4, 1844.
2124. ii.   Harriet Daggett,[8] born Springfield, Mass., October 21, 1829.
2125. iii. Francis Daggett,[8] born Springfield, Mass., April 16, 1832.
2126. iv.   Lovisa Daggett,[8] born Springfield, Mass., June 17, 1834; died Springfield, Mass., October 17, 1848.
2127. v.   Albert Daggett,[8] born Springfield, Mass., May 12, 1836.
2128. vi.   Sarah Elizabeth Daggett,[8] born Springfield, Mass., March 14, 1838.
2129. vii. Daughter —— Daggett,[8] born Springfield, Mass., April 17, 1845; died without name.
2130. viii. —— Daggett,[8] born Springfield, Mass.; died without name.

1472. Ebenezer Daggett [7] (*Ebenezer,*[6] *Samuel,*[5] *Ebenezer,*[4] *John,*[3] *Thomas,*[2] *John* [1]), born Enfield, Mass., June 16, 1798; " carpenter and builder; " died Jordan, N.Y., December 26, 1859; married November 18, 1823, Mary Pope Kennedy, daughter of Lemuel and Rebecca (Pope) Kennedy; born October 22, 1801; died Ottumwa, Iowa, November 22, 1862.

Issue :

2131. i.   Henry Bingham Daggett,[8] born Jordan, N.Y., May 28, 1825.
2132. ii. Rebecca Jennett Daggett,[8] born Jordan, N.Y., October 20, 1827.
2133. iii. William Daggett,[8] born Jordan, N.Y., March 12, 1830.
2134. iv. Calvin Foote Daggett,[8] born Jordan, N.Y., January 24, 1832.

2135. v.   HELEN M. DAGGETT,[8] born Jordan, N.Y., January 12, 1834; died
        Jordan, N.Y., November 12, 1834.
2136. vi. SARAH E. DAGGETT,[8] born Jordan, N.Y., August 7, 1835; died Jor-
        dan, N.Y., November 19, 1861.
2137. vii. MARY L. DAGGETT,[8] born Jordan, N.Y., April 14, 1838; died Jor-
        dan, N.Y., December 7, 1841.
2138. viii. EDWARD H. DAGGETT,[8] born Jordan, N.Y., September 18, 1840; died
        Jordan, N.Y., June 30, 1842.
2139. ix. EMMA M. DAGGETT,[8] born Jordan, N.Y., June 1, 1842; died Jordan,
        N.Y., June 21, 1842.
2140. x.   EDGAR DAGGETT,[8] born Jordan, N.Y., October 9, 1844.

1473. LYDIA DAGGETT [7] (*Ebenezer,*[6] *Samuel,*[5] *Ebenezer,*[4] *John,*[3]
Thomas,[2] *John*[1]), born 1800; died Jordan, N.Y., March, 1862;
married Enfield, Mass., Alonzo Case; born Connecticut, 1800; died
Jordan, N.Y., 1864.

Issue: two children.

1475. PRISCILLA DAGGETT [7] (*Ebenezer,*[6] *Samuel,*[5] *Ebenezer,*[4]
John,[3] *Thomas,*[2] *John*[1]), born 1803; died Jordan, N.Y., August 24,
1815; married Enfield, Mass., Silas Hull.

Issue:

2141. i.   ROSAMOND HULL.[8]
2142. ii. RUFUS HULL.[8]
2143. iii. CHARLES HULL.[8]

1480. LEVI DAGGETT [7] (*Levi,*[6] *Samuel,*[5] *Ebenezer,*[4] *John,*[3]
Thomas,[2] *John*[1]), born Schuylerville, N.Y., November 23, 1796;
died 1874; married Matsy Sanford, of Palmyra, N.Y.; born 1805;
died 1881.

Issue: two daughters, five sons.

2144. i.   J. R. R. DAGGETT,[8] born Arcadia, N.Y., 1835; resides Quincy, Mich.
        (1883).
2145. ii. MARY DAGGETT,[8] married L. B. King; resides Quincy, (Ill. 1883).

1481. DAVID PATTERSON DAGGETT [7] (*Levi,*[6] *Samuel,*[5] *Ebenezer,*[4]
John,[3] *Thomas,*[2] *John*[1]), born Schuylerville, N.Y., July 3, 1799;
died Palmyra, N.Y., September 6, 1861; married 1st, Arcadia, N.Y.,
May 6, 1821, Ruth Hildreth, daughter of Samuel and Phœbe (Cooper)
Hildreth; born Red Creek, L.I., N.Y., June 27, 1803; died Pal-
myra, N.Y., April 11, 1847; married 2d, South Hampton, L.I.,
N.Y., September 19, 1848, Hannah Hildreth, daughter of Samuel
and Phœbe (Cooper) Hildreth; born Bainbridge, N.Y., January 6,
1814; died Palmyra, N.Y., December 14, 1855; married 3d, Jordan,
N.Y., October 1, 1856, Caroline Knowlton, daughter of Joseph and
Priscilla (Howe) Knowlton; born Shrewsbury, Mass., April 20,
1803; died Jordan, N.Y., March 3, 1883.

Issue:

2146. i.   PHILIP D. DAGGETT,[8] born Palmyra, N.Y., July 3, 1822; died Pal-
        myra, N.Y., July 31, 1822.

2147. ii. DEBORAH DAGGETT,[8] born Palmyra, N.Y., September 16, 1823; died
Palmyra, N.Y., May 23, 1845.
2148. iii. LYDIA AMANDA DAGGETT,[8] born Palmyra, N.Y., May 31, 1827; died
Palmyra, N.Y., April 28, 1845.
2149. iv. RUTH ANN DAGGETT,[8] born Palmyra, N.Y., July 3, 1849; died Palmyra, N.Y., February 9, 1855.
2150. v. LYDIA JEANNETTE DAGGETT,[8] born Palmyra, N.Y., May 9, 1852; "a
teacher;" address, care E. A. Bell, 430 Delaware ave., Buffalo,
N.Y. (1892).

David P. Daggett resided in Palmyra, N.Y.; was a manufacturer
and inventor of agricultural implements. The Daggett plows and
cultivators were unrivalled, and showed him to be a man of no
ordinary genius. Deacon Daggett held a prominent position in the
Presbyterian church, and is still remembered in Palmyra.

1482. SARAH DAGGETT [7] (*Levi*,[6] *Samuel*,[5] *Ebenezer*,[4] *John*,[3]
Thomas,[2] *John* [1]), born May 18, 1803; died Aurora, N.Y., October
13, 1859; married Aurora, N.Y., September 5, 1827, Henry Wells
(founder American Express Company); born Vermont, December
12, ——; died Glasgow, Scotland, December 10, 1878.
Issue:

2151. i. CHARLES WELLS,[8] born Palmyra, N.Y., June 19, 1828.
2152. ii. MARY ELIZABETH WELLS,[8] born Palmyra, N.Y., March 27, 1830.
2153. iii. EDWARD WELLS,[8] born Palmyra, N.Y.; died young.
2154. iv. OSCAR ASHBEL WELLS,[8] born Palmyra, N.Y., August 21, 1833.

1483. LYDIA DAGGETT [7] (*Levi*,[6] *Samuel*,[5] *Ebenezer*,[4] *John*,[3]
Thomas,[2] *John* [1]), born September 21, 1805; married Austin Durfee;
removed to Michigan.
Issue:

2155. i. GIDEON DURFEE.[8]
2156. ii. JANE DURFEE,[8] married Mr. Harrison.
2157. iii. HARVEY DURFEE.[8]

1484. AUGUSTUS K. DAGGETT [7] (*Levi*,[6] *Samuel*,[5] *Ebenezer*,[4] *John*,[3]
Thomas,[2] *John* [1]), born March 26, 1808; married Caroline Martin
Patterson.
Issue:

2158. i. TERRESA DAGGETT.[8]
2159. ii. FRANKLIN DAGGETT.[8]
2160. iii. ELIZA DAGGETT.[8]
2161. iv. CALEB DAGGETT.[8]

1485. JULIA JEANNETTE DAGGETT [7] (*Levi*,[6] *Samuel*,[5] *Ebenezer*,[4]
John,[3] *Thomas*,[2] *John* [1]), born May 14, 1810; died May 15, 1890;
married Silas Hull.
Issue:

2162. i. SARAH HULL,[8] died young.

1486. ELIZABETH DAGGETT[7] (*Levi*,[6] *Samuel*,[5] *Ebenezer*,[4] *John*,[3] *Thomas*,[2] *John*[1]), born May 5, 1811; married Harvey Durfee; resided in Michigan.

Issue:

2163. i.   HALSEY DURFEE,[8] resides Wayne, Mich. (1892).
2164. ii. CALISTA DURFEE,[8] married Mr. Dean.
2165. iii. GEORGE DURFEE.[8]
2166. iv. ALANSON DURFEE.[8]
2167. v.   AUGUSTA DURFEE,[8] married Mr. Hollenbeck.

1487. TERRESSA DAGGETT[7] (*Levi*,[6] *Samuel*,[5] *Ebenezer*,[4] *John*,[3] *Thomas*,[2] *John*[1]), born Saratoga, N.Y., September 9, 1812; resides 835 Fifteenth street, Detroit, Mich. (1892); married Livonia, Mich., September 28, 1857, by Rev. Mr. Debois, to Benjamin Pierson, son of Henry and Hannah (Brown) Pierson; born New Jersey, October 21, 1802.

No issue.

Mr. Pierson is a justice of the peace, and has been representative.

1488. MARY DAGGETT[7] (*Levi*,[6] *Samuel*,[5] *Ebenezer*,[4] *John*,[3] *Thomas*,[2] *John*[1]), born Brutus, N.Y., April 23, 1816; resides Mason, Ingham county, Mich. (1892); married Buffalo, N.Y., 1846, by Rev. Mr. Hopkins, to Rev. Hosea Kittredge, son of Kendal (M.D.) and Sarah (Whiting) Kittredge; born Mt. Desert, Me., March 27, 1803; died Mason, Mich., March 30, 1873.

Issue:

2168. i.   SARAH KITTREDGE,[8] born Red Creek, N.Y., September 24, 1849; died
           Red Creek, N.Y., May 15, 1850.
2169. ii. HARRIET KITTREDGE,[8] born Red Creek, N.Y., December 12, 1851.
2170. iii. CALVIN KITTREDGE,[8] born Red Creek, N.Y., March 15, 1854; died
           Mason, Mich., February 25, 1862.

1491. CARLOS DAGGETT[7] (*Ebenezer*,[6] *Ebenezer*,[5] *Ebenezer*,[4] *John*,[3] *Thomas*,[2] *John*[1]), born Wrentham, Mass., December 2, 1793; died West Roxbury, Mass., January 7, 1871; married Weston, Mass., January 19, 1817, by Rev. Joseph Field, to Mary Child, daughter of Edward and Polly (Fiske) Child; born Waltham, Mass., April 5, 1799; died Weston, Mass., January 16, 1867.

Issue:

2171. i.   EDWARD CHILD DAGGETT,[8] born Weston, Mass., August 29, 1817;
           died Mobile, Ala., December 18, 1848.
2172. ii. EBENEZER DAGGETT,[8] born Roxbury, Mass., March 7, 1820; re-
           sided Marysville, Cal., November, 1853.
2173. iii. CHARLES HENRY DAGGETT,[8] born Roxbury, Mass., March 21, 1822;
           died New Boston, N.H., March 23, 1837.
2174. iv. MARY SUSANNA DAGGETT,[8] born Northboro', Mass., July 16, 1824.
2175. v.   ALBERT PLINY DAGGETT,[8] born New Boston, N.H., July 21, 1827;
           died New Boston, N.H., March 26, 1837.
2176. vi. HERMAN DAGGETT,[8] born New Boston, N.H., May 6, 1831; died New
           Boston, N.H., March 18, 1837.

2177. vii.   GEORGE DAGGETT,[8] born New Boston, N.H., April 4, 1834; died New
           Boston, N.H., April 20, 1837.
2178. viii. CHARLES HERMAN DAGGETT,[8] born New Boston, N.H., March 2,
           1838; "soldier;" died Newport News, Va.. February 26, 1863.
2179. ix.   ALBERT PLINY DAGGETT,[8] born New Boston, N.H., April 16, 1841;
           died New Boston, N.H., March 26, 1863.

Carlos Daggett left a will, dated April 11, 1867, in which he
speaks of having been of New Boston, N.H., but now of Weston,
Mass.; "farmer." Names his brother-in-law, Franklin Child, "only
brother of my late beloved wife," executor.

1493. HERMAN DAGGETT [7] (*Ebenezer,*[6] *Ebenezer,*[5] *Ebenezer,*[4] *John,*[3]
Thomas,[2] *John* [1]), born Wrentham, Mass., March 27, 1800; died
Boston, Mass., December 12, 1838; unmarried.

Herman Daggett was a West India goods merchant, of the firm of
Barnes & Daggett, from 1821 to 1827 inclusive, his partner Abel
Barnes, and their office at 42 India street, Boston, Mass.

In 1827 Mr. Daggett resided on Lynde street. From 1828 to 1833
inclusive, he was alone in the same line of business; in 1828 and
1829 at 42 India street, and the rest of the time at 43 India street.

In 1829 he boarded at Milk, cor. Federal street; in 1830 at the
" Sun Tavern," Batterymarch street; and in 1831 on High street.

In 1834 he was associated in business with Marshall Smith at 40
India street, the firm being Herman Daggett & Co.

In 1835, and for the rest of his life, he was alone in the same line
of business, at 43 India street, while he lived in 1836 at the Commercial Coffee-house; and in 1837 and 1838 at the Pearl-street House.

In 1834, April 13, he was made trustee for Louisa Barnes.

Ebenezer Billings petitioned for administration on his estate,
December 17, 1838.

1507. MARY DAGGETT [7] (*Abner,*[6] *Thomas,*[5] *Thomas,*[4] *John,*[3]
Thomas,[2] *John* [1]), born Walpole, Mass., March 23, 1786; died Boston, Mass., August 9, 1861; married Providence, R.I., September
21, 1804, George Monson, born 1771; died New Haven, Conn.,
November 17, 1840.

Issue:

2180. i.   CAROLINE MONSON,[8] born New Haven, Conn., January 17, 1806; died
           Boston, Mass., July 18, 1875.
2181. ii.   HARRIET DAGGETT MONSON,[8] born New Haven, Conn., June 4, 1808.
2182. iii.   GEORGE EDWIN MONSON,[8] born New Haven, Conn., November 23,
           1811.

1510. SUSAN EDWARDS DAGGETT [7] (*David,*[6] *Thomas,*[5] *Thomas,*[4]
John,[3] *Thomas,*[2] *John* [1]), born New Haven, Conn., June 30, 1788;
died New Haven, Conn., August 18, 1839; married New Haven,
Conn., August 28, 1811, by President Dwight, to Sereno Edwards

Dwight, son of President Timothy and Mary (Woolsey) Dwight, of
New Haven; born Greenfield Hill, Conn., May 18, 1786; died Philadelphia, Pa., November 30, 1850.

Issue:

2183. i. CHARLOTTE DWIGHT,[8] born August, 1816; died August, 1816.

President Sereno Edwards Dwight, D.D., graduated at Yale College in 1803.   He taught school at Litchfield, Conn., for a year, and
the next year was his father's amanuensis, and afterward tutor at
Yale for four years — 1806–1810.   While tutor he studied law with
Hon. Charles Chauncey and Nathan Smith, Esq., both eminent
jurists, and practised the profession at New Haven, 1810–1816.

Becoming a Christian in 1815, he renounced the law for the ministry, and on October 8, 1816, was licensed to preach, and was at
once elected chaplain of the United States Senate at Washington.

He afterward, 1817, became pastor of Park-street Church, Boston,
where he remained until 1826.

Resigning from ill-health, he conducted, with his brother Henry, a
large school in New Haven, the " Gymnasium," from 1828 to 1831.

In 1833 he became president of Hamilton College, New York, which
position he held for two and a half years.

Mr. Dwight was remarkable in youth for brilliant talents and force
of character.

He was the author of " Hebrew Life," and edited an edition of
" Works of Jonathan Edwards " in ten volumes.

Mrs. Dwight possessed a vigorous, vivacious, and cultivated
mind.   She was of a slender figure and a bright intellectual aspect,
with large lustrous black eyes, and had very pleasing and graceful
manners.

Her acquaintance with good books was large, and she was earnest
in her religious character.

She was the author of " An Abridgment of the Memoirs of Mrs.
Susan Huntington," her friend.

She aided also her husband, when editing the works of Edwards,
in preparing them for the press.

1511.   LEONARD AUGUSTUS DAGGETT [7] (*David*,[6] *Thomas*,[5] *Thomas*,[4]
John,[3] *Thomas*,[2] *John* [1]), born New Haven, Conn., April 30, 1790;
died New Haven, Conn., April 27, 1867; married 1st, New Haven,
Conn., September 12, 1819, by Rev. Nathl. W. Taylor, to Jennette
Atwater, daughter of Timothy and Susan (Macumber) Atwater;
born New Haven, Conn., March 2, 1799; died New Haven, Conn.,
June 19, 1825; married 2d, New York city, May 13, 1853, by Rev.
G. Spring, to Julia Atwater Raymond, widow, daughter of Timothy

and Susan (Macumber) Atwater; born New Haven, Conn., February 24, 1795; died New Haven, Conn., July 6, 1883.

Issue:

2184. i.   DAVID LEWIS DAGGETT,[8] born New Haven, Conn., June 24, 1820.
2185. ii. SUSAN DWIGHT DAGGETT,[8] born New Haven, Conn., September 5, 1822.
2186. iii. MARY JENNETTE DAGGETT,[8] born New Haven, Conn., October 14, 1823; resides 37 West 25th street, New York city.
2187. iv. LEONARD WALES DAGGETT,[8] born New Haven, Conn., May 3, 1825; died New Haven, Conn., August 12, 1825.

1514. WEALTHY ANN DAGGETT [7] (*David,*[6] *Thomas,*[5] *Thomas,*[4] *John,*[3] *Thomas,*[2] *John* [1]), born New Haven, Conn., November 29, 1796; died December 27, 1860; married September 16, 1822, by Rev. Samuel Merwin, to Joseph Jenkins, of Boston.

No issue.

1521. Rev. OLIVER ELLSWORTH DAGGETT [7] (*David,*[6] *Thomas,*[5] *Thomas,*[4] *John,*[3] *Thomas,*[2] *John* [1]), born New Haven, Conn., January 14, 1810; died Hartford, Conn., September 1, 1880; married Hartford, Conn., July 15, 1840, by Rev. Dr. Hawes, to Elizabeth Watson, daughter of William and Mary (Marsh) Watson; born Hartford, Conn., April 12, 1812; died New Haven, Conn., May 20, 1891.

Issue:

2188. i.   SUSAN ELIZABETH DAGGETT,[8] born Hartford, Conn., December 9, 1841; resides 77 Grove street, New Haven, Conn. (1892).
2189. ii. ELLSWORTH DAGGETT,[8] born Canandaigua, N.Y., May 24, 1845.
2190. iii. MARY DAGGETT,[8] born Canandaigua, N.Y., July 19, 1852; resides 77 Grove street, New Haven, Conn. (1892).
         Three others died in childhood.

Rev. Dr. Oliver E. Daggett graduated from Yale College, 1823; pastor South Congregational Church, Hartford, 1837–1843; pastor Congregational church, Canandaigua, N.Y., 1843–1863; professor divinity, Yale College, 1867–1870; then pastor Second Congregational Church, New London, Conn.; then retired and resided in Hartford, Conn.

He had a reputation as a preacher of great brilliancy, who was not surpassed for magnetic power in the State. He particularly excelled in his command of a clear, graceful, and at the same time vigorous English style. In 1844 he removed to Canandaigua, in the State of New York, where for nearly a quarter of a century he endeared himself to Christians of all denominations throughout western New York, by the cordiality with which he entered into efforts of all kinds, made for the benefit of the community. He was, perhaps by heredity, a conversationalist, like his grandfather, Dr. Æneas Munson, whose name is remembered to this day for his brilliant qualities.

Everything that Dr. Daggett said or did was marked by good taste, and by a cordial and friendly spirit. He was very quick to notice whatever was commendable in others, and was evidently delighted to express his interest and appreciation. With such a character, as might be expected, he was very lenient in his judgment of others, and it is doubtful whether he ever knowingly uttered a word which could hurt the feelings of even the most sensitive.

In 1867, having been appointed a professor in Yale College, to preach in the college chapel, he returned to the home of his boyhood, where the cordial reception which he and his wife received was peculiarly gratifying.

Mrs. Daggett received in early life every advantage that education and acquaintance with the leading literary characters of New England could give. She had a serenity and dignity of manner which were peculiarly beautiful, and, though naturally somewhat reserved, she impressed all who knew her with her sincerity, and with her real friendliness of spirit.

1526. JULIA A. DAGGETT[7] (*Dexter*,[6] *Thomas*,[5] *Thomas*,[4] *John*,[3] *Thomas*,[2] *John*[1]), born November 28, 1805; died Cincinnati, Ohio, August 15, 1875; married Providence, R.I., December 5, 1830, by Elder Toby, to Edward Harwood, son of Edward and Catherine (Sherman) Harwood; born May 6, 1810; died Cincinnati, Ohio, October 15, 1875.

Issue:

2191. i.   GEORGE D. HARWOOD,[8] born Providence, R.I., August 26, 1831; died Cincinnati, Ohio, May 20, 1837.
2192. ii.   EDWARD S. HARWOOD,[8] born Providence, R.I., March 9, 1833; died Cincinnati, Ohio, March 13, 1833.
2193. iii.   HARRIET C. HARWOOD,[8] born Providence, R.I., April 7, 1834.
2194. iv.   WILLIAM S. HARWOOD,[8] born Cincinnati, Ohio, January 5, 1837; died Cincinnati, Ohio, February 19, 1839.
2195. v.   CRAWFORD HARWOOD,[8] born Cincinnati, Ohio, November 27, 1839; died Cincinnati, Ohio, January 25, 1840.
2196. vi.   ADALINE C. HARWOOD,[8] born Cincinnati, Ohio, November 5, 1840.
2197. vii.   ANNA B. HARWOOD,[8] born Cincinnati, Ohio, May 1, 1843; died Cincinnati, Ohio, May 2, 1843.
2198. viii.   GERTRUDE HARWOOD,[8] born Cincinnati, Ohio, June 7, 1845.

1528. ISAAC DAGGETT[7] (*Timothy*,[6] *Brotherton*,[5] *Brotherton*,[4] *Joshua*,[3] *Thomas*,[2] *John*[1]), born Edgartown, Mass., June 25, 1798; "mariner;" died Roxbury, Mass., January 25, 1866; married Cordelia ——.

Issue:

2199. i.   CORDELIA DAGGETT,[8] born 1829.
2200. ii.   CATHERINE F. DAGGETT,[8] born Edgartown, Mass., 1834.
2201. iii.   HELEN JOSEPHINE DAGGETT,[8] born Fairhaven, Mass., October 11, 1843.
2202. iv.   ISAAC HERBERT DAGGETT,[8] born Fairhaven, Mass., April 2, 1849.

Isaac Daggett's will was proved in 1866.   It was dated September 21, 1855, at which time he calls himself of Fairhaven, "mariner." He removed to Roxbury, Mass., and resided on Moreland street at the time of his death.   [Norfolk Probate.]

1532. Brotherton Daggett [7] (*Samuel*,[6] *Thomas*,[5] *Brotherton*,[4] *Joshua*,[3] *Thomas*,[2] *John*[1]), born Tisbury, Mass., January 4, 1778; died Union, Me., November, 1866; married 1st, 1802, Sarah Kimball, of Bristol; married 2d, December, 1838, Emily Marshall, widow (of Thomaston, Me.), daughter of Mr. Chadwick; died Union, Me., October 14, 1844.

Issue :

2203. i.   Eleanor Martin Daggett,[8] born Union, Me., January 7, 1804; married December 29, 1834, John Oakes.
2204. ii.   William Daggett,[8] born Union, Me., August 27, 1805; resides Michigan.
2205. iii. Mary Daggett,[8] born Union, Me., May 18, 1808; died Union, Me., June 4, 1830.
2206. iv.   Sophronia Daggett,[8] born Union, Me., March 4, 1810; married March 5, 1833, Jonathan D. Breck; resided Brighton, Mass. (1851).
2207. v.   Orinda Daggett,[8] born Union, Me., December 26, 1811; married Reuben Sherer; resided Thomaston, Me. (1851).
2208. vi.   Arunah Weston Daggett,[8] born Union, Me., February 16, 1814.
2209. vii. Timothy Kimball Daggett,[8] born Union, Me., February 26, 1816; resided Mobile, Ala.
2210. viii. Eliza Mitchell Daggett,[8] born Union, Me., August 8, 1818.
2211. ix.   Elvira Daggett,[8] born Union, Me., November 17, 1820; married George Hatch, of Thomaston, Me.; had son Charles Hatch,[9] 22 South street, New York city (1892).
2212. x.   Brotherton Daggett,[8] born Union, Me., November 25, 1822; resided Boston, Mass.
2213. xi.   George Bartlett Daggett,[8] born Union, Me., August 23, 1824.
2214. xii. Elisha Harding Daggett,[8] born Union, Me., September 6, 1827; resided Thomaston, Me.

Brotherton Daggett said, though there had been a store on St. George's river, there was not any when he came to Union in 1789.

Mr. Daggett is said to have been something of a poet.

1533. James Daggett [7] (*Samuel*,[6] *Thomas*,[5] *Brotherton*,[4] *Joshua*,[3] *Thomas*,[2] *John*[1]), born Tisbury, Mass., September 9, 1779; died Hodgdon, Me., June 18, 1858; married Waldoboro', Me., August 31, 1800, Deborah Upham, of Bristol; born Massachusetts, April 17, 1784; died Hodgdon, Me., April 28, 1868.

Issue :

2215. i.   James Daggett,[8] born Maine, January 22, 1801; died Amity, Me.
2216. ii.   Isaac Daggett,[8] born Maine, November 28, 1803; drowned Sheyuda Falls, Me., April, 1826.
2217. iii. Jabez Daggett,[8] born Maine, September 9, 1805.
2218. iv.   Deborah Daggett,[8] born Maine, February 3, 1807; died Suntihago, Me., 1834.
2219. v.   Waterman Daggett,[8] born Maine, September 8, 1809.
2220. vi.   Hiram Daggett,[8] born Union, Me., August 16, 1811.

2221. vii. ROBERT DAGGETT,[8] born Maine, May 15, 1813.
2222. viii. ABIGAIL DAGGETT,[8] born Maine, November 15, 1815; married Charles
      Balch; she died Canton, Mass., July 19, 1852.
2223. ix. EBENEZER DAGGETT,[5] born Washington, Me., November 20, 1817.
2224. x. BENJAMIN FRANKLIN DAGGETT,[8] born Wiscasset, Me., September 30,
      1820.
2225. xi. JANE DAGGETT,[8] born Emden, Me., October 1, 1822; died Thomaston,
      Me., June 24, 1842.
2226. xii. WILLIAM DAGGETT,[5] born Emden, Me., September 29, 1825; married;
      resides Haverhill, Mass. (1892).

James Daggett, about 1820, was a pioneer in Aroostook county,
Me., where he lived the rest of his life.

1535. JONATHAN DAGGETT[7] (*Samuel,[6] Thomas,[5] Brotherton,[4]
Joshua,[3] Thomas,[2] John[1]*), born Tisbury, Mass., May 20, 1783; died
Union, Me., 1855; married 1st, 1804, Elizabeth Martin, of St.
George; married 2d. Mary Robinson, of Belmont. Me.

Issue:

2227. i. ATHEARN DAGGETT,[5] born Union, Me., September 1, 1805; died Union,
      Me., July 5, 1806.
2228. ii. JOHN DAGGETT,[5] born Union, Me., August 29, 1806; married Waldo-
      boro', Me.; issue : two children.
2229. iii. WILBERT DAGGETT,[5] born Union, Me., October 30, 1807; married
      Susan Lehr; he died Washington. Me., May 11, 1892.
2230. iv. JULIA ANN DAGGETT,[5] born Union. Me., March 17, 1809; died Union,
      Me., August 21, 1814.
2231. v. RICHARD MARTIN DAGGETT,[5] born Union. Me., January 15. 1811.
2232. vi. SARAH DAGGETT,[5] born Union, Me., February 13, 1813; died Union,
      Me., November 7, 1813.
2233. vii. SILVIA WESTON DAGGETT.[5] born Union, Me., August 6, 1814; mar-
      ried Mr. Wing; resided Belmont. Me. (1851).
2234. viii. AUGUSTUS DAGGETT,[5] married Mary Flanders, of Waldoboro', Me.;
      he died Morrill, Me., February, 1886.
2235. ix. ROBERT L. DAGGETT,[5] born Union. Me., March 12, 1820.
2236. x. THOMAS DAGGETT,[5] born Washington. Me.; died young.
2237. xi. ARAMANDA DAGGETT,[5] born Washington. Me., May 22, 1822.
2238. xii. MARGARET DAGGETT,[5] born Washington. Me.; married Waltham,
      Mass., February 28, 1844, by Rev. John Whitney, to Samuel
      Cousens; resides Boston, Mass. (1886).

1536. WILLIAM DAGGETT[7] (*Samuel,[6] Thomas,[5] Brotherton,[4]
Joshua,[3] Thomas,[2] John[1]*), born Tisbury, Mass., April 9, 1785;
died Bremen. Me., December 19, 1876; married Bristol (now Bremen),
Me., March 15, 1813. Silvia Church Weston, daughter of Arunah
and Sarah (Martin) Weston; born Bristol, Me., March 10, 1790;
died Bremen, Me., March 8, 1888.

Issue:

2239. i. AMELIA DAGGETT,[5] born Union, Me., February 26, 1814.
2240. ii. SARAH ANN DAGGETT,[5] born Union, Me., August 23, 1815; died
      Bremen, Me., August 9, 1890.
2241. iii. JANE TOBEY DAGGETT,[5] born Union, Me., October 9, 1818.
2242. iv. JOSHUA DAGGETT,[5] born Union, Me., September 16, 1820.
2243. v. NANCY ALFORD DAGGETT,[5] born Union, Me., October 25, 1822; died
      Bremen, Me., May 5, 1858.
2244. vi. LUCY WESTON DAGGETT,[8] born Union, Me., January 11, 1825.

2245. vii. MARGERY W. DAGGETT,[8] born Union, Me., June 22, 1827; died
Union, Me., January 8, 1828.
2246. viii. HIRAM DAGGETT,[8] born Belmont, Me., November 30, 1828.
2247. ix. MARGERY WELLS DAGGETT,[8] born Belmont, Me., June 22, 1830.
2248. x. WILLIAM LLEWELLYN DAGGETT,[8] born Belmont, Me., September 26,
1833; died Bremen, Me., May 22, 1863.

1537. SAMUEL DAGGETT[7] (*Samuel,[6] Thomas,[5] Brotherton,[4]
Joshua,[3] Thomas,[2] John[1]*), born Union, Me., October 15, 1792;
died Union, Me., October 11, 1846; married 1st, 1817, Priscilla
Coggan; married 2d, Mrs. Sarah Stetson, widow of Jacob Stetson,
and daughter of Jacob Wade.

Issue:

2249. i. AUGUSTA BACHELDER DAGGETT,[8] born Union, Me., August 24, 1818;
married 1840, George Barter, of Thomaston, Me.
2250. ii. MARTHA DAGGETT,[8] born Union, Me., August 7, 1822; died Union,
Me., September 16, 1823.
2251. iii. HANCEY DAGGETT,[8] born Union, Me., November 6, 1825; died Union,
Me., September 21, 1842.
2252. iv. CYRENUS CHAPIN DAGGETT,[8] born Union, Me., December 13, 1830.
Also two others.

1538. EBENEZER DAGGETT[7] (*Samuel,[6] Thomas,[5] Brotherton,[4]
Joshua,[3] Thomas,[2] John[1]*), born Union, Me., August 2, 1797; died
Washington, Me., August 10, 1887; married 1st, Union, Me., 1819,
by Walter Blake, Esq., to Margaret Miller, daughter of George and
Barbara (Hoffs) Miller, of Waldoboro', Me.; born Waldoboro', Me.;
died Union, Me., May 31, 1830; married 2d, Union, Me., June 9,
1831, by Walter Blake, Esq., to Salome Miller, daughter of George
and Barbara (Hoffs) Miller, of Waldoboro', Me.; born Waldoboro',
Me., 1805; died Union, Me., June 9, 1851; married 3d, Union, Me.,
by Walter Blake, Esq., to Mrs. Frampton, widow, daughter of Mr.
Hipp; divorced.

Issue:

2253. i. CYRUS DAGGETT,[8] born Union, Me., October 22, 1819; resides Sherman, Me. (1892).
2254. ii. THURSTON DAGGETT,[8] born Union, Me., November 28, 1820.
2255. iii. ELZINA DAGGETT,[8] born Union, Me., March 31, 1822; married Reuben
Ghentner, of Waldoboro', Me.; resided Waldoboro' (1851).
2256. iv. BARBARA D. DAGGETT,[8] born Union, Me., November 30, 1823; died
Union, Me., September 5, 1825.
2257. v. MARY MILLER DAGGETT,[8] born Union, Me., June 4, 1825; married
George Robbins, son of Ebenezer Robbins.
2258. vi. ERASTUS DAGGETT,[8] born Union, Me., April 23, 1827; married June
11, 1846, Parnela Ripley, of Appleton, Me.
2259. vii. —— DAGGETT,[8] born Union, Me., May 31, 1830; died Union, Me.,
May 31, 1830.
2260. viii. LYSANDER DAGGETT,[8] born Union, Me., January 10, 1832; died
Union, Me., June 10, 1850.
2261. ix. CHARLES MILLER DAGGETT,[8] born Union, Me., March 8, 1834; resides Terre Haute, Ind. (1892).
2262. x. CLEMENTINE COLE DAGGETT,[8] born Union, Me., October 26, 1835;
married Mr. Lowe; died many years ago (1892).

2263. xi. DARIUS DAGGETT,[8] born Union, Me., March 18, 1838; died in the army.
2264. xii. HARRIET DICKEY DAGGETT,[8] married Mr. Janes; resides Lawrence, Mass. (1892).
2265. xiii. Daughter —— DAGGETT,[8] died.
2266. xiv. LUCIUS CHANDLER DAGGETT,[8] resides Rockland, Me. (1892).
2267. xv.   ANGELIA DAGGETT,[8] born Rockland, Me., 1847.

1539. DANIEL WESTON DAGGETT [7] (*Samuel*,[6] *Thomas*,[5] *Brotherton*,[4] *Joshua*,[3] *Thomas*,[2] *John* [1]), born Union, Me., May 19, 1800; died Union, Me., April 4, 1833; married Union, Me., December 3, 1827, Lydia Jameson, daughter of Brice Jameson, of Warren, Me.; born Warren, Me., 1802.

Issue:

2268. i. OZIAS DAGGETT,[8] born Union, Me., September 29, 1828; died Union, Me., February 2, 1830.
2269. ii. DANIEL O. DAGGETT,[8] born Union, Me., January 18, 1831.

Mrs. Daggett married 2d, Job Casewell, October, 1835. He was born 1787, and was of Minot, Me.

1542. Capt. THOMAS DAGGETT [7] (*Thomas*,[6] *Thomas*,[5] *Brotherton*,[4] *Joshua*,[3] *Thomas*,[2] *John* [1]), born June 4, 1788; died New York city; married New York city, Martha Maidman; born 1796; died Union, Me., August 23, 1818.

Issue:

2270. i. —— DAGGETT,[8] died Union, Me., young.

Capt. Thomas Daggett was a farmer in Searsmont, Me. He went to sea as mate of a vessel, and became acquainted on his voyage from England with an English lady, whom he married in New York and returned with her to his farm. She spent the last weeks of her life at his father's in Union. After the death of his wife, Captain Daggett went to his wife's kindred in New York, where he engaged in business and died.

1544. EDMUND DAGGETT [7] (*Thomas*,[6] *Thomas*,[5] *Brotherton*,[4] *Joshua*,[3] *Thomas*,[2] *John* [1]), born Union, Me., August 23, 1792; married 1818, Deborah Keene, daughter of Josiah Keene, of Camden, Me.

Issue:

2271. i.   FREDERIC K. DAGGETT,[8] born Union, Me., August 13, 1819.
2272. ii. MARTHA DAGGETT,[8] born March 7, 1821; died March 16, 1823.
2273. iii. THOMAS DAGGETT,[8] born May 4, 1822; died Philadelphia, Pa. ·
2274. iv. EPHRAIM GAY DAGGETT,[8] born July 31, 1824; died Roxbury, Mass., June 7, 1851.
2275. v.   FREEMAN LUCE DAGGETT,[8] born Union, Me., February 8, 1827; musician; married; died Boston, Mass., July 12, 1873.
2276. vi. LUCINDA DAGGETT,[8] born March 26, 1828; died October 1, 1831.
2277. vii. JOHN SIBLEY DAGGETT,[8] born February 7, 1830; student at Bowdoin College in 1851.

2278. viii. SARAH GAY DAGGETT,[8] born January 25, 1832; married 1849, John
       Rich; resided Hope, Me. (1851).
2279. ix. PATIENCE HEWETT DAGGETT,[8] born June 1, 1834; died young.
2280. x. ESTHER DAGGETT.[8]
2281. xi. MARY DAGGETT.[8]
2282. xii. HELEN DAGGETT.[8]
2283. xiii. CAROLINE F. DAGGETT,[8] born Hope, Me., 1842.

1547. RUTH DAGGETT [7] (*Aaron*,[6] *Thomas*,[5] *Brotherton*,[4] *Joshua*,[3]
Thomas,[2] *John* [1]), born Union, Me., January 1, 1792; married 1816,
Jacob Kuhn, of Waldoboro', Me.

Issue :

2284. i. WILLIAM HARRIMAN KUHN.[8]
2285. ii. PETER KUHN,[8] died at sea.
2286. iii. ALBERT KUHN.[8]
2287. iv. GILBERT KUHN.[8]
2288. v. ALMOND ORLANDO KUHN.[8]

1548. OLIVE DAGGETT [7] (*Aaron*,[6] *Thomas*,[5] *Brotherton*,[4] *Joshua*,[3]
Thomas,[2] *John* [1]), born Union, Me., February 2, 1794; married January 8, 1818, George Clouse, of Waldoboro', Me.; died November
22, 1825.

Issue :

2289. i. HORATIO NELSON CLOUSE,[8] born Waldoboro' (?), Me., April 22, 1822;
       resides Union, Me.
2290. ii. ANGELICA FRANCES CLOUSE,[8] born Waldoboro' (?), Me., September 2,
       1824.

1549. MARGARET DAGGETT [7] (*Aaron*,[6] *Thomas*,[5] *Brotherton*,[4]
Joshua,[3] *Thomas*,[2] *John* [1]), born Union, Me., July 17, 1796; married
1819, Peleg Wiley.

Issue :

2291. i. ALMIRA WILEY.[8]
2292. ii. AARON DAGGETT WILEY.[8]
2293. iii. EPHRAIM WILEY.[8]
2294. iv. WILLIAM HOVEY WILEY.[8]
2295. v. JACOB KUHN WILEY.[8]
2296. vi. PELEG WILEY.[8]
2297. vii. REBECCA WILEY,[8] died.
2298. viii. CHARLES WILEY,[8] died.
2299. ix. RUTH KUHN WILEY.[8]

1552. LUCY DAGGETT [7] (*Aaron*,[6] *Thomas*,[5] *Brotherton*,[4] *Joshua*,[3]
Thomas,[2] *John* [1]), born Union, Me., November 10, 1802; married
Abraham Gushee, of Hope, Me.

Issue :

2300. i. FREDERICK AUGUSTUS GUSHEE,[8] born August, 1825.
2301. ii. LOUISA GUSHEE,[8] died young.
2302. iii. REBECCA GUSHEE,[8] married Elijah Ripley, of Hope, Me.; issue :
       Frederick Ripley,[9] born July 5, 1847.
2303. iv. ALMOND GUSHEE.[8]
2304. v. AMBROSE GUSHEE.[8]
2305. vi. ELIJAH DAGGETT GUSHEE.[8]

1553. ELIJAH A. DAGGETT[7] (*Aaron,*[6] *Thomas,*[5] *Brotherton,*[4] *Joshua,*[3] *Thomas,*[2] *John*[1]), born Union, Me., March 2, 1806; married Ruth Ann Waters, of Jefferson, Me.

Issue:

2306. i. ANN DAGGETT,[8] born May 28, 1847.
2307. ii. ATHEARN DAGGETT.[8]

Dr. Elijah A. Daggett, a physician in Waldoboro'; M.D. at Bowdoin College, 1833.

1554. AARON ATHEARN DAGGETT[7] (*Aaron,*[6] *Thomas,*[5] *Brotherton,*[4] *Joshua,*[3] *Thomas,*[2] *John*[1]), born Union, Me., December 17, 1808; married Bethiah Thompson, daughter of William Thompson.

Issue:

2308. i. SIMON ELIJAH DAGGETT,[8] born Jefferson, Me.
2309. ii. Daughter —— DAGGETT;[8] died Appleton, Me.
2310. iii. EMELINE OREVILLE DAGGETT,[8] died 1849.
2311. iv. MORRILL STANFORD DAGGETT,[8] born 1845; died 1849.
2312. v. AUGUSTA DAGGETT,[8] died 1849.

1557. HENRY DAGGETT[7] (*Tristram,*[6] *Elijah,*[5] *Brotherton,*[4] *Joshua,*[3] *Thomas,*[2] *John*[1]), born Industry, Me., May 27, 1789; died Wellsville, Pa., April 12, 1857; married Industry, Me., June 22, 1810, by Rev. Mr. Hutchins, to Abigail B. Cleveland, daughter of Jothan and Polly (Burns) Cleveland; born Emden, Me., June 5, 1796; died Bangor, Me., November 2, 1878.

Issue:

2313. i.   JANE DAGGETT,[8] born Industry, Me.
2314. ii. JOTHAN CLEVELAND DAGGETT,[8] born Industry, Me.
2315. iii. TRISTRAM DAGGETT,[8] born Industry, Me.
2316. iv. JAMES DAGGETT,[8] born Industry, Me.; died Industry, Me.
2317. v.   MARY DAGGETT,[8] born Industry, Me.; married Mr. Elliott; resides Garland, Me. (1893); has son William D. Elliott.[9]
2318. vi. JOSEPH DAGGETT,[8] born Industry, Me.
2319. vii. MERCY DAGGETT,[8] born Industry, Me.
2320. viii. ABIGAIL DAGGETT,[8] born Emden, Me.
2321. ix. EDWIN DAGGETT,[8] born Bingham, Me.
2322. x.   EMILY DAGGETT,[8] born Bingham, Me.

Mr. Daggett was a farmer, resided at Levant, Me., and at one time was chairman of the Board of Selectmen.

1559. ABIGAIL DAGGETT[7] (*Tristram,*[6] *Elijah,*[5] *Brotherton,*[4] *Joshua,*[3] *Thomas,*[2] *John*[1]), born Industry, Me., July 22, 1793; died Lee, Me., January 6, 1884; married Industry, Me., October 29, 1814, Capt. Jabez Norton, son of Jabez and Phebe (Luce) Norton; born Edgartown, Mass., August 22, 1777; died Lee, Me., April 9, 1861.

Issue:

2323. i. TRISTRAM NORTON,[8] born Industry, Me.; died aged eleven years.
2324. ii. BENJAMIN NORTON,[8] born Industry, Me., December 25, 1820; married Roxana Patterson; resided, at one time, Brunswick, Minn.

2325. iii. CLEMENTINE NORTON,[8] born Industry, Me.; married Charles Webber; resides Springfield, Me. (1892).

2326. iv. GEORGE BUTLER NORTON,[8] born Industry, Me., March 3, 1826; married December 3, 1854, Minerva Gatchell, daughter of Albert S. and Lydia S. (Staples) Gatchell; he died Pine City, Minn., February 9, 1873. Five children.

2327. v. HANNAH L. NORTON,[8] born Industry, Me., June 29, 1828; married January 9, Rufus W. Noble, son of Isaac and Mary (Coffin) Noble; blacksmith; resides Summer street, Portland, Me. (1892).

2328. vi. HARRISON ALLEN NORTON,[8] born Industry, Me., March 17, 1831; married February 2, 1856, Lucy S. Dwelley, daughter of Allen and Polly (Hodges) Dwelley. She born Springfield, Me., February 4, 1824; farmer; resides Lee, Me. (1892). Five children.

2329. vii. SIMON LOWELL NORTON,[8] born Lee, Me., June 29, 1833; married April, 1858, Angeline Merrill (born Lee, Me., December 13, 1837; died Lee, Me., January 27, 1881), daughter of James and Mary (Hewey) Merrill. Mr. Norton served in the Civil War. Is lumberman and farmer; resides Minnesota. Seven children.

2330. viii. CYRUS DOUGLAS NORTON,[8] born Lee, Me., May 28, 1836; resided, at one time, near Atken, Minn.

Captain Norton, while a resident of Industry, was selectman and captain of the militia. He was one of the best of men, mild in manner, conscientious in the discharge of his duty.

1562. TRISTRAM DAGGETT [7] (*Tristram,*[6] *Elijah,*[5] *Brotherton,*[4] *Joshua,*[3] *Thomas,*[2] *John*[1]), born Industry, Me., June 8, 1799; died Dexter, Me., November 27, 1836; married Maine, April 30, 1823, Martha Luce, daughter of Alsbury and Mary (Burgess) Luce; died Dexter, Me., March, 1873.

Issue:

2331. i. TIMOTHY DAGGETT,[8] born Industry, Me., March 20, 1824.

2332. ii. NATHAN LUCE DAGGETT,[8] born Industry, Me., April 18, 1825.

2333. iii. MARTHA ANN DAGGETT,[8] born St. Albans, Me., October, 1826; died Dexter, Me., about 1840.

2334. iv. LYDIA ANN DAGGETT,[8] born Dexter, Me., 1828; married a sea captain, 1850; died Martha's Vineyard, Mass., December, 1851.

2335. v. SUSAN JANE DAGGETT,[8] born Dexter, Me., 1830.

2336. vi. AMANDA JORDAN DAGGETT,[8] born Dexter, Me., 1832; married November 28, 1872, Rufus Washburn; resides Gloversville, N.Y. (1892); no issue.

Mr. Daggett was a farmer. He lived in Industry, St. Albans, and Dexter.

1563. TIMOTHY DAGGETT [7] (*Tristram,*[6] *Elijah,*[5] *Brotherton,*[4] *Joshua,*[3] *Thomas,*[2] *John*[1]), born Industry, Me., May 26, 1802; died Ripley, Me., July 31, 1879; married Industry, Me., November 29, 1838, Thankful Merry, daughter of Asa and Sally (Bartlett) Merry; born New Vineyard, Me., July 8, 1817; died Parkman, Me., July 13, 1867.

Issue:

2337. i. MARY LUCE DAGGETT,[8] born New Vineyard, Me., August 8, 1839.

2338. ii. TRISTRAM DAGGETT,[8] born New Vineyard, Me., January 2, 1841.

2339. iii. SARAH JANE DAGGETT,[8] born New Vineyard, Me., October 23, 1843; died Parkman, Me., June 11, 1863.

2340. iv. Asa Merry Daggett,[8] born Parkman, Me., July 22, 1845.
2341. v.   Catharine Amanda Daggett,[8] born Parkman, Me., May 31, 1848.
2342. vi. William Merry Daggett,[8] born Parkman, Me., March 24, 1851; resides Pecos, Tex. (1892).
2343. vii. Clara Ella Daggett,[8] born Parkman, Me., June 14, 1854; resides Norway, Me. (1892).

Timothy Daggett, at the age of seventeen, left home to seek his fortune. For thirteen years he followed the sea, alternating with work on a farm.

He owned several pieces of real estate in Industry at different times. He moved to Parkman in 1845, where he owned different farms, and resided there until 1874, when he disposed of his property and moved to Ripley, where he died.

1566. Lucinda Daggett[7] (*Elijah,[6] Elijah,[5] Brotherton,[4] Joshua,[3] Thomas,[2] John[1]*), born Martha's Vineyard, Mass.; died New Vineyard, Me.; married October 2, 1806, Henry Butler, son of Henry and Mehitable (Norton) Butler, of New Vineyard, Me.; "farmer;" died Boston, Mass., aged seventy-four years.

Issue:

2344. i.   Josiah Butler,[8] born New Vineyard, Me., August 28, 1807; married (published March 29, 1834) Lucy Jane Waugh (born Stark, Me., July 25, 1810), daughter of Elijah and Sophia (Ferrand) Waugh, of Stark.
2345. ii. John Gray Butler,[8] born New Vineyard, Me., January 28, 1811; married Dolly Stevens; resides Milo, Me. (1892).
2346. iii. Abigail Daggett Butler,[8] born New Vineyard, Me., February 10, 1813; resides Boston, Mass. (1892).
2347. iv. James Madison Butler,[8] born New Vineyard, Me., March 19, 1815; married November 16, 1844, Sarah Ann Bloomer, of South Sodus, N.Y., daughter of Daniel and Phebe Bloomer; resides Hemlock Lake, N.Y. (1892); one child.
2348. v.   Samuel Daggett Butler,[8] born New Vineyard, Me., July 4, 1817; married Sophronia Williams, of Solon, Me.; went to New York.
2349. vi. Warren Smith Butler,[8] born New Vineyard, Me., July 28, 1821; married Eliza M. Bates (born New Vineyard, October 15, 1831); private, Company D, Seventeenth Regiment Maine Infantry; resided in Lewiston, Me., at one time.
2350. vii. Henry Butler,[8] born New Vineyard, Me.; married (published July 2, 1846) Patience Bray, of Anson; resides Solon, Me. (1892).
2351. viii. Francis Caldwell Butler,[8] born New Vineyard, Me., October 10, 1824; resided, at one time, Eureka, Cal.
2352. ix. Lucinda Butler,[8] born New Vineyard, Me., August 3, 1827; married Samuel Elder.

1568. Sarah Daggett[7] (*Elijah,[6] Elijah,[5] Brotherton,[4] Joshua,[3] Thomas,[2] John[1]*), born Martha's Vineyard, December 7, 1792; went West; married Industry, Me., December 18, 1817, Levi Greenleaf, son of Dea. Levi and Polly (Willard) Greenleaf; born Industry, Me., May 11, 1797.

Issue:

2353. i.   Ann Churchill Greenleaf,[8] born Industry, Me., September 15, 1818; died Industry, Me., September 22, 1840.

JOHN DOGGETT, OF MARTHA'S VINEYARD. 213

2354. ii.   Isaac S. Greenleaf,[8] born Industry, Me., July 2, 1820.
2355. iii. Esther D. Greenleaf,[8] born Industry, Me., January 16, 1822; died
            Industry, Me., June 10, 1841.
2356. iv.   Emma Greenleaf,[8] born Industry, Me., March 5, 1824.
2357. v.   William C. Greenleaf,[8] born Industry, Me., May 31, 1826.
2358. vi.   John Greenleaf,[8] born Industry, Me., April 28, 1828.
2359. vii. Sarah Greenleaf,[8] born Industry, Me., December 19, 1830.
2360. viii. Cordelia W. Greenleaf,[8] born Industry, Me., July 11, 1833.
2361. ix.   Levi Greenleaf,[8] born Industry, Me., June 23, 1835.

1571. Samuel S. Daggett[7] (*Elijah,[6] Elijah,[5] Brotherton,[4]
Joshua,[3] Thomas,[2] John[1]*), born Tisbury, Mass., 1799; "shoe-
maker;" died Edgartown, Mass., September 15, 1879; married 1st,
Nantucket, Mass., July 10, 1823, by Rev. S. F. Swift, to Lydia
Giles; married 2d, —— ; married 3d, Fairhaven, Mass., December
1, 1857, by John A. Hawes, J.P., to Amelia Whitfield, daughter of
Joseph and Parnel Whitfield; born Fairhaven, Mass., 1791; died
Edgartown, Mass., February 19, 1869.
Issue:

2362. i.   Samuel S. Daggett,[8] born Nantucket, Mass., 1825.

Samuel S. Daggett was a man of more than ordinary ability, and
was mate on a brig in the merchant service. Had an accident by
which he injured one of his heels; then learned the shoemaker's trade,
and lived in Nantucket and Edgartown.

1576. Nancy Athearn Daggett[7] (*Matthew,[6] Elijah,[5] Brother-
ton,[4] Joshua,[3] Thomas,[2] John[1]*), born Warren, Me., December 1,
1799; died Union, Me., February 16, 1827; married Warren, Me.,
May 4, 1820, Reuben Alford, son of Dea. Love and Lydia
(Montgomery) Alford; born Warren, Me., March 24, 1800; died
Oldtown, Me., October 7, 1834.
Issue:

2363. i.   Edmund Buxton Alford,[8] born Warren, Me., February 2, 1821.
2364. ii. Lydia North Alford,[8] born Searsmont, Me., June 12, 1823.

1578. Thomas Gilbert Daggett[7] (*James,[6] Jethro,[5] Brotherton,[4]
Joshua,[3] Thomas,[2] John[1]*), born Dighton, Mass., March 2, 1795;
"watchmaker;" died Providence, R.I., February 1, 1871; married
Cumberland, R.I., June 2, 1839, by Rev. Benj. H. Davis, to Frances
C. Streeter.

1580. Jethro Davis Daggett[7] (*James,[6] Jethro,[5] Brotherton,[4]
Joshua,[3] Thomas,[2] John[1]*), born Rehoboth, Mass., August 27, 1802;
"carpenter;" died Providence, R.I., October 22, 1868; married New
Bedford, Mass., January, 1830, by Wm. Cole, to Phebe Maxfield,

daughter of Warren and Ruby Maxfield; born 1810; died New Bedford, Mass., December 10, 1854.

Issue:

2365. i. HANNAH P. DAGGETT,[8] born New Bedford, Mass., 1831.
2366. ii. ELIZABETH DAGGETT,[8] born New Bedford, Mass., 1834.
2367. iii. REBECCA S. DAGGETT,[8] born New Bedford, Mass., 1835.

1589. WILLIAM DAGGETT[7] (*Peter*,[6] *Ebenezer*,[5] [*John*,[4] *Joseph*,[3] *Joseph*,[2] *John*[1]] (?)), born Tisbury, Mass., August 8, 1792; "farmer;" died Phillips, Me., June 25, 1879; married November, 1814, Charity Barker, of New Vineyard; born Bowdoin, Me., 1793.

Issue:

2368. i. AURELIA DAGGETT,[8] born Strong, Me., February 23, 1817; died Phillips, Me., March 7, 1842.
2369. ii. DENNIS DAGGETT,[8] born Phillips, Me., March 11, 1821.
2370. iii. RACHEL DAGGETT,[8] born Phillips, Me., September 30, 1824; married 1st, Shepard Ramsdell; married 2d, December 31, 1870, Ezra R. Wright; born Lewiston, Me., 1829; resides Phillips, Me. (1893).
2371. iv. PAULINA DAGGETT,[8] born Phillips, Me., July 11, 1829.

1590. Capt. PLAMENTIN DAGGETT[7] (*Peter*,[6] *Ebenezer*,[5] [*John*,[4] *Joseph*,[3] *Joseph*,[2] *John*[1]] (?)), born Industry, Me., May 5, 1795; died Strong, Me., March 28, 1866; married Industry, Me., February 21, 1822, Hannah Snow, daughter of Ezekiel and Hannah (Pratt) Snow; born New Vineyard, Me., September 12, 1799; died New Vineyard, Me., September 7, 1862.

Issue:

2372. i. EZEKIEL SNOW DAGGETT,[8] born New Vineyard, Me., February 7, 1823; died New Vineyard, Me., February 25, 1858.
2373. ii. PLAMENTIN DAGGETT,[8] born New Vineyard, Me., May 3, 1825.
2374. iii. ALBERT DAGGETT,[8] born New Vineyard, Me., June 13, 1827.
2375. iv. OLIVER CROMWELL DAGGETT,[8] born New Vineyard, Me., April 20, 1830; died New Vineyard, Me., April 3, 1847.
2376. v. WASHINGTON LIBBEY DAGGETT,[8] born New Vineyard, Me., May 6, 1835.
2377. vi. HANNAH SNOW DAGGETT,[8] born New Vineyard, Me., January 14, 1839.

"Capt. Plamentin Daggett, in early manhood, served in the war of 1812, and subsequently settled in New Vineyard, clearing a large farm, where he made a pleasant home for more than forty years. His wife, a lady of strong mind and sterling qualities, reared a family of five sons and one daughter. He was prominently identified with the growth of his town and its public interests. He held many public offices in the town, and was long regarded as one of its most respected and influential citizens. In the early years of the State militia he was commissioned commander of the New Vineyard Light Infantry, and the name of Captain Daggett became familiar in the military circles of Franklin county. Religiously he was a Methodist; politically an early Democrat, but cast one of the first Free Soil ballots of his town, and was a member of the convention in Strong which organized the Republican party."

1591. JONATHAN LUCE DAGGETT [7] (*Peter*,[6] *Ebenezer*,[5] [*John*,[4] *Joseph*,[3] *Joseph*,[2] *John* [1]] (?)), born Industry, Me., October 11, 1797; married Sally Carle; born Saco, Me., 1793.

Issue:

2378. i. MARY DAGGETT,[8] born Chesterville, Me., October 20, 1821.
2379. ii. JONATHAN DAGGETT,[8] born Chesterville, Me., February 13, 1823.

1592. LEANDER DAGGETT [7] (*Peter*,[6] *Ebenezer*,[5] [*John*,[4] *Joseph*,[3] *Joseph*,[2] *John* [1]] (?)), born Industry, Me., May 15, 1799; died New Vineyard, Me., November 23, 1868; married March 16, 1826, Margaret Anderson, daughter of William Anderson, of New Vineyard; born Lewiston, Me., October 27, 1806.

Issue:

2380. i. MARY ANN DAGGETT,[8] born New Vineyard, Me., March 13, 1827.
2381. ii. WILLIAM ANDERSON DAGGETT,[8] born New Vineyard, Me., April 11, 1831; died New Vineyard, Me., October 31, 1858.
2382. iii. LEANDER DAGGETT,[8] born New Vineyard, Me., October 10, 1841.

1593. ALBERT DAGGETT [7] (*Peter*,[6] *Ebenezer*,[5] [*John*,[4] *Joseph*,[3] *Joseph*,[2] *John* [1]] (?)), born Industry, Me., July 8, 1801; died Manchester, Me., November 25, 1878; married Rochester, Mass., August 1, 1826, Elizabeth S. Cannon; born Rochester, Mass., 1804; died Manchester, Me., June 12, 1861.

Issue:

2383. i. ALBERT DAGGETT,[8] born Rochester, Mass., May 17, 1827.
2384. ii. PLAMENTIN DAGGETT,[8] born Rochester, Mass., December 17, 1828.
2385. iii. ELIZABETH SNOW DAGGETT,[8] born Rochester, Mass., December 25, 1830.
2386. iv. HARRIET SOPHIA DAGGETT,[8] born Rochester, Mass., April 8, 1832; died Rochester, Mass., June 29, 1838.
2387. v. MARTHA JANE DAGGETT,[8] born Rochester, Mass., January 23, 1834.

1596. LAVINA DAGGETT [7] (*Peter*,[6] *Ebenezer*,[5] [*John*,[4] *Joseph*,[3] *Joseph*,[2] *John* [1]] (?)), born Industry, Me., March 23, 1812; died New Vineyard, Me., May 6, 1834; married Industry, Me., December, 1830, Jacob Clark, son of Jacob and Catherine E. (Bean) Clark; "farmer;" born New Vineyard, Me., August 14, 1810; died Lexington, Me., September 7, 1884.

Issue:

2388. i. HANNAH CATHERINE CLARK,[8] married Alfred Pierce; resides New Richmond, Wis. (1892).
2389. ii. CHARLES CLARK,[8] born January 21, 1834; married 1859, Olive Chase; died March 3, 1868.

1597. JONATHAN LUCE [7] (*Hannah Daggett*,[6] *Ebenezer* [5] [*John*,[4] *Joseph*,[3] *Joseph*,[2] *John* [1]] (?)), born Industry, Me., December 12,

1797; died Anson, Me., March 27, 1867; married 1st, May 16, 1821, Eliza Bryar, daughter of Andrew and Ruth Bryar, of Tamworth, N.H.; born 1798; died Anson, Me., August 7, 1838; married 2d, October 2, 1838, Sally B. Merry, daughter of Asa and Sally (Bartlett) Merry; born New Vineyard, Me., 1804.

Issue:

2390. i.   MARY JANE LUCE,[8] born Industry, Me., 1822; died November 3, 1846.
2391. ii.   LEONARD LUCE,[8] born Industry, Me., June 17, 1825; married May 13, 1851, Lois M. Currier, daughter of David and Lydia (Brown) Currier.
2392. iii.   GEORGE LUCE,[8] born Anson, Me.; married Hannah Viles, daughter of Fisher and Hannah (Luce) Viles.
2393. iv.   JOHN P. LUCE,[8] born Anson, Me., July 24, 1829; married March 31, 1857, Melvina O. Viles, daughter of Fisher and Hannah (Luce) Viles.
2394. v.   PHILENA LUCE,[8] born Anson, Me.; married Sanborn L. Viles, son of Fisher and Hannah (Luce) Viles. No. 2410.
2395. vi.   EBEN LUCE,[8] born Anson, Me., November, 1837; died Anson, Me., October 9, 1838.
2396. vii.   CHARLES LLEWELLYN LUCE,[8] born Anson, Me.; married Julia Walker.

1598. LEONARD LUCE[7] (*Hannah Daggett,[6] Ebenezer[5] [John,[4] Joseph,[3] Joseph,[2] John[1]](?)), born Industry, Me., November 17, 1799; died Industry, Me., September 18, 1852; married 1st, September 25, 1827, Susan Butler West, daughter of Peter, Jr., and Anna (Butler) West; born Industry, Me., March 10, 1809; died Industry, Me., November 27, 1843; married 2d, November, 1844, Elizabeth N. Sprague, of Farmington.

Issue:

2397. i.   TAMSON COTTLE LUCE,[8] born Industry, Me., August 15, 1828; married November, 1852, Benjamin G. Eveleth, son of Joseph and Eunice (Gennings) Eveleth.
2398. ii.   JOHN WEST LUCE,[8] born Industry, Me., June 19, 1832; married November 10, 1854, Harriet M. Manny, of Middlebury, Vt.
2399. iii.   LEONARD MURRY LUCE,[8] born Industry, Me., February 20, 1834; died Industry, Me., October 31, 1837.
2400. iv.   HANNAH DAGGETT LUCE,[8] born Industry, Me., October 12, 1836; married Mr. Edwards.
2401. v.   LEONARD HANNIBAL LUCE,[8] born Industry, Me., February 10, —— ; married November 24, 1864, Mary B. Merry, daughter of David and Betsey (Remick) Merry.

1599. ELIZA LUCE[7] (*Hannah Daggett,[6] Ebenezer,[5] [John,[4] Joseph,[3] Joseph,[2] John[1]](?)), born Industry, Me., November 30, 1801; died Stark, Me., December 10, 1885; married May 9, 1822, Jonathan Merry, son of Asa and Sally (Bartlett) Merry; farmer and shoemaker; born New Vineyard, Me., December 29, 1798; died Stark, Me., May 7, 1872.

Issue:

2402. i.   HANNAH DAGGETT MERRY,[8] born Industry, Me., September 29, 1824; married James Rhoety; resides Rockland, Me. (1892).

2403. ii.   CLEMENTINE ALLEN MERRY,[8] born Industry, Me., February 25, 1826; married 1st, Thomas Pelton, son of Thomas and Betsey (Gray) Pelton, of Anson; married 2d, Augustine Crowell or Cromwell; resides Gloucester, Mass. (1892).

2404. iii. ASA MERRY,[8] born Industry, Me., January 2, 1828; married April 13, 1853, Mary Viletta Wood, daughter of Silas and Mary F. (Boyinton) Wood, of Stark, Me.

2405. iv.   EUNICE CHASE MERRY,[8] born Anson, Me., May 22, 1831; married Elias Burrell (?); she died Abington, Mass., April 28, 1852.

2406. v.   ELIZA LUCE MERRY,[8] born Anson, Me., August 11, 1833; married Charles Dill; she died Rockland, Mass., March 12, 1877.

2407. vi.   SOPHIA JANE MERRY,[8] born Anson, Me., August 2, 1835; died Anson, Me., 1838.

2408. vii. JANE CLAGHORN MERRY,[8] born Anson, Me., January 5, 1838; married 1st, Jophanus H. Davis, son of James, Jr., and Abigail (Hobbs-Boardman) Davis; married 2d, Charles Dill, above mentioned.

2409. viii. DEBORAH BUTLER MERRY,[8] born Anson, Me., January 21, 1843; married 1st, March 20, 1862, Menzir B. Merry, son of David and Betsey (Remick) Merry; married 2d, William Tarbox; resides Lewiston, Me. (1892).

1600. HANNAH LUCE[7] (*Hannah Daggett*,[6] *Ebenezer*[5] [*John*,[4] *Joseph*,[3] *Joseph*,[2] *John*[1]](?)), born Industry, Me., July 22, 1804; died October 7, 1877; married (published December 9, 1828) Fisher Viles, son of Joseph and Sarah (Hancock) Viles; farmer; resided in Anson and Industry; born Orland, Me., July 27, 1804; died April 22, 1882.

Issue:

2410. i.   SANBORN LUCE VILES,[8] born 1829; married Philena Luce, *q.v.*; soldier, Company A, Twenty-eighth Maine Regiment; died August 6, 1863.

2411. ii.   SUSAN T. VILES,[8] married October 3, 1849, Joel S. Yeaton, of New Portland; resides Nebraska (1892).

2412. iii. HANNAH VILES,[8] married George Luce, *q.v.* No. 2392.

2413. iv.   MELVIN VILES,[8] married May 18, 1862, M. Ann Bruce, daughter of Hollis and Matilda (Allen) Bruce.

2414. v.   MELVINA O. VILES,[8] married John P. Luce, *q.v.* No. 2393.

2415. vi.   ELIZA VILES,[8] married October 20, 1867, Lorenzo Watson, son of Simeon and Olive (Patterson) Watson, of Stark; resides Industry, Me. (1892).

2416. vii. ADALINE VILES,[8] married William H. Luce, Jr.

1602. SARAH DAGGETT[7] (*John*,[6] *John*[5] [*John*,[4] *Joseph*,[3] *Joseph*,[2] *John*[1]](?)), born New Vineyard, Me., January 5, 1816; resides West's Mills, Me. (1887); married October 24, 1841, Isaac Elder, son of Joseph and Ruth (Quint) Elder; farmer.

Issue:

2417. i.   JOHN DAGGETT ELDER,[8] born New Vineyard, Me., November 10, 1842; "Company I, Ninth Maine Regiment;" died Hilton Head, S.C., June 5, 1863.

2418. ii.   JOSEPH ELDER,[8] born Industry, Me., August 26, 1844; married 1st (published September 4, 1864), Betsey Houghton, of Anson; married 2d, June 1, 1886, Adalaide A. Manter, daughter of Hiram and Jane (Atkinson) Manter; farmer; resides Industry, Me. (1892).

2419. iii. MARY DEBORAH ELDER,[8] born Anson, Me., April 10, 1846; married Charles Jeffers, son of Thomas and Sarah (Kennedy) Jeffers.

2420. iv. DOLLY ELDER,[8] born Anson, Me.; died young.
2421. v.   SARAH LOUISA ELDER,[8] born Anson, Me., June 7, 1852; married
           (published December 23, 1874) Charles W. Shaw, son of Samuel
           and Betsey (Manter) Shaw.
2422. vi. LUCY JANE ELDER,[8] born Anson, Me., April 20, 1856; married Octo-
           ber 10, 1886, Benjamin W. Seavey, son of Alvin and Mary Seavey.

1603. JOHN ATWELL DAGGETT [7] (*John*,[6] *John* [5] [*John*,[4] *Joseph*,[3]
Joseph,[2] *John* [1]] (?)), born New Vineyard, Me., August 24, 1819; re-
sides Industry, Me. (1892); married December 15, 1845, Cynthia P.
Furbush, daughter of Ivory and Sarah (Haskell) Furbush, of Salem.

Issue:

2423. i.   JOHN FRED DAGGETT,[8] born Industry, Me., August 24, 1847.
2424. ii.   Son —— DAGGETT,[8] born Industry, Me., September 10, 1848; died
            December 6, 1848.
2425. iii. I. HOVEY DAGGETT,[8] born Industry, Me., April 8, 1851; died Jan-
            uary 17, 1870.
2426. iv.   C. EMMA DAGGETT,[8] born Temple, Me., February 2, 1856; died
            Salem, Me., February 9, 1862.
2427. v.   FRANK A. DAGGETT,[8] born Salem, Me., November 6, 1859; died
            December 3, 1860.
2428. vi.   MARTHA E. DAGGETT,[8] born Salem, Me., June 22, 1861; married
            March 7, 1885, Ward Burns, son of William and Phebe (Ward)
            Burns; born November 21, 1860. He, farmer, selectman; resides
            Industry, Me. (1892).
2429. vii. MARY JANE DAGGETT,[8] born Industry, Me., October 2, 1864; married
            December 24, 1889, Eugene L. Smith, son of Joseph W. and Lydia
            A. (Daggett) Smith.
2430. viii. CAPITOLA DAGGETT,[8] born Industry, Me., September 8, 1866.

1606. WILLIAM RILEY DAGGETT [7] (*John*,[6] *John* [5] [*John*,[4] *Joseph*,[3]
Joseph,[2] *John* [1]] (?)), born New Vineyard, Me.; resides California,
if living; married (published August 18, 1848) Mary T. Viles,
daughter of Leonard and Annah (Bray) Viles; born May 5, 1832;
resides Lewiston, Me. (1892).

Issue:

2431. i.   WARREN MARSHALL DAGGETT,' born Industry, Me., August 4, 1855;
           married August 25, 1884, Estella Ranger, daughter of Lafayette and
           Sarah (Gardner) Ranger, of Wilton; issue: daughter born Septem-
           ber 4, 1890; resides Farmington, Me. (1892).
2432. ii. CHARLES H. BECK DAGGETT,[8] born Industry, Me., March 25, 1858;
           married Mrs. Sarah Hutchins; resides Livermore Falls, Me. (1892).

1607. WARREN DAGGETT [7] (*John*,[6] *John* [5] [*John*,[4] *Joseph*,[3] *Joseph*,[2]
John [1]] (?)), born New Vineyard, Me., May 1, 1829; died Industry,
Me., January 31, 1883; married New Vineyard, Me., July 15, 1855,
Jane W. Ramsdell, daughter of John and Catherine (Hutchins)
Ramsdell.

Issue:

2433. i.   CASSIA JANE DAGGETT,[8] born Anson, Me., April 1, 18—.
2434. ii. HIRAM DAGGETT,[8] born Anson, Me., June 4, 1862; resides Industry,
           Me. (1892).

2435. iii. Sarah Elder Daggett,[8] born Anson, Me., July 11, 1863; married
              April 27, 1887, Edward A. Hilton, son of Benjamin F. and Mary
              (Furber) Hilton, of Stark, Me.; two children (1892).
2436. iv. Ella Miller Daggett,[8] born Anson, Me., December 28, 1864.
2437. v.   Emma Daggett,[8] born Anson, Me., February 29, 1867; married July
              5, 1886, William C. Watson, son of Joseph and Emma (Coglan)
              Watson.
2438. vi. Anna Love Daggett,[8] born Industry, Me., December 25, 1870; mar-
              ried Charles Haynes; resides Oakland, Me. (1892); children.
2439. vii. Frances Elmira Daggett,[8] born Industry, Me., July 20, 1873.

Mrs. Daggett married 2d, April 26, 1886, Eli Hawes, of Anson.

1608. Ann Cordelia Daggett [7] (*John*,[6] *John*[5] [*John*,[4] *Joseph*,[3]
Joseph,[2] *John* [1]] (?)), born New Vineyard, Me., March 6, 1838; re-
sides Anson, Me. (1893); married 1859, Nelson W. Fish, son of
Nathan and Rhoda (Walker) Fish, of Anson; "farmer."

Issue:

2440. i.   Daughter —— Fish,[8] born Anson, Me.; died young.
2441. ii.   Helen Gusta Fish,[8] born Anson, Me., April 18, 1861; married John
              H. Jeffreys, son of John and Ann D. (Ryant) Jeffreys, of Industry.
2442. iii. Alvin Tinkman Fish,[8] born Anson, Me., May 16, 1865; married
              October 13, 1885, Elvira A. Spencer, daughter of Sylvester and
              Matilda (Watson) Spencer, of Anson.
2443. iv. Nelson John Fish,[8] born Anson, Me., March 6, 1873.
2444. v.   Daughter —— Fish,[8] died in infancy.

JOHN DOGGETT, OF MARTHA'S VINEYARD.

EIGHTH GENERATION.

1610. Edwin Oscar Daggett [8] (*Jefferson*,[7] *Jacob*,[6] *Daniel*,[5]
Israel,[4] *Joseph*,[3] *John*,[2] *John* [1]), born Seekonk, Mass., March 5,
1829; resides Pawtucket, R.I. (1892); married East Providence,
R.I., November 16, 1865, Hannah Elzada Perrin, daughter of Thomas
and Hannah Bliss (Drown) Perrin; born Seekonk, Mass., March
30, 1832.

1611. Anna Judson Daggett [8] (*Jefferson*,[7] *Jacob*,[6] *Daniel*,[5]
Israel,[4] *Joseph*,[3] *John*,[2] *John* [1]), born Seekonk, Mass., March 12,
1830; resides Rumford, R.I. (1892); married Pawtucket, R.I.,
October 8, 1856, by Rev. C. Blodgett, to Ezra Granville French, son
of Ezra and Nancy (Smith) French, of Seekonk; "farmer;" born
Seekonk, Mass., June 23, 1833.

Issue:

2445. i.   Emma Edith French,[9] born Seekonk, Mass., September, 1858; mar-
             ried Mr. Radikin; resides East Providence, R.I. (1892).

2446. ii. Alice Wheaton French,[9] born Pawtucket, R.I., December 23, 1866; married Mr. Kelton; resides Rumford, R.I. (1892).

1615. Mary Knowlton Daggett [8] (*Jefferson,*[7] *Jacob,*[6] *Daniel,*[5] *Israel,*[4] *Joseph,*[3] *John,*[2] *John* [1]), born Pawtucket, R.I., April 29, 1837; resides Pawtucket, R.I. (1892); married Pawtucket, R.I., September 8, 1859, by Rev. James O. Barney, to George William Bliss, son of George W. and Betsey (Bowen) Bliss; "butcher;" born Rehoboth, Mass., October 18, 1836.

Issue :

2447. i. Susie Parkman Bliss,[9] born Pawtucket, R.I., November 18, 1864; married Charles L. Nash; resides Rehoboth, Mass. (1892).
2448. ii. Eva Warren Bliss,[9] born Pawtucket, R.I., September 19, 1869; died there.
2449. iii. George Edwin Bliss,[9] born Pawtucket, R.I., February 9, 1872; died there.
2450. iv. Mary Williams Bliss,[9] born Pawtucket, R.I., March 11, 1876; died there.

1621. Ann Elizabeth Daggett [8] (*Jacob,*[7] *Jacob,*[6] *Daniel,*[5] *Israel,*[4] *Joseph,*[3] *John,*[2] *John* [1]), born Pawtucket, R.I., October 2, 1846; resides Pawtucket, R.I. (1892); married Pawtucket, R.I., January 21, 1873, by Rev. C. Blodgett, to Matthew Jones Leach, of Pawtucket, son of Edwin and Martha (Jones) Leach; "marble-worker;" born Stockport, N.Y., March 5, 1845.

Issue :

2451. i. Angelina Leach,[9] born Pawtucket, R.I., July 5, 1874.
2452. ii. Herbert Allen Leach,[9] born Pawtucket, R.I., July 21, 1875.
2453. iii. Edward Ide Leach,[9] born Pawtucket, R.I., October 17, 1876.
2454. iv. Helen Agnes Leach,[9] born Pawtucket, R.I., April 8, 1879; died Pawtucket, R.I., November 1, 1880.
2455. v. Raymond Jacob Leach,[9] born Pawtucket, R.I., February 17, 1889.

1622. Herbert Sidney Daggett [8] (*Jacob,*[7] *Jacob,*[6] *Daniel,*[5] *Israel,*[4] *Joseph,*[3] *John,*[2] *John* [1]), born Pawtucket, R.I., July 3, 1849; "farmer;" resides Seekonk, Mass. (1892); married Pawtucket, R.I., November 19, 1873, by Rev. George Bullen, to Emily Barton Waterman, daughter of David W. and Eunice M. (Read) Waterman, of Norton, Mass.; born Providence, R.I., August 19, 1850.

Issue :

2456. i. Maud Stearns Daggett,[9] born Seekonk, Mass., November 22, 1876; died Seekonk, Mass., October 5, 1879.
2457. ii. Robert Sidney Daggett,[9] born Seekonk, Mass., October 3, 1880.
2458. iii. Ruth Slack Daggett,[9] born Seekonk, Mass., May 19, 1882.
2459. iv. David Barton Daggett,[9] born Seekonk, Mass., February 16, 1892.

1624. Samuel Sheldon Daggett [8] (*Samuel S.,*[7] *Jacob,*[6] *Daniel,*[5] *Israel,*[4] *Joseph,*[3] *John,*[2] *John* [1]), born Pawtucket, R.I., May 23, 1848; "carpenter;" resides Pawtucket, R.I. (1892); married 1st, East

Greenwich, R.I., May 23, 1868, Hannah Maria Thornley; born Philadelphia, Pa., December 25, 1848; died Pawtucket, R.I., May 4, 1873; married 2d, Pawtucket, R.I., November 16, 1874, by Rev. John C. Gowan, to Maria Louisa Green, widow of Byron Green, and daughter of Rufus and Julia (Buxton) Tift; born Slatersville, R.I., November 7, 1852; died Pawtucket, R.I., March 31, 1879.

No issue.

1625. WILLIAM JAMES DAGGETT [8] (*Samuel S.,*[7] *Jacob,*[6] *Daniel,*[5] *Israel,*[4] *Joseph,*[3] *John,*[2] *John* [1]), born Pawtucket, R.I., January 9, 1851; "carpenter;" resides Pawtucket, R.I. (1892); married Providence, R.I., September 8, 1875, by Rev. Albert H. Heath, to Susan Olive Hazard, daughter of Rowland A. and Amanda L. V. Hazard; born N. Kingston, R.I., August 30, 1853.

Issue:

2460. i. WILLIAM ANSON DAGGETT,[9] born Pawtucket, R.I., April 5, 1876.
2461. ii. LEROY CARR DAGGETT,[9] born Pawtucket, R.I., June 27, 1879.
2462. iii. GEORGE WASHINGTON DAGGETT,[9] born Pawtucket, R.I., November 18, 1881; died Pawtucket, R.I., July 22, 1892.
2463. iv. LUCY BRIGGS DAGGETT,[9] born Pawtucket, R.I., March 19, 1884.

1626. SARAH MATILDA DAGGETT [8] (*Samuel S.,*[7] *Jacob,*[6] *Daniel,*[5] *Israel,*[4] *Joseph,*[3] *John,*[2] *John* [1]), born Pawtucket, R.I., August 25, 1853; resides 49 Sanford street, Pawtucket, R.I. (1892); married Pawtucket, R.I., August 13, 1874, by C. C. Williams, to Edward Henry Reynolds, of Blackstone, Mass., son of Richard and Hannah (Shaw) Reynolds; "beltmaker;" born Bolton, Lancashire, Eng., November 4, 1847.

Issue:

2464. i. CHARLES EDWARD REYNOLDS,[9] born Pawtucket, R.I., September 22, 1875; died Pawtucket, R.I., March 17, 1879.
2465. ii. SAMUEL EDWARD REYNOLDS,[9] born Pawtucket, R.I., May 1, 1886.

1633. ALLEN DAGGETT [8] (*Seth,*[7] *Reuben,*[6] *Reuben,*[5] *Nathaniel,*[4] *Nathaniel,*[3] *John,*[2] *John* [1]), born Jackson, Tioga Co., Pa., October 6, 1811; died Lawrenceville, Pa., March 12, 1886; married Tioga, Pa., March 9, 1844, Clarissa Starkey, daughter of William and Polly (Benjamin) Starkey; born Hector, N.Y., August 21, 1823; resides Bellefont, Center Co., N.Y. (1892).

Issue:

2466. i. INEZ ADELLA DAGGETT,[9] born Tioga, Pa., February 22, 1845.
2467. ii. RICHARD WILLARD DAGGETT,[9] born Tioga, Pa., June 6, 1846; married Elmira, N.Y., August 5, 1873, Celia Metella Fletcher, daughter of John and Debora Teressa (Ramsdale) Fletcher; born Sullivan, Pa., September 20, 1849; resides 214 Franklin street, Elmira, N.Y. (1892).
2468. iii. ORSON STARKEY DAGGETT,[9] born Tioga, Pa., September 28, 1856.

2469. iv. CHARLES ALLEN DAGGETT,[9] born Tioga, Pa., May 1, 1859; married Elmira, N.Y., September 22, 1889, by Rev. Thomas Sharpe, to Maggie Van Druff, daughter of William and Elner (Decker) Van Druff; born New Jersey, April 6, 1868; resides Southport, N.Y. (1892).
2470. v. GEORGE DAGGETT;[9] resides Tioga, Pa. (1892).

1634. GEORGE DAGGETT[8] (Seth,[7] Reuben,[6] Reuben,[5] Nathaniel,[4] Nathaniel,[3] John,[2] John[1]), born Jackson, Pa., July 30, 1813; died Tioga, Pa., March 18, 1850; married 1st, Daggett's Mills, Pa., February, 1836, Harriet Dewey, daughter of Levi and Delighty (Watkins) Dewey; born Columbia, Pa., January 19, 1819; died Daggett's Mills, Pa., October 19, 1839; married 2d, South Creek, Pa., November 14, 1841, Eliza Pettingill, daughter of Samuel and Sally (Taylor) Pettingill; born Tioga county, N.Y.; died December 25, 1880.

Issue:

2471. i. LEVI DAGGETT,[9] born Daggett's Mills, Pa., March 3, 1837.
2472. ii. HARRIET DAGGETT,[9] born Tioga, Pa., July 12, 1844.
2473. iii. FLORENCE DAGGETT,[9] born Tioga, Pa., September 26, 1846.
2474. iv. GEORGE LEWIS DAGGETT,[9] born Tioga, Pa., November 18, 1849; married April, 1891; resides Bradford, Pa. (1892).

1635. LEWIS DAGGETT[8] (Seth,[7] Reuben,[6] Reuben,[5] Nathaniel,[4] Nathaniel,[3] John,[2] John[1]), born Jackson, Pa., May 5, 1816; resides Tioga, Pa. (1892); married March 4, 1839, by Theodore Larrison, Esq., to Ellen Samantha Wells, daughter of Norman and Elizabeth (Coolbaugh) Wells; born Barrington, N.Y., January 30, 1821.

Issue:

2475. i. SETH ORLANDO DAGGETT,[9] born Daggett's Mills, Pa., September 14, 1843.
2476. ii. GEORGIA DAGGETT,[9] born Tioga, Pa., October 26, 1851; died Tioga, Pa., May 5, 1866.
2477. iii. WELLS LEWIS DAGGETT,[9] born Tioga, Pa., April 26, 1854.
Three died young.

1636. CLYMENA E. DAGGETT[8] (Seth,[7] Reuben,[6] Reuben,[5] Nathaniel,[4] Nathaniel,[3] John,[2] John[1]), born Jackson, Pa., March 16, 1818; died Utica, N.Y., 1873; married Jackson, Pa., March, 1841, Rev. Richard L. Stillwell, son of Edward and Sarah (Ferris) Stillwell; born Hector, N.Y., January 27, 1819; resides Bellona, Yates Co., N.Y. (1892).

Issue:

2478. i. SARAH R. STILLWELL,[9] born Rutland, Pa., January 4, 1842; married April, 1863, Brev. Capt. George A. Ludlow, United States Volunteers; she died Elmira, N.Y., April 2, 1882; he resides Wellsboro', Pa. (1892;) issue: two children.
2479. ii. EMMA S. STILLWELL,[9] born May 25, 1844; resides Tioga, Pa. (1892).
2480. iii. ELNORA M. STILLWELL,[9] born February 19, 1847; married Joseph F. Morley; she died February, 1869.
2481. iv. MARY C. STILLWELL,[9] born Bath, N.Y., September 15, 1849; married, 1868, Ranson B. Gay; resides Harrison, Mich. (1892); issue: four children.

2482. v.   AMELIA E. STILLWELL,[9] died in infancy.
2483. vi.   WILLIAM H. STILLWELL,[9] died in infancy.
2484. vii.   RICHARD WELBY STILLWELL,[9] born Tioga, Pa., January 7, 1857; resides Philadelphia, Pa. (1892).

Rev. Richard L. Stillwell, of the Central New York Methodist Episcopal Conference, married 2d, Laura Phelps Whitcomb, and 3d, Julia Welsh Larzelere.

1637.   MINERVA DAGGETT[8] (*Seth,*[7] *Reuben,*[6] *Reuben,*[5] *Nathaniel,*[4] *Nathaniel,*[3] *John,*[2] *John*[1]), born Jackson, Pa., May 19, 1822; resides Tioga, Tioga Co, Pa. (1892); married Jackson, Pa., April 11, 1839, Daniel Dewey, son of Levi and Delighty (Watkins) Dewey; born Columbia, Bradford Co., Pa., September 15, 1816.

Issue:

2485. i.   EVALINE DEWEY,[9] born Jackson, Pa., February 4, 1840.
2486. ii.   HENRY F. DEWEY,[9] born Ridgebury, Pa., April 15, 1842.
2487. iii.   THEODORE DEWEY,[9] born Jackson, Pa., July 17, 1844.
2488. iv.   CHARLES SUMNER DEWEY,[9] born Tioga, Pa., March 4, 1856; married Julia Smith; resides Tioga, Pa. (1892).
2489. v.   FRANK DEWEY,[9] born Tioga, Pa., July 8, 1859.

1638.   ROWENA DAGGETT[8] (*Seth,*[7] *Reuben,*[6] *Reuben,*[5] *Nathaniel,*[4] *Nathaniel,*[3] *John,*[2] *John*[1]), born March 2, 1824; married 1850, W. T. Urell.

Issue:

2490. i.   ROBERT E. URELL,[9] born Tioga, Pa., June 4, 1851; resides there.
2491. ii.   CHARLES A. URELL,[9] born Tioga, Pa., October 16, 1852; resides there.
2492. iii.   MALLIE L. URELL,[9] born Tioga, Pa., 1854; married H. L. Baldwin; issue: one child.
2493. iv.   THOMAS M. URELL,[9] born Tioga, Pa., May 3, 1857; resides there.
2494. v.   RICHARD D. URELL,[9] born June, 1859; married Miss Von Goodne; issue: one child.

1640.   MARY ANN DAGGETT[8] (*Seth,*[7] *Reuben,*[6] *Reuben,*[5] *Nathaniel,*[4] *Nathaniel,*[3] *John,*[2] *John*[1]), born Tioga, Pa., September 11, 1829; resides Elmira, N.Y. (1892); married Tioga, Pa., May 8, 1850, Capt. Hiram Willard Caulking, son of Allen D. and Mary Ann (Willard) Caulking; born Tioga, Pa., August 15, 1817.

Issue:

2495. i.   WILLARD ALLEN CAULKING,[9] born Rodney, Miss., February 11, 1851; "printer;" died Rochester, N.Y., May 6, 1883.
2496. ii.   CATHERINE DORA CAULKING,[9] born Tioga, Pa., July 23, 1853; address, Elmira, N.Y. (1892).
2497. iii.   NETTIE CAULKING,[9] died.
2498. iv.   HIRAM CAULKING,[9] born Tioga, Pa., December 13, 1858; resides Elmira, N.Y. (1892).
2499. v.   CHARLES CAULKING,[9] died.
2500. vi.   EMMA CAULKING,[9] born Tioga, Pa., June 1, 1867; resides Seattle, Wash. (1892).
2501. vii.   THOMAS B. CAULKING,[9] born Tioga, Pa., May 21, 1870; died Mt. Morris, N.Y., January 11, 1891.

1642. SETH Q. KEYES [8] (*Saloma Daggett*,[7] *Reuben*,[6] *Reuben*,[5] *Nathaniel*,[4] *Nathaniel*,[3] *John*,[2] *John* [1]), born Jackson, Pa., July 3, 1810; '' went to sea; '' died Liverpool, Eng., 1852; married Ireland.

Issue:

2502. i. SETH KEYES,[9] lived with his uncle, and after a time went abroad in search of his mother and sister.
2503. ii. MARY KEYES.[9]

1643. WILLIAM B. KEYES [8] (*Saloma Daggett*,[7] *Reuben*,[6] *Reuben*,[5] *Nathaniel*,[4] *Nathaniel*,[3] *John*,[2] *John* [1]), born Jackson, Pa., March 16, 1812; resides Tioga, Pa. (1892); married Tioga, Pa., August 14, 1841, Sarah M. Wells.

Issue:

2504. i.   AUSTIN O. KEYES,[9] born Tioga, Pa., July 9, 1842; died Tioga., Pa., July 17, 1855.
2505. ii.   SARAH M. KEYES,[9] born Tioga, Pa., May 18, 1844; married G. W. Hazelett.
2506. iii. SEVELLON C. KEYES,[9] born Tioga, Pa.. August 14, 1848; married Gertrude Blatchley.
2507. iv.   BELL KEYES,[9] born Tioga, Pa., February 22, 1847; married William Hazelett.
2508. v.   ANNETTE KEYES,[9] born Tioga, Pa., June 16, 1851; married H. W. Lawnsberry.
2509. vi.   ADA M. KEYES,[9] born Tioga, Pa., December 6, 1855.

Mr. Keyes went with his mother and brother to Vermont; but in 1831 returned to Pennsylvania, where he made his home, and became a man of position and substance.

1648. WILLIAM DAGGETT [8] (*Rufus*,[7] *Reuben*,[6] *Reuben*,[5] *Nathaniel*,[4] *Nathaniel*,[3] *John*,[2] *John* [1]), born Pennsylvania, December 26, 1817; died Marinette, Wis., February 21, 1887; married March 19, 1839, Mary Corzatt.

Issue:

2510. i.   ELMER DAGGETT,[9] resides Southport, N.Y. (1888).
2511. ii.   JEROME DAGGETT,[9] resides Minnesota.
2512. iii. EDGAR DAGGETT,[9] resides Wisconsin.
2513. iv.   FRANK DAGGETT,[9] resides Wisconsin.
2514. v.   Daughter —— DAGGETT.[9]
2515. vi.   Daughter —— DAGGETT.[9]

1649. RUFUS DAGGETT [8] (*Rufus*,[7] *Reuben*,[6] *Reuben*,[5] *Nathaniel*,[4] *Nathaniel*,[3] *John*,[2] *John* [1]), born Pennsylvania, February 25, 1819; died January 1, 1864; married July 30, 1842, Rachel Corzatt.

Issue:

2516. i.   IRA DAGGETT,[9] born Tioga County, Pa., November 16, 1844; resides Wells, Bradford Co., Pa. (1892).
2517. ii.   ADAM DAGGETT,[9] born Pennsylvania, February 28, 1848.
2518. iii. ZACH. DAGGETT,[9] born Pennsylvania, March 13, 1850; died Pennsylvania, August 31, 1879.
2519. iv.   LEWIS DAGGETT.[9] born Pennsylvania, July 25, 1851.

2520. v.   Daughter —— DAGGETT,[9] born Pennsylvania.
2521. vi. Daughter —— DAGGETT,[9] born Pennsylvania.
2522. vii. Daughter —— DAGGETT,[9] born Pennsylvania.

1652. CRONELUS C. DAGGETT[8] (*Rufus,*[7] *Reuben,*[6] *Reuben,*[5] *Nathaniel,*[4] *Nathaniel,*[3] *John,*[2] *John*[1]), born Pennsylvania, August 5, 1825; resides Pennsylvania; married March 8, 1846, Jane Seeley.
Issue:

2523. i.   EDWIN DAGGETT.[9]
2524. ii.   MERIT DAGGETT.[9]
2525. iii. WILLIS DAGGETT.[9]
2526. iv.   GEORGE DAGGETT.[9]
2527. v.   FRED DAGGETT.[9]
2528. vi.   LUMAN DAGGETT.[9]
2529. vii. Daughter —— DAGGETT.[9]
2530. viii. Daughter —— DAGGETT.[9]
2531. ix.   Daughter —— DAGGETT.[9]

1656. EMILY BELINDA CONABLE[8] (*Lydia Daggett,*[7] *Reuben,*[6] *Reuben,*[5] *Nathaniel,*[4] *Nathaniel,*[3] *John,*[2] *John*[1]), born Jackson, Pa., January 24, 1818; resides Plainfield, Wis. (1886); married Jackson, Pa., August 9, 1835, Alfred Rozell; "farmer;" died Plainfield, Wis.
Issue: six children, born Jackson, Pa., and all but the third reside in Plainfield, Wis. (1886).

1669. WILLIAM DAGGETT[8] (*John,*[7] *Levi,*[6] *John,*[5] *John,*[4] *Nathaniel,*[3] *John,*[2] *John*[1]), born Seekonk, Mass., June 19, 1824; "farmer;" address, Box 127, East Providence, R.I. (1892); married 1st, Pawtucket, R.I., September 3, 1846, Mercy Ann Wheldon, daughter of John and Ann (Carpenter) Wheldon; born Thompson, Conn., January 26, 1827; died Providence, R.I., December 16, 1872; married 2d, Providence, R.I., September 3, 1873, by Rev. William Phillips, to Caroline Elizabeth Baker Cooper, daughter of William B. and Cecelia A. (Freeman) Cooper; born Pawtucket, R.I., September 16, 1838.
Issue:

2532. i.   AMEY ANN DAGGETT,[9] born Seekonk, Mass., April 29, 1849.
2533. ii. JOHN WHELDON DAGGETT,[9] born Seekonk, Mass., September 5, 1853; died East Providence, R.I., December 12, 1882.
2534. iii. ELSIE MARIA DAGGETT,[9] born East Providence, R.I., March 18, 1864.
2535. iv. CORA MAY DAGGETT,[9] born East Providence, R.I., January 22, 1866.
2536. v.   WILLIAM DAGGETT,[9] born East Providence, R.I., June 11, 1867; died East Providence, R.I., October 16, 1868.

1698. WILLIAM DAGGETT[8] (*William,*[7] *William,*[6] *Seth,*[5] *Samuel,*[4] *Thomas,*[3] *Thomas,*[2] *John*[1]), born Tisbury, Mass., February 20, 1797; married Tisbury, Mass., December 12, 1819, Rebecca Daggett, daughter of Samuel and Rebecca (Daggett) Daggett (No. 1731); born

New Vineyard, Me., November 25, 1796; died Tisbury, Mass., January 28, 1855.

Issue :

2537. i.   WILLIAM DAGGETT,[9] born Tisbury, Mass., August 22, 1825.
2538. ii. EMMA DAGGETT,[9] married Mr. Stone.

1704. HENRY DAGGETT[8] (*William,*[7] *William,*[6] *Seth,*[5] *Samuel,*[4] *Thomas,*[3] *Thomas,*[2] *John*[1]), born Tisbury, Mass., February 8, 1811; " mariner; " died Vineyard Haven, Mass.. January 31, 1873 ; married Mary A. French, daughter of Asa and Rebecca Taber (Hammond) French; born Fairhaven, Mass., September 6, 1815; died Vineyard Haven, Mass., June 25, 1886.

Issue :

2539. i.   REBECCA DAGGETT,[9] died young.
2540. ii.   CARRIE DREW DAGGETT,[9] born Tisbury, Mass., 1839; married Tisbury, Mass., January 6, 1859, by Rev. A. Latham, to William M. Smith, son of James and Mary Smith; " mariner; " born Tisbury, Mass., 1833; resides Vineyard Haven. Mass. (1892).
2541. iii. HENRY CROSWELL DAGGETT,[9] born Tisbury, Mass., May 14, 1843; " mariner; " married Tisbury, Mass., December 17, 1863, by Rev. M. P. Alderman, to Annie Bartlett; born Boston, Mass., 1833.
2542. iv.   JOSIAH TABER DAGGETT,[9] born Tisbury, Mass., December 31, 1844; " mariner; " married Tisbury, Mass., July 9, 1869, by Rev. Edw. Edson, to Alice Ann West, daughter of Charles and Betsey West; born Tisbury, Mass., 1848.
2543. v.   ABRAM ANTHONY DAGGETT,[9] born Tisbury, Mass., May 16. 1847; " mariner; " married Tisbury, Mass., May 31, 1875, by Rev. W. A. Luce, to Sarah Gray Luce, daughter of Lot and Delia Luce; born Tisbury, Mass., 1856.
2544. vi.   FANNIE A. DAGGETT,[9] died; aged two.

1713. Capt. ALONZO DAGGETT[8] (*Seth,*[7] *William,*[6] *Seth,*[5] *Samuel,*[4] *Thomas,*[3] *Thomas,*[2] *John*[1]), born Tisbury, Mass., November 19, 1810; died Gosnold, Mass., March 12, 1889; married 1st, Tisbury, Mass., August 17, 1835, by Rev. Mr. Joselyn, to Eliza Beetle Smith, daughter of Harrison and Anna (Beetle) Smith; born Edgartown, Mass., March 16, 1816; died Tisbury, Mass., June 30, 1864; married 2d, Dartmouth, Mass., June 7, 1866, by Rev. J. L. Pierce, to Addie Matilda Hunt, of Dartmouth, widow of George Hunt and daughter of John and Mary (Hancock) Flanders; born Chilmark, Mass., September 18, 1833; died Taunton, Mass., May 1, 1875; married 3d, New Bedford, Mass., January 8, 1876, Mary Devol Allen, of Gosnold, Mass., widow of Holder Allen and daughter of Charles and Jane (Haskins) Slocum; born Dartmouth, Mass., 1815; resides Cuttyhunk, Mass. (1892).

Issue :

2545. i.   MARY DAGGETT,[9] born Tisbury, Mass., March 23, 1839.
2546. ii.   SETH DAGGETT,[9] born Tisbury, Mass., May 8, 1841; died Tisbury, Mass., June 13, 1841.
2547. iii. ANN ELIZA DAGGETT,[9] born Tisbury, Mass., May 26, 1842.

2548. iv.   GEORGIA DAGGETT,[9] born Tisbury, Mass., November 8, 1845.
2549. v.   LOUISA ATHEARN DAGGETT,[9] born Tisbury, Mass., August 13, 1849;
            died Tisbury, Mass., September 30, 1849.
2550. vi.   CARRIE BRADLEY DAGGETT,[9] born Tisbury, Mass., June 12, 1853.
2551. vii. JOHN LYNES DAGGETT,[9] born Tisbury, Mass., July 11, 1868; drowned
            February 17, 1890.
2552. viii. FRANK WESLEY DAGGETT,[9] born South Dartmouth, Mass., January
            30, 1872; died Taunton, Mass., June 30, 1873.

The early part of the life of Alonzo Daggett was spent in following the sea, but for a few years previous to his death he held the
office of postmaster of Gosnold, Mass.   He was, at one time, a well-
known pilot at Vineyard Haven.

1716. OSCAR DAGGETT[8] (*Seth,*[7] *William,*[6] *Seth,*[5] *Samuel,*[4]
Thomas,[3] *Thomas,*[2] *John*[1]), born Tisbury, Mass., October, 1815;
" mariner; " perished at sea December 2, 1856; married Jane E. Bell;
born Fairhaven, Mass.; perished at sea December 2, 1856.
    Issue :

2553. i.   —— DAGGETT,[9] perished at sea December 2, 1856.
2554. ii.   LIZZIE I. DAGGETT,[9] born New Bedford, Mass., November 14, 1855;
            perished at sea December 2, 1856.

1717. CAROLINE WEST DAGGETT[8] (*Seth,*[7] *William,*[6] *Seth,*[5] *Samuel,*[4] *Thomas,*[3] *Thomas,*[2] *John*[1]), born December 15, 1818; married
August 1, 1839, Henry Bradley, son of Thomas and Hannah Bradley.
    Issue :

2555. i.   LEANDER DAGGETT BRADLEY,[9] born Vineyard Haven, Mass., May 31,
            1841; married Serena Daggett (see No. 1777).

1718. GEORGIANA DAGGETT[8] (*Seth,*[7] *William,*[6] *Seth,*[5] *Samuel,*[4]
Thomas,[3] *Thomas,*[2] *John*[1]), born Tisbury, Mass., December 7, 1827;
resides 24 Vienna street, Cleveland, Ohio (1892); married Tisbury,
Mass., July 30, 1850, by Rev. M. J. Talbot, Jr., to Asa H. Calhoun,
of Harwich, Mass., son of Reuben and Eunice Calhoun; " mariner; "
born Harwich, Mass., 1822.

1727. PETER DAGGETT ELDRIDGE[8] (*Betsey Daggett,*[7] *Peter,*[6] *Seth,*[5]
Samuel,[4] *Thomas,*[3] *Thomas,*[2] *John*[1]), married Ruth Hamlin, of Wellfleet, Mass.
    Issue :

2556. i.   MARY ELDRIDGE,[9] married gentleman from Provincetown, Mass.
2557. ii.   JOSHUA HAMLIN ELDRIDGE,[9] died.
2558. iii. MERY B. ELDRIDGE,[9] married Isaac Rogers; resided Boston (1885);
            issue: J. O. Rogers,[10] with DeWolfe, Fiske & Co., Boston (1885).
2559. iv.   BENJAMIN HAMLIN ELDRIDGE,[9] married lady from Harwich, Mass.

1729. SARAH DAGGETT[8] (*Samuel,*[7] *Samuel,*[6] *Seth,*[5] *Samuel,*[4]
Thomas,[3] *Thomas,*[2] *John*[1]), born Vineyard Haven, Mass., December
29, 1791; died Sodus, N.Y., July, 1832; married New Vineyard,

Me. (published December 19, 1807), Asa Merry Butler, son of Henry and Mehitable (Norton) Butler; died probably in Ohio.

Issue: several children, among whom were:

2560. i.   SARAH BUTLER.[9]
2561. ii. SAMUEL BUTLER.[9]

1730. ISAAC DAGGETT[8] (*Samuel,*[7] *Samuel,*[6] *Seth,*[5] *Samuel,*[4] *Thomas,*[3] *Thomas,*[2] *John*[1]), born New Vineyard, Me., August 5, 1794; "farmer;" died Industry, Me., August 17, 1884; married New Vineyard, Me., March 5, 1818, Sally Butler Norton, daughter of Tristram Gardiner and Sally (Butler) Norton; born New Vineyard, Me., May 7, 1799; died Industry, Me., November 27, 1880.

Issue:

2562. i.   SAMUEL DAGGETT,[9] born New Vineyard (now Industry), Me., November 30, 1818.
2563. ii. TRISTRAM NORTON DAGGETT,[9] born New Vineyard, Me., October 21, 1820.
2564. iii. ISAAC DAGGETT,[9] born New Vineyard, Me., December 2, 1823; died Aroostook county, Me., May 15, 1850.
2565. iv. JOHN TOBEY DAGGETT,[9] born New Vineyard, Me., September 13, 1826.
2566. v.   ANDREW JACKSON DAGGETT,[9] born New Vineyard, Me., November 26, 1829.
2567. vi. FRANCIS MARION DAGGETT,[9] born New Vineyard, Me., April 24, 1833; died Truckee, Cal., July 9, 1868.
2568. vii. WILLIAM HARRISON DAGGETT,[9] born New Vineyard, Me., May 28, 1836; married 1st. Abbie Frost, daughter of John and Olive (Leaver) Frost; married 2d, Angie Coughlin, daughter of Andrew and Ann Coughlin, of New Vineyard, Me.; he died Truckee, Cal., July 27, 1876.
2569. viii. JULIA JONES DAGGETT,[9] born New Vineyard, Me., June 1, 1839.

Isaac Daggett was the second white child born in New Vineyard, Me.

1732. SAMUEL DAGGETT[8] (*Samuel,*[7] *Samuel,*[6] *Seth,*[5] *Samuel,*[4] *Thomas,*[3] *Thomas,*[2] *John*[1]), born New Vineyard, Me., December 24, 1798; "farmer;" died Farmington, Me., June 10, 1859; married New Vineyard, Me., December 2, 1824, Julia Jones, daughter of Ebenezer and Mary (Le Ballister) Jones; born Farmington, Me., June 1, 1807; died Evansville, Ind., July 17, 1887.

Issue:

2570. i.   BRADFORD DAGGETT,[9] born Industry, Me., August 9, 1825; died Industry, Me., July 15, 1841.
2571. ii. JOHN BARNARD DAGGETT,[9] born Industry, Me., May 17, 1827.
2572. iii. MARY JONES DAGGETT,[9] born Industry, Me., December 26, 1830; died Industry, Me., February 9, 1841.
2573. iv. EMILY JONES DAGGETT,[9] born Industry, Me., January 10, 1837.
2574. v.   CHARLES BOARDMAN DAGGETT,[9] born Industry, Me., August 31, 1842; married Derby Line, Can., March 7, 1865, Annie Hill; no issue; First Sergeant, Co. L, Second Maine Cavalry; he died Chicago, Ill., November 6, 1875.
2575. vi. ORRIN DAGGETT (adopted),[9] born New Vineyard, Me., January 7, 1816.

Samuel Daggett was high sheriff of Franklin county from 1842 to 1846; was also a colonel in the militia.

He subsequently removed to Farmington Falls. His widow afterward married Rev. George Webber, and resided in Evansville, Ind.

1736. JOHN TOBEY DAGGETT[8] (*Samuel*,[7] *Samuel*,[6] *Seth*,[5] *Samuel*,[4] *Thomas*,[3] *Thomas*,[2] *John*[1]), born New Vineyard, Me., September 29, 1807; "mariner;" died Tisbury, Mass., March 23, 1876; married Vineyard Haven, Mass., May 26, 1833, Harriet Byron West, daughter of Jeruel and Belinda (Lambert) West; born June 14, 1812; died Tisbury, Mass., December 16, 1886.

Issue:

2576. i.   MARY MERRY DAGGETT,[9] born Tisbury, Mass., May 9, 1834; died
           Tisbury, Mass., April 6, 1841.
2577. ii. BELINDA WEST DAGGETT,[9] born Tisbury, Mass., December 9, 1838.
2578. iii. JOHN TOBEY DAGGETT,[9] born Tisbury, Mass., June 3, 1841; perished
           at sea March 10, 1868.
2579. iv. ABIGAIL BRADFORD DAGGETT,[9] born Tisbury, Mass., February 1,
           1846; address, West Tisbury, Mass. (1892).
2580. v.   MARY MERRY DAGGETT,[9] born Tisbury, Mass., October 19, 1847.
2581. vi. OBED SHERMAN DAGGETT,[9] born Tisbury, Mass., August 22, 1850.
2582. vii. SAMUEL BRADFORD DAGGETT,[9] born Tisbury, Mass., March 22, 1852;
           address, North Tisbury, Mass. (1892).
2583. viii. LUCY ELLEN DAGGETT,[9] born Tisbury, Mass., July 12, 1855.

1738. AMANDA MALVINA DAGGETT[8] (*Samuel*,[7] *Samuel*,[6] *Seth*,[5] *Samuel*,[4] *Thomas*,[3] *Thomas*,[2] *John*[1]), born Tisbury, Mass., August 4, 1815; resides Vineyard Haven, Mass. (1892); married Vineyard Haven, Mass., May 4, 1834, George Bradford Manchester, son of Thomas and Abigail Bradford (Winslow) Manchester; born Vineyard Haven, Mass., December 27, 1813; died Panama, August 23, 1850.

Issue:

2584. i.   REBECCA DAGGETT MANCHESTER,[9] born Vineyard Haven, Mass., De-
           cember 14, 1836.
2585. ii. SOPHRONIA PEAKES MANCHESTER,[9] born Vineyard Haven, Mass.,
           March 17, 1842.
2586. iii. BRADFORD BRUSH MANCHESTER,[9] born Vineyard Haven, Mass., Jan-
           uary 13, 1846; resides Vineyard Haven, Mass. (1892).

1741. LENDAL DAGGETT[8] (*Silas*,[7] *Silas*,[6] *Seth*,[5] *Samuel*,[4] *Thomas*,[3] *Thomas*,[2] *John*[1]), born Tisbury, Mass., October 14, 1804; died Anson, Me., May 13, 1868; married New Vineyard, Me., 1826, Lydia Norton, daughter of Tristram and Sarah (Butler) Norton; born New Vineyard, Me., February 15, 1805; died Industry, Me., December 1, 1885.

Issue:

2587. i.   SETH DAGGETT,[9] born Industry, Me., April 24, 1828; married 1st, Oc-
           tober 14, 1856, Eunice Jane Doyen, daughter of Abbott and Kath-
           erine (Collins) Doyen; born Industry, Me., February 14, 1838;
           divorced; married 2d, Mrs. Jane Morrison; resides Dexter, Me.
           (1892).

2588. ii. SILAS DAGGETT,[9] born Industry, Me., April 24, 1828.
2589. iii. LYDIA ANN DAGGETT,[9] born Industry, Me.. September 19, 1835.
2590. iv. APHIA HARRIET DAGGETT,[9] born Madison, Me., August 16, 1843; married Peter W. Pinkham, son of Winborn and Betsey (Willis) Pinkham; resides Wisconsin (1892).
2591. v.   TRISTRAM GARDNER DAGGETT,[9] born Stark, Me., January 29, 1847.

Mrs. Daggett married 2d, Mr. Tufts, of Kingfield, Me.

1742. ABIGAIL CLEVELAND DAGGETT[8] (*Silas,*[7] *Silas,*[6] *Seth,*[5] *Samuel,*[4] *Thomas,*[3] *Thomas,*[2] *John*[1]), born Industry, Me., May 16, 1807; died Vineyard Haven, Mass., about 1883; married Samuel Tilton, of Chilmark; died Chilmark, Mass., many years before his wife.

No issue.

1744. HIRAM DAGGETT[8] (*Silas,*[7] *Silas,*[6] *Seth,*[5] *Samuel,*[4] *Thomas,*[3] *Thomas,*[2] *John*[1]), died California; married November 3, 1824, Eliza Burnham, daughter of Jeremiah and Julia Burnham; born Strong, Me.

Issue: two sons and two daughters.

1745. JOSEPH DAGGETT[8] (*Silas,*[7] *Silas,*[6] *Seth,*[5] *Samuel,*[4] *Thomas,*[3] *Thomas,*[2] *John*[1]), born Farmington, Me., May 15, 1814; resides Tisbury. Mass. (1893); married Tisbury, Mass., July 5, 1835, by Rev. Mr. Chase, to Sophia Dexter, daughter of Benjamin and Betsey (Hillman) Dexter; born Tisbury, Mass., December 19, 1817.

Issue:

2592. i.   SILAS DAGGETT,[9] born Tisbury, Mass., March 29, 1841; "sea captain;" address, 114 State street, Boston, Mass. (1893).
2593. ii. WILLIAM HENRY DAGGETT,[9] born Tisbury, Mass., January 29, 1844.
2594. iii. ALICE ANN DAGGETT,[9] born Tisbury, Mass., November 11, 1846; died Tisbury. Mass., May 24, 1847.
2595. iv. CHARLES DILLINGHAM DAGGETT,[9] born Tisbury, Mass., July 27, 1848.

1746. ISAAC CHACE DAGGETT[8] (*Silas,*[7] *Silas,*[6] *Seth,*[5] *Samuel,*[4] *Thomas,*[3] *Thomas,*[2] *John*[1]), born New Vineyard, Me., February 6, 1816; "mariner;" died Tisbury, Mass., 1893; married, Tisbury, Mass., March 28, 1844, by B. F. Hedden, to Eliza Nye Robinson, daughter of Hervy and Peggy (Manter) Robinson; born Vineyard Haven, Mass., March 7, 1825.

Issue:

2596. i.   FRANCIS LAWRENCE DAGGETT,[9] born Tisbury, Mass., January 24, 1845; married; resides California (1893).

Isaac C. Daggett, mariner, was member of the Board of Selectmen of Tisbury, 1875–6–7.

1747. DEBORAH DAGGETT[8] (*Silas,*[7] *Silas,*[6] *Seth,*[5] *Samuel,*[4] *Thomas,*[3] *Thomas,*[2] *John*[1]), born Tisbury, Mass., July, 1818; resides 162 Ash street, New Bedford, Mass. (1893); married Tisbury, Mass., 1834, Thomas Tilton, son of Thomas and Fear (Hawks) Tilton; born Chilmark, Mass., 1806; died New Bedford, Mass., 1887.

Issue:

2597. i. HELEN TILTON,[9] born Tisbury, Mass., February 25, 1835; married April 9, 1855, Albert C. Vinson, son of Martin and Sarah Vinson; he born Edgartown, Mass., August 9, 1834; resides New Bedford, Mass. (1893); issue: i. Lizzie Vinson,[10] married Mr. Thompson; ii. Sarah M. Vinson,[10] married Mr. King; iii. Dora T. Vinson,[10] married Mr. Amos.

1748. MARY DAGGETT[8] (*Silas,*[7] *Silas,*[6] *Seth,*[5] *Samuel,*[4] *Thomas,*[3] *Thomas,*[2] *John*[1]), born Maine; died Tisbury, Mass., 1870; married Leander Luce, son of Hovey and Nancy (Clifford) Luce; born Tisbury, Mass.; died there.

Issue:

2598. i. HIRAM LUCE,[9] born Tisbury, Mass.; died there.
2599. ii. JOSIAH PRESBURY LUCE,[9] born Tisbury, Mass.; lost at sea.
2600. iii. IRVING SMITH LUCE,[9] born Tisbury, Mass.; married; removed West.

1767. HENRY WALKER DAGGETT[8] (*Timothy,*[7] *Michael,*[6] *Sylvanus,*[5] *Samuel,*[4] *Thomas,*[3] *Thomas,*[2] *John*[1]), born Tisbury, Mass., April 14, 1853; "seaman;" resides West Chop, Mass. (1892); married Tisbury, Mass., December 24, 1883, by Rev. J. P. Farrar, to Louisa Lee Winslow, daughter of Leander and Jerusha (Hurlbut) Winslow; born Tisbury, Mass., December 24, 1856.

1768. CHARLES NYE DAGGETT[8] (*Charles N.,*[7] *Michael,*[6] *Sylvanus,*[5] *Samuel,*[4] *Thomas,*[3] *Thomas,*[2] *John*[1]), born Edgartown, Mass., December 24, 1843; "blacksmith;" resides 160 Mill street, New Bedford, Mass. (1892); married New Bedford, Mass., February 14, 1867, by Rev. L. B. Bates, to Mary E. Gifford, daughter of Giles and Sarah Gifford, of Westport; born Westport, Mass., 1842.

1777. SERENA DAGGETT[8] (*Franklin,*[7] *Freeman,*[6] *Sylvanus,*[5] *Samuel,*[4] *Thomas,*[3] *Thomas,*[2] *John*[1]), born Tisbury, Mass., November 13, 1849; died Arlington, Mass., June 21, 1893; married Vineyard Haven, Mass., July 31, 1865, Leander Daggett Bradley, son of Henry and Caroline W. (Daggett) Bradley (No. 2555); born Vineyard Haven, Mass., May 31, 1841; resides Arlington, Mass. (1893). No issue.

1780. Capt. GRAFTON LUCE DAGGETT[8] (*Freeman,*[7] *Freeman,*[6] *Sylvanus,*[5] *Samuel,*[4] *Thomas,*[3] *Thomas,*[2] *John*[1]), born Tisbury, Mass., November 24, 1829; "mariner;" resides Vineyard Haven, Mass. (1892); married Taunton, Mass., May 23, 1855, by Rev. H. C. Atwater, to Elizabeth Caroline Luce, widow of George Luce and daughter of Constant and Caroline (Norton) Norton; born Edgartown, Mass., May 23, 1835.

Issue:

2601. i. ANNIE FRANKLIN DAGGETT,[9] born Tisbury, Mass., September 11, 1857.

Captain Grafton L. Daggett is captain of the steamer "Gay Head," running between New Bedford and Nantucket.

1781. MARTHA FERGUSON DAGGETT[8] (*Freeman*,[7] *Freeman*,[6] *Sylvanus*,[5] *Samuel*,[4] *Thomas*,[3] *Thomas*,[2] *John*[1]), born Tisbury, Mass., December 22, 1837; died October 28, 1870; married Tisbury, Mass., December 23, 1863, by Rev. J. L. A. Fish, to Henry B. Martin, son of Henry and Mary Ann Martin; "mariner;" born New Haven, Conn.

Issue:

2602. i. FRANK FERGUSON MARTIN.[9] born Tisbury, Mass., October 21, 1869; resides New Bedford, Mass. (1892).

1784. BETSEY JANE DAGGETT[8] (*Benjamin*,[7] *Thomas*,[6] *Benjamin*,[5] *Benjamin*,[4] *Thomas*,[3] *Thomas*,[2] *John*[1]), born Palmyra, Me., February 26, 1827; resides south-west corner E and Thirteenth streets, Sacramento, Cal. (1892); married Palmyra, Me., May 29, 1850, Zechariah Knox Hersum.

Issue:

2603. i. HENRIETTA MOUNT HERSUM,[9] born California.

1785. HENRIETTA DAGGETT[8] (*Benjamin*,[7] *Thomas*,[6] *Benjamin*,[5] *Benjamin*,[4] *Thomas*,[3] *Thomas*,[2] *John*[1]), born Palmyra, Me., January 19, 1829; died November 22, 1865; married Newport, October 4, 1862, Benjamin Franklin Allin; died March, 1892.

No issue.

1788. CAROLINE DAGGETT[8] (*Benjamin*,[7] *Thomas*,[6] *Benjamin*,[5] *Benjamin*,[4] *Thomas*,[3] *Thomas*,[2] *John*[1]), born Palmyra, Me., December 30, 1839; resides St. Albans, Me. (1892); married Palmyra, Me., January 2, 1864, Daniel Weeks, son of James and Lovey (Carter) Weeks; born Hiram, Me., February 26, 1841.

Issue:

2604. i.   BENJAMIN DAGGETT WEEKS,[9] born St. Albans, Me., August 13, 1866; married; address, 3 Winter street, Boston (1892).
2605. ii.   IDA FRANCES WEEKS,[9] born St. Albans, Me.. June 17, 1868.
2606. iii. SIDNEY PERHAM WEEKS,[9] born St. Albans, Me., August 27, 1871.
2607. iv.   JENNIS LOVEY WEEKS,[9] born St. Albans. Me., February 15, 1872.
2608. v.   CORA BELLE WEEKS,[9] born St. Albans, Me., December 2, 1874.
2609. vi.   HOLLIS WEEKS,[9] born St. Albans, Me., August 10, 1876.
2610. vii. ALBION WEEKS,[9] born St. Albans, Me., July 21, 1879.
2611. viii. WILBUR MOSES WEEKS,[9] born St. Albans, Me., June 17, 1882.

1792. ABIGAIL DAGGETT⁸ (*Darius,*⁷ *Thomas,*⁶ *Benjamin,*⁵ *Benjamin,*⁴ *Thomas,*³ *Thomas,*² *John*¹), born Searsmont, Me., January 30, 1829; resides Ballena, San Diego Co., Cal. (1892); married Skowhegan, Me., May 1, 1856, Benjamin Philbrick Pearson, son of Edmund and Hannah (Philbrick) Pearson; born Kennebunk, Me., October 27, 1824.

Issue:

2612. i. WALTER PEARSON,⁹ born Skowhegan, Me., January 10, 1857; resides Sheridan, Or. (1892).
2613. ii. ELIZABETH HANNAH PEARSON,⁹ born Fond du Lac, Wis., December 2, 1859; resides at home (1892).

1793. HARRIET LOUISA DAGGETT⁸ (*Darius,*⁷ *Thomas,*⁶ *Benjamin,*⁵ *Benjamin,*⁴ *Thomas,*³ *Thomas,*² *John*¹), born Vassalboro', Me., February 8, 1834; resides 1117 West Johnson street, Madison, Wis. (1892); married Madison, Wis., September 22, 1864, Joseph John Stoner, son of John and Elizabeth (Gingrich) Stoner; born Highspire, Pa., December 21, 1829.

Issue:

2614. i. HENRY JOSEPH STONER,⁹ born New Orleans, La., July 12, 1865.
2615. ii. MARY GERTRUDE STONER,⁹ born Madison, Wis., December 25, 1867.

1803. ASBURY MOSES DAGGETT⁸ (*Moses L.,*⁷ *Thomas,*⁶ *Benjamin,*⁵ *Benjamin,*⁴ *Thomas,*³ *Thomas,*² *John*¹), born Palmyra, Me., December 1, 1846; resides Madison, Wis. (1883); married April 4, 1867, Jennie E. Harding, born Manchester, Eng., July 4, 1843; died Madison, Wis., February 14, 1881.

Issue:

2616. i. ASBURY DYSON DAGGETT,⁹ born Madison, Wis., June 20, 1872.
2617. ii. FLORENCE JENNIE DAGGETT,⁹ born Madison, Wis., December 30, 1875.
2618. iii. STANLEY ALLISON DAGGETT,⁹ born Madison, Wis., February 14, 1881.

1806. ALMIRA JANE DAGGETT⁸ (*Samuel B.,*⁷ *Richmond,*⁶ *Benjamin,*⁵ *Benjamin,*⁴ *Thomas,*³ *Thomas,*² *John*¹), born Bangor, Me., June 6, 1839; resides Bangor, Me. (1892); married Garland, Me., September 12, 1858, Llewellyn O. Oakes, son of Rev. John A. and Lucy Ann (Follett) Oakes; born Garland, Me., September 12, 1833.

1807. SAMUEL WESLEY DAGGETT⁸ (*Samuel B.,*⁷ *Richmond,*⁶ *Benjamin,*⁵ *Benjamin,*⁴ *Thomas,*³ *Thomas,*² *John*¹), born Bangor, Me., December 1, 1840; died Davids Island, N.Y., July 1, 1864.

Samuel W. Daggett, of Bangor, was commissioned on the first day of August, 1862, as captain of Company B, First Maine Heavy Artillery, which regiment left the State on the 24th of August, 1862, under Colonel Chaplain, as the Eighteenth Maine Infantry.

Captain Daggett was a member of the Rising Virtue Lodge of

Masons, and before his enlistment was a furniture dealer. The First Maine Heavy Artillery was joined to the Grand Army of the Potomac very soon after that army crossed the Rapidan southward, in the commencement of the summer campaign of 1864, Major-general Meade commanding, and accompanied in person by Lieut.-gen. U. S. Grant.

The first encounter with the enemy resulted in 450 killed, wounded, and missing, out of a regiment of 1,800. Captain Daggett and his gallant Company B were in several other engagements immediately following this one, until that in which he, while gallantly leading on his brave comrades, received the wound which ultimated in his death.

He was at length conveyed to Davids Island Hospital, in New York. The hospital chaplain said of him that he never saw any one in suffering display so great courage and clearness of mind. He was one of the worthiest and bravest of the gallant young officers of the Federal Army.

1808. SUSAN DAGGETT [8] (*Samuel B.*,[7] *Richmond*,[6] *Benjamin*,[5] *Benjamin*,[4] *Thomas*,[3] *Thomas*,[2] *John* [1]), born Bangor, Me., July 30, 1842; died Bangor, Me., June 5, 1882; married Bangor, Me., January 13, 1868, Frank S. Trickey, son of Thomas and Elizabeth (Stilphen) Trickey; born Bangor, Me., January 3, 1837.

1810. LUCY MARIA DAGGETT [8] (*Samuel B.*,[7] *Richmond*,[6] *Benjamin*,[5] *Benjamin*,[4] *Thomas*,[3] *Thomas*,[2] *John* [1]), born Bangor, Me., March 12, 1846; resides Danville, Me. (1892); married Bangor, Me., September 14, 1880, James H. Buckley, son of Barzillia and Mary (Campbell) Buckley; born Danville, Me., April 10, 1826.

1814. JAMES MILTON DAGGETT [8] (*Henry M.*,[7] *Richmond*,[6] *Benjamin*,[5] *Benjamin*,[4] *Thomas*,[3] *Thomas*,[2] *John* [1]), born Bangor, Me., February 7, 1840; "dry goods merchant;" resides 44 Ohio street, Bangor, Me. (1892); married Lowell, Mass., December 13, 1869, by Rev. Horace James, to Harriet Augusta Hadley, daughter of John and Eliza (Bancroft) Hadley; born Lowell, Mass., June 14, 1842.

No issue.

1827. POLLY DAGGETT [8] (*Henry*,[7] *Ichabod*,[6] *Elihu*,[5] *Mayhew*,[4] *John*,[3] *Thomas*,[2] *John* [1]), born Cornwall, Vt., April 15, 1802; died Fort Jackson, N.Y., February 3, 1850; married Stockholm, N.Y., July 19, 1830, Amos Curtis Sheldon; died Fort Jackson, N.Y.

Issue:

2619. i. HOMER HALLOCK SHELDON.[9]
2620. ii. ELMIRA SHELDON,[9] married Charles Loucks; resides Herman, N.Y. (1892).

2621. iii. HENRY M. SHELDON,[9] resides San José, Cal. (1892).
2622. iv. JULIA SHELDON.[9]
2623. v. HARMON SHELDON.[9]

1828. STEPHEN ABBOT DAGGETT[8] (*Henry,[7] Ichabod,[6] Elihu,[5] Mayhew,[4] John,[3] Thomas,[2] John[1]*), born Cornwall, Vt., June 19, 1804; died Cornwall, Vt., December 31, 1871; married 1st, Stockholm, N.Y., September 17, 1837, Olive Battles; died Stockholm, N.Y., April 13, 1842; married 2d, Cornwall, Vt., 1843, Electa Sherwood.

Issue:

2624. i. EMMA DAGGETT,[9] born Stockholm, N.Y., 1838; married Frank K. Daggett (see No. 2633).
2625. ii. FRANCIS DAGGETT,[9] born Stockholm, N.Y.
2626. iii. LEVI DAGGETT,[9] born Stockholm, N.Y., 1845; died 1861.
2627. iv. HOMER DAGGETT,[9] born Cornwall, Vt.
2628. v. ETTA DAGGETT,[9] born Cornwall, Vt.

1830. DAVID DAGGETT[8] (*Henry,[7] Ichabod,[6] Elihu,[5] Mayhew,[4] John,[3] Thomas,[2] John[1]*), born Cornwall, Vt., August 9, 1809; died Parishville, N.Y., May 23, 1891; married Parishville, N.Y., July 2, 1838, Meribah Carr Greene, daughter of Henry Carr and Clarinda (Post) Greene; born Cornwall, Vt., April 1, 1815.

Issue:

2629. i. CLARINDA GREENE DAGGETT,[9] born Hopkinton, N.Y., February 19, 1841.
2630. ii. HENRY LEVI DAGGETT,[9] born Stockholm, N.Y., April 28, 1842.
2631. iii. MARY EMORETTE DAGGETT,[9] born Stockholm, N.Y., November 19, 1844; resides Parishville, N.Y. (1892).
2632. iv. HERBERT MARTIN DAGGETT,[9] born Stockholm, N.Y., October 19, 1846.

1831. LEVI PARSONS DAGGETT[8] (*Henry,[7] Ichabod,[6] Elihu,[5] Mayhew,[4] John,[3] Thomas,[2] John[1]*), born Cornwall, Vt., July 5, 1811; died December 9, 1839; married October 12, 1837, Eunice Fuller, daughter of Joab and Lucy (Daggett) Fuller (No. 1329).

Issue:

2633. i. FRANK K. DAGGETT,[9] born 1838.

1832. ORPHA MANELLA DAGGETT[8] (*Henry,[7] Ichabod,[6] Elihu,[5] Mayhew,[4] John,[3] Thomas,[2] John[1]*), born Cornwall, Vt., May 23, 1816; died Parishville, N.Y., July 14, 1863; married Parishville, N.Y., 1842, Henry Stevens, son of John and Mary (Wescott) Stevens; born Plainfield, N.H.; died January 11, 1875.

Issue:

2634. i. FRANCES STEVENS,[9] born Parishville, N.Y., 1844; resides Minneapolis, Minn. (1892).
2635. ii. CHLOE STEVENS,[9] born Parishville, N.Y.; married S. J. Hyde; resides Lacrosse, Wis. (1892).

2636. iii. LESLIE STEVENS,[9] born Parishville, N.Y.; resides Minneapolis, Minn.
(1892).
2637. iv. ELLA STEVENS,[9] born Parishville, N.Y.; died Parishville, N.Y.,
December 4, 1859.
Remaining children in the far West.

1833. LUCY ELMIRA DAGGETT [8] (*Henry,*[7] *Ichabod,*[6] *Elihu,*[5] *Mayhew,*[4] *John,*[3] *Thomas,*[2] *John*[1]), born Stockholm, N.Y., August 26,
1818; died Parishville, N.Y., August 11, 1879; married Stockholm,
N.Y., Russell F. Welch, of Parishville; died February 28, 1868.
No issue.

1838. ELIZA MARIA DAGGETT [8] (*Benjamin,*[7] *Daniel,*[6] *Elihu,*[5]
Mayhew,[4] *John,*[3] *Thomas,*[2] *John*[1]), born Attleboro', Mass., February
3, 1804; died Attleboro', Mass., May 18, 1887; married Attleboro',
Mass., February 23, 1826, Willard Jillson. son of William and
Betsey (Robinson) Jillson; "carpenter;" born Attleboro', Mass.,
July 3, 1803; died Attleboro', Mass., January 3, 1886.
Issue :

2638. i. JOHN HERVEY JILLSON,[9] born Attleboro', Mass., May 10, 1827; married Sutton, Mass., June 6, 1849, Mrs. Lucy J. Stone; resides North
Attleboro', Mass. (1893); issue : Linda Jillson,[10] Annie Jillson.[10]
2639. ii. WILLIAM HENRY JILLSON,[9] born Attleboro', Mass., August 16, 1829;
married Emily Bullard, of Webster, Mass., 1849; issue: four children; he died Plainville, Mass., February 26, 1858.
2640. iii. ANTOINETTE DEVOE JILLSON,[9] born Attleboro'. Mass., November 13,
1831; married November 14, 1854, Sanford W. Allen, of Bellingham, Mass.; issue : four children; resided Bellingham (1876).
2641. iv. SARAH DAGGETT JILLSON,[9] born Attleboro', Mass., March 28, 1834.
2642. v. GEORGE LEE JILLSON,[9] born Attleboro', Mass., September 23, 1837.
2643. vi. HARRIET HELEN JILLSON,[9] born Attleboro', Mass., September 6, 1840;
died Attleboro', Mass., March 3, 1861.
2644. vii. ELLA M. JILLSON,[9] born Attleboro', Mass., October 21, 1850; married
December 28, 1871, Edward R., son of George Price; resides
Attleboro', Mass. (1893).

1839. CATHERINE BLACKINTON [8] (*Mary Daggett,*[7] *Daniel,*[6] *Elihu,*[5]
Mayhew,[4] *John,*[3] *Thomas,*[2] *John*[1]), born Attleboro', Mass., January
22, 1785; died Attleboro', Mass., August 2, 1862; married Sewell
Stanley; born Attleboro', Mass., July 22, 1787; died Attleboro',
Mass., February 26, 1849.
Issue :

2645. i. OLIVER STANLEY.[9]
2646. ii. SARAH ANN STANLEY,[9] born Attleboro', Mass., February 9, 1817; died
Attleboro', Mass., January 14, 1853.
2647. iii. ELINOR STANLEY.[9]

1841. NANCY BLACKINTON [8] (*Mary Daggett,*[7] *Daniel,*[6] *Elihu,*[5]
Mayhew,[4] *John,*[3] *Thomas,*[2] *John*[1]), born Attleboro', Mass., December 23, 1790; died Attleboro', Mass., October 18, 1868; married 1st,

Attleboro', Mass., July 2, 1811, Lemuel Whiting, son of David and Hannah (Walcott) Whiting; born Attleboro', Mass., December 12, 1776; died Attleboro', Mass., September 30, 1823; married 2d, Ephraim Jewett, son of Jedadiah Jewett; born Attleboro', Mass., May 11, 1800; died Attleboro', Mass., May 17, 1890.

Issue:

2648. i.   MARY ANN WHITING,[9] born Attleboro', Mass., May 7, 1812; married Samuel Kent; she died Seekonk.
2649. ii. WILLIAM DEAN WHITING,[9] born Attleboro', Mass., December 23, 1815.
2650. iii. NANCY WHITING,[9] born Attleboro', Mass., February 4, 1818; died Attleboro', Mass., September 17, 1819.
2651. iv. LEVI WILLARD WHITING,[9] born Attleboro', Mass., 1821; married Nancy Blanchard; issue: Wilhelmine Whiting;[10] he died May 5, 1873.
2652. v.   NANCY M. JEWETT,[9] married 1st, Charles A. Hine; he died September 22, 1854; married 2d, Giles Manchester; issue: Frederick A. Hines, who died April 2, 1854; resides Providence, R.I. (1893).
2653. vi. JOHN JEWETT,[9] married; issue: several children; he died.
2654. vii. HENRY JEWETT,[9] married Catharine Munroe, daughter of Jonas Munroe; resides Providence, R I. (1893).

1843.   OLIVE D. BLACKINTON [8] (*Mary Daggett,*[7] *Daniel,*[6] *Elihu,*[5] *Mayhew,*[4] *John,*[3] *Thomas,*[2] *John* [1]), born Attleboro', Mass., September 7, 1795; died Attleboro', Mass., October 25, 1847; married Calvin Richards, son of Calvin Richards; born 1793; died Attleboro', Mass., April 9, 1873.

Issue:

2655. i.   EMILY RICHARDS.[9]
2656. ii. ANN MARIA RICHARDS,[9] born Attleboro', Mass., August 16, 1819.
2657. iii. FRANCIS B. RICHARDS.[9]

1844.   AZUBA BLACKINTON [8] (*Mary Daggett,*[7] *Daniel,*[6] *Elihu,*[5] *Mayhew,*[4] *John,*[3] *Thomas,*[2] *John* [1]), born Attleboro', Mass., December 15, 1797; died Attleboro', Mass., May 9, 1832; married John Tifft, son of Samuel and Nancy Tifft; born Attleboro', Mass., September 10, 1800; died Attleboro', Mass., June 29, 1851.

Issue:

2658. i.   MARIA TIFFT,[9] married Silas Tyler, of Lowell, son of Silas and Fanny (Stanley) Tyler; both dead; no issue.
2659. ii. FRANK TIFFT,[9] married a French woman (had one son, who was sent to her people in France when she died); he died New York city.
2660. iii. FRANCIS TIFFT,[9] born Attleboro', Mass., November 1, 1824; died Attleboro.' Mass., January 29, 1825.

1855.   ABIGAIL DAGGETT [8] (*Daniel,*[7] *Daniel,*[6] *Elihu,*[5] *Mayhew,*[4] *John,*[3] *Thomas,*[2] *John* [1]), born Attleboro', Mass., March 8, 1795; died Mansfield, Mass., January 31, 1873; married Attleboro', Mass., November 2, 1815, Stephen Richardson, son of Daniel and Chloe

Richardson; born Attleboro', Mass., September 2, 1794; died Mansfield, Mass., September 22, 1885.

Issue:

2661. i.   CHLOE RICHARDSON,[9] born Attleboro', Mass., July 23, 1816.
2662. ii. CYNTHIA ANN RICHARDSON,[9] born Attleboro', Mass.
2663. iii. ABIGAIL RICHARDSON,[9] born Attleboro', Mass.; married Harrison A. Williams; resides Mansfield, Mass. (1892).

1856. RHODA DAGGETT[8] (*Daniel*,[7] *Daniel*,[6] *Elihu*,[5] *Mayhew*,[4] *John*,[3] *Thomas*,[2] *John*[1]), born Attleboro', Mass., November 25, 1797; married Attleboro', Mass., March 25, 1818, Pardon Sheldon, of Cumberland, R.I., son of William and Sarah (Brown) Sheldon; born Cumberland, R.I., May 21, 1790.

Issue:

2664. i.   WILLIAM DAGGETT SHELDON,[9] born May 30, 1819; resides Kerhonkson, N.Y. (1892).
2665. ii. EMILY ANN SHELDON,[9] born September 30, 1821.
2666. iii. STEPHEN BROWN SHELDON,[9] born December 19, 1823.
2667. iv. ABAGAIL RICHARDSON SHELDON,[9] born November 8, 1826.
2668. v.   DANIEL PARDON SHELDON,[9] born November 30, 1828.
2669. vi. GEORGE HENRY SHELDON,[9] born October 28, 1831.

1857. DANIEL DAGGETT[8] (*Daniel*,[7] *Daniel*,[6] *Elihu*,[5] *Mayhew*,[4] *John*,[3] *Thomas*,[2] *John*[1]), born Attleboro', Mass., October 31, 1804; died Milwaukee, Wis., May 5, 1871; married Attleboro', Mass., October 4, 1827, Elizabeth Nichols Franklin, daughter of Ebenezer and Mary (Patt) Franklin; born December 19, 1806.

Issue:

2670. i.   DANIEL CURTIS DAGGETT,[9] born Taunton, Mass., July 11, 1828.
2671. ii. THOMAS HENRY DAGGETT,[9] born Providence, R.I., February 22, 1831; married 1st, July 31, 1856, Mary Raymond; divorced; married 2d, Harriet ——.
2672. iii. MARGARET ELIZEBETH DAGGETT,[9] born Fitchburg, Mass., July 21, 1834; married November 19, 1856, William Chase.
2673. iv. MARY ADELAIDE DAGGETT,[9] born Newburyport, Mass., June 26, 1841; married October 19, 1864, Hiram M. Booth.

Daniel Daggett was a manufacturer. He resided at 608 Walnut street, Milwaukee, Wis. Removed there, from Newburyport, in 1850.

1859. HANNAH DAGGETT[8] (*Daniel*,[7] *Daniel*,[6] *Elihu*,[5] *Mayhew*,[4] *John*,[3] *Thomas*,[2] *John*[1]), born Attleboro', Mass., March 1, 1810; died Attleboro', Mass., July 27, 1846; married Attleboro', Mass., September 6, 1831, by Rev. Nathaniel Wright, to William Henry Robinson, son of Obed and Abigail (Everett) Robinson; born Attleboro', Mass., February 14, 1810; died Attleboro', Mass., November 8, 1868.

Issue:

2674. i.   WILLIAM HENRY ROBINSON,[9] born Attleboro', Mass., June 26, 1833; married 1st, Angie Martin; married 2d, Ellen Blake, daughter of Eliab F. and Abigail E. (Fuller) Blake; issue: several children.

2675. ii. CORNELIUS D. ROBINSON,[9] born Attleboro', Mass., August 28, 1835.
2676. iii. DANIEL H. ROBINSON,[9] born Attleboro', Mass., May 3, 1839.
2677. iv. EDWIN AUGUSTUS ROBINSON,[9] born Attleboro', Mass., November 12, 1842; married 1st, Ida Draper, daughter of George Adams and Lydia Anna (Bishop) Draper; died probably before 1885.
2678. v. HANNAH ELIZABETH ROBINSON,[9] born Attleboro', Mass., August 18, 1845.

1860. SAMUEL SLATER DAGGETT [8] (*Daniel,*[7] *Daniel,*[6] *Elihu,*[5] *Mayhew,*[4] *John,*[3] *Thomas,*[2] *John* [1]), born Attleboro', Mass., April 19, 1812; died Milwaukee, Wis., May 23, 1869; married North Branford, Conn., April 19, 1840, by Rev. John D. Baldwin, D.D., to Ruth Sophronia Bishop, daughter of Neriah and Harriet (Handy) Bishop; born Guilford, Conn., December 6, 1813; resides Pasadena, Cal. (1892).

Issue:

2679. i. CHARLES DANIEL DAGGETT,[9] born Milwaukee, Wis., May 2, 1851.

Samuel S. Daggett was president of the Northwestern Mutual Life Insurance Company.

1862. MINA BRIGGS DAGGETT [8] (*Daniel,*[7] *Daniel,*[6] *Elihu,*[5] *Mayhew,*[4] *John,*[3] *Thomas,*[2] *John* [1]), born Attleboro', Mass., April 7, 1817; " jeweller; " died Mansfield, Mass., December 13, 1874; married Attleboro', Mass., April 7, 1846, by Rev. Reuben Morey, to Anna Maria Huntress, daughter of Nathaniel and Anna M. Huntress; born 1830; resides Winter street, West Somerville, Mass. (1892).

Issue:

2680. i. ANNA MARIA DAGGETT,[9] born Attleboro', Mass., February 12, 1847.
2681. ii. ALIDA MAZELLA DAGGETT,[9] born Attleboro', Mass., August 2, 1848; married Mansfield, Mass., November 21, 1871, by Rev. Welcome Lewis, to Jefferson J. Gray, son of James and Judith Gray; " framemaker; " born Sheffield, Vt., 1836; resides Winter street, West Somerville, Mass. (1892).
2682. iii. MINA EDNAH DAGGETT,[9] born Attleboro', Mass., July 12, 1852; died Attleboro', Mass., Oct. 9, 1863.
2683. iv. FREDERIC W. DAGGETT,[9] born March 23, 1864; died October 6, 1865.

1864. SYLVAN STANLEY [8] (*Betsey Daggett,*[7] *Daniel,*[6] *Elihu,*[5] *Mayhew,*[4] *John,*[3] *Thomas,*[2] *John* [1]), born Attleboro', Mass., April 7, 1798; married Miss Frye.

Issue:

2684. i. ELISABETH STANLEY,[9] married William Trescott; issue: Walter,[10] Annie,[10] Lizzie,[10] Frederic Trescott.[10]
2685. ii. REBECCA STANLEY,[9] married Horace Lincoln, son of William; issue: Edwin H. Lincoln,[10] Jennie A. Lincoln.[10]
2686. iii. SYLVIA A. STANLEY,[9] married Stephen Stanley, son of Stephen Olney and Betsey S. (Stanley) Stanley (see No. 2704); issue: Jesse,[10] Alice Frye.[10]
2687. iv. WILLIAM STANLEY,[9] married; a clergyman; issue: several children.
2688. v. FRANCES STANLEY.[9]

1866. VERNAL STANLEY[8] (*Betsey Daggett*,[7] *Daniel*,[6] *Elihu*,[5] *Mayhew*,[4] *John*,[3] *Thomas*,[2] *John*[1]), born Attleboro', Mass., May 30, 1802; married Louisa Wellman; born 1805; died Attleboro', Mass., May 21, 1863.

Issue:

2689. i.　DANIEL O. STANLEY,[9] born Attleboro', Mass., January 15, 1836.
2690. ii.　GEORGE H. STANLEY,[9] born Attleboro', Mass., August 31, 1837; died Attleboro', Mass., April 26, 1839.
2691. iii.　CAROLINE W. STANLEY,[9] born Attleboro', Mass., October, 1838; died Attleboro', Mass., July 1, 1841.
2692. iv.　JULIA L. STANLEY,[9] born Attleboro', Mass., December, 1840; died Attleboro', Mass., June 22, 1841.
2693. v.　ARTEMAS WOODWARD STANLEY,[9] born Attleboro', Mass., 1842; died Attleboro', Mass., October 1, 1862.
2694. vi.　JOHN F. STANLEY,[9] born Attleboro', Mass., 1844; died Attleboro', Mass., August 21, 1844.

1867. CHLOE READ STANLEY[8] (*Betsey Daggett*,[7] *Daniel*,[6] *Elihu*,[5] *Mayhew*,[4] *John*,[3] *Thomas*,[2] *John*[1]), born Attleboro', Mass., February 25, 1805; died May 25, 1827; married James Cutler Tufts; born 1801; died April 14, 1827.

Issue:

2695. i.　JAMES TUFTS,[9] married; had issue; died.
2696. ii.　WILLIAM CUTLER TUFTS,[9] married Laura J., daughter of Jacob and Deborah (Bates) Capron; issue: four children.
2697. iii.　EMMELINE TUFTS,[9] born 1822; died Attleboro', Mass., July 21, 1844.

1868. OTIS STANLEY[8] (*Betsey Daggett*,[7] *Daniel*,[6] *Elihu*,[5] *Mayhew*,[4] *John*,[3] *Thomas*,[2] *John*[1]), born Attleboro', Mass., March 9, 1807; died Attleboro', Mass., August 9, 1888; married Attleboro' Falls, Mass., January 6, 1847, Harriette Whitney, daughter of Martin and Nancy (Orne) Whitney; born Attleboro', Mass., November 23, 1816; died Attleboro', Mass., February 13, 1877.

Issue:

2698. i.　MARIA STANLEY,[9] married Thomas Patterson; issue: Hattie Patterson.[10]
2699. ii.　EDWARD OTIS STANLEY,[9] married Caroline C. Durfee, of Fall River; issue: Margorie,[10] Robert.[10]

1869. BETSEY SHEPARD STANLEY[8] (*Betsey Daggett*,[7] *Daniel*,[6] *Elihu*,[5] *Mayhew*,[4] *John*,[3] *Thomas*,[2] *John*[1]), born Attleboro', Mass., November 24, 1808; died Attleboro', Mass., June 15, 1886; married Attleboro', Mass., September 28, 1830, Stephen Olney Stanley, son of Stephen and Martha Stanley; born Attleboro', Mass., June 11, 1801; died Attleboro', Mass., April 24, 1876.

Issue:

2700. i.　MARTHA STANLEY,[9] born Attleboro', Mass., February 11, 1836; married Edw. C. Knapp, son of Ephraim; she died Attleboro', Mass., February 2, 1892; issue: Maria,[10] Mabel,[10] Abby,[10] Edward T.,[10] Lizzie,[10] Ephraim,[10] Betsey,[10] Fanny.[10]
2701. ii.　MARY STANLEY,[9] born Attleboro', Mass., February 11, 1836; married Andrew J. Thomas; she died Attleboro', Mass., August 5, 1863.

2702. iii. STEPHEN OLNEY STANLEY,[9] born Attleboro', Mass., 1838; died Attleboro', Mass., November 4, 1838.
2703. iv. ABBY STANLEY,[9] born Attleboro', Mass., 1840; died Attleboro', Mass.,
January 25, 1856.
2704. v. STEPHEN STANLEY,[9] born Attleboro', Mass., June 11, 1842; married
Sylvia A. Stanley (see No. 2686).
2705. vi. BENJAMIN STANLEY,[9] born Attleboro', Mass., June 3, 1848; married
Ella Briggs; issue: Edith,[10] Artemas,[10] Nellie,[10] Percy.[10]

1870. MILTON STANLEY[8] (*Betsey Daggett,[7] Daniel,[6] Elihu,[5] Mayhew,[4] John,[3] Thomas,[2] John[1]*), born Attleboro', Mass., July 15,
1810; married 1st, Abigail K. ——; married 2d, Caroline ——.
Issue:

2706. i. NATHAN STANLEY,[9] resides Boston, Mass.
2707. ii. HARRIETTE STANLEY,[9] married Joseph Orville Fairbanks; died Mansfield, Mass., January, 1892.
2708. iii. OSBORNE STANLEY.[9]

1872. HARRIET EMILY STANLEY[8] (*Betsey Daggett,[7] Daniel,[6]
Elihu,[5] Mayhew,[4] John,[3] Thomas,[2] John[1]*), born Dracut, Mass.,
May 17, 1815; resides Attleboro', Mass. (1893); married Dr. Selem
A. Stanley, son of John and Juliet Stanley; born 1809; died October
18, 1852.
Issue:

2709. i. FRANK STANLEY,[9] married, and had issue, Edward C.,[10] Mary[10]; he
died August 2, 1862.

1875. HENRY DAGGETT BULKLEY[8] (*Amelia M. Daggett,[7] Henry,[6]
Elihu,[5] Mayhew,[4] John,[3] Thomas,[2] John[1]*), born New Haven, Conn.,
April 20, 1803; died New York city, January 4, 1872; married New
York city (?), October 1, 1835, Juliana Barnes, daughter of Wheeler
and Emma White (Olmstead) Barnes, of Rome, N.Y.; born Rome,
N.Y., July 10, 1811; resides Orange, N.J.
Issue:

2710. i. AMELIA MARTHA BULKLEY,[9] born New York city, December 8, 1836;
died March 24, 1841.
2711. ii. JULIA BULKLEY,[9] born New York city, October 1, 1838; married June
10, 1863, J. Cleveland Cady, architect, New York; she died December 19, 1869; issue: ALICE C. CADY.[10]
2712. iii. HENRY WHEELER BULKLEY,[9] born New York city, July 22, 1842.
2713. iv. LUCIUS DUNCAN BULKLEY,[9] born New York city, Jan. 12, 1845.
2714. v. EMMA MATILDA BULKLEY,[9] born New York city, March 22, 1850.
2715. vi. MARY DAGGETT BULKLEY,[9] born New York city, July 25, 1852; resides Brick Church, N.J.

Dr. Henry D. Bulkley graduated at Yale College, 1821, and New
York Medical College in 1829.

He was a physician of high standing, and long connected with New
York Hospital. President of New York Academy of Medicine.

1876. AMELIA MARTHA BULKLEY[8] (*Amelia M. Daggett,[7] Henry,[6]
Elihu,[5] Mayhew,[4] John,[3] Thomas,[2] John[1]*), born New Haven, Conn.,

March 13, 1806; died New York city, August 21, 1834; married New York city, June 30, 1829, Stewart Craig Marsh, "New York merchant."

Issue:

2716. i.   STEWART CRAIG MARSH,[9] born New York city, 1830; died New York city, 1831.
2717. ii.   JOHN ALSTON MARSH,[9] born New York city, June 1, 1832; died London, Eng., about 1860.
2718. iii. STEWART CRAIG MARSH,[9] born New York city, June 19, 1834; died about 1864.

1877. ELISABETH DAGGETT HOOKER [8] (*Elisabeth Daggett,[7] Henry,[6] Elihu,[5] Mayhew,[4] John,[3] Thomas,[2] John [1]*), born Farmington, Conn., May 1, 1813; resides Bloomfield and Hartford, Conn. (1892); married Farmington, Conn., September 10, 1834, Hon. Francis Gillette, son of Rev. Ashbel and Achsah (Francis) Gillette, of Hartford, Conn.; born Windsor, Conn., December 4, 1807; died Hartford, Conn., September 30, 1879.

Issue:

2719. i.   ASHBEL FRANK GILLETTE,[9] born Wintonbury, Conn., May 17, 1836; died California, August 4, 1859.
2720. ii.   ELISABETH HOOKER GILLETTE,[9] born Bloomfield, Conn., December 7, 1838; married September 20, 1864, George H. Warner, son of Justin W. Warner; he born December 21, 1833; secretary American Emigrant Association.
2721. iii. EDWARD HOOKER GILLETTE,[9] born Bloomfield, Conn., October 1, 1840; married June 26, 1866, Sophie Theresa Stoddard, daughter of Joseph Nettleton and Sophia Ives (Buddington) Stoddard, of Milford, Conn.; born New Haven, Conn., March 9, 1845; resides Des Moines, Ia.
2722. iv.   ROBERT HOOKER GILLETTE,[9] born Bloomfield, Conn., August 1, 1842; died Fort Fisher, N.C., Jan. 16, 1865.
2723. v.   MARY HOOKER GILLETTE,[9] born Wintonbury, Conn., June 24, 1845; died Wintonbury, Conn., August 27, 1847.
2724. vi.   WILLIAM HOOKER GILLETTE,[9] born Hartford, Conn., July 24, 1853; married June 1, 1882, Helen Nickels, daughter of David A. Nickels, of Detroit, Mich.; born August 3, 1860.
        Mr. Gillette is an actor and dramatic author; resides Hartford, Conn.

1878. JOHN HOOKER [8] (*Elisabeth Daggett,[7] Henry,[6] Elihu,[5] Mayhew,[4] John,[3] Thomas,[2] John [1]*), born Farmington, Conn., April 19, 1816; resides Hartford, Conn. (1892); married Hartford, Conn., August 5, 1841, Isabella Beecher, daughter of Rev. Lyman and Harriet (Porter) Beecher; born Litchfield, Conn., February 22, 1822.

Issue:

2725. i.   THOMAS BEECHER HOOKER,[9] born Farmington, Conn., September 30, 1842; died Farmington, Conn., September 30, 1842.
2726. ii.   MARY BEECHER HOOKER,[9] born Farmington, Conn., August 15, 1845; married October 4, 1866, Eugene Burton, of Hartford, Conn.; she died January 20, 1886.
2727. iii. ALICE BEECHER HOOKER,[9] born Farmington, Conn., August 26, 1847; married June 17, 1869, John C. Day, lawyer, son of Calvin Day; resides Hartford, Conn.

2728. iv. EDWARD BEECHER HOOKER,[9] born Hartford, Conn., February 26, 1855; married September 18, 1879, Martha C. Kilbourne, daughter of Joseph K. Kilbourne; born Norfolk, Conn., November 11, 1853; "physician;" resides Hartford, Conn.

Mr. and Mrs. Hooker celebrated their golden wedding in 1891. Mrs. Hooker stands at the head of the woman suffragists of the country, and for this reason the celebration assumed largely a sort of jubilee of woman suffragists. Mr. Hooker's connection with the bench of the State attracted many notables of the legal profession.

1880. Commander EDWARD HOOKER,[8] U.S.N. (*Elizabeth Daggett,*[7] *Henry,*[6] *Elihu,*[5] *Mayhew,*[4] *John,*[3] *Thomas,*[2] *John*[1]), born Farmington, Conn., December 25, 1822; resides 289 Gates avenue, Brooklyn, N.Y. (1892); married 1st, Warren. R.I., March 28, 1847, Elizabeth Moore Wardwell, daughter of Capt. Moses H. and Mary (Bushee) Wardwell, of Warren, R.I.; born Warren, R.I., June 22, 1829; died Warren, R.I., February 10, 1849; married 2d, Providence, R.I., May 11, 1851, Esther Ann Smith Battey, daughter of Henry and Susan Townsend (Smith) Battey, of Providence, R.I.; born Providence, R.I., September 8, 1825.

Issue:

2729. i. LILLIE JOSEPHINE HOOKER,[9] born Providence, R.I., January 14, 1854; resides at home.
2730. ii. LUCY COWLES HOOKER,[9] born Providence, R.I., March 17, 1856; died Providence, R.I., October 7, 1856.
2731. iii. ROSABELLE TOWNSEND HOOKER,[9] born Providence, R.I., June 9, 1858.
2732. iv. HENRY DAGGETT HOOKER,[9] born Providence, R.I., April 14, 1859.

Commander Edward Hooker was bred to the sea in the merchant marine, commanding a ship when twenty-three years old. One of the earliest volunteers for the naval service in the Civil War, he was appointed acting master July, 1861. His first service was in the gunboat "Louisiana." He was severely wounded during a boat expedition October 5, 1861. He was the first officer of his grade wounded during the war. He took an active part in the Burnside expedition while in the "Louisiana." At Newberne that vessel fired the first and the last shot of the action. Soon after the capture of Newberne he became the executive officer of the "Louisiana." At the time of the Confederate attack upon Wilmington, N.C., in September, 1862, the ship was fought by Commander Hooker, in the absence of the commanding officer, in a manner which caused high commendation from commanding officers of our own forces. For gallantry on this occasion he was made acting volunteer lieutenant, to date from the day of the action. He was then ordered to a command in the blockade off Wilmington, and soon after to the command of a division of the Potomac flotilla, in which command he continued until the end of the war. Then promoted to acting volunteer lieutenant commander.

After the war he was at the New York Navy Yard. Then took the store-ship "Idaho" to the Asiatic squadron, and while there was transferred from the volunteer to the regular navy list. Commissioned lieutenant March, 1868, and lieutenant commander December, 1868. Captain of the yard at League island until February, 1884. While on duty at the Naval Home, Philadelphia, was promoted to commander. In December, 1884, placed on the retired list. Since then residing in Brooklyn, N.Y.

1882. Samuel Worcester Andrew[8] (*Mary Daggett*,[7] *Henry*,[6] *Elihu*,[5] *Mayhew*,[4] *John*,[3] *Thomas*,[2] *John*[1]), born Woodbury, Conn., June 8, 1822; died December 17, 1849; married January 4, 1848, Fannie Augusta Crafts, daughter of Gen. Chauncey Crafts, of Woodbury, Conn.

Issue:

    i. Samuel Worcester Andrew,[9] agent Fairbanks Lard Co., 5 Central wharf, Boston; resides Jamaica Plain, Mass. (1892).

1889. Charity Galieucia Daggett[8] (*George*,[7] *Elihu*,[6] *Elihu*,[5] *Mayhew*,[4] *John*,[3] *Thomas*,[2] *John*[1]), born Fairfield, Me., September 16, 1800; died Lowell, Mass., November 4, 1866; married Fairfield, Me., March 18, 1824, William Stone Stanley, of Fairfield, Me., son of William and Polly (Stone) Stanley (No. 1366); born Massachusetts, October 12, 1790; died Galesburg, Ill., October 12, 1848.

Issue:

2733. i. Marietta B. Stanley,[9] born West Waterville, Me., May 30, 1826; died in infancy.
2734. ii. Juliette Stanley,[9] born West Waterville, Me., January 12, 1828; died in infancy.
2735. iii. Emily F. Stanley,[9] born West Waterville, Me., October 31, 1830; resides 216 South Garfield avenue, Peoria, Ill. (1892).
2736. iv. Thomas Martin Stanley,[9] born West Waterville, Me., February 6, 1832; died Peoria, Ill., June 16, 1859.

1890. Lydia Tuycross Daggett[8] (*George*,[7] *Elihu*,[6] *Elihu*,[5] *Mayhew*,[4] *John*,[3] *Thomas*,[2] *John*[1]), born Fairfield, Me., January 8, 1805; died Rio, Ill., December 27, 1889; married Stark, Me., October 20, 1830, Eber Stuart Moor, son of John and Susana (Stuart) Moor; born Anson, Me., October 15, 1807; "farmer;" died Rio, Ill., March 4, 1879.

Issue:

2737. i. Nancy Bodfish Moor,[9] born Anson, Me., August 4, 1831; unmarried (1892).
2738. ii. Ellen Daggett Moor,[9] born Anson, Me., March 6, 1833; died Rio, Ill., February 14, 1846.

2739. iii.   ANGUS MOOR,[9] born Anson, Me., February 8, 1835; married Lydia
     F. (Daggett) Stevens (No. 2747).
2740. iv.   URSULA EVELINE MOOR,[9] born Anson, Me., March 22, 1837; married
     Rio, Ill., Daniel Newel Harwood; address, Shelbyville, Ill. (1892).
2741. v.   FRANK NORMAN MOOR,[9] born Anson, Me., February 26, 1839; ad-
     dress, Cedar Bluffs, Neb. (1892).
2742. vi.   CHARLES STUART MOOR,[9] born Anson, Me., January 13, 1841; ad-
     dress, Cedar Bluffs, Neb. (1892).
2743. vii.   CLARA JANE MOOR,[9] born Anson, Me., August 13, 1843; married A.
     A. Rice; died Pine Bluff, Ark., August 3, 1865.

Eber S. Moor was road commissioner one year for Rio township,
and school director several years.

1891.   EMILY APPLETON DAGGETT[8] (*George*,[7] *Elihu*,[6] *Elihu*,[5]
Mayhew,[4] *John*,[3] *Thomas*,[2] *John*[1]), born Fairfield, Me., March 22,
1807; resides Bradford Centre, Me. (1892); married 1st, Fairfield,
Me., October 30, 1830, Seth Webb Kimball, of Fairfield, Me., son of
Frank and Mehitabel (Webb) Kimball; born Deer Island, Me., June
10, 1799; "farmer;" died June 17, 1839; married 2d, Atkinson,
Me., December 25, 1850, Alexander Nelson, son of Roland and
(Fernald) Nelson; born Portsmouth, N.H.; "sea captain;" died
about 1881.
Issue:

2744. i.   MARY ANN KIMBALL,[9] born Fairfield, Me., September 21, 1831; died
     August 27, 1856.
2745. ii.   ALBION PARIS KIMBALL,[9] born Atkinson, Me., August 3, 1837.

1892.   GEORGE RANDOLPH DAGGETT[8] (*George*,[7] *Elihu*,[6] *Elihu*,[5]
Mayhew,[4] *John*,[3] *Thomas*,[2] *John*[1]), born Fairfield, Me., November
18, 1809; died Atkinson, Me., December 12, 1881; married 1st,
Sebec, Me., May 12, 1842, by A. M. Robinson, Esq., to Paulina
King Chase, daughter of Joseph and Comfort (Livermore) Chase;
born Sebec, Me., December 28, 1823; "farmer;" died Atkinson,
Me., September 2, 1856; married 2d, Atkinson, Me., August 21,
1857, by A. M. Robinson, Esq., to Adlenta Jane Chase, daughter of
Ezekiel and Mercy (Livermore) Chase; born Sebec, Me., February
12, 1835; died Atkinson, Me., April 19, 1886.
Issue:

2746. i.   ELLEN MARIA DAGGETT,[9] born Atkinson, Me., March 1, 1843.
2747. ii.   LYDIA FRANCES DAGGETT,[9] born Atkinson, Me., June 17, 1844.
2748. iii.   HENRIETTA ATWOOD DAGGETT,[9] born Atkinson, Me., August 13, 1848.
2749. iv.   ALBERT AUSTIN DAGGETT,[9] born Atkinson, Me., September 30, 1851.
2750. v.   HATTIE EVELYN DAGGETT,[9] born Atkinson, Me., October 13, 1858.
2751. vi.   GEORGE WARREN DAGGETT,[9] born Atkinson, Me., March 11, 1862;
     married Atkinson, Me., October 5, 1887, Hattie Rose McCorrison,
     daughter of Moses and Isabella (Frost) McCorrison; born Atkin-
     son, Me., December 16, 1863; "house carpenter;" resides Milo,
     Me. (1892).
2752. vii.   EDWIN SNOW DAGGETT,[9] born Atkinson, Me., October 11, 1864;
     married Milo, Me., August 3, 1890, Cora Mabel Mooers, daughter
     of David A. and Melissa (Davis) Mooers; born Milo, Me., March

18, 1865; "meat and green groceries;" resides Montague, Me. (1892).

2753. viii. EARL PERCY DAGGETT,[9] born Atkinson, Me., March 6, 1869; "meat and green groceries;" resides Montague, Me. (1892).

1893. MARY ANN DAGGETT[8] (*George,[7] Elihu,[6] Elihu,[5] Mayhew,[4] John,[3] Thomas,[2] John[1]*), born Fairfield, Me., October 7, 1811; died Atkinson, Me., July 29, 1847; married Fairfield, Me., 182$\frac{8}{9}$, Samuel Burrill, of Fairfield, Me., son of Bela Burrill; died Fairfield, Me., 1846.

Issue:

2754. i. AGNES BURRILL.[9]
2755. ii. WILLIAM BURRILL.[9]
2756. iii. BELA BURRILL.[9]
2757. iv. EMILY BURRILL.[9]
2758. v. PAULINA BURRILL.[9]
2759. vi. (Infant) BURRILL,[9] died when a few weeks old.

1894. EARL PERCY DAGGETT[8] (*George,[7] Elihu,[6] Elihu,[5] Mayhew,[4] John,[3] Thomas,[2] John[1]*), born Fairfield, Me., May 30, 1820; "farmer;" resides Medford, Me. (1892); married Atkinson, Me., July 25, 1847, by Rev. Randall Noyes, to Sarah Jane Gould, daughter of James and Sally (Osgood) Gould, of Atkinson; born Atkinson, Me., August 22, 1822.

Issue:

2760. i. JOHN GOULD DAGGETT,[9] born Orneville, Me., June 15, 1849.

1895. ALBION K. PARIS DAGGETT[8] (*George,[7] Elihu,[6] Elihu,[5] Mayhew,[4] John,[3] Thomas,[2] John[1]*), born Fairfield, Me., February 20, 1822; resides Bradford, Me. (1892); married Atkinson, Me., May 28, 1844, Elizabeth Warren Heald, daughter of Warren and Martha (Whitney) Heald, of Winslow, Me.; born Winslow, Me., December 22, 1822.

Issue:

2761. i. MARY ELIZABETH DAGGETT,[9] born Orneville, Me., February 26, 1845.
2762. ii. CHARLES ALBERT DAGGETT,[9] born Orneville, Me., November 24, 1846; soldier in Thirty-second Maine Regiment Volunteers; killed at battle Coal Harbor June 3, 1862.
2763. iii. MARTHA ELLEN DAGGETT,[9] born Orneville, Me., May 20, 1850; died Orneville, Me., March 8, 1854.
2764. iv. ANNIE MARIA DAGGETT,[9] born Orneville, Me., January 22, 1852; died Orneville, Me., April 6, 1854.

Mr. Daggett was a soldier in the Sixteenth Regiment Maine Volunteers; he is a farmer.

1896. Rev. LYMAN WHITE DAGGETT[8] (*Elihu,[7] Elihu,[6] Elihu,[5] Mayhew,[4] John,[3] Thomas,[2] John[1]*), born Attleboro', Mass., July 28, 1812; died North Attleboro', Mass., January 10, 1892; married Wrentham, Mass., June 8, 1842, by Rev. Benj. H. Davis, to Nancy

Grant Fuller, of Newton, daughter of John and Nancy (Grant) Fuller; born Newton, Mass., October 5, 1813; died North Attleboro', Mass., January 19, 1892.

Issue:

2765. i. CORISSANDE LA ROCHE DAGGETT,[9] born Andover, Mass., May 20, 1844; resides Attleboro' Falls, Mass. (1893).
2766. ii. HARRIETTE EVERETT DAGGETT,[9] born Woodstock, Vt., September 1, 1846; died Attleboro', Mass., December 2, 1875.
2767. iii. ADA FULLER DAGGETT,[9] born Attleboro', Mass., September 9, 1848; died Attleboro', Mass., January 2, 1852.

Rev. Lyman W. Daggett received his education in the Attleboro' public schools and Phillips Academy, of Andover.

After teaching for eight years he entered the ministry of the Universalist church, preaching at Holliston and Andover, Mass., and Woodstock and Hartland, Vt.

In 1848 he gave up the ministry and located in North Attleboro'. Mr. Daggett was selectman, overseer of the poor, assessor, town clerk, and member of the school committee, and represented the town in the lower-branch of the Legislature in 1851, 1852, and 1853.

1900. JAMES MADISON DAGGETT [8] (*Jacob,*[7] *Elihu,*[6] *Elihu,*[5] *May-hew,*[4] *John,*[3] *Thomas,*[2] *John*[1]), born Attleboro', Mass., May 10, 1809; "jeweller;" resides Attleboro', Mass. (1892); married Attleboro', Mass., April 28, 1842, Amanda Melvina Coombs, daughter of Ruben and Permelia Marie (Keyes) Coombs; born Shrewsbury, Mass., June 10, 1820; died Attleboro', Mass., April 18, 1874.

Issue:

2768. i. IMOGENE AUGUSTA DAGGETT,[9] born Attleboro', Mass., February 3, 1843.
2769. ii. BYRON ELIHU DAGGETT,[9] born Attleboro', Mass., February 17, 1846; of B. E. Daggett & Co., manufacturing jewellers, Providence, R.I. (1892).

1901. HENRY LEFRELET DAGGETT [8] (*Jacob,*[7] *Elihu,*[6] *Elihu,*[5] *May-hew,*[4] *John,*[3] *Thomas,*[2] *John*[1]), born Attleboro', Mass., August 10, 1812; died Boston, Mass., March 1, 1882; married Boston, Mass., April 6, 1841, by Rev. George Ripley, to Sarah Eliza Williams, daughter of Isaac and Diana (Towne) Williams; born Boston, Mass., October 8, 1824; resides 116 Commonwealth avenue, Boston (1893).

Issue:

2770. i. ISAAC WILLIAMS DAGGETT,[9] born Boston, Mass., April 27, 1845; died Lynn, Mass., July 27, 1864.
2771. ii. HARRIET MCLEOD DAGGETT,[9] born Boston, Mass., February 19, 1848; died Boston, Mass., April 16, 1860.
2772. iii. HENRY LEFRELET DAGGETT,[9] born Boston, Mass., July 19, 1851.
2773. iv. SARA WHITTEMORE DAGGETT,[9] born Boston, Mass., October 2, 1859.
2774. v. ELEANOR WILLIAMS DAGGETT,[9] born Boston, Mass., March 21, 1865.

Henry L. Daggett was one of the stanchest merchants of the shoe and leather business in Boston. From 1834 to 1850 he was located at 202 Washington street, from whence he moved in 1851 to 29 Kilby street. In 1855 he moved to 152 Congress street, and in the following year to 101 and 103 Pearl street. In 1860 the firm became Henry L. Daggett & Co., which form it retained until the end of his business life in 1881.

Thus for almost fifty years he was engaged in the shoe and leather business, a man known to the trade all over the United States, and known as one of the most high-minded and honorable of business men. He held many positions of trust and responsibility, and was a well-known and popular member of the Boston Board of Trade.

1902. MAYHEW FISHER DAGGETT [8] (*Jacob,*[7] *Elihu,*[6] *Elihu,*[5] *Mayhew,*[4] *John,*[3] *Thomas,*[2] *John*[1]), born Attleboro', Mass., December 4, 1814; married 1st, Attleboro', Mass., March 20, 1837, Adeline G. Nott, daughter of —— and Mehitabel (Pond) Nott; born Jersey City, N.J., June 24, 1815; died Wrentham, Mass., August 16, 1867; married 2d, Emma ——; born Woonsocket, R.I.

Issue :

2775. i.   SARAH JANE DAGGETT,[9] born Wrentham, Mass., November 11, 1839.
2776. ii. GEORGE HENRY DAGGETT,[9] born Wrentham, Mass., January 8, 1842; died Taunton, Mass., February 10, 1873.
2777. iii. DANIEL LELAND FLETCHER DAGGETT,[9] born Wrentham, Mass., October 22, 1847.
2778. iv. MAYHEW F. DAGGETT,[9] born Uxbridge, Mass., November 17, 1872; died Wrentham, Mass., June 17, 1873.

1904. WILLARD ELIHU DAGGETT [8] (*Jacob,*[7] *Elihu,*[6] *Elihu,*[5] *Mayhew,*[4] *John,*[3] *Thomas,*[2] *John*[1]), born Attleboro', Mass., February 8, 1818; resides Harvard street, Brookline, Mass. (1893); married Boston, Mass., June 7, 1846, by Rev. Joseph Banvard, to Mary Atwood Wade.

Issue :

2779. i. WILLARD FRANCIS DAGGETT,[9] born Dorchester, Mass., August 7, 1850.
2780. ii. FANNY S. DAGGETT,[9] born Roxbury, Mass., November 22, 1854.

1908. CAROLINE P. DAGGETT [8] (*Milton,*[7] *Elijah,*[6] *Elihu,*[5] *Mayhew,*[4] *John,*[3] *Thomas,*[2] *John*[1]), born Lincoln, Mass., 1820; married 1st, Boston, Mass., September 20, 1838, by Rev. J. W. Downing, to Joseph Shaw; married 2d, Boston, Mass., April 7, 1869, by Seth C. Carey, to Joseph J. Bigelow, son of Isaac and Nancy Bigelow; born Leominster, Mass., 1805; "watchmaker, Boston."

1909. LYMAN DAGGETT [8] (*Milton,*[7] *Elijah,*[6] *Elihu,*[5] *Mayhew,*[4] *John,*[3] *Thomas,*[2] *John*[1]), born Lincoln, Mass., 1821; died Boston,

Mass., January 6, 1890; married 1st, Newton, Mass., December 29, 1844, by Rev. L. Gilbert, to Susan M. Baker, daughter of Eleazer and Susan Baker; born Dorchester, Mass., 1821; died Dorchester, Mass., August 19, 1850; married 2d, Boston, Mass., July 17, 1851, Lydia A. Hill, daughter of Abraham Hill; born Northwood, N.H., 1824.

Issue:

2781. i.   MILTON LYMAN DAGGETT,[9] born Boston, Mass., 1848.
2782. ii. ISABELLA FRANCES DAGGETT,[9] born Boston, Mass., about 1858; died
           Vineland, N.J., about 1874.
2783. iii. WARREN C. DAGGETT,[9] born Boston, Mass., 1862.

1924. MARY ANN DAGGETT[8] (*Otis*,[7] *Joab*,[6] *John*,[5] *Ebenezer*,[4] *John*,[3] *Thomas*,[2] *John*[1]), born Surry, N.H., September 18, 1813; died Penacook, N.H., November 21, 1852; married Attleboro', Mass., April 28, 1836, by Rev. Mr. Forbush, to Henry Hayes Brown, son of David and Eunice (Hayes) Brown; born Seekonk, Mass., June 17, 1805; died Cottage City, Mass., September 24, 1873.

Issue:

2784. i.   HENRY FRANCIS BROWN,[9] born Attleboro', Mass., February 25, 1837;
           married Penacook, N.H., November 6, 1865, Isabel Dyer, daughter
           of William O. and Asenath (Pratt) Dyer; born Mendon, Mass.,
           August 26, 1846; resides Penacook, N.H. (1892).
2785. ii. DAVID ARTHUR BROWN,[9] born Attleboro', Mass., May 14, 1839.
2786. iii. MARY LOUISA BROWN,[9] born Attleboro', Mass., June 25, 1841.
2787. iv. FREDERICK JUDSON BROWN,[9] born Penacook, N.H., July 11, 1844;
           died Penacook, N.H., April 9, 1872.
2788. v.   ELLEN MARIA BROWN,[9] born Penacook, N.H., January 11, 1848.
2789. vi. ISABEL NANCY BROWN,[9] born Penacook, N.H., April 7, 1850.
2790. vii. CHARLES HOWARD BROWN,[9] born Penacook, N.H., October 17, 1852;
           died Penacook, N.H., February 9, 1853.

1925. JOHN GILMAN DAGGETT[8] (*Otis*,[7] *Joab*,[6] *John*,[5] *Ebenezer*,[4] *John*,[3] *Thomas*,[2] *John*[1]), born Surry, N.H., June 21, 1816; "chair manufacturer;" died Sterling, Mass., September 16, 1871; married Brattleboro', Vt., February 3, 1848, by Rev. Mr. King, to Augusta L. Warner, daughter of John and Zernah (Rich) Warner; born Boston, Mass., July 18, 1828; resides 11 Highland avenue, Somerville, Mass. (1892).

Issue:

2791. i.   GRACE DAGGETT,[9] born Princeton, Mass., May 31, 1849; died Prince-
           ton, Mass., April 3, 1850.
2792. ii. JOHN GILMAN DAGGETT,[9] born Princeton, Mass., November 21, 1850.
2793. iii. MARY DAGGETT,[9] born Boston, Mass., October 3, 1860.
2794. iv. MABEL DAGGETT,[9] born Boston, Mass., October 3, 1860.

1931. MARTHA JANE DAGGETT[8] (*Otis*,[7] *Joab*,[6] *John*,[5] *Ebenezer*,[4] *John*,[3] *Thomas*,[2] *John*[1]), born Surry, N.H., February 1, 1836; died Brooklyn, N.Y., July 19, 1878; married Attleboro', Mass., May 8, 1856, by Rev. W. H. Alden, to George Albert Shepardson, of Attleboro', son of George Washington and Juliaette (Richards) Shepardson ; born Attleboro', Mass., September 22, 1835 ; died New York city, December 19, 1887.

Issue :

2795. i. HARRY RICHARDS SHEPARDSON,[9] born Attleboro', Mass., May 19, 1859.

George A. Shepardson was in Battery A, 1st Regiment Rhode Island Light Artillery. Was wounded in first battle of Bull Run. Sunday, July 21, 1861. He left the Battery at Warrenton.

1932. ABIGAIL DAGGETT[8] (*Levi*,[7] *Joab*,[6] *John*,[5] *Ebenezer*,[4] *John*,[3] *Thomas*,[2] *John*[1]), born Troy, N.H., February 11, 1819 ; resides Richland Centre, Wis. (1886) ; married Jaffrey, N.H., May 17, 1847, by Rev. Leonard Tenney, to Benjamin Jewett Tenney, son of Benjamin and Betsey (Taylor) Tenney ; born Groton, Mass., June 6, 1807 ; died Richland Centre, Wis., March 17, 1868.

Issue.

2796. i. ABBY ANN TENNEY,[9] born Beloit, Wis., March 13, 1848 ; died Beloit, Wis., September 6, 1849.
2797. ii. EMMA ELISABETH TENNEY,[9] born Beloit, Wis., November 27, 1849.
2798. iii. HELEN LEORA TENNEY,[9] born Clarence, Wis., December 5, 1852 ; died Richland Centre, Wis., May 18, 1884.

1933. Rev. LEVI DAGGETT[8] (*Levi*,[7] *Joab*,[6] *John*,[5] *Ebenezer*,[4] *John*,[3] *Thomas*,[2] *John*[1]), born Troy, N.H., July 3, 1820 ; died Willimantic, Conn., April 18, 1857 ; married Attleboro', Mass., Nov. 17, 1842, by Rev. Mr. Bailey, to Selah Eleanor Bacon, daughter of George and Avis Bicknell (Fales) Bacon ; born Attleboro', Mass., January 31, 1822 ; resides Plainville, Mass. (1892).

Issue :

2799. i. ABBIE ELEANOR DAGGETT,[9] born East Hartford, Conn., October 30, 1845.
2800. ii. EMMA ADELIA DAGGETT,[9] born Norwich, Conn., June 27, 1849 ; married Attleboro', Mass., November 19, 1873, by Rev. Edwin D. Hall, to Pliny Merton Cobb, son of Samuel C. and Huldah Cobb ; born Mansfield, Mass., 1849 ; he music teacher ; she died May 10, 1874.
2801. iii. ANNA CAROLINE DAGGETT,[9] born Mystic, Conn., January 5, 1855 ; married 1st, Attleboro', Mass., December 23, 1874, by Rev. Edwin D. Hall, to John H. Mathewson, son of John and Eunice Mathewson ; "jeweller ; " born Attleboro', Mass., 1853 ; married 2d, Wrentham, Mass., June 11, 1885, C. N. Moore ; she resides Plainville, Mass. (1892).

Rev. Levi Daggett was a minister of the Methodist Episcopal church, preaching in Massachusetts, Connecticut, and Rhode Island. He was presiding elder when he died.

1934. JOAB DAGGETT[8] (*Levi*,[7] *Joab*,[6] *John*,[5] *Ebenezer*,[4] *John*,[3] *Thomas*,[2] *John*[1]), born Troy, N.H., August 7, 1822 ; "jeweller ; " died Attleboro', Mass., October 31, 1861 ; married Lonsdale, R.I.,

April 21, 1844, Catharine Amanda Peck; born Rehoboth, Mass.;
now Mrs. James Gunn; resides 55 Garden street, Pawtucket, R.I.
(1892).

Issue:

2802. i.   ELLA CATHARINE DAGGETT,[9] born Jaffrey, N.H., September 10, 1846;
      resides Pawtucket, R.I. (1892).
2803. ii. EDMUND JOAB DAGGETT,[9] born Attleboro', Mass., October 29, 1848;
      married Attleboro', Mass., June 22, 1880, by Rev. George Bullen, to
      Mary Ella Dunnell, daughter of Roland B. and Vesta (Ware)
      Dunnell; born Lee, Me., 1859; no issue (1892); he machinist;
      resides Taunton, Mass. (1892).

1940. MARCUS LAFAYETTE DAGGETT [8] (*Marcus,*[7] *Joab,*[6] *John,*[5]
Ebenezer,[4] *John,*[3] *Thomas,*[2] *John*[1]), born Marlboro', N.H., June
15, 1820; "jeweller;" died Pawtucket, R.I., November 22, 1882;
married Martha ———.

Issue:

2804. i.   MARTHA ISABELL DAGGETT,[9] born Attleboro', Mass., January 9, 1846.
2805. ii. CHARLES FREDERICK DAGGETT,[9] born Attleboro', Mass., September 19,
      1849.

1946. ELIZABETH ANN DAGGETT [8] (*Pliny,*[7] *Joab,*[6] *John,*[5] *Eben-*
ezer,[4] *John,*[3] *Thomas,*[2] *John*[1]), born Troy, N.H., March 21, 1826;
died Avoca, Wis., July 21, 1888; married 1st, Attleboro', Mass.,
October 14, 1846, Henry Clay Lucas, of Pawtucket, R.I.; born
Northumberland, N.H., January 6, 1824; died Avoca, Wis., November 26, 1870; married 2d, Avoca, Wis., September 11, 1873, Samuel
Parks, of Saratoga, N.Y., son of Patrick and Abiah (Coon) Parks;
born Saratoga county, N.Y., September 23, 1819; resides Frisco,
Oklahoma territory (1892).

Issue:

2806. i.   ELLA AMANDA LUCAS,[9] born Boston, Mass., September 5, 1847.

1947. ALONZO DAGGETT [8] (*Pliny,*[7] *Joab,*[6] *John,*[5] *Ebenezer,*[4] *John,*[3]
Thomas,[2] *John*[1]), born Troy, N.H., April 20, 1828; resides Jefferson,
Iowa (1892); married Muscoda, Wis., January 17, 1875, Jane
Midling, of Highland, Wis., daughter of James and Matilda (Mc-
Loughlin) Midling; born Canada, February 6, 1854.

Issue:

2807. i.   ALONZO DAGGETT,[9] born Pulaski, Wis., November 6, 1875.
2808. ii. HENRY DAGGETT,[9] born Highland, Wis., March 30, 1878.

1949. MARY JANE DAGGETT [8] (*Pliny,*[7] *Joab,*[6] *John,*[5] *Ebenezer,*[4]
John,[3] *Thomas,*[2] *John*[1]), born Troy, N.H., February 7, 1832; resides Berlin, Wis. (1892); married Dodgeville, Wis., January 1,
1856, Christopher Columbus Jenkins, of Buffalo, N.Y., son of Sam-

uel and Margaret Rogers (Grenell) Jenkins; born Amherst, N.Y., October 29, 1826.

Issue:

2809. i. ANNE CORA JENKINS,[9] born Avoca, Wis., April 21, 1859.

1951. FERDINAND DAGGETT[8] (*Pliny,*[7] *Joab,*[6] *John,*[5] *Ebenezer,*[4] *John,*[3] *Thomas,*[2] *John*[1]), born Attleboro', Mass., May 26, 1836; resides Avoca, Wis. (1892); married Avoca, Wis., September 5, 1860, Anna Knight, of Clyde, Wis., daughter of Darius and Lydia C. (Gile) Knight; born Luzerne county, Pa., January 30, 1842.

Issue:

2810. i. HOMER LUCAS DAGGETT,[9] born Avoca, Wis., July 9, 1861; died Avoca, Wis., January 10, 1863.
2811. ii. PLINY ULYSSES DAGGETT,[9] born Avoca, Wis., May 18, 1867.

1952. PLINY AUGUSTUS DAGGETT[8] (*Pliny,*[7] *Joab,*[6] *John,*[5] *Ebenezer,*[4] *John,*[3] *Thomas,*[2] *John*[1]), born Attleboro', Mass., January 29, 1838; resides 547 Pine street, Spokane, Wash. (1892); married 1st, Dodgeville, Wis., January 1, 1860, Margaret Lucretia Floyd, of Dodgeville, Wis., daughter of Armstead Waltham and Mary Ann (Stiles) Floyd; born Dodgeville, Wis., August 26, 1842; died Minneapolis, Minn., February 26, 1887; married 2d, September 26, 1888, Helen Elthear Merriman, daughter of Samuel Levi and Marion Bradford (Obert) Merriman; born Friendship, N.Y., August 29, 1852.

Issue:

2812. i. FLOYD LORENZO DAGGETT,[9] born Wyoming, Wis., December 15, 1861.
2813. ii. MARION LUCRETIA DAGGETT,[9] born Spokane, Wash., November 2, 1889.
2814. iii. PLINY AUGUSTUS DAGGETT,[9] born Spokane, Wash., September 1, 1891.

Of P. A. Daggett & Co., "insurance," 306 Post street, Spokane (1892).

1957. CLARA LOUISE DAGGETT[8] (*Pliny,*[7] *Joab,*[6] *John,*[5] *Ebenezer,*[4] *John,*[3] *Thomas,*[2] *John*[1]), born Attleboro', Mass., January 8, 1852; resides Kilburn City, Wis. (1892); married Berlin, Wis., June 30, 1877, Chester Smith, of Omro, Wis., son of William Champlin and Sarah (Foote) Smith; born Winnebago county, Wis., April 24, 1851.

Issue:

2815. i. ELLA ROSALIA SMITH,[9] born Berlin, Wis., April 6, 1878.
2816. ii. GRACE SMITH,[9] born Winneconne, Wis., July 7, 1880.
2817. iii. RUSSELL LAWRENCE SMITH,[9] born Winneconne, Wis., March 22, 1884.

1965. JONATHAN MAXCY PECK[8] (*Lydia M. Daggett,*[7] *Ebenezer,*[6] *John,*[5] *Ebenezer,*[4] *John,*[3] *Thomas,*[2] *John*[1]), born Attleboro', Mass., November 25, 1829; died Attleboro', Mass., September 21, 1881; married Oberlin, Ohio, December 16, 1874, Mendora Eliza Wack, daughter of Chauncy and Mary Ann (Brown) Wack; born March 26, 1852; resides Vine street, Oberlin, Ohio (1892).

Issue;

2818. i. DORSEY MAXCY PECK,[9] born February 12, 1877; died May 19, 1880.
2819. ii. MARY LYDIA PECK,[9] born August 22, 1881.

1976. JOHN MAYHEW DAGGETT[8] (*John,*[7] *Ebenezer,*[6] *John,*[5] *Ebenezer,*[4] *John,*[3] *Thomas,*[2] *John* [1]), born Attleboro', Mass., November 16, 1845; resides Marianna, Ark. (1892); married 1st, Stonington, Conn., November 18, 1868, by Rev. John C. Middleton, to Ernestine Rose Brown, of Stonington, Conn., daughter of Thomas Moore and Ann Elizabeth (Chapman) Brown; born Stonington, Conn., March 20, 1849; died Marianna, Ark., December 4, 1876; married 2d, Denton, Tex., October 14, 1879, by Rev. Stephen H. Greene, to Olive May Anderson, daughter of Jesse H. and Martha (Mottley) Anderson; born Lebanon, Tenn., December 14, 1855.

Issue:

2820. i.   JOHN MAYHEW DAGGETT,[9] born Attleboro', Mass., December 31, 1869; died Marianna, Ark., October 11, 1891.
2821. ii.   ERNESTINE ROSE DAGGETT,[9] born Attleboro', Mass., October 14, 1872; died Attleboro', Mass., February 26, 1873.
2822. iii. SAMUEL ANDERSON DAGGETT,[9] born Marianna, Ark., January 19, 1881; died Marianna, Ark., August 23, 1885.
2823. iv.   JESSE BOOMER DAGGETT,[9] born Marianna, Ark., August 24, 1882.
2824. v.   CHARLES EBEN DAGGETT,[9] born Marianna, Ark., April 28, 1885.
2825. vi.   MAXCY DEWITT DAGGETT,[9] born Marianna, Ark., February 28, 1887.
2826. vii. AMELIA DAGGETT,[9] born Marianna, Ark., April 28, 1889.

John M. Daggett (B.U., 1868), attorney at law, has been postmaster of Marianna, Ark., for some years; deputy clerk of Lee county, Ark., for some twelve years previous to 1885. He is also interested in real estate, and acts as loan agent.

1978. AMELIA MAXCY DAGGETT[8] (*John,*[7] *Ebenezer,*[6] *John,*[5] *Ebenezer,*[4] *John,*[3] *Thomas,*[2] *John* [1]), born Attleboro'; Mass., October 23, 1850; resides "Twin Elms Farm," Attleboro', Mass. (1892); married New York city, January 10, 1878, by Rev. Arthur Brooks, to George St. John Sheffield, son of Joseph Earl and Maria (St. John) Sheffield; born New Haven, Conn., April 2, 1842.

No issue.

1984. NANCY ELLA DAGGETT[8] (*Harvey M.,*[7] *Ebenezer,*[6] *John,*[5] *Ebenezer,*[4] *John,*[3] *Thomas,*[2] *John* [1]), born Attleboro', Mass., March 8, 1853; resides North Attleboro', Mass. (1892), on the old homestead; married Attleboro', Mass., June 11, 1884, by Rev. Geo. O. Jenness, to James Bowker Parsons, of Attleboro', son of Fidelio and Rachel

Anne (Bowker) Parsons, of Bangor, Me.; born Bangor, Me., January 1, 1839; postmaster and depot-master, Attleboro' Falls.

Issue:

2827. i. CARROLL DAGGETT PARSONS,[9] born Attleboro', Mass., November 28, 1885.
2828. ii. ARTHUR BOWKER PARSONS,[9] born Attleboro', Mass., December 15, 1889.

1985. JAMES E. MCCLELLAN [8] (*Ama I. Daggett,*[7] *Ebenezer,*[6] *John,*[5] *Ebenezer,*[4] *John,*[3] *Thomas,*[2] *John*[1]), born Sutton, Mass., June 16, 1838; died Harper's Ferry, Md., July 7, 1863.

James E. McClellan enlisted in the Fifty-first Regiment of Massachusetts Volunteers in 1862.

He was stationed at Beaufort, S.C., and there established a school for colored people, teaching it himself at such hours as he could command when off duty.

Just as the term of service of the regiment had expired they were called to join Meade's army, which was moving to repel Lee's invasion of Maryland.

During this forced march Mr. McClellan was accidentally drowned at Harper's Ferry.

Just before his death he was appointed lieutenant in a regiment of colored South Carolina volunteers.

1989. JOHN E. MCCLELLAN [8] (*Ama I. Daggett,*[7] *Ebenezer,*[6] *John,*[5] *Ebenezer,*[4] *John,*[3] *Thomas,*[2] *John*[1]), born Sutton, Mass., September 5, 1847; resides Grafton, Mass. (1892); married 1st, Buffalo, Mo., November 17, 1868, Mary Bartshe; died Springfield, Mo., September, 1881; married 2d, Grafton, Mass., May 16, 1887, S. Elizabeth Dodge.

Issue:

2829. i. JAMES H. MCCLELLAN,[9] born Buffalo, Mo., November 23, 1869.
2830. ii. AMY A. MCCLELLAN,[9] born Buffalo, Mo., May 8, 1871; died Grafton, Mass., July 14, 1891.
2831. iii. LEONARD A. MCCLELLAN,[9] born Buffalo, Mo., March 14, 1873.
2832. iv. MARTHA F. MCCLELLAN,[9] born Grafton, Mass., September 12, 1888.

1997. SHEPARD SILAS EVERETT [8] (*Marcy S. Daggett,*[7] *Ebenezer,*[6] *John,*[5] *Ebenezer,*[4] *John,*[3] *Thomas,*[2] *John*[1]), born Boston, Mass., October 27, 1841; resides Forest Glen, Md. (1892); married Chelsea, Mass., September 23, 1869, by Rev. Chas. J. Baldwin, to Emma Jane Wade, daughter of William and Irene (Nichols) Wade; born Digby, N.S., June 28, 1845.

Issue:

2833. i. ANNIE DAGGETT EVERETT,[9] born Boston, Mass., July 25, 1870; died Chelsea, Mass., September 19, 1870.
2834. ii. WILLIAM WADE EVERETT,[9] born Chelsea, Mass., August 23, 1871.

2835. iii. MARION CLEMENT EVERETT,[9] born Washington, D.C., March 6, 1873.
2836. iv. GEORGE NICHOLS EVERETT,[9] born Washington, D.C., January 2, 1876.
2837. v. WALTER WOODWARD EVERETT,[9] born Falls Church, Va., May 13, 1881; died Falls Church, Va., October 13, 1881.
2838. vi. EDITH EMMA EVERETT,[9] born Washington, D.C., June 30, 1884.

1998. JOSEPHINE SHEPHARD DAGGETT[8] (*Handel N.*,[7] *Ebenezer*,[6] *John*,[5] *Ebenezer*,[4] *John*,[3] *Thomas*,[2] *John*[1]), born Attleboro', Mass., June 21, 1845; resides Attleboro' Falls, Mass. (1892); married Attleboro', Mass., by Rev. F. N. Peloubet, to Harvey Clap, son of Harvey Erastus and Priscilla Barker (Crocker) Clap; "manufacturing jeweller;" born Wrentham, Mass., April 2, 1844.

Issue:

2839. i. EDMUND WRIGHT CLAP,[9] born Attleboro' Falls, Mass., May 30, 1870.
2840. ii. HARVEY ERASTUS CLAP,[9] born Attleboro' Falls, Mass., May 26, 1875.
2841. iii. GEORGE PERCY CLAP,[9] born Attleboro' Falls, Mass., July 5, 1878.

2003. FLORENCE JANE DAGGETT[8] (*Handel N.*,[7] *Ebenezer*,[6] *John*,[5] *Ebenezer*,[4] *John*,[3] *Thomas*,[2] *John*[1]), born Attleboro', Mass., November 25, 1857; resides North Attleboro', Mass. (1892); married Attleboro' Falls, Mass., July 30, 1877, by Rev. F. D. Kelsey, to Henry Francis Barrows, Jr., son of Henry Francis and Henrietta Thompson (Richards) Barrows; "manufacturing jeweller;" born Attleboro', Mass., October 24, 1854.

Issue:

2842. i. MAUD BARROWS,[9] born New York city, February 15, 1878.
2843. ii. LOUIS DAGGETT BARROWS,[9] born North Attleboro', Mass., May 17, 1879.
2844. iii. HELEN BARROWS,[9] born North Attleboro', Mass., November 23, 1880.
2845. iv. DONALD ADAMS BARROWS,[9] born North Attleboro', Mass., October 17, 1887.

2007. HOMER MICAJAH DAGGETT[8] (*Homer M.*,[7] *Ebenezer*,[6] *John*,[5] *Ebenezer*,[4] *John*,[3] *Thomas*,[2] *John*[1]), born Attleboro', Mass., May 22, 1848; resides Attleboro', Mass. (1892); married Providence, R.I., August 17, 1875, by Rev. Geo. Cooper, assisted by Rev. Alexis Caswell, D.D., to Clara Jane Cook, daughter of Otis Mason and Mary Jane (Whipple) Cook, of Providence; born Cumberland, R.I., December 18, 1843.

No issue.

Mr. Daggett is a manufacturing jeweller, and is officially connected with electric street-railway, etc.

2009. SANFORD DAGGETT[8] (*Homer M.*,[7] *Ebenezer*,[6] *John*,[5] *Ebenezer*,[4] *John*,[3] *Thomas*,[2] *John*[1]), born Attleboro', Mass., October 14, 1852; "civil engineer;" resides Attleboro', Mass. (1892); married Woonsocket, R.I., December 28, 1881, by Rev. Eugene Thomas, to

Abbie Medora Jillson, daughter of Allen Bennett and Abbie (Hunt) Jillson; born Woonsocket, R.I., March 20, 1844.

Issue:

2846. i. (Female) Daggett,[9] born Attleboro', Mass., September 7, 1883; died Attleboro', Mass., September 9, 1883.
2847. ii. Handel Allen Daggett,[9] born Attleboro', Mass., August 21, 1885; died Attleboro', Mass., April 5, 1886.

2013. Grace Ann Daggett[8] (*Stephen*,[7] *Henry*,[6] *Naphtali*,[5] *Ebenezer*,[4] *John*,[3] *Thomas*,[2] *John*[1]), born Pontotoc, Miss., September 28, 1842; resides Pontotoc, Miss. (1892); married Pontotoc, Miss., January 15, 1888, Benjamin Randolph Ellis, son of James and Belle (Sullivan) Ellis; born Huntsville, Ala., July, 1842.

No issue (1892).

2014. Harriet Hunt Daggett[8] (*Stephen*,[7] *Henry*,[6] *Naphtali*,[5] *Ebenezer*,[4] *John*,[3] *Thomas*,[2] *John*[1]), born Pontotoc, Miss., August 15, 1844; died Okolona, Miss., October 14, 1878; married Pontotoc, Miss., James Martin Carter, son of James M. and Margret (Courteney) Carter; born Columbia, Tenn., September 28, 1842; resides Pontotoc, Miss. (1892).

Issue:

2848. i. Stephen Daggett Carter.[9] born Pontotoc. Miss., October 4, 1870.
2849. ii. James Martin Carter,[9] born Pontotoc, Miss., June 10, 1872.
2850. iii. Jessie Walton Carter,[9] born Pontotoc, Miss., July 12, 1875.
2851. iv. Hattie Hunt Carter.[9] born Okolona, Miss., October 14, 1878.

2015. Julia Driver Daggett[8] (*Stephen*,[7] *Henry*,[6] *Naphtali*,[5] *Ebenezer*,[4] *John*,[3] *Thomas*,[2] *John*[1]), born Pontotoc, Miss., January 30, 1847; address Neal Store, Miss. (1892); married Algoma, Miss., August 1, 1886, John W. Harris, son of Haden D. and Paulina (Mayes) Harris; born Okolona, Miss.

No issue (1892).

2017. Sarah Hopkins Daggett[8] (*Stephen*,[7] *Henry*,[6] *Naphtali*,[5] *Ebenezer*,[4] *John*,[3] *Thomas*,[2] *John*[1]), born Pontotoc, Miss., March 13, 1853; married Pontotoc, Miss., June 10, 1880, William Holley, son of Samuel and Eliza (Lynn) Holley; born Chester, S.C., March 10, 1849.

Issue:

2852. i. Sarah Holley,[9] born Pontotoc, Miss., May 2, 1881.
2853. ii. William Holley,[9] born Pontotoc, Miss., March 2, 1883.

2018. Charles Walton Daggett[8] (*Stephen*,[7] *Henry*,[6] *Naphtali*,[5] *Ebenezer*,[4] *John*,[3] *Thomas*,[2] *John*[1]), born Pontotoc, Miss., September 9, 1856; resides Pontotoc, Miss. (1892); married Mooreville, Miss., December 21, 1882, Erie Jones, daughter of A. C. and Elizabeth

Arandinta (Hudleson) Jones; born Columbus, Miss., February 3, 1865.

Issue :

2854. i.   ANNIE DAGGETT,[9] born Pontotoc, Miss., January 1, 1884.
2855. ii. STEPHEN DAGGETT,[9] born Pontotoc, Miss., December 25, 1888.

2020.   FRED HUNT DAGGETT [8] (*Horace,*[7] *Henry,*[6] *Naphtali,*[5] *Ebenezer,*[4] *John,*[3] *Thomas,*[2] *John*[1]), born New Haven, Conn., April 2, 1844 ; resides West Point, Miss. (1892) ; married West Point, Miss., April 28, 1869, Bettie Shearer, daughter of Joseph Berry and Susan (Hale) Shearer; born Monroe county, Miss., January 8, 1848.

Issue :

2856. i.   LULA SHEARER DAGGETT,[9] born West Point, Miss., October 10, 1870.
2857. ii.   EVA HALE DAGGETT,[9] born West Point, Miss., March 22, 1872.
2858. iii. HENRY WATTER DAGGETT,[9] born West Point, Miss., July 5, 1874 ; died West Point, Miss., October 3, 1875.
2859. iv.   IRENE GRACE DAGGETT,[9] born West Point, Miss., September 1, 1876.
2860. v.   HORACE EDMUND DAGGETT,[9] born West Point, Miss., May 1, 1879.
2861. vi.   FREDERICK HUNT DAGGETT,[9] born West Point, Miss., August 3, 1881.

2021.   JANE HAWLEY DAGGETT [8] (*Horace,*[7] *Henry,*[6] *Naphtali,*[5] *Ebenezer,*[4] *John,*[3] *Thomas,*[2] *John*[1]), born Mobile, Ala., September 22, 1846 ; resides Water Valley, Miss. (1892) ; married Pontotoc, Miss., December 3, 1869, by Rev. J. J. D. West, to William Early Benson, son of Hardy and Mary Jane (Duke) Benson; born Yalobusha county, Miss., December 9, 1838.

Issue :

2862. i.   MARTHA MARTIN BENSON,[9] born Yalobusha county, Miss., June 13, 1871.
2863. ii.   HATTIE HUNT BENSON,[9] born Yalobusha county, Miss., September 8, 1873.
2864. iii. HARDY HORACE BENSON,[9] born Yalobusha county, Miss., August 27, 1875.
2865. iv.   HENRY BENJAMIN BENSON,[9] born Yalobusha county, Miss., September 16, 1878.
2866. v.   CORA COFFIN BENSON,[9] born Yalobusha county, Miss., November 7, 1880.
2867. vi.   CLARENCE EARLY BENSON,[9] born Water Valley, Miss., September 16. 1883.
2868. vii. JENNIE HUNTINGTON BENSON,[9] born Water Valley, Miss., August 16, 1888.

2023.   IDA HUNTINGTON DAGGETT [8] (*Horace,*[7] *Henry,*[6] *Naphtali,*[5] *Ebenezer,*[4] *John,*[3] *Thomas,*[2] *John*[1]), born Pontotoc, Miss., October 15, 1854 ; resides McComb City, Miss. (1892) ; married Pontotoc, Miss., December 16, 1875, by Rev. J. D. West, to Samuel Miller, son of Robert Alexander and Lizzie (Fumster) Miller; born Pontotoc, Miss., June 17, 1854.

Issue :

2869. i.   EMMA LYDA MILLER,[9] born Pontotoc, Miss., September 28, 1876 ; died McComb City, Miss., February 19, 1892.
2870. ii. ROBERT HORACE MILLER,[9] born Pontotoc, Miss., February 8, 1879.

2030. John Frederick Kensett[8] (*Elizabeth Daggett,*[7] *Naphtali,*[5] *Ebenezer,*[4] *John,*[3] *Thomas,*[2] *John*[1]), born Cheshire, Conn., March 22, 1816 ; died December 14, 1872.

John Frederick Kensett was apprenticed to his uncle, Alfred Daggett, an engraver of bank-note vignettes. In 1840 he went to England, where he studied painting for five years, supporting himself by engraving. At that period he exhibited a view of Windsor Castle in the exhibition of the Society of British Artists, which was selected as the best in the collection. In 1850 he returned to New York and began a series of landscapes of mountain, river, and lake scenery of New York and the Eastern States, with marine views, which had eager purchasers. From this time onward his reputation and success as a landscape painter were great and assured.

No artist was better known, and there is hardly an American art collection of note that does not contain one or more of his pictures.

His works are highly esteemed in France, Belgium, and England, as well as in his native country.

In 1859 he was appointed a member of the " National Art Commission," and engaged to superintend the ornamentation of the national Capitol. His was one of the greatest and most evenly successful of artistic careers. He looked and was a perfect gentleman, of kindly sentiment and genial culture ; a friend to all good men, and an enemy to no one.

2031. Elizabeth Daggett Kensett [8] (*Elizabeth Daggett,*[7] *Ezra,*[6] *Naphtali,*[5] *Ebenezer,*[4] *John,*[3] *Thomas,*[2] *John*[1]), born August 11, 1817 ; married April, 1834, Horatio Nelson Vail.

Issue :

2871. i.   Harriet Vail.[9]
2872. ii.   Horatio Vail.[9]
2873. iii.   Edward Vail.[9]
2874. iv.   Julia Vail.[9]
2875. v.   John Vail.[9]
2876. vi.   Ogden Vail.[9]
2877. vii.   Samuel Vail.[9]

2037. Alfred Daggett [8] (*Smith,*[7] *Ezra,*[6] *Naphtali,*[5] *Ebenezer,*[4] *John,*[3] *Thomas,*[2] *John*[1]), born March 13, 1826 ; resides Ogden, Ill. (1892) ; married Lafayette, Ind., November 1, 1856, Emma Briton ; born Birmingham, Eng., January 20, 1838.

Issue :

2878. i.   Alfred B. Daggett,[9] born September 10, 1857.
2879. ii.   Laura Ann Daggett,[9] born January 12, 1859.
2880. iii. Orion W. Daggett,[9] born January 4, 1861.
2881. iv.   Emma Caroline Daggett,[9] born April 23, 1869.
2882. v.   Mary Godfrey Daggett,[9] born February 21, 1872.

2047. ALFRED DAGGETT [8] (*Alfred,*[7] *Ezra,*[6] *Naphtali,*[5] *Ebenezer,*[4] *John,*[3] *Thomas,*[2] *John* [1]), born New Haven, Conn., August 23, 1837; "druggist;" died New Haven, Conn., August 20, 1878; married New Haven, Conn., November 18, 1863, by Rev. E. L. Drown, to Mary Jane Mason, daughter of James M. and Eliza (Isabell) Mason; born New Haven, Conn., April, 1840; resides 271 Crown street, New Haven, Conn. (1890).

Issue:

2883. i. ALFRED MASON DAGGETT,[9] born New Haven, Conn., August 17, 1864; died New Haven, Conn., March 5, 1865.
2884. ii. EDITH MARY DAGGETT,[9] born New Haven Conn., October 5, 1865.
2885. iii. GRACE ELIZA DAGGETT,[9] born New Haven, Conn., June 19, 1867.
2886. iv. JOHN MAYHEW DAGGETT,[9] born New Haven, Conn., July 5, 1869.
2887. v. JAMES MASON DAGGETT,[9] born New Haven, Conn., February 29, 1872.
2888. vi. EDWARD HERBERT DAGGETT,[9] born New Haven, Conn., November 25, 1873.
2889. vii. Daughter —— DAGGETT,[9] born New Haven, Conn., September 20, 1875; died New Haven, Conn., September 20, 1875.

2048. LAURA DAGGETT [8] (*Alfred,*[7] *Ezra,*[6] *Naphtali,*[5] *Ebenezer,*[4] *John,*[3] *Thomas,*[2] *John*[1]), born New Haven, Conn., October 8, 1839; died New Haven, Conn., December 11, 1872; married New Haven, Conn., October 7, 1869, by Rev. George L. Walker, to Frank Elihu Spencer, son of Elihu and —— (Beecher) Spencer; born Naugatuck, Conn., June 12, 1840; resides New Haven, Conn. (1892).

Issue:

2890. i. ALFRED LAWRENCE SPENCER,[9] born New Haven, Conn., January 6, 1871.
2891. ii. LAURA SPENCER,[9] born New Haven, Conn., November 30, 1872; died New Haven, Conn., August 18, 1873.

2049. HENRY DAGGETT [8] (*Alfred,*[7] *Ezra,*[6] *Naphtali,*[5] *Ebenezer,*[4] *John,*[3] *Thomas,*[2] *John* [1]), born New Haven, Conn., July 12, 1841; resides San Diego, Cal. (1892); married 1st, Cromwell, Conn., May 12, 1868, Harriet Elizabeth Wilcox; born Berlin, Conn., 1842; divorced; married 2d, San Diego, Cal., August 24, 1884, by Rev. H. B. Ristariek, to Rebecca Jenison Cary, daughter of Douglas and Phebe Letteer (Scott) Cary; born Tunkhannock, Pa., November 24, 1859.

Issue:

2892. i. HARRY MAYHEW DAGGETT,[9] born New Haven, Conn., March 10, 1869.
2893. ii. LAURA LETTEER DAGGETT,[9] born San Diego, Cal., June 29, 1885.
2894. iii. ALFRED CARY DAGGETT,[9] born San Diego, Cal., October 31, 1886; died San Diego, Cal., November 10, 1888.
2895. iv. EDITH GERTRUDE DAGGETT,[9] born San Diego, Cal., September 28, 1887.

2052. WILLIAM DAGGETT [8] (*William,*[7] *Ezra,*[6] *Naphtali,*[5] *Ebenezer,*[4] *John,*[3] *Thomas,*[2] *John* [1]), born New Haven, Conn., December 3, 1831; resides Indianapolis, Ind. (1892); married Indianapolis, Ind.,

May 18, 1858, by Rev. James B. Simmons, to Phœbe Eve Webster, daughter of George Chester and Helen (Markle) Webster; born Wooster, Ohio, August 17, 1839.

Issue:

2896. i.   SADA MARIA DAGGETT,[9] born Indianapolis, Ind., June 6, 1859.
2897. ii.   GEORGE WILLIAM DAGGETT,[9] born Indianapolis, Ind., March 12, 1861; died Indianapolis, Ind., May 14, 1862.
2898. iii. WILLIAM HARVEY DAGGETT,[9] born Indianapolis, Ind., September 26, 1864.
2899. iv.   CORA OLIVE DAGGETT,[9] born Indianapolis, Ind., March 8, 1867.

2054. ROBERT PLATT DAGGETT [8] (*William*,[7] *Ezra*,[6] *Naphtali*,[5] *Ebenezer*,[4] *John*,[3] *Thomas*,[2] *John*[1]), born New Haven, Conn., January 13, 1847; resides Indianapolis, Ind. (1892); married New Haven, Conn., December 1, 1869, by Rev. George Newcomb, to Carrie Elizabeth Frost, daughter of Jesse Daniel and Almira Jane (Hawley) Frost; born Waterbury, Conn., November 16, 1847.

Issue:

2900. i.   JESSIE ELIZA DAGGETT,[9] born Indianapolis, Ind., March 16, 1871.
2901. ii.   ELEANOR SARAH DAGGETT,[9] born Indianapolis, Ind., December 6, 1872.
2902. iii. ROBERT HUNT DAGGETT,[9] born Indianapolis, Ind., March 8, 1874.
2903. iv.   ALMIRA FROST DAGGETT,[9] born Indianapolis, Ind., May 9, 1877.
2904. v.   URSULA HUNT DAGGETT,[9] born Indianapolis, Ind., December 6, 1879.

2056. FREDERICK DAGGETT BRADLEY [8] (*Mary Daggett*,[7] *Ezra*,[6] *Naphtali*,[5] *Ebenezer*,[4] *John*,[3] *Thomas*,[2] *John*[1]), born November 22, 1833; died February 6, 1870; married February 18, 1857, Frances Maria Post; died July 20, 1864.

Issue:

2905. i.   ISABELLA EDITH BRADLEY,[9] born February 24, 1859.

2057. JOHN THOMAS BRADLEY [8] (*Mary Daggett*,[7] *Ezra*,[6] *Naphtali*,[5] *Ebenezer*,[4] *John*,[3] *Thomas*,[2] *John*[1]), born August 31, 1835; died January 3, 1868; married October 15, 1862, Elizabeth Naomi Kellogg.

Issue:

2906. i.   JOHN THOMAS BRADLEY,[9] born August 19, 1863; died March 13, 1869.
2907. ii.   CALEB KNEVALS BRADLEY,[9] born February 13, 1865.

2061. EDWIN FRANCIS MERSICK [8] (*Sarah Daggett*,[7] *Ezra*,[6] *Naphtali*,[5] *Ebenezer*,[4] *John*,[3] *Thomas*,[2] *John*[1]), born January 8, 1838; married 1st, November 13, 1862, Emily Augusta Cannon, daughter of Le Grand and Mary Elizabeth (Trowbridge) Cannon; born August 18, 1832; died January 17, 1866; married 2d, May 18, 1870, Emma C. Lewis.

Issue:

2908. i.   SARAH EMILY MERSICK,[9] born August 27, 1863.
2909. ii.   LOUIS MERSICK,[9] died November 20, 1879.

2067. MARY A. DAGGETT[8] (*Frederick,[7] Ezra,[6] Naphtali,[5] Ebenezer,[4] John,[3] Thomas,[2] John[1]*), born New Haven, Conn., December 23, 1850; resides New Haven, Conn. (1892); married 1st, October 14, 1874, Edward Higby; died New Haven, Conn., April 19, 1890; married 2d, New Haven, Conn., July 16, 1891, Isaac Ogden Woodruff.

Issue:

2910. i. GRACE HIGBY.[9] born New Haven, Conn., October, 1878.
2911. ii. FREDERICK WILLIAM HIGBY.[9] born New Haven, Conn., December, 1882.

2068. CATHERINE DAGGETT[8] (*Levi,[7] Samuel,[6] Samuel,[5] Ebenezer,[4] John,[3] Thomas,[2] John[1]*), born Bainbridge, N.Y., May 22, 1820; died Pittsford, N.Y., December 17, 1871; married Newark, N.Y., November 19, 1839, by Rev. Mr. Bennett, to Paul R. Derriter, son of John and Lucinda (Burkette) Derriter; born Easton, N.Y., June 13, 1815; resides Pittsford, N.Y. (1892).

No issue.

2069. GEORGE DAGGETT[8] (*Levi,[7] Samuel,[6] Samuel,[5] Ebenezer,[4] John,[3] Thomas,[2] John[1]*), born Arcada, N.Y., June 27, 1821; " builder and vine-grower; " resides Santa Clara, Cal. (1892); married Alden, N.Y., May 20, 1843, Susannah A. Harrington, daughter of Dr. J. M. and Elizebeth (Halloway) Harrington; born Alden, N.Y., August 12, 1821.

Issue:

2912. i. GEORGE A. DAGGETT.[9] born Cowlesville, N.Y., June 19, 1844.
2913. ii. CAROLINE OPHELIA DAGGETT.[9] born Cowlesville, N.Y.. April 13, 1846; married Kansas City, Mo., April 23, 1865, Lucien W. Pollard.

2070. CAROLINE DAGGETT[8] (*Levi,[7] Samuel,[6] Samuel,[5] Ebenezer,[4] John,[3] Thomas,[2] John[1]*), born Bainbridge, N.Y., April 13, 1824; died Cowlesville, N.Y., December 7, 1845; married Cowlesville, N.Y., December 10, 1844, James Nobles; born Cowlesville, N.Y.

Issue:

2914. i. HENRY NOBLES,[9] born Cowlesville, N.Y., December 10. 1845; resided at one time in Wisconsin.

2071. HANNAH DAGGETT[8] (*Levi,[7] Samuel,[6] Samuel,[5] Ebenezer,[4] John,[3] Thomas,[2] John[1]*), born Campbelltown, N.Y., September 7, 1826; resides Penfield, N.Y. (1892); married Penfield, N.Y., May 20, 1848, by Rev. Mr. Woodard, to George Stearns, son of Relief Stearns; born Pittsfield, Mass., March 12, 1818.

Issue:

2915. i. HELEN S. STEARNS,[9] born Leicester, N.Y., June 19, 1849.
2916. ii. FRANKLIN A. STEARNS,[9] born Leicester, N.Y., May 27, 1852.

2917. iii.   CHARLES A. STEARNS,[9] born Bethany, N.Y., August 10, 1854.
2918. iv.   MARY E. STEARNS,[9] born Penfield, N.Y., November 6, 1857.
2919. v.   JOHN H. STEARNS,[9] born Bristol, N.Y., May 4, 1859; died Bristol,
             N.Y., October 5, 1862.
2920. vi.   GEORGE W. STEARNS,[9] born Bristol, N.Y., October 7. 1861.
2921. vii.   FANNIE E. STEARNS,[9] born Bristol, N.Y., September 4, 1864.
2922. viii. CATHERINE R. STEARNS,[9] born Bristol, N.Y., August 8, 1867.

2076. MARTIN VAN BUREN DAGGETT [8] (*Levi,*[7] *Samuel,*[6] *Samuel,*[5] *Ebenezer,*[4] *John,*[3] *Thomas,*[2] *John* [1]), born Caneadea, N.Y., August 30, 1838; resides Tuscola, Ill. (1884); married October 10, 1867, Emma Dryer.

Issue :

2923. i.   FANNY DAGGETT.[9]
2924. ii.   H. K. DAGGETT.[9]
2925. iii. BELLE DAGGETT.[9]
2926. iv.   GEORGE LEVI DAGGETT.[9]

2080. Hon. JOHN DAGGETT [8] (*John,*[7] *Samuel,*[6] *Samuel,*[5] *Ebenezer,*[4] *John,*[3] *Thomas,*[2] *John* [1]), born Newark, N.Y., May 9, 1833; resides Black Bear, Siskiyou Co., Cal. (1893); married 1870.

Issue : three children.

A thoroughly representative Californian is Hon. John Daggett, of Siskiyou, one of the members of the Board of Commissioners to the Columbian Exposition.

Arriving in California before he had attained to majority, stalwart of frame, genial of disposition, noble in character, buoyant with hope, brave and vigorous in action, and withal industrious, it is not a matter of surprise to his contemporary friends of pioneer days that now, in the meridian of life, he is found a leader of men and a counsellor among the wise. He was educated at the high school in his native village, and left there in May, 1852, for California.

Staying but a few days in San Francisco, where he landed, he went to Sacramento, where he was engineer in a steam flouring-mill, but only for a short time, as the reports of the gold diggings which his friends brought him were so alluring that Mr. Daggett went to the mines, first in El Dorado county, and subsequently to Calaveras county, until the spring of 1853. From this time until June, 1854, he was with his brother David at Marysville, as foreman of his foundry and machine-shop. Mr. Daggett then decided to strike out again for the mines, and this time he selected northern California. Reaching Trinidad by vessel and finding the mines were remote from the coast, he started on foot with his blankets and provisions to last on the journey, over the roughest and wildest of trails, through a region traversed by Indians not very friendly to the white intruders, a distance of one hundred and twenty-five miles, to a place now called Siskiyou county. Here he engaged in placer mining and blacksmithing until 1860, when the first gold-quartz mill was erected there and he became its principal manager.

In 1864 he went to Nevada and remained two years superintending silver mines and mills at Aurora, but returning to Siskiyou county in 1866, he became one-third owner of the Black Bear quartz-mine, which, mainly through his management, became one of the most famous gold-producing mines in the State.

In 1872 the Black Bear mine was sold to a syndicate for a large sum, was incorporated and for some time profitably worked, and then depreciated. Mr. Daggett, however, never lost faith in it, and began purchasing stock, until now (1891) he is owner of five-sixths of it. He has made extensive mining operations, which have opened upon ore bodies of great value and extent, which will again place the mine among the foremost of the State.

Politically Mr. Daggett has ever been a Democrat, and now is a conspicuous figure in the councils of that party. In 1858 he was elected to the Assembly from Klamath and Del Norte counties, and in that session was the youngest member of the House. Being returned the following year, he was made chairman of the Enrolling Committee, and took a prominent part in its proceedings.

In 1880 he was again elected to the Legislature from the counties of Siskiyou and Modoc, and served two sessions, a regular and an extra session.

In 1882 he was elected lieutenant-governor on the Democratic ticket, and presided over the Senate four sessions, — two regular and two extra, — the latter constituting one of the most exciting political periods in the history of the State. The Senate on both occasions was equally divided upon political and corporate legislation, which necessitated the exercise by the presiding officer of a casting vote in numerous instances. Lieutenant-governor Daggett was an able presiding officer. A thorough parliamentarian, his rulings were quickly made and his decisions sustained.

By his prompt methods, his clear conception of measures affecting the interests of the whole people, and his impartial course, in spite of partisan clamor, in averting the enactment of unwise legislation relating to transportation, he exhibited qualifications of superior state-craft; and no scandal has ever been attached to his public acts.

" Daggett " is a station on the Southern Pacific Railroad, named in his honor.

Appointed May 17, 1893, to be superintendent of the United States Mint at San Francisco.

2098. ELISHA JENNINGS [8] (*Priscilla Daggett,*[7] *Samuel,*[6] *Samuel,*[5] *Ebenezer,*[4] *John,*[3] *Thomas,*[2] *John* [1]), born Walworth, N.Y., July 31,

1825; resides Freeport, Mich. (1892); married 1st, May 12, 1849, Hester A. Burroughs; died August 8, 1867; married 2d, May 14, 1868, Susan Whittleton.

Issue :

2927. i.   SARAH L. JENNINGS,[9] born July 30, 1852; died March 14, 1884.
2928. ii. EMMA A. JENNINGS,[9] born October 14, 1854.
2929. iii. MARY E. JENNINGS,[9] born August 25, 1856; died August 8, 1861.
2930. iv. OSCAR E. JENNINGS,[9] born February 12, 1863.

2117. JEREMIAH LUSK[8] (*Sally Daggett,[7] Samuel,[6] Samuel,[5] Ebenezer,[4] John,[3] Thomas,[2] John[1]*), born Walworth, N.Y., January 2, 1834; resides Elmdale, Ionia Co., Mich. (1892); married Lima, Wis., October 30, 1855, Mary E. Smith.

Issue :

2931. i.   ELERY J. LUSK,[9] born Albion, Wis., December 15, 1857; died Lowell, Mich., November 30, 1882.
2932. ii. MARY E. LUSK,[9] born Albion, Wis., April 5, 1861; married Lowell, Mich., July 4, 1880.
2933. iii. SARAH BELL LUSK,[9] born Lowell, Mich., February 2, 1878.

2124. HARRIET DAGGETT[8] (*Moses,[7] Ebenezer,[6] Samuel,[5] Ebenezer,[4] John,[3] Thomas,[2] John[1]*), born Springfield, Mass., October 21, 1829; died Springfield, Mass., July 2, 1870; married Springfield, Mass., August 9, 1853, by Rev. Samuel Osgood, to Henry Grant Shaw, of Springfield, son of William Kingsley and Anna (Barton) Shaw; "armorer;" born Rutland, Vt., March 22, 1830.

Issue :

2934. i.   MARY LOVISA SHAW,[9] born Springfield, Mass., May 20, 1859; died Springfield, Mass., May 4, 1877.
2935. ii. ALBERT HENRY SHAW,[9] born Springfield, Mass., November 5, 1863.
2936. iii. ROBERT GRANT SHAW,[9] born Springfield, Mass., October 8, 1865.

2125. FRANCIS DAGGETT[8] (*Moses,[7] Ebenezer,[6] Samuel,[5] Ebenezer,[4] John,[3] Thomas,[2] John[1]*), born Springfield, Mass., April 16, 1832; "armorer;" resides Springfield, Mass. (1892); married New Britain, Conn., October 27, 1857, by Rev. Henry Glover, to Elizabeth Ann Belden, daughter of Edwin and Mary Ann (Ellis) Belden; born New Britain, Conn., October 2, 1836.

Issue :

2937. i.   WILLIAM HENRY DAGGETT,[9] born Springfield, Mass., October 24, 1858; married Harper's Ferry, W. Va., June 5, 1889. Daisy Pauline Cavalier; she died March 7, 1890; he resides Springfield, Mass. (1892).
2938. ii. CHARLES MARION DAGGETT,[9] born Springfield, Mass., November 5, 1860.
2939. iii. SARAH ELIZABETH DAGGETT,[9] born Springfield, Mass., November 1, 1866; died Leyden, N.Y., September 29, 1868.
2940. iv. GEORGE BELDEN DAGGETT,[9] born Leyden, N.Y., July 18, 1868; died Springfield, Mass., April 17, 1869.

2941. v. James Rogers Daggett,[9] born Springfield, Mass., May 12, 1876;
died Springfield, Mass., July 26, 1876.
2942. vi. Jennie Lee Daggett,[9] born Springfield, Mass., April 15, 1878; died
Springfield, Mass., January 30, 1879.

Artificer Francis Daggett, Company I, Third Regiment, Heavy
Artillery Volunteers. Honorable discharge, September 26, 1865,
given at Gallop's Island.

2127. Albert Daggett [8] (*Moses,*[7] *Ebenezer,*[6] *Samuel,*[5] *Ebenezer,*[4]
John,[3] *Thomas,*[2] *John* [1]), born Springfield, Mass., May 12, 1836.

Corporal Albert Daggett enlisted first with the Providence Marine
Artillery, three months men, in 1861; afterward enlisted with Com-
pany I, Third Heavy Artillery, and was honorably discharged at
Gallop's Island, September 26, 1865.

2128. Sarah Elizabeth Daggett [8] (*Moses,*[7] *Ebenezer,*[6] *Samuel,*[5]
Ebenezer,[4] *John,*[3] *Thomas,*[2] *John* [1]), born Springfield, Mass., March
14, 1838; died Springfield, Mass., July 28, 1864; married Springfield,
Mass., November 23, 1859, by Rev. George DeF. Folsom, to Samuel
Wadsworth Porter, of Springfield, son of George W. and Lucretia H.
(Bodurtha) Porter; "machinist;" born Ware, Mass., August 25,
1834; resides Springfield, Mass. (1878).

Issue:

2943. i. Helen Florence Porter,[9] born Springfield, Mass., July 18, 1862.
2944. ii. Sarah Elizabeth Porter,[9] born Springfield, Mass., July 21, 1864.

2131. Henry Bingham Daggett [8] (*Ebenezer,*[7] *Ebenezer,*[6] *Samuel,*[5]
Ebenezer,[4] *John,*[3] *Thomas,*[2] *John* [1]), born Jordan, N.Y., May 28,
1825; resides Brookfield, Mo. (1892); married Jordan, N.Y., De-
cember 11, 1867, Sarah Stevens, daughter of Thomas and Eliza
(Clark) Stevens; born Jordan, N.Y., June 13, 1836; died Brookfield,
Mo., February 18, 1886.

Issue:

2945. i. Fred Stevens Daggett,[9] born Brookfield, Mo., May 9, 1869; died
San Antonio, Tex., January 18, 1892.
2946. ii. Laura Eliza Daggett,[9] born Brookfield, Mo., November 25, 1871.
2947. iii. Martha Gertrude Daggett,[9] born Brookfield, Mo., September 6,
1873.
2948. iv. Clarence Daggett,[9] born Brookfield, Mo., January 18, 1879.

Henry B. Daggett is of the firm of Daggett, Goldman & Co.,
jobbers of farm implements and hardware, at Brookfield, Mo. (1883),
now called (1892) the "Daggett Hardware Company."

2132. Rebecca Jennett Daggett [8] (*Ebenezer,*[7] *Ebenezer,*[6] *Samuel,*[5] *Ebenezer,*[4] *John,*[3] *Thomas,*[2] *John* [1]), born Jordan, N.Y., October
20, 1827; resides San Mateo, Cal. (1892); married Jordan, N.Y.,

April 11, 1847, by Rev. Mr. Judson, to Lucius Dewitt Morse, son of
Alvah and Amy (Lowell) Morse; born East Poultney, Vt., December 25, 1821.

Issue:

2949. i.   EDITH LEILA MORSE,⁹ born Perth Amboy, N.J., May 28. 1849; died
                  South Amboy, N.J., July 25, 1850.
2950. ii.   FRANK IRVING MORSE,⁹ born South Amboy, N.J., May 2, 1851; died
                  Allenton, Mo., June 1, 1864.
2951. iii.   CHARLES MORGAN MORSE,⁹ born South Amboy, N.J., August 24, 1853.
2952. iv.   MARY EVELINE MORSE,⁹ born Allenton, Mo., October 16, 1861.
2953. v.   JENNETT BODLEY MORSE,⁹ born Kirkwood, Mo., August 11, 1864;
                  died Kirkwood. Mo., August 26, 1864.
2954. vi.   DEWITT MORSE,⁹ born Kirkwood, Mo., January 11, 1867; died Kirk-
                  wood, Mo., January 11, 1867.
2955. vii.   REBECCA MORSE,⁹ born Kirkwood. Mo., February 1, 1868; died
                  Kirkwood, Mo., February 1, 1868.
2956. viii.   LUCIUS DEWITT MORSE,⁹ born Kirkwood. Mo., October 22, 1869.
2957. ix.   WILLIAM HENRY MORSE,⁹ born Kirkwood, Mo., March 25, 1874.

L. D. Morse was surgeon First Regiment Enrolled Missouri Mili-
tia, 1862; commissioner Board of Enrolment, Second District,
Missouri, 1863 to 1865, May 5, Recruiting Service; secretary Missouri
State Board of Agriculture, 1865 to 1869; examiner and appraiser of
Agricultural College lands, State of Missouri, 1870 to 1874; member
of State Constitutional Convention, California, October, 1878, to
March, 1879; horticultural commissioner San Mateo Co., San
Mateo, Cal.

2133. WILLIAM DAGGETT⁸ (*Ebenezer,⁷ Ebenezer,⁶ Samuel,⁵
Ebenezer,⁴ John,³ Thomas,² John¹*), born Jordan, N.Y., March 12,
1830; resides Ottumwa, Iowa (1892); married Seneca Falls, N.Y.,
October 13, 1857, by Rev. J. M. Guion, to Susan Elizabeth Daniels,
daughter of George B. and Mary S. (Giddings) Daniels; born Seneca Falls, N.Y., November 29, 1835.

Issue:

2958. i.   MINNIE ALLINE DAGGETT,⁹ born Seneca Falls. N.Y., December 25,
                  1858.
2959. ii.   MAUD MARY DAGGETT,⁹ born Ottumwa, Iowa, February 17, 1861.
2960. iii.   WALLACE ROSMERANS DAGGETT,⁹ born Ottumwa, Iowa, October 28,
                  1862.
2961. iv.   GEORGE DANIELS DAGGETT,⁹ born Ottumwa, Iowa, July 4, 1865;
                  died Ottumwa. Iowa, May 27, 1868.
2962. v.   AMY MAY DAGGETT,⁹ born Ottumwa, Iowa, January 10, 1868.
2963. vi.   EVA FAY DAGGETT,⁹ born Ottumwa, Iowa, February 10, 1871; mar-
                  ried Ottumwa, Iowa, October 15, 1891, by Rev. J. H. Lloyd, to
                  Otis P. Higlon; resides Ottumwa, Iowa (1892).
2964. vii.   BLANCHE DAGGETT,⁹ born Ottumwa, Iowa, September 11, 1873.
2965. viii.   PHILIP DAGGETT,⁹ born Ottumwa, Iowa, December 25, 1876.

William Daggett went to Ottumwa, Iowa, from his native town, in
1856; engaged in the hardware business in 1857.   February 1, 1873,
he became manager of the Ottumwa Iron Works, firm of Daggett,
Harper & Edgerly.   In the spring of 1875, the oil mills of Daggett

& Harper were established, the factory being built on the C., B. &
Q. R.R. In 1878 their seed-storing capacity was 75,000 bushels,
and their oil tankage and storage capacity, 35,000 gallons. The
flaxseed for the mill has been obtained on the lines of the C., B. & Q.
R.R. and the Central Railroad of Iowa. The oil-cake is nearly all
shipped to Great Britain, in lots of five carloads to each shipment.

Mr. Daggett is vice-president and director of the Iowa National
Bank; president of the Ottumwa Starch Works; vice-president of the
Ottumwa Loan and Building Association, and director of Ottumwa
Water Power Company. Has been alderman of the city two terms.

Mr. and Mrs. Daggett are members of the Episcopal church, Mr.
Daggett being senior warden.

2134. CALVIN FOOTE DAGGETT [8] (*Ebenezer,*[7] *Ebenezer,*[6] *Samuel,*[5]
Ebenezer,[4] *John,*[3] *Thomas,*[2] *John*[1]), born Jordan, N.Y., January 24,
1832; dry-goods salesman; resides 160 Holland street, Syracuse,
N.Y. (1892); married Jordan, N.Y., October 4, 1855, by Rev. John
G. Webster, to Mary Duval, daughter of John B. and Mary (Somers)
Duval; born Port Byron, N.Y., July 7, 1835.

Issue:

2966. i. LURA SARAH DAGGETT,[9] born Jordan, N.Y., September 24, 1857; died
Jordan, N.Y., April 30, 1884.
2967. ii. JOHN DUVAL DAGGETT,[9] born Jordan, N.Y., January 21, 1860.
2968. iii. CAROLINE DAGGETT,[9] born Jordan, N.Y., June 2, 1862; resides 160
Holland street, Syracuse, N.Y. (1892).
2969. iv. HENRY SOMERS DAGGETT,[9] born Jordan, N.Y., November 23, 1867.
2970. v. GEORGE THACHER DAGGETT,[9] born Jordan, N.Y., August 29, 1871.

2140. EDGAR DAGGETT [8] (*Ebenezer,*[7] *Ebenezer,*[6] *Samuel,*[5] *Ebenezer,*[4] *John,*[3] *Thomas,*[2] *John*[1]), born Jordan, N.Y., October 9, 1844;
"dairyman and horseman;" resides Ottumwa, Iowa (1892); mar-
ried Ottumwa, Iowa, March 2, 1865, by Rev. C. F. Coles, to Helen
Hammond, daughter of William H. and Eliza (Baker) Hammond;
born Ottumwa, Iowa, December 30, 1844.

Issue:

2971. i. HENRY DAGGETT,[9] born Ottumwa, Iowa, January 10, 1868.
2972. ii. ERNEST LEE DAGGETT,[9] born Ottumwa, Iowa, September 13, 1870.
2973. iii. FRANK LADD DAGGETT,[9] born Ottumwa, Iowa, June 14, 1874.

2151. CHARLES WELLS [8] (*Sarah Daggett,*[7] *Levi,*[6] *Samuel,*[5] *Ebenezer,*[4] *John,*[3] *Thomas,*[2] *John*[1]), born Palmyra, N.Y., June 19, 1828;
died San Francisco, Cal., May 23, 1891; married New York city,
1851, Louise Burnham, daughter of O. R. Burnham; born New York
city.

Issue:

2974. i. ELLA WELLS,[9] born Syracuse, N.Y., October 21, 1851.

2152. MARY ELIZABETH WELLS [8] (*Sarah Daggett,*[7] *Levi,*[6] *Samuel,*[5] *Ebenezer,*[4] *John,*[3] *Thomas,*[2] *John*[1]), born Palmyra, N.Y., March 27, 1830; died Dansville, N.Y., March 30, 1884; married Aurora, N.Y., September 5, 1854, James H. Welles; born Athens, Pa., May 11, 1819; died New York city, January 8, 1873.

No issue.

2154. OSCAR ASHBEL WELLS [8] (*Sarah Daggett,*[7] *Levi,*[6] *Samuel,*[5] *Ebenezer,*[4] *John,*[3] *Thomas,*[2] *John*[1]), born Palmyra, N.Y., August 21, 1833; resides Brooklyn, N.Y. (1892); married Batavia, N.Y., May 15, 1860, Marion Watrous; born February 26, 1840; died Florida, November, 1883.

Issue :

2975. i. HENRY WELLS,[9] died an infant.

2169. HARRIET KITTREDGE [8] (*Mary Daggett,*[7] *Levi,*[6] *Samuel,*[5] *Ebenezer,*[4] *John,*[3] *Thomas,*[2] *John*[1]), born Red Creek, N.Y., December 12, 1851; resides Mason, Ingham Co., Mich. (1892); married Mason, Mich., December 28, 1875, Charles C. Casterlin.

Issue :

2976. i.   C. GAY CASTERLIN,[9] born Farwell, Mich., February 10, 1877.
2977. ii.   EARL H. CASTERLIN,[9] born Mason, Mich., May 31, 1884.
2978. iii. DON M. CASTERLIN,[9] born Mason, Mich., March 5, 1888.

2174. MARY SUSANNA DAGGETT [8] (*Carlos,*[7] *Ebenezer,*[6] *Ebenezer,*[5] *Ebenezer,*[4] *John,*[3] *Thomas,*[2] *John*[1]), born Northboro', Mass., July 16, 1824; resides Weston, Mass. (1892); married Weston, Mass., February 20, 1847, by Rev. Alanson Rawson, to Nahum Smith, of Weston, son of Samuel and Martha (Stratton) Smith; born Weston, Mass., September 14, 1825.

Issue :

2979. i.   CHARLES EDWARD SMITH,[9] born Weston, Mass., August 25, 1849; resides there (1892).
2980. ii. WALTER LESLIE SMITH,[9] born Weston, Mass., April 8, 1851; resides there (1892).

2181. HARRIET DAGGETT MONSON [8] (*Mary Daggett,*[7] *Abner,*[6] *Thomas,*[5] *Thomas,*[4] *John,*[3] *Thomas,*[2] *John*[1]), born New Haven, Conn., June 4, 1808; died Boston, Mass., January 21, 1887; married Providence, R.I., September 25, 1831, by Rev. Dr. Crocker, to Francis Bullard, son of Jabez and Mary (Hartshorn) Bullard, of Boston; born Boston, Mass., September 22, 1805; died Boston, Mass., June 4, 1887.

Issue :

2981. i.   JAMES BULLARD,[9] born Boston, Mass., September 14, 1832.
2982. ii. ANN DAGGETT BULLARD,[9] born Boston, Mass., November 15, 1833.

2983. iii. MARY MONSON BULLARD,[9] born Boston, Mass., January 7, 1835.
2984. iv. FRANCIS LEWIS BULLARD,[9] born Boston, Mass., November 23, 1836.
2985. v. GEORGE EDWIN BULLARD,[9] born Boston, Mass., March 4, 1839.
2986. vi. CHARLOTTE GUILD BULLARD,[9] born Boston, Mass., October 18, 1842;
resides 77 Mt. Pleasant avenue, Boston, Mass. (1893).
2987. vii. ALFRED MONSON BULLARD,[9] born Boston, Mass., May 21, 1845.

2182.   GEORGE EDWIN MONSON[8] (*Mary Daggett,*[7] *Abner,*[6] *Thomas,*[5] *Thomas,*[4] *John,*[3] *Thomas,*[2] *John*[1]), born New Haven, Conn., November 23, 1811; died July 6, 1874; married Providence, R.I., February 17, 1834, Angeline Taylor.

Issue :

2988. i. MARY ANN MONSON,[9] born Providence, R.I., November 26, 1834;
resides there.
2989. ii. CHARLES HENRY MONSON,[9] born Providence, R.I., June 7, 1836;
died.
2990. iii. JANE MONSON,[9] born Providence, R.I., May 4, 1838; married William Henrys; she died July 20, 1872.
2991. iv. WILLIAM ALLEN MONSON,[9] born Providence, R.I., July 1, 1840;
resides there.
2992. v. CHARLOTTE MONSON,[9] born Providence, R.I., June 22, 1842; resides
there.
2993. vi. THOMAS MONSON,[9] born Providence, R.I., December 10, 1845; died
an infant.
2994. vii. ABNER MONSON,[9] born Providence, R.I., August 22, 1849; died
August 31, 1856.

2184.   Dr. DAVID LEWIS DAGGETT[8] (*Leonard A.,*[7] *David,*[6] *Thomas,*[5] *Thomas,*[4] *John,*[3] *Thomas,*[2] *John*[1]), born New Haven, Conn., June 24, 1820; resides 60 Wall street, New Haven, Conn. (1892); married Wilmington, Del., June 1, 1854, Margaret Donaldson Gibbons, daughter of William and Rebecca (Donaldson) Gibbons, of Wilmington, Del.; born Wilmington, Del., July 24, 1821; died New Haven, Conn., August 11, 1865.

Issue :

2995. i. DAVID DAGGETT,[9] born New Haven, Conn., April 3, 1858; resides at
home (1890).
2996. ii. WILLIAM GIBBONS DAGGETT,[9] born New Haven, Conn., January 8,
1860; resides 236 Crown street, New Haven, Conn. (1890.)
2997. iii. LEONARD MAYHEW DAGGETT,[9] born New Haven, Conn., November 23,
1863; resides at home (1890).

2185.   SUSAN DWIGHT DAGGETT[8] (*Leonard A.,*[7] *David,*[6] *Thomas,*[5] *Thomas,*[4] *John,*[3] *Thomas,*[2] *John*[1]), born New Haven, Conn., September 5, 1822; died New York city, February 25, 1857; married New Haven, Conn., October 21, 1851, Amos Trowbridge Dwight. son of Jabez and Grace (Trowbridge) Dwight; born New Haven, Conn., July 18, 1807; died New York city, February, 1881.

Issue :

2998. 1. JEANNETTE ATWATER DWIGHT,[9] born New York city, October 20, 1852.

Amos Trowbridge Dwight was a wholesale clothing-merchant in New Orleans, La., for several years (1833–1850), and in 1850 established himself in New York, where he was a cotton broker.

Mrs. Dwight was a lady of strong sense, of a genial, generous disposition, and of decided piety.

2189. ELLSWORTH DAGGETT [8] (*Oliver E.,*[7] *David,*[6] *Thomas,*[5] *Thomas,*[4] *John,*[3] *Thomas,*[2] *John*[1]), born Canandaigua, N.Y., May 24, 1845; resides Salt Lake City, Utah (1892); married Salt Lake City, Utah, June 24, 1874, June Knight Spencer, daughter of Orson and Martha (Knight) Spencer, of Salt Lake City, Utah; born Salt Lake City, Utah, June 28, 1855.

Issue:

2999. i. OLIVER ELLSWORTH DAGGETT,[9] born Berlin, Ger., March 9, 1875; died Salt Lake City, Utah, November 23, 1878.
3000. ii. WOODWARD DAGGETT,[9] born Salt Lake City, Utah, August 26, 1879; died Salt Lake City, Utah, December 10, 1879.

2193. HARRIET C. HARWOOD [8] (*Julia A. Daggett,*[7] *Dexter,*[6] *Thomas,*[5] *Thomas,*[4] *John,*[3] *Thomas,*[2] *John*[1]), born Providence, R.I., April 7, 1834; resides 223 Auburn avenue, Mt. Auburn, Cincinnati, Ohio (1892); married Cincinnati, Ohio, July 25, 1854, Edward Y. Robbins.

Issue:

3001. i. EDWARD H. ROBBINS,[9] born Cincinnati, Ohio, May 5, 1855; died Cincinnati, Ohio, November 6, 1860.
3002. ii. SARAH JULIA ROBBINS,[9] born Cincinnati, Ohio, January 3, 1857; married Cincinnati, Ohio, October 2, 1877; died Cincinnati, Ohio, March 30, 1881.
3003. iii. NELLIE S. ROBBINS,[9] born Cincinnati, Ohio, August 2, 1859.
3004. iv. HARWOOD ROBBINS,[9] born Cincinnati, Ohio, January 18, 1868; married May 6, 1891.

2196. ADALINE C. HARWOOD [8] (*Julia A. Daggett,*[7] *Dexter,*[6] *Thomas,*[5] *Thomas,*[4] *John,*[3] *Thomas,*[2] *John*[1]), born Cincinnati, Ohio, November 5, 1840; resides Glendale, Ohio (1891); married Cincinnati, Ohio, February 14, 1865, Maynard French.

Issue:

3005. i. WILLIAM T. FRENCH,[9] born Cincinnati, Ohio, November 18, 1865; married November 18, 1886.
3006. ii. EDWARD H. FRENCH,[9] born Cincinnati, Ohio, April 25, 1868.
3007. iii. ADDIE D. FRENCH,[9] born Cincinnati, Ohio, September 30, 1869.
3008. iv. EDITH B. FRENCH,[9] born Cincinnati, Ohio, December 30, 1872.
3009. v. MAYNARD FRENCH,[9] born Glendale, Ohio, March 4, 1878.
3010. vi. WALLACE P. FRENCH,[9] born Glendale, Ohio, March 13, 1882.

2198. GERTRUDE HARWOOD [8] (*Julia A. Daggett,*[7] *Dexter,*[6] *Thomas,*[5] *Thomas,*[4] *John,*[3] *Thomas,*[2] *John*[1]), born Cincinnati, Ohio, June 7,

1845; resides 712 Prospect street, Cleveland, Ohio (1892); married Cincinnati, Ohio, June 7, 1864, Dr. Oliver F. Gordon.

Issue:

3011. i. FRANK S. GORDON,[9] born Cincinnati, Ohio, May 27, 1865; died Cincinnati, Ohio, July 2, 1865.
3012. ii. CLARA G. GORDON,[9] born Cincinnati, Ohio, September 19, 1866.
3013. iii. EDWARD O. GORDON,[9] born Cincinnati, Ohio, October 29, 1870.
3014. iv. GEORGE GORDON.[9]

2199. CORDELIA DAGGETT[8] (*Isaac,*[7] *Timothy,*[6] *Brotherton,*[5] *Brotherton,*[4] *Joshua,*[3] *Thomas,*[2] *John*[1]), born 1829; married Fairhaven, Mass., May 2, 1849, by Rev. Jacob Roberts, to Alexander F. Gifford, son of Bethuel and Susan Gifford; "clerk;" born 1824.

2200. CATHERINE F. DAGGETT[8] (*Isaac,*[7] *Timothy,*[6] *Brotherton,*[5] *Brotherton,*[4] *Joshua,*[3] *Thomas,*[2] *John*[1]), born Edgartown, Mass., 1834; married Roxbury, Mass., July 7, 1863, by Rev. Henry M. King, to Charles Thacher, son of William and Hannah Thacher; "trader;" born Dartmouth, Mass., 1825.

2201. HELEN JOSEPHINE DAGGETT[8] (*Isaac,*[7] *Timothy,*[6] *Brotherton,*[5] *Brotherton,*[4] *Joshua,*[3] *Thomas,*[2] *John*[1]), born Fairhaven, Mass., October 11, 1843; married Roxbury, Mass., October 15, 1866, by Rev. Henry M. King, to Stephen H. Nichols, of Waverly, Ill., son of Seth and Sally Nichols; born Weathersfield, Vt., 1827; "merchant."

2208. ARUNAH WESTON DAGGETT[8] (*Brotherton,*[7] *Samuel,*[6] *Thomas,*[5] *Brotherton,*[4] *Joshua,*[3] *Thomas,*[2] *John*[1]), born Union, Me., February 16, 1814; "lumberman;" died Bangor, Me., May 13, 1876; married Bangor, Me., February 9, 1848, by Rev. H. R. Nye, to Rachel Smellen Whitney, daughter of Thomas and Susan Randall (Cowing) Whitney; born Orono, Me., March 5, 1828; died Bangor, Me., August 23, 1878.

Issue:

3015. i. ADA WHITNEY DAGGETT,[9] born Bangor, Me., November, 1849; died Bangor, Me., November, 1850.
3016. ii. JAMES WHITNEY DAGGETT,[9] born Bangor, Me., December, 1854; died Bangor, Me., January, 1855.
3017. iii. CORA FRANCES DAGGETT,[9] born Bangor, Me., March 25, 1856; married Bangor, Me., June 15, 1876, by Rev. Arthur M. Knapp, to George Herbert Jackson, son of Joseph Pierce and Mary Lindsay (Skinner) Jackson; born Bangor, Me., December 18, 1854; no issue; resides 65 Broadway, Bangor, Me. (1892).
3018. iv. BELLE WHITNEY DAGGETT,[9] born Bangor, Me., August, 1869; married Bangor, Me., September 20, 1892, Harry Atwood Chapman; resides "Bangor House," Bangor, Me. (1892).

2213. GEORGE BARTLETT DAGGETT[8] (*Brotherton,*[7] *Samuel,*[6] *Thomas,*[5] *Brotherton,*[4] *Joshua,*[3] *Thomas,*[2] *John*[1]), born Union, Me.,

August 23, 1824; died Rockland, Me., October 30, 1887; married Union, Me., November 5, 1847, Mary Jane Burns, daughter of John Burns (originally Bernheimer); born Waldoboro', Me., May 7, 1825; died Rockland, Me., October 10, 1879.

Issue:

3019. i. REUBEN SHERER DAGGETT,[9] born Union, Me., February 1, 1849; died Union, Me., February 16, 1850.
3020. ii. ORINDA SHERER DAGGETT,[9] born Union, Me., November 1, 1850.
3021. iii. LUCINDA DAGGETT,[9] born Union, Me., April 7, 1853; died Union, Me., April, 1859.
3022. iv. GEORGE LORING DAGGETT,[9] born Rockland, Me., September 9, 1855.
3023. v. ELLA DAGGETT,[9] born Rockland, Me., July 2, 1857.
3024. vi. MARY E. DAGGETT,[9] born Rockland, Me., December 1, 1859; died Rockland, Me., September 26, 1864.
3025. vii. MINNIE DAGGETT,[9] born Rockland, Me., October 26, 1861; died Rockland, Me., October 14, 1864.
3026. viii. WILLIAM WESTON DAGGETT,[9] born Rockland, Me., July 20, 1865; resides Rockland, Me. (1892).
3027. ix. MARSHALL MASON DAGGETT,[9] born Rockland, Me., June 27, 1868; married Rockland, Me., December, 1889, Kate Irish, daughter of Fred and Etta (Hart) Irish; resides Rockland, Me. (1892).

2217. JABEZ DAGGETT [8] (*James,*[7] *Samuel,*[6] *Thomas,*[5] *Brotherton,*[4] *Joshua,*[3] *Thomas,*[2] *John*[1]), born Maine, September 9, 1805; died Stockton, Cal., July 15, 1865; married Hodgdon, Me., January, 1830, Emeline Russell, daughter of Jacob and Mercy (Meeker) Russell; born New York city, December 15, 1811; resides Oakland, Cal. (1892).

Issue:

3028. i. EGBERT COFFIN DAGGETT,[9] born Hodgdon, Me., March 28, 1831; died Hodgdon, Me., October 31, 1849.
3029. ii. ISAAC MEEKER DAGGETT,[9] born Hodgdon, Me., June 25, 1833.
3030. iii. ANGELINE MERCY DAGGETT,[9] born Hodgdon, Me., August 18, 1835; died September 29, 1850.
3031. iv. JOHN RANDOLPH DAGGETT,[9] born Hodgdon, Me., March 20, 1838; died Hodgdon, Me., July 28, 1841.
3032. v. JOHN RANDOLPH DAGGETT,[9] born Hodgdon, Me., April 20, 1841; "unmarried;" resides San Francisco, Cal. (1892).
3033. vi. ABBIE JANE DAGGETT,[9] born Hodgdon, Me., September 20, 1843.
3034. vii. TABER WATSON DAGGETT,[9] born Hodgdon, Me., December 6, 1847; married San Francisco, Cal., October 24, 1882, by Rev. Dr. Makencie, to Fannie E. Glasspool, daughter of Thomas and Elizabeth (Phillips) Glasspool; born England, June 29, 1861; no issue (1892); "farmer;" resides Encinitos, Cal. (1892).

2219. WATERMAN DAGGETT [8] (*James,*[7] *Samuel,*[6] *Thomas,*[5] *Brotherton,*[4] *Joshua,*[3] *Thomas,*[2] *John*[1]), born Maine, September 8, 1809; died Hodgdon, Me., March 7, 1880; married Margaret ——.

Issue:

3035. i. BENJAMIN F. DAGGETT,[9] born Hodgdon, Me., 1837; married Boston, Mass., December 23, 1865, by Rev. Phineas Stowe, to Laura F. Rowe, daughter of Samuel C. and Dorothea C. Rowe; born Haverhill, Mass., 1845; address, Daggett Building, Haverhill, Mass. (1892).

2220. HIRAM DAGGETT[8] (*James,[7] Samuel,[6] Thomas,[5] Brotherton,[4] Joshua,[3] Thomas,[2] John[1]*), born Union, Me., August 16, 1811; "ship carpenter and joiner;" died Minneapolis, Minn., December 13, 1881; married 1st, New Castle, Me., December 17, 1840, Sarah Kinsman Little, daughter of Henry and Mary (Kinsman) Little; born New Castle, Me., August 29, 1815; died Canton, Mass., March 24, 1848; married 2d, Bedford, Ohio, March 2, 1867, Calista M. Harvey, daughter of James Harvey; born Hudson, Ohio, August 10, 1840; died Fairhaven, Mass., August 19, 1878.

Issue:

3036. i. CHARLES HENRY DAGGETT,[9] born Canton, Mass., September 19, 1847.
3037. ii. SARAH KINSMAN DAGGETT,[9] born Minneapolis, Minn., June 2, 1870.

2221. ROBERT DAGGETT[8] (*James,[7] Samuel,[6] Thomas,[5] Brotherton,[4] Joshua,[3] Thomas,[2] John[1]*), born May 15, 1813; resides Jackson Brook, Me. (1884); married Sarah ——.

Issue:

3038. i. THOMAS J. DAGGETT,[9] born Hodgdon, Me., 1841.

2223. EBENEZER DAGGETT[8] (*James,[7] Samuel,[6] Thomas,[5] Brotherton,[4] Joshua,[3] Thomas,[2] John[1]*), born Washington, Me., November 20, 1817; "trader;" died Haverhill, Mass., February 19, 1864; married Canton, Mass., October 22, 1850, by Rev. Benjamin Huntoon, to Betsey Tucker, daughter of Samuel and Polly (Upham) Tucker; born Canton, Mass., March 26, 1813; died Haverhill, Mass., September 12, 1888.

Issue:

3039. i. LOLA CAROLINE DAGGETT,[9] born Haverhill, Mass., January 3, 1852.

2224. BENJAMIN FRANKLIN DAGGETT[8] (*James,[7] Samuel,[6] Thomas,[5] Brotherton,[4] Joshua,[3] Thomas,[2] John[1]*), born Wiscasset, Me., September 30, 1820; resides Bowdle, South Dakota (1892); married Limerick, Me., April, 1848, Sylvina Nickerson, daughter of Ephraim and Dorinda Nickerson; born Augusta, Me., 1822.

Issue:

3040. i. ADDIE DAGGETT,[9] born Hodgdon, Me., April, 1852; died Elk River, Minn., August, 1854.
3041. ii. FRED DAGGETT,[9] born Little Falls, Minn., August 13, 1855; resides Bowdle, South Dakota (1892).
3042. iii. OSCAR DAGGETT,[9] born Little Falls, Minn., February 28, 1857; resides Bowdle, South Dakota (1892).
3043. iv. EPHRAIM DAGGETT,[9] born Little Falls, Minn., January 26, 1859; resides Bowdle, South Dakota (1892).
3044. v. ULYSSES L. DAGGETT,[9] born Little Falls, Minn., 1862; resides Bowdle, South Dakota (1892).

2235. ROBERT L. DAGGETT[8] (*Jonathan,[7] Samuel,[6] Thomas,[5] Brotherton,[4] Joshua,[3] Thomas,[2] John[1]*), born Union, Me., March 12, 1820;

" farmer; " resides Morrill, Me. (1892) ; married Washington, Me., January 17, 1840, Adeline Whitehouse, daughter of Daniel and Nancy (Cunningham) Whitehouse; born New Castle, Me., July 14, 1820.

Issue :

3045. i. ELIZA J. DAGGETT,[9] born October 28, 1840.
3046. ii. EDGAR D. DAGGETT,[9] born July 12, 1845 ; died young.
3047. iii. ELLEN E. DAGGETT,[9] born August 27, 1846 ; died young.
3048. iv. BRIGGS C. DAGGETT,[9] born November 27, 1849.

2237. ARAMANDA DAGGETT[8] (*Jonathan,*[7] *Samuel,*[6] *Thomas,*[5] *Brotherton,*[4] *Joshua,*[3] *Thomas,*[2] *John*[1]), born Washington, Me., May 22, 1822; "ship carpenter; " resides Rockland, Me. (1865); married 1st, Washington, Me., September 6, 1848, by Elder Whitehouse, to Arletta Whitehouse, daughter of Daniel and Nancy (Cunningham) Whitehouse; born Jefferson, Me., May 6, 1824; died Rockland, Me., April 23, 1864; married 2d, Rockland, Me., February 22, 1865, by Elder Joseph Keller, to Jane Elizabeth Arff, daughter of Thomas and Syrena (Ludwig) Wagner; born Waldoboro', Me., February 22, 1831; died Rockland, Me., May 7, 1888.

Issue :

3049. i. GEORGE RILEY DAGGETT,[9] born Washington, Me., January 18, 1850 ; died Rockland, Me., November 24, 1884.
3050. ii. WILLARD DEERING DAGGETT,[9] born Morrill, Me., February 18, 1852 ; married Barbara Gness, October 20, 1880, in Scotland ; now (1886) in Australia; no issue (1892).
3051. iii. —— DAGGETT,[9] died.
3052. iv. —— DAGGETT,[9] died.
3053. v. —— DAGGETT,[9] died.

2239. AMELIA DAGGETT[8] (*William,*[7] *Samuel,*[6] *Thomas,*[5] *Brotherton,*[4] *Joshua,*[3] *Thomas,*[2] *John*[1]), born Union, Me., February 26, 1814 ; resides Bremen, Me. (1892) ; married 1st, Bremen, Me., March 28, 1852, by Rev. David Cushman, to Edward Eisenhauer, of Bremen, Me., son of Nicholas and Catherine (Morash) Eisenhauer; born Lunenburg, N.S., May 6, 1799 ; died Bremen, Me., January 13, 1875 ; married 2d, Bremen, Me., June 28, 1885, by Rev. W. W. Ogier, to Isaac Burns, of Waldoboro', Me., son of Cornelius and Catherine (Gross) Burns; born Waldoboro', Me., May 28, 1815.

Issue :

3054. i. CHARLES EDWARD EISENHAUER,[9] born Bremen, Me., June 28, 1855 ; died Bremen, Me., June 4, 1873.

2241. JANE TOBEY DAGGETT[8] (*William,*[7] *Samuel,*[6] *Thomas,*[5] *Brotherton,*[4] *Joshua,*[3] *Thomas,*[2] *John*[1]), born Union, Me., October 9, 1818; died Searsmont, Me., May 24, 1868; married Searsmont, Me., June 24, 1843, Charles Crawford, of Searsmont, Me., son of

James Crawford; born Warren, Me., May 6, 1800; died Surry, Me., January 19, 1884.

Issue:

3055. i. EDWIN WOODHULL CRAWFORD,[9] born Searsmont, Me., March 16, 1845.
3056. ii. JAMES WESTON CRAWFORD,[9] born Searsmont, Me., September 19, 1846; unmarried; resides Searsmont, Me. (1892).
3057. iii. ARTHUR BOHAN CRAWFORD,[9] born Searsmont, Me., November 24, 1847; married Natick, Mass., Abbie Moody; no issue; resides Natick, Mass. (1892).
3058. iv. WILLIAM HARTWELL CRAWFORD,[9] born Searsmont, Me., December 4, 1850.
3059. v. HORATIO HIRAM CRAWFORD,[9] born Searsmont, Me., August 23, 1852; died Boston, Mass., January 15, 1889.
3060. vi. SARAH MEHITABLE CRAWFORD,[9] born Searsmont, Me., August 23, 1854; married Boston, Mass., January 1, 1878, Rev. Caleb Irvin Mills, son of Bailey T. Mills; he pastor M.E. church, Santa Fé, N.M. (1892); she died Boston, Mass., December 23, 1878.

2242. JOSHUA DAGGETT[8] (*William,*[7] *Samuel,*[6] *Thomas,*[5] *Brotherton,*[4] *Joshua,*[3] *Thomas,*[2] *John*[1]), born Union, Me., September 16, 1820; resides Cushing, Me. (1892); married Friendship, Me., May 27, 1866, by Rev. F. L. Farnham, to Ann Church, widow, and daughter of John and Martha (Hutchings) Adams; born Falmouth, Me., July 12, 1829.

Issue:

3061. i. MARGERY ANN DAGGETT,[9] born Friendship, Me., January 28, 1868.

Joshua Daggett, farmer, when residing in Friendship, Me., held the office of second selectman, and was also first assessor, but declined reëlection. He had two mail contracts of four years each, after which he was instrumental in getting a post-office established in East Friendship, of which he was made post-master, but resigned because of removal to Cushing, Me. March 29, 1865, he was drafted into the army. Reported at Augusta, and sent forward to Gallop's island, Boston harbor. Was discharged at the close of the war.

2244. LUCY WESTON DAGGETT[8] (*William,*[7] *Samuel,*[6] *Thomas,*[5] *Brotherton,*[4] *Joshua,*[3] *Thomas,*[2] *John*[1]), born Union, Me., January 11, 1825; resides Cushing, Me. (1892); married Bremen, Me., September 16, 1863, Rev. Frederick Lewis Farnham, son of Noah and Myriam (Brookins) Farnham; born Jefferson, Me., August 1, 1814.

No issue.

2246. Capt. HIRAM DAGGETT[8] (*William,*[7] *Samuel,*[6] *Thomas,*[5] *Brotherton,*[4] *Joshua,*[3] *Thomas,*[2] *John*[1]), born Belmont, Me., November 30, 1828; "mariner;" resides Cottage City, Mass. (1892); married Edgartown, Mass., May 4, 1856, by Rev. Wm. H. Sturtevant, to Charlotte Warren Nye, daughter of Warren Weston and Charlotte (Norton) Nye; born Edgartown, Mass., July 29, 1833.

Issue:

3062. i. NETTIE LOUISE DAGGETT,[9] born North Bridgewater, Mass., October 26, 1861; died Edgartown, Mass., August 4, 1878.

2247. MARGERY WELLS DAGGETT [8] (*William*,[7] *Samuel*,[6] *Thomas*,[5] *Brotherton*,[4] *Joshua*,[3] *Thomas*.[2] *John* [1]), born Belmont, Me., June 22, 1830; died Portland, Me., January 16, 1868; married Saco, Me., June 5, 1856, Benjamin W. Stover; resides Portland, Me. (1892).

Issue:

3063. i. SYLVIA WESTON STOVER,[9] married Frank E. Meserve; resides Portland, Me. (1886).

2254. THURSTON DAGGETT [8] (*Ebenezer*,[7] *Samuel*,[6] *Thomas*,[5] *Brotherton*,[4] *Joshua*,[3] *Thomas*,[2] *John* [1]), born Union, Me., November 28, 1820; died St. George, Me., April 14, 1886; married Union, Me., 1842, Rachel Mitchell, daughter of Andros and Rachel (Pierson) Mitchell; born Union, Me., October 17, 1815; died St. George, Me., June 17, 1883.

Issue:

3064. i. ALONZO DAGGETT,[9] born about 1844 (soldier Twenty-eighth Maine Regiment); resides Rockland, Me. (1892).
3065. ii. GEORGE M. DAGGETT,[9] born Union, Me., March 29, 1845; resides Rockland, Me. (1892).
3066. iii. RACHEL DAGGETT,[9] born Union, Me., March 8, 1847.
3067. iv. EDWIN W. DAGGETT,[9] born St. George, Me., August 27, 1851.
3068. v. SARAH F. DAGGETT,[9] born St. George, Me., August 6, 1853.

Mr. Daggett served in the Civil War in the Twenty-eighth Maine Regiment, nine months' men; was the inventor and proprietor of "Daggett's Bone and Nerve Liniment."

2267. ANGELIA DAGGETT [8] (*Ebenezer*,[7] *Samuel*,[6] *Thomas*,[5] *Brotherton*,[4] *Joshua*,[3] *Thomas*,[2] *John* [1]), born Rockland, Me., 1847; married Lawrence, Mass., July 11, 1867, by Rev. J. J. Twiss, to David P. Stinehour, of Lawrence, son of David P. and Eliza Stinehour; "carpenter;" born Highgate, Vt., 1846.

2271. FREDERIC K. DAGGETT [8] (*Edmund*,[7] *Thomas*,[6] *Thomas*,[5] *Brotherton*,[4] *Joshua*,[3] *Thomas*,[2] *John* [1]), born Union, Me., August 13, 1819; "valise and trunk maker;" died Everett, Mass., February 1, 1879; married 1st, New York city, October 3, 1845, Helen Lauretta Bachelder, daughter of Capt. Lewis and Hannah (Morse) Bachelder; born May 16, 1826; married 2d, Lynn, Mass., August 1, 1858, by Parsons Cooke, to Elizabeth Potter, daughter of Joseph and Ellen

Potter; born Athens, Me., 1832; resides 839 Boylston street, Boston, Mass. (1893).

Issue:

3069. i. FREDERIC LA FORREST DAGGETT,[9] born January 12, 1847; died April 5, 1849.
3070. ii. Son —— DAGGETT,[9] born November, 1850.
3071. iii. HERBERT LINWOOD DAGGETT,[9] born Malden, Mass., July 20, 1861; died Malden, Mass., August 21, 1861.
3072. iv. Son —— DAGGETT, born Malden, Mass., November 10, 1864.
3073. v. HERBERT F. DAGGETT,[9] born Malden, Mass., July 22, 1867; resides 839 Boylston street, Boston, Mass. (1893).

2283. CAROLINE F. DAGGETT[8] (*Edmund,*[7] *Thomas,*[6] *Thomas,*[5] *Brotherton,*[4] *Joshua,*[3] *Thomas,*[2] *John*[1]), born Hope, Me., 1842; married Malden, Mass., March 25, 1869, by Rev. Samuel E. Herrick, to Nathan B. Smith, son of John B. and Sarah Smith; "milkman;" born Malden, Mass., 1838.

2284. WILLIAM HARRIMAN KUHN[8] (*Ruth Daggett,*[7] *Aaron,*[6] *Thomas,*[5] *Brotherton,*[4] *Joshua,*[3] *Thomas,*[2] *John*[1]), married Julia Augusta Groton.

Issue:

3074. i. ANGELINA KUHN,[9] born 1845.
3075. ii. WILLIAM FRANKLIN KUHN,[9] born July, 1847.

2290. ANGELICA FRANCES CLOUSE[8] (*Olive Daggett,*[7] *Aaron,*[6] *Thomas,*[5] *Brotherton,*[4] *Joshua,*[3] *Thomas,*[2] *John*[1]), born Maine, September 2, 1824; resides Worcester, Mass. (1851); married April 13, 1846, Gardner Light, of Waldoboro', Me.

Issue:

3076. i. MARY FRANCES LIGHT,[9] born September 10, 1848.

2331. TIMOTHY DAGGETT[8] (*Tristram,*[7] *Tristram,*[6] *Elijah,*[5] *Brotherton,*[4] *Joshua,*[3] *Thomas,*[2] *John*[1]), born Industry, Me., March 20, 1824; "farmer;" died Dexter, Me., August 10, 1892; married Dexter, Me., November 27, 1851, Mary Jane Fletcher, daughter of Charles and Mary (Smith) Fletcher; born Dexter, Me., September 4, 1827.

Issue:

3077. i. EMELINE ADDIE DAGGETT," born Dexter, Me., September 4, 1852; married Sangerville, Me., September 6, 1879, Wilber Colby Gerry, son of Benjamin Stephens and Miranda (Rowe) Gerry; born Dover. Me., May 30, 1854; "farmer;" resides Dexter, Me. (1892).
3078. ii. CHARLES DAGGETT,[9] born Dexter, Me., June 18, 1854; "jeweller;" resides Lowell, Mass. (1892).
3079. iii. ANN LORETTA DAGGETT,[9] born Dexter, Me., February 28, 1859; married Dexter, Me., August 27, 1886, William Albert Harling, son of Jonas and Elizabeth (Heigh) Harling; born Meltham, Yorkshire, Eng., September 3, 1853; resides Garland, Me. (1892).

3080. iv. NATHAN DAGGETT,[9] born Dexter, Me., June 2, 1860; married Dexter, Me., June 20, 1892, Idella May True, daughter of George Bradbury and Caroline Frances (Maxim) True; born Dexter, Me., January 7, 1868; "boots and shoes;" resides Dexter, Me. (1892).
3081. v. MARY ELIZABETH DAGGETT,[9] born Dexter, Me., March 20, 1861; resides Lowell, Mass. (1892).
3082. vi. AMANDA DAGGETT,[9] born Dexter, Me., July 12, 1866; resides Dexter, Me. (1892).

2332. NATHAN LUCE DAGGETT[8] (*Tristram,*[7] *Tristram,*[6] *Elijah,*[5] *Brotherton,*[4] *Joshua,*[3] *Thomas,*[2] *John*[1]), born Industry, Me., April 18, 1825; "bootmaker;" died West Boylston, Mass., December 6, 1887; married 1st, West Boylston, Mass., July 25, 1847, by Rev. L. Tracy, to Eunice H. Perry, daughter of James and Harriet (Osgood) Perry; born Boylston, Mass., May 29, 1829; died West Boylston, Mass., December 27, 1854; married 2d, West Boylston, Mass., November 1, 1855, Harriet Frances Pierce; born West Boylston, Mass.; resides West Boylston, Mass. (1892).

Issue :

3083. i. NATHAN WALDO DAGGETT,[9] born West Boylston, Mass., March 22, 1849; died West Boylston, Mass., December 31, 1855.
3084. ii. JONAS TRISTRAM DAGGETT,[9] born Shrewsbury, Mass., July 16, 1850; died West Boylston, Mass., December 22, 1855.
3085. iii. EUNICE HELEN DAGGETT,[9] born West Boylston, Mass., January 13, 1852; died West Boylston, Mass., January 14, 1856.
3086. iv. MARTHA ANN DAGGETT,[9] born West Boylston, Mass., August 12, 1853; died West Boylston, Mass., November 16, 1853.

2335. SUSAN JANE DAGGETT[8] (*Tristram,*[7] *Tristram,*[6] *Elijah,*[5] *Brotherton,*[4] *Joshua,*[3] *Thomas,*[2] *John*[1]), born Dexter, Me., 1830; died Dexter, Me., December 31, 1861; married James Brown, son of Samuel and —— (Luce) Brown.

Issue :

3087. i. NETTIE BROWN,[9] born Dexter, Me., 1848; died Dexter, Me., September, 1858; also several others, who died in infancy.

2337. MARY LUCE DAGGETT[8] (*Timothy,*[7] *Tristram,*[6] *Elijah,*[5] *Brotherton,*[4] *Joshua,*[3] *Thomas,*[2] *John*[1]), born New Vineyard, Me., August 8, 1839; resides Dexter, Me. (1893); married Dexter, Me., June 14, 1862, Edward Freeman Libby, son of Joseph Weeks and Mary (Jordan) Libby; "farmer;" born Dexter, Me., April 3, 1832. No issue.

2338. TRISTRAM DAGGETT[8] (*Timothy,*[7] *Tristram,*[6] *Elijah,*[5] *Brotherton,*[4] *Joshua,*[3] *Thomas,*[2] *John*[1]), born New Vineyard, Me., January 2, 1841; died Ripley, Me., January 30, 1879; married 1st, Ripley, Me., September, 1866, Hannah Woodcock, daughter of Theodore and Deborah (Bessy) Woodcock; born 1847; died Ripley, Me., August 17, 1871; married 2d, Ripley, Me., May 24, 1872, Mrs. Phebie Cummings Libby, daughter of Nehemiah and Polly (Drake) Leavitt; now (1892) Mrs. Phebie C. Eldridge, Pittsfield, Me.

Issue:

3088. i.   TRISTRAM LINWOOD DAGGETT,[9] born Ripley, Me., March 28, 1869; resides Guilford, Me. (1892).
3089. ii. CHARLES DELBERT DAGGETT,[9] born Ripley, Me., July 13, 1873; resides Cambridge, Me. (1892).
3090. iii. FRED DAGGETT,[9] born Ripley, Me., July 10, 1875; died Ripley, Me., October 30, 1876.
3091. iv. FRED EUGENE DAGGETT,[9] born Ripley, Me., July 31, 1877; resides Pittsfield, Me. (1892).

Tristram Daggett enlisted in Third Battery, First Regiment Artillery, December 11, 1861. December 24, 1863, he reënlisted for the remainder of the war. Mustered out June 17, 1865.

The following spring he purchased a farm and settled in Ripley, where the remainder of his life was spent.

2340. ASA MERRY DAGGETT[8] (*Timothy,*[7] *Tristram,*[6] *Elijah,*[5] *Brotherton,*[4] *Joshua,*[3] *Thomas,*[2] *John*[1]), born Parkman, Me., July 22, 1845; died West New Portland, Me., May 19, 1889; married New Portland, Me., December 18, 1870, Rhoda Merry Williams, daughter of Henry and Catharine (Merry) Williams; born East New Portland, Me., 1853; resides West New Portland, Me. (1892).

Issue:

3092. i.   CARROLL LINWOOD DAGGETT,[9] born New Portland, Me., April 30, 1872; resides West New Portland, Me. (1892).
3093. ii. ELSIE MAE DAGGETT,[9] born New Portland, Me., November 15, 1874; died West New Portland, Me., April 29, 1889.
3094. iii. ARTHUR EARL DAGGETT,[9] born New Portland, Me., April 23, 1882.
3095. iv. LENA ALICE DAGGETT,[9] born West New Portland, Me., January 26, 1887.

Mr. Daggett, near the close of the war, enlisted at Bangor, as a substitute, and was a member of the Twelfth Company Unassigned Infantry.

2341. CATHARINE AMANDA DAGGETT[8] (*Timothy,*[7] *Tristram,*[6] *Elijah,*[5] *Brotherton,*[4] *Joshua,*[3] *Thomas,*[2] *John*[1]), born Parkman, Me., May 31, 1848; died Ripley, Me., March 24, 1877; married Guilford, Me., January 8, 1871, Henry True Woodcock, son of Theodore and Deborah (Bessy) Woodcock; born Winthrop, Me., October 6, 1840; resides Ripley, Me. (1892).

Issue:

3096. i.   MINNIE MAY WOODCOCK,[9] born Ripley, Me., January 24, 1872; resides Norway, Me. (1892).

2363. EDMUND BUXTON ALFORD[8] (*Nancy A. Daggett,*[7] *Matthew,*[6] *Elijah,*[5] *Brotherton,*[4] *Joshua,*[3] *Thomas,*[2] *John*[1]), born Warren, Me., February 2, 1821; died Boston, Mass., November, 1887; married

Waldoboro', Me., June 24, 1850, Sarah Russell, daughter of Thomas and Sarah (Engley) Russell; born Waldoboro', Me.

Issue:

3097. i. FLORA R. ALFORD,[9] born Warren, Me., August 31, 1851.
3098. ii. MARIA H. ALFORD,[9] born Warren, Me., July, 1854.

2364. LYDIA NORTH ALFORD [8] (*Nancy A. Daggett,*[7] *Matthew,*[6] *Elijah,*[5] *Brotherton,*[4] *Joshua,*[3] *Thomas,*[2] *John* [1]), born Searsmont, Me., June 12, 1823; resides Warren, Me. (1892); married Warren, Me., April 10, 1850, Lawrence Crawford French, son of William and Mary (Crawford) French; born Warren, Me., August 30, 1821.

Issue:

3099. i. MARY E. FRENCH,[9] born Warren, Me., April 19, 1851.
3100. ii. CHARLES A. FRENCH,[9] born Warren, Me., November 22, 1854.
3101. iii. DORA E. FRENCH,[9] born Warren, Me., October 27, 1857.

2365. HANNAH P. DAGGETT ` (*Jethro D.,*[7] *James,*[6] *Jethro,*[5] *Brotherton,*[4] *Joshua,*[3] *Thomas,*[2] *John* [1]), born New Bedford, Mass., 1831; married New Bedford, Mass., December 12, 1850, by Rev. R. M. Hatfield, to William C. Stoddard, son of John H. and Catherine Stoddard; " carpenter; " born Newport, R.I., 1821.

2366. ELIZABETH DAGGETT ` (*Jethro D.,*[7] *James,*[6] *Jethro,*[5] *Brotherton,*[4] *Joshua,*[3] *Thomas,*[2] *John* [1]), born New Bedford, Mass., 1834; married New Bedford, Mass., April 16, 1852, by Rev. James Taylor, to Davis Kelley, son of Coleman and Peace Kelley; " painter; " born Dartmouth, Mass., 1826.

2367. REBECCA S. DAGGETT ` (*Jethro D.,*[7] *James,*[6] *Jethro,*[5] *Brotherton,*[4] *Joshua,*[3] *Thomas,*[2] *John* [1]), born New Bedford, Mass., 1835; married Dartmouth, Mass., August 25, 1852, by Joseph Gifford, J.P., to George Kelley, son of Coleman and Peace Kelley; " mariner; " born Dartmouth, Mass., 1827.

2369. DENNIS DAGGETT [8] (*William,*[7] *Peter,*[6] *Ebenezer* [5] [*John,*[4] *Joseph,*[3] *Joseph,*[2] *John* [1]] (?)), born Phillips, Me., March 11, 1821; resides Phillips, Me. (1893); married February 20, 1845, Mary Wright; born Strong, Me., 1823.

Issue:

3102. i. LEANDER A. DAGGETT,[9] born Phillips, Me., April 3, 1846; married September 22, 1875, Florence Worthley; she born Strong, Me., 1853.
3103. ii. WILLIAM J. DAGGETT,[9] born Phillips, Me., October 26, 1851.

2371. PAULINA DAGGETT [8] (*William,*[7] *Peter,*[6] *Ebenezer* [5] [*John,*[4] *Joseph,*[3] *Joseph,*[2] *John* [1]] (?)), born Phillips, Me., July 11, 1829;

died Phillips, Me., August 12, 1864; married October 31, 1859, Ezra R. Wright; born Lewiston, Me., 1829.

Issue:

3104. i. FRED A. WRIGHT,[9] born Lewiston, Me., November 18, 1860.

2373. PLAMENTIN DAGGETT[8] (*Plamentin*,[7] *Peter*,[6] *Ebenezer*[5] [*John*,[4] *Joseph*,[3] *Joseph*,[2] *John*[1]] (?)), born New Vineyard, Me., May 3, 1825; died Strong, Me., December 12, 1884; married Strong, Me., October 1, 1856, Nancy Thomas Vining, daughter of David and Jane Chase (Thomas) Vining; born Strong, Me., May 2, 1835.

Issue:

3105. i. WALTER SNOW DAGGETT,[9] born Strong, Me., February 11, 1860.
3106. ii. GEORGE FRANKLIN DAGGETT,[9] born Strong, Me., May 26, 1866; married Trenton, N.J., September 26, 1891, Margaret Sweeny, daughter of Dr. Barnabas and Elizabeth Williamson (Robinson) Sweeny; born Brookville, Pa., October 28, 1864; resides 1100 New Hampshire avenue, Washington, D.C. (1893).
3107. iii. FRED HERBERT DAGGETT,[9] born Strong, Me., November 25, 1867; married Strong, Me., November 29, 1890, Susie Louisa Carr, daughter of Charles W. and Louisa (Earle) Carr; born Phillips, Me., October 4, 1872; resides Strong, Me. (1893).

2374. ALBERT DAGGETT[8] (*Plamentin*,[7] *Peter*,[6] *Ebenezer*[5] [*John*,[4] *Joseph*,[3] *Joseph*,[2] *John*[1]] (?)), born New Vineyard, Me., June 13, 1827; resides Strong, Me. (1893); married 1st, Strong, Me., April 2, 1857, Sarah Montgomery Porter, daughter of Ezekiel and Eunice (Hitchcock) Porter; born Strong, Me., July 21, 1836; died Strong, Me., May 3, 1886; married 2d, Strong, Me., June 13, 1888, Ada Eldora Pottle; born Freeman, Me., December 23, 1853.

Issue:

3108. i. WILLIAM DAGGETT,[9] born Strong, Me., December 17, 1868; died Strong, Me., August 26, 1870.
3109. ii. MINNIE WARREN DAGGETT,[9] born Strong, Me., August 31, 1873; died Strong, Me., September 4, 1873.

Mr. Daggett is of the firm of Daggett Bros., general merchandise, Strong, Me.

2376. Hon. WASHINGTON LIBBEY DAGGETT[8] (*Plamentin*,[7] *Peter*,[6] *Ebenezer*[5] [*John*,[4] *Joseph*,[3] *Joseph*,[2] *John*[1]] (?)), born New Vineyard, Me., May 6, 1835; resides Strong, Me. (1893); married Strong, Me., September 20, 1868, Reliance Collier Dickey, daughter of John and Lucy (Collier) Dickey, born Avon, Me., October 27, 1841.

No issue.

Hon. W. L. Daggett is of the firm of Daggett Bros., general merchandise, Strong, Me. He is among the very best Sunday-school workers, and long an office-bearer in the State association.

Mr. Daggett has completed twenty-five years of unbroken service as superintendent of the Methodist Episcopal Sunday-school of Strong. His enthusiasm and devotion are greatly appreciated in the whole region. Mr. Daggett was one of the representatives of Maine at the World's Sunday-school Convention at London.

2377. HANNAH SNOW DAGGETT[8] (*Plumentin*,[7] *Peter*,[6] *Ebenezer*[5] [*John*,[4] *Joseph*,[3] *Joseph*,[2] *John*[1]] (?)), born New Vineyard, Me., January 12, 1839; resides 95 Hamilton avenue, Columbus, Ohio (1893); married Farmington, Me., June 25, 1867, George Washington Luce, son of John Tilton and Betsey (Wendell) Luce; "jeweller;" born New Vineyard, Me., April 17, 1834.

Issue:

3110. i. GEORGE ERNEST LUCE,[9] born Xenia, Ohio. January 17, 1872; resides 95 Hamilton avenue, Columbus, Ohio (1893).

2378. MARY DAGGETT[8] (*Jonathan L.*,[7] *Peter*,[6] *Ebenezer*[5] [*John*,[4] *Joseph*,[3] *Joseph*,[2] *John*[1]] (?)), born Chesterville, Me., October 20, 1821; died Salem, Me., June 19, 1888; married January 18, 1839, Frederick Richards; born Leeds. Me., 1815.

Issue:

3111. i.   BENJAMIN F. RICHARDS,[9] born Salem, Me., November 3, 1839; died Salem, Me., March 15, 1846.
3112. ii. VELZORA RICHARDS,[9] born Salem. Me., October 21, 1841.
3113. iii. WINFIELD S. RICHARDS,[9] born Salem, Me., April 27, 1855; died Salem, Me., January 23, 1862.
3114. iv. AFFIE T. RICHARDS,[9] born Salem, Me., January 2, 1862.

2379. JONATHAN DAGGETT[8] (*Jonathan L.*,[7] *Peter*,[6] *Ebenezer*[5] [*John*,[4] *Joseph*,[3] *Joseph*,[2] *John*[1]] (?)), born Chesterville, Me., February 13, 1823; resides Strong, Me. (1893); married June 19, 1853, Adeline Curtis; born Salem, Me., 1832.

Issue:

3115. i. ELLA F. DAGGETT,[9] born Salem, Me., April 2, 1854; married January 1, 1884, Stephen W. Mayo; he born Freeman, Me., 1841.

2380. MARY ANN DAGGETT[8] (*Leander*,[7] *Peter*,[6] *Ebenezer*[5] [*John*,[4] *Joseph*,[3] *Joseph*,[2] *John*[1]] (?)), born New Vineyard, Me., March 13, 1827; died New Vineyard, Me., August 22, 1886; married (published December 17, 1846) Columbus Harvey, son of Columbus and Esther (Stafford) Harvey; born Anson, Me., 1825.

Issue:

3116. i.   EMILY L. HARVEY,[9] born Industry, Me., 1847; married William H. Look; he born Georgetown, Me. (1849).
3117. ii. MARGARET D. HARVEY,[9] born New Vineyard, Me., 1851; died 1855.
3118. iii. BRADFORD C. HARVEY,[9] born New Vineyard, Me., 1854; married Harriet S. Daggett (see No. 3123).

3119. iv. ORLAND C. HARVEY,[9] born New Vineyard, Me., 1857; died 1859.
3120. v. WILLIAM M. HARVEY,[9] born New Vineyard, Me., 1859.
3121. vi. MABEL L. HARVEY,[9] born New Vineyard, Me., 1863.
3122. vii. CHARLES S. HARVEY,[9] born New Vineyard, Me., 1866.

2382. LEANDER DAGGETT [8] (*Leander*,[7] *Peter*,[6] *Ebenezer* [5] [*John*,[4] *Joseph*,[3] *Joseph*,[2] *John* [1]] (?)), born New Vineyard, Me., October 10, 1841; resides Strong, Me. (1893); married April 4, 1865, Amelia P. Butler, daughter of Philander and Mary (Norton) Butler; born New Vineyard, Me., October 10, 1844.

2383. ALBERT DAGGETT [8] (*Albert*,[7] *Peter*,[6] *Ebenezer* [5] [*John*,[4] *Joseph*,[3] *Joseph*,[2] *John* [1]] (?)), born Rochester, Mass., May 17, 1827; resides Manchester, Me. (1893); married May 17, 1854, Abbie B. Fifield; born Readfield, Me., 1829.

Issue:

3123. i. HARRIET S. DAGGETT,[9] born Manchester, Me., October 28, 1855; married Bradford C. Harvey (see No. 3118), December 25, 1878.
3124. ii. EMOGENE W. DAGGETT,[9] born Manchester, Me., September 23, 1857; died Manchester, Me., June 11, 1873.
3125. iii. OREANA F. DAGGETT,[9] born Manchester, Me., July 29, 1859; died Manchester, Me., October 22, 1862.
3126. iv. LIZZIE C. DAGGETT,[9] born Manchester, Me., October 30, 1861; died Manchester, Me., November 16, 1878.
3127. v. EFFIE A. DAGGETT,[9] born Manchester, Me., December 5, 1863; died Manchester, Me., December 2, 1865.
3128. vi. JOHN A. DAGGETT,[9] born Manchester, Me., May 9, 1866.
3129. vii. CHARLES E. DAGGETT,[9] born Manchester, Me., September 13, 1869.

2384. PLAMENTIN DAGGETT [8] (*Albert*,[7] *Peter*,[6] *Ebenezer* [5] [*John*,[4] *Joseph*,[3] *Joseph*,[2] *John* [1]] (?)), born Rochester, Mass., December 17, 1828; resides 7 Woodstock avenue, Rutland, Vt. (1893); married December 14, 1853, Elvira A. Capen; born Winthrop, Me., 1832.

Issue:

3130. i. CORA A. DAGGETT,[9] born Manchester, Me., October 10, 1863.

2385. ELIZABETH SNOW DAGGETT [8] (*Albert*,[7] *Peter*,[6] *Ebenezer* [5] [*John*,[4] *Joseph*,[3] *Joseph*,[2] *John* [1]] (?)), born Rochester, Mass., December 25, 1830; resides 702½ Cherry street, Camden, N.J. (1893); married August 21, 1851, Proctor S. Gilbert; born Greene, Me., 1824.

Issue:

3131. i. ELLA B. GILBERT,[9] born Manchester, Me., September 4, 1854; married November 8, 1876, Eugene H. Furbush; he born Rome, Me., 1855; she died February 15, 1877.
3132. ii. EDWIN S. GILBERT,[9] born Turner, Me., July 26, 1856; married October 31, 1883, Sarah J. Bealer; she born Lower Marion, Pa., 1855.
3133. iii. MANLY A. GILBERT,[9] born Turner, Me., March 21, 1858.
3134. iv. JENNIE F. GILBERT,[9] born Manchester, Me., March 4, 1863; married July 23, 1881, Wm. H. Gearheart; he born Doylestownborough, Pa., 1858.
3135. v. WILLIAM A. GILBERT,[9] born Manchester. Me., October 3, 1865.

2387. MARTHA JANE DAGGETT [8] (*Albert,*[7] *Peter,*[6] *Ebenezer*[5] [*John,*[4] *Joseph,*[3] *Joseph,*[2] *John*[1]] (?)), born Rochester, Mass., January 23, 1834; resides Augusta, Me. (1893); married October 12, 1858, William G. Fifield; born Augusta, Me., 1835.

Issue:

3136. i. JOHN A. FIFIELD,[9] born Augusta, Me., July 31, 1861; died 1863.
3137. ii. WALTER L. FIFIELD,[9] born Augusta, Me., October 16, 1867.
3138. iii. IRVINE D. FIFIELD,[9] born Augusta, Me., February 25, 1873.

2423. JOHN FRED DAGGETT [8] (*John A.,*[7] *John,*[6] *John*[5] [*John,*[4] *Joseph,*[3] *Joseph,*[2] *John*[1]] (?)), born Industry, Me., August 24, 1847; resides New Sharon, Me. (1892); married January 19, 1871, Clara L. Flood, daughter of James and Caroline (Lothrop) Flood, of Farmington; born June 20, 1840.

Issue:

3139. i. INEZ CAROLINE DAGGETT,[9] born Farmington, Me., June 1, 1871.
3140. ii. BESSIE LENA DAGGETT,[9] born Farmington, Me., September 9, 1872; married December 1, 1889, Frank Lane; resides New Sharon, Me. (1892); issue: Clara Belle Lane,[10] born New Sharon, Me., May 9, 1890; died May 21, 1890.

Mr. Daggett was in Co. A, Twenty-ninth Maine Regiment, in 1864–5. He is a travelling salesman.

2430. CAPITOLA DAGGETT [8] (*John A.,*[7] *John,*[6] *John*[5] [*John,*[4] *Joseph,*[3] *Joseph,*[2] *John*[1]] (?)), born Industry, Me., September 8, 1866; resides Dixfield, Me. (1892); married February 14, 1885, William Henry Durrell, son of Hiram P. and Lucy (Hanson) Durrell; born Industry, Me., December 28, 1858.

Issue:

3141. i. MATTIE MAY DURRELL,[9] born New Sharon, Me., November 27, 1885.
3142. ii. BERNICE BELLE DURRELL,[9] born New Sharon, Me., April 4, 1888.

2433. CASSIA JANE DAGGETT [8] (*Warren,*[7] *John,*[6] *John*[5] [*John,*[4] *Joseph,*[3] *Joseph,*[2] *John*[1]] (?)), born Anson, Me., April 1, 18—; resides Industry, Me. (1892); married January 7, 1878, Orrin Leeman, son of John and Betsey (Stover) Leeman, of Stark, Me.

Issue:

3143. i. JENNIE MAUD LEEMAN,[9] born Industry, Me., March 16, 1878.
3144. ii. BESSIE ELLA LEEMAN,[9] born Industry, Me., June 21, 1879.
3145. iii. HATTIE BLANCHE LEEMAN,[9] born Stark, Me.

2436. ELLA MILLER DAGGETT [8] (*Warren,*[7] *John,*[6] *John*[5] [*John,*[4] *Joseph,*[3] *Joseph,*[2] *John*[1]] (?)), born Anson, Me., December 28, 1864; married November 24, 1886, James Tucker Staples, son of Daniel Staples.

Issue:

3146. i. WARREN DAGGETT STAPLES,[9] born Industry, Me., May 15, 1887.
3147. ii. JAMES TUCKER STAPLES,[9] born Oakland, Me., July 1, 1888.

JOHN DOGGETT, OF MARTHA'S VINEYARD.

NINTH GENERATION.

2466. INEZ ADELLA DAGGETT [9] (*Allen,*[8] *Seth,*[7] *Reuben,*[6] *Reuben,*[5] *Nathaniel,*[4] *Nathaniel,*[3] *John,*[2] *John*[1]), born Tioga, Pa., February 22, 1845; resides Lawrenceville, Tioga Co., Pa. (1892); married Lawrenceville, Pa., August 10, 1869, Fred David Fletcher, son of John and Debora Terressa (Ramsdale) Fletcher; born Sullivan, Pa., September 26, 1847.

Issue:

3148. i. BERTIE LEE FLETCHER,[10] born Cohocton, N.Y., March 9, 1870.
3149. ii. OSCAR CHARLES FLETCHER,[10] born Wellsboro', Pa., August 18, 1876.

2468. ORSON STARKEY DAGGETT [9] (*Allen,*[8] *Seth,*[7] *Reuben,*[6] *Reuben,*[5] *Nathaniel,*[4] *Nathaniel,*[3] *John,*[2] *John*[1]), born Tioga, Pa., September 28, 1856; resides Oak street, Corning, Steuben Co., N.Y. (1892); married East Charleston, Pa., September 12, 1875, Laura A. Palmer, daughter of Reuben T. and Mary (Ayers) Palmer; born Middlebury, Pa., December 11, 1856.

Issue:

3150. i. JAY ALLEN DAGGETT,[10] born Stokesdale, Pa., March 24, 1876.
3151. ii. ADA MAY DAGGETT,[10] born Niles Valley, Pa., February 10, 1878.
3152. iii. CHARLES D. DAGGETT,[10] born Stokesdale, Pa., February 5, 1880.
3153. iv. LUCIEN P. DAGGETT,[10] born Dallas City, Pa., January 13, 1882.
3154. v. ELIZA K. DAGGETT,[10] born Harrison Valley, Pa., July 14, 1884.

2471. LEVI DAGGETT [9] (*George,*[8] *Seth,*[7] *Reuben,*[6] *Reuben,*[5] *Nathaniel,*[4] *Nathaniel,*[3] *John,*[2] *John*[1]), born Daggett's Mills, Pa., March 3, 1837; resides Tioga, Tioga Co., Pa. (1892); married Tioga, Pa., January 1, 1857, Frances Smartwood.

Issue:

3155. i. EFFIE DAGGETT.[10]
3156. ii. NELLIE DAGGETT.[10]
3157. iii. NORMAN DAGGETT.[10]
3158. iv. ANNIE DAGGETT.[10]
3159. v. MAY DAGGETT.[10]
3160. vi. BIRDIE DAGGETT.[10]
3161. vii. DAISY DAGGETT.[10]

2472. HARRIET DAGGETT [9] (*George,*[8] *Seth,*[7] *Reuben,*[6] *Reuben,*[5] *Nathaniel,*[4] *Nathaniel,*[3] *John,*[2] *John*[1]), born Tioga, Pa., July 12, 1844; resides Tioga, Tioga Co., Pa. (1892); married Tioga, Pa.,

November 13, 1866, Henry Wheeler, son of Royal and Sarah J. (Miller) Wheeler; born Lawrenceville, Pa., August 15, 1843.

Issue:

3162. i.   H. Fay Wheeler,[10] born Lawrenceville, Pa., March 6, 1868.
3163. ii. George R. Wheeler,[10] born Tioga, Pa., December 27, 1873.
3164. iii. Royal P. Wheeler,[10] born Tioga, Pa., October 12, 1876.

2473. Florence Daggett[9] (*George,*[8] *Seth,*[7] *Reuben,*[6] *Reuben,*[5] *Nathaniel,*[4] *Nathaniel,*[3] *John,*[2] *John*[1]), born Tioga, Pa., September 26, 1846; resides Addison, N.Y. (1892); married Tioga, Pa., 1879, Oscar Dudley.

Issue:

3165. i. Ethel Dudley,[10] born Addison, N.Y., August 24, 1882.
3166. ii. Dora Dudley,[10] born Addison, N.Y., February 13, 1884.

2475. Seth Orlando Daggett[9] (*Lewis,*[8] *Seth,*[7] *Reuben,*[6] *Reuben,*[5] *Nathaniel,*[4] *Nathaniel,*[3] *John,*[2] *John*[1]), born Daggett's Mills, Pa., September 14, 1843; "proprietor Park Hotel;" resides Tioga, Pa. (1892); married 1st, Havana, N.Y., June 9, 1878, Ella Boynton, daughter of Eben B. and Helen (Miller) Boynton; born Reading, N.Y., December 22, 1861; died Wellsboro', Pa., October 2, 1885; married 2d, Watkins, N.Y., March 14, 1888, Jessie D. Brown, daughter of S. B. and Mary (Gevero) Brown; born Watkins, N.Y., August 13, 1867.

Issue:

3167. i. Georgia Daggett,[10] born Tioga, Pa., July 21, 1880.
3168. ii. Leah Daggett,[10] born Tioga, Pa., January 22, 1882.

2477. Wells Lewis Daggett[9] (*Lewis,*[8] *Seth,*[7] *Reuben,*[6] *Reuben,*[5] *Nathaniel,*[4] *Nathaniel,*[3] *John,*[2] *John*[1]), born Tioga, Pa., April 26, 1854; resides Bellefonte, Pa. (1892); married Wellsboro', Pa., January, 1886, Carrie Boynton, daughter of Eben B. and Helen (Miller) Boynton; born Millerton, Pa., December 10, 1863.

Issue:

3169. i. Lewis Daggett,[10] born Lawrenceville, Pa., August 9, 1887.

Wells Lewis Daggett was proprietor of the "Daggett House," Lawrenceville, Tioga Co., Pa., 1888.

2532. Amey Ann Daggett[9] (*William,*[8] *John,*[7] *Levi,*[6] *John,*[5] *John,*[4] *Nathaniel,*[3] *John,*[2] *John*[1]), born Seekonk, Mass., April 29, 1849; resides East Providence, R.I. (1892); married East Providence, R.I., October 31, 1867, Benjamin P. Branch, son of Joseph and Lucy (Beaverstalk) Branch; born Providence, R.I., July 4, 1838.

Issue:

3170. i. Benjamin Branch,[10] born East Providence, R.I., October 18, 1868.
3171. ii. Amey Drucilla Branch,[10] born East Providence, R.I., November 15, 1871.

3172. iii. WILLIAM DAGGETT BRANCH,[10] born East Providence, R.I., December 14, 1877; died East Providence, R.I., December 8, 1879.

2537. WILLIAM DAGGETT [9] (*William*,[8] *William*,[7] *William*,[6] *Seth*,[5] *Samuel*,[4] *Thomas*,[3] *Thomas*,[2] *John* [1]), born Tisbury, Mass., August 22, 1825; " merchant; " resides Fresno, Cal.; married 1st, Tisbury, Mass., August 11, 1848, by Rev. O. S. Walker, to Harriet Merry, daughter of William and Harriet (Manter) Merry; born Tisbury, Mass., 1827; married 2d, ——.

Issue (three sons, three daughters by first wife) :

3173. i. IDA E. DAGGETT,[10] born Tisbury, Mass., August 10, 1849.

2545. MARY DAGGETT [9] (*Alonzo*,[8] *Seth*,[7] *William*,[6] *Seth*,[5] *Samuel*,[4] *Thomas*,[3] *Thomas*,[2] *John* [1]), born Tisbury, Mass., March 23, 1839; died at sea, on passage Havana to New York, July 9, 1875; married Tisbury, Mass., July 9, 1860, by Rev. F. A. Loomis, to Rodney Joshua Conary, son of Joshua and Pamelia Andrus (Carter) Conary, of Surry, Me.; " mariner; " born Surry, Me., September 17, 1834; at sea (1892).

Issue :

3174. i.   ADELIA MELVILLE CONARY,[10] born Vineyard Haven, Mass., June 9, 1861; died Vineyard Haven, Mass., August 16, 1861.
3175. ii.   GEORGE HOUGH CONARY,[10] born Vineyard Haven, Mass., November 17, 1863; resides Taunton, Mass. (1892).
3176. iii.   OLITA MAY CONARY,[10] born Vineyard Haven, Mass., November 8, 1868; resides Taunton, Mass. (1892).

2547. ANN ELIZA DAGGETT [9] (*Alonzo*,[8] *Seth*,[7] *William*,[6] *Seth*,[5] *Samuel*,[4] *Thomas*,[3] *Thomas*,[2] *John* [1]), born Tisbury, Mass., May 26, 1842; resides Taunton, Mass. (1892); married Tisbury, Mass., October 3, 1864, by Rev. W. V. Morrison, to William McCready Conary, of Tisbury, son of Joshua and Pamelia Andrus (Carter) Conary, of Surry, Me.; " mariner;" born Surry, Me., June 29, 1839.

Issue :

3177. i. ALONZO DAGGETT CONARY,[10] born Vineyard Haven, Mass., September, 1865; died Vineyard Haven, Mass., June, 1866.

2548. GEORGIA DAGGETT [9] (*Alonzo*,[8] *Seth*,[7] *William*,[6] *Seth*,[5] *Samuel*,[4] *Thomas*,[3] *Thomas*,[2] *John* [1]), born Tisbury, Mass., November 8, 1845; resides 2 Foster street, New Bedford, Mass. (1892); married Tisbury, Mass., December 12, 1866, by Rev. John F. Sheffield, to Vernal Clifford, of Tisbury, son of Nathan and Elizabeth (Clifford) Clifford; " farmer; " born Chilmark, Mass., March 6, 1837.

Issue :

3178. i. MABEL EDSON CLIFFORD,[10] born Vineyard Haven, Mass., February 6, 1873.

2550. CARRIE BRADLEY DAGGETT [9] (*Alonzo*,[8] *Seth*,[7] *William,
Seth*,[5] *Samuel*,[4] *Thomas*,[3] *Thomas*,[2] *John*[1]), born Tisbury, Mass.,
June 12, 1853; resides New Bedford, Mass. (1892); married Tis-
bury, Mass., October 13, 1875, by Rev. E. Tirrell, to Osander Gilberts
Hammett, of New Bedford, son of Hiram and Mary Ann (Tilton)
Hammett; "mariner;" born Chilmark, Mass., September 19, 1853.
Issue:

3179. i. MAYE GILBERTS HAMMETT,[10] born Woods Holl, Mass., April 13, 1878;
died New Bedford, Mass., Aug. 15, 1891.

2562. SAMUEL DAGGETT [9] (*Isaac*,[8] *Samuel*,[7] *Samuel*,[6] *Seth*,[5]
Samuel,[4] *Thomas*,[3] *Thomas*,[2] *John*[1]), born New Vineyard, Me.,
November 30, 1818; "farmer;" removed to Iowa, 1883; resides
Sanborn, Iowa (1892); married 1st, Louisa W. Pennel; born 1825;
died January 20, 1848; married 2d (published September 30, 1848),
Lydia Norton, daughter of Samuel and Susannah Wade (Davis)
Norton; born Eustis, Me., October 28, 1827.
Issue:

3180. i. SARAH N. DAGGETT,[10] born September, 1847; died January 6, 1848.
3181. ii. ANDREW JACKSON DAGGETT,[10] born Industry, Me., May 25, 1849;
married; resides California (1892).
3182. iii. AMANDA W. DAGGETT,[10] born Industry, Me., November 19, 1852;
married (published January 15, 1873) John W. Keith, of Farmington,
Me.; she died there, January 22, 1889.
3183. iv. LYDIA JANE DAGGETT,[10] born Industry, Me.; married Mark Bunker,
son of Ichabod Bunker, of Anson, Me.; divorced; resides Sanborn,
Iowa (1892).

2563. TRISTRAM NORTON DAGGETT [9] (*Isaac*,[8] *Samuel*,[7] *Samuel*,[6]
Seth,[5] *Samuel*,[4] *Thomas*,[3] *Thomas*,[2] *John*[1]), born New Vineyard, Me.,
October 21, 1820; died New Vineyard, Me., March 3, 1891; married
1st, New Portland, Me., June 9, 1846, by Tobias Churchill, to Lucy
Churchill, daughter of Tobias and Jane (Everett) Churchill; born
New Portland, Me., November 6, 1822; married 2d, July 11, 1866,
Caroline E. Thomas, divorced wife of Hovey Thomas, and daughter
of Philander and Mary (Norton) Butler; born New Vineyard, Me.,
April 19, 1825.
Issue:

3184. i. ORRAVILLE DAGGETT,[10] born New Vineyard, Me., June 19, 1847; died
New Vineyard, Me., August 3, 1863.
3185. ii. ORINGTON DAGGETT,[10] born New Vineyard, Me., June 19, 1847; died
New Vineyard, Me., July 1, 1863.
3186. iii. ISAAC W. DAGGETT,[10] born New Vineyard, Me., January 2, 1851.
3187. iv. SARAH ELIZABETH DAGGETT,[10] born New Vineyard, Me., February
28, 1853; died New Vineyard, Me., June 16, 1863.
3188. v. RUSSELL EVERETT DAGGETT,[10] born New Vineyard, Me., September
28, 1855; died New Vineyard, Me., July 12, 1863.
3189. vi. WARREN TRISTRAM DAGGETT,[10] born New Vineyard, Me., July 21,
1858; died New Vineyard, Me., June 25, 1863.

3190. vii. Lucy Annah Daggett,[10] born New Vineyard, Me., August 11, 1860;
died New Vineyard, Me., September 4, 1863.

Mr. Daggett, farmer, resided in Industry, New Vineyard, and Iowa.

2565. John Tobey Daggett [9] (*Isaac,*[8] *Samuel,*[7] *Samuel,*[6] *Seth,*[5]
Samuel,[4] *Thomas,*[3] *Thomas,*[2] *John* [1]), born New Vineyard, Me.,
September 13, 1826; " farmer; " died Farmington, Me., December
23, 1891; married 1st, Industry, Me., January 31, 1856, Caroline
Norton, daughter of Benjamin Warren and Amy Allen (Manter)
Norton; born New Vineyard, Me., December 9, 1833; died Industry,
Me., April 14, 1878; married 2d, November 16, 1879, Eleanor
Greenwood, widow of Hannibal Greenwood, and daughter of Daniel
H. and Betsey (Spencer) Fish; born Industry, Me., March 14, 1848.

Issue :

3191. i.   William Harrison Daggett,[10] born Industry, Me., August 14, 1857.
3192. ii.   Charles Manter Daggett,[10] born Industry, Me., November 21,
             1861; died Industry, Me., July 20, 1863.
3193. iii.   Emma Allen Daggett,[10] born Industry, Me., October 29, 1864.
3194. iv.   James Norton Daggett,[10] born Industry, Me., June 7, 1867.
3195. v.   Abbie Norton Daggett,[10] born Industry, Me., August 11, 1872.
3196. vi.   Julia Jones Daggett,[10] born Industry, Me., October 6, 1876.
3197. vii.   Blanche M. Daggett,[10] born Industry, Me., December 31, 1880.
3198. viii. John M. Daggett,[10] born Industry, Me., May 13, 1882.
3199. ix.   Delia F. Daggett,[10] born Industry, Me., January 31, 1884.

2566. Andrew Jackson Daggett [9] (*Isaac,*[8] *Samuel,*[7] *Samuel,*[6]
Seth,[5] *Samuel,*[4] *Thomas,*[3] *Thomas,*[2] *John* [1]), born New Vineyard,
Me., November 26, 1829; died Industry, Me., April 21, 1860; mar-
ried August 14, 1852, Susan Tinkham, daughter of Ariel and Susan
(Bray) Tinkham, of Anson, Me. ; address, Anson, Me. (1892).

Issue :

3200. i.   Francis A. Daggett,[10] born Industry, Me., January 1, 1853; died
           Industry, Me., July 16, 1861.
3201. ii. Susie M. Daggett,[10] born Industry, Me., February 19, 1860.

2569. Julia Jones Daggett [9] (*Isaac,*[8] *Samuel,*[7] *Samuel,*[6] *Seth,*[5]
Samuel,[4] *Thomas,*[3] *Thomas,*[2] *John*[1]), born New Vineyard, Me., June
1, 1839; resides Sanborn, O'Brien Co., Ia. (1892); married Industry, Me., July 3, 1859, by Phineas Libby, to Benjamin Warren
Norton, son of Benjamin Warren and Amy Allen (Manter) Norton,
of Industry, Me. ; born New Vineyard, Me., July 3, 1836.

Issue :

3202. i.   Sarah Ellen Norton,[10] born Industry, Me., April 4, 1862; married
            February 6, 1885, Henry E. Hodgkins, son of Henry T. and Ann
            Greeley (Stinchfield) Hodgkins; issue: Ernest Warren,[11] born
            April 24, 1889; resides N. Chesterfield, Me. (1892).
3203. ii.   David Merry Norton,[10] born Industry, Me., February 23, 1864;
            married November 22, 1890, Orie Woolworth, daughter of William
            and Mary (Taylor) Woolworth; resides Sanborn, Ia. (1892).
3204. iii. Emily Daggett Norton,[10] born Industry, Me., September 20, 1869;
            resides Sanborn, Ia. (1892).

Benjamin W. Norton, farmer, settled in Industry, Me., was representative in the State Legislature, and town treasurer. Moved to Iowa in 1886.

2571. JOHN BARNARD DAGGETT[9] (*Samuel*,[8] *Samuel*,[7] *Samuel*,[6] *Seth*,[5] *Samuel*,[4] *Thomas*,[3] *Thomas*,[2] *John*[1]), born Farmington Falls, Me., May 17, 1827; "merchant and farmer;" died Wesley, Ia., March 12, 1879; married Farmington Falls, Me., June 14, 1856, Cornelia Russ, daughter of Henry and Mary (Clark) Russ; born Me., March 1, 1830.

Issue:

3205. i. ALICE DAGGETT,[10] born Farmington Falls, Me., October 30, 1858; married Mason City, Ia., April 1, 1885, Mr. Heal; resides Wesley, Ia. (1892).
3206. ii. BRADFORD BRUSH DAGGETT,[10] born Farmington Falls, Me., November 27, 1864; of "Daggett & Schwie," stoves and plumbing supplies, Mason City, Ia. (1892).

2573. EMILY JONES DAGGETT[9] (*Samuel*,[?] *Samuel*,[7] *Samuel*,[6] *Seth*,[5] *Samuel*,[4] *Thomas*,[3] *Thomas*,[2] *John*[1]), born Industry, Me., January 10, 1837; resides Evansville, Ind. (1892); married Farmington, Me., July 30, 1862, by Rev. Horatio Q. Butterfield, to Charles H. Butterfield, son of Asa and Hannah (Jordan) Butterfield; born Farmington, Me., May 17, 1833.

No issue.

Hon. Charles H. Butterfield served in the Civil War three years, as major and lieutenant-colonel, Ninety-first Indiana Infantry. In 1870 he was judge of the Criminal Court; 1872, mayor of the city of Evansville; 1886–91, county attorney, Vanderburg county, Ind.

2575. ORRIN DAGGETT[9] (*Samuel*,[?] *Samuel*,[7] *Samuel*,[6] *Seth*,[5] *Samuel*,[4] *Thomas*,[3] *Thomas*,[2] *John*[1]), born New Vineyard, Me., January 7, 1816; resides Presque Isle, Me. (1892); married New Vineyard, Me., February 23, 1839, by Rev. Thomas Smith, to Mary Perkins, daughter of Levi H. and Bethia (Dunbar) Perkins; born North Anson, Me., January 11, 1820.

Issue:

3207. i.   LEVI HOOPER DAGGETT,[10] born Industry, Me., February 21, 1840.
3208. ii. PHEDELIA W. DAGGETT,[10] born New Vineyard, Me., September 8, 1843; died East Greenwich, R.I., October 18, 1872.
3209. iii. SAMUEL DAGGETT,[10] born Industry, Me., May 29, 1846.
3210. iv. EMMA A. DAGGETT,[10] born New Sharon, Me., April 23, 1854; died Wilbraham, Mass., May 4, 1877.
3211. v.   CHARLES F. DAGGETT,[10] born New Sharon, Me., September 9, 1856.

Orrin Daggett is a farmer at Presque Isle. He has been selectman and assessor of the town, sheriff of the county four years, and member of the State Legislature.

2577. BELINDA WEST DAGGETT [9] (*John T.,*[8] *Samuel,*[7] *Samuel,*[6] *Seth,*[5] *Samuel,*[4] *Thomas,*[3] *Thomas,*[2] *John*[1]), born Tisbury, Mass., December 9, 1838; died New Bedford, Mass.; married Tisbury, Mass., November 30, 1856, Allen Willcox, of New Bedford, Mass.

Issue:

3212. i. FRANK WILLCOX,[10] born April 22, 186¾.

2581. OBED SHERMAN DAGGETT [9] (*John T.,*[8] *Samuel,*[7] *Samuel,*[6] *Seth,*[5] *Samuel,*[4] *Thomas,*[3] *Thomas,*[2] *John*[1]), born Tisbury, Mass., August 22, 1850; resides Tisbury, Mass. (1892); married Marshfield, Mass., February 12, 1884, by Rev. T. P. Gurney, to Maria Roberts Gurney, daughter of Theophilus B. and Rebecca (Newcomb) Gurney; born East Hartford, Conn., March 19, 1860.

Issue:

3213. i.   EMMA SHERMAN DAGGETT,[10] born Tisbury, Mass., August 23, 1886.
3214. ii.   JOHN TOBEY DAGGETT,[10] born Tisbury, Mass., November 26, 1887.
3215. iii. ROBERT GURNEY DAGGETT,[10] born Tisbury, Mass., October 10, 1889.

2583. LUCY ELLEN DAGGETT [9] (*John T.,*[8] *Samuel,*[7] *Samuel,*[6] *Seth,*[5] *Samuel,*[4] *Thomas,*[3] *Thomas,*[2] *John*[1]), born Tisbury, Mass., July 12, 1855; resides North Tisbury, Mass. (1892); married 1st, Tisbury, Mass., December 5, 1875, by Rev. Charles E. Stokes, to Erford W. Burt, of Taunton, Mass., son of William A. and Salome S. Burt; born Taunton, Mass., 1853; "carpenter;" died Taunton, Mass., March, 1878; married 2d, Tisbury, Mass., May 5, 1885, by Rev. John Fish, to Shubart Weeks Gray, son of William and Viann (Weeks) Gray.

Issue:

3216. i. OTIS E. BURT,[10] born Taunton, Mass., December 13, 1876.

2584. REBECCA DAGGETT MANCHESTER [9] (*Amanda M. Daggett,*[8] *Samuel,*[7] *Samuel,*[6] *Seth,*[5] *Samuel,*[4] *Thomas,*[3] *Thomas,*[2] *John*[1]), born Vineyard Haven, Mass., December 14, 1836; resides Vineyard Haven, Mass. (1892); married 1st, Vineyard Haven, Mass., Benjamin Franklin Norton, son of Constant and Caroline Elizabeth (Norton) Norton; born Farmington, Me., September 21, 1833; perished at sea, autumn of 1856; married 2d, Vineyard Haven, Mass., March 27, 1865, Alfred Elijah Getchell, son of Parker and Rosanna (Lamb) Getchell; born Haverhill, N.H., July 1 or 2, 1822; died April 28, 1875.

No issue.

2585. SOPHRONIA PEAKES MANCHESTER [9] (*Amanda M. Daggett,*[8] *Samuel,*[7] *Samuel,*[6] *Seth,*[5] *Samuel,*[4] *Thomas,*[3] *Thomas,*[2] *John*[1]), born Vineyard Haven, Mass., March 17, 1842; resides Vineyard Haven,

Mass. (1892) ; married Vineyard Haven, Mass., October 8, 1863, Ellis Hamilton Dean, of Glasgow, Scot., son of Charles and Jessie (Keir) Dean; born Scotland, August 27, 1835.

Issue :

3217. i. GEORGE HAMILTON DEAN,[10] born Vineyard Haven, Mass., April 1, 1865; address, 38 Pearl street, Boston, Mass. (1892).
3218. ii. HENRY MANTER DEAN,[10] born Cambridgeport, Mass., December 2, 1869; address, 33½ India street, Boston, Mass. (1892).

2588. SILAS DAGGETT[9] (*Lendal*,[8] *Silas*,[7] *Silas*,[6] *Seth*,[5] *Samuel*,[4] *Thomas*,[3] *Thomas*,[2] *John*[1]), born Industry, Me., April 24, 1828; " farmer; " resides Harwood, N. Dak. (1892) ; married Anson, Me., October 16, 1855, by Asa Moor, Esq., to Mellison Pinkham, daughter of Nahum and Nancy (Nash) Pinkham; born Stark, Me., June 19, 1835.

Issue :

3219. i. IRA P. DAGGETT,[10] born Stark, Me., August 22, 1856; died Anson, Me., January 8, 1865.

2589. LYDIA ANN DAGGETT[9] (*Lendal*,[8] *Silas*,[7] *Silas*,[6] *Seth*,[5] *Samuel*,[4] *Thomas*,[3] *Thomas*,[2] *John*[1]), born Industry, Me., September 19, 1835; resides West's Mills, Me. (1892) ; married February 26, 1857, Joseph Warren Smith, son of Peter B. and Eleanor (Spencer) Smith; " farmer, blacksmith; " born New Vineyard, Me., December 22, 1833.

Issue :

3220. i. ELLEN MARY SMITH,[10] born Industry, Me., January 6, 1858; married William H. Daggett (see No. 3191).
3221. ii. FRANK WEBSTER SMITH,[10] born Industry, Me., August 8, 1859; married October 29, 1885, Augusta Brackett, daughter of Franklin and Florilla (Woodcock) Brackett; resides Stark, Me. (1892) ; issue : Ellen Frances Smith, born Stark, Me., April 18, 1886.
3222. iii. EUGENE LENDAL SMITH,[10] born Industry, Me., May 11, 1861; married Mary J. Daggett.
3223. iv. CHARLES GARDINER SMITH,[10] born Industry, Me., April 5, 1867; died Industry, Me., August 16, 1869.
3224. v. FRED WARREN SMITH,[10] born Industry, Me., March 17, 1869.
3225. vi. CHARLES MARSHALL SMITH,[10] born Industry, Me., August 25, 1874.

2591. TRISTRAM GARDNER DAGGETT[9] (*Lendal*,[8] *Silas*,[7] *Silas*,[6] *Seth*,[5] *Samuel*,[4] *Thomas*,[3] *Thomas*,[2] *John*[1]), born Stark, Me., January 29, 1847; resides Anson, Me. (1892) ; married Stark, Me., January 20, 1868, by Elder John Spinney, to Sarah Maria Gilman, daughter of Stephen and Sarah (Brown) Gilman; born Anson, Me., December 28, 1847.

Issue :

3226. i. BERTICE ALBERT DAGGETT,[10] born Stark, Me., December 20, 1868.
3227. ii. MAUD EUGENIE DAGGETT,[10] born Stark, Me., June 24, 1876.

Mr. Daggett is in the cardroom of the Indian Spring Woollen Mill, Madison, Me.

2593. WILLIAM HENRY DAGGETT[9] (*Joseph,*[8] *Silas,*[7] *Silas,*[6] *Seth,*[5] *Samuel,*[4] *Thomas,*[3] *Thomas,*[2] *John*[1]), born Tisbury, Mass., January 29, 1844; resides 696 Washington street, Brighton, Mass. (1893); married Goffstown Centre, N.H., November 23, 1870, by Rev. Watson W. Smith, to Nellie Iantha Hills, daughter of Albert and Sarah (Shaw) Hills; born Manchester, N.H., January 4, 1849.
Issue :

3228. i. FRED WALLACE DAGGETT,[10] born Boston, Mass., July 26, 1877.

2595. CHARLES DILLINGHAM DAGGETT[9] (*Joseph,*[8] *Silas,*[7] *Silas,*[6] *Seth,*[5] *Samuel,*[4] *Thomas,*[3] *Thomas,*[2] *John*[1]), born Tisbury, Mass., July 27, 1848; resides Bayswater street, Boston, Mass. (1893); married Boston, Mass., February 21, 1872, by Rev. S. J. B. House, to Emily Jane Norton, daughter of Richard and Caroline Love (Cottle) Norton; born Tisbury, Mass., January 24, 1845; died Boston, Mass., February 22, 1893.
Issue :

3229. i. VENETIA INIS DAGGETT,[10] born Tisbury, Mass., October 4, 1873.

Mr. Daggett has been connected with the " Boston Journal " for many years.

2601. ANNIE FRANKLIN DAGGETT[9] (*Grafton L.,*[8] *Freeman,*[7] *Freeman,*[6] *Sylvanus,*[5] *Samuel,*[4] *Thomas,*[3] *Thomas,*[2] *John*[1]), born Tisbury, Mass., September 11, 1857; resides Franklin, Pa. (1892); married Tisbury, Mass., May 21, 1885, by Rev. J. P. Farrar, to Charles Edwin Lord, of Newport, R.I., son of Albert E. and Caroline Elizabeth (Furber) Lord; " teacher; " born Woodstock, Vt., July 15, 1852.
Issue :

3230. i. CONSTANCE LORD,[10] born Tisbury, Mass., October 20, 1886.
3231. ii. ELISABETH DAGGETT LORD,[10] born Franklin, Pa., June 3, 1890.

2629. CLARINDA GREENE DAGGETT[9] (*David,*[8] *Henry,*[7] *Ichabod,*[6] *Elihu,*[5] *Mayhew,*[4] *John,*[3] *Thomas,*[2] *John*[1]), born Hopkinton, N.Y., February 19, 1841; resides Potsdam, N.Y. (1892); married Parishville, N.Y., August 16, 1864, John A. Vance, son of John and Aner (Hill) Vance; born Osnabruck, Ont., Can., October 8, 1836.
Issue :

3232. i. CARROLL HERBERT VANCE,[10] born Parishville, N.Y., September 14, 1866.
3233. ii. ETHEL METTE VANCE,[10] born Potsdam, N.Y., February 15, 1871.

2630. HENRY LEVI DAGGETT [9] (*David*,[8] *Henry*,[7] *Ichabod*,[6] *Elihu*,[5] *Mayhew*,[4] *John*,[3] *Thomas*,[2] *John*[1]), born Stockholm, N.Y., April 28, 1842; resides Parishville, N.Y. (1892); married Potsdam, N.Y., November 24, 1869, Marion Church, daughter of Calvin Colton and Elizabeth Bradbury (Follett) Church; born Crary's Mills, N.Y., May 9, 1849.

Issue:

3234. i. GRACE ELIZABETH DAGGETT,[10] born Parishville, N.Y., May 3, 1873.
3235. ii. ARTHUR DAVID DAGGETT,[10] born Parishville, N.Y., August 27, 1876.

2632. HERBERT MARTIN DAGGETT [9] (*David*,[8] *Henry*,[7] *Ichabod*,[6] *Elihu*,[5] *Mayhew*,[4] *John*,[3] *Thomas*,[2] *John*[1]), born Stockholm, N.Y., October 19, 1846; address, 159 Baldwin street, Elmira, N.Y. (1892); married Parishville, N.Y., December 15, 1869, Myra Shepard Smith, daughter of Ansel Sowles and Susan Zerniah (Shepard) Smith; born Parishville, N.Y., September 4, 1851.

Issue:

3236. i. MABEL CORNELIA DAGGETT,[10] born Parishville, N.Y., June 12, 1873.
3237. ii. MYRON HERBERT DAGGETT,[10] born Parishville, N.Y., April 20, 1875.
3238. iii. CLARA MAY DAGGETT,[10] born Parishville, N.Y., October 17, 1877.
3239. iv. HENRY DAVID DAGGETT,[10] born Potsdam, N.Y., January 20, 1884.

Mr. Daggett is of the " Elmira Portrait Company."

2633. FRANK K. DAGGETT [9] (*Levi P.*,[8] *Henry*,[7] *Ichabod*,[6] *Elihu*,[5] *Mayhew*,[4] *John*,[3] *Thomas*,[2] *John*[1]), born 1838; died Litchfield, Minn., October, 1876; married Stockholm, N.Y., 1860, Emma Daggett, daughter of Stephen Abbot and Olive (Battles) Daggett (No. 2624); born Stockholm, N.Y., 1838; died August 4, 1883.

No issue.

2641. SARAH DAGGETT JILLSON [9] (*Eliza M. Daggett*,[8] *Benjamin*,[7] *Daniel*,[6] *Elihu*,[5] *Mayhew*,[4] *John*,[3] *Thomas*,[2] *John*[1]), born Attleboro', Mass., March 28, 1834; resides Attleboro', Mass. (1893); married Attleboro', Mass., November 24, 1858, Albert D. Dean, son of Dorrance and Sepha (Whittaker) Dean.

Issue:

3240. i. RUSSELL DEAN.[10]
3241. ii. EVALINE DEAN,[10] married Frederic Fogg; issue: two sons.

2642. GEORGE LEE JILLSON [9] (*Eliza M. Daggett*,[8] *Benjamin*,[7] *Daniel*,[6] *Elihu*,[5] *Mayhew*,[4] *John*,[3] *Thomas*,[2] *John*[1]), born Attleboro', Mass., September 23, 1837; resides North Attleboro', Mass. (1892); married 1st, Frances Stanley, daughter of Charles and Margaret (Montgomery) Stanley; married 2d, May 30, 1867, Estelle A. Bosworth, daughter of Pliny Bosworth; born Newton, Mass., September

7, 1843; married 3d, Ella Aldrich, daughter of Silas and Salome (Foster) Aldrich.

Issue : three children, 1876.

2645. OLIVER STANLEY[9] (*Catherine Blackinton,*[8] *Mary Daggett,*[7] *Daniel,*[6] *Elihu,*[5] *Mayhew,*[4] *John,*[3] *Thomas,*[2] *John*[1]), resides North Attleboro', Mass. (1893); married 1st, Attleboro' Falls, Mass., February 26, 1842, Emily Whitney, daughter of Martin and Nancy (Orne) Whitney; born Attleboro', Mass., February 6, 1813; died Attleboro', Mass., April 1, 1852; married 2d, Mary Perry, daughter of John Perry.

Issue :

3242. i. FREDERIC M. STANLEY,[10] born Attleboro', Mass., March 15, 1843; married; no issue; died Attleboro', Mass., August 15, 1877.
3243. ii. ANNIE FRANCES STANLEY,[10] married W. W. Pratt; issue : Stanley Pratt.[11]
3244. iii. EMILY STANLEY,[10] born Attleboro', Mass., 1852.

2647. ELINOR STANLEY[9] (*Catherine Blackinton,*[8] *Mary Daggett,*[7] *Daniel,*[6] *Elihu,*[5] *Mayhew,*[4] *John,*[3] *Thomas,*[2] *John*[1]), married Isaac Bailey; born Attleboro', Mass., May 11, 1814; died Attleboro', Mass., June 28, 1856.

Issue :

3245. i. IRVING I. BAILEY,[10] born Attleboro', Mass., January 17, 1846; died Attleboro', Mass., May 10, 1854.
3246. ii. CATHARINE BAILEY.[10]
3247. iii. ANNIE BAILEY.[10]

2649. WILLIAM DEAN WHITING[9] (*Nancy Blackinton,*[8] *Mary Daggett,*[7] *Daniel,*[6] *Elihu,*[5] *Mayhew,*[4] *John,*[3] *Thomas,*[2] *John*[1]), born Attleboro', Mass., December 23, 1815; died Attleboro', Mass., November 24, 1891; married December 17, 1839, Rebecca Damon Butterfield, daughter of Pitt and Lucy (Damon) Butterfield; born Dedham, Mass., May 8, 1818.

Issue :

3248. i. WILLIAM OSBORNE WHITING,[10] born September 30, 1846; drowned April 28, 1851.
3249. ii. FRANK MORTIMER WHITING,[10] born 1847; married Florence Hancock, daughter of Timothy E. and Harriett (Doane) Hancock; he died Attleboro', Mass., May 28, 1892; issue : two daughters; widow resides North Attleboro' (1893).
3250. iii. JOSEPHINE S. WHITING.[10]
3251. iv. FLORENCE R. WHITING.[10]

2655. EMILY RICHARDS[9] (*Olive D. Blackinton,*[8] *Mary Daggett,*[7] *Daniel,*[6] *Elihu,*[5] *Mayhew,*[4] *John,*[3] *Thomas,*[2] *John*[1]), married David

Capron; born December, 1811; died Attleboro', Mass., March 18, 1879.

Issue:

3252. i.   HENRY CAPRON,[10] married Josephine Mason; issue: two children.
3253. ii.   FRANK CAPRON,[10] married Emmeline Goodwin, daughter of Wallace and Angeline Goodwin.
3254. iii.   LOUISE CAPRON.[10]

2656. ANN MARIA RICHARDS[9] (*Olive D. Blackinton*,[8] *Mary Daggett*,[7] *Daniel*,[6] *Elihu*,[5] *Mayhew*,[4] *John*,[3] *Thomas*,[2] *John*[1]), born Attleboro', Mass., August 16, 1819; married Attleboro', Mass., October 28, 1841, Abiel Codding, son of Abiel and Chloe (Daggett) Codding; born Rehoboth, Mass., January 29, 1817.

Issue:

3255. i.   ARTHUR E. CODDING,[10] married Alice, daughter of Lucius and Amelia (Robinson) Chamberlin; issue: Alice,[11] Arthur,[11] daughter.[11]
3256. ii.   ELLA M. CODDING,[10] born Attleboro', Mass., February 26, 1845; died Attleboro', Mass., July 4, 1846.
3257. iii.   JAMES A. CODDING,[10] married Agnes Adele, daughter of Benjamin Stanley and Ann (Robinson) Freeman; issue: James A.,[11] Annie,[11] Josephine.[11]
3258. iv.   EDWIN A. CODDING,[10] married Jeanie, daughter of Joseph Jackson and Sarah A. (Tisdale) Freeman; issue: Joseph.[11]
3259. v.   ELLEN L. CODDING,[10] born Attleboro', Mass., November, 1860; died Attleboro', Mass., January 27, 1879.

2657. FRANCIS B. RICHARDS[9] (*Olive D. Blackinton*,[8] *Mary Daggett*,[7] *Daniel*,[6] *Elihu*,[5] *Mayhew*,[4] *John*,[3] *Thomas*,[2] *John*[1]), resides No. Attleboro', Mass. (1893); married 1st, Julia M. Peck; born 1828; died Attleboro', Mass., September 7, 1853; married 2d, Mrs. Short.

Issue:

3260. i.   HATTIE OLIVE RICHARDS,[10] married George Cheever, son of William and Betsy (Allen) Cheever; issue: one child.[11]
3261. ii.   ANNIE RICHARDS,[10] married Orin Clifford; issue: one child.[11]

2661. CHLOE RICHARDSON[9] (*Abigail Daggett*,[8] *Daniel*,[7] *Daniel*,[6] *Elihu*,[5] *Mayhew*,[4] *John*,[3] *Thomas*,[2] *John*[1]), born Attleboro', Mass., July 23, 1816; died Attleboro' Falls, Mass., February 5, 1854; married Guilford Fuller, son of Ezekiel and —— (Thayer) Fuller; born 1811; died Wrentham, Mass., January 17, 1889.

Issue:

3262. i.   ANSON FULLER.[10]
3263. ii.   CORNELIA FULLER.[10]
3264. iii.   ARTHUR FULLER.[10]
3265. iv.   SARAH FULLER.[10]

2662. CYNTHIA ANN RICHARDSON[9] (*Abigail Daggett*,[8] *Daniel*,[7] *Daniel*,[6] *Elihu*,[5] *Mayhew*,[4] *John*,[3] *Thomas*,[2] *John*[1]), born Attleboro', Mass., 1816; died Attleboro', Mass., September 19, 1888; married

Thomas Gully; born England, 1812; died Attleboro', Mass., May 24, 1892.

Issue:

3266. i. THOMAS GULLY,[10] born January 27, 1860.

2670. DANIEL CURTIS DAGGETT[9] (*Daniel*,[8] *Daniel*,[7] *Daniel*,[6] *Elihu*,[5] *Mayhew*,[4] *John*,[3] *Thomas*,[2] *John*[1]), born Taunton, Mass., July 11, 1828; "machinist;" died March 22, 1883; married Newburyport, Mass., August 28, 1851, by Rev. Nicholas Medbury, to Mary E. Brown, daughter of Charles and Lydia Brown; born Newburyport, Mass., 1833.

Issue:

3267. i. GEORGE H. DAGGETT,[10] resides Minneapolis, Minn. (1892).

2675. CORNELIUS D. ROBINSON[9] (*Hannah Daggett*,[8] *Daniel*,[7] *Daniel*,[6] *Elihu*,[5] *Mayhew*,[4] *John*,[3] *Thomas*,[2] *John*[1]), born Attleboro', Mass., August 28, 1835; died December 29, 1863; married Eva Barrows, daughter of Aaron and Evaline (Norris) Barrows.

Issue:

3268. i. EVA ROBINSON,[10] born April 13, 1863; died December 28, 1863.

2676. DANIEL H. ROBINSON[9] (*Hannah Daggett*,[8] *Daniel*,[7] *Daniel*,[6] *Elihu*,[5] *Mayhew*,[4] *John*,[3] *Thomas*,[2] *John*[1]), born Attleboro', Mass., May 3, 1839; resides West Attleboro', Mass. (1892); married Clara Ellis, daughter of Joel and Mary (Walcott) Ellis.

Issue: several children.

3269. i. JENNIE E. ROBINSON,[10] born July, 1883; drowned March 1, 1889.
3270. ii. DANIEL O. ROBINSON,[10] born September, 1884; drowned March 1, 1889.

2679. CHARLES DANIEL DAGGETT[9] (*Samuel S.*,[8] *Daniel*,[7] *Daniel*,[6] *Elihu*,[5] *Mayhew*,[4] *John*,[3] *Thomas*,[2] *John*[1]), born Milwaukee, Wis., May 2, 1851; resides Pasadena, Cal. (1892); married Milwaukee, Wis., September 7, 1875, Mary Stewart, daughter of Rev. J. B. (D.D.) and Nancy (Macgreger) Stewart; born Morristown, Ohio, May 30, 1854.

Issue:

3271. i. RUTH DAGGETT,[10] born Milwaukee, Wis., July 28, 1876.
3272. ii. HELEN DAGGETT,[10] born Milwaukee, Wis., November 6, 1877.
3273. iii. JOHN STEWART DAGGETT,[10] born Kansas City, Mo., November 5, 1878.
3274. iv. MAUD DAGGETT,[10] born Kansas City, Mo., February 10, 1883.

2680. ANNA MARIA DAGGETT[9] (*Mina B.*,[8] *Daniel*,[7] *Daniel*,[6] *Elihu*,[5] *Mayhew*,[4] *John*,[3] *Thomas*,[2] *John*[1]), born Attleboro', Mass., February 12, 1747; died Cumberland, R.I., June, 1887; married Attleboro', Mass., August 13, 1878, by Rev. W. Henry

King, to Charles Herbert Jencks, son of Liberty Whipple and Ann *
Elizabeth (Razee) Jencks, of Cumberland, R.I.; "farmer;" born
Cumberland, R.I., May 23, 1853.

Issue: four children.

3275. i. HALSEY BAXTER JENCKS,[10] born June 5, 1879.
3276. ii. LESTER MINA JENCKS,[10] born September 6, 1881.

2689. DANIEL O. STANLEY [9] (*Vernal Stanley,*[8] *Betsey Daggett,*[7]
Daniel,[6] *Elihu,*[5] *Mayhew,*[4] *John,*[3] *Thomas,*[2] *John* [1]), born Attleboro',
Mass., January 15, 1836; died Attleboro', Mass., June 16, 1886;
married 1st, Nancy D. Rounds, daughter of Enon and Nancy Rounds,
of Mansfield; born 1837; died Attleboro', Mass., November 12,
1857; married 2d, Eliza C. Gay, daughter of Jabez J. R. Gay;
born 1836; died Attleboro', Mass., November 14, 1878; married
3d, ——.

Issue: three children.

2712. HENRY WHEELER BULKLEY [9] (*Henry D.,*[8] *Amelia M. Dag-
gett,*[7] *Henry,*[6] *Elihu,*[5] *Mayhew,*[4] *John,*[3] *Thomas,*[2] *John* [1]), born New
York city, July 22, 1842; resides Orange, N.J. (1887); married
April 26, 1881, Isabella Cassard, of Baltimore, Md.

Issue:

3277. i. HENRY DAGGETT BULKLEY.[10]
3278. ii. GEORGE CASSARD BULKLEY.[10]

Henry Wheeler Bulkley is a mechanical engineer by profession, and
an extensive inventor. He was educated at New York College.

2713. Dr. LUCIUS DUNCAN BULKLEY [9] (*Henry D.,*[8] *Amelia M.
Daggett,*[7] *Henry,*[6] *Elihu,*[5] *Mayhew,*[4] *John,*[3] *Thomas,*[2] *John* [1]), born
New York city, January 12, 1845; resides 4 East Thirty-seventh
street, New York city (1889); married May 28, 1872, Kate Mellick,
of Bergen Point, N.J.

Issue:

3279. i.   LILLIE A. BULKLEY.[10]
3280. ii. JULIA BULKLEY.[10]
3281. iii. L. CONSTANT BULKLEY.[10]
3282. iv. H. DUNCAN BULKLEY.[10]
3283. v.   KATHLEEN BULKLEY.[10]
3284. vi. KENNETT BULKLEY.[10]

Lucius Duncan Bulkley, M.D., graduated at Yale and the New
York College of Physicians and Surgeons.

2714. EMMA MATILDA BULKLEY [9] (*Henry D.,*[8] *Amelia M. Daggett,*[7]
Henry,[6] *Elihu,*[5] *Mayhew,*[4] *John,*[3] *Thomas,*[2] *John* [1]), born New York

ьcity, March 22, 1850; resides New York city; married J. Cleveland
Cady, whose first wife was Julia Bulkley.

Issue:

3285. i. JULIA BULKLEY CADY.[10]
3286. ii. CLEVELAND CADY.[10]

2731. ROSABELLE TOWNSEND HOOKER [9] (*Edward*,[8] *Elisabeth
Daggett*,[7] *Henry*,[6] *Elihu*,[5] *Mayhew*,[4] *John*,[3] *Thomas*,[2] *John* [1]), born
Providence, R.I., June 9, 1858; resides Des Moines, Ia.; married
Philadelphia, Pa., March 28, 1882, John Lorenz, son of Jacob and
Christiana (Leupold) Lorenz; born Weissenstadt, Ger.

Issue:

3287. i. LUCY HOOKER LORENZ,[10] born Des Moines, Ia., April 7, 1884.
3288. ii. EDWARD HOOKER LORENZ,[10] born Des Moines, Ia., September 13,
1886.
3289. iii. PHILIP BATTEY LORENZ,[10] born Des Moines, Ia., January 2, 1889.
3290. iv. MAUD ESTHER LORENZ,[10] born Des Moines, Ia., July 11, 1891.

2732. HENRY DAGGETT HOOKER [9] (*Edward*,[8] *Elisabeth Daggett*,[7]
Henry,[6] *Elihu*,[5] *Mayhew*,[4] *John*,[3] *Thomas*,[2] *John* [1]), born Providence,
R.I., April 14, 1859; "architect;" resides 20 Sefferts place, Brooklyn,
N.Y. (1892); married Brooklyn, N.Y., January 7, 1886, Mary
Theodora Davenport, daughter of Julius and Mary Ann (Bates)
Davenport; born Brooklyn, N.Y., June 25, 1856.

Issue:

3291. i. DAVENPORT HOOKER,[10] born Brooklyn, N.Y., May 13, 1887.
3292. ii. HENRY DAGGETT HOOKER,[10] born Brooklyn, N.Y., January 25, 1892.

2745. ALBION PARIS KIMBALL [9] (*Emily A. Daggett*,[8] *George*,[7]
Elihu,[6] *Elihu*,[5] *Mayhew*,[4] *John*,[3] *Thomas*,[2] *John* [1]), born Atkinson,
Me., August 3, 1837; "farmer;" resides Bradford Centre, Me.
(1892); married Atkinson, Me., 1863, Margaret Blether, daughter of
Eben and Margaret (Coombs) Blether: born Atkinson. Me., March
31, 1845.

Issue:

3293. i. CHARLES EDWIN KIMBALL,[10] born Charleston, Me., January 31, 1866.
3294. ii. EBEN BLETHER KIMBALL,[10] born Bradford. Me., May 6, 1879.

2746. ELLEN MARIA DAGGETT [9] (*George R.*,[8] *George*,[7] *Elihu*,[6]
Elihu,[5] *Mayhew*,[4] *John*,[3] *Thomas*,[2] *John* [1]), born Atkinson, Me.,
March 1, 1843; resides Dover, Me. (1892); married Atkinson, Me.,
February 21, 1863, by Elisha L. Hammond, Esq., to Alanson Mellen
Warren, son of Elbridge G. and Phebe Celestia (Nason) Warren, of
Old Town, Me.; born Old Town, Me., June 1, 1838.

Issue:

3295. i. LELAND TINDALL WARREN,[10] born Atkinson, Me., July 8, 1864; died
Dover, Me., January 13, 1887.

3296. ii. VICTOR LISLE WARREN,[10] born Orneville, Me., December 8, 1865; student "Shaw's Commercial College," Portland, Me. (1892).

3297. iii. FRED GERRY WARREN,[10] born Orneville, Me., March 23, 1867; married Sebec, Me., January 1, 1890, by Rev. Mr. Taylor, to Effie Levensalor, daughter of Thomas and Vesta (Battles) Levensalor; born Sebec, Me., May 24, 1876; "boots and shoes;" resides Dover, Me. (1892).

3298. iv. BERNARD JEROME WARREN,[10] born Orneville, Me., June 25, 1869; married Dover, Me., September 18, 1889, by Rev. A. G. Hill, to Hester Frances Foss, daughter of John and Sophia (Johnson) Foss; born Milo, Me., February 3, 1867; "hair-dresser;" resides Dover, Me. (1892).

3299. v. MELLEN EDWIN WARREN,[10] born Orneville, Me., November 4, 1874; "clerk;" resides Sebec, Me. (1892).

3300. vi. ELLEN ALWILDA WARREN,[10] born Orneville, Me., March 1, 1879.

Mr. Warren was orderly sergeant of Company M, First Maine Cavalry, and was severely wounded at the battle of Aldie, June 17, 1863.

He was for many years a teacher and farmer; now (1892) register of deeds, Piscataquis county, Me.

2747. LYDIA FRANCES DAGGETT[9] (*George R.,*[8] *George,*[7] *Elihu,*[6] *Elihu,*[5] *Mayhew,*[4] *John,*[3] *Thomas,*[2] *John*[1]), born Atkinson, Me., June 17, 1844; resides Ontario, Knox county, Ill. (1892); married 1st, South Sebec, Me., October 23, 1863, by Theodore Wyman, to Jesse Frank Stevens, of Sebec, Me., son of Judge Jesse and Glaphyra (Lovejoy) Stevens; born Wayne, Me., July 22, 1831; died Rockton, Ill., September 11, 1878; married 2d, Galesburg, Ill., December 23, 1882, by Thomas McKee, to Angus Moor,[9] son of Eber Stuart and Lydia T.[8] (Daggett) Moor (No. 2739); born Anson, Me., February 8, 1835; "farmer."

Issue:

3301. i. CONRAD FRANK STEVENS,[10] born Sebec, Me., August 7, 1864.

3302. ii. JESSIE PAULINA STEVENS,[10] born Sebec, Me., May 19, 1866.

3303. iii. GEORGE DAGGETT STEVENS,[10] born Sebec, Me., February 24, 1868; married Aledo, Ill., April 15, 1881; address, Ontario, Ill. (1892).

3304. iv. HOWARD WARREN STEVENS,[10] born Rockton, Ill., March 1, 1872.

3305. v. HARRY WALLACE STEVENS,[10] born Rockton, Ill., March 1, 1872.

3306. vi. JAY FRED STEVENS,[10] born Rockton, Ill., February 7, 1879.

3307. vii. DON ANGUS MOOR,[10] born Rio, Ill., April 28, 1885.

Jesse F. Stevens was enrolled September 24, 1864, and assigned to the Seventeenth Regiment, Maine Infantry, but was detailed to write in quartermaster's department. Discharged May 13, 1865, at Portland, Me. Appointed justice of the peace, April 20, 1867, for a term of seven years. Was school director in Rockton, Ill., several terms.

2748. HENRIETTA ATWOOD DAGGETT[9] (*George R.,*[8] *George,*[7] *Elihu,*[6] *Elihu,*[5] *Mayhew,*[4] *John,*[3] *Thomas,*[2] *John*[1]), born Atkinson, Me., August 13, 1848; resides Milo, Me. (1892); married 1st, Orne-

ville, Me., January 1, 1867, by Alanson M. Warren, Esq., to Lewis
Melvin Porter, son of William and Persis (Hamlin) Porter; born
Orneville, Me., February 12, 1845; "carpenter;" died Jacksonville,
Fla., January 8, 1888; married 2d, Dover, Me., March 4, 1889, by
Alanson M. Warren, Esq., to Amos Perkins Morse, of Milo, Me.,
son of Aaron and Olive (White) Morse; "farmer;" born Old Town,
Me., March 23, 1837.

No issue.

Mr. Porter was a soldier during the Civil War. He served in the
Fourth and Sixteenth Maine Regiments; was eight months a prisoner
at Libby Prison, and released only a short time before the close of
the war.

2749. ALBERT AUSTIN DAGGETT[9] (*George R.,*[8] *George,*[7] *Elihu,*[6]
Elihu,[5] *Mayhew,*[4] *John,*[3] *Thomas,*[2] *John*[1]), born Atkinson, Me.,
September 30, 1851; "farmer;" resides Atkinson, Me. (1892);
married Atkinson, Me., June 21, 1873, Hattie Orissa Turner,
daughter of Joseph and Sarah Scovill (Stocker) Turner; born Dover,
Me., December 22, 1855; postmistress at Maple, Me. (town of
Atkinson), (1892).

Issue:

3308. i. ANNIE PAULINE DAGGETT,[10] born Atkinson, Me., February 1, 1874.
3309. ii. HENRY WORTH DAGGETT,[10] born Atkinson, Me., March 4, 1879.
3310. iii. HELEN LYDIA DAGGETT,[10] born Atkinson, Me., December 27, 1880.
3311. iv. MARY ETTA DAGGETT,[10] born Atkinson, Me., October 27, 1886; died
Atkinson, Me., August 25, 1887.
3312. v. EVA ALBERTA DAGGETT,[10] born Atkinson, Me., April 17, 1889.

2750. HATTIE EVELYN DAGGETT[9] (*George R.,*[8] *George,*[7] *Elihu,*[6]
Elihu,[5] *Mayhew,*[4] *John,*[3] *Thomas,*[2] *John*[1]), born Atkinson, Me.,
October 13, 1858; resides Atkinson, Me. (1892); married Atkinson,
Me., May 26, 1877, by Rev. S. S. Goss, to Charles Barney Noyes,
son of David Jewett and Nancy (Barney) Noyes; "farmer;" born
Atkinson, Me., May 2, 1845.

Issue:

3313. i. ALICE MARY NOYES,[10] born Atkinson, Me., October 22, 1878.
3314. ii. EDITH HENRIETTA NOYES,[10] born Atkinson, Me., September 15, 1880.
3315. iii. EDWIN DAGGETT NOYES,[10] born Atkinson, Me., August 17, 1882.
3316. iv. CARL B. NOYES,[10] born Atkinson, Me., December 12, 1883.
3317. v. WILLIAM MORREN NOYES,[10] born Atkinson, Me., May 6, 1887.
3318. vi. FRED A. NOYES,[10] born Atkinson, Me., March 12, 1889.

2760. JOHN GOULD DAGGETT[9] (*Earl P.,*[8] *George,*[7] *Elihu,*[6] *Elihu,*[5]
Mayhew,[4] *John,*[3] *Thomas,*[2] *John*[1]), born Orneville, Me., June 15,
1849; "cook;" resides Medford, Me. (1892); married Medford,
Me., March 30, 1876, by Rev. Mr. Palmer, to Manilla E. Emery,

daughter of Joseph and Harriet (Boobar) Emery; born Medford, Me., February 20, 1857.

Issue:

3319. i. JOHN HENRY DAGGETT,[10] born Medford, Me., August 24, 1879.
3320. ii. PERLEY LOWE DAGGETT,[10] born Medford, Me., December 27, 1881: drowned January 4, 1890.
3321. iii. EARL BYRON DAGGETT,[10] born Medford, Me., August 20, 1886.

2761. MARY ELIZABETH DAGGETT [9] (*Albion K. P.,*[8] *George,*[7] *Elihu,*[6] *Elihu,*[5] *Mayhew,*[4] *John,*[3] *Thomas,*[2] *John* [1]), born Orneville, Me., February 26, 1845; resides Bradford, Me. (1892); married Bradford, Me., January 1, 1866, Daniel Waterman King, of Bradford, son of Rice and Bridget (Cowan) King; "farmer;" born Bradford, Me., September 12, 1844.

Issue:

3322. i. CHARLES HENRY KING,[10] born Bradford, Me., October 31, 1866.
3323. ii. ANNIE MABEL KING,[10] born Bradford, Me., July 14, 1870.

2772. HENRY LEFRELET DAGGETT [9] (*Henry L.,*[8] *Jacob,*[7] *Elihu,*[6] *Elihu,*[5] *Mayhew,*[4] *John,*[3] *Thomas,*[2] *John* [1]), born Boston, Mass., July 19, 1851; resides Commonwealth avenue, Boston, Mass. (1892); married Boston, Mass., October 15, 1873, by Rev. Alexander H. Vinton, to Evelyn W. Fay, daughter of Franklin L. and Hannah S. Fay; born Malden, Mass., 1852.

Issue:

3324. i. HENRY LEFRELET DAGGETT.[10] born Boston, Mass., December 24, 1874.

2779. WILLARD FRANCIS DAGGETT [9] (*Willard E.,*[8] *Jacob,*[7] *Elihu,*[6] *Elihu,*[5] *Mayhew,*[4] *John,*[3] *Thomas,*[2] *John* [1]), born Dorchester, Mass., August 7, 1850; "clerk;" died Boston, Mass., April 11, 1875; married Boston, Mass., October 29, 1872, by Rev. John O. Means, to Mary J. Lee, daughter of James and Frances Lee; born Norwich, Conn., 1854.

Issue:

3325. i. HARRY LEE DAGGETT,[10] born Boston, Mass., September 15, 1873; died Boston, Mass., May 5, 1874.

2781. MILTON LYMAN DAGGETT [9] (*Lyman,*[8] *Milton,*[7] *Elijah,*[6] *Elihu,*[5] *Mayhew,*[4] *John,*[3] *Thomas,*[2] *John* [1]), born Boston, Mass., 1848; "photographer;" resides Taunton, Mass. (1885); married 1st, Charlestown, Mass., July 3, 1873, by Rev. Mark Trafton, to Mary A. Ames, widow, daughter of Francis A. and Mary G. Curtis; born Surry, Me., March 14, 1847; died Taunton, Mass., April 16, 1878; married 2d, Taunton, Mass., June 10, 1880, by Rev. J. W. Ballantine, to Hattie L. Becker, daughter of William and Mary A. Becker; born Dorchester, Mass., 1861.

2783. WARREN C. DAGGETT[9] (*Lyman,*[8] *Milton,*[7] *Elijah,*[6] *Elihu,*[5] *Mayhew,*[4] *John,*[3] *Thomas,*[2] *John* [1]), born Boston, Mass., 1862; "printer;" address, 39 Arch street, Boston, Mass. (1893); married Malden, Mass., May 10, 1882, by Rev. J. W. Wellman, to Bessie P. Stafford, daughter of William W. and Elizabeth Stafford; born Newton, Mass., 1865.

Issue:

3326. i. ISABELLA STAFFORD DAGGETT,[10] born Boston, Mass., August 18, 1883.

2785. DAVID ARTHUR BROWN[9] (*Mary A. Daggett,*[8] *Otis,*[7] *Joab,*[6] *John,*[5] *Ebenezer,*[4] *John,*[3] *Thomas,*[2] *John* [1]), born Attleboro', Mass., May 14, 1839; resides Penacook, N.H. (1892); married Concord, N.H., December 22, 1864, Susan Malvina Follansbee, daughter of John Pettee and Sarah Ann (Jacobs) Follansbee; born Grafton, N.H., March 18, 1842.

Issue:

3327. i. HENRY ARTHUR BROWN,[10] born Penacook, N.H., February 8, 1868.

Mr. Brown is treasurer of the Concord Axle Company, and president of the Archibald Wheel Company (1892).

2786. MARY LOUISA BROWN[9] (*Mary A. Daggett,*[8] *Otis,*[7] *Joab,*[6] *John,*[5] *Ebenezer,*[4] *John,*[3] *Thomas,*[2] *John* [1]), born Attleboro', Mass., June 25, 1841; resides Penacook, N.H. (1892); married Penacook, N.H., July 10, 1866, William Henry Caldwell, son of Benjamin F. and Pamelia (Symonds) Caldwell; born Nashua, N.H., May 23, 1842.

Issue:

3328. i. MARY GRACE CALDWELL,[10] born Penacook, N.H., May 6, 1867.

2788. ELLEN MARIA BROWN[9] (*Mary A. Daggett,*[8] *Otis,*[7] *Joab,*[6] *John,*[5] *Ebenezer,*[4] *John,*[3] *Thomas,*[2] *John* [1]), born Penacook, N.H., January 11, 1848; died Winchester, Mass., July 10, 1884; married Penacook, N.H., January 16, 1873, Rev. Joseph Flanders Fielden, son of Samuel and Betsy (Scott) Fielden; born Somersworth, N.H., October 23, 1844; resides Newport, N.H. (1892).

Issue:

3329. i. HENRY BROWN FIELDEN,[10] born Penacook, N.H., June 29, 1874.

2789. ISABEL NANCY BROWN[9] (*Mary A. Daggett,*[8] *Otis,*[7] *Joab,*[6] *John,*[5] *Ebenezer,*[4] *John,*[3] *Thomas,*[2] *John* [1]), born Penacook, N.H., April 7, 1850; resides Penacook, N.H. (1892); married Penacook, N.H., June 8, 1874, John Howard Moore, son of John S. and Hannah (Dow) Moore; born Canterbury, N.H., May 22, 1852.

Issue:

3330. i. HERBERT FISHER MOORE,[10] born Penacook, N.H., July 10, 1875.

3331. ii. Mary Belle Moore,[10] born Penacook, N.H., July 21, 1876; died
    Penacook, N.H., September 11, 1876.
3332. iii. Howard Brown Moore,[10] born Penacook, N.H., August 8, 1883.

2792. John Gilman Daggett [9] (*John G.,*[8] *Otis,*[7] *Joab,*[6] *John,*[5]
Ebenezer,[4] *John,*[3] *Thomas,*[2] *John* [1]), born Princeton, Mass., November 21, 1850; of " De Butts & Daggett; " resides Somerville, Mass.
(1891); married Boston, Mass., December 6, 1882, by Rev. E. E.
Hale, to Eva Pickering Goodwin, daughter of Henry and Eveline S.
Goodwin; born Salem, Mass., 1853.
Issue:

3333. i. Ethel Goodwin Daggett,[10] born Boston, Mass., March 27, 1884.
3334. ii. Harold Pickering Daggett,[10] born Boston, Mass., August 3, 1885;
    died Boston, Mass., September 21, 1885.

2793. Mary Daggett [9] (*John G.,*[8] *Otis,*[7] *Joab,*[6] *John,*[5] *Ebenezer,*[4]
John,[3] *Thomas,*[2] *John* [1]), born Boston, Mass., October 3, 1860;
married October 17, 1886, Capt. Walter Francis Thorndike, of
Rockport, Me., son of Joseph Wallace and Margaret Williams (Colley) Thorndike.
Issue:

3335. i. Warner Thorndike,[10] born Somerville, Mass., November 17, 1891.

2794. Mabel Daggett [9] (*John G.,*[8] *Otis,*[7] *Joab,*[6] *John,*[5] *Ebenezer,*[4] *John,*[3] *Thomas,*[2] *John* [1]), born Boston, Mass., October 3, 1860;
resides Farmington, Conn. (1892); married Somerville, Mass., August 12, 1886, Charles Brandegee, of Berlin, Conn.
Issue:

3336. i. Hildegarde Brandegee,[10] born Leavenworth, Kan., April 12, 1887.

2795. Harry Richards Shepardson [9] (*Martha J. Daggett,*[8]
Otis,[7] *Joab,*[6] *John,*[5] *Ebenezer,*[4] *John,*[3] *Thomas,*[2] *John* [1]), born Attleboro', Mass., May 19. 1859; manager " New Star Laundry; "
address, 406 So. State street, Chicago, Ill. (1892); married Keokuk,
Ia., May 12, 1885.
Issue:

3337. i. Elizabeth Daggett Shepardson,[10] born Keokuk, Ia., March 2,
    1886.
3338. ii. Charlotte Shepardson,[10] born Chicago, Ill., March 28, 1888.
3339. iii. Dorothy Conant Shepardson,[10] born Boston, Mass., December 28,
    1889.

2797. Emma Elisabeth Tenney [9] (*Abigail Daggett,*[8] *Levi,*[7] *Joab,*[6]
John,[5] *Ebenezer,*[4] *John,*[3] *Thomas,*[2] *John* [1]), born Beloit, Wis., November 27, 1849; resides Richland Centre, Wis. (1892); married Richland Centre, Wis., November 25, 1874, Edgar Van Winter, son of

Michael and Margrett (Oliver) Van Winter; born Poynette, Wis.,
March 27, 1847.

Issue:

3340. i.   EDGAR TENNEY VAN WINTER.[10]
3341. ii. CARL BENJAMIN VAN WINTER.[10]
3342. iii. WALTER BAILEY VAN WINTER.[10]
3343. iv. HERBERT VAN WINTER.[10]

2799.   ABBIE ELEANOR DAGGETT [9] (*Levi*,[8] *Levi*,[7] *Joab*,[6] *John*,[5]
Ebenezer,[4] *John*,[3] *Thomas*,[2] *John* [1]), born East Hartford, Conn.,
October 30, 1845; resides East Attleboro', Mass. (1892); married
Providence, R.I., April 18, 1867, J. S. Richards.

Issue:

3344. i.   HERBERT L. RICHARDS,[10] born Mansfield, Mass., April 2, 1868; mar-
           ried Mansfield, Mass., June 20, 1889.
3345. ii. IDA SYLVIA RICHARDS,[10] born Mansfield, Mass., September 16, 1869;
           died Attleboro', Mass., January 2, 1879.
3346. iii. ANNIE EMELINE RICHARDS,[10] born Attleboro', Mass., May 21, 1883;
           died Attleboro', Mass., November 5, 1883.

2806.   ELLA AMANDA LUCAS [9] (*Elizabeth A. Daggett*,[8] *Pliny*,[7]
Joab,[6] *John*,[5] *Ebenezer*,[4] *John*,[3] *Thomas*,[2] *John* [1]), born Boston,
Mass., September 5, 1847; resides Frisco, Oklahoma territory (1892);
married Avoca, Wis., December 7, 1871, William Henry Morey, of
Pulaski, Wis., son of Thomas Jefferson and Maria (Antnette)
Morey; born Avoca, Wis., April 6, 1845.

Issue:

3347. i.   ELIZABETH MARIE MOREY,[10] born Avoca, Wis., June 5, 1874.
3348. ii. GUY ALLEN MOREY,[10] born Avoca, Wis., September 24, 1877.
3349. iii. ELLA ETTA MOREY,[10] born Avoca, Wis., July 25, 1879.
3350. iv. FRANK PARKS MOREY,[10] born Luverne, Minn., October 3, 1883.
3351. v.   RAYMOND AUGUSTUS MOREY,[10] born August 7, 1891: died January 11,
           1892.

2809.   ANNE CORA JENKINS [9] (*Mary J. Daggett*,[8] *Pliny*,[7] *Joab*,[6]
John,[5] *Ebenezer*,[4] *John*,[3] *Thomas*,[2] *John* [1]), born Avoca, Wis., April
21, 1859; resides St. Paul, Minn. (1892); married La Crosse, Wis.,
December 31, 1890, John Louis Townley, son of Manley and Elizabeth (Loyhed) Townley; born Ludlowville, N.Y., November 24,
1854; "lawyer."

Issue:

3352. i.   FLORENCE ELIZABETH TOWNLEY,[10] born St. Paul, Minn., February 2,
           1892.

2812.   FLOYD LORENZO DAGGETT [9] (*Pliny A.*,[8] *Pliny*,[7] *Joab*,[6]
John,[5] *Ebenezer*,[4] *John*,[3] *Thomas*,[2] *John* [1]), born Wyoming, Wis.,
December 15, 1861; resides Spokane, Wash. (1892); married June

6, 1886, Christeena McIntyre, daughter of Jno. B. and Cynthia (Allison) McIntyre; born Muscoda, Wis., October 5, 1868.

Issue:

3353. i. GORDON FLOYD DAGGETT,[10] born Muscoda, Wis., August 9, 1889.
3354. ii. GUSSIE MAC DAGGETT,[10] born Spokane, Wash., August 12, 1891.

Of the firm of P. A. Daggett & Co., " insurance," 306 Post street, Spokane (1892).

2901. ELEANOR SARAH DAGGETT [9] (*Robert P.*,[8] *William*,[7] *Ezra*,[6] *Naphtali*,[5] *Ebenezer*,[4] *John*,[3] *Thomas*,[2] *John* [1]), born Indianapolis, Ind., December 6, 1872; resides Bloomington, Ind. (1892); married Indianapolis, Ind., March 24, 1891, Prof. Gustaf Karsten, of Petershagenfeld, West Prussia, Ger.

Issue:

3355. i. CARL ROBERT GUSTAF KARSTEN,[10] born Bloomington, Ind., December 25, 1891.

2908. SARAH EMILY MERSICK [9] (*Edwin F.*,[8] *Sarah Daggett*,[7] *Ezra*,[6] *Naphtali*,[5] *Ebenezer*,[4] *John*,[3] *Thomas*,[2] *John* [1]), born August 27, 1863; married June 14, 1887, Fred Bradley.

Issue:

3356. i. SEYMOUR MERSICK BRADLEY,[10] born April 25, 1888.
3357. ii. MILDRED BRADLEY,[10] born May 1, 1890.

2912. GEORGE A. DAGGETT [9] (*George*,[8] *Levi*,[7] *Samuel*,[6] *Samuel*,[5] *Ebenezer*,[4] *John*,[3] *Thomas*,[2] *John* [1]), born Cowlesville, N.Y., June 19, 1844; married Kansas City, Mo., April 30, 1868, Lillie G. Carter.

Issue:

3358. i. WILLIAM A. DAGGETT,[10] married San Francisco, Cal., June 27, 1889, Rebecca Dunn.
3359. ii. CAROLINE BIRD DAGGETT,[10] married Stockton, Cal., November, 1890, W. S. Towson.

George A. Daggett enlisted in the Seventh Missouri Volunteer Cavalry, September 1, 1862. Was in the engagement at Prairie Grove, Ark., December 7, and at the siege of Vicksburg, Miss. Commissioned first lieutenant, Company A, Fortieth Missouri Volunteer Infantry, August 25, 1864, and was in engagements at Columbia, Franklin, and Nashville, Tenn.; also at the siege of Mobile, Ala.

2915. HELEN S. STEARNS [9] (*Hannah Daggett*,[8] *Levi*,[7] *Samuel*,[6] *Samuel*,[5] *Ebenezer*,[4] *John*,[3] *Thomas*,[2] *John* [1]), born Leicester, N.Y., June 19, 1849; resides Academy, N.Y. (1892); married Bristol, N.Y., November 18, 1875, Henry Stid.

Issue:

3360. i. FANNY R. STID,[10] born Bristol, N.Y., January 28, 1876.
3361. ii. EDWARD F. STID,[10] born Bristol, N.Y., December 20, 1881.

2916. FRANKLIN A. STEARNS [9] (*Hannah Daggett,*[8] *Levi,*[7] *Samuel,*[6] *Samuel,*[5] *Ebenezer,*[4] *John,*[3] *Thomas,*[2] *John*[1]), born Leicester, N.Y., May 27, 1852; resides Tescott, Kan. (1892); married Tescott, Kan., April 8, 1886.

Issue :

3362. i. PERRY R. STEARNS,[10] born Tescott, Kan., February 26, 1887.
3363. ii. HARVEY C. STEARNS,[10] born Tescott, Kan., August 5, 1890.

2917. CHARLES A. STEARNS [9] (*Hannah Daggett,*[8] *Levi,*[7] *Samuel,*[6] *Samuel,*[5] *Ebenezer,*[4] *John,*[3] *Thomas,*[2] *John*[1]), born Bethany, N.Y., August 10, 1854; resides E. Syracuse, N.Y. (1892); married Penfield, N.Y., February 13, 1890.

Issue :

3364. i. MARGUERITE C. STEARNS,[10] born E. Syracuse, N.Y., February 4, 1891.

2918. MARY E. STEARNS [9] (*Hannah Daggett,*[8] *Levi,*[7] *Samuel,*[6] *Samuel,*[5] *Ebenezer,*[4] *John,*[3] *Thomas,*[2] *John*[1]), born Penfield, N.Y., November 6, 1857; resides Penfield, N.Y. (1892); married 1st, Emerson Corner; married 2d, Albert Mutschler.

Issue :

3365. i. ALICE M. CORNER,[10] born Bristol, N.Y., May 8, 1877.
3366. ii. HELEN M. CORNER,[10] born Canandaigua, N.Y., February 3, 1879.

2938. CHARLES MARION DAGGETT [9] (*Francis,*[8] *Moses,*[7] *Ebenezer,*[6] *Samuel,*[5] *Ebenezer,*[4] *John,*[3] *Thomas,*[2] *John*[1]), born Springfield, Mass., November 5, 1860; resides Aspen, Col. (1892); married Dallas, Tex., December 8, 1882, Lizzie Caldwell.

Issue :

3367. i. FRANK MONROE DAGGETT,[10] born San Antonio, Tex., September 8, 1883; resides Springfield, Mass. (1892).

2951. CHARLES MORGAN MORSE [9]. (*Rebecca J. Daggett,*[8] *Ebenezer,*[7] *Ebenezer,*[6] *Samuel,*[5] *Ebenezer,*[4] *John,*[3] *Thomas,*[2] *John*[1]), born South Amboy, N.J., August 24, 1853; resides San Mateo, Cal. (1892); married Kirkwood, Mo., February 8, 1876, Della Rogers.

Issue :

3368. i. FRANK KYLE MORSE,[10] born Kirkwood, Mo., November 30, 1876.

2960. WALLACE ROSMERANS DAGGETT [9] (*William,*[8] *Ebenezer,*[7] *Ebenezer,*[6] *Samuel,*[5] *Ebenezer,*[4] *John,*[3] *Thomas,*[2] *John*[1]), born Ottumwa, Ia., October 28, 1862; resides Englewood, Kan. (1892); married Englewood, Kan., April 26, 1888, by Rev. M. L. Mun, to Jennie Mair Beach, daughter of James Hutchins and Jennie (Gould) Beach; born Lockport, N.Y., March 17, 1869.

Issue :

3369. i. GENEVIEVE GOULD DAGGETT,[10] born Englewood, Kan., October 6, 1890.

2974. ELLA WELLS [9] (*Charles,*[8] *Sarah Daggett,*[7] *Levi,*[6] *Samuel,*[5] *Ebenezer,*[4] *John,*[3] *Thomas,*[2] *John* [1]), born Syracuse, N.Y., October 21, 1851; resides Oakland, Cal. (1892); married New York city, 1873, Byron F. Stone.

Issue:

3370. i.   BYRON F. STONE,[10] born Oakland, Cal.
3371. ii. CHARLES W. STONE,[10] born Oakland, Cal.
3372. iii. LOUISE B. STONE,[10] born Oakland, Cal.

2981. JAMES BULLARD [9] (*Harriet D. Monson,*[8] *Mary Daggett,*[7] *Abner,*[6] *Thomas,*[5] *Thomas,*[4] *John,*[3] *Thomas,*[2] *John* [1]), born Boston, Mass., September 14, 1832; resides Farmington, N.H. (1893); married Boston, Mass., January 22, 1874, by Rev. C. C. Carpenter, to Mary Elizabeth Souther, daughter of William and Mary Souther; born Boston, Mass., 1835; died Boston, Mass., February 26, 1888.

Issue:

3373. i. MARIA BULLARD,[10] born Claremont, N.H., December 8, 1877; died Claremont, N.H., December 8, 1877.

2982. ANN DAGGETT BULLARD [9] (*Harriet D. Monson,*[8] *Mary Daggett,*[7] *Abner,*[6] *Thomas,*[5] *Thomas,*[4] *John,*[3] *Thomas,*[2] *John* [1]), born Boston, Mass., November 15, 1833; resides 77 Mt. Pleasant avenue, Boston, Mass. (1893); married Boston, Mass., September 1, 1853, by Rev. George M. Randall, to Lemuel Nichols Ide, son of Simeon and Evelina Pamela (Goddard) Ide, of Claremont, N.H.; born Windsor, Vt., August 29, 1825.

Issue:

3374. i.   HARRIET FRANCES IDE,[10] born Boston, Mass., July 27, 1854; married Claremont, N.H., October 19, 1882, by Rev. Charles S. Hale, to George Manton Randall, son of Bishop George M. and Eliza (Hoar) Randall; born Boston, Mass., April, 1853; resides Plainfield, N.J. (1893).
3375. ii.   ALICE BULLARD IDE,[10] born Boston, Mass., December 20, 1857.
3376. iii. ARTHUR WILSON IDE,[10] born Claremont, N.H., June 12, 1860; married Manchester, N.H., December 26, 1889, Lilian June Ricker; resides Helena, Mont. (1893).
3377. iv.   HENRY JORDAN IDE,[10] born Claremont, N.H., September 18, 1862.
3378. v.   FRANCIS LEMUEL IDE,[10] born Claremont, N.H., August 26, 1864; married Fort Missoula, Mont., August 10, 1893, Frances Stillson Brown, daughter of Johnson Butler Brown; resides Missoula, Mont. (1893).
3379. vi.   EDWIN BULLARD IDE,[10] born Claremont, N.H., July 22, 1869.
3380. vii. ANNA LOUISE IDE,[10] born Claremont, N.H., March 15, 1871.
3381. viii. HORTON GREGORY IDE,[10] born Claremont, N.H., July 24, 1873.

Mr. Ide was for many years engaged in the manufacture of paper in Claremont, where he also conducted a printing and binding establishment. He is now in the book trade in Boston.

2983. MARY MONSON BULLARD [9] (*Harriet D. Monson,*[8] *Mary Daggett,*[7] *Abner,*[6] *Thomas,*[5] *Thomas,*[4] *John,*[3] *Thomas,*[2] *John* [1]), born

Boston, Mass., January 7, 1835; resides Parade street, Providence, R.I. (1893); married Boston, Mass., February 10, 1858, by Dr. Geo. M. Randall, to Herbert Augustus Richards, son of Henry and Fanny (Holmes) Richards; born Attleboro', Mass., February 8, 1832.

Issue:

3382. i.   ANN BULLARD RICHARDS,[10] born Providence, R.I.. March 2, 1859.
3383. ii.   MARY FLORENCE RICHARDS,[10] born Providence, R.I., September 30, 1860.
3384. iii. CHARLOTTE GUILD RICHARDS,[10] born Providence, R.I., June 20, 1863.
3385. iv.   ELLEN LOUISA RICHARDS,[10] born Providence, R.I., May 1, 1865.
3386. v.   CAROLINE FRANCES RICHARDS,[10] born Providence, R.I., August 4, 1868.
3387. vi.   HERBERT AUGUSTUS RICHARDS,[10] born Providence, R.I., August 29, 1870; graduated Brown University, 1893.
3388. vii. WALTER HOLMES RICHARDS,[10] born Attleboro', Mass., June 26, 1872; died Attleboro', Mass., November 24, 1874.
3389. viii. FRANCIS BULLARD RICHARDS,[10] born Attleboro', Mass., November 24, 1874.

Mr. Richards is engaged in the wholesale dry-goods business, of the firm of Hartwell, Richards & Co.

2984. FRANCIS LEWIS BULLARD [9] (*Harriet D. Monson*,[8] *Mary Daggett*,[7] *Abner*,[6] *Thomas*,[5] *Thomas*,[4] *John*,[3] *Thomas*,[2] *John* [1]), born Boston, Mass., November 23, 1836; resides Wellesley, Mass. (1893); married Boston, Mass., September 25, 1862, by Rev. E. E. Hale, to Ellen M. Hinkley, daughter of Holmes and Mary Hinkley; born Boston, Mass., 1839.

Issue:

3390. i.   MARY ADAMS BULLARD.[10] born Boston, Mass., January 9, 1866; married Boston. Mass., November 18, 1886, by Rev. Edward A. Horton, to William Dart Sheldon, son of Nicholas Sheldon; he born July 9, 1865; died Providence, R.I., June 23, 1893; no issue; she resides Providence, R.I. (1893).
3391. ii.   ALFRED MACKENZIE BULLARD,[10] born Boston, Mass., March 22, 1874; died Boston, Mass., August 28, 1874.
3392. iii. LEWIS HINKLEY BULLARD,[10] born Boston, Mass., August 15, 1878.

Mr. Bullard was for many years treasurer of the Hinkley Locomotive Works, afterward of the Rhode Island Locomotive Works, and now interested in trust estates in Boston.

2985. GEORGE EDWIN BULLARD [9] (*Harriet D. Monson*,[8] *Mary Daggett*,[7] *Abner*,[6] *Thomas*,[5] *Thomas*,[4] *John*,[3] *Thomas*,[2] *John* [1]), born Boston, Mass., March 4, 1839; resides Highland street, Boston, Mass. (1893); married Boston, Mass., October 6, 1881, by Rev. J. G. Brooks, to Mrs. Josephine H. Binney, widow of George Binney, and daughter of Joseph H. and Mary (Davenport) Hayward, of Boston; born Boston, Mass., 1836.

Mr. Bullard is Boston agent of Brown Bros. & Co., bankers.

2987. Alfred Monson Bullard [9] (*Harriet D. Monson,*[8] *Mary Daggett,*[7] *Abner,*[6] *Thomas,*[5] *Thomas,*[4] *John,*[3] *Thomas,*[2] *John* [1]), born Boston, Mass., May 21, 1845; resides Winthrop street, Boston, Mass. (1893); married Boston, Mass., February 27, 1878, by Rev. C. C. Carpenter, to Florence Emeline Todd, daughter of Frederick A. and Emeline Todd; born Roxbury, Mass., 1847.

Issue:

3393. i. Lawrence Bullard,[10] born Boston, Mass., May 14, 1879.

Mr. Bullard is of the firm of Bullard & Davenport, insurance agents.

2998. Jeannette Atwater Dwight [9] (*Susan D. Daggett,*[8] *Leonard A.,*[7] *David,*[6] *Thomas,*[5] *Thomas,*[4] *John,*[3] *Thomas,*[2] *John*[1]), born New York city, October 20, 1852; resides 37 West Twenty-fifth street, New York city; married New York city, February 12, 1879, George Theodore Bliss, son of George Bliss.

Issue:

3394. i. Susan Dwight Bliss,[10] born New York city, January, 1882.

George T. Bliss, of the firm of Morton & Bliss, bankers.

3020. Orinda Sherer Daggett [9] (*George B.,*[8] *Brotherton,*[7] *Samuel,*[6] *Thomas,*[5] *Brotherton,*[4] *Joshua,*[3] *Thomas,*[2] *John* [1]), born Union, Me., November 5, 1850; resides Rockland, Me. (1892); married Rockland, Me., January 15, 1870, Michael Jacob Achorn (originally " Eichhorn "), son of Michael and Celinda (Gregory) Achorn; born Rockland, Me., August 8, 1845; died Dark Harbor, Me., June 6, 1892.

Issue.

3395. i. Kate Murray Achorn,[10] born Rockland, Me., September 20, 1871; died Rockland, Me., November 10, 1878.
3396. ii. Davis Tillson Achorn,[10] born Rockland, Me., March 14, ——.
3397. iii. Luella Achorn,[10] born Rockland, Me., June 18, 1882.

3022. George Loring Daggett [9] (*George B.,*[8] *Brotherton,*[7] *Samuel,*[6] *Thomas,*[5] *Brotherton,*[4] *Joshua,*[3] *Thomas,*[2] *John* [1]), born Rockland, Me., September 9, 1855; resides Rockland, Me. (1892); married Rockland, Me., December 25, 1885, Lena E. Ulmer, daughter of Edward and Lucinda (Overlock) Ulmer.

Issue:

3398. i. Ralph Bartlett Daggett,[10] born Rockland, Me., May 29, 1887.

3023. Ella Daggett [9] (*George B.,*[8] *Brotherton,*[7] *Samuel,*[6] *Thomas,*[5] *Brotherton,*[4] *Joshua,*[3] *Thomas,*[2] *John* [1]), born Rockland, Me., July 2, 1857; resides Rockland, Me. (1892); married Rockland, Me., August, 1890, Herbert Eugene Bowden, son of Silas and Vesta (Hallowell) Bowden.

Issue :

3399. i. MARY MELINDA BOWDEN,[10] born Rockland, Me., May 12, 1891.

3029. ISAAC MEEKER DAGGETT [9] (*Jabez*,[8] *James*,[7] *Samuel*,[6] *Thomas*,[5] *Brotherton*,[4] *Joshua*,[3] *Thomas*,[2] *John* [1]), born Hodgdon, Me., June 25, 1833; address, 1296 Madison avenue, corner Ninety-second street, New York city (1892); married 1st, Boston, Mass., May 16, 1855, Mary Elizabeth Rowe, daughter of Nathan and Mary (Murry) Rowe; born Haverhill, Mass., August, 1837; died Haverhill, Mass., May 16, 1861; married 2d, Chicago, Ill., December 2, 1869, Sarah Elizabeth Dake, daughter of Joseph M. and Mary (Poge) Dake; born West Greenfield, N.Y., April 27, 1846.

Issue :

3400. i. IDA FLORENCE DAGGETT,[10] born Groton, Mass., July 28, 1855.
3401. ii. HARRY EGBERT DAGGETT,[10] born Haverhill, Mass., January 9, 1857.
3402. iii. JOSEPH MORY DAGGETT,[10] born Chicago, Ill., April 2, 1873.

3033. ABBIE JANE DAGGETT [9] (*Jabez*,[8] *James*,[7] *Samuel*,[6] *Thomas*,[5] *Brotherton*,[4] *Joshua*,[3] *Thomas*,[2] *John* [1]), born Hodgdon, Me., September 20, 1843; resides Oakland, Cal. (1892); married Stockton, Cal., September 12, 1867, by Rev. David Deal, to Alfred Wilson Root, son of David and Luanna (Pulling) Root; born Saratoga county, N.Y., February 2, 1827.

Issue :

3403. i. ISORA EMELINE ROOT,[10] born Stockton, Cal., December 8, 1872.
3404. ii. MAUD ROOT,[10] born Stockton, Cal., February 19, 1876.
3405. iii. ALFRED LESLIE ROOT,[10] born Stockton, Cal., September 6, 1879.

3036. CHARLES HENRY DAGGETT [9] (*Hiram*,[8] *James*,[7] *Samuel*,[6] *Thomas*,[5] *Brotherton*,[4] *Joshua*,[3] *Thomas*,[2] *John* [1]), born Canton, Mass., September 19, 1847; address, 317 Hennepin avenue, Minneapolis, Minn. (1889); married Minneapolis, Minn., July 7, 1873, Sarah Marilla Bidwell, daughter of Marcius De Count and Elvira (Hall) Bidwell; born Sandisfield, Mass., April 27, 1845.

Issue :

3406. i. HUBERT LINDSLEY DAGGETT,[10] born Minneapolis, Minn., September 29, 1877.

3038. THOMAS J. DAGGETT [9] (*Robert*,[8] *James*,[7] *Samuel*,[6] *Thomas*,[5] *Brotherton*,[4] *Joshua*,[3] *Thomas*,[2] *John* [1]), born Hodgdon, Me., 1841, " teamster;" resided 112 Chelsea street, East Boston (1869); married Boston, Mass., January 21, 1867, by Rev. W. H. Cudworth, to

Ella F. York, daughter of George N. and Dolly H. York; born Boston, Mass., 1848.

Issue :

3407. i. GEORGE NORTON DAGGETT,[10] born Boston, Mass., June 23, 1867; died Boston, Mass., April 5, 1875.

3039. LOLA CAROLINE DAGGETT [9] (*Ebenezer*,[8] *James*,[7] *Samuel*,[6] *Thomas*,[5] *Brotherton*,[4] *Joshua*,[3] *Thomas*,[2] *John* [1]), born Haverhill, Mass., January 3, 1852; resides 35 Vine street, Haverhill, Mass. (1892); married Haverhill, Mass., August 11, 1873, by Rev. E. B. Fairchild, to Daniel Forest Sprague, son of Daniel L. and Mary Pierce (Hadley) Sprague; born Stoneham, Mass., August 3, 1851.

Issue :

3408. i. BESSIE HADLEY SPRAGUE,[10] born Haverhill, Mass., May 20, 1874; died Haverhill, Mass., January 6, 1892.
3409. ii. ADELBERT DAGGETT SPRAGUE,[10] born Haverhill, Mass., October 12, 1875.
3410. iii. FOREST OTTEO SPRAGUE,[10] born Haverhill, Mass., May 2, 1883.
3411. iv. CHANDLER SPRAGUE,[10] born Haverhill, Mass., May 26, 1886.

3045. ELIZA J. DAGGETT [9] (*Robert L.*,[8] *Jonathan*,[7] *Samuel*,[6] *Thomas*,[5] *Brotherton*,[4] *Joshua*,[3] *Thomas*,[2] *John* [1]), born October 28, 1840; died May 11, 1892; married Morrill, Me., July 20, 1862, by Rev. Ira Brown, to George Erskine.

Issue :

3412. i. OSCAR ERSKINE,[10] born January 3, 1865; "physician" (1892).
3413. ii. EDGAR ERSKINE,[10] born April 9, 1873; "farmer" (1892).

3048. BRIGGS C. DAGGETT [9] (*Robert L.*,[8] *Jonathan*,[7] *Samuel*,[6] *Thomas*,[5] *Brotherton*,[4] *Joshua*,[3] *Thomas*,[2] *John* [1]), born November 27, 1849; "farmer;" married 1st, Morrill, Me., December 6, 1878, Sarah Jackson; died April 9, 1888; married 2d, December 4, 1888, by Rev. George Tufts, to Eliza Simmons.

Issue :

3414. i. ANNABELL DAGGETT,[10] born December 2, 1879.
3415. ii. GEORGIA DAGGETT,[10] born April 21, 1882; died 1888.
3416. iii. ADDIE DAGGETT,[10] born November 2, 1885.

3055. EDWIN WOODHULL CRAWFORD [9] (*Jane T. Daggett*,[8] *William*,[7] *Samuel*,[6] *Thomas*,[5] *Brotherton*,[4] *Joshua*,[3] *Thomas*,[2] *John* [1]), born Searsmont, Me., March 16, 1845; address, Boylston Market, Boston, Mass. (1892); married Boston, Mass., November 1, 1868, Mary Frances Allen, daughter of Philip and Susan Allen.

Issue :

3417. i. JENNIE ALLEN CRAWFORD,[10] born Boston, Mass., March 10, 1870; died Hull, Mass., August 1, 1889.
3418. ii. EVERETT WESTON CRAWFORD,[10] born Medford, Mass., June 16, 1878.

3058. Rev. WILLIAM HARTWELL CRAWFORD [9] (*Jane T. Daggett,*[8] *William,*[7] *Samuel,*[6] *Thomas,*[5] *Brotherton,*[4] *Joshua,*[3] *Thomas,*[2] *John* [1]), born Searsmont, Me., December 4, 1850; resides Pittsford, Vt. (1892); married Bucksport, Me., June 6, 1876, by Rev. Charles A. Plumer, to Emma Marshall Foye, daughter of James and Joanna (Decker) Foye; born Wiscasset, Me., June 23, 1852.

Issue:

3419. i. RALPH FOSTER CRAWFORD,[10] born Tremont, Me., June 28, 1877.
3420. ii. HITTIE MILLS CRAWFORD,[10] born Millbridge, Me., March 16, 1879.
3421. iii. PERSIS MOORE CRAWFORD,[10] born Millbridge, Me., May 1, 1881.
3422. iv. HORATIO HIRAM CRAWFORD,[10] born Surry, Me., October 29, 1882.
3423. v. GUY FOYE CRAWFORD,[10] born Surry, Me., November 30, 1883.

Rev. William H. Crawford was supervisor of schools in Searsmont in 1873. Is now (1892) pastor Methodist Episcopal church in Pittsford, Vt. He has in his possession a cane given him by his grandfather, William Daggett, which is said to have been brought to this country by his Daggett ancestor.

3103. WILLIAM J. DAGGETT [9] (*Dennis,*[8] *William,*[7] *Peter,*[6] *Ebenezer* [5] [*John,*[4] *Joseph,*[3] *Joseph,*[2] *John* [1]] (?)), born Phillips, Me., October 26, 1851; married September 22, 1879, Lizzie S. Higgins; born Augusta, Me., 1855.

Issue:

3424. i. HAROLD L. DAGGETT,[10] born Augusta, Me., April 3, 1883.

3105. WALTER SNOW DAGGETT [9] (*Plamentin,*[8] *Plamentin,*[7] *Peter,*[6] *Ebenezer* [5] [*John,*[4] *Joseph,*[3] *Joseph,*[2] *John* [1]] (?)), born Strong, Me., February 11, 1860; resides Strong, Me. (1893); married Strong, Me., November 12, 1882, Louisa Lottie Parsons, daughter of Benjamin Burgess and Almira Jane (Wilbur) Parsons; born Medford, Mass., December 15, 1862.

Issue:

3425. i. SARAH ALBERTA DAGGETT,[10] born Strong, Me., April 16, 1887; died Strong, Me., July 13, 1889.

3112. VELZORA RICHARDS [9] (*Mary Daggett,*[8] *Jonathan L.,*[7] *Peter,*[6] *Ebenezer* [5] [*John,*[4] *Joseph,*[3] *Joseph,*[2] *John* [1]] (?)), born Salem, Me., October 21, 1841; married December 15, 1861, John Hodgman; born Litchfield, Me., 1839.

Issue:

3426. i. FRED R. HODGMAN,[10] born Salem, Me., May 12, 1864.
3427. ii. FRANK R. HODGMAN,[10] born Salem, Me., February 11, 1870.
3428. iii. CHARLES L. HODGMAN,[10] born Salem, Me., August 13, 1872.

3114. AFFIE T. RICHARDS [9] (*Mary Daggett,*[8] *Jonathan L.,*[7] *Peter,*[6] *Ebenezer* [5] [*John,*[4] *Joseph,*[3] *Joseph,*[2] *John* [1]] (?)), born Salem,

Me., January 2, 1862; married February 29, 1880, George F. Briggs; born Salem, Me., 1846.

Issue:

3429. i. ADDIE M. BRIGGS,[10] born Salem, Me., August 17, 1882.

JOHN DOGGETT, OF MARTHA'S VINEYARD.

3186. ISAAC W. DAGGETT [10] (*Tristram N.,*[9] *Isaac,*[8] *Samuel,*[7] *Samuel,*[6] *Seth,*[5] *Samuel,*[4] *Thomas,*[3] *Thomas,*[2] *John*[1]), born New Vineyard, Me., January 2, 1851; resides Sanborn, Ia. (1892); married Hampton, Ia., October 29, 1872, by W. J. Mitchell, to Emma A. Ward, daughter of William and Emily (Olds) Ward; born Springfield, Pa., June 18, 1851.

Issue:

3430. i. ARTHUR ELVIN DAGGETT,[11] born Hampton, Ia., July 30, 1874; died Primghar, Ia., August 20, 1876.
3431. ii. NELLIE MAY DAGGETT,[11] born Primghar, Ia., September 18, 1878.
3432. iii. EMMA ROSEMOND DAGGETT,[11] born Sanborn, Ia., January 1, 1881.

Isaac W. Daggett is attorney at law, banker and merchant.

3191. WILLIAM HARRISON DAGGETT [10] (*John T.,*[9] *Isaac,*[8] *Samuel,*[7] *Samuel,*[6] *Seth,*[5] *Samuel,*[4] *Thomas,*[3] *Thomas,*[2] *John*[1]), born Industry, Me., August 14, 1857; resides West's Mills, Me. (1892); married 1st, Industry, Me., April 14, 1883, Ellen Mary Smith, daughter of Joseph Warren and Lydia Ann (Daggett) Smith (No. 3220); born Industry, Me., January 6, 1858; died Industry, Me., March 17, 1888; married 2d, August 4, 1889, Frances M. Brackett, daughter of Franklin and Florilla (Woodcock) Brackett, of Stark.

Issue:

3433. i. CLIFFORD DAGGETT,[11] born Industry, Me., June 17, 1890.
3434. ii. RUBY EMMA DAGGETT,[11] born Industry, Me., April 24, 1892.

Mr. Daggett is a merchant at West's Mills, also postmaster, town clerk, treasurer, etc.

3193. EMMA ALLEN DAGGETT [10] (*John T.,*[9] *Isaac,*[8] *Samuel,*[7] *Samuel,*[6] *Seth,*[5] *Samuel,*[4] *Thomas,*[3] *Thomas,*[2] *John*[1]), born Industry, Me., October 29, 1864; resides Oakland, Me. (1892) married January 4, 1884, Charles E. Crowell, son of Calvin C. and Cordelia

(Blair) Crowell; "machinist;" born Oakland, Me., August 30, 1850.

Issue :

3435. i. Mildred Louise Crowell,[11] born Oakland, Me., February 3, 1889.

3207. Levi Hooper Daggett[10] (*Orrin,*[9] *Samuel,*[8] *Samuel,*[7] *Samuel,*[6] *Seth,*[5] *Samuel,*[4] *Thomas,*[3] *Thomas,*[2] *John*[1]), born Industry, Me., February 21, 1840 ; resides 23 Hudson street, Somerville, Mass. (1892) ; married Farmington Falls, Me., March 6, 1864, by Rev. W. W. Dow, to Mary Carrie Delano, daughter of Calvin and Lucretia (Richards) Delano, born Livermore, Me., February 26, 1839.

Issue :

3436. i. Fred Levi Daggett,[11] born Jay, Me., December 1, 1869; married East Boston, Mass., July 13, 1891, Alice W. Anglin; resides 21 Hudson street, Somerville, Mass. (1893).
3437. ii. Emma Carrie Daggett,[11] born Jay, Me., July 30, 1875.
3438. iii. Orrin Elmer Daggett,[11] born Deering, Me., June 3, 1877; died East Boston, Mass., October 19, 1886.

L. H. Daggett served four years in the Civil War, enlisting as a private in the First Maine Cavalry, and holding all the non-commissioned offices in the company. He returned after the close of the war as captain of the company. He is now (1892) a commission merchant.

3209. Samuel Daggett[10] (*Orrin,*[9] *Samuel,*[8] *Samuel,*[7] *Samuel,*[6] *Seth,*[5] *Samuel,*[4] *Thomas,*[3] *Thomas,*[2] *John*[1]), born Industry, Me., May 29, 1846 ; resides Sprague's Mills, Me. (1892) ; married Kent's Hill, Me., April 11, 1868, Lizzie A. Smith.

Issue :

3439. i. Edwin H. Daggett,[11] born Presque Isle, Me., January 22, 1872; died June 3, 1881.
3440. ii. Walter S. Daggett,[11] born Presque Isle, Me., August 27, 1879.

3211. Charles F. Daggett[10] (*Orrin,*[9] *Samuel,*[8] *Samuel,*[7] *Samuel,*[6] *Seth,*[5] *Samuel,*[4] *Thomas,*[3] *Thomas,*[2] *John*[1]), born New Sharon, Me., September 9, 1856 ; resides Presque Isle, Me. (1892) ; married Presque Isle, Me., February 10, 1881, Alifair Dyer.

Issue :

3441. i. Helen A. Daggett,[11] born Presque Isle, Me., November 13, 1883.

3226. Bertice Albert Daggett[10] (*Tristram G.,*[9] *Lendal,*[8] *Silas,*[7] *Silas,*[6] *Seth,*[5] *Samuel,*[4] *Thomas,*[3] *Thomas,*[2] *John*[1]), born Stark, Me., December 20, 1868; resides South Norridgewock, Me. (1892) ; married Skowhegan, Me., September 18, 1886, Lilla Attella Devoll, daughter of David and —— (Young) Devoll.

Issue :

3442. i. Omer Gardner Daggett,[11] born Stark, Me., June 13, 1887.
3443. ii. Daughter —— Daggett.[11] born South Norridgewock, Me., May 27, 1891; died South Norridgewock, Me., July 24, 1891.

3301. CONRAD FRANK STEVENS[10] (*Lydia F. Daggett,*[9] *George R.,*[8] *George,*[7] *Elihu,*[6] *Elihu,*[5] *Mayhew,*[4] *John,*[3] *Thomas,*[2] *John*[1]), born Sebec, Me., August 7, 1864; died November 14, 1888; married Aledo, Ill., October 13, 1885, Madora ——; resides Millersburg, Ill. (1892).

Issue:

3444. i. JESSE FRANK STEVENS,[11] born Beloit, Wis., September 17, 1886.
3445. ii. Daughter —— STEVENS,[11] born Hamlin, Wis., Oct., 1888; died an infant.

3302. JESSIE PAULINA STEVENS[10] (*Lydia F. Daggett,*[9] *George R.,*[8] *George,*[7] *Elihu,*[6] *Elihu,*[5] *Mayhew,*[4] *John,*[3] *Thomas,*[2] *John*[1]), born Sebec, Me., May 19, 1866; resides Galesburg, Ill. (1892); married Galesburg, Ill., January 29, 1885, Charles Osgood.

Issue:

3446. i. FRED CHARLES OSGOOD,[11] born Sparta, Ill., July 19, 1886.
3447. ii. GRACE OSGOOD,[11] born Sparta, Ill., January 31, 1888.
3448. iii. HENRY STANLEY OSGOOD,[11] born Sparta, Ill., January 6, 1890.

3322. CHARLES HENRY KING[10] (*Mary E. Daggett,*[9] *Albion K. P.,*[8] *George,*[7] *Elihu,*[6] *Elihu,*[5] *Mayhew,*[4] *John,*[3] *Thomas,*[2] *John*[1]), born Bradford, Me., October 31, 1866; "farmer;" resides Bradford, Me. (1892); married Bradford, Me., September 21, 1889, Louise Hathorn Salley, daughter of Samuel Livingston and Annie Colby (Spaulding) Salley; born Carmel, Me., April 29, 1872.

Issue:

3449. i. RAY CLIFFORD KING,[11] born Bradford, Me., June 14, 1891.

3323. ANNIE MABEL KING[10] (*Mary E. Daggett,*[9] *Albion K. P.,*[8] *George,*[7] *Elihu,*[6] *Elihu,*[5] *Mayhew,*[4] *John,*[3] *Thomas,*[2] *John*[1]), born Bradford, Me., July 14, 1870; resides Bradford, Me. (1892); married Bradford, Me., July 14, 1888, Farrington James Salley, of Bradford, son of Samuel Livingston and Annie Colby (Spaulding) Salley; "farmer;" born Madison, Me., October 22, 1863.

Issue:

3450. i. WAYLAND RAY SALLEY,[11] born Bradford, Me., January 11, 1891; died Bradford, Me., January 13, 1891.

PROBABLY DESCENDED FROM JOHN DOGGETT, OF MARTHA'S VINEYARD.

3451. JOHN DAGGETT,[1] born 1762; died Farmington, Me., 1822; married 1st, Edgartown, Mass., January 26, 1784, Susanna Stewart; died Tisbury, Mass., 1799; married 2d, Tisbury, Mass., October 31, 1804, Betty Crowell, of Tisbury.

Issue:

3452. i. ELIJAH DAGGETT,[2] bapt. Edgartown, Mass., November 6, 1799; died Martha's Vineyard, 1828.
3453. ii. SUSAN DAGGETT,[2] born Edgartown, Mass., August 11, 1790.
3454. iii. HOLMES STEWART DAGGETT,[2] born Edgartown, Mass., May 11, 1793.
3455. iv. SARAH DAGGETT,[2] born Edgartown, Mass. (bapt. November 6, 1799).
3456. v. THOMAS DAGGETT,[2] bapt. Edgartown, Mass., November 6, 1799.

John Daggett, about 1810, left the Vineyard with his three youngest children and Hugh Stewart, his brother-in-law, and settled in Farmington, Me. He was a sea captain in early life. His will, made September 16, 1821, was probated July 8, 1822.

3453. SUSAN DAGGETT [2] (*John* [1]), born Edgartown, Mass., August 11, 1790; died Farmington, Me., April 22, 1879; married Farmington, Me., October 22, 1826, William Holley, son of John and Hephzibah (Marchant) Holley; born Martha's Vineyard, Mass., April 7, 1786; died Farmington, Me., February 16, 1859.

Issue:

3457. i. HARRIET ANN HOLLEY,[3] born Farmington, Me., August 18, 1829; married Farmington, Me., July 21, 1853, Charles M. Holley; issue: six children.
3458. ii. GEORGE HOLLEY,[3] born Farmington, Me., July 22, 1831.

3454. HOLMES STEWART DAGGETT [2] (*John* [1]), born Edgartown, Mass., May 11. 1793; died Linn county, Ia., May 9, 1858; married Farmington, Me. (published October 31, 1815), Mary Hartson Smith, daughter of William Smith; born Oromucto, N.B.; died Linn county, Ia., January 4, 1859.

Issue:

3459. i. WILLIAM SMITH DAGGETT,[3] born Farmington, Me., August 24, 1816; died Houlton, Me., May 14, 1851.
3460. ii. JOHN MINOT DAGGETT,[3] born Temple, Me., June 25, 1818.
3461. iii. HOLMES STEWART DAGGETT,[3] born Strong, Me., July 26, 1820.
3462. iv. MARY SEWALL DAGGETT,[3] born Strong, Me., October 19, 1824; married Linn county, Iowa, Alva Lucon; resides Traer, Tama Co., Ia.

Holmes S. Daggett was private in Captain Morrison's company of militia, called out for the defence of the seacoast, and waiting orders at Farmington from September 14 to September 18, 1814.

He moved from Farmington to Houlton, Me., about 1836. In 1853 he removed with his family to Linn county. Ia.

3455. SARAH DAGGETT[2] (*John[1]*), born Edgartown, Mass. (bapt. November 6, 1799) ; died Farmington, Me., April 15, 1826 ; married Farmington, Me., May 5, 1811, William Holley, son of John and Hephzibah (Marchant) Holley ; born Martha's Vineyard, Mass., April 7, 1786 ; died Farmington, Me., February 16, 1859.

Issue :

3463. i. HENRY HOLLEY,[3] born Farmington, Me., November 18, 1813.
3464. ii. SUSAN HOLLEY,[3] born Farmington, Me., May 29, 1815 ; married Farmington, Me., January 22, 1839, Marchant Holley ; resides Farmington, Me. (1886).
3465. iii. HIRAM HOLLEY,[3] born Farmington, Me., April 29, 1817.
3466. iv. SARAH HOLLEY,[3] born Farmington, Me., September, 1821 ; married February 28, 1841, John C. Stewart ; she died January 15, 1856.

William Holley was a farmer, and acquired a large estate. He was remarkable for his untiring industry.

3456. THOMAS DAGGETT[2] (*John[1]*), bapt. Edgartown, Mass., November 6, 1799 ; "farmer ;" died Farmington, Me., April 10, 1871 ; married Farmington, Me., September 2, 1829, Mary Fisher Caswell, of New Vineyard, daughter of Salmon and Mary (Fisher) Caswell ; born Mansfield, Mass., February 12, 1806 ; resides Farmington, Me. (1891).

Issue :

3467. i. SAMUEL DAGGETT,[3] born Farmington, Me., June, 1829.
3468. ii. JOHN DAGGETT,[3] born Farmington, Me., January, 1831 ; married Mary Moore ; he killed in battle at Gettysburg, July, 1863.
3469. iii. SUSAN DAGGETT,[3] born Farmington, Me., November, 1834 ; resides Farmington, Me. (1892).
3470. iv. EDWARD DAGGETT,[3] born Farmington, Me., July, 1836 ; married Mary McFarland ; he died Michigan, January 23, 1873.
3471. v. ABIGAIL MELVINA DAGGETT,[3] born Farmington, Me., October, 1842 ; married Stephen Davis ; afterwards divorced ; had daughter Alice Davis,[4] born May 5, 1861, who married George Bragg, of Fairbanks, Me. ; Mrs. Davis resided at Mt. Vernon, Me.
3472. vi. EMILY MARY DAGGETT,[3] born Farmington, Me., October 30, 1848 ; died Farmington, Me., July 4, 1872.

3458. GEORGE HOLLEY[3] (*Susan Daggett,[2] John[1]*), born Farmington, Me., July 22, 1831 ; married Farmington, Me., September 8, 1859, Rachel Emeline Backus, daughter of Nathan William and Rachel (Hatch) Backus ; born Farmington, Me., September 24, 1836 ; died Farmington, Me., January 2, 1892.

Issue :

3473. i. AUGUSTA BACKUS HOLLEY,[4] born Farmington, Me., April 21, 1861 ; married Farmington, Me., June 20, 1885, Llewellyn M. Felch, of Linneus, Me. : resides Houlton, Me. (1892) ; issue : two children.
3474. ii. ANNIE ABBOTT HOLLEY,[4] born Farmington, Me., August 4, 1864.
3475. iii. FLORENCE EMMA HOLLEY,[4] born Farmington, Me., November 29, 1869.

George Holley succeeded to the homestead, and is a large and successful farmer.

3460. JOHN MINOT DAGGETT [3] (*Holmes S.,*[2] *John*[1]), born Temple, Me., June 25, 1818; resides 155 East Congress street, St. Paul, Minn. (1893); married Houlton, Me., November 23, 1852, Martha Matilda Cates, daughter of Sewall and Rebecca (Bolton) Cates; born Houlton, Me., July 14, 1832.

Issue:

3476. i.   CARMEN BELMONT DAGGETT,[4] born Linn county, Ia., Oct. 15, 1853.
3477. ii. HARRY BERTRAM DAGGETT,[4] born Linn county, Ia., Feb. 25, 1857.
3478. iii. WALTER SCOTT DAGGETT,[4] born Linn county, Ia., March 25, 1859; died Dunleith, Ill., April 8, 1864.
3479. iv. WILLIAM SMITH DAGGETT,[4] born Dunleith, Ill., January 2, 1864; married and has one son; address, Fargo, N. Dak., care U.S. Marshal's office (1893).
3480. v.   WALLACE MINOTT DAGGETT,[4] born Dunleith, Ill., March 25, 1869; resides 155 East Congress street, St. Paul, Minn. (1893).

John M. Daggett left Farmington in 1836 and went to New Bedford, Mass., where he engaged in the whaling business for a number of years.

In 1851 he went to Houlton, and in 1853 moved with the rest of the family to Linn county, Ia.

3461. HOLMES STEWART DAGGETT [3] (*Holmes S.,*[2] *John*[1]), born Strong, Me., July 26, 1820; "farmer;" died Linn county, Ia., December 21, 1862; married Plymouth, Me., September 19, 1847, Sarah J. Jordan, daughter of Rishworth and Charlotte (Chase) Jordan; born Hartland, Me., September 1, 1823; resides Paw Paw, Kan. (1886).

Issue:

3481. i.   MARY HELEN DAGGETT,[4] born Houlton, Me., October 12, 1848; died Houlton, Me., January 28, 1850.
3482. ii. FRANCES EMMA DAGGETT,[4] born Houlton, Me., December 8, 1851.
3483. iii. FRED E. DAGGETT,[4] born Linn county, Ia., June 16, 1854; died Linn county, Ia., November 8, 1854.
3484. iv. CHARLES S. DAGGETT,[4] born Linn county, Ia., November 4, 1856; resides Paw Paw, Kan. (1886).
3485. v.   SARAH DAGGETT,[4] born Linn county, Ia., December 24, 1858; died Linn county, Ia., April 15, 1859.
3486. vi. FRANK B. DAGGETT,[4] born Linn county, Ia., December 18, 1861; resides Paw Paw, Kan. (1886).

Mrs. Daggett married 2d, January 13, 1867, Emery White, of Iowa.

3463. HENRY HOLLEY [3] (*Sarah Daggett,*[2] *John*[1]), born Farmington, Me., November 18, 1813; died Farmington, Me., March 27, 1861; married 1st, Farmington, Me., January 1, 1838, Dulcina D. Higgins; born 1819; died Farmington, Me., October 15, 1855; married 2d, April 8, 1856, Mrs. Eliza F. Wade, daughter of Mr. Smith; born April 15, 1813; died December, 1885.

Issue:

3487. i.   CHARLES HENRY HOLLEY,[4] born Farmington, Me., November 6, 1838; died Farmington, Me., April 26, 1840.

3488. ii.   LIZZIE HIGGINS HOLLEY,[4] born Farmington, Me., July 30, 1840; married 1873, Hiram Wright; she died September 19, 1876.
3489. iii.   CHARLES HENRY HOLLEY,[4] born Farmington, Me., January 6, 1842; died Kansas, 1866.
3490. iv.   JULIA HORTENSE HOLLEY,[4] born Farmington, Me., February 7, 1844; married March 4, 1866, Abner Corbett; he died October 16, 1879; she died April 1, 1883.
3491. v.   SUSAN COLUMBIA HOLLEY,[4] born Farmington, Me., September 2, 1845; married June 22, 1867, Lucellus Timberlake, of Livermore, Me.; she died November 23, 1879.
3492. vi.   APPHIA GILL HOLLEY,[4] born Farmington, Me., August 4, 1848; married February 16, 1870, Herbert A. Millett, of Campello, Mass.
3493. vii.   FRANK FIELD HOLLEY,[4] born Farmington, Me., December 10, 1850; married October, 1875, Maria Dolbier, of Kingfield; he died November, 1877.
3494. viii. GEORGIANA HOLLEY,[4] born Farmington, Me., June 21, 1853; died September 18, 1875.

Henry Holley was a shoemaker and farmer, and resided on the Davis farm in the " Holley neighborhood," so called. He was respected for honesty and integrity of character.

3465. HIRAM HOLLEY[3] (*Sarah Daggett,*[2] *John* [1]), born Farmington, Me., April 29, 1817; died Farmington, Me., October 11, 1859; married Farmington, Me., December 31, 1838, Sophia Ann Butler, daughter of Freeman Butler.
   Issue:

3495. i.   SARAH MEHITABLE HOLLEY,[4] born Farmington, Me., January 6, 1840; died Farmington, Me., August 4, 1855.
3496. ii.   ELIZABETH WENDELL HOLLEY,[4] born Farmington, Me., January 20, 1842; married December 19, 1861, Wesley R. Cothren.
3497. iii.   ELLEN CAROLINE HOLLEY,[4] born Farmington, Me., July 19, 1844; married May 26, 1864, Benjamin F. Atkinson; issue: Leroy Atkinson,[5] born June 29, 1882.
3498. iv.   CLARENCE EUGENE HOLLEY,[4] born Farmington, Me., March 19, 1847; resides Fort Fairfield, Me.
3499. v.   LOUISE BUTLER HOLLEY,[4] born Farmington, Me., January 14, 1850; married July 10, 1870, R. Hanley Smith.
3500. vi.   WARREN GILMAN HOLLEY,[4] born Farmington, Me., August 19, 1852; died Farmington, Me., March 24, 1873,
3501. vii.   ALICE ELVIRA HOLLEY,[4] born Farmington, Me., December 31, 1856; died June 8, 1872.
3502. viii. ANNIE PAGE HOLLEY,[4] born Farmington, Me., July 9, 1859; married October 9, 1880, Leonard B. Bangs.

Hiram Holley was a shoemaker as well as farmer. He was distinguished by his honest dealings and industrious habits.

3467. SAMUEL DAGGETT[3] (*Thomas,*[2] *John* [1]), born Farmington, Me., June, 1829; resides Dead River, Me. (1892); married 1st, Olive Pullen; married 2d, Mary Washburn.
   Issue:

3503. i.   JOHN P. DAGGETT,[4] resides Dead River, Me. (1892); married 1883, Ada Maria Greenwood, daughter of Hannibal and Eleanor (Fish) Greenwood; born Industry, Me., December 19, 1865; issue: Olive May Daggett,[5] born Dead River, September, 1884.

3476. CARMEN BELMONT DAGGETT[4] (*John M.*,[3] *Holmes S.*,[2] *John*[1]), born Linn county, Ia., October 15, 1853 ; resides Marshalltown, Ia. (1893) ; married Allison, Ia., May 23, 1883, William K. Conaughy.

Issue :

3504. i.   CLARENCE CONAUGHY,[5] born Allison. Ia., February 23, 1885.
3505. ii. LOUIS CONAUGHY.[5]
3506. iii. LAURA CONAUGHY.[5]
3507. iv. CHARLES CONAUGHY.[5]

3477. HARRY BERTRAM DAGGETT[4] (*John M.*,[3] *Holmes S.*,[2] *John*[1]), born Linn county, Ia., February 25, 1857 ; resides Hampton, Ia. (1893) ; married Hampton, Ia., May 22, 1882, Fanny Thompson.

Issue :

3508. i.   MARY DAGGETT,[5] born Hampton, Ia., April 4, 1884.
3509. ii. JAMES DAGGETT,[5] born Sheffield, Ia., December 27, 1885.
3510. iii. JOHN MINOTT DAGGETT,[5] born Hampton, Ia., August 26, 1887.

3482. FRANCES EMMA DAGGETT[4] (*Holmes S.*,[3] *Holmes S.*,[2] *John*[1]), born Houlton, Me., December 8, 1851; resides Paw Paw, Kan. (1886) ; married Cedar Rapids, Ia., January 2, 1872, John W. McCalley.

Issue :

3511. i.   GRACE A. McCALLEY,[5] born Waubeck, Ia., November 28, 1872; died June 27, 1874.
3512. ii. GUY PERRY McCALLEY,[5] born Marion, Ia., July 6, 1874; died October 20, 1876.
3513. iii. MYRTH M. McCALLEY,[5] born Marion, Ia., July 10, 1884.

PROBABLY DESCENDED FROM JOHN DOGGETT, OF MARTHA'S VINEYARD.

3514. HENRY DAGGETT[2] (*Nathan*[1]), born Martha's Vineyard, Mass., 1788; died ——— ; married Nantucket, Mass., March 29, 1818, by Rev. James Gurney, to Dina Ames, daughter of Benjamin and Sally Ames ; born Nantucket, Mass., December 4, 1791; died Nantucket, Mass., January 2, 1859.

Issue :

3515. i.   WILLIAM HENRY DAGGETT,[3] born Nantucket, Mass., 1819.
3516. ii. BENJAMIN F. DAGGETT,[3] born Nantucket, Mass., August, 1822.
3517. iii. JAMES DAGGETT,[3] born Nantucket. Mass., November, 1825.
3518. iv. CHARLES A. DAGGETT,[3] born Nantucket, Mass., August, 1828 : went whaling.
3519. v.   EDWARD DAGGETT,[3] born Nantucket, Mass., February 11, 1831.

3515. WILLIAM HENRY DAGGETT[3] (*Henry*,[2] *Nathan*[1]), born Nantucket, Mass., 1819; "laborer; " died Nantucket, Mass., De-

cember 17, 1862; married Nantucket, Mass., February 13, 1842, by
Benjamin Gardner, J.P., to Mary Courtney, of New York; born
Ireland.

Issue:

3520. i. (Female) DAGGETT,[4] born Nantucket, Mass., September 14, 1850; died
Nantucket, Mass., October 14, 1850.

3516. BENJAMIN F. DAGGETT[3] (*Henry,[2] Nathan[1]*), born Nan-
tucket, Mass., August, 1822; "stable-keeper;" died Nantucket,
Mass., December 19, 1854; married Nantucket, Mass., April 11,
1841, by Benjamin Gardner, J.P., to Phœbe S. Higgins, daughter of
George and Mary Higgins; born September, 1821; died Nantucket,
Mass., October 18, 1880.

Issue:

3521. i. ELIZA B. DAGGETT,[4] born Nantucket, Mass., July, 1841; probably
died young.
3522. ii. REBECCA M. DAGGETT,[4] born Nantucket, Mass., December, 1842.
3523. iii. ELIZABETH B. DAGGETT,[4] born Nantucket, Mass., September 21,
1843; married Nantucket, Mass., November 16, 1864, to Emanuel
Rogey, son of Charles and Clarett Rogey; "mariner;" born Belgium, 1843.
3524. iv. ARTHUR DAGGETT,[4] born Nantucket, Mass., September, 1846.
3525. v. ABBY B. DAGGETT,[4] born Nantucket, Mass., April 6, 1848.
3526. vi. BENJAMIN F. DAGGETT,[4] born Nantucket, Mass., March 6, 1850;
died at sea.
3527. vii. GEORGE H. DAGGETT,[4] born Nantucket, Mass., January 2, 1853.

Mrs. Phœbe (Higgins) Daggett, married Nantucket, Mass., Au-
gust 17, 1856, Seth S. Pinkham, son of George C. and Phebe S.
Pinkham; born Nantucket, Mass., 1822. They were married by
William C. Folger, J.P.

3517. JAMES DAGGETT[3] (*Henry,[2] Nathan[1]*), born Nantucket,
Mass., November, 1825; "laborer;" married Nantucket, Mass.,
November 7, 1847, by George Cobb, J.P., to Phœbe E. Norton,
daughter of Daniel and Hannah Norton, of Edgartown; born Edgartown, Mass., 1826.

Issue:

3528. i. (Male) DAGGETT,[4] born Nantucket, Mass., June 19, 1850; probably
died young.
3529. ii. ELLA C. DAGGETT,[4] born New Bedford, Mass., November 22, 1858.

3519. EDWARD DAGGETT[3] (*Henry,[2] Nathan[1]*), born Nantucket,
Mass., February 11, 1831; "laborer;" died in battle at Kingston,
December, 1862; married Mary Ann Curran; born Ireland, 1833.

Issue:

3530. i. CHARLES I. DAGGETT,[4] born Nantucket, Mass., June 4, 1853.
3531. ii. WILLIAM H. DAGGETT,[4] born Nantucket, Mass., 1855.
3532. iii. EDWARD H. DAGGETT,[4] born Nantucket, Mass., 1858.

3522. Rebecca M. Daggett [4] (*Benjamin F.,[3] Henry,[2] Nathan[1]*), born Nantucket, Mass., December, 1842; died Nantucket, Mass., June 2, 1876; married 1st, Nantucket, Mass.. September 20, 1860, by William Cobb, J.P., to James Wilkinson, of Nantucket, son of Thomas and Margrett Wilkinson, of Liverpool, Eng.; "mariner;" born Liverpool, Eng., 1837; died ——; married 2d, New Bedford, Mass., July 17, 1862, by James D. Butler, to Irving H. Backus, of Nantucket, son of Ichabod and Sophronia Backus; "farmer;" born Nantucket, Mass., March 7, 1835.

Issue:

3533. i. George A. Backus,[5] born Nantucket, Mass., March 26, 1863.
3534. ii. Lucy C. Backus,[5] born Nantucket, Mass.; died young.
3535. iii. Ida Lewis Backus,[5] born Nantucket, Mass.

3532. Edward H. Daggett [4] (*Edward,[3] Henry,[2] Nathan[1]*), born Nantucket, Mass., 1858; "puddler;" married Wareham, Mass., November 20, 1880, by William L. Chipman, J.P., to Alice Mitchell, daughter of Owen and Alice (Harvey) Mitchell; born Wareham, Mass., 1864.

Issue:

3536. i. Mary Alice Daggett,[5] born Wareham, Mass., February 16, 1881.
3537. ii. Edward H. Daggett,[5] born Wareham, Mass., May 22, 1882.
3538. iii. Nellie May Daggett,[5] born Wareham, Mass., July 23, 1884.
3539. iv. (Male) Daggett,[5] born Wareham, Mass., December 29, 1885.

POSSIBLY DESCENDED FROM JOHN DOGGETT, OF MARTHA'S VINEYARD.

3540. George Daggette,[1] born Erie county, Pa. (?), 1798; died Buena Vista, Allegheny Co., Pa., April 15, 1826; married Allegheny county, Pa., 1823, Rachel Morton.

Issue:

3541. i. Diana Daggette,[2] born Allegheny county, Pa., 1824; married E. H. Kiehl; she died Washington county, Pa., 1860.
3542. ii. John Morton Daggette,[2] born Allegheny county, Pa., April 29, 1826.

- About 1820 or 1821 George Daggette, an only son, fled from the tyranny of a step-mother, from Erie county to Allegheny county, Pa., where he married, in 1823, a niece of Thomas Morton, of Revolutionary fame. Being a fine scholar, George Daggette after coming to Allegheny county engaged in teaching, which vocation he followed until one month before his death. The family still (1883) own and live on the place where George Daggette settled.

3542. JOHN MORTON DAGGETTE [2] (*George* [1]), born Allegheny county, Pa., April 29, 1826; died Allegheny county, Pa., March 25, 1883; married 1853, M. M. Kelly.

Issue: two sons, four daughters.

3543. i. A. S. DAGGETTE, [3] graduated Medical College, Cleveland; address, Yohoghany, Pa. (1883).
3544. ii. F. S. DAGGETTE. [3]
3545. iii. OLIVE DAGGETTE, [3] born 1859; died Allegheny county, Pa., July 28, 1881.

POSSIBLY DESCENDED FROM JOHN DOGGETT, OF MARTHA'S VINEYARD.

3546. CHARLES DAGGETT, [1] married Mary ——.

Issue:

3547. i. CHARLES A. DAGGETT, [2] born Boston, Mass., 1815.

3547. CHARLES A. DAGGETT [2] (*Charles* [1]), born Boston, Mass., 1815; "junk-dealer;" married 1st, Lucy A. Waterhouse, daughter of Enoch and Abigail Waterhouse; born Machias, Me.; died East Boston, Mass., January 15, 1873; married 2d, Boston, Mass., May 19, 1874, by Rev. J. V. Hilton, to Emma Powers, of Boston, widow, daughter of George and Margaret Tryder; born Halifax, N.S., 1835.

Issue:

3548. i. CHARLES A. DAGGETT, [3] born Sandwich, Mass., 1837; married New Bedford, Mass., November 20, 1865, by Rev. Timothy Stowe, to Rebecca H. Eldred, widow, daughter of Henry and Mary Tobey; born Falmouth, Mass., 1836.
3549. ii. MOSES W. DAGGETT, [3] born Sandwich, Mass., 1839.

3549. MOSES W. DAGGETT [3] (*Charles A.,* [2] *Charles* [1]), born Sandwich, Mass., 1839; "painter;" married Boston, Mass., January 4, 1865, by Rev. W. H. Cudworth, to Aurelia B. Mallowes, daughter of Samuel and Aurelia Mallowes; born Chatham, Mass., 1846.

Issue:

3550. i. HARRY BEARSE DAGGETT, [4] born Boston, Mass., June 16, 1866; died Boston, Mass., April 29, 1874.

DOGGETT-DAGGETT.

THOMAS DOGGETT, OF MARSHFIELD, MASS.

FIRST GENERATION.

3551. THOMAS DOGGETT[1] (spelled also with one "t," and at times with one "g"), born England, 1607; removed to New England in the "Marey Anne," of Yarmouth, Eng., William Goose, master, May, 1637; died Marshfield, Mass., August 18, 1692; married 1st (date, place, and to whom not found), who died Concord, Mass., 23, 6 mo., 1642; married 2d, Weymouth, Mass., 1643, Elizabeth Fry, widow of William Fry, of Weymouth, and daughter of Jonas and Frances Humphrey, of Dorchester, Mass.; born probably England; died Weymouth, Mass., 1652; married 3d, Marshfield, Mass., August 17, 1654, Joane Chillingsworth, widow of Thomas Chillingsworth, of Marshfield, Mass.; born probably England; died Marshfield, Mass., September 4, 1684.

Issue:

3552. i. JOHN DOGGETT,[2] born Concord (?), Mass., 1642.
3553. ii. HANNAH DOGGETT,[2] born Weymouth, Mass., 1646.
3554. iii. SARAH DOGGETT,[2] born Weymouth, Mass., 1650.
3555. iv. SAMUEL DOGGETT,[2] born Weymouth, Mass., 1652.
3556. v. REBECCA DOGGETT,[2] born Marshfield, Mass., July 29, 1655.

Thomas Doggett, of Marshfield, was previously a resident of Weymouth, and before that, of Concord, Mass. Of these facts the records now extant seem to offer sufficient evidence; but of his life previous to arrival at Concord there is more uncertainty. Authorities on the subject express the opinion that Thomas who came in the "Marey Anne," in 1637, was the Thomas afterward of Marshfield, and finding no evidence to prove or disprove this theory, the writer has followed it as a possible truth. It is hoped that the points here made known may lead to positive proof of his parentage and home in England.

In the Rolls Office, in London, Eng., is a small parchment volume occupied with a record of persons " desirous to passe beyond seas." It consists of but sixteen written leaves, and much the greater portion of them is taken up with names of persons going into Holland. The several entries relating to those who came to New England are printed in the N.E. Hist. Gen. Register, Vol. XIV., page 328. What is not destroyed of the title of the volume is:

A Register of the . . . . . .
of such persons a . . . .
and upwards and have . . . . . .
to passe into forraigne partes . . .
March 1637 to the 29th day of Sept.
by vertu of a commission granted to
Mr Thomas Mayhew, gentleman.

The people whose names are here recorded as bound for New England came, with but few exceptions, from the counties of Norfolk and Suffolk, England. They were very many of them cloth workers, of Norwich, others were " cordwayners," " coopers," " joyners," and a few were husbandmen. Some came in the " John and Dorethay," of Ipswich, others in the " Rose," of Yarmouth, while " these people went to New England with William Goose, Mr of the ' Marey Anne ' of Yarmouth."

May the 13, 1637. The examinaction of Thomas Olliuer of Norwich, Calinder,[1] ageed 36 yeares and Marey his wife, aged 34 yeares, with 2 children: Thomas and John and 2 sernants:[2] THOMAS DOGED aged 30 yeares and Marey Sape ageed 12 yeares ar desirous to passe for N.E. to inhabitt.

Thomas Oliver settled in Salem, Mass., and Thomas Doggett may have stayed there in his employ long enough to pay for his passage to this country.

It was a common thing for gentlemen of some means in leaving England for America to take an apprentice or servant, paying the expenses of his passage, and after their arrival employing him to work to repay the amount. In this way many young and poor persons made their passage to this country.

This being customary, men of distinction were enabled to escape to America as servants to those permitted to come, who would have been prevented if they had attempted to come in their own name. Such was the strictness of the laws, and the vigilance of the officers, that many found it necessary to resort to this means to accomplish their object. Possibly Thomas Doggett may have engaged himself

---

[1] Calendering is the last operation to which dyed and printed cottons are sometimes subjected to render the surface smooth, compact, and uniform.

[2] The term " servant," as used by the early settlers. did not have the sense of a menial, but that of apprentice. They were immigrants whose passage was paid generally by some relative or friend in consideration of a stated term of service.

to Thomas Oliver in order to obtain permission to leave England, for among those who wished to come in the same company was one John Yonge, a minister of " St. Margretts, Suffolk," who, after he was examined and the answers recorded, was mentioned in the place of the date as — "This man was forbyde passage by the commissioners and went not from Yarmouth." Although this may have been Thomas Doggett's reason for thus calling himself, I am of the opinion he engaged himself as apprentice in order to pay his passage to New England, where he wished to come, either for religious freedom, or because he felt he could better his condition; having much the same idea as a young man of the present day who leaves New England for the West.

As there seem to be no evidences of property in his hands for several years after his arrival in New England, there is every reason to believe he was without means when he arrived.

The exact date of the departure of the "Marey Anne" is not known, nor the length of her voyage; neither is it known to what port she came, whether to Boston or Salem. Voyages across the Atlantic at that time took many weeks, so it was probably mid-summer, 1637, when they first caught sight of the New England shores.

Between this time and 1642 we lose sight of him, and it would be only conjecture to suggest where he may have lived during these years.

In 1642, the 23d of the 6th month, the records of Concord, Mass., record the death of the wife of Thomas Doggett, but a search of the town records reveals nothing more regarding them.

When or where he was married, or how long he had resided in Concord, is unknown.

Even the Christian name of his wife has not been found, after much search; or whether his oldest son, John, who was born about this time, was her son, or a son by his second wife. I am inclined, however, to believe him to be her son, and born at Concord, Mass. Shattuck, in his history of Concord, after speaking of the death of Mrs. Thomas Doggett, says, " Mr. Doggett removed from town," so that our interest in Concord is in the period previous to 1642, when he was a resident there.

Walcott, in " Concord in the Colonial Period," says : " Concord was the first settlement above tide water.

" It adjoined the towns of Watertown, Cambridge Farms, and Sudbury, and is nineteen miles from Boston.

" This tract of land, about six miles square, was occupied, in a sense, by two or three hundred Indians, and was called Musketaquid.

" The meadows traversed by the sluggish rivers that ran by devious windings to the northward were bordered by tracts of upland that had been burned over and brought under rude cultivation by the natives, and afforded a large area of cleared land that was very attractive to the English settlers. The woodland was for the most part covered with pine. Shad, salmon, and alewives abounded in the rivers and brooks, which were also the haunts of fur-bearing animals."

As the " Old Towne Booke of Concord " is lost, it cannot be told in what part of the town Thomas Doggett lived, whether he was granted or bought lands, when or to whom he sold the same, or what part he may have taken in the town affairs during his residence there.

Walcott says : " It cannot be doubted that there once was a town book which contained the records of the earliest grants of land and probably the other proceedings of the inhabitants, meeting together in general assembly." " A book of this character is referred to in ancient deeds and other documents, as well as the records that remain to us." The church of Concord was formally gathered at Cambridge, July 5, 1636, and was organized April 6, 1637, with Rev. Peter Bulkley as teacher, and Rev. John Jones pastor, and the town dates from the previous year. Mr. Bulkley and Mr. Flint had some property, but the rest of the Concord company were plain people, of humble station in England, and of small means, who hoped in the New World to better their condition, and to enjoy unmolested the simpler forms of religious worship that their tastes and consciences approved. Thomas Doggett may have been inclined to settle in Concord because John Doggett had been living in the adjoining town of Watertown for several years, and he would seem to have gone there more from this reason than because of any relatives or friends already there, when it is known that there is no reason to suppose that the Concord settlers ever came together on English soil. There was no transplanting of a church and its pastor, like the removal of John Robinson and his flock to Holland, or like the settlement of Plymouth and Dorchester. The first houses were humble structures with thatched roofs, and, very likely, wooden chimneys, oiled paper serving in place of window glass. Emerson says of them :

> " Beneath low hills, in broad interval,
> Through which at will our Indian rivulet
> Winds mindful still of sannup and of squaw,
> Whose pipe and arrow oft the plough unburies :
> Here in pine houses, built of new fallen trees,
> Supplanters of the tribe, the farmers dwell."

It is impossible to overestimate the trials and actual suffering that were endured by the pioneer families. Here as elsewhere in the colony, a close grappling with the facts was followed by inevitable disappointment. The meadows were wet, the soil was found to require hard labor to make and keep it productive, and it is written that the people were " forced to cut their bread very thin for a long season." It cannot be wondered that some sickened and died by reason of the unaccustomed hardships and severity of the winter weather, while others lost all faith in the success of the enterprise, sold their estates for a little, and departed.

Leaving Concord, Thomas Doggett removed to Weymouth, Mass., which is, next to Plymouth, the oldest English settlement in Massachusetts. Just when he moved there is not known, as there is a total absence of all church records for the first hundred and more years; and the town records of births, marriages, and deaths are v'ry incomplete. The property records are full and well preserved, as well as the records of town affairs, which, until 1651, seem to have been kept·by the townsmen, or selectmen, as since called. Weymouth, the old settlement of Wessagusset, was quite advanced in 1642, as compared with Concord.

In 1642 Rev. Samuel Newman was the minister, having been called to the church in Weymouth in 1639, where he remained four or five years. He was followed by Rev. Thomas Thacher, who was ordained pastor of the church January 2, 164$\frac{4}{3}$, where he remained for about twenty years, when he removed to Boston.

Weymouth was more advanced than any other place in New England except Plymouth in having the priority as to the presence of a physician, Dr. Nicholas Byram, who came to Weymouth in 1638, and remained there twenty-four years. The town is bounded on the east side by Hingham, on the west by Braintree, and has on the north a well-protected water frontage on an arm of Massachusetts bay, about twelve miles from Boston; so it was considered a most desirable location at the time of the removal there of Thomas Doggett.

Here it probably was he married, in 1643, as his second wife, Elizabeth, the widow of William Fry. William Fry had died here October 26, 1642, leaving a wife Elizabeth and daughters Elizabeth and Mary. His noncup. will is found in Suffolk Probate, 1–29, and was "deposed by Thomas Baily and John Barge before the Courte the 9 of the 9 mo. 1643." By it " he did give unto his wife after his decease his house and foure acres of land being his home lot and after her decease to his two daughters Elizabeth and Mary," to both of whom he makes other bequests. Elizabeth Fry was born December 20, 1639, and Mary Fry was born January 9, 1642, probably at Weymouth, as their father was a freeman and had twelve acres of land allotted to him there as early as 1636.

Thomas Doggett by his marriage with Mrs. Fry became one of the proprietors of Weymouth, and the property records, which are not

dated, but which were written at some time between his marriage and
May 21, 1644, speak of his lands as:

The Land of *[signature: Thomas Doget]* during the life of his wife and
afterwards to   Elizabeth and Mary ffrie the
daughters of   William ffrie deceased.

ffower acres in the west ffield first giuen to William ffrie bounded on the
East with the land of Edward Smith and John Hardinge, the land of John
Rogeres on the south, of John Whitman on the north, a highwaie on the south.

Twelue acres amongst the greate lotes bounded on the East with the greate
pond on the west with the comon the north with the land of Thomas White of
Robert Louell on the south.

In the will of Elder Bate, Suffolk Probate, Book 11, page 13, 20th
October, 1683, mention is made of " Doggett's lot," locating it at
East Weymouth, near the Hingham line.   Here it was his children,
Hannah, Sarah, and Samuel, were probably born ; but a careful search
of the records at Weymouth gives no insight into his family affairs
nor the dates of birth of his children.

Between the time of the record of land in his name, 1643–4, until
1648, the records at Weymouth do not mention the name, but in 1648
his fellow townsmen show their appreciation of his judgment and
ability by electing him to the office of townsman or selectman.

The following records of meetings of the townsmen are all that
is contained in the Weymouth town books relating to Thomas
Doggett :

Weymouth Town Records, page 17, " The 1st day of the 1st mo.
(March) 1648 ":

At a meeting of the Townsmen they having taken into consideration the
destruction of Pine and Cedar which are every year destroyed notwithstanding
there was order to the contrary to pay for it if they find it.   It is therefore
ordered that from this day forward whosoever do intend to fall any such tree of
Pine or Cedar for any use they shall come to Thomas Dyer and give cation to
him for as much as they shall fall.   For commoner one shilling three pence
a thousand under the penalty of 20s. a thousand.   And for those inhabitants
that are not commoners 2s 6d a thousand and whosoever shall fall any Pine or
Cedar Tree that might make boards, if it were employed to it, shall be liable by
this order to pay to the towns use 20s for every parcell that have the substance
of a 1000 of Boards in it.   But by this order wee doe not deny any man that is a
commoner to fall for his owne use.

And he that can make the breach of this to appeare, shall have one quarter of
the fines for his labour, and the other three quarters to be returned to the Towns
use.

Townsmen.

JOHN HOLBROOK   JOHN ROGERS
HENRY KINGMAN   THOMAS DOGGETT
JAMES BAYLEY   THOMAS HOLBROOK

Page 50, " The last day of the last month (Feb) 1648 ":

It was ordered that all swine that is above a quarter of a year old within this
Towne, shall be sufficiently Ringed and Yoked by the 14th day of the next month
uppon penalty of 3d a peese.   And wee do appoint John Randal and Hugh Roe

to be Hogwards, who shall carefully look to the execution of this order, and whosoever shall neglect to ring or yoke his swine as aforesaid it shall be lawfull for the hogwards, or either of them, to recover for their owne proper use the aforesaid 3^d of the owners of every such swine as shall be unwrung as often as they shall find them unringed. Always provided the owners have due notice, and that it be not demanded twis in one day, and if any person shall refuse to pay the foresayd 3^d it shall be lawfull for the Hogwards or either of them to pound the sayd swine, and keepe them according to the law til they satisfie them as aforesaid but in case any hoggs or swine looste their yokes or rings the owners of any such swine shall not be liable to this penalty aforesaid.

Townsmen —

NICHOLAS PHILLIPS
ROBERT TUCKER
MICATH PRATT

Thom Dogget

JOHN HOLBROOK
RICHARD PORTER

Page 58, " 26th day of the 9th mo (Nov.) 1651 ":

Voted — That there shall be but 5 Townsmen chosen this year ensueing and that there power shall be the same that it was the last year with those alterations and additions therein exprest.

Voted — That Serg^t Holbrook shall be authorized to procure a surveyor to run the lines between Hingham and Braintree and to attend that surveyor together with those that are made choyse of for that end viz John Whitman, Thomas Pratt for Hingham line and John Kinge and Edward Kingman for the other line.

Wee whose names are here subscribed in the 1st meeting do chowese Deken Rogers for to be the recorder for this year 165$\frac{2}{1}$

JOHN HOLBROOK   HENRY KINGMAN
THOMAS HOLBROOK   JAMES BAYLEY
             JAMES SMITH.

The names of the Townsmen
HENRY KINGMAN   JOHN HOLBROOK
THOMAS HOLBROOK   JAMES SMITH
JAMES BAYLEY   JOHN ROGERS
             THOMAS DOGGETT

Page 59, " At a meeting of the Townsmen the 2nd of the 12th mo. (Feb.) 1651 ":

It was then and there ordered by the Townsmen that a great lotts that mentioned in the old Towne Booke that were formerly given and also lotts drawne shall be layde out on the E side of the fresh Pond next to Mrs Richards her mill joyning to those small lotts that were formerly layde out butting uppon the fresh Pond and to run 18 rod toward Hingham lyne. And in case these lotts under written doth run beyond the Pond in weidth that then it shall front uppon a straight lyne as the Pond hath. The names of those that are to have lotts in order as followeth : [Then follows the division.]

The names of the Townsmen
             THOMAS DOGGETT
             JOHN ROGERS
             JOHN HOLBROOK.

Page 61, " The 14th the 10th mo (Dec) 1652 ":

At a general towne meeting there were chosen townsmen Deacon Rogers, Serg^t Holbrook — Thomas Doggett — Thomas Dyer John Bicknell Serg^t Hunt and William Torrey and the same power is hereby given them that the last Townsmen had, as also further that they shall take some care for Mr Lowman that she shall be provided for in respect of a house and also to do what they shall judge present necessity requires about the meeting house and that may make it more comfortable and prevent any further decay.

Page 62, "The 7th of the 1st mo (March) 1653":

At a meeting of the Townsmen it was ordered that Thomas Doggett should take care for the burning of the woods for wich he is to have due satisfaction.

In 1652 Elizabeth, the second wife of Thomas Doggett, died, probably in Weymouth, and in the following year he changed his home for the last time, by moving to Marshfield, Mass.

In an article on Marshfield, by William T. Davis, Esq., in the " History of Plymouth County," he says: " The town of Marshfield, together with Duxbury, its adjoining town on the south, shares with Plymouth the interest which attaches to the home of the Pilgrims. Its fertile lands and broad marshes early attracted the attention of the first settlers, and were eagerly sought for homesteads and farms. Watered by North river on its northerly border, by South river in its central section, and by Green's Harbor river in its southerly, its territory was admirably adapted to those agricultural pursuits which were the chief support of the Pilgrims. The township, slightly increased in size since its original incorporation, covers an area of about twenty-five square miles, and is bounded easterly by the ocean and the town of Duxbury; southerly by Duxbury and Pembroke; westerly by Duxbury, Pembroke, and the North river; and northerly by the North River and the ocean." This territory has been called Missaucatucket, Oxford, Green's Harbor, Rexham, and Marshfield, was made a township March 2, 1640, and is about thirty miles south-east of Boston. Among the first settlers was Thomas Chillingsworth, who was quite a prominent man in public matters. After a short residence at Lynn, in 1637, and afterward at Sandwich, he settled in Marshfield, where he was a large landholder, and was representative 1648 and 1652. Administration on his estate was granted March, 1652–3, to his widow Joanna, who married August 17, 1654, Thomas Doggett.

Mr. Chillingsworth had four daughters, but no son.

Elizabeth died unmarried, September 28, 1655.

Mehitabel married May 2, 1661, Justus Eames.

Mary married Deacon John Foster.

Sarah married Samuel Sprague, the last secretary of Plymouth Colony.

The Bible of Mr. Chillingsworth Miss Thomas mentions as still in existence, printed by Christopher Barker, 1589.

The maiden name of his wife is not known, nor the date or place of their marriage.

The interest of Thomas Doggett in the widow Chillingsworth is first noticed in a record at Plymouth:

The widow, Joan Chillingsworth, in like manner came into court 7 March 1653 and acknowledged that she hath given unto her four daughters 10£ a piece to be delivered to them on their day of marriage or within three months after same and in case any of them die, the survivors to have their part divided equally between them and for performance thereof Thomas Doged and the said Joane Chillingsworth have jointly given security to the court.

"July 3, 1654. Upon desire of Arthur Howland for the ending of controversies regarding bounds of lands, that he and Thomas Doged be acquainted with the bounds of lands according to original grant."

In 1655 Thomas Doggett serves on the jury at Plymouth, and October 4 of the same year:

The court have ordered that Mr. Arthur Howland and Thomas Doged shall procure a surveyor to lay out the land in controversy betwixt Thomas Doged and him who shall do it according to decision and testimony from Captain Standish and Mr. Alden and to lay out the line of division betwixt them according to the evidence and to return what is done unto the court and the charges thereof to be equally borne betwixt them. [Court Orders, 3–89.]

May 6, 1656 — In answer to a petition preferred to the court by Thomas Doged of Marshfield wherein the said Thomas Doged proposed that a Jury might be impannelled to make division of a certain part of land sold by Mr Edmond ffreeman of Cambridge Point unto Mr Arthur howland and Thomas Chillingsworth deceased lying at the south bridge in the Town of Marshfield. The court have ordered there shall be a jury of 12 men that shall determine the laying out of the said land and shall fully end the controversy betwixt said Arthur howland and Thomas Doged about the said land the said jury to be impannelled at the next general court. [Court Orders, 3–97.]

At the town meeting 1656, May 19, Thomas Dogget and John Rouse were chosen grand jurymen for the present year ensuing.

June 18, 1656 an agreement was made in regard to the land in controversy, before Mr John Alden Capt Cudworth and the Jury appointed, and the division line decided upon. The agreement was signed by Arthur howland and Thomas _T_ Doged
his   marke.   [Court Orders, 3–103.]

At the town meetings May 18 and August 13, 1657, Thomas Dogget was absent the first hour, and in each case was fined 6d.

During this year Thomas Doggett took the oath of fidelity at Marshfield.

November 16, 1657, town meeting, Goodman Dogget and John Rouse for grand juryship, £1.

Rev. George Leonard says of this, in a letter dated April 9, 1852, "I have already transcribed about a thousand names, including repetitions, to my list of town officers, and this is the only instance in which the title 'Goodman'[1] is used."

1658, October 11, town meeting, Thomas Dogget, 1s. 0d., being his town rate. This year he serves on a coroner's jury.

The Rev. Edward Bulkley, son of Rev. Peter Bulkley, of Concord, was the pastor at Marshfield, and held an estate independent of the minister's land. His father dying in 1659, he succeeded him as pastor of the church at Concord, and was succeeded in the pastoral office at Marshfield by Rev. Samuel Arnold, of Yarmouth.

---

[1] The term "goodman" was used as a slight appellation of civility. The Puritans, strictly speaking, gave the title "Goodman" to a specially prominent church-member of mature years.

As the first volume of church records at Marshfield does not begin until 1696, there is an absence here as well as at Weymouth and Concord of all evidence to show what may have been the church relations of Thomas Doggett.

At a town meeting May 16, 1659, he gave "one barrel of beef" toward the purchase of the lands of Mr. Bulkley in Marshfield.

May, 1659, on the jury.

He bought this year (1659) the farm to which he afterward removed, and which adjoined the farm of Peregrine White, near the junction of North and South rivers.

Indenture made the 11th day of October A.D. 1659 between Comfort Starr of Boston in County of Suffolk in New England, Chirurgeon on the one part and Thomas Dogget of Marshfield on the other part.   120 acres in Marshfield with buildings thereon, the same being now leased to William Sherman and Edmond Hindsman.   [O.C. Deeds, 6–23.]

Comfort Starr deceased before the sale was completed, and among the amounts due the estate as recorded in Suffolk Probate is one from "Good Doggett," as he is called.

March 15, 1659–60, We whose names are under written are testators of the possession given by John Starr sole executor of Comfort Starr deceased of Boston, To Thomas Dogget of Marshfield according to usual custom By twig and turf. with all and singular the privileges and immunities mentioned in the deed.

Testators   PEREGRINE WHITE
                                         EDMUND HINKMAN, Sen.

This deed of sale on the other side sold by Comfort Starr unto Thomas Dogget the truth whereof was acknowledged by John Starr his son and that the said John Starr hath received in full what was behind at his fathers death this John Starr acknowledges before me.   SIMON WILLARD Asst.
2–4mo 1663.   [O.C. Deeds, 6–25.]

The exact location of Thomas Doggett's house on this land is not known, but is presumed to be in a field back of a house now occupied by Capt. Asa Sherman, at Centre Marshfield.   In this field, overlooking the marshes, the two rivers, and the ocean, on the side of the hill, yet protected by it, near a spring of clear, cold water, is an old cellar which the oldest inhabitants of the vicinity call the site of the "Doggett House."   This and the fact that the cellar is on a line with the house of Peregrine White, and not very far from it, both near the old highway, long since closed, would lead one to believe this was the site of the house of Thomas Doggett.   The stones would indicate a house about thirty feet square, and a barn not far from it. Out on the marsh is an oasis of cedar trees, old and gnarled, called "Doggett's Cedars," and beyond, where the surf breaks on the beach, is "Doggett's Beach," names which have clung to the spot to the present time among a few of the older inhabitants.

1660, May 14, Thomas Dogget chosen one of a jury.

1660, July 15, at said town meeting the town have chosen Thomas Dogget constable, who then refused the taking the oath to serve as constable.

1661, October 14, at said town meeting Thomas Dogget, constable, formally gave in his account and is fully discharged.

1661, June 4, Mr. Anthony Eames acknowledged before the court that his son, Justus Eames, hath received £13 6s. 8d. of Thomas Doged, of Marshfield, in full of his wife's portion.

1662, on the jury.

1663, May 18, town meeting, Thomas Dogget surveyor for the year.

1663, July 6. At town meeting the inhabitants chose a committee to view land by request of Lieut. Peregrine White and Thomas Dogget.

1663–1664. On the jury each year.

166¾, March 8. Town meeting, Thomas Dogget chosen on a committee.

1664, October 4. One of a committee to settle a dispute regarding a debt of Edward Bumpas.

Among the papers of the Massachusetts Historical Society is one superscribed " Namaskett Proprs names." The record was made about 1664. Thomas Dogget is named as the grantee of the 27th lot, the first at Whetstone's Vineyard.

In the papers at Plymouth, relating to the settlement of the estate of Thomas Bourn, whose will was dated May 2, 1664, the inventory was taken by " Serg^t Joseph Riddle, A. Snow, and Thomas Doged."

February 13, 166⅘. Town meeting. The inhabitants have chosen five selectmen, viz. :

Lieut. PEREGRINE WHITE.   Ensign MARK EAMES.
JOSEPH BEADLE.   THOMAS DOGGET.
                ANTHONY SNOW.

March 1, 1664. Peregrine White, of Marshfield, sells Thomas Dogged, of Marshfield, meadow ground lying on the north side of a great brook, running to said White's now dwelling-house. [O.C. Deeds, 3–215.]

1666, May 28. Thomas Dogget, grand juryman.

1667, April 5. On a jury to lay out the highway.

August 5. The rate as follows : Thomas Dogget, grand juryman, £1 2s. 6d.

1668, September 23. At said town-meeting the inhabitants have given liberty to Thomas Dogget, Lieut. Peregrine White, William Ford, Jr., Samuel Sprague, John Foster, and Justus Eames, to use and make improvements of all the lands at the head of their lots.

In 1671, he is appointed to collect the ordinary or taxes in Marshfield, as also to collect for the minister's maintenance.

On March 3, 1671, William Turning, of Eastham, sells him a one-hundred-acre lot at Namakasett, for £28. [O.C. Deeds, 3–207.]

1671, June 5. For the prevention of the great abuse by the excessive use of liquors, two or three men are appointed in every town in the jurisdiction of Plymouth, to have the inspection of the ordinary or in any other places suspected, and Thomas Doged is named for Marshfield.

In 1672, he begins the distribution of his estate among his children, by giving them land for house and farm just previous to their marriages. The first such gift is:

April 20, 1672 — Thomas Dogget of Marshfield, planter, to my well beloved son John Dogget, one half of all my uplands and meadow which was formerly land of Comfort Starr deceased. [O.C. Deeds, 4–50.]

Thomas Doggett owned a share in "Cedar Swamp," and October 14, 1672, the swamp was divided in seven lots of five shares each, his share being one in the third lot. This swamp was in what was called "Majors Purchase." Windsor, in his "History of Duxbury," says, near "Mattekesett ponds, alias Namasakesett." The ponds thus named are that collection which now are within the bounds of Pembroke and Hanson.

May 5, 1673. At town meeting, Thomas Dogget is chosen surveyor.

June 9, 1673, occurs the second instance of his giving land to his children, this time to his son-in-law, Samuel Sherman, in consideration of his marriage with his daughter Sarah. [O.C. Deeds, 4–90.] The original deed was shown the writer by one of the descendants of Samuel Sherman, it having been handed down and always highly valued by its possessor.

1674, May 13. The town chose Thomas Dogget as grand juryman.

1675, May 6. Town meeting, Thomas Dogget chosen constable.

1675, Aug. 23. Town meeting, rate as follows:

Thomas Dogget, 16s. 3d.

In the will of William Ford, Sen., of Marshfield, aged about seventy-two years, dated 12th September, 1676, he says: "I appoint my son William to be my executor and request Thomas Doggett if God so dispose that he survive my wife to be my overseer."

May 30, 1677. An agreement is made regarding a division of land granted at a meeting at Marshfield. The whole tract is divided into six lots, of which the second lot falls to Peregrine White, Thomas Dogget, William Ford, Justus Eames, John Dogget, Samuel Sherman, and John Ford, Sen. [O.C. Deeds, 6–114.]

May 30, 1677. Town meeting. "At said town meeting the inhabitants have voted Anthony Snow, Thomas Dogget and John Bourne to look into and improve the Poor stock in the town for the benefit of the poor and upholding the stock to their discretion."

August 13, 1677. Town meeting. "At said meeting the town did vote Thomas Dogget and Ensign Eames to lay out Edward

Stevens, his land formerly granted and then it is to be recorded and also fully committed to him and his heirs forever."

During this year he was appointed to enforce the liquor law.

March 20, 1681.   He makes an agreement with his son John regarding the division of lands which he had formerly given him, and on the same date gives land to his son Samuel, making the third instance of gifts of this nature to his children.

An extract of this last deed is as follows:

March 20 1681 Thomas Dogget of Marshfield, in consideration of the tender love and fatherly affection which I have and bear to my natural and well beloved son Samuel Dogget of Marshfield, one half of all my lands in Middleboro and places adjacent which said share of land formerly purchased of William Twining of Eastham as by deed Mar. 7, 1671.   [O.C. Deeds, 6-27.]

On the same date he gives his son John Doggett the other half of land in Middleboro'; also gives him land in the valley in Marshfield.

1682, May 22.   At the town meeting Thomas Doggett is mentioned for the last time on the records of the town of Marshfield, and is chosen surveyor of highways.

Feb. 6, 1683 — Thomas Dogget of Marshfield in the Colony of New Plymouth in New England, sendeth greeting. In consideration of the love and fatherly affection I have for my natural and loving son Samuel Dogget as also for divers other good causes All my land both upland and meadow which I now have in Marshfield, that is to say more particularly the moiety of all that farm that I formerly purchased of Mr Comfort Starr being that part of said farm whereon I now live according as it is marked 40 and bounded between my son John Dogget and myself as may appear by indenture of part under our hands and seals, reserving the use during life, also all that tract of land purchased of Leut Peregrine White lying north of a great brook next adjoining to the southerly part of my other meadows with the same reserved, with the moiety of one half part of the land granted to me and others of my neighbors at the heads of our lots by the town aforesaid.   [O.C. Deeds, 6-26.]

June 3, 1684.   The court named him as constable for Marshfield.

Retired from active pursuits and positions of public trust, with his lands distributed among his children, the records examined do not show that he is again mentioned, and during the remaining years of his long and busy life we think of him in the words of Mrs. Sigourney:

> " While moving on thro' Marshfield's vales,
>   Mid the balm of her summer breeze,
> With a peaceful smile on his honor'd brow,
>   A fair old man she sees:
> Full many a change in the Mother Land,
>   From the cottage to the throne,
> As well as here, in this younger sphere,
>   That reverend sire hath known."

He died August 18, 1692, and is supposed to have been buried among his fellow-townsmen, in the old First Burial Ground, sometimes called the Winslow Ground, among whose honored dead Daniel Webster, by his special request, was interred.

There are many stones whose inscriptions are long since illegible, but among those which can be read none has been found to mark the spot where Thomas Doggett lies.

In the Probate Records of Plymouth County, Vol. I., page 154, is found the will of Thomas Doggett, as follows:

I Thomas Dogget, of Marshfield, being grown aged, yet of sound mind, and memory, praysed be God. Do make this my last will, and testament, in manor and forme following: first I comit my soul unto ye hands of God, my saviour, and my Body to desent Buriall, when it shall pleased God to take me hense, with sure and certain hope of a joy full resurrection, and reunion of Soul and Body to Eternall Glory through the gracious merits of Christ, our Lord our onely saviour.

And for the disposall of my outward estate my mind and will is, it shall be disposed as followeth: I having formerly given unto my son John Dogget, the one half of my farm, and divided the same unto him as by one instrument bearing date the 20th day of March 1681 may appear which he is in possession of.

And having also given to my sonn Samuel Dogget, a deed of the other half of my farm I live upon with other lands.

And to avoid all other controverces as concerning the Lands intended to be granted by the aforesaid Deed to my son Samuel, I do hereby declare and hereby give and confirm unto my said son Samuel Dogget, all that half of ye aforesaid farm which I am in possession of, viz: house, out houses orchard, half Barns and Lands, whatsoever, both divided and undivided or lying in common with my son John or otherwise.

To have and to hold to him the said Samuel Dogget his heirs and assigns for ever.

Item — my debts and funerall expenses being first paid, I give and bequeath to my daughter Sarah Sherman's children, viz: to Prudence Sarah and Susanna, ten shillings apiece and all the remainder of my estate to be divided amongst the rest of my children viz: to my sons John, Samuel, and Hannah Blanchers children, and Rebecka Wilder, my son John to have two fifths parts thereof, or double to any other of my children, and my son Samuel to have one fifth part thereof, and my daughter Rebeckah one fifth part thereof, and my daughter Hannah's children one fifth part thereof.

Lastly I nominate and appoint my son Samuel to be sole executor of this my last will and testament. In witness whereof I have hereunto set my hand and seal the twentieth day of January 1689.

THOMAS T DOGET [Seal.]
his   marke

We under written did see the above named Thomas Dogett sign seal and deliver the above written instrument.

SAMUEL ARNOLD
NATHANIEL THOMAS
MEHETABEL TRUANT
her w T marke

memo. Jan 3, 1692/3 — Captain Nathaniel Thomas and Mr Samuel Arnold two of the witnesses herein named made oath before William Bradford Esq commissionated judge for Granting Probate of wills. That they were present and did see and hear the above named Thomas Dogget sign seal and deliver the above written Instrument to be his last will and Testament and that to the best of their judgment he was of sound mind and memory when he did ye same.

Attest SAMUEL SPRAGUE, Regis.

On the following page is a tracing from the original will, which is in the Probate Office at Plymouth, Mass. It is interesting to note that the name is spelled in three different ways in this small portion of the document.

In Wittnes whereof

Set my hand & Seale the 20th Day of January 1682

Thomas

his [mark]

Dogett

his marke

Sealed and Delivered in the presence of us

Samuel Ramsey

Nathaniel Thomas

Capt Nath Thomas Sen.t

&

[illegible]

Memorand January 3d 1693

[several lines illegible]

On the back of the will it is indorsed :

Vol. I., page 155.

William Bradford Esq. commissionated by his Excellency Sr William Phips Kn't, Captain Generall & Governor in Chief in and over their Majesties Province of ye Massachusetts Bay in New England with the advice and consent of ye council for ye granting probate of wills and Letters of Administration within ye county of Plymouth — Know ye that on the third day of January 1692 or 3 before me at Marshfield the will of Thomas Dogget late of Marshfield aforesaid to those presents annexed was proved, approved and allowed his will in any manor concerning was comitted unto his son Samuel Dogget executor in the same named will, and to administer the same and to make a true and perfect inventory. . . . In testimony whereof I have hereunto set my hand and the seal of said office.

WILLIAM BRADFORD.

Dated at Marshfield ye 3rd day of Jan., 169$\frac{2}{3}$.

SAMUEL SPRAGUE. Regis.

Vol. I., page 155.

Inventory of " ye goods and chattels of Thomas Dogget, late of Marshfield, deceased," taken and appraised August 23, 1692 :

	£	s.	d.
Item — To his Cash	2	7	6
Wearing apparel	3	7	0
4 cows at 38s. Ye head	7	12	0
1 — 2 year old heiffer	1	4	0
1 horse Bridle & saddle	4	0	0
2 swine	1	0	0
A feather bed and furniture	6	10	6
Towels and table linen	1	9	0
2 remnants of homespun cloth and shrouds	0	15	3
Saws and wedges and other tools	0	14	0
A chest two bedsteads and cords	1	4	0
1 tray and ½ doz spoons	0	2	9
Vessels of Pewter	0	18	8
Vessels of Brass	0	18	0
Vessels of Iron	0	15	6
2 chains and a trammel	0	17	0
A whelot rod chain	0	2	0
Vessels of wood	0	5	0
To his Books	0	6	0
Cob irons, spit tongs and sh'td	0	10	0
A chain, ditching knife and grindstone	0	10	0
The estate Indebted ye bill	7	0	0
Charge	1	1	0

SAMUEL SPRAGUE,
THOMAS MACOMBER.

Samuel Dogget executor to ye last will of Thomas Dogget late of Marsh-field deceased appointed Jan. 3, 169$\frac{2}{3}$ before William Bradford Judge and made oath that ye above written is a true Inventory of ye goods and chattels of said deceased so far as he knows and that when more shall come to his knowl-edge he will discover it.

Attest   SAMUEL SPRAGUE. Regis.

THOMAS DOGGETT, OF MARSHFIELD, MASS.

SECOND GENERATION.

3552. JOHN DOGGETT [2] (*Thomas* [1]), born Concord (?), Mass., 1642; died Marshfield, Mass., 1718; married 1st, Hingham, Mass., 1673, Persis Sprague, daughter of William and Milicent (Eames) Sprague, of Hingham, Mass.; born Hingham, Mass., November 12, 1643; died Marshfield, Mass., 1684; married 2d, Marshfield, Mass., September 3, 1691, Mehitabel Truant, daughter of Maurice and Jane Truant, of Duxbury, Mass.; married 3d, Newbury, Mass., June 22, 1697, Rebecca Brown, widow of Isaac Brown, of Newbury, Mass., and daughter of Mr. Bailey; born 1640; died Newbury, Mass., August 25, 1731.

Issue:

3557. i. JOHN DOGGETT,[3] born Marshfield, Mass., June 28, 1674; died Marsh-field, Mass., March 11, 167$\frac{8}{9}$.
3558. ii. THOMAS DOGGETT,[3] born Marshfield, Mass., 1676.
3559. iii. JOHN DOGGETT,[3] born Marshfield, Mass., February 26, 1678; probably died unmarried before 1716.
3560. iv. ISAAC DOGGETT,[3] born Marshfield, Mass., June 7, 1692; died Marsh-field, Mass., September 21, 1692.
3561. v. HANNAH DOGGETT,[3] born Marshfield. Mass., December 28, 1693.

John Doggett spent the greater part of his life in Marshfield.

In 1662 he was in Hingham, where he witnessed an Indian deed.

April 20, 1672, his father gives him one-half of the home-farm in Marshfield, and on May 13, of the same year, he is admitted a towns-man.

In 1677, May 30, his landed estate is increased by the addition of land allotted to certain proprietors by the town, and again, in 168$\frac{1}{2}$, March 20, by the gift from his father of land in Middleboro' and Marshfield.

The town records show that he was interested in town affairs, and chosen by the town in 1682 as constable. In 1684 he was made sur-veyor of the highways, and August 4, of the same year, had distributed rate as constable.

April 1, 1686, he purchased from Justus Eames for £10 land adjoining the head of his house-lot and that of his father; Peregrine White and Samuel Sherman being witnesses to the deed. [Plymouth Deeds, 6–31.]

On August 2, 1686, he and his brother Samuel hired the flats on the South river of the town, for that year, probably for the salt hay which they could cut there, as he was, like his father, a planter or husbandman. June, 1689, he was received and admitted as freeman at a court at Plymouth.

May 18, 1691, he was chosen grand juryman. In 1692 a jury, consisting of John Rogers, Thomas Macomber, John Foster, John Hewett, John Rose, John Barker, John Doggett, Joseph Waterman, Isaac Holmes, Anthony Eames, Ephraim Little, Michael Ford, Joseph Crocker, John Thomas, and Nathaniel Thomas, Jr., laid out the highways of the town as follows:

We whose names are subscribed being chosen and sworn as a jury at Marshfield on the first day of June 1692, to lay out and remove such highways in the said town as are needful according as the law directed, in order thereunto having met together on the sixteenth day of June aforesaid, do declare as followeth:

That part which relates to the highway through the Doggetts' land is:

And also from the aforesaid way which leadeth from Benjamin Phillips, beginning at the north west corner of said Phillips field and so turning southward up the hill by his field, and so on as the way now lieth, through the land of the Sherman's and the Doggett's, and Mr. White's down the hill as the way hath been lately dug, and so on the old way through the land of Ensign Ford, Anthony Eames, and Samuel Sprague, and so over the brook as the way now leadeth between the house and shop of John Foster, and so through the land of Arthur Howland as the way now lieth until it come to John Walker's land, and then upon the range between said Howland's and Walker's land north westward into the other way.

July 28, 1692, again chosen surveyor of the highways, and the following year, March 20, to the same office, and the additional one of viewer of fences. As grand juror, at the same meeting he receives from the town 15s. for his services.

In those days the tithingman was an all-important personage; he was a parish officer who preserved order at public worship, and enforced the observance of the Sabbath.

For three successive years John Doggett filled this office, he being chosen thereto March 10, 169¾, March 11, 169⅘, and March 16, 169⅝.

From the first volume of records of the first church in Marshfield: "John Doggett admitted into this church May 30, 1697."

170⁰⁄₁, February 24. Grand juryman.

170⅞, February 9. John Doggett chosen grand juryman, but excused at his request.

170⅞, March 22. Chosen surveyor of the highways.

1708, December 13.   Chosen on a jury of trial at Plymouth.

At a meeting of the proprietors of Marshfield, 3d day of April, 1710, the rate for each proprietor's share in the common lands is given, John Dogget being 13s.

October 9, 1710.   John and Thomas Doggett drew lot No. 51 in the first division, and No. 38 in the second division.

The exact date of death of John Doggett is not known, neither is the place of his interment, as no stone has been found to his memory, although he is supposed to have been buried in the old Winslow Ground.

The will of John Doggett is recorded in Plymouth Probate, 4–120:

In the name of God, Amen. The twenty first day of January 1716. I, John Dogget of Marshfield in the County of Plymouth in New England, Husbandman, being aged and infirm of body but of perfect mind and memory thanks be given to God and calling to mind the mortality of my body and knowing that it is appointed for all men once to die do make and ordain this my last will and testament.

That is to say. Principaly and first of all I recommend my soul into the hands of God that gave it and my body to the earth to be buried in a decent christian burial at the discretion of my executor herein after named.

And as touching such worldly goods and estate as the Lord in mercy hath been pleased to bless me with in this life (my just debts being first paid and funeral charges defrayed) I give demise and dispose of the residue of the same in manner and form following:

Imprimis — I give and bequeath to my beloved wife Rebeckah Dogget the use and improvement of the westerly end of the Leanto standing on the back side or northerly side of my dwelling house, That is to say the Chamber, Lower room and the seller under it and also a liberty to set a bed in the chamber in the westerly end of my said dwelling house and lodge herselfe or others in it as she shall have ocation also I give to my said wife free liberty to take and fetch water out of my well and out of the brook on the back side of my house and carry it through the Great Room of my said house as she may have ocation and also the use and Improvement of the half acre of land or thereabouts that is fenced in at the north westerly end of the said house and also the garden at the west end of said house.

Also I give to my said wife the use and Improvement of my 2 feather beds, bedsteds and beding and all the furniture belonging to them and also the use of the utensils of household stuff in the house to wit: of pewter, brass and Iron and dishes and spoons — 2 washing tubs, the tongs and 2 barrells, only my son Thomas Dogget shall have liberty to use the great Brass Kettle when he shall have ocation.

Also I give to my said wife Liberty to take Apples out of the orchard what she shall have ocasion for to spend in the house. That is to say all the perticulers and things and privilidges above said I give my said wife the use and Improvement off during her natural Life for her support and maintenance also I give unto my said wife her firewood to be brought to her door and cut fit for her fire so much as she shall stand in need of and 2 barrells of sider to be filled into her barrells as hereafter in this my will I shall order during her natural Life. Also I give unto my s'd wife the sum of 8 pounds a year to be paid to her yearly and every year during the whole time of her natural life ½ thereof in corn and provisions at the currant money in price and the other half in money or bills of credit of the province as hereafter in this my will I shall order.

Item — I give and bequeath unto my son Thomas Dogget all that my farm and lands or tenement whereon I now dwell both that which I had of my father and that which I purchased of my uncle Justice Eames with all the salt marsh and meadow adjoining and belonging to it Lying and being in Marshfield aforesaid with all the housing, outhousing and buildings orchard and fences standing upon and belonging to it excepting the interest and improvements given to my said wife as above expressed.

Item — I give unto my said son Thomas Dogget all my right and interest in the allotment or division of the common lands formerly called the upper part of Marshfield now Lying in the Town of Pembroke and also all my right and interest in the cedar swamp lying in that part of land called the Majors purchase in pembroke aforesaid and also all my part and interest in the 60 acre lot of land lying in the Majors purchase in Pembroke aforesaid which I have and hold in partnership with my brother Samuel Dogget, all the within and above mentioned farm housing and buildings and several parcels of lands expressed to be given to my said son Thomas Dogget. I give the same and every part and parcell thereof the priveleges and appurtenances to all or any part thereof belonging, unto him said Thomas Dogget, his heirs and assigns forever (excepting as within excepted) he and they paying the sum of 8£ to my said wife yearly and every year half in corn and provisions at the currant money price and one half in money or bills of this province during her natural life and finding and providing her firewood and filling her 2 barrells of cider yearly during her life as within expressed for her to have.

Item — I give and bequeath to my daughter Hannah White 2 cows and it is my mind and will that after my said wifes decease my said daughter Hannah shall have one of the feather beds bedstead beding and furniture belonging to it and all my pewter and Iron pots which my said wife is to have the improvement of during life as aforesaid which with what I have formerly given to said Hannah I judge sufficient for her portion of my estate.

Item — I give and bequeath to my grandson John Dogget all my right and interest in the allotment or division of the common lands in the Lower part of Marshfield aforesaid Lying near or adjoining to the land of Samuel Rogers

To have and to hold the same with the privileges and appurtenances thereunto belonging unto him the said John Dogget his heirs and assigns forever.

Item — I give to my grandson Thomas Dogget 2 cows.

Item — I give to my granddaughters Persis Dogget Sarah Dogget and Experience Dogget each of them 2 ewe sheep and farther it is my mind and will that all that estate which I have given my said wife the improvement of during her life as within expressed, after her decease all of it except what I have given to my daughter Hannah as aforesaid shall be and belong to my said son Thomas Dogget.

And all the rest of my estate of what kind or nature soever and wheresoever Lying and being not before in this my will disposed of I give and bequeath the same unto my said son Thomas Dogget his heirs and assigns forever.

Lastly I hereby nominate and appoint my son Thomas Dogget to be sole executor to this my last will and testament and in testimony that above and within written in the several pages thereof is my last will and testament I have hereunto set my hand and seal the day and year first above written

John   Dogget ◇

Signed sealed published and declared by the said John Dogget to be his last will and testament In the presence of
JOHN CUSHING SR.
JOHN CUSHING JR
JOSHUA LORING
ELIZABETH HOLMES   Proved July 2, 1718

"An inventory of the goods chattels and credits of John Dogget of Marshfield, appraised July 2, 1718":

Some of the items are as follows:

	£	s	d
In purse and bills of credit .	2	2	10
Wearing apparell	18		
Books .	3		
Arms .	1	4	
Bed and furniture in great room .	14		
" " " " leanto			

4 pair of sheets and other small linen
Coverlid, Blanket, Rug and Canvas Bed
Sheeps' wool, Brass Kettle, Skillet and warming pan Iron Pots, Kettle,
Trammels, frying pan, tongs, Spit, Pewter spoons and Knives, chains, chests,
spinning wheels, Bellows, Tubs, Trays, pails, barrels Indian corn, powdering
tub and meat, Saddle Bridle, Pillion, Carpenters tools, old Lumber in house, 3
stocks of bees, Cart wheels & yoak, Plow, Cleaver, 3 old axes, Beetle and
wedges A dung fork, shovel and Sythe, Tackling. Horse traces, 1 Hod,

	£		£
4 Cows	17	2 Oxen	13
2 Heifers 1 yr old . .	8	1 Horse	8
5 swine	3 – 10	20 sheep & 5 lambs	9
Iron letters	0 – 5 – 0	Grindstone, Looking Glass and fowls.	

Appraisers John Kent, John Barker, John Little. [Plymouth Probate, 4-122.]

3553. HANNAH DOGGETT [2] (*Thomas* [1]), born Weymouth, Mass.,
1646; died Andover, Mass., July 10, 1725; married Charlestown,
Mass., June 24, 1673, by Richard Russell, magistrate, to Samuel
Blanchard, of Charlestown, Mass., son of Thomas Blanchard; born
County Hants, Eng., August 6, 1627; died Andover, Mass., April
22, 1707.

Issue:

3562. i. THOMAS BLANCHARD,[3] born Charlestown, Mass., April 28, 1674.
3563. ii. JOHN BLANCHARD,[3] born Charlestown, Mass., July 3, 1677; married
 Billerica, Mass., August 7, 1701, Mary Crosby, daughter of Simon
 and Rachel (Brackett) Crosby; she died Billerica, Mass., May 7,
 1748; he died Billerica, Mass., April 10, 1750.
3564. iii. SAMUEL BLANCHARD,[3] born Charlestown, Mass., June 4, 1680; married
 Andover, Mass., March 31, 1708, Sarah Johnson; she died Andover,
 Mass., August 19, 1769; he died Andover, Mass., April 17, 1754.
3565. iv. HANNAH BLANCHARD,[3] born Charlestown, Mass., September 26, 1681;
 married Andover, Mass., May 24, 1699, Stephen Osgood; she died
 Andover, Mass., March, 1774.

Thomas Blanchard, who was the ancestor of the larger part of the
New England families of the name of Blanchard, came from London
in the year 1639. It is supposed he settled in Braintree, Mass.,
where he is known to have lived from 1646 to 1651. In 1651 he
purchased a house and farm of two hundred acres, on Mystic side,
Charlestown, Mass., to which place he removed the same year, and
where he died 1654. His son Nathaniel, born in England 1636, married 1658, in Charlestown, Susanna Bates, and removed to Weymouth,
Mass. (Hobart's History of Abington, 1866.) An older son, Samuel
Blanchard, of Charlestown, was constable 1657, and admitted to the
church, 25 (7) 1681.

An old manuscript book, the property of Mr. Abel Blanchard, of
Andover, Mass. (now, 1869, with the Bible Society, Astor place, New
York), is in the handwriting of several parties, but evidently com-
menced by the first Samuel Blanchard, of Andover.

In this book he says: "Samuel Blanchard was married to his wife
Mary (Sweetser) in the year 165$\frac{3}{4}$ upon the 3rd day of January."
They had Samuel, Sarah, Mary, Jonathan, Joshua, and Abigail.
Following the list of children is:

" My wife died 20 Feb 166⅞."

" I Samuel Blanchard was marred to my wif hanah vpon the 24 day of juen in the yer 1673."

" I Samuel Blanchard landed in New ingland on the 23 day of Jun in the year 1639."

" I Samuel Blanchard came to Andover with my family upon the 10th June 1686."

The record, continued by their son Thomas :

" My mother Hannah Blanchard departed this life July 10, 1725, and as wee reseve it, in the 79th year of her age."

George D. B. Blanchard, Esq., of Malden, Mass., writes from that place as follows, regarding Hannah (Doggett) Blanchard :

" After her marriage, which evidently took place at Charlestown, she lived thirteen years within a short distance from the spot where I am now writing, and I can see plainly from my window the ground where her home was, and where all of her children were born. They all lived till maturity, and I have a pretty full record of each one of them, three sons and a daughter Hannah, named for her.

" She (the mother) died in 1725, and among her descendants are some worthy names.

" I visited her grave at Andover in 1863, and copied at that time the inscription upon the headstone, as follows :

> " ' Here Lyes ye Body of Mrs Hannah
> Blanchard Relict of Mr Samuel
> Blanchard Who Dec'd July 10th 1725
> in ye 79th . . . f Her Age.'

" The stone was then broken, the upper part of it lying on the ground, but all the lettering could be read except what I have marked."

3554. SARAH DOGGETT[2] (*Thomas*[1]), born Weymouth, Mass., 1650; died Marshfield, Mass., July, 1680; married Marshfield, Mass., 1673, Samuel Sherman, son of William and Prudence (Hill) Sherman; born Mass., 1644½; died Marshfield, Mass., July 2, 1718.

Issue :

3566. i. PRUDENCE SHERMAN,[3] born Marshfield, Mass., 1674; married February 2, 174½, Robert Cushman. son of Thomas and Ruth (Howland) Cushman; he born Oct. 4, 1664 ; died Kingston, Mass., Sept. 7, 1757.

3567. ii. SARAH SHERMAN,[3] born Marshfield, Mass., 1676; married Josiah Foster, son of Deacon John and Mary (Chillingsworth) Foster; he born Marshfield, Mass., 1669 ; they died Pembroke (?), Mass.

3568. iii. SUSANNA SHERMAN,[3] born Marshfield, Mass., 1678.

Sarah Doggett, on her marriage with Samuel Sherman, brought with her, as a marriage gift from her father, the deed to her husband of six acres of upland in Marshfield, the deed bearing date June 9, 1673.

Samuel Sherman was a farmer, holding a part of the homestead given by deed from his father before his death. In the deed his father calls him "My noble son." He married 2d, Hannah, by whom he had nine children: Hannah, Samuel, Mary, Joshua, Desire, Patience, William, Gershom, and Caleb.

3555. SAMUEL DOGGETT [2] (*Thomas* [1]), born Weymouth, Mass., 1652; died Marshfield, Mass., September 15, 1725; married 1st, Marshfield, Mass., January 24, 1682, Mary Rogers, daughter of John Rogers; died Marshfield, Mass., April 15, 1690; married 2d, Marshfield, Mass., January 21, 1691, Bathsheba Holmes, daughter of Abraham and Elizabeth (Arnold) Holmes, and granddaughter of Rev. Samuel Arnold; died Marshfield, Mass., April 17, 1747.

Issue:

3569. i. SAMUEL DOGGETT,[3] born Marshfield, Mass., Dec. 24, 1683; died young.
3570. ii. SAMUEL DOGGETT,[3] born Marshfield, Mass., April 7, 1685.
3571. iii. MARY DOGGETT,[3] born Marshfield, Mass., April 26, 1687.
3572. iv. SARAH DOGGETT,[3] born Marshfield, Mass., April 7, 1689.
3573. v. ELIZABETH DOGGETT,[3] born Marshfield, Mass., November 3, 1691; married Marshfield, Mass., January 13, 172⅔, by Rev. James Gardner, to Sylvanus Hall, of Plymouth, son of Elisha and Lydia Hall; born Yarmouth, Mass., May 17, 1693.
3574. vi. EBENEZER DOGGETT,[3] born Marshfield, Mass., November 22, 1693.
3575. vii. BATHSHEBA DOGGETT,[3] born Marshfield, Mass., June 18, 1695.
3576. viii. JOHN DOGGETT,[3] born Marshfield, Mass., March 29, 1697.
3577. ix. ISAAC DOGGETT,[3] born Marshfield, Mass., February 6, 1699.
3578. x. LYDIA DOGGETT,[3] born Marshfield, Mass., October 26, 1703.
3579. xi. SETH DOGGETT,[3] born Marshfield, Mass., October 22, 1705.
3580. xii. ABIGAIL DOGGETT,[3] born Marshfield, Mass., March 14, 17½½.

Samuel Doggett, although born in Weymouth, was probably taken to Marshfield when an infant.

The town of Marshfield paid him 1s. 6d. on August 8, 1673, as a witness fee.

June 15, 1676, the town of Marshfield makes the following record:

At the said townsmeeting the inhabitants have voted Christopher Winter, constable, and he did refuse, being sent to, by the Governor by Samuel Doggett and the inhabitants have voted Mr. Nathaniel Thomas constable.

March 20, 1681, Samuel Doggett receives from his father one-half of all his lands in Middleboro' and places adjacent, and in the instrument is called "my natural and well beloved son." [Plymouth Deeds, 6–27.]

Early in the following year he married Mary Rogers, whose father appears to have been proprietor of much landed estate.

February 6, 1683, his father deeds to him all his land which he then has in Marshfield, reserving to himself "the use during life;" in consideration of the love and fatherly affection he has for his natural and loving son. [Plymouth Deeds, 9–74.]

1683, Samuel Doggett, "Transcribed on list of Freemen for Marshfield," is a memorandum from a correspondent. The town records, giving the names of the townsmen, 1684, mention Samuel Doggett as one of the number.

June 2, 1685, constable for Marshfield.

June, 1689, he was received and admitted as freeman at a court held at Plymouth.

August 23, 1689. Town meeting in Marshfield:

In pursuance of the order of the last court for the raising money for the present expedition against the barbarous enemy Indians, Samuel Doggett, Anthony Eames, Ephraim Little and John Foster promised to lend the town 20s apiece to be repaid again by the next town rate.

The Marshfield church records show: "Samuel Doggett adm. into this church Feb 22, 170$\frac{1}{2}$." "Bathsheba Doggett wife of Samuel Doggett bapt and adm. into this church July 26, 1702."

Boston June 28, 1695 — Received of Daniel White Constable of Marshfield 26£ 2s 6d in full of a warrant of same, by the hands of Mr Samuel Doggett, I say received for Mr James Taylor, Treas.   DAVID JENNER.

Aug. 17, 1702, Samuel and brother John, "yeomen," sell land in Middleboro' to Dr Francis Le Barron, chirurgeon. [Plymouth Deeds, 8–258.]

Samuel Doggett was chosen tithingman March 20, 170$\frac{3}{4}$. February 25, 170$\frac{5}{6}$, chosen grand juryman.

In 1708 he owned sloop "Swan," twenty tons.

April 3, 1710. The proprietors' records of Marshfield show his rate for the proportioning of each proprietor's share in the common lands as 16s. 3d.

Feb 26, 17$\frac{10}{11}$ Samuel Doggett, sen. Joseph Waterman, Joseph Rogers and John Truant, sell 4 lots of land, to Samuel Doggett Jr, for 13£ 10s. [Plymouth Deeds, 8–162.]

April 15, 1713 Samuel and his brother, sell 100 acres land in Plympton, to Wm Shurtleff, for 44£. [Plymouth Deeds, 11–67.]

Part owner in sloop "Seaflower," in 1714.

March 19, 17$\frac{15}{16}$, elected constable.

March 13, 1717. Town meeting. Samuel Doggett, collector of several persons' rates:

"Voted That Samuel Doggett be collector in north side of the South River for gathering 2 rates."

September 2, 1717. Town meeting:

At said meeting the town accept of Samuel Doggett to serve in the stead of his son Samuel Doggett Jr in the office of constable in said town for the present year also that there be 1£ 5s added to the town rate forthwith to be made and paid to Samuel Doggett.

July 5, 1718. Samuel Doggett, Sen., and John Rogers, of Marshfield, joint owners of land originally belonging to right of Thomas

Dogget, deceased, in 16s. purchase in Middleboro', agree to divide and each take their portion equally. [Plymouth Deeds, 16–179.]

December 4, 1718. Samuel Doggett, Sen., and Thomas Doggett, of Marshfield, and Thomas Barker, of Pembroke, owners of the fifth lot in Major's purchase, now in Pembroke, agree to divide. [Plymouth Deeds, 18–167.]

1720, Samuel Doggett on grand jury.

In the burying-ground about the Congregational church at Marshfield, called Cedar Grove Cemetery, stands the gravestone of Samuel Doggett. It is of slate stone, about two inches thick, and stands on a knoll about twenty feet from the road and about one hundred feet from the church and facing it, on the side toward the railway station.

The head and foot stones are both in excellent state of preservation, and the headstone inscribed as follows :

> Here lyse ẙe
> Interred Body
> of Mr Samuel
> Doggett who
> dyed Septtem^br
> ẙ 15th 1725
> aged 73 yea^re

In Plymouth Probate, 5–97, is found his will, as follows :

Marshfield Jan. 13, 1724, I. Samuel Doggett of Marshfield in ye county of Plymouth, Yeoman, being in a good measure of health at present blessed be God for ye same, calling to mind ye uncertainty of my life and willing to settle ye estate which God hath been pleased of his goodness to bless me with all, Do make this my last will and testament in manner and form following.

First I commit my soul to God who gave it and my body to a decent buriall in hope of a Joyfull Resurrection to Eternal life through ye precious merits of my Lord and Savior Jesus Christ and for ye disposal of my outward estate my mind and will is that it shall be bestowed in such manner as in this my last will is set down.

Imprimis — I give and Bequeath ye use and improvement of all my Housing and lands whereon I now dwell and also my vally Lotts and my Cedar Swamp in ye Township of Pembroke to my beloved wife Bathsheba towards her livelyhood for and during her widdowhood and also all my moveable estate whatsoever to be at her dispose for ye Payment of my Debts and funeral charges and what shall remain at her decease or second marriage to be by her disposed amongst my children as she shall see meet.

Item — I give and Bequeath to my son Samuel Doggett fourty and two acres of Land Lying in ye Township of Middleboro in ye 16 Shilling Purchase being ye 93rd lott to Him and His heirs and assigns forever in full of his part or portion of my estate.

Item — I give and Bequeath to my son John Doggett and to his Heirs and assigns forever all my thirty and eight acres of Land in ye Township of Middleboro being ye lott in ye 16 Shilling Purchase.

Item — I give and Bequeath to my sons Ebenezer Isaac and Seth Doggett and to their Respective Heirs and assigns forever in Equal Parts after ye second marriage or decease of my said wife all my Housing and Lands in Marshfield and also my Cedar Swamp in ye Township of Pembroke, they Paying ye severall sums of money and other things hereafter expressed after my said wife's decease or second marriage (that is to say)

To my daughter Mary White ye sum of 20s.

To my daughter Sarah Allen ye sum of 20s and to my daughter Bathsheba Kent ye sum of 5£ and to my daughters, Elizabeth, Lydiah and Abigail Doggett, ye sum of 10£ apiece.

Isaac and Seth Doggett shall find their three sisters Elizabeth, Lydiah and Abigail Doggett convenient Housing (that is to say) fire Room and firewood to all or such of them as shall remain unmarried as long as they shall live unmarried, and if any of them should be sick or Lame so as not to be capable to maintain themselves that they be maintained out of that real estate which I have given to my three sons, viz to Ebenezer, Isaac and Seth Doggett so long as they shall remain unmarried.

Lastly I nominate and appoint my said wife and my son Ebenezer Doggett to be executors of this my last will and testament hereby giving them full power to make sale of and give deeds of conveyance of all that my one halfe of a 60 acre Lott of Land Lying near to Joseph Stetson in ye Township of Pembroke toward ye payment of my debts and also it is my will that if either Ebenezer, Isaac or Seth Doggett should dye without Issue that his or their part of ye housing and Land I have given them shall belong to ye survivor or survivors of these three. In witness whereof I have hereonto set my hand and seal ye day and year above written

Samuel Doggett [Seal.]

Signed sealed and declared by ye said Samuel Doggett to be His last will and Testament.

In presence of us.
NATHAN M. THOMAS
      her
PRISCILLA PT THOMAS
      marke
ROBERT HOPKINS.

Oct 4, 1725.

The above named N. Thomas, Priscilla Thomas and Robert Hopkins made oath that they saw ye above named Samuel Doggett sign, seal and heard him declare ye above and within written Instrument to be his last will and testament and at the same time they sett their hands as witnesses and that according to ye best of their observation He was then of sound and disposing mind and memory Before

                  ISAAC WINSLOW, Judge of Probate.

Oct. 4, 1725.

Isaac Winslow confirms will and orders them to make Inventory.

Plymouth Probate, 5–120:

" Inventory of all and singular the goods and Chattels and Credits of Samuel Doggett, gentleman, deceased, Nov. 5, 1725 ":

His purse and apparell. £21 10d; Arms and ammunition, £1 11s; Books, £1 6s; Cloth and mow hair, 13s 6d; Indian corn 14£ English corn 5£ 6s., £20 7s; To Tobacco, £1 15s; To weaving gears and worsted combs, £5 13s; Wheels, salt, yarn, Rope, a chest and 6 Barrels worsted, £4 14s: Yarn and old Iron, £3 2s; To Pewter 2£ 16s Brass 3£ 15s Potts and Iron ware 6£ 17s, £13 8s; Earthern 1£ Nails and other small things 18s Salver 1£, £2 18s; Hand Saw, Hamers, Pott Hooks, chairs, Tables and stool, £2 18s; Chests, Boxes 1£ 8s Nails & Scales 12s, £2; To beds and bedding, £45 2s; Wool and lumber, £3; Cyder 1£ 16s Casks 1£ beef 5£ 11s, £8 7s; Pork 4£ To Linnen 5£ 17s, £9 17s; Flax and other small things, £2 1s; Sheep 4£ 8s Horse 4£ Tackling £1 5s, £9 13s; Swine 11£ Oxen 16£ Steers 15£ 5 Cows 25£ 4 Young cattle 7£ 10s, £74 10s; Yoakes, chains, grinding stone, spade and plow, £2 15s; Cast wheels, horse gears, £3 13s; 18 Loads of Hay, £22 10s; Trees 1£ Turnips 10s, To flax in ye sheaf 5s, all £1 15s; To a Bond of his son's John Doggett, £40; Cordwood, £13; ½ of a 60 acre Lott at Pembroke, £30; ½ share in ye 16s Purchase in ye Last division in Middleboro, £3; To a desperate debt of John Haskell, £11 4s 4d; total, £361 15s 8d.

JOHN BARKER.
THOMAS DOGGETT.
JAMES SPRAGUE.

Dec 23, 1725 Acknowledged as a perfect inventory.

3556. REBECCA DOGGETT[2] (*Thomas*[1]), born Marshfield, Mass., July 29, 1655; died Hingham, Mass., October 4, 1728; married Marshfield, Mass., November 30, 1675, John Wilder, son of Edward and Elizabeth (Eames) Wilder; born Marshfield, Mass. (?), 1653; died Hingham, Mass., April 11, 1724.

Issue:

3581. i. HANNAH WILDER,[3] born Hingham, Mass., November 12, 1676; died Hingham, Mass., January 12, 1682.
3582. ii. ELIZABETH WILDER,[3] born Hingham, Mass., April 27, 1679; married Josiah Sprague, May 17, 1705; he born Hingham, April 23, 1680; died March 23, 1760; she died Hingham, October 21, 1755.
3583. iii. HANNAH WILDER,[3] born Hingham, Mass., May 3, 1683; died Hingham, Mass., November 17, 1756.
3584. iv. REBECCA WILDER,[3] born Hingham, Mass., February 27, 1687; died Hingham, Mass., June 13, 1743.
3585. v. MARY WILDER,[3] born Hingham, Mass., July 30, 1692; married Hingham, Mass., October 9, 1740, Daniel Waters; she died Hingham, November 10, 1756.
3586. vi. EPHRAIM WILDER,[3] born Hingham, Mass., August 25, 1696.
3587. vii. ISAAC WILDER,[3] born Hingham, Mass., 1700.

From the "Wilder Family" published in 1878 we find that John Wilder, who married Rebecca Doggett, was a farmer of Hingham, Mass.

His father was Edward Wilder, son of Thomas and Martha Wilder, of Shiplock Oxon, Eng., presumed to be the Thomas who was proprietor of the Sulham estate, in Berkshire county, Eng. Edward Wilder was born in England in 1623, and came with his mother to New England in May, 1633. He lived in Hingham till his mother's death, in 1652, after which he resided in Marshfield, Mass.

THOMAS DOGGETT, OF MARSHFIELD, MASS.

THIRD GENERATION.

3558. THOMAS DOGGETT[3] (*John*,[2] *Thomas*[1]), born Marshfield, Mass., 1676; died Marshfield, Mass., January 5, 173⅔; married 1st, Marshfield, Mass., January 18, 169⅜, by Rev. Edward Tompson, to Experience Ford, daughter of William Ford, of Marshfield, Mass., born 1676; died Marshfield, Mass., October 25, 1728; married 2d (between 1728 and 1732), Sarah Phillips.

Issue:

3588. i. WILLIAM DOGGETT,[4] born Marshfield, Mass., October 30, 1699; died Marshfield, Mass., February 16, 1699/1700.

3589. ii. JOHN DOGGETT,[4] born Marshfield, Mass., 1702.
3590. iii. PERSIS DOGGETT,[4] born Marshfield, Mass., May (?), 1704.
3591. iv. THOMAS DOGGETT,[4] born Marshfield, Mass., 1706.
3592. v. SARAH DOGGETT,[4] born Marshfield, Mass., 1709; baptized November
       7, 1709; resided in Marshfield — unmarried — September 30, 1745.
3593. vi. EXPERIENCE DOGGETT,[4] born Marshfield, Mass., 1714; died Lebanon,
       Conn. (previous to November 12), 1736.

February 27, 170½. John Doggett gives his son Thomas part of his upland whereon he dwells. [Plymouth Deeds, 13–157.]

May 10, 1708. At town meeting at Marshfield: Thomas Doggett is chosen on a trial jury at Plymouth.

March 21, 170⅜, he is chosen field director.

January 10, 1710, Thomas Doggett and Isaac Little sell land above Mattakeesett to Josiah and Joseph Ford. [Plymouth Deeds, 17–78.]

February 26, 1710, chosen grand juryman.

The proprietors' records show the rate of Thomas Doggett for the proportioning of his share in the common lands is 8s. 8d., at a meeting April 3, 1710; at a later meeting, October 9, 1710, when the lots were drawn, he drew lots in the first and second divisions.

March 20, 17$\frac{16}{17}$:

Thomas Macomber and Thomas Doggett were chosen officers to see the due observing of the law relating to swine — also — Joseph Taylor and Thomas Doggett were chosen to serve on the Grand Jury at the superior court to be holden at Plymouth on the last Tuesday of this inst march.

At the town meeting September 7, 1719, appointed clerk for the day.

1720 he is chosen with Joseph Taylor and John Little as surveyor of the highways, and at the same meeting to serve on the grand jury.

William Ford's will, dated 1720, appoints his son-in-law, Thomas Doggett, to act as executor.

March 27, 1721, he is chosen with Samuel Thomas and Timothy Rogers as constable.

At the town meeting May 15, 1727:

Thomas Doggett chosen on Jury of Trials at Inferior Court of Common Pleas to be held at Plymouth the 3rd Tuesday of June next. Thomas Doggett for expences in attending the committee last fall, 1£ 0s 0d.

March 25, 1728. Chosen, with Nathaniel Winslow and John Carver, as surveyor of highways.

March 31, 1729. Town meeting: Thomas Doggett, Samuel Thomas, and Ebenezer Sherman, surveyors of highways.

February 10, 1729. John Kent and Thomas Doggett chosen to serve on grand jury for year ensuing.

September 20, 1731:

At said town meeting Mr. Thomas Doggett being chosen the moderator thereof refused the same, then Mr. John Thomas Jr was chosen, who accepted thereof.

January 26, 1732.   Thomas Doggett sells land joining to a place called " Doggetts Cedars," to Cornelius White.   [Plymouth Deeds, 27–184.]

March 1, 173¾, Thomas Doggett on a jury of trials at the Inferior Court at Plymouth, first Tuesday of this inst. March.

March 24, 173⅘, the town chooses him surveyor of highways.

April 14, 1736. A vote being called, whether the town would raise 20£ with the ministers rate, to assist constable Isaac Phillips, in defending an action commenced by Thomas Doggett against him, and it past in the negative.

May 10, 1736. To Constable Isaac Phillips for time and charge, in defending his action against Thomas Doggett, deducting out thereof his bill or bills of cost when ascertained, 21£ 4s 6d.

October 13, 1736.   He buys of Thomas Phillips the fifty-fifth lot in second division of Marshfield.   [Plymouth Deeds, 31–88.]

Living in Marshfield all his life, with his occupation that of a farmer, there is some reason to think he may have also been interested in the shipping interests on the North river, which during his lifetime began to increase.   In 1736 occurred the death of his youngest daughter, which is mentioned in a short letter from James Barker, who married Bethiah Ford, a sister of Experience Doggett, dated at Lebanon, November 12, 1736, in which he says to Brother Doggett that his daughter Experience died of the prevailing sickness there. This daughter Experience was baptized at the First Church in Marshfield, August 1, 1714.

His death occurred at Marshfield, January 5, 173⅚, and his remains were deposited in the Cedar Grove Cemetery, about twenty-eight feet back of his uncle Samuel, and a few feet farther from the road.

His first wife was buried next to the grave in front of his, and their gravestones, in excellent preservation, are of slate stone, and inscribed as follows:

Here Lyes Buried	Here lyes ye body
the body of Mr	of Mrs Experience
Thomas Doggett	Doggett wife to Mr
who deceased	Thomas Dog
Jan ye 5	gett who dyed
1736	Oct the 25
ye 60th yeare	1728 and aged
of his age	about 52 years.

Sarah Doggett, the second wife of Thomas Doggett, married at Pembroke, September 7, 1737, Joseph Ford, of Pembroke, by Rev. Daniel Lewis.

October 3, 1743.   The court orders to be set off to Mrs. Sarah Ford, late widow of Thomas Doggett, her thirds in the real estate. [Plymouth Probate, 14–194.]

The will of Thomas Doggett, of Marshfield, dated April 19, 1736, may be found in Plymouth Probate, 7–282.   The following are the items:

Sarah Doggett dearly beloved wife, use of house &c; Son John Doggett ½ cedar swamp in Pembroke and 30£:

son Thomas Doggett, his sword, belt, house and land, mansion I dwell in with 30£:

Well beloved daughters Persis Kent, Sarah Doggett, and Experience Doggett, "all the rest of my moveable estate, except my long gun, which I give to my grandson Thomas Doggett who bears my name":

Persis Kent his daughter 40£:

Sarah Doggett 60£,
Experience Doggett 50£: } unmarried

son Thomas Executor.

Leaves his mulatto servant to executor, he finding her a new Bible, at the expiration of her time.   Proved Jan 31, 1736.

witness
    WM SHERMAN
    JOSEPH WHITE
    JAMES SPRAGUE

The "Inventory of the real and personal estate of Thomas Doggett," recorded in Plymouth Probate, 7–311, nets £278 10s. 4d. personal estate; £910 0s. 0d. real estate; with debts, £150 17s. 8d; so the valuation of his estate was £1,037 12s. 8d.

The items are as follows:

Purse and apparel 17£; 1 Bed and furniture Bedstead; 2 Beds and bedding Bedstead and cord; 1 Bed; Feathers; Sword; 4 yds of all wool cloth; Knives and forks; Silver Buckle; Linen; Flannel Sheet; 1 Rig; Candles & Bray Tallow; Shears; Bible; old Pewter; Bed Pan; Box Iron and Heaters; Button mold; Small pieces of Buckram; Cheese Press; Wheel; Bedstead and Cord; a chair table; Cupboard; Pork & Tub; Cheesee Hoops & felloes; Beer cask; Churn; Sundry things in chest; Castile soap and other small wares; Shoe leather Thread &c; Small box with what is in it; Sugar and what it is in; Earthern Pot & Honey; Shots or bullets; Glass Bottles; Hour Glass and other glasses; Earthern ware; Warming Pan; Silver headed cane; Mug Porringer & Cup; Looking Glass;

Gun; Earthern Pots; Great Bible, 1£ 15s; Books, 1£ 16s; Brass Kittle & Skillett; Pots, Pot Hooks, Kettle & frying pan; Hand Irons; Fire shovel & tongs; Spit & Grid Iron; Trammel; Tin ware; Six Plats Brasses & Tan Card; Cards; Warping Brass spool & frame; Tub; Oil Jar; Small old wheel; Iron Tools; Old wheel; The Indian Girl, 7£ 10s; Old cradle; Shingles; Chain Yokes, Cop Sled & Plough; Grindstone & crank; Ham, Sheep Shears; Pillion; Cyder; Chest; Small wheel; Cheeses; Indian corn; Wheat, Leather bag; Beans; Butter & Tub; A loom; Forks Pole & Rake; Cast Rope; Iron wedges; Cast & wheels; An old Gun; One pair of oxen; 3 Cows; 1 Bull; Calf; House & furniture; Swine; Geese; Dunghil fowls; Horse Gears; Old Cast wheels; Tub & 2 Pails; Cheese Tongs; Trays & Keeler; Chest & Table; Old Iron; Iron Tools; Board nails; Chains; Hog fat, Sewett; Meal troughs & meal; Meat tub &c; Towe yarn; Old wheel tubs &c; Baskets; Homestead & Buildings, £810; One wood lot, 55£; One small lot, 13£; Cedar swamp, 32£.

Marshfield Mass.
May 24, 1737

3561. HANNAH DOGGETT [3] (*John,*[2] *Thomas*[1]), born Marshfield, Mass., December 28, 1693; married Marshfield, Mass., March 9, 17¹²⁄₁₃, by Rev. James Gardner, to Ebenezer White, son of Daniel and Hannah (Hunt) White, and grandson of Peregrine White; born Marshfield, Mass., August 3, 1691.

Issue:

3594. i.   OBADIAH WHITE,[4] born Marshfield, Mass., March 27, 1716.

3595. ii. REBECCA WHITE,[4] born Marshfield, Mass., November 17, 1718.
3596. iii. HANNAH WHITE,[4] born Marshfield, Mass., March 13, 17$\frac{2}{2}\frac{9}{0}$.
3597. iv. CHOSEN WHITE,[4] born Marshfield, Mass., July 16, 1722.

3562. THOMAS BLANCHARD[3] (*Hannah Doggett,[2] Thomas[1]*), born Charlestown, Mass., April 28, 1674; died Andover, Mass., March 17, 1759; married 1st, Andover, Mass., March 22, 169$\frac{8}{9}$, Rose Holmes, daughter of Abraham and Elizabeth (Arnold) Holmes, of Marshfield, Mass.; born 1674; died Andover, Mass., August 27, 1714; married 2d, Andover, Mass., September 21, 1715, Hannah Gowen, widow of Mr. Gowen, of Linn (Reading), Mass.; died Andover, Mass., June 25, 1724; married 3d, Malden, Mass., February 21, 172$\frac{5}{6}$, Judith Hill, widow of Zechary Hill, of Malden, Mass.; born 1677; died December 1, 1767.

3568. SUSANNA SHERMAN[3] (*Sarah Doggett,[2] Thomas[1]*), born Marshfield, Mass., 1678; died Marshfield, Mass., December 22, 1766; married Marshfield, Mass., February 18, 1700, John White, son of Daniel and Hannah (Hunt) White, and grandson of Peregrine White; born Marshfield, Mass., April 26, 1675; died Marshfield, Mass., September 7, 1753.

Issue:

3598. i. HANNAH WHITE,[4] born Marshfield, Mass., March 28, 1702; "first school dame of which there is record;" died unmarried.
3599. ii. JOHN WHITE,[4] born Marshfield, Mass., August 17, 1704; married Joanna Sprague, 1729; he died Marshfield, Mass.
3600. iii. ABIJAH WHITE,[4] born Marshfield, Mass., October 8, 1706; married Anna Little, and had William[5] and Sylvanus;[5] Abijah died Boston, October 29, 1775; buried "King Chapel Yard;" widow died Marshfield, March 11, 1791.
3601. iv. SARAH WHITE,[4] born Marshfield, Mass., May 31, 1710; married Isaac Phillips, January 25, 1727; she died Marshfield, Mass., February, 1788; he died Marshfield, Mass., September, 1787.
3602. v. REBECCA WHITE,[4] born Marshfield, Mass., December, 1713; died Marshfield, Mass., 1716.
3603. vi. SYLVANUS WHITE,[4] born Marshfield, Mass., July 24, 1718; died Marshfield, Mass., December 19, 1742.
3604. vii. JESSE WHITE,[4] born Marshfield, Mass., December 7, 1720; married Catherine Charlotte Wilhelmina Sybellina Warner, a German lady; he lived on the Peregrine White estate; died Marshfield, Mass.

3570. SAMUEL DOGGETT[3] (*Samuel,[2] Thomas[1]*), born Marshfield, Mass., April 7, 1685; died Boston, Mass., September(?), 1745; married Marshfield, Mass., February 20, 17$\frac{0}{1}\frac{9}{0}$, by Rev. James Gardner, to Bethia Waterman, daughter of Joseph and Sarah (Snow) Waterman; born Marshfield, Mass., August 20, 1687; died Boston, Mass., November 28, 1746.

Issue:

3605. i. AMOS DOGGETT,[4] born Marshfield, Mass., May 25, 1710.
3606. ii. LYDIA DOGGETT,[4] born Marshfield, Mass., —— 3, 1712.

3607. iii. ZILPHA DOGGETT,[4] born Marshfield, Mass., November 3, 1714.
3608. iv. SARAH DOGGETT,[4] born Marshfield, Mass., October, 1716.
3609. v. BETHIA DOGGETT,[4] born Marshfield, Mass., 1718.
3610. vi. SAMUEL DOGGETT,[4] born Marshfield, Mass., 1720.
3611. vii. JOSEPH DOGGETT,[4] born Marshfield, Mass., 1722.
3612. viii. NOAH DOGGETT,[4] born Marshfield, Mass., 1727.

The records at Marshfield do not mention Samuel Doggett, until we find the record of his marriage to Bethia Waterman. She belonged to that family of Waterman of whom we read in " We and our Kinsfolk ": " We have it by tradition that the Waterman family came from Germany to Wales, and from Wales to Norwich, England." " Many hundred years ago they were famous seamen." " Robert, who was at Salem 1636, at Plymouth 1638, and at Marshfield 1642, true to the family tradition, did more or less business on the deep." " He married 1638, Elizabeth, daughter of Thomas Bourne, and at his death in 1653 left, under the guardianship of Anthony Snow and his uncle Josias Winslow, three sons, John, Joseph, and Robert." Joseph married the daughter of his guardian, and was the father of Bethia, who married Samuel Doggett. Joseph Waterman's will, dated August 6, 1709, proved March 12, 1710, shows he left an estate valued at £2,500, of which his daughter Bethia received £100.

October 9, 1710. At a meeting of the proprietors of Marshfield, Samuel Doggett, Jr., drew lot No. 55 in the first division, and No. 57 in the second division, and thus became a landholder in his native town.

Whether his connection with the Waterman family had an influence in his choice of a vocation, or whether the growth of the business of shipbuilding drew his attention to the sea, is not known; but we find him the first of the family to follow the callings suggested in the following extracts:

Jan 1, 1710/11 Samuel Doggett Jr of Marshfield "boatman" buys of Joshua Cushing for 323£, piece of upland containing 30 acres and salt marsh containing 5 acres, with all the housing, out housing buildings and orchards, bounded on the north by the North river, beginning at " Ye mouth of ye great creek." [Plymouth Deeds, 8–165.]

Jan 26, 1710 Samuel Doggett Jr of Marshfield "Mariner" for 39£ paid by James Gardner of Marshfield 2 lots of land in Marshfield adjacent to Pudder Wharf Brook, about 50 acres. [Plymouth Deeds, 10–605.]

The first deed is probably that of the land on which he lived during the rest of the time he made Marshfield his home; it is located near East Marshfield, and now called Bryant's pasture.

On the upland, not far from the river, are some old apple-trees and the walls of an ancient cellar, which was surrounded by bushes and small trees in 1886, and supposed to be the site of his house.

The view from this spot overlooking the river is one of quiet, restful beauty, and it is difficult to picture it as it looked in former days, when, as we read in the " History of Plymouth County," it was the scene of busy industry. The North river, which forms the boundary of a portion of Marshfield in its winding way of twenty miles through the meadows, from Ludden's ford to the sea, is one of surpassing beauty. The tide rose and fell many feet, while its banks were lined with shipyards, and more shipbuilding was carried on here than upon any other river in New England. At Little's bridge, once Doggett's ferry, vessels were built at one time on the Marshfield side of the river. Below this point the river expands greatly in width, the salt meadows form a vast expanse, and the scenery takes on grand proportions of beauty. The river near its mouth between that and the Fourth Cliff was sometimes called New Harbor, and vessels wintered there from earliest times.

Commerce with the West Indies has been carried on from thence, and there is reason to believe that Samuel Doggett was one of those interested in that trade.

December 10, 1711. Town meeting: Samuel Doggett, Jr., on a jury of trials at the next Inferior Court at Plymouth, third Tuesday of the list.

In an account book of Arthur Howland, now (1888) in possession of Miss Thomas, of Marshfield, under date July 24, 1714, — charge to Samuel Doggett for writing a bond, bill of sale, and five bonds, settled by paper, jack-knife, logwood, copper.

February 21, 17$\frac{14}{15}$. Town meeting: He was chosen on jury of trial at next Inferior Court at Plymouth.

March 20, 17$\frac{16}{17}$. Town meeting: Samuel Doggett, Jr., Constable.

In the will of John Rogers, of Marshfield, dated May 9, 1718 (Plymouth Probate, 4–130), is the following:

" Item I give to my grandson Samuel Doggett 20£ in money to be paid him within two years after my decease."

March 23, 172$\frac{3}{4}$. On trial jury.

May 16, 1726. Town meeting: " Voted and agreed with Samuel Doggett to keep the town stock of ammunition, and to make it good whenever the town shall demand it of him, and the town to allow him 10s. a year for the keeping the same."

September 7, 1726. On the jury.

March 27, 1727, Samuel Doggett chosen one of the selectmen of Marshfield. February 24, 172$\frac{8}{9}$, on grand jury. March 25, 172$\frac{8}{9}$, Samuel Doggett, tithingman, and on the same date grand juryman.

During these years Samuel Doggett had been extending his business relations, and his vessels, either commanded by himself or those in his employ, sailed from the North river or the port of Boston, in the coasting trade, and also across the Atlantic. At that time the territory now comprised in the State of Maine was attracting attention as a new settlement, and a number of Boston capitalists, securing a tract of land, formed the Wiscasset Company, which settled the town now bearing that name.

Samuel Doggett was interested in the settlement of the territory; and :

Feb 8, 1730   At a meeting of the Wiscasset Proprietors at the Royal Exchange Boston.

Voted Mr Samuel Doggett, Twenty five acres of land in the 2nd division for every family that he shall settle on our land at Sheepscot within the term of 24 months from this time to the number of 40 families which settlements shall be agreeable to our articles of agreement.   Above 25 acres of Land is given as a gratuity for all the charge and trouble the said Doggett is or shall be at, in settling the same.

Jan 18, 1731   Voted Mr Samuel Doggett to get a good surveyor to lay out the above township directly at the charge of the Proprietors.

Jan 11, 173$\frac{2}{3}$ Voted Mr Samuel Doggett and Mr Andrew Tyler to go to the Records in order to compare Robert's deeds with ours.   Voted to lay out the 74, hundred acre lots, according to the discretion of Mr Samuel Doggett.

1738   At a meeting held, the lots which have been laid out are drawn. Samuel Doggett, 1 lot.

Feb 22 173$\frac{4}{5}$ He pays 53£ for land at Sheepscott.

April 13, 1730. Samuel Doggett, " yeoman," buys of Daniel Mac-Lucas, of Pembroke, two lots containing about thirty acres. [Plymouth Deeds, 25–218.]

The growing interest in the vicinity of Sheepscott river evidently made that a promising field for investment.

Nov 2, 1730, Samuel Doggett of Marshfield, mariner, buys of Jonathan Loring of Boston, currier for 25£ one full 64th part of all that land called George Davies Right of land in Sheepscott River, reference being had to the several Indian Deeds for bounderies.   [York Deeds, 20–158.]

Nov 2, 1730   He also buys another 64th part of the same tract from John Burt of Boston, Goldsmith, for the same amount.   [York Deeds, 20–158.]

January 25, 1731.   In Arthur Howlands account book, already referred to, he says : " This day paid Samuel Doggett all I owed him on my own account and all that was due him on M. Eames her account."

The residents at East and North Marshfield were rather distant from the church, and this led to a demand for a church nearer home. In 1730 several, among whom was Samuel Doggett, were members who paid for preaching at North Marshfield, as appears from a paper in possession of Miss Thomas.

The first church records show : " Nov. 7, 1731 — Bethia wife of Samuel Doggett taken into the church at Marshfield."

March 24, 173$\frac{4}{5}$.   Marshfield town meeting : Samuel Doggett chosen town treasurer.

The treasurer's account-book kept by Samuel Doggett when in that office, now (1885) in the possession of Miss Thomas, shows entries in his handwriting beginning February 7, 1734, and extending through the year 1739.

March 22, 173⅚, }
March 21, 173⁶⁄₇, } Samuel Doggett chosen town treasurer.

May 10, 1737 Voted — That the sums hereafter mentioned be raised by way of rate and paid to the persons hereafter named as followeth,
To Mr Samuel Doggett for keeping of Joseph Rose and his wife 25£ 0s 0d.

March 27, 1738. Samuel Doggett was chosen town treasurer, who accepted of said trust, and in open meeting agreed with the town to serve in that office for 30s. this year.

May 22, 1738. Voted that the selectmen be desired to make up the town accounts with Mr. Samuel Doggett, their treasurer.

March 1, 173⅜. Samuel Doggett town treasurer.

May 14, 1739 — Samuel Doggett and Jedidiah Bourne were chosen and appointed agreeably to Province Law to serve on the Jury of Trials at the next Court of Session of the Peace and Inferior Court of Common Pleas to be held at Plymouth on the third Tuesday of May instant.

May 21, 1739. Samuel Doggett for being treasurer four years last past at 30s. = £6.

May 25, 1741. Voted, To allow to Samuel Doggett £1 10s. 0d. for his service as town treasurer, 1739.

The growth of Boston and the consequent centring of business interests there made it necessary that Samuel Doggett, with his interest in shipping, should be there much of the time.

In making voyages himself he would naturally start and return there, and this probably decided him to leave his native town and make his home in Boston.

The first move in that direction we find in the sale of his lands in Marshfield, April 19, 1742. The deed (Plymouth Deeds, 35–80) says:

Samuel Doggett of Marshfield, yeoman for 1800£ paid by Seth Bryant of Scituate, shipwright all that my farm whereon I now dwell in Marshfield containing about 60 acres of upland and meadow land lying on both sides the highway, bounded partly to the North River on the N., the highway that goes from said river toward the Precinct Meeting House to the E: another lot of 6 acres near the south end of the farm: the 20th lot in the 1st Division; the 35th and 45th lots in the 2nd Division of Marshfield Common lands.

After the sale of the estate in Marshfield it appears they still lived there for two years, at which time Mrs. Doggett came to Boston. By a law which obliged every one moving to Boston to prove they should not become a charge on the town, we are enabled to show just when Mrs. Doggett came to Boston.

In the Boston Selectmen's Minutes, p. 101, report of meeting June 6, 1744:

Mrs Bethia Doggett from Marshfield lodges at Mr Wheelers, has been in Town about 25 Days. Ordered That She be Warned to depart the Town in Fourteen Days unless She give Security to Indemnify the Town from any Charge upon her Acc^t as the Law directs.

About this time (1744) arrangements were being made by the Province of Massachusetts Bay to make an expedition against Louisburg, and among the vessels engaged by the government to aid in the attack were those of Samuel Doggett. The expedition sailed from Boston, bearing three thousand men, to attack a stronghold which had been called the Gibraltar of America, and whose very fortifications were said to have cost five million dollars. On April 30, 1745, the fleet, with additions from England, New Hampshire, and Connecticut, came in sight of Louisburg, and found its strength not exaggerated. The walls were twenty or thirty feet high and forty feet thick, surrounded by a ditch eighty feet wide, defended by one hundred and eighty-three pieces of artillery, besides sixty more in the two outlying batteries.

For six weeks Louisburg was besieged, and on June 17 the fort surrendered.

Voltaire, in his "Siècle de Louis XV.," ranks among the great events of the period this capture of a strong fortress by the husbandmen of New England. In the Massachusetts State Archives, Vol. LXXII., p. 778, is found:

Account of the charge of the transport vessels employed in his Majesties Service in the expedition against Cape Breton, and for the service of his Majestys Garrison at Louisburg exclusive of such as were Laden with stores, by express orders from the Admiral and General.

Among the list of vessels:

Sloop Dolphin, S. Doggett, master — 6 men — time of entry Feb 18, 1745, discharge Nov 28, sailors wages 102£ 9s 7d, hire of vessel 169£ 13s 0d.

Whether the sloop Dolphin returned to Boston previous to the time of her discharge has not been ascertained, but it is probable Samuel Doggett was in Boston when he died, in September, 1745.

The Boston papers of September 23 mention the arrival of sixty sick men from Louisburg on September 19, and it may have been Samuel Doggett was one of the number.

The family were then living in Boston, between King street (now State street) and Dock square, and here it is probable he died.

His estate paid for a gravestone, but it has not been located, so it is not known exactly when he died or where he was buried, and the city or church records examined contain no note to assist in the search. His widow Bethia died the following year, and was buried in the Granary Burial-ground, in Boston, where a stone erected to her memory, standing about half-way back from Tremont street, and not far from the side of Park-street Church, is inscribed as follows :

Here lyes buried
the Body of M^{rs}
Bethiah Doggett
wife to Mr Samuel
Doggett aged 60
years died Nov
ye 28. 1746.

In Suffolk Probate (38–155) Josiah Willard, Esq., grants letters of administration to Bethiah Doggett on the estate of her husband, Samuel Doggett, mariner, deceased, dated September 28, 1745.

Boston, October 1, 1745.   An inventory of the estate of Mr. Samuel Doggett, deceased.   [Suffolk Probate, 38–370.]

30¼ lbs of Pewter @ 6s 6d, £9 16s 4½d, 11½ lbs of old Pewter @ 4s 6d, 15s 9d, £12 8s 1½d ; 27½ lbs Brass @ 5s, £6 2s 6d ; 12 lb Brass 7s, 84s, £10 6s 6d ; an old pan 3s, Iron Potts & Kittles, £5 5s, £5 8s ; an old pan & flesh fork 2s, a pewter still £5, £5 2 ; andirons & Trammels £5, Tongs & Firepan 12s, £5 12s ; a pair of Bellows 5s, a looking Glass 5s, 10s ; Knives & forks & candle-stick, 15s, old iron, £5, £5 15s ; Axes 53s, Betle & wedges 8s, a cross cut saw 50s, £5 11s ; 32 oz 15 dwt Silver @ 33s, £52 16s ; Scailes & weights 60s, a pr of stil-yards 35s, £4 15s ; old BB & tubs £8, Pails & woodenware 40s, £10 ; 3 wheel-barrows 45s, bottles & earthen ware 14s, £2 19s ; The Books 80s, a pocket compas 10s, £4 10s ; Shott Bullets Flints Razors buttons etc £2 ; a parcel of coopers tools £4 9s ; old canvas £8, Logwood 30s, 3 lbs Goose feathers 12s, 2 beds and blankets, £27 10s ; an old side saddle 20s, 5 Shirts £6 10s, 2 Hatts 50s, £10 ; wearing apparell, £13 ; Spy Glass 40s, 5 Guns & 2 Pistells £15, £17 ; 2 Mackeril led and a cod line, £1 ; a bed & cloaths £20, 1 Ditto £25, £45 ; Button & Mohair 25s, 6 Chairs 48s, 6 Ditto 30s, £5 3 ; 1 Bed & Cloaths £25, 3 pr Sheets £6, £31 ; Table Linen 77s, 3 Tables 60s, £6 17s ; a cask of rice £8, 4 Chests 80s, £12 ; a small hammer 5s, a tin tunnel & 3 Brishes 15s, £1 ; The Sloop "Swan" with cables anchors Sails Rigging, Boat & all stores to her belonging £750 ; The Sloop "Dolphin" & appurtenances, £1100.   Old Tenor, £2132 11s 10d

a just and true appraisement of the estate of Mr Samuel Doggett deceased.

JON^A TILDEN — JABEZ HATCH — JOHN OTIS —

N.B.   There is a bond of Luther Bryants for the sum of £100 in Bills of the Province of the last emission to be paid at the Decease of Bethiah, the deceaseds now widow.

There is also a Tract of Land at Sheepscott the value unknown.

This inventory was presented to the court by Bethiah Doggett and recorded December 26, 1745.

November 25, 1746.   Bethiah Doggett presents an account of her administration to date (Suffolk Probate, 39–252), which is as follows :

Suffolk S.S.   The account of Bethiah Doggett administratrix of the estate of her late husband Samuel Doggett late of Boston, mariner, deceased.

The said accountant chargeth herself with all and singular the Goods and chattels of the said deceased specifyd in an inventory thereof by her exhibited into the Probate office on the 26 day of Dec. 1745, amounting to the sum of £2132 11s 10d as also with Sundries since Rec'd viz. of the Honble Com^{tee} of Warr &c £674 6s 5d ; of Mr Belnap 14s ; of Mrs Dwelley 8s, £1 2s ; of Mr Isaiah Barrett £3 5s ; of Mr Gam^l Smith money due on a whale voyage £200 ; of Mr Isaac Smith £30 ; of Mr Jonathan Tilden £30 10s ; £60 10s.   Old tenor, £3071 15s 3d.

And the said accountant prays allowance for sundries by her paid as follows : viz.

To John Hooker for Burial per acct, £6 9s ; To the Coffin, £8 ; Paid for 6 pair of Gloves, 72s : £11 12s ; Paid Horse hire for a man to go to Marshfield to acquaint the deceased Friends of his death, £3 ; Paid Jabez Hatch his Ballance, £42 4s ; Peleg Perry his ditto, £1 17s 6d ; Philip Bougardeen for Rent, £13 15s ; John Erving Esq a Bond dated May 2, 1745, £246 1s 7d ; Wifford Fisher in full, £3 8s ; Edward Gray his ballance, £24 11s 9d ; Mich¹ Seive in full, £4 ; To an allowance to the Honble Committee of war for a Cable they supplyed the Sloop " Dolphin " with as per Certificate, £159 14s 4d ; Paid Ebenezer Damon & Receipt, £3 ; Thomas Palfrey in full, £110 3s ; James Bowdoin Esq on acct, £87 ; ditto in full of two Bonds, £230 2s ; ditto in full of all accts, £100 ; Doc⁺ Eleazer Harlow, £1 18s ; James Beighton in full, £18 5s ; William Thomas in full, £3 ; Oxenbridge Thacher in full, £29 15s 3d ; Susanna Decrow in full, £6 10 ; Abigail Foster in full for Susanna Callender, £3 1s ; Peleg Bryant in full, £11 ; William Snoden in full, £56 5s 2d ; Samuel Sturgis in full, £33 : £89 5s 2d ; Jos. Grant in full, £14 ; Wm Wheeler in full, £13 18s 6d : £27 18s 6d ; Henry Ames for Grave Stones, £2 ; William Palfrey, £6 7s 10d ; Benjamin Barnard in full, 91s 2d : £10 19s ; John Hall of Marshfield, 17s 6d ; Jn Hubbard in full, £10 : £10 17s 6d ; Joseph Doggett a debt, £399 18s 5d ; Samuel Doggett his disbursements, £57 ; John Sprague, £87 18s ; Paid Thos Savage, £60 : £147 18s ; For Letters of Admincon &c, £1 9s ; Record of the Inventory etc, 16s ; To the administratrix for necessary Implements of Household, £40 ; To the administratrix for her time and trouble, £10 ; Drawing allowing & recording this account &c, £1 15s. Old tenor, £1920 4s.

Bethiah Doggett died a few days after the above account was returned to the Probate Court, and before she had fully administered on the estate of her husband. May 20, 1747, Kenelm Winslow, of Boston, brazier, was appointed to complete the administration of the estate, the letters being granted to him by request of two of the children, Lydia Cliff and Bethiah Doggett. The Suffolk Probate records contain no return of administration on said estate by Kenelm Winslow.

3571. MARY DOGGETT³ (*Samuel*,² *Thomas*¹), born Marshfield, Mass., April 26, 1687 ; married Marshfield, Mass., September 29, 1712, by Rev. James Gardner, to Eleazer White, son of Daniel and Hannah (Hunt) White, and grandson of Peregrine White ; born Marshfield, Mass., November 8, 1686.

Issue :

3613. i. NEHEMIAH WHITE,⁴ born Marshfield, Mass., January 14, 1713.
3614. ii. PEREGRINE WHITE,⁴ born Marshfield, Mass., September 18, 1715.
3615. iii. ELEAZER WHITE,⁴ born Marshfield, Mass., March 8, 1717.
3616. iv. ELKANAH WHITE,⁴ born Marshfield, Mass., December 10, 1719.
3617. v. MARY WHITE,⁴ born Marshfield, Mass., March 23, 17²⁰⁄₂₁.
3618. vi. BENAIAH WHITE,⁴ born Marshfield, Mass., September 19, 1724.
3619. vii. PENELOPE WHITE,⁴ born Marshfield, Mass., June 13, 1727.
3620. viii. THOMAS WHITE,⁴ born Marshfield, Mass., June 29, 1729.
3621. ix. REBECCA WHITE,⁴ born Marshfield, Mass., August 18, 1731 ; married John Hyland.

3572. SARAH DOGGETT³ (*Samuel*,² *Thomas*¹), born Marshfield, Mass., April 7, 1689 ; married Marshfield, Mass., January 12, 1710, by Rev. James Gardner, to John Allen, son of Joseph and Rebecca Allen ; born Braintree, Mass., July 8, 1686.

Issue :

3622. i. JOHN ALLEN,⁴ born Braintree, Mass., May 19, 1711.

HOUSE OF CAPT. EBENEZER DOGGETT, PLYMOUTH, MASS.

1720 - 1743

3623. ii. Isaac Allen,[4] born Braintree, Mass., October 26, 1713; married 1st, Braintree, February 16, 173⅞, Deborah Hayward; married 2d, Braintree, 1756, Hannah Hayward.
3624. iii. Bethiah Allen,[4] born Braintree, Mass., March 23, 1716; married Braintree, December 12, 1734, Jonathan Nash, of Weymouth, Mass.
3625. iv. Sarah Allen,[4] born Braintree, Mass., March 4, 17⅒.

3574. Capt. Ebenezer Doggett[3] (*Samuel,*[2] *Thomas*[1]), born Marshfield, Mass., November 22, 1693; died Boston, Mass., December (?), 1746; married 1st, Plymouth, Mass., June 9, 1720, by Mr. Little, to Elizabeth Rickard, daughter of John and Mary Rickard, of Plymouth; died Plymouth, Mass., December 7, 1731; married 2d, Plymouth (?), Mass., September (?), 1733. Desire Rickard.

Issue:

3626. i. Ebenezer Doggett,[4] born Plymouth, Mass., July 5, 1722; died Plymouth, Mass., December 20, 1722.
3627. ii. John Doggett,[4] born Plymouth, Mass., February 6, 172¾; possibly removed to Liverpool, N.S., and had wife Dorcas, who administered on his estate, August 27, 1781; if so, some items credited to John (No. 3673) may belong here.
3628. iii. Ebenezer Doggett,[4] born Plymouth, Mass., July 17, 1726.
3629. iv. Samuel Doggett,[4] born Plymouth, Mass., January 20, 172⅞.
3630. v. —— Doggett,[4] born Plymouth, Mass., October 23, 1730; died Plymouth, Mass., November, 1730.
3631. vi. Elizabeth Doggett,[4] born Marshfield, Mass., May 14, 1738.

Ebenezer Doggett was baptized September 27, 1702, at the First Church in Marshfield. Like his brother Samuel, he is called at different times "yeoman" and "mariner." Early Boston newspapers mention his sailing from that port to the Carolinas and to Newfoundland, and it is probable he made voyages to the West Indies and possibly across the Atlantic. Captain Doggett married a Plymouth lady for his first wife, and made his home in Plymouth, where he bought of Ignatius Cushing (husband of Mrs. Doggett's sister) a dwelling-house, which Mr. Cushing had just built.

The house was deeded to him May 16, 1720, and in the deed Captain Doggett is called "late of Marshfield, now of Plymouth." [Plymouth Deeds, 15-27.]

This house he made his home until after his second marriage, when he removed to Marshfield, sometime between December 14, 1734, and May 14, 1738, and sold the house to Thomas Foster, February 3, 1743, for £230, and with it his pew in the meeting-house in Plymouth. [Plymouth Deeds, 36-103.]

This pew had been hired May 26, 1740, by Samuel Clarke, of Plymouth. [Plymouth Deeds, 34-218.]

The Doggett house, after being owned and occupied by many Plymouth families, became the property of Mr. Chas. T. Holmes, of Plymouth, who had it torn down during the winter of 1884-5. During the previous summer it was my privilege to see the house, which had retained its original style and finish, and was located on the town square, the lot having adjoined the town house. The house set back about twenty feet from the square, the front toward the town house, and overlooking the bay. Entering the front door, the hall was found to be of good size, and the sides dadoed to a height of about four feet, with panels which divided the space above the baseboard into a series of small square panels over the same number of long ones. The parlor on the right, which was rather higher studded than the rest of the ground floor, was about eight feet high, and contained an open fireplace, high dado, and windows looking toward the square and the water. The next room of importance, the kitchen or living-room, was of large size, and entered from the end of the hall or from the other rooms.

Here was the large fireplace, and in the back the iron fireback, on which was the English coat of arms.

This fireback weighs one hundred and fifty-seven pounds, is about three feet long, supposed to have been cast in England, and is now in the possession of the writer. The quaint staircase. the panelling, the small window-panes, all attracted one's attention, and the second story was as interesting as the first.

August 8, 1727. Ebenezer Doggett bought of his brother, Isaac Doggett, his interest in the estate of their father, Samuel Doggett. [Plymouth Deeds, 22–72.]

As Seth Doggett died without issue, Ebenezer became possessed of the real estate of his father, according to the will, and with his mother began the sale of the Marshfield and Pembroke lands. Ten transfers were made by him, which are recorded in Plymouth county, between 1734 and 1745, besides the purchase and sale of his house in the town of Plymouth, previously mentioned. In all there is deeded fully two hundred and fifty acres of land. amounting to about £1,400.

The town records of Marshfield contain only the following items regarding Captain Doggett. and it does not appear that he held any offices in the town during his residence there :

" March 1, 173$\frac{8}{9}$. Chosen to serve on the Grand Jury on Tuesday preceding the last Tuesday of April.

" March 29, 1742. Chosen to serve on the Grand Jury at Plymouth 2nd Tuesday of April next.

" June 28, 1742. Chosen on Grand Jury at the Superior Court at Plymouth 2nd Tuesday in July next."

After the final sale of land in Marshfield on November 5, 1745, Captain Doggett probably soon removed to Boston as more central for a place of residence, and as it was the port from which he had sailed as early as 1727, and possibly before.

During the following year he died, but the exact date of his death has not been found.

His widow, Desire Doggett, and his son, John Doggett, were appointed administrators of his estate, Boston, December 9, 1746. [Suffolk Probate, 39–276.]

(39–298.) Inventory of estate of Ebenezer Doggett, appraised December 16, 1746:

A parcel of new earthern ware, £7; 5 yds new Broad Cloth @ 75s, £18 15s; A Gun & Bayonet £5 a small pistol 15s, £5 15s; wearing apparel viz: a great coat, 3 close bodyed coats — 4 jackets — a pair of breeches a pair Kersey ditto — 4 shirts — a hat and wig, 5 pair stockings, £64; 1 Brass Kittle & Skillet, £9; Sundry Pewter platers, plates etc w^t. 43 @ 5s, £10 15s; 2 Iron Pots — 5 skillets — a dripping pan & spit & frying pan, £6; 5 candlesticks, 16s; 1 pr Tongs & fire shovel, 3 Trammels & chafing dish, £4; 2 pr Andirons tongs & fire shovel & a toasting iron, £3; 4 axes 50s a pair Brass Scales & weights & carpenters adze 20s, £3 10s; 2 old pr stilyards 15s earthern & glassware Knives & forks 65s, £4; Sundry Tin & Glass & earthern ware, £5; Sundry tubs & pails 20s 2 Kitchen tables & 10 chairs 55s, £3 15s; an old oval oak table and joint stool 25s 6 chairs 20s, £2 5s; 5 chairs 18s 2 pair bellows 12s, £1 10; 2 saws, 2 whale irons 70s 1 warming pan 25s, £4 15s; A box, 2 chests & a trunk 50s a table & trunk 30s, £4; a box Iron & heaters 20s a small stand & candlestick 3s, £1 3s; a case of 5 bottles 15s sundry old books 50s, £3 5s; 4 small looking glasses 85s a quadrant & nocturnal £6, £10 5s; 2 Cod lines and ledds, £2; 1 feather bed, bedstead & bed-clothing, £28; 3 feather beds & 1 Hammock, £60; an old under bed & bedding £5 12 pr Sheets £20, £25; 13 pillow biers, £5 4s; 1 doz Napkins & towels 50s 4 Table Cloths 90s, £7; 1½ BB flour ½ bushels pears & a barrel Pork, £25; 2 live hogs, £6; 25 oz 11 pwt Silver @ 42s, £53 13s 1d; 6 pwt Gold @ £32 per oz, £9 12s; Bills of old tenor, £68 13s 2d; A bond of Isaac Smith & others, £400; old tenor, £862 11s 3d.

JAMES GOLD
DANIEL INGERSOL
JOHN MARSHALL

Desire Doggett appeared & made oath that the above was a full account of estate of her late husband Dec 30, 1746.

June 8, 1747, an intention of marriage between John Frazier and Desire Doggett, of Boston, is recorded, and July 30, 1747, they were married by the minister of the New South Church.

Suffolk Probate, 41–99. Account of Desire Frazier and John Doggett, administrators of Ebenezer Doggett, late of Boston, mariner, deceased.

charge themselves with £862 11s 3d; Rec'd since of Susannah Howland, £1 7s 6d; Isaac Phillips, £1 17s 7d; Barnabas Rayment, 8s 5d; John Whites estate, £10 10s; Thomas Eames, £1 2s; Thomas Church, £36; Cushing, 19s 2d; old tenor, £916 15s. 3d.
and the said accountants pray allowance as follows viz. Paid for letters of administration, £1 15s; paid for exhib. Inventory, oaths, 16s; Allowance to Isaac Smith out of his bond being previously received but not receipted for £70; Paid for funeral charges & mourning for widow & children, £145 19s 8d; Daniel Johonnot. £8 6s; Brattle Oliver, £5 10s; Mary Hubbard, a quarters rent, £15; Jonathan Cushing of Kingston his acct., £9 5s; Peleg Ford, £3; Thomas Murdock, £4 11d; Anthony Winslow, 9s 4d; Michael Foord for rate due 1745, £6 18s; Samuel Foster, £5 11s 6d; Oxenbridge Thacher, £3 6s 10d; Thacher & Bois, £11 11s. To Bathsheba Doggett the deceased mother's Lodging & board from Dec 16 to Apr 17, 1747 @ 80s per week, ye greatest part

of which time she was sick ye dec'd being bound to maintain her, £68; To funeral charges of said Bathsheba, £34 19s 6d; Bethiah Doggett, £2; Paid for Drawing, allowing & recording this acct. &c, £1 7s 6d; allowed & approved, £397 16s 3d.

April 21, 1748.

3575. BATHSHEBA DOGGETT[3] (*Samuel,*[2] *Thomas*[1]), born Marshfield, Mass., June 18, 1695; died Milton, Mass., January 30, 1776; married 1st, Marshfield, Mass., September 17, 1719, by Rev. James Gardner, to Capt. John Kent, son of John and Sarah (Smith) Kent, of Marshfield; died Kingston, Jamaica, W.I., 1731½; married 2d, Boston, Mass., July 30, 1740, by Rev. Joseph Sewall, D.D., to Oxenbridge Thacher, Esq., of Boston, Mass., son of Rev. Peter and Theodora (Oxenbridge) Thacher, of Milton, Mass.; born May 17, 1681; died Milton, Mass., October 22, 1772.

Issue:

3632. i. BATHSHEBA KENT,[4] born Marshfield, Mass., May 21, 1721; died Boston, Mass., 1729.
3633. ii. JOHN KENT,[4] born Marshfield, Mass., January 26, 17$\frac{29}{30}$; died Boston, Mass., October 31, 1737.

And probably others.

February 15, 1732, administration was granted on estate of Capt. John Kent to Bathsheba Kent. [Suffolk Probate, 31–286.]

The inventory dated May 12, 1733, mentions: "1 Negro Girl £80; 1 Indian Girl & child £80; ½ Pew in New South Brick." [Suffolk Probate, 31–468.]

The inventory amounted to £1,340 9s. 10d., and in the account mention is made of payments to son and daughter, also for "Tombstone and carrying and setting up at Jamaica £19." The account is dated October 29, 1734. [Suffolk Probate, 30–398.]

Oxenbridge Thacher graduated Harvard College, 1698. He was selectman of Boston for many years, and representative for that place and Milton, to which latter town he removed.

He devoted some part of his early days to the ministry, and preached the first sermon ever delivered in Stoughton.

He died 1772, but his more famous son of the same name more than filled his place.

3576. Dea. JOHN DOGGETT[3] (*Samuel,*[2] *Thomas*[1]), born Marshfield, Mass., March 29, 1697; died Lebanon, Conn., February 19, 1764; married Marshfield, Mass., November 5, 1719, by Rev. James Gardner, to Margery Eames, daughter of Anthony and Grace (Oldham) Eames; born Marshfield, Mass.; died after January 25, 1771.

Issue:

3634. i. MARY DOGGETT,[4] born Marshfield, Mass., November 14, 1720; married Azariah Smith.

3635. ii. SAMUEL DOGGETT,[4] born Marshfield, Mass., February 3, 172⅔.
,3636. iii. JOHN DOGGETT,[4] born Lebanon, Conn., September 5, 1725.
3637. iv. SARAH DOGGETT,[4] born Lebanon, Conn., April 12, 1728; married Mr. Chipman.
3638. v. HANNAH DOGGETT,[4] born Lebanon, Conn., March 26, 1732.
3639. vi. MARGERY DOGGETT,[4] born Lebanon, Conn., February 21, 173⅜; married Joseph Griswold.
3640. vii. BATHSHEBA DOGGETT,[4] born Lebanon, Conn., January 3, 173⅘.

The church records of Marshfield include among the children of Samuel Doggett, who were baptized September 27, 1702, his son, John Doggett. His boyhood was spent in Marshfield, but as a young man he went first to Rochester, Mass.

Among the early settlers of Rochester, Mass., were Rev. Samuel Arnold and Abraham Holmes, both relatives of John Doggett. There were also other Marshfield people who had settled there, and this fact doubtless led him to first seek his home among them. A search of the town records of Rochester does not show any particulars of his residence there. A brook which runs through the town has the name "Doggett's brook," but it is not known for whom it was named, although, as he was probably the earliest settler of the name, it may have been so called because of his living in the vicinity.

It is not known when he went to Rochester, but the record of his marriage at Marshfield, in 1719, calls him John Doggett, of Rochester.

How long he remained in Rochester after his marriage is also uncertain; but his two oldest children, Mary and Samuel, were born in Marshfield, the latter in 1723.

Soon after the birth of Samuel he removed to Lebanon, Conn., and it is an interesting fact that he had his marriage recorded in that town, as well as the birth of his two children, who were born in Marshfield. The record in Lebanon agrees with that in Marshfield in every particular, excepting the name of his wife, who in Lebanon is called Ames, instead of Eames.

Walter G. Kingsley, Esq., of Lebanon, writes (1888) the name is usually spelled "Dogget" on the records at Lebanon; and he also says in regard to the children and descendants calling the name Daggett that he was told about thirty-five years ago, while teaching in Bolton, that "the name was only a change from Dogget to Daggett."

The earliest conveyance of real estate to him occurred September 16, 1725, and he was then described as of Lebanon, and continued to make purchases of land until about 1750 or 1760.

The locality where the family owned farms was very close to the town limits of both Coventry and Hebron.

From the Lebanon town-meeting records, "John Doged appointed constable Dec 4, 1727," but no subsequent appointment to office.

The church records show that John and his wife united with the Second Society in 1727 (this parish in 1806 became an incorporated town, " Columbia ").

A rate bill for the North Parish of Lebanon (now Columbia) for the year 1741, which was made to pay the salary of the minister, and dated December, 1741, shows the whole amount raised £330 16s. 9d., of which " John Dogit paid £3 9s 2d."

The will of Samuel Doggett, of Marshfield, gives his son, John Doggett, thirty-eight acres of land in Middleboro', " being ye lot in 16 shilling purchase," and from the records at Plymouth we find the sale of this lot as follows : " John Doggett of the Town of Lebanon in County Windham in Connecticut in New England for 25£ paid by John Booth of Middleboro in County Plymouth, sells him 38 acres land in 16 shilling purchase in Middleboro, laid out originally to Thomas Doggett No. 104 lot.   Oct 8, 1736." [Plymouth Deeds, 30–210.]

In the Windham Probate District, at Willimantic, Conn., is recorded the will of Dea. John Doggett, Vol. VI., page 503, as follows :

In the name of God Amen, the 10th day of Feb. A.D. 1764. I, John Doggett of Lebanon in the County of Windham, and Colony of Conn. in New England being weak and in a low declining state of body, of a disposing mind and memory, thanks be given to God.   Therefore, Calling into minde the mortality of my body and knowing that it is appointed for all men once to die, do make and ordain this my Last will and testament (that is to say).   Principally and first of all, I give and recomend my soul into the hands of God that gave it, and my body I recomend to the earth to be buried in decent Christian burial at the Disiscretion of my executors, nothing doubting but at the general resurrection I shall receive the same again by the mighty Power of God, and as touching such worldly Estate wherewith it hath pleased God to bless me in this Life.   I give demise and dispose of the same in the Following manner after my Just debts and funeral expenses are discharged.

Imprimis ; I give and bequeath to Margery my well beloved wife one third part of my household goods, also one Cow and twelve sheep, and a quarter part of what shall be found due to me at my decease, by note or by book, which I give her forever to be at her dispose, likewise I give her the use of my dwelling house so long as she shall remain my widow, except some privileges which I shall hereafter mention.   Together with the use of one third of my barn, and likewise one third part of the improvement of my Farm which Lyeth in Lebanon, which third part shall be sett off to her on the eastward of the highway to be improved by her during Life, and also I give her the privilege of getting firewood on my wood Land, so Long as she continues my widow.

Item, I give and bequeath to my well beloved son Samuel Doggett, and to his heirs and assigns forever, all my lands Lying in Coventry, excepting twenty acres in farm, as I shall hereafter describe, he paying if need so require as I shall herein order.

Likewise I give him one halfe of my wearing apparel, except a certain part otherwise disposed of, in this my will.   Together with a halving plow, a cornish and onstile.

Item : I give and bequeath to my well beloved son John Doggett, his heirs and assigns forever, all my lands Lying in Lebanon with all the appurtenances thereto belonging, he paying if need so require as I shall order in this my will, two thirds of said farm to fall into his hands at my Decease, and so much of the house as to stow away his ware, which he may make, and to have the use of the garrett as he used to have, to stow his corn and grain, and likewise he shall have the whole benefit of my shop adjoining to my dwelling house at my decease, to work in, and the third part of my farm which my wife shall improve as above said, and her right in the house.   Together with a privilege which I do hereby allow my two Daughters when they and last of them have done with them according to the intent of this my will they shall Fall into the possession of him the said John Doggett as they each of them quit their rights severally.   Also I give him all my Tools and utencels for husbandry, as carts, plows, chains, hoes &c with my grindstone, also all my Carpenters and Joyners Tools Except which I have given to my son Samuel, I give him one gun and a sword with my best suit of apparel From Top to toe.   Including my best great Coat and the remaining halfe of my wearing apparel and Furthermore, I give to my son Doggett his heirs and assigns forever, twenty acres of my land Lying in Coventry begin the bounds namely at ye westerly corner of the land which my son Samuel had of me by deed at the highway.   From thence running by said highway westwardly to Bolton Line, and is to Extend so wide as to containe twenty acres, being of one width at each end, making a parrelel Line on the south side with said highway on the north, and whereas their is a dispute between me and Capt Leach, and others, where the line between me and they shall be, and thereby said highway may be removed from where it is now which if it should be one way or the other, said Land which I give to my son John shall conform to said highway.

Item — I give and bequeath to my loving daughter Mary the wife of Azariah Smith, the sum of one pound Lawful money, she having already received the other part of her Legacey.

Item — I give to my well beloved daughter Margery the wife of Joseph Griswold, the sum of three pounds lawful money, she also having already received the other part of her Legacy.

Item — I give to my well beloved daughters Hannah, and Bethiah Doggett, the sum of Fourty Pounds lawful money that is to Hannah Twenty pounds, and to Bethiah twenty pounds, and whereas these my two daughters Hannah and Bethiah, as yet continue unmarried, and have constantly Lived with me, it is therefore my will that they shall still have the privilege to Live in my house, so long as they continue unmarried, and have ye benefit of so much room therein, as to Labour and do there necessary bussiness they may ingage in, and to stow away their house goods, and whereas I have given them some few things heretofore exclusive of this my will, but they by their own Labour and industry have acquired many things as household goods &c, to themselves, which are not my estate and I have no right To, altho they may be found in my house, those goods or estate which they are able to shew, I order to remain their own property, and not to be brought Into my Inventory, and Furthermore it is my will that these my daughters shall have a right to so much of my provissions as they have heretofore had in my Lifetime, so as to support them through this year, without making any allowance therefore, and also the same privilege of Provissions I do allow to my wife as I have to my daughters in this my will.

Item — Furthermore it is my will that my Executors shall pay the above said Legacies to each one of my daughters out of my moveable estate, if it be sufficient, but if it be insufficient then it is my will that my son John pay ye remainder thereof to them after the decease of my wife but if my moveable Estate shall be more than sufficient to pay said Legacys what remains thereof shall be equally divided between my daughters Sarah, Hannah, Margery, and Bethiah or their heirs.

Item — It is my will that if what I have given to my wife for the support of her maintenance during the span or time she shall continue my widow, shall not be sufficient therefor, then it is my will that my sons Samuel, and John shall afford her sutable and comfortable support so long as she is my widow at their equal expence.

Again whereas I say that the above Legacys shall be so much in Lawful money it is my will that my executors shall have liberty if they see fit to pay them in bills of Credit of this Government Emition or any Coin money that passes Current in this Colony if my moveable Estate be not sufficient.

Item: whereas I have a right in what we call the Delievare Purchase of Land, and as Y^t not Known whether it will be obtained, Therefore if it be obtained to the advantage of my estate so that I have a right or share therein, then it is my will that my son John Doggett shall have half thereof as his proper due and right by our private agreement when I put in for said right as that he hath heretofore carried one halfe the cost until this time which he and I. agreed that he should do, so that one half said right is his property altho affixed to my name which give and demise to him and his heirs and assigns forever, and the other one half if obtained is my property which I do hereby give unto my two sons Samuel and John and to my five daughters Mary, Sarah, Hannah, Margery and Bethiah to be divided in eight shears, and my son Samuel to have two shears and the other of my children each of them one sheare, and whereas there may yet arise cost on said Land it is my will that they shall bear equal costs according to their several quantities or shears, and if any one of them shall refuse to support the cost thereon arising, then his or her part so refusing shall be equally divided among so many of them as shall support said charge.

It is my will that Margery my beloved wife, and my son John Doggett be executors to my will whom I do hereby make constitute appoint and ordain to be executors to this my last will and testament and I do hereby revoke and disannull all other Former wills Legacies bequests, and executors heretofore named or made by me.

In witness Confirmation, hereof I have hereunto set my hand and seal the day and year first above written.

John Doggett [Seal]

Signed Sealed Published and proclaimed by the above said John Doggett to be his last will and Testament, In presence of us.

ISRAEL WOODWARD
BENJAMIN LAMB
WILLIAM SIMES

Windham County Feb 28, 1764, the witnesses appeared & proved the will before Joseph Clark, J.P.

March 19, 1764, Lebanon, John Doggett appeared and accepted the trust as executor.

Apr 4, 1764 The executrix appeared and accepted the trust.

The inventory was taken the 6th, 7th, and 14th days of March, 1764, and amounted to £387 13s. 6d.

Among the items are :

73 acres Land in Lebanon by est. 50 per acre, £182 10s ; 50 acres Land in Coventry 20 acre, £50; making value of land, £232 10s; moveables, £155 3s 6d.

Among the many items classed under the head of moveables we notice 4 Tables, 13 chairs, 1 great wheel, 1 side saddle, 1 ox, 2 cows, 1 hundred sheep, horse kind, 1 Tooth Drawing Instrument &c.

3577. ISAAC DOGGETT [3] (*Samuel,*[2] *Thomas*[1]), born Marshfield, Mass., February 6, 1699 ; died Braintree (?), Mass., between February 24, 1762, and September, 1763 ; married Braintree, Mass., September 9, 1725, by Rev. Samuel Niles, to Abigail Allen, daughter of Samuel and Abigail (Webb) Allen ; born Braintree, Mass., November 2, 1700 ; died Braintree, Mass., between Jan. 22 and May 23, 1785.

Issue :

3641. i. BATHSHEBA DOGGETT,[4] born Braintree, Mass., June 12, 1726; died Braintree, Mass., June 26, 1726.
3642. ii. SAMUEL DOGGETT,[4] born Marshfield, Mass., May 30, 1727.
3643. iii. ABIGAIL DOGGETT,[4] born Braintree, Mass., December 5, 1728.
3644. iv. ISAAC DOGGETT,[4] born Braintree, Mass., December 12, 1732; probably the Isaac who " mar Boston Mass January 8, 1761 by Rev Andrew Eliot to Alice Cates."
3645. v. BATHSHEBA DOGGETT,[4] born Braintree, Mass., February 5, 173⅔; probably the Bathsheba whose intention of marriage, October 31, 1757, is recorded in Boston, to Jonathan Brown.
3646. vi. SETH DOGGETT,[4] born Braintree, Mass., November 9, 1737; " cord-

wainer;" was paid 8d. for killing birds January 20, 1755, Braintree; impressed for Fort William Henry expedition on roll of
Capt. Nathaniel Blake, of Milton, August 7, 1756.

3647. vii. EUNICE DOGGETT,[4] born Dorchester, Mass., December 25, 1741;
bapt. by Rev. John Taylor at Milton, January 3, 1742.

3648. viii. ELIZABETH DOGGETT,[4] born 1748; bapt. Milton, Mass., Aug. 7, 1748.

September 27, 1702. Isaac Doggett baptized in the First Church,
Marshfield.

March 20, 17$\frac{16}{17}$, Marshfield town meeting:

At said meeting voted that Isaac Dogget and eleven others, these or so many
suitable persons have liberty to banister the back seat of the men's end gallery
so that they do not raise it higher than that in the front and that there be so
many owners at least constantly belonging to it.

Isaac Doggett, like his older brothers, is called both "mariner"
and "yeoman," the first being his occupation when he lived at
Marshfield, and the latter after he had married and settled in
Braintree.

He removed to Braintree in 1727 or 1728, and preparatory to
moving there sold out his property in Marshfield and secured land in
Braintree, as appears in the following deeds:

Rebeckah Allen of Braintree in County Suffolk spinster, daughter of Samuel
Allen of Braintree wheelwright, deceased intestate. Whereas a certain tract
of land at Bendall's Farm containing 100 acres was divided between her
and Isaac Doggett in the right of Abigail his wife, daughter of Samuel Allen
and is now held by both in joint tenancie. Said Rebeckah for 110£ paid by
Isaac Doggett now of Marshfield, County Plymouth, mariner, sells him her
moiety. May 12, 1727. [Suffolk Deeds, 41–182.]

Isaac Doggett of Marshfield, mariner, for 100£ paid by his brother Ebenezer
Doggett of Plymouth and also by paying Isaac's proportion of such bequests
and legacies as by will of his honored Father Samuel Doggett late of Marshfield
deceased, his third part of housing and land in Marshfield & Cedar Swamp in
Pembroke and also the one half of Seth Doggett's interest, provided he die
without issue, to hold the same after the death or 2nd marriage of his mother
Bathsheba Doggett, Aug 8, 1727. [Plymouth Deeds, 22–72.]

Abigail, wife of Isaac Doggett, joined the church in the Middle
Precinct, Braintree, in 1729.

March 27, 1732. At a town meeting in Braintree the various town
ways were laid out and described, one of the highways running:

Thence to the southerly corner of Dogget's Garden, the way to ly as it is
now Improved: thence to the southerly corner of Dogget's Field and so along
side of the Fence as it now stands till we come to the line between Benjamin
Hayward and said Dogget &c The ways as laid down were accepted, only with
the following amendment at the desire of Isaac Dogget abovenamed viz: that
from the way against Mr Dogget's House the way aforesaid shall go over a
Shoalplace in the corner of a Pond in his land and along the north side of the
Pond to Mr Haywards Barrs and thence directly to said Haywards Door.

Isaac Doggett probably resided in that part of Braintree, now
Randolph, as he connected himself with the church in that precinct
in 1733. June 25, 1734, Mary Spear's mulatto child was bound to

Isaac Doggett, and an order was drawn to pay him £25 for keeping it until it should become of age.

The following from the Braintree records, March 1, $173\frac{5}{6}$: "Isaac Dogget chosen surveyor of Highways."

March 7, $173\frac{6}{7}$, "Isaac Doged chosen Tithingman."

March 26, 1739, "Isaac Doggett chosen constable and sworn."

Said Dogget then applyed to the meeting for some allowance for to serve ye Town, In s^{d} office above s^{d} and after some Debate in s^{d} meeting, voted that six pounds be allowed out of the Treasury of this Town and to be equally divided between the three constables &c.

February 28, 1753, Isaac Doggett was paid for teaching school in the Middle Precinct two months. April 16, 1753, Isaac Doggett was paid for teaching school.

February 24, 1762. Isaac Doggit, yeoman, and Abigail his wife, of Braintree, sell land in Braintree. [Suffolk Deeds, 97–156.]

Isaac Doggett died between this time and September, 1763, at which time Mrs. Doggett is called "widow."

3578. LYDIA DOGGETT^{3} (*Samuel*,^{2} *Thomas*^{1}), born Marshfield, Mass., October 26, 1703; married Plymouth, Mass., August 10, 1730, by Rev. Nathaniel Leonard, to Nicholas Drew, son of John and Hannah (Churchill) Drew; born Plymouth, Mass., 1684.

Issue:

3649. i. REBECCA DREW,^{4} born Plymouth, Mass., 1731.
3650. ii. LYDIA DREW.^{4}

3579. SETH DOGGETT^{3} (*Samuel*,^{2} *Thomas*^{1}), born Marshfield, Mass., October 22, 1705; died 1734; married Plymouth, Mass., September 9, 1729, by Rev. Nathaniel Leonard, to Elizabeth Delano.

Seth Doggett was a "mariner," and perhaps lost at sea. He married at Plymouth, and doubtless made that his home, as his wife calls herself of Plymouth, in applying for letters of administration. The following from the probate office at Plymouth relate to his estate. To Capt. Ebenezer Doggett, mariner, and Mrs. Elizabeth Doggett, widow of Capt. Seth Doggett, mariner, deceased, both of Plymouth, letter of administration on estate of Capt. Seth Doggett, December 14, 1734 (7–82). An inventory of the estate of Mr. Seth Doggett, of Plymouth, March 10, $173\frac{5}{6}$ (7–172):

6 Books — 5 Mariners books — 1 Seal skin trunk & chest 6 wigs — 4 silver spoons — 1 Blanket — 7 knives & 2 forks 1 Picture — 1 case — 8 Bottles — 42 Bottles — 1 Great Bottle 1 Bed & Rug — 1 Pillow Bier &c —
To 5 pces of 8 he gave his wife when he went off ye last time.

(7–172.) Inventory of Mr. Seth Doggett, late of Plymouth, March 11, $173\frac{5}{6}$. Necessary utensils set to Elizabeth Doggett, widow, relict of Seth Doggett, late of Plymouth, deceased:

Seal skin trunk & chest — 1 pr Andirons and Chafing dish — table — 7 pewter plates and platters 2 Glasses — 2 small bowls — 2 white mugs — 2 earthern plates — 2 salt sellers — 1 Earthern mug — a spinning wheel and pair cards — 1 Blanket — 7 Knives & 2 forks — bed bolster — 2 pillows — 3 pr sheets — 1 Coverlid — 1 Bedstead & cord — 2¼ lbs Linnen yarn — Iron skillet — 1 pillow bier — 1 Earthern plate — 6 books — (5 pieces eight given to ye widow by her husband when going off, allowed).

May 16, 1737, Mrs. Elizabeth Doggett and Thomas Murdoch were married at Plymouth.

3580. ABIGAIL DOGGETT [3] (*Samuel*,[2] *Thomas* [1]), born Marshfield, Mass., March 14, 17¹¹⁄₁₂; married Marshfield, Mass., January 18, 1728, by Rev. James Gardner, to Joshua Eames, son of Anthony Eames, of Marshfield, Mass. ; born November, 1704.

Issue :

3651. i. LUCY EAMES,[4] born Marshfield, Mass., October 9, 1729; married Timothy Sylvester.
3652. ii. AMOS EAMES,[4] married Sarah ——.
3653. iii. BATHSHEBA EAMES,[4] born 1731.
3654. iv. SARAH EAMES,[4] married Mr. Randall.
3655. v. ABIGAIL EAMES,[4] married Joshua Keen.
3656. vi. JOSHUA EAMES,[4] baptized 1735; married Deborah Doty, Aug. 28, 1755.

3586. EPHRAIM WILDER [3] (*Rebecca Doggett*,[2] *Thomas* [1]), born Hingham, Mass., August 25, 1696; died Abington, Mass., about 1770; married Hingham, Mass., July 30, 1723, Mary Lane, daughter of John and Tabitha (Stodder) Lane.

Issue :

3657. i. EPHRAIM WILDER,[4] born Hingham, Mass., June 30, 1724.
3658. ii. LYDIA WILDER,[4] born Hingham, Mass., November 24, 1725; married May 15, 1745, Matthew Tower.
3659. iii. JOHN WILDER,[4] born Hingham, Mass., March 25, 1727.
3660. iv. DAVID WILDER,[4] born Hingham, Mass., May 12, 1729.
3661. v. HANNAH WILDER,[4] born Hingham, Mass.. May 20, 1730; died there November, 1756.
3662. vi. MARY WILDER,[4] born Hingham, Mass.. August 12, 1731; died there, August 28, 1731.
3663. vii. MARY WILDER,[4] born Hingham, Mass., June 12, 1732; married July 30, 1752, Jonathan Anderson.
3664. viii. ABEL WILDER,[4] born Hingham, Mass., April 9, 1736; died in the army, October 31, 1756.
3665. ix. SETH WILDER,[4] born Hingham, Mass., February 3, 1739; married August 27, 1761, Miriam Beal.

3587. ISAAC WILDER [3] (*Rebecca Doggett*,[2] *Thomas* [1]), born Hingham, Mass., 1700; married 1st, 1744, Bathsheba Damon; married 2d, 1756, Letitia Chubbuck.

Issue :

3666. i. BATHSHEBA WILDER,[4] born Hingham, Mass., November 23, 1746; died there, 1746.
3667. ii. ISAAC WILDER,[4] born Hingham, Mass., January 12, 1748; married February 2, 1775, Abigail Cushing; he died December 18, 1839.
3668. iii. REBECCA WILDER,[4] born Hingham, Mass., December 28, 1749; married November 23, 1775, William Barrell.

3669. iv. ELIZABETH WILDER,[4] born Hingham, Mass., March 25, 1752; married
        June 19, 1783, Joseph Nash.
3670. v. DANIEL WILDER,[4] born Hingham, Mass., May 17, 1754; married
        twice; he died Hingham, October 30, 1838.
3671. vi. BATHSHEBA WILDER,[4] born Hingham, Mass., November 8, 1756; mar-
        ried May 19, 1780, Zenas Wilder.
3672. vii. LUCY WILDER.[4] born Hingham, Mass., May 9, 1760; married June 30,
        1780, John Jones.

THOMAS DOGGETT, OF MARSHFIELD, MASS.

FOURTH GENERATION.

3589. JOHN DOGGETT [4] (*Thomas*,[3] *John*,[2] *Thomas* [1]), born Marsh-
field, Mass., 1702; died Scituate, Mass. (?), April, 1751; married
Scituate, Mass., October 5, 1726, by Rev. Nathaniel Eells, to Jemima
Turner, daughter of Thomas and Hannah Turner, of Scituate.

Issue:

3673. i. JOHN DOGGETT,[5] born Scituate, Mass., 1730.
3674. ii. DAVID DOGGETT,[5] born Scituate, Mass., 1734.

John Doggett was baptized in the First Church in Marshfield, June
4, 1704.   He was a "mariner," and according to Deane's History
of Scituate kept the ferry on North river, in 1730, called Doggett's
ferry (now Little's Bridge).

His wife was daughter of Thomas Turner, a lawyer of Scituate,
and after their marriage they removed there, probably after a residence in Marshfield of about a year, as would appear by the following deeds:

> Thomas Turner of Scituate, currier, for 10£ paid by John Doggett of Marsh-
> field, mariner, 5 acres of land whereon he now dwells in Scituate, bounded N
> by highway and strip of land laid out in 2nd Division of Scituate common, with
> houses & buildings, Nov. 14, 1727. [Plymouth Deeds, 22–134.]
> Thomas Turner of Scituate, conveys land in Scituate provided John Dog-
> gett takes care of his mother Hannah Turner, during her life, Nov 18, 1727.
> [Plymouth Deeds, 22–135.]
> David Turner of Rehoboth in County Bristol clerk, and Thomas Turner of
> Scituate, currier, executors to last will of Thomas Turner late of Scituate, for
> 90£ paid by John Doggett of Scituate mariner, ⅔ part of 5 acres, whereon the
> said Doggett now dwells.   Oct 9, 1731. [Plymouth Deeds, 30–209.]

"Jan 22, 1737   Thomas Doggett, yeoman, of Marshfield, for
18£ paid by my brother John Doggett of Scituate, in County
Plymouth, mariner, all that my cedar Swamp in Pembroke, being all
the cedar swamp which my father Thomas Doggett gave me by his
will, and therein mentioned to be one half of his cedar swamp in said
Pembroke." [Plymouth Deeds, 40–39.]

The other half of the swamp was given to John Doggett by his father's will, so by this purchase he owned the whole of his father's cedar swamp in Pembroke.

March 14, 1738. John Doggett of Scituate mariner, sells Samuel Jenkins of Scituate, land in Scituate, provided he support his Honored mother Hannah Eames at the house on this land in sickness and in health, during her life. Jemima Doggett wife of John releases her dower. [Plymouth Deeds, 33–125.]

March 19, 172⅝. The decked sloop " Patience," about sixty tons, Capt. John Doggett, is mentioned as now filled for sea and at anchor in North river.

Captain Doggett probably made his headquarters in Boston soon after March, 1738.   From the Massachusetts State Archives, 64–132, we have the following :

Whereas Andrew Oliver of Boston, within said Province aforesaid, Esq ; one of the owners of the sloop " Swan " John Dogget, master, has represented to me that the said Sloop in her passage from Jamaica to Boston, by reason of bad weather, ran ashore at the mouth of the said Harbour & has thereby suffered great damage both as to vessel and cargo, upon which Insurance was made, and hath requested that I would appoint suitable persons to survey said vessel and estimate the damage come to her and her cargo, by the said disaster, or otherwise by stormy weather in her said passage, &c.
Given at Boston Dec 9, 1741   SHIRLEY. Gov.

Damage estimated at 1020£ 17s 4d New Eng Currency Jan 16, 1741. Among the charges are the following : Breakfasting the people Bread sugar, cyder &c. To Capt Dogget for dining the men To damage of cables, riggin & flying jib, 15£.   To 3124½ Gal: molasses lost, cost in Jamaica 11ᵈ = 143£ 4s 2d.   Exchange 300 per cent.

" The Fellowship Club began in Boston, June 1, 1742, designed to promote the interest of each other in all things in their power, as well as to relieve such members of this society who by misfortunes and losses shall become proper objects, according to the ability of the box. The members to consist of such persons only who now are or have been commanders of vessels, and admitted by approval of a majority of the company."   Among the founders of this society was Capt. John Doggett, and in the application for incorporation as the Boston Marine Society (Massachusetts State Archives, 64–521), May 5, 1752, a circular containing all the members' names is added, his name being among those who had deceased previous to date.

Captain Doggett seems to have been somewhat unfortunate as a mariner, as appears from his letter which was printed in the Boston " Evening Post," of January 30, 1744 : " An extract of a letter of John Doggett of this town (who sailed in a brigantine for Jamaica the 1st of Nov. last) dated at Antigua Dec 25, 1743 " :

The 25ᵗʰ of Nov. in sight of Antigua, we had the misfortune to be taken by a Spanish privateer sloop with 75 men belonging to Sᵗ Domingo.
There was one of our men of war in sight when I was taken but by her mismanagement she neither took the privateer, nor retook my brig.

Three days after they took me, they marooned me and two of my men, with another master they had taken about a month before and one of his men, five of us in all, they gave us two pieces of beef and 20 lbs of bread.   They striped me almost naked and some of the villians attempted to kill me, but running to the bushes, I got a club that was my friend, and should certainly destroyed all those that put us ashore, would my companion have stood by me, but as it was they did not all go away with whole skins. We were taken off the island by a vessel bound to St Thomas and 2 days after, we met with the " Lively " man of war of 20 guns, and informed them where the privateer lay, for we heard them talking of going to that place. The Captain of the Man of war said if I was willing to go with him, he would go and destroy him.

We bore away after him and met with an English Privateer who went with us.

We soon found the Spaniard out at 3 o'clock in the morning, who weighed anchor and ran into shoal water, where neither our man of war nor Privateer could go.

At 8 o'clock in the morning the 1st of Dec. we began to fire, the man of war fired 350 shots and our Privateer 170 shots before the Spaniard would quit his vessel. We killed 3 men, and wounded 3 more. The Spaniard fired at the English Privateer, and did him some damage but neither killed nor wounded any of his men. At 3 P.M. we concluded to man all the boats from the man of war and Privateer, and board the Spaniard at all events, but they seeing us coming with resolution, the cowardly Dogs left their sloop (after running her ashore) and hid themselves in the bushes.

We destroyed the sloop, and then made the best of our way for the Island.

I hope to be home in a short time by the way of Statia.

" This is the 2nd time Capt. Doggett has had the misfortune to be taken by the Spaniards since the commencement of the war."

Joseph Tolman, of Scituate, is appointed administrator of the estate of John Doggett, late of Scituate, mariner, deceased, April 18, 1751. [Plymouth Probate, 12–313.]

The inventory of John Doget, of Scituate, deceased, is dated May 21, 1751, and among other things mentions the following :

Purse & apparrell 55£ 5s old tenor, Best Bible 6£ 10s other books 3£ 5 silver spoons, 1 walking cane, china, earthern and glass, case drawers, Desk, 1 pce English Cotton Striped dark culer, Bag holland, Sadle & side saddle, spinning wheel, foot wheel brooken pallet Bedstead, other brooken bedstead, best bed bolster, pillows, white blankets, callico, quilt, green chaney curtain, rods, bedstead cord & mat, Brass Kettle, Red chairs, other chairs, and great chair, Rought iron ware, cast iron doggs, iron skellet, case & 5 bottles, pewter, Knives & forks & the box, 2 Iron Pots and a Keetle, 2 frying pans, grid iron & candlesticks, old chest, old Trunk, old Trough, old caske, small desk, old baskets, copper ladle, bed, bedsteads & coverlid &c. amounting to 780£ 10s 1d or Lawful, 104£ 4s 4d.

The inventory was made by Thomas Stockbridge, David Bryant, and Benjamin Randal. [Plymouth Probate, 12–369.]

On May 2, 1751 (Plymouth Probate, 12–374), the estate of John Doggett, of Scituate, was rendered insolvent, and on March 2, 1752 (Plymouth Probate, 13–118), further time was allowed to examine claims on the estate. After this date there are no further records of the settlement of the estate in the Probate Court, but in the Registry of Deeds, 42–199 :

Joseph Tolman of Scituate in Co. Plymouth in N.E. gent, by virtue of the power and authority granted by the Justices of the Supreme Court at Plymouth in July 1752, as I am administrator on the estate of John Doggett late of said

Scituate mariner, deceased, for 4£ 5s 4d paid for ye discharging of ye dec'd just debts by Paul White of Marshfield, mariner, do convey unto him ⅔ parts of ye 55th Lot in the 2nd Division of Marshfield Common, the whole of which 55th Lot is about 39 acres, March 4, 1754.

March 8, 1792 — Joseph Tolman of Scituate adm. on estate of John Doggett late of said Scituate dec'd, sells a certain piece of Cedar Swamp in Pembroke viz : the whole of the 2nd share or division of the 5th great lot in the swamp called the Major's purchase except a strip of land through said share 6 rods & 3 ft wide formerly set off to Samuel Doggett and Thomas Barker on the one part and Thomas Doggett on the other part, for 18£ to Zacheriah and Noah Whitman Seth Pratt, Joshua Alden & Perez Waterman, all of Bridgewater. [Plymouth Deeds, 73–8.]

3590. PERSIS DOGGETT[4] (*Thomas,*[3] *John,*[2] *Thomas*[1]), born Marshfield, Mass., May (?), 1704 ; married Marshfield, Mass., October 31, 1723, by Rev. James Gardner, to Benjamin Kent ; born Marshfield, Mass.

Issue :

3675. i. PENELOPE KENT,[5] born Marshfield, Mass., July 9, 1724.

Persis Doggett was baptized at the First Church in Marshfield, June 4, 1704.

" May 13, 1717. Persis Doggett and others have liberty to banister up the hind seat of the womens end gallery and to set therein." [Marshfield Town Records.]

In 1718 her grandfather's will leaves her two ewe sheep. Benjamin Kent and wife removed to Boston, Mass.

3591. THOMAS DOGGETT[4] (*Thomas,*[3] *John,*[2] *Thomas*[1]), born Marshfield, Mass., 1706 ; died Middleboro', Mass., Aug. 11, 1788 ; married Marshfield, Mass., Dec. 11, 1728, by Rev. James Gardner, to Joanna Fuller, a descendant of Samuel Fuller, of the " Mayflower."

Issue :

3676. i. JOHN DOGGETT,[5] born Marshfield, Mass., 1729 ; baptized October 11, 1731 ; constable at Middleboro', 1752 ; unmarried ; died 1754.
3677. ii. THOMAS DOGGETT,[5] born Marshfield, Mass., 1731 ; died an infant.
3678. iii. MARK DOGGETT,[5] born Marshfield, Mass., 1733 ; died when a child.
3679. iv. JABEZ DOGGETT,[5] born Marshfield, Mass., March 3, 1734.
3680. v. SETH DOGGETT,[5] born Marshfield, Mass., February 15, 1736.
3681. vi. SIMEON DOGGETT,[5] born Marshfield, Mass., January 4, 1738.
3682. vii. EXPERIENCE DOGGETT,[5] born Marshfield, Mass., May 16, 1740 ; baptized April 23, 1741 ; died Middleboro', Mass., 1830.
3683. viii. JOANNA DOGGETT,[5] born Marshfield, Mass., March 16, 1742.

Thomas Doggett was a " yeoman," of Marshfield, and afterward of Middleboro'. He was executor of his father's estate, and received among other things his father's " sword, belt, &c."

January 12, 173⅔, was part owner of sloop " Middleboro'."

In the year 1741 he takes the first step toward removing to Middleboro', by selling the homestead in Marshfield, as appears by the following deed :

Thomas Doggett yeoman and Joanna his wife of Marshfield for 850£ paid by Cornelius White of Marshfield, Gentleman, 50 acres of upland and meadow in

Marshfield, bounded N.E. thereof by ye old channel of the South River and bounded E by the said river as ye same runs to the meadow of Ebenezer Doggett, then running with the fence across the Beach (called Doggett's Beach) to ye said Whites meadow that he bought of Thomas Doggett late of Marshfield deceased by land of Samuel Sherman. The same being the homestead farm lately belonging to our Honored father Thomas Doggett, deceased, also 10 acres of Pasture called Valley lot, bounded E & W by land of Ebenezer Doggett also ⅔ of the wood lot in Marshfield containing 39 acres March 26, 1741. [Plymouth Deeds, 34–93.]

He next adds to his lands in Middleboro' by the purchase of a farm, which was probably the one to which he afterward removed, and which is described in the following deed:

David and Susanna Miller. of Middleboro for 450£ paid by Thomas Doggett of Marshfield, our homestead land containing 88 acres in Middleboro, whereon we now dwell, May 7, 1741. [Plymouth Deeds, 34–123.]

Thomas Doggett removed to Middleboro', between this date and September 14, 1741.

Oct. 25, 1765. Thomas Doggett, of Middleboro in County Plymouth, Yeoman, sells 3 acres of his homestead land, to his son Simeon. and also by deed dated Oct 26, 1765 land in Middleboro to his son Simeon, lying in the purchase of lands called the little Lot Mens Purchase, and is about ½ of the homestead farm that I now live on, bounded beginning at the middle of my said farm at the country road that leads towards Dartmouth, thence by parallel line with NE side of said farm down to Namasket River. [Plymouth Deeds, 52–56.]

The will of Thomas Doggett, of Middleboro' (Plymouth Probate, 30–456), is dated August 30, 1785, and was proved October 6, 1788.

Gives son Seth Doggett ⅔ of the home farm, adjoining land belonging to ye heirs of Mr Read dec'd, also ½ the buildings thereon, all the meadow lying on Nemasket River bounded by land of Simeon Doggett. also right and title to certain rights of wood bought of Ebenezer Blackman of Middleboro except ½ of said lot:
Daughter Experience Doggett ⅓ of the homestead farm, ½ wood right bought of E. Blackman, and ½ buildings:
Daughter Joanna Pierce wife of William Pierce of Taunton, County Bristol, 2£ 2s:
Six grand children, William, Ephraim. Joanna. Samuel, Benajah, & Experience, children of William and Joanna Pierce 1£ 10s each;
Son Jabez Doggett, ½ lot in 16 shilling purchase;
Gives Son Simeon Doggett, all the other real estate not disposed of and all my rights to Iron ore in Assawamscott Pond and elsewhere in Middleboro.
witnessed by Sylvanus, Andrew & Ichabod Wood.

3605. AMOS DOGGETT[4] (*Samuel*,[3] *Samuel*,[2] *Thomas*[1]), born Marshfield, Mass.. May 25, 1710; died Marshfield, Mass. (?), May (?), 1737.

Capt. Amos Doggett, the oldest son of Samuel and Bethia Doggett, was born in Marshfield. He was a "mariner," and died at the age of twenty-seven years.

June 2, 1737. The judge of probate appoints Mr. Samuel Doggett, of Marshfield, administrator on the estate of his son Amos Doggett. [Plymouth Probate, 7–363.]

Marshfield, May 28, 1739. Then we the subscribers made an appraisement of these things underwritten of Capt. Amos Doggett, deceased, viz.:

To one Cloath Coat 300s, £15; Cloath Britches 37s, £1 17s; 1 Banyan Coat 100s, £5; 1 Cloth Coat 70s, £3 10s; 1 West coat 15s, 15s; 1 pr silk stockings 20s, £1; 1 pr old silk stockings 8s; 1 Wigg 40s, £2; 1 Flowered Westcoat 100s, £5; 1 pr Thread Stockings 20s, £1; 1 pr old silk Stockings 10s, 10s; 2 Caps 15s. 15s; 2 Neckings 12s, 12s; 1 Holland Shirt 30s, £1 10s; 1 Shirt 80s, £4; 1 Trunck 12s, 12s: £43 9s.

May 28, 1739.

Samuel Rogers, Thomas White & John Tilden oath as to just appraisment.

before JOHN CUSHING Judge of Probate.

May 28, 1739.

Samuel Doggett administrator on the estate of Amos Doggett, made oath that the above Inventory is all the estate of ye deceased that he Knows of.

3606. LYDIA DOGGETT[4] (*Samuel*,[3] *Samuel*,[2] *Thomas*[1]), born Marshfield, Mass., —— 3, 1712; died Plainfield, Conn. (?), March 8, 1790; married Marshfield, Mass. (?), 1732, Samuel Clift, son of William and Lydia Clift; born Marshfield, Mass., October 22, 1709; died Griswold, Conn., August 22, 1794.

Issue:

3684. i. RHODA CLIFT,[5] born Marshfield, Mass., August 29, 1733; died Marshfield, Mass., December 22, 1737.

3685. ii. RHODA CLIFT,[5] born Marshfield, Mass., April 29, 1735; died Marshfield, Mass., September 5, 1739.

3686. iii. AMOS CLIFT,[5] born Marshfield, Mass., September 20, 1737; married 1st, February 12, 1761, Mary Coit; she died July 20, 1790; married 2d, Mrs. Anna Avery, widow, daughter of John and Abigail Denison, of Stonington, Conn.; he died Griswold, Conn., July 29, 1806.

3687. iv. MARY CLIFT,[5] born Marshfield, Mass., October 7, 1738.

3688. v. LEMUEL CLIFT,[5] born Marshfield, Mass., April 20, 1740; died Marshfield, Mass., February 14, 1741.

3689. vi. WATERMAN CLIFT,[5] born Marshfield, Mass., December 28, 1741.

3690. vii. BETHIAH CLIFT,[5] born Marshfield, Mass., February 21, 1744; married Elias Woodward, of Plainfield, Conn.; issue: thirteen children; she died February 5, 1795.

3691. viii. WILLS CLIFT,[5] born Marshfield, Mass., July 18, 1745; married 1st, Mary Shepherd, of Plainfield, Conn.; married 2d, Hannah Benedict; married 3d, Mrs. Mary Hazard; he died Westport, Conn., April 29, 1810.

3692. ix. DEBORAH CLIFT,[5] born Plainfield, Conn. (?), June 6, 1749; probably died young.

3693. x. JOSEPH CLIFT,[5] born Plainfield, Conn. (?), September 13, 1750.

3694. xi. LEMUEL CLIFT,[5] born Plainfield, Conn. (?), October 10, 1755.

William Clift, Esq., of Stonington, Conn., says: " Samuel Clift removed to Plainfield, Conn., probably about 1745, as Wills is the last child baptized in Marshfield. He lived on the Jerry Kinsman place, and died at the house of his son Amos, in Griswold. Samuel and Lydia Clift are buried in the old burial-ground in Plainfield, Conn., near the south wall."

3608. SARAH DOGGETT[4] (*Samuel*,[3] *Samuel*,[2] *Thomas*[1]), born Marshfield, Mass., October, 1716; died Marshfield, Mass., Jan. 22,

1794 ; married Marshfield, Mass. (?), previous to 1738, Edward Oakman, son of Tobias and Elizabeth (Doty) Oakman, of Marshfield ; born Marshfield, Mass., 1716 ; died Marshfield, Mass., May 28, 1791.

Issue :

3695. i.   ELIZABETH OAKMAN,[5] born Marshfield, Mass., September 20, 1738 ; died Marshfield, Mass.
3696. ii.   BETHIAH OAKMAN,[5] born Marshfield, Mass., Dec. 10, 1739 ; married Marshfield, Mass., Jan. 22, 1761, William, son of William Stevens.
3697. iii. SARAH OAKMAN,[5] born Marshfield, Mass., October 12, 1741 ; married Samuel Lothrop.
3698. iv.   JOHN OAKMAN,[5] born Marshfield, Mass., June 29, 1743 ; died.
3699. v.   SAMUEL OAKMAN,[5] born Marshfield, Mass., September 18, 1745.
3700. vi.   JOSEPH OAKMAN,[5] born Marshfield, Mass., April 28, 1749 ; " sea captain ; " died and was buried on Arrowsic island, Me., 1776.
3701. vii. TOBIAS OAKMAN,[5] born Marshfield, Mass., March 13, 1751 ; " sea captain," privateer in Revolution, and taken prisoner, 1778 ; in Boston, 1784 (see " Boston Globe," Jan. 1, 1884) ; married Olive Little.
3702. viii. ALICE OAKMAN,[5] born Marshfield, Mass., June 10, 1753 ; died Pembroke, Mass.
3703. ix.   ABIAH OAKMAN,[5] born Marshfield, Mass., April 26, 1756 ; married December 13, 1781, Asa Rogers.
3704. x.   AMOS OAKMAN,[5] born Marshfield, Mass., January 26, 1759.

Edward Oakman and Sarah, his wife, are buried near the church, in the cemetery of the Second Congregational Society of Marshfield, near the village of East Marshfield.

Their gravestones are in a good state of preservation, and the inscriptions were kindly copied by Col. H. A. Oakman, of Marshfield :

> In memory of Mr Edward Oakman who died
> May 28, 1791, in the 75th year of his age.
>
> Old age with all her dismal train,
>   Invades our golden years,
> With sighs and groans and raging pains,
>   And death which never spares.
>
> In memory of Mrs Sarah Oakman wife of
> Mr Edward Oakman, who died Jan. 22, 1794 in the
> 78th year of her age.
>
> Stoop down my tho'ts that used to rise
>   Converse awhile with death,
> Think how a gasping mortal lies,
>   And pants away his breath.

3609. BETHIA DOGGETT[4] (*Samuel*,[3] *Samuel*,[2] *Thomas*[1]), born Marshfield, Mass., 1718 ; married Boston, Mass., September 27, 1749, by Rev. Andrew Eliot, D.D., to Robert Kinsman, of Norwich, Conn., son of Robert and Rebecca (Burley) Kinsman, of Norwich ; born Ipswich, Mass., May 3, 1713 ; died December 16, 1788.

Issue (possibly) :

3705. i. PELATIAH KINSMAN,[5] born 1750 ; died Boston, Mass., April 2, 1797.

3610. Capt. SAMUEL DOGGETT[4] (*Samuel*,[3] *Samuel*,[2] *Thomas*[1]), born Marshfield, Mass., 1720 ; died Boston, Mass., April 24, 1781 ;

married Boston, Mass., June 21, 1753, by Rev. Charles Chauncy, to Esther Fairfield, daughter of William and Elizabeth (White) Fairfield, of Boston, Mass.; born Wenham, Mass., February 5, 1729; died Boston, Mass., January, 1812.

Issue:

3706. i. BETHIAH DOGGETT,[5] born Boston, Mass., February, 1754; bapt. First Church, February 24, 1754; died young.
3707. ii. SAMUEL DOGGETT,[5] born Boston, Mass., May 16, 1755.
3708. iii. WILLIAM DOGGETT,[5] born Boston, Mass., April 3, 1757.
3709. iv. ELIZABETH DOGGETT,[5] born Boston, Mass., May 22, 1759.
3710. v. SARAH DOGGETT,[5] born Boston. Mass., December 31, 1761; bapt. First Church, January 3, 1762; died young.
3711. vi. SARAH DOGGETT,[5] born Boston, Mass., October 1, 1767.

Capt. Samuel Doggett, mariner and merchant, married, in 1753, Esther Fairfield, of Boston, granddaughter of William Fairfield, of Wenham, Mass., who was a representative for twenty-seven years, and in 1741 speaker of the House.

Her brother, Rev. John Fairfield, H.C., 1757, was for many years minister at Saco.

After 1757 they lived for several years in a house which Captain Doggett bought on Marlboro' street, now a part of Washington street, Boston; an extract of the deed of which is as follows:

Henderson Inches of Boston, merchant, for 240£ sells Samuel Doggett of Boston, mariner, Dwelling house on Marlboro St in Southerly part of Boston, 17 ft 11 in on Marlboro St, Aug 6, 1757. [Suffolk Deeds, 91–26.]

Captain Doggett seems to have inherited his father's interest in the Wiscasset Company, and in the settlement of their lands at Sheepscott. January 26, 1762, the company's records mention: "Samuel Doggett paid for his lot letter A."

As a mariner he was doubtless well posted in the country near the coast of Maine, and invested in land which at that time seemed a most promising locality (the neighborhood of the Kennebec), as appears in the following extract:

Francis Whitmore of Medford in County of Middlesex Mass, Merchant for 390£ lawful money paid by Samuel Doggett of Boston, County of Suffolk, mariner, land in Bowdoinham, west side of Kennebec, near Swan Island, 800 acres, Feb. 21, 1765. [Lincoln Deeds, 4–32.]

The records indicate that from this time until his death he devoted much time and money to the development of this land.

He had houses and barns built, and it is possible his family spent a portion of each season there.

At the meetings of the Wiscasset Company, in Boston, October 20 and 27, November 21, and December 29, 1767, Capt. Samuel Doggett is mentioned as present; and at the October 27 meeting as being elected collector of taxes for the company.

At the company's meetings in 1768 he is mentioned as present January 5 and 19, March 10, 22, and 29, April 1 and 6, June 21, July 14 and 26, August 9, and October 5. At the April 6 meeting the following vote was passed, which explains itself:

> April 6, 1768 Whereas it appears by the clerks account that Capt. Samuel Doggett now deceased stands charged with the sum of 10£ O.T. for sundry Taxes. of his Lands and as it has been suggested by his heirs that the same has been paid although they cannot find a Receipt therefor, and there being some reason to think that by some mistake credit was not given for it when paid, Voted that the heirs of said Capt Doggett and his estate be discharged of said sum of 10£.
>
> At the same meeting it was also voted that A. Johonnot be paid by Capt. Samuel Doggett to be sent to Mr. James Sullivan, &c.

Capt. Samuel Doggett was present at the company's meetings in Boston, in 1769, April 26, August 9 and 10, November 14, 17, and 21, and December 12. At the meeting August 10 a sale of land of delinquent proprietors was held, at which he bought Lot No. 33, containing one hundred and twelve acres and one hundred and thirty-four rods, which belonged to the heirs of Charles Frost.

At the meetings in 1770 he was present January 2, March 12 and 13, May 1, October 23 and 26, November 19, 23, and 27, and December 25.

In 1771, present on March 6 and 18, June 4, 12, 17, 18, 22, and 24, July 19, August 29, September 12, November 12 and 25, acting as moderator at the meeting March 18.

At the meetings in 1772, present February 17, March 11, May 19, July 20 and 23, September 1, October 20, and November 30, acting as moderator March 11 and November 30, and being mentioned May 19 as follows: "Voted Taxes must be paid to Capt Samuel Doggett collector of Taxes for the Company."

In 1773, present January 19 and 25, February 2, 16, and 26, May 5, 10, and 31, August 24 and 30, and September 2. At the February 16 meeting it was "Voted, that 2½ % be allowed Capt Samuel Doggett, collector of Taxes for the Company, for all monies he has collected." At the meeting May 5 he acted as moderator.

In 1774, present January 4, February 1, March 1 and 29, May 17, September 27, and November 29; at all of which meetings, excepting the first and last, he acted as moderator. The last meeting at which he was present was the one held in Boston January 3, 1775.

By the will of William Fairfield (his father-in-law), dated May 11, 1770, he was named as one of the executors. [Suffolk Probate, 69–116.]

It was the custom in those days for the selectmen, accompanied by the governor, school committee, and prominent citizens, to make periodical visits to inspect the public schools, and it is in this connection that we first find his name on the town records as visiting the several public schools on Wednesday, July 10, 1771.

At a town meeting held at Faneuil Hall March 14, 1774, twelve wardens were chosen for the ensuing year, among whom is the name of Capt. Samuel Doggett. Monday, November 11, 1776, at a town meeting, sixty persons were chosen for collecting an account of the damages sustained since the Boston Port Bill, of whom from Ward 10 was Capt. Samuel Doggett. Captain Doggett's house, on Marlboro' street, was built of wood and called in the records his "Mansion House." He attended church at the "Old Brick" or First Church, which was then located where Rogers Building now stands. His wife received the covenant there, February 10, 1754.

In the Suffolk Probate, 80–206, is the will of Capt. Samuel Doggett. It is as follows:

In the name of God, Amen, I, Samuel Doggett of Boston in the county of Suffolk and Commonwealth of Mass. Mariner, being sick and weak in Body but through the Goodness of God of sound and disposing mind and memory and considering that I must shortly Die, Do make and ordain this my last Will as follows, that is to say,

First and Principally, I commend my precious and immortal Soul into the hands of God who gave it relying Solely on his mercy through the Merits and Satisfaction of my only Lord and Saviour Jesus Christ for the Pardon of all my sins and Gracious acceptance with him, My Body I commit to the earth to be decently Interred at the discretion of my executors hereinafter named, nothing doubting but at the General Resurrection I shall receive the same again by the mighty power of God. And as for such Worldly Estate as it hath pleased God to bless me with I will and order that the same be disposed of in the following manner, That is to say —

Imprimis, I will and order that all my Just debts and Funeral Expences be well and truly paid by my Executors with all convenient speed after my decease.

Item — I give to my wife Esther the Income, use and Improvement of one third part of all the Remainder of my Estate both Real and Personal whatsoever and wheresoever the same is, shall or may be found for and during the Term of her Natural Life.

Item — I give devise and Bequeath unto my youngest daughter Sarah, Two fifths part of all of my estate both real and personal whatsoever and wheresoever the same is, shall or may be found to be holden by her, her heirs and assigns forever.

Item — The remaining three fifths parts of all my estate both real and personal whatsoever and wheresoever the same is, shall or may be found, I give Devise and Bequeath to among my other three children, namely Samuel and William Doggett and Elizabeth Miers wife of Marcus Miers to be holden by them, their heirs and assigns in equal third parts forever.

Item — I do hereby appoint my said wife Esther and my said two sons Samuel and William to be the executors of this my will, hereby revoking all other wills by me at any time heretofore made, declaring this and no other to be my last will and Testament.

In Witness whereof, I the said Samuel Doggett have hereunto set my hand and seal, the 23rd day of April, In the year of our Lord 1781.

SAMUEL DOGGETT (Seal)

Signed sealed published and
declared by the said Samuel Doggett
the testator to be his last will and
testament in the presence of

ISAAC GREENWOOD.
JOHN CLARKE.
HENRY ALLINE.

Proved, May 8, 1781.

May 22, 1781, an inventory of the estate of Capt. Samuel Doggett in the county of Suffolk was taken [Suffolk Probate, 80–234], which amounted to £651 6s. 1d.

This inventory of the personal effects in the " Mansion House " on Marlboro' street enables one to note the style of furnishing at that day.

A return of the inventory of all the estate that could be found in the county of Lincoln belonging to Capt. Samuel Doggett late of Boston was made June 10, 1782, and amounted to £1057 13s. 4d. [Suffolk Probate, 84–242.]

August 30, 1782. The real estate of Samuel Doggett was divided by setting off to the widow her dower. [Suffolk Probate, 82–699.]

Two accounts were afterward returned in relation to the settlement of the estate [Suffolk Probate, 84–243 and 85–738], the last one including the sale of 521 acres of land, which was sold at auction April 10, 1786, and the return dated April 27, 1786.

Esther Doggett, the wife of Capt. Samuel Doggett, sold all her rights in the estate on Hanover street, near Friend street, which she inherited from her father, on July 13, 1780. [Suffolk Deeds, 131–228.]

Benjamin White, of Brookline, Mass., the son of Edward White, by his wife Hannah Wiswall, was born October 5, 1724.

His first wife was Elizabeth Aspinwall, by whom he had four sons and one daughter.

January 17, 1783. Benjamin White bought of his cousin Esther Doggett the estate on Devonshire street which she inherited from her father. [Suffolk Deeds, 160–48.]

April 11, 1787. She makes over to Benjamin White, of Brookline, her dower in the estate of her late husband Samuel Doggett, on account of a note given said White by her, dated October 7, 1784. [Suffolk Deeds, 160–48.]

August 5, 1788. Marriage settlement between Esther Doggett and Benjamin White, she to have the use of house in Devonshire and Marlboro streets in case said White dies. [Suffolk Deeds, 168–109.]

Benjamin White and Esther Doggett were married in Brookline, Oct. 27, 1788, at the First Church. Benjamin White died in Brookline, May 10, 1790.

Esther his widow remained in Brookline until 1791 or 1792, when she removed to Boston, where she resided until her death.

3611. JOSEPH DOGGETT[4] (*Samuel*,[3] *Samuel*,[2] *Thomas*[1]), born Marshfield, Mass., 1722.

" Account of the charges of the Transport vessels employed in the service of his Majesties Garrison at Louisburg after the reduction of the place exclusive of such as were Laden with stores by orders from the Admiral & General.

" Sloop Dolphin. J. Doggett, 6 men, July 8 to Nov 8 54£ wages of sailors, 24 days term of victualling 80£ paid for hire of vessel.

" Approved Nov 19, 1746." [State Archives of Mass., 72–737.]

3612. Capt. NOAH DOGGETT[4] (*Samuel*,[3] *Samuel*,[2] *Thomas*[1]), born Marshfield, Mass.. 1727; died Boston, Mass., October 18,

1805; married 1st, Boston, Mass., November 8, 1753, by Rev. Samuel Cooper, to Mary Clark, daughter of James and Rebecca (Newmarsh) Clark; born Boston, Mass., July 8, 1733; died Boston, Mass., March 8, 1761; married 2d, Boston, Mass., October 10, 1762, by Rev. Samuel Checkley, to Mary Alline, daughter of Henry and Jane (Swett) Alline; born Boston, Mass., May 25, 1735; died Boston, Mass., August 11, 1824.

Issue:

3712. i.   JOSEPH DOGGETT,[5] born Boston, Mass., August 16, 1754.
3713. ii.   BETHIAH DOGGETT,[5] born Boston, Mass., August 22, 1756.
3714. iii. NOAH DOGGETT,[5] born Boston, Mass., April 6, 1758; died young.
3715. iv. AMOS DOGGETT,[5] born Boston, Mass., January 7, 1764; died young.
3716. v.   MARY DOGGETT,[5] born Boston, Mass., March 12, 1765; died Boston, Mass., October 29, 1777.
3717. vi. HENRY DOGGETT,[5] born Boston, Mass., February 15, 1767.
3718. vii. JANE DOGGETT,[5] born Boston, Mass., January 27, 1769; died Boston, Mass , September 24, 1769.
3719. viii. NOAH DOGGETT,[5] born Boston, Mass., October 1, 1770.
3720. ix. SAMUEL DOGGETT,[5] born Boston, Mass., August 31, 1772.
3721. x.   LYDIA DOGGETT,[5] born Newburyport, Mass., October 14, 1775; died Boston, Mass., August 7, 1815.

Capt. Noah Doggett, son of Capt. Samuel Doggett, inherited from his father that love for travel which led him to become what was then called a mariner.

His father died when he was but eighteen years of age, and two years afterward he had the misfortune to lose his mother, so he was left an orphan at twenty.

He constitutes his uncle Kenelm Winslow, of Boston, brazier, as his guardian during his minority, which instrument is recorded in Suffolk Probate, 39–279. In this paper he says:

I, Noah Doggett, a minor aged about 19 years, son of Samuel Doggett late of Boston in the County of Suffolk in N.E. mariner, deceased — and — signed and sealed May 5, 1747.

The bond was for £100, and was signed by Kenelm Winslow, brazier, Jacob Hurd, goldsmith, and William Baker, shop-keeper. The records at the Boston Custom House having been removed by the British when they evacuated the town, they are not at present accessible to enable one to search for papers to show in what vessels Captain Doggett sailed, to what ports, and at what dates. January 21, 1750 or 1752, he was in London, Eng., and bought a book, now in the possession of the writer, on the fly-leaf of which he wrote his name, "bought in London on Tower Hill, price 10£," and the date (one of the dates named above). The title of the book is "The English Pilot, the 4th book, Describing the West India Navigation from Hudson's Bay to the River Amazones, Pub London. Printed for W. & T. Mount and T. Page on Tower Hill, MDCCXLIX."

A memorandum on one of the pages gives latitude and longitude against the date May 3, 1760, which might indicate he was near the Azores at that time. The family Bible in the possession of the writer is inscribed " Noah Doggett, his Bible, bought in Bristol, Sept 21, 1764, price 20/." It was printed by " Thomas Baskett, Oxford, MDCCLXI," and shows that he was again across the water.

As an indication of what may have been a portion of his cargo on his return trip in 1764, the writer has in his possession a glass seal which was given him in 1886 by Mrs. Elizabeth D. Clapp, of Dedham, Mass. It was found about 1864 in the garden of Jesse Clap, who married Betsey Doggett, High street, Dedham, Mass.

The seal is about one and a half inches in diameter, of olive green, and indicates that it once formed a portion of a bottle. On it is :

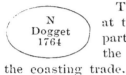

The chart book shows evidence of having been used at the pages giving the coasts of the Carolinas, and particularly off Hatteras, which would seem to prove the family tradition that he engaged at one time in the coasting trade.

Regarding his home life, he is supposed to have lived during the life of his first wife in the northerly part of Boston. Her family attended the Brattle-street Church, and they were married by its minister, Rev. Samuel Cooper, whose diary speaks of the marriage, and that he received a fee of $1 for his services.

In the Granary Burial-ground in Boston, near the spot where his mother was buried, is a gravestone to the memory of this first wife, and inscribed as follows :

Here lies the Body of
Mrs Mary Doggett
wife of Mr Noah
Doggett who died
March ye 18, 1761
In the 27th year
of her age.

Captain Doggett married 2d, Mary Alline, who belonged to an old Boston family, and whose father and brother were for many years registers of deeds for Suffolk county. The family lived on Sea street, now called Federal street, nearly opposite where now stands the New York & New England station. May 13, 1767, Captain Doggett bought a house and land just beyond that occupied by the Allines, on Sea street, the house standing on the site of the present Essex-street extension. He bought the estate of William Faris, for £240 (Suffolk Deeds, 110–164), but although owned by Faris it was still occupied by the family of Knox, who had previously owned it.

Henry Knox, the seventh of ten sons, was born in this house, and became prominent as a general in the Revolution.

Captain Doggett and family moved to the house as soon as the

HOUSE OF CAPT. NOAH DOGGETT, SEA ST., BOSTON, MASS., 1767

Knox family had removed, and it was his home for the rest of his life.

It was then a most delightful spot, the lawn in front extending to the roadway some thirty feet, while the house itself, several feet higher than the street, overlooked the beach and harbor beyond. The neighborhood was the best, and the house situated quite near the New South Church, where the family attended worship.

December 11, 1763, Mary (Alline) Doggett entered into full communion at this church, and Captain Doggett did the same May 2, 1784. September 21, 1784, he bought pew No. 57, for £9 lawful, of Dea. John Preston, and received his deed from a committee of the proprietors.

The period of the Revolution proved very disastrous to Captain Doggett, and tradition tells of the loss of his vessels by seizure and decay.

During the siege of Boston, his house was in such an exposed position the family closed it, and visited in Newburyport.

Some of the British officers, finding the house deserted, used it as their headquarters until the evacuation. After the war, Captain Doggett, owing to his losses, was unable to again take up his vocation of "mariner," and therefore established himself as a shop-keeper. The Boston Directory for 1796, 1798, 1800, 1805, mentions him as Noah Doggett, captain, Sea street.

Captain Noah Doggett, personally, is spoken of as a man of commanding presence; his face had a stern expression; he had great will-power.

He was a man of but few words, very careful that all his expressions were true, an upright and just man, beloved and respected by his fellow-men. In his declining years he was comforted by his wife and children in his mansion house overlooking the sea, where he died in 1805. He was buried in a tomb, probably in the Granary Burial-ground, as appears by a bill of Edward Vannevar, in the possession of the writer, which makes a charge for opening the tomb, tolling the bells, and for the interment.

His wife, Mary (Alline) Doggett, died in 1824, at the house of her son, corner of Hollis and Tremont streets, and was buried in tomb No. 182 in the Granary Ground.

In Suffolk Probate, No. 22,501, is the will of Capt. Noah Doggett, as follows:

In the name of God Amen, I Noah Doggett of Boston in the County of Suffolk and Commonwealth of Massachusetts, shop keeper, being in good health of Body and through the goodness of God, of sound disposing mind and memory and considering the uncertainty of life do make and ordain this my last Will and Testament as follows,

Imprimis, I will and order that all my just debts and funeral expenees be well and truly paid by my Executrix with all convenient speed after my decease.

Item, I give to my six children, namely Joseph, Bethia, Henry, Noah, Samuel & Lydia two dollars each.

Item, All the rest, residue and remainder of my estate, Real, and Personal whatsoever and wheresoever the same is shall or may be found, I give devise and bequeath to my well beloved wife Mary, to be holden by her, her heirs and assigns forever.

Item : I do hereby nominate and appoint my said wife Mary to be the sole Executrix of this my last will, hereby revoking, making null and void, all former and other wills by me at any time heretofore made, declaring this and no other to be my last Will and Testament.

In witness, whereof I the said Noah Doggett have hereunto set my hand and seal, this tenth day of April in the year of our Lord one thousand eight hundred.

Noah Doggett [Seal].

Signed, sealed, published, pronounced and declared by the said Noah Doggett the testator, to be his last Will and Testament, in presence of us, who in his presence and in the presence of each other hereto subscribe our names.

Joshua Thaxter, Elisha Hunt, Thomas Somes.   Proved Dec. 16, 1805.

3622. JOHN ALLEN [4] (*Sarah Doggett*,[3] *Samuel*,[2] *Thomas* [1]), born Braintree, Mass., May 19, 1711 ; married 1st, Rebecca ——— ; died Braintree, Mass., August 14, 1739 ; married 2d, Braintree, Mass., December 20, 1739, Mary Bushnel.

Issue :

3722. i. SILENCE ALLEN,[5] born Braintree, Mass., February 12, 173⅞.
3723. ii. JOHN ALLEN,[5] born Braintree, Mass., June 19, 1742.

3625. SARAH ALLEN [4] (*Sarah Doggett*,[3] *Samuel*,[2] *Thomas* [1]), born Braintree, Mass., March 4, 17$\frac{18}{19}$; married Braintree, Mass., November 21, 1734, Benjamin Copeland.

Issue :

3724. i. BENJAMIN COPELAND,[5] born Braintree, Mass., 1736.
3725. ii. SARAH COPELAND,[5] born Braintree, Mass., 1738.
3726. iii. WILLIAM COPELAND,[5] born Norton, Mass.
3727. iv. MOSES COPELAND,[5] born Norton, Mass.
3728. v. SAMUEL COPELAND,[5] born Norton, Mass.
3729. vi. ASA COPELAND,[5] born Norton, Mass.

3628. EBENEZER DOGGETT [4] (*Ebenezer*,[3] *Samuel*,[2] *Thomas* [1]), born Plymouth, Mass., July 17, 1726 ; died Liverpool, N.S. (?) ; married Plymouth, Mass., January 5, 174$\frac{8}{9}$, Elizabeth Brace, of Plymouth.

Issue :

3730. i. ELIZABETH DOGGETT,[5] born Plymouth, Mass., November 9, 1749.
3731. ii. BATHSHEBA DOGGETT,[5] born Plymouth, Mass., August 4, 1751; died Plymouth, Mass., October 6, 1751.
3732. iii. EBENEZER DOGGETT,[5] born Plymouth, Mass., August 25, 1754 ; married Plymouth, Mass., May 6, 1778, by Rev. Chandler Robbins, to Lydia Holmes.

3733. iv. THOMAS DOGGETT,[5] born Boston, Mass., December 19, 1756; bapt.
First Church, December 26, 1756.
3734. v. WILLIAM DOGGETT,[5] born Boston. Mass., August 3, 1759; bapt. First
Church, August 12, 1759; will dated September 3, 1795; leaves his
property to his brother, Seth Doggett; "tailor;" bond dated July
10, 1798. [Suffolk Probate.]
3735. vi. SETH DOGGETT.[5]

Mr. Ebenezer Doggett moved from Plymouth to Boston about
1756. They had belonged to the church in Plymouth, and on arriving in Boston attended the First Church. They lived in a house
toward "Oliver's Dock," where they were burned out in the great
Boston fire of March 10, 1760.

About 1761 Ebenezer Doggett removed with his family to Liverpool, N.S., to which place his brother Samuel had previously gone.

The grant of the township of Liverpool was not passed until
November 20, 1764, and was then made to one hundred and forty-two
proprietors, one share being reserved for the Church of England and
one for schools.

The eighth name in this list is Ebenezer Doggett.

A letter written by him is dated Liverpool, March 1, 1767 (now
in the possession of George Sampson, Esq., 1889). It relates to his
daughter Elizabeth, and will be found under her name.

Ebenezer Doggett witnessed a deed at Liverpool Feb 3, 1767 and again Feb
24, 1768.
Feb 25, 1768 exchanges 30 acre lots with John Wall. [Queens Deeds, 1–191.]
Oct. 10, 1770 Ebenezer Doggett, Gentleman buys of William Hadley, Gent, a
lot in town of Liverpool. [Queens Deeds, 1–292.]
Oct 17, 1770 Ebenezer Doggett of Liverpool, Joiner, sells Benj. Gerrish of
Halifax, ½ acre land on King St. [Queens Deeds, 1–350.]

3629. SAMUEL DOGGETT [4] (*Ebenezer,*[3] *Samuel,*[2] *Thomas* [1]), born
Plymouth, Mass., January 20, 172⅜; died Liverpool, N.S. (?), previous to November 9, 1773; married Plymouth, Mass., May 6, 1756,
by Rev. Jacob Bacon, to Deborah Foster, of Plymouth, daughter of
Thomas and Lois (Fuller) Foster; born Plymouth, Mass., 1737.

Issue:

3736. i. DEBORAH DOGGETT,[5] born Plymouth. Mass., August 8, 1758; married
Mr. Gardner; resided cor. Front and Wolff streets, Liverpool, N.S.
3737. ii. SAMUEL DOGGETT,[5] born Liverpool, N.S.; of Liverpool; "mariner;"
August 21, 1788.
3738. iii. THOMAS FOSTER DOGGETT,[5] born Liverpool, N.S.; of Liverpool;
"yeoman:" August 21, 1788.
3739. iv. CATHARINE DOGGETT,[5] born Liverpool, N.S.
3740. v. BETSEY DOGGETT,[5] born Liverpool. N.S., September 24, 1767.
3741. vi. LOIS DOGGETT,[5] born Liverpool, N.S.; married Israel Cole; resided
Liverpool, N.S.

Samuel Doggett, a minor, aged about nineteen years, son of Ebenezer Doggett, late of Boston, in County of Suffolk, in New England,

mariner, appoints Jesse White, of Marshfield, in county of Plymouth, mariner, his guardian, June 22, 1747. [Suffolk Probate, 40–10.]

Soon after his marriage he removed to Liverpool, N.S., of which place he was one of the first settlers. In 1759 a warrant of survey was issued by Governor Lawrence, the wording of which begins as follows:

" Whereas John Doggett, Elisha Freeman, Samuel Doggett and Thomas Foster on behalf of themselves and the other persons hereinafter mentioned, have made application to me for a township within this Province, and have undertaken a speedy and effectual settlement of said township," etc. In 1761 he was one of a committee of five appointed to lay out the lands.

The grant of the township to one hundred and forty-two persons was made November 20, 1764, and he is named the fourth one in the list.

Soon after the decease of Samuel Doggett, his widow wrote a letter which is now (1889) in the possession of Benj. Drew, Esq., and which was found in the house of his grandfather, of the same name:

LIVERPOOL Nov 26, 1773

DEAR SISTER:

I having an opportunity, embrace it, to let you know that I am well and the children that are with me but how it is with them that are there with you God only knows. I have been much distressed about my dear child that is with you but I hope he is recovered. My father and my brother wrote that you was all very tender of him for which I return you my thanks and hope God will reward you for your goodness to him, it is not in my power to make you any satisfaction. Do write to me by Capt. Drew and let me know how he has been if still alive or if God has taken him from me, be very particular in telling me how he was, Oh! Betsey I hope you will never see such a day of darkness and sorrow as I now see. What a sweet, kind, pleasant companion I have lost but I must be dumb and not open my mouth for it is the Lord that has done it I am so overwhelmed with my trouble that I know not what I have written but I know you will excuse me. With my duty to your mother and love to your spous and self so I conclude. Your loving sister

DEBORAH DOGGETT.

A search of the county records at Liverpool, N.S., shows the following items regarding Samuel Doggett:

Edward Doten sells Samuel Doggett, mariner, 30 acre lot in Liverpool March 29, 1762. [Queens Deeds, 1–206.]

Samuel Doggett of Liverpool sells $\frac{1}{16}$th part of 100 acres of land granted by the proprietors of Liverpool, part of Sawmill, dam, iron, timber, to Simeon Perkins Nov. 10, 1764. [Queens Deeds, 1–183.]

Robt Slocombe of Liverpool sells Samuel Doggett, Gentleman, $\frac{1}{6}$th of a saw mill Dec 8, 1766. [Queens Deeds, 1–187.] also the same parties for lot of land at Moose Harbor, a 30 acre lot in Liverpool Feb 24, 1768. [Queens Deeds, 1–189.]

Samuel Doggett of Liverpool Gentleman, sells Mr Hawkins of Liverpool, merchant lot in Liverpool 29 April 1768. [Queens Deeds, 1–208.]

Samuel Doggett of Liverpool, Gentleman, sells a fish lot in Liverpool to S. Perkins April 1, 1771. [Queens Deeds, 1–312.] Samuel Doggett of Liverpool

Esquire sells, ⅙ Saw mill in Liverpool to Samuel Saunders of Salem, N.E. 29 Sept, 1772. [Queens Deeds, 1–371.]

Samuel Doggett died in 1773, and his widow was appointed administratrix of his estate.

9 Nov 1773 — Administration granted to widow Deborah Doggett on goods &c of Samuel Doggett Esq. [Queens Probate, 1–33.]

11 June 1775 Allowance to Mrs Deborah Doggett widow and administratrix to the intestate Estate of Samuel Doggett late of Liverpool deceased, of personal effects. [Queens Probate, 1–37.]

16 August 1776 ⅓rd rent or profit of ⅙ part of a saw mill at East side of main river in Liverpool allowed to Deborah Doggett widow of Samuel Doggett as her dower. [Queens Probate, 1–43.]

The widow Deborah Doggett then began the sale of a large amount of land in her possession, and between June 14, 1775, and May 10, 1797, recorded in the Records of Deeds, at Liverpool, N.S., the sale of eleven different tracts, nearly one thousand acres in all.

The house and land which she deeds to her sons is described as once the property built and occupied by Samuel Doggett, Esq., late of Liverpool, deceased, located below Fore street, in Liverpool, in which she is then residing, and in deeding it reserves right to certain rooms during life.

3631. Elizabeth Doggett [4] (*Ebenezer,*[3] *Samuel,*[2] *Thomas*[1]), born Marshfield, Mass., May 14, 1738; died Plymouth, Mass., December 6, 1798; married Plympton, Mass., November 22, 1764, Benjamin Drew.

Issue:

3742. i.   Elizabeth Drew,[5] born Plymouth, Mass., December 2, 1765.
3743. ii.   Benjamin Drew,[5] born Plymouth, Mass., February 7, 1767.
3744. iii. Bathsheba Drew,[5] born Plymouth, Mass., March 17, 1768; died Plymouth, Mass., March 29, 1768.
3745. iv.   Ebenezer Drew,[5] born Plymouth, Mass., December 21, 1769; died Plymouth, Mass., August 27, 1771.
3746. v.   Margaret Drew,[5] born Plymouth, Mass., July 30, 1771.
3747. vi.   Ebenezer Drew,[5] born Plymouth, Mass., May 1, 1773; married March or April. 1799, Deborah Ransom, of Carver, Mass.; he died Plymouth, Mass., January 6, 1851; no issue.
3748. vii. Malachi Drew,[5] born Plymouth, Mass., November 10, 1774; died Plymouth, Mass., February 22, 1863.
3749. viii. Desire Drew,[5] born Plymouth, Mass., September 21, 1776; died Plymouth, Mass., November 15, 1805.
3750. ix.   Simeon Drew,[5] born Plymouth, Mass., May 24, 1780; died Plymouth, Mass., November 1, 1815.

Elizabeth Doggett, whose birth is recorded at Marshfield as Bethia, had a guardian, Isaac Smith, of Boston, wharfinger, appointed April 1, 1748.

Miss Fanny Drew, of Plymouth, writes of her grandmother: " I used to hear that before her marriage she and her mother lived in Plympton." They resided after marriage on North street, near Cole's Hill, Plymouth.

3635. SAMUEL DOGGETT[4] (*John,*[3] *Samuel,*[2] *Thomas*[1]), born Marshfield, Mass., February 3, 172⅔; died Coventry, Conn., August 24, 1798; married Lebanon, Conn., April 17, 1754, Ann Bushnell; born April 28, 1733; died Andover, Conn., January 28, 1832.

Issue (called Daggett):

3751. i. ASENATH DAGGETT,[5] born Coventry, Conn., January 2, 1755.
3752. ii. TABITHA DAGGETT,[5] born Coventry, Conn., April 5, 1757.
3753. iii. ISAIAH DAGGETT,[5] born 1759.

The church records of Marshfield contain the baptism of Samuel, as follows: "March 6, 172⅔ John Dogget and his wife had a son baptized called Samuel."

The town records of Lebanon give the date of his marriage and his name spelled "Dogget," while the town records of Coventry, which contain the births of his children as returned to me by the town clerk, spell the name in all cases "Daggett."

Mr. Doggett was in the army and stationed near the State House in New London in May, 1777.

After Mrs. Doggett was eighty years old she worked a bed spread for each of her grandchildren, in crewels of her own make and coloring. One of her great-grandchildren, Mrs. Phelps, of Atlantic City, N.J., in speaking of her and of the spread, now in her possession, which was made for her mother, says: "The spread is beautiful, and although made so long ago can be admired still. I well remember my great-grandmother, a noble woman; her name and fame will never die, but generation after generation arise and call her blessed; ' Her price above rubies,' a great-grandchild's testimony."

3636. JOHN DOGGETT[4] (*John,*[3] *Samuel,*[2] *Thomas*[1]), born Lebanon, Conn., September 5, 1725; married Lebanon, Conn., August 30, 1749, Sarah Ellis; she died aged 101 years, 3 months, 11 days.

Issue:

3754. i. ELIZABETH DOGGETT,[5] born Lebanon, Conn., February 21, 1750.
3755. ii. JOHN DOGGETT,[5] born Lebanon, Conn., September 11, 1754.
3756. iii. ELEAZER DOGGETT,[5] born Lebanon, Conn., April 20, 1764; died Lebanon, Conn., November 19, 1767.
3757. iv. SAMUEL DOGGETT,[5] born Lebanon, Conn., December 3, 1768.

The Lebanon land records show that John Doggett, Jr., made several purchases of land there until as late as 1774.

3642. SAMUEL DOGGETT[4] (*Isaac,*[3] *Samuel,*[2] *Thomas*[1]), born Marshfield, Mass., May 30, 1727; died Dedham, Mass., March 6, 1794; married Dorchester, Mass., September 7, 1749, Abigail Davenport, daughter of Ambrose and Rachel (Searle) Davenport;

born Dorchester, Mass., August 30, 1727; died Dedham, Mass., September 1, 1803.

Issue :

3758. i. JONATHAN DOGGETT,[5] born Dedham, Mass., August 30, 1750; died Dedham, Mass., September 10, 1750.
3759. ii. SAMUEL DOGGETT,[5] born Dedham, Mass., October 5, 1751.
3760. iii. EUNICE DOGGETT,[5] born Dedham, Mass., May 30, 1753; married Joseph Sampson; issue: Betsey Sampson;[6] Eunice died Attleboro', Mass., Jan. 20, 1789; he died Attleboro', Mass., Dec. 6, 1793.
3761. iv. MARY DOGGETT,[5] born Dedham, Mass., November 9, 1755.
3762. v. ISAAC DOGGETT,[5] born Dedham, Mass., January 11, 1758.
3763. vi. JESSE DOGGETT,[5] born Dedham, Mass., January 12, 1761.
3764. vii. ELISHA DOGGETT,[5] born Dedham, Mass., May 10, 1767.
3765. viii. JOHN DOGGETT,[5] born Dedham, Mass., April 15, 1771; died Dedham, Mass., June 29, 1771.

July 9, 1727. " Isaac Dogget his wife had a son baptized whose name was Samuel." [Marshfield Church Records.]

Samuel Doggett lived in Braintree and Milton until he went to Dorchester, where he learned the trade of a " millwright," as a young man. At the age of twenty-two he married in Dorchester and removed to Dedham, where he became a " housewright."

Aug. 11, 1751, he and his wife were admitted to the First Church, Dedham.

July 24, 1753 bought of Joseph Fisher of Walpole for 13£ 6s 8d 20 rods of land in Dedham, with house and well. [Suffolk Deeds, 99–261.]
March 13, 1762, Samuel Doggett of Dedham "housewright" bought of Samuel Richards of Dedham for 53£ 6s 8d ¼ of an acre of land with house, near the meeting house. [Suffolk Deeds, 99–262]
March 17, 1778 Samuel Doggett and wife Abigail to son Samuel land and part of house in Dedham. [Suffolk Deeds, 129–63.]
Dec 29, 1784 Samuel Doggett and Abigail his wife of Dedham sell Elisha Davenport their rights in land in Dorchester. [Suffolk Deeds, 160–60.]

Mrs. Elizabeth D. Clapp, of Dedham, had in her possession the cane used by Abigail Doggett.

Samuel Doggett died in Dedham and lies buried in the old cemetery there. His gravestone has the following inscription :

Memento Mori
In memory of
MR SAMUEL DOGGETT
who died March 6, 1794
Æ 67
This grave contains the
feeble mouldering clay :
The spirit triumphs in
eternal day.

3643. ABIGAIL DOGGETT[4] (*Isaac*,[3] *Samuel*,[2] *Thomas*[1]), born Braintree, Mass., December 5, 1728; married Braintree, Mass., January 6, 1753, by Rev. Samuel Niles, to Jacob Copeland.

Issue :

3766. i. OLIVE COPELAND,[5] bapt. Braintree, Mass., February 15, 1756.

3767. ii.   Asa Copeland,[5] bapt. Braintree, Mass., February 15, 1756.
3768. iii. Jacob Copeland,[5] bapt. Braintree, Mass., November 6, 1757.
3769. iv.   Susanna Copeland,[5] bapt. Braintree. Mass., January 6, 1760.
3770. v.   Abigail Copeland,[5] bapt. Braintree, Mass., April 19, 1761.

3653.   Bathsheba Eames [4] (*Abigail Doggett,*[3] *Samuel,*[2] *Thomas* [1]),
born 1731; died Buckfield, Me., August 17, 1806; married Marshfield, Mass., October 31, 1754, John Lapham; born 1731; died
Buckfield, Me., August 18, 1804.

They lived in Marshfield and Pembroke, and in 1793 removed to
Buckfield, Me.

THOMAS DOGGETT, OF MARSHFIELD, MASS.

FIFTH GENERATION.

3673.   Capt. John Doggett [5] (*John,*[4] *Thomas,*[3] *John,*[2] *Thomas* [1]),
born Scituate, Mass., 1730; died Liverpool, N.S., previous to April
17, 1772; married Scituate, Mass. (intention, September 24, 1748),
Abigail House. daughter of Benjamin and Abigail House, of Scituate; died Liverpool, N.S., after 17th February, 1805.

Issue:

3771. i.   Abner Doggett,[6] born Scituate, Mass., August 16, 1749.
3772. ii.   Ebenezer Doggett,[6] born Scituate, Mass., July 9, 1752.
3773. iii. Abigail Doggett [6]
3774. iv.   Samuel Doggett.[6]   October 29, 1774, Israel Chewer appointed guar-
            dian. [Queens Probate, 1–35.]
3775. v.   Ichabod Doggett,[6] born 1771.

Capt. John Doggett is mentioned by Deane in his History of
Scituate as keeping Doggett's ferry (now Little's bridge) 1755, and
subsequently.

Dec. 20, 1756 Hannah Woodworth of Scituate widow, administratrix of the
estate of Benjamin Woodworth late of said Scituate, mariner, for 36£ paid by
John Doggett of Scituate. mariner, 3¾ acres land in Scituate. [Plymouth
Deeds. 44–54.]
Dec. 20, 1756 John Doggett of Scituate, mariner, for 19£ paid by Hannah
Woodworth of Scituate widow, gives her the use and improvement of the easterly
great lower Room in the house where she now dwells with ½ chamber over same
and ½ the buttery and ½ the cellar and also the yard at the east end excepting the
liberty of fetching water from the well in said yard as occasion may require also
the privilege of baking in the oven as occasion may require, as long as she lives.
[Plymouth Deeds. 54–262.]
May 3, 1769 John Doggett of Liverpool in County Queens and Province of
Nova Scotia Esquire, for 36£ 3s 7d paid by Benjamin House of Scituate in
County Plymouth, sells him 3¾ acres of land in Scituate with buildings thereon
which he purchased of Hannah Woodworth of said Scituate in 1756. [Plymouth
Deeds, 55–43.]

These extracts show that between the purchase and sale of this
land Captain Doggett had removed to Liverpool, N.S.

From the "History of the County of Queens, by James F. More, Esq., Halifax, 1873," we read: "The New England fishermen, being largely engaged in prosecuting the fisheries during the summer months, were, after the expulsion of the Acadians, attracted by the munificent offers of the Government, and readily consented to become permanent settlers. To further this object they petitioned by a committee appointed from among themselves and asked that a township might be granted to them on the southern coast of Nova Scotia to the eastward of Cape Sable and around port Rossignol. In 1759 a warrant of survey was issued by Governor Lawrence to John Doggett, Elisha Freeman, Samuel Doggett, and Thomas Foster, on behalf of themselves, and the other persons after named, to lay out a township to be called Liverpool, bounded by the sea coast of Cape Sable shore, extending fourteen miles into the country and containing according to the bounds about 100,000 acres.

"John Doggett, who came with the first settlers from New England in 1759, was one of the most prominent men among the first applicants, and had it not been for his exertions in persuading the settlers to remain the whole number would have returned. As it was many of the young men returned. Those whom he persuaded to remain he kept at his own house during the first winter, and provided for them as best he could, at a considerable outlay, for which the government, in acknowledgment of his patriotic sacrifices, partially reimbursed him."

He was one of the first appointed to office in Liverpool township; first, as truck-master, to have the management of the trade with the Indians; and in 1764 he was appointed justice of the Inferior Court of Common Pleas for Queens County, justice of the peace, and a militia officer.

"His dwelling-house was situated on Doggett's point, in front of the old town plot.

"He was considered a very trustworthy and respectable man.

"He had, no doubt, been frequently on the coast previous to his becoming a settler at Liverpool. In 1764, the population of Liverpool was five hundred. May, 1761, Capt. John Doggett was instructed to hire a vessel for the purpose of removing to the township twenty families and sixty head of cattle. This last for the use of the settlers.

"The expense incurred in this undertaking was to be defrayed by the government. In this same year a committee was appointed to lay out the lands under the first warrant. This committee consisted of John Dogget, Elisha Freeman, Samuel Doggett, Nathan Tory, and Nathan Tupper.

"In 1763 petitions began to be presented asking for grants of land outside of the township, and among these one from John Doggett, Esq., for Port Mouton island, which he had previously held under license and improved. The grant was issued to him, and a portion of the island is still in the possession of the family. In 1770 John Doggett was elected as the member for Liverpool to the House of Assembly, and held the office till his death, in 1772, when Seth Harding took his place."

Nathaniel Godfrey of Liverpool sells John Dogget ½ Sawmill on Millbrook Sept 27, 1762. [Queens Deeds, 1–3.]

This ½ sawmill Dogget sells to Lemuel Drew Oct. 24, 1767. [Queens Deeds, 1–115.]

Nov. 8, 1766, John Doggett became bound to Joshua Mager which bond was released to Ichabod Doggett, and Joseph Verge, by J. Brook Watson of London Eng. Nov 10, 1797 acting as executor of Mr Mager. [Queens Deeds, 4–284.]

The first register of deeds in the township of Liverpool was John Doggett, and his writing, clear and distinct, may be seen on the Queens county records; the first deed entered being April, 1764, and the last in his handwriting, 18th November, 1771.

17 April 1772. Letter of adm. was granted on the Estate of John Dogget Esq. to Abner Dogget [Queens Probate, 1–24]. The final settlement occurs 15 Oct 1793 when John Thomas Esq. atty. to Abner Dogget adm. to the estate of the late John Dogget Esq dec'd, exhibits his account in selling said estate since his appointment as adm. The whole demand by a debt due Job Prim as appears by an order of council Dec 11, 1788.   Principal £60-0-0
                                                                  Int. 16 years 57–12–0
Real estate sold in pursuance to order of council amounted to £124–4–0 less expenses £12–4–0 which the court ordered paid to Prim. [Queens Probate, 1–140.]

Joseph Verge, Esq., attorney for Abigail Doggett, of Liverpool, Queens Co., N.S., receives £279, being a legacy paid under the will of her father Benjamin House, by her brother Benjamin House, Jr., and also for land which came by their mother Abigail House, deceased, dated September 27, 1784. [O.C. Records, 29–188.]

The final disposal of land in Scituate does not take place until 1798, when "Abigail Doggett of Liverpool, Queens Co. N.S. widow of the late John Doggett Esq. of said Liverpool dec'd puts her son Ichabod Doggett of Liverpool, mariner, as her attorney especially to sell land in Scituate, Aug. 23, 1798." [Plymouth Deeds, 85–20.]

Acting under this authority Ichabod Doggett sells ½ of 2 pieces of salt marsh lying in Scituate near the 3rd Cliff and in common and undivided with heirs of Thomas Mann dec'd to Nathan Brooks Jr & Simeon Brooks, Sept 12, 1798 [Plymouth Deeds, 85–21] and also to Leonard Clapp 2 pieces of land containing 5 acres 2 quarters & 38 rods near Clapps dwelling house. Sept 12, 1798. [Plymouth Deeds, 89–128.]

Abigail Doggett, of Liverpool, widow of John Doggett, late of Liverpool, sells all her dower in an island, once called "Doggetts Island," in town of Guysborough, to Benomi Gardner, 17th February, 1805. [Queens Deeds, 5–271.]

3679. JABEZ DOGGETT [5] (*Thomas,*[4] *Thomas,*[3] *John,*[2] *Thomas*[1]), born Marshfield, Mass., March 3, 1734; married 1st, Plymouth, Mass., Jan. 24, 1760, by Rev. Jacob Bacon, to Rebecca Rich, daughter of Walter and Rebecca Rich, of Plymouth; married 2d, Middleboro', Mass., Oct. 20, 1783, Jael Caswell; died Middleboro', Mass., Nov. 16, 1805; married 3d, Middleboro', Mass., May 25, 1807, Sarah Caswell.

Issue:

3776. i. JOHN DOGGETT,[6] born Middleboro', Mass., April 12, 1761; died Grand Manan, N.B.
3777. ii. NATHANIEL DOGGETT,[6] born Middleboro', Mass., October 5, 1763; probably lost at sea, 1783.
3778. iii. SUSANA DOGGETT,[6] born Middleboro', Mass., April 20, 1765; married Mr. Chamberlain; she died Kennebec, Me.
3779. iv. JABEZ DOGGETT,[6] born Middleboro', Mass., September 13, 1766; married; settled Kennebec, Me.: issue: three sons.
3780. v. MARK DOGGETT,[6] born Middleboro', Mass., August 28, 1768.
3781. vi. REBECCA DOGGETT,[6] born Middleboro', Mass., February 18, 1770.
3782. vii. JOANNA DOGGETT,[6] born Middleboro', Mass., March 28, 1772; married Joel Hereford; she died New York.
3783. viii. PEREZ DOGGETT,[6] born Middleboro', Mass., August 22, 1776.

Jabez Doggett was baptized in the First Church in Marshfield, September 22, 1734.

In 1758, in the French and Indian war, Capt. Benjamin Pratt, of Middleboro', gathered a company among which was Jabez Doggett. He was at Oneida Station (now Ticonderoga), September 28, 1758, and in an unsuccessful attempt to take it July 8, 1758, he was among the wounded. In 1759 he was a member of Capt. Ephraim Holmes's company, of Plymouth county, which was stationed at Lunenburg.

May 5, 1773. Rebecca Rich of Plymouth having deceased, her estate is divided among her heirs [Plymouth Deeds, 57-150], and June 18, 1773, Jabez Doggett and his wife (dau. of Mrs Rich) sell the share which came to them, to Elijah Daman, and Richard Holmes. [Plymouth Deeds, 57-151.]

June 29, 1799. He sells all his homestead land situate in Middleboro being same he bought of Cornelius Bennet January 2, 1759, to his son Perez Doggett of Middleboro. [Plymouth Deeds, 89-90.]

3680. SETH DOGGETT [5] (*Thomas,*[4] *Thomas,*[3] *John,*[2] *Thomas*[1]), born Marshfield, Mass., February 15, 1736; died Middleboro', Mass., August 19, 1816.

The church records of the First Church of Marshfield mention the baptism of Seth Doggett, May 23, 1736. Removing when a child to Middleboro', he spends his life in that town.

June 24, 1791, he sells part of the homestead farm of Thomas Doggett, his late father, deceased, to Ephraim Pierce, of Middleboro', carpenter, and in the instrument speaks of himself as "yeoman." [Plymouth Deeds, 80-219.]

The will of Seth Doggett, of Middleboro', is dated July 19, 1815, and proved November 6, 1816.

In it he gives Daniel Macomber his part of the wood lot; mentions sister Experience Doggett; brother Simeon Doggett; niece Experience Pierce; gives Mark Doggett his wearing apparel. [Plymouth Probate, 48–230.]

3681. SIMEON DOGGETT [5] (*Thomas,*[4] *Thomas,*[3] *John,*[2] *Thomas*[1]), born Marshfield, Mass., January 4, 1738; died Middleboro', Mass., May 6, 1823; married February 28, 1760, Abigail Pratt, daughter of David Pratt, born North Carolina.

Issue:

3784. i. THOMAS DOGGETT,[6] born Middleboro', Mass., April 14, 1761.
3785. ii. ELKANAH DOGGETT,[6] born Middleboro', Mass., October 27, 1762.
3786. iii. SIMEON DOGGETT,[6] born Middleboro', Mass., March 6, 1765.
3787. iv. ABIGAIL DOGGETT,[6] born Middleboro', Mass., March 4, 1775.

Simeon Doggett was baptized in the First Church in Marshfield, August 20, 1738. When four years old he was taken to Middleboro', which was afterward his home.

He was with his brother Jabez in the French and Indian war, and served with him in Capt. Benjamin Pratt's company, being at Oneida Station, N.Y., September 28, 1758.

He and his wife sold 7 acres of land and meadow in Middleboro April 28, 1762 which was described as part of the homestead of Eleazer Lewis deceased. [Plymouth Deeds, 52–184.]
Dec. 30, 1789 Simeon and Jabez Doggett sell the 93rd lot in the 3rd allotment in the 16 shilling purchase to Elijah Macomber. [Plymouth Deeds, 74–152.]

Simeon Doggett was a farmer in Middleboro', also carpenter, or " joyner."

In the Revolution he did not feel that it was right for the colonies to rebel against the mother country, and, as a result, was forbidden to leave his farm. One of his descendants, speaking of this mandate, says: " He and a neighbor Tory, under like prohibition, obeyed by walking daily to the bounds of their adjoining farms, and there holding friendly talks upon the grave situation."

Simeon Doggett, the Tory farmer, was a staunch Episcopalian, and built the house on the highway from Plymouth to Taunton, in the town of Middleboro', which was long occupied by his descendants.

3683. JOANNA DOGGETT [5] (*Thomas,*[4] *Thomas,*[3] *John,*[2] *Thomas*[1]), born Marshfield, Mass., March 16, 1742; married William Pierce, of Taunton.

Issue:

3788. i. WILLIAM PIERCE.[6]
3789. ii. EPHRAIM PIERCE.[6]
3790. iii. JOANNA PIERCE.[6]
3791. iv. SAMUEL PIERCE.[6]
3792. v. BENJAMIN PIERCE.[6]
3793. vi. EXPERIENCE PIERCE.[6]

3687. MARY CLIFT [5] (*Lydia Doggett,[4] Samuel,[3] Samuel,[2] Thomas[1]*), born Marshfield, Mass., October 7, 1738; died Plainfield, Conn., July 9, 1781; married Joseph Kimball, of Plainfield, Conn., son of Joseph and Hannah (Morgan) Kimball; born Preston, Conn., December 29, 1731; died Plainfield, N.H., October 22, 1822.

Issue :

3794. i. WILLS KIMBALL,[6] born Plainfield, Conn., March 31, 1760.
3795. ii. HANNAH KIMBALL,[6] born Plainfield, Conn., September 6, 1761.
3796. iii. BENJAMIN A. KIMBALL,[6] born Plainfield, Conn., March 6, 1763.
3797 iv. ELISHA KIMBALL,[6] born Plainfield. Conn , March 1, 1765.
3798. v. MARY CLIFT KIMBALL,[6] born Plainfield, Conn., November 30, 1767.
3799. vi. SARAH KIMBALL,[6] born Plainfield, Conn., July 15, 1769.
3800. vii. LYDIA KIMBALL,[6] born Plainfield, Conn., April 3, 1771.
3801. viii. JOSEPH KIMBALL,[6] born Plainfield, Conn., September 9, 1775.

Joseph Kimball and Mary his wife lived on the homestead of Samuel Clift, known as the "Kimball place."

Mary Clift was the second wife of Joseph Kimball, and after her decease he again married, and removed to Plainfield, N.H.

3689. WATERMAN CLIFT [5] (*Lydia Doggett,[4] Samuel,[3] Samuel,[2] Thomas[1]*), born Marshfield, Mass., December 28, 1741; died Windham, Conn., September 17, 1828; married 1st, 1767 (?), Hannah Farnham; married 2d, Keziah Bradford; married 3d, Clarissa Fitch.

Waterman Clift had four daughters by his first wife, and five daughters and two sons by his second.

He lived and died in Windham, Conn., and has numerous descendants. He was a major in the Revolutionary army.

3693. JOSEPH CLIFT [5] (*Lydia Doggett,[4] Samuel,[3] Samuel,[2] Thomas[1]*), born Plainfield, Conn., September 13, 1750; died Skaneateles, N.Y., May 9, 1827; married 1774, Elizabeth Stanton.

Joseph Clift lived in Griswold, Conn., removed to Shaftsbury, Vt., thence to Onondaga county, N.Y.; died and was buried at Skaneateles, N.Y. They had six children, whose descendants are numerous in New York State.

3694. LEMUEL CLIFT [5] (*Lydia Doggett,[4] Samuel,[3] Samuel,[2] Thomas[1]*), born Plainfield, Conn., October 10, 1755; died South East, N.Y., September 13, 1821; married December 5, 1778, Sarah Hall, of Plainfield, Conn.

Lemuel Clift had nine children. He died and was buried on his farm in South East, N.Y. The farm now owned (1884) by Daniel Drew or his heirs.

3699. SAMUEL OAKMAN [5] (*Sarah Doggett,[4] Samuel,[3] Samuel,[2] Thomas[1]*), born Marshfield, Mass., September 18, 1745; died Pittston, Me., December 18, 1822; married Hannah Agry, daughter of

Thomas and Annar (Demmick) Agry, of Pittston, Me., born 1755; died Pittston, Me., April 16, 1788.

Issue:

3802. i. HANNAH OAKMAN,[6] born Pittston, Me., 1774; married Capt. Freeborn Groves; he died Aug. 4, 1854, aged 84; she died Nov. 3, 1822, aged 48.
3803. ii. JOSEPH OAKMAN,[6] born Pittston, Me., 1776; died Pittston, Me., November 4, 1788.
3804. iii. SAMUEL OAKMAN,[6] born Pittston, Me., 1778; " captain;" married Mary Reed, of Maine, 1802; she died September 24, 1819, aged 41; he died December 28. 1807, aged 29.
3805. iv. ELIZABETH OAKMAN,[6] born Pittston, Me., 1781; married Francis Flitner, son of Dr. Zachariah and Lucy (Colburn) Flitner; he born August 1, 1774; married December 2, 1804; died April 3, 1850; she died October 18, 1850.
3806. v. SARAH OAKMAN,[6] born Pittston, Me., 1782; married December, 1812, Rev. Daniel Kendrick; he born Hollis, N.H., 1786; died Wilton, Me., May 4, 1868; she died Cambridge, Mass., July 10, 1871.
3807. vi. MARY OAKMAN,[6] born Pittston, Me., May 10, 178⅜; married July 1, 1816, James Cary, son of James and Sarah (Roberts) Cary; he born June 22, 1790; died August 25, 1865; she died Brunswick, Me., November 9, 1850.

Samuel Oakman moved to Pittston, Me., about 1771. He was a mariner and shipbuilder.

3704. Capt. AMOS OAKMAN [5] (*Sarah Doggett,*[4] *Samuel,*[3] *Samuel,*[2] *Thomas*[1]), born Marshfield, Mass., January 26, 1759; died Lunenburg, Mass., June 17, 1805; married Marshfield, Mass., 1787, Silvina Thomas; born Marshfield, Mass., 1765; died Lunenburg, Mass., December 1, 1814.

Issue:

3808. i. SARAH OAKMAN,[6] born Marshfield, Mass., June 30. 1789.
3809. ii. AMOS OAKMAN,[6] born Marshfield, Mass., July 16, 1795.
3810. iii. ELIZA OAKMAN,[6] born Marshfield, Mass., January 2, 1797.
3811. iv. JOSEPH OAKMAN,[6] born Marshfield, Mass., June 23, 1799.
3812. v. NANCY OAKMAN,[6] born Marshfield, Mass., March 1, 1801.
3813. vi. JANE OAKMAN,[6] born Marshfield, Mass.. January 26, 1804; married Benjamin Clark; had son Hiram Clark.[7]

Capt. Amos Oakman was a sea captain sailing from Boston. After retiring from the sea he moved to Fitchburg, and then to Lunenburg, Mass.

Captain Oakman as a sea captain was very severe, and exercised the very strictest discipline on board his vessel. Among his voyages was one to Liverpool, where, on July 15, 1791, he wrote a letter to his uncle, Noah Doggett, regarding his cousin Samuel Doggett, who had made the voyage with him, from which we learn he arrived there June 21, and intended to sail for Boston in ten or twelve days.

In 1793 he was captured, and his vessel conveyed to a Spanish port, where he and his crew were for some time confined, and the ship and a cargo of manufactured French goods confiscated.

3707. SAMUEL DOGGETT [5] (*Samuel,*[4] *Samuel,*[3] *Samuel,*[2] *Thomas*[1]), born Boston, Mass., May 16, 1755; died Boston, Mass., May 26, 1817.

Samuel Doggett was baptized in the First Church in Boston, May 18, 1755.

He entered Harvard College, and graduated in the class of 1775.

John L. Sibley, Librarian Emeritus of Harvard College, wrote of him: " Samuel Doggett was twenty years old when he graduated. He appears from my memoranda to have resided at one time in Maine, and his father to have been ' Capt.' This is everything I know about him."

Samuel Doggett studied law, and April 29, 1780, upon motion of Mr. Morton, it was voted that Mr. Samuel Doggett be recommended to the Inferior Court of Common Pleas, this day to be admitted to the oath of an attorney of that court.   [Historical Society Collection, Vol. XIX., p. 153.]

As one of the executors of his father's estate he was active in its settlement.

In 1787 he began the sale of eight hundred acres of land in Bowdoinham, Me., which had belonged to his father, and in each deed styles himself as of Brookline, gentleman.

In a deed recorded in Suffolk Deeds, November 25, 1793, Samuel Doggett calls himself of Bowdoinham, gentleman.

The Fairfield family at Saco, Me., speak of their cousin, Samuel Doggett, as visiting them there, possibly on some of his trips to or from Bowdoinham.

March 18, 1805, he was of Boston, and appointed attorney to sell, let, or demise land in Newburyport, and also in Newton, for " Sarah Mulvany now of Boston, widow."   [Essex Deeds, 176–21.]

Acting under this power he sold land in Newburyport, March 21, 1805 [Essex Deeds, 176–19], and March 27, 1805, five acres bounded by road leading to Newton.   [Essex Deeds, 179–103.]

In each of these cases he is called of Boston, as also in Suffolk Deeds, 212–3, when he mortgages estate on Tremont street, Boston, adjoining Mr. Pemberton, as attorney to Sarah Mulvany, May 1, 1805.

His name occurs in two of the Boston Directories, 1813 and 1816, both of which give his address as Fleet street, and one of them as No. 22.   He died of consumption in 1817, and was buried in the Fairfield tomb.

3708. William Doggett [5] (*Samuel,*[4] *Samuel,*[3] *Samuel,*[2] *Thomas* [1]), born Boston, Mass., April 3, 1757; died Boston, Mass., March 19, 1818.

William Doggett was baptized in the First Church, April 10, 1757.

After the death of his father, he assists his mother and brother in the settlement of the estate, and seems to have represented the family at the meetings of the Wiscasset Company.

In 1784 he was present at meetings of the company in Boston on August 31, September 13 and 17.

In 1788, at the meeting June 23, and in 1789, December 31. At this last meeting it was " Voted — that William Doggett go down to Wiscasset [1] upon the companys business."

In 1791 he was present at the meeting October 31, and in 1792, October 22 and 26, and December 11.

The affairs of the company were closed in 1798.

The Fairfield family at Saco, Me., speak of their cousin, William Doggett, as visiting them there.

June 2, 1788, William Doggett is called of Boston, trader. [Suffolk Deeds, 153–274.]

The Boston Directory for 1789 says : " William Doggett, housewright & printers furniture maker, Milk St."

November 24, 1790, as attorney for his sister, he with others sells land in Bowdoinham, Me., and styles himself of Boston, trader. [Lincoln Deeds, 26–262.]

November 25, 1793, he is called of Brookline, gentleman. [Suffolk Deeds, 165–231.]

June 6, 1805, William Doggett and William Taylor made a survey for a road from Boston to Worcester via Northboro'. [Wm. Taylor's Note-book.]

He died in Boston, and was buried in the South Ground.

3709.   Elizabeth Doggett [5]   (Samuel,[4]   Samuel,[3]   Samuel,[2] Thomas [1]), born Boston, Mass., May 22, 1759 ; married Boston (?), Mass. (intention, July 27, 1780), Mark Myers.

Elizabeth Doggett was baptized in the First Church, May 27, 1759.

After the death of her father the family begin the sale of the land in Bowdoinham, Me.

Marcus Myers of Biddeford, County York, Innholder, and Elizabeth his wife, with others, sell land in Bowdoinham May 31, 1787. [Lincoln Deeds, 21–143.]

Nov 24, 1790 Marcus Myers of Demerara, in the West Indies, Trader, and Elizabeth Myers wife of said Marcus by our Atty's said Samuel and William Doggett of Boston in said County, Trader. Atty. recorded Oct. 2, and 25 Dec, 1788 to dispose of 800 acres belonging to our father Samuel Doggett of Boston, merchant, deceased, sell George Thomas 75 acres. [Lincoln Deeds, 26–262.]

Aug 29, 1796 Marcus Myers of the Colony of Demerara in the West Indies, trader, and Elizabeth Myers wife of said Marcus by our atty, said Samuel Doggett with others sell 111½ acres land in Bowdoinham. [Lincoln Deeds, 43–28.]

---

[1] A point of land opposite Wiscasset was once called " Doggett's Point," and a bold cliff on the Sheepscott river, about three miles below the town, is still known as " Doggett's Castle," from the tradition that the Doggetts traded with the Indians from this rock in early times.

A letter of inquiry was addressed to J. Thomson, Esq., of George-town, Demerara, the editor of the "Argosy," as to whether any de-scendants of Marcus and Elizabeth Myers were living in the colony, or whether he could tell anything of them. His reply, dated Demerara, July 6, 1886, says: "I have published your request for information in the 'Argosy' and also in the 'West India Quarterly.' If any information reaches me, it will be a pleasure to me to for-ward it."

3711. SARAH DOGGETT[5] (*Samuel,[4] Samuel,[3] Samuel,[2] Thomas[1]*), born Boston, Mass., October 1, 1767; married Thomas Johnston.

Sarah Doggett was baptized in the First Church, October 27, 1767.

She joins with her brothers and sister in the sale of land in Bowdoinham, and she and her husband are spoken of as "Thomas Johnston (or Johnson) Gentleman, & Sarah wife of Thomas, of Brookline, County Suffolk," on the following dates: 31 May, 1787; 15 October, 1787; 15 September, 1790; while her husband is called "yeoman," with the same residence, in transfers 24th November, 1790, and 29th August, 1796.

In a letter written May 20, 1792, Mr. and Mrs. Johnston are spoken of as having gone to Demerara, evidently on a visit to her sister, Mrs. Myers, as they are again of Brookline in 1796.

3712. JOSEPH DOGGETT[5] (*Noah,[4] Samuel,[3] Samuel,[2] Thomas[1]*), born Boston, Mass., August 16, 1754; died Newburyport, Mass., March 15, 1833; married Newburyport, Mass., August 24, 1780, by Rev. Thomas Cary, to Sarah Akerman; born Boxford (?), Mass.; died January 28, 1813.

Issue :

3814. i.   JOSEPH DOGGETT,[6] born Newburyport, Mass., January 30, 1785.
3815. ii. NOAH DOGGETT,[6] born Newburyport, Mass., January 8, 1787; died at sea, August 16, 1803.
3816. iii. SAMUEL DOGGETT,[6] born Newburyport. Mass., September 18, 1789.
3817. iv. SARAH DOGGETT,[6] born Newburyport, Mass., February 1, 1792.
3818. v. HENRY DOGGETT,[6] born Newburyport, Mass., November 24, 1793.
3819. vi. THOMAS BISPHAM DOGGETT,[6] born Newburyport, Mass., Oct. 22, 1797.
3820. vii. DANIEL JACKSON DOGGETT,[6] born Newburyport, Mass., May 11, 1799.

Joseph Doggett either preceded or went with his father's family when they visited Newburyport, at the time of the siege of Boston, in 1775.

He was by trade a cooper, and married and settled in Newburyport.

October 13, 1784, he purchased land in Newburyport, probably on Ash Lane, where he made his home. [Essex Deeds, 146–227.]

December 14, 1790, Joseph Doggett, cooper, and Sarah his wife, of New-buryport, sell land in Portsmouth to Abner Blasdel. [Rockingham Deeds, 128–426.]

April 21, 1814 [Essex Deeds, 204–127] and May 2, 1826 [Essex Deeds, 240–209] he sells his land in Newburyport, the last deed being to his son Henry Doggett, of Boston.

3713. Bethiah Doggett [5] (*Noah*,[4] *Samuel*,[3] *Samuel*,[2] *Thomas* [1]), born Boston, Mass., August 22, 1756; died Greensboro', Vt., December 31, 1828; married January 24, 1780, Samuel Huntington, M.D., son of Nathan and Amy (Brown) Huntington, of Shaftesbury, Vt.; born Norwich (now Griswold), Conn., June 3, 1759; died Greensboro', Vt., December 7, 1823.

Issue:

3821. i. Robert Huntington,[6] born Plainfield, Conn., October 21, 1780; died Shaftesbury, Vt., February 14, 1784.
3822. ii. Bethia Huntington,[6] born Plainfield, Conn., October 21, 1780.
3823. iii. John Huntington,[6] born Shaftesbury, Vt., March 20, 1782.
3824. iv. Henry Huntington,[6] born Shaftesbury, Vt., March 20, 1782.
3825. v. Betsey Huntington,[6] born Shaftesbury, Vt., January 17, 1784; died Shaftesbury, Vt., March 12, 1795.
3826. vi. Mary Huntington,[6] born Greensboro', Vt., Nov. 3, 1785; married Capt. David Stone; she died Greensboro', Vt., March 1, 1809.
3827. vii. Robert Huntington,[6] born Shaftesbury (?), Vt., June 28, 1787; lawyer; married; died Mississippi.
3828. viii. Roxana Huntington,[6] born Greensboro', Vt., December 15, 1788; died Greensboro', Vt., June 16, 1809.
3829. ix. Nathan Huntington,[6] born Shaftesbury, Vt., April 25, 1792; died Shaftesbury, Vt., March 30, 1796.
3830. x. Sophia Huntington,[6] born Shaftesbury, Vt., May 15, 1794.
3831. xi. Elizabeth Huntington,[6] born Greensboro', Vt., December 6, 1797; died Greensboro', Vt., May 19, 1809.

" Aug 29. 1756 Bethiah daughter of Noah and Mary Doggett in Covenant at O. North, baptized." [New South Church Records.]

Bethiah Doggett after her marriage lived in Vermont, and at her husband's decease visited her daughter Sophia, with the idea of spending her remaining years with her. The change of scene from Vermont to Ohio at that time was too much for one of her age, and she longed for the old home in Greensboro'. Her son Henry went to Ohio and brought her back to his home in Greensboro', much to her gratification, and she died at his house in 1828, and was buried near her husband in the cemetery there, where a stone stands to her memory.

Her descendants speak of her as always active, and as one who could not tolerate an idle person.

Dr. Samuel Huntington retained to the close of his life a high reputation as a physician and surgeon. He settled in Shaftesbury, Vt., and in 1797 removed to Greensboro'.

He was a surgeon in the army during the war, and a custom-house officer in 1812.

3717. Henry Doggett [5] (*Noah*,[4] *Samuel*,[3] *Samuel*,[2] *Thomas* [1]), born Boston, Mass., Feb. 15, 1767; died Boston, Mass., August 10, 1828; married Charleston, S.C., 1789, Nancy Hyslup; born 1773; died Georgetown, S.C., June 29, 1807.

Issue:

3832. i. John Hooper Doggett,[6] born Charleston, S.C., January 10, 1790; died Charleston, S.C., April 6, 1791.

Noah Doggett

3833. ii.   HENRY DOGGETT,[6] born Charleston, S.C., March 6, 1792; died young, probably soon after 1802.
3834. iii. JOSEPH ENNALLS DOGGETT,[6] born Daniels Island, S.C., February, 1794; died November 7, 1802.
3835. iv.   NOAH DOGGETT,[6] died October 27, 1799.
3836. v.   JOHN RALPH DOGGETT,[6] born Charleston, S.C., November 16, 1799.
3837. vi.   MARY AMELIA DOGGETT,[6] born Charleston, S.C., February 2, 1802.
3838. vii. ROBERT HYSLUP DOGGETT,[6] born Charleston, S.C., February 2, 1802.

Henry Doggett was baptized in the New South Church, February 22, 1767. Previous to 1789 he removed to Charleston, S.C., where he married and settled.

In a letter to his parents, dated November 25, 1802, he says of himself:

HONORED PARENTS

. . . I am still in the planting line and conceive it more profitable than the mercantile as it is carried on in Charleston at present, . . . We have had seven children four only are now alive. Your daughter writes by this opportunity. My love to Lydia, Noah, and his family, and all our Relations.

I pray God to have you in his holy keeping and am, Your dutiful son

I have ten slaves which bring in about 300£ a year, all of which it takes to bring up the children and for our expences.

Another letter, dated Charleston, S.C., March 10, 1813, to his mother and sister, speaks of receiving their letter of January 17, 1813, on the twenty-second of February following, also that:

On 8th Inst, at Evening we had an illumination of this City, and the vessels in the Harbor on account of our Naval victory, &c. the Houses and vessels made a most brilliant appearance, and was gratifying to every eye. About 900 persons dined together, and the greatest order and tranquility prevailed the whole time.

Henry Doggett returned to Boston about 1824, where he first visited his brother Noah, and afterward made his home on Sea street, where his parents had previously lived.

He died in 1828, and was buried in the Granary Burial-ground.

3719. NOAH DOGGETT [5] (*Noah,*[4] *Samuel,*[3] *Samuel,*[2] *Thomas*[1]), born Boston, Mass., October 1, 1770; died Boston, Mass., August 9, 1842; married 1st, Boston, Mass., May 5, 1793, by Rev. Samuel Stillman, to Ruth Lyne; born 1773; died Boston, Mass., July 19, 1809; married 2d, Boston, Mass., September 15, 1810, by Rev. Horace Holley, to Elizabeth Bradlee, daughter of Nathaniel and Ann

(Dunlap) Bradlee; born Boston, Mass., October 12, 1781; died Boston, Mass., January 25, 1869.

Issue:

3839. i. HENRY DOGGETT,[6] born Boston, Mass., January 22, 1794; died Boston, Mass., January 23, 1794.
3840. ii. MARY DOGGETT,[6] born Boston, Mass., December 12, 1794; died Boston, Mass., July 24, 1797.
3841. iii. HENRY DOGGETT,[6] born Boston, Mass., February 16, 1797; died Boston, Mass., February 16, 1797.
3842. iv. MARY ALLINE DOGGETT,[6] born Boston, Mass., October 12, 1798.
3843. v. ANN BRADLEE DOGGETT,[6] born Boston, Mass., August 18, 1811.
3844. vi. NATHANIEL BRADLEE DOGGETT,[6] born Boston, Mass., October 30, 1813; died Boston, Mass., October 31, 1813.
3845. vii. ELIZABETH DOGGETT,[6] born Boston, Mass., June 16, 1816; died Boston, Mass., May 3, 1818.
3846. viii. NATHANIEL BRADLEE DOGGETT,[6] born Boston, Mass., Nov. 28, 1818.
3847. ix. NOAH ALLINE DOGGETT,[6] born Boston, Mass., May 26, 1821.

October 7, 1770. Noah Doggett was baptized in the New South Church, Boston, by Dr. Whitaker, of Salem.

After receiving a common-school education he learned the carpenter's trade, and commenced business as a " housewright."

The Boston Directory for 1796 calls him " housewright," and his address " Daggett's Alley."

In 1798 this alley became Battery alley, and the Directory shows he had added to his business that of " cistern maker."

During these years he was associated in business with Shubael Bell, the combination being " Bell & Doggett."

From the nature of his business he became interested early in real estate, and his first venture was the purchase of an estate in Battery alley. He made some improvements on the estate, and sold it in parts, the final disposal being September 14, 1824.

In 1800 and 1803 he was a " housewright," Edward's wharf, Back street, with house North square.

In 1801 he was interested in securing a building on Clark square, and in the latter part of the year devoted his evenings to the study of mensuration and gauging, with Osgood Carleton as his teacher.

January 4, 1803, he received his degree as a member of St. John's Lodge of Masons, of which lodge his partner Shubael Bell was also a member.

In 1805 and 1806 he was on Jarvis row, Newbury street, which was opposite the Lamb tavern, now the Adams house, and still a " housewright," but the following year (1807) he retired from the carpenter's trade, and became a " surveyor of lumber," with his headquarters at his house on Sea street.

His first wife, Ruth Doggett, died in 1809, but her mother, who resided in Boston, lived several years after her death, and was visited by her granddaughter, Mary A. Doggett, at her home in Boston; but aside from this fact, I have found no positive information as to the

parentage of Ruth Lyne; she may have been of the Marblehead family of that name, but that is only conjecture.

In 1810 Noah Dogget married his second wife, Elizabeth Bradlee, a descendant in the fifth generation from Nathan Bradley, of Dorchester, Mass., through Nathaniel,[4] Samuel,[3] Nathan,[2] Nathan.[1]

They resided in Sea street until their removal in the spring of 1823 to the family mansion, corner of Hollis and Tremont streets, which had been built by her father in 1771, and was purchased of the heirs in 1822 by Noah Doggett.

During these years he had been otherwise interested in real estate, in 1814 by the purchase of land in Roxbury on the Dorchester road, and in the same year by the purchase of an estate on Pleasant street, near the present site of the Providence station.

This latter estate ran to low-water mark in the Back Bay, and his remarks regarding this territory are worthy of record as they showed a keen foresight of the events of to-day, with the bay filled and covered with costly structures.

Interested in the building of the milldam on the other side of the bay, and one of the earliest stockholders in the Boston and Roxbury Mill Corporation, he had an opportunity to observe the closeness of the district to the centre of the town, and often said with much emphasis, "That territory must be utilized, filled up and built on, it must come into the market." Noah Doggett attended the New South Church during his boyhood, but after his second marriage became a member of the First Church, of which he was one of the "standing committee" in 1836-7-8-9.

The volunteer fire department of the city numbered among its members many of our best citizens, and for several years Noah Doggett acted as "captain" of Engine No. 11. From this position he was called "captain" to the end of his life.

He was a member of the Bunker Hill Monument Association.

During the last ten years of his life he retired from surveying, and occupied himself with the care of his private affairs.

In appearance and bearing Noah Doggett was commanding, about five feet eleven inches in height, and well proportioned; his expression stern; his features large.

Until after his second marriage he wore the dress of that day, the queue and knee breeches.

He died widely known and respected, and was buried in the Central Burial Ground, Tomb No. 53.

3720. SAMUEL DOGGETT[5] (*Noah,[4] Samuel,[3] Samuel,[2] Thomas[1]*), born Boston, Mass., August 31, 1772.

Samuel Doggett was baptized in the New South Church by Doctor

Chauncy, September 13, 1772. At an early age he had a desire to follow the sea, and went on a voyage to Liverpool with Capt. Amos Oakman.

The following extract is from a letter in the possession of the writer, and is all that has been found concerning him:

LIVERPOOL 15 July 1791

HONORED SIR:

I arrived here the 21st of June and shall sail for Boston in the course of 10 or 12 days. I must inform you of this unwelcome news, Since I have been in port Sam entered on board the tender in this port and it is out of my power to get him out. . . . I remain yours

AMOS OAKMAN

Samuel Doggett was never afterward heard from. Inquiry at the admiralty office, London, brings the reply that nothing further can be told without the name of the tender, and the authorities at Liverpool, Eng., say their records will not supply that.

3730. ELIZABETH DOGGETT [5] (*Ebenezer,*[4] *Ebenezer,*[3] *Samuel,*[2] *Thomas*[1]), born Plymouth, Mass., November 9, 1749; died Liverpool, N.S., February 5, 1767; married 1766.

Elizabeth Doggett died in Liverpool, N.S., and the following is an extract of a letter written by her father soon after her death.

LIVERPOOL March ye 1st 1767

HONORED MOTHER:

After our duty to you and love to sister Betsey, I send these, hoping they will meet you in good health but must acquaint you that we have met with a heavy stroke of Providence in taking away our only daughter by death. . . . She was blest with a very agreeable partner while she lived with him which was but a little while, not quite 11 months. She died the 5th of February 1767. The first day appointed for her funeral the people accordingly met but meeting with difficulty in digging the Grave it was put by, then we had her brought over to our house in order for her funeral from there the next day. Accordingly the people met again but the same difficulty happened so that it was put by again until ye next Day, which seemed remarkable that the people were obliged to meet 3 days one after another before her funeral was accomplished but it was great satisfaction to us that it happened so for it was very hard for us to part with her. Although she was dead she seemed only like one asleep with her child by her side. She being well but the day before she died.

Please to remember our love to Brother Drew & all inquiring friends. Please to remember us to your brothers, Sisters and Mother if living.

These from Your Dutiful Son in law

EBENEZER DOGGET

3735. SETH DOGGETT [5] (*Ebenezer,*[4] *Ebenezer,*[3] *Samuel,*[2] *Thomas*[1]), married Plymouth, Mass., April 15, 1792, Jane Harlow, daughter of Samuel and Remembrance (Holmes) Harlow; born Plymouth, Mass., 1768; died Plymouth, Mass., May 31, 1794.

Issue:

3848. i. Daughter DOGGETT,[6] born Plymouth, Mass., May 31, 1794; died there same day.

Seth Doggett was a "tailor" in Plymouth.

His brother William lived in Boston, and at his decease left all his property to his "brother Seth Doggett of Plymouth." This was in 1798.

Jane Doggett, the wife of Seth, was very beautiful, a fact which has been handed down in several families of that branch of the Doggetts. She died in the twenty-sixth year of her age, and lies buried on Burial Hill, Plymouth, close beside the path leading from Town square, and on top of the hill. The stone has the following inscription:

> To the memory of the
> Amiable Mrs Jane
> Dogget consort of Mr
> Seth Dogget who died
> May 31, 1794
> In the 26th year of her
> age also an infant
> daughter by her side.
>
> Come view the scene twill
> fill you with surprise
> Behold the loveliest form
> in nature dies.
> At noon she flourished
> blooming fair and gay
> At evening an extended
> corpse she lay.

3739. CATHARINE DOGGETT[5] (*Samuel,*[4] *Ebenezer,*[3] *Samuel,*[2] *Thomas*[1]), born Liverpool, N.S.; married Mr. Little; resided Liverpool, N.S., Market lane.

July 4, 1795, buys land at Liverpool, and then called Catharine Doggett.

July 8, 1795, sells land at "Doggett's Point," Liverpool.

3740. BETSEY DOGGETT[5] (*Samuel,*[4] *Ebenezer,*[3] *Samuel,*[2] *Thomas*[1]), born Liverpool, N.S., September 24, 1767; married Liverpool, N.S., June 14, 1789, Thomas Kempton; born Liverpool, N.S., November 24, 1767; resided Milton, N.S.

Issue:

3849. i. ELISABETH KEMPTON,[6] born Liverpool, N.S., June 5, 1790.
3850. ii. DEBORAH KEMPTON,[6] born Liverpool, N.S., March 19, 1792.
3851. iii. RICHARD KEMPTON,[6] born Liverpool, N.S., November 7, 1794.
3852. iv. MARY KEMPTON,[6] born Liverpool, N.S., June 5, 1796.
3853. v. HANNAH KEMPTON,[6] born Liverpool, N.S., May 19, 1798.
3854. vi. CATHARINE KEMPTON,[6] born Liverpool, N.S., June 21, 1800.
3855. vii. CHARLOTTE KEMPTON,[6] born Liverpool, N.S., June 20, 1802.
3856. viii. SAMUEL DOGGETT KEMPTON,[6] born Liverpool, N.S., March 20, 1805.
3857. ix. CAROLINE KEMPTON,[6] born Liverpool, N.S., July 4, 1807.
3858. x. SIMEON KEMPTON,[6] born Liverpool, N.S., July 31, 1809.
3859. xi. SOPHIA KEMPTON,[6] born Liverpool, N.S., December 6, 1813.

3742. ELIZABETH DREW[5] (*Elizabeth Doggett,*[4] *Ebenezer,*[3] *Samuel,*[2] *Thomas*[1]), born Plymouth, Mass., December 2, 1765; died Plymouth, Mass., October 9, 1849; married Plymouth, Mass., November 23, 1794, by Rev. Chandler Robbins, to William Sherman, son of Samuel and Betty (Sears) Sherman; born Plymouth, Mass., November 23, 1764; died at sea January 9, 1796.

Issue:

3860. i. ELISABETH SHERMAN,[6] born Plymouth, Mass., June 19, 1795.

3743. BENJAMIN DREW [5] (*Elizabeth Doggett,*[4] *Ebenezer,*[3] *Samuel,*[2] *Thomas* [1]), born Plymouth, Mass., February 7, 1767; died Plymouth, Mass., January 1, 1850; married Sophia Bartlett.

Issue:

3861. i. MARTHA B. DREW,[6] born Plymouth, Mass., January 23, 1798; married Lewis Weston, November 11, 1818; issue: Horace Weston, of Weston & Putnam, Province street, Boston; she died Oct. 17, 1877.
3862. ii. ELIZABETH DREW,[6] born Plymouth, Mass., September 29, 1799.
3863. iii. BENJAMIN DREW,[6] born Plymouth, Mass., December 6, 1800; died Plymouth, Mass., July 8, 1802.
3864. iv. SOPHIA DREW,[6] born Plymouth, Mass., August 29, 1802; died Plymouth, Mass., August 19, 1803.
3865. v. SOPHIA B. DREW,[6] born Plymouth, Mass., October 8, 1803; died Plymouth, Mass., November 2, 1806.
3866. vi. FANNY DREW,[6] born Plymouth, Mass., November 10, 1805; died Plymouth, Mass., January 14, 1887.
3867. vii. SOPHIA B. DREW,[6] born Plymouth, Mass., September 28, 1807; died Plymouth, Mass., September 2, 1821.
3868. viii. MARY DREW,[6] born Plymouth, Mass., September 9, 1810; married Sylvanus Harvey, October 23, 1845; no issue.
3869. ix. BENJAMIN DREW,[6] born Plymouth, Mass., November 28, 1812.

3746. MARGARET DREW [5] (*Elizabeth Doggett,*[4] *Ebenezer,*[3] *Samuel,*[2] *Thomas* [1]), born Plymouth, Mass., July 30, 1771; married 1st, Anselm Rickard; married 2d, Plymouth, Mass., October 26, 1812, Barnabas Holmes.

Issue:

3870. i. ANSELM RICKARD,[6] born Plymouth, Mass., June 4, 1798; died without issue.

3751. ASENATH DAGGETT [5] (*Samuel,*[4] *John,*[3] *Samuel,*[2] *Thomas* [1]), born Coventry, Conn., January 2, 1755; died Cazenovia, N.Y., September 26, 1823; married Nathaniel Kingsbury, of Andover, son of Dea. Jabez Kingsbury; born October 15, 1751; died Feb. 5, 1829.

Issue:

3871. i. ALLEN KINGSBURY,[6] born February 9, 1779; married and died Cazenovia, N.Y., leaving descendants.
3872. ii. WEALTHY KINGSBURY,[6] born October 24, 1783.
3873. iii. ASENATH KINGSBURY,[6] born October 17, 1785.
3874. iv. JABEZ KINGSBURY,[6] born October 9, 1788.

3752. TABITHA DAGGETT [5] (*Samuel,*[4] *John,*[3] *Samuel,*[2] *Thomas* [1]), born Coventry, Conn., April 5, 1757; married Joseph Carver, of Bolton.

Issue:

3875. i. TABITHA CARVER.[6]

3876. ii.   NANCY CARVER.[6]
3877. iii. JOSEPH CARVER.[6]
3878. iv.   AUGUSTUS CARVER.[6]
3879. v.   CYNTHIA BUSHNELL CARVER,[6] born Bolton, Conn., March 5, 1791;
            married Chester Daggett (see No. 3885).
3880. vi.   PROSPER CARVER.[6]
3881. vii. CALVIN CARVER.[6]
3882. viii. SAMUEL CARVER.[6]

3753.   Dea. ISAIAH DAGGETT[5] (*Samuel,*[4] *John,*[3] *Samuel,*[2]
Thomas[1]), born 1759; died Coventry, Conn., August 24, 1835;
married Coventry, Conn., December 9, 1784, Esther English, daughter of Richard and Freedom (Strong) English, of Hebron, Conn.

Issue:

3883. i.   ISAIAH DAGGETT,[6] born Coventry, Conn., August 1, 1785.
3884. ii.   CHESTER DAGGETT,[6] born Coventry, Conn., September 25, 1786; died
            Coventry, Conn., February 21, 1795.
3885. iii. CHESTER DAGGETT,[6] born Coventry, Conn., September 25, 1787.
3886. iv.   ANNA DAGGETT,[6] born Coventry, Conn., November 22, 1791; died
            Coventry, Conn., February 12, 1795.
3887. v.   BETSEY DAGGETT,[6] born Coventry, Conn., July 13, 1794; died
            Andover, Conn., August 19, 1861.
3888. vi.   CALVIN DAGGETT,[6] born Coventry, Conn., August 16, 1797; died July
            28, 1880.
3889. vii. SAMUEL BUSHNELL DAGGETT,[6] born Coventry, Conn., Oct. 7, 1800.

3754.   ELIZABETH DOGGETT[5] (*John,*[4] *John,*[3] *Samuel,*[2] *Thomas*[1]),
born Lebanon, Conn., February 21, 1750; died December 3, 1844;
married Lebanon, Conn., February 16, 1775, Azariah Bill, son of
Elisha and Lydia (Woodward) Bill; born Lebanon, Conn., April 27,
1751; died Columbia, Conn., January 31, 1829.

Issue:

3890. i.   CYNTHIA BILL,[6] born Lebanon, Conn., May 22, 1776; died Lebanon,
            Conn., August 1, 1780.
3891. ii.   BETSEY BILL,[6] born Lebanon, Conn., March 8, 1799; married 1st,
            Dudley Williams; 2d, Mr. Doolittle.
3892. iii. AARON BILL,[6] born Lebanon, Conn., March 22, 1781; married Sally
            Savory and had Sally,[7] Lydia Ann,[7] and Caroline;[7] Lydia Ann[7]
            married Mr. Hutchinson and had Ida Z. Hutchinson[8] (see No. 4526).
3893. iv.   CYNTHIA BILL,[6] born Lebanon, Conn., May 1, 1783; married William
            Carver.
3894. v.   ELEAZER BILL,[6] born Lebanon, Conn., September 14, 1785; married
            Nancy Richardson, April 19, 1805.
3895. vi.   LYDIA BILL,[6] born Lebanon, Conn., May 11, 1788; married Wm.
            Hazard.
3896. vii. HORACE BILL,[6] born Lebanon, Conn., May 10, 1791; died Lebanon,
            Conn., April 23, 1793.

Azariah Bill spent his life chiefly in Lebanon, his native town,
though for a number of years he lived in Hebron, but finally removed to Columbia, north of Lebanon. He was a man much respected, and for several years filled the offices of grand juror,
collector, etc.

3755. JOHN DOGGETT[5] (*John,*[4] *John,*[3] *Samuel,*[2] *Thomas*[1]), born Lebanon, Conn., September 11, 1754; called his name Daggett; died Girard, Erie Co., Pa., February 12, 1837; married 1st, 1772, Sarah Hawkins; died Sharzee, Vt.; married 2d, Greenfield, Pa., Polly Smith; born Greensburg, Pa.; died Girard, Pa.; married 3d, Fairview, Pa., Nancy Smith; born Greensburg, Pa.; died Girard, Pa., 1827; married 4th, Girard, Pa., 1828, Mrs. Hannah Sanford, widow of Darius Sanford, and daughter of Mr. Jackson; born N.Y., March 26, 1766; divorced; died Girard, Pa., April 6, 1837; married 5th, Girard, Pa., 1835, by John Davis, J.P., to Mrs. Huldah Bills; born 1801; died Springfield, Pa., 1840.

Issue :

3897. i.   PAMELA DAGGETT,[6] born Vergennes, Vt., June 3, 1774.
3898. ii.   SEBRA DAGGETT,[6] born Hebron, Conn., November 25, 1775.
3899. iii.   ETHAN ALLEN DAGGETT,[6] born Vergennes, Vt., May 13, 1783.
3900. iv.   DON DELANCE DAGGETT,[6] born Hartford, Conn., 1780.
3901. v.   CHARLES DAGGETT.[6]
3902. vi.   ELEAZER DAGGETT,[6] born Vergennes, Vt., 1788.
3903. vii.   RODERIC DAGGETT,[6] born Vergennes, Vt.; died aged 7.
3904. viii.   —— DAGGETT,[6] died aged three months.

John Daggett in the fall of 1802 settled in Greenfield, Erie Co., Pa., within three miles of Colt's station. He was one of the first settlers in the county, there being at that time but three houses in Erie, where now dwell thirty thousand people. He bought two hundred acres of land, on which he made his home, and the land is still in the possession of his descendants. When he first settled here there were no roads laid out, and the path to Erie was marked by blazed trees.

John Daggett was five feet ten inches in height, stood very erect, had black eyes and hair of the same color. He spent much time hunting and fishing. He was a man that everybody liked.

He speaks of himself in his application for a pension, on account of services rendered during the Revolution : "Born in 1753 in Lebanon, now in New London Co., Conn., removed in 1780 to Vermont, where, in 1784, settled in Vergennes, Addison Co."

In 1802 he removed with his family to Erie county, Pa., and in September, 1828, his residence was at Fairview, and September, 1832, it was at Girard, both in Erie Co.

He enlisted in April, 1775, with Capt. James Clark, who immediately marched to Cambridge, Mass., where he joined the Connecticut regiment commanded by Colonel Starr. In the siege of Boston, a part of the company was detached for service at Bunker Hill; but at the time of the battle there, Daggett was on guard at Cambridge.

He was discharged the last of December, 1775.

In May, 1776, he entered the service with Capt. James Clark, marched to Norwich, Conn., to embark on board the brig " Naney," Captain Pierce, for New York city, where on their arrival they were stationed on Broadway, in the command of Colonel Sage, of Connecticut, for a few days, and then ordered to Governor's island, where they remained until after the battle on Long island, August 27, 1776, at which time the army on Long island made a midnight retreat across the East river to New York city, where his company was ordered to occupy their former post on Broadway.

The continued advance of the enemy was followed by the evacuation of the city, September 15, 1776, and his regiment retreated to Turtle bay and Harlem heights. He was in the engagements in that vicinity, Harlem plains, September 16, 1776, then to White plains, where he was in the battle October 28, 1776, after which he marched to Phillips manor and Crum pond, fourteen miles below Peekskill, N.Y., where they encamped until his discharge in January, 1777.

In June, 1777, he enlisted for six months under Capt. John Skinner, who was attached to the regiment commanded by Colonel Lattimer, of Connecticut, and he proceeded from Lebanon by way of Berkshire county, Mass., Albany, N.Y., to Stillwater, Saratoga Co., and was stationed on Bemis heights, where he was in the battles of September 19 and October 7, 1777, which preceded the surrender of General Burgoyne at Saratoga, October 17, 1777.   After his removal to Vermont he served as sergeant under Captain Sexton and Colonel Walbridge, from June, 1782, at Skeenboro', now Whitehall, at the head of Lake Champlain, and soon after the British had evacuated Crown Point, he was, in December, 1782, discharged.

In a supplemental statement he stated that he resided in Vergennes twenty years, then removed to Greenfield, Erie Co., Penn.

He died in Girard township, in what is now called Fairplain.

3757. Gen. SAMUEL DOGGETT [5] (*John,*[4] *John,*[3] *Samuel,*[2] *Thomas*[1]), born Lebanon, Conn., December 3, 1768; called his name Daggett; died Coventry, Conn., April 15, 1832; married Sallie Bill; died after 1832.

No issue.

3759. Lieut. SAMUEL DOGGETT [5] (*Samuel,*[4] *Isaac,*[3] *Samuel,*[2] *Thomas*[1]), born Dedham, Mass., October 5, 1751; died Dedham, Mass., November 19, 1831; married Dedham, Mass., June 1, 1777,

Elizabeth Badlam, daughter of Stephen and Hannah (Clapp) Badlam; born Stoughton, Mass., December 20, 1753; died Dedham,
Mass., December 22, 1832.

Issue :

3905. i.   BETSEY DOGGETT,[6] born Dedham, Mass., June 24, 1778.
3906. ii. JOHN DOGGETT,[6] born Dedham, Mass., September 15, 1780.
3907. iii. SAMUEL DOGGETT,[6] born Dedham, Mass., February 12, 1794.

Samuel Doggett on the commencement of hostilities in 1775
entered the American army, and served in the eight months' service
in 1775.

January 23, 1776, he again entered the service as lieutenant in
Captain Stevens's company, in Col. Henry Knox's regiment of
artillery. After having served for one year he was honorably discharged in consequence of the expiration of the term of service for
which he had engaged. October 2, 1778, he was again commissioned as lieutenant of the second company, Capt. Ebenezer Battle,
of the First Regiment of Militia in the county of Suffolk. They
were in service in Rhode Island from July 29 to September 16, 1778,
inclusive. The pay-roll of this company at that time was preserved
by his descendants, who presented it to the town of Dedham at the
time of the Dedham centennial. His commission as lieutenant is in
possession of his granddaughter, Emily Doggett Crafts.

Under the Pension Act passed by Congress March 18, 1818, he
became a pensioner January 30, 1819, for services in the year 1776
as lieutenant in Captain Stevens's company. In pursuance of the Act
of Congress, May 1, 1820, he exhibited a schedule of his whole
estate and income, which was appraised at the sum of $3,590. In
consequence of the possession of this property, his name was stricken
from the pension list.

It was restored, however, April 23, 1828, in answer to his petition
of the February preceding, he having been obliged during the interval
of eight years to dispose of nearly all of his property for his support.
He continued to draw a pension until his death, November 19, 1831.

He was born and always lived in Dedham, and took a great interest
in all movements for its welfare. He was by occupation a millwright and housewright, or carpenter, and later in life was jailer of
Dedham jail.

Mr. and Mrs. Doggett dwelt together in wedlock for fifty-four
years. Their old mansion-house in Dedham is still standing, and in
possession of Dr. Southgate. Their portraits finely executed in oil
by Gilbert Stuart are held in the family. They were painted in 1815.

3761.   MARY DOGGETT[5] (*Samuel,*[4] *Isaac,*[3] *Samuel,*[2] *Thomas*[1]),
born Dedham, Mass., November 9, 1755; died Dedham, Mass.,

LIEUT. SAMUEL DOGGETT.

ELIZABETH (BADLAM) DOGGETT.

March 15, 1836; married Dedham, Mass., October 10, 1774, by
Rev. Jason Haven, to Daniel Baker, son of Daniel and Mary
(Wight) Baker; born Dedham, Mass., October 10, 1752; died Ded-
ham, Mass., May 7, 1806.

Issue:

3908. i.   ABIGAIL BAKER,[6] born Dedham, Mass., August 13, 1775.
3909. ii. CATHERINE BAKER,[6] born Dedham, Mass., January 9, 1777.
3910. iii. JOHN BAKER.[6]

3762. ISAAC DOGGETT[5] (*Samuel,*[4] *Isaac,*[3] *Samuel,*[2] *Thomas*[1]),
born Dedham, Mass., January 11, 1758; died Dedham, Mass., May
31, 1807; married Dedham, Mass., December 7, 1784, by Rev.
Jason Haven, to Rebeca Ellis, daughter of Abel and Abigail
(Guild) Ellis; born Dedham, Mass., January 11, 1757; died Dedham, Mass., December 16, 1811.

Issue:

3911. i. SETH DOGGETT,[6] born Dedham, Mass., February 14, 1786; died Dedham, Mass., March 4, 1820.

They always lived in Dedham, his house being next to that of his
brother, Samuel Doggett.

3763. JESSE DOGGETT[5] (*Samuel,*[4] *Isaac,*[3] *Samuel,*[2] *Thomas*[1]),
born Dedham, Mass., January 12, 1761; died Roxbury, Mass.,
August 10, 1813; married Roxbury, Mass., December 1, 1790,
Elizabeth Sumner, daughter of Samuel and Susannah (Boylston)
Sumner; born Roxbury, Mass., June 22, 1770; died Roxbury, Mass.,
December 17, 1858.

Issue:

3912. i.   ELIZABETH SUMNER DOGGETT,[6] born Roxbury, Mass., Sept. 12, 1791.
3913. ii.   SAMUEL SUMNER DOGGETT,[6] born Roxbury, Mass., October 26, 1795;
died Roxbury, Mass., April 25, 1802.
3914. iii. JESSE DOGGETT,[6] born Roxbury, Mass., September 11, 1797; died
Roxbury, Mass., October 4, 1815.
3915. iv.   INCREASE SUMNER DOGGETT,[6] born Roxbury, Mass., November 22,
1799; died Roxbury, Mass., November 8, 1820.
3916. v.   SUSANNAH DOGGETT,[6] born Roxbury, Mass., May 25, 1802; died Roxbury, Mass., July 1, 1805.
3917. vi.   ABIGAIL WHITING DOGGETT,[6] born Roxbury, Mass., March 8, 1804;
died Roxbury, Mass., October 5, 1822.
3918. vii. SAMUEL SUMNER BOYLSTON DOGGETT,[6] born Roxbury, Mass., May
9, 1808; died Roxbury, Mass., January 3, 1854.

Jesse Doggett, of Roxbury, gentleman, bought land there of Jonathan Davis, December 1, 1787. [Suffolk Deeds, 161–286.]

On Washington street, Roxbury, near the burying-ground, at the
corner of Eustis street, is "an old house formerly a tavern, with the
sign of the 'Ball and Pin,' kept by Capt. Jesse Doggett. 'A train-
band captain eke was he,' who often marshalled his men along this
dusty highway, and after a hot day's exercise doubtless threw wide

his hospitable doors, and regaled the thirsty heroes with cool and refreshing beverages." [Drake's Roxbury, p. 87.]

He was attorney for Sampson Reed, of Boston, August 23, 1788 [Suffolk Deeds, 153–278]; executor of Jonathan Williams, October 2, 1799 [Essex Deeds, 165–124], and in both instruments called of Roxbury, gentleman.

Besides being an " Innkeeper," he is called " Leather Dresser " in an instrument dated April 13, 1807.   [Essex Deeds, 180–116.]

3764. ELISHA DOGGETT [5] (*Samuel,* [4] *Isaac,* [3] *Samuel,* [2] *Thomas* [1]), born Dedham, Mass., May 10, 1767; died Salem, Mass., April 29, 1810; married 1st, 1789, Miss Mason; died February 23, 1795; married 2d, March 6, 1796, Elizabeth Holland; born Salem, Mass.; died Boston, Mass., January 5, 1837.

Issue :

3919. i.   EUNICE DOGGETT,[6] born July 26, 1790.
3920. ii.   ELIZABETH DOGGETT,[6] born August 17, 1792.
3921. iii. ELISHA DOGGETT,[6] born August 27, 1794; died August 29, 1795.
3922. iv.   CATHARINE DOGGETT,[6] born February 23, 1797.
3923. v.   MARGARET DOGGETT,[6] born Salem, Mass., July 23, 1798; died Cambridgeport, Mass., August 24, 1882.
3924. vi.   MARY DOGGETT,[6] born April 16, 1800; died October 29, 1806.
3925. vii. NANCY THORNDIKE DOGGETT,[6] born November 3, 1803.
3926. viii. LYDIA DOGGETT,[6] born April 20, 1805; died November 9, 1818.
3927. ix.   MARY DOGGETT,[6] born October 13, 1807.

Elisha Doggett removed to Salem, Mass., where he was at one time (1807) a hair-dresser, having a shop on Washington street.

THOMAS DOGGETT, OF MARSHFIELD, MASS.

SIXTH GENERATION.

3771. ABNER DOGGETT [6] (*John,* [5] *John,* [4] *Thomas,* [3] *John,* [2] *Thomas* [1]), born Scituate, Mass., August 16, 1749.

Abner Doggett was appointed administrator on the estate of his father, 17th April, 1772.

He may have resided at that time in Liverpool, but as the final settlement, October 15, 1793, is exhibited by John Thomas as his attorney, and the records examined do not in any other case mention his name, he possibly removed between these two dates, but no records have been found to indicate to what place.

Abner Doggett, of Truro, N.S., may be his son (No. 5587), but no facts have come to light to substantiate this suggestion.

3773. ABIGAIL DOGGETT [6] (*John,* [5] *John,* [4] *Thomas,* [3] *John,* [2] *Thomas* [1]), married Liverpool, N.S., Joseph Verge.

Joseph Verge, cooper, acted as attorney for his mother-in-law to receive certain money which was due her, and also made several real-estate transfers in the settlement of the Doggett estate.

11 May 1798. Joseph Verge sells dwelling house formerly the property of John Doggett Esq dec'd, in Liverpool. [4–321.]
28 Aug 1799. Joseph Verge and Ichabod Doggett sell Lemuel Drew 3rd, land in Liverpool. [5–5.]

Port Matoon island was left unoccupied for many years by the Doggett family, and was taken possession of by a man named Bushen.

Ichabod Doggett endeavored to dispossess him, but failed to do so, as he had had it over twenty years. Mrs. Verge being a married woman was enabled to hold her half according to law.

3775. ICHABOD DOGGETT [6] (*John*,[5] *John*,[4] *Thomas*,[3] *John*,[2] *Thomas*[1]), born 1771; died White Point, N.S., March 8, 1856; married Liverpool, N.S., Priscilla Freeman; born Liverpool, N.S., 1775; died White Point, N.S., March 11, 1835.

Issue :

3928. i. JOHN DOGGETT,[7] born Liverpool, N.S., September 20, 1799.
3929. ii. LATHROP DOGGETT,[7] born Liverpool, N S., October 5, 1801.
3930. iii. JAMES DOGGETT,[7] born Liverpool, N.S., September 15, 1805; died White Point, N.S., October 29, 1834.
3931. iv. JOSEPH DOGGETT,[7] born White Point, N.S., April 30, 1808.
3932. v. SAMUEL DOGGETT,[7] born White Point, N.S., September 10, 1812; died Halifax, N.S., September 15, 1828.
3933. vi. PENINAH DOGGETT,[7] born White Point, N.S., September 10, 1815.
3934. vii. EBENEZER DOGGETT,[7] born White Point, N.S., September 6, 1817.

3780. MARK DOGGETT [6] (*Jabez*,[5] *Thomas*,[4] *Thomas*,[3] *John*,[2] *Thomas*[1]), born Middleboro', Mass., August 28, 1768; died Grand Manan, N.B., February 23, 1838; married Bridgewater, Mass., Portia Keith; born 1770; died Grand Manan, N.B., May 17, 1846.

Issue :

3935. i. ELIPHALET DOGGETT,[7] born Middleboro', Mass., November 13, 1793.
3936. ii. SHEPARD DOGGETT,[7] born Middleboro', Mass., May 6, 1796.
3937. iii. MARTIN KEITH DOGGETT,[7] born Middleboro', Mass., March 23, 1800.
3938. iv. NATHANIEL DOGGETT,[7] born Middleboro', Mass., May 8, 1802.
3939. v. PHILO DOGGETT,[7] born Middleboro', Mass., February 13, 1805.
3940. vi. MARK DOGGETT,[7] born Middleboro', Mass., May 18, 1807.
3941. vii. JOHN DOGGETT,[7] born Middleboro', Mass., February 24, 1810.
3942. viii. ELIZA DOGGETT,[7] born Middleboro,' Mass., January 24, 1814.

Mr. Doggett removed from Massachusetts to New Brunswick in 1817.

3781. REBECCA DOGGETT [6] (*Jabez*,[5] *Thomas*,[4] *Thomas*,[3] *John*,[2] *Thomas*[1]), born Middleboro', Mass., February 18, 1770; died Grand Manan, N.B.; married Edmund Cheney.

Issue :

3943. i. WILLIAM CHENEY.[7]
3944. ii. JOHN CHENEY.[7]

3945. iii. SAMUEL CHENEY.[7]
3946. iv. EDMUND CHENEY.[7]
3947. v. HARRIET CHENEY.[7]
3948. vi. PEREZ CHENEY.[7]
3949. vii. ELIZABETH CHENEY.[7]

3783. PEREZ DOGGETT[6] (*Jabez*,[5] *Thomas*,[4] *Thomas*,[3] *John*,[2] *Thomas*[1]), born Middleboro', Mass., August 22, 1776; died Middleboro', Mass., January 14, 1849; married Middleboro', Mass., November 28, 1799, Griselle Townsend; born 1779; died Middleboro', Mass., September 28, 1863.

No issue.

"Mr. Doggett, 'farmer,' lived on his father's farm in Middleboro'. He had in his possession a bureau which was brought over in the 'Mayflower' by Samuel Fuller."

3784. THOMAS DOGGETT[6] (*Simeon*,[5] *Thomas*,[4] *Thomas*,[3] *John*,[2] *Thomas*[1]), born Middleboro', Mass., April 14, 1761; died Middleboro', Mass., June 15, 1831; married (published March 16, 1788), Phœbe Dean, of Taunton, Mass.; born Taunton, Mass., 1764; died Middleboro', Mass., August 4, 1837.

Issue:

3950. i. ELKANAH DOGGETT,[7] born Middleboro', Mass., October 4, 1790.
3951. ii. PHŒBE DEAN DOGGETT,[7] born Middleboro', Mass., November 1, 1795.
3952. iii. THOMAS DOGGETT,[7] born Middleboro', Mass., September 24, 1801.

Thomas Doggett was a respected farmer in Middleboro'.

At the time of his marriage his father built an addition to the homestead, and gave the first-built portion to the newly married pair.

3785. ELKANAH DOGGETT[6] (*Simeon*,[5] *Thomas*,[4] *Thomas*,[3] *John*,[2] *Thomas*[1]), born Middleboro', Mass., October 27, 1762; died between August 7 and December 9, 1789; married Wareham (?), Mass. (published March 16, 1789), Lucy Fearing; born Wareham (?), Mass.; died Pittsfield (?), Mass.

No issue.

Elkanah Doggett, of Middleboro', gentleman, merchant, purchased with Abiel Washburn two lots of land; one deeded July 26, 1789, of sixty-six and three-fourths acres, which they bought of Silas Fearing, of Wareham, Paul Fearing, of the city of Marietta, in county Washington and territory of the United States, north-west of the river Ohio, and Hannah Fearing, wife of Silas [Plymouth Deeds, 71–33]; and the other deeded August 7, 1789, for woodland in the sixteen-shilling purchase in Middleboro', bought of Paul Fearing, of Marietta, Ohio. [Plymouth Deeds, 69–274.]

December 9, 1789, administration on the estate of Elkanah Doggett was granted to Simeon Doggett of Middleboro', yeoman. [Plymouth Probate, 27–307.]

Dec 28, 1789   The Inventory of the estate of Elkanah Doggett amounted to 1,038£ 4s 4¾d. [Plymouth Probate, 31–109.]

May 17, 1790   Simeon Doggett and Abiel Washburn make an equal division of the land bought July 26, 1789. [Plymouth Deeds, 71–43.]

Aug 2, 1790 Simeon Doggett renders his acct. from which it appears that there remained after paying 322£ 1s 10¼d the sum of 504£ 12s 7½d. [Plymouth Probate, 31–241.]

Lucy Doggett, the widow of Elkanah Doggett, married January 26, 1791, Hon. Nathan Willis, by whom she had Lucy Willis, who married George Elkanah Watson.

3786.   Rev. Simeon Doggett [6] (*Simeon*,[5] *Thomas*,[4] *Thomas*,[3] *John*,[2] *Thomas*[1]), born Middleboro', Mass., March 6, 1765; died Raynham, Mass., March 20, 1852; married October 29, 1797, Nancy Fobes, daughter of Rev. Perez Fobes, LL.D., and Prudence (Wales) Fobes; born Raynham, Mass., September 8, 1769; died Raynham, Mass., December 14, 1854.

Issue:

3953. i.   John Locke Doggett,[7] born Taunton, Mass., September 8, 1798.
3954. ii.   Samuel Wales Doggett,[7] born Taunton, Mass., July 9, 1800.
3955. iii. Simeon Doggett,[7] born Taunton, Mass., November 11, 1802; died Georgia, July 21, 1826.
3956. iv.   Prudence Wales Doggett,[7] born Raynham, Mass., September 30, 1804; died Raynham, Mass., December 27, 1854.
3957. v.   Perez Fobes Doggett,[7] born Taunton, Mass., June 2, 1806.
3958. vi.   Theophilus Pipon Doggett,[7] born Taunton, Mass., January 20, 1810.
3959. vii. Abigail Doggett,[7] born Taunton, Mass., November 8, 1812.
3960. viii. William Paley Doggett,[7] born Taunton, Mass., June 29, 1814; died Raynham, Mass., November 25, 1836.

Rev. Simeon Doggett was born in Middleboro', Mass., March 6, 1765.   His early associations were those of an orderly, industrious, and pious Puritan home.

His mother, a native of North Carolina, had brought with her from her southern birthplace the prepossessions of an Episcopal training, and took care early to indoctrinate the mind of her son with the tenets of the English church.   The sterner influences of Calvinism in his home were softened by the graces of the Arminian liturgy; and while a heretical bias was thus given to the faith of the child, an attachment to the English ritual was fostered, which no length of years, no change of opinions, no constant use of other methods, could weaken.

It was the tradition of his childhood, and the memory of his mother, that led one who had been for more than half a century a Congregational preacher, annually to the altar of the Episcopal church, on the Saviour's birthday.

The father of Mr. Doggett, though not rich, was in easy circumstances, and was able to prepare his son for college and maintain him there.

Mr. Doggett was entered at Brown University in 1785, and graduated in 1788 at the age of twenty-three. His collegiate course was marked throughout by great earnestness in study, and the most scrupulous propriety of demeanor. Though not intending to follow permanently the profession of a teacher, Mr. Doggett had gained, both before and during his college course, an interest and an experience in that vocation. In the town of Charlton, where he taught one year, he had learned to see the importance of rightly guiding the principles and the habits of childhood. While he was in college, he was led to examine for himself the various systems of church government and discipline, and especially to inquire if the form in which he had been brought up was justified by Scripture.

The result of a careful scrutiny was that the Congregational and not the Episcopal order seemed to him the original form of church polity.

In obedience to his conviction he gave up at once the prejudice of his training, and worshipped afterward in the Puritan way. An inquiry concerning scriptural doctrine seemed to him to prove that the Christian view of nature and of grace was that of Arminius and not that of Calvin. His views were such that, on examination by a deacon of Mr. Barker's church, in Middleboro', he, not being willing to fall in with their views, was rejected, and was welcomed at Rev. Dr. Hitchcock's church, in Providence.

Before leaving college he had become a decided Unitarian in his views, though the influence around him all tended to an opposite faith.

On graduating, Mr. Doggett commenced at once, in his father's house, the study of theology. For the first year or two his studies were interrupted by various causes, among other things being obliged to settle the estate of his deceased brother.

Through the good offices of President Manning he was able to reside some six months in a planter's family in Virginia. In 1790 he went to live with the celebrated Dr. West, of Dartmouth, and prosecuted vigorously the study of his profession under the direction of that eccentric and able divine.

In the summer of 1791, Mr. Doggett was chosen to be a tutor in Brown University. In that office he continued five years. In May, 1793, he received from the Rhode Island Convention of Congregational Ministers a license to preach the gospel, and commenced at once to supply vacant pulpits as they might invite him.

One of his early sermons was liked so well it was asked for publication. This sermon was one of the first published sermons in the United States which openly defended Unitarian views.

In teaching others in the pulpit and lecture-room, Mr. Doggett was not unmindful to teach himself. No man was more close in self-scrutiny.

In the month of July, 1796, Bristol Academy, in Taunton, one of the oldest institutions in New England, and the oldest that has been from the beginning free from sectarian influence, was opened, with Mr. Doggett as its first preceptor. It was a highly desirable position. On the day of the opening, Mr. Doggett delivered the inaugural address. The town was full of strangers, and all were delighted at the broad, vigorous, and noble views upon education which were here for the first time publicly advanced. That address was the pioneer of liberal education in the Old Colony.

In April, 1813, his resignation, which he had requested some time before, was accepted, and he was at once chosen a member of the Board of Trustees.

He immediately settled at Mendon, Mass., where he was ordained, January 17, 1815. The society at Mendon was large, influential, and supposed to be orthodox. Yet they called him unanimously, and did not rescind their call when he at a special meeting stated his belief, and required, if he accepted the post, that the church creed and covenant, which he neither believed nor understood, should be altered. Mr. Doggett remained in the ministry of Mendon until January, 1831, having been dismissed at his own request, December 4, 1830. He was called to preach at Raynham, in Bristol county.

At Raynham he wished to spend his declining years, as the father and grandfather of his wife for more than three-quarters of a century illustrated the ministers calling here. His pecuniary means were adequate to his desires, and placed him quite above the fear of want. He had a choice library, gathered and inherited, of the old standard theological works, and he had leisure to use it.

The success of his children could bring joy to his heart, and though they were widely separated from his home their frequent letters kept the family union unbroken.

The youngest child had scarcely commenced the practice of law in his own village when he was suddenly removed by death. In the winter of 1834–5 he made a visit south. In the cities of Charleston, St. Augustine, Jacksonville, and Savannah he was treated with marked attention, and invited in the last-mentioned city to preach at the dedication of the new Unitarian church. The ministry of Mr. Doggett at Raynham continued until the year 1845, when he felt the necessity of retiring from active labor. On his eighty-seventh birthday his friends gathered at his house to offer congratulations.

It was a glad occasion. He died March 20, 1852. [Sketch of Rev. Simeon Doggett, by Chas. H. Brigham, 1852.]

Mr. Doggett and his wife made their will June 8, 1849, beginning with the following words:

Impressed with the Prophets words to Hezekiah — Set thy house in order for
thou shalt die and not live We Simeon Doggett and Nancy his wife of Raynham in the County of Bristol make and publish this our last will and testament.
[Bristol Probate.]

3787. ABIGAIL DOGGETT[6] (*Simeon*,[5] *Thomas*,[4] *Thomas*,[3] *John*,[2]
Thomas[1]), born Middleboro', Mass., March 4, 1775; died Middle-
boro', Mass., August 14, 1830; married Middleboro', Mass., Septem-
ber 30, 1798, Thomas Weston, son of Col. Thomas and Abigail
(Tinkham) Weston; born Middleboro', Mass., March 21, 1770; died
Middleboro', Mass., June 17, 1834.

Issue:

3961. i.   ABIGAIL WESTON,[7] born Middleboro', Mass., March 15, 1801; married
            H. G. Wood; she died Middleboro', Mass., June 7, 1854.
3962. ii.   BETHANIA WESTON,[7] born Middleboro', Mass., October 27, 1802;
            died Middleboro', Mass., December 4, 1803.
3963. iii. THOMAS WESTON,[7] born Middleboro', Mass., February 27, 1804.
3964. iv.   MARY WESTON,[7] born Middleboro', Mass., July 14, 1805; died.
3965. v.   BETHANIA WESTON,[7] born Middleboro', Mass., June 30, 1807.
3966. vi.   SARAH WESTON,[7] born Middleboro', Mass., April 25, 1810; died.
3967. vii. HENRY WESTON,[7] born Middleboro', Mass., May 18, 1812; died
            Middleboro', Mass., June 28, 1813.
3968. viii. LAVINIA WESTON.[7]
3969. ix.   HENRY WESTON,[7] born Middleboro', Mass., June 20, 1817.

Thomas Weston, of Middleboro', purchased, about 1798, a portion
of the estate at Muttock, before Revolutionary times owned by Peter
Oliver, and a few years later purchased the remaining portion of it.

Judge Oliver used to make this place his summer residence, and it
was regarded as the finest estate in the colonies. In 1809, and for
five successive years, Mr. Weston was representative to the General
Court.

In 1815 and 1816 he was a member of the Senate, and elected to
the House again in 1819. In 1820 he was chosen a member of the
convention to revise the Constitution of Massachusetts. From 1823
to 1827 he was a member of the Governor's Council. Judge Weston
was a gentleman of the old school, dignified, but always courteous and
polite. He was a man of strong character and firm principles, scorn-
ing everything mean or dishonest. As a merchant he was enterprising, careful, and of exact business habits. His judgment on the
ordinary matters of life was much sought after by his acquaintances,
and the value of his strong common-sense early recognized. He was
very happy in his domestic life, with a large family of children, most
of whom he lived to see grow to manhood and womanhood, and com-
fortably settled in life. His house was always open, and he enter-
tained with a generous hospitality. His wife, a lady of culture,
presided with a quiet dignity over his household, and her rare conver-
sational powers added much to the pleasure of his guests. [History
Plymouth County.]

In her school days she was sent away from home to school, which was not a common thing in those days.

3808. SARAH OAKMAN[6] (*Amos,*[5] *Sarah Doggett,*[4] *Samuel,*[3] *Samuel,*[2] *Thomas*[1]), born Marshfield, Mass., June 30, 1789; married 1817, Elnathan Gibson.

Issue:

3970. i. EDWIN GIBSON,[7] born Fitchburg, Mass.
3971. ii. ELNATHAN GIBSON,[7] born Fitchburg, Mass.
3972. iii. SARAH GIBSON,[7] born Fitchburg, Mass.

3809. AMOS OAKMAN[6] (*Amos,*[5] *Sarah Doggett,*[4] *Samuel,*[3] *Samuel,*[2] *Thomas*[1]), born Marshfield, Mass., July 16, 1795; died Fitchburg, Mass., June 10, 1860; married Lunenburg, Mass., May 12, 1819, Sally Jones.

Issue:

3973. i. AMOS THOMAS OAKMAN,[7] born Lunenburg, Mass., March 29, 1820; married Mary Carlton, June 7, 1847.
3974. ii. ELIZA J. OAKMAN,[7] born July 18, 1822; died September 2, 1861.
3975. iii. JOHN OAKMAN,[7] born January 22, 1825; died August 19, 1826.
3976. iv. SARAH S. OAKMAN,[7] born July 29, 1829; married November 10, 1846, Cyrus L. Eastman.
3977. v. LEONARD J. OAKMAN,[7] born January 19, 1830.
3978. vi. GEORGE OAKMAN,[7] born July 2, 1832; died June 3, 1837.

3810. ELIZA OAKMAN[6] (*Amos,*[5] *Sarah Doggett,*[4] *Samuel,*[3] *Samuel,*[2] *Thomas*[1]), born Marshfield, Mass., January 2, 1797; died Fitchburg, Mass., June 26, 1835; married 1822, Asa Perley.

Issue:

3979. i. ELIZA JANE PERLEY,[7] married and resides Acton, Mass. (1884).

3811. JOSEPH OAKMAN[6] (*Amos,*[5] *Sarah Doggett,*[4] *Samuel,*[3] *Samuel,*[2] *Thomas*[1]), born Marshfield, Mass., June 23, 1799; died Illinois, August 27, 1839; married Abby Carter.

Issue:

3980. i. JOSEPH OAKMAN,[7] resided New York city.
3981. ii. Son —— OAKMAN,[7] resided Troy, N.Y.

3812. NANCY OAKMAN[6] (*Amos,*[5] *Sarah Doggett,*[4] *Samuel,*[3] *Samuel,*[2] *Thomas*[1]), born Marshfield, Mass., March 1, 1801; died Cottage City, Mass., September 6, 1887; married June 17, 1825, Elijah G. Hutchinson.

Issue:

3982. i. SUSAN G. HUTCHINSON,[7] resides Boston, Mass. (1893).
3983. ii. CALVIN G. HUTCHINSON,[7] born February 17, 1836; resides Wales street, Dorchester, Mass. (1893).
3984. iii. GEORGE O. HUTCHINSON,[7] resides Boston, Mass. (1893).

3814. Joseph Doggett[6] (*Joseph*,[5] *Noah*,[4] *Samuel*,[3] *Samuel*,[2] *Thomas*[1]), born Newburyport, Mass., January 30, 1785; died Newburyport, Mass., March 13, 1832; married 1808, Ednah Haskell, daughter of Caleb and Ednah (Hale) Haskell; born Deer Isle, Me., April 27, 1788; died Newburyport, Mass., January 6, 1868.

Issue:

3985. i. Samuel Doggett,[7] born Newburyport, Mass., April 13, 1809; name changed to Brainard, 1822–3; married Haverhill, Mass., June 3, 1833, Abigail P. Sawyer, of Hampstead, N.H.; born October 8, 1803; no issue; resides Campbell, Ia. (1893).
3986. ii. Joseph Doggett,[7] born Newburyport, Mass., October 5, 1811; name changed to Joseph Brainard, 1822–3; died Newburyport, Mass., November 13, 1831.
3987. iii. Nathan Haskell Doggett,[7] born Newburyport, Mass., Oct. 28, 1813.
3988. iv. Charles Henry Doggett,[7] born Newburyport, Mass., Oct. 11, 1817.
3989. v. Amos Hale Doggett,[7] born Newburyport, Mass., March 27, 1824.

3816. Capt. Samuel Doggett[6] (*Joseph*,[5] *Noah*,[4] *Samuel*,[3] *Samuel*,[2] *Thomas*[1]), born Newburyport, Mass., September 18, 1789; died Boston, Mass., April 9, 1836; married Boston, Mass., November 29, 1821, by Rev. Ephraim Wiley, to Laura P. Foster, daughter of Jacob Foster, of Andover, Mass.; born 1804; died January 10, 1873.

Issue:

3990. i. Samuel Foster Doggett,[7] born January 8, 1823; died April 6, 1824.
3991. ii. John Dorr Doggett,[7] born November 2, 1824; died April 17, 1837.
3992. iii. Jacob Foster Doggett,[7] born September 21, 1827; "captain," making many voyages to Valparaiso; captain of a United States steamer during the war; never married; died San Francisco, Cal., Sept. 30, 1877.

Capt. Samuel Doggett at first made only short voyages, but after he became captain was gone three years at a time.

Mrs. Laura P. Doggett married 2d, David Alden, Boston, October 19, 1847.

3817. Sarah Doggett[6] (*Joseph*,[5] *Noah*,[4] *Samuel*,[3] *Samuel*,[2] *Thomas*[1]), born Newburyport, Mass., February 1, 1792; died Boston, Mass., July 17, 1870; married Boston, Mass., October 20, 1824, by Rev. Sebastian Streeter, to William Setchell.

Issue:

3993. i. William Frederic Setchell,[7] born Boston, Mass., June 16, 1825.
3994. ii. Edward Henry Setchell,[7] born Boston, Mass., October 12, 1826.
3995. iii. Timothy Coffin Setchell,[7] born Boston, Mass., January 28, 1828; died Boston, Mass., April 12, 1828.
3996. iv. Daniel Setchell,[7] born Boston, Mass., February 7, 1831.

3818. Henry Doggett[6] (*Joseph*,[5] *Noah*,[4] *Samuel*,[3] *Samuel*,[2] *Thomas*[1]), born Newburyport, Mass., November 24, 1793; called his name Daggett; died New Haven, N.Y., May 6, 1870; married Newburyport, Mass., June 6, 1824, by Rev. Josiah Houghton, to

Mary Bartlett; born Bangor, Me., December 20, 1800; died New Haven, N.Y., September 13, 1871.

Issue:

3997. i.   WILLIAM HENRY DAGGETT,[7] born Boston, Mass., May 19, 1825; died Newburyport, Mass., July 19, 1825.
3998. ii. HENRY JEFFERSON DAGGETT,[7] born Boston, Mass., August 11, 1826.
3999. iii. GEORGE FRANKLIN DAGGETT,[7] born New York city, September 8, 1830; died New York city, November 1, 1832.
4000. iv. GEORGE WILLIAM DAGGETT,[7] born New York city, February 1, 1833.
4001. v.   EMILIE AUGUSTA DAGGETT,[7] born Oswego, N.Y., June 28, 1835; died Newburyport, Mass., July 11, 1836.
4002. vi. MARY EMILIE DAGGETT,[7] born New Haven, N.Y., August 11, 1837.
4003. vii. LAURA FOSTER DAGGETT,[7] born New Haven, N.Y., August 26, 1846.

Henry Daggett in early life was a mechanic; later became engaged in mercantile pursuits in the cities of Boston, New York, and Oswego, N.Y. He removed from Boston to New York city, November 15, 1827, and a few years later to Oswego. Failing health obliged him to leave business, and he became a farmer in New Haven, N.Y., where he resided until his death.

3819. THOMAS BISPHAM DOGGETT [6] (*Joseph,*[5] *Noah,*[4] *Samuel,*[3] *Samuel,*[2] *Thomas*[1]), born Newburyport, Mass., October 22, 1797; died Jalapa, Mexico, September 7, 1834; married Newburyport, Mass., April 5, 1820, by Rev. Charles W. Milton, to Salome Bartlett, daughter of Ezekiel Bartlett, of Newburyport; born Bangor, Me., March 24, 1798; died Newburyport, Mass., December 19, 1868.

Issue:

4004. i.   SARAH ANN DOGGETT.[7] born Newburyport, Mass., October 22, 1821; died February 26. 1843.
4005. ii. THOMAS DOGGETT,[7] born Newburyport, Mass., November 3, 1823; died August 30, 1825.
4006. iii. MARY LAPISH DOGGETT,[7] born Oct. 7, 1826; died Sept. 5, 1828.
4007. iv. HARRIET MARIA DOGGETT,[7] born Sept. 3, 1829; died Aug. 11, 1830.
4008. v.   THOMAS DOGGETT,[7] born October 21, 183-; died June 11, 1854.

3820. DANIEL JACKSON DOGGETT [6] (*Joseph,*[5] *Noah,*[4] *Samuel,*[3] *Samuel,*[2] *Thomas*[1]), born Newburyport, Mass., May 11, 1799; name changed to Akerman March 13, 1832; died Ipswich, Mass., November 22, 1868; married Ipswich, Mass., July 21, 1820, by Rev. D. T. Kimball, to Lucy Lord; born Ipswich, Mass., March 8, 1804; died Ipswich, Mass., March 10, 1882.

Issue:

4009. i.   JOSEPH LORD DOGGETT,[7] born Ipswich, Mass., January 14, 1821.
4010. ii. SARAH LORD DOGGETT,[7] born Ipswich, Mass., February 21, 1826.
4011. iii. LUCY MARIA DOGGETT,[7] born Ipswich, Mass.; name changed to Akerman March 13, 1832; married Ipswich, Mass., May 4, 1851, Daniel Rogers Rutherford, of Ipswich; no issue.
4012. iv. SUSAN LORD DOGGETT,[7] born Ipswich, Mass., March 25, 1829.
4013. v.   WALTER PHILLIPS DOGGETT,[7] born Ipswich, Mass., July 20, 1831; name changed to Akerman March 13, 1832; died Ipswich, Mass., November 4, 1833.

4014. vi.   EDNAH BRAINARD AKERMAN,[7] born Ipswich, Mass., May 14, 1835; died Ipswich, Mass., December 17, 1836.
4015. vii. SAMUEL THOMAS AKERMAN,[7] born Ipswich, Mass., May 6, 1837; died Ipswich, Mass., September 23, 1838.
4016. viii. MARY EDNAH AKERMAN,[7] born Ipswich, Mass., March 23, 1842.

3822. BETHIA HUNTINGTON [6] (*Bethiah Doggett,*[5] *Noah,*[4] *Samuel,*[3] *Samuel,*[2] *Thomas*[1]), born Plainfield, Conn., Oct. 21, 1780; died Lansingburg, N.Y., Oct. 27, 1851; married 1799, Elisha Janes, son of Elijah and Lucy (Crooker) Janes; born Brimfield, Mass., June 9, 1774.

Issue:

4017. i.   HARRIET JANES,[7] born December 1, 1800.
4018. ii. ELIJAH JANES,[7] born 1803.
4019. iii. LAURA JANES,[7] born 1805.
4020. iv. MARY JANE JANES,[7] born 1809.
4021. v.   OLIVE JANES,[7] born 1812; a teacher South, afterward went West.

3823. JOHN HUNTINGTON [6] (*Bethiah Doggett,*[5] *Noah,*[4] *Samuel,*[3] *Samuel,*[2] *Thomas*[1]), born Shaftesbury, Vt., March 20, 1782; died Perry, N.Y., October 8, 1840; married Hardwick, Vt., Martha Bailey, daughter of Charles and Martha Bailey; born Hardwick, Vt., March, 1778; died Perry, N.Y., September, 1850.

Issue.

4022. i.   ELIZA HUNTINGTON,[7] born Greensboro', Vt.; died Greensboro', Vt., aged fifteen months.
4023. ii.   ELIZA HUNTINGTON,[7] born Greensboro', Vt., July 21, 1808.
4024. iii. NATHAN HUNTINGTON,[7] born Greensboro'. Vt., September 8, 1810.
4025. iv.   MARY HUNTINGTON,[7] born Greensboro', Vt.. February 11, 1813.
4026. v.   SAMUEL HUNTINGTON,[7] born Greensboro', Vt., February 22, 1815; died Peru, Ill., October 17. 1838.
4027. vi.   JOHN BAILEY HUNTINGTON,[7] born Greensboro'. Vt., January 1, 1818.
4028. vii. CHARLES B. HUNTINGTON,[7] born Greensboro', Vt., Dec. 23, 1820.
4029. viii. ABIGAIL HUNTINGTON,[7] born Greensboro', Vt., August 21, 1823; died Greensboro', Vt., November 12, 1855.
4030. ix.   MARTHA HUNTINGTON,[7] born Greensboro', Vt., August 21, 1825.

John Huntington was a man honored for his intelligence and social worth, and especially for his overflowing benevolence.

3824. HENRY HUNTINGTON [6] (*Bethiah Doggett,*[5] *Noah,*[4] *Samuel,*[3] *Samuel,*[2] *Thomas*[1]), born Shaftesbury, Vt., March 20, 1782; died Greensboro', Vt., May 16, 1852; married January 24, 1807, Elizabeth Parmale; born January 8, 1787; died Greensboro', Vt., April 7, 1830.

Issue:

4031. i.   CAROLINE HUNTINGTON,[7] born Greensboro', Vt., February 4, 1808.
4032. ii.   ROXANA HUNTINGTON,[7] born Greensboro', Vt., June 14, 1810.
4033. iii. BETSEY HUNTINGTON,[7] born Greensboro', Vt., October 6, 1812.
4034. iv.   BETHIA ESTHER HUNTINGTON,[7] born Greensboro', Vt., Oct. 20, 1815.
4035. v.   HENRY HUNTINGTON,[7] born Greensboro', Vt., June 3, 1818.
4036. vi.   ELLEN S. HUNTINGTON,[7] born Greensboro', Vt., December 11, 1820.
4037. vii. FARNHAM PARMELEE HUNTINGTON,[7] born Greensboro', Vt., July 4, 1825.
4038. viii. EUNICE CARTER HUNTINGTON,[7] born Greensboro', Vt., March 31, 1829.

Henry Huntington was a useful and honored man, and held offices of trust in the town where he resided.

3830. Sophia Huntington [6] (*Bethiah Doggett,* [5] *Noah,* [4] *Samuel,* [3] *Samuel,* [2] *Thomas* [1]), born Shaftesbury, Vt., May 15, 1794; died Ingleside, near Cincinnati, Ohio, May 27, 1867; married Greensboro', Vt., 1822, Dr. Thomas Wright, son of John and Elizabeth (Lee) Wright, of Scotland; born County Tyrone, Province of Ulster, Ire., March, 1797; died Ingleside, Ohio, February 27, 1877.

Issue:

4039. i. Noah Doggett Wright,[7] born Reading, Ohio, February 22, 1823.
4040. ii. Thomas Lee Wright,[7] born Windham, Ohio, August 7, 1825.
4041. iii. Elizabeth Ann Wright,[7] born Reading, Ohio, November 10, 1827.
4042. iv. Samuel Huntington Wright,[7] born Windham, Ohio, May 15, 1828.
4043. v. Sophia Huntington Wright,[7] born Windham, Ohio.
4044. vi. Mary Angelina Wright,[7] born Carthage, Ohio, July 12, 1834.
4045. vii. John Eberly Wright,[7] born Carthage, Ohio, December 20, 1839.

Sophia Huntington came to Boston, Mass., to be educated, about 1812, making her home with the family of her uncle Noah Doggett.

After completing her education she returned to Greensboro', where she married, in 1822, Dr. Thomas Wright.

About the year 1823 Dr. and Mrs. Wright travelled in a two-horse spring wagon, accompanied by their baggage team and driver, from Greensboro', Vt., to Reading, near Cincinnati, Ohio. Subsequently they removed to Windham, Ohio, then back to Reading; thence again to Windham, soon after which they returned to southern Ohio, settling in Carthage. About the year 1849 Dr. Wright retired from his professional practice, and they planned and built for themselves a residence upon a beautiful tract of thirty-eight acres of land (then seven miles from Cincinnati), which they had long held for that purpose, called Ingleside, where they both permanently resided to the time of their death. Mrs. Wright was a lady of care, culture, and intellectual endowments, of whom it was said by one of the most eminent scholars and divines of the age, " She is the best educated and most intelligent lady I have seen in America." To her aid and superior wisdom her husband attributed much of his financial and professional success in life; and although a most devoted wife and mother, her influence for good in all relating to the improvement of the human race was widely felt and recognized by a large circle of acquaintances.

3836. John Ralph Doggett [6] (*Henry,* [5] *Noah,* [4] *Samuel,* [3] *Samuel,* [2] *Thomas* [1]), born Charleston, S.C., November 16, 1799; died Sapelo island, near Darien, Ga., March 6, 1850; married Charleston, S.C., April 26, 1821, by Rev. Dr. Gadashant, to Marie Johnson; born Goshen, N.Y., November 3, 1798; died Darien, Ga., June, 1869.

Issue:

4046. i. Ann Marie Doggett,[7] born Charleston, S.C., January, 1822.
4047. ii. Margaret Doggett,[7] born Charleston, S.C., December 2, 1823; died June 22, 1825.

4048. iii. WILLIAM J. DOGGETT,[7] born Darien, Ga., December 22, 1825.
4049. iv. ELIZA ELLEN DOGGETT,[7] born Darien, Ga., October 15, 1830; died
         Darien, Ga., September 20, 1836.
4050. v. MARGARET JANE DOGGETT,[7] born Darien, Ga., March 13, 1833; mar-
         ried Darien, Ga., December 22, 1860, Rufus Murphy; she died
         Beaufort, S.C., May 14, 1865.

3837. MARY AMELIA DOGGETT[6] (*Henry*,[5] *Noah*,[4] *Samuel*,[3]
Samuel,[2] *Thomas*[1]), born Charleston, S.C., February 2, 1802; died
Camden, S.C., March 4, 1864; married Columbia, S.C., March 15,
1832, by Rev. Dr. Gouldin, to Rev. William Edward Hughson, of
Camden, son of John and Martha [Williamson (Roach)] Hughson;
born Camden, S.C., April 18, 1809; died Sumter, S.C., May 22, 1877.

Issue:

4051. i. ANN REBECCA HUGHSON,[7] born Camden, S.C., December 13, 1839;
        died Camden, S.C., December 14, 1839.
4052. ii. JOHN SCOTT HUGHSON,[7] born Camden, S.C., October 1, 1841.

Dr. Hughson, writing of his mother, says: "She was a noble
woman, one loved by all; a kind, affectionate disposition, always
engaged in some charitable work; the poor always looked upon her
as their friend and benefactor. No charitable undertaking was ever
inaugurated in our town that she was not among the leaders. During
the war many families whose sons and husbands were in the army
would have suffered but for the charity of the ladies. I remember
being at home on furlough in the winter of 1862, and going one afternoon with my mother in her rounds to find out the wants and needs
of the dependent families. Taking our carriage we rode all the
afternoon from house to house, and the next day one family would
find a barrel or sack of flour, left at their door, another meal or meat,
or perhaps a load of wood would be quietly deposited in the yard."

3838. ROBERT HYSLUP DOGGETT[6] (*Henry*,[5] *Noah*,[4] *Samuel*,[3]
Samuel,[2] *Thomas*[1]), born Charleston, S.C., February 2, 1802; died
Griffin, Ga., March, 1860; married near Charleston, S.C., Emity
Pippin, daughter of Solomon Pippin; born North Carolina; died
Butt county, Ga., May 7, 1878.

Issue:

4053. i. SARAH JANE DOGGETT,[7] born Lee county, Ga., May 16, 1824.
4054. ii. MARY DOGGETT,[7] born Lee county, Ga., September 28, 1836; married
        1st, 1858, John Shaw; he died March 5, 1868; married 2d, Henry
        county, Ga., November 12, 1878, Green Austin, born Franklin
        county, Tenn., January 13, 1816; resides Wynn's Mill, Ga. (1884).
4055. iii. LAURA VICY DOGGETT,[7] born Lee county, Ga., October 26, 1838.

3842. MARY ALLINE DOGGETT[6] (*Noah*,[5] *Noah*,[4] *Samuel*,[3] *Samuel*,[2]
Thomas[1]), born Boston, Mass., October 12, 1798; died Boston,
Mass., March 17, 1838; married Boston, Mass., January 11, 1821,
by Rev. N. L. Frothingham, to Charles Cole, Jr., son of Charles and

Nathaniel B Doggett

Esther (Clapp) Cole; born Scituate, Mass., March 4, 1799; died Stamford, Conn., September 5, 1884.

Issue:

4056. i. CHARLES DOGGETT COLE,[7] born Boston, Mass., September 30, 1823.
4057. ii. NOAH DOGGETT COLE,[7] born Dorchester, Mass., April 21, 1828; died Boston, Mass., February 21, 1833.
4058. iii. MARY ANN COLE,[7] born Boston, Mass., April 1, 1830; resides Scituate, Mass. (1893).
4059. iv. CAROLINE MATILDA COLE,[7] born Boston, Mass., July 20, 1833; married Albany, N.Y., February 15, 1872, by Judge Van Alstine, to Joseph Isaac Pierce, son of Isaac and Sarah (Weeks) Pierce; born Mt. Pleasant, N.Y., Jan. 11, 1820; no issue; resides Albany, N.Y. (1893).
4060. v. ELIZABETH DOGGETT COLE,[7] born Boston, Mass., April 28, 1835.
4061. vi. NOAH DOGGETT COLE,[7] born Boston, Mass., September 20, 1836; resides (1893) East Boston, Mass.
4062. vii. Daughter COLE,[7] born Boston, Mass., March 17, 1838; died Boston, Mass., March 17, 1838.

3843. ANN BRADLEE DOGGETT [6] (*Noah*,[5] *Noah*,[4] *Samuel*,[3] *Samuel*,[2] *Thomas*[1]), born Boston, Mass., August 18, 1811; died Boston, Mass., May 28, 1842; married Boston, Mass., April 7, 1836, by Rev. N. L. Frothingham, to Daniel Goodnow, son of Asher and Fanny (Goodnow) Goodnow; born Sudbury, Mass., April 4, 1804; died Boston, Mass., August 4, 1890.

Issue:

4063. i. ELIZABETH DOGGETT GOODNOW,[7] born Boston, Mass., March 12, 1837; died Boston, Mass., June 11, 1871.
4064. ii. DANIEL GOODNOW, Jr.,[7] born Boston, Mass., July 9, 1839.
4065. iii. ESTHER OPHELIA GOODNOW,[7] born Boston, Mass., September 24, 1841; died Boston, Mass., July 30, 1842.

Daniel Goodnow came to Boston in 1825, and soon after opened a retail grocery store at the corner of Washington and Hollis streets, under the firm name of A. & D. Goodnow.

Afterward the firm became D. & G. Goodnow, and the location Washington street, opposite Oak.

From thence he removed to South Market street, with his partner George Goodnow, and they formed a partnership with John Goodnow, under the style of J. D. & G. Goodnow, wholesale grocers.

Retiring from this partnership he removed to Commercial street to a building of his own, where he continued in the wholesale grocery business under the name of D. Goodnow & Co.

Mr. Goodnow did a very large business, and its cares, together with real-estate interests in which he had invested, took so much of his time that he retired from the grocery trade in 1880, and devoted the rest of his life to the development of his real estate.

3846. NATHANIEL BRADLEE DOGGETT [6] (*Noah*,[5] *Noah*,[4] *Samuel*,[3] *Samuel*,[2] *Thomas*[1]), born Boston, Mass., November 28, 1818; resides Hollis street, corner Tremont, Boston, Mass. (1893); married Boston, Mass., April 30, 1857, by Rev. Edward Everett Hale, D.D., to Caroline Bullard, daughter of Jabez and Dorothy [Clement (Quincy)] Bullard; born Boston, Mass., January 31, 1819.

Issue:

4066. i. SAMUEL BRADLEE DOGGETT,[7] born Boston, Mass., May 29, 1858.

Nathaniel B. Doggett was born in the Doggett homestead, on Sea street, in 1818, but removed to Hollis street, corner of Tremont, at the age of five years. From this spot he began his school life, going, after the fashion of the day, to private schools not far from home. Mrs. Starkweather, Mr. Allen, and Mr. Dow were among his early teachers whose instructions prepared him for the public school, then on Mason street.

November, 1832, at the early age of 'fourteen, Mr. Doggett entered the employ of Mr. William Taylor, Jr., a hardware merchant, at 408 Washington street, nearly opposite the Boylston market.

Mr. Taylor was a gentleman of the old school, kind, affectionate, and gentle to a remarkable degree, and a friend and visitor of the Doggetts during the greater part of a life of over eighty years.

Having learned the business, Mr. Doggett purchased the stock and stand of Mr. Taylor, and on January 1, 1840, the sign, Nathaniel B. Doggett, appeared over the door of the store.

Although thus making a change, Mr. Taylor continued to make his headquarters at the store, retaining his desk, and spending much of his time there when in town. Thus the strong attachment between the two continued like that of father and son.

On March 1, 1842, the firm became N. B. & N. A. Doggett by the admission of Noah A. Doggett.

Hardware, at first entirely imported, began to be manufactured in this country, and the trade changed from time to time, but the business increased and prospered until 1868, when the owner of the building decided to rebuild, and the firm, not finding quarters in the vicinity to suit their requirements, concluded to retire.

Since that time Mr. Doggett has devoted himself to the care of his private affairs.

Interested in the preservation of family records, he has kept for many years the records of the nearest relatives, and his collection was the nucleus from which the history of the family was started; while his ready and valued advice and kindly interest have been a constant inspiration to the writer.

3847. NOAH ALLINE DOGGETT[6] (*Noah,*[5] *Noah,*[4] *Samuel,*[3] *Samuel,*[2] *Thomas*[1]), born Boston, Mass., May 26, 1821; died Boston, Mass., December 26, 1869.

Noah A. Doggett, like his elder brother, entered the hardware

Noah A. Doggett

business at an early age, and March 1, 1842, became a partner under the style of " N. B. & N. A. Doggett."

Mr. Doggett possessed much mechanical ability, which showed itself at an early age.

One of his first works was a clock, which he constructed without instruction, and his taste developing in that direction he taught himself to repair watches, which he did so successfully that many friends preferred to have him attend to valuable watches rather than carry them to those who had learned the trade.

His ingenuity led him to construct and improve many articles, among which might be mentioned the " rattle." This had previously been a very clumsy affair, but by his changes it was greatly improved, and was adopted by the police department. Mr. Doggett was never strong, but his spare moments from business were always devoted to some work of an inventive nature. He constructed a burglar alarm, by which three burglars were caught in the store by the night watch, who were attracted to the spot by the noise.

He was interested in music and a player on the flute; a man of upright character and sterling integrity, of pleasing presence, and an interesting conversationalist.

3860. ELISABETH SHERMAN [6] (*Elizabeth Drew,* [5] *Elizabeth Doggett,* [4] *Ebenezer,* [3] *Samuel,* [2] *Thomas* [1]), born Plymouth, Mass., June 19, 1795; died Plymouth, Mass., Feb. 22, 1885; married Plymouth, Mass., Jan. 1, 1822, by Dr. James Kendall, to Isaac Sampson.

Issue :

4067. i.   ELISABETH SAMPSON,[7] born Plymouth, Mass., January 15, 1824; married Plymouth, Mass., June 4, 1848, John Kneeland; she died Roxbury, Mass., December 19, 1857.
4068. ii. GEORGE SAMPSON,[7] born Plymouth, Mass., May 28, 1825; married Boston, Mass., June 19, 1855, to Rebecca Francis Hovey; resides 26 Sherman street, Roxbury (1892); of the firm of Sampson, Murdock & Co., " Boston Directory."
4069. iii. ISAAC SAMPSON,[7] born Plymouth, Mass., April 4, 1830; died Plymouth, Mass., December 11, 1833.

3862. ELIZABETH DREW [6] (*Benjamin,* [5] *Elizabeth Doggett,* [4] *Ebenezer,* [3] *Samuel,* [2] *Thomas* [1]), born Plymouth, Mass., September 29, 1799; died January 24, 1869; married May 3, 1826, Nathaniel Freeman, of Sandwich.

Issue :

4070. i.   WESTON G. FREEMAN.[7]
4071. ii. BENJAMIN D. FREEMAN.[7]
4072. iii. NATHANIEL FREEMAN,[7] resides Winthrop, Mass.
4073. iv. GEORGE FREEMAN.[7]
4074. v.   ABNER FREEMAN.[7]

3869. BENJAMIN DREW [6] (*Benjamin,* [5] *Elizabeth Doggett,* [4] *Ebenezer,* [3] *Samuel,* [2] *Thomas* [1]), born Plymouth, Mass., November 28,

1812; resides Plymouth, Mass. (1892); married January 19, 1842,
Caroline Bangs, of Brewster.

Issue:

4075. i.   EDWARD B. DREW,[7] born August 24, 1843.
4076. ii.   FRANCIS B. DREW,[7] born April 1, 1845; died aged 3 years 6 months.
4077. iii. HELEN E. DREW,[7] born December 5, 1846.
4078. iv.   CHARLES A. DREW,[7] born October 9, 1848; married Harriet (Jaquith)
            Clark, of Billerica; issue: Bertha V. Drew;[8] born July 10, 1876.
4079. v.   CAROLINE B. DREW,[7] born October 26, 1852.

3872. WEALTHY KINGSBURY [6] (*Asenath Daggett,*[5] *Samuel,*[4] *John,*[3]
Samuel,[2] *Thomas* [1]), born October 24, 1783; married Coventry,
Conn., Zachariah Cone; born May 8, 1774.

Issue:

4080. i.   MARY CONE,[7] born March 10, 1805; married Reuben Rowley, Decem-
            ber 25, 1829; she died Hebron, Conn.
4081. ii.   WALTER CONE,[7] born August 7, 1807.
4082. iii. HUBBEL B. CONE,[7] born February 15, 1809.
4083. iv.   ALBERT G. CONE,[7] born June 2, 1811; died Arizona, December, 1884.
4084. v.   NATHANIEL K. CONE,[7] born July 14, 1813.
4085. vi.   SALMON G. CONE,[7] born August 6, 1815.
4086. vii. HARRIET M. CONE,[7] born June 5, 1818.

3883. ISAIAH DAGGETT [6] (*Isaiah,*[5] *Samuel,*[4] *John,*[3] *Samuel,*[2]
Thomas [1]), born Coventry, Conn., August 1, 1785; died Andover,
Conn., April 21, 1853; married 1st, Middletown, Conn., 1812 (?),
Lucy Graves, daughter of Rev. Benjamin and Lucy (Arnold) Graves,
of Middletown, Conn.; born 1793; died Andover, Conn., July 31,
1819; married 2d, Middletown, Conn., July 20, 1820, by Rev. Eli
Barr, to Harriet Graves, daughter of Rev. Benjamin and Lucy
(Arnold) Graves; born East Haddam, Conn., June 19, 1802; died
Hartford, Conn., March 2, 1885.

Issue:

4087. i.   WILLIAM HENRY HARRISON DAGGETT,[7] born Coventry, Conn., De-
            cember 13, 1820.
4088. ii.   LUCY HARRIET ARNOLD DAGGETT,[7] born Coventry, Conn., December
            15, 1826.
4089. iii. NORMAN SMITH DAGGETT,[7] born Coventry, Conn., July 8, 1834; died
            Hartford, Conn., February 29, 1854.

" Isaiah Daggett, Jr., kept a private school at his house in Andover.

" His first scholar was Roswell Graves, of Middletown, whose
father wanted Mr. Daggett to educate the boy at his (Daggett's) own
house, and not allow him to go to a district school under any circumstances. Very soon his scholars increased, and for twenty years and
more his school-room was crowded. If his accommodations had been
ampler his school would have been much larger: as it was, the number
was quite sufficient for one teacher.

" Mr. Daggett was an anti-Mason, and afterwards an Abolitionist.
In religion he was a Methodist, and sometimes had Methodist evening

meetings (but they were not crowded) in his school-room. Mr. Daggett had a large fund of anecdotes and jokes, which were sometimes related with cutting effect. He did not always spoil a story for relations' sake. He always appreciated favors, and rendered good for good. He talked sometimes of rendering good for evil, a proceeding which may occur occasionally, but not often, either in Andover or elsewhere.

" Daggett finally abandoned the orthodox faith of his father, and became a heretic, which requires both intelligence and courage, and he was not deficient in either. He was neither a hypocrite nor a slave ; he wore neither mask nor collar. It is certainly refreshing to meet such a man anywhere and at any time."

Writing at another time, one of his pupils says :

" He kept school from 1820 to 1850, and had scholars from Hartford and Middletown, and from many towns in Tolland and Hartford counties. Many of his pupils afterward became distinguished in the different professions and occupations.

" He was well informed and able in debate.

' He was independent, anti-Mason, Free Soil, Whig, and Abolitionist. Such a man would have enemies, but all conceded his ability as a teacher. He had Methodist meetings at his house, a daring, reckless proceeding at that early day, for a man who expected to get his living in Andover and vicinity by teaching school in a place where all were Orthodox."

3885. Col. CHESTER DAGGETT [6] (*Isaiah*,[5] *Samuel*,[4] *John*,[3] *Samuel*,[2] *Thomas* [1]), born Coventry, Conn., September 25, 1787 ; " tavern-keeper ; " died Bolton, Conn., March 25, 1846 ; married Bolton, Conn., 1822, by Rev. Philander Parmelee, to Cynthia Bushnell Carver, daughter of Joseph and Tabitha (Daggett) Carver (No. 3879) ; born Bolton, Conn., March 5, 1791 ; died Hartford, Conn., March 4, 1869.

Issue :

4090. i. CHESTER LA FAYETTE DAGGETT,[7] born Coventry, Conn., April 25, 1824; resides Middletown, Conn. (1893).
4091. ii. AUGUSTUS LAVALETTE DAGGETT,[7] born Bolton, Conn., October 27, 1828.

3889. SAMUEL BUSHNELL DAGGETT [6] (*Isaiah*,[5] *Samuel*,[4] *John*,[3] *Samuel*,[2] *Thomas* [1]), born Coventry, Conn., October 7, 1800 ; died Andover, Conn., October 17, 1890 ; married Bolton, Conn., November 9, 1826, by Rev. Lavius Hyde, to Amelia Amadon Skinner, daughter of Zenas and Mary (Loomis) Skinner ; born Bolton, Conn., October 26, 1808 ; died Andover, Conn., May 12, 1891.

Issue :

4092. i. SAMUEL HENRY DAGGETT,[7] born Coventry, Conn., December 23, 1829.

3897. PAMELA DAGGETT[6] (*John,*[5] *John,*[4] *John,*[3] *Samuel,*[2] *Thomas*[1]), born Vergennes, Vt., June 3, 1774; died Cass county, Mich., September, 1848; married probably Vergennes, Vt., August 30, 1792, Ezra Chilson.

Issue:

4093. i.   LODENIA CHILSON,[7] born Vergennes, Vt., April 1, 1793; died Vergennes, Vt., May 4, 1793.
4094. ii. CHARLOTTE CHILSON,[7] born Vergennes, Vt., April 21, 1794.
4095. iii. HIRAM CHILSON,[7] born Cooperstown, N.Y., January 15, 1797.
4096. iv. JOHN WESLEY CHILSON,[7] born Vergennes, Vt., April 30, 1799; married Electa Bates.
4097. v.   MILO CHILSON,[7] born Vergennes, Vt., June 27, 1801.
4098. vi. MANDANA CHILSON,[7] born Vergennes, Vt., April 17, 1804.
4099. vii. THERON CHILSON,[7] born Vergennes, Vt., November 4, 1806.
4100. viii. CHARLES CHILSON,[7] born Vergennes, Vt., May 17, 1809.
4101. ix. CAROLINE CHILSON,[7] born Vergennes, Vt., January 21, 1812.
4102. x.   OLIVER I. CHILSON,[7] born Vergennes, Vt., August 28, 1814; died Vergennes, Vt., July 28, 1818.
4103. xi. LAURA LAVINA CHILSON,[7] born Vergennes, Vt., May 9, 1817.

3898. SEBRA DAGGETT[6] (*John,*[5] *John,*[4] *John,*[3] *Samuel,*[2] *Thomas*[1]), born Hebron, Conn., November 25, 1775; died Girard, Pa., June 17, 1860; married Vergennes, Vt., 1801, Annis Pete, daughter of Abraham and Hannah (Burroughs) Pete, of N. Milford, Conn.; born Stafford, Conn.; died Girard, Pa., February 3, 1868.

Issue:

4104. i.   ALICE DAGGETT,[7] born Greenfield, Pa., July 3, 1799.
4105. ii. LAURA DAGGETT,[7] born Greenfield, Pa., September 17, 1803.
4106. iii. AUSTIN DAGGETT,[7] born Greenfield, Pa., May 27, 1805.
4107. iv. DARIUS DAGGETT,[7] born Greenfield, Pa., February 3, 1807.
4108. v.   REUBEN DAGGETT,[7] born Greenfield, Pa., July 24, 1809.
4109. vi. JOHN DAGGETT,[7] born Greenfield, Pa., 1811; died Fairview, Pa., January 21, 1892.
4110. vii. SALLY DAGGETT,[7] born Greenfield, Pa., 1813; died Greenfield, Pa., 1815.
4111. viii. ELEANOR DAGGETT,[7] born Greenfield, Pa., August 30, 1814.
4112. ix. HIRAM DAGGETT,[7] born Fairview, Pa., May 3, 1816.
4113. x.   PHILANDER DAGGETT,[7] born Fairview, Pa., October 5, 1819.

In 1814, Sebra Daggett and his sons entered the land in Girard township which has since been known as the Daggett homestead.

3899. ETHAN ALLEN DAGGETT[6] (*John,*[5] *John,*[4] *John,*[3] *Samuel,*[2] *Thomas*[1]), born Vergennes, Vt., May 13, 1783; died Harbour Creek, Pa., October 11, 1853; married 1st, Canada, Fannie Heindrich; divorced; died Canada, 1868; married 2d, Denmark, N.Y., 1818, by Rev. Mr. Dutton, to Mrs. Sally Sage, widow, and daughter of Daniel and Susanna (Wilcox) Beckley; born Winsted, Conn., June 8, 1786; died Denmark, N.Y., September 22, 1848; married 3d, Harbour Creek, Pa., July or August, 1849, by Elder Job Leach, to Mrs. Betsey Burroughs, widow of Joseph Burroughs, and daughter of Amariah and

Elizabeth (Olds) Wheelock; born Vermont, 1793; died Harbour Creek, Pa., March 3, 1861.

Issue:

4114. i. GEORGE LANGLEY DAGGETT,[7] born Toronto, Can., August 25, 1809.
4115. ii. ERASTUS PORTER DAGGETT,[7] born Denmark, N.Y., July 5, 1819.
4116. iii. ADALINE DAGGETT,[7] born Denmark, N.Y., January 13, 1825.

3900. DON DELANCE DAGGETT [6] (*John*,[5] *John*,[4] *John*,[3] *Samuel*,[2] *Thomas*[1]), born Hartford, Conn., 1780; died Buckfield, Me., June, 1858; married Putney, Vt., 1801, Susan Root, daughter of Isaac Root.

Issue:

4117. i. HORACE DAGGETT,[7] born Putney, Vt., May 11, 1802.
4118. ii. HENRY TRASK DAGGETT,[7] born Buckfield, Me., 1808; murdered Lake Providence, La., May 21, 1837.
4119. iii. FLORILLA DAGGETT,[7] born Buckfield, Me., August 9, 1810.
4120. iv. ESTHER M. DAGGETT,[7] born Buckfield, Me., September 3, 1811.
4121. v. NELSON DAGGETT,[7] born Buckfield, Me., 1812; died Blake, Fla., October 27, 1884.
4122. vi. JOHN R. DAGGETT,[7] born Buckfield, Me., October 5, 1816.
4123. vii. EVELINE A. DAGGETT,[7] born Buckfield, Me., February 21, 1818.
4124. viii. ISAAC ROOT DAGGETT,[7] born Buckfield, Me., April 16, 1819.
4125. ix. WILLIAM DAGGETT,[7] born Buckfield, Me., 1822; died San Francisco, Cal., 1850.
4126. x. CHARLES DAGGETT,[7] born Buckfield, Me., March 1, 1825.

3902. ELEAZER DAGGETT [6] (*John*,[5] *John*,[4] *John*,[3] *Samuel*,[2] *Thomas*[1]), born Vergennes, Vt., 1788; died Shelby county, Tex., October 6, 1850; married Queenstown, Can., 1809, Elizabeth Cronk, of Queenstown, Can.; born Philadelphia, Pa., 1790; died Fort Worth, Tex., February 8, 1867.

Issue:

4127. i. EPHRAIM MERRILL DAGGETT,[7] born Queenstown, Can., June 3, 1810.
4128. ii. CHARLES BIGGERS DAGGETT,[7] born Queenstown, Can., July 15, 1812.
4129. iii. WILLIAM DAGGETT,[7] born Lewiston, N.Y., 1814; died Terre Haute, Ind., 1821.
4130. iv. HENRY CLAY DAGGETT,[7] born Lewiston, N.Y., February, 1820.
4131. v. HELLEN MAR DAGGETT,[7] born Terre Haute, Ind., December 3, 1824.
4132. vi. SARAH ANN DAGGETT,[7] born Terre Haute, Ind., November 3, 1830.

Eleazer Daggett ran away from home when he was fourteen years old. He went to Upper Canada, where he learned the saddler's trade. After his marriage he lived at St. Davies and its vicinity until the war of 1812. Being a true Yankee, he and fourteen others crossed the Niagara river.

He was at Lundy's Lane battle, and Black Rock; also at the blowing up of Fort Brown, and various other battles. Mr. Daggett was first lieutenant.

His property in Canada was confiscated, but he drew land warrants in this country, and located his claim in Indiana. After the war he moved from Batavia to Lewiston, where he could supply his old acquaintances among the British officers with their fine harness and saddlery. In 1820 he moved to Vigo county, Ind., where he owned one hundred and sixty acres near Terre Haute. This was sold for two hundred and fifty dollars per acre, where now stand large brick houses.

In 1840, Mr. Daggett removed to Shelby county, Tex., where he died. He was a member of the Legislature in 1850.

3905. BETSEY DOGGETT[6] (*Samuel,*[5] *Samuel,*[4] *Isaac,*[3] *Samuel,*[2] *Thomas*[1]), born Dedham, Mass., June 24, 1778; died Dedham, Mass., December 20, 1850; married Dedham, Mass., December 15, 1796, by Rev. Jason Haven, to Jesse Clap, son of Seth and Elizabeth (Everett) Clap; born Walpole, Mass., January 5, 1772; died Dedham, Mass., January 19, 1823.

Issue:

4133. i. MARY ANN CLAP,[7] born Dedham, Mass., October 31, 1798; died Dedham, Mass., October 3, 1800.
4134. ii. ELIZABETH DOGGETT CLAP,[7] born Dedham, Mass., July 24, 1801; died Dedham, Mass., June 24, 1810.
4135. iii. JOHN DOGGETT CLAP,[7] born Dedham, Mass., August 25, 1803; died Chelsea, Mass., February 11, 1878.
4136. iv. MARY ANN CLAP,[7] born Dedham, Mass., February 20, 1806; died Dedham, Mass., July 15, 1816.
4137. v. ELEANOR CLAP,[7] born Dedham, Mass., November 11, 1809.
4138. vi. ELIZABETH DOGGETT CLAP,[7] born Dedham, Mass., July 2, 1811.

" Jesse Clap removed to Dedham prior to his marriage. He was by trade a baker, and was a man of excellent business capacity and very upright character.

" He erected a house in Dedham, on what was afterward the site of the Phœnix House, and when Dedham was made the shire town he ran it for a short time as a hotel for the accommodation of the judges and officers of the court. He afterwards bought a large tract of land in Dedham, in connection with Major Newell, and together they built a large double house upon it, and he went back to his former trade of a cracker baker. He afterward kept a dry-goods store there for a time.

" At about this time he also had a large farm in Needham. The last several years of his life he devoted his attention to the manufacture of chip bonnets of poplar wood, split, shaved, and braided.

" He carried on the straw-bonnet business for some years prior to his death." The following is one of his advertisements of that period:

Willow Bonnets. The subscriber offers for Sale a large assortment of willow bonnets from 4 6 to 10.6.
Dedham April 9, 1819.   JESSE CLAP.

In all his business enterprises he was greatly assisted by his estimable wife, who was a woman of sterling worth and great force of character.

JOHN DOGGETT.

She outlived her husband nearly thirty years, during a part of which time she carried on the store and large farm in Dedham, and died respected by all at the age of seventy-two.

After the death of their daughter Mary Ann Clap, the well-known little tract of thirty-six pages, concerning her religious character and godly sayings, written by Rev. Joshua Bates, D.D., was published, entitled "Happy Death of Mary Ann Clap"—afterwards reproduced by the American Tract Society.

3906. JOHN DOGGETT[6] (*Samuel*,[5] *Samuel*,[4] *Isaac*,[3] *Samuel*,[2] *Thomas*[1]), born Dedham, Mass., September 15, 1780; died Dedham, Mass., June 17, 1857; married 1st, Charlestown, Mass., March 29, 1804, by Rev. Dr. Morse, to Sophia Miller, daughter of Dea. Hezekiah N. and Jane (Field) Miller, of Milton, Mass.; born Dorchester, Mass., July 28, 1783; died Boston, Mass., May 15, 1829; married 2d, Boston, Mass., October 15, 1829, by Rev. Dr. Lyman Beecher, to Mrs. Mary Jones, widow; died Boston, Mass., August 24, 1838; married 3d, Boston, Mass., July 9, 1840, by Rev. Hubbard Winslow, to Mrs. Ann Eliza Webster, widow, daughter of Edward and Mary Cushing; born Boston, Mass., 1797; died Dedham, Mass., October 4, 1849.

Issue:

4139. i.   SOPHIA DOGGETT,[7] born Roxbury, Mass., May 23, 1805.
4140. ii.   JANE MILLER DOGGETT,[7] born Roxbury, Mass., December 13, 1806.
4141. iii.   JOHN DOGGETT,[7] born Roxbury, Mass., June 7, 1809.
4142. iv.   ELIZABETH DOGGETT,[7] born Roxbury, Mass., October 26, 1811.
4143. v.   FRANCIS MILLER DOGGETT,[7] born Roxbury, Mass., September 28, 1813; died Roxbury, Mass., October 8, 1813.
4144. vi.   SAMUEL DOGGETT,[7] born Roxbury, Mass., October 15, 1814.
4145. vii.   WILLIAM FRANCIS DOGGETT,[7] born Boston, Mass., March 15, 1817.
4146. viii. STEPHEN BADLAM DOGGETT,[7] born Boston, Mass., November 18, 1819; died San Francisco, Cal., December 27, 1850.
4147. ix.   MARIA DOGGETT,[7] born Boston, Mass., February 14, 1822; died Boston, Mass., September 8, 1838.
4148. x.   BENJAMIN FRANKLIN DOGGETT,[7] born Boston, Mass., Feb. 17, 1824.

"John Doggett was born in Dedham, 15th September, 1780. As was the custom of that day he learned a trade when a boy, choosing that of a carver, and became very ingenious in working in wood, horn, and shell. From an English artisan he also learned the trade of a gilder, $25 being the price paid for the instruction given. He plied his trade of carver and gilder in Roxbury, and was the first gilder who ever practised his trade in the vicinity. His thorough workmanship caused his business to increase to large proportions, and among the many apprentices were representatives of several of the leading Roxbury families. Among those who learned the trade were his brother Samuel Doggett and Samuel Sprague Williams, who were taken into partnership under the style of 'John Doggett & Co.,' their factory being on the corner of Washington and Williams streets, Roxbury. About this time a knowledge of weaving was obtained from a travelling English artisan, who had obtained a meal at the factory, and the manufacture of rugs was begun, which soon came into general use and laid the foundation for an extensive carpet-business.

"Another and earlier branch of the business was that of looking-glasses and mirrors, which had its origin in the embargo laws of 1812. Importations being then forbidden, they quicksilvered window glass, which met with a ready sale.

" In later years large quantities of looking-glass plate were imported, which they framed; and with this they also imported large invoices of carpets.

" The small factory at Roxbury was replaced with a commodious one on the same site, on the Washington-street front of which was a balcony, reached by a flight of steps, from which opened a large wareroom for displaying goods; and in 1818 a warehouse was opened at 28 Market street; then, in 1822, at 12, 14, and 16 Market street, now Cornhill, Boston. Their reputation for a high standard of goods being sustained, and business increasing, a branch house was established in 1830 in Philadelphia, under the style of Doggett, Farnsworth & Co.

" In 1837 the Boston warerooms were removed to 37 Tremont row (now 55 Tremont street).

" At this time (1837), in consequence of business reverses, they were obliged to suspend payment.

" With the high sense of honor for which the firm were noted, they eventually paid their creditors in full, although released from payment. Mr. Samuel Doggett making a trip to England and Scotland for this purpose; and it was stated that this act went far to strengthen American credit among English manufacturers. In 1845 he retired from the firm, the business being continued by his brother, Samuel Doggett, and Mr. Samuel S. Williams, who removed from Tremont row to 234 Washington street, into the building which stood on the site now occupied by Messrs. A. Shuman & Co. In 1854 Mr. Samuel Doggett retired from the firm, and the business was reorganized, the manufacture of mirror and picture frames being continued under the style of ' Williams & Everett,' who added the branch of paintings, etc., and who are now located on Boylston street, Boston (1893).

" John Doggett resided in Roxbury after his marriage until 1814, when he removed to No. 52 Boylston street, Boston, and continued to live there until 1838, when he removed in 1839 to 4 Bowdoin street; then to 61 Hancock street, 1840. In 1833 he was a member of the Boston City Council. In 1830 he went to England and Scotland

LOIS (CURRIER) DOGGETT.

SAMUEL DOGGETT.

to make purchases of carpets, and again in 1839; on the latter trip being accompanied by his daughter Jane. On his return he gave up his house in Boston, and a few years later removed to Dedham, where he passed the remaining years of his life in the house formerly his father's, where he died 17th June, 1857."

3907. SAMUEL DOGGETT[6] (*Samuel*,[5] *Samuel*,[4] *Isaac*,[3] *Samuel*,[2] *Thomas* [1]), born Dedham, Mass., February 12, 1794; died Roxbury, Mass., August 18, 1856; married 1st, Roxbury, Mass., November 28, 1816, by Rev. Eliphalet Porter, to Lois Currier, daughter of John and Elizabeth (Bartlett) Currier; born South Hampton, N.H., November 14, 1795; died Roxbury, Mass., November 23, 1839; married 2d, Stockbridge, Mass., September 12, 1842, by Rev. Mark Hopkins, to Mrs. Electa Webster, widow of Nelson Webster, U.S.N., and daughter of John Sergeant and Lucinda (Fellows) Hopkins; born Stockbridge, Mass., September 26, 1802; died Stockbridge, Mass., July 13, 1848.

Issue :

4149. i.   MARY ANN CLAP DOGGETT,[7] born Roxbury, Mass., February 2, 1818.
4150. ii. EMILY DOGGETT,[7] born Roxbury, Mass., July 29, 1822.

"Samuel Doggett was born in Dedham, Mass., 12th February, 1794. He early learned the trade of a carver and gilder, and was associated with his brother John (fourteen years his senior) and Mr. Samuel S. Williams, in partnership, under the style of John Doggett & Co. They manufactured mirror and picture frames and rugs at their factory at Roxbury, and imported looking-glass plate from France, and carpets from England and Scotland.

"The history of this house is given under the previous record of his brother John, and is the record of an honorable and successful business career of over forty years. The house was widely known in this country, and favorably regarded by the foreign manufacturers of whom they purchased.

"In the importation of these goods it became necessary to make trips abroad to purchase goods, and he made trips to England and Scotland in 1825, again in 1831, and a third time in 1837 or 1839.

"These trips were of course made at that time in sailing-vessels, and the journals and letters descriptive of the voyages and travels are preserved, and are highly interesting. In 1830 a branch house was established at Philadelphia, under the style of 'Doggett, Farnsworth & Co.,' and he went there to assume its management, Mr. Williams taking charge of the manufactory at Roxbury; but his brother going abroad, he returned at once to Boston, Mr. Jacob Farnsworth taking his place there. In 1845, on the retirement of his brother John from the firm, he succeeded him as senior partner, and with Mr. Williams continued under the old style of 'John Doggett & Co.'

" Eight years later he also retired from the firm, and the business was continued so far as it related to mirrors and frames by ' Messrs. Williams & Everett.'

" Samuel Doggett lived in Roxbury, purchasing in 1821 the large square mansion-house which stood until recently at 19 Warren street. He resided there until 1839, and during the eighteen years he made it his residence he took especial pride in beautifying the house and grounds, and in entertaining with old-fashioned hospitality in its spacious rooms and halls. He inherited from his father an interest in military life, and early joined the Norfolk Guards, of which he was commissioned a lieutenant February 26, 1818. On the 1st September, 1819, he was commissioned as captain of the company.

" He held this office over four years, when an increasing business requiring his making a trip to England, he tendered his resignation, which was accepted January 12, 1824.

" While in command of this company it was frequently his custom to assemble them for drill in the second story of his house on Warren street, it offering a capital hall for the purpose. He was also chief engineer of the Roxbury Fire Department for many years, and made an active and efficient officer.

" In 1839 he sold his residence on Warren street, and the remainder of his life resided at different places in Roxbury and Boston, and died at the residence of his daughter Emily, August 18, 1856."

3908. ABIGAIL BAKER[6] (*Mary Doggett,*[5] *Samuel,*[4] *Isaac,*[3] *Samuel,*[2] *Thomas*[1]), born Dedham, Mass., August 13, 1775; married Dedham, Mass., August 13, 1794, Josiah Bumstead.

Issue :

4151. i. FREEMAN BUMSTEAD;[7] one of the descendants is E. W. Bumstead, 87 Milk street, room 34, Boston (1892).

3909. CATHERINE BAKER[6] (*Mary Doggett,*[5] *Samuel,*[4] *Isaac,*[3] *Samuel,*[2] *Thomas*[1]), born Dedham, Mass., January 9, 1777 ; married Dedham, Mass., Oct. 1, 1794, Samuel Kelton, of Wrentham, Mass.

Issue :

4152. i. MARY KELTON,[7] married Mr. Partridge.

3912. ELIZABETH SUMNER DOGGETT[6] (*Jesse,*[5] *Samuel,*[4] *Isaac,*[3] *Samuel,*[2] *Thomas*[1]), born Roxbury, Mass., September 12, 1791 ; died Roxbury, Mass., September 9, 1874 ; married Roxbury, Mass., August 5, 1819, by Rev. Eliphalet Porter, D.D., to Elijah Lewis, son of James Hawkes and Lydia (Pratt) Lewis ; born Canton, Mass., March 3, 1773 ; died Roxbury, Mass., December 15, 1858.

Issue :

4153. i. GEORGE LEWIS,[7] born Roxbury, Mass., May 25, 1820.

Elijah Lewis was born in Canton, Mass., where his father owned a farm of one hundred acres on Ponkapoag pond.

When eighteen years of age he went to Roxbury, Mass., where he entered the store of Charles and Aaron Davis, with whom he was afterward associated in business.

He was first married in Roxbury November 14, 1803, to Fanny, daughter of Edward and Rebecca (Payson) Sumner, of Roxbury. She was born in Roxbury December 22, 1785, and died there May 16, 1810, leaving two children.

3919. EUNICE DOGGETT[6] (*Elisha,*[5] *Samuel,*[4] *Isaac,*[3] *Samuel,*[2] *Thomas*[1]), born July 26, 1790; died Waterford, Me., March 15, 1846; married Boston, Mass., June 3, 1818, by Rev. Thomas Baldwin, to John Carter, son of Abijah Carter; "trader;" born Waterford, Me., 1788; died Waterford, Me., April 24, 1827.

Issue:

4154. i. KATE CARTER,[7] born Waterford, Me., June 4, 1820.
4155. ii. JOHN CARTER,[7] born Waterford, Me.

3920. ELIZABETH DOGGETT[6] (*Elisha,*[5] *Samuel,*[4] *Isaac,*[3] *Samuel,*[2] *Thomas*[1]), born August 17, 1792; died Jan. 25, —; married Boston, Mass., Dec. 5, 1815, by Rev. Thomas Baldwin, to Daniel Cummings.

Issue:

4156. i. ELIZABETH CUMMINGS.[7]

3922. CATHARINE DOGGETT[6] (*Elisha,*[5] *Samuel,*[4] *Isaac,*[3] *Samuel,*[2] *Thomas*[1]), born February 23, 1797; died September 4, 1847; married 1st, Boston, Mass., March 5, 1816, by Rev. Paul Dean, to John C. Masters; married 2d, Edmund Estes.

Issue:

4157. i. MARY MASTERS,[7] resides Deerfield, Mass.
4158. ii. EDMUND ESTES.[7]

3925. NANCY THORNDIKE DOGGETT[6] (*Elisha,*[5] *Samuel,*[4] *Isaac,*[3] *Samuel,*[2] *Thomas*[1]), born November 3, 1803; married Boston, Mass., October 23, 1823, by Rev. Thomas Baldwin, to Frederick Clapp, son of William and Sarah (Smith) Clapp; born Scituate, Mass., April 10, 1794; he died December 9, 1868.

Issue:

4159. i. FREDERICK CLAPP,[7] born August 11, 1824.
4160. ii. JAMES KNOWLES CLAPP,[7] born November 21, 1826; died Oct. 18, 1828.
4161. iii. ELIZABETH DOGGETT CLAPP,[7] born June 9, 1830; resides Brookline, Mass.
4162. iv. EDWARD AUGUSTUS CLAPP,[7] born April 28, 1834.
4163. v. MARY COOK CLAPP,[7] born May 22, 1839; died May 8, 1851.
4164. vi. GEORGE WALTER CLAPP,[7] born June 10, 1841.
4165. vii. ANNIE ISADORA CLAPP,[7] born August 5, 1845.

Frederick Clapp was in active business in Boston for over fifty years; first on Exchange street in the grocery business, afterward commenced the wooden-ware business in Dock square, and was the pioneer in this particular branch. He soon after associated himself with Daniel Cummings, on South Market street, until 1867, when he went into the metal trade with his son George Walter Clapp.

3927. MARY DOGGETT[6] (*Elisha*,[5] *Samuel*,[4] *Isaac*,[3] *Samuel*,[2] *Thomas*[1]), born Salem, Mass., October 13, 1807; died Boston, Mass., July 7, 1842; married Boston, Mass., March 22, 1830, by Rev. James K. Knowles, to Charles Flint Eaton, son of Charles and Elizabeth (Flint) Eaton; born Reading, Mass., April 15, 1809; died Salem, Mass., September, 1877.

Issue:

4166. i. MARY ELIZABETH EATON,[7] born Boston, Mass., April 17, 1831.
4167. ii. JAMES FLINT EATON,[7] born Boston, Mass., May 15, 1832.
4168. iii. MARGARET DOGGETT EATON,[7] born Boston, Mass., June 8, 1834; married Danvers, Mass., 1860, Charles F. Wyman, son of Abraham G. Wyman; no issue; he resides 744 Main street, Cambridge, Mass.; she died 1874.
4169. iv. LOUISA BECKFORD EATON,[7] born Boston, Mass., January 27, 1836.
4170. v. LYDIA ELLEN EATON,[7] born Boston, Mass., August 17, 1838.

THOMAS DOGGETT, OF MARSHFIELD, MASS.

SEVENTH GENERATION.

3928. JOHN DOGGETT[7] (*Ichabod*,[6] *John*,[5] *John*,[4] *Thomas*,[3] *John*,[2] *Thomas*[1]), born Liverpool, N.S., September 20, 1799; died White Point, N.S., October 20, 1857; married White Point, N.S., December 15, 1830, by Rev. Mr. Moody, to Mary Louisa Loring, daughter of Charles and Elizabeth (Tupper) Loring; born Lunenburg, N.S., September 24, 1808; resides (1890) White Point, N.S.

Issue:

4171. i. JOHN DOGGETT,[8] born White Point, N.S., May 2, 1832.
4172. ii. PENINAH DOGGETT,[8] born White Point, N.S., September 2, 1834.
4173. iii. WILLIAM DOGGETT,[8] born White Point, N.S., October 9, 1836.
4174. iv. MARY DOGGETT,[8] born White Point, N.S., August 22, 1841.
4175. v. ELIZA DOGGETT,[8] born White Point, N.S., July 4, 1845.
4176. vi. ALFRED DOGGETT,[8] born White Point, N.S., August 10, 1847; died White Point, N.S., September 3, 1876.
4177. vii. LEANDER DOGGETT,[8] born White Point, N.S., July 29, 1850.
4178. viii. ROBERT DOGGETT,[8] born White Point, N.S., September 30, 1854.

3929. LATHROP DOGGETT[7] (*Ichabod*,[6] *John*,[5] *John*,[4] *Thomas*,[3] *John*,[2] *Thomas*[1]), born Liverpool, N.S., October 5, 1801; died

Provincetown, Mass., September 30, 1882; married Hunt's Point, N.S., December 28, 1827, Jennett Huffman, daughter of Jacob and Elizabeth (Martin) Huffman.

Issue :

4179. i.   FREDERIC THOMAS DOGGETT,[8] born White Point, N.S., May 15, 1828.
4180. ii.   JAMES DOGGETT,[8] born White Point. N.S.
4181. iii.   ELIZABETH DOGGETT,[8] born White Point, N.S.
4182. iv.   PRISCILLA DOGGETT,[8] born White Point, N.S.
4183. v.   MARY JANE DOGGETT,[8] born White Point, N.S., 1840.
4184. vi.   SELINA DOGGETT,[8] born White Point, N.S., 1846.
4185. vii.   SUSAN DOGGETT,[8] born White Point, N.S.
4186. viii.   EXPERIENCE DOGGETT,[8] born White Point, N.S.

The will of Lathrop Doggett, dated October 2, 1880, and proved February 13, 1883, mentions his house on Bradford street, Provincetown. [Barnstable Probate, 127–151.]

3931. JOSEPH DOGGETT [7] (*Ichabod,*[6] *John,*[5] *John,*[4] *Thomas,*[3] *John,*[2] *Thomas*[1]), born White Point, N.S., April 30, 1808; died White Point, N.S., April 30, 1860; married Brookfield, N.S., December 15, 1838, by Rev. Mr. Cranswick, to Peninah Cardess, daughter of Thomas Cardess; born Brookfield, N.S., June 10, 1813; died White Point, N.S., February 19, 1890.

Issue :

4187. i.   RALPH DOGGETT,[8] born White Point, N.S., December 14, 1840.
4188. ii.   CECILIA DOGGETT,[8] born White Point, N.S., March 14, 1843; died White Point, N.S., January 25, 1866.
4189. iii.   MERCY DOGGETT,[8] born White Point, N.S., May 14, 1845:
4190. iv.   JABEZ DOGGETT,[8] born White Point, N.S., August 14, 1847.
4191. v.   ALMOND DOGGETT,[8] born White Point, N.S., March 14, 1849.
4192. vi.   CHARLES DOGGETT,[8] born White Point, N.S., December 14, 1851.
4193. vii.   ANNIE DOGGETT,[8] born White Point, N.S., May 6, 1855; resides (1890) White Point, N.S.

3933. PENINAH DOGGETT [7] (*Ichabod,*[6] *John,*[5] *John,*[4] *Thomas,*[3] *John,*[2] *Thomas*[1]), born White Point, N.S., September 10, 1815; died White Point, N.S., May 25, 1848; married White Point, N.S., May 18, 1836, Simeon Lavender, son of Robert and Annie (Spearwater) Lavender; born White Point, N.S., September 8, 1812; died Provincetown, Mass., August 25, 1854.

Issue :

4194. i.   ADELINE DOGGETT LAVENDER,[8] born White Point, N.S., Oct. 3, 1841.

3934. EBENEZER DOGGETT [7] (*Ichabod,*[6] *John,*[5] *John,*[4] *Thomas,*[3] *John,*[2] *Thomas*[1]), born White Point, N.S., September 6, 1817; died White Point, N.S., September 1, 1876; married 1st, Milton, N.S., September 17, 1840, by Rev. Mr. Ran, to Martha Tupper, daughter of Oliver and Lydia (Freeman) Tupper; born Milton, N.S., August 17, 1822; died White Point, N.S., November 26, 1864;

married 2d, White Point, N.S., October 3, 1872, by Rev. Mr. Marton, to Mary Cook, daughter of George and Annie (Ball) Cook; born Hunt's Point, N.S., February 6, 1828; resides White Point, N.S. (1890).

Issue:

4195. i.   ADELAIDE DOGGETT,[8] born White Point, N.S., October 3, 1841.
4196. ii. SIMEON DOGGETT,[8] born White Point, N.S., May 2, 1844; died at sea
           April 3, 1867.
4197. iii. ABIGAIL HOWE DOGGETT,[8] born White Point, N.S., August 27, 1846;
           resides White Point, N.S. (1890).

3935. ELIPHALET DOGGETT[7] (*Mark,*[6] *Jabez,*[5] *Thomas,*[4] *Thomas,*[3] *John,*[2] *Thomas*[1]), born Middleboro', Mass., November 13, 1793; died New Bedford, Mass., July 25, 1880; married 1st, Westport, Mass., September 16, 1816, Sybil Peabody, daughter of Isaac and Phebe (Craw) Peabody; born Dartmouth, Mass., 1791; died New Bedford, Mass., April 24, 1839; married 2d, New Bedford, Mass., April 29, 1842, by Rev. S. Holmes, to Lapira Larrabee Nightingale, widow of Abijah Edward Nightingale, and daughter of Mr. Larrabee, of Hanover, N.H.; born New York, August 4, 1794; died New Bedford, Mass., June 4, 1885.

Issue: all called Daggett.

4198. i.   CATHARINE GRACE DAGGETT,[8] born Middleboro', Mass., October 14,
           1818; married Newport, R.I., July 21, 1852, Noah Clark, of Middle-
           boro'; no issue; he, son of Noah Clark; born Middleboro', 1808;
           died February 3, 1879; she died Middleboro', Mass., Aug. 28, 1874.
4199. ii. DANIEL THOMAS DAGGETT,[8] born Middleboro', Mass., Jan. 21, 1820.
4200. iii. SAMUEL PERRY DAGGETT,[8] born Middleboro', Mass., July 11, 1823.
4201. iv. JANE MARIA DAGGETT,[8] born West Bridgewater, Mass., February 4,
           1825; resides 164 North street, New Bedford, Mass.
4202. v.   SYBIL DAGGETT,[8] born West Bridgewater, Mass., May 23, 1827.

Mr. Doggett removed from West Bridgewater to New Bedford, June, 1830. He served in the war of 1812, twenty days.

3936. SHEPARD DOGGETT[7] (*Mark,*[6] *Jabez,*[5] *Thomas,*[4] *Thomas,*[3] *John,*[2] *Thomas*[1]), born Middleboro', Mass., May 6, 1796; called his name Daggett; died Charleston, S.C., October 14, 1864; married New Bedford, Mass., August 2, 1818, by Rev. Sylvester Holmes, to Mary West, daughter of John Pinkham West; born New Bedford, Mass., October 31, 1800; died Charleston, S.C., October 2, 1849.

Issue:

4203. i.   ELIZABETH WEST DAGGETT,[8] born New Bedford, Mass., Nov. 4, 1820.
4204. ii.   LEMUEL WEST DAGGETT,[8] born New Bedford, Mass., May 11, 1822.
4205. iii. WILLIAM LAFAYETTE DAGGETT,[8] born New Bedford, Mass., August
            6, 1824.
4206. iv.   ABIGAIL DAGGETT,[8] born New Bedford, Mass., October 24, 1827.
4207. v.   THOMAS WEST DAGGETT,[8] born New Bedford, Mass., Oct. 24, 1829.
4208. vi.   SHEPARD DAGGETT,[8] born New London, Conn., August 27, 1833.
4209. vii. JOHN WILBUR DAGGETT,[8] born New Bedford, Mass., April 29, 1835;
            died New Bedford, Mass., October 14, 1836.

4210. viii. JOHN WILBUR DAGGETT,[8] born New Bedford, Mass., Aug. 22, 1837.
4211. ix. MARY CAROLINE DAGGETT,[8] born Charleston, S.C., Feb. 2, 1842; married James John McLean; he died New Orleans, La.; she died Charleston, S.C., June 22, 1861; issue: Maggie McLean;[9] resides Charleston. S.C. (1893).
4212. x. THEODORE DOUGHTY DAGGETT,[8] born Charleston, S.C., May 31, 1844; died Charleston, S.C., 1864.
4213. xi. ALEXANDER CURRANS DAGGETT,[8] born Charleston, S.C., May 9, 1847; died Charleston, S.C., August 11, 1848.

Mr. Daggett removed from New Bedford to Charleston in 1838.

3937. MARTIN KEITH DOGGETT [7] (*Mark*,[6] *Jabez*,[5] *Thomas*,[4] *Thomas*,[3] *John*,[2] *Thomas* [1]), born Middleboro', Mass.. March 23, 1800; called his name Daggett; died Grand Manan, N.B., January 1, 1870; married Grand Manan, N.B., January 9, 1824, Eliza Gatcomb.

Issue:

4214. i. LAURA A. DAGGETT,[8] born Grand Manan, N.B., May 24, 1826.
4215. ii. JEROME P. DAGGETT,[8] born Grand Manan, N.B., June 22, 1828; died Grand Manan, N.B., December 24, 1829.
4216. iii. AMANDA DAGGETT,[8] born Grand Manan, N.B., November 13, 1830; died Grand Manan, N.B., December 10, 1851.
4217. iv. JOHN A. DAGGETT,[8] born Grand Manan, N.B., December 10, 1832.
4218. v. JULIET DAGGETT,[8] born Grand Manan, N.B., September 15, 1836; married 1853, W. Osborn; resided 22 Hammond st., Waltham, Mass.
4219. vi. EMILY J. DAGGETT,[8] born Grand Manan, N.B., March 6, 1840; married 1865, Robert Carson, "carpenter."
4220. vii. MATILDA DAGGETT,[8] born Grand Manan, N.B., December 6, 1842; died Grand Manan, N.B., February 6, 1861.
4221. viii. CATHARINE S. DAGGETT,[8] born Grand Manan, N.B., February 7, 1845.
4222. ix. ABIGAIL DAGGETT,[8] born Grand Manan, N.B., April 15, 1848.
4223. x. OLIVER DAGGETT,[8] born Grand Manan, N.B., April 7, 1851; died Grand Manan, N.B., March 6, 1862.
4224. xi. JEROME DAGGETT,[8] born Grand Manan, N.B., June 23, 1854.

3938. NATHANIEL DOGGETT [7] (*Mark*,[6] *Jabez*,[5] *Thomas*,[4] *Thomas*,[3] *John*,[2] *Thomas* [1]), born Middleboro', Mass., May 8, 1802; called his name Daggett; died Grand Manan, N.B., September 24, 1852; married 1st, 1826, Harriet Cheney; died Grand Manan, N.B., June 30, 1842; married 2d, March 20, 1844, Temperance Burke.

Issue:

4225. i. THOMAS W. DAGGETT,[8] born Grand Manan, N.B., January 11, 1828.
4226. ii. SHEPARD DAGGETT,[8] born Grand Manan, N.B., August 16, 1830; died.
4227. iii. HORATIO N. DAGGETT,[8] born Grand Manan, N.B., Aug. 28, 1832; died.
4228. iv. JAMES DAGGETT,[8] born Grand Manan, N.B., August 17, 1833; U.S.N.; removed to California.
4229. v. EDMUND DAGGETT,[8] born Grand Manan, N.B., September 6, 1835.
4230. vi. HARRIET O. DAGGETT,[8] born Grand Manan, N.B., October 2, 1837; removed to California.
4231. vii. ELIPHALET DAGGETT,[8] born Grand Manan, N.B., October 1, 1839; died.
4232. viii. CAROLINE L. DAGGETT,[8] born Grand Manan, N.B., Mar. 31, 1841; died.
4233. ix. NATHANIEL DAGGETT,[8] born Grand Manan, N.B., June 20, 1842; died.
4234. x. MAY N. DAGGETT,[8] born Grand Manan, N.B., Dec. 5, 1846; died.
4235. xi. HENRY E. DAGGETT,[8] born Grand Manan, N.B., June 21, 1848; removed to Avon, Skagit Co., Wash.
4236. xii. ANNIE R. DAGGETT,[8] born Grand Manan, N.B., March 5, 1852; removed to Avon, Skagit Co., Wash.

3939. PHILO DOGGETT[7] (*Mark,*[6] *Jabez,*[5] *Thomas,*[4] *Thomas,*[3] *John,*[2] *Thomas*[1]), born Middleboro', Mass., February 13, 1805; called his name Daggett; died Grand Manan, N.B., September 10, 1877; married 1827, Marie Ellenwood; born 1806; died Grand Manan, N.B., June 15, 1852.

Issue:

4237. i.   DRUCILLA DAGGETT,[8] born Grand Manan, N.B., January 8, 1834.
4238. ii.   NATHANIEL DAGGETT,[8] born Grand Manan, N.B.; died ——.
4239. iii.   SIMEON DAGGETT,[8] born Grand Manan, N.B., October, 1836; died Grand Manan, N.B., November, 1837.
4240. iv.   ELIZA DAGGETT,[8] born Grand Manan, N.B., June 15, 1838.
4241. v.   ANNE DAGGETT,[8] born Grand Manan, N.B., May, 1840; died Grand Manan, N.B., February, 1848.
4242. vi.   SILAS DAGGETT,[8] born Grand Manan, N.B.; died Grand Manan, N.B., January, 1848.
4243. vii.   MARTIN DAGGETT,[8] born Grand Manan, N.B., February 22, 1843.
4244. viii.   ANDREW DAGGETT,[8] born Grand Manan, N.B., 1844; died Grand Manan, N.B., May, 1862.
4245. ix.   DANIEL DAGGETT,[8] born Grand Manan, N.B., 1846; died Grand Manan, N.B., May, 1862.
4246. x.   PHEBE M. DAGGETT,[8] born Grand Manan, N.B., March 19, 1850; died Boston, Mass., December 10, 1872.

3940. MARK DOGGETT[7] (*Mark,*[6] *Jabez,*[5] *Thomas,*[4] *Thomas,*[3] *John,*[2] *Thomas*[1]), born Middleboro', Mass., May 18, 1807; called his name Daggett; died Grand Manan, N.B., February 11, 1885; married Grand Manan, N.B., 1826, Elizabeth Cheney, daughter of Edmund Cheney; born 1811; died Grand Manan, N.B., Dec. 7, 1858.

Issue:

4247. i.   REBECCA DAGGETT,[8] born Grand Manan, N.B., June 4, 1829.
4248. ii.   SAMUEL DAGGETT,[8] born Grand Manan, N.B.; "farmer;" married Campobello, N.B., Olivia Gillian; no issue.
4249. iii.   MARY DAGGETT,[8] born Grand Manan, N.B.
4250. iv.   URANIA DAGGETT,[8] born Grand Manan, N.B., January 3, 1833.
4251. v.   LOUISA DAGGETT,[8] born Grand Manan, N.B., December 20, 1834.
4252. vi.   MARK DAGGETT,[8] born Grand Manan, N.B., October 10, 1836.
4253. vii.   SIMEON DAGGETT,[8] born Grand Manan, N.B., October 20, 1840.
4254. viii.   EVELINE DAGGETT,[8] born Grand Manan, N.B., 1842; died Grand Manan, N.B., December 6, 1851.
4255. ix.   DANIEL DAGGETT,[8] born Grand Manan, N.B., 1846; died Grand Manan, N.B., February 24, 1847.
4256. x.   WILLIAM DAGGETT,[8] born Grand Manan, N.B.
4257. xi.   SARAH DAGGETT,[8] born Grand Manan, N.B., August 5, 1847.
4258. xii.   ABIGAIL W. DAGGETT,[8] born Grand Manan, N.B., June 8, 1850.

3941. JOHN DOGGETT[7] (*Mark,*[6] *Jabez,*[5] *Thomas,*[4] *Thomas,*[3] *John,*[2] *Thomas*[1]), born Middleboro', Mass., February 24, 1810; called his name Daggett; died Grand Manan, N.B., September 20, 1876; married 1838, Sarah Bancroft; born 1820; died Grand Manan, N.B., July 1, 1872.

Issue:

4259. i.   LORING DAGGETT,[8] born Grand Manan, N.B., January 11, 1841.
4260. ii.   CYNTHIA DAGGETT,[8] born Grand Manan, N.B.
4261. iii.   MARIETTA DAGGETT,[8] born Grand Manan, N.B., February 25, 1852.

3942. ELIZA DOGGETT[7] (*Mark*,[6] *Jabez*,[5] *Thomas*,[4] *Thomas*,[3] *John*,[2] *Thomas*[1]), born Middleboro', Mass., January 24, 1814; died Eastport, Me., April 5, 1886; married St. John, N.B., April 20, 1845, John O'Grady, son of Michael and Honora (McCormick) O'Grady; born Limerick, Ire., April 28, 1814; died Eastport, Me., March 17, 1883.

Issue:

4262. i. JOHN CADWALADER O'GRADY,[8] born Eastport, Me., October 8, 1847.
4263. ii. JAMES B. O'GRADY,[8] born Eastport, Me., July 20, 1849.
4264. iii. GEORGE O'GRADY,[8] born Eastport, Me., March 14, 1851.
4265. iv. DANIEL O'GRADY,[8] born Eastport, Me., May 25, 1853; died Eastport, Me., October 15, 1857.
4266. v. WILLIAM O'GRADY,[8] born Eastport, Me., May 25, 1855; called his name Grady; married New York city, February 14, 1893, Mary Agnes Russell, daughter of Michael and Bridget (Geoghegan) Russell; born New York, October 2, 1867; resides Eastport, Me. (1893).
4267. vi. ELIZA PORTIA O'GRADY,[8] born Eastport, Me., March 21, 1859; called her name Grady; resides Eastport, Me. (1893).

3950. ELKANAH DOGGETT[7] (*Thomas*,[6] *Simeon*,[5] *Thomas*,[4] *Thomas*,[3] *John*,[2] *Thomas*[1]), born Middleboro', Mass., October 4, 1790; died Chicago, Ill., May 22, 1858; married Middleboro', Mass., Oct. 23, 1816, by Rev. Emerson Payne, to Eunice Barker, daughter of Rev. Joseph and Eunice (Stebbins) Barker; born Middleboro', Mass., Dec. 29, 1789; died Chicago, Ill., Sept. 10, 1851.

Issue:

4268. i. EUNICE STEBBINS DOGGETT,[8] born Assonet, Mass., August 20, 1817; resides 5617 Monroe avenue, Hyde Park, Ill. (1893).
4269. ii. WILLIAM ELKANAH DOGGETT,[8] born Assonet, Mass., Nov. 20, 1820.
4270. iii. JOSEPH BARKER DOGGETT,[8] born Assonet, Mass., February 16, 1823.
4271. iv. THOMAS DOGGETT,[8] born Assonet, Mass., November 15, 1827.
4272. v. SON DOGGETT,[8] born Assonet, Mass.; died there an infant.

Elkanah Doggett settled as a merchant in the village of Assonet, a part of Freetown, in 1816; afterward removed to Chicago with his wife, two children, Eunice S. and William E., and wife's sister, Miss E. Barker.

3951. PHŒBE DEAN DOGGETT[7] (*Thomas*,[6] *Simeon*,[5] *Thomas*,[4] *Thomas*,[3] *John*,[2] *Thomas*[1]), born Middleboro', Mass., November 1, 1795; died Lakeville, Mass., April 20, 1865; married Middleboro', Mass., October 11, 1821, John Sampson, son of John and Deborah (Torrey) Sampson; born Middleboro', Mass., August 23, 1796; died Lakeville, Mass., May 7, 1865.

Issue:

4273. i. EMMELINE SAMPSON,[8] born Lakeville, Mass., August 12, 1822; died Lakeville, Mass., February 3, 1826.
4274. ii. PHŒBE DOGGETT SAMPSON,[8] born Lakeville, Mass., March 5, 1824.
4275. iii. MARY TURNER SAMPSON,[8] born Lakeville, Mass., January 1, 1826; married Lakeville, Mass., November 24, 1864, John Winslow; he died Freetown, Mass., April 6, 1889; no issue; she resides Freetown, Mass. (1889).

4276. iv. JOHN HENRY SAMPSON,[8] born Lakeville, Mass., May 27, 1830; married 1st, Ypsilanti, Mich., December 1, 1858, Cynthia M. Blackmer;
she died Ypsilanti. Mich., November 28, 1864; married 2d, Athol,
Mass., May 29, 1866, Elizabeth A. Frye; no issue; resides Escondido, San Diego Co., Cal. (1890).
4277. v. FRANCIS EARL SAMPSON,[8] born Lakeville, Mass., January 22, 1832.
4278. vi. EVELINE LEONARD SAMPSON,[8] born Lakeville, Mass., February 2, 1835.
4279. vii. JAMES BOWEN SAMPSON,[8] born Lakeville, Mass., August 19, 1836;
died N. Bridgewater, Mass., February 11, 1865.

John Sampson resided in that part of Middleboro' now called Lakeville.   He held town offices at different times.

3952. THOMAS DOGGETT [7] (*Thomas,*[6] *Simeon,*[5] *Thomas,*[4] *Thomas,*[3]
John,[2] *Thomas* [1]), born Middleboro', Mass., September 24, 1801; died
Lakeville, Mass., January 18, 1865; married Middleboro', Mass.,
October 31, 1824, Eveline Leonard, daughter of George and Mary
Leonard; born Middleboro', Mass., August 6, 1802; died New Bedford, Mass., May 20, 1885.

No issue.

Thomas Doggett was one of the selectmen of Middleboro' from
1838 to 1846, inclusive.   He was a representative to the General
Court in 1840 and 1841.   Was appointed justice of the peace, January 4, 1853, and served as selectman of Lakeville, 1859 and 1860.

3953. Hon. JOHN LOCKE DOGGETT [7] (*Simeon,*[6] *Simeon,*[5] *Thomas,*[4]
Thomas,[3] *John,*[2] *Thomas* [1]), born Taunton. Mass., September 8,
1798; died Jacksonville, Fla., January 8, 1844; married Mendon,
Mass., November 9, 1823, Maria Fairbanks, of Mendon, Mass.;
died previous to 1874.

Issue:

4280. i. JOHN LOCKE DOGGETT,[8] born Massachusetts; died 1867.
4281. ii. JUNIUS DOGGETT,[8] born Florida; died Florida.
4282. iii. ARISTIDES DOGGETT,[8] born Jacksonville, Fla., July 30, 1830.
4283. iv. FORES DOGGETT,[8] "lawyer;" resides Jacksonville, Fla. (1893).
4284. v. MARIA CATHARINE DOGGETT,[8] born Jacksonville, Fla., Oct. 12, 1840.

Judge John Locke Doggett graduated from Brown University in
1821; studied law, and was admitted to the bar of Massachusetts.

He was one of the earliest settlers of Florida after its purchase by
the United States, and founded with Col. Isaiah D. Hart the city of
Jacksonville, which he named in honor of President Jackson, from
whom he received the appointment of territorial judge.

Judge Doggett was a man of keen intellect, high culture, fine
physique, and austere manners.

As a lawyer he had few equals; as a judge, no superior.

3954. SAMUEL WALES DOGGETT [7] (*Simeon,*[6] *Simeon,*[5] *Thomas,*[4]
Thomas,[3] *John,*[2] *Thomas* [1]), born Taunton, Mass., July 9, 1800;
died Mendon, Mass., August 27, 1872; married Charleston, S.C.,

March 12, 1824, by Rev. Dr. Henry, to Harriet Wotton, daughter of
Capt. James and Chloe (Campbell) Wotton; born Charleston, S.C.,
April 2, 1804; died Manchester, Ia., February 7, 1892.

Issue :

4285. i. SAMUEL WALES DOGGETT,[8] born Charleston, S.C., Dec. 23, 1824.
4286. ii. JULIA HARRIET DOGGETT,[8] born Charleston, S.C., January 13, 1827.
4287. iii. SIMEON LOCKE DOGGETT,[8] born Charleston, S.C., March 29, 1829.
4288. iv. MALVINA CAMPBELL DOGGETT,[8] born Charleston, S.C., April 12, 1831.
4289. v. THEOPHILUS MELANCTHON DOGGETT,[8] born Charleston, S.C., August 28, 1833.
4290. vi. NARCISSA NEWTON DOGGETT,[8] born Charleston, S.C., March 28, 1836.
4291. vii. WILLIAM ALFRED DOGGETT,[8] born Mendon, Mass., February 9, 1839.
4292. viii. GERTRUDE GLORVINA DOGGETT.[8] born Mendon, Mass., May 20, 1841.
4293. ix. LAWRENCE BRYANT DOGGETT,[8] born Mendon, Mass., April 30, 1845;
soldier Twenty-second Regiment Massachusetts Volunteers; died
Andersonville, Ga., August 13, 1864.

" Samuel Wales Doggett was a man of fine scholastic attainments,
rare manly beauty, undaunted courage, with the address of a Chesterfield, and unrivalled colloquial powers. He settled, about the year
1822, in Abbeville, S.C., and there commenced the practice of law,
but soon after removed to Charleston, where he founded a seminary
of learning, in which were educated the daughters of the most refined,
aristocratic, and opulent families of that then justly proud and arro-
gant city. He at the same time did much to foster and develop the
system of free schools, then in its infancy, and at the time, with a
distinguished cotemporary educator, Jno. A. Wotton, whose sister was
his wife, managed the only free schools established in the city and
the suburb called ' Hempstead.' For half a generation he conducted
the ' Female Seminary,' and his name became a household word and
a synonym of honor and true nobility in homes of wealth, refinement,
and true chivalry. Few men were ever endowed with nobler instincts.
His mind was one of striking originality, and his favorite study the
British classics.

" In politics he was ever a consistent, sincere, and uncompromis-
ing Democrat, thoroughly indoctrinated and imbued with the great
political principles of the school of Jefferson, Monroe, and Jackson.
As an extemporaneous speaker without a specialty, he had but few
superiors. whether in voice, diction, oratorical style, or philosophical
research.

" In 1838, owing to the ravages of the cholera, he removed with
his family to Massachusetts, where he bought of his father the Mendon farm.

" Mr. Doggett's residence at the South having made him pro-
slavery in politics, he was unpopular among the New England
Abolitionists, and so never attained that position in public life for
which he was eminently fitted.

" In 1840 he was a nominee as representative to the General Court;

was chosen, but declined to serve, as a member of the School Committee in 1845, and in 1846 served on one of the committees of the town.   He visited his daughter, Mrs. Norris, in Chicago, from 1869 to 1872, when he returned to Mendon, and soon afterward died.

"His wife, Miss Harriet Wotton, was a native of Charleston, a woman who to rare personal charms united a superior mind and deep sensibility."

3957.   Dr. PEREZ FOBES DOGGETT [7] (*Simeon,* [6] *Simeon,* [5] *Thomas,* [4] *Thomas,* [3] *John,* [2] *Thomas* [1]), born Taunton, Mass., June 2, 1806; died Wareham, Mass., June 28, 1875; married Wareham, Mass., November 26, 1832, Lucy Maria Fearing, daughter of William and Elizabeth (Nye) Fearing; born Wareham, Mass., August 27, 1807; died Wrentham, Mass., October 2, 1885.

Issue:

4294. i.   CHARLES SEYMOUR DOGGETT, [8] born Wareham, Mass., March 9. 1836.
4295. ii.   WILLIAM SEDLEY DOGGETT, [8] born Wareham, Mass., Nov. 9, 1837.
4296. iii.   ANNA MARIA DOGGETT, [8] born Wareham, Mass., November 5, 1839; married Sandwich, Mass., November 25, 1858, by Rev. Nathan P. Philbrook, to Walter Danforth Burbank, son of Samuel Burbank; born Sandwich, Mass., 1834; resides Wareham, Mass. (1893); no issue; she died Wareham, Mass., March 16, 1870.

"Dr. Perez Fobes Doggett spent his early life upon his father's large farm, and his early education seems to have been largely obtained in his father's library.

"For two years we find him in Florida, assisting an older brother in a mercantile business.   Returning thence to New England, by the well-considered advice of both his parents, and following his own inclinations, he entered upon the study of medicine with Dr. Usher Parsons, a distinguished member of the profession, and in large practice in Providence, R.I.

"Two years later he entered at the Jefferson Medical School, Philadelphia, graduating therefrom. after the usual three years' course, at the age of twenty-five, and soon after began the practice of his profession in Wareham, Mass.   Dr. Doggett seems to have sprung at once into a good practice, and thereafter for forty-four years went in and out among his friends, neighbors, and patrons in his own and surrounding towns, meeting with the success which a man well equipped for his business may command; falling, at the end, upon the street, a professional call just made, in apparently full possession of physical and mental health, and at the age of sixty-nine.

"Dr. Doggett was not a brilliant man, and in some directions he was as simple-minded as a child; but it is believed few men bring to the study and practice of their profession more of those peculiar and varied mental and physical qualifications which help to make up the true physician or surgeon.

" Timid and slow in some departments of life, in everything relating to his profession he was always on the alert, quick to see and
prompt to act.

" Proving himself the well-trained, patient, conscientious physician, whose judgment was not often at fault, he also demonstrated by
delicate operations, skilfully performed, that a brilliant surgeon was
only concealed by his narrow field and lack of opportunity."

3958.   Rev. THEOPHILUS PIPON DOGGETT [7] (*Simeon,*[6] *Simeon,*[5]
Thomas,[4] *Thomas,*[3] *John,*[2] *Thomas* [1]), born Taunton, Mass., January
20, 1810; died Arlington, Mass., May 18, 1875; married Bridge-
water, Mass., November 30, 1843, Elizabeth Bates, daughter of Benjamin and Mary (Hooper) Bates, of Boston, Mass.; born Boston,
Mass., January 3, 1820; died Boston, Mass., July 27, 1882.

Issue:

4297. i.   SOLON DOGGETT,[8] born Bridgewater, Mass., April 1, 1845; married
Scituate, Mass., August 12, 1873, Sarah Harris Otis, daughter of
Daniel and Mary (Greene) Otis; born South Scituate, Mass.; no
issue; resides 13 Union street, Quincy, Mass. (1893).
4298. ii.   FREDERIC FOBES DOGGETT,[8] born Barnstable, Mass., Feb. 22, 1855.
4299. iii.   CHILTON LATHAM DOGGETT,[8] born Barnstable, Mass., Oct. 1, 1858.

" Rev. Theophilus Pipon Doggett graduated from Brown University, 1829.   He was the fifth minister of the First Church in Bridgewater, and was ordained November 13, 1833, as successor of Rev.
Mr. Hodges.

" Mr. Doggett continued the pastor for eleven years, when by
reason of bronchial disease he was disqualified for the duties of the
pulpit, and resigned his pastorate.

" In 1844 he was appointed preceptor of Bridgewater Academy,
which office he held until 1846.   He subsequently was settled as minister in Ashby, in 1847, continuing there for six years, and then
removed to Barnstable, where he preached for seven years.   He then
preached at Pembroke, Mass., for thirteen years, from 1861 to 1874."

3959.   ABIGAIL DOGGETT [7] (*Simeon,*[6] *Simeon,*[5] *Thomas,*[4] *Thomas,*[3]
John,[2] *Thomas* [1]), born Taunton, Mass., November 8, 1812; died
Brookline, Mass., May 6, 1861; married Raynham, Mass. (intention,
April 26, 1834), William Reed Deane, of Boston, son of Jacob
Deane; born Mansfield, Mass.

Issue:

4300. i.   WILLIAM ROSCOE DEANE,[8] born Boston, Mass., April 15, 1835; married
July 14, 1858, Ellen M. Underwood, daughter of Hon. Abel Underwood, of Wells River, Vt.; he died Chicago, Ill., August 31, 1861.
4301. ii.   SAMUEL BLAIR DEANE,[8] of Lacon, Ill. (1864); died before 1875.
4302. iii.   ABBY WESTON DEANE,[8] born Boston, Mass., September 28, 1839;
died Davos, Switzerland, December 14, 1888.
4303. iv.   HENRY WARE DEANE,[8] born Boston, Mass., December, 1848; graduated
Harvard, 1869, medical student; died April 7, 1875.

"Abigail Doggett, who married William Reed Deane, possessed elements of character which fill our ideal of a true Christian lady.

"She was almost a model mother in disciplining her children, moulding their minds and habits, and impressing the principles of Christian duty. Intelligent and literary without being pedantic, she was always found a genial companion for the lovers of literature and the products of genius.

"Her love, however, for these things never became so absorbing as to lift her above or take her out of the sphere of those necessary but less intellectual occupations and duties that belong to home life.

"In rendering home attractive to husband, children, and visiting friends, in giving it the inviting aspect of neatness, order, and comfort, and in everything pertaining to the whole circle of domestic duty, few were more successful, few were her equals." [Gen. Register, Vol. XV.]

Her husband was greatly interested in genealogical matters, and made collections relating to the Doggett family. After his death these collections were deposited by his heirs in the library of the New England Historic Genealogical Society.

The daughter, Abby Weston Deane (No. 4302), was early in life given a position as teacher. For about twenty-five years she continued to teach, all the time searching literature, availing herself of any accessible lectures on the subjects she taught, and seeking instruction from professors and private teachers. Twice, to improve her knowledge of French, she went to Paris. She also took a course of study in the Harvard Annex for women, at Cambridge. So much and more was she doing to perfect herself as a teacher.

Her great success may be shown by the affectionate mention and sweet memory of her in every family where she was known, and in the public memorial service which was held when the news of her death reached Brookline.

3963. THOMAS WESTON [7] (*Abigail Doggett,*[6] *Simeon,*[5] *Thomas,*[4] *Thomas,*[3] *John,*[2] *Thomas*[1]), born Middleboro', Mass., February 27, 1804; died Lakeville, Mass., February 12, 1888; married Middleboro', Mass., December 25, 1832, Thalia Eddy, daughter of Joshua Eddy; born Middleboro', Mass., September 23, 1806; died Middleboro', Mass., December 7, 1889.

Issue:

4304. i.   THOMAS WESTON,[8] born Middleboro', Mass., June 14, 1834.
4305. ii.   MARY WESTON,[8] married J. T. Higgins, of Wellfleet, Mass.
4306. iii.   THALIA WESTON,[8] married Sprague S. Stetson, of Lakeville, Mass.

"Col. Thomas Weston was engaged in the early part of his life with his father, in general mercantile business, and as an iron manufacturer. Upon the death of his father, in 1843, he continued in the business at Muttock, in Middleboro'. During these years he employed a large number of men, probably more than any other establishment in the county. Afterward he retired to a farm which had been in his family for several generations, and upon which he resided until shortly before his death.

"He was always deeply interested in agriculture, and at the time of his decease was the oldest member of the Plymouth County Agricultural Society. For many years he was one of its trustees. In his early life he was very active in the militia of his county, and held the office of colonel for some years in the Fourth Regiment of the First Brigade of Massachusetts Volunteer Militia.

"He was a member of the First Congregational Church of Middleboro' for more than sixty years, and was always active in promoting its temporal and spiritual interests.

"Colonel Weston was an unassuming man of great strength of character, of positive convictions, of sterling integrity, of great industry, and an earnest and devout Christian man."

3965. BETHANIA WESTON [7] (*Abigail Doggett,*[6] *Simeon,*[5] *Thomas,*[4] *Thomas,*[3] *John,*[2] *Thomas* [1]), born Middleboro', Mass., June 30, 1807; died Middleboro', Mass., December 3, 1877; married Earle Sproat; born Middleboro', Mass.; died May 9, 1864.
Issue:
4307. i.   MARY SPROAT.[8]
4308. ii. HENRY H. SPROAT,[8] resides Freetown, Mass. (1890).
4309. iii. THOMAS C. SPROAT.[8]

3968. LAVINIA WESTON [7] (*Abigail Doggett,*[6] *Simeon,*[5] *Thomas,*[4] *Thomas,*[3] *John,*[2] *Thomas* [1]), died Middleboro', Mass.; married Middleboro', Mass., Reeland Tinkham; born Middleboro', Mass.
Issue:
4310. i.   ALICE TINKHAM,[8] born Middleboro', Mass.; married Rev. Edward M. Williams; resides Minneapolis, Minn. (1880.)

3969. HENRY WESTON [7] (*Abigail Doggett,*[6] *Simeon,*[5] *Thomas,*[4] *Thomas,*[3] *John,*[2] *Thomas* [1]), born Middleboro', Mass., June 20, 1817; died Middleboro', Mass., June 10, 1863; married 1st, Middleboro', Mass., Harriet Murdock, daughter of Calvin and Polly (Leonard) Murdock; born Middleboro', Mass., May 3, 1818; died Lowell, Mass., March 18, 1847; married 2d, ———.
Issue:
4311. i.   HENRY WESTON,[8] born 1840; resides California.
4312. ii. HARRIET WESTON,[8] born Rochester, N.Y., 1843.
4313. iii. EDWARD WESTON,[8] born January, 1845; died Middleboro', Mass., July 19, 1849.

3987. NATHAN HASKELL DOGGETT [7] (*Joseph,*[6] *Joseph,*[5] *Noah,*[4] *Samuel,*[3] *Samuel,*[2] *Thomas* [1]), born Newburyport, Mass., October

28, 1813; name changed to Edward Haskell Brainard, 1822–3; died
South Boston, Mass., June 3, 1888; married Danvers, Mass., September 7, 1834, Mary Ann Loud; born Methuen, Mass.; resides
371 West Fourth street, South Boston, Mass. (1893).

Issue:

4314. i. ELIZA McDONALD BRAINARD,[8] born Methuen, Mass., Nov. 11, 1835.
4315. ii. EMMA WILLARD BRAINARD,[8] born South Boston, Mass., Aug. 1, 1839.
4316. iii. JOSEPH EARL BRAINARD,[8] born South Boston, Mass., June 17, 1842;
      married 1877, Augusta Davies, of London, Eng.
4317. iv. GRACE BRAINARD,[8] born South Boston, Mass., July 31, 1849; died 1858.
4318. v. DANIEL HALE BRAINARD,[8] born South Boston, Mass., April 5, 1852;
      died 1857.
4319. vi. ANNIE BRAINARD,[8] born South Boston, Mass., March 7, 1855.

Mr. Edward H. Brainard when quite young came to Boston, and
was employed in the express business. Later he entered the carriage-
making business, continuing in it for many years, and having a
manufactory on the corner of Dorchester avenue and Sixth street,
South Boston. During the war he built a great many ambulances of
a superior pattern. He was very prominent in the Masonic order.
He was a member of the Common Council, 1854–1855, and was also
a member of the School Committee for a number of years. He was
connected with the Ancient and Honorable Artillery Company, and
was a member of the Charitable Mechanic Association.

3988. CHARLES HENRY DOGGETT[7] (*Joseph,*[6] *Joseph,*[5] *Noah,*[4]
Samuel,[3] *Samuel,*[2] *Thomas*[1]), born Newburyport, Mass., October 11,
1817; name changed to Brainard, 1822–3; died Washington, D.C.,
February 4, 1885; married New York city, June 24, 1856, Angelia
C. Sawyer, daughter of Nathan and Lydia (Dyer) Sawyer; born
Medford, Mass.; resides Melrose, Mass. (1893).

Issue:

4320. i. LILIAN MAY BRAINARD,[8] born Medford, Mass., March 12, 1857; mar-
      ried Medford, Mass., September 30, 1885, Charles E. Anderson;
      born Lynn, Mass.; no issue; she died Lynn, Mass., March 2, 1886.
4321. ii. GRACE LEIGH BRAINARD,[8] born Medford, Mass., March 20, 1859;
      resides Melrose, Mass. (1893).
4322. iii. ANGELA BRAINARD,[8] born Boston, Mass., November 5, 1862; died
      Medford, Mass., August 28, 1867.
4323. iv. CHARLES SUMNER BRAINARD,[8] born Jamaica Plain, Mass., February 3,
      1865; married Brockton, Mass., November 24, 1891, Mary Augusta
      Sproul, daughter of Charles L. and Mary A. (Wood) Sproul; born
      Brockton, Mass.; resides Melrose, Mass. (1893).
4324. v. ALBERT SAWYER BRAINARD,[8] born Medford, Mass., January 6, 1870;
      died Medford, Mass., August 3, 1870.

"Mr. Brainard was a self-educated man, and was possessed of
great versatility. He began business life about 1841 as a messenger
for Alvin Adams, running between Boston and New York.

"Subsequently he was a photographer, an auctioneer, and a lect-
urer. He had a powerful, well-modulated voice and great elocu-
tionary skill.

"His readings of Whittier's poetry were particularly fine. For several years he was engaged in carrying on an art gallery in Boston. During his life he spent much time in Washington. He possessed a remarkably retentive memory, and his fund of anecdotes relating to distinguished men was a very choice one. As a writer he possessed talent of a superior order. His last work was a memorial volume, containing a biographical sketch of the life of John Howard Payne, prepared under the auspices of Mr. Corcoran. He had been in the Pension Office from 1881 to the end of his life.

"He was much interested in a project to establish a free public library in Washington."

3989. AMOS HALE DOGGETT[7] (*Joseph,[6] Joseph,[5] Noah,[4] Samuel,[3] Samuel,[2] Thomas[1]*), born Newburyport, Mass., March 27, 1824; name changed to Brainard; resides River street, Hyde Park, Mass. (1893); married 1st, Boston, Mass., October 5, 1845, Christiana C. Delano, daughter of Asa and —— (Covel) Delano; born Boston, Mass.; died Boston, Mass., April 22, 1854; married 2d, Boston, Mass., October 28, 1854, Elizabeth Curran, daughter of James and Elizabeth (Cammack) Curran; born Granby, Can., 1831.

Issue:

4325. i.   GENEVIEVE BRAINARD,[8] born Boston, Mass., June 9, 1847; resides Hyde Park, Mass. (1893).
4326. ii. FLORENCE BRAINARD,[8] born Brookline, Mass., April 22, 1849.
4327. iii. AMOS DAGGETT BRAINARD,[8] born Boston, Mass., September 12, 1850; married Hyde Park, Mass., April 24, 1876, Maria Louisa Gridley, daughter of George Augustus and Susan Payson (Smallpeace) Gridley; born Boston, Mass.; no issue; resides Hyde Park, Mass. (1893).
4328. iv. JOSEPHINE BRAINARD,[8] born Boston, Mass., August 7, 1855.
4329. v.   EDITH ISABEL BRAINARD,[8] born Boston, Mass., May 7, 1857.
4330. vi. MARION BRAINARD,[8] born Hyde Park, Mass., December 25, 1859; resides Hyde Park, Mass. (1893).
4331. vii. EDNAH ELIZABETH BRAINARD,[8] born Hyde Park, Mass., Jan. 7, 1861.
4332. viii. IDA AUGUSTA BRAINARD,[8] born Hyde Park, Mass., October 24, 1865.

Mr. Brainard is the inventor of the "Brainard Milling Machine."

3993. WILLIAM FREDERIC SETCHELL[7] (*Sarah Doggett,[6] Joseph,[5] Noah,[4] Samuel,[3] Samuel,[2] Thomas[1]*), born Boston, Mass., June 16, 1825; resides Fitchburg, Mass.; married 1st, West Cambridge, Mass., April 12, 1849, Rebecca Ann Fletcher; born September, 1830; died April 7, 1857; married 2d, West Cambridge, Mass., January 7, 1863, Mrs. Augusta Parker, widow.

Issue:

4333. i.   AUGUSTA ANNA SETCHELL,[8] born West Cambridge, Mass., Nov. 3, 1850.
4334. ii. CHARLES WILLIAM SETCHELL,[8] born West Cambridge, Mass., October 18, 1852; died Fitchburg, Mass., June 11, 1877.
4335. iii. CHRISTIANNA CORA SETCHELL,[8] born West Cambridge, Mass., December 13, 1854.
4336. iv. ELIZA SETCHELL,[8] born Brooklyn, N.Y., March 27, 1864.

3994. EDWARD HENRY SETCHELL [7] (*Sarah Doggett,*[6] *Joseph,*[5] *Noah,*[4] *Samuel,*[3] *Samuel,*[2] *Thomas*[1]), born Boston, Mass., October 12, 1826; resides 189 I street, South Boston, Mass. (1892); married October 30, 1853, Sophia E. Foster.

Issue:

4337. i.   DANIEL EDWARD SETCHELL,[8] born Boston, Mass., August 21, 1854.
4338. ii. FRANK WENDELL SETCHELL,[8] born Boston, Mass., June 21, 1859; resides 189 I street, South Boston, Mass. (1892).
4339. iii. LAURA SOPHIA SETCHELL,[8] born Malden, Mass., June 25, 1861; died South Boston, Mass., November 13, 1882.
4340. iv. HERMAN LINCOLN SETCHELL,[8] born Malden, Mass., August 6, 1863; resides 189 I street, South Boston, Mass. (1892).
4341. v.   MARY SALINA SETCHELL,[8] born Malden, Mass., March 25, 1865.
4342. vi. ANNA FOSTER SETCHELL,[8] born Medford, Mass., November 16, 1868.
4343. vii. MORTON ELERY SETCHELL,[8] born Hyde Park, Mass., March 17, 1871; resides 189 I street, South Boston, Mass. (1892).

3996. DANIEL SETCHELL [7] (*Sarah Doggett,*[6] *Joseph,*[5] *Noah,*[4] *Samuel,*[3] *Samuel,*[2] *Thomas*[1]), born Boston, Mass., February 7, 1831; died probably at sea in 1866.

Mr. Setchell was a play-actor by profession, becoming well known and travelling as a star in the various cities of the country. His specialty was low comedy. After playing a successful engagement at San Francisco in 1865, he took passage on a bark for Australia in 1866 to fulfil an engagement at Melbourne, since which time nothing has been heard of the vessel or those on board.

3998. Capt. HENRY JEFFERSON DAGGETT [7] (*Henry,*[6] *Joseph,*[5] *Noah,*[4] *Samuel,*[3] *Samuel,*[2] *Thomas*[1]), born Boston, Mass., August 11, 1826; resides New Haven, N.Y. (1893); married New Haven, N.Y., March 12, 1857, Frances Lucy Hanley, daughter of Philander and Lucy (Wells) Hanley, of New Haven, N.Y.; born New Haven, N.Y., December 5, 1831.

No issue.

In early life Mr. Daggett left the farm for the lakes, and was rapidly promoted to the rank of captain. He continued in this business for several years, when, becoming somewhat tired of a sailor's life, he turned his attention to agricultural pursuits. He served his town as supervisor for several years, and in the winter of 1876–7 represented his district in the State Legislature. In the summer of 1880 he returned to the lakes as captain of the steamer "City of Toronto," running between the city of that name and Niagara City.

4000. GEORGE WILLIAM DAGGETT [7] (*Henry,*[6] *Joseph,*[5] *Noah,*[4] *Samuel,*[3] *Samuel,*[2] *Thomas*[1]), born New York city, February 1, 1833; "farmer;" died New Haven, N.Y., May 4, 1885; married Canton Centre, Conn., September 10, 1856, Mary Jane Merrill, daughter of Alanson and Lucy (Mills) Merrill; born Canton Centre, Conn., January 18, 1837.

Issue :

4344. i.   LILLIAN MARIA DAGGETT,[8] born New Haven, N.Y., May 16, 1858; married New Haven, N.Y., February 3, 1892, Irvine Keaff, son of Arthur and Sarah (Jerrett) Keaff; born New Haven, N.Y., May 28, 1860; resides New Haven, N.Y. (1893).
4345. ii. LOUISE VIOLA DAGGETT,[8] born New Haven, N.Y., April 17, 1860.
4346. iii. SARAH ADELAIDE DAGGETT,[8] born New Haven, N.Y., July 15, 1862.
4347. iv. GEORGE WILLIAM DAGGETT,[8] born New Haven, N.Y., September 1, 1865; resides Canton Centre, Conn. (1893).

4002. MARY EMILIE DAGGETT [7] (*Henry,[6] Joseph,[5] Noah,[4] Samuel,[3] Samuel,[2] Thomas [1]*), born New Haven, N.Y., August 11, 1837; resides Sioux Falls, S.D. (1893) ; married New Haven, N.Y., March 16, 1863, Capt. George Herbert Snow, son of Daniel and Betsy (Utter) Snow, of New Haven, N.Y.; lost with schooner "Corsair," on Lake Huron, September 29, 1872.

Issue :

4348. i.   GERTRUDE DAGGETT SNOW,[8] born New Haven, N.Y., September 21, 1865; resides Yankton, S.D. (1893).
4349. ii. GEORGE HERBERT SNOW,[8] born Oswego, N.Y., April 21, 1872; resides Sioux Falls, S.D. (1893).

4003. Dr. LAURA FOSTER DAGGETT [7] (*Henry,[6] Joseph,[5] Noah,[4] Samuel,[3] Samuel,[2] Thomas [1]*), born New Haven, N.Y., August 26, 1846; resides Yankton, S.D. (1893).

Dr. Daggett graduated from the Woman's Medical College of Chicago, February 28, 1882; practised at Oswego, N.Y.; removed to Sioux Falls, S.D., May 12, 1885; thence to Yankton, March 15, 1892, where she at present practises.

4009. JOSEPH LORD DOGGETT [7] (*Daniel J.,[6] Joseph,[5] Noah,[4] Samuel,[3] Samuel,[2] Thomas [1]*), born Ipswich, Mass., January 14, 1821; name changed to Akerman, March 13, 1832; died Worcester, Mass., June 6, 1870; married Ipswich, Mass., December 15, 1842, Mary Dodge, of Ipswich, Mass. ; resides Ipswich, Mass.

Issue :

4350. i.   SAMUEL THOMAS AKERMAN,[5] born Ipswich, Mass., May 16, 1843; died.
4351. ii. JOSEPHINE AKERMAN,[8] born Ipswich, Mass., February 16, 1859.

4010. SARAH LORD DOGGETT [7] (*Daniel J.,[6] Joseph,[5] Noah,[4] Samuel,[3] Samuel,[2] Thomas [1]*), born Ipswich, Mass., Feb. 21, 1826; name changed to Akerman, March 13, 1832; married Ipswich, Mass. (intention, Oct. 26, 1844), Benjamin Newman, of Ipswich, Mass.

Issue :

4352. i.   BRAINARD B. NEWMAN,[8] died May 12, 1872.
4353. ii. CLARENCE W. NEWMAN,[8] born April 5, 1860.
4354. iii. SARAH ANNE NEWMAN,[8] born April 18, 1863.

4012. SUSAN LORD DOGGETT[7] (*Daniel J.,*[6] *Joseph,*[5] *Noah,*[4] *Samuel,*[3] *Samuel,*[2] *Thomas*[1]), born Ipswich, Mass., March 25, 1829; name changed to Akerman, March 13, 1832; resides Ipswich, Mass.; married Ipswich, Mass., February 9, 1852, Charles M. Arthur, of Inverary, Scot.

Issue:

4355. i. SUSAN ISABEL ARTHUR,[8] born Ipswich, Mass., June 4, 1859.
4356. ii. FANNIE WHITE ARTHUR,[8] born Ipswich, Mass., February 18, 1861.
4357. iii. JESSIE PARKINSON ARTHUR,[8] born Ipswich, Mass., September 27, 1867.

4016. MARY EDNAH AKERMAN[7] (*Daniel J.,*[6] *Joseph Doggett,*[5] *Noah,*[4] *Samuel,*[3] *Samuel,*[2] *Thomas*[1]), born Ipswich, Mass., March 23, 1842; resides Cheshire street, Jamaica Plain, Boston, Mass. (1893); married Ipswich, Mass., November 2, 1862, Edward M. Foster, born North Reading, Mass., November 4, 1840.

Issue:

4358. i. HERBERT ARTHUR FOSTER,[8] born Jamaica Plain, Mass., Jan. 17, 1865.
4359. ii. EDWARD MANSFIELD FOSTER,[8] born Jamaica Plain, Mass., August 20, 1870; died Jamaica Plain, Mass., September 25, 1877.
4360. iii. EVA MAY FOSTER,[8] born Jamaica Plain, Mass., February 5, 1875; died Jamaica Plain, Mass., December 21, 1879.

4018. ELIJAH JANES[7] (*Bethia Huntington,*[6] *Bethiah Doggett,*[5] *Noah,*[4] *Samuel,*[3] *Samuel,*[2] *Thomas*[1]), born 1803; married ——.

4361. i. ELISHA JANES.[8]
4362. ii. OLIVE JANES.[8]
4363. iii. MARY JANES.[8]
4364. iv. ELIJAH JANES.[8]

4023. ELIZA HUNTINGTON[7] (*John,*[6] *Bethiah Doggett,*[5] *Noah,*[4] *Samuel,*[3] *Samuel,*[2] *Thomas*[1]), born Greensboro', Vt., July 21, 1808; died Key West, Fla., September 1, 1858; married Perry, N.Y., April 21, 1831, Chauncey Langdon Hatch, of Hardwick, Vt.; born Norwich, Vt., Feb. 24, 1799; died Key West, Fla., Dec. 3, 1872.

Issue:

4365. i. MARY ELIZA HATCH,[8] born Perry, N.Y., January 16, 1832.
4366. ii. CHAUNCEY LANGDON HATCH,[8] born Perry, N.Y., July 9, 1834; died there an infant.
4367. iii. CHAUNCEY LANGDON HATCH,[8] born Perry, N.Y., December 14, 1835; died Key West, Fla., October 2, 1874.
4368. iv. EMILY HATCH,[8] born Perry, N.Y., May, 1838; died there an infant.
4369. v. ISABEL STANLEY HATCH,[8] born Jacksonville, Fla., July 15, 1846; married Wichita, Kan., April 13, 1881, Cyrus Burnap Pulver, born Pine Plains, N.Y., April 18, 1835; resides Newport, Cal. (1883).

4024. NATHAN HUNTINGTON[7] (*John,*[6] *Bethiah Doggett,*[5] *Noah,*[4] *Samuel,*[3] *Samuel,*[2] *Thomas*[1]), born Greensboro', Vt., September 8, 1810; "mason;" died Boston, Mass., May, 1842; married Boston, Mass., Ann Sanders; died previous to 1883.

Issue:

4370. i. ANNETTE HUNTINGTON,[8] born Boston, Mass.; died previous to 1883.

4025. Mary Huntington [7] (*John,*[6] *Bethiah Doggett,*[5] *Noah,*[4] *Samuel,*[3] *Samuel,*[2] *Thomas*[1]), born Greensboro', Vt., February 11, 1813; died St. Joseph, Mich., October 10, 1874; married Hardwick, Vt., January 7, 1835, by Rev. Kiah Bailey, to Benjamin Comings, of East Berkshire, Vt.; died St. Joseph, Mich., October 26, 1872.

Issue :

4371. i. Ann Elizabeth Comings,[8] born East Hardwick, Vt., October 24, 1835; married Burlington, Vt., December, 1861, Calvin B. Anderson; she died Enosburgh, Vt., May 2, 1863.

4372. ii. Charles Andrew Comings,[8] born East Hardwick, Vt., December 12, 1837; died East Berkshire, Vt., May 27, 1838.

4373. iii. Samuel Huntington Comings,[8] born Greensboro', Vt., August 4, 1839; married Flint, Mich., March 7, 1864, Sarah E. Pierson; "lumber;" resides St. Charles, Mich.

4374. iv. Lucy Jane Comings,[8] born Greensboro', Vt., September 30, 1841; resides 446 Maria avenue, St. Paul, Minn.

4375. v. Mary Sarepta Comings,[8] born Greensboro', Vt., October 12, 1844.

4376. vi. Ella Fidelia Comings,[8] born Greensboro', Vt., October 28, 1846; resides 446 Maria avenue, St. Paul, Minn.

4377. vii. George Fisher Comings,[8] born Greensboro', Vt., March 18, 1849.

4378. viii. Abbie Frances Comings,[8] born Greensboro', Vt., April 9, 1851.

4379. ix. Andrew Benjamin Comings,[8] born Greensboro', Vt., June 16, 1853; died Greensboro', Vt., August 12, 1855.

4380. x. Charles Sumner Comings,[8] born Greensboro', Vt., July 3, 1855; died Greensboro', Vt., January 15, 1857.

4027. John Bailey Huntington [7] (*John,*[6] *Bethiah Doggett,*[5] *Noah,*[4] *Samuel,*[3] *Samuel,*[2] *Thomas*[1]), born Greensboro', Vt., January 1, 1818; resides Des Moines, Ia.; married Taunton, Mass., 1844, Rachel Loring.

Issue :

4381. i. Samuel Averill Huntington,[8] born Taunton, Mass., 1847; married Perry, N.Y., 1868, Jane Elizabeth Huntington (see No. 4383); resides Des Moines, Ia. (1883).

4382. ii. Isabel Huntington,[8] born 1849; married Samuel Webb; resides Des Moines, Ia. (1883).

4028. Charles B. Huntington [7] (*John,*[6] *Bethiah Doggett,*[5] *Noah,*[4] *Samuel,*[3] *Samuel,*[2] *Thomas*[1]), born Greensboro', Vt., December 23, 1820; " breeder of Cotswold sheep; " died Perry, N.Y., August 12, 1887; married 1st. Perry, N.Y., 1842, Lucy Olin; died 1842; married 2d, Perry, N.Y., November 19, 1846, Mary Buell; born Shaftsbury, Vt., January 2, 1824.

Issue :

4383. i. Jane Elizabeth Huntington,[8] born Perry, N.Y., March 30, 1850; married Samuel A. Huntington (see No. 4381).

4384. ii. Ella E. Huntington,[8] born Perry, N.Y., April 2, 1853.

4385. iii. Henrietta Huntington,[8] born Perry, N.Y., June 26, 1856.

4386. iv. Buell C. Huntington,[8] born Perry, N.Y., February 9, 1860; died Perry, N.Y., January 28, 1861.

4387. v. Charles E. Huntington,[8] born Perry, N.Y., March 18, 1863.

4388. vi. Arthur R. Huntington,[8] born Perry, N.Y., July 6, 1866.

4030. MARTHA HUNTINGTON [7] (*John,*[6] *Bethiah Doggett,*[5] *Noah,*[4] *Samuel,*[3] *Samuel,*[2] *Thomas*[1]), born Greensboro', Vt., August 21, 1825; resides Brightwood, Springfield, Mass. (1892); married North Chelmsford, Mass., October 5, 1847, by Rev. Mr. Clark, to Charles Smith, son of Seth and Wealthy (Cook) Smith; born Winchester, N.H., February 13, 1808; died Hinsdale, N.H., December 19, 1884.

Issue:

4389. i.   MYRON SMITH,[8] born Boston, Mass., September 2, 1848; died East Boston, Mass., September 2, 1850.
4390. ii. CLARA SMITH,[8] born Boston, Mass., January 17, 1850; married Hinsdale, N.H., 1883, by Rev. Mr. Sinclair, to Olcott B., son of Warren and Mary Tyler; issue: Charles Warren Tyler,[9] born September 2, 1885; resides Hinsdale, N.H. (1892).
4391. iii. MARY AUGUSTA SMITH,[8] born East Boston, Mass., September 21, 1851.
4392. iv. MARTHA SMITH,[8] born East Boston, Mass., November 29, 1853; died East Boston, Mass., February 22, 1854.
4393. v.   SARAH ADELAIDE SMITH,[8] born East Boston, Mass., January 11, 1856; married Brattleboro', Vt., January 14, 1885, Melvin R. Warner; no issue; resides Brightwood, Springfield, Mass. (1892).
4394. vi. EDWARD EVERETT SMITH,[8] born East Boston, Mass., March 4, 1859; died East Boston, Mass., August 18, 1859.
4395. vii. CHARLES HUNTINGTON SMITH,[8] born East Boston, Mass., July 26, 1860; graduated Amherst College; resides Chicago, Ill.
4396. viii. ANNETT SMITH,[8] born Hinsdale, N.H., July 24, 1862; died Hinsdale, N.H., October 30, 1890.
4397. ix. HATTIE LOUISE SMITH,[8] born Hinsdale, N.H., March 29, 1868; resides Springfield, Mass. (1892).

4031. CAROLINE HUNTINGTON [7] (*Henry,*[6] *Bethiah Doggett,*[5] *Noah,*[4] *Samuel,*[3] *Samuel,*[2] *Thomas*[1]), born Greensboro', Vt., February 4, 1808; died Hanover, N.H., December 13, 1857; married Greensboro', Vt., 1830, Charles Cook; born Greensboro', Vt., January 1, 1804; died Greensboro', Vt., February 17, 1868.

Issue:

4398. i.   BETSEY PARMALEE COOK,[8] born Greensboro', Vt., May 19, 1834; married Greensboro', Vt., December 31, 1868, John A. Goss; she died Greensboro', Vt., July 23, 1880.
4399. ii. JOHN BRAY COOK,[8] born Greensboro', Vt., July 4, 1836.
4400. iii. EDWARD BURBECK COOK,[8] born Greensboro', Vt., November 15, 1839; died Greensboro', Vt., January 23, 1842.
4401. iv. CHARLES HENRY COOK,[8] born Greensboro', Vt., April 10, 1845; married Barre, Vt., January 10, 1878, Rosa S. Perkins; he a physician; resides Natick, Mass. (1883).

4032. ROXANA HUNTINGTON [7] (*Henry,*[6] *Bethiah Doggett,*[5] *Noah,*[4] *Samuel,*[3] *Samuel,*[2] *Thomas*[1]), born Greensboro', Vt., June 14, 1810; died Newbury, Pa., January 16, 1874; married Greensboro', Vt., January 30, 1833, Josiah Nelson Stevens, of Greensboro', Vt.; resides Newbury, Pa.

Issue:

4402. i.   LEVI NELSON STEVENS,[8] born Greensboro', Vt., May 9, 1834; married June 6, 1860, Emma Elizabeth Roberts; resides Chateaugay, N.Y. (1883).

4403. ii.   HENRY HUNTINGTON STEVENS,⁵ born Greensboro', Vt., May 24, 1836 ; died July 3, 1866.
4404. iii. DAN STEVENS,⁵ born Greensboro', Vt., December 16, 1838 ; resides Newbury, Pa.
4405. iv.   CAROLINE EMILY STEVENS,⁵ born Greensboro', Vt., June 18, 1842 ; married July 9, 1861, James Rice ; resides Pueblo, Col. (1883).
4406. v.   HELEN ESTHER STEVENS,⁵ born Greensboro', Vt.. July 17, 1844 ; married January 15, 1868, Charles Frederick Blossom ; resides National City, Cal. (1883).
4407. vi.   PARMALEE AUGUSTUS STEVENS.⁵ born Greensboro', Vt., April 6, 1846 ; married August 29, 1874, Ellen R. Doane ; resides Newbury, Pa. (1883).
4408. vii. ABBY MARIA STEVENS.⁵ born Greensboro'. Vt.. May 7, 1848 ; married Oct. 5, 1876, Henry A. Babbitt ; resides East Hardwick. Vt. (1883).
4409. viii. JOSIAH NELSON STEVENS,⁵ born Greensboro', Vt., July 20, 1849 ; resides Newbury, Pa. (1883).
4410. ix.   SUSAN ESTELLE STEVENS,⁵ born Greensboro', Vt., July 23. 1854 ; married October 5, 1876, Samuel G. Updegroff ; resides Newbury, Pa. (1883).

4033. BETSEY HUNTINGTON⁷ (*Henry,*⁶ *Bethiah Doggett,*⁵ *Noah,*⁴ *Samuel,*³ *Samuel.*² *Thomas*¹). born Greensboro', Vt.. October 6, 1812 ; died Cedar Rapids. Ia.. Nov. 26, 1882 ; married Greensboro', Vt.. June 19. 1831. Josiah Hale ; resides Cedar Rapids. Ia. (1883).

Issue :

4411. i.   AGNES CLARISSA HALE,⁵ born Greensboro', Vt., 1832 ; died an infant.
4412. ii.   ASHBEL HUNTINGTON HALE,⁵ born Greensboro', Vt., February 5, 1834 ; died Cedar Rapids, Ia., August 27, 1858.
4413. iii. GEORGE WEEKS HALE.⁵ born Greensboro', Vt., December 5, 1838.
4414. iv.   ELLEN S. HALE,⁵ born Greensboro', Vt., January 12, 1841 ; resides Cedar Rapids, Ia. (1883).
4415. v.   EDWARD J. HALE.⁵ born Greensboro', Vt., December 20, 1843 ; resides Cedar Rapids, Ia. (1883).
4416. vi.   JOHN P. HALE.⁵ born Greensboro', Vt.. August 27, 1848.

4034. BETHIA ESTHER HUNTINGTON⁷ (*Henry,*⁶ *Bethiah Doggett,*⁵ *Noah,*⁴ *Samuel,*³ *Samuel,*² *Thomas*¹), born Greensboro', Vt., October 20, 1815 ; resides Canon City. Col. (1883) ; married Greensboro', Vt., May 7, 1837, Franklin Blake ; died Leavenworth. Kan.. April 18. 1857.

Issue :

4417. i.   SYLVIA BLAKE,⁵ born Greensboro'. Vt., March 23. 1838 ; married Cedar Rapids, Ia.. August 7, 1862. Edmund H. Dewey.
4418. ii.   BERTHA BLAKE,⁵ born Greensboro', Vt.. May 29, 1840 : married Mapleton. Kan.. May 1. 1859. Leander Martin.
4419. iii. FLORA BLAKE,⁵ born Greensboro'. Vt.. June 18, 1842 ; married St. Louis. Mo., Nov. 5. 1860, Joshua W. Jewell : she died Feb. 3, 1872.
4420. iv.   HENRY DWIGHT BLAKE.⁵ born Greensboro', Vt., December 26. 1844 ; died January 10. 1845.
4421. v.   HENRY HUNTINGTON BLAKE.⁵ born Greensboro', Vt.. March 14, 1846.
4422. vi.   FRANKLIN BLAKE.⁵ born Greensboro'. Vt., April 17, 1848 ; married Louisville. Ky.. July 3. 1875. Wilhelmine Bell.
4423. vii. ESTHER BLAKE.⁵ born Greensboro', Vt., May 25, 1850 : died October 26. 1854.
4424. viii. ALICE BLAKE.⁵ born Greensboro', Vt.. April 30, 1852 ; died July 5, 1852.
4425. ix.   MARY ELLEN BLAKE,⁵ born Greensboro', Vt., August 2. 1853.
4426. x.   CAROLINE BLAKE.⁵ born Parkville. Mo.. April 30. 1857 ; died May 14. 1857.

4035. Dr. HENRY HUNTINGTON [7] (*Henry,*[6] *Bethiah Doggett,*[5] *Noah,*[4] *Samuel,*[3] *Samuel,*[2] *Thomas* [1]), born Greensboro', Vt., June 3, 1818; resides North Craftsbury, Vt. (1883); married Craftsbury, Vt., October 5, 1847, Martha Matilda Dustan; born Craftsbury, Vt., July 10, 1825.

Issue:

4427. i.   CHARLES DUSTAN HUNTINGTON,[8] born Champlain, N.Y., August 9, 1848; died Champlain, N.Y., August 16, 1849.
4428. ii. HENRY D. HUNTINGTON,[8] born Craftsbury, Vt., July 16, 1850.
4429. iii. LAURA CORBIN HUNTINGTON,[8] born Albany, Ga., April 9, 1853; died Albany, Ga., July 12, 1857.
4430. iv. FREDERIC WALTER HUNTINGTON,[8] born Albany, Ga., November 27; 1858; died Albany, Ga., July 6, 1859.
4431. v.   DANIEL N. HUNTINGTON,[8] born Atlanta, Ga., January 13, 1861; died Colorado Springs, Col., March 23, 1880.
4432. vi. WILLIAM CRAFTS HUNTINGTON,[8] born Atlanta, Ga., April 7, 1864; died Meridian, Miss., August 27, 1864.
4433. vii. PLINY CORBIN HUNTINGTON,[8] born Des Moines, Ia., June 23, 1868.

Henry Huntington took his medical diploma at Albany, N.Y., in 1846, and followed the profession of medicine five years, when a bronchial difficulty obliged him to abandon it. He went south in 1851, and there resided in Albany, Ga., where he was a dentist.

Removed to Des Moines, Ia., in January, 1865, where he practised his profession until January, 1879.

From that date until 1882 he spent in Colorado and Montana, for his health, and in May, 1883, removed with his family to Craftsbury, Vt.

4037. FARNHAM PARMELEE HUNTINGTON [7] (*Henry,*[6] *Bethiah Doggett,*[5] *Noah,*[4] *Samuel,*[3] *Samuel,*[2] *Thomas* [1]), born Greensboro', Vt., July 4, 1825; resides Huntington, W. Va. (1883); married Champlain, N.Y., January 19, 1858, Frances Mary Savage.

Issue:

4434. i.   NELLY M. HUNTINGTON,[8] born Cedar Rapids, Ia., December 8, 1859.
4435. ii. CHARLES PARMELEE HUNTINGTON,[8] born Cedar Rapids, Ia., November 28, 1861.
4436. iii. CYRUS SAVAGE HUNTINGTON,[8] born Champlain. N.Y., July 24, 1865; died October 8, 1866.

4038. EUNICE CARTER HUNTINGTON [7] (*Henry,*[6] *Bethiah Doggett,*[5] *Noah,*[4] *Samuel,*[3] *Samuel,*[2] *Thomas* [1]), born Greensboro', Vt., March 31, 1829; died Cedar Rapids, Ia., September 26, 1865; married Greensboro', Vt., July 19, 1855, Edwin Derby.

Issue:

4437. i.   EDWIN DERBY,[8] died an infant.
4438. ii. —— DERBY,[8] died ——.
4439. iii. CLARA DERBY,[8] born February 10, 1859.

4039. NOAH DOGGETT WRIGHT [7] (*Sophia Huntington,*[6] *Bethiah Doggett,*[5] *Noah,*[4] *Samuel,*[3] *Samuel,*[2] *Thomas* [1]), born Reading, Ohio,

February 22, 1823; died Covington, Ky., July 7, 1893; married Cincinnati, Ohio, September 3, 1845, Maria L. Ferris; born Cincinnati, Ohio, January 9, 1826.

Issue:

4440. i. ANNA HUNTINGTON WRIGHT,[8] born June 12, 1846.
4441. ii. HELEN MARIA WRIGHT,[8] born June 26, 1848.
4442. iii. SOPHIA LEE WRIGHT,[8] born August 6, 1850; resides Carthage, Ohio.
4443. iv. MARY FRANCES WRIGHT,[8] born November 3, 1852.
4444. v. VIRGINIA IRENE WRIGHT,[8] born May 28, 1855.
4445. vi. ELIZABETH WRIGHT,[8] born July 22, 1860; died July 25, 1860.
4446. vii. CATHERINE BERTHA WRIGHT,[8] born June 1, 1863..
4447. viii. GEORGE LEE WRIGHT,[8] born August 31, 1864.
4448. ix. URSULA ISABEL WRIGHT,[8] born April 15, 1867; married Mr. Clark.

4040. Dr. THOMAS LEE WRIGHT [7] (*Sophia Huntington,*[6] *Bethiah Doggett,*[5] *Noah,*[4] *Samuel,*[3] *Samuel,*[2] *Thomas* [1]), born Windham, Ohio, August 7, 1825; died Bellefontaine, Ohio, June 22, 1893; married Bellefontaine, Ohio, March 31, 1846, Lucinda Lord, daughter of Abiel H. and Letitia (McCloud) Lord; resides Bellefontaine, Ohio (1893).

Issue:

4449. i. ABIEL LORD WRIGHT,[8] born Bellefontaine, Ohio, April 3, 1847.
4450. ii. THOMAS HUNTINGTON WRIGHT,[8] born Bellefontaine, Ohio, April 30, 1849; "lawyer;" resides there.

Dr. Thomas Lee Wright attended the "Miami University" four years, and afterward graduated in medicine from the Medical College of Ohio in 1846.

He made his home chiefly in Bellefontaine since that time. He resided from January, 1851, to December, 1854, in Kansas City, Mo., where he practised medicine mainly among the Wyandotte Indians, just over the Kansas river. He was a member of the "American Association for the Cure of Inebriety."

In 1891 he went as one of two delegates from the United States to London to the international meeting of the Society for the treatment of Alcoholism. No resident of Bellefontaine was better known than was Dr. Wright, and none was more highly respected and admired for intellect and general worth.

4041. ELIZABETH ANN WRIGHT [7] (*Sophia Huntington,*[6] *Bethiah Doggett,*[5] *Noah,*[4] *Samuel,*[3] *Samuel,*[2] *Thomas* [1]), born Reading, Ohio, November 10, 1827; died Chicago, Ill., November 24, 1889; married "Ingleside," Ohio, 1852, Rev. Charles Burton Phillips, son of —— and Elizabeth (Lyon) Phillips; born 1807.

Issue:

4451. i. THOMAS WRIGHT PHILLIPS,[8] born Ingleside, Ohio, February 6, 1854.
4452. ii. MARY ELIZABETH PHILLIPS,[8] born Chicago, Ill., May 16, 1857; resides Hinsdale, Ill. (1893).
4453. iii. IDA HUNTINGTON PHILLIPS,[8] born Jonesboro', Ill., May 31, 1860; resides Hinsdale, Ill. (1893).

4042. Judge SAMUEL HUNTINGTON WRIGHT[7] (*Sophia Hunting-ton*,[6] *Bethiah Doggett*,[5] *Noah*,[4] *Samuel*,[3] *Samuel*,[2] *Thomas*[1]), born Windham, Ohio, May 15, 1828; resides Oakland, Cal. (1892); married California, Dec. 19, 1849, Sarah Maria Derby, of St. Louis, Mo.

Issue:

4454. i.   MARY ELIZABETH WRIGHT,[8] born Marysville, Cal., May 11, 1852; married 1874, Mr. Clark; two children.
4455. ii.   EDWARD HUNTINGTON WRIGHT,[8] born Marysville, Cal., January 24, 1856; married 1879.
4456. iii.   WILLARD ROODE WRIGHT,[8] born Santa Clara, Cal., June 9, 1859; married June 7, 1884.
4457. iv.   STANLEY HERBERT WRIGHT,[8] born Santa Clara, Cal., Sept. 16, 1861.
4458. v.   GARRETT DERBY WRIGHT,[8] born Carson. Nev., October 31, 1863.
4459. vi.   HOWARD WRIGHT,[8] born Carson, Nev.. October 16, 1866.
4460. vii.   LESLIE WRIGHT,[8] born Carson, Nev., October 16, 1866.
4461. viii.   CURTIS WRIGHT,[8] born Carson, Nev., February 10, 1869.

Judge Samuel H. Wright crossed the plains to California in 1849. He is a lawyer of good standing and reputation. Has been probate judge under the territorial organization of Nevada, and district judge under the State organization.

4043. SOPHIA HUNTINGTON WRIGHT[7] (*Sophia Huntington*,[6] *Bethiah Doggett*,[5] *Noah*,[4] *Samuel*,[3] *Samuel*,[2] *Thomas*[1]), born Windham, Ohio; died 1863 or 1864; married Michael Stevenson Williams, son of Michael Anthony and Elizabeth Lee (Demster) Williams; born Cincinnati, Ohio, March 27, 1828; died Cincinnati, Ohio, November 6, 1870.

Issue:

4462. i.   JOHN EBERLE WILLIAMS,[8] born Reading, Ohio. January 9, 1853; died Cincinnati, Ohio, April 21, 1884.
4463. ii.   ECKLEN WILLIAMS,[8] born Dearborn county, Ind., September 18, 1855.
4464. iii.   THOMAS WRIGHT WILLIAMS,[8] born Dearborn county, Ind., September 3, 1859; address, 141 Ridley street, San Francisco, Cal. (1891).
4465. iv.   STELLA HUNTINGTON WILLIAMS,[8] born Ingleside, Ohio, August 9, 1860; resides Hinsdale, Ill. (1893).
4466. v.   LOUIS WILLIAMS,[8] born Reading, Ohio, May 6, 1862; married Cincinnati, Ohio, October 30, 1889, Matilda Von Hagel; resides 55 Pendleton street, Cincinnati, Ohio (1891).

4044. MARY ANGELINA WRIGHT[7] (*Sophia Huntington*,[6] *Bethiah Doggett*,[5] *Noah*,[4] *Samuel*,[3] *Samuel*,[2] *Thomas*[1]), born Carthage, Ohio, July 12, 1834; resides 143 Park avenue, Chicago, Ill. (1891); married 1st, Bellefontaine, Ohio, March 18, 1863, Richard S. C. Lord, son of Abiel H. and —— (McCloud) Lord; born Bellefontaine, Ohio, October, 1832; died Bellefontaine, Ohio, October 15, 1866; married 2d, Ingleside, Ohio, December 10, 1877, James Kissam Goodwin, son of James Kissam and Rebecca Ann Hart (Ulstick) Goodwin; born Cincinnati, Ohio, December 10, 1834.

Issue:

4467. i.   RICHARD STANTON LORD,[8] born Ingleside, Ohio, April 9, 1864; died Ingleside, Ohio, May 27, 1867.

4468. ii. EDITH LORD,[8] born Ingleside, Ohio, May, 1865; died Ingleside, Ohio, September, 1865.

4045. JOHN EBERLY WRIGHT[7] (*Sophia Huntington,*[6] *Bethiah Doggett,*[5] *Noah,*[4] *Samuel,*[3] *Samuel,*[2] *Thomas*[1]), born Carthage, Ohio, December 20, 1839; resides 647 Washington boulevard, Chicago, Ill. (1893); married Lockland, Ohio, July 7, 1864, Irene Parker, daughter of Benjamin Franklin and Catherine (Carr) Parker; born June 7, 1845.
Issue:

4469. i. KATHERINE LAURA WRIGHT,[8] born Lockland, Ohio, April 11, 1865.
4470. ii. FRANK PARKER WRIGHT,[8] born Lockland, Ohio, November 11, 1867.
4471. iii. CLARENCE HUNTINGTON WRIGHT,[8] born Lockland, Ohio, Mar. 20, 1869.

John E. Wright was connected with some of the Cincinnati banks for over twenty years, but owing to impaired health he removed to Chicago in 1877, and became the financial manager of the " Friend & Fox Paper Company."

4046. ANN MARIE DOGGETT[7] (*John R.,*[6] *Henry,*[5] *Noah,*[4] *Samuel,*[3] *Samuel,*[2] *Thomas*[1]), born Charleston, S.C., January, 1822; died " The Thicket," near Darien, Ga., June 13, 1874; married Darien, Ga., July 4, 1853, Aaron Nelson, of Norway; died November 19, 1874.
Issue:

4472. i. JOHN DOGGETT NELSON,[8] born Black Bearce Island, Ga., July 20, 1854; died Darien. Ga., July 1, 1855.
4473. ii. MARGARET MARIE NELSON,[8] born Darien, Ga., May 30, 1858.

4048. WILLIAM J. DOGGETT[7] (*John R.,*[6] *Henry,*[5] *Noah,*[4] *Samuel,*[3] *Samuel,*[2] *Thomas*[1]), born Darien, Ga., December 22, 1825; resides Darien, Ga. (1881); married 1879.
Issue:

4474. i. ELIZA ELLEN DOGGETT,[8] born Darien, Ga., 1881.

4052. Dr. JOHN SCOTT HUGHSON[7] (*Mary A. Doggett,*[6] *Henry,*[5] *Noah,*[4] *Samuel,*[3] *Samuel,*[2] *Thomas*[1]), born Camden. S.C., October 1, 1841; resides Sumter, S.C. (1893); married 1st, March 15, 1864, Eliza Randolph Turner, daughter of Capt. Shirley Carter and Sarah Legare (Bascom) Turner, of Virginia; born Charleston, S.C., July 4, 1843; died Sumter. S.C., Jan. 21, 1876; married 2d, May 22, 1879, Celeste Elizabeth Quattlebaum, daughter of Dr. Joseph and Lucy Ann (Merritt) Quattlebaum, of Fairfield county, S.C.; born Orangeburg county, S.C., Nov. 25, 1853; died Sumter, S.C., Aug. 30, 1893.
Issue:

4475. i. MARY AMELIA HUGHSON,[8] born Camden, S.C., May 29, 1865; resides Sumter, S.C. (1893).
4476. ii. SHIRLEY CARTER HUGHSON,[8] born Camden, S.C., February 15, 1867; " student; " resides New York city (1893).
4477. iii. ZADAH BASCOM HUGHSON,[8] born Sumter. S.C.. September 30, 1872.

4478. iv.   WILLIAM EDWARD HUGHSON,[8] born Sumter, S.C., December 6, 1875;
                  died Sumter, S.C., December 17, 1875.
4479. v.   LUCILE HUGHSON,[8] born Sumter, S.C., June 4, 1880.
4480. vi.   EDNA HUGHSON,[8] born Sumter, S.C., September 26, 1881.
4481. vii. CLARA BESSIE HUGHSON,[8] born Sumter, S.C., March 8, 1884.
4482. viii. CELESTE HUGHSON,[8] born Sumter, S.C., January 6, 1886.
4483. ix.   IVA BELLE HUGHSON,[8] born Sumter, S.C., October 1, 1889.
4484. x.   ELEANOR HUGHSON,[8] born Sumter, S.C., October 22, 1891.

Dr. John S. Hughson was educated at the Furman University,
Greenville, S.C.; graduated in medicine at Medical College of South
Carolina, at Charleston, in 1867, and has practised in Sumter, S.C.,
since 1869. The father of Dr. Hughson's first wife was a cousin
and intimate friend of Gen. Robert E. Lee, while her grandmother
was a Legare, of South Carolina.

4053.   SARAH JANE DOGGETT [7]   (*Robert H..[6] Henry.[5] Noah,[4]
Samuel,[3] Samuel,[2] Thomas[1]*), born Lee county, Ga., May 16, 1824;
died Monroe county, Ga., January 13, 1881; married Jasper county,
Ga., October 27, 1842, B. J. Norris; born March 4, 1820.

Issue:

4485. i.   JOHN G. NORRIS,[8] born February 19, 1846; resides Brushy, Spalding
                  Co., Ga. (1881).
4486. ii.   MARTHA ANN NORRIS,[8] born July 16, 1849.
4487. iii. WILLIAM A. NORRIS,[8] born October 25, 1852.
4488. iv.   MARY E. NORRIS,[8] born February 19, 1855.
4489. v.   EDMAND F. NORRIS,[8] born April 16, 1858.
4490. vi.   SARAH J. NORRIS,[8] born November 10, 1860.

4055.   LAURA VICY DOGGETT [7]   (*Robert H.,[6] Henry,[5] Noah,[4]
Samuel,[3] Samuel,[2] Thomas[1]*), born Lee county, Ga., October 26,
1838; resides (1884) De Kalb county, Ala.; married 1st, October
5, 1858, Andrew Jackson Bankston; born Georgia, November 20,
1835; died Virginia, January 10, 1863; married 2d, February 22,
1865, Samuel Collins; born Delaware, September 22, 1785; died
November 25, 1878; married 3d, Monroe county, Ga., April 6, 1879,
T. J. Morgan; born March 17, 1829.

Issue:

4491. i.   ROBERT J. W. COLLINS.[8] born December 29, 1867.

4056.   CHARLES DOGGETT COLE [7]   (*Mary A. Doggett,[6] Noah,[5]
Noah,[4] Samuel,[3] Samuel,[2] Thomas[1]*), born Boston, Mass., September
30, 1823; resides Highland avenue, Cambridge, Mass. (1893);
married Boston, Mass., November 14, 1844, by Rev. Edward N.
Kirk, to Mary Sophia Jeffers, daughter of Ebenezer and Mary B.
(Tucker) Jeffers; born Boston, Mass., February 22, 1820; died
Cambridgeport, Mass., November 8, 1887.

Issue:

4492. i.   Daughter COLE,[8] born Boston, Mass., October 15, 1845; died Boston,
                  Mass., October 15, 1845.
4493. ii. MARY ELIZABETH COLE.[8] born Boston. Mass., January 16, 1852.

Charles D. Cole was engaged in the flour and West India goods business in early life, afterwards interested in publishing.

His whole attention for many years has been given to the Independent Order of Odd Fellows, of which society he has held the offices, since 1856, of Grand Secretary of the Grand Lodge of Massachusetts, and Grand Scribe of the Grand Encampment, with office in the Odd Fellows Building, Boston.

4060. ELIZABETH DOGGETT COLE [7] (*Mary A. Doggett,*[6] *Noah,*[5] *Noah,*[4] *Samuel,*[3] *Samuel,*[2] *Thomas* [1]), born Boston, Mass., April 28, 1835; resides Grand street, Albany, N.Y. (1893); married Albany, N.Y., February 29, 1856, by Rev. Dr. Halley, to Robert Barclay Wing, son of Barnabas and Ruth (Wilbur) Wing; born Quaker Springs, N.Y., May 3, 1833.

Issue :

4494. i. CHARLES COLE WING,[8] born Albany, N.Y., November 27, 1856; resides Grand street, Albany. N.Y., 1893.
4495. ii. CHARLOTTE ADELAIDE WING,[8] born Albany, N.Y., December 15, 1858.

4064. DANIEL GOODNOW, JR.[7] (*Ann B. Doggett,*[6] *Noah.*[5] *Noah,*[4] *Samuel,*[3] *Samuel,*[2] *Thomas* [1]), born Boston, Mass.. July 9, 1839 ; resides Chestnut Hill avenue, Boston, Mass. (1893) ; married Boston, Mass., June 29, 1871, by Rev. C. D. Bradlee, to Elizabeth Augusta Welch, daughter of John J. and Mary Elizabeth (Adams) Welch; born Boston, Mass., November 24, 1852.

Issue :

4496. i. HOLLIS BRADLEE GOODNOW,[8] born Boston, Mass., April 13, 1872; died Boston, Mass., February 16, 1890.
4497. ii. RUSSELL JARVIS GOODNOW,[8] born Boston, Mass., August 3, 1873; married Melrose, Mass., June 1, 1893, Florence Louise, daughter of John C. Maker.
4498. iii. ELIZABETH GOODNOW,[8] born Boston, Mass., December 27, 1874.
4499. iv. FANNY GOODNOW,[8] born Boston, Mass., March 6, 1876.

Daniel Goodnow, Jr., after graduating from the public schools, entered the employ of Messrs. A. J. Wilkinson & Co., hardware merchants, Washington street, corner of Wilson's lane.

Of an inventive inclination, he devoted his spare hours to the development of his genius in that direction, and, leaving Messrs. A. J. Wilkinson & Co., began the manufacture of several articles which he had invented or improved.

In addition to the factory thus established, he opened a hardware and tool store at 23 Cornhill, and soon after associated with him Mr. Luther H. Wightman, under the style of Goodnow & Wightman, importers, manufacturers, and dealers in tools and hardware.

Business having greatly increased, they enlarged by adding the next store, and in 1878 removed to still larger quarters at 176 Washington street. An annual edition of a catalogue free to any address, which was extensively advertised, brought in time a trade from every part of the world.

In 1890 the firm removed to 63 Sudbury street, with increased facilities for handling the business.

Owing to private business which came to him by the death of his father, he retired from the partnership March 1, 1892. He still retains his office at 63 Sudbury street.

4066. SAMUEL BRADLEE DOGGETT [7] (*Nathaniel B.,*[6] *Noah,*[5] *Noah,*[4] *Samuel,*[3] *Samuel,*[2] *Thomas*[1]), born Boston, Mass., May 29, 1858; resides Hollis, corner Tremont street, Boston, Mass. (1893).

The writer was educated in the public schools of Boston, graduating from the English High School in 1876.

Entering the employ of Messrs. Goodnow & Wightman, October, 1877, he was book-keeper the first three years, and afterward engaged in looking after some of the outside interests of the firm, as well as details of correspondence and different departments in the inside work.

Other cares and prospects developing resulted in his retiring from the hardware business in June, 1892.

Born and always living in a family mansion with a history of the stirring times of the Revolution, and associated in early life with those who could tell of those times, he developed an interest in ancestry, which resulted first in a short account of the Bradlee family, printed in 1878, and since that time in the accumulation of material for the present work.

4075. EDWARD B. DREW [7] (*Benjamin,*[6] *Benjamin,*[5] *Elizabeth Doggett,*[4] *Ebenezer,*[3] *Samuel,*[2] *Thomas*[1]), born August 24, 1843; married June 25, 1871, Anna Davis, of Medfield.

Issue :

4500. i. CHARLES DAVIS DREW,[8] born September 13, 1875.
4501. ii. DORA MAY DREW,[8] born August 22, 1877.
4502. iii. ELSA CAROLINE DREW,[8] born March 11, 1881.
4503. iv. LUCY BARTLETT DREW,[8] born March 22, 1884.
4504. v. KATHLEEN DREW,[8] born June 24, 1886.

4077. HELEN E. DREW [7] (*Benjamin,*[6] *Benjamin,*[5] *Elizabeth Doggett,*[4] *Ebenezer,*[3] *Samuel,*[2] *Thomas*[1]), born December 5, 1846; married August 2, 1873, Abbott Bassett, of Chelsea.

Issue :

4505. i. MARION DREW BASSETT,[8] born November 1, 1877.
4506. ii. HELEN A. BASSETT,[8] born July 13, 1885.

4079. CAROLINE B. DREW [7] (*Benjamin,*[6] *Benjamin,*[5] *Elizabeth Doggett,*[4] *Ebenezer,*[3] *Samuel,*[2] *Thomas*[1]), born October 26, 1852;

Samuel B. Doggett

resides Providence, R.I. (1889) ; married Sacramento, Cal., November 7, 1876, Herbert D. Nickerson.

Issue :

4507. i.   EDWARD DREW NICKERSON,[8] born February 6, 1880.
4508. ii. CHESTER BARTLETT NICKERSON,[8] born August 3, 1881.
4509. iii. —— NICKERSON,[8] born June 1, 1889.

4082. HUBBEL B. CONE[7] (*Wealthy Kingsbury,*[6] *Asenath Daggett,*[5] *Samuel,*[4] *John,*[3] *Samuel,*[2] *Thomas*[1]), born February 15, 1809 ; died Chicago, Ill. ; married Mary M. Skelton, of Litchfield South Farms, Conn., daughter of Henry Skelton ; born Bethlehem, Conn., December 6, 1814.

Issue :

4510. i.   PINCKNEY S. CONE,[8] born Wetumpka, Ala., January 25, 1838.
4511. ii.   EVA M. CONE,[8] born Harris Hill, N.Y., September 20, 1840.
4512. iii. SALMON FULTON CONE,[8] born Harris Hill, N.Y., October 7, 1842.
4513. iv.   GEORGE H. CONE,[8] born Harris Hill, N.Y., September 12, 1844.
4514. v.   MARSHALL H. CONE,[8] born Harris Hill, N.Y., June 15, 1847.
4515. vi.   JOSEPHINE M. CONE,[8] died Chicago.
4516. vii. ALBERT G. CONE,[8] born Chicago, Ill., September 30, 1852.
4517. viii. IRVING H. CONE,[8] born Chicago, Ill., March 22, 1856.

4084. NATHANIEL K. CONE[7] (*Wealthy Kingsbury,*[6] *Asenath Daggett,*[5] *Samuel,*[4] *John,*[3] *Samuel,*[2] *Thomas*[1]), born July 14, 1813 ; died Batavia, 1886 ; married East Hartford, Conn., October 9, 1840, Adaline Brewer, daughter of Samuel Brewer.

Issue :

4518. i.   HOBART BREWER CONE,[8] born March 3, 1843.
4519. ii. HARRIET MARY CONE,[8] born March 18, 1857.

4085. SALMON G. CONE[7] (*Wealthy Kingsbury,*[6] *Asenath Daggett,*[5] *Samuel,*[4] *John,*[3] *Samuel,*[2] *Thomas*[1]), born August 6, 1815 ; died Unadilla, N.Y., April 7, 1890 ; married 1st, Mercy Ann Cone, daughter of Gardner Cone ; married 2d, Julia Fowler.

Issue :

4520. i.   ALASKA F. CONE.[8]
4521. ii. SALMON CONE.[8]

4086. HARRIET M. CONE[7] (*Wealthy Kingsbury,*[6] *Asenath Daggett,*[5] *Samuel,*[4] *John,*[6] *Samuel,*[2] *Thomas*[1]), born June 5, 1818 ; resides 167 Ocean avenue, Atlantic City, N.J. (1890) ; married Batavia, N.Y., January 7, 1841, by Rev. Dr. James A. Bolles, to William Redfield Phelps, of Hebron, Conn.

Issue :

4522. i.   GERTRUDE REDFIELD PHELPS,[8] born Hartford, Conn., March 4, 1845.
4523. ii.   HELEN MARIA PHELPS,[8] born Hartford, Conn., August 17, 1848 ; married Charles Malcom Gudknecht, at Atlantic City, N.J., Dec. 9, 1886.
4524. iii. HARRIET AUGUSTA PHELPS,[8] born Brooklyn, N.Y., December 29, 1853 ; married Harvey K. Hinchman, at Philadelphia, Pa., November 16, 1881 ; she died September 26, 1883.

4087. WILLIAM HENRY HARRISON DAGGETT [7] (*Isaiah,*[6] *Isaiah,*[5] *Samuel,*[4] *John,*[3] *Samuel,*[2] *Thomas* [1]), born Coventry, Conn., December 13, 1820; resides Hartford, Conn. (1893); married East Hartford, Conn., 1844, by Rev. Samuel Spring, to Lucy Ann Pratt, daughter of Solomon and Pamelia (Porter) Pratt; born East Hartford, Conn., August 18, 1824; died May 31, 1892.

Issue:

4525. i. MARY PRATT DAGGETT,[8] born Andover, Conn., January 25, 1846.
4526. ii. GEORGE EDWIN DAGGETT,[8] born East Hartford, Conn., Nov. 3, 1854.
4527. iii. ESTHER PAMELIA DAGGETT,[8] born Andover, Conn., January 7, 1858.
4528. iv. NELLIE LUCY ANN DAGGETT,[8] born Andover, Conn., July 18, 1864; married Andover, Conn., June 21, 1883, by Rev. F. D. Avery, to Charles F. Lincoln; she died Andover, Conn., September 21, 1887.

4088. LUCY HARRIET ARNOLD DAGGETT [7] (*Isaiah,*[6] *Isaiah,*[5] *Samuel,*[4] *John,*[3] *Samuel,*[2] *Thomas* [1]), born Coventry, Conn., December 15, 1826; resides (1890) Sigourney street, Hartford, Conn.; married Andover, Conn., October 20, 1847, by Rev. Mr. Ely, to Henry Ensign, son of Harry and Abigail (Abbey) Ensign; born East Hartford, Conn., November 5, 1825.

Issue:

4529. i. FRANK HENRY ENSIGN,[8] born Hartford, Conn., April 7, 1852.
4530. ii. ROSELLA LUCY ENSIGN,[8] born Hartford, Conn., November 11, 1853; died Hartford, Conn., June 4, 1860.
4531. iii. EARL ENGLISH ENSIGN,[8] born Hartford, Conn., September 5, 1857; died Hartford, Conn., December 12, 1859.

4091. AUGUSTUS LAVALETTE DAGGETT [7] (*Chester,*[6] *Isaiah,*[5] *Samuel,*[4] *John,*[3] *Samuel,*[2] *Thomas* [1]), born Bolton, Conn., October 27, 1828; resides Port Orange, Volusia Co., Fla. (1893); married Coventry, Conn., April 21, 1852, by George A. Calhoun, to Almira Long, daughter of Asahel and Patience (Hopkings) Long; born Coventry, Conn., April 27, 1832.

Issue:

4532. i. JOSEPH AUGUSTUS DAGGETT,[8] born Coventry, Conn., September 30, 1853; resides Quarryville, Conn. (1893).
4533. ii. CLAYTON DAGGETT,[8] born Coventry, Conn., Sept., 1856; "a cowboy."

4092. SAMUEL HENRY DAGGETT [7] (*Samuel B.,*[6] *Isaiah,*[5] *Samuel,*[4] *John,*[3] *Samuel,*[2] *Thomas* [1]), born Coventry, Conn., December 23, 1829; resides (1893) Andover, Conn.; married Colchester, Conn., June 2, 1858, by Rev. John Avery, to Cornelia Louisa Brown, daughter of John M. and Louisa (Lombard) Brown; born Franklin, Conn., September 16, 1833.

Issue:

4534. i. HENRY CALVIN DAGGETT,[8] born Andover, Conn., April 9, 1861.

4094. Charlotte Chilson [7] (*Pamela Daggett,*[6] *John,*[5] *John,*[4] *John,*[3] *Samuel,*[2] *Thomas*[1]), born Vergennes, Vt., April 21, 1794 ; died August 6, 1829 ; married 1820, William T. Foster.

Issue :

4535. i. Ezra Foster,[8] resides near Sacramento, Cal.

4095. Hiram Chilson [7] (*Pamela Daggett,*[6] *John,*[5] *John,*[4] *John,*[3] *Samuel,*[2] *Thomas*[1]), born Cooperstown, N.Y., January 15, 1797 ; died Niles, Mich., 1890 ; married Painesville, Ohio, Mary Ann Parks.

Issue :

4536. i. Charlotte Chilson,[8] married Amos Shepherdson ; resides Dakota.
4537. ii. Melvin Chilson,[8] resides Niles, Mich.

4097. Milo Chilson [7] (*Pamela Daggett,*[6] *John,*[5] *John,*[4] *John,*[3] *Samuel,*[2] *Thomas*[1]), born Vergennes, Vt., June 27, 1801 ; supposed killed by Indians, 1848 ; married Girard, Penn., 1822, by Rev. Mr. Stuntz, to Nancy Martin, daughter of Agrippa and Ann (Jefferson) Martin ; born Fredonia, N.Y., 1806 ; died Conneaut, Ohio, 1884.

Issue :

4538. i. Ezra Chilson,[8] born Girard, Penn., 1826.

4098. Mandana Chilson [7] (*Pamela Daggett,*[6] *John,*[5] *John,*[4] *John,*[3] *Samuel,*[2] *Thomas*[1]), born Vergennes, Vt., April 17, 1804 ; married 1st, Vergennes, Vt., July 4, 1831, Justin Hobart ; born New York ; died Niles, Mich., Feb. 29, 1839 ; married 2d, Niles, Mich., 1841, by Philemon Samson, to George Clark Case, of St. Joseph, Mich.

Issue :

4539. i. Harvey Justin Hobart,[8] born Vt., April 15, 1832 ; died Cal., 1861.
4540. ii. Tryphena Caroline Hobart,[8] born Vermont, September 1, 1833.
4541. iii. Harriet Lovina Hobart,[8] born Niles, Mich., February 2, 1835.
4542. iv. Nelson Landon Hobart,[8] born Niles, Mich., December 24, 1836.
4543. v. Olive Jane Hobart,[8] born Niles, Mich., August 17, 1838 ; died November 25, 1838.
4544. vi. Samuel H. Case,[8] born September 29, 1842.
4545. vii. Charles Delancy Case,[8] born November 19, 1843.
4546. viii. George Alfred Case,[8] born March 20, ——.

4099. Theron Chilson [7] (*Pamela Daggett,*[6] *John,*[5] *John,*[4] *John,*[3] *Samuel,*[2] *Thomas*[1]), born Vergennes, Vt., November 4, 1806 ; "wheelwright" at Niles, Mich. ; died Bertrand, Mich., January 18, 1850 ; married New York, 1830, Martha Sophia Arthur, daughter of Thomas and Theodosia (Strong) Arthur ; born Keeserville, N.Y., December 25, 1810 ; died Niles, Mich., December 26, 1849.

Issue : seven children ; five died infants.

4547. i. Charles Chilson,[8] died California, November 28, 1857.
4548. ii. Mariette Chilson.[8]

4100. Charles Chilson [7] (*Pamela Daggett,*[6] *John,*[5] *John,*[4] *John,*[3] *Samuel,*[2] *Thomas*[1]), born Vergennes, Vt., May 17, 1809 ; married

1st, Amy Laneworthy; married 2d, Dayton, Ohio, March 11, 1841, by Esquire Fowler, to Mary Brush, daughter of Edward and Margret (Wooley) Brush; born New Jersey, March 6, 1818; she resides Montgomery, Ohio (1893).

Issue:

4549. i. VICTORIA JANE CHILSON,[8] born Dayton, Ohio, February 7, 1842; married Cincinnati, Ohio, September 14, 1889, by Rev. G. W. Mackley, to Thompson B. Smith; he born 1837; divorced; she resides Montgomery, Ohio (1893).
4550. ii. THERON CHILSON,[8] born Dayton, Ohio, July 14, 1844; died Dayton, Ohio, August 3, 1844.
4551. iii. JOHN WESLEY CHILSON,[8] born Dayton, Ohio, October 2, 1845; died Dayton, Ohio, September 17, 1865.
4552. iv. CHARLES CHILSON,[8] born Urbana, Ohio, June 7, 1849; resides Montgomery, Ohio (1893).

4101. CAROLINE CHILSON[7] (*Pamela Daggett,[6] John,[5] John,[4] John,[3] Samuel,[2] Thomas[1]*), born Vergennes, Vt., January 21, 1812; died Glidden, Ia., September 7, 1882; married Niles, Mich., September 6, 1835, Henry Drew; born Woodstock, Vt., December 4, 1807; died Glidden, Ia., November 27, 1874.

Issue:

4553. i. WILLIAM HENRY DREW,[8] born Niles, Mich., July 13, 1836.
4554. ii. OLIVE EMILY DREW,[8] born Niles, Mich., February 27, 1842.
4555. iii. FRANK EZRA DREW,[8] born Niles, Mich., April 30, 1850; married Lamoille, Ill., October 13, 1876, Martha Ann Long, daughter of Abram and Elizabeth (Flatt) Long; she born Watertown, Can., October 18, 1848; no issue: resides Pierce, Neb. (1893).

4103. LAURA LAVINA CHILSON[7] (*Pamela Daggett,[6] John,[5] John,[4] John,[3] Samuel,[2] Thomas[1]*), born Vergennes, Vt., May 9, 1817; died Black Lake, Mich., October 25, 1888; married 1st, Edwardsburg, Mich., April 19, 1840, by Barak Mead, J.P., to Samuel Ross Henderson, son of Henry Henderson; born State Line, between Vermont and New Hampshire, November 27, 1797; died Cass county, Mich., October 15, 1864; married 2d, Cooper, Mich., May 3, 1868, Lowell Nelson White; born Keene, N.H., 1822.

Issue:

4556. i. GEORGE HENRY HENDERSON,[8] born Dowagiac, Mich., Nov. 22, 1840.
4557. ii. HELEN MARIA HENDERSON,[8] born Cass county, Mich., April 10, 1842.
4558. iii. PITT MOORE HENDERSON,[8] born Cass county, Mich., November 7, 1844; died Cass county, Mich., April 22, 1858.
4559. iv. ROYAL RANSOM HENDERSON,[8] born Cass county, Mich., July 25, 1847; died Cass county, Mich., January 21, 1848.
4560. v. LAURA ETTA HENDERSON,[8] born Wayne, Cass Co., Mich., Jan. 18, 1853.
4561. vi. SAMUEL ERWIN HENDERSON,[8] born Cass county, Mich., September 8, 1854; died Cass county, Mich., July 11, 1866.
4562. vii. ARTHUR McCLELLAND HENDERSON,[8] born Cass county, Mich., March 25, 1864; married Muskegon, Mich., September 21, 1889, Ann Eliza Wells, daughter of Joseph and Mary (Wheater) Wells; born Yorkshire, Eng., February 3, 1864; died Black Lake, Mich., April 9, 1890; he died Black Lake, Mich., April 20, 1892.

4104. ALICE DAGGETT [7] (*Sebra*,[6] *John*,[5] *John*,[4] *John*,[3] *Samuel*,[2] *Thomas*[1]), born Greenfield, Pa., July 3, 1799; died Girard, Pa., October 1, 1876; married 1st, Fairview, Pa., May 24, 1820, by Esquire Hall, to Benjamin Easterbrook, son of Oliver and Mary Easterbrook; born Danbury, Conn.; died Ohio, 1827; married 2d, Greenfield, Pa., May, 1840, Adolphus Draper; born Worcester, Mass., August 27, 1778; died Girard, Pa., May 25, 1868.

Issue :

4563. i. WILLIAM EASTERBROOK,[3] born Girard, Pa., January, 1821; died Albion. Pa., August, 1828.
4564. ii. OLIVER EASTERBROOK,[8] born Girard, Pa., February 3, 1825.

4105. LAURA DAGGETT [7] (*Sebra*,[6] *John*,[5] *John*,[4] *John*,[3] *Samuel*,[2] *Thomas*[1]), born Greenfield, Pa., September 17, 1803; died Erie, Pa., August 2, 1893; married Fairview, Pa., January 6, 1828, by Rev. Mr. Davis, to Lewis Wildman, son of Jonathan Wildman; born Homer, N.Y., Dec. 26, 1801; died Gasconade, Mo., Sept. 17, 1864.

Issue :

4565. i. SEBRA WILDMAN,[8] born Greenfield, Pa., December 8, 1830; died Greenfield, Pa., October 26, 1874.
4566. ii. WILLIS THOMAS WILDMAN,[8] born Greenfield, Pa., March 28, 1832.
4567. iii. ARMINDA JANE WILDMAN,[8] born Greenfield. Pa., October 25, 1835; married Henry G. Daggett. (See No. 4598.)
4568. iv. LUCINDA WILDMAN,[8] born Greenfield, Pa.. March 3, 1837.
4569. v. PHILANDER WILDMAN,[8] born Greenfield, Pa., July 14, 1839; married 1st, Greenfield, Pa., August 27, 1862, by Rev. Mr. Masters, to Mary Ann Ellsworth, daughter of John and Mary Ann (Goodsell) Ellsworth; born Monroe, Ohio; divorced 1865; married 2d, South Wales, Pa., 1878, by Rev. Mr. Adams, to Kate Hetrick, daughter of Charles and Kate (Hath) Hetrick; born West Greene, Pa.; divorced 1879; he resides Boscobel, Pa. (1893).
4570. vi. HIRAM ALBERT WILDMAN,[8] born Greenfield, Pa., January 13, 1841.
4571. vii. ANNIS WILDMAN,[8] born Greenfield, Pa., September 5, 1843.
4572. viii. JONATHAN WILDMAN,[8] born Greenfield, Pa., February 25, 1834; died Greenfield, Pa., April 25, 1847.

4106. Capt. AUSTIN DAGGETT [7] (*Sebra*,[6] *John*,[5] *John*,[4] *John*,[3] *Samuel*,[2] *Thomas*[1]), born Greenfield, Pa., May 27, 1805; died Fairview, Pa., January 19, 1889; married Amboy, Ohio, June 3, 1830, by Rev. Rodney Viets, to Elvira Green, daughter of Joab and Rebecca (Johnson) Green; born Herkimer, N.Y., June 9, 1808; died Fairview, Pa., February 26, 1889.

Issue :

4573. i. CYRUS SERVETUS DAGGETT,[8] born Girard, Pa., July 11, 1831.
4574. ii. JULIUS ALONZO OGEDA DAGGETT,[8] born Girard, Pa., June 2, 1833.
4575. iii. ANNIS REBECCA DAGGETT,[8] born Girard, Pa., August 30, 1835.
4576. iv. ALMEDA ELECTA DAGGETT,[8] born Girard, Pa., January 3, 1837.
4577. v. HELEN MARIAN DAGGETT,[8] born Girard, Pa., March 10, 1840.
4578. vi. MELLISSA LOVERNIA DAGGETT,[8] born Girard, Pa., Nov. 29, 1842.
4579. vii. FLORENCE VOLUTIA DAGGETT,[8] born Girard, Pa., Dec. 28, 1844.
4580. viii. JOSEPHINE HARRIET DAGGETT,[8] born Girard, Pa., February 15, 1846.
4581. ix. RUEA SILVIA SOPHRONIA DAGGETT,[8] born Girard, Pa., Aug. 12, 1849.
4582. x. THEODOSIA ANNETTE DAGGETT,[8] born Girard, Pa., March 22, 1851; died Girard, Pa., October 11, 1863.

In 1814 Mr. Daggett entered Girard township with his father, and eventually by division became possessed of ninety-five of the original one hundred and twenty-five acres.   He was inured to all the hardships and privations of pioneer life, clearing away the virgin forest from his land to prepare it for cultivation, and through laborious effort, working by gradual and slow stages, up to a point where in his old age he had become independent.   He served in the militia for twenty years, and held a captain's commission.

4107.   Darius Daggett [7] (*Sebra,*[6] *John,*[5] *John,*[4] *John,*[3] *Samuel,*[2] *Thomas*[1]), born Greenfield, Pa., February 3, 1807; died W. Millcreek, Pa., November 14, 1886; married Girard, Pa., November 14, 1833, Louisa Prosser, daughter of John and Nancy (Moon) Prosser, of Farmington, Ohio; born Cottage, N.Y., May 30, 1817; died Girard, Pa., March 18, 1876.

Issue :

4583. i.   Mary Adelia Daggett,[8] born Girard, Pa., February 25, 1835.
4584. ii.   Henry Bascom Daggett,[8] born Girard, Pa., July 19, 1836; died Girard, Pa., September 28, 1847.
4585. iii. Esther Elizabeth Daggett,[8] born Girard, Pa., July 10, 1838.
4586. iv.   Emma Celestia Daggett,[8] born Girard, Pa., November 13, 1840; died Girard, Pa., March 7, 1842.
4587. v.   Ursula Florence Daggett,[8] born Girard, Pa., September 15, 1842.
4588. vi.   Lorenzo Dow Daggett,[8] born Girard, Pa., July 19, 1845.
4589. vii. William Earnest Daggett,[8] born Girard, Pa., November 10, 1846.
4590. viii. Nancy Emma Daggett,[8] born Girard, Pa., January 17, 1849.
4591. ix.   David Olin Daggett,[8] born Girard, Pa., July 15, 1854; died Girard, Pa., March 26, 1856.
4592. x.   John Prosser Daggett,[8] born Girard, Pa., July 15, 1854; died Girard, Pa., March 6, 1856.
4593. xi.   John Wesley Daggett,[8] born Girard, Pa., November 6, 1858; died Girard, Pa., October 14, 1863.
4594. xii. Wellington Daggett,[8] born Girard, Pa., December 3, 1860; died Girard, Pa., July 3, 1863.
4595. xiii. Isaac Daggett,[8] born Girard, Pa., 1862; died Girard, Pa., September 17, 1864.
4596. xiv. Adelaide Elouise Daggett,[8] born Girard, Pa., February 18, 1865.

4108.   Reuben Daggett [7] (*Sebra,*[6] *John,*[5] *John,*[4] *John,*[3] *Samuel,*[2] *Thomas*[1]), born Greenfield, Pa., July 24, 1809; died Erie, Pa., Oct. 26, 1891; married Girard, Pa., Feb. 3, 1832, by Rev. John Prosser, to Martha McCumber, daughter of George McCumber; born Orangeville, N.Y., Aug. 25, 1813; died Fairview, Pa., July 25, 1847.

Issue :

4597. i.   Emeline Daggett,[8] born Fairview, Pa., July 3, 1833; died Fairview, Pa., September 10, 1856.
4598. ii.   Henry George Daggett,[8] born Fairview, Pa., January 20, 1835.
4599. iii. Lucinda Daggett,[8] born Fairview, Pa., July 20, 1836; died Fairview, Pa., May 21, 1838.
4600. iv.   Harriet Daggett,[8] born Fairview, Pa., December 13, 1838; married Marshall, Mich., March 8, 1872, by Rev. W. M. Byrows, to Christopher Mason Child, son of Christopher and Harriet Newell (Wright) Child; born Smithfield, Pa., August 4, 1846; no issue; resides Billings, Mont. (1893).

·4601. v. WELLINGTON HARRY DAGGETT,[8] born Fairview, Pa., July 19, 1839.
4602. vi. FRANKLIN ADELBERT DAGGETT,[8] born Fairview, Pa., November 3, 1846; married Ravenna, Ohio, March 9, 1875. by Rev. Mr. Darsey, to Nelly Hopkins, daughter of Bradford and Tirza (Wildman) Hopkins; born Rochester, N.Y., January 1, 1856; divorced; no issue; he resides Brainerd, Minn. (1893).

4111. ELEANOR DAGGETT[7] (*Sebra,[6] John,[5] John,[4] John,[3] Samuel,[2] Thomas[1]*), born Greenfield, Penn., August 30, 1814; died South Saybrook, Ohio, February 20, 1891; married Fairview, Penn., July 9, 1835, by Rev. Mr. Eaton, to Jacob Williams, son of David and Mollie (Yerlette) Williams; born Lancaster, Pa., March 19, 1812; died Girard, Penn., November 15, 1881.

Issue:

4603. i. ADELIA ANNIS WILLIAMS,[8] born Girard, Penn., July 28, 1836.
4604. ii. AMELIA WILLIAMS.[8] born Girard, Penn., November 21, 1837; died Girard, Penn., September 27, 1864.
4605. iii. CHESTER DAVID WILLIAMS,[8] born Girard, Penn., December 13, 1839; died near Delta. Ga., May 27, 1864.
4606. iv. SYLVESTER ABRAHAM WILLIAMS,[8] born Girard, Penn., Oct. 21, 1841.
4607. v. HARRIET WILLIAMS,[8] born Girard, Penn., May 18, 1843; died Girard, Penn., February 3. 1856.
4608. vi. WATSON E. WILLIAMS,[8] born Girard. Penn., January 28, 1848; married Girard, Penn., February 6, 1879, by Henry Ball, J.P., to Sophia Schlofke, daughter of Henry and Ellena (Smeel) Schlofke; born Luxemburg, January 16, 1852; no issue; address Box 180, Oil City. Penn. (1893).
4609. vii. ADELBERT ISAAC WILLIAMS,[8] born Girard, Penn., April 16, 1847; died Girard. Pa., August. 1847.
4610. viii. SARAH JANE WILLIAMS,[8] born Girard, Penn., September 17, 1848.
4611. ix. EUGENE CASS WILLIAMS.[8] born Girard, Penn., March 29, 1850.
4612. x. NELLY WILLIAMS,[8] born Girard, Penn., October 15, 1853.

4112. HIRAM DAGGETT[7] (*Sebra,[6] John,[5] John,[4] John,[3] Samuel,[2] Thomas[1]*), born Fairview, Penn., May 3, 1816; died Fairview, Penn., January 9, 1889; married Clymer, N.Y., September 6, 1840, by Rev. Ira Gleason, to Patience Gillson, daughter of Gideon and Mary (Dailey) Gillson, of Jamestown, N.Y.; born Ellicott, N.Y., 1819; died Girard, Penn., January 15, 1885.

Issue:

4613. i. CHARLES WINFIELD DAGGETT,[8] born Girard, Penn., Jan. 31, 1841.
4614. ii. BYRON HIRAM DAGGETT,[8] born Girard. Penn., January 27, 1842.
4615. iii. CLAYTON GRISWOLD DAGGETT,[8] born Girard, Penn., July 7. 1848.
4616. iv. FENTON GILSON DAGGETT,[8] born Girard, Penn., March 11, 1855.

4113. PHILANDER DAGGETT[7] (*Sebra,[6] John,[5] John,[4] John,[3] Samuel,[2] Thomas[1]*), born Fairview, Penn., October 5, 1819; died Fairview, Penn., August 6, 1846; married Girard, Penn., May 13, 1843, by Elder Barrett, to Mary Gillson, daughter of Gideon and Mary (Dailey) Gillson; born Ellicott, N.Y., 1817; died Coloma, Mich., May 11, 1893.

Issue:

4617. i. CLIFTON DAGGETT,[8] born Girard, Penn., October 3, 1845; died Fairview, Penn., March 6, 1857.

4114. GEORGE LANGLEY DAGGETT [7] (*Ethan A.,*[6] *John,*[5] *John,*[4] *John,*[3] *Samuel,*[2] *Thomas*[1]), born Toronto, Can., August 25, 1809; died Palestine, West Va., March 13, 1886; married Fort Madison, Ia., August 14, 1836, by Theophilus Bullard, Esq., to Delilah Aldridge, daughter of Elikeney and Elizabeth (Capwell) Aldridge; born Otsego county, Ia., December 25, 1819.

Issue:

4618. i.   ELIZABETH ADALINE DAGGETT.[8] born Fort Madison, Ia., Dec. 11, 1840.
4619. ii. ERASTUS PORTER DAGGETT,[8] born Lee county, Ia., June 6, 1843.
4620. iii. BERTHA JANE DAGGETT,[8] born Limestone Hill, West Va., March 25, 1849.
4621. iv. CATHERINE MINERVA DAGGETT,[8] born Wirt county, West Va., January 16, 1855.
4622. v.   GEORGE WILLIAM DAGGETT,[8] born Wirt county, West Va., July 22, 1857.

Mr. Daggett entered the army July 5, 1833. In 1834 was ordered to Fort Gibson, Ark., from whence he with his company proceeded against three tribes of Indians, with whom treaties were made. In 1835 he was at Fort Des Moines, Ia., and again proceeding to make Indian treaties. Honorably discharged July 5, 1836.

4115. ERASTUS PORTER DAGGETT [7] (*Ethan A.,*[6] *John,*[5] *John,*[4] *John,*[3] *Samuel,*[2] *Thomas*[1]), born Denmark, N.Y., July 5, 1819; died Copenhagen, N.Y., March 27, 1876; married 1st, Denmark, N.Y., March 13, 1849, by Elder Curtis, to Sarah Bethiah Lawton, daughter of William Clark and Eunice Eliza (Tuttle) Lawton; born Denmark, N.Y., Jan. 25, 1826; died Denmark, N.Y., July 14, 1852; married 2d, Adams, N.Y., May 3, 1860, by Rev. Mr. Dox, to Adedia Lyons, daughter of Reuben and Annie (Lanphere) Lyons; born Adams, N.Y., May 29, 1827; resides Copenhagen, N.Y. (1893).

Issue:

4623. i. SIDNEY BENTON DAGGETT,[8] born Copenhagen, N.Y., June 26, 1852.
4624. ii. ADA DAGGETT,[8] born Copenhagen, N.Y., November 23, 1866.

4116. ADALINE DAGGETT [7] (*Ethan A.,*[6] *John,*[5] *John,*[4] *John,*[3] *Samuel,*[2] *Thomas*[1]), born Denmark, N.Y., January 13, 1825; resides Pinckney, N.Y. (1893); married Denmark, N.Y., April 20, 1851, by Rev. Horace Rogers, to Curtis Joshua Austin, son of Joshua and Irene (Anderson) Austin; born Denmark, N.Y., December 20, 1828; died Carthage, N.Y., April 6, 1884.

Issue:

4625. i.   IDA SARA AUSTIN,[8] born Copenhagen, N.Y., February 12, 1858.
4626. ii. FRANK DEWITT AUSTIN,[8] born Copenhagen, N.Y., July 14, 1860.
4627. iii. GEORGE PUTNAM AUSTIN,[8] born Copenhagen, N.Y., March 28, 1867.

4117. HORACE DAGGETT [7] (*Don Delance,*[6] *John,*[5] *John,*[4] *John,*[3] *Samuel,*[2] *Thomas*[1]), born Putney, Vt., May 11, 1802; died Auburn, Me., November, 1891; married 1st, Skowhegan, Me., February 26,

1827, Jane Coburn, of Greene, Me.; married 2d, Randolph, Mass., April 2, 1846, Sarah L. Sawyer, of Madison, Me.

Issue:

4628. i. HORACE VIRGIL DAGGETT,[8] born Norridgewock, Me., January 4, 1828; died Mayfield, Cal., November 23, 1880.

4629. ii. FRANCIS AUGUSTUS DAGGETT,[8] born Norridgewock, Me., July 27, 1829; died Madison, Me., May 11, 1879.

4630. iii. NANCY JANE DAGGETT,[8] born Mercer, Me., November 5, 1831; resides Auburn, Me. (1893).

4631. iv. FREDERICK DELANCE DAGGETT,[8] born New Sharon, Me., April 18, 1835; resides Auburn, Me. (1893).

4632. v. LEONARD R. DAGGETT,[8] born Madison, Me., 1837; died young.

4633. vi. RUSSELL DAGGETT,[8] born Madison, Me., May 5, 1840; resides Lewiston, Me.

4634. vii. MARSELL O. DAGGETT,[8] born Lewiston, Me., October 11, 1847; died Auburn, Me., April 9, 1853.

4635. viii. ELLA M. DAGGETT,[8] born Auburn, Me., October 7, 1852; resides Auburn, Me. (1893).

4636. ix. HENRY W. DAGGETT,[8] born Auburn, Me., March 21, 1859; died July 21, 1859.

4637. x. CAROLINE L. DAGGETT,[8] born Auburn, Me., September 1, 1863; resides Lewiston, Me. (1893).

4119. FLORILLA DAGGETT[7] (*Don Delance,*[6] *John,*[5] *John,*[4] *John,*[3] *Samuel,*[2] *Thomas*[1]), born Buckfield, Me., August 9, 1810; died Hartford, Conn., July 24, 1884; married 1st, Buckfield, Me., 1830, James E. Young; married 2d, Edmund Irish.

Issue:

4638. i. GEORGE I. YOUNG,[8] born Buckfield, Me., December 7, 1831; died in battle, September 30, 1864.

4639. ii. CHARLES YOUNG,[8] born Byron, Me., December 18, 1834; in Utah on U.S. Service, 1857; no further reported.

4640. iii. ISANNA YOUNG,[8] born Byron, Me., February 21, 1836; married Charles Emerson; resides Auburn, Me. (1893).

4641. iv. JAMES E. YOUNG,[8] born Byron, Me., September 13, 1837; died Alexandria, Va., December 8, 1862.

4642. v. HENRY YOUNG,[8] born Byron, Me., Nov. 24, 1838; died Oct. 9, 1841.

4643. vi. DON DELANCE YOUNG,[8] born Byron, Me., November 14, 1840.

4644. vii. ELLEN S. YOUNG,[8] born Byron, Me., March 19, 1842.

4645. viii. HENRY YOUNG,[8] born Byron, Me., February 8, 1844.

4646. ix. VOLNEY E. YOUNG,[8] born Byron, Me., April 29, 1847.

4647. x. HORACE N. YOUNG,[8] born Byron, Me., July 25, 1850; went West, 1872; no further reported.

4648. xi. RICHARD YOUNG,[8] born Byron, Me., October 4, 1854.

4120. ESTHER M. DAGGETT[7] (*Don Delance,*[6] *John,*[5] *John,*[4] *John,*[3] *Samuel,*[2] *Thomas*[1]), born Buckfield, Me., September 3, 1811; married Buckfield, Me., January 14, 1831, Thomas Chase, son of Nathaniel and Jemima (Haskell) Chase; born Buckfield, Me., June 6, 1808; died Buckfield, Me., March 13, 1866.

Issue:

4649. i. ESTHER MELONA CHASE,[8] born Buckfield, Me., July 17, 1835.

4650. ii. ROSCOE G. CHASE,[8] born Buckfield, Me., November 3, 1837; resides Geneva, N.Y. (1893).

4651. iii. ABBIE F. CHASE,[8] born Buckfield, Me., October 23, 1839; resides So. Braintree, Mass. (1893).

4652. iv.   CHARLES CHASE,[8] born Buckfield, Me., July 18, 1841; died Cold Harbor, Va., June 3, 1864.
4653. v.   GEORGE H. CHASE,[8] born Buckfield, Me., May 5, 1844; 23 Pemberton square, Boston; resides Malden, Mass. (1892).
4654. vi.   HOWARD AQUILA CHASE,[8] born Buckfield, Me., October 15, 1846; resides Philadelphia, Penn. (1893).
4655. vii.   LUCY A. CHASE,[8] born Buckfield, Me., May 20, 1849; died Buckfield, Me., November 22, 1860.
4656. viii.   WILLIAM D. CHASE,[8] born Buckfield, Me., August 26, 1852; resides Geneva, N.Y. (1893).
4657. ix.   HOMER N. CHASE,[8] born Buckfield, Me., September 30, 1855; resides Auburn, Me. (1893).

Thomas Chase lived on the homestead in Buckfield, and died there March 13, 1866. He was a member of the State Senate at the time of his death.

4122. JOHN R. DAGGETT [7] (*Don Delance,*[6] *John,*[5] *John,*[4] *John,*[3] *Samuel,*[2] *Thomas* [1]), born Buckfield, Me., October 5, 1816; resides 5 Franklin street, Neponset, Mass. (1893); married Stoughton, Mass., September 5, 1835, Lucy Ann Alden, daughter of Calvin and Martha Alden; born Randolph, Mass., August 11, 1819.

Issue:

4658. i.   HENRY TRASK DAGGETT,[8] born Randolph, Mass., April 22, 1836.
4659. ii.   JOHN CODMAN DAGGETT,[8] born Randolph, Mass., January 29, 1838.
4660. iii.   MARTHA HAYDEN DAGGETT,[8] born Randolph, Mass., Feb. 28, 1840.
4661. iv.   GEORGIANA DAGGETT,[8] born Randolph, Mass., November 4, 1842; died Neponset, Mass., January 24, 1886.
4662. v.   WILLIAM ALDEN DAGGETT,[8] born Randolph, Mass., January 5, 1846.

4123. EVELINE A. DAGGETT [7] (*Don Delance,*[6] *John,*[5] *John,*[4] *John,*[3] *Samuel,*[2] *Thomas* [1]), born Buckfield, Me., February 21, 1818; resides Buckfield, Me. (1893); married Buckfield, Me., September 6, 1835, Thomas Irish, son of Thomas and —— (Roberts) Irish; born Buckfield, Me., March 3, 1800; died Rumford, Me., March 16, 1879.

Issue:

4663. i.   HENRY DAGGETT IRISH,[8] born Buckfield, Me., July 19, 1836.
4664. ii.   JONATHAN NELSON IRISH,[8] born Buckfield, Me., January 23, 1838; resides Buckfield, Me. (1893).
4665. iii.   EMILY STETSON IRISH,[8] born Buckfield, Me., January 20, 1841; died Rumford, Me., April 24, 1870.
4666. iv.   PHŒBE MORTON IRISH,[8] born Buckfield, Me., September 4, 1843; died Buckfield, Me., September 6, 1847.

4124. ISAAC ROOT DAGGETT [7] (*Don Delance,*[6] *John,*[5] *John,*[4] *John,*[3] *Samuel,*[2] *Thomas* [1]), born Buckfield, Me., April 16, 1819; " cordwainer; " died Brockton, Mass., Aug. 6, 1890; married East Stoughton, Mass., Oct. 24, 1841, Arethusa Melissa Snell, daughter of Samuel and Ruth Gurney (Reed) Snell, of North Bridgewater, Mass.; born Levant, Me., Nov. 16, 1823; resides Florida (1893).

Issue:

4667. i.   SUSAN MARION DAGGETT,[8] born Randolph, Mass., July 8, 1844; died South Weymouth, Mass., October 7, 1849.

4668. ii. MARION EVELYN DAGGETT,⁸ born South Weymouth, Mass., September 30, 1849; married Boston, Mass., June 21, 1870, by Dr. William R. Alger, to Capt. Charles William Hastings, son of Elijah and Rebecca (Smith) Hastings; born Schenectady, N.Y., January 19, 1831; no issue; resides South Weymouth, Mass. (1893).

4669. iii. EMMA LOUISE DAGGETT,⁸ born South Weymouth, Mass., January 23, 1851; resides Whitman, Mass. (1893).

4670. iv. IDA FLORENCE DAGGETT,⁸ born South Weymouth, Mass., July 24, 1853; married Weymouth, Mass., May 20, 1873, by Rev. Jacob Baker, to Thomas Henry Reed, son of Theodore and Lydia (Gurney) Reed; "farmer;" born Abington, Mass., July 24, 1852; no issue; resides Rockland, Mass. (1893).

4671. v. VOLNEY CHAPIN DAGGETT,⁸ born South Weymouth, Mass., May 8, 1859; married Rockland, Mass., May 17, 1883, by Rev. C. L. Ferris, to Ione Chase, daughter of Henry and Phebe (Dend) Chase; born Abington, Mass., August 21, 1859; "druggist," of "Daggett & Ramsdell," 328 Fifth avenue, New York city (1893).

4672. vi. HELEN ESTHER DAGGETT,⁸ born South Weymouth, Mass., July 17, 1860.

4126. CHARLES DAGGETT ⁷ (*Don Delance,⁶ John,⁵ John,⁴ John,³ Samuel,² Thomas¹*), born Buckfield, Me., March 1, 1825; resides 165 Franklin street, Portland, Me.; married Susan L. Lakeman.

Issue:

4673. i. ALTON C. DAGGETT,⁸ born Portland, Me., October 2, 1857; died.

4674. ii. ALICE M. DAGGETT,⁸ born Portland, Me., February 10, 1862; died Portland, Me., June 1, 1866.

4675. iii. WILLIAM L. DAGGETT,⁸ born Portland, Me., 1863; resides Portland, Me. (1893).

4127. Capt. EPHRAIM MERRILL DAGGETT ⁷ (*Eleazer,⁶ John,⁵ John,⁴ John,³ Samuel,² Thomas¹*), born Queenstown, Can., June 3, 1810; died Fort Worth, Tex., April 19, 1883; married 1st, Montezuma, Ind., November, 1835, Faribo Hays, daughter of Captain Hays; born Chillicothe, Ohio, 1818; married 2d, Shelby county, Tex., 1842, Caroline Matilda Adams, widow, daughter of Mr. Noris; born Charleston, S.C.; died Fort Worth, Tex., November 7, 1872.

Issue:

4676. i. JOSEPH DAGGETT.⁸

4677. ii. EPHRAIM BECK DAGGETT,⁸ born Independence, Mo., August, 23, 1838.

Capt. Ephraim M. Daggett, founder of Fort Worth, Tex., started out into the world when he reached his twenty-first year. In 1837 we find him in what was then the post of Chicago, trading with the Indian tribes. Texas, then a province of Mexico, soon attracted his attention, and he not only went there himself, but took his father's family with him. In the spring of 1840 they entered the Republic of Texas, and commenced farming in Shelby county. In those days the farmer went to work in the field with his gun on his shoulder. Mexico was bending every energy to conquer the Republic of Texas, and she was energetically and desperately making resistance.

Mr. Daggett entered the army, joining the regiment of Col. John Hays. In this service he served as captain, making a judicious but at the same time a dashing officer. With his company he succeeded in capturing Santa Anna's chief, General Valentia, who was not hated as was his superior officer, but who was a great power among the enemy. For this service Captain Daggett received the thanks of Colonel Hays and General Houston.

One night Captain Daggett's company came upon the camp of Mexicans, with whom was General Santa Anna, at the time in bed. The alarm was given, and the haughty Santa Anna managed to get away, but he was bareheaded and coatless, these trophies falling into the hands of the young captain. The great Mexican sent a courier to Captain Daggett to give him a sum of money something in excess of $1,000 if he would but return the coat with its elegant trappings, and the cap of the general. The young captain refused the offer, reported his capture, and turned over the trophies. Captain Daggett was next sent to operate against Taranta, chief of a band of cutthroats, who was met in two engagements, in both of which he drove the enemy back, killed several, and made a number of prisoners. He did not reach the City of Mexico until December 23, 1847.

Writing of himself he said : " I have served two terms in the Texas Legislature, have been cotton planter, merchant, and cattle raiser. I once weighed two hundred and seventy-three pounds."

In 1854 he settled in Tarrant county. When it looked dark for Fort Worth he was always cheerful, always active in the work of building up the city, and confident it would become what it is to-day. Fully one-half of the city stands on his land. Regarding it he said : " I came here while the Indians were here, and have given the Texas & Pacific Railroad ninety-six acres of my land, while to others I have given large donations, and have succeeded in founding one of the finest and most flourishing inland cities in Texas."

4128. CHARLES BIGGERS DAGGETT [7] (*Eleazer,*[6] *John,*[5] *John,*[4] *John,*[3] *Samuel,*[2] *Thomas*[1]), born Queenstown, Can., July 15, 1812 ; died Fort Worth, Tex., October 29, 1888 ; married Henderson, Tex., July 14, 1844, by Judge Watkins, to Mary Ferguson, daughter of Isaac and Elizabeth (Johnson) Ferguson, of Lexington, Ky. ; born Marine, Madison Co., Ill., July 14, 1822 ; resides Fort Worth, Tex. (1893).

Issue :

4678. i.   SARAH ELIZABETH DAGGETT,[8] born Shelbyville, Tex., July 15, 1845.
4679. ii.   CHARLES ANNA DAGGETT,[8] born Henderson, Tex., September 17, 1847 ; married Fort Worth, Tex., January, 1865, by Rev. Mr. Vance, to Thomas Anderson, son of Abraham and —— (Tucker) Anderson ; born Kentucky. Charles Anna died Fort Worth, Tex., Oct. 6, 1866. Mr. Anderson resides Vineyard City, Tex. (1893).
4680. iii. EPHRAIM MERRILL DAGGETT,[8] born Shelbyville, Tex., Jan. 22, 1850.
4681. iv.   HENRY WILLIAM DAGGETT,[8] born Shelbyville, Tex., April 2, 1852 ; died Fort Worth, Tex., April 30, 1872.
4682. v.   JOHN PURVIS DAGGETT,[8] born Fort Worth, Tex., April 23, 1855 ;

married Girard, Pa., Nov. 8, 1892, by Rev. C. L. Shipman, to Stella
Elvira Zahn (see No. 5208) ; resides Fort Worth, Tex. (1893).

4683. vi.   MOLLIE HELLEN DAGGETT,[8] born Fort Worth, Tex., Sept. 15, 1857.
4684. vii. JUSTINA MELISSA DAGGETT,[8] born Fort Worth, Tex., July 12, 1860.
4685. viii. JOSEPHINE MALINDA DAGGETT,[8] born Fort Worth, Tex., April 20, 1863.
4686. ix.   CHARLES BIGGERS DAGGETT,[8] born Fort Worth, Tex., March 12, 1867.

Charles Biggers Daggett was ever noted for a certain way of making haste slowly, but ever did things after a fashion to make sure of what he did.

He with his kindred marched to the grand plaza of our sister republic on the west, and opened the hall doors of that last race of the Aztecs, the Montezumas, which led the way to California, New Mexico, and the golden shores of the Pacific.

4130. HENRY CLAY DAGGETT [7] (*Eleazer,*[6] *John,*[5] *John,*[4] *John,*[3] *Samuel,*[2] *Thomas* [1]), born Lewiston, N.Y., February, 1820; resides Birdville, Tex. (1893); married Dallas, Tex., 1851, by Rev. Mr. Smith, to Sarah Ellen Marsh, daughter of Harrison County and Mary Ann (Raymond) Marsh; born Cynthiana, Ky., 1833.

Issue :

4687. i. CHARLES BIGGERS DAGGETT,[8] born Fort Worth, Tex., Aug. 20, 1852.
4688. ii. THOMAS HARRISON DAGGETT,[8] born Fort Worth, Tex., January 11,
          1855; died Birdville, Tex., October 11, 1891.

4131. HELLEN MAR DAGGETT [7] (*Eleazer,*[6] *John,*[5] *John,*[4] *John,*[3] *Samuel,*[2] *Thomas* [1]), born Terre Haute, Ind., December 3, 1824; married 1st, Shelby county, Tex., January 8, 1844, by Hon. Mr. Hammond, to Col. C. W. Moorman; born 1823; assassinated February 14, 1850; married 2d, Ellis county, Tex., November 15, 1865, by Rev. Mr. Hill, to W. M. McKee; born Bourbon county, Ky., 1830; died October 9, 1882.

Issue :

4689. i. MARY VIRGINIA MOORMAN,[8] born November 14, 1845; married Ellis
         county, Tex., March 22, 1867, by Rev. Mr. Denison, to George Harris,
         son of Arno Love and Elizabeth Abanatha (Farrer) Harris; born
         Grand Stage Stand, Ark., August 2, 1844; no issue; resides Fort
         Worth, Tex. (1893).

4132. SARAH ANN DAGGETT [7] (*Eleazer,*[6] *John,*[5] *John,*[4] *John,*[3] *Samuel,*[2] *Thomas* [1]), born Terre Haute, Ind., November 3, 1830; died Ellis county, Tex., June 24, 1855; married Shelby county, Tex., 1848, Simon Bowdon Farrer, son of James and Jane (Bowdon) Farrer, of Mississippi; born Alabama, March 10, 1827; resides Palmer, Tex. (1893).

Issue :

4690. i.   WILLIAM HENRY FARRER,[8] born Shelby county, Tex., March 29, 1849.
4691. ii. EPHRAIM FARRER,[8] born Shelby county, Tex., June 23, 1851; died
           Shelby county, Tex., November 18, 1852.
4692. iii. JANE FARRER,[8] born Ellis county, Tex., October 24, 1853; died Ellis
           county, Tex., October 14, 1868.

4137. ELEANOR CLAP [7] (*Betsey Doggett,*[6] *Samuel,*[5] *Samuel,*[4] *Isaac,*[3] *Samuel,*[2] *Thomas* [1]), born Dedham Mass., November 11, 1809; died Boston, Mass., December 16, 1876; married Dedham, Mass., November 13, 1831, by Rev. Alvan Lamson, to Joseph Francis Trott, son of Jonathan and Eliza (Francis) Trott; born Boston, Mass., June 16, 1807; died Newton, Mass., July 15, 1892.

Issue:

4693. i. CHARLES PARKER TROTT,[8] born Nashua, N.H., September 20, 1832; in the "merchant service;" died San Francisco, Cal., Feb. 23, 1861.

4694. ii. ELIZABETH ANN TROTT,[8] born Nashua, N.H., December 19, 1833; married Lowell, Mass., October 14, 1858, by Rev. Frederic Hinkley, to George Edward Alden, son of George and Hannah (Eaton) Alden; born Dedham, Mass., April 3, 1833; no issue; resides Newton, Mass. (1891).

4695. iii. JOSEPH FRANCIS TROTT,[8] born Lowell, Mass., August 17, 1836; married Boston, Mass., September 10, 1872, by Rev. George A. Thayer, to Mary Beal, daughter of Warren Stedman and Mary (McIntire) Beal; born Boston, Mass., March 22, 1843; no issue; he died St. Thomas, W.I., April 18, 1876; she resides Chester park, Boston, Mass. (1890).

4696. iv. ELEANOR CLAP TROTT,[8] born Lowell, Mass., March 19, 1838.

4697. v. JOHN CLAP TROTT,[8] born Lowell, Mass., February 18, 1840.

4698. vi. FREDERICK HENRY DORR TROTT,[8] born Lowell, Mass., November 12, 1842; died Lowell, Mass., August 6, 1843.

4699. vii. MARY ANN CUNNINGHAM TROTT,[8] born Lowell, Mass., July 24, 1845.

They were located in Nashua, N.H., for a few years after marriage, then removed to Lowell, Mass., where they resided for about thirty years. Here for many years Mr. Trott was paymaster for the Boott Cotton Mills. About 1866 they removed to South Boston, where he retired from all active business.

After the death of his wife he removed to his daughter's house in Newton.

4138. ELIZABETH DOGGETT CLAP [7] (*Betsey Doggett,*[6] *Samuel,*[5] *Samuel,*[4] *Isaac,*[3] *Samuel,*[2] *Thomas* [1]), born Dedham, Mass., July 2, 1811; died Dedham, Mass., September 13, 1892; married Dedham, Mass., October 7, 1830, by Rev. Alvan Lamson, to Nathaniel Clapp, son of Levi and Elizabeth (Wallace) Clapp; born Walpole, Mass., September 14, 1802; died Dedham, Mass., July 27, 1889.

Issue:

4700. i. SAMUEL WALLACE CLAPP,[8] born Dedham, Mass., February 18, 1832.

4701. ii. HENRY FRANCIS CLAPP,[8] born Dedham, Mass., February 5, 1834; died Dedham, Mass., January 2, 1862.

4702. iii. JOHN DOGGETT CLAPP,[8] born Dedham, Mass., January 30, 1835; died Dedham, Mass., October 4, 1836.

4703. iv. JOHN DOGGETT CLAPP,[8] born Dedham, Mass., August 8, 1836; died Dedham, Mass., January 21, 1843.

4704. v. MARY ANN CLAPP,[8] born Dedham, Mass., August 24, 1838; died Dedham, Mass., April 2, 1839.

4705. vi. JANE DOGGETT CLAPP,[8] born Dedham, Mass., May 28, 1840; died Dedham, Mass., January 4, 1841.

4706. vii. ELIZABETH DOGGETT CLAPP,[8] born Dedham, Mass., Nov. 15, 1841.

4707. viii.   CHARLES WARREN CLAPP,[8] born Dedham, Mass., May 29, 1844; died
        Dedham, Mass., May 17, 1876.
4708. ix.   ELEANOR TROTT CLAPP,[8] born Dedham, Mass., March 1, 1846.
4709. x.   MARY BADLAM CLAPP,[8] born Dedham, Mass., March 12, 1848; died
        Dedham. Mass., September 13, 1872.
4710. xi.   FREDERICK EVERETT CLAPP,[8] born Dedham, Mass., October 22, 1851;
        married Roxbury, Mass., July 5, 1893, by Rev. Charles R. Tenney,
        to Grace Hermione Bredeen, daughter of Samuel Naramore and
        Mary (Lewis) Bredeen; born Charlestown, Mass., July 26, 1861;
        resides Dedham, Mass. (1893).
4711. xii.   JANE DOGGETT CLAPP,[8] born Dedham, Mass., June 8, 1854; died
        Dedham, Mass., October 22, 1873.

After his marriage Mr. Clapp settled in Dedham, Mass., and engaged in the manufacture of ladies' bonnets and artificial flowers, which business he continued for a number of years. He also manufactured carmine saucers for services and ornaments, and discovered a process by which to color raw cotton pink. In 1871 he started a factory in Dedham for its manufacture, and its use becoming general in the jewelry trade it was known as jewellers' cotton.

Ten years later he invented a process for making what is known as "absorbent cotton," which is used very extensively for surgical use in all sections of the country. In 1885 he retired from active business, and the manufacture of these cottons was afterward carried on by his widow, and his son Fred. E. Clapp, and nephew John C. Trott, at Dedham, under the style of F. E. Clapp & Co., with the Dennison Manufacturing Company as selling agents.

In all his business enterprises he was greatly assisted by his estimable wife, who inherited the Doggett capability for thrift and business management. They resided together in wedlock over fifty years, celebrating their golden wedding in Dedham October 7, 1880.

Mrs. Clapp was known and loved by all for her thoughtfulness for others, and her wish to do all the good she could in life. Of a cheerful and sunny disposition, she took an active interest in all affairs of the day, and has been of very valuable assistance in collecting records and biographies. She had a large collection of family heirlooms, among them being two pocket-books and a copy-book which belonged to her grandmother Elizabeth Badlam, the latter dated 1768.

She also owned the silver knee and shoe buckles which were worn by her grandfather Samuel Doggett, and a curious cane which her great-grandmother Abigail (Davenport) Doggett used. Many silver teaspoons which belonged to her grandparents are also among the heirlooms, and some rare old china. She had also the wedding shoes and a part of the wedding dress worn by her mother at the time of her marriage in 1796. Mrs. Clapp always took a very active interest in the Unitarian church of Dedham, and was one of its most earnest supporters. She was possessed of a vast amount of information of events of an earlier generation, and has contributed many interesting and valuable papers to historical magazines and societies.

4139. Sophia Doggett [7] (*John,*[6] *Samuel,*[5] *Samuel,*[4] *Isaac,*[3] *Samuel,*[2] *Thomas* [1]), born Roxbury, Mass., May 23, 1805; died Dedham, Mass., January 13, 1878; married Roxbury, Mass., September 26, 1822, by Rev. Eliphalet Porter, D.D., to Jonathan Holmes Cobb, son of Jonathan and Sybil (Holmes) Cobb; born Sharon, Mass., July 8, 1799; died Dedham, Mass., March 12, 1882.

Issue :

4712.	i.	Sophia Jane Cobb,[8] born Dedham, Mass., July 12, 1823.
4713.	ii.	Maria Elizabeth Cobb,[8] born Dedham, Mass., August 13, 1826.
4714.	iii.	Jonathan Cobb,[8] born Dedham, Mass., March 2, 1829.
4715.	iv.	Samuel Doggett Cobb,[8] born Dedham, Mass., August 15, 1831.
4716.	v.	Isabelle Frances Cobb,[8] born Dedham, Mass., April 19, 1835.
4717.	vi.	Abby Cobb,[8] born Dedham, Mass., May 17, 1837.
4718.	vii.	John Doggett Cobb,[8] born Dedham, Mass., April 28, 1840.
4719.	viii.	William Austin Cobb,[8] born Dedham, Mass., August 4, 1845.

Mr. Cobb was educated at Harvard College, graduating in the class of 1817. After leaving college he entered the law office of William Dunbar, Esq., of Canton, where he remained until October 9, 1818, when he went to Charleston, S.C., and entered the office of Benjamin S. Dunkin, then a celebrated lawyer of that city. In 1819 he returned to Massachusetts, and entered the law office of Jabez Chickering, Esq., of Dedham, remaining there until he was admitted to the bar in 1820. When twenty-one years of age he opened a law office in Dedham.

Subsequently for a few years he was the editor of "The Village Register," published in Dedham, and also had a law office in Boston. In 1831 he was actively instrumental in establishing the Dedham Institution for Savings, of which he was the first secretary and treasurer. About this time he engaged in the manufacture of silk, and published a work on the subject. In February, 1831, the Legislature of Massachusetts requested Governor Lincoln to procure the compilation of a manual on the mulberry tree and the manufacture of silk, and Mr. Cobb prepared the work, of which several editions were printed, and which was afterward republished by Congress, and distributed throughout the country.

In 1837 he established a manufactory of sewing-silk, of which he was superintendent and principal proprietor, but which was burned in 1845, at a great loss to him.

On the retirement of Judge Haven in 1833, he was appointed register of deeds for Norfolk county, which position he held until 1878, when his term expired. He was for thirty consecutive years town clerk of Dedham, and declined a reëlection in 1875. He was for forty years deacon of the Unitarian church of Dedham, and for some years a magistrate for Norfolk county. His wife was a woman of great amiability, cheerful disposition, excellent judgment, and high moral standard.

4140. JANE MILLER DOGGETT [7] (*John,*[6] *Samuel,*[5] *Samuel,*[4] *Isaac,*[3] *Samuel,*[2] *Thomas*[1]), born Roxbury, Mass., December 13, 1806; died Dedham, Mass., October 14, 1868.

She was a woman of a remarkably beautiful character, amiable and unselfish, and was always engaged in some good work, living always for others.

She was devoted to her father during his entire life, especially in his later years. She always resided with him, with the exception of a few years with her brother William at Dayton, Ohio, and a short time in Philadelphia with her niece Mrs. Frederick H. French. She was not married.

4141. JOHN DOGGETT [7] (*John,*[6] *Samuel,*[5] *Samuel,*[4] *Isaac,*[3] *Samuel,*[2] *Thomas*[1]), born Roxbury, Mass., June 7, 1809; died New York city, March 21, 1852.

John Doggett lived in Boston when a boy, but the greater part of his life was passed in New York city. He was the compiler of Doggett's directories of New York city, which he published for many years. He was a man of enterprise and energy of character, and the business community of New York are deeply indebted to him for his unwearied labors in bringing to a perfect system a directory of that city.

4142. ELIZABETH DOGGETT [7] (*John,*[6] *Samuel,*[5] *Samuel,*[4] *Isaac,*[3] *Samuel,*[2] *Thomas*[1]), born Roxbury, Mass., October 26, 1811; died Boston, Mass., July 5, 1835; married Boston, Mass., October 4, 1832, by Rev. Hubbard Winslow, to Joseph Babcock Lyon, born Boston, Mass., March 4, 1811; died Baltimore, Md., March 23, 1847.

Issue :

4720. i.   JOSEPH BABCOCK LYON,[8] born Boston, Mass., October 12, 1833; died Boston, Mass., May 31, 1837.
4721. ii.   ELIZABETH DOGGETT LYON,[8] born Boston, Mass., November 30, 1834; died Boston, Mass., October 23, 1835.

They resided in Boston, where he was engaged with a dry-goods house on Kilby street. They resided on Boylston place, where Mrs. Lyon died. He afterward went to New York, thence to Baltimore, Md.

4144. SAMUEL DOGGETT [7] (*John,*[6] *Samuel,*[5] *Samuel,*[4] *Isaac,*[3] *Samuel,*[2] *Thomas*[1]), born Roxbury, Mass., October 15, 1814; died Boston, Mass., July 13, 1876.

When quite a young man he left home and went to sea on a whaler, and most of his early life was passed on the ocean. After he left the sea he was in the carpet business in New York city and Brooklyn for some years. He then went to Dayton, Ohio, where he lived upwards of ten years. He was not married.

4145. WILLIAM FRANCIS DOGGETT [7] (*John,* [6] *Samuel,* [5] *Samuel,* [4] *Isaac,* [3] *Samuel,* [2] *Thomas* [1]), born Boston, Mass., March 15, 1817; died Chicago, Ill., July 2, 1874; married September 5, 1838, Elizabeth Borlander, of Mason, Ohio; born near Lima, Ohio; resides 1090 North Tennessee street, Indianapolis, Ind. (1891).

Issue:

4722. i. STEPHEN SYLVESTER DOGGETT, [8] born September 6, 1839; married Dayton, Ohio, February 25, 1860, Emma Harris; he died Dayton, Ohio, February 25, 1860.
4723. ii. JOHN DOGGETT, [8] born near Pisgah, Ohio, June 3, 1844.
4724. iii. JANE MILLER DOGGETT, [8] born Mason, Ohio, February 15, 1846.
4725. iv. SAMUEL JACKSON DOGGETT, [8] born Kenton, Ohio, March 16, 1850.
4726. v. ELIZABETH DOGGETT, [8] born Dayton, Ohio, March 14, 1852.

4148. BENJAMIN FRANKLIN DOGGETT [7] (*John,* [6] *Samuel,* [5] *Samuel,* [4] *Isaac,* [3] *Samuel,* [2] *Thomas* [1]), born Boston, Mass., February 17, 1824; died New York city, March 15, 1853.

When a young man he went to sea, and made a voyage to China. He lived for several years in Hong-Kong. He was afterward in Boston for a year or two, about 1851 or 1852. Just prior to his death he went to New York, with the intention of returning to China. His death was very sudden. He was buried in Dedham, Mass.

4149. MARY ANN CLAP DOGGETT [7] (*Samuel,* [6] *Samuel,* [5] *Samuel,* [4] *Isaac,* [3] *Samuel,* [2] *Thomas* [1]), born Roxbury, Mass., February 2, 1818; died Boston, Mass., April 7, 1853; married Roxbury, Mass., June 27, 1839, by Rev. George Putnam, to Jared Burritt Curtis, son of Jared and Thankful (Ashley) Curtis, of Charlestown, Mass.; born Stockbridge, Mass., December 11, 1810; died Somerville, Mass., August 23, 1858.

Issue:

4727. i. MARY CURTIS, [8] born Roxbury, Mass., December 21, 1840.
4728. ii. FANNIE CURTIS, [8] born Roxbury, Mass., March 7, 1843.
4729. iii. CAROLINE CURTIS, [8] born Roxbury, Mass., May 27, 1845; married Boston, Mass., May 20, 1869, by Rev. Mr. Bolles, to Augustus Life Evans, son of Daniel and Lucy (Young) Evans; born Winona, Minn.; no issue; "lawyer;" 230 La Salle street, Chicago, Ill. (1890); she died Winona, Minn., December 26, 1869.

After his marriage Mr. Curtis lived in Roxbury, and was engaged in the dry-goods business in Boston, of the firm of Kimball, Jewett & Co. He then went to New York, and afterwards went West, and was interested in railroad enterprises. He returned to Boston shortly before he died.

4150. EMILY DOGGETT [7] (*Samuel,* [6] *Samuel,* [5] *Samuel,* [4] *Isaac,* [3] *Samuel,* [2] *Thomas* [1]), born Roxbury, Mass., July 29, 1822; resides 1679 Tremont street, Roxbury, Mass. (1893); married, 1842, William Augustus Crafts, son of Major Ebenezer and Sarah Heath (Spooner) Crafts, of Roxbury; born Roxbury, Mass., Oct. 28, 1819.

Issue:

4730. i. LOUISE AUGUSTA CRAFTS,[8] born Roxbury, Mass., Feb. 21, 1843.
4731. ii. SAMUEL DOGGETT CRAFTS,[8] born Roxbury, Mass., August 29, 1848; married New York city, December 1, 1892, by Rev. J. Franklin Carter, to Mary Virginia Bostwick, daughter of Charles Edmund and Mary (Terhune) Bostwick; born New York city, March 25, 1859; resides New York city (1893).
4732. iii. MARY ELIZABETH CRAFTS,[8] born Roxbury, Mass., August 21, 1851; died Roxbury, Mass., February 5, 1873.
4733. iv. WILLIAM FRANCIS CRAFTS,[8] born Roxbury, Mass., August 24, 1855; one of the compilers of the " Crafts Family History," and a contributor to the present work of many records regarding his branch.
4734. v. EMILY ALICE CRAFTS,[8] born Roxbury, Mass., December 26, 1861.

Mr. Crafts was educated in the somewhat famous schools of Gideon F. Thayer, in Brookline, and Stephen M. Weld, at Jamaica Plain, Mass., in the last of which he prepared for college. He was class poet, and graduated at Harvard in 1840. He studied law in the Dane Law School, at Cambridge, and in the office of Phillips & Robins, in Boston, and for several years practised in Boston and Roxbury.

Being somewhat interested in politics, he was induced in 1849 to establish the " Norfolk County Journal," a Whig paper, of which he was editor till 1857. From 1847 to 1851 he was a member of the Common Council of the city of Roxbury, and for the last three years its president. He was also for twelve years a member of the school committee. He was a representative to the General Court, from Roxbury, in 1853 and 1854, and again in 1861. Subsequently for several years he was assistant clerk of the House of Representatives. In 1869 when the Board of Railroad Commissioners was established he was appointed its clerk, and with the exception of a brief interval has held the office till the present time (1893).

His wife inherits in a marked degree the Doggett family traits, and is known and loved by all for her sunny, cheerful disposition, her way of seeing the bright side always, of looking for the good in every one, and of always thinking of others first, herself last.

They reside on the old Crafts estate, in Roxbury, which has been held in the Crafts family since 1705, at which time it came into possession of his great-great-grandfather Ensign Ebenezer Craft, a grandson of Lieut. Griffin Craft, who settled in Roxbury in 1630.

4153. GEORGE LEWIS[7] (*Elizabeth S. Doggett,*[6] *Jesse,*[5] *Samuel,*[4] *Isaac,*[3] *Samuel,*[2] *Thomas* [1]), born Roxbury, Mass., May 25, 1820; died Boston, Mass., October 8, 1887; married Roxbury, Mass., June 12, 1850, by Rev. George Putnam, to Susan Minns Wheelwright, daughter of William and Susan Cunningham (Minns) Wheelwright;

born New York city, April 16, 1827; died Roxbury, Mass., October 8, 1876.

Issue:

4735. i. ELIZABETH SUMNER LEWIS,[8] born Roxbury, Mass., April 24, 1851.
4736. ii. WILLIAM WHEELWRIGHT LEWIS,[8] born Roxbury, Mass., July 29, 1853; died Roxbury, Mass., December 30, 1859.
4737. iii. ADELINE WHEELWRIGHT LEWIS,[8] born Roxbury, Mass., Nov. 22, 1858.
4738. iv. GEORGE LEWIS,[8] born Roxbury, Mass., July 7, 1860.

George Lewis was a resident of Roxbury during the greater part of a long and honored life. He was a member of the Common Council of Roxbury in 1852 and 1853, and a member of the Board of Aldermen of Roxbury in 1857, 1858, 1859. He was elected mayor of Roxbury in 1863, during the trying times of the war of the Rebellion, and was reëlected in 1864, 1865, 1866, and 1867, serving until the annexation of Roxbury to Boston, January 6, 1868.

After annexation he served several years in the Boston Water Board, and was for years the treasurer of the Forest Hills Cemetery Corporation, and of the Granite Railway Company. He was a director for the People's National Bank and for the Roxbury Gas Light Company for several years.

His residence was at 42 Highland street, Roxbury, but a few years prior to his death he removed to 125 Marlboro' street, Boston, where he was living at the time of his death. He bore a reputation for the strictest integrity, and was held in the highest esteem, as was evinced by the many offices which he was called upon to fill.

4154. KATE CARTER [7] (*Eunice Doggett,[6] Elisha,[5] Samuel,[4] Isaac,[3] Samuel,[2] Thomas[1]*), born Waterford, Me., June 4, 1820; resides (1891) 5 Suffolk street, Chelsea, Mass.; married Chelsea, Mass., January 1, 1851, by Rev. J. M. Sykes, to John T. Hadaway, son of John T. and Mary (Crocker) Hadaway; born Philadelphia, Pa., June 29, 1824.

Issue:

4739. i. JOHN MASON HADAWAY,[8] born Chelsea, Mass., June 18, 1853.
4740 ii. DANIEL HADAWAY,[8] born Chelsea, Mass., March 11, 1856.
4741. iii. MARY HADAWAY,[8] born Chelsea, Mass., April 26, 1860.

4155. JOHN CARTER [7] (*Eunice Doggett,[6] Elisha,[5] Samuel,[4] Isaac,[3] Samuel,[2] Thomas[1]*), of "Carter & Haskell," Blackstone street, Boston; married Phœbe McBride.

Issue:

4742. i. JOHN CARTER.[8]
4743. ii. MARY CARTER.[8]
4744. iii. CHARLES CARTER.[8]
4745. iv. GRACE CARTER.[8]

4156. ELIZABETH CUMMINGS[7] (*Elizabeth Doggett,*[6] *Elisha,*[5] *Samuel,*[4] *Isaac,*[3] *Samuel,*[2] *Thomas*[1]), married H. K. W. Palmer.
Issue:
4746. i. WILLIAM CUMMINGS PALMER,[8] with "Tidewater Oil Company;" resides New York city.
4747. ii. ELLA PALMER.[8]
4748. iii. EVA PALMER,[8] married Mr. Upham; resides Coffeyville, Kan. (1890).
4749. iv. JESSIE ELIZABETH PALMER,[8] died.
4750. v. GEORGE LINCOLN PALMER,[8] died.

4158. EDMUND ESTES[7] (*Catharine Doggett,*[6] *Elisha,*[5] *Samuel,*[4] *Isaac,*[3] *Samuel,*[2] *Thomas*[1]), died Cohasset, Mass.; married ——.
Issue:
4751. i. ANNA ESTES.[8]
4752. ii. EDMUND ESTES.[8]

4159. FREDERICK CLAPP[7] (*Nancy Thorndike Doggett,*[6] *Elisha,*[5] *Samuel,*[4] *Isaac,*[3] *Samuel,*[2] *Thomas*[1]), born August 11, 1824; died June 16, 1863; married Lois S. Evans.
Issue:
4753. i. MARY COOK CLAPP,[8] resides Newton street, Brookline, Mass.
4754. ii. FANNY LOIS CLAPP,[8] married Frank E. Bradish.
4755. iii. EMMA CINDERELLA CLAPP,[8] resides Beacon street, Boston, Mass.

4162. EDWARD AUGUSTUS CLAPP[7] (*Nancy Thorndike Doggett,*[6] *Elisha,*[5] *Samuel,*[4] *Isaac,*[3] *Samuel,*[2] *Thomas*[1]), born April 28, 1834; married Ellen M. Wheelock.
Issue:
4756. i. ANNA LOUISE CLAPP,[8] married Walter Abbott; resides Salem, Mass.

4164. GEORGE WALTER CLAPP[7] (*Nancy Thorndike Doggett,*[6] *Elisha,*[5] *Samuel,*[4] *Isaac,*[3] *Samuel,*[2] *Thomas*[1]), born June 10, 1841; resides Cambridge, Mass.; married May 9, 1871, Emma C. Hinman.
Issue:
4757. i. FREDERICK CLAPP,[8] born February 25, 1872.
4758. ii. WALTER CLAPP,[8] born September 5, 1878.
4759. iii. GEORGE CLAPP,[8] born September 5, 1878; died ——.

4165. ANNIE ISADORA CLAPP[7] (*Nancy Thorndike Doggett,*[6] *Elisha,*[5] *Samuel,*[4] *Isaac,*[3] *Samuel,*[2] *Thomas*[1]), born August 5, 1845; married June 7, 1870, Albert I. Sands.
Issue:
4760. i. FREDERICK IVORY SANDS.[8]
4761. ii. ANNIE THORNDIKE SANDS,[8] died.
4762. iii. SUMNER REDWAY MASON SANDS,[8] resides Pembroke, Mass.

4166. MARY ELIZABETH EATON[7] (*Mary Doggett,*[6] *Elisha,*[5] *Samuel,* *Isaac,*[3] *Samuel,*[2] *Thomas*[1]), born Boston, Mass., April 17, 1831; died Columbia, S.C., March, 1876 or 1877; married Boston, Mass.,

April 17, 1850, Rev. Benjamin Bosworth Babbitt, son of Jacob and
Abbie Eliza (Briggs) Babbitt; born Bristol, R.I., September, 1827;
died Columbia, S.C., December 20, 1889.

Issue:

4763. i. CHARLES JACOB BABBITT,[8] born Providence, R.I., 1854.
4764. ii. EDWARD MILES BABBITT,[8] born Providence, R.I., 1856; resides there.

4167. JAMES FLINT EATON[7] (*Mary Doggett,*[6] *Elisha,*[5] *Samuel,*[4]
Isaac,[3] *Samuel,*[2] *Thomas*[1]), born Boston, Mass., May 15, 1832;
resides Maplewood, Malden, Mass. (1892); married Malden, Mass.,
November 30, 1854, by Rev. W. F. Stubberts, to Helen Mar Web-
ster, daughter of Joshua and Elizabeth B. (Chase) Webster; born
Boston, Mass., Dec. 17, 1834; died Malden, Mass., July 31, 1886.

Issue:

4765. i. MARY DOGGETT EATON,[8] born Malden, Mass., September 12, 1855;
died Malden, Mass., September 29, 1859.
4766. ii. PERCIVAL JAMES EATON,[8] born Malden, Mass., February 13, 1862;
married Crafton, Pa., June 11, 1891, Emily Miltenberger Craft,
daughter of Charles Cathral and Mary Ellen (Mallery) Craft, of
Crafton, Pa.; born Pittsburg, Pa., April 14, 1868; "physician;"
resides 5945 Pennsylvania avenue, E. E. Pittsburg, Pa. (1890).
4767. iii. FREDERICK WEBSTER EATON,[8] born Malden, Mass., April 5, 1864;
married Haverhill, Mass., April 22, 1890, Annie Otis George,
daughter of Henry Otis and Loise Ann (Eaton) George; born Bradford, Mass., August 22, 1862; resides Maplewood, Mass. (1891).

James F. Eaton has been a grocer. He was chairman of the Board
of Selectmen in Malden in 1876.

4169. LOUISA BECKFORD EATON[7] (*Mary Doggett,*[6] *Elisha,*[5]
Samuel,[4] *Isaac,*[3] *Samuel,*[2] *Thomas*[1]), born Boston, Mass., January
27, 1836; died Boston, Mass., January 17, 1865; married Salem,
Mass., September 24, 1861, by Rev. B. B. Babbitt, to Dr. Francis
Henry Brown, son of Francis and Caroline Matilda (Kuhn) Brown;
born Boston, Mass., August 8, 1835; resides 75 Westland avenue,
Boston, Mass. (1892).

Issue:

4768. i. Daughter BROWN,[8] born Cambridge, Mass., December 2, 1862; died
Cambridge, Mass., December 4, 1862.
4769. ii. LOUIS FRANCIS BROWN,[8] born Boston, Mass., December 16, 1864.

4170. LYDIA ELLEN EATON[7] (*Mary Doggett,*[6] *Elisha,*[5] *Samuel,*[4]
Isaac,[3] *Samuel,*[2] *Thomas*[1]), born Boston, Mass., August 17, 1838;
resides Cambridge, Mass. (1891); married Cambridge, Mass.,
March 12, 1867, George Henry Pierce, son of George and Eliza
(Mitchell) Pierce; born Portland, Me., September 19, 1837; died
Cairo, Egypt, March 6, 1874.

Issue:

4770. i. GEORGE JAMES PIERCE,[8] born Manilla, Philippine Islands, March 13,
1868; resides Cambridge, Mass. (1891).

THOMAS DOGGETT, OF MARSHFIELD, MASS.

EIGHTH GENERATION.

4171. John Doggett [8] (*John*,[7] *Ichabod*,[6] *John*,[5] *John*,[4] *Thomas*,[3] *John*,[2] *Thomas* [1]), born White Point, N.S., May 2, 1832; died at sea, September 12, 1870; married White Point, N.S., January 1, 1855, by Rev. Mr. Moore, to Louisa Mullins, daughter of William and Ellen (Mitchell) Mullins; born Mills Village, N.S., September 10, 1835; died White Point, N.S., October 10, 1874.

Issue:

4771. i.   William Doggett,[9] born White Point, N.S., February 20, 1857.
4772. ii.   Andrew Doggett,[9] born White Point, N.S., October 1, 1858; married Sadie Inman; born Prince Edward Island; resides South Portland, Me. (1891).
4773. iii. Isaac Doggett,[9] born White Point, N.S., August 14, 1860; married 1882, Emma Hameon, of Lockport, N.S.; no issue; he died at sea, probably West Indies, January 1, 1885.
4774. iv.   Ella Doggett,[9] born White Point, N.S., February 18, 1862; married 1st, 1883, Harding, son of James and Hannah (West) Huphman; he died 1884; married 2d, 1886, Neil McLeod; no issue; resides Portland, Me. (1891).
4775. v.   Joshua Doggett,[9] born White Point, N.S., 1863; died young.
4776. vi.   Simeon Doggett,[9] born White Point, N.S., May 12, 1865; resides White Point, N.S. (1890).
4777. vii. Martha Doggett,[9] born White Point, N.S., October 27, 1867; married Portland, Me., September, 1888, Reuben Pulk; resides Portland, Me. (1891).
4778. viii. Joseph Doggett,[9] born White Point, N.S., Nov. 5, 1868; died young.
4779. ix.   George Garvey Doggett,[9] born White Point, N.S., Dec. 22, 1869.

4172. Peninah Doggett [8] (*John*,[7] *Ichabod*,[6] *John*,[5] *John*,[4] *Thomas*,[3] *John*,[2] *Thomas* [1]), born White Point, N.S., September 2, 1834; resides Mills Village, N.S. (1891); married White Point, N.S., December 10, 1857, by Rev. Mr. Addie, to William Mullins, son of John Mullins; born Liverpool, N.S., October 10, 1810; died Mills Village, N.S.

Issue:

4780. i.   Ada Mullins,[9] born Mills Village, N.S., October 2, 1858; married Captain Sparks; resides Provincetown, Mass. (1890).
4781. ii.   Clara Mullins,[9] born Mills Village, N.S., July 20, 1859; married Howard Allen; resides Lockport, N.S. (1890).
4782. iii. Elizabeth Mullins,[9] born Mills Village, N.S., September 27, 1860; resides Boston, Mass.
4783. iv.   Emma Mullins,[9] born Mills Village, N.S., September 15, 1864; married Mr. Bezanson; resides Cambridge, Mass. (1890).
4784. v.   Sophronia Mullins,[9] born Mills Village, N.S., May 20, 1866; resides Campello, Mass.
4785. vi.   Alivelda Mullins,[9] born Mills Village, N.S., March 20, 1869; resides Campello, Mass.
4786. vii. Doren Mullins,[9] born Mills Village, N.S., December 24, 1870; resides Mills Village, N.S. (1890).

4173. WILLIAM DOGGETT [8] (*John*,[7] *Ichabod*,[6] *John*,[5] *John*,[4] *Thomas*,[3] *John*,[2] *Thomas*[1]), born White Point, N.S., October 9, 1836; resides White Point, N.S. (1891); married White Point, N.S., January 25, 1862, by Rev. J. Burns, to Eunice Huphman, daughter of James and Hannah (West) Huphman; born Hunt's Point, N.S., November 9, 1841.

Issue:

4787. i. ELIZABETH DOGGETT,[9] born White Point, N.S., January 13, 1863; married Leonard Dyer; no issue; she died 1886.
4788. ii. CLARA JANE DOGGETT,[9] born White Point, N.S., June 23, 1864; married Edward Inness; resides Portland, Me. (1891).
4789. iii. JOHN DOGGETT,[9] born White Point, N.S., November 23, 1865; died at sea, July 6, 1884.
4790. iv. EVA DOGGETT,[9] born White Point, N.S., February 26, 1869; resides there (1891).
4791. v. NETTIE DOGGETT,[9] born White Point, N.S., February 20, 1871; married Leonard Dyer (since 1886): resides Portland, Me. (1891).
4792. vi. HATTIE DOGGETT,[9] born White Point, N.S., February 20, 1871; resides there (1891).
4793. vii. ARCHIE FRANCIS DOGGETT,[9] born White Point, N.S., December 14, 1871; died White Point, N.S., October 27, 1890.
4794. viii. CLARENCE FREEMAN DOGGETT,[9] born White Point, N.S., April 17, 1873; died White Point, N.S., April 24, 1882.
4795. ix. ANGUS MCRITCHIE DOGGETT,[9] born White Point, N.S., November 6, 1874; resides there (1891).
4796. x. ALFRED DOGGETT,[9] born White Point, N.S., January 12, 1876; died White Point, N.S., December 20, 1876.
4797. xi. IDA SPARKS DOGGETT,[9] born White Point, N.S., March 19, 1877.
4798. xii. FREDERICK JAMES DOGGETT,[9] born White Point, N.S., July 2, 1878.
4799. xiii. GILBERT SELMA DOGGETT,[9] born White Point, N.S., September 27, 1879; died White Point, N.S., December 19, 1879.
4800. xiv. GERTRUDE MAY DOGGETT,[9] born White Point, N.S., Oct. 18, 1880.
4801. xv. KATE ALLEN DOGGETT,[9] born White Point, N.S., March 25, 1883; died White Point, N.S., July 2, 1883.

4174. MARY DOGGETT [8] (*John*,[7] *Ichabod*,[6] *John*,[5] *John*,[4] *Thomas*,[3] *John*,[2] *Thomas*[1]), born White Point, N.S., August 22, 1841; resides 228 Shawmut avenue, Boston, Mass. (1893); married Boston, Mass., December 20, 1869, by Rev. B. H. Davis, to Francis Marion Freeman, son of Hatsuld and Elizabeth (Eldridge) Freeman; born Provincetown, Mass., January 24, 1830.

Issue:

4802. i. CLARENCE NEWTON FREEMAN,[9] born Provincetown, Mass., Jan. 11, 1870.
4803. ii. ELDRIDGE CHAPMAN FREEMAN,[9] born Provincetown, Mass., Jan. 6, 1871.
4804. iii. FRANCIS MARION FREEMAN,[9] born Provincetown, Mass., December 14, 1871; died Provincetown, Mass., June 14, 1875.
4805. iv. MABEL FREEMAN,[9] born Provincetown, Mass., February 9, 1876; died Provincetown, Mass., February 9, 1876.
4806. v. MARION LOUISE FREEMAN,[9] born Provincetown, Mass., April 20, 1877.
4807. vi. ALFRED DOGGETT FREEMAN,[9] born Provincetown, Mass., March 22, 1880.
4808. vii. CHESTER CROWEL FREEMAN,[9] born Provincetown, Mass., March 2, 1883.

4175. ELIZA DOGGETT [8] (*John*,[7] *Ichabod*,[6] *John*,[5] *John*,[4] *Thomas*,[3] *John*,[2] *Thomas*[1]), born White Point, N.S., July 4, 1845; died Provincetown, Mass., May 11, 1886; married Provincetown, Mass., November 9, 1868, Angus McRitchie; born Prince Edward Island, 1838; resides Provincetown, Mass. (1890).

Issue:

4809. i. EDDIE BERT McRITCHIE,[9] born Provincetown, Mass., 1869; died White Point, N.S., 1875.
4810. ii. EDDIE COOK McRITCHIE,[9] born Provincetown, Mass., 1880; resides there.

4177. LEANDER DOGGETT[8] (*John*,[7] *Ichabod*,[6] *John*,[5] *John*,[4] *Thomas*,[3] *John*,[2] *Thomas*[1]), born White Point, N.S., July 29, 1850; died White Point, N.S., February 10, 1890; married White Point, N.S., November 1, 1877, by Rev. J. Johnson, to Elmira Campbell, daughter of Donald and Susan (Gardner) Campbell; born Port Matoon, N.S., April 10, 1850; resides White Point, N.S. (1890).

Issue:

4811. i. EDWARD HERBERT DOGGETT,[9] born White Point, N.S., April 7, 1878.
4812. ii. SUSIE MAY DOGGETT,[9] born White Point, N.S., November 25, 1880.
4813. iii. LILLIAN DOGGETT,[9] born White Point, N.S., December 12, 1881.
4814. iv. SADDIE MARIA DOGGETT,[9] born White Point, N.S., May 17, 1882.
4815. v. CLARENCE NEWTON DOGGETT,[9] born White Point, N.S., July 21, 1883.
4816. vi. ADDIE ELLEN DOGGETT,[9] born White Point, N.S., May 27, 1885.

4178. ROBERT DOGGETT[8] (*John*,[7] *Ichabod*,[6] *John*,[5] *John*,[4] *Thomas*,[3] *John*,[2] *Thomas*[1]), born White Point, N.S., September 30, 1854; resides White Point, N.S. (1890); married White Point, N.S., February 9, 1880, by Rev. Mr. Atwater, to Clara Smith, daughter of George and Clarissa (McGowan) Smith; born Hunt's Point, N.S., July 10, 1854.

Issue:

4817. i. MARY FREEMAN DOGGETT,[9] born White Point, N.S., Dec. 17, 1880.
4818. ii. ELIZA DOGGETT,[9] born White Point, N.S.; died.
4819. iii. ELIZA DOGGETT,[9] born White Point, N.S., April 4, 1883; died ——.
4820. iv. GORHAM FREEMAN DOGGETT,[9] born White Point, N.S., Dec. 4, 1886.
4821. v. GEORGE FARRISH DOGGETT,[9] born White Point, N.S., Sept. 4, 1889.

4179. FREDERIC THOMAS DOGGETT[8] (*Lathrop*,[7] *Ichabod*,[6] *John*,[5] *John*,[4] *Thomas*,[3] *John*,[2] *Thomas*[1]), born White Point, N.S., May 15, 1828; " mariner; " resides Provincetown, Mass. (1890); married Provincetown, Mass., May 30, 1858, Helen F. Snow; born Provincetown, Mass., December 11, 1828.

Issue:

4822. i. JOHN L. DOGGETT,[9] died.
4823. ii. FREDERIC W. DOGGETT,[9] born Provincetown, Mass., September 19, 1863; married Boston, Mass., June 17, 1887, Nettie B. Freeman.
4824. iii. ALTON L. DOGGETT.[9]
4825. iv. SARAH S. DOGGETT.[9]
4826. v. CORA M. DOGGETT,[9] born Provincetown, Mass., December 2, 1872.

4180. JAMES DOGGETT [8] (*Lathrop,*[7] *Ichabod,*[6] *John,*[5] *John,*[4] *Thomas,*[3] *John,*[2] *Thomas* [1]), born White Point, N.S.; resides Provincetown, Mass. (1890); married Liverpool, N.S., Mary Snow.

Issue:

4827. i.   FRANK F. DOGGETT,[9] born Provincetown, Mass., September 4, 1865; died Provincetown, Mass., December 7, 1865.
4828. ii. JOSEPH ATKINS DOGGETT,[9] born Provincetown, Mass., March 1, 1867.
4829. iii. FRANK E. DOGGETT,[9] resides Boston, Mass. (1890).

4181. ELIZABETH DOGGETT [8] (*Lathrop,*[7] *Ichabod,*[6] *John,*[5] *John,*[4] *Thomas,*[3] *John,*[2] *Thomas* [1]), born White Point, N.S.; resides Provincetown, Mass. (1890); married Provincetown, Mass., January 1, 1858, Capt. Joseph Pinckney; born Boston, Mass.; died Provincetown, Mass.

Issue:

4830. i.   LEWIS B. PINCKNEY.[9]
4831. ii. ADDIE A. PINCKNEY.[9]
4832. iii. WILLIAM O. PINCKNEY.[9]

4182. PRISCILLA DOGGETT [8] (*Lathrop,*[7] *Ichabod,*[6] *John,*[5] *John,*[4] *Thomas,*[3] *John,*[2] *Thomas* [1]), born White Point, N.S.; resides Provincetown, Mass.; married White Point, N.S., Joseph Frellick.

Issue:

4833. i.   JANE W. FRELLICK,[9] died.
4834. ii. ANNA B. FRELLICK.[9]
4835. iii. JAMES F. FRELLICK.[9]
4836. iv. LOTTY D. FRELLICK.[9]
4837. v.   JENNETT W. FRELLICK.[9]

4183. MARY JANE DOGGETT [8] (*Lathrop,*[7] *Ichabod,*[6] *John,*[5] *John,*[4] *Thomas,*[3] *John,*[2] *Thomas* [1]), born White Point, N.S., 1840; married North Bridgewater, Mass., March 2, 1859, by Rev. C. L. Mills, to John Garland, of Provincetown; "mechanic;" born Boston, Mass., 1830.

Issue:

4838. i.   T. L. GARLAND.[9]
4839. ii. WINNY F. GARLAND.[9]
4840. iii. EDITH E. GARLAND.[9]

4184. SELINA DOGGETT [8] (*Lathrop,*[7] *Ichabod,*[6] *John,*[5] *John,*[4] *Thomas,*[3] *John,*[2] *Thomas* [1]), born White Point, N.S., 1846; married Provincetown, Mass., November 28, 1866, by Rev. Thomas Audas, to Reuben N. Mayo, son of Stephen A. and Jerusha Mayo; "mariner;" born Provincetown, Mass., 1840.

Issue:

4841. i.   IDA F. MAYO.[9]
4842. ii. ALFRED S. MAYO.[9]
4843. iii. ETHEL S. MAYO.[9]
4844. iv. ANNIE F. MAYO.[9]
4845. v.   FRANK L. MAYO.[9]

4185. Susan Doggett[8] (*Lathrop,*[7] *Ichabod,*[6] *John,*[5] *John,*[4] *Thomas,*[3] *John,*[2] *Thomas*[1]), born White Point, N.S.; married 1st, White Point, N.S., Lockwood Frellick; married 2d, Alec Livingstone.

Issue:

4846. i. NELLIE FRELLICK.[9]
4847. ii. ELIZABETH L. LIVINGSTONE.[9]
4848. iii. BESSIE MAY LIVINGSTONE.[9]
4849. iv. ADDIE A. LIVINGSTONE.[9]

4186. EXPERIENCE DOGGETT[8] (*Lathrop,*[7] *Ichabod,*[6] *John,*[5] *John,*[4] *Thomas,*[3] *John,*[2] *Thomas*[1]), born White Point, N.S.; married Provincetown, Mass., Oct. 15, 1871, by Rev. Charles Young, to Archie W. Dowling, son of John and Elizabeth Dowling; born Cape Breton, 1841.

Issue:

4850. i. BESSY S. DOWLING,[9] died.
4851. ii. SADY B. DOWLING,[9] died.

4187. RALPH DOGGETT[8] (*Joseph,*[7] *Ichabod,*[6] *John,*[5] *John,*[4] *Thomas,*[3] *John,*[2] *Thomas*[1]), born White Point, N.S., December 14, 1840; resides White Point, N.S. (1891); married Mills Village, N.S., July 11, 1877, by Rev. Mr. Pickels, to Mary Jane Manthorn, daughter of James and Mary (Smith) Manthorn; born Mills Village, N.S., August 12, 1846.

No issue; one child, adopted.

4852. i. LYDIA MACK DOGGETT,[9] born Mills Village, N.S., August 31, 1876.

4189. MERCY DOGGETT[8] (*Joseph,*[7] *Ichabod,*[6] *John,*[5] *John,*[4] *Thomas,*[3] *John,*[2] *Thomas*[1]), born White Point, N.S., May 14, 1845; died White Point, N.S., December 2, 1867; married White Point, N.S., December 30, 1866, by Rev. Robert Warson, to Elijah Frellick, son of George and Ellen (Smith) Frellick; born Hunt's Point, N.S., May 10, 1840; resides Hunt's Point, N.S. (1890).

No issue.

4190. JABEZ DOGGETT[8] (*Joseph,*[7] *Ichabod,*[6] *John,*[5] *John,*[4] *Thomas,*[3] *John,*[2] *Thomas*[1]), born White Point, N.S., August 14, 1847; resides Black Point, N.S. (1891); married Liverpool, N.S., May 23, 1883, by Rev. Mr. Parkson, to Eliza Wynot, daughter of Jacob and Elizabeth (Conrod) Wynot; born Port Medway, N.S., September 6, 1864.

Issue:

4853. i. FRANK DOGGETT,[9] born Liverpool, N.S., July 5, 1884.
4854. ii. FLORENCE DOGGETT,[9] born Liverpool, N.S., May 20, 1886.
4855. iii. BERTHA DOGGETT,[9] born Liverpool, N.S., September 9, 1888.
4856. iv. AGNES DOGGETT,[9] born Liverpool, N.S., November 10, 1890.

4191. ALMOND DOGGETT[8] (*Joseph,*[7] *Ichabod,*[6] *John,*[5] *John,*[4] *Thomas,*[3] *John,*[2] *Thomas*[1]), born White Point, N.S., March 14,

1849; resides White Point, N.S. (1891); married White Point, N.S., May 7, 1878, by Rev. John Johnson, to Jane Fitzgerald, daughter of William and Catherina (Hagan) Fitzgerald; born Summerville, N.S., June 3, 1854.

Issue:

4857. i.   LENNIE DOGGETT,[9] born White Point, N.S., November 30, 1878.
4858. ii. WILLAS DOGGETT,[9] born White Point, N.S., September 21, 1880.
4859. iii. LIZZIE DOGGETT,[9] born White Point, N.S., June 13, 1885.
4860. iv. VERNIE EARL DOGGETT,[9] born White Point, N.S., February 23, 1890.

4192.   CHARLES DOGGETT[8] (*Joseph,*[7] *Ichabod,*[6] *John,*[5] *John,*[4] *Thomas,*[3] *John,*[2] *Thomas*[1]), born White Point, N.S., December 14, 1851; resides White Point, N.S. (1891); married Mills Village, N.S., November 30, 1876, by Rev. Mr. Addie, to Ella Mullins, daughter of William and Ellen (Mitchell) Mullins; born Mills Village, N.S., August 25, 1856.

Issue:

4861. i.   MERCY DOGGETT,[9] born White Point, N.S., October 26, 1877.
4862. ii. FLORA MAY DOGGETT,[9] born White Point, N.S., October 29, 1878.
4863. iii. ELDRIDGE DOGGETT,[9] born White Point, N.S., December 21, 1880.
4864. iv. ARCHIE DOGGETT,[9] born White Point, N.S., June 13, 1884.
4865. v.   ROBERT DOGGETT,[9] born White Point, N.S., May 10, 1886.
4866. vi. JOHN HARVEY DOGGETT,[9] born White Point, N.S., April 14, 1888.
4867. vii. HERBERT FRANCIS DOGGETT,[9] born White Point, N.S., Nov. 8, 1890.

4195.   ADELAIDE DOGGETT[8] (*Ebenezer,*[7] *Ichabod,*[6] *John,*[5] *John,*[4] *Thomas,*[3] *John,*[2] *Thomas*[1]), born White Point, N.S., October 3, 1841; resides White Point, N.S. (1890); married White Point, N.S., January 20, 1870, by Rev. Andrew Gray, to Jacob West, son of Oliver and Nancy (Huphman) West; born White Point, N.S., April 1, 1840; died White Point, N.S.

Issue:

4868. i. ANNIE BORDEN WEST,[9] born White Point, N.S., January 23, 1874; died White Point, N.S., July 25, 1885.

4199.   DANIEL THOMAS DAGGETT[8] (*Eliphalet,*[7] *Mark,*[6] *Jabez,*[5] *Thomas,*[4] *Thomas,*[3] *John,*[2] *Thomas*[1]), born Middleboro', Mass., January 21, 1820; "housewright;" died Stockton, Cal., July 13, 1881; married New Bedford, Mass., October 4, 1840, by Thomas M. Smith, to Sarah Louisa Alden, daughter of Humphrey and Mary (Pitman) Alden; born New Bedford, Mass., February 22, 1822; resides Stockton, Cal. (1893).

Issue:

4869. i.   WILLIAM COFFIN DAGGETT,[9] born New Bedford, Mass., October 20, 1842; married Sacramento, Cal., April 28, 1862, Alice Gray, daughter of Nathaniel and Lois (Leeland) Gray; born Seville, Ohio, July 1, 1843; no issue; resides Stockton, Cal. (1893).
4870. ii. JOHN PITMAN DAGGETT,[9] born New Bedford, Mass., July 20, 1843; died Stockton, Cal., March 28, 1879.
4871. iii. SARAH LOUISA DAGGETT,[9] born Cambridgeport, Mass., September 17, 1848; died Stockton, Cal., September 23, 1858.

4200. Samuel Perry Daggett[8] (*Eliphalet,*[7] *Mark,*[6] *Jabez,*[5] *Thomas,*[4] *Thomas,*[3] *John,*[2] *Thomas*[1]), born Middleboro', Mass., July 11, 1823; died Auburn, Cal., May 17, 1869.

A California paper, speaking of the death of Samuel P. Daggett, says:

He was an old resident of Placer and one of our truest and best men. Of more than ordinary intelligence and the highest integrity, he possessed the respect and confidence of all who knew him. Mr. Daggett filled several important offices in the township where he has resided for years past, and was always prompt and faithful in the discharge of his duties. He was a true and loyal man, and one of the most earnest and efficient friends of the Union cause in the county during the Rebellion. Mr. Daggett left no family, but his memory will be cherished by all who enjoyed his acquaintance.

4202. Sybil Daggett[8] (*Eliphalet,*[7] *Mark,*[6] *Jabez,*[5] *Thomas,*[4] *Thomas,*[3] *John,*[2] *Thomas*[1]), born West Bridgewater, Mass., May 23, 1827; died North Dartmouth, Mass., May 28, 1878; married Dartmouth, Mass., July 4, 1860, by Rev. Gould Anthony, to William Campbell Jones, of North Dartmouth, son of Jeremiah M. and Lucy (Maxfield) Jones; "farmer;" born Dartmouth, Mass., 1834; resides North Dartmouth, Mass. (1893).

Issue:

4872. i. Lucy Portia Jones,[9] born North Dartmouth, Mass., January 15, 1862.

4203. Elizabeth West Daggett[8] (*Shepard,*[7] *Mark,*[6] *Jabez,*[5] *Thomas,*[4] *Thomas,*[3] *John,*[2] *Thomas*[1]), born New Bedford, Mass., Nov. 4, 1820; died Charleston, S.C., Jan. 6, 1890; married Charleston, S.C., Dec. 24, 1844, Vincent Wyld; born Eastwood, Nottinghamshire, Eng., April 12, 1804; died Charleston, S.C., June 10, 1856.

Issue:

4873. i. Mary Elizabeth Wyld,[9] born Charleston, S.C., October 5, 1845; died Charleston, S.C., September 15, 1847.
4874. ii. Vincent William Wyld,[9] born Charleston, S.C., October 29, 1846; died Charleston, S.C., July 7, 1851.
4875. iii. Joseph Doley Wyld,[9] born Charleston, S.C., July 17, 1848.
4876. iv. Robert James Wyld,[9] born Charleston, S.C., December 29, 1849; died Charleston, S.C., May 8, 1851.
4877. v. Joanna Portia Wyld,[9] born Charleston, S.C., January 6, 1852; resides Charleston, S.C. (1893).
4878. vi. Isabella Jane Wyld,[9] born Charleston, S.C., October 8, 1854; died Charleston, S.C., February 22, 1863.

4204. Lemuel West Daggett[8] (*Shepard,*[7] *Mark,*[6] *Jabez,*[5] *Thomas,*[4] *Thomas,*[3] *John,*[2] *Thomas*[1]), born New Bedford, Mass., May 11, 1822; died near Georgetown, S.C., July 5, 1867; married Charleston, S.C., ——.

Issue:

4879. i. Edgar Daggett,[9] born Charleston, S.C., January 23, 1854; died Charleston, S.C., June 4, 1855.

4205. WILLIAM LAFAYETTE DAGGETT ⁸ (*Shepard,*⁷ *Mark,*⁶ *Jabez,*⁵ *Thomas,*⁴ *Thomas,*³ *John,*² *Thomas* ¹), born New Bedford, Mass., August 6, 1824; died Charleston, S.C., August 11, 1890; married Charleston, S.C., May 28, 1844, Eliza Lambert, of England; born about 1812; resides Charleston, S.C. (1893).

Issue:

4880. i.   LEANORA HENRIETTA DAGGETT,⁹ born Charleston, S.C., April 18, 1845; resides Charleston, S.C. (1893).
4881. ii.   MARY ANN DAGGETT,⁹ born Charleston, S.C., November 21, 1846.
4882. iii. ELIZA JANE DAGGETT,⁹ born Charleston, S.C., August 24, 1848; resides Charleston, S.C. (1893).
4883. iv.   VALINTIA DAGGETT,⁹ born Charleston, S.C., February 14, 1850; died Charleston, S.C., August 10, 1850.
4884. v.   EMILY DAGGETT,⁹ born Charleston, S.C., September 15, 1851; resides Charleston, S.C. (1893).
4885. vi.   WALTER LAMBERT DAGGETT,⁹ born Charleston, S.C., May 4, 1854.

Mr. Daggett was for some years superintendent of the printing establishment of "The News and Courier."

4206. ABIGAIL DAGGETT ⁸ (*Shepard,*⁷ *Mark,*⁶ *Jabez,*⁵ *Thomas,*⁴ *Thomas,*³ *John,*² *Thomas* ¹), born New Bedford, Mass., October 24, 1827; resides Charleston, S.C. (1893); married 1st, Charleston, S.C., September 3, 1846, A. T. Curans; born Mississippi; died Havre, France; married 2d, Charleston, S.C., April 26, 1855, Irvine Jones Corby, son of John and Ann (Jones) Corby; born Charleston, S.C.; died Charleston, S.C., September 15, 1892.

Issue:

4886. i.   MARY ANN ELIZABETH CORBY,⁹ born Charleston, S.C., March 21, 1856; died Charleston, S.C., March 22, 1856.
4887. ii.   IRVINE JONES CORBY,⁹ born Charleston, S.C., November 12, 1857; married Charleston, S.C., February 3, 1886, Marion P. Spidy; resides Charleston, S.C. (1893).
4888. iii. MARY ANN ELIZABETH CORBY,⁹ born Charleston, S.C., July 18, 1859; died Charleston, S.C., June 27, 1861.
4889. iv.   CAROLIN AMELIA CORBY,⁹ born Charleston, S.C., May 22, 1862; died Charleston, S.C., September 12, 1866.
4890. v.   OTTO TIEDEMAN CORBY,⁹ born Charleston, S.C., July 28, 1864; married Savannah, Ga., February 26, 1888, Anna Acken; resides Savannah, Ga. (1893).
4891. vi.   ISABELLA MISSCALLY CORBY,⁹ born Charleston, S.C., April 5, 1867; died Charleston, S.C., October 11, 1889.

4207. THOMAS WEST DAGGETT ⁸ (*Shepard,*⁷ *Mark,*⁶ *Jabez,*⁵ *Thomas,*⁴ *Thomas,*³ *John,*² *Thomas* ¹), born New Bedford, Mass., October 24, 1829; died Conway, S.C., January 10, 1893; married 1st, Charleston, S.C., 1850, Mary Elizabeth Kruse; died Charleston, S.C.; married 2d, Charleston, S.C., 1851, Lucretia Kruse; died September. 1855; married 3d, Green Hill, Waccamaw Neck, S.C., April 15, 1857, Mary A. Tillman, daughter of Benjamin A.

and Sarah Adeline (Singleton) Tillman; born Waserly, Waccamaw River, S.C., November 27, 1841; resides Conway, S.C. (1893).

Issue:

4892. i.   JOSHUA DAGGETT,[9] born Charleston, S.C., November 23, 1851; died Charleston, S.C., March, 1852.

4893. ii.   MARY ELIZABETH DAGGETT,[9] born Charleston, S.C., September 7, 1852; died Charleston, S.C., November 25, 1854.

4894. iii.   ADELINE DAGGETT,[9] born Waccamaw, S.C., May 30, 1858; died Black River, S.C., January 20, 1863.

4895. iv.   MARY ELIZABETH DAGGETT,[9] born Magnolia Beach, S.C., July 4, 1860; resides Conway, S.C. (1893).

4896. v.   HARRIET AGNES DAGGETT,[9] born Black River, S.C., Sept. 22, 1862; married Conway, S.C., December 19, 1886, Walter E. Porter; resides Conway, S.C. (1893).

4897. vi.   THOMAS SHEPARD DAGGETT,[9] born Black River, S.C., December 28, 1864; resides Georgetown, S.C. (1893).

4898. vii.   BENJAMIN TILLMAN DAGGETT,[9] born Longbay Beach, S.C., October 5, 1867; married Hovey county, S.C., April 24, 1890, Charlotte F. Vereene; resides Conway, S.C. (1893).

4899. viii.   LULA ABIGAIL DAGGETT,[9] born Pee Dee, S.C., February 7, 1870; married Conway, S.C., January 22, 1888, Albert J. Bants; resides Marlow, S.C. (1893).

4900. ix.   SUSAN WEST DAGGETT,[9] born Pee Dee, S.C., July 30, 1872; resides Conway, S.C. (1893).

4901. x.   MABEL DAGGETT,[9] born Conway, S.C., December 2, 1876; died Conway, S.C., April 29, 1883.

4208. SHEPARD DAGGETT[8] (*Shepard,*[7] *Mark,*[6] *Jabez,*[5] *Thomas,*[4] *Thomas,*[3] *John,*[2] *Thomas*[1]), born New London, Conn., August 27, 1833; died Charleston, S.C., November 23, 1862; married Charleston, S.C., September 6, 1853, Sophia Ann Syfan, daughter of John and Mary P. (Gould) Syfan; born Charleston, S.C., February 27, 1831; resides Charleston, S.C. (1893).

Issue:

4902. i.   ALEXANDER WESTMAN DAGGETT,[9] born Charleston, S.C., October 16, 1854; died Charleston, S.C., October 21, 1880.

4903. ii.   MARY FRANCIS DAGGETT,[9] born Charleston, S.C., July 24, 1856; died Charleston, S.C., September 16, 1858.

4904. iii.   FRANCIS SYFAN DAGGETT,[9] born Charleston, S.C., September 16, 1858; died Charleston, S.C., July 25, 1859.

4905. iv.   LAURA EUGENIA DAGGETT,[9] born Charleston, S.C., June 22, 1862; died Charleston, S.C., August 16, 1884.

4210. JOHN WILBUR DAGGETT[8] (*Shepard,*[7] *Mark,*[6] *Jabez,*[5] *Thomas,*[4] *Thomas,*[3] *John,*[2] *Thomas*[1]), born New Bedford, Mass., August 22, 1837; died Charleston, S.C., March 23, 1864; married Savannah, Ga., March 6, 1859, Josephine Espey, daughter of William and Caroline Ratcliffe (Gardner) Espey; born Beaufort, S.C., June 5, 1840; resides Charleston, S.C. (1893).

Issue:

4906. i.   JOHN ELLIOTT DAGGETT,[9] born Charleston, S.C., September 11, 1860; died Charleston, S.C., September 16, 1860.

4907. ii.   MARY CAROLINE DAGGETT,[9] born Charleston, S.C., September 3, 1862; died Charleston, S.C., April 9, 1864.

4214. LAURA A. DAGGETT [8] (*Martin K.*,[7] *Mark*,[6] *Jabez*,[5] *Thomas*,[4] *Thomas*,[3] *John*,[2] *Thomas*[1]), born Grand Manan, N.B., May 24, 1826; married Grand Manan, N.B., Jan. 29, 1845, by Rev. J. Neales, to Asa Foster, son of Asa Foster; born July 21, 1819.

Issue:

4908. i. HIRAM FOSTER,[9] born Grand Manan, N.B.. November 9, 1847.
4909. ii. JOHN FOSTER,[9] born Grand Manan, N.B., October 29, 1849.
4910. iii. ASA FOSTER,[9] born Grand Manan, N.B., February 22, 1852.
4911. iv. HOWARD FOSTER,[9] born Grand Manan, N.B., June 23, 1853.
4912. v. GERTRUDE FOSTER,[9] born Grand Manan, N.B., June 19, 1857.
4913. vi. WARREN FOSTER,[9] born Grand Manan, N.B., September 12, 1861.
4914. vii. LAURA FOSTER,[9] born Maine, October 12, 1866.

4221. CATHARINE S. DAGGETT [8] (*Martin K.*,[7] *Mark*,[6] *Jabez*,[5] *Thomas*,[4] *Thomas*,[3] *John*,[2] *Thomas*[1]), born Grand Manan, N.B., February 7, 1845; resides Madison, Conn. (1893); married Boston, Mass., May 1, 1869, by Rev. W. H. H. Murray, to Charles A. Bartlett, son of Samuel and Louisa Bartlett; "artist;" born Madison, Conn., 1831.

Issue:

4915. i. VICTORIA BARTLETT,[9] born May 7, 1870.
4916. ii. ELIZA BARTLETT,[9] born June 13, 1873.
4917. iii. WALTER BARTLETT,[9] born November 27, 1878.

4222. ABIGAIL DAGGETT [8] (*Martin K.*,[7] *Mark*,[6] *Jabez*,[5] *Thomas*,[4] *Thomas*,[3] *John*,[2] *Thomas*[1]), born Grand Manan, N.B., April 15, 1848; married Grand Manan, N.B., 1866, by Rev. G. T. Carey, to Charles Cheney, son of Samuel Cheney; "carpenter."

Issue:

4918. i. EUGENE CHENEY,[9] born Grand Manan, N.B., January 27, 1867.
4919. ii. KATIE CHENEY,[9] born Grand Manan, N.B., May 10, 1869.
4920. iii. HELEN CHENEY.[9] born Grand Manan, N.B.. November 24, 1879.

4224. JEROME DAGGETT [8] (*Martin K.*,[7] *Mark*,[6] *Jabez*,[5] *Thomas*,[4] *Thomas*,[3] *John*,[2] *Thomas*[1]), born Grand Manan, N.B.. June 23, 1854; "farmer;" resides Grand Manan, N.B. (1893); married Grand Manan, N.B., October 26, 1884, by Rev. Wm. Downey, to Annie McDowell, daughter of John McDowell; born Pennfield, ——, January 21, 1858.

Issue:

4921. i. MAGGIE DAGGETT,[9] born Grand Manan, N.B., July 24, 1885.
4922. ii. JOHN DAGGETT,[9] born Grand Manan, N.B., October 27, 1886.
4923. iii. JAMES DAGGETT,[9] born Grand Manan, N.B., December 25, 1887.
4924. iv. BEATRICE DAGGETT,[9] born Grand Manan, N.B., May 19, 1889.
4925. v. HAZEN DAGGETT,[9] born Grand Manan, N.B., July 19, 1891.

4229. EDMUND DAGGETT [8] (*Nathaniel*,[7] *Mark*,[6] *Jabez*,[5] *Thomas*,[4] *Thomas*,[3] *John*,[2] *Thomas*[1]), born Grand Manan, N.B., September 6, 1835; resides Grand Manan, N.B. (1893); married Grand Manan,

N.B., 1857, Susan Sinclair, daughter of John Sinclair ; born April 2, 1836.

Issue :

4926. i. MARINA DAGGETT,[9] born Grand Manan, N.B., June 29, 1860; died Grand Manan, N.B., April 16, 1862.
4927. ii. ELDON E. DAGGETT,[9] born Grand Manan, N.B., January 21, 1862; died Grand Manan, N.B., February 9, 1868.
4928. iii. LAURA A. DAGGETT,[9] born Grand Manan, N.B., September 24, 1863.
4929. iv. ELLA W. DAGGETT,[9] born Grand Manan, N.B., September 18, 1865.
4930. v. BOLTON DAGGETT,[9] born Grand Manan, N.B., May 24, 1869 ; "minister."
4931. vi. EDNA I. DAGGETT,[9] born Grand Manan, N.B., August 16, 1871.
4932. vii. WELLINGTON L. DAGGETT,[9] born Grand Manan, N.B., March 17, 1873.
4933. viii. RALPH S. DAGGETT,[9] born Grand Manan, N.B., March 17, 1873.

Mr. Daggett is a justice of the peace. He is proprietor of the "Sea View House."

4240. ELIZA DAGGETT[8] (*Philo,*[7] *Mark,*[6] *Jabez,*[5] *Thomas,*[4] *Thomas,*[3] *John,*[2] *Thomas*[1]), born Grand Manan, N.B., June 15, 1838; resides Grand Manan, N.B. (1893); married Grand Manan, N.B., January 17, 1859, by Rev. George Carey, to William B. Green, son of William Green; "fisherman."

Issue :

4934. i. ADAVILLA GREEN,[9] born Grand Manan, N.B., March 24, 1860.
4935. ii. OWEN GREEN,[9] born Grand Manan, N.B., May 26, 1861.
4936. iii. EMMIETTA GREEN,[9] born Grand Manan, N.B., August 16, 1866.
4937. iv. LORING GREEN,[9] born Grand Manan, N.B., May 27, 1869.
4938. v. MINNIE GREEN,[9] born Grand Manan, N.B., August 21, 1872 ; died Grand Manan, N.B., June 19, 1876.
4939. vi. ARNOLD W. GREEN,[9] born Grand Manan, N.B., February 26, 1878.
4940. vii. MINERVA GREEN,[9] born Grand Manan, N.B., April 4, 1882.

4247. REBECCA DAGGETT[8] (*Mark,*[7] *Mark,*[6] *Jabez,*[5] *Thomas,*[4] *Thomas,*[3] *John,*[2] *Thomas*[1]), born Grand Manan, N.B., June 4, 1829 ; resides Grand Manan, N.B.; married Grand Manan, N.B., December 17, 1852, by Rev. George Carey, to William Benson, son of Caleb Benson ; "fisherman; " born August 22, 1830.

Issue :

4941. i. LEONARD H. BENSON,[9] born Grand Manan, N.B., October 19, 1853; died Grand Manan, N.B.. ——.
4942. ii. NELLIE BENSON,[9] born Grand Manan. N.B., November 27, 1855.
4943. iii. FRANK BENSON,[9] born Grand Manan. N.B., June 8, 1859.
4944. iv. ALICE BENSON,[9] born Grand Manan, N.B., November 10, 1864.

4249. MARY DAGGETT[8] (*Mark,*[7] *Mark,*[6] *Jabez,*[5] *Thomas,*[4] *Thomas,*[3] *John,*[2] *Thomas*[1]), born Grand Manan, N.B.; married Grand Manan, N.B.. by Rev. G. T. Carey, to Benjamin Flagg, son of Winslow Flagg; "carpenter."

Issue :

4945. i. ARTHUR FLAGG,[9] born Grand Manan, N.B.

4946. ii. WILLIAM FLAGG,[9] born Grand Manan, N.B.
4947. iii. FRANK FLAGG,[9] born Grand Manan, N.B.
4948. iv. ANNIE FLAGG,[9] born Grand Manan, N.B.

4250. URANIA DAGGETT[8] (*Mark*,[7] *Mark*,[6] *Jabez*,[5] *Thomas*,[4] *Thomas*,[3] *John*,[2] *Thomas*[1]), born Grand Manan, N.B., January 3, 1833; resides Grand Manan, N.B.; married Grand Manan, N.B., April 2, 1856, by Rev. G. T. Carey, to Alexander Cheney, son of Samuel Cheney; "carpenter."

Issue:

4949. i. GEORGE CHENEY,[9] born Grand Manan, N.B., January 22, 1857.
4950. ii. HENRY CHENEY,[9] born Grand Manan, N.B., May 8, 1859; died Grand Manan, N.B.
4951. iii. LIZZIE CHENEY,[9] born Grand Manan, N.B., September 19, 1861.
4952. iv. SARAH CHENEY,[9] born Grand Manan, N.B., September 16, 1863; died Grand Manan, N.B., April 17, 1884.
4953. v. TEMPERANCE CHENEY,[9] born Grand Manan, N.B., July 25, 1865.
4954. vi. HANNAH CHENEY,[9] born Grand Manan, N.B., September 20, 1866.
4955. vii. CLARENCE CHENEY,[9] born Grand Manan, N.B., October 1, 1869; died Grand Manan, N.B., September 20, 1870.
4956. viii. MARK CHENEY,[9] born Grand Manan, N.B., September 11, 1871.
4957. ix. EMSLEY CHENEY,[9] born Grand Manan, N.B., December 30, 1873.

4251. LOUISA DAGGETT[8] (*Mark*,[7] *Mark*,[6] *Jabez*,[5] *Thomas*,[4] *Thomas*,[3] *John*,[2] *Thomas*[1]), born Grand Manan, N.B., December 20, 1834; resides Avon, Skagit Co., Wash. (1893); married Grand Manan, N.B., by Rev. George Carey, to Capt. Charles Ingalls, son of William Ingalls; lost at sea, November 2, 1867.

Issue:

4958. i. FRANK INGALLS.[9] born Grand Manan. N.B.
4959. ii. ROSS INGALLS,[9] born Grand Manan, N.B.
4960. iii. GRACE INGALLS,[9] born Grand Manan. N.B.; died Grand Manan, N.B.
4961. iv. CARRIE INGALLS.[9] born Grand Manan, N.B.

4252. MARK DAGGETT[8] (*Mark*,[7] *Mark*,[6] *Jabez*,[5] *Thomas*,[4] *Thomas*,[3] *John*,[2] *Thomas*[1]), born Grand Manan, N.B., October 10, 1836; "light-keeper;" resides Grand Manan, N.B. (1893); married Wickham, N.B., December 9, 1865, by Rev. J. N. Barnes, to Mary C. Huggard, daughter of John Huggard; born Wickham, N.B., August 6, 1842.

Issue:

4962. i. ERNEST A. DAGGETT,[9] born Grand Manan, N.B., Oct. 5, 1867; "farmer."
4963. ii. SARAH E. DAGGETT,[9] born Grand Manan, N.B., September 18, 1869; "teacher;" resides Grand Harbour, Grand Manan, N.B. (1893).
4964. iii. D. HERBERT DAGGETT,[9] born Grand Manan, N.B.,, October 22, 1872.
4965. iv. HARRY M. DAGGETT,[9] born Grand Manan, N.B., November 9, 1880.

4253. SIMEON DAGGETT[8] (*Mark*,[7] *Mark*,[6] *Jabez*,[5] *Thomas*,[4] *Thomas*,[3] *John*,[2] *Thomas*[1]), born Grand Manan, N.B., October 20, 1840; "carpenter;" "justice of the peace;" resides Somerville,

Mass. (1893) ; married Grand Manan, N.B., by Rev. J. N. Barnes, to Julia Ingersoll, daughter of Anson Ingersoll.

Issue :

4966. i.   GEORGE DAGGETT,[9] born Grand Manan, N.B., February 7, 1866.
4967. ii. EDITH DAGGETT,[9] born Grand Manan, N.B.

4256. WILLIAM DAGGETT[8] (*Mark*,[7] *Mark*,[6] *Jabez*,[5] *Thomas*,[4] *Thomas*,[3] *John*,[2] *Thomas*[1]), born Grand Manan, N.B. ; "farmer;" resides Avon, Skagit Co.. Wash. (1893) ; married Grand Manan, N.B., November, 1880, by Rev. J. N. Barnes, to Jeannette Flagg, daughter of Josiah Flagg.

Issue : four children.

4968. i.   BESSIE DAGGETT,[9] born Grand Manan, N.B.
4969. ii. REDMOND DAGGETT,[9] born Grand Manan, N.B.

4257. SARAH DAGGETT[8] (*Mark*,[7] *Mark*,[6] *Jabez*,[5] *Thomas*,[4] *Thomas*,[3] *John*,[2] *Thomas*[1]), born Grand Manan, N.B., August 5, 1847 ; resides 28 Prescott street, Everett, Mass. (1893) ; married Grand Manan, N.B., January 14, 1869, by Thomas Connor, to George W. Benson, son of Cyrus Benson; "carpenter;" born Grand Manan, N.B., September 18, 1844.

Issue :

4970. i.   GRACE W. BENSON,[9] born Grand Manan, N.B., August 18, 1870.
4971. ii. MINNIE E. BENSON,[9] born Grand Manan, N.B., March 7, 1887.

4258. ABIGAIL W. DAGGETT[8] (*Mark*,[7] *Mark*,[6] *Jabez*,[5] *Thomas*,[4] *Thomas*,[3] *John*,[2] *Thomas*[1]), born Grand Manan, N.B., June 8, 1850 ; resides Grand Manan, N.B. (1893) ; married Curtis Ingalls, son of David Ingalls ; "fisherman."

Issue :

4972. i.   ALBERT C. INGALLS,[9] born Grand Manan, N.B., December 5, 1867.
4973. ii.   CHARLES H. INGALLS,[9] born Grand Manan, N.B., June 26, 1869.
4974. iii. WALTER G. INGALLS.[9] born Grand Manan, N.B., April 2, 1874.
4975. iv.   MAGGIE M. INGALLS,[9] born Grand Manan, N.B., July 6, 1878.
4976. v.   ALICE E. INGALLS,[9] born Grand Manan, N.B., July 24, 1886.

4259. LORING DAGGETT[8] (*John*,[7] *Mark*,[6] *Jabez*,[5] *Thomas*,[4] *Thomas*,[3] *John*,[2] *Thomas*[1]), born Grand Manan, N.B., January 11, 1841 ; "fisherman ;" resides Grand Manan, N.B. ; married St. Andrews, N.B., November 8, 1860, by Rev. Mr. Brownwell, to Kate Burnham, daughter of Abraham Burnham ; born 1840.

Issue :

4977. i.   ANTOINETTE DAGGETT,[9] born Grand Manan, N.B., August 26, 1861.
4978. ii.   CLARA C. DAGGETT,[9] born Grand Manan, N.B., December 16, 1862.
4979. iii. LUCY I. DAGGETT,[9] born Grand Manan, N.B., April 13, 1864.
4980. iv.   MANFORD L. DAGGETT,[9] born Grand Manan, N.B., April 2, 1869.
4981. v.   SARAH J. DAGGETT,[9] born Grand Manan, N.B., January 6, 1871.
4982. vi.   KATIE J. DAGGETT,[9] born Grand Manan, N.B., June 23, 1875; died Grand Manan, N.B., July 23, 1884.

4260. Cynthia Daggett [8] (*John,*[7] *Mark,*[6] *Jabez,*[5] *Thomas,*[4] *Thomas,*[3] *John,*[2] *Thomas*[1]), born Grand Manan, N.B.; resides South Lubec, Me. (1893); married Grand Manan, N.B., by Rev. G. T. Carey, to Lemuel N. Benson, son of Henry Benson; "fisherman."

Issue:

4983. i. Arthur Benson,[9] born Grand Manan, N.B.
4984. ii. Cora Benson,[9] born Grand Manan, N.B.

4261. Marietta Daggett [8] (*John,*[7] *Mark,*[6] *Jabez,*[5] *Thomas,*[4] *Thomas,*[3] *John,*[2] *Thomas*[1]), born Grand Manan, N.B., February 25, 1852; resides Grand Manan, N.B. (1893); married Grand Manan, N.B., Dec. 3, 1871, by Rev. G. T. Carey, to Abraham Burnham, son of Abraham Burnham; "fisherman;" born Grand Manan, N.B., Oct. 31, 1846.

Issue:

4985. i. Sarah D. Burnham,[9] born Grand Manan, N.B., August 16, 1873; died Grand Manan, N.B., April 20, 1884.
4986. ii. Rupert C. Burnham,[9] born Grand Manan, N.B., March 12, 1874.
4987. iii. Oscar J. Burnham,[9] born Grand Manan, N.B., June 17, 1876.
4988. iv. Helen A. Burnham,[9] born Grand Manan, N.B., November 28, 1877.
4989. v. John L. Burnham,[9] born Grand Manan, N.B., October 27, 1879.
4990. vi. Faustina Burnham.[9] born Grand Manan, N.B., April 12, 1882.
4991. vii. Alice S. Burnham.[9] born Grand Manan. N.B., August 26, 1886.
4992. viii. Ralph A. Burnham.[9] born Grand Manan. N.B., May 3, 1889.

4262. John Cadwalader O'Grady [8] (*Eliza Doggett,*[7] *Mark,*[6] *Jabez,*[5] *Thomas,*[4] *Thomas,*[3] *John,*[2] *Thomas*[1]), born Eastport, Me., October 8, 1847; called his name Grady; address, 812 Girard building, Philadelphia, Pa. (1893); married Philadelphia, Pa., November 4, 1875, Anna Clark, daughter of James Wilson and Hannah E. (McFarland) Clark; born Danville, Pa., October 2, 1854.

Issue:

4993. i. Willie Leeds Grady,[9] born Philadelphia, Pa., December 5, 1876; died Philadelphia, Pa., November 21, 1882.
4994. ii. George Balwin Grady.[9] born Philadelphia, Pa., October 11, 1878; died Philadelphia, Pa., November 26, 1882.
4995. iii. Anna Portia Grady.[9] born Philadelphia, Pa., April 3, 1880; died Philadelphia, Pa., November 25, 1882.
4996. iv. Helen Grady,[9] born Philadelphia, Pa., January 5, 1884.
4997. v. Stanley Quay Grady.[9] born Philadelphia. Pa., April 28, 1886.
4998. vi. Marie Cadwalader Grady,[9] born Philadelphia, Pa., April 8, 1889.
4999. vii. Elizabeth Grady,[9] born Philadelphia, Pa., November 4, 1890.

4263. Dr. James B. O'Grady [8] (*Eliza Doggett,*[7] *Mark,*[6] *Jabez,*[5] *Thomas,*[4] *Thomas,*[3] *John,*[2] *Thomas*[1]), born Eastport, Me., July 20, 1849; called his name Grady; resides Eastport. Me. (1893); married Portland, Me., May 27, 1891, Mary Kennedy Dawson, daughter of Gen. Samuel Kennedy and Jane Nelson (Weston) Dawson; born Eastport, Me., August 28, 1861.

Issue:

5000. i. John Weston Grady,[9] born Columbia, S.C., March 18, 1892.

4264. George O'Grady [8] (*Eliza Doggett,*[7] *Mark,*[6] *Jabez,*[5] *Thomas,*[4] *Thomas,*[3] *John,*[2] *Thomas*[1]), born Eastport, Me., March 14, 1851; called his name Grady; resides Eastport, Me. (1893); married Eastport, Me., February 14, 1888, Mary Ann Barry, daughter of Edward and Bridget (Lawler) Barry; born St. John, N.B., March 2, 1853.

Issue:

5001. i. George Grady,[9] born Eastport, Me., December 27, 1891.

4269. William Elkanah Doggett [8] (*Elkanah,*[7] *Thomas,*[6] *Simeon,*[5] *Thomas,*[4] *Thomas,*[3] *John,*[2] *Thomas*[1]), born Assonet, Mass., November 20, 1820; died Palatka, Fla., April 3, 1876; married Cleveland, Ohio, February 22, 1858, by Rev. Lewis Burton, to Kate Newell, daughter of George and Caroline (Hubbell) Newell, of Cleveland, Ohio; born Charlotte, Vt., November 5, 1827; died Havana, Cuba, March 12, 1885.

Issue:

5002. i. George Newell Doggett,[9] born Chicago, Ill., December 19, 1858.

William Elkanah Doggett, Esq., of Chicago, was in 1846 junior member of the firm of Ward, Doggett & Co., of that city, he with Mr. George Ward, of Lakeville, Mass., having founded a boot and shoe house, and established himself in Chicago. The firm was changed in 1852 to Ward, Doggett & Co., on the admission of H. D. Bassett, and so remained till 1857, when, by the death of Mr. Ward, D. H. Hills became a member of the house, under the style of Doggett, Bassett & Hills.

On the news of Mr. Doggett's death reaching Chicago, one of the newspapers says of him:

To the deep surprise and grief of this city, William E. Doggett died a few days since in Palatka, Fla. He had gone South, as most persons supposed, only to recruit, and to enjoy the more attractive climate. The telegraphic despatch announcing his death was a most painful shock to all the older families of the city. A quick consumption removed him from earth. Mr. Doggett was such a combination of virtues of mind and heart that when we call him a gentleman we satisfy the feelings of even his nearest friends. His worth is revealed by the fact that all the paths of our city life now mourn his loss. There have been men whose death has called only tradesmen together, or only fellows of the church or the club, but when this man passed away, the places of business, and the rooms of science, and art and literature, and the church, and the social circle, showed their grief in the same moment, for he was eminent everywhere. Educated, conscientious, active, broad, kind, and religious, he has left a place that must long remain empty.

Mrs. Doggett was a brilliant and accomplished woman, well known in literary and scientific circles, in the woman's rights movement, and as president of the " Woman's Congress."

At one of the sessions of this congress, which was held in Boston, in October, 1880, Mrs. Doggett is mentioned as

A lady who has both represented and infused a higher culture in the West than has any other Western woman. It is the aroma of education, so to speak, that Mrs. Doggett represents. She is, in Chicago, the apostle, par excellence, of belles-lettres — of all that makes up polite culture; and she would perhaps be surprised to know how her influence radiates through the Western States. An author, an art connoisseur, an elegant woman of society, Mrs. Doggett is indeed preëminently fitted to be the president of the American Woman's Congress.

4270. JOSEPH BARKER DOGGETT [8] (*Elkanah,*[7] *Thomas,*[6] *Simeon,*[5] *Thomas,*[4] *Thomas,*[3] *John,*[2] *Thomas*[1]), born Assonet, Mass., February 16, 1823; died Chicago, Ill., July 20, 1893; married Cleveland, Ohio, April 2, 1845, by Rev. Cyrus L. Watson, to Lydia Anna Burton, daughter of Isaac and C. Lorinda (Lewis) Burton, of Cleveland, Ohio; born Malone, N.Y., February 17, 1827; resides 5617 Monroe avenue, Hyde Park, Ill. (1893).

Issue:

5003. i. FRANK LEWIS DOGGETT,[9] born Chicago, Ill., July 14, 1847; married Chicago, Ill., November 7, 1872, by Rev. Arthur Mitchell, to Elizabeth Mary Corwith, daughter of Nathan and Mary (Campbell) Corwith; born May 28, 1851; no issue; he died Chicago, Ill., October 14, 1876; she married 2d, October 2, 1883, M. D. Wells; resides Chicago, Ill.

5004. ii. RICHARD MATHER DOGGETT,[9] born Chicago, Ill., July 2, 1851; died Chicago, Ill., September 11, 1852.

5005. iii. CAROLINE WARD DOGGETT,[9] born Chicago, Ill., November 27, 1853; died Chicago, Ill., August 8, 1854.

5006. iv. FREDERIC STERLING DOGGETT,[9] born Chicago, Ill., March 1, 1856; married Kansas City, Mo., April 30, 1884, by Rev. Henry Hopkins, to Mrs. Alice Matteson, widow of Arthur Ogden Matteson, and daughter of George Newton and Elisabeth (Allport) Blossom; born Scriba, N.Y.; resides Kansas City, Mo.

5007. v. LEWIS CHITTENDEN DOGGETT,[9] born Chicago, Ill., October 5, 1858.

5008. vi. ROBERT WILLIAMS DOGGETT,[9] born Chicago, Ill., December 3, 1862; died Chicago, Ill., August 26, 1864.

Joseph B. Doggett removed to Chicago, and engaged in business as a broker. Mr. Doggett was one of the trustees mentioned in the act of incorporation of the Hahnemann College, in Chicago, in 1855.

4271. Rev. THOMAS DOGGETT [8] (*Elkanah,*[7] *Thomas,*[6] *Simeon,*[5] *Thomas,*[4] *Thomas,*[3] *John,*[2] *Thomas*[1]), born Assonet, Mass., November 15, 1827; resides (1892) Bryan, Ohio; married Andover, Mass., September 28, 1853, by Rev. Prof. Elijah P. Barrows, to Frances Lee Barrows, daughter of Rev. Prof. Elijah Porter and Sarah Maria (Lee) Barrows, of Andover, Mass.; born Hartford, Conn., May 24, 1831.

Issue:

5009. i. WILLIAM ELKANAH DOGGETT,[9] born Madison, Wis., March 17, 1855.

5010. ii. CHARLES STEBBINS DOGGETT,[9] born Groveland, Mass., Nov. 27, 1858.

5011. iii. ALLEN BARROWS DOGGETT,[9] born Groveland, Mass., June 18, 1860.

5012. iv. FRANCES MARIA DOGGETT,[9] born Niagara Falls, N.Y., Jan. 15, 1866.

5013. v. ANNA BURTON DOGGETT,[9] born Niagara Falls, N.Y., Sept. 18, 1870.

Rev. Thomas Doggett was baptized in infancy, and united with the First Congregational Church of Cleveland, Ohio, in 1843.

Mr. Doggett graduated at Western Reserve College in 1848, and at

Western Reserve Theological Seminary in 1852. He was licensed by the Portage Presbytery, Ohio, September 3, 1850, and was ordained at Groveland, Mass., as colleague with Rev. Dr. Perry, March 4, 1857 ; dismissed April 20, 1864, to accept a call from the Presbyterian Church at Niagara Falls, N.Y., where he was installed by the Presbytery of Niagara, July 20, 1864.

4274. PHŒBE DOGGETT SAMPSON [8] (*Phœbe D. Doggett,*[7] *Thomas,*[6] *Simeon,*[5] *Thomas,*[4] *Thomas,*[3] *John,*[2] *Thomas* [1]), born Lakeville, Mass., March 5, 1824 ; resides Lakeville, Mass. ; married Lakeville, Mass., Sept. 16, 1845, Frederic Leonard ; died Lakeville, Mass., Aug. 4, 1869.
Issue :

5014. i.   SALLIE MURDOCK LEONARD,[9] born Lakeville, Mass., July 13, 1846; married Jackson, Mich., March 18, 1875, Frederic J. Brown, of New Baltimore, Mich.; no issue; resides New Baltimore, Mich. (1890).
5015. ii.   HORACE FREDERIC LEONARD,[9] born Lakeville, Mass., May 26, 1848.
5016. iii.   MARY SAMPSON LEONARD,[9] born Lakeville, Mass., July 27, 1851.
5017. iv.   FRANK HERBERT LEONARD,[9] born Lakeville, Mass., October 16, 1852; married Iowa, November, 1873.
5018. v.   LLOYD OAKES LEONARD,[9] born Lakeville, Mass., January 16, 1854 ; resides Lakeville, Mass.
5019. vi.   LOUISA MARIA LEONARD,[9] born Lakeville, Mass., December 2, 1858; died Lakeville, Mass., October 9, 1863.
5020. vii.   CHARLES LEONARD,[9] born Lakeville, Mass., January 10, 1860; married three times.
5021. viii.   FANNIE BELLE LEONARD,[9] born Lakeville, Mass., May 30, 1861.
5022. ix.   EVELINE LEONARD,[9] born Lakeville, Mass., May 29, 1863; married New Bedford, Mass., May 28, 1885, Elbert E. Winslow, of Freetown, Mass. ; resides Freetown, Mass. (1890).
5023. x.   LIZZIE MARIA LEONARD,[9] born Lakeville, Mass., July 6, 1866; resides Lakeville, Mass.

4277. FRANCIS EARL SAMPSON [8] (*Phœbe D. Doggett,*[7] *Thomas,*[6] *Simeon,*[5] *Thomas,*[4] *Thomas,*[3] *John,*[2] *Thomas* [1]), born Lakeville, Mass., January 22, 1832 ; resides (1890) Lakeville, Mass. ; married Lowell, Mass., August 30, 1865, Emma Peary, of Lowell, Mass.
Issue :

5024. i.   BERTHA MAY SAMPSON,[9] born Lakeville, Mass., August 29, 1866; resides there.

4278. EVELINE LEONARD SAMPSON [8] (*Phœbe D. Doggett,*[7] *Thomas,*[6] *Simeon,*[5] *Thomas,*[4] *Thomas,*[3] *John,*[2] *Thomas* [1]), born Lakeville, Mass., February 2, 1835 ; resides (1890) New Baltimore, Mich. ; married Saline, Mich., Aug. 15, 1859, James S. P. Hatheway, of New Baltimore, Mich. ; died New Baltimore, Mich., Jan. 12, 1887.
Issue :

5025. i.   MABEL GILBERT HATHEWAY,[9] born New Baltimore, Mich., May 3, 1860; married Detroit, Mich., December 27, 1880, Oren Dunham, of Paw Paw, Mich.; she died Paw Paw, Mich., March 24, 1881; he resides Summerdale, Ill. (1890).

4282. ARISTIDES DOGGETT [8] (*John L.,*[7] *Simeon,*[6] *Simeon,*[5] *Thomas,*[4] *Thomas,*[3] *John,*[2] *Thomas* [1]), born Jacksonville, Fla., July

30, 1830; died Jacksonville, Fla., April 29, 1890; married Lake City, Fla., February, 1865, Mrs. Anna Timothy Howe, widow of Colonel Howe, and daughter of John Clifton and Maria (Holland) Cleland; born Montigua Bay, Isle of Jamaica, June 26, 1823; resides Jacksonville, Fla. (1890).

Issue:

5026. i. JOHN LOCKE DOGGETT,[9] born Jacksonville, Fla., March 14, 1868; "lawyer and clerk of the Criminal Court of Record, Duval county;" married Jacksonville, Fla., June 10, 1890, by Rev. Frederick Pasco, to Carrie May Van Deman, daughter of Erskine Burton and Louisa (Forster) Van Deman; born Washington Court House, Ohio, June 20, 1870; resides Jacksonville, Fla. (1890).

" As the faint rays of a beautiful dawn began to struggle through the twilight of July 30, 1830, Aristides Doggett was sent into the world to do his part, have his share, and participate in the rush and hum of the world's onward march.

" Jacksonville was at that period in its infancy (there being only a dozen houses), and his father, Judge John Locke Doggett, having but little means at his disposal, sent him to the little school where now stands the courthouse of Duval county.

" Getting there what might be termed an elementary education, he was placed under a private tutor who fitted him for college. He then went first to Bridgewater, Mass., and thence to Peoria, Ill., but before he finished this college education he was called home by the death of his father.

" About this time (his age being seventeen years), recruits were being sent to Mexico, and he, having the aspirations that so frequently are found embedded in the hearts of youths of his age, enlisted in the regiment that was sent from this portion of Florida (having to stand on his tiptoes to reach the required height, five feet two inches, at the muster).

" Serving all through the war with Mexico, he witnessed the blood streaming down the gory hills of Chapultepec, and took an active part in the fierce struggles of Vera Cruz, Resaca, Molina del Rey, and finally in the capture of the City of Mexico.

" He returned home, youth as he was, styled by the soldiers ' Baby Brave,' and with the chevrons of a sergeant implanted on his arm.

" He became clerk of the United States Circuit Court shortly after, and studied law in the office of Hon. Philip Frazier, late judge of that court.

" He was admitted to practice law in 1857. He was appointed inspector and deputy collector of customs at the port of St. Johns, which office he held for several years.

" But now the cannons of civil strife were beginning to be heard, and a nation of brothers were very soon to crimson their nation's soil with fraternal blood.   His patriotic spirit again asserting itself, he was instrumental in raising a company of young men in the city of Jacksonville, and very shortly becoming their captain he gave the command ' Forward,' and again launched out upon the bloody field of battle and distinction.   Then followed the baptisms of blood at Perry-ville, Vicksburg, Chickamauga, Murfreesborough, Missionary Ridge, Peach-tree creek, and Franklin, into all of which battles he led his command with that intrepid bravery and fortitude which characterized him through to the end of this civil strife.   The war being over, he returned home and again began the practice of law.   He held the several offices of alderman of the city of Jacksonville, county commis-sioner, city attorney, and judge of the Probate Court, all of which offices he retired from with the emblematic titles of truth, veracity, and honor stamped upon his name.

"But following the course of all flesh, like a weary child who falls asleep in its mother's arms he laid down the burden of life and passed away peacefully, just as the shadows of noon on April 29, 1890, were beginning to lengthen.   Being the soul of courtesy, fidelity, and trust, the announcement of his death was met with grief all over the State and in many places beyond its borders.   It ended a life that was heroic and good; full of chivalry and adventure, loyal and just, and in the folds of whose heart was implanted and embodied as its watchword that motto of a fulfilled destiny — ' Honor.' "

4284.   MARIA CATHARINE DOGGETT [8] (*John L.,*[7] *Simeon,*[6] *Simeon,*[5] *Thomas,*[4] *Thomas,*[3] *John,*[2] *Thomas* [1]), born Jacksonville, Fla., Oct. 12, 1840; died Jacksonville, Fla., Jan. 13, 1879; married Jackson-ville, Fla., April 25, 1871, by Rev. R. H. Weller, to Rev. Frederick Pasco, son of John and Amelia (Nash) Pasco; born Rustico, Prince Edward Island, May 4, 1844; resides Jacksonville, Fla. (1890).

Issue :

5027. i.   FREDERICK LOCKE PASCO,[9] born Jacksonville, Fla., February 2, 1872.
5028. ii. SAMUEL NASH PASCO,[9] born Jacksonville, Fla., August 4, 1874.
5029. iii. SIDNEY DOGGETT PASCO,[9] born Jacksonville, Fla., September 3, 1877; died Jacksonville, Fla., March 11, 1878.

Rev. Frederick Pasco graduated from Harvard College in the class of 1865.   He enlisted May 16, 1864, as private in the Twelfth Unattached Company Massachusetts Volunteer Infantry, and was mustered out August 15, 1864.

In February, 1867, he joined the Methodist Episcopal Church, in April, 1867, receiving a license to preach, and in September, 1867, joined the Illinois Conference of the Methodist Episcopal Church. He remained connected with the Illinois Conference until September, 1869, when he joined the Methodist Episcopal Church South and was ordained elder, having been ordained deacon while in Illinois.   He began preaching in Florida January, 1870, and is a member of the Florida Conference. He commenced teaching school in 1871, in connection with his ministerial duties, and continued to teach until 1874. At the conference in 1874, the term of his pastorate at Jacksonville having expired, he was appointed presiding elder of the Jacksonville District of the Methodist Episcopal Church South. Still resides in Jacksonville. Is a Master Mason and chaplain of Duval Lodge, No. 18, at Jacksonville. He has been superintendent of public instruction, Duval county, Fla., 1877–1880, and councilman of the city of Jacksonville, 1889.

4285. SAMUEL WALES DOGGETT[8] (*Samuel W.*,[7] *Simeon*,[6] *Simeon*,[5] *Thomas*,[4] *Thomas*,[3] *John*,[2] *Thomas*[1]), born Charleston, S.C., December 23, 1824; address (1891), 608 Sacramento street, San Francisco, Cal.; married Miss Sierra; born Illapel, Chili.

Issue:

5030. i. BOLIVAR DOGGETT,[9] born Diamond Springs, Eldorado Co., Cal., April 4, 1855.
5031. ii. DANTON C. DOGGETT,[9] born San Francisco, Cal., November 5, 1858.
5032. iii. SUMPTER E. DOGGETT,[9] born San Francisco, Cal., July 3, 1862.
5033. iv. GERTRUDE MARY DOGGETT,[9] born San Francisco, Cal., May 6, 1878.

" Samuel Wales Doggett was prepared for college in his native city. About the year 1837 he went to Massachusetts with his father and family, and resided at Mendon, Worcester county. He taught school in Raynham and Bridgewater, but returned to Charleston in 1844. In 1845 Mr. Doggett opened a first-class seminary in Jacksonville, studied law, and was admitted to practice before Judge McCray, of the Circuit Court of Florida. In 1847 he ran for the clerkship of the Circuit Court for Duval county on the Democratic ticket, but was beaten by his Whig opponent, Oscar Hart (afterward governor of the State), in consequence of some irregularity in the election returns, and, pending a *quo-warranto* contest on appeal to the Supreme Court at Tallahassee, he went to New Orleans, La., where he was connected with the Public School Department of the Third Municipality of that city for nearly three years, when he resigned, and emigrated to California in the spring of 1850.

" Engaging in various mining enterprises in Eldorado county, as well as practising his profession there, he so continued until 1856, when he removed to San Francisco, where he was similarly engaged until the breaking out of the civil war. He declined to take the oath required by the legislation of that time, as it was entirely contrary to his ideas, but chose rather to retire from court practice, and take up office and Spanish law, loans, sales, and general negotiations in lands and land titles. Although Mr. Doggett never graduated from any college, he was deemed a better classical and English scholar at eighteen than most of the great army of alumni, and he well merited the favorable criticism of the friends of his youth in the matter of scholarship. In 1864 he was unanimously elected secretary of the Board of Education of the city and county of San Francisco, a position which he did not solicit, and from which he resigned after serving a brief term."

In writing of his sons, Mr. Doggett says, "They have proved themselves to be upright, industrious, temperate, trustworthy and brave, filially loyal to an exceptional degree, endowed with vigorous constitutions, mental and physical, and of striking personal appearance;" and of their mother that "She is a woman of sterling worth, possessing the peculiar beauty to be found only among Spanish-American women, of a poetical temperament, slightly tinged with melancholy, and a manifest representative of the haughty land of her birth."

4286. JULIA HARRIET DOGGETT [8] (*Samuel W.*,[7] *Simeon*,[6] *Simeon*,[5] *Thomas*,[4] *Thomas*,[3] *John*,[2] *Thomas*[1]), born Charleston, S.C., January 13, 1827; resides (1890) West Swanzey, N.H.; married Milford, Mass., July 4, 1849, by Rev. Adin Ballou, to Benjamin S. Wheeler, of Templeton, son of Russell and Irena (Boyce) Wheeler; born Royalston, Mass., April 23, 1826.

Issue:

5034. i.   SAMUEL B. WHEELER,[9] born Northumberland, N.Y., August 5, 1850; married Winchendon, Mass., April 18, 1878, by Rev. C. Hanaford, to Emogene Bickford, daughter of Walter and Abigail (Phillips) Bickford; born Gardner, Mass., December 19, 1854; resides Winchendon, Mass. (1890).

5035. ii. HARRIET ALICE WHEELER,[9] born Royalston, Mass., December 7, 1851; died Fitzwilliam, N.H., December 27, 1861.

5036. iii. CLARENCE EDWARD WHEELER,[9] born Royalston, Mass., February 19, 1857; married South Royalston, Mass., May 1, 1879, by Rev. C. L. Tomblin, to Amelia Isora Day, daughter of David Walker and Amanda Elvira (Wheeler) Day; born Winchendon, Mass., November 5, 1856; resides South Royalston, Mass. (1890).

5037. iv. HARRY ARTHUR WHEELER,[9] born Fitzwilliam, N.H., August 30, 1861.

5038. v.   FRANCIS EUGENE WHEELER,[9] born Fitzwilliam, N.H., July 28, 1864; resides West Swanzey, N.H. (1890).

4287. SIMEON LOCKE DOGGETT [8] (*Samuel W.*,[7] *Simeon*,[6] *Simeon*,[5] *Thomas*,[4] *Thomas*,[3] *John*,[2] *Thomas*[1]), born Charleston, S.C., March 29, 1829; resides (1893) Manchester, Ia.; married Dubuque, Ia., July 15, 1857, by Rev. Mr. Griffith, to Mary Ann White, daughter of Moses and Roxanna (Newton) White; born Walpole, Mass., August 4, 1830.

Issue:

5039. i.   WALTER WOTTON DOGGETT,[9] born Manchester, Ia., January 1, 1861; died Manchester, Ia., November 13, 1862.

5040. ii. LAURENCE LOCKE DOGGETT,[9] born Manchester, Ia., Dec. 22, 1865; Ohio State Secretary Y.M.C.A.; resides Cleveland, Ohio (1893).

5041. iii. MARY LIZZEE DOGGETT,[9] born Manchester, Ia., December 22, 1865; graduated New England Conservatory of Music, 1893.

Simeon L. Doggett is a lawyer; has been a justice. He and his wife were early settlers of Manchester, and its intellectual and social growth owes much to them.

4288. MALVINA CAMPBELL DOGGETT [8] (*Samuel W.,[7] Simeon,[6] Simeon,[5] Thomas,[4] Thomas,[3] John,[2] Thomas[1]*), born Charleston, S.C., April 12, 1831; resides (1893) Winchendon, Mass.; married Mendon, Mass., October 8, 1856, by Rev. Elijah Demond, to Oren S. Hale, son of Nathaniel W. and Sarah (Guy) Hale; born Winchendon, Mass., October 22, 1829; died Winchendon, Mass., February, 1893.

Issue:

5042. i. ROSE DOGGETT HALE,[9] born Winchendon, Mass., May 29, 1858; died Winchendon, Mass., September 20, 1858.
5043. ii. GERTRUDE HARRIET HALE,[9] born Winchendon, Mass., June 13, 1864.

4289. THEOPHILUS MELANCTHON DOGGETT [8] (*Samuel W.,[7] Simeon,[6] Simeon,[5] Thomas,[4] Thomas,[3] John,[2] Thomas[1]*), born Charleston, S.C., Aug. 28, 1833; died Shiloh, April 6, 1862; married Pawtucket, R.I., July 2, 1860, by Rev. Joseph Thayer, to Sarah Elizabeth Nelson, daughter of Samuel and Lavinia (Thayer) Nelson, of Milford, Mass.; born Mendon, Mass., 1841; died Boston, Mass., July 26, 1881.

Issue:

5044. i. HARRIET WOTTON DOGGETT,[9] born Chicago, Ill., May 2, 1861; died Chicago, Ill., August 2, 1861.

Lieut. Theophilus Melancthon Doggett was a lawyer in Chicago. He was killed in the service of his country at the battle of Shiloh, as lieutenant in the Fifty-seventh Illinois Volunteers.

4290. NARCISSA NEWTON DOGGETT [8] (*Samuel W.,[7] Simeon,[6] Simeon,[5] Thomas,[4] Thomas,[3] John,[2] Thomas[1]*), born Charleston, S.C., March 28, 1836; resides (1892) Shelton, Buffalo Co., Neb.; married Milford, Mass., October 9, 1852, by Rev. Lyman Maynard, to William G. Carleton, of Mendon, Mass., son of Franklin and Mary C. Carleton; born Derby, Vt., 1829; died ——.

Issue:

5045. i. EVA CARLETON.[9]
5046. ii. ELLA CARLETON,[9] married William M. Allister; resides 174 Forty-seventh street, Chicago, Ill. (1892).
5047. iii. GEORGE CARLETON.[9] resides Shelton, Neb. (1892).
5048. iv. ANNA CARLETON.[9]
5049. v. IDA CARLETON.[9]
5050. vi. FRANK CARLETON.[9]
5051. vii. CHARLES CARLETON.[9]

4291. WILLIAM ALFRED DOGGETT [8] (*Samuel W.,*[7] *Simeon,*[6] *Simeon,*[5] *Thomas,*[4] *Thomas,*[3] *John,*[2] *Thomas* [1]), born Mendon, Mass., Feb. 9, 1839; resides (1892) Lincoln, Neb. ; married Emma ——.

Issue :

5052. i. DOUGLAS D. DOGGETT,[9] married; resides Chicago, Ill. (1892).

4292. GERTRUDE GLORVINA DOGGETT [8] (*Samuel W.,*[7] *Simeon,*[6] *Simeon,*[5] *Thomas,*[4] *Thomas,*[3] *John,*[2] *Thomas* [1]), born Mendon, Mass., May 20, 1841; resides (1892) 1822 Sacramento street, San Francisco, Cal.; married Chicago, Ill., May 27, 1867, by Rev. Robert Collyer, to Benjamin Franklin Norris, son of Josiah and Lois (Colton) Norris, of Ann Arbor, Mich. ; born Ann Arbor, Mich., January 10, 1836.

Issue :

5053. i. GRACE COLTON NORRIS,[9] born Chicago, Ill., December 28, 1868; died Chicago, Ill., April 20, 1869.
5054. ii. BENJAMIN FRANKLIN NORRIS,[9] born Chicago, Ill., March 5, 1870; author of " Yvernelle," published by Lippincott, Philadelphia (1892).
5055. iii. FLORENCE COLTON NORRIS,[9] born Chicago, Ill., September 11, 1871; died Chicago, Ill., September 9, 1872.
5056. iv. ALBERT LESTER NORRIS,[9] born Chicago, Ill., April 29, 1877; died San Francisco, Cal., January 18, 1887.
5057. v. CHARLES GILMAN NORRIS,[9] born Chicago, Ill., April 23, 1881.

Miss Gertrude Glorvina Doggett made her début at McVicker's theatre, in Chicago, in the character of Elvira, in Pizarro, and subsequently in Shakespearean characters at the same theatre.

She was received with great favor, and many regrets were expressed by the public when she retired into domestic bliss, as wife of B. F. Norris, Esq.

The Chicago papers, speaking of her début, say :

It may be beside the fact to say that she quite exceeded the expectations of her friends, for apparently much was expected of her by those to whom her abilities were previously known. But she fairly took by surprise the audience at large (and a very large audience it was), who had come, perhaps, with a kind of pitying encouragement in their thoughts for a novice in the dramatic art, who might probably be seized with a stage fright at the first glare of the footlights.

The young artist who made her début soon showed that she stood in need of no such encouragement. From her very first entrance all through the succeeding scene in the somewhat arduous assumption she had chosen, Miss Doggett manifested a degree of self-possession which at once set at rest any fear of failure, and stamped her as a thorough artiste. Miss Doggett's entree was the signal for a unanimous, cordial burst of applause. Her form is singularly graceful and dignified, and recalls somewhat of Helen Faucitt to whom Miss Doggett bears no very remote resemblance.

Her countenance and the tones of her voice are indicative of deep and fine sensibilities, and admirably qualified to express either sentimental feeling or tragic passion. She was dressed in a rich crimson velvet robe over white silk, and trimmed with gold lace and fringe. and wore on her head a coronet of velvet and gold.

Her rendition of " Elvira " evinced, besides a natural adaptedness to the part, much careful study, and a correct conception of the character.

Her reading is particularly fine, and she has asserted herself as an artiste of no ordinary promise, of no ordinary talent. It would be but due to a young debutante to treat with leniency, even if she fell below the mark. Miss Doggett's acting, however, will be found to bear a strict critical examination.

Her merits are great; her shortcomings are those which it would be unjust not to expect and make allowances for. In some of her situations last night there was a want of freedom in her movements, and occasionally she failed to do full justice to her excellent voice. These are drawbacks which could not well be avoided. We cordially indorse the sentiments of the audience, which induced them to call her three times before the curtain, and predict for her a distinguished career.

Mr. and Mrs. Norris resided at the corner of Michigan avenue and Park row in Chicago, from whence they removed to San Francisco. In 1887 their son Albert Lester died in San Francisco, and as a tribute to his memory the "Lester Norris Memorial Kindergarten School," of that city, has been endowed by his parents.

4294. CHARLES SEYMOUR DOGGETT [8] (*Perez F.,*[7] *Simeon,*[6] *Simeon,*[5] *Thomas,*[4] *Thomas,*[3] *John,*[2] *Thomas*[1]), born Wareham, Mass., March 9, 1836; resides (1893) Walpole, Mass.; married Utica, N.Y., June 19, 1861, by Rev. Dr. A. B. Goodrich, to Margareta Bowers Hall, daughter of James B. and Elizabeth B. (Cooper) Hall; born Middletown, Conn., June 21, 1834.

Issue:

5058. i. ROBERT SEDLEY DOGGETT,[9] born Auburn, N.Y., October 3, 1863; died Utica, N.Y., May 19, 1869.
5059. ii. ELIZABETH COOPER DOGGETT,[9] born Utica, N.Y., October 12, 1865; died Utica, N.Y., March 29, 1866.
5060. iii. WALTON HALL DOGGETT,[9] born Utica, N.Y., August 29, 1867; "Episcopal clergyman;" resides Green River, Wyoming (1893).

Charles S. Doggett was for fifteen years a woollen manufacturer, later a farmer, at present retired.

4295. WILLIAM SEDLEY DOGGETT [8] (*Perez F.,*[7] *Simeon,*[6] *Simeon,*[5] *Thomas,*[4] *Thomas,*[3] *John,*[2] *Thomas*[1]), born Wareham, Mass., November 9, 1837; resides (1893) Clinton, Mass.; married Auburn, N.Y., June 21, 1866, Frances Pomeroy Willson, daughter of Harvey and Fanny (Pomeroy) Willson; born Auburn, N.Y., July 5, 1842.

Issue:

5061. i. LUCY FEARING DOGGETT,[9] born Auburn, N.Y., August 7, 1867.
5062. ii. ANNA FRANCES DOGGETT,[9] born Warren, N.H., May 3, 1871.
5063. iii. AMY WILLSON DOGGETT,[9] born Clinton, Mass., August 31, 1884.

William Sedley Doggett was in business on Milk street, Boston, in 1857, 1858, and 1859, since then engaged in the dry-goods business in Clinton.

4298. Dr. FREDERIC FOBES DOGGETT [8] (*Theophilus P.,*[7] *Simeon,*[6] *Simeon,*[5] *Thomas,*[4] *Thomas,*[3] *John,*[2] *Thomas*[1]), born Barnstable, Mass., February 22, 1855; "physician;" resides 805 East Broadway, South Boston, Mass. (1893) ; married Dartmouth, N.S., July 7, 1880, Mary Chipman DeWolf, daughter of Thomas Leonard and Amelia (Allison) DeWolf; born Cambridge, Mass., February 28, 1855.

Issue :

5064. i. ELIZABETH DEWOLF DOGGETT,[9] born Boston, Mass., Oct. 29, 1882.
5065. ii. ARTHUR LATHAM DOGGETT,[9] born Boston, Mass., November 8, 1884.
5066. iii. ELLEN DOGGETT,[9] born Boston, Mass., December 3, 1885; died Boston, Mass., January 20, 1886.
5067. iv. LEONARD ALLISON DOGGETT,[9] born Boston, Mass., November 10, 1888.

Dr. Doggett is a graduate of Harvard College and Harvard Medical School, and has also studied his profession in Germany.

4312. HARRIET WESTON [8] (*Henry*,[7] *Abigail Doggett*,[6] *Simeon*,[5] *Thomas*,[4] *Thomas*,[3] *John*,[2] *Thomas* [1]), born Rochester, N.Y., 1843; resides 2893 Delmar avenue, St. Louis, Mo. (1885) ; married Middleboro', Mass., December 12, 1865, by Rev. L. A. Abbott, to Fred A. Leonard, son of Thomas Nelson and Betsey (Wood) Leonard; born Middleboro', Mass., 1840.

Issue :

5068. i. FREDERIC WARD LEONARD,[9] born St. Joseph, Mo., June 17, 1867.
5069. ii. LUCY DOGGETT LEONARD,[9] born St. Joseph, Mo., May 30, 1872.
5070. iii. HARRY WESTON LEONARD,[9] born Middleboro', Mass., April 8, 1874.
5071. iv. GRACE LEONARD,[9] born St. Louis, Mo., April 1, 1882.

4315. EMMA WILLARD BRAINARD [8] (*Nathan H. Doggett*,[7] *Joseph*,[6] *Joseph*,[5] *Noah*,[4] *Samuel*,[3] *Samuel*,[2] *Thomas* [1]), born South Boston, Mass., August 1, 1839 ; died Yonkers, N.Y., July 6, 1876; married South Boston, Mass., January 1, 1868, Samuel S. Hepworth.

Issue :

5072. i. ADA HEPWORTH.[9]
5073. ii. GERTRUDE HEPWORTH.[9]

4326. FLORENCE BRAINARD [8] (*Amos H. Doggett*,[7] *Joseph*,[6] *Joseph*,[5] *Noah*,[4] *Samuel*,[3] *Samuel*,[2] *Thomas* [1]), born Brookline, Mass., April 22, 1849; address, 47 Temple place, Boston, Mass. (1893) ; married Hyde Park, Mass., October 28, 1867, George Dudley Thayer, son of Isaiah Warren and Ann Elizabeth (Dudley) Thayer; born Roxbury, Mass., 1845.

Issue :

5074. i. LILA GENEVIEVE THAYER,[9] born 1870.
5075. ii. HARRY BRAINARD THAYER,[9] born 1872.

Mr. Thayer is of the firm of Thayer, McNeil & Hodgkins, Temple place, Boston.

4328. JOSEPHINE BRAINARD [8] (*Amos H. Doggett*,[7] *Joseph*,[6] *Joseph*,[5] *Noah*,[4] *Samuel*,[3] *Samuel*,[2] *Thomas* [1]), born Boston, Mass., August

7, 1855; resides Hyde Park, Mass. (1893); married Hyde Park, Mass., June 20, 1878, Randolph Perrault Moseley, son of Thomas William Henry Harrison and Mary (Beckner) Moseley; born Columbus, Ohio, 1842.

Issue:

5076. i. ROBERT BRAINARD MOSELEY,[9] born Hyde Park, Mass., 1880.
5077. ii. EDNAH ELIZABETH MOSELEY,[9] born Nashua, N.H., 1883.

4329. EDITH ISABEL BRAINARD [8] (*Amos H. Doggett,*[7] *Joseph,*[6] *Joseph,*[5] *Noah,*[4] *Samuel,*[3] *Samuel,*[2] *Thomas*[1]), born Boston, Mass., May 7, 1857; resides Hyde Park, Mass. (1893); married Hyde Park, Mass., December 16, 1885, by Rev. John T. Magrath, to John Lincoln Barry, Jr., son of John Lincoln and Frances Augusta (Hearsey) Barry; born Boston, Mass., 1862.

Issue:

5078. i. CONSTANCE BARRY,[9] born Hyde Park, Mass., 1886; died ——.
5079. ii. MARGARET LINCOLN BARRY,[9] born Hyde Park, Mass., 1888.
5080. iii. JOHN LINCOLN BARRY,[9] born Hyde Park, Mass., 1890.

Mr. Barry is of the firm of Barry & Keyes, shoe manufacturers' goods, 44 High street, Boston.

4331. EDNAH ELIZABETH BRAINARD [8] (*Amos H. Doggett,*[7] *Joseph,*[6] *Joseph,*[5] *Noah,*[4] *Samuel,*[3] *Samuel,*[2] *Thomas*[1]), born Hyde Park, Mass., January 7, 1861; died Montreal, Can., May 29, 1892; married Hyde Park, Mass., September 22, 1885, by Rev. J. T. Magrath, to Ebenezer McAdam, son of James and Elizabeth (Robertson) McAdam; born Montreal, Can.; resides Montreal, Can. (1893).

Issue:

5081. i. LINDA McADAM,[9] born Montreal, Can., 1888.
5082. ii. EDITH GENEVIEVE McADAM,[9] born Montreal, Can., 1892.

4332. IDA AUGUSTA BRAINARD [8] (*Amos H. Doggett,*[7] *Joseph,*[6] *Joseph,*[5] *Noah,*[4] *Samuel,*[3] *Samuel,*[2] *Thomas*[1]), born Hyde Park, Mass., October 24, 1865; resides Hyde Park, Mass. (1893); married Hyde Park, Mass., February 19, 1891, by Rev. W. J. Harris, D.D., to Orsemus Stillman Hyde, son of Theophilus and Fanny Brown (Hazard) Hyde; born Stonington, Conn., 1851.

Issue:

5083. i. STILLMAN BRAINARD HYDE,[9] born Hyde Park, Mass., 1892.

Mr. Hyde is a wool broker, 19 High street, Boston.

4345. LOUISE VIOLA DAGGETT [8] (*George W.,*[7] *Henry,*[6] *Joseph,*[5] *Noah,*[4] *Samuel,*[3] *Samuel,*[2] *Thomas*[1]), born New Haven, N.Y., April 17, 1860; resides Demster, N.Y. (1893); married New Haven,

N.Y., December 25, 1879, Calvin Ellis Leavitt, son of Samuel and Jane (Kenyon) Leavitt; born Albion, N.Y., August 19, 1854.

Issue:

5084. i. WARREN ELLIS LEAVITT,[9] born New Haven, N.Y., Dec. 16, 1882.
5085. ii. GEORGE HOWARD LEAVITT,[9] born New Haven, N.Y., April 30, 1888.

4346. SARAH ADELAIDE DAGGETT[8] (*George W.*,[7] *Henry*,[6] *Joseph*,[5] *Noah*,[4] *Samuel*,[3] *Samuel*,[2] *Thomas*[1]), born New Haven, N.Y., July 15, 1862; resides Canton Centre, Conn. (1893); married New Haven, N.Y., June 16, 1891, Edward Mills Beckwith, son of Austin and Charlotte (Mills) Beckwith; born Canton Centre, Conn., June 26, 1867.

Issue:

5086. i. WILLIAM HALLOCK BECKWITH,[9] born Canton Centre, Conn., July 22, 1892.

4365. MARY ELIZA HATCH[8] (*Eliza Huntington*,[7] *John*,[6] *Bethiah Doggett*,[5] *Noah*,[4] *Samuel*,[3] *Samuel*,[2] *Thomas*[1]), born Perry, N.Y., January 16, 1832; resides St. Louis, Mo. (1883); married Belvidere, Ill., August 18, 1859, William H. Mixer; born Brantford, Can., August 18, 1837.

Issue:

5087. i. HELEN ISABEL MIXER,[9] born Burlington, Ia., September 24, 1861.
5088. ii. WILLIAM MIXER,[9] born Illinois. November 7, 1865; died Aurora, Ill., June 6, 1873.

4375. MARY SAREPTA COMINGS[8] (*Mary Huntington*,[7] *John*,[6] *Bethiah Doggett*,[5] *Noah*,[4] *Samuel*,[3] *Samuel*,[2] *Thomas*[1]), born Greensboro', Vt., October 12, 1844; resides Berkeley, Cal. (1883); married Oberlin, Ohio, July 31, 1871, Cornelius B. Bradley.

Issue:

5089. i. BERTHA T. BRADLEY,[9] born Bangkok, Siam, December 15, 1872.
5090. ii. HAROLD C. BRADLEY,[9] born Oakland, Cal., November 25, 1878.

Mr. Bradley is a missionary, now holding a position in the State University of California.

4377. GEORGE FISHER COMINGS[8] (*Mary Huntington*,[7] *John*,[6] *Bethiah Doggett*,[5] *Noah*,[4] *Samuel*,[3] *Samuel*,[2] *Thomas*[1]), born Greensboro', Vt., March 18, 1849; "fruit-raiser;" resides St. Joseph, Mich. (1883); married Barre, Vt., Oct. 12, 1874, Emma F. Currier.

Issue:

5091. i. MARY HUNTINGTON COMINGS,[9] born St. Joseph, Mich., Sept. 3, 1877.
5092. ii. ALICE TENNEY COMINGS,[9] born St. Joseph, Mich., November 23, 1879.
5093. iii. ELLEN COPELAND COMINGS,[9] born St. Joseph, Mich., October 29, 1881.
5094. iv. BENJAMIN HUNTINGTON COMINGS,[9] born St. Joseph, Mich., April 7, 1883.

4378. ABBIE FRANCES COMINGS[8] (*Mary Huntington*,[7] *John*,[6] *Bethiah Doggett*,[5] *Noah*,[4] *Samuel*,[3] *Samuel*,[2] *Thomas*[1]), born Greensboro', Vt., April 9, 1851 ; resides 446 Maria avenue, St. Paul, Minn. (1883) ; married Des Moines, Ia., July 6, 1876, Charles D. Parker; " freight agent Traders Despatch."

Issue :

5095. i. ISABELLE PARKER,[9] born Chicago, Ill., May 13, 1877.
5096. ii. EDWARD CARY PARKER,[9] born St. Paul, Minn., August 4, 1881.

4391. MARY AUGUSTA SMITH[8] (*Martha Huntington,*[7] *John,*[6] *Bethiah Doggett,*[5] *Noah,*[4] *Samuel,*[3] *Samuel,*[2] *Thomas*[1]), born East Boston, Mass., September 21, 1851 ; resides Fort Valley, Ga. (1891) ; married Winchester, N.H., February 15, 1873, by Rev. Mr. Foster, to Alfred Sabin Martin, son of ———— and Mary (Gould) Martin ; born Springfield, Vt., December 5, 1850.

Issue :

5097. i. NOEL MARTIN,[9] born Hinsdale, N.H., September 18, 1875.
5098. ii. CHARLES HUNTINGTON MARTIN,[9] born Hinsdale, N.H., March 2, 1878.
5099. iii. HARRY SABIN MARTIN,[9] born Hinsdale, N.H., August 6, 1881; died Eufaula, Ala., August 15, 1883.
5100. iv. ROLAND MARTIN,[9] born Fort Valley, Ga., October 8, 1887.

4399. JOHN BRAY COOK[8] (*Caroline Huntington,*[7] *Henry,*[6] *Bethiah Doggett,*[5] *Noah,*[4] *Samuel,*[3] *Samuel,*[2] *Thomas*[1]), born Greensboro', Vt., July 4, 1836 ; resides Greensboro', Vt. (1883) ; married Sioux City, Ia., November 14, 1865, Katherine Kallmyer; born Pensacola, Fla., October 23, 1846.

Issue :

5101. i. ANNA C. COOK,[9] born September 25, 1866.
5102. ii. CHARLES B. COOK,[9] born January 25, 1868.
5103. iii. GEORGE S. COOK,[9] born September 14, 1877.

4413. GEORGE WEEKS HALE[8] (*Betsey Huntington,*[7] *Henry,*[6] *Bethiah Doggett,*[5] *Noah,*[4] *Samuel,*[3] *Samuel,*[2] *Thomas*[1]), born Greensboro', Vt., December 5, 1838; died Cedar Rapids, Ia., August 26, 1875 ; married Cedar Rapids. Ia.. April 4, 1865, Amanda McDowell.

Issue :

5104. i. CARRIE HALE,[9] born Cedar Rapids, Ia., January 6, 1866.
5105. ii. ADELA HALE,[9] born Cedar Rapids, Ia., February 20, 1872.
5106. iii. MARY EMMA HALE,[9] born Cedar Rapids, Ia. ; died in infancy.

4416. JOHN P. HALE[8] (*Betsey Huntington,*[7] *Henry,*[6] *Bethiah Doggett,*[5] *Noah,*[4] *Samuel,*[3] *Samuel,*[2] *Thomas*[1]), born Greensboro', Vt., August 27, 1848; married Cedar Rapids, Ia., December 23, 1869, Lucy Berry.

Issue :

5107. i. EDWARD J. HALE,[9] born Cedar Rapids, Ia., February 10, 1871.
5108. ii. LIDA HALE,[9] born Cedar Rapids, Ia., January 14, 1874.
5109. iii. CHARLES HALE,[9] born Cedar Rapids, Ia., December 5, 1878.

4428. HENRY D. HUNTINGTON [8] (*Henry,*[7] *Henry,*[6] *Bethiah Doggett,*[5] *Noah,*[4] *Samuel,*[3] *Samuel,*[2] *Thomas*[1]), born Craftsbury, Vt., July 16, 1850; resides (1883) Fort Custer, Mont.; married Des Moines, Ia., January 16, 1877, Jennie M. McKay.

Issue:

5110. i. CHARLES M. HUNTINGTON,[9] born Des Moines, Ia., February 7, 1882.

Henry D. Huntington graduated West Point, 1874.

4440. ANNA HUNTINGTON WRIGHT [8] (*Noah D.,*[7] *Sophia Huntington,*[6] *Bethiah Doggett,*[5] *Noah,*[4] *Samuel,*[3] *Samuel,*[2] *Thomas*[1]), born June 12, 1846; resides Covington, Ky. (1890); married April 15, 1869, Nathan L. Young; "grocer."

Issue:

5111. i. KATE YOUNG,[9] born February 17, 1870.
5112. ii. HELEN SANTMYER YOUNG,[9] born June 10, 1872.
5113. iii. JAMES LEBINS YOUNG,[9] born May 30, 1875.

4441. HELEN MARIA WRIGHT [8] (*Noah D.,*[7] *Sophia Huntington,*[6] *Bethiah Doggett,*[5] *Noah,*[4] *Samuel,*[3] *Samuel,*[2] *Thomas*[1]), born June 26, 1848; resides Carthage, Ohio (1890); married December 10, 1868, Capt. Charles A. Santmyer, son of Joseph Santmyer.

Issue:

5114. i. JOSEPH WRIGHT SANTMYER,[9] born May 8, 1870.
5115. ii. JESSIE SANTMYER,[9] born January 8, 1876.
5116. iii. HELEN SANTMYER,[9] born September 24, 1877.
5117. iv. LOUISE SANTMYER,[9] born December 27, 1879.
5118. v. HAIDEE SANTMYER,[9] born January 2, 1882.
5119. vi. REUBEN SANTMYER,[9] born June 8, 1883.
5120. vii. RUTH SANTMYER,[9] died 1890.

4444. VIRGINIA IRENE WRIGHT [8] (*Noah D.,*[7] *Sophia Huntington,*[6] *Bethiah Doggett,*[5] *Noah,*[4] *Samuel,*[3] *Samuel,*[2] *Thomas*[1]), born May 28, 1855; resides Carthage, Ohio (1890); married June 30, 1880, George H. Hutton.

Issue:

5121. i. HARRY HUTTON,[9] born July 24, 1881.

4449. Dr. ABIEL LORD WRIGHT [8] (*Thomas L.,*[7] *Sophia Huntington,*[6] *Bethiah Doggett,*[5] *Noah,*[4] *Samuel,*[3] *Samuel,*[2] *Thomas*[1]), born Bellefontaine, Ohio, April 3, 1847; resides Bellefontaine, Ohio (1890); married Bellefontaine, Ohio, March 4, 1869, Clara Gregg, daughter of Israel and Roxcy (Olds) Gregg; born Lithopolis, Ohio, Aug. 27, 1849.

Issue:

5122. i. THOMAS LEE WRIGHT,[9] born Bellefontaine, Ohio, November 29, 1869.
5123. ii. WILLIAM LORD WRIGHT,[9] born Bellefontaine, Ohio, Nov. 14, 1879.

Abiel L. Wright graduated in medicine from the Miami Medical College, of Cincinnati, but ill-health prevented him from active practice. He is reporter, land agent, and coroner for Logan county, Ohio.

4451. THOMAS WRIGHT PHILLIPS [8] (*Elizabeth A. Wright,*[7] *Sophia Huntington,*[6] *Bethiah Doggett,*[5] *Noah,*[4] *Samuel,*[3] *Samuel,*[2] *Thomas*[1]), born Ingleside, Ohio, February 6, 1854; resides Hinsdale, Ill. (1893); married Chicago, Ill., March 29, 1886, Sallie Jane Rae, daughter of Robert and Hattie (Coburn) Rae; born Chicago, Ill., Dec. 6, 1863.

Issue :

5124. i. ELIZABETH PHILLIPS,[9] born Chicago, Ill., April 6, 1887; died Chicago, Ill., April 8, 1887.
5125. ii. THOMAS WRIGHT PHILLIPS,[9] born Chicago, Ill., April 9, 1888.
5126. iii. MARIE ANGELITA PHILLIPS,[9] born Chicago, Ill., July 29, 1889.
5127. iv. PAUL PHILLIPS,[9] born Hinsdale, Ill., January 22, 1893; died Hinsdale, Ill., January 29, 1893.

4463. ECKLEN WILLIAMS [8] (*Sophia H. Wright,*[7] *Sophia Huntington,*[6] *Bethiah Doggett,*[5] *Noah,*[4] *Samuel,*[3] *Samuel,*[2] *Thomas*[1]), born Dearborn county, Ind., September 18, 1855; address, 141 Ridley street, San Francisco, Cal. (1891); married Cincinnati, Ohio, September 6, 1882, Delia McLaughlin, daughter of Patrick and Ann McLaughlin; born Quebec, Can., February 2, 1859.

Issue :

5128. i. ANNIE ESTELLA WILLIAMS,[9] born Cincinnati, Ohio, October 26, 1883.
5129. ii. ETHEL MAY WILLIAMS,[9] born Cincinnati, Ohio, May 9, 1887.

4473. MARGARET MARIE NELSON [8] (*Ann M. Doggett,*[7] *John R.,*[6] *Henry,*[5] *Noah,*[4] *Samuel,*[3] *Samuel,*[2] *Thomas*[1]), born Darien, Ga., May 30, 1858; resides Darien, Ga. (1881); married June 6, 1874, William H. Quigley, of Liverpool, Eng.; died April, 1877.

Issue :

5130. i. WILLIAM H. QUIGLEY,[9] born August, 1877.

4493. MARY ELIZABETH COLE [8] (*Charles D.,*[7] *Mary A. Doggett,*[6] *Noah,*[5] *Noah,*[4] *Samuel,*[3] *Samuel,*[2] *Thomas*[1]), born Boston, Mass., January 16, 1852; resides Highland ave., Cambridge, Mass. (1893); married Cambridgeport, Mass., February 26, 1880, by Rev. J. S. Hoyt, to William F. Hurter, son of William and Sophia Hartwell (Kimball) Hurter; born Mobile, Ala., February 19, 1849.

Issue :

5131. i. CHARLES COLE HURTER,[9] born Cambridgeport, Mass., November 30, 1880; died Cambridgeport, Mass., November 30, 1880.
5132. ii. ANNIE BELL HURTER,[9] born Cambridgeport, Mass., April 18, 1884.
5133. iii. CHARLES COLE HURTER,[9] born Cambridgeport, Mass., August 21, 1890.

4495. CHARLOTTE ADELAIDE WING [8] (*Elizabeth D. Cole,*[7] *Mary A. Doggett,*[6] *Noah,*[5] *Noah,*[4] *Samuel,*[3] *Samuel,*[2] *Thomas*[1]), born Albany, N.Y., December 15, 1858; resides 208 Jay street, Albany, N.Y. (1891); married Albany, N.Y., June 2, 1886, by Rev. S. T. Ford,

to Harry Carpenter Parsons, son of Seth Edward and Sarah Ann (Carpenter) Parsons; born Albany, N.Y., January 5, 1859.
Issue:

5134. i. CHARLES WING PARSONS,[9] born Albany, N.Y., June 3, 1887.
5135. ii. MARION BETTMAN PARSONS,[9] born Albany, N.Y., October 27, 1889.

4522. GERTRUDE REDFIELD PHELPS [8] (*Harriet M. Cone,*[7] *Wealthy Kingsbury,*[6] *Asenath Daggett,*[5] *Samuel,*[4] *John,*[3] *Samuel,*[2] *Thomas*[1]), born Hartford, Conn., March 4, 1845; resides Atlantic City, N.J. (1887); married June 22, 1871, Dr. William Boardman Reed.
Issue:

5136. i. HARMON PHELPS REED,[9] born Atlantic City, N.J., October 1, 1883.
5137. ii. HELEN FRANCES KINGSBURY REED,[9] born Atlantic City, N.J., February 4, 1887.

4525. MARY PRATT DAGGETT [5] (*William H. H.,*[7] *Isaiah,*[6] *Isaiah,*[5] *Samuel,*[4] *John,*[3] *Samuel,*[2] *Thomas*[1]), born Andover, Conn., January 25, 1846; resides (1890) South Windsor, Conn.; married Andover, Conn., December 26, 1867, by Rev. F. D. Avery, to J. Milton Elmore; born South Windsor, Conn., September 10, 1842; died South Windsor, Conn., February 18, 1885.
Issue:

5138. i. MARIETTE MALENCE ELMORE,[9] born South Windsor, Conn., November 24, 1868.
5139. ii. HATTIE GERTRUDE ELMORE,[9] born South Windsor, Conn., Aug. 24, 1873.
5140. iii. GRACE MAY ELMORE,[9] born South Windsor, Conn., December 1, 1882.

4526. GEORGE EDWIN DAGGETT [8] (*William H. H.,*[7] *Isaiah,*[6] *Isaiah,*[5] *Samuel,*[4] *John,*[3] *Samuel,*[2] *Thomas*[1]), born East Hartford, Conn., November 3, 1854; resides (1893) Stamford, Conn.; married Andover, Conn., June 20, 1877, by Rev. B. F. Chapman, to Ida Zitella Hutchinson, daughter of —— and Lydia Ann (Bill) Hutchinson (No. 3892); born Andover, Conn., January 24, 1852.
Issue:

5141. i. BESSIE ENGLISH DAGGETT,[9] born Willimantic, Conn., April 28, 1885.

4527. ESTHER PAMELIA DAGGETT [8] (*William H. H.,*[7] *Isaiah,*[6] *Isaiah,*[5] *Samuel,*[4] *John,*[3] *Samuel,*[2] *Thomas*[1]), born Andover, Conn., January 7, 1858; resides (1890) Hartford, Conn.; married Andover, Conn., November 18, 1874, by Rev. Mr. Smith, to Roscoe Bishop, son of Walter Bishop; born Andover, Conn., November, 1854; died Manchester, Conn., April 30, 1888.
Issue:

5142. i. ALONZO R. BISHOP,[9] born Andover, Conn., January 24, 1878.
5143. ii. NELLIE L. BISHOP,[9] born Andover, Conn., March 13, 1882.

4529. FRANK HENRY ENSIGN [8] (*Lucy H. A. Daggett,*[7] *Isaiah,*[6] *Isaiah,*[5] *Samuel,*[4] *John,*[3] *Samuel,*[2] *Thomas*[1]), born Hartford, Conn.,

April 7, 1852; died Hartford, Conn., 1886; married Kingston, N.Y., March 15, 1883, Katherine M. Smith; resides Kingston, N.Y. (1890).

Issue:

5144. i. HARRY SMITH ENSIGN,[9] born June 19, 1884.

4534. HENRY CALVIN DAGGETT[8] (*Samuel H.,*[7] *Samuel B.,*[6] *Isaiah,*[5] *Samuel,*[4] *John,*[3] *Samuel,*[2] *Thomas*[1]), born Andover, Conn., April 9, 1861; resides 240 View street, New Haven, Conn. (1893); married Andover, Conn., June 30, 1887, by Rev. B. F. Chapman, to Estella Maria Fleming, daughter of Elliot and Louisa Elizabeth (Newell) Fleming; born East Windsor, Conn., February 5, 1855.

Issue:

5145. i. HENRY ELLIOT DAGGETT,[9] born Andover, Conn., April 12, 1889.

4538. EZRA CHILSON[8] (*Milo,*[7] *Pamela Daggett,*[6] *John,*[5] *John,*[4] *John,*[3] *Samuel,*[2] *Thomas*[1]), born Girard, Pa., 1826; resides Amboy, Ohio (1893); married Fairview, Pa., 1853, Louisa Curtis, daughter of Myron and Elmira (Clemens) Curtis.

Issue:

5146. i. FRANK CHILSON,[9] born Fairview, Pa., January 11, 1855.
5147. ii. HATTIE CHILSON.[9]
5148. iii. JENNIE CHILSON,[9] born Girard, Pa., September 13, 1859.
5149. iv. EDWARD CHILSON.[9]
5150. v. HARRIE CHILSON.[9]
5151. vi. AGNES CHILSON.[9]
5152. vii. JOHN CHILSON.[9]

4548. MARIETTE CHILSON[8] (*Theron,*[7] *Pamela Daggett,*[6] *John,*[5] *John,*[4] *John,*[3] *Samuel,*[2] *Thomas*[1]), resides Dowagiac, Mich. (1893); married 1st, Mr. Hatfield; married 2d, Dowagiac, Mich., by Rev. Seward McKedsie, to Charles Larzelere, son of William Larzelere.

Issue:

5153. i. IDA SOPHIA HATFIELD,[9] born Niles, Mich., November 25, 1852; married Charles Hubbard; no issue; address, Dowagiac, Mich. (1893).
5154. ii. ELLA FRANCES HATFIELD,[9] born Niles, Mich., February 1, 1855.
5155. iii. CHARLES WESLEY HATFIELD,[9] born Niles, Mich., January 25, 1857; married Lista Simpson; resides Dowagiac, Mich. (1893); issue: Cecil Catherine Hatfield,[10] born 1887.
5156. iv. RICHARD WILSON LARZELERE,[9] born Dowagiac, Mich., Nov. 5, 1874.

4553. WILLIAM HENRY DREW[8] (*Caroline Chilson,*[7] *Pamela Daggett,*[6] *John,*[5] *John,*[4] *John,*[3] *Samuel,*[2] *Thomas*[1]), born Niles, Mich., July 13, 1836; resides Glidden, Ia. (1893); married Summerville, Mich., January 24, 1859, Caroline Frost, daughter of Elijah and Prudy Ann (Cary) Frost; died.

Issue:

5157. i. OLIVER LINCOLN DREW,[9] born Casseopolis, Mich.; resides Lake City, Ia. (1893).
5158. ii. JOHN DREW,[9] born Niles, Mich.; died September 24, 1879.

5159. iii. MARY JANE DREW,[9] born Glidden, Ia.
5160. iv. ROBERT DREW,[9] born Glidden, Ia., March, 1873.
5161. v. ELLA DREW,[9] born Glidden, Ia., July, 1876.

4554. OLIVE EMILY DREW [8] (*Caroline Chilson,*[7] *Pamela Daggett,*[6] *John,*[5] *John,*[4] *John,*[3] *Samuel,*[2] *Thomas* [1]), born Niles, Mich., February 27, 1842; resides Neligh, Neb. (1893); married, Niles, Mich., February 27, 1864, by Rev. I. E. Henny, to Robert Fox, son of Jonas Fox; born Ascension, Ind., October 4, 1838.

Issue :

5162. i. FRANK EZRA FOX,[9] born Cameron, Ill., September 1, 1866.
5163. ii. LINFORD FOX,[9] born Galesburg, Ill., January 1, 1868.
5164. iii. MAY FOX,[9] born Galesburg, Ill., October 9, 1869.

4556. GEORGE HENRY HENDERSON [8] (*Laura L. Chilson,*[7] *Pamela Daggett,*[6] *John,*[5] *John,*[4] *John,*[3] *Samuel,*[2] *Thomas* [1]), born Dowagiac, Mich., November 22, 1840; resides Copenish, Mich. (1893); married Sharon, Wis., February 21, 1870, by Rev. J. G. Schaeffer, to Frances Tucker, daughter of William Lincoln and Mary Ann (Lewis) Tucker; born Walworth, Wis., May 22, 1849.

Issue :

5165. i. JESSE ROSS HENDERSON,[9] born Dowagiac, Mich., Sept. 30, 1871.
5166. ii. LEWIS ERWIN HENDERSON,[9] born Dowagiac, Mich., Dec. 23, 1872.
5167. iii. GEORGE LESLIE HENDERSON,[9] born Volinia, Mich., Sept. 28, 1874.
5168. iv. ETTA BELLE HENDERSON,[9] born Volinia, Mich., March 16, 1876.
5169. v. MINNIE FRANCES HENDERSON,[9] born Volinia, Mich., June 6, 1878; died Volinia, Mich., March 10, 1879.
5170. vi. ELBERT GARD HENDERSON,[9] born Volinia, Mich., February 4, 1880.
5171. vii. MILDRED ALICE HENDERSON,[9] born Volinia, Mich., March 5, 1882.
5172. viii. MARY ANN HENDERSON,[9] born Cleon, Mich., August 31, 1885.

4557. HELEN MARIA HENDERSON [8] (*Laura L. Chilson,*[7] *Pamela Daggett,*[6] *John,*[5] *John,*[4] *John,*[3] *Samuel,*[2] *Thomas* [1]), born Cass county, Mich., April 10, 1842; resides 508 North West street, Kalamazoo, Mich. (1893); married Wayne, Cass Co., Mich., September 4, 1860, by Rev. William Sprague, to Sylvester Fuller, son of Obadiah and Elizabeth (Crossett) Fuller; born Genesee county, N.Y., January 18, 1834.

Issue :

5173. i. LESLIE FULLER,[9] born October 2, 1861; died Montcalm, Mich., September 3, 1863.
5174. ii. ELIZABETH MAUD FULLER,[9] born Dowagiac, Mich., July 8, 1864.
5175. iii. FRED ERWIN FULLER,[9] born Dowagiac, Mich., June 17, 1868.
5176. iv. DAISY RUTH FULLER,[9] born Dowagiac, Mich., December 8, 1878.

4560. LAURA ETTA HENDERSON [8] (*Laura L. Chilson,*[7] *Pamela Daggett,*[6] *John,*[5] *John,*[4] *John,*[3] *Samuel,*[2] *Thomas* [1]), born Wayne, Cass Co., Mich., January 18, 1853; resides Black Lake, Mich. (1893); married Wayne, Mich., December 8, 1878, by Rev. T. N. Glover, to

Edson Danford Amidon, son of Moses Pool and Sophia (Starr) Amidon; born Onondaga county, N.Y., August 14, 1834.

Issue:

5177. i.   RUBY ETTIE AMIDON,[9] born Wayne, Mich., October 19, 1880.
5178. ii.   PEARL SOPHIA AMIDON,[9] born Fruitport, Mich., July 31, 1882.
5179. iii. HARRY ROY AMIDON,[9] born Fruitport, Mich., January 20, 1885.
5180. iv.   ELIZABETH MARIE AMIDON,[9] born Fruitport, Mich., June 4, 1887.
5181. v.   WINNIE RUTH AMIDON,[9] born Fruitport, Mich., December 11, 1891.

4564. OLIVER EASTERBROOK [8] (*Alice Daggett,*[7] *Sebra,*[6] *John,*[5] *John,*[4] *John,*[3] *Samuel,*[2] *Thomas*[1]), born Fairview, Pa., February 3, 1825; died Girard, Pa., November 24, 1872; married Girard, Pa., November 15, 1853, by Rev. Mr. Stephens, to Sarah Lowry Gallowhur, daughter of George and Eliza (Lowry) Gallowhur; born Girard, Pa., February 7, 1830; resides Girard, Pa. (1893).

Issue:

5182. i.   SUSIE GALLOWHUR EASTERBROOK,[9] born Girard, Pa., July 17, 1855.
5183. ii.   BENJAMIN F. EASTERBROOK,[9] born Girard, Pa., January 25, 1868.

4566. WILLIS THOMAS WILDMAN [8] (*Laura Daggett,*[7] *Sebra,*[6] *John,*[5] *John,*[4] *John,*[3] *Samuel,*[2] *Thomas*[1]), born Greenfield, Pa., March 28, 1832; resides Boscobel, Pa. (1893); married Union, Pa., April 23, 1856, by Rev. Mr. Rice, to Phebe Alzina Nason, daughter of Ezra Washburn and Phebe (Brown) Nason; born Greenfield, Pa., March 27, 1832.

Issue:

5184. i.   HARRIET LODEMA WILDMAN,[9] born Greenfield, Pa., January 8, 1859.
5185. ii.   WILLIS BERT WILDMAN,[9] born Greenfield, Pa., August 5, 1870.

4568. LUCINDA WILDMAN [8] (*Laura Daggett,*[7] *Sebra,*[6] *John,*[5] *John,*[4] *John,*[3] *Samuel,*[2] *Thomas*[1]), born Greenfield, Pa., March 3, 1837; resides Boscobel, Pa. (1893); married Wesleyville, Pa., March 27, 1865, by Rev. N. W. Jones, to Allanson Loomis Randal, son of George and Sally S. (Loomis) Randal, of Charlotte, Mich.; born Summit, Pa., January 28, 1839; died Greenfield, Pa., Jan. 28, 1882.

Issue:

5186. i.   LEWIS LEVATOR RANDAL,[9] born Greenfield, Pa., December 25, 1865.
5187. ii.   GEORGE IRA RANDAL,[9] born Greenfield, Pa., September 20, 1867.
5188. iii. WALTER BENJAMIN RANDAL,[9] born Greenfield, Pa., October 14, 1871.
5189. iv.   LAURA LODEMA RANDAL,[9] born Greenfield, Pa., January 23, 1880.

4570. HIRAM ALBERT WILDMAN [8] (*Laura Daggett,*[7] *Sebra,*[6] *John,*[5] *John,*[4] *John,*[3] *Samuel,*[2] *Thomas*[1]), born Greenfield, Pa., January 13, 1841; resides Greenfield, Pa. (1893); married 1st, Greenfield, Pa., January 12, 1860, by Jesse R. Prindle, Esq., to Mary Smith, daughter of John Harvey and Eliza (Tate) Smith; born East Greene,

Pa., September 5, 1844 ; died December 23, 1861 ; married 2d, December 24, 1868, Caroline Henry ; born 1852 ; divorced 1877.

Issue :

5190. i.   FRED WILDMAN,[9] born Greenfield, Pa., October 29, 1869; resides Rockford, Ill. (1893).

5191. ii.   FRANKLIN ADELBERT WILDMAN,[9] born Greenfield, Pa., September 23, 1872 ; resides Greenfield, Pa. (1893).

5192. iii.   LOTTIE WILDMAN,[9] born Greenfield, Pa., April 16, 1876.

4571. ANNIS WILDMAN[8] (*Laura Daggett,*[7] *Sebra,*[6] *John,*[5] *John,*[4] *John,*[3] *Samuel,*[2] *Thomas*[1]), born Greenfield, Pa., September 5, 1843 ; resides Boscobel, Pa. (1893) ; married Greenfield, Pa., September 4, 1862, by William Yost, Esq., to William Harrison Ellsworth, son of John and Mary Ann (Goodsell) Ellsworth ; born Monroe, Ohio, Oct. 19, 1839 ; died Greenfield, Pa., Jan. 16, 1875.

Issue :

5193. i.   WILLIS MELVIN ELLSWORTH,[9] born Greenfield, Pa., Aug. 6, 1863.

5194. ii.   LEWIS JOHN ELLSWORTH,[9] born Greenfield, Pa., July 31, 1864.

5195. iii.   FRANK ADOLPHUS ELLSWORTH,[9] born Greenfield, Pa., July 11, 1867.

5196. iv.   ARTHUR WILLIAM ELLSWORTH,[9] born Greenfield, Pa., October 23, 1868 ; died Greenfield, Pa., February 2, 1870.

5197. v.   ROWENA ELLSWORTH,[9] born Greenfield, Pa., June 31, 1870 ; died Greenfield, Pa., April 11, 1871.

5198. vi.   OLIVER ESTA ELLSWORTH,[9] born Greenfield, Pa., Feb. 14, 1872.

5199. vii.   IRA SHADDOCK ELLSWORTH,[9] born Greenfield, Pa., Aug. 12, 1873.

5200. viii.   BRADFORD HARRISON ELLSWORTH,[9] born Greenfield, Pa., April 20, 1875.

4573. CYRUS SERVETUS DAGGETT[8] (*Austin,*[7] *Sebra,*[6] *John,*[5] *John,*[4] *John,*[3] *Samuel,*[2] *Thomas*[1]), born Girard, Pa., July 11, 1831 ; died Genesee, Ill., November 24, 1865 ; married 1st, Fairview, Pa., April 5, 1856, by Rev. L. D. Prosser, to Kathrina Myers, daughter of Henry and Elizabeth (Allgier) Myers ; born Fairview, Pa., October 13, 1838 ; divorced September, 1860 ; died Beebeetown, Ia., May 13, 1887 ; married 2d, Osco, Ill., Oct. 7, 1860, by Rev. Wm. Batcheller, to Mary Hamilton, daughter of Levi and Mary (Walker) Hamilton ; born Brookfield, Mass., Jan. 11, 1842 ; resides Chicago, Ill. (1893).

Issue :

5201. i.   LILLY MARTHA DAGGETT,[9] born Girard, Pa., October 26, 1856.

5202. ii.   CARRIE DAGGETT,[9] born Genesee, Ill., October 29, 1861 ; married Des Moines, Ia., Feb. 15, 1888, by Rev. Dr. Ames, to William Clokey Dinwiddie, son of John A. and Edith J. (Bulsford) Dinwiddie ; born Springfield, Ohio, Aug. 10, 1862 ; no issue ; resides Chicago, Ill. (1893).

4574. JULIUS ALONZO OGEDA DAGGETT[8] (*Austin,*[7] *Sebra,*[6] *John,*[5] *John,*[4] *John,*[3] *Samuel,*[2] *Thomas*[1]), born Girard, Pa., June 2, 1833 ; resides Avonia, Pa. (1893) ; married Girard, Pa., April 10, 1860, by Rev. L. D. Prosser, to Fidelia Melinda Weeks, daughter of Amory and Huldah Cooper (Sawyer) Weeks ; born Georgia, Vt., Jan. 20, 1834.

Issue :

5203. i.   CHLOE MELISSA DAGGETT,[9] born Girard, Pa., September 21, 1861 ; died Girard, Pa., December 6, 1865.

5204. ii.   SARAH BELL DAGGETT,[9] born Girard, Pa., September 29, 1864.
5205. iii. NINA ETHEL DAGGETT,[9] born Girard, Pa., October 28, 1867.
5206. iv.   DON AMORY DAGGETT,[9] born Girard, Pa., August 15, 1869; married
            Erie, Pa., June 28, 1893, by Rev. Margaret Brennan, to Myrtis Emily
            Haven, daughter of Cassius and Julia (Wright) Haven; she born
            Franklin, Pa., Feb. 3, 1873; resides Girard, Pa. (1893).
5207. v.   GUY HAROLD DAGGETT,[9] born Girard, Pa., March 10, 1874.

In the grove east of the residence of Mr. Daggett was held a Daggett reunion, August 9, 1883.

4575. ANNIS REBECCA DAGGETT [8] (*Austin,*[7] *Sebra,*[6] *John,*[5] *John,*[4] *John,*[3] *Samuel,*[2] *Thomas*[1]), born Girard, Pa., August 30, 1835; resides Avonia, Pa. (1893); married Girard, Pa., November 4, 1856, by Rev. L. D. Prosser, to John Christian Zahn, son of Christian and Barbara (Hostetler) Zahn, of Berne, Switz.; born Atlantic Ocean, September 27, 1833.

Issue:

5208. i.   STELLA ELVIRA ZAHN,[9] born Linwood Farm, Erie, Pa., March 16, 1861;
            married John P. Daggett (see No. 4682).
5209. ii.   ANNETTE FLORENCE DAGGETT ZAHN,[9] born Linwood Farm, Erie, Pa.,
            September 12, 1862. Miss Zahn has been much interested in the family
            history, and this branch of the family are indebted to her for her kind
            aid in perfecting the details; resides Avonia, Pa. (1893).

4576. ALMEDA ELECTA DAGGETT [8] (*Austin,*[7] *Sebra,*[6] *John,*[5] *John,*[4] *John,*[3] *Samuel,*[2] *Thomas*[1]), born Girard, Pa., January 3, 1837; died Girard, Pa., August 3, 1866; married Girard, Pa., November 4, 1855, by Rev. L. D. Prosser, to Philip Bowen, son of Abraham and Betsey (Palmer) Bowen; born Richmond, Can., July 27, 1820; resides Miles' Grove, Pa. (1893).

Issue:

5210. i.   ZADIA BOWEN,[9] born Girard, Pa., August 4, 1858.
5211. ii.   EMERSON DRAPER BOWEN,[9] born Fairview, Pa., May 28, 1862.
5212. iii. AUSTIN DAGGETT BOWEN,[9] born Fairview, Pa., May 16, 1864.

4577. Dr. HELEN MARIAN DAGGETT [8] (*Austin,*[7] *Sebra,*[6] *John,*[5] *John,*[4] *John,*[3] *Samuel,*[2] *Thomas*[1]), born Girard, Pa., March 10, 1840; resides Fairview, Pa. (1893); married 1st, Springfield, Pa., November 18, 1857, by Rev. L. D. Prosser, to Samuel Bates Pollay, son of James Madison and Adaline (Eaton) Pollay; born Ithaca, N.Y., November 11, 1839; died battle of Antietam, September 17, 1862; married 2d, Girard, Pa., March 14, 1867, by Rev. Albino Hall, to Welcome Joshua Weeks, son of Amory and Huldah (Sawyer) Weeks; born Milton, Vt., March 23, 1838.

No issue.

A Daggett reunion was held on the lawn of Dr. Weeks, August 9, 1888, a company of one hundred and seventy-five being present.

4578. MELISSA LOVERNIA DAGGETT [8] (*Austin,*[7] *Sebra,*[6] *John,*[5] *John,*[4] *John,*[3] *Samuel,*[2] *Thomas*[1]), born Girard, Pa., November 29,

1842; resides Coldwater, Mich. (1893); married Girard, Pa., April 13, 1864, by Revs. Mr. Carleton and C. L. Shipman, to Richard Thomas Tuckey, son of Thomas Richard and Jane (Carr) Tuckey; born Franklin, Pa., March 9, 1836.

Issue:

5213. i.   MARY ELVIRA TUCKEY,[9] born Girard, Pa., April 26, 1865; died Coldwater, Mich., September 12, 1869.
5214. ii. RICHARD THOMAS TUCKEY,[9] born Girard, Pa., October 15, 1867; died Coldwater, Mich., April 3, 1872.
5215. iii. FRANCIS BYRON TUCKEY,[9] born Coldwater, Mich., Sept. 22, 1870.
5216. iv. CHARLES EDWIN TUCKEY,[9] born Coldwater, Mich., April 26, 1872; died Coldwater, Mich., February 14, 1883.
5217. v.   SUSIE LUELLA TUCKEY,[9] born Coldwater, Mich., January 11, 1875.
5218. vi. RICHARD GLADIUS TUCKEY,[9] born Coldwater, Mich., October 26, 1878; died Coldwater, Mich., September 6, 1881.
5219. vii. JAY DAGGETT TUCKEY,[9] born Coldwater, Mich., July 21, 1882.
5220. viii. PHEBE LOVERNIA TUCKEY,[9] born Coldwater, Mich., Sept. 5, 1884.

4579. FLORENCE VOLUTIA DAGGETT[8] (*Austin*,[7] *Sebra*,[6] *John*,[5] *John*,[4] *John*,[3] *Samuel*,[2] *Thomas*[1]), born Girard, Pa., December 28, 1844; resides Fairview, Pa. (1893); married 1st, Girard, Pa., March 14, 1867, by Rev. C. L. Shipman, to James Hanlin, son of Mary (Grace) Hanlin; born Cork, Ire., November 8, 1841; died Rochester, N.Y., December 8, 1869; married 2d, Erie, Pa., January 19, 1881, by Rev. A. A. Thayer, to William Mainard Anderson, son of Mathew and Emily (Mainard) Anderson; born Girard, Pa.; divorced March 11, 1886.

Issue:

5221. i. GEORGE LUCAS HANLIN.[9] born Moscow, Ohio, January 27, 1869.
5222. ii. ROSS ELTON ANDERSON,[9] born Fairplain, Pa., September 2, 1882.

Mrs. Anderson has aided in the work of compiling the family history, and in the perfection of the details of her branch.

4580. JOSEPHINE HARRIET DAGGETT[8] (*Austin*,[7] *Sebra*,[6] *John*,[5] *John*,[4] *John*,[3] *Samuel*,[2] *Thomas*[1]), born Girard, Pa., Feb. 15, 1846; resides Coldwater, Mich. (1893); married Girard, Pa., July 26, 1865, by Rev. C. L. Shipman, to James Bowen Tuckey, son of Thomas Richard and Jane (Carr) Tuckey; born Franklin, Pa., Jan. 9, 1841.

Issue:

5223. i.   CLAUDIA BEATRICE TUCKEY,[9] born Girard, Pa., December 11, 1869; married Coldwater, Mich., November 8, 1890, by Rev. H. P. Collins, to James Madison Brown, son of David and Maggretta (McKay) Brown; born Illiopolis, Ill., July 25, 1867; resides Coldwater, Mich. (1893); no issue.
5224. ii. MABEL OLIVE TUCKEY,[9] born Girard, Pa., January 29, 1873.
5225. iii. EARL ZAHN TUCKEY,[9] born Girard, Pa., December 5, 1875.

4581. RHEA SILVIA SOPHRONIA DAGGETT[8] (*Austin*,[7] *Sebra*,[6] *John*,[5] *John*,[4] *John*,[3] *Samuel*,[2] *Thomas*[1]), born Girard, Pa., August 12, 1849; died Erie, Pa., Jan. 27, 1882; married Girard, Pa., Sept. 17,

1873, by Rev. C. L. Shipman, to George Moorhead Moore, son of Montgomery and Katherine (Moorhead) Moore; born Moorheadville, Pa., Sept. 13, 1848; resides 326 West Twenty-third street, Erie, Pa. (1893).

Issue:

5226. i. CHARLES LAWRENCE MOORE,[9] born Erie, Pa., March 18, 1878; died Erie, Pa., August 8, 1878.

4583. MARY ADELIA DAGGETT [8] (*Darius,*[7] *Sebra,*[6] *John,*[5] *John,*[4] *John,*[3] *Samuel,*[2] *Thomas* [1]), born Girard, Pa., February 25, 1835; resides Norwalk, Cal. (1893); married Girard, Pa., January 10, 1854, by Rev. D. E. Day, to Charles Gaillard, son of Charles and Mary Ann (Trissler) Gaillard; born Lancaster, Pa., Jan. 10, 1829.

Issue:

5227. i. ELIZABETH TRISSLER GAILLARD.[9] born Fairview, Pa., Oct. 7, 1854.
5228. ii. CHARLES LESLIE GAILLARD,[9] born Fairview, Pa., May 1, 1856; married Girard, Pa., March 16, 1882, by Rev. R. S. Borland, to Eva Ryman, daughter of Theodore and Julia (Brewer) Ryman; born Girard, Pa., October 17. 1854; resides Girard, Pa. (1893); no issue.
5229. iii. JULIUS THEODORE GAILLARD,[9] born Sterrettania, Pa., May 30, 1858.
5230. iv. GERTRUDE AGNES GAILLARD,[9] born Fairview, Pa., October 11, 1860.
5231. v. HARRY DAGGETT GAILLARD,[9] born West Millcreek, Pa., July 20, 1875; resides Norwalk, Cal. (1893).

4585. ESTHER ELIZABETH DAGGETT [8] (*Darius,*[7] *Sebra,*[6] *John,*[5] *John,*[4] *John,*[3] *Samuel,*[2] *Thomas* [1]), born Girard, Pa., July 10, 1838; resides Girard, Pa. (1893); married Girard, Pa., September 18, 1860, by Rev. John Prosser, to Charles Bennett, son of Caleb and Sophia (Hinds) Bennett; born Oneonta. N.Y.. June 8, 1836.

Issue:

5232. i. LOUISA SOPHIA BENNETT,[9] born Fairview, Pa., March 21, 1863.
5233. ii. WILLIE WESLEY BENNETT,[9] born Girard. Pa., September 17, 1864; died Girard, Pa., September 10. 1887.
5234. iii. JESSIE EMMA BENNETT,[9] born Girard, Pa., September 19, 1869; married Girard, Pa., Sept. 1, 1892, by Rev. A. A. Horton. to Edward Marzell Hatheway, son of Edward Butler and Lovina (Brown) Hatheway; born Lansing. Mich., March 30, 1869; resides Girard, Pa. (1893).
5235. iv. ARTHUR LEE BENNETT,[9] born Girard. Pa., July 22, 1871; married Chicago, Ill., June 28, 1892, by Rev. C. H. Kees. to Estella Vivian Ward. daughter of Cyrus Joseph and Anna (Tiffin) Ward; born Cedar Rapids. Ia., January 6, 1872; resides Girard, Pa. (1893).
5236. v. ELMER LESLIE BENNETT,[9] born Girard. Pa., August 10, 1875.

4587. URSULA FLORENCE DAGGETT [8] (*Darius,*[7] *Sebra,*[6] *John,*[5] *John,*[4] *John,*[3] *Samuel,*[2] *Thomas* [1]), born Girard. Pa., September 15, 1842; resides Girard, Pa. (1893); married Girard, Pa.. Nov. 7. 1861. by Rev. J. Prosser, to John Gaillard, of Fairview, Pa.. son of Charles and Mary Ann (Trissler) Gaillard; born Fairview, Pa., Aug. 8, 1838.

Issue:

5237. i. CHARLES DARIUS GAILLARD,[9] born Fairview, Pa., February 15, 1863; resides Cleveland. Ohio (1893).

5238. ii. IMOGENE GAILLARD,[9] born Girard, Pa., January 1, 1873; resides Fairview, Pa. (1893).
5239. iii. JOHN KARL GAILLARD,[9] born Girard, Pa., March 6, 1884.

4588. LORENZO DOW DAGGETT [8] (*Darius*,[7] *Sebra*,[6] *John*,[5] *John*,[4] *John*,[3] *Samuel*,[2] *Thomas* [1]), born Girard, Pa., July 19, 1845; resides San Antonio, Tex. (1893); married Alexandria, Minn., May 20, 1871, by Rev. H. F. Kingsland, to Mary Frank Reynolds, daughter of Judge Reuben and Lucia Aurora (Tucker) Reynolds; born Grand Rapids, Mich., December 26, 1849.

Issue:

5240. i. EMMA LOUISA DAGGETT,[9] born Otter Tail City, Minn., April 3, 1872.
5241. ii. FRED DILLON DAGGETT,[9] born Girard, Pa., June 28, 1876.
5242. iii. LORENZO DOW DAGGETT,[9] born Girard, Pa., December 1, 1877.
5243. iv. ANSORA MARTHEDUS DAGGETT,[9] born Erie, Pa., January 18, 1884.

Mr. Daggett enlisted in the navy for one year in 1864.

4589. WILLIAM EARNEST DAGGETT [8] (*Darius*,[7] *Sebra*,[6] *John*,[5] *John*,[4] *John*,[3] *Samuel*,[2] *Thomas* [1]), born Girard, Pa., Nov. 10, 1846; resides Miles' Grove, Pa. (1893); married Girard, Pa., June 25, 1868, by Rev. John Prosser, to Helen Emma Taylor, daughter of Eleazer and Ann Eliza (Seeley) Taylor; born Girard, Pa., Oct. 8, 1850.

Issue:

5244. i. EARNEST DAGGETT.[9] born Girard, Pa., October 8, 1868; married Erie, Pa., September 6, 1892, by Rev. J. O. Baker, to Cora Bell Sweet, daughter of John and Lulie Maud (Smith) Sweet; born East Springfield, Pa., August 11, 1874; resides Conneaut, Ohio (1893).
5245. ii. HARRY DAGGETT,[9] born Girard, Pa., September 19, 1871.
5246. iii. ROY DAGGETT,[9] born Girard, Pa., July 4, 1873.
5247. iv. CARL DAGGETT,[9] born Girard, Pa., November 6, 1875.
5248. v. ROBERT BENJAMIN DAGGETT,[9] born Girard, Pa., December 19, 1881.

4590. NANCY EMMA DAGGETT [8] (*Darius*,[7] *Sebra*,[6] *John*,[5] *John*,[4] *John*,[3] *Samuel*,[2] *Thomas* [1]), born Girard, Pa., January 17, 1849; resides Avonia, Pa. (1893); married Girard, Pa., Sept. 25, 1867, by Rev. Albino Hall, to Isaac Spence, son of Abraham and Lucinda (Webster) Spence; born West Millcreek, Pa., Jan. 16, 1845.

Issue:

5249. i. LULU MAY SPENCE,[9] born Fairview, Pa., June 8, 1868.
5250. ii. MILLICENT LUCINDA SPENCE,[9] born Girard, Pa., June 5, 1871.
5251. iii. MARY ISABEL SPENCE,[9] born Girard, Pa., December 4, 1874.
5252. iv. HARVEY REED SPENCE,[9] born Girard, Pa., June 25, 1878; died Avonia, Pa., April 15, 1888.
5253. v. FRANK MYRA SPENCE,[9] born Girard, Pa., April 20, 1881.
5254. vi. GRACE GERTRUDE SPENCE,[9] born Girard, Pa., January 22, 1886.

4596. ADELAIDE ELOUISE DAGGETT [8] (*Darius*,[7] *Sebra*,[6] *John*.[5] *John*,[4] *John*,[3] *Samuel*,[2] *Thomas* [1]), born Girard, Pa., February 18, 1865; died Erie, Pa., May 10, 1890; married Erie, Pa., November 14, 1886, by Rev. J. L. Stratton, to George Earnest Riblet, son of

John Ebersole and Eliza Jane (Collins) Riblet; born **Erie, Pa.,** May 15, 1864; resides Erie, Pa. (1893).

Issue:

5255. i. GEORGE ARCHIBALD RIBLET,[9] born Erie, Pa., May, 1889; died Erie, Pa., August, 1889.

Mrs. Riblet possessed a voice of remarkable sweetness and power, and was much sought in musical entertainments.

4598. HENRY GEORGE DAGGETT [8] (*Reuben,*[7] *Sebra,*[6] *John,*[5] *John,*[4] *John,*[3] *Samuel,*[2] *Thomas*[1]), born Fairview, Pa., January 20, 1835; died Oil City, Pa., August, 1865; married Girard, Pa., December 15, 1859, by Rev. D. E. Day, to Arminda Jane Wildman, daughter of Lewis and Laura (Daggett) Wildman (No. 4567); born Greenfield, Pa., October 25, 1835; died Erie, Pa., November 11, 1878.

Issue:

5256. i. MARTHA ELIZABETH DAGGETT,[9] born Girard, Pa., October 9, 1860.
5257. ii. ABRAHAM LINCOLN DAGGETT,[9] born Girard, Pa., May 5, 1862; died Girard, Pa., November 11, 1862.

4601. WELLINGTON HARRY DAGGETT [8] (*Reuben,*[7] *Sebra,*[6] *John,*[5] *John,*[4] *John,*[3] *Samuel,*[2] *Thomas*[1]), born Fairview, Pa., July 19, 1839; resides Salem, Ohio (1893); married Erie, Pa., December 19, 1871, by Rev. E. A. Stone, to Ida Weeks.

Issue:

5258. i. FRED HAYS DAGGETT,[9] born Erie, Pa., September 19, 1872.
5259. ii. CHARLES HILTON DAGGETT,[9] born Erie, Pa., May 27, 1874.
5260. iii. JESSIE MAY DAGGETT,[9] born Erie, Pa., July 8, 1882.
5261. iv. GEORGE BYRON DAGGETT,[9] born Salem, Ohio, May 16, 1885.

4603. ADELIA ANNIS WILLIAMS [8] (*Eleanor Daggett,*[7] *Sebra,*[6] *John,*[5] *John,*[4] *John,*[3] *Samuel,*[2] *Thomas*[1]), born Girard, Pa., July 28, 1836; resides South Saybrook, Ohio (1893); married 1st, Girard, Pa., December 5, 1857, by Rev. D. Prosser, to Alfred Smith; born Springfield, Mass.; married 2d, Amboy, Ohio, November 28, 1865, by Rev. John Robinson, to Armenius Eli Viets, son of Zophei and Lacy (Hylier) Viets; born Granby, Conn., June 18, 1817; died Amboy, Ohio, August 30, 1881; married 3d, Amboy, Ohio, April 19, 1883, by Rev. W. H. King, to George Bates, son of Solomon and Susan (Fields) Bates; born Saybrook, Ohio, February 12, 1822.

Issue:

5262. i. ALFRED SMITH,[9] born Girard, Pa., September 9, 1858; died Girard, Pa., September 14, 1859.
5263. ii. GEORGE SMITH,[9] born Girard, Pa., September 13, 1859; died Girard, Pa., December 6, 1859.
5264. iii. IVA ETHLYN VIETS,[9] born Amboy, Ohio, March 6, 1871; died Amboy, Ohio, October 8, 1882.
5265. iv. ARMENIUS ELMER VIETS,[9] born Amboy, Ohio, May 2, 1875; died Amboy, Ohio, October 5, 1882.

THOMAS DOGGETT, OF MARSHFIELD. 531

4606. Sylvester Abraham Williams [8] (*Eleanor Daggett,*[7] *Sebra,*[6] *John,*[5] *John,*[4] *John,*[3] *Samuel,*[2] *Thomas* [1]), born Girard, Pa., October 21, 1841; resides 148 W. Sixteenth street, Erie, Pa. (1893); married Girard, Pa., April 2, 1867, by Rev. D. E. Day, to Fidelia McDonald, daughter of James and Clarissa (Cole) McDonald; born Girard, Pa., September 27, 1851.

Issue:

5266. i. Clara Bell Williams,[9] born Girard, Pa., February 7, 1868; died Erie, Pa., August 1, 1892.
5267. ii. Earl Williams,[9] born Girard, Pa., November 2, 1874.
5268. iii. Forrest Williams,[9] born Girard, Pa., September, 1888.

4610. Sarah Jane Williams [8] (*Eleanor Daggett,*[7] *Sebra,*[6] *John,*[5] *John,*[4] *John,*[3] *Samuel,*[2] *Thomas* [1]), born Girard, Pa., September 17, 1848; resides Miles' Grove, Pa. (1893); married Fairview, Pa., July 25, 1870, Frederic August Schutte, son of Frederic August and Caroline (Stille) Schutte; born Hanover, Ger., August 6, 1848.

Issue:

5269. i. Frederic August Schutte,[9] born Girard, Pa., July 15, 1871.
5270. ii. Benjamin Franklin Schutte,[9] born Girard, Pa., October 22, 1872; died Girard, Pa., February 11, 1878.
5271. iii. Nina Schutte,[9] born Girard, Pa., Dec. 8, 1873; died Girard, Pa., Oct. 4, 1874.
5272. iv. George Watson Schutte,[9] born Girard, Pa., January 19, 1875.
5273. v. Adelia Annis Schutte,[9] born Girard, Pa., August 26, 1878.

4611. Eugene Cass Williams [8] (*Eleanor Daggett,*[7] *Sebra,*[6] *John,*[5] *John,*[4] *John,*[3] *Samuel,*[2] *Thomas* [1]), born Girard, Pa., March 29, 1850; resides Hickernell, Pa. (1893); married Hickernell, Pa., Oct. 29, 1877, by Elder Hake, to Sarah Melissa Jossling, daughter of James and Mary (Hickernell) Jossling; born Hickernell, Pa., April 11, 1855.

Issue:

5274. i. Stella May Williams,[9] born Girard, Pa., November 7, 1878.
5275. ii. Rolla Eugene Williams,[9] born Girard, Pa., February 1, 1880.
5276. iii. Ernest Watson Williams,[9] born Girard, Pa., January 5, 1882.
5277. iv. Minta Adelia Williams,[9] born Spring, Pa., February 16, 1884.
5278. v. Lorenzo Williams,[9] born Spring, Pa., March 18, 1886.

4612. Nelly Williams [8] (*Eleanor Daggett,*[7] *Sebra,*[6] *John,*[5] *John,*[4] *John,*[3] *Samuel,*[2] *Thomas* [1]), born Girard, Pa., Oct. 15, 1853; resides Miles' Grove, Pa. (1893); married Amboy, Ohio, Jan. 24, 1872, by Squire Dibble, to John Skivington, son of William and Maria (Coleman) Skivington; born Toronto, Can., Nov. 6, 1855.

Issue:

5279. i. Harley Skivington,[9] born Girard, Pa., March 2, 1875.
5280. ii. Gardie Skivington,[9] born Girard, Pa., March 4, 1877.
5281. iii. Ada Skivington,[9] born Girard, Pa., March 1, 1879.
5282. iv. John Skivington,[9] born Erie, Pa., April 13, 1887.
5283. v. Pearl Skivington,[9] born Miles' Grove, Pa., October 3, 1888.

4613. CHARLES WINFIELD DAGGETT[8] (*Hiram,*[7] *Sebra,*[6] *John,*[5] *John,*[4] *John,*[3] *Samuel,*[2] *Thomas*[1]), born Girard, Pa., January 31, 1841; resides Girard, Pa. (1893); married Girard, Pa., July 4, 1864, by Rev. D. E. Day, to Sally Boughton, daughter of Joseph and Julia (Bailey) Boughton; born Girard, Pa., January 1, 1846.

Issue:

5284. i.   CHARLOTTA GILSON DAGGETT,[9] born Girard, Pa., April 30, 1865.
5285. ii.   JULIA DAGGETT,[9] born Girard, Pa., February 3, 1867.
5286. iii.   CHARLES DAGGETT,[9] born Girard, Pa., September 10, 1869.
5287. iv.   RICHARD DAGGETT,[9] born Girard, Pa., September 3, 1873.
5288. v.   BURTON DAGGETT,[9] born Girard, Pa., August 4, 1875.
5289. vi.   DAISY DAGGETT,[9] born Girard, Pa., March 12, 1877.
5290. vii.   HENRY DAGGETT,[9] born Girard, Pa., September 30, 1880.
5291. viii.   JOSEPH DAGGETT,[9] born Girard, Pa., November 29, 1882.
5292. ix.   EDNA DAGGETT,[9] born Girard, Pa., January 8, 1885.

4614. Dr. BYRON HIRAM DAGGETT[8] (*Hiram,*[7] *Sebra,*[6] *John,*[5] *John,*[4] *John,*[3] *Samuel,*[2] *Thomas*[1]), born Girard, Pa., January 27, 1842; resides 258 Franklin street, Buffalo, N.Y. (1893); married Holyoke, Mass., June 14, 1869, by Rev. Dr. Peet, to Sarah Yale Long, daughter of Dr. Lawson and Lonisa S. (Allen) Long; born Shelburne Falls, Mass., June, 1844.

Issue:

5293. i.   B. BYRON DAGGETT,[9] born Buffalo, N.Y., June 26, 1870; married Buffalo, N.Y., April 19, 1892, by Rev. Dr. Chevers, to Lulu Mary Choate, daughter of Rufus Mortimer and Ellen (Strickler) Choate; resides 215 Hudson street, Buffalo, N.Y. (1893).
5294. ii.   ALLEN FENTON DAGGETT,[9] born Buffalo, N.Y., December 17, 1879.

4615. CLAYTON GRISWOLD DAGGETT[8] (*Hiram,*[7] *Sebra,*[6] *John,*[5] *John,*[4] *John,*[3] *Samuel,*[2] *Thomas*[1]), born Girard, Pa., July 7, 1848; resides Girard, Pa. (1893); married Girard, Pa., Feb. 16, 1872, by Rev. C. L. Shipman, to Ida Blanch Drury, daughter of William Sherman and Ann Elizabeth (Hart) Drury; born Girard, Pa., Dec. 30, 1851.

Issue:

5295. i.   OLIVER WOODFORD DAGGETT,[9] born Girard, Pa., July 20, 1875.
5296. ii.   FRANK GILSON DAGGETT,[9] born Girard, Pa., February 19, 1885.

4616. FENTON GILSON DAGGETT[8] (*Hiram,*[7] *Sebra,*[6] *John,*[5] *John,*[4] *John,*[3] *Samuel,*[2] *Thomas*[1]), born Girard, Pa., March 11, 1855; died Girard, Pa., October 16, 1877; married Erie, Pa., May 11, 1876, by Rev. A. H. Carrier, to Jennie May Ball, daughter of Henry and Martha (Chesebro) Ball; born Girard, Pa., February 26, 1857; resides Girard, Pa. (1893).

Issue:

5297. i.   FENTON GILSON DAGGETT,[9] born Girard, Pa., October 29, 1877.
    (Daughter named for her father.)

4618. ELIZABETH ADALINE DAGGETT[8] (*George L.,*[7] *Ethan A.,*[6] *John,*[5] *John,*[4] *John,*[3] *Samuel,*[2] *Thomas*[1]), born Fort Madison, Ia.,

December 11, 1840; resides Reedy Ripple, W. Va. (1893); married 1st, Wirt county, W. Va., by Rev. Mr. Newbanks, to Jacob Brookover, son of Jacob and Jane Brookover; born Monongahela county, W. Va., June 15, 1836; died Wirt county, W. Va., July 19, 1865; married 2d, Wirt county, W. Va., March 28, 1867, by David Province, to William Lockhart, son of John M. and Nancy Lockhart; born Wirt county, W. Va., February 10, 1822.

Issue:

5298. i. DELILAH JANE BROOKOVER,[9] born Wirt county, W. Va., September 23, 1857; died Wirt county, W. Va., October 2, 1890.
5299. ii. ELIZABETH R. BROOKOVER,[9] born Wirt county, W. Va., October 19, 1860; died Wirt county, W. Va., August 16, 1862.
5300. iii. ERASTUS G. BROOKOVER,[9] born Wirt county, W. Va., May 8, 1864; died Wirt county, W. Va., October 9, 1865.
5301. iv. EZRA B. LOCKHART,[9] born Wirt county, W. Va., September 24, 1868; died Wirt county, W. Va., April 6, 1883.
5302. v. NOBLE LOCKHART,[9] born Wirt county, W. Va., October 19, 1871.
5303. vi. ANNIE V. LOCKHART,[9] born Wirt county, W. Va., July 17, 1874; died Wirt county, W. Va., November 3, 1876.

4619. ERASTUS PORTER DAGGETT [8] (*George L.,*[7] *Ethan A.,*[6] *John,*[5] *John,*[4] *John,*[3] *Samuel,*[2] *Thomas*[1]), born Lee county, Ia., June 6, 1843; resides Reedy Ripple, W. Va. (1893); married Wood county, W. Va., December 10, 1865, by Rev. Ozias Stephens, to Abbie Vanvlack, daughter of Theodore and Maria (Aldridge) Vanvlack; born Cook county, Ill., March 19, 1847.

Issue:

5304. i. EDWARD B. DAGGETT,[9] born Wirt county, W. Va., Dec. 16, 1867.
5305. ii. LEWIS V. DAGGETT,[9] born Wood county, W. Va., June 6, 1869.
5306. iii. ELORA M. DAGGETT,[9] born Wirt county, W. Va., August 9, 1871.
5307. iv. ROSA M. DAGGETT,[9] born Wirt county, W. Va., September 21, 1873.
5308. v. CORA B. DAGGETT,[9] born Wirt county, W. Va., May 14, 1876.
5309. vi. MARIA D. DAGGETT,[9] born Wirt county, W. Va., October 25, 1878.
5310. vii. CHARLES A. DAGGETT,[9] born Wirt county, W. Va., Sept. 17, 1880.
5311. viii. CARRIE E. DAGGETT,[9] born Wirt county, W. Va., October 22, 1882.
5312. ix. CLARENCE E. DAGGETT,[9] born Wirt county, W. Va., December 15, 1884; died Wirt county, W. Va., April 14, 1886.

Mr. Daggett enlisted at Parkersburg, W. Va., September, 1861, in Company II, Seventh Virginia Infantry Volunteers; discharged September, 1864.

4620. BERTHA JANE DAGGETT [8] (*George L.,*[7] *Ethan A.,*[6] *John,*[5] *John,*[4] *John,*[3] *Samuel,*[2] *Thomas*[1]), born Limestone Hill, W. Va., March 25, 1849; resides Reedy Ripple, W. Va. (1893); married Wirt county, W. Va., December 3, 1878, by Rev. George A. Burdet, to Caleb Wiseman, son of Caleb and Susan (Coe) Wiseman; born Wirt county, W. Va., May 12, 1850.

Issue:

5313. i. CLARA MABEL WISEMAN,[9] born Wirt county, W. Va., January 3, 1880; died Wirt county, W. Va., January 12, 1882.
5314. ii. CLARENCE BURLEY WISEMAN,[9] born Wirt Co., W. Va., March 24, 1883.

4621. CATHERINE MINERVA DAGGETT[8] (*George L.,*[7] *Ethan A.,*[6] *John,*[5] *John,*[4] *John,*[3] *Samuel,*[2] *Thomas*[1]), born Wirt county, W. Va., January 16, 1855; resides Reedy Ripple, W. Va. (1893); married Wirt county, W. Va., March 5, 1871, by Charles W. Owens, to John Ames Chevvrout, son of Perry and Nancy (Lockhart) Chevvrout; born Wirt county, W. Va., April 9, 1853.

Issue :

5315.	i.	ANNIE CHEVVROUT,[9] born Wirt county, W. Va., January 16, 1872.
5316.	ii.	CHARLES CHEVVROUT.[9] born Wirt county, W. Va., December 1, 1874; died Wirt county, W. Va., August 15, 1875.
5317.	iii.	WINONA MAY CHEVVROUT,[9] born Wirt county, W. Va., June 2, 1877.
5318.	iv.	JEANNETTE CHEVVROUT,[9] born Wirt county, W. Va., October 9, 1879; died Wirt county, W. Va., November 23, 1880.
5319.	v.	BERTHA CHEVVROUT,[9] born Wirt county, W. Va., October 17, 1881; died Wirt county, W. Va., January 9, 1882.
5320.	vi.	VINNIE CHEVVROUT,[9] born Wirt county, W. Va., January 23, 1883.
5321.	vii.	ROSCA CHEVVROUT,[9] born Wirt county, W. Va., May 16, 1886.
5322.	viii.	GILBERT CHEVVROUT,[9] born Wirt county, W. Va., August 19, 1888.

4622. GEORGE WILLIAM DAGGETT[8] (*George L.,*[7] *Ethan A.,*[6] *John,*[5] *John,*[4] *John,*[3] *Samuel,*[2] *Thomas*[1]), born Wirt county, W. Va., July 22, 1857; resides Reedy Ripple, W. Va. (1893); married Wirt county, W. Va., November 20, 1879, by Rev. M. Wells, to Harriet Virginia Lockhart, daughter of Isaiah and Margret Lockhart.

Issue :

5323.	i.	ADDIE DAGGETT,[9] born Wirt county, W. Va., August 15, 1880.
5324.	ii.	LAURA BELL DAGGETT,[9] born Wirt county, W. Va., Nov. 5, 1882.
5325.	iii.	DELLA DAGGETT,[9] born Wirt county, W. Va., March 22, 1884.
5326.	iv.	WALTER ANDREW DAGGETT,[9] born Wirt county, W. Va., Oct. 26, 1887.
5327.	v.	LIGA DAGGETT,[9] born Wirt county, W. Va., August 31. 1890.

4623. SIDNEY BENTON DAGGETT[8] (*Erastus P.,*[7] *Ethan A.,*[6] *John,*[5] *John,*[4] *John,*[3] *Samuel,*[2] *Thomas*[1]), born Copenhagen, N.Y., June 26, 1852; died Carthage, N.Y., May 8, 1888; married Brockville, Can., April 30, 1878, by Rev. Father Isaac McCarthy, to Agnes Manley, daughter of William and Bridget Massealieu (Fealey) Manley; born Brockville, Can., June 23, 1861; resides Carthage, N.Y. (1893).

Issue :

5328.	i.	CATHERINE MANLEY DAGGETT,[9] born Brockville, Can., June 30, 1879.
5329.	ii.	EMILY LOUISE DAGGETT,[9] born Alexandria Bay, N.Y., Aug. 11, 1881.
5330.	iii.	MARY BENTON DAGGETT,[9] born Copenhagen, N.Y., August 19, 1883.
5331.	iv.	AGNES LORETTA DAGGETT,[9] born Copenhagen, N.Y., March 10, 1886.
5332.	v.	SARA LAWTON DAGGETT,[9] born Carthage, N.Y., February 28, 1888.

4625. IDA SARA AUSTIN[8] (*Adaline Daggett,*[7] *Ethan A.,*[6] *John,*[5] *John,*[4] *John,*[3] *Samuel,*[2] *Thomas*[1]), born Copenhagen, N.Y., February 12, 1858; died Denmark, N.Y., October 29, 1882; married Copenhagen, N.Y., November 17, 1880, by Silas Slater, to Richard

Sheldon, son of Ansel and Malinda (Elliott) Sheldon; born Denmark, N.Y., June 17, 1853; resides Denmark, N.Y. (1893).

Issue:

5333. i. LEON CURTIS SHELDON,[9] born Denmark, N.Y., October 4, 1882.

4649. ESTHER MELONA CHASE [8] (*Esther M. Daggett,[7] Don Delance,[6] John,[5] John,[4] John,[3] Samuel,[2] Thomas [1]*), born Buckfield, Me., July 17, 1835; resides Woodstock, Me. (1878); married Buckfield, Me., April 26, 1854, Dr. Charles D. Bradbury.

Issue:

5334. i.   THOMAS BRADBURY,[9] born Buckfield, Me., April 16, 1855.
5335. ii. CHARLES D. BRADBURY,[9] born Buckfield, Me., July 9, 1858.
5336. iii. ROLFE BRADBURY,[9] born Buckfield, Me., March 12, 1861.
5337. iv. ABBY L. BRADBURY,[9] born Buckfield, Me., January 7, 1864.

4658. HENRY TRASK DAGGETT [8] (*John R.,[7] Don Delance,[6] John,[5] John,[4] John,[3] Samuel,[2] Thomas [1]*), born Randolph, Mass., April 22, 1836; "clerk;" died Boston, Mass., July 31, 1877; married South Braintree, Mass., October 9, 1867, by Rev. Calvin R. Fitts, to Hannah Elizabeth Perkins, daughter of Marcus and Elizabeth (Bowditch) Perkins; born Braintree, Mass., 1839.

Issue:

5338. i. CHARLES HENRY DAGGETT,[9] born North Abington, Mass., Oct. 20, 1868.
5339. ii. WILLIAM PERKINS DAGGETT,[9] born Springvale, Me., October 19, 1876; died Merrimac, Mass., August 10, 1877.

4659. JOHN CODMAN DAGGETT [8] (*John R.,[7] Don Delance,[6] John,[5] John,[4] John,[3] Samuel,[2] Thomas [1]*), born Randolph, Mass., January 29, 1838; "clerk;" resides Neponset, Mass. (1892); married Braintree, Mass., February 8, 1859, by Rev. Jonas Perkins, to Almira A. Sawin, daughter of Benjamin and Almira Sawin; born Randolph, Mass., October 3, 1839.

Issue:

5340. i.   GILBERT ALDEN DAGGETT,[9] born South Braintree, Mass., July 27, 1859.
5341. ii. JESSIE KIMBALL DAGGETT,[9] born South Braintree, Mass., November 30, 1867; died Neponset, Mass., November 20, 1881.
5342. iii. JOHN CHURCHILL DAGGETT,[9] born Wollaston, Mass., Sept. 11, 1872.

4660. MARTHA HAYDEN DAGGETT [8] (*John R.,[7] Don Delance,[6] John,[5] John,[4] John,[3] Samuel,[2] Thomas [1]*), born Randolph, Mass., February 28, 1840; married Neponset, Mass., February 25, 1873, by Rev. D. W. Waldron, to Samuel Ervin Chase, son of Benjamin B. and Lydia L. Chase; born Braintree, Vt., 1843.

Issue:

5343. i. LYDIA LOUISE CHASE,[9] born Neponset, Mass., January 29, 1874.
5344. ii. JOHN ALDEN CHASE,[9] born West Randolph, Vt., June 20, 1877.

4662. William Alden Daggett [8] (*John R.*,[7] *Don Delance*,[6] *John*,[5] *John*,[4] *John*,[3] *Samuel*,[2] *Thomas* [1]), born Randolph, Mass., January 5, 1846; "salesman;" resides Hingham, Mass. (1892); married Hingham, Mass., January 5, 1875, by Rev. Calvin Lincoln, to Eliza Jane Hersey, daughter of Henry M. and Eliza J. (Brown) Hersey; born Hingham, Mass., February 12, 1846.

Issue:

5345. i. Louis Alden Daggett,[9] born Hingham, Mass., September 20, 1875; died Hingham, Mass., September 26, 1877.
5346. ii. William Alden Daggett,[9] born Hingham, Mass., July 21, 1878.

4672. Helen Esther Daggett [8] (*Isaac R.*,[7] *Don Delance*,[6] *John*,[5] *John*,[4] *John*,[3] *Samuel*,[2] *Thomas* [1]), born South Weymouth, Mass., July 17, 1860; resides Rockland, Mass. (1893); married Weymouth, Mass., February 23, 1882, by Rev. Anson Titus, Jr., to Henry Wallace Chase, of Rockland, son of Henry and Phebe (Dend) Chase; born Abington, Mass., March 23, 1854.

Issue:

5347. i. Linda Hastings Chase,[9] born Rockland, Mass., March 1, 1884.

4677. Ephraim Beck Daggett [8] (*Ephraim M.*,[7] *Eleazer*,[6] *John*,[5] *John*,[4] *John*,[3] *Samuel*,[2] *Thomas* [1]), born Independence, Mo., August 23, 1838; resides Fort Worth, Tex. (1893); married Dallas county, Tex., February 4, 1864, by Rev. Mr. Livingstone, to Elizabeth Marsh, daughter of Harrison County and Mary (Raymond) Marsh; born Independence, Mo., October 9, 1843.

Issue:

5348. i. Frank B. Daggett,[9] born Tarrant county, Tex., February 2, 1866.
5349. ii. Harrison Marsh Daggett,[9] born McLennan county, Tex., Dec. 1, 1871.
5350. iii. Helen McKee Daggett,[9] born Hill county, Tex., February 26, 1874.
5351. iv. Thomas Corbin Daggett,[9] born Dallas county, Tex., April 6, 1876.
5352. v. Ephraim Merrill Daggett,[9] born Fort Worth, Tex., Oct. 30, 1879.

4680. Ephraim Merrill Daggett [8] (*Charles B.*,[7] *Eleazer*,[6] *John*,[5] *John*,[4] *John*,[3] *Samuel*,[2] *Thomas* [1]), born Shelbyville, Tex., Jan. 22, 1850; resides Fort Worth, Tex. (1893); married Fort Worth, Tex., Jan. 14, 1880, by Rev. W. W. Brimm, to Laura Alice Palmer, daughter of William and Sabina L. (Miller) Palmer; born Tennessee, Nov. 14, 1863.

Issue:

5353. i. Mary Sabina Daggett,[9] born Fort Worth, Tex., November 11, 1880.
5354. ii. Cora Josephine Daggett,[9] born Fort Worth, Tex., Nov. 21, 1882.
5355. iii. Justina Daggett,[9] born Fort Worth, Tex., December 23, 1884.
5356. iv. Charles William Daggett,[9] born Fort Worth, Tex., July 6, 1888.
5357. v. E. M. Daggett,[9] born Fort Worth, Tex., April 2, 1891.
5358. vi. John Palmer Daggett,[9] born Fort Worth, Tex., August 6, 1893.

4683. Mollie Hellen Daggett [8] (*Charles B.*,[7] *Eleazer*,[6] *John*,[5] *John*,[4] *John*,[3] *Samuel*,[2] *Thomas* [1]), born Fort Worth, Tex., September

15, 1857; resides Fort Worth, Tex. (1893); married Daggett's Point, Tex., February 24, 1881, by Rev. W. P. Wilson, to Charles Wilson McDougall, son of Duncan and Anna E. (White) McDougall; born Port Gibson, Miss., April 19, 1844.

Issue:

5359. i. CHARLES HARRISON McDOUGALL,[9] born Fort Worth, Tex., November 16, 1881; died Fort Worth, Tex., November 11, 1882.
5360. ii. JOHN DAGGETT McDOUGALL,[9] born Fort Worth, Tex., Dec. 18, 1883.
5361. iii. MARY KATIE McDOUGALL,[9] born Fort Worth, Tex., January 16, 1890.

4684. JUSTINA MELISSA DAGGETT [8] (*Charles B.,*[7] *Eleazer,*[6] *John,*[5] *John,*[4] *John,*[3] *Samuel,*[2] *Thomas* [1]), born Fort Worth, Tex., July 12, 1860; resides Fort Worth, Tex. (1893); married Fort Worth, Tex., Feb. 13, 1879, by H. C. Renfro, to Forney Davis Smyth, son of John and Harriet (Howell) Smyth; born Calhoun Co., Ala., July 13, 1853.

Issue:

5362. i. CHARLES CURREY SMYTH,[9] born Fort Worth, Tex., April 5, 1880.
5363. ii. JOSEPH MERRELL SMYTH,[9] born Fort Worth, Tex., January 26, 1882.
5364. iii. JOSHUA DAGGETT SMYTH,[9] born Cleburn, Tex., April 7, 1885.
5365. iv. JOHN McKEE SMYTH,[9] born Tarrant county, Tex., August 1, 1888.

4685. JOSEPHINE MALINDA DAGGETT [8] (*Charles B.,*[7] *Eleazer,*[6] *John,*[5] *John,*[4] *John,*[3] *Samuel,*[2] *Thomas* [1]), born Fort Worth, Tex., April 20, 1863; resides Fort Worth, Tex. (1893); married Fort Worth, Tex., September 28, 1887, by Judge Furman, to Ernest Vinton Barre, son of Bazil Vinton and Kate (Cobb) Barre; born Virginia City, Nev., August 20, 1863.

Issue:

5366. i. PERCY DOUGLAS BARRE,[9] born Coronado Beach, Cal., April 5, 1888.
5367. ii. JOHN DAGGETT BARRE,[9] born Coronado Beach, Cal., Dec. 21, 1889.
5368. iii. ERNEST VINTON BARRE,[9] born Fort Worth, Tex., March 30, 1892.

4687. CHARLES BIGGERS DAGGETT [8] (*Henry C.,*[7] *Eleazer,*[6] *John,*[5] *John,*[4] *John,*[3] *Samuel,*[2] *Thomas* [1]), born Fort Worth, Tex., August 20, 1852; resides San Diego, Cal. (1893); married 1st, Lewiston, Mo., June 14, 1874, by Rev. James Penn, to Addie Zimmerman, daughter of John Zimmerman; born Missouri, 1851; died Fort Worth, Tex., Nov. 20, 1876; married 2d, Murray, Ky., Oct. 23, 1877, by Rev. Wm. Shelton, to Sallie Ann Ryan, daughter of William and Sarah Vidne (McAtee) Ryan; born Murray, Ky., Feb. 21, 1858.

Issue:

5369. i. THOMAS MARK DAGGETT,[9] born Fort Worth, Tex., March 13, 1876; died Fort Worth, Tex., October 12, 1876.
5370. ii. MAUDE VIDNE DAGGETT,[9] born Murray, Ky., August 30, 1878.
5371. iii. RYAN McKEE DAGGETT,[9] born Fort Worth, Tex., March 30, 1880; died Fort Worth, Tex., March 29, 1883.
5372. iv. HENRY AUSTIN DAGGETT,[9] born Fort Worth, Tex., Dec. 17, 1881.
5373. v. CHARLES BIGGERS DAGGETT,[9] born Fort Worth, Tex., Feb. 10, 1884.

4690. WILLIAM HENRY FARRER [8] (*Sarah A. Daggett,* [7] *Eleazer,* [6] *John,* [5] *John,* [4] *John,* [3] *Samuel,* [2] *Thomas* [1]), born Shelby county, Tex., March 29, 1849; resides Palmer, Tex. (1893); married Ellis county, Tex., Oct. 6, 1878, Nannie Steveanna Runnals, daughter of Stephen and Mary (Turner) Runnals; born Shelby county, Tex., Dec. 14, 1855.

Issue :

5374. i. MAGGIE KATIE FARRER,[9] born Palo Pinto county, Tex., Sept. 29, 1879.
5375. ii. EPHRAIM DAGGETT FARRER,[9] born Palmer, Tex., May 26, 1882.
5376. iii. HELEN ELIZABETH FARRER,[9] born Palmer, Tex., April 21, 1885.
5377. iv. SIMON BOWDON FARRER,[9] born Palmer, Tex., June 30, 1887.

4696. ELEANOR CLAP TROTT [8] (*Eleanor Clap,* [7] *Betsey Doggett,* [6] *Samuel,* [5] *Samuel,* [4] *Isaac,* [3] *Samuel,* [2] *Thomas* [1]), born Lowell, Mass., March 19, 1838; resides Newton, Mass. (1891); married Lowell, Mass., November 3, 1859, by Rev. Frederic Hinckley, to John Eaton Alden, son of George and Hannah (Eaton) Alden, of Dedham, Mass. ; born Dedham, Mass., June 13, 1835.

Issue :

5378. i. MARY ELEANOR ALDEN,[9] born Boston, Mass., February 13, 1861.
5379. ii. MARTHA ELIZABETH ALDEN,[9] born Boston, Mass., January 8, 1865.
5380. iii. JOHN TROTT ALDEN,[9] born Boston, Mass., July 26, 1874.
5381. iv. PRISCILLA ENDICOTT ALDEN,[9] born Boston, Mass., Nov. 28, 1877.

Mr. Alden was connected for some years with the Suffolk Bank, and afterward with the Glendon Iron Company, of Boston, with which he is still associated.

4697. JOHN CLAP TROTT [8] (*Eleanor Clap,* [7] *Betsey Doggett,* [6] *Samuel,* [5] *Samuel,* [4] *Isaac,* [3] *Samuel,* [2] *Thomas* [1]), born Lowell, Mass., February 18, 1840; resides Dedham, Mass. (1891); married Boston, Mass., January 10, 1877, by Rev. George A. Thayer, to Sallie Sturgis Crocker, daughter of Samuel Sturgis and Mary Crocker; born Barnstable, Mass., 1842.

Issue :

5382. i. JOHN ALDEN TROTT,[9] born Boston, Mass., March 16, 1878.

When a young man Mr. Trott entered the United States navy, and held the office of paymaster for many years. While in the service he visited almost every quarter of the globe, but in 1888, being disabled by an accident, he resigned his position. The following year he associated himself with his cousin at Dedham in the manufacture of absorbent cotton, under the style of F. E. Clapp & Co.

4699. MARY ANN CUNNINGHAM TROTT [8] (*Eleanor Clap,* [7] *Betsey Doggett,* [6] *Samuel,* [5] *Samuel,* [4] *Isaac,* [3] *Samuel,* [2] *Thomas* [1]), born Lowell, Mass., July 24, 1845; died Newton, Mass., March 5, 1885; married Lowell, Mass., November 10, 1864, by Rev. Frederic Hinckley, to Frank Henry Kimball, son of William Nelson and Priscilla Kimball

(Hopkinson) Kimball; born Bradford, Mass., October 12, 1843; resides Haverhill, Mass. (1891).

Issue:

5383. i. FRANK HENRY KIMBALL,[9] born Boston, Mass., July 31, 1867; died Boston, Mass., December 6, 1867.
5384. ii. GEORGE ALDEN KIMBALL,[9] born Boston, Mass., July 30, 1869; resides Boston, Mass. (1890).
5385. iii. ELLEN SARGEANT KIMBALL,[9] born Boston, Mass., January 12, 1873; died Boston, Mass., August 17, 1873.
5386. iv. ELEANOR TROTT KIMBALL,[9] born Bradford, Mass., June 26, 1875; died Bradford, Mass., September 17, 1875.
5387. v. CHARLES TROTT KIMBALL,[9] born Bradford, Mass., June 7, 1880; resides Newton, Mass. (1890).

4700. SAMUEL WALLACE CLAPP[8] (*Elizabeth D. Clap,[7] Betsey Doggett,[6] Samuel,[5] Samuel,[4] Isaac,[3] Samuel,[2] Thomas [1]*), born Dedham, Mass., February 18, 1832; resides Fort Scott, Kan. (1891); married St. Joseph, Mo., June 28, 1866, by Rev. B. B. Parsons, to Alice Seymour Lyon, daughter of Harvey and Laura (Seymour) Lyon; born Ogdensburg, N.Y., June 19, 1846.

Issue:

5388. i. ALICE ELIZABETH CLAPP,[9] born St. Joseph, Mo., April 26, 1867.
5389. ii. GRACE SEYMOUR CLAPP,[9] born Sparta, Wis., April 9, 1872; died Racine, Wis., June 24, 1874.
5390. iii. JOHN LYON CLAPP,[9] born Dedham, Mass., February 25, 1876; died Baxter Springs, Kan., September 22, 1879.

Mr. Clapp is by profession a civil engineer and railroad contractor. When the Hannibal & St. Joseph Railroad was built, he went West and superintended its construction. He then located in St. Joseph, Mo., and afterward settled in Fort Scott, Kan., being one of the pioneer settlers of the latter town, and investing largely in real estate there.

4706. ELIZABETH DOGGETT CLAPP[8] (*Elizabeth D. Clap,[7] Betsey Doggett,[6] Samuel,[5] Samuel,[4] Isaac,[3] Samuel,[2] Thomas [1]*), born Dedham, Mass., November 15, 1841; resides Dedham, Mass. (1891); married Dedham, Mass., March 30, 1869, by Rev. Jonathan Edwards, to Freeman Fisher, son of Joshua and Eliza W. (Furnald) Fisher; born Dedham, Mass., Aug. 20, 1841; died Dedham, Mass., March 14, 1876.

Issue:

5391. i. MIRIAM BURGESS FISHER,[9] born Dedham, Mass., October 15, 1870; died Dedham, Mass., January 22, 1882.
5392. ii. KATE PHILLIPS FISHER,[9] born Dedham, Mass., November 27, 1871.
5393. iii. NATHANIEL CLAPP FISHER,[9] born Dedham, Mass., November 4, 1874.
5394. iv. HENRY FREEMAN FISHER,[9] born Dedham, Mass., June 14, 1875; died Dedham, Mass., January 13, 1882.

Mr. Fisher carried on a dairy and milk farm in Dedham, and had established a large trade at the time of his death.

4708. Eleanor Trott Clapp [8] (*Elizabeth D. Clap,* [7] *Betsey Dog-gett,* [6] *Samuel,* [5] *Samuel,* [4] *Isaac,* [3] *Samuel,* [2] *Thomas* [1]), born Dedham, Mass., March 1, 1846; resides Dedham, Mass. (1891); married Dedham, Mass., November 15, 1866, by Rev. Benjamin Bailey, to Ferdinand Clark Field, son of Ozias and Charlotte (Whiting) Field; born Roxbury, Mass., November 24, 1843.

Issue:

5395. i. Eleanor Louise Field, [9] born Dedham, Mass., August 20, 1868; died Dedham, Mass., July 27, 1885.
5396. ii. Edwin Henry Field, [9] born Dedham, Mass., December 10, 1871; died Dedham, Mass., May 30, 1885.
5397. iii. Mary Elizabeth Field, [9] born Dedham, Mass., June 7, 1878; died Dedham, Mass., January 28, 1890.

4712. Sophia Jane Cobb [8] (*Sophia Doggett,* [7] *John,* [6] *Samuel,* [5] *Samuel,* [4] *Isaac,* [3] *Samuel,* [2] *Thomas* [1]), born Dedham, Mass., July 12, 1823; resides Jamaica Plain, Mass. (1891); married Dedham, Mass., March 17, 1842, by Rev. Alvan Lamson, to Abram French, son of Ephraim and Rebecca (Abrams) French; born Chelmsford, Mass., February 13, 1815; died Jamaica Plain, Mass., January 13, 1884.

Issue:

5398. i. William Abram French, [9] born Boston, Mass., October 17, 1843.
5399. ii. Samuel Waldo French, [9] born Boston, Mass., July 14, 1845; treasurer "The Abram French Company;" resides Jamaica Plain, Mass. (1891).
5400. iii. Sophia Jane French, [9] born Dedham, Mass., April 11, 1847; died Boston, Mass., August 17, 1849.
5401. iv. Arthur Burrage French, [9] born Boston, Mass., April 30, 1849.
5402. v. Isabelle Maria French, [9] born Dedham, Mass., September 5, 1854; resides Jamaica Plain, Mass. (1891).
5403. vi. Mary Rosabelle French, [9] born Boston, Mass., September 26, 1856.
5404. vii. Henry Cormerais French, [9] born Boston, Mass., March 21, 1860.
5405. viii. Elizabeth Sophia French, [9] born Boston, Mass., October 23, 1862; resides Jamaica Plain, Mass. (1891).

Mr. French was born in Chelmsford, Mass., whither his parents had removed temporarily from their Winter-street (Boston) home during the hostilities with England. He commenced his business life as a clerk for Samuel B. Pierce, a large crockery merchant on Broad street, in 1831.

In 1846 he formed the firm of French, Wells & Co., and succeeded to the business of Andrew T. Hall, corner of Milk and Batterymarch streets. In 1860 the style was changed to "Bassett & French," and afterward became Abram French & Co. For over twenty-five years he remained in this location, but in 1873 the business had increased to such an extent that a removal was made to the large building corner of Devonshire and Franklin streets, where the business is still conducted under the old style of Abram French & Co.

He was the oldest merchant in his line in New England, if not in the United States, and throughout his long business career maintained his high reputation for honorable dealings.

His success as a merchant was remarkable. Thoroughly familiar with the business in all its details, and with the confidence of every one, his firm had reached the foremost position in the trade. As the requirements and demands changed, the business had been enlarged so as to include all the finest grades of china and glassware, bric-à-brac, and silver-plated ware, and branch houses had been established in Chicago and other cities.

Socially Mr. French was much beloved and respected — genial, cordial, and hospitable, with a remarkably even temper which made him hosts of friends. He never sought for, nor desired, public office, but was devoted to his home and family. During all of his earlier married life he lived in Boston, but afterward purchased the extensive estate at Jamaica Plain known as "Parley Vale," formerly the residence of Peter Parley.

The last twenty years of his life were passed there, and the estate continues to be occupied by the family.

4713. MARIA ELIZABETH COBB [8] (*Sophia Doggett,*[7] *John,*[6] *Samuel,*[5] *Samuel,*[4] *Isaac,*[3] *Samuel,*[2] *Thomas*[1]), born Dedham, Mass., August 13, 1826; died Dedham, Mass., February 24, 1855; married Dedham, Mass., March 22, 1853, by Rev. C. A. Bartol, to Henry Cormerais, son of John and Sarah (Belknap) Cormerais; born Boston, Mass., April 24, 1820; died Dedham, Mass., September 4, 1876.

Issue:

5406. i. ELIZABETH CORMERAIS,[9] born Dedham, Mass., January 17, 1854; died Dedham, Mass., September 5, 1855.

Mr. Cormerais married 2d, Dedham, Mass., May 12, 1857, Mary Otis Sampson, by whom he had four children.

4714. JONATHAN COBB [8] (*Sophia Doggett,*[7] *John,*[6] *Samuel,*[5] *Samuel,*[4] *Isaac,*[3] *Samuel,*[2] *Thomas*[1]), born Dedham, Mass., March 2, 1829; resides Dedham, Mass. (1892); married Dedham, Mass., July 27, 1857, by Rev. Alvan Lamson, to Martha Sigourney Wales, daughter of Samuel and Martha (Sigourney) Wales; born Boston, Mass., March 24, 1832; died Dedham, Mass., June 29, 1877.

Issue:

5407. i. EDWARD SIGOURNEY COBB,[9] born Nashville, Tenn., May 21, 1859.
5408. ii. BENJAMIN WALES COBB,[9] born Dedham, Mass., July 15, 1860; resides there (1891).
5409. iii. CHARLES AUGUSTINE COBB,[9] born Dedham, Mass., April 11, 1863; resides there (1891).
5410. iv. FREDERICK COPELAND COBB,[9] born Dedham, Mass., October 10, 1868; resides there (1891).
5411. v. HENRY WORCESTER COBB,[9] born Dedham, Mass., November 22, 1872; died Dedham, Mass., June 8, 1874.

Jonathan Cobb entered a store in Boston as clerk in 1844, remaining there until January, 1849, when he went overland to California by way of Mexico.

In 1851 he returned to Dedham, and soon afterward went into the store of French, Wells & Co., of Boston, as clerk.   In 1855 he went into business in Nashville, Tenn., under the style of Campbell & Cobb.   In March, 1859, he returned to Dedham and entered the probate office.

He was appointed assistant register of probate and insolvency in January, 1862, and was elected register for the term of five years in 1878, 1883, and 1888.   Was clerk of the First Parish in Dedham about twenty years.

4715.   SAMUEL DOGGETT COBB[8] (*Sophia Doggett*,[7] *John*,[6] *Samuel*,[5] *Samuel*,[4] *Isaac*,[3] *Samuel*,[2] *Thomas*[1]), born Dedham, Mass., August 15, 1831; resides Dedham, Mass. (1892); married Dedham, Mass., March 5, 1867, by Rev. Benjamin Bailey, to Mary Thwing Shumway, daughter of Erastus and Harriet Newell (Gunn) Shumway; born Dedham, Mass., February 18, 1844.

Issue:

5412. i.   NELLIE FANNIE COBB,[9] born Dedham, Mass., September 14, 1867.
5413. ii.   MARY SIBYL COBB,[9] born Dedham, Mass., January 8, 1869; married Dedham, Mass., Nov. 4, 1891, by Rev. William H. Fish, Jr., to Frank Turnbull, son of David F. and Mary (McMillen) Turnbull; born Boston, Mass., Dec. 2, 1867; resides West Roxbury, Mass. (1892).
5414. iii.   WALLACE ERASTUS COBB,[9] born Dedham, Mass., August 24, 1870.
5415. iv.   CARRIE SHUMWAY COBB,[9] born Dedham. Mass., February 9, 1873.
5416. v.   ALICE EVERETT COBB,[9] born Dedham, Mass., October 28, 1876.
5417. vi.   JENNIE ELIZABETH COBB,[9] born Dedham, Mass., August 4, 1879; died Dedham, Mass., February 14, 1883.

Mr. Cobb attended the schools of his native town, mostly of a private character, and studied market gardening in Arlington, Mass. In 1853 he went West with a corps of civil engineers to construct the Hannibal & St. Joseph Railroad.   August 25, 1862, he enlisted in Company D, Forty-third Regiment Massachusetts Volunteer Militia, then forming at Readville. Mass.   The regiment was ordered to North Carolina.

He was engaged in no great or decisive battle, but in constant skirmishes.   He served as color corporal throughout his term of service.   Was mustered out at Readville, Mass., July 30, 1863.

He then went into the employ of his brother-in-law Abram French, in Boston, where he remained nearly twenty-one years.   He has resided in Dedham since his marriage in 1867, where he is now (1892) engaged in carrying on a small farm.

4716.   ISABELLE FRANCES COBB[8] (*Sophia Doggett*,[7] *John*,[6] *Samuel*,[5] *Samuel*,[4] *Isaac*,[3] *Samuel*,[2] *Thomas*[1]), born Dedham,

Mass., April 19, 1835; resides Dedham, Mass. (1892); married Dedham, Mass., May 2, 1860, by Rev. Benjamin Bailey, to Frederic Halverson French, son of William and Anna Rosetta (Halverson) French; born Baltimore, Md., Oct. 24, 1819; died Henderson, Ky., Aug. 16, 1881.

Issue reside at Dedham, excepting F. D. French.

5418. i.   ISABEL COBB FRENCH,[9] born Philadelphia, Pa., March 10, 1862.
5419. ii.   MARION HOBAN FRENCH,[9] born Nashville, Tenn., February 20, 1864.
5420. iii.   ANNA ROSETTA FRENCH,[9] born Nashville, Tenn., April 22, 1866.
5421. iv.   FRANK DANE FRENCH,[9] born Nashville, Tenn., September 18, 1868; married Denver, Col., September 3, 1891, by Rev. Charles Marshall, to Mary Emilé Walther; resides Denver, Col. (1892).
5422. v.   FREDERIC HALVERSON FRENCH,[9] born Nashville, Tenn., Sept. 5, 1870.
5423. vi.   JOHN DUFF FRENCH,[9] born Owensboro', Ky., September 24, 1873.
5424. vii.   ABRAM FRENCH,[9] born Owensboro', Ky., April 10, 1876.

Mr. French was educated at Georgetown College, which he left when he was sixteen years of age and went into the employ of Messrs. Whelan & Co., of Philadelphia. He afterward became a member of the firm and remained there twenty-seven years. He continued to reside in Philadelphia until 1862, when he was appointed as aid on the staff of his brother, Gen. William H. French, U.S.A.

He decided, however, to go to Nashville, Tenn., where he engaged in the shoe business, and removed his family from Philadelphia in 1862. He was a well-known merchant in the business circles of Philadelphia and Nashville, where his integrity, intelligence, activity, and enterprise placed him in the front rank in promoting all that related to the prosperity of these cities. The National Agricultural and Tennessee Horticultural Societies were revived by him.

He founded the Nashville Life Insurance Company, inaugurated the Exposition, and was president of the Board of Trade.

In Nashville he established a manufactory of wheels, spokes, etc., but easy access to better material induced a removal to Owensboro', Ky., in June, 1873, where he had the misfortune to lose two large factories by fire.

In 1880 he went to Henderson, Ky., formed a copartnership under the style of French, Mayer & Co., and successfully started another factory, when an accident there necessitated the amputation of his arm; and from the effects of this shock he died Aug. 16, 1881. After his death his widow and family removed to Dedham, Mass.

4717.   ABBY COBB[8] (*Sophia Doggett,[7] John,[6] Samuel,[5] Samuel,[4] Isaac,[3] Samuel,[2] Thomas[1]*), born Dedham, Mass., May 17, 1837; resides Dedham, Mass. (1891); married Dedham, Mass., January 23, 1860, by Rev. Alvan Lamson, to George Austin Guild, son of Francis and Caroline Elizabeth (Covell) Guild; born Dedham, Mass., June 6, 1836.

Issue:

5425. i.   ABBY ELIZABETH GUILD,[9] born Dedham, Mass., September 8, 1861.

5426. ii. GEORGE COBB GUILD,[9] born Dedham, Mass., December 28, 1863; died Dedham, Mass., January 5, 1869.
5427. iii. SOPHIA DOGGETT GUILD,[9] born Dedham, Mass., December 12, 1865.
5428. iv. JONATHAN FRANCIS GUILD,[9] born Dedham, Mass., September 24, 1871; resides there (1891).

4718. JOHN DOGGETT COBB [8] (*Sophia Doggett,*[7] *John,*[6] *Samuel,*[5] *Samuel,*[4] *Isaac,*[3] *Samuel,*[2] *Thomas*[1]), born Dedham, Mass., April 28, 1840; resides Dedham, Mass. (1891).

Mr. Cobb is not married. He resides in the old homestead. Is assistant register of probate for Norfolk county. He entered the high school in Dedham in 1853, and prepared for Harvard College, from which he graduated A.B. 1861. He continued his studies at the Harvard Law School, and graduated LL.B. in 1866. He served in the war, enlisting August 16, 1862, as sergeant of Company I, Thirty-fifth Regiment Massachusetts Volunteer Militia, and was made captain November 29, 1864. His regiment was in the Army of the Potomac, and he was present in fourteen battles. He is the author of a history of the Thirty-fifth Massachusetts Regiment. He represented Dedham in the General Court in 1876 and 1877.

4719. WILLIAM AUSTIN COBB [8] (*Sophia Doggett,*[7] *John,*[6] *Samuel,*[5] *Samuel,*[4] *Isaac,*[3] *Samuel,*[2] *Thomas*[1]), born Dedham, Mass., August 4, 1845; resides Concord, N.H. (1891); married 1st, Boston, Mass., November 2, 1879, by Rev. C. C. Grafton, to Anna Theresa Sullivan, daughter of Cornelius J. and Mary T. Sullivan; born London, Eng., January 4, 1861; died Haverhill, N.H., January 5, 1887; married 2d, Newbury, Vt., September 24, 1889, by Rev. S. L. Bates. to Mary Elvira Rollins, daughter of Henry G. and Harriet J. (Waddell) Rollins; born Newbury, Vt., March 5, 1859.

Issue :

5429. i. WILLIAM HOLMES COBB,[9] born Plymouth, N.H., August 17, 1880.
5430. ii. JAMES HAROLD COBB,[9] born Plymouth, N.H., March 19, 1882.
5431. iii. SOPHIA DOGGETT COBB,[9] born Plymouth, N.H., December 6, 1884.
5432. iv. WENDELL ROLLINS COBB,[9] born Concord, N.H., November 1, 1890.

Mr. Cobb served his country in the late war, enlisting July 18, 1864, when but nineteen years of age, as private in the Forty-second Regiment Massachusetts Volunteer Militia, and continued in the service until his discharge on November 11 following. He dwelt in Boston until 1871, filling positions of entry clerk and book-keeper. He was chief clerk of the Pemigewasset House, Plymouth, N.H., in the summer of 1871, and then entered the employ of the Boston, Concord & Montreal Railroad, continuing with that road until its lease in 1884. He filled the following positions with that railroad, in the order named : Superintendent's clerk, car accountant, assistant cashier, head of freight department, 1875 to 1883; general freight agent, promoted to paymaster, cashier, and assistant treasurer, 1883–4.

In 1885 he was elected register of deeds for Grafton county, N.H., serving two terms of two years each.   He has been treasurer of Grafton County Agricultural Society from 1881 to the present time (1891).   In 1889 he was appointed accountant of the freight department of the Concord & Montreal Railroad, which position he now holds, and resides in Concord, N.H.   He takes an active interest in Grand Army affairs, and is adjutant of E. E. Sturtevant Post, No. 2, Department of New Hampshire, at Concord.

4723.   John Doggett[8] (*William F.,*[7] *John,*[6] *Samuel,*[5] *Samuel,*[4] *Isaac,*[3] *Samuel,*[2] *Thomas*[1]), born near Pisgah, Ohio, June 3, 1844; resides Plain City, Ohio (1891); married Lima, Ohio, November 1, 1877, by Rev. Thomas P. Johnston, to Mary Larrissa Martin, daughter of Hon. Andrew J. and Sarah Ann (Stagg) Martin; born ten miles east of Columbus, Ohio, December 2, 1853.

Issue :

5433. i.   Birdie Pearl Doggett,[9] born Lima, Ohio, July 15, 1878.
5434. ii.   Ritta Pleasant Doggett,[9] born Lima, Ohio, August 12, 1879.
5435. iii. Leslie Russell Doggett,[9] born Lima, Ohio, October 18, 1880.
5436. iv.   Jane Ethel Doggett,[9] born Lima, Ohio, June 20, 1882.
5437. v.   Etta Elizabeth Doggett,[9] born Lima, Ohio, March 17, 1884.
5438. vi.   Talmage Martin Doggett,[9] born Plain City, Ohio, Aug. 14, 1888.

John Doggett was for twenty years in a railway office with his father, since which time he has been inventing and improving several kinds of instruments, among others a combined telegraph key and sounder.   Mrs. Doggett's father is (1891) mayor of Plain City.

4724.   Jane Miller Doggett[8] (*William F.,*[7] *John,*[6] *Samuel,*[5] *Samuel,*[4] *Isaac,*[3] *Samuel,*[2] *Thomas*[1]), born Mason, Ohio, February 15, 1846; resides 1090 North Tennessee street, Indianapolis, Ind. (1893); married Columbus, Ohio, April 25, 1866, by Rev. Wm. R. Marshall, to Wallace Foster, son of Riley and Sarah J. (Wallace) Foster; born Vernon, Ind., June 22, 1837.

Issue :

5439. i.   William Edgar Foster,[9] born Indianapolis, Ind., February 13, 1867.
5440. ii.   Lucia Shriver Foster,[9] born Indianapolis, Ind., October 20, 1871; died Indianapolis, Ind., September 6, 1881.

Wallace Foster was a druggist in Indianapolis at the breaking out of the Rebellion, and a member of the Independent Zouaves.   He enlisted on the day of President Lincoln's first call for volunteers, April 16, 1861, and was commissioned lieutenant, Company H, Eleventh Indiana Infantry, three months' campaign.   He reënlisted in the Thirteenth Indiana Infantry (Old Guard), and was promoted respectively lieutenant and captain of Company H.

Later he was appointed aid-de-camp to Brig.-Gen. Jerry C. Sullivan and Maj.-Gen. Robert S. Foster.

At the close of the Rebellion he was connected with the United States Pay Department, later commissioned on special service at Cairo, Ill., and Memphis, Tenn. He is a charter member of George H. Thomas Post, No. 17, G.A.R., of Indianapolis. He is now (1892) record clerk of the Consumers Natural Gas Trust Company, of Indianapolis.

4725. SAMUEL JACKSON DOGGETT [8] (*William F.,* [7] *John,* [6] *Samuel,* [5] *Samuel,* [4] *Isaac,* [3] *Samuel,* [2] *Thomas* [1]), born Kenton, O., March 16, 1850; died Chicago, Ill., December 1, 1887; married New Orleans, La., December 13, 1871, by Rev. Benjamin Palmer, to Mary Elizabeth Harlan, daughter of Samuel Dawson and Sarah Martha (McGregor) Harlan; born Washington, Tex., September 29, 1853; resides 3936 Indiana avenue, Chicago, Ill. (1891).

Issue:

5441. i. HARRY HARLAN DOGGETT,[9] born Chicago, Ill., September 16, 1872.
5442. ii. WILLIAM FRANCIS DOGGETT,[9] born Chicago, Ill., September 16, 1872.
5443. iii. ANNA ISABEL DOGGETT,[9] born Chicago, Ill., August 29, 1874; died Chicago, Ill., October 9, 1874.
5444. iv. EDWIN WALKER DOGGETT,[9] born Chicago, Ill., December 1, 1877.
5445. v. BENJAMIN DOGGETT,[9] born Chicago, Ill., June 5, 1879; died Chicago, Ill., June 5, 1879.
5446. vi. FLORENCE DOGGETT,[9] born Chicago, Ill., October 24, 1881; died Chicago, Ill., October 25, 1881.

4726. ELIZABETH DOGGETT [8] (*William F.,* [7] *John,* [6] *Samuel,* [5] *Samuel,* [4] *Isaac,* [3] *Samuel,* [2] *Thomas* [1]), born Dayton, Ohio, March 14, 1852; resides 337 Parsons avenue, Columbus, Ohio (1891); married Columbus, Ohio, April 22, 1869, by Rev. J. Beck, to John Bowman, son of George and Elizabeth (Auspach) Bowman; born Reading, Ohio, January 6, 1843.

Issue:

5447. i. WILLIAM WALLACE BOWMAN,[9] born Columbus, Ohio, June 20, 1870.
5448. ii. ALICE JANET BOWMAN,[9] born Columbus, Ohio, November 3, 1874.
5449. iii. HARRY LEROY BOWMAN,[9] born Chicago, Ill., June 11, 1877.
5450. iv. IDA FLORENCE BOWMAN,[9] born Columbus, Ohio, September 18, 1880.

4727. MARY CURTIS [8] (*Mary A. C. Doggett,* [7] *Samuel,* [6] *Samuel,* [5] *Samuel,* [4] *Isaac,* [3] *Samuel,* [2] *Thomas* [1]), born Roxbury, Mass., Dec. 21, 1840; resides Washington, D.C. (1891); married Somerville, Mass., Oct. 26, 1865, by Rev. E. Porter Dyer, to Samuel Fay Rugg, son of Hosea and Rebecca (Sanderson) Rugg; born Northboro', Mass., Jan. 29, 1834.

Issue:

5451. i. FRANK CURTIS RUGG,[9] born Charlestown, Mass., September 16, 1866; died Cambridge, Mass., August 8, 1881.
5452. ii. JENNIE THAYER RUGG,[9] born Cambridge, Mass., April 22, 1869.
5453. iii. ELLEN MARSHALL RUGG,[9] born Cambridge, Mass., December 1, 1871.
5454. iv. LURA CURRIER RUGG,[9] born Cambridge, Mass., June 21, 1876.

4728. FANNIE CURTIS[8] (*Mary A. C. Doggett,*[7] *Samuel,*[6] *Samuel,*[5] *Samuel,*[4] *Isaac,*[3] *Samuel,*[2] *Thomas*[1]), born Roxbury, Mass., March 7, 1843; resides Somerville, Mass. (1891); married Somerville, Mass., Oct. 22, 1862, by Rev. D. T. Packard, to Frederic William Jacques, son of William and Adaline Jane (Carter) Jaques, of "Ten Hills," Somerville, Mass.; born Somerville, Mass., Feb. 22, 1840.

Issue:

5455. i. LOUIS CURTIS JAQUES,[9] born Somerville, Mass., November 27, 1868.
5456. ii. SIDNEY HARRIS JAQUES,[9] born Somerville, Mass., July 18, 1870.
5457. iii. MARIAN ASHLEY JAQUES,[9] born Somerville, Mass., December 18, 1872; died Somerville, Mass., May 23, 1873.

They reside at Somerville, Mass., on a part of the old "Ten Hills" farm, which has been in the Jaques family for several generations. He was engaged with his father for many years in the manufacture of bricks, and was for some time superintendent of the Bay State Brick Company, of which his father was president.

4730. LOUISE AUGUSTA CRAFTS[8] (*Emily Doggett,*[7] *Samuel,*[6] *Samuel,*[5] *Samuel,*[4] *Isaac,*[3] *Samuel,*[2] *Thomas*[1]), born Roxbury, Mass., February 21, 1843; resides Roxbury, Mass. (1893); married Boston, Mass., October 30, 1866, by Rev. E. E. Hale and Rev. George Putnam, to Henry Watson Gore, son of Watson and Charlotte Louisa (White) Gore, of Boston; born Roxbury, Mass., June 17, 1842.

Issue:

5458. i. HENRY WATSON GORE,[9] born Roxbury, Mass., October 9, 1871.

Mr. Gore served in the civil war, enlisting May 26, 1862, and serving until December 30, 1865, with the exception of the year 1863, during which he resigned, and was in business in Chicago.

Since the war he has resided in Chicago, Grand Rapids, and Boston.

4735. ELIZABETH SUMNER LEWIS[8] (*George,*[7] *Elizabeth S. Doggett,*[6] *Jesse,*[5] *Samuel,*[4] *Isaac,*[3] *Samuel,*[2] *Thomas*[1]), born Roxbury, Mass., April 24, 1851; resides 429 Marlboro' street, Boston, Mass. (1891); married Roxbury, Mass., Jan. 8, 1874, by Rev. H. W. Foote, to Thorndike Nourse, son of John Frederick and Annie Thorndike (Rand) Nourse, of Boston; born Beverly, Mass., Dec. 29, 1847.

Issue:

5459. i. ANNIE ENDICOTT NOURSE,[9] born Detroit, Mich., May 4, 1875.
5460. ii. GEORGE LEWIS NOURSE,[9] born Roxbury, Mass., July 9, 1877; died Detroit, Mich., June 4, 1881.

4737. ADELINE WHEELWRIGHT LEWIS[8] (*George,*[7] *Elizabeth S. Doggett,*[6] *Jesse,*[5] *Samuel,*[4] *Isaac,*[3] *Samuel,*[2] *Thomas*[1]), born Roxbury, Mass., November 22, 1858; resides Medford, Mass. (1891); married Boston, Mass., December 15, 1887, by Rev. James DeNormandie, to John Heard, Jr., son of Augustine and Jane Leep (De-Cormick) Heard, of Ipswich, Mass. ; born Paris, France, May 4, 1859.

Issue :

5461. i. Albert Farley Heard,[9] born Medford, Mass., April 20, 1889.

4738. George Lewis[8] (*George,*[7] *Elizabeth S. Doggett,*[6] *Jesse,*[5] *Samuel,*[4] *Isaac,*[3] *Samuel,*[2] *Thomas*[1]), born Roxbury, Mass., July 7, 1860 ; resides Dorchester, Mass. (1892) ; married Roxbury, Mass., October 14, 1884, by Rev. James DeNormandie, to Marian Gray, daughter of William and Katherine H. (Cunningham) Gray ; born Dorchester, Mass., March 8, 1863.

Issue :

5462. i. Marian Lewis,[9] born Dorchester, Mass., July 22, 1885.
5463. ii. George Lewis,[9] born Dorchester, Mass., August 30, 1887.

Mr. Lewis is a member of the firm of Wheelwright, Eldredge & Co., woollens, Boston.

4739. John Mason Hadaway[8] (*Kate Carter,*[7] *Eunice Doggett,*[6] *Elisha,*[5] *Samuel,*[4] *Isaac,*[3] *Samuel,*[2] *Thomas*[1]), born Chelsea, Mass., June 18, 1853; resides 5 Suffolk street, Chelsea, Mass. (1891) ; married Chelsea, Mass., November 24, 1875, by Rev. C. P. H. Nason, to Ella Eva Cora Kibby, daughter of Charles Kibby.

Issue :

5464. i. Lewella Hadaway,[9] born Chelsea, Mass., September, 1878.

4740. Daniel Hadaway[8] (*Kate Carter,*[7] *Eunice Doggett,*[6] *Elisha,*[5] *Samuel,*[4] *Isaac,*[3] *Samuel,*[2] *Thomas*[1]), born Chelsea, Mass., March 11, 1856; resides (1891) Newton Highlands, Mass.; married Chelsea, Mass., Jan. 18, 1882, by Rev. John Love, to Florence S. Lees.

Issue :

5465. i. Ralph Lees Hadaway,[9] born Newton Highlands, Mass., June 24, 1890.

4747. Ella Palmer[8] (*Elizabeth Cummings,*[7] *Elizabeth Doggett,*[6] *Elisha,*[5] *Samuel,*[4] *Isaac,*[3] *Samuel,*[2] *Thomas*[1]), resides Bayonne, N.J. (1891) ; married William Leeman.

Issue :

5466. i. Herbert Leeman.[9]
5467. ii. Louise Leeman.[9]

4763. Charles Jacob Babbitt[8] (*Mary E. Eaton,*[7] *Mary Doggett,*[6] *Elisha,*[5] *Samuel,*[4] *Isaac,*[3] *Samuel,*[2] *Thomas*[1]), born Providence, R.I., 1854; married Cornelia J. Snow.

Issue :

5468. i. Cora Babbitt.[9]

4769. Louis Francis Brown[8] (*Louise B. Eaton,*[7] *Mary Doggett,*[6] *Elisha,*[5] *Samuel,*[4] *Isaac,*[3] *Samuel,*[2] *Thomas*[1]), born Boston,

Mass., Dec. 16, 1864 ; resides Chicago, Ill. (1892) ; married Boston, Mass., March 20, 1888, by Rev. E. A. Horton, to Jennie Brigham Boyd.
Issue :

5469. i. Roger Francis Brown,[9] born July, 1889 ; died September 14, 1889.

THOMAS DOGGETT, OF MARSHFIELD, MASS.

NINTH GENERATION.

4771. William Doggett [9] (*John*,[8] *John*,[7] *Ichabod*,[6] *John*,[5] *John*,[4] *Thomas*,[3] *John*,[2] *Thomas* [1]), born White Point, N.S., February 20, 1857; resides White Point, N.S. (1891) ; married by Rev. Mr. Bigny, to Sophia Fitzgerald, daughter of William and Catherine (Magan) Fitzgerald ; born Hunt's Point, N.S.
Issue :

5470. i. William Alexander Doggett,[10] born White Point, N.S., July 8, 1883.
5471. ii. Effie Bond Doggett,[10] born White Point, N.S., July 10, 1890.

4875. Joseph Doley Wyld [9] (*Elizabeth W. Daggett*,[8] *Shepard*,[7] *Mark*,[6] *Jabez*,[5] *Thomas*,[4] *Thomas*,[3] *John*,[2] *Thomas* [1]), born Charleston, S.C., July 17, 1848 ; resides Charleston, S.C. (1893) ; married Charleston, S.C., Dec. 1, 1872, Anna Sigwald, daughter of Christian Baker and Eliza Mary (Burch) Sigwald ; born Charleston, S.C., Sept. 8, 1854.
Issue :

5472. i.   Vincent Sigwald Wyld,[10] born Charleston. S.C., October 21, 1873.
5473. ii. Edward Christopher Wyld,[10] born Charleston, S.C., Sept. 19, 1875.
5474. iii. Joseph Percival Rutledge Wyld,[10] born Charleston, S.C., November 24, 1877.
5475. iv. Eliza Mary Wyld,[10] born Charleston, S.C., October 4, 1879 ; died Charleston, S.C., October 5, 1879.
5476. v.   George Doley Wyld,[10] born Charleston, S.C., September 10, 1881.

4881. Mary Ann Daggett [9] (*William L.*,[8] *Shepard*,[7] *Mark*,[6] *Jabez*,[5] *Thomas*,[4] *Thomas*,[3] *John*,[2] *Thomas* [1]), born Charleston, S.C., November 21, 1846; resides Charleston, S.C. (1893) ; married 1st, Charleston, S.C., December 27, 1870, William Henry Keckeley, son of George Washington and Caroline Elizabeth (Shaffer) Keckeley ; born Columbia, S.C., December 27, 1845; died Charleston, S.C., March 2, 1876; married 2d, Charleston, S.C., October 23, 1888, Henry William Sigwald, son of Mary (Syfan) Sigwald ; born Charleston, S.C., May 28, 1825; died Charleston, S.C., July 19, 1890.
Issue :

5477. i. William Lafayette Keckeley,[10] born Charleston, S.C., December 23, 1871 ; died Charleston, S.C., February 26, 1878.
5478. ii. George Washington Keckeley,[10] born Charleston, S.C., May 31, 1872 ; resides Charleston, S.C. (1893).

4885. WALTER LAMBERT DAGGETT[9] (*William L.*,[8] *Shepard*,[7] *Mark*,[6] *Jabez*,[5] *Thomas*,[4] *Thomas*,[3] *John*,[2] *Thomas*[1]), born Charleston, S.C., May 4, 1854; manager "Daggett Printing Company," 153 East Bay, Charleston, S.C. (1893); married Charleston, S.C., May 4, 1881, Angela Eva Salvo, daughter of Vincent Marinith and Marie Eloise (Lafourcade) Salvo; born Charleston, S.C., March 10, 1864.

Issue:

5479. i. INA ELOISE DAGGETT,[10] born Charleston, S.C., March 2, 1882.
5480. ii. MARY CANNON FALES DAGGETT,[10] born Charleston, S.C., June 21, 1884.
5481. iii. LENONORA EULALIE DAGGETT,[10] born Charleston, S.C., Dec. 28, 1886.
5482. iv. EVA LAMBERT DAGGETT,[10] born Charleston, S.C., Jan. 24, 1888.
5483. v. LILIEN OCTAVIA DAGGETT,[10] born Charleston, S.C., Feb. 26, 1890.
5484. vi. WALTER LAFAYETTE DAGGETT,[10] born Charleston, S.C., March 26, 1893; died Charleston, S.C., April 21, 1893.

4966. GEORGE DAGGETT[9] (*Simeon*,[8] *Mark*,[7] *Mark*,[6] *Jabez*,[5] *Thomas*,[4] *Thomas*,[3] *John*,[2] *Thomas*[1]), born Grand Manan, N.B., February 7, 1866; "carpenter;" resides Somerville, Mass. (1893); married Grand Manan, N.B., January 23, 1885, by Rev. W. S. Covert, to Helena Russell, daughter of William Russell; born Grand Manan, N.B., April 19, 1868.

Issue:

5485. i. DONALD C. DAGGETT,[10] born Grand Manan, N.B., April 27, 1890.

5002. GEORGE NEWELL DOGGETT[9] (*William E.*,[8] *Elkanah*,[7] *Thomas*,[6] *Simeon*,[5] *Thomas*,[4] *Thomas*,[3] *John*,[2] *Thomas*[1]), born Chicago, Ill., December 19, 1858; died Fredericksburg, Va., January 15, 1887; married Fredericksburg, Va., February 22, 1885, Hughgenia Sally Doggett, daughter of Lee Roy Benjamin and Lucy Frances (Jerrell) Doggett (see No. 6186); born Fredericksburg, Va., Sept. 5, 1867; resides 2951 Prairie avenue, Chicago, Ill. (1893).

Issue:

5486. i. ETHEL NEWELL DOGGETT,[10] born November 27, 1885.

5007. LEWIS CHITTENDEN DOGGETT[9] (*Joseph B.*,[8] *Elkanah*,[7] *Thomas*,[6] *Simeon*,[5] *Thomas*,[4] *Thomas*,[3] *John*,[2] *Thomas*[1]), born Chicago, Ill., October 5, 1858; superintendent Fairbanks & Co.'s Lard Refinery, St. Louis, Mo. (1893); married Chicago, Ill., March 16, 1882, by Rev. L. P. Mercer, to Grace Miriam Mülheim, daughter of Charles and Grace Letitia (Lander) Mülheim; born Nashville, Ill., February 17, 1865.

Issue:

5487. i. MARGARET BURNET DOGGETT,[10] born St. Louis, Mo., Feb. 13, 1883.
5488. ii. HENRY COURTRIGHT DOGGETT,[10] born St. Louis, Mo., Oct. 11, 1885.

5009. WILLIAM ELKANAH DOGGETT[9] (*Thomas*,[8] *Elkanah*,[7] *Thomas*,[6] *Simeon*,[5] *Thomas*,[4] *Thomas*,[3] *John*,[2] *Thomas*[1]), born Madison, Wis., March 17, 1855; resides Flatbush, Long Island, N.Y. (1893); married 1st, Niagara Falls, N.Y., August 21, 1883, Cora Delle Pierce, daughter of John Spencer and Laura (Smith) Pierce; born Niagara Falls, N.Y., December 30, 1861; died Brooklyn, N.Y., January 19, 1888; married 2d, Bramley, Eng., July 16, 1890, Lucy Verity, daughter of John Kirk and Sarah (Young) Verity; born Bramley, Eng., January 16, 1867.

Issue:

5489. i. MARTHA ALICE DOGGETT,[10] born Flemington, N.J., March 25, 1885; died Flemington, N.J., November 27, 1885.
5490. ii. ALLEN THOMAS DOGGETT,[10] born Brooklyn, N.Y., August 4, 1886.
5491. iii. JOSEPH PIERCE DOGGETT,[10] born Brooklyn, N.Y., December 6, 1887.

Mr. Doggett is instructor in mathematics and commercial law at the Boys' High School, Marcy and Putnam avenues, Brooklyn, N.Y. (1893).

5010. CHARLES STEBBINS DOGGETT[9] (*Thomas,*[8] *Elkanah,*[7] *Thomas,*[6] *Simeon,*[5] *Thomas,*[4] *Thomas,*[3] *John,*[2] *Thomas*[1]), born Groveland, Mass., November 27, 1858; resides 342 Meridian street, East Boston, Mass. (1893); married Bramley, Eng., August 25, 1886, by Rev. J. Robinson, to Sara Anne Verity, daughter of John Kirk and Sarah (Young) Verity; born Bramley, Eng., December 1, 1864.

Issue:

5492. i. MARGUERITE VERITY DOGGETT,[10] born Walpole, Mass., Dec. 22, 1887.
5493. ii. LUCY LEE DOGGETT,[10] born Walpole, Mass., November 22, 1889.

Charles S. Doggett is a chemical engineer. He is at present (1893) with Messrs. William H. Swift & Co., of Boston, Mass.

He has been with the Willimantic Company in Connecticut, and with the Walpole Dye and Chemical Company at Walpole, Mass., and has spent a year in study and experiment in Manchester, Eng.

5011. ALLEN BARROWS DOGGETT[9] (*Thomas,*[8] *Elkanah,*[7] *Thomas,*[6] *Simeon,*[5] *Thomas,*[4] *Thomas,*[3] *John,*[2] *Thomas*[1]), born Groveland, Mass., June 18, 1860; resides Flatbush, Long Island, N.Y. (1893); married Montclair, N.J., Feb. 26, 1885, by Rev. Amory H. Bradford, D.D., to Mary Letitia Rogers, daughter of Marvin Newton and Mary Elizabeth (Spence) Rogers; born Georgetown, Tex., Dec. 4, 1863.

Issue:

5494. i. ALLEN BARROWS DOGGETT,[10] born Munich, Ger., October 23, 1887.
5495. ii. MARVIN ROGERS DOGGETT,[10] born Bryan, Ohio, November 7, 1889.
5496. iii. EUNICE DOGGETT,[10] born 1891.

Allen B. Doggett was for some years with the Forbes Lithograph Manufacturing Company, Boston, Mass., and resided at Charlestown, Mass. His talent for artistic work was there developed, and he left Boston for study in Europe in 1887.

He was accepted by the "Royal Academy of Fine Arts, Munich," which was highly complimentary to his ability, as there were but ten vacancies and one hundred and twenty-five contestants for them. He returned to America in the summer of 1889, after which he remained in Bryan, Ohio, until September, 1890, when he opened a studio on Fourteenth street, near Fifth avenue, in New York city.

5015. HORACE FREDERIC LEONARD [9] (*Phœbe D. Sampson*,[8] *Phœbe D. Doggett*,[7] *Thomas*,[6] *Simeon*,[5] *Thomas*,[4] *Thomas*,[3] *John*,[2] *Thomas*[1]), born Lakeville, Mass., May 26, 1848; resides Marshall, Mich. (1890); married Marshall, Mich., June 7, 1870, Flora Gray, of Marshall, Mich.

Issue:

5497. i. INEZ LOUISA LEONARD,[10] born Marshall, Mich., April 21, 1872; died Marshall, Mich., September, 1872.
5498. ii. FREDERIC GRAY LEONARD,[10] born Marshall, Mich., April 28, 1879.

5016. MARY SAMPSON LEONARD [9] (*Phœbe D. Sampson*,[8] *Phœbe D. Doggett*,[7] *Thomas*,[6] *Simeon*,[5] *Thomas*,[4] *Thomas*,[3] *John*,[2] *Thomas*[1]), born Lakeville, Mass., July 27, 1851; resides (1890) New Baltimore, Mich.; married Lakeville, Mass., December 25, 1871, Emmett Gordon, of New Baltimore, Mich.

Issue:

5499. i. NORA ISABEL GORDON,[10] born New Baltimore, Mich., Nov. 14, 1872.

5021. FANNIE BELL LEONARD [9] (*Phœbe D. Sampson*,[8] *Phœbe D. Doggett*,[7] *Thomas*,[6] *Simeon*,[5] *Thomas*,[4] *Thomas*,[3] *John*,[2] *Thomas*[1]), born Lakeville, Mass., May 30, 1861; resides Lakeville, Mass. (1890); married Lakeville, Mass., November 6, 1882, William F. Harlow, of Lakeville, Mass.

Issue:

5500. i. CLYDE LEONARD HARLOW,[10] born Lakeville, Mass., August 17, 1884.

5030. BOLIVAR DOGGETT [9] (*Samuel W.*,[8] *Samuel W.*,[7] *Simeon*,[6] *Simeon*,[5] *Thomas*,[4] *Thomas*,[3] *John*,[2] *Thomas*[1]), born Diamond Springs, Eldorado Co., Cal., April 4, 1855; died San Francisco, Cal., April, 1886; married June 11, 1875, Catherine McNeeve; born California; died San Francisco, Cal., February, 1890.

Issue:

5501. i. MARY DOGGETT,[10] born San Francisco, Cal., 1876.
5502. ii. WINETTA DOGGETT,[10] born San Francisco, Cal., 1878.
5503. iii. RALPH DOGGETT,[10] born San Francisco, Cal., 1880.
5504. iv. ALFRED DOGGETT,[10] born San Francisco, Cal., 1882.

Bolivar Doggett received a public-school education, and was a first-class mechanic, having learned the trade of plumbing and gas-fitting.   His father in speaking of his sons' career in life as mechanics says : " It resulted in no manner from their lack of intellectuality, nor was it of their own volition ; but on the contrary it was according to my judgment and election, the former based upon a long and cosmopolitan experience, and observation of the human family and its life-struggles."

Bolivar Doggett married Catherine McNeeve, a native of California, and daughter of Irish parents, born in Roscommon county. Mr. Doggett was a man of good physique, standing over six feet, and weighing one hundred and seventy-six pounds.

5031.   DANTON C. DOGGETT [9] (*Samuel W.*,[8] *Samuel W.*,[7] *Simeon*,[6] *Simeon*,[5] *Thomas*,[4] *Thomas*,[3] *John*,[2] *Thomas* [1]), born San Francisco, Cal., November 5, 1858 ; resides 1823 Greenwich street, San Francisco, Cal. ; married Celina Neulens, daughter of Jules Buessard and Marguerite (Le Loudec) Neulens.

Issue :

5505. i.   CALHOUN JULES DOGGETT,[10] born San Francisco, Cal., May 9, 1881.

Danton C. Doggett received a common-school education, and was indentured at the age of sixteen to Messrs. Bacon & Co., book and job printers, and is now (1884) their principal foreman, in charge of the steam presses of this extensive printing-company.   He married Celina Neulens, daughter of Jules Buessard Neulens, born in Noure, Belgium, and graduate of " Conservatoire Royal des Arts et Metiers," and Marguerite Le Loudec, born in Paimpol, Brittany, France.

5032.   SUMPTER E. DOGGETT [9] (*Samuel W.*,[8] *Samuel W.*,[7] *Simeon*,[6] *Simeon*,[5] *Thomas*,[4] *Thomas*,[3] *John*,[2] *Thomas* [1]), born San Francisco, Cal., July 3, 1862 ; resides 1517 Mason street, San Francisco, Cal. ; married San Francisco, Cal., April 27, 1883, Bertha Margaret Corneps ; born San Francisco, Cal., 1862.

Sumpter E. Doggett was educated in the public schools of San Francisco.   He married Bertha Margaret Corneps, whose parents both are natives of Hanover, Ger.   He learned the trade of a pressman, and is now (1884) superintendent of the press department of Messrs. Francis Valentine & Co., of San Francisco, though but a year past his majority.

5037.   HARRY ARTHUR WHEELER [9] (*Julia H. Doggett*,[8] *Samuel W.*,[7] *Simeon*,[6] *Simeon*,[5] *Thomas*,[4] *Thomas*,[3] *John*,[2] *Thomas* [1]), born Fitzwilliam, N.H., August 30, 1861 ; resides Grand Rapids, Mich. (1890) ; married Grand Rapids, Mich., December 17, 1884, by William G. Saunders, J.P., to Elizabeth Frances Gallaway, daughter of Alexander and Matilda (Keetham) Gallaway; born Grandville, Mich., June 16, 1868.

Issue:

5506. i. ARTHUR WHEELER,[10] born Grand Rapids, Mich., November 18, 1885.
5507. ii. HAZEL PEARL WHEELER,[10] born Grand Rapids, Mich., May 11, 1886; died in infancy.

5146. FRANK CHILSON [9] (*Ezra,*[8] *Milo,*[7] *Pamela Daggett,*[6] *John,*[5] *John,*[4] *John,*[3] *Samuel,*[2] *Thomas* [1]), born Fairview, Pa., Jan. 11, 1855; resides Conneaut, Ohio (1893); married Monroe, Ohio, Aug. 19, 1879, by Rev. Mr. Bliss, to Jennie May Laird, daughter of Horace and Mary (Minneley) Laird; born Monroe, Ohio, Feb. 27, 1859.

Issue:

5508. i. CARL CHILSON,[10] born Amboy, Ohio, July 11, 1880.
5509. ii. BIRDIE BENTON CHILSON,[10] born Conneaut, Ohio, April 27, 1882.

5148. JENNIE CHILSON [9] (*Ezra,*[8] *Milo,*[7] *Pamela Daggett,*[6] *John,*[5] *John,*[4] *John,*[3] *Samuel,*[2] *Thomas* [1]), born Girard, Pa., September 13, 1859; died Amboy, Ohio, September 28, 1881; married Amboy, Ohio, April 29, 1877, by Rev. O. P. Wyman, to Lee Green, son of Alonzo and Mary Elizabeth (McCreary) Green; born Fairview, Pa., May 5, 1854; resides Amboy, Ohio (1893).

Issue:

5510. i. MINNIE GREEN,[10] born Amboy, Ohio, December 14, 1877.
5511. ii. GERTRUDE GREEN,[10] born Amboy, Ohio, June 10, 1879.
5512. iii. NELLIE GREEN,[10] born Amboy, Ohio, April 29, 1881.

5154. ELLA FRANCES HATFIELD [9] (*Mariette Chilson,*[8] *Theron,*[7] *Pamela Daggett,*[6] *John,*[5] *John,*[4] *John,*[3] *Samuel,*[2] *Thomas* [1]), born Niles, Mich., February 1, 1855; resides Marion, Ind. (1893); married Frank E. Alward.

Issue:

5513. i. BESSIE MARY ALWARD,[10] born Niles, Mich., June 29, 1878.
5514. ii. FLORENCE ELLA ALWARD,[10] born Niles, Mich., June 2, 1880.
5515. iii. IDA MAY ALWARD,[10] born Niles, Mich., July 20, 1882.

5174. ELIZABETH MAUD FULLER [9] (*Helen M. Henderson,*[8] *Laura L. Chilson,*[7] *Pamela Daggett,*[6] *John,*[5] *John,*[4] *John,*[3] *Samuel,*[2] *Thomas* [1]), born Dowagiac, Mich., July 8, 1864; resides Kalamazoo, Mich. (1893); married Fruitport, Mich., May 15, 1883, by Rev. James F. Hill, to Frank Graham Plews, son of Thomas and Emma Wilder (Hagerman) Plews; born Northumberland county, Ontario, Can.

Issue:

5516. i. HARRY SYLVESTER PLEWS,[10] born Kalamazoo, Mich., July 13, 1885.
5517. ii. ETTIE GRACE PLEWS,[10] born Kalamazoo, Mich., March 27, 1887.
5518. iii. LESLIE GRAHAM PLEWS,[10] born Kalamazoo, Mich., March 3, 1891.

5184. Harriet Lodema Wildman [9] (*Willis T.,*[8] *Laura Daggett,*[7] *Sebra,*[6] *John,*[5] *John,*[4] *John,*[3] *Samuel,*[2] *Thomas* [1]), born Greenfield, Pa., January 8, 1859 ; resides Boscobel, Pa. (1893) ; married Greenfield, Pa., September 15, 1877, by Rev. William H. Adams, to Francis Orlando Cardot, son of Francis and Sarah Jane (Burnham) Cardot; born Arkwright, N.Y., January 21, 1852.

Issue :

5519. i.   Charles Willis Cardot,[10] born Greenfield, Pa., June 11, 1879.
5520. ii. Clayton Francis Cardot,[10] born Greenfield, Pa., July 21, 1883.
5521. iii. Bertha May Cardot,[10] born Greenfield, Pa., May 10, 1889.

5186. Lewis Levator Randal [9] (*Lucinda Wildman,*[8] *Laura Daggett,*[7] *Sebra,*[6] *John,*[5] *John,*[4] *John,*[3] *Samuel,*[2] *Thomas* [1]), born Greenfield, Pa., Dec. 25, 1865 ; married Findley's Lake, N.Y., Dec. 24, 1885, by Rev. A. H. Bowers, to Ella Dunlap, daughter of John and Jeannette (Nutting) Dunlap; born Spring Creek, Pa., April 21, 1871.

Issue :

5522. i.   Floyd Clayton Randal,[10] born Venango, Pa., March 24, 1887.
5523. ii. Edith Blanche Randal,[10] born Greenfield, Pa., August 12, 1888.
5524. iii. Glen Allanson Randal,[10] born Greenfield, Pa., February 25, 1891.

5193. Willis Melvin Ellsworth [9] (*Annis Wildman,*[8] *Laura Daggett,*[7] *Sebra,*[6] *John,*[5] *John,*[4] *John,*[3] *Samuel,*[2] *Thomas* [1]), born Greenfield, Pa., August 6, 1863; resides Phillipsville, Pa. (1893) ; married Phillipsville, Pa., April 30, 1890, by Rev. J. P. Hicks, to Mary Agnes Young, daughter of Albert and Sylvia (Tompkins) Young; born Seneca Falls, N.Y., May 21, 1871.

Issue :

5525. i.   Floyd Harrison Ellsworth,[10] born Phillipsville, Pa., Jan. 6, 1891.
5526. ii. Lena May Ellsworth,[10] born Phillipsville, Pa., December 17, 1892.

5201. Lilly Martha Daggett [9] (*Cyrus S.,*[8] *Austin,*[7] *Sebra,*[6] *John,*[5] *John,*[4] *John,*[3] *Samuel,*[2] *Thomas* [1]), born Girard, Pa., Oct. 26, 1856 ; resides Beebeetown, Ia. (1893) ; married Beebeetown, Ia., March 31, 1875, by Rev. Preston Doty, to Edward Young, son of George and Phebe (Mendenhall) Young; born Cadiz, Ohio, June 25, 1846.

Issue :

5527. i.   Gertrude L. Young,[10] born Beebeetown, Ia., July 5, 1876.
5528. ii. Cora Anna Young,[10] born Beebeetown, Ia., April 8, 1880.
5529. iii. Frank Edward Young,[10] born Beebeetown, Ia., July 31, 1885.

5205. Nina Ethel Daggett [9] (*Julius A. O.,*[8] *Austin,*[7] *Sebra,*[6] *John,*[5] *John,*[4] *John,*[3] *Samuel,*[2] *Thomas* [1]), born Girard, Pa., Oct. 28, 1867 ; resides Miles' Grove, Pa. (1893) ; married Dunkirk, N.Y., July 21, 1886, by Rev. Thos. Kreuger, to James Taylor, son of Eleazer and Ann Eliza (Seeley) Taylor; born Girard, Pa., Jan. 11, 1866.

Issue :

5530. i.   Kittie Bell Taylor,[10] born Girard, Pa., March 26, 1887.

5531. ii. MARION ELVIRA TAYLOR,[10] born Girard, Pa., April 3, 1890.
5532. iii. JAMES DAGGETT TAYLOR,[10] born Girard, Pa., March 11, 1892.

5210. ZADIA BOWEN [9] (*Almeda E. Daggett,*[8] *Austin,*[7] *Sebra,*[6] *John,*[5] *John,*[4] *John,*[3] *Samuel,*[2] *Thomas* [1]), born Girard, Pa., August 4, 1858; resides cor. Twelfth and Parade streets, Erie, Pa. (1893); married Girard, Pa., by Rev. C. L. Shipman, to Charles Napoleon Gross, son of Charles Bonaparte and Tressa (Nyernhaus) Gross; born Erie, Pa., April 12, 1851.

Issue:
5533. i. RHEASILVIA ELVIRA GROSS,[10] born Girard, Pa., November 2, 1879.

5211. EMERSON DRAPER BOWEN [9] (*Almeda E. Daggett,*[8] *Austin,*[7] *Sebra,*[6] *John,*[5] *John,*[4] *John,*[3] *Samuel,*[2] *Thomas* [1]), born Fairview, Pa., May 28, 1862; resides Girard, Pa. (1893); married Miles' Grove, Pa., February 2, 1889, by Rev. Father Briody, to Elizabeth Agnes Lartsch, daughter of John Adam and Bridget (Inglisbee) Lartsch; born Miles' Grove, Pa., July 1, 1861.

Issue:
5534. i. SUSIE EASTERBROOK BOWEN,[10] born Girard, Pa., November 9, 1889.
5535. ii. WILL CARLTON BOWEN,[10] born Girard, Pa., February 24, 1893.

5212. AUSTIN DAGGETT BOWEN [9] (*Almeda E. Daggett,*[8] *Austin,*[7] *Sebra,*[6] *John,*[5] *John,*[4] *John,*[3] *Samuel,*[2] *Thomas* [1]), born Fairview, Pa., May 16, 1864; resides Ashtabula, Ohio (1893); married Ashtabula Harbor, Ohio, December 19, 1888, by Rev. Mr. Davidson, to Mary Selina Cole, daughter of Charles and Ann (Hollick) Cole; born Ashtabula Harbor, Ohio, January 21, 1862.

Issue:
5536. i. ALMEDA BOWEN,[10] born Ashtabula, Ohio, November 4, 1889.
5537. ii. CHARLES COLE BOWEN,[10] born Ashtabula, Ohio, May 8, 1891.

5221. Capt. GEORGE LUCAS HANLIN [9] (*Florence V. Daggett,*[8] *Austin,*[7] *Sebra,*[6] *John,*[5] *John,*[4] *John,*[3] *Samuel,*[2] *Thomas* [1]), born Moscow, Ohio, January 27, 1869; resides Avonia, Pa. (1893); married Lockport, N.Y., July 14, 1891, by Rev. T. T. Rowe, to Nettie Forshee, daughter of Silas Walker and Clara (Reed) Forshee; born Austinburgh, Ohio, September 8, 1873.

Issue:
5538. i. TREVA FLORENCE HANLIN,[10] born Erie, Pa., September 21, 1891.

5227. ELIZABETH TRISSLER GAILLARD [9] (*Mary A. Daggett,*[8] *Darius,*[7] *Sebra,*[6] *John,*[5] *John,*[4] *John,*[3] *Samuel,*[2] *Thomas* [1]), born Fairview, Pa., October 7, 1854; resides 354 West Twenty-second street, Erie, Pa. (1893); married West Millcreek, Pa., November 14, 1876, by Rev. J. O. Osborn, to Mathias Brindle Bigger, son of

Joseph Hassler and Mary Ann (Brindle) Bigger; born Erie, Pa., October 22, 1844; divorced Erie, Pa., June 5, 1884.

Issue:

5539. i. GEORGE FRANCIS BIGGER,[10] born West Millcreek, Pa., Nov. 24, 1877.
5540. ii. RAWLE ALLISON BIGGER,[10] born West Millcreek, Pa., Feb. 19, 1880.

5230. GERTRUDE AGNES GAILLARD [9] (*Mary A. Daggett,*[8] *Darius,*[7] *Sebra,*[6] *John,*[5] *John,*[4] *John,*[3] *Samuel,*[2] *Thomas*[1]), born Fairview, Pa., October 11, 1860; resides 144 East Eighth street, Erie, Pa. (1893); married West Millcreek, Pa., May 30, 1881, by Rev. G. W. Staples, to Henry Michael Riblet, son of Jonathan and Sophia (Fluke) Riblet; born Erie, Pa., November 6, 1845.

Issue:

5541. i. CHARLES GAILLARD RIBLET,[10] born West Millcreek, Pa., June 14, 1882; died West Millcreek, Pa., November 9, 1883.
5542. ii. MARY GERTRUDE RIBLET,[10] born May 16, 1884; died October 8, 1884.
5543. iii. HARRY GAILLARD RIBLET,[10] born August 12, 1885.

5232. LOUISA SOPHIA BENNETT [9] (*Esther E. Daggett,*[8] *Darius,*[7] *Sebra,*[6] *John,*[5] *John,*[4] *John,*[3] *Samuel,*[2] *Thomas*[1]), born Fairview, Pa., March 21, 1863; resides Girard, Pa. (1893); married McLane, Pa., July 1, 1885, Allen Alonzo Alden, son of Alonzo Alden; born about 1838.

Issue:

5544. i. CHARLES ALLEN WESLEY ALDEN,[10] born November 9, 1886.

5245. HARRY DAGGETT [9] (*William E.,*[8] *Darius,*[7] *Sebra,*[6] *John,*[5] *John,*[4] *John,*[3] *Samuel,*[2] *Thomas*[1]), born Girard, Pa., Sept. 19, 1871; resides Conneaut, Ohio (1893); married Erie, Pa., April 26, 1892, by Rev. A. H. Bowers, to Irene Anna Snadeker, daughter of William and Polly Ann (Pease) Snadeker; born Lockport, Pa., March 7, 1872.

Issue:

5545. i. ANSON DAGGETT,[10] born Conneaut, Ohio, May 3, 1893.

5249. LULU MAY SPENCE [9] (*Nancy E. Daggett,*[8] *Darius,*[7] *Sebra,*[6] *John,*[5] *John,*[4] *John,*[3] *Samuel,*[2] *Thomas*[1]), born Fairview, Pa., June 8, 1868; resides Avonia, Pa. (1893); married Erie, Pa., by C. Swalley, J.P., to Frank T. Fisher, son of Thomas Jefferson and Ann Eliza (Shannon) Fisher; born Fairview, Pa., May 2, 1868.

Issue:

5546. i. FOSTER HENDERSON FISHER,[10] born Fairview, Pa., December 4, 1891; died Fairview, Pa., October 4, 1892.
5547. ii. ROBERT DAMON FISHER,[10] born Fairview, Pa., July 8, 1892.

5250. MILLICENT LUCINDA SPENCE [9] (*Nancy E. Daggett,*[8] *Darius,*[7] *Sebra,*[6] *John,*[5] *John,*[4] *John,*[3] *Samuel,*[2] *Thomas*[1]), born Girard, Pa., June 5, 1871; resides Miles' Grove, Pa. (1893); married Avonia,

Pa., July 23, 1891, by Rev. R. S. Borland, to George Andrew Campbell, son of Andrew Jackson and Jennett Elizabeth (Dunning) Campbell; born Lundy's Lane, Pa., December 27, 1866.

Issue:

5548. i. MAMIE ISABEL CAMPBELL,[10] born Miles' Grove, Pa., October 17, 1891.
5549. ii. HELEN EMMA CAMPBELL,[10] born Miles' Grove, Pa., March 15, 1893.

5256. MARTHA ELIZABETH DAGGETT[9] (*Henry G.*,[8] *Reuben*,[7] *Sebra*,[6] *John*,[5] *John*,[4] *John*,[3] *Samuel*,[2] *Thomas*[1]), born Girard, Pa., October 9, 1860; died Greenfield, Pa., March 30, 1893; married Findley's Lake, N.Y., Oct. 19, 1885, by Rev. Charles Boorman, to John Blackman, son of Benjamin and Elizabeth (Graham) Blackman; born Cambridge, Eng., Sept. 10, 1854; resides Greenfield, Pa. (1893).

Issue:

5550. i. BENJAMIN BLACKMAN,[10] born Greenfield, Pa., July 13, 1887.
5551. ii. BLANCHE BLACKMAN,[10] born Greenfield, Pa., March 4, 1889.
5552. iii. ANNIE BLACKMAN,[10] born Greenfield, Pa., July 21, 1892.

5284. CHARLOTTA GILSON DAGGETT[9] (*Charles W.*,[8] *Hiram*,[7] *Sebra*,[6] *John*,[5] *John*,[4] *John*,[3] *Samuel*,[2] *Thomas*[1]), born Girard, Pa., April 30, 1865; resides Girard, Pa. (1893); married Fairview, Pa., October 4, 1883, Frank Henry Halstead, son of George Henry and Murilla (Smith) Halstead.

Issue:

5553. i. IDA BELLE HALSTEAD,[10] born Lockport, Pa., August 25, 1884; died April 25, 1885.
5554. ii. CLARENCE ELMER HALSTEAD,[10] born Girard, Pa., April 23, 1886.

5285. JULIA DAGGETT[9] (*Charles W.*,[8] *Hiram*,[7] *Sebra*,[6] *John*,[5] *John*,[4] *John*,[3] *Samuel*,[2] *Thomas*[1]), born Girard, Pa., February 3, 1867; resides Fairview, Pa. (1893); married Girard, Pa., March 25, 1885, by Rev. Mr. Moore, to Daniel Kreider, son of Benjamin and Katherine (Ruhl) Kreider; born Sterrettania, Pa., Nov. 20, 1865.

Issue:

5555. i. BESSIE MAY KREIDER,[10] born Fairview, Pa., January 29, 1886.
5556. ii. OLIVER LEROY KREIDER,[10] born Girard, Pa., March 19, 1887.

5340. GILBERT ALDEN DAGGETT[9] (*John C.*,[8] *John R.*,[7] *Don Delance*,[6] *John*,[5] *John*,[4] *John*,[3] *Samuel*,[2] *Thomas*[1]), born South Braintree, Mass., July 27, 1859; "musician;" resides 5 Franklin street, Neponset, Mass. (1893); married Boston, Mass., June 23, 1884, by Rev. C. D. Bradlee, to Elizabeth J. Hayward, daughter of Jonathan N. and Margaret Hayward; born Dorchester, Mass., 1857.

Issue:

5557. i. PARKER HAYWARD DAGGETT,[10] born Boston, Mass., April 5, 1885.

5348. FRANK B. DAGGETT[9] (*Ephraim B.*,[8] *Ephraim M.*,[7] *Eleazer*,[6] *John*,[5] *John*,[4] *John*,[3] *Samuel*,[2] *Thomas*[1]), born Tarrant county,

Tex., February 2, 1866; resides Fort Worth, Tex. (1893); married Brenham, Tex., December 6, 1887, by Rev. Mr. Goodwin, to Mary Lou Smith, daughter of Edward Morris and Callie Josephine (Walker) Smith; born Lebanon, Tenn., January 26, 1868.

Issue:

5558. i. RAYMOND DAGGETT,[10] born Fort Worth, Tex., October 13, 1888.

5378. MARY ELLEN ALDEN [9] (*Eleanor C. Trott*,[8] *Eleanor Clap*,[7] *Betsey Doggett*,[6] *Samuel*,[5] *Samuel*,[4] *Isaac*,[3] *Samuel*,[2] *Thomas* [1]), born Boston, Mass., February 13, 1861; resides Newton, Mass. (1891); married Newton, Mass., June 21, 1883, by Rev. Francis B. Hornbrooke, to Samuel Sturges Crocker, son of Daniel Chipman and Charlotte (Howes) Crocker; born Barnstable, Mass., August 24, 1858; with F. W. Nickerson & Co. (1891).

Issue:

5559. i. ELANOR CROCKER,[10] born Newton, Mass., June 29, 1885.
5560. ii. SAMUEL STURGES CROCKER,[10] born Newton, Mass., March 29, 1890.

5379. MARTHA ELIZABETH ALDEN [9] (*Eleanor C. Trott*,[8] *Eleanor Clap*,[7] *Betsey Doggett*,[6] *Samuel*,[5] *Samuel*,[4] *Isaac*,[3] *Samuel*,[2] *Thomas* [1]), born Boston, Mass., January 8, 1865; resides Brookline, Mass. (1891); married Newton, Mass., September 29, 1887, by Rev. Francis B. Hornbrooke, to Alpheus Stetson Baker, son of Joseph Francis and Sarah Williams Kent (Stetson) Baker; born Boston, Mass., Feb. 6, 1860; "book-keeper," 50 Bromfield street, Boston.

Issue:

5561. i. FRANCES JOSEPHINE BAKER,[10] born Newton, Mass., October 13, 1888.

5388. ALICE ELIZABETH CLAPP [9] (*Samuel W.*,[8] *Elizabeth D. Clap*,[7] *Betsey Doggett*,[6] *Samuel*,[5] *Samuel*,[4] *Isaac*,[3] *Samuel*,[2] *Thomas* [1]), born St. Joseph, Mo., April 26, 1867; resides Fort Scott, Kan. (1891); married Fort Scott, Kan., March 6, 1890, by Rev. Henry Mackey, to William Worthington Read, son of Hiram E. and Angelina A. (Combs) Read; born Evansville, Ind., February 11, 1864; "commission merchant."

Issue:

5562. i. SHIRLEY WALLACE READ,[10] born Fort Scott, Kan., June 3, 1891.

5398. WILLIAM ABRAM FRENCH [9] (*Sophia J. Cobb*,[8] *Sophia Doggett*,[7] *John*,[6] *Samuel*,[5] *Samuel*,[4] *Isaac*,[3] *Samuel*,[2] *Thomas* [1]), born Boston, Mass., October 17, 1843; resides Jamaica Plain, Mass. (1891); married Canton, Mass., October 1, 1868, by Rev. S. K. Lothrop, to Olivia Chapman, daughter of Oliver and Elizabeth (Everett [Otis]) Chapman; born Canton, Mass.

Issue:

5563. i. ELIZABETH SOPHIA FRENCH,[10] born Canton, Mass., Sept. 21, 1869.

5564. ii.   HELEN OLIVIA FRENCH,[10] born Canton, Mass., July 10, 1871.
5565. iii. WILLIAM CHAPMAN FRENCH,[10] born Jamaica Plain, Mass., Nov. 23, 1873.
5566. iv.   HAROLD WALDO FRENCH,[10] born Jamaica Plain, Mass., Aug. 25, 1878.

William A. French was associated with his father in the firm of Abram French & Co., and on his father's death succeeded him in the management of the business. The "Abram French Company" was formed in 1891, with William A. French as president. He is also president of the Massachusetts National Bank of Boston, and treasurer of the American Spool, Bobbin, and Shuttle Company, of Boston. He is often called upon in the settlement of estates.

5401. ARTHUR BURRAGE FRENCH[9] (*Sophia J. Cobb,*[8] *Sophia Doggett,*[7] *John,*[6] *Samuel,*[5] *Samuel,*[4] *Isaac,*[3] *Samuel,*[2] *Thomas*[1]), born Boston, Mass., April 30, 1849; resides Salem, Mass. (1892); married Salem, Mass., April 15, 1885, by Rev. Benjamin McDaniels, to Minnie Kendrick Felt, daughter of George Ropes and Elizabeth (Kendrick) Felt; born Salem. Mass., February 22, 1858.

Issue:

5567. i.   GEORGE BREWER FRENCH,[10] born Pittsburg, Pa., March 17, 1887.
5568. ii. MARGARET FRENCH,[10] born Pittsburg, Pa., December 19, 1890.

Mr. French learned the china and glassware business in his father's establishment, and in 1886 removed to Pittsburg, Pa., where he established the china house of French, Kendrick & Co. In the summer of 1890 he sold out his interest in the firm of French, Kendrick & Co., and removed to Salem, Mass., where he now resides (1892).

5403. MARY ROSABELLE FRENCH[9] (*Sophia J. Cobb,*[8] *Sophia Doggett,*[7] *John,*[6] *Samuel,*[5] *Samuel,*[4] *Isaac,*[3] *Samuel,*[2] *Thomas*[1]), born Boston, Mass., Sept. 26, 1856; resides Newtonville, Mass. (1891); married Jamaica Plain, Mass., Feb. 21, 1883, by Rev. Charles F. Dole, to Charles Sumner Dennison, son of Eliphalet Whorf and Lydia Anne (Beals) Dennison; born Newtonville, Mass., June 20, 1858.

Issue:

5569. i.   FLORENCE LYDIA DENNISON,[10] born London, Eng., November 30, 1884.
5570. ii. OLIVIA BELLE DENNISON,[10] born Newtonville, Mass., Nov. 28, 1888.
5571. iii. ELIZABETH WILLARD DENNISON,[10] born Cataumet, Mass., Aug. 24, 1891.

Mr. Dennison is a member of the well-known firm of the Dennison Manufacturing Company, established by his father in Boston, and now having branch houses in most of the leading cities of the United States, and in London, Eng. For a few years after his marriage they resided in London, he having charge of the London house. He returned to Boston just prior to his father's death, and has since been connected with the main house.

5404. HENRY CORMERAIS FRENCH[9] (*Sophia J. Cobb,*[8] *Sophia Doggett,*[7] *John,*[6] *Samuel,*[5] *Samuel,*[4] *Isaac,*[3] *Samuel,*[2] *Thomas*[1]), born

Boston, Mass., March 21, 1860; resides Chicago, Ill. (1892); married Monkstown, County Cork, Ire., June 22, 1892, at St. John's Church, to Margaret Elizabeth Taylor, daughter of John P. Taylor.

Mr. French graduated from Harvard University, 1882. He entered mercantile life with the Pairpoint Manufacturing Company, of New Bedford, Mass. (silver-ware manufacturers), for whom his father's firm was selling agent in Boston and Chicago. He afterward settled in Chicago, and is now treasurer of the French & Potter Company, of that city.

5407. EDWARD SIGOURNEY COBB [9] (*Jonathan,*[8] *Sophia Doggett,*[7] *John,*[6] *Samuel,*[5] *Samuel,*[4] *Isaac,*[3] *Samuel,*[2] *Thomas* [1]), born Nashville, Tenn., May 21, 1859; "mechanical engineer;" resides Dallas, Tex. (1891); married Hyde Park, Mass., January 5, 1881, by Rev. W. N. Richardson, to Charlotte Lucina Whitney, daughter of Luther Warren and Ruth Eliza (Tefft) Whitney; born Boston, Mass., August 28, 1860; resides Walnut Hill, Dedham, Mass. (1891).
Issue:

5572. i. EDWARD WHITNEY COBB,[10] born Hyde Park. Mass., Nov. 30, 1881.
5573. ii. IRENE MABEL COBB,[10] born Terre Haute, Ind., July 10, 1883.

5425. ABBY ELIZABETH GUILD [9] (*Abby Cobb,*[8] *Sophia Doggett,*[7] *John,*[6] *Samuel,*[5] *Samuel,*[4] *Isaac,*[3] *Samuel,*[2] *Thomas* [1]), born Dedham, Mass., September 8, 1861; resides Everett, Mass. (1891); married Dedham, Mass., November 3, 1887, by Rev. S. C. Beach, to Walter Herbert Cutter, son of John and Esther Elizabeth (Capen) Cutter; born Littleton, Mass., May 6, 1855.
Issue:

5574. i. HERBERT GUILD CUTTER,[10] born Everett, Mass., March 31, 1889.
5575. ii. ABBOTT SANFORD CUTTER,[10] born Everett, Mass., September 20, 1890.

5427. SOPHIA DOGGETT GUILD [9] (*Abby Cobb,*[8] *Sophia Doggett,*[7] *John,*[6] *Samuel,*[5] *Samuel,*[4] *Isaac,*[3] *Samuel,*[2] *Thomas* [1]), born Dedham, Mass., December 12, 1865; resides Dedham. Mass. (1891); married Dedham, Mass., June 13, 1889, by Rev. S. C. Beach, to Eugene Webb Smith, son of Philander Webb and Almira Susan (Brown) Smith, of Claremont. N.H.; born Cornish, N.H., December 31, 1861.
Issue:

5576. i. CONSTANCE SMITH.[10] born Dedham. Mass., January 10, 1892.

PROBABLY DESCENDED FROM THOMAS DOGGETT, OF MARSHFIELD, MASS.

5577. Capt. JOHN DOGGETT,[1] born 1772; died Boston, Mass., May 23, 1809; married Boston, Mass., April 10, 1799, by Rev. Samuel Stillman, to Marcy Hall, daughter of Zachariah and Mary Hall; born Boston, Mass., February 11, 1781; died West Roxbury, Mass., September 5, 1869.

Issue:

5578. i. JOHN DOGGETT,[2] born Boston, Mass., June 25, 1800; died Boston, Mass., June 14, 1804.
5579. ii. THOMAS DOGGETT,[2] born Boston, Mass., November 1, 1801; died Boston, Mass., March 13, 1814.
5580. iii. MARY DOGGETT,[2] born Boston, Mass., September 13, 1804.
5581. iv. ELIZA ANN DOGGETT,[2] born Boston, Mass., August 8, 1806; died Boston, Mass., May 24, 1808.

Captain Doggett had in his possession a Doggett coat of arms: two greyhounds rampant, combatant, or; crest — a greyhound's head; with "1686 of Norfolk" printed on the sheet. These arms are now held by Mr. Jackson, of Roxbury.

Captain Doggett resided in 1800 on North square. In 1803 he lived at 53 Prince street, and continued to live there until his death.

His widow remained there during the next year and then moved to North street. In 1823 she was living at 11 Fleet street, in 1826 at 240 Hanover street, and continued to reside in the immediate vicinity until 1856.

5580. MARY DOGGETT[2] (*John*[1]), born Boston, Mass., September 13, 1804; died Boston, Mass., May 10, 1882; married Boston, Mass., November 13, 1833, by Rev. Paul Dean, to Samuel Jackson; born January 15, 1803; died Boston, Mass., November 7, 1873.

Issue:

5582. i. ALONZO D. JACKSON,[3] born Boston, Mass., April 17, 1835; died Boston, Mass., December 11, 1875.
5583. ii. EUGENE A. JACKSON,[3] born Boston, Mass., April 6, 1837.
5584. iii. SAMUEL JACKSON,[3] born Boston, Mass., January 14, 1843; "trunk manufacturer;" married December 15, 1862, Marion C. Bird; resides 65 Clifford street, Roxbury, Mass. (1892).

5583. EUGENE A. JACKSON[3] (*Mary Doggett,*[2] *John*[1]), born Boston, Mass., April 6, 1837; "real estate;" died December 21, 1891; married January 17, 1871, Harriet A. Stevens; resides 196 Green street, Jamaica Plain, Mass. (1892).

Issue:

5585. i. MINNIE EUGENIE JACKSON,[4] born Boston, Mass., November 20, 1871.
5586. ii. SAMUEL WARD JACKSON,[4] born Boston, Mass., December 29, 1875.

PROBABLY DESCENDED FROM THOMAS DOGGETT, OF MARSHFIELD, MASS.

5587. ABNER DOGGETT,[1] born 1775; died Truro, N.S., January 26, 1807; married Truro, N.S., January 30, 1800, Mary Logan, daughter of John and Mary (Cox) Logan; born Truro, N.S., April 20, 1774; died Truro, N.S., June 23, 1850.

Issue:

5588. i. REBECCA COLWELL DOGGETT,[2] born Truro, N.S., November 3, 1800.
5589. ii. JOHN LOGAN DOGGETT,[2] born Truro, N.S., June 8, 1805.

Abner Doggett went to Truro, N.S., in company with his brother Ebenezer Doggett and sister Betsey Doggett. The brother and sister remained but a short time when they removed to one of the New England States, and the descendants of Abner have no further information regarding them.

5588. REBECCA COLWELL DOGGETT [2] (*Abner* [1]), born Truro, N.S., November 3, 1800; died Truro, N.S., July 18, 1848; married Truro, N.S., February 2, 1819, David Forbes, of Truro.

Issue:

5590. i.   JOHN D. FORBES,[3] born Truro, N.S., July 4, 1820; married Maitland, N.S., November 22, 1843, Elmira, daughter of John Douglas.
5591. ii. MARY FORBES,[3] born Truro, N.S., October 30, 1822; married Truro, N.S., April, 1846, John Sanderson, son of William Sanderson, of Clifton, N.S.; she died Clifton, N.S., November 24, 1849; he resides Princeport, N.S. (1885).
5592. iii. WILLIAM FORBES,[3] born Truro, N.S., December 22, 1824; married 1st, Cordelia Curtis, of East Abington, Mass.; married 2d, Mary Curtis, daughter of John Curtis; resides Rockland, Mass. (1885).
5593. iv. SAMUEL FORBES,[3] born Truro. N.S., Nov. 7, 1826; lost at sea, 1852.
5594. v.   RENEW NELSON FORBES,[3] born Truro, N.S., April 24, 1828; died Truro, N.S., January 5, 1885.
5595. vi. SARAH FORBES,[3] born Truro, N.S., November 5, 1832; married July 24, 1865, Francis Kimball Pemberton, son of William Pemberton; born 1814; died March 12, 1880; she resides Peabody, Mass. (1885).
5596. vii. ABNER FORBES,[3] born Truro, N.S., November 29, 1834; married Eliza Daniels, of Charlestown, Mass.; resides Lowell, Mass. (1885).
5597. viii. HANNAH FORBES,[3] born Truro, N.S., December 5, 1836; died young.
5598. ix. HENRY FORBES,[3] born Truro, N.S., March 2, 1839; married Jane, daughter of Isaac Dart, of Maitland, N.S.; he was lost at sea.
5599. x.   ELIZABETH FORBES,[3] born Truro, N.S., Aug. 7, 1841; married Robert McBurnie, of Tatmagouche, N.S.; resides Clifton, N.S. (1885).

5589. JOHN LOGAN DOGGETT [2] (*Abner* [1]), born Truro, N.S., June 8, 1805; died Truro, N.S., January 18, 1892; married Truro, N.S., December 4, 1828, Esther Smith Pearson, widow of Robert Pearson, and daughter of William and Esther (Hunter) Smith; born Truro, N.S., February 13, 1799; died Truro, N.S., March, 1876.

Issue:

5600. i. ABNER DOGGETT,[3] born Truro, N.S., July 16, 1829; married St. John,

N.B., April 26, 1877, Amelia Pervis McHay, daughter of John P. and Maria (Henderson) McHay ; born St. John, N.B., 1848 ; died Truro, N.S., November 29, 1889 ; no issue ; he resides Truro, N.S. (1893).

5601. ii.   DANIEL DOGGETT,[3] born Truro, N.S., Feb. 20, 1834 ; resides there (1893).
5602. iii. ALEXANDER DOGGETT,[3] born Truro, N.S., June 20, 1836 ; resides there (1893).
5603. iv.   ALBERT DOGGETT,[3] born Truro, N.S., July 14, 1840 ; resides there (1893).
5604. v.   MARTHA DOGGETT,[3] born Truro, N.S., Dec. 16, 1843 ; resides there (1893).

DOGGETT-DAGGETT.

WILLIAM DAGGETT, OF SACO, ME.

5605. WILLIAM DAGGETT[1] (spelled also with one "t" and at times with one "g"), born 1661; died Marblehead (?), Mass., previous to January 7, 1695; married Saco, Me., about 1681, Rebecca Wormstall, daughter of Arthur and Rebecca (Scadlock) Wormstall, of Winter Harbor, Me.; born about 1663; died Sutton (?), Mass., after 1727.

Issue : *

5606. i.   SUSANNA DAGGETT,[2] born Saco (?), Me., about 1685; married Lynn, Mass. (intention, January 13, 170$\frac{4}{5}$), John Collins, Jr., of Lynn. They were of Westerly, R.I., May 16, 1730, when they sold their interest in their father's estate (William Daggett's estate in Biddeford) to Samuel Daggett, of Sutton. [York Deeds, 14–39.]
5607. ii.   WILLIAM DAGGETT,[2] born Saco (?), Me., about 1687.
5608. iii. EBENEZER DAGGETT,[2] born Marblehead (?), Mass., about 1693.
5609. iv.   SAMUEL DAGGETT,[2] born Salem, Mass., January 7, 1695.

Of the birth or parentage of William Daggett nothing has been found. There is a tradition that he came from Scotland.

His name first appears at Saco, Me., December 3, 1681, when he is granted ten acres of land at the head of his father Wormstall's lot.

William Daggett may be descended from (5610) William Dogget, who "28 2nd mo 1647" bought house and land at Rehoboth, Mass.; but this is only conjecture, and the writer has not found any further record of William of Rehoboth, or earlier record of William of Saco, to aid in proving or disproving this theory.

"The early settlers of Saco and vicinity were not like the other fathers of New England, religious sectarians flying from the intolerance of their native land.

"They were emigrants from motives of interest, brought hither by the same impulse that even at the present day carries men of an

---

* Possibly Thomas Daggett (No. 6041) was the oldest child, born about 1683.

enterprising character to the very corners of the earth." [Folsom's
Saco.]

The employments of the colonists were chiefly agriculture, fishing,
and trade with the natives. Most of them combined these pursuits,
and were styled husbandmen, or planters.

Fishing was the most common occupation, as it was both easy and
profitable to barter the products of this business for corn from Virginia, and other stores from England.

" May 10, 1684, At a town meeting legally held by the free-
holders of Saco, W. Daget chosen constable for this year."

Nov 16, 1684 Arthur Wormestall of the town of Sacoe In the province of
Mayne, fisherman, for divers good causes and considerations unto me moveing
and more especially for and in consideration of that love and affection which I
do unreservably beare unto my sonn in law William Daggett, Carpenter, now
dwelling in the said town as a part of that filiall portion which I give unto my
daughter now wife of said Daggett — two acres of upland and four acres of
meadow. [York Deeds, 4–27.]

William Daggett continued to reside in Saco until some time between 1685 and 1689, when he removed to Marblehead, Mass.

In 1691 he gave his evidence in regard to will of Robert Bennet,
and was then, according to the evidence, upwards of thirty years of
age, and of Marblehead. June 11, 1691, he is mentioned in account with the estate of Jona. Gatchell. [Essex Probate, III., 544
and 556.]

In 1692 James Beale had small-pox at Marblehead, and William
Daggett of Marblehead was his nurse.

March 25, 1693, he executed a mortgage on his cattle and goods
for four years' rent of a house and land, as follows :

Know all men by these presents that I William Daggott of Marblehead in the
County of Essex in New England, House Carpenter and Husbandman for and in
consideration of a perfect debt that I do acknowledge to owe with Mr. Erasmus
James of ye same town aforesaid merchant and also for the rent of a house and
land that I hired of ye said Erasmus James of ye full term of 4 years which said
debt and the rent aforesaid for ye term as above mentioned is to the value of 25£.

I the said William Daggett have and do by these presents freely clearly and
absolutely without any fraud or deceit clearly make over and confirm unto the
above Erasmus James for his security for ye true payment of ye above James,
and have delivered unto the said Erasmus James the cattle and goods following,
viz : 1 Red Cow above 4 years old marked with a top cut and a half penny cut
under her ear ; 1 Black Cow about 7 years old with a white star in her forehead
and white under her belly with an up cut and a half penny cut on her near ear ;
A heifer 2 years old 4 white feet, a white tail and a white speck on her fore
shoulder with a half penny cut on her near ear ; a heifer a year old and a white
spot in her forehead and half penny cut under her near ear ; 1 great Iron Pot
and 2 Iron pots smaller ; 5 small pewter platters ; 3 or four little small casons ;
3 feather beds with the rugs blankets and pillows belonging to them and 3 or 4
chests all and which cattle, and goods, and everything, or things whatsoever is
above named I have delivered and made over unto the said Erasmus James
without fraud or deceit to him the said Erasmus James to his own proper use
and behoof and as his own property to have and to hold and for his security till

such times as ye said Erasmus James is' full satisfied for the sum of money above named.

In witness hereunto I have set to my hand and seal this 25 day of March 1693.

his
WILLIAM   W   DAGGETT   (Seal)
mark

Signed sealed & delivered
in presence of us
BENJ. JAMES,
EDWARD HUMPHREY.   [Essex Deeds, 9–274.]

April 15, 1706, Rebecca Daggett, of Salem, widow, buys six acres of land in Salem, of William and Samuel Upton. [Essex Deeds, 22–212.]

April 8, 1717, she sold the six acres to Benj. Prescott, and was then of Salem, widow. [Essex Deeds, 33–103.]

Mrs. Daggett removed to Sutton, Mass., to the home of her sons, Ebenezer and Samuel, and October 27, 1727, sold her rights in her father's estate, the deed of which says:

Rebecca Dagget of Sutton, County Suffolk for 20£ paid by Ebenezer and Samuel Dagget both of Sutton husbandmen, all that my part or share in the lands tenements or hereditaments goods chattels &c in and unto the estate of my late honoured father Arthur Wormstall late of Saco, in the Province of Maine [now called Biddeford in County York in Province of Mass Bay in New England] fisherman, deceased either within the said town of Biddeford or elsewhere within the Province of Mass. Bay, Province of Maine or elsewhere with houses, buildings, edifices, fences, marsh, upland, commons, out division, bills, bonds &c.

her
REBECCA   R   DAGGET
[York Deeds, 12–329.]   mark

WILLIAM DAGGETT, OF SACO, ME.

SECOND GENERATION.

5607. WILLIAM DAGGETT [2] (*William* [1]), born Saco (?), Me., about 1687; died Salem, Mass., January, 172⁴⁄₅; married Salem, Mass., Nov. 29, 1711, by Rev. Joseph Green, to Mary Nurse, daughter of Samuel and Mary (Smith) Nurse; born Salem, Mass., May 25, 1685.

Issue:

5611. i. SUSANNA DAGGETT,[3] born Salem, Mass., October 11, 1712.
5612. ii. MARY DAGGETT,[3] born Salem, Mass., November 1, 1713; married Salem, Mass., May 6, 1736, by Rev. Peter Clark, to John How, of Middleton.
5613. iii. REBECCA DAGGETT,[3] born Salem, Mass., July 20, 1716; married Salem, Mass., June 7, 1737, by Rev. Benj. Presiot, to Jonathan Moulton.

5608. EBENEZER DAGGETT [2] (*William* [1]), born Marblehead (?), Mass., about 1693; died Sutton, Mass., April 8, 1762; married 1st, Aug. 10, 1722, Hannah Sibley; died Sutton, Mass., Feb. 8, 1731;

married 2d, Reading, Mass., Nov. 25, 1731, by Rev. Richard Brown, to Mrs. Hannah Burnap, widow, daughter of Dea. Samuel Lilley.

Issue:

5614. i. EBENEZER DAGGETT,[3] born Sutton, Mass., April 21, 1723; "physician;" died Mendon, Mass., 1761 (before August 3). Dr. Daggett settled first in Smithfield, R.I. Samuel Daggett appointed administrator of his estate, August 3, 1761. [Worcester Probate.]
5615. ii. THOMAS DAGGETT,[3] born Sutton, Mass., April 25, 1725.
5616. iii. WILLIAM DAGGETT,[3] born Sutton, Mass., August 15, 1727.
5617. iv. ARTHUR DAGGETT,[3] born Sutton, Mass., January 30, 1729.
5618. v. SAMUEL DAGGETT,[3] born Sutton, Mass., October 11, 1732.
5619. vi. HANNAH DAGGETT,[3] born Sutton, Mass., August 25, 1736.
5620. vii. REBECCA DAGGETT,[3] born Sutton, Mass., February 1, 1739; married Sutton, Mass., July 15, 1762, Benjamin Rich.

Ebenezer Daggett, carpenter, was of Salem, Mass., February 13, 1716–17, at which time Jona. King, of Salem, sells Ebenezer Daggett, carpenter, and Samuel Daggett, husbandman, both of Salem, in equal one-half parts, one-fifteenth part of one-tenth of a tract of land in township called Sutton, in County Suffolk, containing two hundred acres, for £26. [Suffolk Deeds, 31–29.]

"Samuel and Ebenezer Daggett were among the original thirty families who settled in the town of Sutton, and the proprietors of the four thousand acres." [Tracy's Sutton.]

Ebenezer Daggett was of Salem, April 8, 1717, when he witnessed a deed, and removed to Sutton between this time and December 1, 1718, when he and his brother Samuel, husbandmen, of Sutton, sell land there. [Suffolk Deeds, 33–156.]

Oct 19, 1727 he and his brother Samuel buy the right of their aunt, the wife of Robert Darby of Lancaster Mass, in the estate of her father Arthur Wormstall of Saco. [York Deeds, 12–189.]

Oct 27, 1727 buys with his brother Samuel, his mothers rights in her fathers estate. [York Deeds, 12–329.]

Oct 11, 1831 Ebenezer and Samuel Daggett of Sutton sell 118 acres of land in Biddeford which belonged to Arthur Wormstall to Richard Simpson of Biddeford. [York Deeds, 15–98.]

The will of Ebenezer Daggett, of Sutton, County Worcester, husbandman, was dated April 7, 1762, and proved April 26, 1762.

Wife Hannah; heirs of son Thomas Daggett deceased 10£ 13s 6d (that is to say his sons John, and David, and 4 daughters Mary, Hannah, Polly, Lydia,); son William; 2 sons William, and Arthur, what household stuff he had in his first wifes days; his wearing apparel to 3 sons William, Arthur and Samuel; Arthur and Samuel lands in Sutton, and Petersham; daughters Hannah Dwinel, and Rebecca Daggett; 2 youngest sons Arthur and Samuel executors. [Worcester Probate, 1761–1762, 492.]

5609. SAMUEL DAGGETT[2] (*William*[1]), born Salem, Mass., January 7, 1695; died Sutton, Mass., August 24, 1756; married April 10, 1740, Mrs. Martha Sibley, widow of Samuel Sibley.

Issue:

5621. i. JOHN DAGGETT,[3] born Sutton, Mass., December 17, 1741.
5622. ii. STEPHEN DAGGETT,[3] born Sutton, Mass., February 12, 1745.

Samuel Daggett was of Salem, husbandman, and removed with his brother Ebenezer to Sutton, Mass., about 1718. They were among the original thirty families who settled the town, and his transactions in real estate there, as well as at Biddeford, are referred to in connection with his brother Ebenezer.

In May, 1728, he was administrator of the estate of Arthur Wormstall.

May 16, 1730 he bought his sisters interest in their fathers estate for 9£ 14s. [York Deeds, 14-39.]

Oct 20, 1731 he sells 10 acres of land in Biddeford to Benj. Haley for 10£ "which was granted to my father William Dagat and is staked at his father Wormstalls head of his land and was given in the year 1681 which will fully appear by the town book of Saco." [York Deeds, 16-209.]

Nov 3, 1732 he buys of Richard Simpson of Biddeford estate transferred to said Simpson by Samuel and Ebenezer, Oct 11, 1731. [York Deeds, 15-98.]

June 18, 1739 Samuel Daggett of Sutton, yeoman, makes Mr John Stackpole, his attorney, to take possession and sell 100 acres of land in Biddeford as also to receive all rearearages of rent. [York Deeds, 22-110.]

Sept 26, 1740 John Stackpole sells 100 acres of land and also marsh which belonged to Arthur Wormstall by right of power of attorney granted by Samuel Daggett, for 400£ bills of credit. [York Deeds, 22-110.]

The will of Samuel Daggett, of Sutton, County Worcester, yeoman, was dated August 25, 1756, and proved September 4, 1756.

Funeral charges to be paid by Nath[l] Sibley: Mentions wife Martha, that her son Nath[l] Sibley is to provide for her as he has given him deed of $\frac{1}{2}$ of his estate in Sutton: Kinsman Samuel Daggett Jr son of my brother Ebenezer, whom he appoints as executor. [Worcester Probate, 1756-1758, 100.]

WILLIAM DAGGETT, OF SACO, ME.

THIRD GENERATION.

5611. Susanna Daggett[3] (*William*,[2] *William*[1]), born Danvers, Mass., October 11, 1712; married Danvers, Mass., November 2, 1732, James Upton, son of William and Mary (Maber) Upton; born Danvers, Mass., January 5, 170$\frac{7}{8}$; died Danvers, Mass., between January 30 and August 4, 1778.

Issue:

5623. i. Tamasin Upton,[4] born Danvers, Mass., September 1, 1733.
5624. ii. Stephen Upton,[4] born Danvers, Mass., April 23, 1735; died probably young.
5625. iii. Hannah Upton,[4] born Danvers, Mass., June 26, 1737.
5626. iv. Mary Upton,[4] born Danvers, Mass., March 11, 1738; died Danvers, Mass., August 4, 1746.
5627. v. James Upton,[4] born Danvers, Mass., March 29, 1744; died probably young.
5628. vi. John Upton,[4] born Danvers, Mass., November 19, 1746.
5629. vii. Daniel Upton,[4] born Danvers, Mass., April 6, 1749; died probably young.

James Upton was a " cordwainer," well to do, but not wealthy.
He and his wife resided in what is now the town of Peabody, formerly
South Danvers, all their days.

Some of the posterity of James Upton still live on the lot purchased by him, in conjunction with his father, of Ezekiel Goldthwait,
January 10, 1733. It is on Main street, Peabody. His will is dated
January 30, 1778; proved August 4, 1778; recorded Essex Probate, 53–97.

He mentions his wife Susanna; son John Upton who after the wifes decease
is to have the dwelling house and land contiguous; daughter Tamasin Felton;
daughter Hannah Sprague; granddaughter Mary Sprague : Inventory: dwelling house and a quarter of an acre adjoining 160£. 5 acres of land called " the
field " 56£ 13s 4d. Whole estate real and personal 344£.

Susanna Daggett was baptized in Salem Village, now North Parish,
Danvers, October 19, 1712.

5615. Thomas Daggett³ (*Ebenezer*,² *William*¹), born Sutton,
Mass., April 25, 1725; died Petersham, Mass., previous to November 28, 1758; married May 14, 1747, Martha Stockwell.

Issue :

5630. i.   John Daggett,⁴ born Sutton, Mass., September 15, 1748.
5631. ii. Mary Daggett,⁴ born Sutton, Mass., March 29, 1750.
5632. iii. David Daggett,⁴ born about 1752.
5633. iv. Hannah Daggett.⁴
5634. v.   Polly Daggett.⁴
5635. vi. Lydia Daggett.⁴

Martha Dagget was appointed administratrix on the estate of
Thomas Dagget, late of Petersham, cordwainer, November 28, 1758.
The inventory amounted to £18 5s. 1d.

A few things at N. Salem not apprised.
About 80 acres of land in N. Salem, Co. Hampshire.
June 12, 1759 she makes a further account. [Worcester Probate, 1758–1761,
65–434.]

5616. William Daggett³ (*Ebenezer*,² *William*¹), born Sutton,
Mass., August 15, 1727; died Westmoreland, N.H., January 13,
1813; married Petersham, Mass., December 27, 1759, Thankful
Gleason ; died Westmoreland, N.H., December 28, 1813.

Issue :

5636. i.   Asa Daggett,⁴ born Petersham, Mass , July 7, 1760; July 5, 1779,
             enlisted in Revolution.
5637. ii. Anna Daggett,⁴ born Petersham, Mass., September 11, 1762; married
             Westmoreland, N.H., October 12, 1788, by Samuel Works, Esq., to
             William Esty, of Westmoreland.
5638. iii. Phineas Daggett,⁴ born Petersham, Mass., August 22, 1764.
5639. iv. Nathaniel Daggett.⁴
5640. v.   Sarah Daggett.⁴
5641. vi. Hannah Daggett,⁴ married Mr. Horton, of New York; no issue.
5642. vii. Amos Daggett,⁴ went to Vermont.
5643. viii. Daughter Daggett,⁴ married Mr. Ide.

5617. ARTHUR DAGGETT [3] (*Ebenezer,* [2] *William* [1]), born Sutton, Mass., Jan. 30, 1729; died Sutton, Mass., Aug. 23, 1775; married Sutton, Mass., Jan. 28, 1751, Mehitable Marsh, daughter of Benjamin and Mehitable (King) Marsh; born Sutton, Mass., May 8, 1731.

Issue:

5644. i.   ARTHUR DAGGETT,[4] born Sutton, Mass., April 23, 1751.
5645. ii. MEHITABLE DAGGETT,[4] born Sutton, Mass., October 10, 1752.
5646. iii. SIMEON DAGGETT,[4] born Sutton, Mass., March 7, 1757; July 22, 1777, of Westmoreland, N.H., and in the Revolution; reported as died in or soon after the war.
5647. iv. GIDEON DAGGETT,[4] born Sutton, Mass., December 21, 1759.
5648. v.   BETTY DAGGETT,[4] born Sutton, Mass., February 23, 1763; married December 12, 1782, Thomas Todd.
5649. vi. TAMAR DAGGETT,[4] born Sutton, Mass., March 24, 1767; married January 4, 1787, Eliphalet Holman, of Auburn.

The estate of Arthur Daggett was divided May 24, 1778. In the division were mentioned:

The widow Mehitable; Eldest son and administrator Arthur Daggett, land in Petersham; daughter Mehitable Rich wife of Jon. Rich; Follensbie Chase guardian to Gideon, Betty and Tamar Daggett; Simeon Daggett 2nd son of deceased.
The Inventory of the estate of Arthur Daggett amounted to 647£ 10s 5d. [Worcester Probate, 1778-1779, 23, and 1779-1781, 93-475.]

5618. SAMUEL DAGGETT [3] (*Ebenezer,* [2] *William* [1]), born Sutton, Mass., Oct. 11, 1732; died 1784; married May 6, 1755, Lydia Sibley.

Issue:

5650. i.   SAMUEL DAGGETT,[4] born Sutton, Mass., August 20, 1756; died in Revolution.
5651. ii.   ANNA DAGGETT,[4] born Sutton, Mass., July 4, 1758; died Sutton, Mass., November 13, 1759.
5652. iii. ANNA DAGGETT,[4] born Sutton, Mass., April 3, 1760.
5653. iv.   LYDIA DAGGETT,[4] born Sutton, Mass., April 23, 1762.
5654. v.   JUDITH DAGGETT,[4] born Sutton, Mass., April 12, 1764; died Sutton, Mass., July 28, 1782.
5655. vi.   JACOB DAGGETT,[4] born Sutton, Mass., May 30, 1766.
5656. vii. EBENEZER DAGGETT,[4] born Sutton, Mass., April 8, 1770.
5657. viii. RUTH DAGGETT,[4] born Sutton, Mass., August 8, 1773.
5658. ix.   REBECKAH DAGGETT,[4] born Sutton. Mass., September 8, 1775; died Sutton, Mass., September 24, 1851.
5659. x.   HANNAH DAGGETT,[4] born Sutton, Mass., September 8, 1780.

June 1, 1784, Lydia Daggett was appointed administratrix of the estate of Samuel Daggett, late of Sutton, deceased. Among the accounts is the item, paid "Lydia Daggett for nursing and support of Hannah Daggett, mother of said deceased, whom estate was obliged to support." There is also mention of land in Petersham. [Worcester Probate, 1781-5, 163-348, and 1777-86, 203-638.]

5619. HANNAH DAGGETT [3] (*Ebenezer,* [2] *William* [1]), born Sutton, Mass., August 25, 1736; married April 26, 1757, Henry Dwinel, son of Jonathan and Mehitable (Kennay) Dwinel, of Sutton; born 1732.

Issue:

5660. i.   SOLOMON DWINEL,[4] born Sutton, Mass., October 1, 1757.

5661. ii.   Moses Dwinel,[4] born Sutton, Mass., January 22, 1760.
5662. iii.   Henry Dwinel,[4] born Sutton, Mass., February 22, 1762.
5663. iv.   Jonathan Dwinel,[4] born Sutton, Mass., March 5, 1764; died.
5664. v.   John Dwinel,[4] born Sutton, Mass., July 5, 1766; died.
5665. vi.   Hannah Dwinel,[4] born Sutton, Mass., May 16, 1768.
5666. vii.   Samuel Dwinel,[4] born Sutton, Mass., September 28, 1770.
5667. viii. Abraham Dwinel,[4] born Sutton, Mass., September 25, 1773.
5668. ix.   Remark Dwinel,[4] born Sutton, Mass., July 13, 1775; died.
5669. x.   Thankful Dwinel,[4] born Sutton, Mass., 1779; died.
5670. xi.   Isaac Dwinel,[4] born Sutton, Mass., March 5, 1782.

Henry Dwinel was a soldier in the French and Indian war.

He married as second wife Mrs. Mehitable Daggett, the widow of Arthur Daggett.

WILLIAM DAGGETT, OF SACO, ME.

FOURTH GENERATION.

5630.   Capt. John Daggett [1] (*Thomas*,[3] *Ebenezer*,[2] *William* [1]), born Sutton, Mass., September 15, 1748; "husbandman;" died Greene, Me., 1816; married 1st, Charlton, Mass., ——; died Charlton, Mass., ——; married 2d, Charlton, Mass., Mary Stevens.

Issue:

5671. i.   Thomas Daggett,[5] born Charlton, Mass., August 5, 1776.
5672. ii.   John Daggett,[5] born Charlton, Mass., October 14, 1778.
5673. iii. Sarah Daggett,[5] born Charlton, Mass., April 2, 1780.
5674. iv.   Simeon Daggett,[5] born Greene, Me.; died, age 21 years.
5675. v.   Aaron Daggett,[5] born Greene, Me., March 4, 1787.
5676. vi.   Mary Daggett,[5] born Greene, Me.; married Deacon Luther Robbins, of Greene, Me., son of Luther Robbins; issue: i. Louisana Robbins;[6] ii. Survetus Robbins;[6] iii. Mary Robbins;[6] iv. John Robbins;[6] v. Clementine Robbins.[6]

Capt. John Daggett removed from Charlton, Mass., to Greene, Me., about 1780. He was the first military captain in the town of Greene, the first school teacher, member of the first and every succeeding board of selectmen for twenty-two years, and chairman of the board thirteen of those years.

He was member of the General Court about 1810.

5632.   David Daggett [4] (*Thomas*,[3] *Ebenezer*,[2] *William* [1]), born about 1752; married Azuba ——.

Issue:

5677. i.   Lyman Daggett,[5] born Charlton, Mass., August 22, 1775.
5678. ii.   David Daggett,[5] born Charlton, Mass., January 31, 1776; he or his father died Charlton, Mass., May 14, 1777.

March 9, 1781, Azuba Daggett admitted to First Baptist Church, Charlton.

5638. PHINEAS DAGGETT [4] (*William,*[3] *Ebenezer,*[2] *William*[1]), born Petersham, Mass., August 22, 1764; died Westmoreland, N.H., October 5, 1842; married 1st, Westmoreland, N.H., September 24, 1788, by Samuel Works, Esq., to Betsey Wilson; born 1769; died Westmoreland, N.H., August 11, 1791; married 2d, Westmoreland, N.H., September 7, 1794, by George Aldrich, Esq., to Mercy Pierce; born 1771; died Westmoreland, N.H., June 29, 1850.

Issue:

5679. i.   WILLIAM DAGGETT,[5] born Westmoreland, N.H., December 21, 1788.
5680. ii.   ARTEMAS DAGGETT,[5] born Westmoreland, N.H., July 17, 1790; married Sally Smith, of Hawley, N.Y.; he died Hawley, N.Y., 1835; issue: three daughters.
5681. iii.   POLLY DAGGETT,[5] born Westmoreland, N.H.; died Westmoreland, N.H., August 6, 1802.
5682. iv.   HIRAM DAGGETT,[5] born Westmoreland, N.H., August 9, 1797; died Westmoreland, N.H., January 1, 1832.
5683. v.   BETSEY DAGGETT,[5] born Westmoreland, N.H., December 31, 1799.
5684. vi.   HOLLIS DAGGETT,[5] born Westmoreland, N.H., November 4, 1802.
5685. vii.   LEWIS DAGGETT,[5] born Westmoreland, N.H., August 15, 1804.
5686. viii.   PRENTISS DAGGETT,[5] born Westmoreland, N.H., August 26, 1807; married Esther M. Hall; no issue; she died Westmoreland, N.H., 1889; he died there, October 29, 1881.
5687. ix.   MARY DAGGETT,[5] born Westmoreland, N.H., 1809.
5688. x.   LOUISA DAGGETT,[5] born Westmoreland, N.H., December 10, 1812.

5639. NATHANIEL DAGGETT [4] (*William,*[3] *Ebenezer,*[2] *William*[1]), married.

Issue:

5689. i.   SAMUEL DAGGETT,[5] born Vermont.

5640. SARAH DAGGETT [4] (*William,*[3] *Ebenezer,*[2] *William*[1]), married John Rice, of Walpole, N.H., son of Phineas and Abigail (Livermore) Rice; born Walpole, N.H., 1764–5; died Walpole, N.H., 1841.

Issue:

5690. i.   NANCY RICE,[5] born Walpole, N.H., 1789; married Luther Dennison, 1810, and Jeremiah Robbins, 1827.
5691. ii.   JOHN RICE,[5] born 1791; married Eliza Burke; resided Sandy Hill, N.Y., and died 1822.
5692. iii.   POLLY RICE,[5] born 1793; married Samuel Nichols, 1813; she died Walpole. N.H., 1854.
5693. iv.   LEWIS RICE,[5] born 1796; died Walpole, N.H., 1835.
5694. v.   LOUISA RICE,[5] born 1798; married Gilman Esty, 1826; resided Brownington, Vt.
5695. vi.   FANNY RICE,[5] born 1800.
5696. vii.   LUCINDA RICE,[5] born 1802; married John Bryant, 1829; resided Brownington, Vt.
5697. viii.   HORACE RICE,[5] born 1804.
5698. ix.   GEORGE RICE,[5] born 1807; married Caroline Esty, 1838; resided Brownington, Vt.
5699. x.   EMILY RICE,[5] born 1809; married Truman Richardson, 1834; resided Brownington, Vt.
5700. xi.   SUSAN RICE,[5] born 1811; married Calvin B. Meads, 1832; resided Barton, Vt.

5644. ARTHUR DAGGETT [4] (*Arthur,*[3] *Ebenezer,*[2] *William*[1]), born Sutton, Mass., April 23, 1751; died Montpelier, Vt., August 25,

1835; married December 10, 1772, Lucy Cutler; born 1752; died Montpelier, Vt., February 23, 1813.

Issue:

5701. i.   ARTHUR DAGGETT,[5] born Sutton, Mass., 1775.
5702. ii.   STEPHEN DAGGETT,[5] born Sutton, Mass., March 7,·1776.
5703. iii. JOHN DAGGETT,[5] born Sutton, Mass., December 12, 1777.
5704. iv.   SIMEON DAGGETT,[5] born Sutton, Mass., June 11, 1779; married Mrs. Sallie Putnam; no issue.
5705. v.   POLLY DAGGETT,[5] born Sutton, Mass., February 14. 1781.
5706. vi.   KATE DAGGETT,[5] born Sutton, Mass., April 4, 1786; died young, Montpelier, Vt.
5707. vii. LUCY DAGGETT,[5] born Sutton. Mass., September 27, 1789; died young, Montpelier, Vt.
5708. viii. MEHITABLE DAGGETT,[5] born 1793; died Montpelier, Vt., Aug. 14, 1844.

5645. MEHITABLE DAGGETT [4] (*Arthur,*[3] *Ebenezer,*[2] *William* [1]), born Sutton, Mass., Oct. 10, 1752; married Sutton, Mass., July 7, 1774, Jonathan Rich, son of Samuel Rich, of Sutton; born July 20, 1747.

Issue:

5709. i.   REUBEN RICH,[5] born April 26, 1775.
5710. ii.   ARTHUR RICH,[5] born October 13, 1777.
5711. iii. SIMEON RICH,[5] born March 6, 1780.
5712. iv.   JONATHAN RICH,[5] born November 19, 1782.
5713. v.   PAUL RICH,[5] born August 16, 1785.
5714. vi.   BARNABAS RICH,[5] born October 13, 1787.

5647. GIDEON DAGGETT [4] (*Arthur,*[3] *Ebenezer,*[2] *William* [1]), born Sutton, Mass., December 21, 1759; died Licking county, Ohio, Aug. 27, 1838; married Elizabeth Child; died Poultney, Vt., 1822.

Issue:

5715. i.   GARDNER DAGGETT,[5] born Sutton, Mass., October 12, 1788.
5716. ii.   WILLIAM KING DAGGETT,[5] born Sutton, Mass., August 24, 1792.
5717. iii. NANCY DAGGETT,[5] born 1793; living with her father, December, 1824.
5718. iv.   HARVEY DAGGETT,[5] born 1797; resided Knox county, Ohio, Dec., 1824.
5719. v.   GIDEON DAGGETT,[5] born 1800.

Gideon Daggett during the Revolutionary war was living in Sutton, Mass., where he enlisted February, 1777, for three years, with Capt. Thomas Fish. He was discharged at Budd's Highlands, near West Point, N.Y.. February, 1780. In his application for a pension, which is on file at Washington, he mentions no battles, or other incidents or places of his service, or that he was in a previous or subsequent service.

After the war he moved to Poultney, Vt., where he was the owner of one hundred and twelve acres of land, with a house and barn. In 1820 he speaks of being unable from infirmities to labor on his farm, and his wife had also been an invalid for many years. To add to his misfortunes a violent storm unroofed and otherwise injured both his house and barn.

In November, 1822, he sold his land, and took in part payment one hundred acres of woodland in Knox county. Ohio.

In 1827 he was living with his son William, in Potsdam, N.Y., and removed with him to Licking county, Ohio, where he died in 1838.

5653. LYDIA DAGGETT [4] (*Samuel*,[3] *Ebenezer*,[2] *William* [1]), born Sutton, Mass., April 23, 1762; married March 24, 1785, Amos Gould, son of Amos and Desire (King) Gould.

Issue: apparently none.

Amos Gould lived in Sutton, Charlton, and afterward in New York State, but most probably he did not move during the life of his first wife. He married 2d, 1796, May 18, Martha Dresser.

5659. HANNAH DAGGETT [4] (*Samuel*,[3] *Ebenezer*,[2] *William* [1]), born Sutton, Mass., September 8, 1780; died Sutton, Mass., February 11, 1871; married Sutton, Mass., October 14, 1806, Simeon Hall, son of Stephen and Abigail (Spring) Hall; '' farmer; '' born Sutton, Mass., May 27, 1780; died Sutton, Mass., July 29, 1827.

Issue:

5720. i. FREDERIC AUGUSTUS HALL,[5] born Sutton, Mass., December 4, 1816; married August 30, 1846, Emma Carlton; two children; resides Shrewsbury, Mass. (1883).
5721. ii. ELIZA HALL,[5] born Sutton, Mass., March 18, 1818; married January 1, 1838, Elijah Thomson, of East Douglas, Mass.; resides Millbury, Mass. (1883); two children.

5660. SOLOMON DWINEL [4] (*Hannah Daggett*,[3] *Ebenezer*,[2] *William* [1]), born Sutton, Mass., October 1, 1757; died Millbury, Mass., July 26, 1830; married Sutton, Mass., April 1, 1783, Mrs. Hannah Singletary Gould, widow of Capt. Jonathan Gould, and daughter of Hon. Amos and Mary (Curtis) Singletary; born Sutton, Mass., March 15, 1753.

Issue:

5722. i. SOLOMON DWINEL,[5] born Sutton, Mass., November 24, 1783; married Mary Ashley.
5723. ii. REMARK DWINEL,[5] born Sutton, Mass., December 10, 1785; married Abigail Miller.
5724. iii. SALMON DWINEL,[5] born 1788; died 1803.
5725. iv. SIMEON DWINEL,[5] born 1790: died unmarried, 1859.
5726. v. LUTHER DWINEL,[5] born 1792; died 1808.
5727. vi. ABIJAH LEGG DWINEL,[5] born 1795; married Rebecca ——.

Solomon Dwinel served in the army through the whole war of the Revolution. He fought at Boston; in the battle on Long Island; at White Plains; was under Stark at Bennington; at the capture of Burgoyne, and at the capture of Cornwallis, at Yorktown, under Lafayette.

5661. MOSES DWINEL [4] (*Hannah Daggett*,[3] *Ebenezer*,[2] *William* [1]), born Sutton, Mass., January 22, 1760; died Sutton, Mass.; married Sarah Paine.

Issue:

5728. i. LEONARD DWINEL,[5] born 1800.
5729. ii. SARAH DWINEL,[5] died young.

5730. iii. JANE DWINEL,[5] died aged 14.
5731. iv. HANNAH DWINEL,[5] married Mr. Garside.

Moses Dwinel, "husbandman," lived and died in the part of Sutton now Millbury.   He served several years in the Revolutionary army.

5662.   HENRY DWINEL [4] (*Hannah Daggett*,[3] *Ebenezer*,[2] *William* [1]), born Sutton, Mass., February 22, 1762; died Albany, N.Y., October 17, 1805; married 1790, Tamar Gale, daughter of Nehemiah Gale.

Issue :

5732. i.   ELBRIDGE GERRY DWINEL,[5] born July 25, 1791; married Sarah S. Nichols.
5733. ii. HANNAH DWINEL,[5] born November 23, 1793; married Enos Baldwin, of Albany, N.Y.
5734. iii. HARRIET DWINEL,[5] born 1795; married Stephen Van Schaick, of Albany, N.Y.
5735. iv. NANCY DWINEL,[5] born 1796; married John L. D. Matthies, of Rochester, N.Y.
5736. v.   HENRY GALE DWINEL,[5] born Albany, N.Y., September 17, 1804; married Anna Maria Newcomb.

Henry Dwinel, "husbandman," of Sutton, went into the Revolutionary army when sixteen years of age; was at the battle of Stony Point, and at West Point when André was hung.   Afterward served in the South until the end of the war.   In 1800 they removed from Sutton to Albany, N.Y.

5666.   SAMUEL DWINEL [4] (*Hannah Daggett*,[3] *Ebenezer*,[2] *William* [1]), born Sutton, Mass., September 28, 1770; died Guilford, Vt., February 21, 1847; married Polly Dudley, daughter of David Dudley, of Sutton; died Guilford, Vt., October 12, 1842.

Issue :

5737. i.   FANNY DWINEL,[5] born September 5, 1793; married James Faulkner; lived in Michigan.
5738. ii. HARVEY DWINEL,[5] born July 4, 1796; married Sarah Babbit.
5739. iii. ORRIGEN DWINEL,[5] born July 21, 1798.
5740. iv. BESSY DWINEL,[5] born September 21, 1801; died 1807.
5741. v.   LUTHER DUDLEY DWINEL,[5] born July 14, 1803.
5742. vi. SALLY DWINEL,[5] born July 3, 1806; married Seth Sherman.
5743. vii. LUCY DWINEL,[5] born August 4, 1808; died 1830.
5744. viii. POLLY DWINEL,[5] born May 28, 1810; married Chanceles L. Eddy.
5745. ix. DAVID DWINEL,[5] born May 28, 1812.
5746. x.   JULIA DWINEL,[5] born February 21, 1814; married Ebenezer Camp, of Guilford, Vt.
5747. xi. IRZOLA DWINEL,[5] born November 12, 1817; married Elbridge G. Minns, of Leyden, Mass.

Samuel Dwinel, or Dunnel, farmer, removed from Sutton to Whittingham, Vt., thence to Colerain, and thence to Guilford, Vt.

5667.   ABRAHAM DWINEL [4] (*Hannah Daggett*,[3] *Ebenezer*,[2] *William* [1]), or "Dunnel," born Sutton, Mass., September 25, 1773; "yeoman;" died March 5, 1814; married Mehitable Rich.

Issue :

5748. i.   CYRUS DWINEL,[5] born Aug. 2, 1797; of Cleveland, Ohio, 1854.

5749. ii. POLLY DWINEL,[5] born November 17, 1799; married Leonard Davis, of Oxford, Mass.
5750. iii. LUCY DWINEL,[5] born March 8, 1802; married Wm. Wilson, of Shoreham, Vt.
5751. iv. HIRAM DWINEL,[5] born February 28, 1808; married Charlotte A. Willard, of Ashburn.
5752. v. SALEM DWINEL,[5] born March 3, 1810; died young.
5753. vi. ALICE DWINEL,[5] born June 10, 1813; married James M. Bailey, of Ticonderoga.
5754. vii. ELIZA DWINEL,[6] born May 20, 1815; married Wm. G. Wilson, of Shoreham, Vt.

5670. Rev. ISAAC DWINEL [4] (*Hannah Daggett*,[3] *Ebenezer*,[2] *William* [1]), born Sutton, Mass., March 5, 1782; died Tolland Conn., November 11, 1857; married 1st, Millbury, Mass., Roxa Marble, daughter of Dea. Solomon Marble, of Millbury; died Tolland, Conn., October, 1848; married 2d, Lucretia Martin, daughter of Henry and Mary Martin, of Woodstock, Conn.

Issue:

5755. i. MARCUS DWINEL,[5] born August 2, 1818.
5756. ii. LUCIUS DWINEL,[5] born December 10, 1821.
5757. iii. SUMNER DWINEL,[5] born July 16, 1824; died 1843.

Rev. Elder Isaac Dwinel was a Baptist elder, and in the habit of frequently preaching, but most of the time cultivated his farm; resided the latter part of his days in Tolland, Conn.

WILLIAM DAGGETT, OF SACO, ME.

FIFTH GENERATION.

5671. Rev. THOMAS DAGGETT [5] (*John*,[4] *Thomas*,[3] *Ebenezer*,[2] *William* [1]), born Charlton, Mass., August 5, 1776; married daughter of Dea. Thomas Record, of Minot, Me.

Issue:

5758. i. ELISHA DAGGETT,[6] born Greene, Me.
5759. ii. RUTH DAGGETT,[6] married; died Foxcroft, Me., 1881.
5760. iii. THOMAS DAGGETT.[6]

5672. JOHN DAGGETT [5] (*John*,[4] *Thomas*,[3] *Ebenezer*,[2] *William* [1]), born Charlton, Mass., Oct. 14, 1778; died Greene, Me., 1824; married Sarah Record, daughter of Dea. Thomas Record, of Minot, Me.

Issue:

5761. i. BETSEY DAGGETT.[6]
5762. ii. CALVIN DAGGETT.[6]
5763. iii. LUCY DAGGETT.[6]
5764. iv. ANNIE DAGGETT.[6]

5765. v. JOHN DAGGETT.[6]
5766. vi. SILAS DAGGETT.[6]

Rev. John Daggett was pastor of the Baptist church in Greene, Me., from 1810 to 1820. He was a patriotic citizen and a sound philanthropist.

5673. SARAH DAGGETT[5] (*John,*[4] *Thomas,*[3] *Ebenezer,*[2] *William*[1]), born Charlton, Mass., April 2, 1780; died St. Albans, Me., 1873; married Greene, Me., Capt. Samuel Bates, of Greene, Me.

Issue:

5767. i. FLORENTINE BATES.[6]
5768. ii. SIMEON BATES.[6]
5769. iii. MARILLA BATES.[6]
5770. iv. SARAH BATES.[6]

5675. Capt. AARON DAGGETT[5] (*John,*[4] *Thomas,*[3] *Ebenezer,*[2] *William*[1]), born Greene, Me., March 4, 1787; died Greene, Me., Feb. 1, 1862; married 1st, Monmouth, Me., Aug., 1817, Almira Dearborn, daughter of Simon and Molly (Blake) Dearborn; born Monmouth, Me., May 7, 1789; died Greene, Me., March 11, 1830; married 2d, Monmouth, Me., Nov., 1830, Dorcas Christiana Dearborn, daughter of Simon and Molly (Blake) Dearborn; born Monmouth, Me., June 13, 1796; died Greene, Me., March 24, 1869.

Issue:

5771. i. GREENLIEF DEARBORN QUINCY ADAMS DAGGETT,[6] born Greene, Me., November 10, 1818.
5772. ii. CONVERSE ROLLIN DAGGETT,[6] born Greene, Me., March 14, 1820.
5773. iii. SIMON DEARBORN ALFRED PIERCE DAGGETT,[6] born Greene, Me., September 19, 1822; died Greene, Me., August 11, 1840.
5774. iv. MOLLY DEARBORN DAGGETT,[6] born Greene, Me., April 13, 1826; died Greene, Me., April 23, 1826.
5775. v. ALMIRA AUGUSTA DAGGETT,[6] born Greene, Me., September 28, 1827; married January, 1865, Isaac Cotton Merrill, of Lewiston, Me.; she died March 27, 1865, Greene, Me.; no issue.
5776. vi. EBENEZER SANBORN DAGGETT,[6] born Greene, Me., September 30, 1831; died Greene, Me., October 14, 1831.
5777. vii. JOHN CARROL DAGGETT,[6] born Greene, Me., July 29, 1833.
5778. viii. MARY ELIZA DAGGETT,[6] born Greene, Me., January 9, 1835; died Greene, Me., October 1, 1861.
5779. ix. AARON SIMON DAGGETT,[6] born Greene, Me., June 14, 1837.

Capt. Aaron Daggett was many years member of the board of selectmen and school committee of Greene, Me.

He served a term in the Maine House of Representatives, was justice of the peace and military captain, serving in the war of 1812 for a short time. He was universally esteemed. He died in the house where he was born seventy-five years before.

5679. WILLIAM DAGGETT[5] (*Phineas,*[4] *William,*[3] *Ebenezer,*[2] *William*[1]), born Westmoreland, N.H., Dec. 21, 1788; died Westmoreland, N.H., June 2, 1818; married Westmoreland, N.H., March 20,

1813, by Rev. Allen Pratt, to Clarissa Wait, daughter of Maj. Jason Wait; born Westmoreland, N.H., 1791; died Springville, N.Y., 1862.

Issue :

5780. i. WILLIAM DAGGETT,[6] born Westmoreland, N.H., 1813; died Troy, N.Y., May 16, 1860.
5781. ii. CLARISSA DAGGETT,[6] born Westmoreland, N.H., March 6, 1815.
5782. iii. ELIZA DAGGETT,[6] born Westmoreland. N.H., October 2, 1817.
5783. iv. GEORGE WAIT DAGGETT,[6] born Westmoreland, N.H., June 30, 1818.

5683. BETSEY DAGGETT[5] (*Phineas*,[4] *William*,[3] *Ebenezer*,[2] *William*[1]), born Westmoreland, N.H., December 31, 1799; died Lockport, N.Y., 1877; married Westmoreland, N.H., October 17, 1833, by Rev. Ebenezer Chase, to Broughton Knight, of Lockport, N.Y.

Issue :

5784. i. GEORGE KNIGHT,[6] resides Church street, Lockport, N.Y. (1892).
5785. ii. Daughter KNIGHT.[6]

5684. HOLLIS DAGGETT[5] (*Phineas*,[4] *William*,[3] *Ebenezer*,[2] *William*[1]), born Westmoreland, N.H., November 4, 1802; died Brighton, N.Y., 1882; married Flora Jackman.

Issue :

5786. i. FREDERIC DAGGETT,[6] resides Lockport, N.Y.
5787. ii. Daughter DAGGETT.[6]

5685. LEWIS DAGGETT[5] (*Phineas*,[4] *William*,[3] *Ebenezer*,[2] *William*[1]), born Westmoreland, N.H., August 15, 1804, died Lockport, N.Y., May 10, 1884; married 1st, McGrawville, N.Y., September, 1832, Harriet Haughton, daughter of John and Thankful (Penny) Haughton; born Palenville, N.Y., August 7, 1807; died August 10, 1866; married 2d, Cordelia ——; resides Hinsdale, N.H. (1893).

Issue :

5788. i. HIRAM SIBLEY DAGGETT,[6] born Cambria, N.Y., February 3, 1833; died Cambria, N.Y., November 25, 1861.
5789. ii. CAROLINE LOUISA DAGGETT,[6] born Cambria, N.Y., June 7, 1837; died Cambria. N.Y., February 14, 1839.
5790. iii. HENRY TALMADGE DAGGETT,[6] born Cambria, N.Y., February 8, 1840.
5791. iv. CHARLES PRENTISS DAGGETT,[6] born Cambria, N.Y., October 5, 1843; died Cambria, N.Y., January 14, 1846.
5792. v. CHARLES LEWIS DAGGETT.[6] born Cambria, N.Y., January 14, 1851; died Cambria, N.Y., February 25, 1869.

" Lewis Daggett was deacon of the Congregational church at Cambria for thirty years, and was looked up to and respected by rich and poor; the latter he never turned away empty-handed from his door. He was the poor man's friend, a staunch temperance man, and a reformer in his way. He was justice of the peace, also town superintendent of common schools, and settled several estates. He was elected superintendent of the poor, and kept the county house for several terms.

" He removed to Lockport about a year before his death."

5687. MARY DAGGETT[5] (*Phineas*,[4] *William*,[3] *Ebenezer*,[2] *William*[1]), born Westmoreland, N.H., 1809; died Hawley, N.Y., 1841; married Westmoreland, N.H., November 18, 1834, by Rev. Ebenezer Chase, to Daniel Pierce, of Hawley, N.Y.

Issue:

5793. i. DARWIN PIERCE,[6] died Andersonville prison.
5794. ii. HORACE PIERCE,[6] resided Hawley, N.Y.

5688. LOUISA DAGGETT[5] (*Phineas*,[4] *William*,[3] *Ebenezer*,[2] *William*[1]), born Westmoreland, N.H., December 10, 1812; resides Belvidere, Ill. (1892); married Westmoreland, N.H., March 24, 1842, by Rev. R. W. Fuller, to Moses Knapp Pratt, son of Josiah and Jane (Knapp) Pratt; born Westmoreland, N.H., January 1, 1813; died Spring, Ill., March 15, 1884.

Issue:

5795. i. FREDERIC KNIGHT PRATT,[6] born Westmoreland, N.H., May 25, 1843.

5701. ARTHUR DAGGETT[5] (*Arthur*,[4] *Arthur*,[3] *Ebenezer*,[2] *William*[1]), born Sutton, Mass., 1775; died Montpelier, Vt., January 11, 1855; married Mrs. Azuba West, widow of Freeman West, and daughter of Mr. Haskell; born New Bedford, Mass., 1771; died Montpelier, Vt., May 15, 1843.

Issue:

5796. i. ARTHUR DAGGETT,[6] born Montpelier, Vt., March, 1803.
5797. ii. FREEMAN DAGGETT,[6] born Montpelier, Vt., June 20, 1807.

5702. STEPHEN DAGGETT[5] (*Arthur*,[4] *Arthur*,[3] *Ebenezer*,[2] *William*[1]), born Sutton, Mass., March 7, 1776; died Montpelier, Vt.; married Mary Doty, daughter of Capt. Barnabas Doty; born Rochester (?), Mass.; died Calais, Vt.

Issue:

5798. i. LUCY DAGGETT,[6] born Montpelier, Vt., January 28, 1805.
5799. ii. CATHARINE DAGGETT,[6] born Montpelier, Vt., January 16, 1807.
5800. iii. JAMES SULLIVAN DAGGETT,[6] born Montpelier, Vt., September 20, 1808.
5801. iv. MORRITTA DAGGETT,[6] born Montpelier, Vt., Sept. 9, 1810; died Calais, Vt.

5703. JOHN DAGGETT[5] (*Arthur*,[4] *Arthur*,[3] *Ebenezer*,[2] *William*[1]), born Sutton, Mass., December 12, 1777; died near Madison, Ind., August, 1820; married 1st, Loruhanah Nealy; born August 5, 1782; died Mayville, N.Y., 1814; married 2d, Abigail Durfee; born New York; died near Madison, Ind., August, 1820.

Issue:

5802. i. NEALY DAGGETT,[6] born Montpelier, Vt., April 17, 1803; died Leavenworth, Ind., August 24, 1824.
5803. ii. KATHERINE DAGGETT,[6] born Montpelier, Vt., January 9, 1805.
5804. iii. JOHN SCOTT DAGGETT,[6] born Mayville, N.Y., February 22, 1808.
5805. iv. ORPHA DAGGETT,[6] born Mayville, N.Y., May 24, 1810.

5806. v. STEPHEN DAGGETT,[6] born Mayville, N.Y., October 11, 1816; died Crawford, Ind., 1833.
5807. vi. SIMEON DAGGETT,[6] born Madison, Ind., August 14, 1818.

5705. POLLY DAGGETT [5] (*Arthur,*[4] *Arthur,*[3] *Ebenezer,*[2] *William* [1]), born Sutton, Mass., February 14, 1781; died Plainfield, Vt., November 1, 1813; married Montpelier, Vt., 1800 or 1801, Amasa Bancroft, son of John and Ruth (Watrous) Bancroft; "blacksmith;" born Oxford, Mass., 1779; died Plainfield, Vt., February 6, 1812.

Issue:

5808. i. LUCY BANCROFT,[6] born Montpelier, Vt., March 30, 1802.
5809. ii. NANCY BANCROFT,[6] born Montpelier, Vt., 1804; died Montpelier, Vt., April 4, 1834.
5810. iii. CORNELIUS WATROUS BANCROFT,[6] born Montpelier, Vt., 1808.
5811. iv. CARLOS BANCROFT,[6] born Montpelier, Vt., March 20, 1809.
5812. v. AMASA BANCROFT,[6] born Montpelier, Vt.

5715. GARDNER DAGGETT [5] (*Gideon,*[4] *Arthur,*[3] *Ebenezer,*[2] *William* [1]), born Sutton, Mass., October 12, 1788; died Brunersburg, Ohio, October, 1843; married Heath, Mass., 1811, Eunice White, daughter of Luke and Eunice (White) White; born Heath, Mass., 1786; died Richville, N.Y., June 15, 1833.

Issue:

5813. i. SOPHRONIA DAGGETT,[6] born Heath, Mass., July 15, 1812; married May, 1835, Amos Stoddard, of Massachusetts; she died Defiance, Ohio, October 14, 1888; no issue living.
5814. ii. DIANA DAGGETT,[6] born Heath, Mass., December, 1814; married Gideon Marihugh, of Connecticut; she died Defiance, Ohio, fall of 1866; no issue living.
5815. iii. EUNICE DAGGETT,[6] born Heath, Mass., December, 1816; died Brunersburg, Ohio, fall of 1841.
5816. iv. ELIZABETH ANN DAGGETT,[6] born Poultney, Vt., July 4, 1818.
5817. v. WILLIAM DAGGETT,[6] born Poultney, Vt., 1821; died Richville, N.Y., May, 1835.
5818. vi. GARDNER DAGGETT,[6] born Poultney, Vt.; died Richville, N.Y., young.
5819. vii. ARTHUR DAGGETT,[6] born Poultney, Vt.; died Richville, N.Y., young.
5820. viii. HARRIET DAGGETT,[6] born Poultney, Vt., April, 1827.
5821. ix. ESTHER SMITH DAGGETT,[6] born Richville, N.Y., September 27, 1829.
5822. x. ROLLIN MALLORY DAGGETT,[6] born Richville, N.Y., Feb. 22, 1831.

5716. WILLIAM KING DAGGETT [5] (*Gideon,*[4] *Arthur,*[3] *Ebenezer,*[2] *William* [1]), born Sutton, Mass., Aug. 24, 1792; died Antwerp, Ohio, Feb. 6, 1862; married Middlebury, Vt., Feb. 15, 1819, Betsey Johnson, daughter of Libeus and Annie (Claghorn) Johnson; born Rutland, Vt., Sept. 20, 1791; died Richville, N.Y., Nov. 6, 1835.

Issue:

5823. i. NANCY DAGGETT,[6] born Middlebury, Vt., December 9, 1819.
5824. ii. WILLIAM KING DAGGETT,[6] born Middlebury, Vt., May 4, 1822.
5825. iii. ANN DAGGETT,[6] born Middlebury, Vt., July 1, 1824.
5826. iv. CAROLINE DAGGETT,[6] born Potsdam, N.Y., June 26, 1826; married Antwerp, Ohio, July 14, 1850, Jedediah Banks, son of William and Hester (Cassabone) Banks; he born Delhi, Ohio, August 16, 1826; died Dec. 13, 1872; no issue; she resides Antwerp, Ohio (1892).

5827. v. LOUISA DAGGETT,[6] born Potsdam, N.Y., April 22, 1828.
5828. vi. SAMANTHA DAGGETT,[6] born Potsdam, N.Y., November 28, 1830; resides
        Antwerp, Ohio (1892).

5719. GIDEON DAGGETT [5] (*Gideon*,[4] *Arthur*,[3] *Ebenezer*,[2] *William* [1]), born 1800; died Lockport, Ind., 1862; married ———.
Issue:

5829. i. EDWARD DAGGETT.[6]
5830. ii. EDWIN DAGGETT.[6]
5831. iii. LAURA DAGGETT,[6] married Jackson Moorman; had son, Rev. Charles
        E. Moorman, Bryan, Ohio (1892).

WILLIAM DAGGETT, OF SACO, ME.

SIXTH GENERATION.

5758. ELISHA DAGGETT [6] (*Thomas*,[5] *John*,[4] *Thomas*,[3] *Ebenezer*,[2] *William* [1]), born Greene, Me.; "carpenter;" died Foxcroft, Me., about 1881; married 1st. Turner, Me., Evelina Thayer, daughter of Abner and Persis (Turner) Thayer; born Turner, Me., October 17, 1803; died Foxcroft, Me., October 2, 1831; married 2d, Foxcroft, Me., December 6, 1832, Augusta Bolster, daughter of Abraham and ——— (House) Bolster; resides Foxcroft, Me. (1893).
Issue:

5832. i.   MARY THAYER DAGGETT,[7] born Foxcroft, Me., March 13, 1828; mar-
           ried Rev. Cyrus Cunningham; resides Hotel Warwick, Boston,
           Mass. (1893).
5833. ii. MATILDA DAGGETT,[7] born Foxcroft, Me., May 17, 1829; resides Hotel
           Warwick, Boston, Mass. (1893).
5834. iii. EVELINA DAGGETT,[7] born Foxcroft, Me., June 1, 1831; died 1839.
5835. iv. ALBION DAGGETT,[7] born Foxcroft, Me., September 4, 1832; married
           ———; has several children; resides Illinois (1893).
5836. v.   FRANKLIN HENRY DAGGETT,[7] born Frankfort, Me., October 21, 1837;
           married; no issue; died Foxcroft, Me., 1865.
5837. vi. HENRY FRANKLIN DAGGETT,[7] born Frankfort, Me., October 21, 1837.
5838. vii. RUTH AUGUSTA DAGGETT,[7] born Frankfort, Me., April 16, 1841; mar-
           ried Salmon Briggs; resides Urbana, Ill. (1893).
5839. viii. THOMAS DAGGETT,[7] born Foxcroft, Me., December 25, 1843.
5840. ix. SIMEON ROSCOE DAGGETT,[7] born Foxcroft, Me., September, 1846;
           died Foxcroft, Me., 1865.

5760. THOMAS DAGGETT [6] (*Thomas*,[5] *John*,[4] *Thomas*,[3] *Ebenezer*,[2] *William* [1]), died Attleboro', Mass.; married.
Issue:

5841. i. HENRY DAGGETT,[7] resides Attleboro', Mass. (1893).

5771. Dr. GREENLIEF DEARBORN QUINCY ADAMS DAGGETT [6] (*Aaron*,[5] *John*,[4] *Thomas*,[3] *Ebenezer*,[2] *William* [1]), born Greene, Me.,

A. S. Daggett.

November 10, 1818; died Boonton, N.J., July 23, 1854; married New Jersey, Miss Robinson.

Issue:

5842. i. —— Daggett,[7] born Boonton, N.J.; died Boonton, N.J., soon after 1854.

G. D. Q. A. Daggett, M.D., graduated at the College of Physicians and Surgeons, New York city, and was afterward a year in Bellevue Hospital.

He then settled in Boonton, N.J., where he was president of the County Medical Society and trustee of Boonton Academy.

5772. Rev. Converse Rollin Daggett [6] (*Aaron,*[5] *John,*[4] *Thomas,*[3] *Ebenezer,*[2] *William*[1]), born Greene, Me., March 14, 1820; resides Greene, Me. (1893); married Cambridge, Me., June 11, 1871, Anna F. Packard Bailey, daughter of Sands and Nancy Anna (Mayhew) Bailey; born Cambridge, Me., June 11, 1845.

Issue:

5843. i. Emma Rose Daggett,[7] born Greene, Me., December 4, 1880.

Rev. C. R. Daggett studied at the Bangor Theological Seminary, and was ordained a minister in Bangor, Me., September 6, 1862.

Enlisted in August, 1862, in the Twenty-third Maine Regiment; mustered out in June, 1863.

Member of the Maine House of Representatives in the winter of 1864. In the spring of 1864 he became pastor of the Congregational church in South Solon and East Madison, Me. Has worked for Athens, Cambridge, and Greene churches.

5777. John Carrol Daggett [6] (*Aaron,*[5] *John,*[4] *Thomas,*[3] *Ebenezer,*[2] *William*[1]), born Greene, Me., July 29, 1833; resides Greene Corner, Me. (1893); married Greene, Me., May, 1871, Abbie Fogg; born Greene, Me.

Issue:

5844. i. Aaron Dagglit,[7] born Greene, Me.
5845. ii. Augusta Daggett.[7] born Greene, Me.
5846. iii. Simon Dearborn Daggett,[7] born Greene, Me.

5779. Gen. Aaron Simon Daggett [6] (*Aaron,*[5] *John,*[4] *Thomas,*[3] *Ebenezer,*[2] *William*[1]), born Greene, Me., June 14, 1837; stationed at Fort Sill, Oklahoma territory (1893); married Turner, Me., June 14, 1865, Martha Rosetta Bradford, daughter of Gen. Phillips and Mary Brett (Bird) Bradford; born Turner, Me., September 11, 1840.

Issue:

5847. i. Mary Augusta Daggett,[7] born Atlanta, Ga., October 21, 1868.
5848. ii. Royal Bradford Daggett,[7] born Auburn, Me., November 13, 1870.
5849. iii. Alice Southworth Daggett,[7] born Auburn, Me., August 11, 1872.
5850. iv. Helen Daggett,[7] born Auburn, Me., September 1, 1881.

Gen. Aaron S. Daggett enlisted as a private in the Fifth Maine

Regiment in the spring of 1861, served three years, and was mustered out as brevet brigadier-general.

He enlisted again in Hancock's Veteran Corps as captain, and remained till the close of the war. He was then commissioned as captain in the regular service, and continues in the army with the present rank of brevet lieutenant-colonel. He was not an applicant for a position in the regular army, the appointment being made without solicitation, by recommendation of General Grant.

Colonel Daggett was brevetted colonel and brigadier-general of volunteers, March 2, 1867, for "gallant and meritorious services during the war," and received the brevets of major United States army for "gallant and meritorious services at the battle of Rappahannock Station, Va., November 7, 1863," and lieutenant-colonel for "gallant and meritorious services in the battle of the Wilderness, Va."

Immediately after the battle of Rappahannock Station, the captured trophies, flags, cannon, etc., were escorted to General Meade's headquarters, Colonel Daggett being in command of the battalion of his brigade, he having been chosen by General Upton, the escort being selected from those who had taken the most conspicuous part in that battle. General Upton wrote as follows regarding Colonel Daggett:

"In the assault at Rappahannock Station, Col. Daggett's regiment captured over five hundred prisoners."

"In the assault at Spottsylvania Court House. May 10, his regiment lost six out of seven captains, the seventh being killed on the 12th of May, at 'the angle,' or the point where the tree was shot down by musketry, on which ground the regiment fought from 9.30 A.M. until 5 30 P.M., when it was relieved. On all these occasions, Colonel Daggett was under my immediate command, and fought with distinguished bravery. Throughout his military career in the army of the Potomac he maintained the character of a good soldier and an upright man, and his promotion would be but a simple act of justice, which would be commended by all those who desire to see courage rewarded."

At another time General Upton said: "His promotion would be a great benefit to the service, while the honor of the State could scarcely be intrusted to safer hands."

Generals Hancock, Meade, Wright, and Russell also recommended him for promotion.

General Daggett is not only a soldier, but has ability outside of his profession; is a fine speaker, and distinguished for courteous and gentlemanly bearing, strict integrity, frank courtesy, and sterling worth.

5781. CLARISSA DAGGETT [6] (*William,*[5] *Phineas,*[4] *William,*[3] *Ebenezer,*[2] *William* [1]), born Westmoreland, N.H., March 6, 1815; died

Westminster West, Vt., November 10, 1890; married Westmoreland, N.H., September 18, 1834, Sidney Smith Campbell, son of Dr. Edward Raymond and Anna (Norton) Campbell, of Chesterfield, N.H.; born Westminster West, Vt., March 3, 1810.

Issue: four children.

5851. i. MARY ELIZABETH CAMPBELL,[7] married Jason Holman, Hinsdale, N.H.; she died March 16, 1871.
5852. ii. CHARLES SIDNEY CAMPBELL,[7] resides Chesterfield Factory, N.H. (1892).
5853. iii. CLARA ANNA CAMPBELL,[7] married J. H. Clark; resides Westminster West, Vt. (1892).

5782. ELIZA DAGGETT[6] (*William,*[5] *Phineas,*[4] *William,*[3] *Ebenezer,*[2] *William*[1]), born Westmoreland, N.H., October 2, 1817; resides Cuba, N.Y. (1871); married Westmoreland, N.H., July 15, 1838, Stephen Kimball Cutter, son of Stephen and Mehitable Cutter; born Jaffrey, N.H., March 12, 1815; " carpenter."

Issue:

5854. i. FRANCES EVELINE CUTTER,[7] born Springville, N.Y., April 18, 1839; married September 14, 1859, Veranes Bemis Coleman; he born January 21, 1837; resides Belmont, N.Y. (1871).
5855. ii. JUDSON CHARLES CUTTER,[7] born Cuba, N.Y., July 30, 1842.
5856. iii. ADDISON ADOLPHUS CUTTER,[7] born Cuba, N.Y., April 20, 1845; died Cuba, N.Y., June 26, 1845.
5857. iv. ADDISON ADOLPHUS CUTTER,[7] born Cuba, N.Y., October 5, 1846.
5858. v. ELLA ELIZA CUTTER,[7] born Cuba, N.Y., March 30, 1849.

5783. GEORGE WAIT DAGGETT[6] (*William,*[5] *Phineas,*[4] *William,*[3] *Ebenezer,*[2] *William*[1]), born Westmoreland, N.H., June 30, 1818; died Westmoreland, N.H., June 25, 1834; married Westmoreland, N.H., September 7, 1847, by Rev. Stephen Rodgers, to Sarah Laurette Cole, daughter of Heber and Sally (Bennett) Cole, of Vermont; born Westmoreland, N.H., March 7, 1821; resides Westmoreland, N.H. (1892).

Issue:

5859. i. GEORGE MARSHALL DAGGETT,[7] born Worcester, Mass., October 16, 1848; died Westmoreland, N.H., July 11, 1862.
5860. ii. SARAH LOUISE DAGGETT,[7] born Worcester, Mass., May 19, 1850.
5861. iii. CLARA ESTHER DAGGETT,[7] born Westmoreland, N.H., March 3, 1852.
5862. iv. WALTER SIDNEY DAGGETT,[7] born Westmoreland, N.H., May 17, 1853; resides Westmoreland Depot, N.H. (1892).
5863. v. ELIZA ISABELL DAGGETT,[7] born Westmoreland, N.H., July 1, 1857; died Westmoreland, N.H., July 22, 1862.

5790. HENRY TALMADGE DAGGETT[6] (*Lewis,*[5] *Phineas,*[4] *William,*[3] *Ebenezer,*[2] *William*[1]), born Cambria, N.Y., February 8, 1840; died Ridgeway, N.Y., October 13, 1888; married 1st, Cambria, N.Y., July 3, 1867, Mary Elton, daughter of William and Mary (Gaskill) Elton; born Cambria, N.Y., June 27, 1840; died April 28, 1884; married 2d, Milton, Pa., January 1, 1885, by Rev. William Gotwalt, to Mrs. Martha Matilda Slater, widow, daughter of James and Mary (Hause) Brass; born near Comly, Pa., July 3, 1843; resides 83 Prospect street, Lockport, N.Y. (1893).

Issue:

5864. i. FRANKIE DAGGETT,[7] born June 8, 1869; died September 3, 1869.
5865. ii. WILLIAM L. DAGGETT,[7] born August 1, 1871.
5866. iii. MARY HARRIET DAGGETT,[7] born March 5, 1884.
5867. iv. HARRY NESBITT DAGGETT,[7] born October 30, 1886.

Mr. Daggett lived quietly on the farm in Cambria until the war began, when he enlisted, November 4, 1861, Company C, Twenty-eighth New York Volunteers. Discharged from the hospital June 18, 1862. As soon as he was well he reënlisted, Second Mounted Rifles, New York Volunteers, as sergeant, Company I. Enrolled October 24, 1863; discharged at close of war, August 10, 1865, at Petersburg. He was a stanch Republican, Free Mason, also member of the G.A.R. Was customs inspector at Suspension Bridge for one term. Removed to Ridgeway in March, 1887.

5795. FREDERIC KNIGHT PRATT [6] (*Louisa Daggett*,[5] *Phineas*,[4] *William*,[3] *Ebenezer*,[2] *William* [1]), born Westmoreland, N.H., May 25, 1843; resides Belvidere, Ill. (1892); married Bonus, Ill., January 20, 1875, Marion B. Turnure.

Issue:

5868. i. FRANK HOLLIS PRATT,[7] born Spring, Ill., November 25, 1877.
5869. ii. RALPH TURNURE PRATT,[7] born Spring, Ill., April 22, 1884.

5796. ARTHUR DAGGETT [6] (*Arthur*,[5] *Arthur*,[4] *Arthur*,[3] *Ebenezer*,[2] *William* [1]), born Montpelier, Vt., March, 1803; died East Montpelier, Vt., September 15, 1882; married Barre, Vt., Nancy Farewell, daughter of Lemuel and Patience (Walker) Farewell; born Barre, Vt., May 1, 1807; died East Montpelier, Vt., March 30, 1881.

Issue:

5870. i. ABBIE BILLINGS DAGGETT,[7] born East Montpelier, Vt., January 30, 1831.
5871. ii. ARTHUR DAGGETT,[7] born East Montpelier, Vt., May 15, 1843; died East Montpelier, Vt., January 20, 1844.

5797. FREEMAN DAGGETT [6] (*Arthur*,[5] *Arthur*,[4] *Arthur*,[3] *Ebenezer*,[2] *William* [1]), born Montpelier, Vt., June 20, 1807; died East Montpelier, Vt., September 11, 1865; married Barre, Vt., Calista Ingalls, daughter of Samuel and Hannah (Raymond) Ingalls; born Barre, Vt., January 9, 1809; died Winooski, Vt., August 31, 1886.

Issue:

5872. i. GEORGE DAGGETT,[7] born Montpelier, Vt., September 18, 1835.

5798. Lucy Daggett [6] (*Stephen*,[5] *Arthur*,[4] *Arthur*,[3] *Ebenezer*,[2] *William* [1]), born Montpelier, Vt., January 28, 1805; died Calais, Vt.; married Calais, Vt., Alpheus Bliss; died Calais, Vt.

Issue:

5873. i.   CATHARINE AMELIA BLISS,[7] died Calais, Vt., February, 1892; married 1st, Orlando Morse; he died Calais, Vt.; married 2d, John Van Rensselaer Kent, in Calais; he died Calais, Vt., February, 1892; issue: Charles Van Kent,[8] resides Calais, Vt. (1893).

5874. ii. CAROLINE ELIZABETH BLISS,[7] resides Calais, Vt. (1893); married Calais, Vt., William Robinson; he died Calais, Vt., October, 1875; issue: Ina Lucy Robinson,[8] born April 19, 1869; resides Calais, Vt. (1893).

5799. CATHARINE DAGGETT [6] (*Stephen*,[5] *Arthur*,[4] *Arthur*,[3] *Ebenezer*,[2] *William* [1]), born Montpelier, Vt., January 16, 1807; died Calais, Vt., May 15, 1881; married Calais, Vt., May 24, 1832, Levi Robinson, son of Joel and Rachel (Stevens) Robinson; born Calais, Vt., September 18, 1803; died Calais, Vt., Sept. 7, 1863.

Issue:

5875. i.   JOEL EMERY ROBINSON,[7] born Calais, Vt., February 18, 1834; served Thirteenth Regiment Vermont Volunteers; mustered out July 21, 1863; died Calais, Vt., July 28, 1863.

5876. ii. JULIUS SULLIVAN ROBINSON,[7] born Calais, Vt., March 9, 1836.

5877. iii. OTIS VINTON ROBINSON,[7] born Calais, Vt., July 25, 1838; died Calais, Vt., September 15, 1863.

5878. iv. MARY CHERILL ROBINSON,[7] born Calais, Vt., August 24, 1845.

5800. JAMES SULLIVAN DAGGETT [6] (*Stephen*,[5] *Arthur*,[4] *Arthur*,[3] *Ebenezer*,[2] *William* [1]), born Montpelier, Vt., September 20, 1808; died Calais, Vt.; married 1st, Middleboro', Mass., October 10, 1837, Elizabeth Vinton, daughter of Capt. William and Abigail (Otis) Vinton; born East Bridgewater, Mass., July 15, 1812; died Holliston, Mass., June 12, 1850; married 2d, Holliston, Mass., December 10, 1850, Mrs. Fidelia Pratt; resides Calais, Vt. (1893).

Issue:

5879. i.   ABBIE ELIZABETH DAGGETT,[7] born Holliston, Mass., November 22, 1851; married Calais, Vt., William Daley; resides Calais, Vt. (1893).

James S. Daggett, shoemaker, of Calais, Vt., resided there for some time; afterward at East Medway, Mass.

5803. KATHERINE DAGGETT [6] (*John*,[5] *Arthur*,[4] *Arthur*,[3] *Ebenezer*,[2] *William* [1]), born Montpelier, Vt., January 9, 1805; died Kirkwood, Ill., March 15, 1887; married Madison, Ind., February 1, 1827, Ebenezer Chapin, son of Samuel and Susannah (Walbridge) Chapin; born Burlington, N.Y., May 1, 1800; died Oquawka, Ill., Jan. 29, 1874.

Issue:

5880. i.   NEALY ADOLPHUS CHAPIN,[7] born Leavenworth, Ind., January 29, 1828.

5881. ii. PATRICK HENRY CHAPIN,[7] born Greenville, Ind., August 22, 1834.

5882. iii. MARY ANN CHAPIN,[7] born Henderson, Ill., November 4, 1836; married Oquawka, Ill., December 19, 1862, John Adams Pence, son of John and Elizabeth (Heaton) Pence; born Oquawka, Ill., August 12, 1830; no issue; resides Oquawka, Ill. (1893).
5883. iv. JOHN EBENEZER CHAPIN,[7] born Oquawka, Ill., March 10, 1840.
5884. v. ANDREW GREGG CHAPIN,[7] born Oquawka, Ill., September 13, 1845; died Oquawka, Ill., August 10, 1846.

5804. JOHN SCOTT DAGGETT[6] (*John,*[5] *Arthur,*[4] *Arthur,*[3] *Ebenezer,*[2] *William*[1]), born Mayville, N.Y., February 22, 1808; died Columbus, Mo., January 14, 1890; married Leavenworth, Ind., March 25, 1830, Sally Chapin, daughter of Joseph Chapin; born New York; died Galesburg, Ill., August 8, 1865.

Issue:

5885. i. NEALY DAGGETT,[7] has son Elbert O. Daggett;[8] and daughter Alta Daggett,[8] born December 6, 1880; resides Columbus, Johnson Co., Mo. (1892).
5886. ii. ANN ELIZA DAGGETT,[7] married Mr. Richardson; resides Avon, Fulton Co., Ill. (1892).
5887. iii. ALMIRON DAGGETT,[7] resides Alto, Wash. (1892).
5888. iv. SAMUEL DAGGETT,[7] resides Panama, Ia. (1892).
5889. v. LORUHANNA DAGGETT,[7] married Mr. Williams; resides Panama, Ia. (1892).
5890. vi. MARY S. DAGGETT,[7] married Mr. Powell; resides Meadow Grove, Neb. (1892).
5891. vii. SARAH DAGGETT,[7] married Mr. Johnson; resides Liberty, Mo. (1892).
5892. viii. AMELIA DAGGETT,[7] married Mr. Ericson; resides Goodland, Kan. (1892).
5893. ix. CORNELIA DAGGETT,[7] married Mr. Culver; resides Columbus, Mo. (1892).

5805. ORPHA DAGGETT[6] (*John,*[5] *Arthur,*[4] *Arthur,*[3] *Ebenezer,*[2] *William*[1]), born Mayville, N.Y., May 24, 1810; married 1st, Mr. Edson; married 2d, Ira Woods.

Issue:

5894. i. HANNAH EDSON.[7]
5895. ii. WILLIS EDSON,[7] "grain and feed merchant;" resides Topeka, Kan. (1892).
5896. iii. WILLIAM EDSON.[7]
5897. iv. CLARISSA WOODS,[7] married Mr. McGowan; resides Newton, Kan. (1892).
5898. v. NEALY C. WOODS,[7] resides San Buena Ventura, Cal. (1892).
5899. vi. PHEBE WOODS,[7] died California.
5900. vii. ORPHA WOODS,[7] married Mr. Foster; resides San Buena Ventura, Cal. (1892).

5807. SIMEON DAGGETT[6] (*John,*[5] *Arthur,*[4] *Arthur,*[3] *Ebenezer,*[2] *William*[1]), born Madison, Ind., August 14, 1818; resides Corning, Ia. (1892); married Jefferson county, Ind., February 14, 1839, by Rev. E. B. Mann, to Martha Rea, daughter of Silas and Elizabeth (Patton) Rea; born Jefferson county, Ind., March 30, 1822.

Issue:

5901. i. EDMOND M. DAGGETT,[7] born Jefferson county, Ind., January 1, 1840; died Oquawka, Ill., October 20, 1866.
5902. ii. LOUISA JANE DAGGETT,[7] born Jefferson county, Ind., July 24, 1841.

5903. iii. ELIZABETH M. DAGGETT,[7] born Jefferson county, Ind., January 8, 1844; died aged 8 months.
5904. iv. SIMEON TAYLOR DAGGETT,[7] born Jefferson county, Ind., Dec. 22, 1846.
5905. v. JOHN SCOTT DAGGETT,[7] born Jefferson county, Ind.; died aged 2 years.
5906. vi. MARTHA SELONA DAGGETT,[7] born Oquawka, Ill., August 26, 1859; married March 10, 1880, Adams county, Iowa, to Lewis F. Davis; resides Lake View, Sac Co., Ia. (1892).
5907. vii. SILAS CLARK DAGGETT.[7]
5908. viii. FRANK SMITH DAGGETT,[7] born Henderson county, Ill., May 18, 1864.

Simeon Daggett enlisted October 20, 1861, Company G, Tenth Illinois, serving eleven months. Reënlisting March 22, 1865, he served in Company F, Sixteenth Illinois, to the close of the war. He is now (1892) a wagon-maker.

5808. LUCY BANCROFT[6] (*Polly Daggett,[5] Arthur,[4] Arthur,[3] Ebenezer,[2] William[1]*), born Montpelier, Vt., March 30, 1802; resides 24 Barre street, Montpelier, Vt. (1892); married Montpelier, Vt., October 20, 1822, Barnabas Hammett Snow, of Montpelier, Vt., son of Jonathan and Lydia (Hammett) Snow; born Montpelier, Vt., October 28, 1796; died Montpelier, Vt., May 31, 1873.
Issue :

5909. i. POLLY BANCROFT SNOW,[7] born Montpelier, Vt., November 28, 1823.
5910. ii. KATE DAGGETT SNOW,[7] born Montpelier, Vt., October 11, 1826.
5911. iii. EMELINE SNOW,[7] born Montpelier, Vt., September 20, 1829.
5912. iv. AVIS FRENCH SNOW,[7] born Montpelier, Vt., March 17, 1832; married Montpelier, Vt., June 8, 1870, Luther Cree, son of Moses and Patty (Dennis) Cree; born Troy, N.H., August 21, 1820; no issue; resides Montpelier, Vt. (1892).

5810. CORNELIUS WATROUS BANCROFT[6] (*Polly Daggett,[5] Arthur,[4] Arthur,[3] Ebenezer,[2] William[1]*), born Montpelier, Vt., 1808; died January 22, 1856; married 1st, Lucy Howard; born 1808; died Montpelier, Vt., February 24, 1852; married 2d, Mrs. Elizabeth Field.
Issue :

5913. i. HOWARD C. BANCROFT,[7] married Mary Greenlief; resides Columbus, Ohio (1892).
5914. ii. LUCY H. BANCROFT,[7] married Leander Hurd, of Boston; he died; she resides 8 Gordon terrace, Buena park, Chicago, Ill. (1892).

5811. CARLOS BANCROFT[6] (*Polly Daggett,[5] Arthur,[4] Arthur,[3] Ebenezer,[2] William[1]*), born Montpelier, Vt., March 20, 1809; died October 24, 1876; married 1st, Berlin, Vt., December 19, 1839, Mary E. Johnston; born July 4, 1813; died September 15, 1856; married 2d, February 3, 1858, Mrs. Margarette Wallace McLean.
Issue :

5915. i. JANE SOPHIA BANCROFT,[7] born Montpelier, Vt., Oct. 4, 1841; married Charles Scott, Montpelier, Vt., Feb. 26, 1856; she died Feb. 8, 1867.
5916. ii. ARTHUR DAGGETT BANCROFT,[7] born Montpelier, Vt., August 29, 1843; married Juliette Camp, Montpelier, Vt., June 16, 1869; he died April 11, 1881.
5917. iii. CARLOS AMASA BANCROFT,[7] born Sept. 15, 1845; died Aug. 23, 1846.

5918. iv. Charles Eastman Bancroft,[7] born Apr. 23, 1848; died Aug. 5, 1848.
5919. v. Carlos Johnston Bancroft,[7] born May 18, 1852; died Aug. 6, 1863.
5920. vi. Frederick Wallace Bancroft,[7] born September 15, 1855; resides Montpelier, Vt. (1892).

5812. Amasa Bancroft [6] (*Polly Daggett,*[5] *Arthur,*[4] *Arthur,*[3] *Ebenezer,*[2] *William* [1]), born Montpelier, Vt., ——; died July 7, 1856; married Danby, Vt., Lydia Hadwin; resides Danby, Vt. (1892).

Issue :

5921. i. Nancy Bancroft,[7] married Mr. Lillie; resides Danby, Vt. (1892).
5922. ii. Emma Bancroft,[7] married Edward Read; resides Danby, Vt. (1892).
5923. iii. Elizabeth Bancroft,[7] married Marinus Pratt; resides Bolton or Lake George (1892).
5924. iv. Edward Bancroft,[7] resides Batavia, Ill. (1892).

5816. Elizabeth Ann Daggett [6] (*Gardner,*[5] *Gideon,*[4] *Arthur,*[3] *Ebenezer,*[2] *William* [1]), born Poultney, Vt., July 4, 1818; resides Defiance, Ohio (1892); married Brunersburg, Ohio, November 3, 1839, William Carter, son of William and Abigail (Blackman) Carter; "lawyer;" born Chenango county, N.Y., December 15, 1812.

Issue :

5925. i. Emma Elizabeth Carter,[7] born Defiance, Ohio, February 3, 1844.
5926. ii. Florence Adell Carter,[7] born Defiance, Ohio, August 15, 1850; resides there (1892).
5927. iii. William Carter,[7] born Defiance, Ohio, December 31, 1856.
5928. iv. Elbert Eugene Carter,[7] born Defiance, Ohio, December 9, 1860; "banker;" resides Defiance, Ohio (1892).

5820. Harriet Daggett [6] (*Gardner,*[5] *Gideon,*[4] *Arthur,*[3] *Ebenezer,*[2] *William* [1]), born Poultney, Vt., April, 1827; died Defiance county, Ohio, October, 1876; married 1st, Haze Luce; married 2d, Mr. Marks.

Issue :

5929. i. Emma Melissia Luce.[7]
5930. ii. Sarah Luce.[7]
5931. iii. Harriet Luce.[7]
5932. iv. John Luce.[7]
5933. v. Moses Luce.[7]
5934. vi. Della Marks,[7] died.

5821. Esther Smith Daggett [6] (*Gardner,*[5] *Gideon,*[4] *Arthur,*[3] *Ebenezer,*[2] *William* [1]), born Richville, N.Y., September 27, 1829; resides 201 Francis street, Defiance, Ohio (1892); married Defiance, Ohio, October 9, 1853, Edward Henry Gleason, son of Alonso and Irena Gleason; born Diberry, Pa., December 12, 1823; died Defiance, Ohio, November 24, 1889.

Issue :

5935. i. Rollin Henry Gleason,[7] born Defiance, Ohio, December 24, 1854; resides there (1892).
5936. ii. Irene May Gleason,[7] born Defiance, Ohio, February 3, 1858; died Defiance, Ohio, February 24, 1858.
5937. iii. Emie Bell Gleason,[7] born Defiance, Ohio, May 10, 1860; died Defiance, Ohio, April 1, 1886.

5938. iv. STANLEY GLEASON,[7] born Defiance, Ohio, January 31, 1863; died Defiance, Ohio, March 30, 1863.
5939. v. ADRIENNA GLEASON,[7] born Defiance, Ohio, May 1, 1864; resides there (1892).
5940. vi. GRACE GLEASON,[7] born Defiance, Ohio, October 8, 1866; died Defiance, Ohio, August 12, 1868.
5941. vii. HELEN GLEASON,[7] born Defiance, Ohio, November 13, 1869; died Defiance, Ohio, June 30, 1883.
5942. viii. CLAUD GLEASON,[7] born Defiance, Ohio, February 28, 1873; resides there (1892).
5943. ix. MAUD GLEASON,[7] born Defiance, Ohio, February 28, 1873; died Defiance, Ohio, August 11, 1874.

5822. Hon. ROLLIN MALLORY DAGGETT [6] (*Gardner,*[5] *Gideon,*[4] *Arthur,*[3] *Ebenezer,*[2] *William* [1]), born Richville, N.Y., February 22, 1831; resides San Diego, Cal. (1892); married 1st, Virginia, Nev., December 30, 1868, Maggie Curry, daughter of William and Kate (Henderson) Curry; born Philadelphia, Pa., March 19, 1851; died Philadelphia, Pa., March 21, 1877; married 2d, Oakland, Cal., October 1, 1883, Lizzie Mabel Hinds, daughter of Sumner B. and Ellen M. (Andrews) Hinds; born Seattle, Wash. Ter., April 12, 1863.
Issue :

5944. i. GRACE DAGGETT,[7] born Virginia, Nev., October 30, 1869.
5945. ii. KATE DAGGETT,[7] born Virginia, Nev., November 29, 1870.

Hon. Rollin M. Daggett, United States Senator, United States minister to the Sandwich islands, edited, with an introduction, in 1888, "The Legends and Myths of Hawaii, The Fables and Folk-lore of a Strange People, by his Hawaiian majesty Kalakaua."

5823. NANCY DAGGETT [6] (*William K.,*[5] *Gideon,*[4] *Arthur,*[3] *Ebenezer,*[2] *William* [1]), born Middlebury, Vt., December 9, 1819; resides Antwerp, Ohio (1892); married September 19, 1847, Joseph Clark; born Pennsylvania, 1817; died Antwerp, Ohio, 1873.
Issue: all reside Antwerp, Ohio (1892).

5946. i. WILLIAM CLARK,[7] born Antwerp, Ohio, August 5, 1848.
5947. ii. LOUISA B. CLARK,[7] born Antwerp, Ohio, December 26, 1849.
5948. iii. VERRES A. CLARK,[7] born Antwerp, Ohio, December 24, 1852.
5949. iv. FLORRAS V. CLARK,[7] born Antwerp, Ohio, December 24, 1852.
5950. v. JOSEPH E. CLARK,[7] born Antwerp, Ohio, August 15, 1854.
5951. vi. ELLA S. CLARK,[7] born Antwerp, Ohio, April 4, 1857.

5824. WILLIAM KING DAGGETT [6] (*William K.,*[5] *Gideon,*[4] *Arthur,*[3] *Ebenezer,*[2] *William* [1]), born Middlebury, Vt., May 4, 1822; resides Antwerp, Ohio (1892); married Antwerp, Ohio, June 6, 1855, Eliza Middleton, daughter of John and Lydia (Phillips) Middleton.
Issue: all reside Antwerp, Ohio (1892).

5952. i. EMMA DAGGETT,[7] born Antwerp, Ohio.
5953. ii. WILLIAM KING DAGGETT,[7] born Antwerp, Ohio.
5954. iii. CAROLINE DAGGETT,[7] born Antwerp, Ohio.
5955. iv. EDWARD DAGGETT,[7] born Antwerp, Ohio.
5956. v. ELIZA DAGGETT,[7] born Antwerp, Ohio.

5957. vi. Netta Daggett,[7] born Antwerp, Ohio.
5958. vii. John Daggett,[7] born Antwerp, Ohio.

5825. Ann Daggett[6] (*William K.*,[5] *Gideon*,[4] *Arthur*,[3] *Ebenezer*,[2] *William*[1]), born Middlebury, Vt., July 1, 1824; resides Antwerp, Ohio (1892); married Antwerp, Ohio, Sept. 8, 1850, John S. Snook, son of William C. and Lumbertha (DeHort) Snook; born Deerfield, Ohio, Dec. 5, 1815; died Champion Mills, Miss., May 16, 1863.

Issue:

5959. i. William D. Snook,[7] born Antwerp, Ohio, June 8, 1851; died Antwerp, Ohio, September 18, 1851.
5960. ii. Inez C. Snook,[7] born Antwerp, Ohio, September 13, 1852; died Antwerp, Ohio, October 12, 1882.
5961. iii. Ione L. Snook,[7] born Antwerp, Ohio, Dec. 8, 1854; resides there (1892).

John S. Snook enlisted in the army; was lieutenant-colonel of Sixty-eighth Regiment Ohio Volunteer Infantry. He was killed at Champion Mills, Miss., May 16, 1863.

5827. Louisa Daggett[6] (*William K.*,[5] *Gideon*,[4] *Arthur*,[3] *Ebenezer*,[2] *William*[1]), born Potsdam, N.Y., April 22, 1828; resides Antwerp, Ohio (1892); married Antwerp, Ohio, June 7, 1855, Robert Filley, son of Libby and Rosanna (Murphy) Filley; died 1890.

Issue:

5962. i. William S. Filley,[7] born Antwerp, Ohio, January 8, 1858; resides there (1892).

WILLIAM DAGGETT, OF SACO, ME.

SEVENTH GENERATION.

5837. Henry Franklin Daggett[7] (*Elisha*,[6] *Thomas*,[5] *John*,[4] *Thomas*,[3] *Ebenezer*,[2] *William*[1]), born Frankfort, Me., October 21, 1837; "grist mill;" resides Milo, Me. (1893); married ——.

Issue:

5963. i. May Daggett,[8] died.
5964. ii. Clinton Daggett.[8]
5965. iii. Florence Daggett.[8]

5839. Thomas Daggett[7] (*Elisha*,[6] *Thomas*,[5] *John*,[4] *Thomas*,[3] *Ebenezer*,[2] *William*[1]), born Foxcroft, Me., Dec. 25, 1843; married.

Issue:

5966. i. Herbert Chapin Daggett,[8] resides Lowell, Mass. (1893).
5967. ii. Elizabeth Mabel Daggett.[8]
5968. iii. Sumner Daggett.[8]
5969. iv. Grace Daggett.[8]

5860. Sarah Louise Daggett[7] (*George W.*,[6] *William*,[5] *Phineas*,[4] *William*,[3] *Ebenezer*,[2] *William*[1]), born Worcester, Mass., May 19,

1850; died Belvidere, Ill., December 23, 1881; married Westmoreland, N.H., March 7, 1870, Thomas Smith Merrill, of Belvidere, Ill., son of Asel and Auretta (Smith) Merrill; born Herkimer county, N.Y., September 8, 1836; resides Belvidere, Ill. (1892).

Issue:

5970. i. MAUD EVYLIN MERRILL,[8] born Belvidere, Ill., March 26, 1873; resides there (1892).
5971. ii. BLANCHE AURETTA MERRILL,[8] born Belvidere, Ill., October 12, 1875; resides there (1892).

5861. CLARA ESTHER DAGGETT[7] (*George W.*,[6] *William*,[5] *Phineas*,[4] *William*,[3] *Ebenezer*,[2] *William*[1]), born Westmoreland, N.H., March 3, 1852; resides Walpole, N.H. (1892); married Walpole, N.H., April 26, 1876, Willie Graves Leonard, of Walpole, N.H., son of Rufus and Sarah Elizabeth (Graves) Leonard; born Walpole, N.H., February 3, 1853.

Issue:

5972. i. WALLACE COLE LEONARD,[8] born Walpole, N.H., March 20, 1877; resides there (1892).
5973. ii. EVA LOUISE LEONARD,[8] born Walpole, N.H., June 25, 1879; died Walpole, N.H., March 21, 1880.

5870. ABBIE BILLINGS DAGGETT[7] (*Arthur*,[6] *Arthur*,[5] *Arthur*,[4] *Arthur*,[3] *Ebenezer*,[2] *William*[1]), born East Montpelier, Vt., January 30, 1831; resides East Montpelier, Vt. (1892); married East Montpelier, Vt., December 4, 1850, James Allen Coburn, son of Larned and Lovisia (Allen) Coburn; born East Montpelier, Vt., 1828.

Issue:

5974. i. LARNED COBURN,[8] born East Montpelier, Vt., April 2, 1852; resides Fulda, Minn. (1892).
5975. ii. ARTHUR DAGGETT COBURN,[8] born East Montpelier, Vt., August 31, 1855; resides East Montpelier, Vt. (1892).
5976. iii. FLORA COBURN,[8] born East Montpelier, Vt., June 25, 1858; married Mr. Kelton; resides East Montpelier, Vt. (1892).
5977. iv. JAMES LEE COBURN,[8] born East Montpelier, Vt., November 3, 1859; resides Lime Creek, Minn. (1892).

5872. GEORGE DAGGETT[7] (*Freeman*,[6] *Arthur*,[5] *Arthur*,[4] *Arthur*,[3] *Ebenezer*,[2] *William*[1]), born Montpelier, Vt., September 18, 1835; resides Winooski, Vt. (1892); married 1st, Montpelier, Vt., December 23, 1863, Sarah Emeline Hamblin, daughter of Marcus B. and Philuro (Gray) Hamblin; born Montpelier, Vt., November 12, 1839; died New York city, October 22, 1885; married 2d, Winooski, Vt., April 27, 1892, Mary Frances Dudley, daughter of Frank W. and Susan (Celley) Dudley; born Brighton, Mass., October 21, 1853.

5876. JULIUS SULLIVAN ROBINSON[7] (*Catharine Daggett*,[6] *Stephen*,[5] *Arthur*,[4] *Arthur*,[3] *Ebenezer*,[2] *William*[1]), born Calais, Vt., March 9, 1836; resides Calais, Vt. (1893); married 1st, Montpelier, Vt., 1861, Mary Amelia Pierce, daughter of David and Mary (Bancroft) Pierce;

born Montpelier, Vt., May 31, 1840; died Calais, Vt., September 11, 1872; married 2d, Calais, Vt., August 16, 1874, Harriet Louisa Persons, widow of Marshall K. Persons, and daughter of Rev. J. B. H. and Thirsa (Cate) Norriss; born Lisbon, N.H., May 17, 1837.

Issue:

5978. i. IRVING GEORGE ROBINSON,[8] born Calais, Vt., January 22, 1864.
5979. ii. ILDA G. ROBINSON,[8] born Calais, Vt., April 17, 1865; died Calais, Vt., 1882.
5980. iii. INDA MARY ROBINSON,[8] born Calais, Vt., April 13, 1867.
5981. iv. LUCY C. ROBINSON,[8] born Calais, Vt., April 7, 1878.

5878. MARY CHERILL ROBINSON[7] (*Catharine Daggett,[6] Stephen,[5] Arthur,[4] Arthur,[3] Ebenezer,[2] William[1]*), born Calais, Vt., August 24, 1845; resides 6 Kent street, Montpelier, Vt. (1893); married Calais, Vt., January 1, 1870, James Kelton Tobey, son of Richard West and Hannah Clarisa (Dodge) Tobey; born Calais, Vt., June 17, 1845; died Calais, Vt., April 21, 1883.

Issue:

5982. i. LELIA MARY TOBEY,[8] born Calais, Vt., October 7, 1873.
5983. ii. LAURA CATHERINE TOBEY,[8] born Calais, Vt., August 9, 1875.
5984. iii. CLARA LEONE TOBEY,[8] born Calais, Vt., October 8, 1879.

5880. NEALY ADOLPHUS CHAPIN[7] (*Katherine Daggett,[6] John,[5] Arthur,[4] Arthur,[3] Ebenezer,[2] William[1]*), born Leavenworth, Ind., January 29, 1828; resides Kirkwood, Ill. (1892); married near Swan Creek, Ill., January 28, 1852, Cordelia Olive Perry, daughter of Jonathan Childs and Phebe Maria (Dodge) Perry; born Lewiston, N.Y., July 29, 1829.

Issue:

5985. i. WILLIS ADOLPHUS CHAPIN,[8] born Oquawka, Ill., October 31, 1852; died Kirkwood, Ill., September 4, 1868.
5986. ii. EBEN HUBERT CHAPIN,[8] born Oquawka, Ill., November 21, 1854.
5987. iii. FLORENCE CHAPIN,[8] born Oquawka, Ill., December 9, 1856.
5988. iv. KATIE BERTHA CHAPIN,[8] born Kirkwood, Ill., September 29, 1859.
5989. v. FRED LINCOLN CHAPIN,[8] born Kirkwood, Ill., June 16, 1863; married Jan. 19, 1893, Grace M. Seldon, of Erie, Pa.; ensign, United States Navy, steamship "Patterson," Mare island, San Francisco (1893).
5990. vi. JENNIE MARY CHAPIN,[8] born Kirkwood, Ill., December 11, 1865.
5991. vii. LAURA ANNA CHAPIN,[8] born Kirkwood, Ill., April 4, 1869.
5992. viii. WILLIAM ROBERT CHAPIN,[8] born Kirkwood, Ill., March 24, 1875; resides there (1893).

5881. PATRICK HENRY CHAPIN[7] (*Katherine Daggett,[6] John,[5] Arthur,[4] Arthur,[3] Ebenezer,[2] William[1]*), born Greenville, Ind., Aug. 22, 1834; died Medicine Lodge, Kan., 1886; married Oquawka, Ill., April 9, 1860, Mary Louise Wadleigh, daughter of Luke and Phebe (Rowell) Wadleigh; born Compton, Lower Canada, March 16, 1837; resides 1309 Seventeenth avenue, Denver, Col. (1893).

Issue:

5993. i. FRANK BEVERLY CHAPIN,[8] born Oquawka, Ill., November 28, 1862; married Chicago, Ill., September 2, 1891, to Agnes L. Samuel; resides Medicine Lodge, Kan. (1893).

5994. ii. MAUD CHAPIN,[8] born Oquawka, Ill., June 11, 1864; died Oquawka, Ill., May 5, 1866.
5995. iii. LUKE CHAPIN,[8] born Oquawka, Ill., March 10, 1867; married Denver, Col., March 18, 1891, to Viola Hardin; resides Medicine Lodge, Kan. (1893).
5996. iv. WILLIS CHAPIN,[8] born Oquawka, Ill., February 23, 1870; died Oquawka, Ill., June 29, 1874.
5997. v. NEALY CHAPIN,[8] born Oquawka, Ill., September 8, 1875; resides Denver, Col. (1893).

5883. JOHN EBENEZER CHAPIN [7] (*Katherine Daggett,[6] John,[5] Arthur,[4] Arthur,[3] Ebenezer,[2] William [1]*), born Oquawka, Ill., March 10, 1840; resides 907 Florida avenue, Washington, D.C. (1893); married Chicago, Ill., May 16, 1872, Sarah Sevilla Russell, daughter of Gideon and Sarah (Halsey) Russell; born Oquawka, Ill., December 15, 1845.
Issue:

5998. i. MARY KATHARINE CHAPIN,[8] born Oquawka, Ill., March 5, 1873.
5999. ii. OLIVE RUSSELL CHAPIN,[8] born Oquawka, Ill., May 31, 1876.
6000. iii. ERNEST CHAPIN,[8] born Medicine Lodge, Kan., August 21, 1882.

5902. LOUISA JANE DAGGETT [7] (*Simeon,[6] John,[5] Arthur,[4] Arthur,[3] Ebenezer,[2] William [1]*), born Jefferson county, Ind., July 24, 1841; died Oquawka, Ill., December 3, 1863; married August 26, 1860, John Digby; resides in Canada (1892).
Issue:

6001. i. FLORA DIGBY,[8] born 1860; resides Canada (1892).
Two children died young.

5904. SIMEON TAYLOR DAGGETT [7] (*Simeon,[6] John,[5] Arthur,[4] Arthur,[3] Ebenezer,[2] William [1]*), born Jefferson county, Ind., December 22, 1846; "farmer;" resides Prescott, Ia. (1892); married Henderson county, Ill., December 24, 1867, Nancy M. Watson.
Issue:

6002. i. NEALY ELLIS DAGGETT,[8] born Henderson county, Ill., November 6, 1868; "carpenter."
6003. ii. JOHN SCOTT DAGGETT,[8] born Henderson county, Ill., August 28, 1870; "carpenter."
6004. iii. EDWARD TAYLOR DAGGETT,[8] born Henderson county, Ill., July 12, 1872; "farmer."
6005. iv. WILLIS EBEN. DAGGETT,[8] born Adams county, Ia., April 11, 1874; "farmer."
6006. v. CLARA ELNORA DAGGETT,[8] born Adams county, Ia., March 14, 1876.
6007. vi. CHARLES WALTER DAGGETT,[8] born Adams county, Ia., December 15, 1878; "farmer."
6008. vii. OLIVE SELONA DAGGETT,[8] born Adams county, Ia., Jan. 12, 1881.
6009. viii. GEORGE WESLEY DAGGETT,[8] born Adams county, Ia., March 18, 1883.
6010. ix. CLARENCE ALBERT DAGGETT,[8] born Adams county, Ia., June 14, 1887; died Adams county, Ia., May 15, 1888.
6011. x. MILLIE GRACE DAGGETT,[8] born Adams county, Ia., May 13, 1889.
6012. xi. HENRY WARD BEECHER DAGGETT,[8] born Adams county, Ia., February 4, 1892.

Mr. Daggett enlisted in Company F, Sixteenth Illinois, March 22, 1865, serving to the close of the war.

5907. SILAS CLARK DAGGETT [7] (*Simeon*,[6] *John*,[5] *Arthur*,[4] *Arthur*,[3] *Ebenezer*,[2] *William* [1]), resides Corning, Ia. (1892) ; married Henderson county, Ill., February 15, 1873, Lucy Shields.

Issue :

6013. i.   ETTA MAY DAGGETT,[8] born Henderson county, Ill., January 20, 1874.
6014. ii.   FLORENCE ELLA DAGGETT,[8] born Adams county, Ia., Dec. 6, 1875.
6015. iii.   BENJAMIN HENRY DAGGETT,[8] born Adams county, Ia., March 14, 1879.
6016. iv.   RUTH ELIZABETH DAGGETT,[8] born Adams county, Ia., January 5, 1881.
6017. v.   VIVA PERL DAGGETT,[8] born Adams county, Ia., September 25, 1888.

5908. FRANK SMITH DAGGETT [7] (*Simeon*,[6] *John*,[5] *Arthur*,[4] *Arthur*,[3] *Ebenezer*,[2] *William* [1]), born Henderson county, Ill., May 18, 1864 ; married Adams county, Ia., February 23, 1887, Lizzy Bell Burget.

Issue :

6018. i.   MARTHA EDNA DAGGETT,[3] born Sac county, Ia., February 2, 1889.
6019. ii.   CARL DAGGETT,[8] born Adams county, Ia., June 24, 1891.

5909. POLLY BANCROFT SNOW [7] (*Lucy Bancroft*,[6] *Polly Daggett*,[5] *Arthur*,[4] *Arthur*,[3] *Ebenezer*,[2] *William* [1]), born Montpelier, Vt., Nov. 28, 1823 ; died Baltimore, Md., Sept. 7, 1860 ; married Montpelier, Vt., Jan. 14, 1846, Mark R. Putnam, of Montpelier, son of John Putnam ; born Montpelier, Vt. ; died Baltimore, Md., May 13, 1873.

Issue :

6020. i.   CLARENCE FRANCIS PUTNAM,[8] born E. Montpelier, Vt., March 7, 1848 ; resides Cheyenne, Wyoming (1892).

5910. KATE DAGGETT SNOW [7] (*Lucy Bancroft*,[6] *Polly Daggett*,[5] *Arthur*,[4] *Arthur*,[3] *Ebenezer*,[2] *William* [1]), born Montpelier, Vt., October 11, 1826 ; resides 24 Barre street, Montpelier, Vt. (1892) ; married Montpelier, Vt., April 9, 1850, George Henry Watson, of Williamstown, Vt., son of David and Anna (Elliot) Watson ; born Williamstown, Vt., December 24, 1820 ; died February 24, 1880.

Issue :

6021. i.   MARTHA SEAVER WATSON,[3] born Williamstown, Vt., March 29, 1851 ; resides Montpelier, Vt. (1892).

5911. EMELINE SNOW [7] (*Lucy Bancroft*,[6] *Polly Daggett*,[5] *Arthur*,[4] *Arthur*,[3] *Ebenezer*,[2] *William* [1]), born Montpelier, Vt., September 20, 1829 ; resides there (1892) ; married Montpelier, Vt., March 12, 1862, Nathaniel Cutler Tabor, of Montpelier, son of Elihu and Laura (Cutler) Tabor ; born Montpelier, Vt., January 7, 1823.

Issue :

6022. i.   HARRY SNOW TABOR,[8] born Montpelier, Vt., February 7, 1870 ; resides there (1892).

5925. EMMA ELIZABETH CARTER [7] (*Elizabeth A. Daggett*,[6] *Gardner*,[5] *Gideon*,[4] *Arthur*,[3] *Ebenezer*,[2] *William* [1]), born Defiance, Ohio,

February 3, 1844; resides Charlotte, Mich. (1888) ; married Defiance, Ohio, August 5, 1868, Frank Arthur Hooker; " lawyer," " judge."
Issue :

6023. i. HARRY EUGENE HOOKER,[8] born Charlotte, Mich., April 27, 1870.
6024. ii. CHARLES EGGLESTON HOOKER,[8] born Charlotte, Mich., April 18, 1872.

5927. WILLIAM CARTER [7] (*Elizabeth A. Daggett,[6] Gardner,[5] Gideon,[4] Arthur,[3] Ebenezer,[2] William [1]*), born Defiance, Ohio, December 31, 1856; " lawyer;" resides there (1888) ; married Defiance, Ohio, April 30, 1878, Emma A. Houghton.
Issue :

6025. i. ABBIE CARTER,[8] born Defiance, Ohio, April 9, 1879.
6026. ii. WILLIAM CARTER,[8] born Defiance, Ohio, December 19, 1881.
6027. iii. ELIZABETH CARTER,[8] born Defiance, Ohio, February 22, 1887.

WILLIAM DAGGETT, OF SACO, ME.

EIGHTH GENERATION.

5978. IRVING GEORGE ROBINSON [8] (*Julius S.,[7] Catharine Daggett,[6] Stephen,[5] Arthur,[4] Arthur,[3] Ebenezer,[2] William [1]*), born Calais, Vt., January 22, 1864; resides Calais, Vt. (1893) ; married Montpelier, Vt., October 12, 1887, Nellie Rich Swasey, daughter of Samuel H. and Laura A. (Rich) Swasey; born Morristown, Vt., Feb. 10, 1864.
Issue :

6028. i. MINNIE SWASEY ROBINSON,[9] born Calais, Vt., November 19, 1889.
6029. ii. Daughter ROBINSON,[9] born Calais, Vt., April 7, 1893.

5980. INDA MARY ROBINSON [8] (*Julius S.,[7] Catharine Daggett,[6] Stephen,[5] Arthur,[4] Arthur,[3] Ebenezer,[2] William [1]*), born Calais, Vt., April 13, 1867; resides Calais, Vt. (1893) ; married Calais, Vt., September 24, 1889, Simon Wheeler, son of Henry and Adeline (Ainsworth) Wheeler; born Calais, Vt.
Issue :

6030. i. JULIUS H. WHEELER,[9] born Calais, Vt., August 18, 1890.

5986. EBEN HUBERT CHAPIN [8] (*Nealy A.,[7] Katherine Daggett,[6] John,[5] Arthur,[4] Arthur,[3] Ebenezer,[2] William [1]*), born Oquawka, Ill., November 21, 1854; resides 1132 H street, Lincoln, Neb. (1893) ; married Meriden, Conn., October 18, 1883, Kate Anne Mathews, daughter of William Sylvester and Laura Anne (Mack) Mathews; born Meriden, Conn., June 5, 1861.
Issue :

6031. i. CHARLES MATHEWS CHAPIN,[9] born Lincoln, Neb., Sept. 19, 1884.

6032. ii. ELSA CHAPIN,[9] born Lincoln, Neb., May 28, 1886.
6033. iii. RUTH CHAPIN,[9] born Lincoln, Neb., September 20, 1887.

5987. FLORENCE CHAPIN [8] (*Nealy A.,*[7] *Katherine Daggett,*[6] *John,*[5] *Arthur,*[4] *Arthur,*[3] *Ebenezer,*[2] *William* [1]), born Oquawka, Ill., December 9, 1856; resides Kirkwood, Ill. (1893); married 1st, January 31, 1881, George W. Ellis, son of Benjamin and Jane (Houston) Ellis; born Canton, Me., December 10, 1848; died Medicine Lodge, Kan., October 29, 1888; married 2d, Kirkwood, Ill., November 27, 1890, William H. Hartwell, son of Derrick B. and Marianne (Rice) Hartwell; born Langdon, N.H., August 28, 1844.

Issue :

6034. i. NEALY PERES ELLIS,[9] born Bonanza, Col., March 15, 1882.
6035. ii. JAMES GLENN ELLIS,[9] born Medicine Lodge, Kan., December 18, 1884.
6036. iii. JOHN ROBERT ELLIS,[9] born Medicine Lodge, Kan., November 8, 1887.
6037. iv. MARIAN HARTWELL,[9] born Kirkwood, Ill., September 23, 1891.

5988. KATIE BERTHA CHAPIN [8] (*Nealy A.,*[7] *Katherine Daggett,*[6] *John,*[5] *Arthur,*[4] *Arthur,*[3] *Ebenezer,*[2] *William* [1]), born Kirkwood, Ill., September 29, 1859; resides 1229 Wilcox avenue, Chicago, Ill. (1893); married June 3, 1879, James Franklin Morgan, son of Andrew and Nancy Weddell (Collins) Morgan; born Monongahela City, Pa., December 6, 1852.

Issue :

6038. i. BESSIE MORGAN,[9] born Chicago, Ill., July 16, 1880.
6039. ii. OLIVE MYRTLE MORGAN,[9] born Chicago, Ill., February 12, 1884.

5990. JENNIE MARY CHAPIN [8] (*Nealy A.,*[7] *Katherine Daggett,*[6] *John,*[5] *Arthur,*[4] *Arthur,*[3] *Ebenezer,*[2] *William* [1]), born Kirkwood, Ill., December 11, 1865; resides 425 East Superior street, Chicago, Ill. (1893); married Kirkwood, Ill., May 24, 1888, John McGaw Glenn, son of John G. and Mary Jane (McGaw) Glenn; born Fort Wayne, Ind., November 14, 1859.

Issue :

6040. i. MARY GLENN,[9] born Monmouth, Ill., July 5, 1889.
6041. ii. HELEN GLENN,[9] born Chicago, Ill., June 9, ——.

5991. LAURA ANNA CHAPIN [8] (*Nealy A.,*[7] *Katherine Daggett,*[6] *John,*[5] *Arthur,*[4] *Arthur,*[3] *Ebenezer,*[2] *William* [1]), born Kirkwood, Ill., April 4, 1869; resides Kirkwood, Ill. (1893); married Monmouth, Ill., November 6, 1889, Harry D. Flewhart, son of Fred and Margaret D. (Smith) Flewhart; born Kokomo, Ind., February 2, 1861.

Issue :

6042. i. PAUL GILBERT FLEWHART,[9] born Des Moines, Ia., October 6, 1890.
6043. ii. FRED CHAPIN FLEWHART,[9] born Monmouth, Ill., November 23, 1891.

CAPT. THOMAS DAGGETT

POSSIBLY SON OF WILLIAM DAGGETT,
OF SACO, ME.

6044. Capt. Thomas Daggett,[1] born about 1683; died probably May, 1730; married Boston, Mass., October 27, 1709, by Rev. Cotton Mather, to Lydia Scolly.

Issue:

6045. i. Lydia Daggett,[2] born ——; baptized Second Church, Boston, January 31, 1713–14; died Boston, Mass.; buried February 19, 1713.
6046. ii. Lydia Daggett,[2] born Boston, Mass., January 27, 1715.
6047. iii. Rebecca Daggett,[2] born Boston, Mass., September 24, 1719 (married Mr. Cathcart ?).
6048. iv. Susanna Daggett,[2] born Boston, Mass., October 9, 1721; married Boston, Mass., January 12, 1740, to Richard Bore or Bone.
6049. v. Hannah Daggett,[2] born Boston, Mass., July 22, 1725; married (intention, Boston, November 22, 1746) Thomas Armstrong; he died before December 3, 1760; on which date she sells ten-acre lot in North Yarmouth, in front of the town, "which descended to me by the death of my late Hon[d] Father." [Cumberland Deeds, 2–89.]

Tradition says Captain Daggett came from Scotland.

Thomas Dagget, of Salem, mariner, buys of Robert Moulton, of Salem, for £80, thirty acres of land, with dwelling-house and barn; also six acres of swamp land bounded south by the Town Common of Salem, September 12, 1709. [Essex Deeds, 21–129.]

This land he sold to Thomas Mackentire, of Salem, September 20, 1717, and in the deed calls himself "late of Salem now of Boston in County Suffolk, mariner." [Essex Deeds, 33–66.]

November 10, 1719, he buys of Joshua Gee, brick house and land one hundred and three feet on Battery lane. [Suffolk Deeds, 34–117.]

January 3, 1713, Lydia Daggett was "received into Covenant" at the Second Church, Boston.

"Thomas Dogget one of the founders of the New Brick Church, Boston, 1718. The picture of Thomas Daggett is from an oil portrait which is now owned by Mrs. Rogers, of Boston, who inherited it from her mother, Mrs. Cushing Stetson (No. 6066). It represents him dressed in a brown coat and wearing a wig, while to the left in the background is a globe. The portrait is in excellent preservation.

"Inventory of the estate of Capt. Thomas Daggett, deceased, taken by us the subscribers this 8th day of June, 1730":

His Late Dwelling house and outhouses Garden &c., £1130; Sundry Shop Goods as per acct. of particulars herewith presented to be filed, £5614 11s 3d; a Negro Man called "Pompey," £90; a Negro Lad called "Boston," £90; a Negro woman called "Moll" and child "Sippeo," £70; a Negro girl called "Mareah," £50. — In the Hall, — vizt: a clock & case £28, a couch & furniture £10, £38; a Glass and 2 pr Glass Sconces, £12; a Screwtore £5, 9 leather chairs @ 20s £9, £14; 5 Large Pictures with Gilt frames, £6 5s; 5 Small Pictures 50s, a oval Table 45s, £4 15s; a cross faced andirons & shovel & tongs, £2 10s; a Fuzee peice 45s, 2 small arm 75s, £6; Sundry small things with a case, and some empty bottles in a clossett, £2; a board gammon table, Coffee mill and sugar box and two brishes. £2 10; a parcell of earthern ware in a clossett, £3; 96 oz of Plate @ £19 6s, £93 12s. — In the entry and staircase, — vizt: 5 Pictures, a lanthorn and a bell, £2. — In the Dining Room — viz: 4 Tables £3 10s, a looking glass & 6 small pictures £7, £10 10s; 3 Large Pictures 45s, a pr Dogs and a stand candlestick 50s, £4 15s; China ware and some glass in Boffatt, £10; 7 cain chairs, broken and old, £2. — In the Hall Chamber, — vizt: a bedstead with Red Curtains and vallions, £10; a bead, bolster & 2 pillows 56 lbs @ 3s, £8 8s; a small Silk quilt 70s, a glass & pr Sconces £6 10s, £10; 8 small pictures 30s, 4 basketts 22s, £2 12s; 6 Cain Chairs £6 10s, 1 Twilight & Table 50s, £9; a old tea table & some chiney, £5; a chest of Drawers £5, a parcel of glassware upon it 70s, £8 10s; a parcell of earthern ware in a clossett, £5; a parcell of raisins 80s, his waring apparel particularly valued £61 14s, £65 14s; 15 Shirts, £16, 10 neck cloaths £5, 13 pr sheets £20 10s, £41 10s; 12 pr Pillow Biers £6, 13 Table Cloths £13, £19; 3 doz Napkins £10 10s, a quilted coverlid 50s, £13; a Empty Trunk 8s, a muff, a cain, and 3 Baskets, £5 13s; 1 pr Bellows and tongs, £1. — In the Entry Chamber, — vizt.: a looking glass 90s. a screwtore 80s, £8 10s; a Bible Psalm Book £10, a spy glass & Quadrant, £29 10s; a Gun, a Remnant of Duck and sundry small things, £5 5s; a old silver watch, £8. — In the Middle Chamber, — vizt: a Beadstead & suit of calico curtains, £6; a bead and two pillows, w't, 76 lbs @ 3s, £16 8s; a looking glass and table, £6; 7 small pictures and 2 baskets, £1 5s; a parcell of Earthern ware, £3 15s. — In the Upper Chamber, — vizt: 3 feather beads, Pillars & Bolsters, w't, 180 lbs @ 2s 9d, £24 15s; 2 old beadsteads 30s a stove, a compass & glass 10s. £2; a Cotton Hammock & Coverlid, £2 10s; 3 old coverlids £3, a old calico quilt 30s, £4 10s; 3 Blankets 70s, 8 small blankets 60s, £6 10s; a sea chest with some Powder & Shott, £2. — In the Kitchen, — vizt: a Jack, 4 Iron Potts & a Kittle, £4 10s; 3 Iron Trammels & a fender & gridiron, £2 7s; 2 pr Iron Dogs, 2 pr Tongs & Chafin dish, £2 15s; a pr Bellows, Chopping Knife & pr stilyards, £1 5s; a Brass Warming pan & a pr tobacco tongs, £1 10s; 2 Candle boxes, a tea Kettle & stand, £3 5s; 2 Coffee Potts & 2 pr Brass Candlesticks, £2; a spitt, frying pan, skimmer & dripping pan, £2 10s; 2 Kitchen tables and a joint stool, £1 5s; 2 Iron Boxes & heaters, £1 6s; a parcell of Tinware, £1; a pr of Brass Andirons, £1 10s; 3 Morters & pestles 15s, a stew pan & 4 skillets 60s, £3 15s; a bell mettle skillett 50s, 82 lbs Pewter @ 3s £12 6s, £14 16s; 2 Brass Kittle £7 10s, a parcell empty bottles & 2 stone jugs £3, £10 10s; Empty Cask & Lumbring stuff, £4; a bridle, saddle & portmanteau, £3; £7645 17s 3d; Cash in the house, £100; £7745 17s 3d; a tract of land at North Yarmouth.

> ISAAC WHITE
> JOHN CARNES
> EBENEZER HOUGH   allowed July 6, 1730
> [Suffolk Probate, 28–90.]

Lydia Daggett, the administratrix, in her first account, July 7, 1732, mentions the receipt of proceeds of 3,263 gallons molasses by the brigantine "Susannah," £377 10s. 0d.; and amount of proceeds of silk and salt per the "Lydia," £225 9s. 1½d. Mr. Hicks, her son-in-law, having no objections, the account was allowed. [Suffolk Probate, 31–46.]

Lydia Daggett, widow of Capt. Thomas Daggett, married 2d (intention, Boston, Mass., May 18, 1732), Thomas Parker.

6046. LYDIA DAGGETT[2] (Thomas[1]), born Boston, Mass., January 27, 1715; baptized Second Church, February 5, 1715–16; married Boston, Mass., December 2, 1731, by Mr. William Welsted, to Zachariah Hicks; "Boston school-master."

Issue:

6050. i. LYDIA HICKS,[3] born Boston, Mass., October 31, 1732.

6051. ii. HANNAH HICKS,[3] married, and died with first child.
6052. iii. Son HICKS,[3] died.
6053. iv. Son HICKS,[3] died.

6050. LYDIA HICKS [3] (*Lydia Daggett,*[2] *Thomas* [1]), born Boston, Mass., October 31, 1732; died January 8, 1812; married April 12, 1753, William Atwill, of Lynn.

Issue:

6054. i. LYDIA ATWILL,[4] married William Tarbox.
6055. ii. ZACHARIAH ATWILL,[4] born 1755; married Elizabeth Breed.
6056. iii. ANNA ATWILL,[4] married Mr. Ramsdill.
6057. iv. MARY ATWILL,[4] died young.
6058. v. HANNAH HICKS ATWILL,[4] married James Alley and had daughter Sally.
6059. vi. WILLIAM ATWILL,[4] died young.
6060. vii. SALLY ATWILL,[4] married Aaron Breed, brother of Elizabeth.
6061. viii. JOHN DAGGETT ATWILL,[4] married 1st, Martha Ingalls, of Lynn; married 2d, Hannah Palfrey, of Salem.
6062. ix. BETSEY ATWILL.[4]
6063. x. THOMAS HICKS ATWILL,[4] married Miss Mansfield.

6062. BETSEY ATWILL [4] (*Lydia Hicks,*[3] *Lydia Daggett,*[2] *Thomas* [1]), married 1st, Boston, Mass., December 23, 1792, by Rev. John Eliot, to Joseph Fullerton; he died Boston, Mass., 1795; married 2d, Sept. 22, 1797, William Burrows, sea captain; born Woodbridge, Eng.

Issue:

6064. i. BETSEY FULLERTON,[5] died young.
6065. ii. MARY B. FULLERTON,[5] married William Thompson, of Boston.
6066. iii. FRANCES ELIZABETH BURROWS,[5] married 1st, William Bowles; married 2d, Cushing Stetson.

PROBABLY DESCENDED FROM WILLIAM DAGGETT, OF SACO, ME.

6067. SAMUEL DAGGETT [2] (*Samuel* [1] (?)), married Lydia ——.
Issue:

6068. i. WILLIAM DAGGETT,[3] born Putney, Vt., November 15, 1788; supposed died Manchester, Vt., 1809.
6069. ii. PORZINA DAGGETT,[3] born Putney, Vt., May 5, 1790; married Putney, Vt., February 27, 1823, Curtis Lord; issue four children; removed to Wisconsin (1844).
6070. iii. SARAFINA DAGGETT,[3] born Putney, Vt., December 5, 1790; removed to Wisconsin 1844.
6071. iv. LINDSEY DAGGETT,[3] born Putney, Vt., August 15, 1792.
6072. v. NANCY DAGGETT,[3] born Putney, Vt., April 15, 1793.
6073. vi. SAMUEL DAGGETT,[3] born Putney, Vt., October 7, 1795.
6074. vii. LYDIA DAGGETT,[3] born Putney, Vt., Feb. 18, 1798; died Massachusetts.

6071. LINDSEY DAGGETT [3] (*Samuel* [2] [*Samuel* [1]] (?)), born Putney, Vt., August 15, 1792; died Westminster West, Vt., September 22, 1869; married Westminster West, Vt., January 1, 1836, Sarah

Hudson, daughter of Benjamin and Sarah (Power) Hudson; born Athens, Vt., May 11, 1817; died Pomfret, Vt., August 6, 1885.

Issue:

6075. i.   MAIRA PHEBE DAGGETT,[4] born Putney, Vt., June 28, 1838.
6076. ii. SAMUEL LINDSEY DAGGETT,[4] born Townsend, Vt., January 7, 1839.
6077. iii. DAVID OREN DAGGETT,[4] born Winhall, Vt., February 16, 1841; unmarried; resides Port Gamble, Wash. (1892).
6078. iv. BENJAMIN SILAS DAGGETT,[4] born Westminster West, Vt., November 2, 1844; unmarried; resides West Hartford, Vt. (1892).
6079. v.   ROYAL DAGGETT,[4] born Athens, Vt., June, 1846; died Westminster, Vt., 1847.
6080. vi. WALTER HERBERT DAGGETT,[4] born Westminster, Vt., July 23, 1849.
6081. vii. WALLACE DAGGETT,[4] born Westminster, Vt., July 23, 1849; died Westminster, Vt., 1859.
6082. viii. HENRY WALLACE DAGGETT,[4] born Westminster, Vt., Dec. 25, 1850.
6083. ix. ALICE JULIA DAGGETT,[4] born Saxton's River, Vt., January 9, 1855.

6072. NANCY DAGGETT [3] (*Samuel* [2] [*Samuel* [1]] (?)), born Putney, Vt., April 15, 1793; died Westminster West, Vt., November 25, 1879; married Asa Wellman.

Issue:

6084. i.   ASA WELLMAN,[4] born Putney, Vt., November 7, 1814; married Eliza M. Daggett (see No. 6085).

6073. SAMUEL DAGGETT [3] (*Samuel* [2] [*Samuel* [1]] (?)), born Putney, Vt., October 7, 1795; "stable-keeper;" died Charlestown, Mass., April 4, 1854; married Charlestown, Mass., April 18, 1822, by Rev. Warren Fay, to Lucy Winn Kendall, daughter of Daniel and Keziah (Winn) Kendall; born Burlington, Mass., October 7, 1800; died Charlestown, Mass., January 12, 1877.

Issue:

6085. i.   ELIZA MARIA DAGGETT,[4] born Charlestown, Mass., March 9, 1823.
6086. ii.   COOLEDGE CLARK DAGGETT,[4] born Watertown, Mass., Jan. 1, 1825.
6087. iii. LUCY JANE DAGGETT,[4] born Watertown, Mass., September 5, 1826.
6088. iv.   SAMUEL OTIS DAGGETT,[4] born Charlestown, Mass., April 13, 1828.
6089. v.   CRAWFORD DAGGETT,[4] born Charlestown, Mass., March 9, 1830; resides 4 Cross street, Charlestown, Mass. (1893).
6090. vi.   GEORGE DAGGETT,[4] born Charlestown, Mass., January 1, 1832; died Charlestown, Mass., October 24, 1834.
6091. vii. GEORGIANA DAGGETT,[4] born Charlestown, Mass., July 11, 1835.
6092. viii. GEORGE HENRY DAGGETT,[4] born East Wilton, Me., Dec. 17, 1837.
6093. ix.   TYLER HUNTINGTON DAGGETT,[4] born Charlestown, Mass., January 27, 1840; married Boston, Mass., June 13, 1864, by Rev. A. A. Miner, to Addie M. Brown, daughter of William and Eliza Brown; born Wilton, Me., 1841; no issue; he died E. Wilton, Me., July 25, 1887.
6094. x.   FOSTER MASON DAGGETT,[4] born Charlestown, Mass., July 23, 1842; married Bradford, Mass., September 16, 1872, by Rev. W. F. Crafts, to Clara Estelle Parker, daughter of Henry F. and Sarah J. Parker; born Bradford, Mass., 1851; resides 4 Cross street, Charlestown, Mass. (1893).

6075. MAIRA PHEBE DAGGETT [4] (*Lindsey*,[3] *Samuel* [2] [*Samuel* [1]] (?)), born Putney, Vt., June 28, 1838; resides 29 Henry street, Bellows Falls, Vt. (1892); married Saxton's River, Vt.,

February 19, 1855, Marshall Conant Ladd, son of Nathaniel and Sallie (Gilbert) Ladd; born Pomfret, Vt., June 29, 1828.

Issue:

6095. i.   CHARLES WALLACE LADD,[5] born Bellows Falls, Vt., May 22, 1856; address, 145 Nassau street, Brooklyn, N.Y. (1892).
6096. ii.   WILLIE CLAYTON LADD,[5] born Bellows Falls, Vt., September 27, 1859; died Bellows Falls, Vt., July 16, 1864.
6097. iii. JENNIE ALICE LADD,[5] born Bellows Falls, Vt., October 27, 1863; died Bellows Falls, Vt., July 2, 1874.
6098. iv.   HATTIE MAY LADD,[5] born Bellows Falls, Vt., October 19, 1867; resides there (1892).

6076. SAMUEL LINDSEY DAGGETT [4] (*Lindsey,*[3] *Samuel* [2] [*Samuel* [1]] (?)), born Townsend, Vt., January 7, 1839; resides Bellows Falls, Vt. (1892); married Delia Ellison, daughter of Barney and Sarah (Nash) Ellison.

Issue:

6099. i.   HERBERT ELLISON DAGGETT,[5] born Saxton's River, Vt., January 20, 1867; died Saxton's River, Vt., November 7, 1879.
6100. ii.   MINNIE MAIRA DAGGETT,[5] born Saxton's River, Vt., June 7, 1868; died Saxton's River, Vt., April 9, 1881.
6101. iii. JENNIE MAY DAGGETT,[5] born Saxton's River, Vt., January 12, 1878.
6102. iv.   CARRIE EMMA DAGGETT,[5] born Saxton's River, Vt., August 10, 1880.

6080. WALTER HERBERT DAGGETT [4] (*Lindsey,*[3] *Samuel* [2] [*Samuel* [1]] (?)), born Westminster, Vt., July 23, 1849; " machinist; " resides 88 Fountain street, Fall River, Mass. (1892); married Boston, Mass., June 10, 1877, by Rev. M. F. Higgins, to Josephine M. Poulin, daughter of Mark and Sophia Poulin; born Montreal, Can., 1853.

Issue:

6103. i.   SARAH JOSEPHINE DAGGETT,[5] born Boston, Mass., March 10, 1878.
6104. ii.   WALTER H. DAGGETT,[5] born Fall River, Mass., September 29, 1879.
6105. iii. FRANK O. DAGGETT,[5] born Fall River, Mass., January 18, 1881; died Fall River, Mass., July 31, 1881.
6106. iv.   MARY M. DAGGETT,[5] born Fall River, Mass., June 5, 1884.

6082. HENRY WALLACE DAGGETT [4] (*Lindsey,*[3] *Samuel* [2] [*Samuel* [1]] (?)), born Westminster, Vt., December 25, 1850; married Ella Clapp.

Issue:

6107. i.   KENNETH DAGGETT,[5] born about 1874.
6108. ii.   LOTTIE DAGGETT,[5] born about 1878.

6083. ALICE JULIA DAGGETT [4] (*Lindsey,*[3] *Samuel* [2] [*Samuel* [1]] (?)), born Saxton's River, Vt., January 9, 1855; resides West Hartford, Vt. (1892); married 1st, George Story; married 2d, Woodstock, Vt., April 9, 1890, Herman Barrows.

Issue:

6109. i.   DAISEY STORY,[5] born June 29, 1878; resides West Hartford, Vt. (1892).
6110. ii.   HAROLD BARROWS,[5] born May 19, 1891.

6085. ELIZA MARIA DAGGETT [4] (*Samuel*,[3] *Samuel* [2] [*Samuel* [1]] (?)), born Charlestown, Mass., March 9, 1823; resides 4 Cross street, Charlestown, Mass. (1892); married Boston, Mass., May 23, 1845, by Rev. S. Streeter, to Asa Wellman, son of Asa and Nancy (Daggett) Wellman (No. 6084); born Putney, Vt., November 7, 1814; died Charlestown, Mass., August 16, 1858.

No issue.

6086. COOLEDGE CLARK DAGGETT [4] (*Samuel*,[3] *Samuel* [2] [*Samuel* [1]] (?)), born Watertown, Mass., January 1, 1825; "ticket agent, Fitchburg railroad;" resides Somerville, Mass. (1893); married Boston, Mass., July 27, 1853, by Rev. S. Streeter, to Sarah Rich Holman, daughter of Cyrus and Lydia (Stow) Holman; born Royalston, Mass., November 18, 1828.

Issue:

6111. i. WILLIAM HALE DAGGETT,[5] born Somerville, Mass., September 18, 1854; resides Somerville, Mass. (1893).
6112. ii. CORA GEORGIANNA DAGGETT,[5] born Somerville, Mass., August 17, 1857; resides Somerville, Mass. (1893).

6087. LUCY JANE DAGGETT [4] (*Samuel*,[3] *Samuel* [2] [*Samuel* [1]] (?)), born Watertown, Mass., September 5, 1826; died Charlestown, Mass., April 23, 1857; married 1st, Charlestown, Mass., July 14, 1853, by Rev. William I. Budington, to Francis Timothy Eaton Bryant, son of Timothy and Sophia (Eaton) Bryant; "provision dealer;" born Charlestown, Mass., 1828; died Charlestown, Mass.; married 2d, Charlestown, Mass., Arthur Bennett, son of Jonas and Selina (Grover) Bennett.

Issue: three children.

6113. i. JANE SOPHIA.[5]

6088. SAMUEL OTIS DAGGETT [4] (*Samuel*,[3] *Samuel* [2] [*Samuel* [1]] (?)), born Charlestown, Mass., April 13, 1828; died Charlestown, Mass., May 4, 1879; married Boston, Mass., December 30, 1858, by Rev. S. Streeter, to Anne Eliza Richards, daughter of Joseph and Susan T. (Shelton) Richards; born Boston, Mass., July 18, 1832; resides 47 Mystic street, Charlestown, Mass. (1893).

Issue:

6114. i. ANNE OTIS DAGGETT,[5] born Charlestown, Mass., October 8, 1859.
6115. ii. LUCY GORE DAGGETT,[5] born Charlestown, Mass., September 18, 1864; resides Somerville, Mass. (1893).

6091. GEORGIANA DAGGETT [4] (*Samuel*,[3] *Samuel* [2] [*Samuel* [1]] (?)), born Charlestown, Mass., July 11, 1835; resides Charlestown, Mass. (1892); married Charlestown, Mass., March 24, 1861, by Rev. H.

C. Graves, to Caleb Drew, son of Caleb and Harriet (Elliott) Drew; "ice-dealer;" born Charlestown, Mass., March 24, 1829.

Issue:

6116. i. WILLIAM FRANCIS DREW,[5] born Charlestown, Mass., June 17, ——; married Annie Hawthorn, and has Lilian Gertrude Drew,[6] and Edwin Hawthorn Drew.[6]

6092. GEORGE HENRY DAGGETT [4] (*Samuel,*[3] *Samuel* [2] [*Samuel* [1]] (?)), born East Wilton, Me., December 17, 1837; resides 8 Wesley street, Charlestown, Mass. (1893); married Charlestown, Mass., November 24, 1861, by Rev. Geo. E. Ellis, to Marie Elizabeth Parker, daughter of Warren B. and Elizabeth Allen (Edmands) Parker; born Charlestown, Mass., June 18, 1839.

Issue:

6117. i. HENRY WARREN DAGGETT,[5] born Charlestown, Mass., June 26, 1863.

6114. ANNE OTIS DAGGETT [5] (*Samuel O.,*[4] *Samuel,*[3] *Samuel,*[2] [*Samuel* [1]] (?)), born Charlestown, Mass., October 8, 1859; resides East Somerville, Mass. (1892); married Boston, Mass., February 28, 1880, by Charles F. Lee, to Robert Hugh Riddell, son of Henry G. and Emily (Crosby) Riddell; born Wilmington, Vt., March, 1857.

Issue:

6118. i. GUY CROSBY RIDDELL,[6] born Charlestown, Mass., February 27, 1892.

6117. HENRY WARREN DAGGETT [5] (*George H.,*[4] *Samuel,*[3] *Samuel,*[2] [*Samuel* [1]] (?)), born Charlestown, Mass., June 26, 1863; resides Charlestown, Mass. (1893); married Boston, Mass., October 22, 1882, by Rev. W. F. Perrin, to Dora Ellard, daughter of George and Margaret Ellard; born Charlestown, Mass., November 17, 1864.

Issue:

6119. i. FLORENCE ELIZABETH DAGGETT,[6] born Charlestown, Mass., May 4, 1886.

DOGGETT-DAGGETT.

REV. BENJAMIN DOGGETT, OF LANCASTER, VA.

FIRST GENERATION.

6120. Rev. BENJAMIN DOGGETT,[1] died Lancaster, Va., 1681; married Jane ———.

Issue:

6121. i. BENJAMIN DOGGETT,[2] born England about 1664.
6122. ii. JANE DOGGETT,[2] born England about 1666; living in England 1681.
6123. iii. RICHARD DOGGETT,[2] born Virginia about 1670.
6124. iv. WILLIAM DOGGETT,[2] born Virginia about 1676.
6125. v. ANNE DOGGETT,[2] born Virginia about 1678.

Rev. Benjamin Doggett was a clergyman in the Established Church of England, who immigrated to America previous to 1670, the exact date not being found, or the location in England from which he came. One of his descendants reports him as coming from near London, and this seems very probable after following that London branch of which some of the members are known to have come to America, and in which the names Benjamin, William, and Richard often occur. (See descendants of John Dogett, of Groton, No. 65.)

Mr. Doggett settled in what is known as the "Northern Neck of Virginia," and founded the church near Chesapeake Bay, in what is now called Lancaster county, Va.

The church of which he was rector he called White Chapel, and when he died directed that he should be buried before the pulpit in the Chapel church. The main body of the old White Chapel church-edifice still remains, having once or twice been repaired, and the building reconstructed.

The old walls are still standing, and are of substantial masonry, reared in colonial times, of brick imported from the mother country. These walls mark the spot of Rev. Benjamin Doggett's interment.

In a visit to the old church, the writer was escorted by the present rector and privileged to see its quaint interior. Its acoustic properties are remarkably fine, its walls plain, excepting only the tablets,

CHRIST CHURCH, LANCASTER CO., VIRGINIA.

u

which were presented to the church by David and William Fox in 1702. The font, made of dark-colored stone, and having the appearance of great age, is most interesting.

In the churchyard are the graves and tombs of the principal families of the neighborhood, many of them quite old, and some which must have been of very beautiful workmanship.

The whole, situated on a knoll surrounded by the beautiful verdure of Virginia, made a picture of perfect peace and harmony, which seemed a most fitting resting-place for the founder of our race in that portion of America, and a monument to his zeal in the good work which still continues there for the welfare of our fellow-men.

Christ Church and White Chapel were built from the same plans, and the first named has remained in its original form to the present time.

The first vestry-book or parish-record of Lancaster county has been lost or destroyed, and the rector has been unable to obtain any definite information regarding it. It has disappeared since the early part of this century. " Rev. Benjamin Doggett is stated to have been stationed in Lancaster county, in 1670." [R. A. Brock, Esq.]

June 30, 1680. In a list of the churches and rectors in the various counties, Lancaster county has " Christ Church" and " White Chapple," Mr. Benjamin Doggett, rector. [State Papers, Colonial Virginia, Vol. LX., No. 410.]

Aug 4, 1680 George Flowers, merchant, sells Benjamin Doggett, minister of Lancaster County all that Plantation whereon the said George Flowers lately lived, together with all buildings &c thereunto belonging, title &c according to the true patent thereof — 350 acres land.
Witness, Thomas Marshall — Thomas Touse. Mary Flowers wife of George Flowers releases dower. [Lancaster Deeds, 4–364.]
Feb 4, 1681 Benjamin Doggett of the County of Lancaster mortgages land to Robert Griggs, the land situated in White Chapel Parish, also land bought of George Flowers. [Lancaster Deeds, 4–428.]

Book of Wills and Inventories of Lancaster County, Va., p. 87 :

In the name of God Amen: I, Benjamin Doggett, minister, of Lancaster County, being sick and weake in boddy but of sound and perfect memory, do make this my last will and testament, as follows :
1st I bequeath my soul and boddy to God the giver and my body to be decently buried before the pulpit in the Chapel Church.
2nd I give unto my eldest son Benjamin Doggett, a hundred and fifty acres of land, beginning at the water side and to run right across from the line that parts me and Thomas Tomson, to Jon Crooke, and in case he dyes without issue male, then the land to be equally divided with the orchard, between my two sons Richard and William and in case my son Benjamin shall mary before he arrives to ye age of two and twenty, he shall thereby forfeit all his title and interest in said land and the land to be divided as above mentioned.
3rd I give unto my son Richd Doggett, one hundred acres of land and in case he dyes without issue male or marries before he arrives to the age of twenty-two then the land to descend to my son William Doggett, the shares . . . without of his share in my personal estate as will purchase him a part the land to be . . . for him. sarbts afterward to be bought for him as his estate

will admit of. if sar^bts cannot be purchased the Tobb to be disposed to ye best advantage.

4th I give to my son William Doggett, one hundred acres of land and in case he dyes without issue male or marries before he arrives at the age of twenty two, then ye land to be divided between my two daughters Jane and Anne Doggett, a part to be purchased for him out of his share in my personal estate the land seated and other parts to be bought for him as his estate will admit of, if sarb^ts cannot be purchased then the Tobb to be disposed of, to ye best advantage, those two hundred acres given between my two sons Richard and William to be devided at the discretion of my Executor.

5th I give unto my daughter Jane Doggett in England, twenty shillings and no more because she have been detained from me and is surely provided for.

6th I give unto my daughter Anne Doggett, fifteen thousand pounds of Tobb, six young cows, six breeding sows to be paid her by my 3 sons Benjamin, Richard and William provided she doth not marry before she arrives at the age of eighteen, ye lott to be at two yearly payments, one half the first year and the other half the next year, her name and age to be registered in the book of Crist Church parish and likewise my two sons borne in Virginia. their agge you must have from their Mother.

7th Because there remains six thousand pounds of Tobb to be paid Mr. Flower and some other lott if the Tobb allowed me by ye parishes and with my sarb^ts make will not dephrey them. then so much to be sould out of my personal estate to be equally divided between my wife and children only debaring my son Benjamin any share amid share in ye cattell because he have a good stock of his own.

8th My wife to have her accommodation as long as she continues a widow but if she marries, she shall desert the plantation, my two sons and my daughter An to have their accomidation with my son Benjamin till they are capable to live on their own.

9th The pipe stands to be sold for money . . . Sawers to be employed to saw two just planks to be sold for money to pay Mr Griggs.

10th My books to be aprised, a great chest to be bought, ye books to be packed up and sent for England to be sold, ye overplus of monies that remains when Mr Griggs is paid, I give unto my loving wife Jane Doggett desiring her to buy mourning ring with this purpose. following more.

11th I do constitute and appoint Mr Shraphoard, Mr ffirmsold, Mr Atkins, Mr Wilkes ye apprisers of my estate. Mr Thomas Marlin Mr Jo^th Mullis executors to this my last will and testament and for their trouble I give unto both my executors 20£ to buy the mourning rings.

In witness whereof I have hereunto put my hand and seal this fourteenth Day of March in ye year 1681

BENJAMIN DOGGETT [Seal]

Signed sealed and delivered in the presence of
  JON DABIN pr sig.
  ST WILLIAM KELLY & sig.

Probated in Crist Court, Lancaster Jan. 1682 by Sar. Jon Dabin and St William Kelly.

REV. BENJAMIN DOGGETT, OF LANCASTER, VA.

SECOND GENERATION.

6121. BENJAMIN DOGGETT² (*Benjamin¹*), born England, about 1664 ; married 1st, Mary ——— ; married 2d, Ann Emerson, daughter of John Emerson, of Lancaster county : she died before 1771.

Issue :

6126. i. THOMAS DOGGETT.³
6127. ii. ELIZABETH DOGGETT,³ married Philip Ffrond, of Lancaster county.

6128. iii. BENJAMIN (?) DOGGETT.[3]
6129. iv. MARY ANN DOGGETT.[3]
6130. v. MARGARET DOGGETT,[3] married John Edwards.
6131. vi. LEANNA DOGGETT,[3] married Richard Hutchings.
6132. vii. BETTY DOGGETT,[3] married William Doggett (No. 6134).

January 9, 1722, Benjamin Doggett, of Lancaster county, wife Mary; on account of love and affection bear to son Thomas Doggett, gives him negro boy three years old, called "Wingo." [Lancaster Deeds, 11–220.]

Same date, gives Elizabeth, his daughter, now wife of Philip Ffrond of same county, negro boy called "Tom," five years old. [Lancaster Deeds, 11–221.]

6123. RICHARD DOGGETT [2] (*Benjamin* [1]), born Virginia, about 1670; married Richmond county, Va., Ann Ascough, daughter of Thomas Ascough, of Richmond county.

Issue:

6133. i. GEORGE DOGGETT.[3]

October 31, 1727, Richard Doggett, of Richmond county, and Ann, his wife, who was Ann Ascough, the only daughter of Thomas Ascough, of Richmond county, convey one hundred acres land to Marmaduke Beckwith. [Richmond Deeds.]

November 5, 1729, Richard Doggett, now of Westmoreland county, and Ann, his wife, convey seventy acres land to John Champe. [Richmond Deeds.]

6124. WILLIAM DOGGETT [2] (*Benjamin* [1]), born Virginia, about 1676; died between 1771 and 1776; married ——.

Issue:

6134. i. WILLIAM* DOGGETT,[3] born Lancaster county, Va.
6135. ii. COLEMAN DOGGETT,[3] born Lancaster county, Va., February 7, 1736.

"The old family homestead, four miles south of Lancaster Court House, now standing and habitable, was the home of William Doggett, the son of Benjamin (as my father John informed me), and was handed down, by hereditary descent, to the oldest surviving son, with the strict injunction that it should never be sold out of the family, until it reached myself (that is, Cyrus Doggett). In the last bequest this injunction was not imposed. The rigid adherence to descent, and the scrupulous preservation of family relics, is manifested in the fact that many pieces of household furniture, of old English mould, descended through the intervening generations to the writer." [Rev. Cyrus Doggett, in Sketch of Bishop Doggett, Nashville, 1882.]

---

* William and Coleman have been reported as sons of William and grandsons of Benjamin, and are so placed, but this arrangement seems not fully proved.

REV. BENJAMIN DOGGETT, OF LANCASTER, VA.

THIRD GENERATION.

6126.   Thomas Doggett [3] (*Benjamin,*[2] *Benjamin*[1]),   married
Bathsheba ——.

Sept 9, 1748   Thomas Doggett of the parish of St. Mary's, White Chapel, Lancaster County, Planter Exchanges land near mouth of Corotoman River with James Gordon, Bathsheba Doggett releases her dower. [Lancaster Deeds, 14–215.]

Nov 16, 1753   Thomas Doggett and Bathsheba his wife of Lancaster County sell land to Solomon Ewell. [Lancaster Deeds, 15–157.]

July 24, 1756.   James Gordon sells land purchased of Thomas Doggett late of the county. [Lancaster Deeds, 15–282.]

6133.   George Doggett [3] (*Richard,*[2] *Benjamin*[1]).
George Doggett sells one hundred acres of land between branches of Corotoman river, bounded as by draft made for a certain Richard Doggett, September 9, 1748.   [Lancaster Deeds, 14–215.]

6134.   William Doggett [3] (*William,*[2] *Benjamin*[1]),   born Lancaster county, Va.; married Betty Doggett, daughter of Benjamin and Ann (Emerson) Doggett (No. 6132).

Issue :

6136. i.   Sarah M. Doggett,[4] born Lancaster county, Va., 1790.
6137. ii.   Samuel B. Doggett,[4] born Lancaster county, Va.
6138. iii.   Mary Doggett,[4] married Hugh Stephens.

William Doggett owned the Kilmanock farm, in Lancaster county, about two and a half miles from the first church in that part of Virginia.

6135.   Coleman Doggett [3] (*William,*[2] *Benjamin*[1]),   born Lancaster county, Va., February 7, 1736; died March, 1782; married Mary King; born November 19, 1739; died November, 1789.

Issue :

6139. i.   John Doggett,[4] born Lancaster county, Va., January 4, 1761.
6140. ii.   Mary Doggett,[4] born Lancaster county, Va., September 5, 1765.
6141. iii.   William Doggett,[4] born Lancaster county, Va., July 27, 1769.
6142. iv.   Dennis Doggett,[4] born Lancaster county, Va., January, 1776; died Lancaster county, Va., 1818.
6143. v.   Priscilla Doggett.[4]
6144. vi.   Ann Doggett.[4]

REV. BENJAMIN DOGGETT, OF LANCASTER, VA.

FOURTH GENERATION.

6136. SARAH M. DOGGETT[4] (*William*,[3] *William*,[2] *Benjamin* [1]), born Lancaster county, Va., 1790; died Woodstock, Va., February 13, 1866; married Lancaster county, Va., 1810, Lemuel Doggett, son of William Doggett; born Lancaster county, Va., 1789; died near Fredericksburg, Va., August, 1871.

Issue:

6145. i.   HUGH STEPHENS DOGGETT,[5] born Fredericksburg, Va., May 11, 1816.
6146. ii.   OLIVIA ANN DOGGETT,[5] born Fredericksburg, Va., March 30, 1818.
6147. iii.   LEE ROY BENJAMIN DOGGETT,[5] born Fredericksburg, Va., January 11, 1820.
6148. iv.   GEORGE FLOWERS DOGGETT,[5] born Spottsylvania county, Feb. 9, 1828.

6139. Rev. JOHN DOGGETT[4] (*Coleman*,[3] *William*,[2] *Benjamin* [1]), born Lancaster county, Va., January 4, 1761; died Lancaster county, Va., December 3, 1825; married Philadelphia, Pa., August 27, 1782, Mary Smith; born 1766.

Issue:

6149. i.   COLEMAN DOGGETT,[6] born Lancaster county, Va., December 20, 1783; died young.
6150. ii.   JOHN DOGGETT,[5] born Lancaster county, Va., August 24, 1785; died young.
6151. iii.   SARAH DOGGETT,[5] born Lancaster county, Va., November 2, 1787.
6152. iv.   MARY SMITH DOGGETT,[5] born Lancaster county, Va., Nov. 7, 1789.
6153. v.   ANN COLEMAN DOGGETT,[5] born Lancaster county, Va., December 12, 1791; died young.
6154. vi.   ELIZABETH DOGGETT,[5] born Lancaster county, Va., March 10, 1794; died young.
6155. vii.   WILLIAM SMITH DOGGETT,[5] born Lancaster county, Va., August 18, 1796; died young.
6156. viii. CHARLES WESLEY DOGGETT,[5] born Lancaster county, Va., September 27, 1798; died young.
6157. ix.   CYRUS DOGGETT,[5] born Lancaster county, Va., March 12, 1801.
6158. x.   LE ROY COLEMAN DOGGETT,[5] born Lancaster county, Va., February 17, 1804; died young.
6159. xi.   JOSEPH SMITH DOGGETT,[5] born Lancaster county, Va., April 18, 1807; died young.
6160. xii.   DAVID SETH DOGGETT,[5] born Lancaster county, Va., Jan. 23, 1810.

" John Doggett lived and died on the paternal estate in Lancaster county, Va. He was long a justice of the peace in that county, and a local minister in the Methodist Episcopal church. He was well read in law and theology, a man of decided ability and extensive influence. It was the intention of his father, who died when he was young, to educate him for a clergyman." [Bishop Doggett, February 5, 1879.]

6141. William Doggett[4] (*Coleman*,[3] *William*,[2] *Benjamin*[1]), born Lancaster county, Va., July 27, 1769; died Newburyport, Mass., July 23, 1812; married Gloucester, Mass., Mary Lane, daughter of Caleb Lane, of Gloucester, Mass.; died before 1835.

Issue:

6161. i.   David Doggett.[5]
6162. ii. Priscilla Doggett.[5]
6163. iii. William Doggett,[5] born Gloucester, Mass., April 13, 1792.
6164. iv. John Doggett,[5] removed to Ipswich.
6165. v.   Elias Doggett,[5] removed to Canada.

REV. BENJAMIN DOGGETT, OF LANCASTER, VA.

FIFTH GENERATION.

6145. Capt. Hugh Stephens Doggett[5] (*Sarah M.*,[4] *William*,[3] *William*,[2] *Benjamin*[1]), born Fredericksburg, Va., May 11, 1816; resides Fredericksburg, Va. (1893); married Caroline county, Va., November 28, 1844, by Rev. Larrance Battaile, to Sarah Adaline Burruss, daughter of William C. and Elizabeth (Cocke) Burruss; born Caroline county, Va., April 14. 1814; died Fredericksburg, Va., January 13, 1885.

Issue:

6166. i.   Mary E. Doggett,[6] born Fredericksburg, Va., October 6, 1845; died Fredericksburg, Va., October 6, 1846.
6167. ii. Susanna A. Doggett,[6] born Fredericksburg, Va., February 20, 1847; died Fredericksburg, Va., June 28, 1848.
6168. iii. Fannie A. Doggett,[6] born Fredericksburg, Va., December, 1848.
6169. iv. Hugh Stephens Doggett,[6] born Fredericksburg, Va., March 13, 1851; died Fredericksburg, Va., September 8, 1854.
6170. v.   Huberta Stephens Doggett,[6] born Fredericksburg, Va., December 17, 1856; died Fredericksburg, Va., September 6, 1857.

Capt. Hugh S. Doggett has long been identified with the best interests of his native town.

He was captain of infantry in the Confederate army, and since the war has been mayor of the city of Fredericksburg four years, and member of the town council. He is a general grocer, of the firm "Doggett & Scott."

6146. Olivia Ann Doggett[5] (*Sarah M.*,[4] *William*,[3] *William*,[2] *Benjamin*[1]), born Fredericksburg, Va., March 30, 1818; died Lancaster county, Va., September 10, 1882; married Spottsylvania county, Va., November 14, 1839, Dr. James Simmonds, son of

William and Frances (Robb) Simmonds; born Lancaster county, Va., September 17, 1812; resides Merry Point, Va. (1893).

Issue:

6171. i.   OSCAR MONROE SIMMONDS,[6] born Lancaster county, Va., September 9, 1840; died Lancaster county, Va., October 8, 1850.

6172. ii.   BINOZA ULRICA SIMMONDS,[6] born Lancaster county, Va., April 7, 1843; died Lancaster county, Va., July 28, 1846.

6173. iii.   IWANONA ADELINE SIMMONDS,[6] born Lancaster county, Va., December 17, 1844.

6174. iv.   ULRICA OLIVIA SIMMONDS,[6] born Lancaster county, Va., Oct. 25, 1847.

6175. v.   FANNIE FLOWERS SIMMONDS,[6] born Lancaster county, Va., October 15, 1851.

6176. vi.   JAMES CYRUS SIMMONDS,[6] born Lancaster county, Va., December 18, 1855; died Lancaster county, Va., September 17, 1856.

6177. vii.   JAMES OSCAR BURTON SIMMONDS,[6] born Lancaster county, Va., February 20, 1859.

6178. viii.   SIDNEY JOHNSTON SIMMONDS,[6] born Lancaster county, Va., June 3, 1862; resides there.

Dr. James Simmonds has been commissioner in chancery of the circuit and county courts of Lancaster county; physician to the county poorhouse; enlisted in the home guard in the Confederate service.

6147. Capt. LEE ROY BENJAMIN DOGGETT[5] (*Sarah M.,*[4] *William,*[3] *William,*[2] *Benjamin*[1]), born Fredericksburg, Va., January 11, 1820; resides 2951 Prairie avenue, Chicago, Ill. (1893); married Stafford county, Va., November 5, 1848, by Rev. John Lanahan, to Lucy Frances Jerrell, daughter of James S. and Rachel (Wright) Jerrell, of Caroline county; born Fauquier county, Va., Dec. 7, 1829.

Issue:

6179. i.   JAMES LEMUEL DOGGETT,[6] born Fredericksburg, Va., March 6, 1848.

6180. ii.   OCEOLA JACKSON DOGGETT,[6] born Fredericksburg, Va., November 17, 1850; formerly of the firm of Doggett & Son, Fredericksburg; resides Chicago, Ill. (1893).

6181. iii.   ANDREW CAPEN DOGGETT,[6] born Fredericksburg, Va., Sept. 20, 1852.

6182. iv.   WILLIAM LEE DOGGETT,[6] born Fredericksburg, Va., August 18, 1854; of "Doggett Brothers," real estate; resides 2951 Prairie avenue, Chicago, Ill. (1893).

6183. v.   VIRGINIA EMMA DOGGETT,[6] born Fredericksburg, Va., March 9, 1858; resides 2951 Prairie avenue, Chicago, Ill. (1893).

6184. vi.   HERBERT EDMAND LEE DOGGETT,[6] born Fredericksburg, Va., December 1, 1862; of "Doggett Brothers," real estate; resides 2951 Prairie avenue, Chicago, Ill. (1893).

6185. vii.   LUTHER WESLEY DOGGETT,[6] born Fredericksburg, Va., March 20, 1865; in 1889 rector of Grace Protestant Episcopal Church at Petersburg, Va.; now (1893) rector of St. Philip's, Philadelphia, Pa.; married Petersburg, Va., April 21, 1892, Fannie Collier Hinton, daughter of Judge Drury A. and —— (Collier) Hinton.

6186. viii.   HUGHGENIA SALLY DOGGETT,[6] born Fredericksburg, Va., September 5, 1867; married George N. Doggett (see No. 5002).

6187. ix.   CARRIE MAY DOGGETT,[6] born Fredericksburg, Va., May 21, 1870.

6188. x.   ARTHUR MERREY DOGGETT,[6] born Fredericksburg, Va., May 18, 1872.

Three sons died at birth unnamed.

Capt. L. B. Doggett was for many years a commission merchant, of the firm of L. B. Doggett & Son, of Fredericksburg, Va. He was captain in the Confederate army.

6148. George Flowers Doggett⁵ (*Sarah M.*,⁴ *William*,³ *William*,² *Benjamin* ¹), born Spottsylvania county, Va., Feb. 9, 1828; died Fredericksburg, Va., April 27, 1889; married Petersburg, Va., Aug. 25, 1859, by Rev. James H. Joyner, to Mrs. Virginia Sara Françoise Hughes, widow of James Crawford Hughes, and daughter of Capt. Joseph and Rebekah Heath (Simmons) Boisseau; born Prince George county, Va., Nov. 9, 1838; resides Fredericksburg, Va. (1893).

Issue:

6189. i. Sarah Rebekah Doggett,⁶ born Hessee Castle, Northampton Co., Va., September 1, 1860; married Dr. A. C. Doggett (see No. 6181).

George F. Doggett was Commonwealth's attorney for the city of Petersburg; United States commissioner, United States cotton inspector for the port of Petersburg; magistrate; member of the Common Council of the city of Petersburg; chairman of the School Board of the city, and chairman of the Finance Committee. He was a lawyer, a graduate of the University of Virginia, and practised in Petersburg for a number of years, from whence, on important occasions, he was called out of his State to other bars. At the age of eighteen he taught school in Charlestown, W. Va., and elsewhere. For a time, and until 1860, he was teaching in Washington, D.C. He was confirmed by Bishop Johns, and joined the Protestant Episcopal church at Petersburg in 1865.

At one time he was director in the Norfolk & Western Railroad.

6151. Sarah Doggett⁵ (*John*,⁴ *Coleman*,³ *William*,² *Benjamin* ¹), born Lancaster county, Va., November 2, 1787; married (her cousin?) James Doggett (perhaps brother of Lemuel).

Issue:

6190. i. Robert Doggett,⁶ died without issue.
6191. ii. Mary Doggett,⁶ died without issue.
6192. iii. Emily Doggett,⁶ married Thomas Pitman, Lancaster county; had two daughters, who married.
6193. iv Nancy Doggett.⁶

6152 Mary Smith Doggett⁵ (*John*,⁴ *Coleman*,³ *William*,² *Benjamin* ¹), born Lancaster county, Va., November 7, 1789; married George Payne.

Issue: removed to Missouri 1829.

6194. i. Maria Payne,⁶ died.
6195. ii. Penelope Payne,⁶ married Charles Hicks, Howard county, Mo.
6196. iii. Eliza Payne,⁶ died.
6197. iv. Fannie Payne,⁶ married Mr. Woods; resides Huntsville, Mo. (1886).
6198. v. Cyrus Payne,⁶ married and died, leaving widow and children; widow married again, and lives Saline county, Mo. (1886).
6199. vi. David Payne,⁶ resides near Huntsville, Mo. (1886).

6157. Rev. Cyrus Doggett⁵ (*John*,⁴ *Coleman*,³ *William*,² *Benjamin* ¹), born Lancaster county, Va., March 12, 1801; died Fincastle,

Va., August 2, 1883; married Northumberland county, Va., September 4, 1824, Elizabeth Larkey, daughter of Rev. John T. and Mary (Conway [Kenna]) Larkey; born Fairfield, Northumberland Co., Va., October 12, 1805; died Fincastle, Va., January 27, 1888.

Issue:

6200. i. MARY ANN DOGGETT,[6] born Lancaster county, Va., October 10, 1825; died Lancaster county, Va., October 1, 1826.

6201. ii. ARABELLA DOGGETT,[6] born Lancaster county, Va., August 29, 1827; resides Suffolk, Va. (1892).

6202. iii. NARCISSA DOGGETT,[6] born Lancaster county, Va., October 4, 1829; died Lancaster county, Va., September 5, 1832.

6203. iv. ROWLAND DOGGETT,[6] born Lancaster county, Va., October 31, 1831.

6204. v. ALMIRA DOGGETT,[6] born Lancaster county, Va., October 15, 1833; married Bedford, Va., 1866, Hugh French, of Cumberland county; she died Powhatan county, Va., November, 1866.

6205. vi. JOHN LARKEY DOGGETT,[6] born Lancaster county, Va., July 23, 1835.

6206. vii. ELLA MARGUERITE DOGGETT,[6] born Lancaster county, Va., April 25, 1837; died Lancaster county, Va., August 25, 1837.

6207. viii. CYRUS DOGGETT,[6] born Lancaster county, Va., September 18, 1838.

6208. ix. ELIZABETH LARKEY DOGGETT,[6] born Lancaster county, Va., July 3, 1840; died Lancaster county, Va., 1852.

6209. x. ROBERT EMORY DOGGETT,[6] born Lancaster county, Va., Feb. 28, 1845.

6210. xi. JOSEPHINE DOGGETT,[6] born Lancaster county, Va., November 19, 1846; died Boydton, Mecklenburg Co., Va., October, 1847.

" Rev. Cyrus Doggett professed religion and joined the Methodist church when he was about sixteen years old. In his eighteenth year he was licensed to preach, and was an active local preacher all the early part of his life.

" He filled the highest positions of honor and trust in his county, such as magistrate, high sheriff, and clerk of the county and circuit courts.

" At that day the magistrates were appointed by the governor of the State, and three of them presided at the county courts, and the oldest magistrate was sheriff. About the year 1856 he resigned his position as county and circuit clerk of Lancaster county, and engaged in the active work of the ministry.

" He joined the Virginia Conference, Methodist Episcopal Church South, and became a Methodist itinerant preacher. Continuing his connection with the Virginia Conference after the war, he was then transferred to the Missouri Conference, Methodist Episcopal Church South, and remained there until his age put him on the superannuated list, and he returned to Virginia, where he was actively engaged in preaching till just before his last sickness, and on August 2, 1883, he passed calmly to his reward. So ended a long and useful life. His great idea of life was to live for the benefit of his race.

" He sacrificed the pleasures and emoluments of this life for the noble employment of advancing his species."

6160. Bishop DAVID SETH DOGGETT, D.D.[5] (*John*,[4] *Coleman*,[3] *William*,[2] *Benjamin*[1]), born Lancaster county, Va., January 23,

1810; died Richmond, Va., October 27, 1880; married 1834, Martha Ann Gwathmey, of Lynchburg, Va.; born Lynchburg, Va., 1812; died Richmond, Va., February 19, 1882.

Issue:

6211. i.   ANNIE DOGGETT,[6] died young.
6212. ii. DAVID SETH DOGGETT.[6]
6213. iii. MATTIE GWATHMEY DOGGETT,[6] married Tazewell Fitzgerald; issue: four children.
6214. iv. GEORGE BROOKE DOGGETT,[6] born Lynchburg, Va., October 30, 1847.
6215. v.   JOHN MARSHALL DOGGETT,[6] born January 30, 1852; "professor;" resides 206 E. Clay street, Richmond, Va.
6216. vi. LUCY B. DOGGETT.[6]

"David Seth Doggett was born in the old family homestead, and received his elementary education at the neighboring schools in Lancaster county, Va. After the death of his father he was placed in the Northumberland Academy. 'Among the testamentary arrangements of our father,' says the Rev. Cyrus Doggett, 'he desired that David should be trained for the profession of the law. Providence, however, designed another sphere in which he should exercise his talents.' The conversion of David S. Doggett in his seventeenth year, and his union with the Methodist Episcopal church, which was soon followed by the conviction that it was his duty to devote himself to the work of the Christian ministry, deflected him from the line of life which had been projected by his father, and for which his education was intended to prepare him. His church membership was held at the old White Marsh church in Lancaster circuit, then in the bounds of the old Baltimore Conference. On leaving the academy he spent a year in teaching school in Orange county, Va. While engaged in teaching he diligently pursued a course of theological reading, exercised his gifts as an exhorter, attended class meeting, and rapidly developed himself into a singularly rounded and symmetrical character for one of his years, distinguished alike for his piety and his intelligence.

"He was admitted on trial into the Virginia Conference, held in Lynchburg, February, 1829, and appointed junior preacher on Roanoke circuit, in North Carolina, a large portion of that State then being in the bounds of the Virginia Conference. He was young and handsome, with agreeable manners and winning address, and withal was a fervid, earnest, and eloquent preacher for one of his age. He soon acquired unbounded popularity, and became a universal favorite among the people. In 1830 he was sent to Mattamuskeet circuit, in the lowlands of North Carolina, as the preacher in charge. He was cordially received, and soon became exceedingly popular, and had a year of great success in the ministry. In 1831 he was appointed to the Petersburg station. His wonderful eloquence captivated the people, and the revival commenced under his ministry continued

D. S. Doggett.

almost without interruption during the whole year.   After two years' service in Petersburg, Mr. Doggett was appointed in 1833 to Lynch-burg.   Here again his popularity and success continued without abatement.

" In 1834 he was stationed at Trinity, in Richmond. Again, in 1835, he was returned to Petersburg.   In 1836-7 he was appointed to Nor-folk, where he achieved a great success.   Once more, in 1838, he was returned to Lynchburg.   In 1839 he was appointed to Charlottes-ville, and acted as chaplain to the University of Virginia, while he performed his duties as pastor of the Methodist church in the town.

" In 1840 he was appointed chaplain to Randolph-Macon College. In 1841 and onward till 1846, by successive appointment, he filled the chair of mental and moral philosophy in Randolph-Macon Col-lege.   In 1847-8 he fell back into regular pastoral work at Lynch-burg, in 1849-50 at Petersburg.   In 1850 he was appointed editor of the 'Southern Methodist Quarterly Review,' a position he filled for seven or eight years.

" In 1851-52 he was pastor of Centenary Church in Richmond, in addition to his editorial work ; then in 1853-54 in Norfolk, in charge of Granby-street Church.

" In 1855 his time was exclusively devoted to the 'Review.'   In 1856-57 he was in charge of the church in Washington, where he won for himself the reputation of a great preacher.   In 1858-61 he was presiding elder of the Richmond district; 1862-63 at Broad-street Church, in Richmond, and here during the war he preached some of the most powerful and eloquent sermons of his life.   In 1864-66 he was again appointed to the Centenary charge in Richmond.

" At the General Conference held in the city of New Orleans, May, 1866, Dr. Doggett was elected to the Episcopacy of the Methodist Episcopal Church South, by a flattering vote of that body, and here began a new epoch in his ministerial life.

" Bishop Doggett's work and official administration as one of the bishops of the Methodist Episcopal Church South has gone to record ; and we may safely say that no man has occupied that posi-tion who has filled it with more honor to himself, or more credit to the church, than he.

" His escutcheon is untarnished, his administration has passed the General Conference with approval, and he has gone down to his honored grave with the affection of his colleagues clustering around him, and the benediction of the whole church, which he served with fidelity, following him to the last breath of his mortal life, and to his last resting-place in the grave.   In his episcopal visitations he traversed the entire domain of Southern Methodism, and whether in California or Texas, in Missouri or Virginia, in Kansas or Georgia, he bound his church — ministry and laity — to him, and to his precious memory, as with hooks of steel.

" Bishop Doggett, in his prime, and before incessant toil and advancing age had undermined his constitution and robbed him of his manly vigor and vivacity, was an unusually handsome and courtly man in port and physique. His complexion was bright and ruddy, his features delicately chiselled, his eye a lustrous blue, and his hand and head a model for the sculptor.

" As a public speaker he had a finely modulated voice, with striking facial expression and graceful gesture, all of which was rendered doubly effective by the genuine and unaffected goodness that beamed in every feature and shone out so conspicuously in every utterance of his lips.

" Bishop Doggett for many years was a member of the Board of Trustees of Randolph-Macon College, and from it he received his honorary degree of doctor of divinity. During the last two years of his life he was president of the Virginia Bible Socie'y."

6163. WILLIAM DOGGETT[5] (*William*,[4] *Coleman*,[3] *William*,[2] *Benjamin*[1]), born Gloucester, Mass., April 13, 1792; "fisherman;" died Gloucester, Mass., August 13, 1868; married 1st, Gloucester, Mass., December 15, 1816, by Rev. Ezra Leonard, to Mary York, daughter of Joseph York; born 1801; died Gloucester, Mass., May 6, 1822; married 2d, Gloucester, Mass., December 30, 1827, Ann J. Robinson, daughter of Jonathan and Lydia Robinson; born Gloucester, Mass., April 10, 1800; died Gloucester, Mass., August 24, 1867.

Issue :

6217. i.   WILLIAM DOGGETT,[6] born Gloucester, Mass., October 16, 1817.
6218. ii.   HENRIETTA DOGGETT,[6] married Gloucester, Mass., October 24, 1843, by Rev. Maxcy B. Newell, to John Newman, Jr.; "fisherman;" he died; she resides Gloucester, Mass. (1892).
6219. iii.   MARY DOGGETT,[6] born 1821; married Mr. Sargent; she died Gloucester, Mass.
6220. iv.   JOHN DOGGETT,[6] born Gloucester, Mass., 1823.
6221. v.   ELIAS DOGGETT,[6] born Gloucester, Mass., 1829.
6222. vi.   LYDIA DOGGETT,[6] died.
6223. vii.   LYDIA ANN DOGGETT,[6] born Gloucester, Mass., 1832.
6224. viii. HENRY DOGGETT,[6] born Gloucester, Mass., May 12, 1835.
6225. ix.   SAMUEL DOGGETT,[6] born Gloucester, Mass., September 18, 1837; died Gloucester, Mass., April 18, 1844.
6226. x.   HANNAH DOGGETT,[6] born Gloucester, Mass., February 8, 1842; died Gloucester, Mass., April 8, 1844.
6227. xi.   JAMES DOGGETT,[6] died.
6228. xii.   HANNAH MORRIS DOGGETT,[6] born Gloucester, Mass., 1846.

REV. BENJAMIN DOGGETT, OF LANCASTER, VA.

SIXTH GENERATION.

6168. FANNIE A. DOGGETT[6] (*Hugh S.,*[5] *Sarah M.,*[4] *William,*[3] *William,*[2] *Benjamin*[1]), born Fredericksburg, Va., December, 1848; resides Fredericksburg, Va. (1893); married Fredericksburg, Va., April 4, 1867, by Dr. Thomas S. Dunaway, to William Scott, son of John Scott; born Rappahannock, Va., June 10, 1838.

Issue:

6229. i.   ANNIE HUGH SCOTT,[7] born Fredericksburg, Va., July 11, 1868; married Fredericksburg, Va., June 27, 1889, Thomas Norman Cunningham, son of Thomas N. and Lizzie (Hume) Cunningham; born 1861; resides Fredericksburg, Va. (1893).
6230. ii. JOHN HUGH SCOTT,[7] born Fredericksburg, Va., April 12, 1871; died Fredericksburg, Va., May 7, 1873.
6231. iii. HUGH DOGGETT SCOTT,[7] born Fredericksburg, Va., Sept. 17, 1873.
6232. iv. DAVID WILLIAM SCOTT,[7] born Fredericksburg, Va., April 19, 1876.
6233. v.   SIDNEY L. SCOTT,[7] born Fredericksburg, Va., April 14, 1879.
6234. vi. CA LEE SCOTT,[7] born Fredericksburg, Va., May 6, 1881.
6235. vii. MALLER MARVIN SCOTT,[7] born Fredericksburg, Va., June 24, 1883; died Fredericksburg, Va., April 19, 1886.
6236. viii. HARRY BISSETT SCOTT,[7] born Fredericksburg, Va., June 16, 1885; died Fredericksburg, Va., June 12, 1887.
6237. ix. GEORGE ARMSTEAD SCOTT,[7] born Fredericksburg, Va., Sept. 1, 1887.

6173. IWANONA ADELINE SIMMONDS[6] (*Olivia A. Doggett,*[5] *Sarah M.,*[4] *William,*[3] *William,*[2] *Benjamin*[1]), born Lancaster county, Va., Dec. 17, 1844; resides Petersburg, Va. (1893); married Lancaster county, Va., August 12, 1868, Spencer Vaughan, of Petersburg.

Issue:

6238. i.   ROSA VAUGHAN.[7]
6239. ii. DAISY VAUGHAN.[7]
6240. iii. CARRIE VAUGHAN.[7]
6241. iv. NELLIE VAUGHAN.[7]
6242. v.   INES VAUGHAN.[7]
6243. vi. JAMES VAUGHAN.[7]

6174. ULRICA OLIVIA SIMMONDS[6] (*Olivia A. Doggett,*[5] *Sarah M.,*[4] *William,*[3] *William,*[2] *Benjamin*[1]), born Lancaster county, Va., Oct. 25, 1847; died Charlotteville, Va., Dec. 20, 1892; married Lancaster county, Va. May 21, 1873, John M. Godwin, of Charlottesville, Va.

Issue:

6244. i.   Son GODWIN,[7] died.
6245. ii. ANNIE GODWIN.[7]
6246. iii. NETTIE GODWIN.[7]

6175. FANNIE FLOWERS SIMMONDS[6] (*Olivia A. Doggett,*[5] *Sarah M.,*[4] *William,*[3] *William,*[2] *Benjamin*[1]), born Lancaster Co., Va.,

Oct. 15, 1851; resides Chase's Wharf, Lancaster Co., Va. (1893); married Lancaster county, Va., Aug. 7, 1879, William H. Flowers.

Issue:

6247. i. JOSEPHINE FLOWERS.[7]
6248. ii. GRACE FLOWERS.[7]
6249. iii. ANNIE FLOWERS.[7]

6177. JAMES OSCAR BURTON SIMMONDS [6] (*Olivia A. Doggett,*[5] *Sarah M.,*[4] *William,*[3] *William,*[2] *Benjamin* [1]), born Lancaster county, Va., Feb. 20, 1859; resides Lancaster Court House, Va. (1893); married Lancaster county, Va., Sept 9, 1886, Mary Alice Robinson.

Issue:

6250. i. JAMES HENRY ROBINSON SIMMONDS,[7] born June 17, 1887.
6251. ii. SIDNEY GORDON SIMMONDS.[7]

6179. JAMES LEMUEL DOGGETT [6] (*Lee Roy B.,*[5] *Sarah M.,*[4] *William,*[3] *William,*[2] *Benjamin* [1]), born Fredericksburg, Va., March 6, 1848; resides McKinney, Colin Co., Tex. (1893); married Caroline county, Va., August 17, 1876, Bettie Burruss Wright, daughter of James D. and Susan (Burruss) Wright.

Issue:

6252. i. LUCY FRANCES DOGGETT,[7] born McKinney, Tex.
6253. ii. EDWIN BURRUSS DOGGETT.[7] born McKinney, Tex.
6254. iii. SARA DURRETT DOGGETT,[7] born McKinney, Tex.
6255. iv. ELIZABETH DOGGETT,[7] born McKinney, Tex.
6256. v. RACHEL DOGGETT,[7] born McKinney, Tex.

Mr. Doggett graduated at the University of Virginia; resides at McKinney, where he is a lawyer; has been mayor and member of the Legislature.

6181. Dr. ANDREW CAPEN DOGGETT [6] (*Lee Roy B.,*[5] *Sarah M.,*[4] *William,*[3] *William,*[2] *Benjamin* [1]), born Fredericksburg, Va., September 20, 1852; resides Fredericksburg, Va. (1893); married Petersburg, Va., March 30, 1880, Sarah Rebekah Doggett, daughter of George Flowers and Virginia S. F. (Hughes [Boisseau]) Doggett (No. 6189); born Hessee Castle, Northampton Co., Va., September 1, 1860; died Fredericksburg, Va., March 15, 1893.

Issue:

6257. i. KATE NEWELL DOGGETT,[7] born Fredericksburg, Va., April 15, 1881.

Dr. A. C. Doggett graduated at the University of Virginia, and completed his education as a physician at the Bellevue College and Hospital in New York city.

"Mrs. Doggett had great musical talent. Her summers were for the most part spent at the White Sulphur Springs, West Va., and there she formed friends from nearly every part of the country. There she could call from five hundred to a thousand people together at will to hear the music from her lips.

"Her voice, a strong, clear contralto, reached into one's heart, and stirred the best impulses and awakened the best emotions.

> "'We heard far off the siren's song,
> We caught the gleam of sea-maid hair;
> The glimmering isles and rocks among,
> We moved through sparkling purple air.'

"Mrs. Doggett was gifted with rare beauty, her disposition very attractive, as happy as a child, and filled with bright sunshine which she lavishly scattered everywhere. Mrs. Doggett was confirmed in St. Paul's Episcopal Church, Petersburg, just before her twelfth birthday, and was known for her devotion to her church and for her many acts of kindness to those in need."

6193. NANCY DOGGETT[6] (*Sarah,*[5] *John,*[4] *Coleman,*[3] *William,*[2] *Benjamin*[1]), married Lancaster county, Va., Warner Lunsford.

Issue :

6258. i. LEMUEL L. LUNSFORD,[7] died without issue.
6259. ii. SARAH LUNSFORD,[7] married Robert Perceful; had daughter Roberta,[8] who married Landon Treakle ; issue : two or three children.

6203. REV. ROWLAND DOGGETT[6] (*Cyrus,*[5] *John,*[4] *Coleman,*[3] *William,*[2] *Benjamin*[1]), born Lancaster county, Va., October 31, 1831 ; resides Suffolk, Va. (1892) ; married 1st, Norfolk, Va., August 7, 1856, Martha Rebecca Olivia Portlock, daughter of William and Sophia (Nash) Portlock ; born Norfolk county, Va., 1832 ; died Fairview, Mo., December 7, 1870 ; married 2d, Brunswick, Mo., July 26, 1877, Mattie A. Woods, daughter of James and Mildred Ann Perkins (Jones) Woods, of Albemarle county, Va. ; born Albemarle county, Va., June 19, 1839.

Issue :

6260. i. AURELIUS DOGGETT,[7] born Churchland, Va., October 4, 1859.
6261. ii. BETTIE LARKEY DOGGETT,[7] born Oak Forest, Va., August 7, 1861 ; died Suffolk, Va., May 24, 1889.
6262. iii. LALLA LEIGH DOGGETT,[7] born Oak Forest, Va., June 1, 1863.
6263. iv. ROBERT LEE DOGGETT,[7] born Palmyra, Va., July 15, 1865 ; died Fincastle, Va., October 9, 1887.
6264. v. SALLIE ROUTH DOGGETT,[7] born Lisbon, Va., April 9, 1867 ; resides Suffolk, Va. (1892).

6205. DR. JOHN LARKEY DOGGETT[6] (*Cyrus,*[5] *John,*[4] *Coleman,*[3] *William,*[2] *Benjamin*[1]), born Lancaster county, Va., July 23, 1835 ; "dentist ; " resides Bedford City, Va. (1892) ; married Junction Stores, Va., May 10, 1867, Octavia Mays, daughter of Fletcher H. and Mary Lewis (Jones) Mays ; born Botetourt county, Va., July 24, 1843.

Issue :

6265. i. MARY MAYS DOGGETT,[7] born Junction Stores, Va., May 10, 1869 ; died Fincastle, Va., October 9, 1882

6266. ii. FLORENCE HUTT DOGGETT,[7] born Troy, Mo., May 1, 1871.
6267. iii. OCTAVIA MAYS DOGGETT,[7] born Miami, Mo., September 19, 1872.

6207. Dr. CYRUS DOGGETT [6] (*Cyrus,*[5] *John,*[4] *Coleman,*[3] *William,*[2] *Benjamin* [1]), born Lancaster county, Va., September 18, 1838; "physician;" resides Fincastle, Va. (1892); married Junction Stores, Va., Jan. 16, 1866, Isabella Ellen Mays, daughter of Fletcher H. and Ellen (Ferguson) Mays; born Fincastle Va., June, 1838.

Issue:

6268. i. FLETCHER MAYS DOGGETT,[7] born Junction Stores, Va., December 16, 1866; died Fincastle, Va., December 8, 1890.
6269. ii. BESSIE EWING DOGGETT,[7] born Junction Stores, Va., September 11, 1868; died August 24, 1870.
6270. iii. FRANK GRANT DOGGETT,[7] born Moberly, Mo., July 3, 1871; resides New Orleans, La. (1892).
6271. iv. NELLIE BELLE DOGGETT,[7] born Fincastle, Va., August 2, 1878; died fall of 1888.

6209. ROBERT EMORY DOGGETT [6] (*Cyrus,*[5] *John,*[4] *Coleman,*[3] *William,*[2] *Benjamin* [1]), born Lancaster county, Va., February 28, 1845; "lawyer;" resides Russellville, Ark. (1892); married Wright City, Mo., March 10, 1869, Ella Pendleton, of Wright City, Mo.; born Warren county, Mo.

Issue:

6272. i. MYRA DOGGETT,[7] born December 24, 1869; married Horace Bradley, December 24, 1888; issue: two sons (1892).
6273. ii. ETHEL DOGGETT,[7] born May 19, 1881.
6274. iii. ROBERT EMORY DOGGETT,[7] born Russellville, Mo., June, 1887.

6212. DAVID SETH DOGGETT [6] (*David S.,*[5] *John,*[4] *Coleman,*[3] *William,*[2] *Benjamin* [1]), resides 317 East Franklin street, Richmond, Va. (1892); married Annie Curtiss Jones.

Issue:

6275. i. ANNIE CURTISS DOGGETT.[7]

6214. GEORGE BROOKE DOGGETT [6] (*David S.,*[5] *John,*[4] *Coleman,*[3] *William,*[2] *Benjamin* [1]), born Lynchburg, Va., Oct. 30, 1847; resides Park avenue and Lombardy street, Richmond, Va. (1892); married " Oak Grove " farm, Essex Co., Va., Aug. 13, 1890, by Rev. Dr. McDonnall, to Georgia Anderson, daughter of William H. and Sarah (Keeser) Anderson; born Oak Grove, Essex Co., Va., March 12, 1859.

Issue:

6276. i. Son DOGGETT,[7] born May 21, 1891; died May 21, 1891.

6217. WILLIAM DOGGETT [6] (*William,*[5] *William,*[4] *Coleman,*[3] *William,*[2] *Benjamin* [1]), born Gloucester, Mass., Oct. 16, 1817; " mariner; " " fisherman ; " died Gloucester, Mass., Aug. 16, 1872;

married Judith Robinson, daughter of Daniel and Judith Robinson; born Gloucester, Mass., 1816; died Gloucester, Mass., Feb. 14, 1879.

Issue:

6277. i.   MARY ELLA DOGGETT,[7] born Gloucester, Mass., 1839; married Gloucester, Mass., December 9, 1856, by Nathaniel Richardson, to William A. Ryder, son of William and Frances Ryder; "mariner;" born New York, 1835.

6278. ii. HARRIET DOGGETT,[7] born Gloucester, Mass., 1843; married Gloucester, Mass., August 8, 1864, by Rev. S. Chapin, to Fitz Edward Elwell, son of Fitz W. and Caroline (Robinson) Elwell; born Gloucester, Mass., 1838; "fisherman."

6279. iii. GEORGE W. DOGGETT,[7] born Gloucester, Mass., November 1, 1843.

6280. iv. ABBA JANE DOGGETT,[7] born Gloucester, Mass., Nov. 16, 1845; died.

6281. v.   Daughter DOGGETT,[7] born Gloucester, Mass., June 15, 1846.

6282. vi. EMILY DOGGETT,[7] born Gloucester, Mass., August 4, 1849; married Rockport, Mass., March 30, 1868, by Rev. Lewis Holmes, to Abram O. Lane, son of Cyrus and Sarah Lane; "fisherman;" born Gloucester, Mass., 1843.

6283. vii. WARREN E. DOGGETT,[7] born Gloucester, Mass., June 6, 1851.

6220.   JOHN DOGGETT [6] (*William*,[5] *William*,[4] *Coleman*,[3] *William*,[2] *Benjamin* [1]), born Gloucester, Mass., 1828; "quarryman;" resides 646 Washington street, Bayview, Gloucester, Mass. (1892); married Gloucester, Mass., September 7, 1865, by Rev. W. F. LaCount, to Charlotte A. Riggs, daughter of James and Almira Riggs; born Gloucester, Mass.. 1843.

Issue:

6284. i.   LYDIA ANN DOGGETT,[7] born Gloucester, Mass., March 21, 1868; married 1892, Frank Sylvester; resides Riverdale, Mass. (1893).

6221.   ELIAS DOGGETT [6] (*William*,[5] *William*,[4] *Coleman*,[3] *William*,[2] *Benjamin* [1]), born Gloucester, Mass., 1829; "mariner;" "laborer;" resides 22 Gee avenue, Riverdale, Gloucester, Mass. (1892); married Gloucester, Mass., August 14, 1853, by Rev. E. W. Coffin, to Catherine Lewis, widow, and daughter of Nehemiah and Catherine Stanwood; born Gloucester, Mass., 1828.

Issue:

6285. i.   HENRIETTA DOGGETT,[7] born Gloucester, Mass., May 6, 1854; married Francis Tucker; issue: 6 children; resides Riverdale, Mass. (1893).

6286. ii. ADALINE P. DOGGETT,[7] born Gloucester, Mass., November 23, 1856; died Gloucester, Mass., December 10, 1863.

6287. iii. CAROLINE AMANDA DOGGETT,[7] born Gloucester, Mass., March 10, 1861; died Gloucester, Mass., February 9, 1864.

6288. iv. CHARLES DOGGETT,[7] "contractor;" married Jennie —— ; issue: three children; resides Gloucester, Mass. (1893).

6289. v.   EVERETT DOGGETT,[7] "butcher;" resides Gloucester, Mass. (1893).

6223.   LYDIA ANN DOGGETT [6] (*William*,[5] *William*,[4] *Coleman*,[3] *William*,[2] *Benjamin* [1]), born Gloucester, Mass., 1832; resides 146 Leonard street, Annisquam, Gloucester, Mass. (1893); married Gloucester, Mass., November 10, 1853, by Rev. A. D. Mayo, to

Warren Harvey, son of Joseph and Nancy Harvey; " farmer;" born Gloucester, Mass., 1832.

Issue:

6290. i.   GEORGE HARVEY,[7] "stock-raiser;" resides Amherst, N.H. (1893).
6291. ii.   CAROLINE HARVEY,[7] married Alden Kilpatrick; issue: Sydney,[8] Essie;[8] resides Annisquam, Mass. (1893).
6292. iii. CHARLES HARVEY,[7] " stable-keeper;" resides Lanesville, Mass. (1893).
6293. iv.   SYDNEY HARVEY,[7] married Miss Charde; " stable-keeper;" issue: one child; resides Lanesville, Mass. (1893).
6294. v.   FRANK HARVEY,[7] married; "teamster;" issue: one child (1892); resides Annisquam, Mass. (1893).

6224. HENRY DOGGETT[6] (*William*,[5] *William*,[4] *Coleman*,[3] *William*,[2] *Benjamin*[1]), born Gloucester, Mass., May 12, 1835; " United States soldier;" "freighter;" resides Rockport, Mass. (1892); married Gloucester, Mass., December 11, 1857, by Nathaniel Richardson, to Emily Richardson Grimes, daughter of Thomas and Tammy (Davis) Grimes; born Rockport, Mass., December 20, 1841.

Issue:

6295. i.   THOMAS GRIMES DOGGETT,[7] born Rockport, Mass., August 20, 1858.
6296. ii.   JOHN HENRY DOGGETT,[7] born Rockport, Mass., July 16, 1861; resides there (1892).
6297. iii. EMMA FRANCES DOGGETT,[7] born Rockport, Mass., January 20, 1864; died Rockport, Mass., October 23, 1880.
6298. iv.   CARRIE MARIA DOGGETT,[7] born Rockport, Mass., November 19, 1868.
6299. v.   WILLIAM CHESTER DOGGETT,[7] born Rockport, Mass., October 16, 1871; married Ida Phillips; issue: Fred Osborn Doggett;[8] resides Rockport, Mass. (1893).
6300. vi.   FRED ELMER DOGGETT,[7] born Rockport, Mass., September 27, 1875; resides there (1892).
6301. vii. EMMA FRANCES DOGGETT,[7] born Rockport, Mass., November 4, 1880; resides there (1892).
6302. viii. EFFIE JANE DOGGETT,[7] born Rockport, Mass., October 29, 1882; resides there (1892).

6228. HANNAH MORRIS DOGGETT[6] (*William*,[5] *William*,[4] *Coleman*,[3] *William*,[2] *Benjamin*[1]), born Gloucester, Mass., 1846; resides Lanesville, Gloucester, Mass. (1892); married Gloucester, Mass., November 28, 1868, by Rev. W. H. Pierson, to Charles Morris, of Gloucester, son of William and Elizabeth Morris; " stone-cutter;" born Mount Sorrel, Eng., 1833.

Issue: thirteen children.

6303. i. Son MORRIS,[7] born Gloucester, Mass., November 25, 1875.

REV. BENJAMIN DOGGETT, OF LANCASTER, VA.

SEVENTH GENERATION.

6260. AURELIUS DOGGETT [7] (*Rowland,*[6] *Cyrus,*[5] *John,*[4] *Coleman,*[3] *William,*[2] *Benjamin* [1]), born Churchland, Va., October 4, 1859; resides 1317 East Twenty-second street, Kansas City, Mo. (1892); married Carrollton, Mo., March 23, 1886, Caroline Reid, widow of William Reid, and daughter of John Shoupe; born Harrisonburg, Rockingham Co., Va.

Issue:

6304. i. PATTIE VIRGINIA DOGGETT,[8] born March 26, 1887.
6305. ii. ROBERT SHOUPE DOGGETT,[8] died December, 1888.

6262. LALLA LEIGH DOGGETT [7] (*Rowland,*[6] *Cyrus,*[5] *John,*[4] *Coleman,*[3] *William,*[2] *Benjamin* [1]), born Oak Forest, Va., June 1, 1863; resides Dardanelle, Ark. (1892); married Dardanelle, Ark., November 16, 1882, Rufus H. Howell; born Dardanelle, Ark.

Issue:

6306. i. ELLENE HOWELL,[8] born Dardanelle, Ark., August 26, 1883.
6307. ii. ANNIE DOGGETT HOWELL,[8] born October 14, 1888; died Dec. 29, 1889.
6308. iii. BETTIE LEE HOWELL,[8] born December 26, 1890.

6279. GEORGE W. DOGGETT [7] (*William,*[6] *William,*[5] *William,*[4] *Coleman,*[3] *William,*[2] *Benjamin* [1]), born Gloucester, Mass., November 1, 1843; "fisherman;" "paving-cutter;" resides 4 Albion court, Gloucester, Mass. (1892); married Gloucester, Mass., January 1, 1873, by Rev. William Hooper, to Susan Elwell, daughter of Fitz W. and Caroline (Robinson) Elwell; born Gloucester, Mass., 1836.

Issue:

6309. i. GEORGIANA DOGGETT,[8] born Gloucester, Mass., June 26, 1874.
6310. ii. DAISY F. DOGGETT,[8] born Gloucester, Mass., April 13, 1880.

6295. THOMAS GRIMES DOGGETT [7] (*Henry,*[6] *William,*[5] *William,*[4] *Coleman,*[3] *William,*[2] *Benjamin* [1]), born Rockport, Mass., August 20, 1858; "machinist;" resides Damon street, Readville, Mass. (1893); married Hyde Park, Mass., Dec. 21, 1882, by Rev. Jesse Wagner, to Harriet Emma Stevens, of Hyde Park, daughter of John P. and Mary Elizabeth (Fuller) Stevens; born Whitam, Eng., Dec. 26, 1858.

Issue:

6311. i. JULIA EMMA DOGGETT,[8] born Hyde Park, Mass., April 20, 1884.

6298. CARRIE MARIA DOGGETT [7] (*Henry,*[6] *William,*[5] *William,*[4] *Coleman,*[3] *William,*[2] *Benjamin* [1]), born Rockport, Mass., November 19, 1868; resides Rockport, Mass. (1892); married Rockport, Mass.,

November 16, 1884, by Calvin W. Pool, J.P., to James Allen, of Rockport, son of William and Laura (Kimball) Allen; " fisherman ; " " stone-cutter ; " born North Berwick, Me., December 14, 1862.

Issue :

6312. i.   JAMES ELMER ALLEN,[8] born Rockport, Mass., February 3, 1885.
6313. ii. IDA LAVINIA ALLEN,[8] born Rockport, Mass., November 28, 1886.
6314. iii. WILLIE CHESTOM ALLEN,[8] born Rockport, Mass., January 3, 1888.
6315. iv. ERNEST LOYD ALLEN,[8] born Rockport, Mass., December 17, 1891.

PROBABLY DESCENDED FROM REV. BENJAMIN DOGGETT, OF LANCASTER, VA.

Issue :

6316. i. THOMAS DOGGETT,[2] born Lancaster county, Va.
6317. ii. ELMORE DOGGETT,[2] born Lancaster county, Va.

6316.   THOMAS DOGGETT,[2] born Lancaster county, Va. ; married.
Issue :

6318. i.   REUBEN DOGGETT,[3] born Lancaster county, Va., 1739.
6319. ii.   THOMAS DOGGETT.[3]
6320. iii. GEORGE DOGGETT.[3]
6321. iv.   BENJAMIN DOGGETT.[3]
6322. v.   WILLIAM DOGGETT.[3]
6323. vi.   PRESLEY DOGGETT.[3]
6324. vii. JOHN DOGGETT.[3]
6325. viii. JAMES DOGGETT.[3]
            And eight daughters.

6317.   ELMORE DOGGETT,[2] born Lancaster county, Va. ; married.
Issue :

6326. i. JOHN DOGGETT.[3]
6327. ii. WILLIAM DOGGETT.[3]

April 14, 1777.   Elmore Doggett, of Christ Church, gives son John Doggett one hundred and sixty acres land. [Lancaster Deeds, 19–174.]

October 21, 1779.   Indenture between Elmore Doggett, of County Lancaster, and William Doggett, son of said Elmore Doggett, on account of love and fatherly affection, gives him land. [Lancaster Deeds, 19–212.]

6318.   REUBEN DOGGETT[3] (*Thomas*[2]), born Lancaster county, Va., 1739 ; died Virginia, 1826 ; married Mary Browne.
Issue :

6328. i.   THOMAS DOGGETT,[4] born Virginia.
6329. ii. REUBEN DOGGETT,[4] married and had issue ; died Virginia.
6330. iii. DANIEL BROWN DOGGETT,[4] born Virginia, September 13, 1787.
6331. iv. BENJAMIN F. DOGGETT,[4] born Culpeper county, Va., Aug. 4, 1790.
6332. v.   GEORGE ROSWELL DOGGETT,[4] born Virginia.
6333. vi. NELLIE DOGGETT,[4] married Daniel Johnson, Harper's Ferry, Va. ;
           issue : Gen. Joe E. Johnson.

6334. vii. Daughter Doggett,[4] married Mr. Stypes; lived near Harper's Ferry.
6335. viii. Daughter Doggett,[4] married Philip Cook; removed to Nicholasville, Jessamine Co., Ky.

6319. Thomas Doggett[3] (*Thomas*[2]), enlisted and died in the army; married Nancy Browne.

Issue:

    i. Armstead Doggett,[4] "colonel."
    ii. George Doggett,[4] "captain."
    iii. William Doggett.[4]
    iv. Lucy Doggett.[4]

6328. Thomas Doggett[4] (*Reuben*,[3] *Thomas*[2]), born Virginia; died Culpeper county, Va., about 1826 or 1827; married ——; she removed to Warren county, Ohio, with her family, about 1828.

Issue:

6336. i. Reuben Doggett,[5] born Culpeper county, Va.
6337. ii. Daniel Doggett,[5] born Culpeper county, Va.
6338. iii. Thomas Doggett,[5] born Culpeper county, Va.
    iv. Susan Doggett,[5] born Culpeper county, Va.
    v. Alziah Doggett,[5] born Culpeper county, Va.
    vi. Julia Ann Doggett,[5] born Culpeper county, Va.
    vii. Sarah Doggett,[5] born Culpeper county, Va.
    viii. Mary Doggett,[5] born Culpeper county, Va.

6330. Daniel Brown Doggett[4] (*Reuben*,[3] *Thomas*[2]), born Virginia, September 13, 1787; married Virginia, Catharine Brimmer; born 1780; died Hawkins county, Tenn.

Issue:

6339. i. Alexander Doggett,[5] born Virginia, July 18, 1808.
6340. ii. Susan Doggett,[5] born Virginia, 1810; married Sullivan county, Tenn., James Anderson; born Sullivan county, Tenn.; he died California, Mo.; issue: several children.
6341. iii. Edwin Doggett,[5] born Virginia, August 31, 1812.
6342. iv. Phinella Doggett,[5] born Virginia, August 31, 1312; married Samuel Crawford; issue: a large family; he born Sullivan county, Tenn.; died Moniteau county, Mo.; she resides California, Mo. (1892).
6343. v. Mary Doggett,[5] born Virginia, 1814.
6344. vi. Marshall Wellington Doggett,[5] born Virginia, March 31, 1816.
6345. vii. Arthur Jackson Doggett,[5] born Culpeper county, Va., July 18, 1820.

6331. Capt. Benjamin F. Doggett[4] (*Reuben*,[3] *Thomas*[2]), born Culpeper county, Va., August 4, 1790; died near Tranquility, Ohio, May 1, 1885; married Stafford county, Va., July 20, 1809, Polly Brimmer, daughter of John Brimmer; born Stafford county, Va.; died Winchester, Ohio, April 20, 1863.

Issue:

6346. i. Richard Doggett,[5] born Virginia, 1810.
6347. ii. Ellen Doggett,[5] born Virginia, 1811; married Madison county, Va., 1832, Alfred R. Skinner.
6348. iii. George W. Doggett,[5] born Virginia, October 8, 1813; married Hillsboro', Ohio, January 28, 1836, Sarah Ann Gossett; resides Tranquility, Ohio (1893).

6349. iv.   MARY DOGGETT,[5] born Virginia, 1816; married Winchester, Ohio,
                1846, David Young.
6350. v.   BENJAMIN DOGGETT,[5] born Virginia, 1818; died Hillsboro', Ohio, 1835.
6351. vi.   REUBEN DOGGETT,[5] born Virginia, 1822; married Youngsville, Ohio,
                about 1851, Mary Hays; died Missouri; buried Chillicothe.
6352. vii.   THOMAS DOGGETT,[5] born Virginia, 1828; died Winchester, Ohio,
                October, 1848.

Benjamin F. Doggett was at different times deputy sheriff of
Adams county, Ohio, captain of militia, etc.

6332.   GEORGE ROSWELL DOGGETT [4] (*Reuben,*[3] *Thomas*[2]), born
Virginia; removed to Clinton county, Ohio; married.
   Issue:

     i.   AGNES DOGGETT,[5] married George Johnson; resides Sabina, Ohio (1893).
     ii. ELLEN DOGGETT,[5] married Robert Snow; both deceased.
     iii. SARAH DOGGETT,[5] died.
     iv. BENJAMIN ROSWELL DOGGETT,[5] died young.
     v.   WESLEY DOGGETT,[5] died in Indiana.
     vi. GEORGE DOGGETT,[5] resided in Clinton county, Ohio.

6339.   ALEXANDER DOGGETT [5] (*Daniel B.,*[4] *Reuben,*[3] *Thomas*[2]),
born Virginia, July 18, 1808; died ——; married 1st, Sullivan
county, Tenn., October 6, 1830, Jane Rhea; married 2d, ——.
   Issue: three by 1st, two by 2d.

6353. i.   JOSEPH DOGGETT.[6]
6354. ii.   WILLIAM DOGGETT.[6]
6355. iii. CATHARINE DOGGETT.[6]
6356. iv.   SMITH DOGGETT.[6]
6357. v.   SUSAN DOGGETT.[6]

6341.   EDWIN DOGGETT [5] (*Daniel B.,*[4] *Reuben,*[3] *Thomas*[2]), born
Virginia, August 31, 1812; died California, Mo.. ——; married Miss
Eads; died California, Mo.
   Issue:

6358. i.   HESTER DOGGETT,[6] married Mr. Gladson.
6359. ii.   WILLIAM DOGGETT,[6] became blind when a boy.
6360. iii. MOLLIE DOGGETT,[6] married Mr. Job.

6343.   MARY DOGGETT [5] (*Daniel B.,*[4] *Reuben,*[3] *Thomas*[2]), born
Virginia, 1814; resides Pinckneyville, Ill. (1892); married Sullivan
county, Tenn., William Lindsey Gladson.
   Issue:

6361. i.   WILLIAM GLADSON,[6] married.
6362. ii.   DANIEL GLADSON,[6] married.
6363. iii. BROWN GLADSON,[6] married.
6364. iv.   MARY KATE GLADSON,[6] married Frank Cloud; resides Perry county,
                Mo. (1892).

6344.   MARSHALL WELLINGTON DOGGETT [5] (*Daniel B.,*[4] *Reuben,*[3]
Thomas[2]), born Virginia, March 31, 1816; resides Green Ridge,

Mo. (1892); married Sullivan county, Tenn., Caroline Steel; born Sullivan county, Tenn.

Issue:

6365. i.   MARY CATHARINE DOGGETT,[6] married Noah Minter.
6366. ii. SARAH A. DOGGETT,[6] married James H. Brim.
6367. iii. ARTHUR JACKSON DOGGETT.[6]
6368. iv. MATTIE E. DOGGETT,[6] married Samuel Aldridge.
6369. v.   ANNA BELL DOGGETT,[6] married Cumberland Dodd.
6370. vi. EDWIN H. DOGGETT.[6]
6371. vii. HARVEY S. DOGGETT.[6]

6345. ARTHUR JACKSON DOGGETT[5] (*Daniel B.,*[4] *Reuben,*[3] *Thomas*[2]), born Culpeper county, Va., July 18, 1820; died Morell's Mill, Tenn., July 12, 1887; married Morell's Mill, Tenn., October 6, 1842, Eliza Jane Drake, daughter of Jacob and —— (Foust) Drake; born Sullivan county, Tenn., September 5, 1822.

Issue:

6372. i.   JAMES POLK DOGGETT,[6] born Sullivan county, Tenn., Jan. 4, 1844.
6373. ii. JOHN HARR DOGGETT,[6] born Sullivan county, Tenn., December 10, 1850; married White Store, Tenn., August 18, 1891, Josie Latture, daughter of Samuel and —— (Jones) Latture; resides Morell's Mill, Tenn. (1892).
6374. iii. MARSHALL WELLINGTON DOGGETT,[6] born Sullivan county, Tenn., April 14, 1855.
6375. iv. REBECCA JANE DOGGETT,[6] born Sullivan county, Tenn., October 24, 1857; resides Marietta, Ga. (1892).
6376. v.   LIZZIE MALVINA DOGGETT,[6] born Sullivan county, Tenn., May 18, 1860; resides Marietta, Ga. (1892).
6377. vi. SALLIE ELIZA DOGGETT,[6] born Sullivan county, Tenn., September 29, 1862; resides Marietta, Ga. (1892).

6372. Rev. JAMES POLK DOGGETT[6] (*Arthur J.,*[5] *Daniel B.,*[4] *Reuben,*[3] *Thomas*[2]), born Sullivan county, Tenn., January 4, 1844; resides Jonesboro', Tenn. (1892); married Arcadia, Tenn., February 18, 1872, Ellen Anderson Newland, daughter of Joseph and Rebecca Hall (Anderson) Newland; born Sullivan county, Tenn., Oct. 14, 1844.

Issue:

6378. i.   LIDA BEATRICE DOGGETT,[7] born Bristol, Tenn., February 26, 1873.
6379. ii. REBECCA HALL ANDERSON DOGGETT,[7] born Bristol, Tenn., Oct. 6, 1875.
6380. iii. FANNIE LINN DOGGETT,[7] born Bristol, Tenn., April 30, 1877.
6381. iv. JOSEPH NEWLAND DOGGETT,[7] born Bristol, Tenn., May 21, 1879.
6382. v.   MARGARET ELLEN DOGGETT,[7] born Bristol, Tenn., April 16, 1885.

Mr. Doggett was at one time a teacher at Bristol, Tenn.; now (1892) a Presbyterian minister, preaching at Jonesboro'.

6374. Rev. MARSHALL WELLINGTON DOGGETT[6] (*Arthur J.,*[5] *Daniel B.,*[4] *Reuben,*[3] *Thomas*[2]), born Sullivan county, Tenn., April 14, 1855; resides Marietta, Ga. (1892); married Wytheville, Va., June 4, 1887, Berta Carter, daughter of Walter C. and Lucy Ann (Jennings) Carter; born Hillsville, Va., April 11, 1865.

Issue:

6383. i.   ARTHUR JACKSON DOGGETT,[7] born March 22, 1890.
6384. ii. ANNIE HOUSTON DOGGETT,[7] born Marietta, Ga., March 27, 1892.

PROBABLY DESCENDED FROM REV. BENJAMIN DOGGETT, OF LANCASTER, VA.

6385. BENJAMIN DOGGETT,[1] died Mecklenburg county, Va.; married Miss Garner.

Issue:

6386. i.   WILLIAM DOGGETT,[2] born Mecklenburg county, Va.
6387. ii.   GEORGE DOGGETT,[2] born Mecklenburg county, Va.
6388. iii. JOHN DOGGETT,[2] born Mecklenburg county, Va.
6389. iv.   BENJAMIN DOGGETT,[2] born Mecklenburg county, Va.
6390. v.   TAPLEY DOGGETT,[2] born Mecklenburg county, Va.
6391. vi.   LUCY DOGGETT,[2] born Mecklenburg county, Va.
6392. vii. HANNAH DOGGETT,[2] born Mecklenburg county, Va.; married Mr. Gregory.
6393. viii. LEANNAH DOGGETT,[2] born Mecklenburg county, Va.
6394. ix.   BETTIE DOGGETT,[2] born Mecklenburg county, Va.
6395. x.   REBECCA DOGGETT,[2] born Mecklenburg county, Va.; married Thomas Gregory; issue: four children.

6388. JOHN DOGGETT[2] (*Benjamin*[1]), born Mecklenburg county, Va.; died Mecklenburg county, Va., July 7, 1826; married Mildred Clark; died North Carolina.

Issue:

6396. i.   JAMES DOGGETT,[3] born near Clarksville, Va., October 7, 1813.
6397. ii.   GEORGE THOMAS DOGGETT,[3] born Charlotte county, Va., July 21, 1816.
6398. iii. JOHN DOGGETT,[3] born Charlotte county, Va., March 26, 1819.
6399. iv.   REBECCA DOGGETT,[3] born Mecklenburg county, Va.
6400. v.   Infant DOGGETT,[3] born Mecklenburg county, Va.; died.
6401. vi.   Infant DOGGETT,[3] born Mecklenburg county, Va.; died.

6389. BENJAMIN DOGGETT[2] (*Benjamin*[1]), born Mecklenburg county, Va.; married Mary Clark.

Issue:

6402. i.   GRESSETT DOGGETT.[3]
6403. ii.   JORDAN DOGGETT.[3]
6404. iii. WILLIAM DOGGETT.[3]
6405. iv.   DAVID DOGGETT.[3]
6406. v.   EDWIN DOGGETT,[3] married in Virginia, Mrs. Redd; issue: several children; resided Virginia (1888).
6407. vi.   DUREL DOGGETT.[3]
6408. vii. ELIZABETH DOGGETT.[3]
6409. viii. MARTHA DOGGETT.[3]
6410. ix.   JOSEPH DOGGETT.[3]
6411. x.   Son DOGGETT.[3]

6396. JAMES DOGGETT[3] (*John*,[2] *Benjamin*[1]), born near Clarksville, Va., October 7, 1813; moved to North Carolina, 1835; resides Brown's Summit, N.C. (1888); married near Greensboro', N.C., March 17, 1842, by Rev. John Lambeth, to Mary Lambeth, daughter of Joseph and Levina (Flack) Lambeth; born near Greensboro', N.C., September 18, 1822.

Issue:

6412. i.   MARY DOGGETT,[4] born near Brown's Summit, N.C., August 29, 1843.

6413. ii.   AMANDA DOGGETT,[4] born near Brown's Summit, N.C., June 28, 1845.
6414. iii. TAYLOR DOGGETT,[4] born near Brown's Summit, N.C., June 3, 1847;
            died near Brown's Summit, N.C., February 13, 1879.
6415. iv.   C. RUSSELL DOGGETT,[4] born near Brown's Summit, N.C., September
            4, 1849; resides Brown's Summit, N.C. (1888).
6416. v.   WESLEY DOGGETT,[4] born near Brown's Summit, N.C., January 29,
            1852; married Caswell county, N.C., November 28, 1883, Lalula
            Chandler, daughter of William Chandler; born North Carolina,
            1863; resides Brown's Summit, N.C. (1888).
6417. vi.   LIZZIE DOGGETT,[4] born near Brown's Summit, N.C., Oct. 12, 1854.
6418. vii. JOHN DOGGETT,[4] born near Brown's Summit, N.C., January 16, 1857;
            died near Brown's Summit, N.C., October 3, 1883.

6397. GEORGE THOMAS DOGGETT[3] (*John,*[2] *Benjamin*[1]), born
Charlotte county, Va., July 21, 1816; "farmer;" died Hightown,
Miss., 1881; married 1st, Guilford county, N.C., January 10, 1840,
by Rev. William Postley, to Eliza Wharton, daughter of Elisha
Wharton; born Guilford county, N.C., October 18, 1819; died Rock-
ingham county, N.C., October 17, 1853; married 2d, Tishomingo
county, Miss., October 8, 1857, by Rev. Thomas Savage, to Sophia
M. Moses, daughter of Rev. M. F. and Lucinda (Dunlap) Moses;
born Mooresville, Ala., 1838; resides Elmont, Tex. (1889).
  Issue :

6419. i.   JOHN DOGGETT,[4] born Rockingham county, N.C., February 19, 1842.
6420. ii.   MARTHA DOGGETT,[4] born Rockingham county, N.C., July 26, 1844.
6421. iii. NANCY ANN DOGGETT,[4] born Rockingham county, N.C., May 23, 1846.
6422. iv.   WORTH WINFIELD DOGGETT,[4] born Rockingham county, N.C., May
            6, 1848.
6423. v.   CAROLINE DOGGETT,[4] born Rockingham county, N.C., Oct. 5, 1850.
6424. vi.   ELLEN DOGGETT,[4] born Rockingham county, N.C., October 5, 1850;
            married November, 1869, Franklin Thinton; "farmer;" issue:
            five sons, two daughters; resides Corinth, Miss. (1888).
6425. vii. JAMES WILLIAM DOGGETT,[4] born Tishomingo county, Miss., January
            25, 1861.
6426. viii. BAXTER FORREST DOGGETT,[4] born Tishomingo county, Miss., Febru-
            ary 27, 1870; resides Elmont, Tex. (1889).

  George T. Doggett was born in Virginia; removed with his mother
and the others of the family, after the death of his father, to the
State of North Carolina, from whence he removed to Mississippi.
  Mrs. Sophia Doggett married 2d, November 5, 1885, Samuel
Chamber, of Tippah county, Miss. Mr. Chamber died Sept. 10, 1888.

6398. JOHN DOGGETT[3] (*John,*[2] *Benjamin*[1]), born Charlotte
county, Va., March 26, 1819; resides Guilford county, N.C. (1888);
married Guilford county, N.C., March 26, 1845, by Rev. John Lambeth, to Mary Ann Cobb, daughter of Valentine and Betsey (May)
Cobb; born Guilford county, N.C., April 25, 1820.
  Issue :

6427. i.   REBECCA JANE DOGGETT,[4] born Guilford county, N.C., May 31, 1846;
            died Guilford county, N.C., August 31, 1869.
6428. ii.   MARTHA ANN DOGGETT,[4] born Guilford county, N.C., Nov. 10, 1848.
6429. iii. SARAH EMMA DOGGETT,[4] born Guilford county, N.C., April 12, 1851;

married Guilford county, N.C., June 20, 1876, by Rev. J. A. Alexander, to James W. Peay, son of G. W. and Harriet (Wall) Peay; merchant; born Rockingham county, N.C., December 8, 1848; no issue; resides Reidsville, N.C. (1888).

6430. iv. WILLIAM THORINGTON DOGGETT,[4] born Guilford county, N.C., July 7, 1853; married Spiceland, Ind., November 15, 1888, by Rev. I. M. Hughes, D.D., to Sarah Ellen Bogue, daughter of Alfred and Charity (Bogue) Bogue; born Spiceland, Ind., July 31, 1857; "Presbyterian minister;" resides North Danville, Va. (1888).

6431. v. FRANKLIN WELKER DOGGETT,[4] born Guilford county, N.C., January 26, 1857.

6432. vi. THOMAS BADGER DOGGETT,[4] born Guilford county, N.C., April 6, 1859; "railroad agent and telegraph operator;" resides Benaja, N.C. (1888).

6433. vii. JAMES FISHER DOGGETT,[4] born Guilford county, N.C., December 1, 1863; "farmer;" resides Guilford county, N.C. (1888).

John Doggett entered the Confederate army in 1861, as second lieutenant in Captain Scott's company. Having served for an indefinite time, he joined Major Chisman's department at Greensboro', N.C., where he served until the close of the war. Mr. Doggett has since then been a farmer at Brown's Summit, N.C.

6399. REBECCA DOGGETT [3] (*John,*[2] *Benjamin*[1]), born Mecklenburg county, Va.; died Virginia, July, 1845; married 1833, John Lambeth.

Issue:

6434. i. JOSIAH LAMBETH.[4]
6435. ii. WILLIAM LAMBETH.[4]
6436. iii. EDWIN LAMBETH.[4]
6437. iv. ALBERT LAMBETH.[4]
6438. v. HILORY LAMBETH.[4]
6439. vi. JAMES LAMBETH.[4]
6440. vii. JENNINGS LAMBETH.[4]
6441. viii. CORNELIUS LAMBETH.[4]

6403. JORDAN DOGGETT [3] (*Benjamin,*[2] *Benjamin*[1]), born Virginia; resided North Carolina; married 1st, North Carolina, ——; married 2d, North Carolina, ——.

Issue: one by each wife.

6442. i. ADDISON DOGGETT,[4] died.
6443. ii. MARY DOGGETT,[4] married; issue several children (1888).

6412. MARY DOGGETT [4] (*James,*[3] *John,*[2] *Benjamin*[1]), born near Brown's Summit, N.C., August 29, 1843; resides Brown's Summit, N.C. (1888); married near Brown's Summit, N.C., October 18, 1866, Rufus Evans, of Caswell county, N.C.; died soon after marriage.

Issue:

6444. i. IDA EVANS,[5] born Caswell county, N.C., August 24, 1867.

6413. AMANDA DOGGETT [4] (*James,*[3] *John,*[2] *Benjamin*[1]), born near Brown's Summit, N.C., June 28, 1845; resides Monroeton,

N.C. (1888) ; married near Brown's Summit, N.C., February 17, 1880, Thomas W. Hopkins, of Rockingham county, N.C.

Issue :

6445. i. MITTIE HOPKINS,[5] born near Reidsville, N.C., November 28, 1880.
6446. ii. ARTURA HOPKINS,[5] born near Reidsville, N.C., December 1, 1886.

6417. LIZZIE DOGGETT [4] (*James*,[3] *John*,[2] *Benjamin* [1]), born near Brown's Summit, N.C., October 12, 1854 ; resides Kernersville, N.C. (1888) ; married Brown's Summit, N.C., June 5, 1883, Joseph Kerner, of Kernersville, N.C.

Issue :

6447. i. LEGGETT KERNER,[5] born Kernersville, N.C., May 23, 1884.
6448. ii. OSRIC LeVOY KERNER,[5] born Kernersville, N.C., August 21, 1888.

6419. JOHN DOGGETT [4] (*George T.*,[3] *John*,[2] *Benjamin* [1]), born Rockingham county, N.C., February 19, 1842 ; died Franklin, Tenn., —— ; married December 28, 1860, ——.

Issue :

6449. i. JOHN WILLIAM DOGGETT,[5] born Alcorn county, Miss., Nov. 17, 1861.

John Doggett joined the Confederate army, and was killed in a charge on the Federal breastworks at Franklin, Tenn.

6420. MARTHA DOGGETT [4] (*George T.*,[3] *John*,[2] *Benjamin* [1]), born Rockingham county, N.C., July 26, 1844 ; resides Alcorn county, Miss. (1888) ; married Alcorn county, Miss., March 7, 1860, by Rev. H. G. Savage, to Thomas Evans, son of John and Sallie (Anderson) Evans ; born Halifax county, Va., September 23, 1834 ; died Mobile, Ala., April, 1864.

Issue :

6450. i. BENJAMIN FRANKLIN EVANS,[5] born February 6, 1861.
6451. ii. GEORGE WASHINGTON EVANS,[5] born January 15, 1863.

Thomas Evans was a farmer at the commencement of the war. He joined the Confederate army, and was killed near Mobile, Ala.

6421. NANCY ANN DOGGETT [4] (*George T.*,[3] *John*,[2] *Benjamin* [1]), born Rockingham county, N.C., May 23, 1846 ; resides Keeter, Tex. (1888) ; married Rienzi, Miss., February 12, 1867, by Rev. H. G. Savage, to William Wilkinson, son of John R. and Sarah C. (Wilkinson) Wilkinson ; born Booneville, Miss., April 21, 1844.

Issue :

6452. i. COLLIE WILKINSON,[5] born Rienzi, Miss., January 2, 1868.
6453. ii. JOHN T. WILKINSON,[5] born Rienzi, Miss., March 26, 1869 ; died Rienzi, Miss., ——.
6454. iii. WILLIAM WINFIELD WILKINSON,[5] born Booneville, Miss., September 21, 1870; died Booneville, Miss., ——.
6455. iv. JAMES M. WILKINSON,[5] born Rienzi, Miss., December 20, 1871.
6456. v. ALPHEUS FORREST WILKINSON,[5] born Corinth, Miss., Jan. 27, 1874.

6457. vi. MATTIE FRANCES WILKINSON,[5] born Corinth, Miss., March 6, 1876.
6458. vii. CORRENIA SANFORD WILKINSON,[5] born Corinth, Miss., Nov. 25, 1878.
6459. viii. GEORGIA CILE WILKINSON,[5] born Corinth, Miss., November 11, 1881.
6460. ix. DELONIA WORTEN WILKINSON,[5] born Corinth, Miss., May 22, 1885; died Keeter, Tex., ——.
6461. x. KEESIE WILKINSON,[5] born Keeter, Tex., November 5, 1886.

Mr. William Wilkinson served as a private in the Confederate army from 1861 to April 24, 1865.

6422. WORTH WINFIELD DOGGETT[4] (*George T.,*[3] *John,*[2] *Benjamin*[1]), born Rockingham county, N.C., May 6, 1848; resides Ravenna, Tex. (1888); married Fannin county, Tex., Dec. 23, 1875, by William Anderson, to Mary Lizzie Corzina, daughter of W. R. and S. A. (Anderson) Corzina; born Hunt county, Tex., Jan. 11, 1859.
Issue:

6462. i. WILLIAM WORTH DOGGETT,[5] born Fannin county, Tex., Oct. 7, 1876.
6463. ii. THOMAS EDWIN DOGGETT,[5] born Fannin county, Tex., Oct. 5, 1878; died Fannin county, Tex., September 13, 1880.
6464. iii. SALLIE EVA DOGGETT,[5] born Fannin county, Tex., June 2, 1880.
6465. iv. JOEL DOGGETT,[5] born Fannin county, Tex., March 21, 1882.
6466. v. FANNIE DOGGETT,[5] born Fannin county, Tex., March 20, 1884.
6467. vi. JOHN WINFIELD DOGGETT,[5] born Fannin county, Tex., Dec. 21, 1886.

6423. CAROLINE DOGGETT[4] (*George T.,*[3] *John,*[2] *Benjamin*[1]), born Rockingham county, N.C., October 5, 1850; resides Kossuth, Alcorn Co., Miss. (1888); married Alcorn county, Miss., August 26, 1868, by Rev. M. F. Moses, to James Melvin, son of Elis and Neonia (Cook) Melvin; born Guilford county, N.C., Aug. 7, 1832.
Issue:

6468. i. EDDIE ROSALIE MELVIN,[5] born Alcorn county, Miss., Oct. 10, 1869.
6469. ii. MITTIE MINER MELVIN,[5] born Alcorn county, Miss., July 4, 1871.
6470. iii. THEODOSIA MELVIN,[5] born Alcorn county, Miss., May 21, 1873.
6471. iv. ANNA FLORENCE MELVIN,[5] born Alcorn county, Miss., Aug. 1, 1875.
6472. v. JAMES ELIS MELVIN,[5] born Alcorn county, Miss., October 7, 1877.
6473. vi. WILLIAM THOMAS MELVIN,[5] born Alcorn county, Miss., Nov. 2, 1881.

James Melvin served four years in the Confederate army. He is a farmer in Alcorn county, Miss.

6425. JAMES WILLIAM DOGGETT[4] (*George T.,*[3] *John,*[2] *Benjamin*[1]), born Tishomingo county, Miss., January 25, 1861; "farmer;" resides Elmont, Tex. (1888); married Alcorn county, Miss., November 1, 1882, by Rev. G. Savage, to Fannie Parish, daughter of William and Catherine (Savage) Parish; born Tishomingo county, Miss., November 1, 1863.
Issue:

6474. i. WILLIAM THOMAS DOGGETT,[5] born Grayson county, Tex., Aug. 8, 1883.
6475. ii. JAMES DOGGETT,[5] born Grayson county, Tex., August 8, 1885.
6476. iii. AGNES GERTRUDE DOGGETT,[5] born Grayson county, Tex., Jan. 29, 1888.

6428. MARTHA ANN DOGGETT[4] (*John,*[3] *John,*[2] *Benjamin*[1]), born Guilford county, N.C., Nov. 10, 1848; resides Alamance county,

N.C. (1888) ; married Guilford county, N.C., Dec. 12, 1872, by Rev.
J. A. Alexander, to Andrew Summers, son of Peter and Barbara
(Gerringer) Summers; born Guilford county, N.C., Jan. 1, 1835.
Issue :

6477. i. EVERETTE DOGGETT SUMMERS,[5] born Guilford county, N.C., August
30, 1878.
6478. ii. WILLETTA BLANCHE SUMMERS,[5] born Alamance county, N.C., May 28,
1881.

Andrew Summers entered the Confederate army in 1861 as third
lieutenant in Captain Scott's company, and came out at the close of
the war with the rank of major. Major Summers is now engaged in
farming.

6431. FRANKLIN WELKER DOGGETT[4] (*John,[3] John,[2] Benjamin[1]*),
born Guilford county, N.C., January 26, 1857; "farmer;" resides
Guilford county, N.C. (1888) ; married Monticello, N.C., February
8, 1881, Mollie Rudd, daughter of Hezekiah and Mary (McKenney)
Rudd ; born Caswell county, N.C., February 26, 1860.
Issue :

6479. i. CARLOS DOGGETT,[5] born Guilford county, N.C., March 9, 1882.
6480. ii. JOHN CLARK DOGGETT,[5] born Guilford county, N.C., Nov. 26, 1883.
6481. iii. OSCAR WILLIAM DOGGETT,[5] born Guilford county, N.C., July 27, 1886.

6449. JOHN WILLIAM DOGGETT[5] (*John,[4] George T.,[3] John,[2] Benjamin[1]*), born Alcorn county, Miss., November 17, 1861; "merchant;" resides Hightown, Miss. (1888) ; married Alcorn county,
Miss., December 6, 1883, by Rev. H. G. Savage, to Lida Armaneila
Hill, daughter of Lanson Alexander and Barbara (Whisunant) Hill;
born York county, S.C., May 24, 1864.
Issue :

6482. i. JOHN JOSEPH DOGGETT,[6] born December 6, 1884.
6483. ii. MARY EFFIE DOGGETT,[6] born November 12, 1886.
6484. iii. ROBERT ALEXANDER DOGGETT,[6] born November 27, 1888.

6450. BENJAMIN FRANKLIN EVANS[5] (*Martha Doggett,[4] George T.,[3]
John,[2] Benjamin[1]*), born February 6, 1861; resides Hightown, Miss.
(1888) ; married December 6, 1882.
Issue :

6485. i. JAMES RUSSELL EVANS,[6] born January 2, 1884.

6451. GEORGE WASHINGTON EVANS[5] (*Martha Doggett,[4] George T.,[3]
John,[2] Benjamin[1]*), born January 15, 1863 ; resides Hightown, Miss.
(1888) ; married December 22, 1886.
Issue :

6486. i. LEWELLA EVANS,[6] born October 7, 1887.

6468. EDDIE ROSALIE MELVIN [5] (*Caroline Doggett,*[4] *George T.,*[3] *John,*[2] *Benjamin*[1]), born Alcorn county, Miss., October 10, 1869; resides Kossuth, Miss. (1888); married January 13, 1887, Mr. Mills.
Issue:
6487. i. ALBERT REED MILLS,[6] born October 26, 1887; died July 25, 1888.

PROBABLY DESCENDED FROM REV. BENJAMIN DOGGETT, OF LANCASTER, VA.

6488. —— DOGGETT,[1] married.
Issue:
6489. i. WILLIAM DOGGETT,[2] born Northumberland county, Va., 1767.
6490. ii. ELIZABETH DOGGETT,[2] died.
6491. iii. Daughter DOGGETT,[2] married Mr. Flint, of Northumberland county, Va.
6492. iv. CLEMENT DOGGETT,[2] died.

Mr. Doggett had a brother George Doggett who was in the navy during the Revolution.

6489. WILLIAM DOGGETT,[2] born Northumberland county, Va., 1767; "ship-master;" died January, 1839; married Elizabeth Totterdell, of Norfolk county, Va.
Issue:
6493. i. WILLIAM HENRY DOGGETT,[3] born Portsmouth, Va., April 2, 1815.
6494. ii. Son DOGGETT,[3] died a child.
6495. iii. Daughter DOGGETT,[3] married Mr. McRea; has grandson Edwin P. Parker; resides Wytheville, Va. (1892).
6496. iv. Daughter DOGGETT,[3] married.
6497. v. Daughter DOGGETT,[3] died.

Bishop David Seth Doggett said to be a distant cousin.

6493. WILLIAM HENRY DOGGETT [3] (*William*[2]), born Portsmouth, Va., April 2, 1815; died Jersey City, N.J., April 25, 1890; married New York city, October 4, 1847, Hannah Elizabeth Judkins, daughter of Loraine Moody and Mary Dunn (Clark) Judkins; born Readfield, Me., April 16, 1818; resides 100 Jewett avenue, Jersey City, N.J. (1892).
Issue:
6498. i. WILLIAM BROOKS DOGGETT,[4] born Augusta, Me., August 12, 1848.
6499. ii. GEORGE TAIT DOGGETT,[4] born Jersey City, N.J., June, 1850; died Jersey City, N.J., November, 1851.
6500. iii. GEORGE HENRY TAIT DOGGETT,[4] born Jersey City, N.J., April 2, 1852.
6501. iv. VIRGINIA ADAMS DOGGETT,[4] born Jersey City, N.J., February 10, 1855; resides Jersey City, N.J. (1892).

6502. v. INDIANA McREA DOGGETT,[4] born Jersey City, N.J., February 17, 1859; died Jersey City, N.J., December 20, 1882.
6503. vi. MARY ELIZABETH DOGGETT,[4] born Jersey City, N.J., January 26, 1862; died Jersey City, N.J., July, 1864.

6498. WILLIAM BROOKS DOGGETT[4] (*William H.,*[3] *William*[2]), born Augusta, Me., August 12, 1848; resides 228 Monticello avenue, Jersey City, N.J. (1892); married 1st, Newark, N.J., July, 1871, Sarah Ann Street, daughter of William Street; married 2d, New York city, July, 1881, Laura Virginia Ring, daughter of Leonard and Mary F. (Hawley) Ring; born Brooklyn, N.Y., Dec. 25, 1851.
Issue:

6504. i. MINNIE DOGGETT,[5] born Jersey City, N.J., September 20, 1872.
6505. ii. GEORGE LOUIS DOGGETT,[5] born Jersey City, N.J., August 6, 1882.
6506. iii. HAZEL ADAMS DOGGETT,[5] born Jersey City, N.J., January 3, 1889.

6500. GEORGE HENRY TAIT DOGGETT[4] (*William H.,*[3] *William*[2]), born Jersey City, N.J., April 2, 1852; resides Rutherford, N.J. (1892); married Jersey City, N.J., October 17, 1888, Lelia Clara Phillips, daughter of Benjamin and Josephine Adelaide (Losee) Phillips; born Jersey City, N.J., February 5, 1865.
Issue:

6507. i. RUTH JOSEPHINE DOGGETT,[5] born Rutherford, N.J., Nov. 22, 1892.

PROBABLY DESCENDED FROM REV. BENJAMIN DOGGETT, OF LANCASTER, VA.

6508. —— DOGGETT,[1] died before 1806; married ——.
Issue:

6509. i. ASA DOGGETT,[2] born Virginia, 1770.
6510. ii. JESSIE DOGGETT,[2] died Columbia county, Ga.
6511. iii. WILLIAMSON DOGGETT,[2] died Columbia county, Ga.
6512. iv. JOHN DOGGETT,[2] died Jasper county, Ga.
6513. v. REUBEN DOGGETT,[2] died Columbia county, Ga.
6514. vi. GARNER DOGGETT,[2] died Jasper county, Ga.
6515. vii. REBECCA DOGGETT,[2] died Columbia county, Ga.
6516. viii. HANNAH DOGGETT,[2] married Mr. Clyton; died Columbia county, Ga.
6517. ix. ORPHEY DOGGETT,[2] died Jasper county, Ga.

6509. ASA DOGGETT,[2] born Virginia, 1770; died Columbia county, Ga., 1814; married Elizabeth Eubank.
Issue:

6518. i. NANCY DOGGETT,[3] born Columbia county, Ga., 1804; married Columbia county, Ga., Watt Dunn; no issue; she died Columbia county, Ga.
6519. ii. RICHARD E. DOGGETT,[3] born October 25, 1806.
6520. iii. ELIZA FRANCES DOGGETT,[3] born 1808; married Columbia county, Ga., J. Cotton Rawls; issue: nine or ten children; moved to Huntsville, Tex.; she died Texas.

6521. iv. JOHN W. DOGGETT,[3] born Columbia county, Ga., 1810.
6522. v. NAOMI DOGGETT,[3] born 1812.

6519. RICHARD E. DOGGETT[3] (*Asa*[2]), born October 25, 1806; resides Hernando, Miss. (1883); married 1st, Columbia county, Ga., Oct. 17, 1833, E. T. Yarbrough; died March 22, 1854; married 2d, Mrs. Martha M. Huddleston, widow, and daughter of Mr. Baldwin.

Issue:

6523. i. ASA B. DOGGETT,[4] born December 8, 1834.
6524. ii. ANN ELIZABETH DOGGETT,[4] born April 18, 1837; died De Soto county, Miss., May 17, 1843.
6525. iii. RICHARD E. DOGGETT,[4] born December 8, 1838; "in Southern army;" died Chattanooga, Tenn., April 18, 1863.
6526. iv. ARABELLA DOGGETT,[4] born September 22, 1840; died Nov. 24, 1859.
6527. v. WILLIAM L. Y. DOGGETT,[4] born December 15, 1845.
6528. vi. E. T. DOGGETT,[4] born December 15, 1848; married November, 1865, Mr. A. W. Huddleston; issue: two boys and two girls.
6529. vii. MARY A. DOGGETT,[4] born January 18, 1851; married 1869, John R. Totmand; he died September, 1878; issue: girl and boy.
6530. viii. NAOMI DOGGETT,[4] born January 7, 1854.
6531. ix. —— DOGGETT,[4] died an infant.
6532. x. LILLIAN DOGGETT,[4] born October 2, 1859; died May 5, 1883.
6533. xi. LORA DOGGETT,[4] born January 1, 1862.
6534. xii. LENA EUBANK DOGGETT,[4] born August 31, 1865.
6535. xiii. LENNARD DOGGETT,[4] born February 13, 1872.

6521. JOHN W. DOGGETT[3] (*Asa*[2]), born Columbia county, Ga., 1810; died Alabama, 1853; married Harris county, Ga., March 1, 1838, Mary Ann Lyon; died 1858.

Issue:

6536. i. ASA EDMUND DOGGETT,[4] born Harris county, Ga., Dec. 29, 1838.
6537. ii. MARY ELIZABETH DOGGETT,[4] born near Columbus, Ga., April 11, 1840; married; died.
6538. iii. ANN ELIZA DOGGETT,[4] born near Columbus, Ga., August 29, 1842; married; died.
6539. iv. SARAH ESTHER DOGGETT,[4] born Notasulga, Ala., March 18, 1844; died young.
6540. v. NAOMI FRANCES DOGGETT,[4] born Notasulga, Ala., January 11, 1846; married; died.
6541. vi. EUGENIA FREDONIA DOGGETT,[4] born Notasulga, Ala., November 17, 1847; married; died.
6542. vii. JOHN R. DOGGETT,[4] resides Norwoodville, Ark. (1881).
6543. viii. GEORGE W. DOGGETT.[4]

6522. NAOMI DOGGETT[3] (*Asa*[2]), born 1812; died Columbia county, Ga.; married Columbia county, Ga., Joseph A. Marshall; resides Columbia county, Ga.

Issue: three boys, two girls.

6544. i. JABEZ MARSHALL.[4]
6545. ii. JOSEPH MARSHALL.[4]
6546. iii. JOHN MARSHALL.[4]

6523. ASA B. DOGGETT[4] (*Richard E.,*[3] *Asa*[2]), born December 8, 1834; resides Hernando, Miss. (1882); married 1st, De Soto county, Miss., November 27, 1855, Mattie E. Nichols; died October 1, 1856; married 2d, De Soto county, Miss., December 4, 1867, Sarah E. Ellis ; died July 8, 1871.

Issue :

6547. i. Daughter Doggett,[5] born De Soto county, Miss.
6548. ii. Daughter Doggett,[5] born De Soto county, Miss.

6527. William L. Y. Doggett[4] (*Richard E.,*[3] *Asa*[2]), born Dec. 15, 1845 ; died Aug., 1878 ; married 1872, Jane E. McClanahan.

Issue :

6549. i. Asa Doggett.[5]
6550. ii. Richard Doggett.[5]

6536. Asa Edmund Doggett[4] (*John W.,*[3] *Asa*[2]), born Harris county, Ga., December 29, 1838; address, Box 513, Weatherford, Tex. (1892) ; married Paraclifta, Ark., December 24, 1866, Sarah Frances Clement, daughter of Abel Beaufort and Ann (Perkins) Clement; born Nashville, Ark., September 3, 1844.

Issue :

6551. i. Richard James Doggett,[5] born Paraclifta, Ark., November 10, 1867.
6552. ii. Asa Edmund Doggett,[5] born Brownstown, Ark., July 31, 1871.
6553. iii. John Beaufort Doggett,[5] born Brownstown, Ark., August 30, 1873.
6554. iv. Martha Ann Doggett,[5] born Fulton, Ark., October 4, 1876.

Asa E. Doggett moved to Alabama with his parents when about five years old. After their death he spent one year in Louisiana, and in 1859 went back to Alabama, from whence he moved to Arkansas in January, 1860.

At the commencement of the war he entered the Confederate army. After participating in the battle at Oak Hill or Wilson Creek, in Missouri, August 10, 1861, he was transferred to the Mississippi river, where he was in battle at New Madrid, Mo., and Island No. 10, where he was captured. After remaining a few months in prison at Camp Douglas, Chicago, he was exchanged at Vicksburg, Miss. He was in battle at Corinth, Miss., and stationed at Port Hudson, La., during the long siege of General Banks at that place in 1863. At the surrender he went to prison in North Carolina ; then to Gouverneur's island, N.Y. ; then to Johnson's island, near Sandusky, Ohio ; then to Baltimore ; then to Point Lookout, Md. ; then to Fort Delaware prison, till June, 1865, when he was released, and returned to Arkansas in December, 1865.

He has been a farmer ; more recently engaged in steam milling and sawing lumber.

PROBABLY DESCENDED FROM REV. BENJAMIN DOGGETT, OF LANCASTER, VA.

6555. Reuben Doggett,[1] married Mary ——.

Issue :

6556. i. Thomas Doggett,[2] born Virginia, June 10, 1780.

6556. Thomas Doggett [2] (*Reuben* [1]), born Virginia, June 10, 1780; died near Culpeper Court House, Va., September 17, 1823; married Virginia, September 28, 1802, Sarah Harding, daughter of Hal and Elizabeth Harding; born Virginia, February 13, 1782; died Morrisville, Ohio, January 16, 1866.

Issue :

6557. i.   Reuben Ellis Doggett,[3] born Harper's Ferry, Va., Aug. 6, 1803.
6558. ii.   Daniel Brown Doggett,[3] born Harper's Ferry, Va., January 10, 1805; died Delphi, Ind., June 15, 1860.
6559. iii.   Susan Ann Stewart Doggett,[3] born Harper's Ferry, Va., August 21, 1807.
6560. iv.   Julia Ann Doggett,[3] born Harper's Ferry, Va., June 13, 1810.
6561. v.   Alzira Doggett,[3] born Harper's Ferry, Va., December 19, 1813.
6562. vi.   Thomas Andrew Doggett,[3] born Culpeper Court House, Va., August 16, 1816.
6563. vii.   Sarah Elizabeth Doggett,[3] born Harper's Ferry, Va., November 13, 1818.
6564. viii.   Martha Ellenor Doggett,[3] born Harper's Ferry, Va., January 12, 1821; died Virginia.
6565. ix.   Mary Staley Doggett.[3] born Harper's Ferry, Va., Sept. 27, 1823.

6557. Reuben Ellis Doggett [3] (*Thomas,*[2] *Reuben* [1]), born Harper's Ferry, Va., August 6, 1803; died Madison county, Ind., March 6, 1874; married Clark county, Ohio, March 25, 1828, Rachel Ann Strain, daughter of —— (Moore) Strain; born Virginia, 1806; died Madison county, Ind., January 28, 1861.

Issue :

6566. i.   John William Doggett,[4] born Green county, Ohio, February 6, 1829; married Miami county, Ohio, July 15, 1856, Isabella M. Day, daughter of Thomas and Hannah (Johnston) Day; born Warren county, Ohio, Sept 5, 1834; no issue; resides Troy, Ohio (1892).
6567. ii.   Sarah Ann Doggett,[4] born Green county, Ohio, December 6, 1830; married Miami county, Ohio, September 28, 1856, Rudolph Billet; she died Miami county, Ohio, August 5, 1868.
6568. iii.   Horace Rittenhouse Doggett,[4] born Miami county, Ohio, June 15, 1838; married; resides Coursen's Grove, Mitchell Co., Kan. (1892).
6569. iv.   Caroline Egerton Doggett,[4] born Miami county, Ohio, October 24, 1840; married Madison county, Ind., April 12, 1857, Peter Fair; she died Allen county, Ind., April 6, 1880.
6570. v.   Mary Columbia Doggett,[4] born Miami county, Ohio, September 18, 1843; died Miami county, Ohio, January 17, 1856.
6571. vi.   Samantha Kelley Doggett,[4] born Miami county, Ohio, September 30, 1846; married Allen county, Ind., September 20, 1863, Andrew Fair; she died March, 1888.

6559. Susan Ann Stewart Doggett [3] (*Thomas,* [2] *Reuben* [1]), born Harper's Ferry, Va., August 21, 1807; died Morrisville, Ohio, February 16, 1877; married 1st, Culpeper county, Va., December 24, 1824, John Hodge Perley, son of Ebenezer and —— (Bacon) Perley; born Massachusetts, 1803; died Smithland, Ky., 1838; married 2d, 1840–41, Mr. Cowgill.

Issue:

6572. i.   Benjamin Franklin Perley,[4] born Deerfield, Ohio, Oct. 22, 1825.
6573. ii. Sarah Frances Perley,[4] died.
6574. iii. Ellen Perley,[4] died.
6575. iv. Amos T. Cowgill [4] (Rev.), address, Newtown, Ohio (1892).

6560. Julia Ann Doggett [3] (*Thomas,* [2] *Reuben* [1]), born Harper's Ferry, Va., June 13, 1810; died Rock Island county, Ill., December 14, 1877; married Lebanon, Ohio, July 5, 1836, Jacob Glenn, son of James and Sarah (Shoafstall) Glenn; born Lexington, Ky., November 8, 1809; died Rock Island county, Ill., May 25, 1882.

Issue:

6576. i.   Sarah Elisa Glenn,[4] born Martinsville, Ohio, December 14, 1837; married J. W. Briggs, October 7, 1856; resides Colorado (1892).
6577. ii.   Mary Elisabeth Glenn,[4] born Martinsville, Ohio, December 14, 1837; married A. R. Harper, July 13, 1856; she died June 2, 1866.
6578. iii. Louisa Jane Glenn,[4] born Martinsville, Ohio, February 9, 1840; married J. W. Stearns, July 18, 1867; resides Orion, Henry county, Ill. (1893).
6579. iv.   Adaline Glenn,[4] born Martinsville, Ohio, December 27, 1841; died Martinsville, Ohio, September 8, 1843.
6580. v.   Emma Ellen Glenn,[4] born Martinsville, Ohio, August 21, 1843; married James Craig, October 22, 1863; resides Coal Valley, Rock Island county, Ill. (1892).
6581. vi.   Samantha Ann Glenn,[4] born Martinsville, Ohio, Nov. 19, 1844; married John Huntoon, March 12, 1864; she died May 30, 1892.
6582. vii. Thomas William Glenn,[4] born Martinsville, Ohio, November 30, 1846; married Mary Holshoe, March 28, 1869; resides Gothenburg, Neb. (1892).
6583. viii. Henrietta Glenn,[4] born Martinsville, Ohio, October 30, 1849; married William O. Rugh, July 12, 1868; died January 1, 1883.

6561. Alzira Doggett [3] (*Thomas,* [2] *Reuben* [1]), born Harper's Ferry, Va., Dec. 19, 1813; died Lebanon, Ohio, Dec. 27, 1847; married Lebanon, Ohio, May 12, 1842, Richard B. Campbell; born Cranstown, Ire., Aug. 25, 1810; died Lebanon, Ohio, Aug. 8, 1845.

Issue:

6584. i. Anna Eliza Campbell,[4] born Lebanon, Ohio, July 13, 1842; married Morrisville, Ohio, October 31, 1861, David Ellis Foreman, son of Abraham and Anna (Shields) Foreman; he born Morrisville, Ohio, October 29, 1838; resides Morrisville, Ohio (1892).

6562. Thomas Andrew Doggett [3] (*Thomas,* [2] *Reuben* [1]), born Culpeper Court House, Va., August 16, 1816; died Delphi, Ind., January 19, 1878; married Addison, Ohio, February 14, 1836, Eliza

Curtis, daughter of Elisha and Anna (Moses) Curtis; born Rutland
Corner, Vt., September 19, 1815; resides Delphi, Ind. (1892).

Issue:

6585. i.   SILAS BROWN DOGGETT,[4] born Addison, Ohio, February 10, 1837.
6586. ii. LEANDER HARDIN DOGGETT,[4] born Addison, Ohio, August 18, 1838.
6587. iii. ELIZA CARRIE DOGGETT,[4] born Addison, Ohio, October 30, 1840.
6588. iv. SAMUEL CAMPBELL DOGGETT,[4] born Addison, Ohio, Sept. 15, 1842.
6589. v.   AMANDA JANE DOGGETT,[4] born Addison, Ohio, October 18, 1845;
           married Delphi, Ind., October 14, 1868, Samuel Barnett, son of
           William and Julia (McElhaney) Barnett; born Delphi, Ind., Sep-
           tember 16, 1845; resides Delphi, Ind. (1892).

Thomas A. Doggett was born in Culpeper Court House, near
what is known as the Raccoon Ford; removed to the State of Ohio, to
a small village called at that time Christiansburg, but now Addison.
He was a carpenter by trade, and moved to Delphi, Ind., where he
died, and was honorably buried by the Odd Fellows in their cemetery
at that place.

6563. SARAH ELIZABETH DOGGETT[3] (*Thomas,*[2] *Reuben*[1]), born
Harper's Ferry, Va., November 13, 1818; died Lebanon, Ohio,
August 1, 1848; married Benjamin Mikesell.

Issue:

6590. i. MARY ELIZABETH MIKESELL,[4] married Mr. Phillips; resides Morris-
          ville, Ohio (1892).
6591. ii. EMMA J. MIKESELL,[4] married Mr. Holmes; resides Columbus, Ohio
          (1892).

6565. MARY STALEY DOGGETT[3] (*Thomas,*[2] *Reuben*[1]), born Harper's Ferry, Va., September 27, 1823; resides Morrisville, Ohio
(1892); married Martinsville, Ohio, March 20, 1845, John Strick-
land Cowgill, son of Henry and Mary (McDaniel) Cowgill; born
Morrisville, Ohio, September 24, 1824; died February 19, 1864.

Issue:

6592. i. GEORGE SHIELDS COWGILL,[4] born Morrisville, Ohio, February 24,
          1846; resides there (1892).
6593. ii. SARAH EMILY COWGILL,[4] born Morrisville, Ohio, February 27, 1855;
          married Mr. Cashman; resides there (1892).

6572. BENJAMIN FRANKLIN PERLEY[4] (*Susan A. S. Doggett,*[3]
Thomas,[2] *Reuben*[1]), born Deerfield, Ohio, October 22, 1825; resides
Alexandria, La. (1892); married 1st, St. Francisville, June 24, 1851,
Mydelphine Mary Guthrie, daughter of Lartigue Guthrie; died
November 4, 1853; married 2d, Louisiana, April 10, 1857, Cicilly
Ann Lyons.

Issue:

6594. i. JOHN HENRY PERLEY,[5] born June 13, 1852; died August 15, 1852.
6595. ii. WILLIAM FRANKLIN PERLEY,[5] born Dec. 10, 1859; died Aug. 4, 1861.

6585. SILAS BROWN DOGGETT[4] (*Thomas A.,*[3] *Thomas,*[2] *Reuben*[1]),
born Addison, Ohio. February 10, 1837; resides Delphi, Ind. (1892);

married Lane's Prairie, Mo., July 12, 1868, Rhoda Elizabeth Walker; born November 14, 1843 ; died Seneca, Mo., March 29, 1872.

Issue :

6596. i. BUSNICE BELINDA ELIZA DOGGETT,[5] born Lane's Prairie, Mo., May 26, 1869.

6586. LEANDER HARDIN DOGGETT [4] (*Thomas A.,*[3] *Thomas,*[2] *Reuben* [1]), born Addison, Ohio, August 18, 1838 ; died Logansport, Ind., October 14, 1881 ; married Logansport, Ind., July 20, 1868, Susan McElhaney, daughter of Thomas and Amanda (Archer) McElhaney ; born Logansport, Ind., September 17, 1844 ; resides 423 Market street, Logansport, Ind. (1892).

Issue :

6597. i. CHARLES DOGGETT,[5] born Pittsburg, Ind., July 8, 1869 ; died Logansport, Ind., June 6, 1875.
6598. ii. ADA DOGGETT,[5] born Logansport, Ind., March 23, 1871 ; resides there (1892).
6599. iii. HARRY DOGGETT,[5] born Logansport, Ind., September 23, 1872.
6600. iv. FREDERICK DOGGETT,[5] born Logansport, Ind., May 24, 1874.
6601. v. MABEL DOGGETT,[5] born Logansport, Ind., December 21, 1876.
6602. vi. EDITH DOGGETT,[5] born Logansport, Ind., July 8, 1879.

6587. ELIZA CARRIE DOGGETT [4] (*Thomas A.,*[3] *Thomas,*[2] *Reuben* [1]), born Addison, Ohio, October 30, 1840; died Delphi, Ind., Jan. 17, 1878 ; married Delphi, Ind., Oct. 20, 1861, Joseph Sampson.

Issue :

6603. i. CLARRIE ELDORA SAMPSON,[5] born Pittsburg, Ind., July 24, 1863 ; resides Indianapolis, Ind. (1892).
6604. ii. ANNA ELIZA SAMPSON,[5] born Pittsburg, Ind., May 19, 1866 ; resides Brownsville, Mo. (1886).
6605. iii. JAMES SAMPSON.[5] born Pittsburg, Ind., June 26, 1869 ; resides Delphi, Ind. (1886).

6588. SAMUEL CAMPBELL DOGGETT [4] (*Thomas A.,*[3] *Thomas,*[2] *Reuben* [1]), born Addison, Ohio, September 15, 1842 ; resides Clinton, Mo. (1893) ; married Monticello, Ind., January 26, 1866, Isabelle La Fleur, daughter of Joseph and Anna (Allen) La Fleur ; born Delphi, Ind., March 2, 1842.

Issue :

6606. i. HEBER LA FLEUR DOGGETT,[5] born Pittsburg, Ind., April 21, 1869.
6607. ii. ANNA DOGGETT,[5] born Black River, Saline Co., Mo., July 23, 1875.
6608. iii. JOSEPHINE DOGGETT,[5] born Saline county, Mo., August 26, 1877 ; died Saline county, Mo., December 5, 1878.
6609. iv. DAISY DEAN DOGGETT,[5] born Sweet Springs, Saline Co., Mo., January 30, 1882.

Samuel C. Doggett worked for his father until he was twenty-two years old, when he settled in Pittsburg, Ind., and started a cooper's shop. In the fall of 1869 he moved to Lane's Prairie, Mo., where he bought a home, and lived there for two years. He next moved to St. James, Mo., and opened a dry-goods store, in which he did a good business until the panic of 1872, when he sold out and bought eighty acres of land in Saline county, Mo., where he engaged in farming for four years. Not finding farming profitable, he moved to Brownsville, Mo., thence to Clinton, Mo. (1892).

PROBABLY DESCENDED FROM REV. BENJAMIN DOGGETT, OF LANCASTER, VA.

6610. Mr. Doggett,[1] married Sarah Ann Doggett; born Virginia; died North Carolina.

Issue:

6611. i. Bushrod Doggett.[2]

Sarah Ann Doggett married 2d, William Byers, a Revolutionary soldier, by whom she had seven children. Mr. Byers died in the war, and she married 3d, Joel Blackwell, by whom there was no issue.

6611. Bushrod Doggett,[2] " Revolutionary soldier," " arm broken in service; " died North Carolina, July 25, 1829; married Susannah Davis.

Issue:

6612. i.   William Doggett,[3] born North Carolina, March 10, 1785.
6613. ii.   George Doggett.[3]
6614. iii. Richard Doggett.[3]
6615. iv.   Sally Doggett.[3]
6616. v.   Nancy Doggett.[3]
6617. vi.   Polly Doggett.[3]
6618. vii. Betsy Doggett.[3]
6619. viii. Patsy Doggett.[3]

6612. William Doggett[3] (*Bushrod*[2]), born North Carolina, March 10, 1785; died North Carolina, March 31, 1852; married Masa Bedford.

Issue:

6620. i.   George Doggett.[4]
6621. ii.   Peter Doggett,[4] born North Carolina.
6622. iii. James Lewis Doggett,[4] born North Carolina, July 25, 1829.
6623. iv.   John Doggett,[4] born North Carolina.
6624. v.   Susanna Doggett,[4] born North Carolina.
6625. vi.   Nancy Doggett,[4] born North Carolina.
6626. vii. Patsy Doggett,[4] born North Carolina.
6627. viii. Betsy Doggett.[4]

6620. George Doggett[4] (*William*,[3] *Bushrod*[2]), married 1st, Betsy Watkins; married 2d, Mary McDaniel.

Issue:

6628. i.   Micajah Doggett.[5]

6629. ii.　JAMES DOGGETT.⁵
6630. iii.　WILLIAM DOGGETT.⁵
6631. iv.　JOHN DOGGETT.⁵
6632. v.　RUFUS DOGGETT.⁵
6633. vi.　GEORGE DOGGETT.⁵
6634. vii.　MARY DOGGETT.⁵
6635. viii.　SALLIE DOGGETT.⁵

6621.　PETER DOGGETT⁴ (*William,*³ *Bushrod*²), born North Carolina; married Miss Fancier.

Issue :

6636. i.　WILLIAM DOGGETT.⁵
6637. ii.　JOHN DOGGETT.⁵
6638. iii.　JAMES DOGGETT.⁵
6639. iv.　NANNIE DOGGETT.⁵

6622.　JAMES LEWIS DOGGETT⁴ (*William,*³ *Bushrod*²), born North Carolina, July 25, 1829; resides Forest City, N.C. (1889); married Cemantha Tanner.

Issue :

6640. i.　WILLIAM DOGGETT,⁵ born North Carolina; married Mary Groves.
6641. ii.　NANNIE DOGGETT,⁵ married John Moore.
6642. iii.　DORA DOGGETT,⁵ married D. P. Tate.
6643. iv.　RICHARD DOGGETT,⁵ resides Forest City, N.C. (1889).
6644. v.　MARY DOGGETT,⁵ resides Forest City, N.C. (1889).
6645. vi.　HORACE DOGGETT,⁵ resides Forest City, N.C. (1889).

6623.　JOHN DOGGETT⁴ (*William,*³ *Bushrod*²), born North Carolina; married Sallie Harris.

Issue :

6646. i.　MASA DOGGETT,⁵ born North Carolina; married Ira Phillips.
6647. ii.　BUSHROD DOGGETT.⁵
6648. iii.　BIRCH DOGGETT.⁵
6649. iv.　MATTIE DOGGETT.⁵
6650. v.　VIRGINIA DOGGETT.⁵
6651. vi.　SIMPSON DOGGETT.⁵
6652. vii.　JOSEPH DOGGETT.⁵

6624.　SUSANNA DOGGETT⁴ (*William,*³ *Bushrod*²), born North Carolina; married Barnabas King.

Issue :

6653. i.　MASA KING.⁵
6654. ii.　NANCY KING.⁵
6655. iii.　KATY KING.⁵
6656. iv.　PATSY KING.⁵
6657. v.　MARGARET KING.⁵
6658. vi.　MARY KING.⁵
6659. vii.　JUDITH KING.⁵
6660. viii.　DANIEL KING.⁵
6661. ix.　THOMAS KING.⁵
6662. x.　BARNABAS KING.⁵
6663. xi.　PINKNEY KING.⁵

6625. NANCY DOGGETT[4] (*William*,[3] *Bushrod*[2]), born North Carolina; married Edmund Durham.

Issue:

6664. i. SUSAN DURHAM.[5]
6665. ii. ZULA DURHAM.[5]

6626. PATSY DOGGETT[4] (*William*,[3] *Bushrod*[2]), born North Carolina; married George Byers.

Issue:

6666. i. JOHN BYERS.[5]
6667. ii. GEORGE BYERS.[5]
6668. iii. MASA BYERS.[5]
6669. iv. CARSES BYERS.[5]
6670. v. MISSOURI BYERS.[5]

PROBABLY DESCENDED FROM REV. BENJAMIN DOGGETT, OF LANCASTER CO., VA.

6671. ELMORE DOGGETT[2] (*Elmore*[1]) (?), born probably Lancaster county, Va.; died Mason county, Ky., 1806; married Elizabeth ——.

Issue:

6672. i. NEWTON DOGGETT,[3] born Mason county, Ky., February 2, 1787.
6673. ii. FANNIE DOGGETT.[3]
6674. iii. POLLY DOGGETT.[3]
6675. iv. LUCINDA DOGGETT.[3]
6676. v. JULIA DOGGETT.[3]
6677. vi. ELMORE DOGGETT.[3]

Among the descendants of Elmore Doggett is the tradition that he came to this country from Scotland in 1770 and settled in Lancaster county, Va.; that he married in Scotland, and that his father's name was probably Elmore. The writer believes him to be a descendant of Rev. Benjamin Doggett.

6672. NEWTON DOGGETT[3] (*Elmore*[2] [*Elmore*[1]] (?)), born Mason county, Ky., February 2, 1787; died Hillsboro', Ohio, April 2, 1839; married Maysville, Ky., September 7, 1808, Mary Mitchell, daughter of John and Nancy (Boone) Mitchell; born Maysville, Ky., February 26, 1793; died Hillsboro', Ohio, October 7, 1845.

Issue:

6678. i. WASHINGTON DOGGETT,[4] born Hillsboro', Ohio, May 28, 1811.
6679. ii. NANCY DOGGETT,[4] born Hillsboro', Ohio, March 29, 1813; died young.
6680. iii. ELMORE DOGGETT,[4] born Hillsboro', Ohio, Aug. 16, 1814; died young.
6681. iv. ELMORE DOGGETT,[4] born Hillsboro', Ohio, October 15, 1816.
6682. v. JOHN MITCHELL DOGGETT,[4] born Hillsboro', Ohio, Feb. 17, 1819.
6683. vi. WILLIAM DOGGETT,[4] born Hillsboro', Ohio, June 27, 1821.
6684. vii. WESLEY DOGGETT,[4] born Hillsboro', Ohio, July 13, 1823.
6685. viii. ELIZABETH ANN DOGGETT,[4] born Hillsboro', Ohio, October 19, 1825.

6686. ix. NEWTON DOGGETT,[4] born Hillsboro', Ohio, December 30, 1827; died
      in infancy.
6687. x. MARY DOGGETT,[4] born Hillsboro', Ohio, August 28, 1829; died Hills-
      boro', Ohio, August 2, 1879.
6688. xi. NEWTON DOGGETT,[4] born Hillsboro', Ohio, February 21, 1832.

Mr. Doggett moved to Hillsboro' in 1809. Twelve years county
commissioner; twenty years member Methodist Episcopal church, and
trustee of same; was cabinet-maker and undertaker. Mrs. Doggett
was granddaughter of Jacob Boone, a brother of Daniel Boone, of
Kentucky fame.

6678. WASHINGTON DOGGETT [4] (*Newton,*[3] *Elmore* [2] [*Elmore* [1]] (?)),
born Hillsboro', Ohio, May 28, 1811; died Hillsboro', Ohio, April 1,
1878; married 1st, near Hillsboro', Ohio, January, 1837, Milly
Saunders, daughter of Thomas Saunders; died Hillsboro', Ohio,
February 3, 1857; married 2d, August 30, 1859, Sarah R. Kerr,
widow of Alexander Kerr, and daughter of Alvin and Eliza Priscilla
(Winchell) Foote; born Granville, Ohio, February 16, 1829; died
Hillsboro', Ohio, April, 1876.
  Issue:

6689. i. MARY DOGGETT,[5] born Hillsboro', Ohio; died Hillsboro', Ohio.
6690. ii. HENRY DOGGETT,[5] born Hillsboro', Ohio; died Hillsboro', Ohio.
6691. iii. THOMAS NEWTON DOGGETT,[5] born Hillsboro', Ohio, January, 1844;
      died Hillsboro', Ohio, October 16, 1845.
6692. iv. MATTIE W. DOGGETT,[5] born Hillsboro', Ohio, 1847.
6693. v. JOSEPH NEWTON DOGGETT,[5] born Hillsboro', Ohio, 1853; died Hills-
      boro', Ohio, July 25, 1862.
6694. vi. SAMUEL C. DOGGETT,[5] born Hillsboro', Ohio, July 23, 1855; died
      Hillsboro', Ohio, January 6, 1872.
6695. vii. MARY ELIZABETH DOGGETT,[5] born Hillsboro', Ohio, December 18,
      1862; died Hillsboro', Ohio, February 21, 1865.

Washington Doggett was justice of the peace in Hillsboro' about
thirty-five years; mayor of the city several terms; trustee of the
Methodist Episcopal church, and of Hillsboro' Female College.

6681. ELMORE DOGGETT [4] (*Newton,*[3] *Elmore* [2] [*Elmore* [1]] (?)),
born Hillsboro', Ohio, Oct. 15, 1816; died Hillsboro', Ohio, Aug. 7,
1859; married 1st, Frances Rhoads; married 2d, Mary Glasscock.
  Issue:

6696. i. SALLIE MARY DOGGETT,[5] born Hillsboro', Ohio, September 15, 1848;
      married John Freshour; resides Chillicothe, Ohio (1893).
6697. ii. WILLIAM DOGGETT,[5] born Hillsboro', Ohio, about 1854; died in Dakota
      about 1892.
6698. iii. FRANK DOGGETT,[5] born Hillsboro', Ohio, about 1856; resides Dakota
      (1893).

6682. JOHN MITCHELL DOGGETT [4] (*Newton,*[3] *Elmore* [2] [*Elmore* [1]] (?)), born Hillsboro', Ohio, February 17, 1819; resides Linwood, Ohio (1893); married Hillsboro', Ohio, January 12, 1843, by

Bishop Randolph Foster, to Elma Barrere Parker, daughter of Isaac C. and Sarah E. (Fenner) Parker; born Hillsboro', Ohio, Oct. 6, 1825.

Issue:

6699. i.   CHARLES L. DOGGETT,⁵ born Hillsboro', Ohio, August 14, 1846.
6700. ii.   ANNA P. DOGGETT,⁵ born Hillsboro', Ohio, January 22, 1849; died
            Hillsboro'. Ohio, June 6, 1849.
6701. iii. SALLIE M. DOGGETT,⁵ born Hillsboro', Ohio, May 6, 1850.
6702. iv.   MADISON W. DOGGETT,⁵ born Hillsboro', Ohio. March 20, 1853; with
            the "Consolidated Coal and Mining Company," 99 West Fourth
            street, Cincinnati, Ohio (1893).
6703. v.   JOHN KIRBY DOGGETT,⁵ born Hillsboro', Ohio, June 10, 1856.
6704. vi.   WASHINGTON PARKER DOGGETT,⁵ born Hillsboro', Ohio, May 25,
            1861; died Hillsboro', Ohio, March 5, 1862.
6705. vii. LIZZIE L. DOGGETT,⁵ born Hillsboro', Ohio, July 7, 1865; died Cin-
            cinnati, Ohio, March 6, 1870.
6706. viii. JAMES C. DOGGETT,⁵ born Cincinnati, Ohio, May 7, 1869; died Cin-
            cinnati, Ohio, March 12, 1870.

When in Hillsboro' Mr. Doggett was undertaker, furniture dealer, and builder; at present retired.

6683. WILLIAM DOGGETT⁴ (*Newton,³ Elmore²* [*Elmore¹*] (?)), born Hillsboro', Ohio, June 27, 1821; resides Hillsboro', Ohio (1893); married Hillsboro', Ohio, November 17, 1846, by Rev. William McRunnels, to Eliza Jane Henton, daughter of Evan and Maria (Inskeep) Henton; born Connersville, Ind., October 4, 1823; died Hillsboro', Ohio, December 2, 1872.

Issue:

6707. i.   MARIA DOGGETT,⁵ born Hillsboro', Ohio, January 15, 1848; died
            Hillsboro', Ohio, January 15, 1864.
6708. ii.   CLINT DOGGETT,⁵ born Hillsboro', Ohio, February 4, 1852.
6709. iii. EMMA DOGGETT,⁵ born Hillsboro', Ohio, November 4, 1856; died Hills-
            boro', Ohio, October 31, 1861.
6710. iv.   JESSIE DOGGETT,⁵ born Hillsboro'. Ohio, January 30, 1862; resides
            there (1893).

Mr. Doggett is a tanner and butcher. At one time held the office of assessor in Liberty township, and was in former years constable of Hillsboro'.

6684. WESLEY DOGGETT⁴ (*Newton,³ Elmore²* [*Elmore¹*] (?)), born Hillsboro', Ohio, July 13, 1823; died Hillsboro', Ohio, August, 1863; married Hillsboro', Ohio, July, 1856, Martha Kent.

Issue:

6711. i. NELSON DOGGETT,⁵ born 1857.
6712. ii. EDWARD DOGGETT,⁵ born 1859.

6685. ELIZABETH ANN DOGGETT⁴ (*Newton,³ Elmore²* [*Elmore¹*] (?)), born Hillsboro', Ohio, October 19, 1825; died Ottumwa, Ia., December 15, 1889; married Hillsboro', Ohio, February 18, 1846,

Charles Lawrence; born Crewkerne, Somersetshire, Eng., January 29, 1822; resides Ottumwa, Ia. (1893).

Issue:

6713. i. JOSEPH NEWTON LAWRENCE,[5] born Hillsboro', Ohio, Nov. 19, 1846.
6714. ii. MARY REBECCA LAWRENCE,[5] born Hillsboro', Ohio, September 13, 1848: died Ottumwa, Ia., January 17, 1852.
6715. iii. ELLA D. LAWRENCE,[5] born Ottumwa, Ia., January 7, 1853.
6716. iv. HESTER LAWRENCE,[5] born Ottumwa, Ia., February 7, 1861; died Ottumwa, Ia., April 12, 1862.

Mr. Lawrence is of the firm of Lawrence & Garner, wholesale dealers in dry goods, notions, etc., at Ottumwa, Ia. He moved to Hillsboro' in 1835, and to Cincinnati in 1844. After two years he returned to Hillsboro', and then moved to Ottumwa in April, 1849.

6688. NEWTON DOGGETT [4] (*Newton*,[3] *Elmore* [2] [*Elmore* [1]] (?)), born Hillsboro', Ohio, Feb. 21, 1832; died Keokuk, Ia., 1865 or 1866.

Mr. Doggett was recorder of the city of Ottumwa in 1858; enlisted as sergeant August 8, 1863, Co. L, Eighth Cavalry; captured at Newnan, Ga.; promoted to second lieutenant August 28, 1865; presented with a gold-mounted sword by the citizens of Ottumwa, Ia.

6692. MATTIE W. DOGGETT [5] (*Washington*,[4] *Newton*,[3] *Elmore*,[2] [*Elmore* [1]] (?)), born Hillsboro', Ohio, 1847; died Los Anamos, Col., March 3, 1874; married John Sinclair Harman; born Hillsboro', Ohio; resides Tecumseh, Neb. (1893).

Issue:

6717. i. HARRY S. HARMAN,[6] born November, 1871; died Tecumseh, Neb., April 26, 1873.

6699. CHARLES L. DOGGETT [5] (*John M.*,[4] *Newton*,[3] *Elmore*,[2] [*Elmore* [1]] (?)), born Hillsboro', Ohio, August 14, 1846; resides Cincinnati, Ohio (1893); married Cincinnati, Ohio, August 13, 1868, Nannie Durrell; died June 24, 1886.

Issue:

m18. i. CHARLES L. DOGGETT,[6] born 1869.
6,19. ii. FORREST DOGGETT,[6] born 1871.
6720. iii. JOSEPH DOGGETT,[6] born 1873.
6721. iv. ALICE DOGGETT,[6] born 1875.
6722. v. ELMA DOGGETT,[6] born 1878.
6723. vi. CLARENCE DOGGETT,[6] born 1881.

6701. SALLIE M. DOGGETT [5] (*John M.*,[4] *Newton*,[3] *Elmore* [2] [*Elmore* [1]] (?)), born Hillsboro', Ohio, May 6, 1850; died Linwood, Ohio, November 30, 1891; married Cincinnati, Ohio, May 30, 1871, Oscar B. Grant; resides Linwood, Ohio (1893).

Issue:

6724. i. ARTHUR D. GRANT,[6] born 1875.
6725. ii. FRANK D. GRANT,[6] born 1879.
6726. iii. WILLIAM D. GRANT,[6] born 1885.

6703. JOHN KIRBY DOGGETT [5] (*John M.,* [4] *Newton,* [3] *Elmore* [2] [*Elmore* [1]] (?)), born Hillsboro', Ohio, June 10, 1856; resides 3907 Washington avenue, St. Louis, Mo. (1893); married November 17, 1882, Jennie Lindsay.

Issue:

6727. i. ANDREW LINDSAY DOGGETT,[6] born 1883.
6728. ii. ANNA WISE DOGGETT,[6] born 1885.

6708. CLINT DOGGETT [5] (*William,* [4] *Newton,* [3] *Elmore* [2] [*Elmore* [1]] (?)), born Hillsboro', Ohio, February 4, 1852; resides Hillsboro', Ohio (1893); married Hillsboro', Ohio, January 27, 1875, Eliza Lavinia Murphy.

Issue:

6729. i. NELLIE LEE DOGGETT,[6] born Hillsboro', Ohio, January 8, 1876; died Hillsboro', Ohio, January 7, 1893.
6730. ii. MARY ELIZA DOGGETT,[6] born Hillsboro', Ohio, September 11, 1880.
6731. iii. WALTER LINN DOGGETT,[6] born Hillsboro', Ohio, July 16, 1881.

6713. JOSEPH NEWTON LAWRENCE [5] (*Elizabeth A. Doggett,* [4] *Newton,* [3] *Elmore* [2] [*Elmore* [1]] (?)), born Hillsboro', Ohio, November 19, 1846; resides Ottumwa, Ia. (1893); married 1st, Ottumwa, Ia., October 11, 1869, Eunice Harrington Field; born Worcester, Mass., Oct. 17, 1849; died Ottumwa, Ia., Dec. 1, 1871; married 2d, April 2, 1891, Ella Caisman; born Meredosia, Ill., May 3, 1869.

Issue:

6732. i. ELLA FIELD LAWRENCE,[6] born Ottumwa, Ia., November 21, 1871.

6715. ELLA D. LAWRENCE [5] (*Elizabeth A. Doggett,* [4] *Newton,* [3] *Elmore* [2] [*Elmore* [1]] (?)), born Ottumwa, Ia., January 7, 1853; died March 19, 1883; married September 17, 1872, Edward Coffin Loomis; born Ravenna, Ohio, February 10, 1852; resides Red Oak, Ia. (1893).

Issue:

6733. i. CHARLES LOOMIS,[6] born 1874; died 1874.
6734. ii. JOSEPH MATTHEWS LOOMIS,[6] born January 2, 1875.
6735. iii. ELIZABETH ANN LOOMIS,[6] born September 17, 1879.

PROBABLY DESCENDED FROM REV. BENJAMIN DOGGETT, OF LANCASTER, VA.

6736. JAMES WILLIAM DOGGETT [2] (*George* [1]), born Virginia; Revolutionary soldier; died from wounds received in battle; married.

Issue:

6737. i. GEORGE WASHINGTON DOGGETT,[3] born Culpeper county, Va., 1788.
6738. ii. WILLIAM DOGGETT,[3] born Culpeper county, Va., 1790.

6739. iii. ARMSTEAD DOGGETT,[3] born Culpeper county, Va., 1792.
6740. iv. PRESLEY DOGGETT,[3] born Culpeper county, Va., 1794.
6741. v. BENJAMIN DOGGETT,[3] born Culpeper county, Va., 1796.
6742. vi. JUDITH DOGGETT,[3] born Culpeper county, Va., 1798; married; issue: nineteen children.

6737. GEORGE WASHINGTON DOGGETT [3] (*James W.,*[2] *George*[1]), born Culpeper county, Va., 1788; died Hillsboro', Ohio, 1885; married Winchester, Ky., 1816, Lucy Shepherd, daughter of William Shepherd; born Winchester, Ky.; died Hillsboro', Ohio, 1837.

Issue:

6743. i. JULIA DOGGETT,[4] born Winchester, Ky., 1817; married Joseph Bently, 1836; no issue; resides Hillsboro', Ohio (1893).
6744. ii. JAMES WILLIAM DOGGETT,[4] born Winchester, Ky., July 11, 1819.
6745. iii. BENJAMIN FRANKLIN DOGGETT,[4] born Winchester, Ky., 1821.
6746. iv. MARY DOGGETT,[4] born Hillsboro', Ohio, 1826; died Hillsboro', Ohio, 1830.

George W. Doggett was coroner of Highland county, Ohio. Served in the war of 1812.

6744. JAMES WILLIAM DOGGETT [4] (*George W.,*[3] *James W.,*[2] *George*[1]), born Bourbon county, Ky., July 11, 1819; resides State Soldiers' Home, Ohio (1893); married Hillsboro', Ohio, September 7, 1852, by Rev. Wm. McRannells, to Hester Ann Fitzpatrick, daughter of Robert and Nancy (Curtis) Fitzpatrick; born Highland county, Ohio, 1823.

Issue:

6747. i. ROBERT BENTLY DOGGETT,[5] born Hillsboro', Ohio, June 27, 1853; died Hillsboro', Ohio, 1880.
6748. ii. GEORGE CRUMBAUGH DOGGETT,[5] born Hillsboro', Ohio, 1855; died Hillsboro', Ohio, 1882.
6749. iii. INDIANA DOGGETT,[5] born Hillsboro', Ohio, 1857; died Hillsboro', Ohio, 1878.
6750. iv. EMMA JANE DOGGETT,[5] born Hillsboro', Ohio, January 17, 1859.

Mr. Doggett in early life was a hatter; subsequently United States marshal for eighteen years.

6745. BENJAMIN FRANKLIN DOGGETT [4] (*George W.,*[3] *James W.,*[2] *George*[1]), born Winchester, Ky., 1821; killed in battle, Benton Cross Roads, N.C., 1865; married Greenfield, Ohio, Elizabeth Dean; died Greenfield, Ohio, 1886.

Issue:

6751. i. JOHN DOGGETT,[5] died Greenfield, Ohio, 1884.
6752. ii. GEORGE DOGGETT,[5] resides Greenfield, Ohio (1893).

6750. EMMA JANE DOGGETT [5] (*James W.,*[4] *George W.,*[3] *James W.,*[2] *George*[1]), born Hillsboro', Ohio, January 17, 1859; address, care Hoyt & Co., Chicago, Ill. (1893); married Hillsboro', Ohio, June

29, 1882, Charles Newton Holmes, son of Newton and Phebe Ann (Lewis) Holmes; born Sugar Tree Ridge, Ohio, February 14, 1860.

Issue:

6753. i.   GEORGE EDWARD HOLMES,[6] born Hillsboro', Ohio, May 21, 1884.
6754. ii. FAITH HOLMES,[6] born Hillsboro', Ohio, April 26, 1887.

PROBABLY DESCENDED FROM REV. BENJAMIN DOGGETT, OF LANCASTER, VA.

6755. GEORGE DOGGETT,[1] born Culpeper county, Va.; died Cleveland county, N.C.; married Culpeper county, Va., Sarah Ann Yancy; died Cleveland county, N.C., about 1840.

Issue:

6756. i.   COALMAN DOGGETT,[2] born Culpeper county, Va., Jan. 6, 1801.
6757. ii.   GEORGE DOGGETT.[2]
6758. iii. ELIZABETH DOGGETT.[2]
6759. iv.   FANNIE DOGGETT,[2] married Mr. McBryer; removed to Missouri.
6760. v.   SARAH DOGGETT,[2] married John B. Goudalock; several children.
6761. vi.   CHARLES DOGGETT,[2] married; two children.
6762. vii. RICHARD DOGGETT,[2] died.
6763. viii. JAMES DOGGETT,[2] born Cleveland county, N.C.; married.

George Doggett was wounded in the knee in the Revolution. He married Sarah A. Yancy, a sister of Major Yancy, who died near Culpeper, Va. Mr. Doggett removed from Virginia to Rutherford county, N.C. (now called Cleveland county), in 1802 or 1803.

6756. COALMAN DOGGETT [2] (*George* [1]), born Culpeper county, Va., January 6, 1801; died near Shelby, Cleveland county, N.C., Jan. 6, 1853; married Cleveland county, N.C., 1834, by Rev. Drury Dobbins, to Mary Smith, daughter of Miner and Jane (Rigsby) Smith.

Issue:

6764. i.   SARAH ANN DOGGETT,[3] born near Shelby, Cleveland Co., N.C., March 10, 1835.
6765. ii. FRANCES CAROLINE DOGGETT,[3] born near Shelby, Cleveland Co., N.C., January 1, 1838.
6766. iii. MINER WINN DOGGETT,[3] born near Shelby, Cleveland Co., N.C., August 16, 1840.
6767. iv. JAMES RINEHART DOGGETT,[3] born near Shelby, Cleveland Co., N.C., April 18, 1843; Co. E, Twelfth Regiment, North Carolina, Confederate Army; died Richmond, Va., July 10, 1862.
6768. v.   GEORGE WILLIAM DOGGETT,[3] born near Shelby, Cleveland Co., N.C., May 14, 1848.

6757. GEORGE DOGGETT [2] (*George* [1]), married.
Issue: three sons.

6769. i. WILLIAM A. DOGGETT,[3] resides Gaffney City, S.C. (1888).

6758. ELIZABETH DOGGETT[2] (*George*[1]), married Mr. Elliott.
Issue :
6770. i. ROBERT ELLIOTT,[3] resides Waco, N.C. (1890).

6764. SARAH ANN DOGGETT[3] (*Coalman*,[2] *George*[1]), born near
Shelby, N.C., March 10, 1835; resides Polkville, N.C. (1888);
married Cleveland county, N.C., September 28, 1854, by Rev. David
Byars, to Andrew Jackson Elliott, son of John C. and Mary
(Donaho) Elliott; born Cleveland county, N.C., April 11, 1822.
Issue :
6771. i.   COALMAN DOGGETT ELLIOTT,[4] born Cleveland county, N.C., October
            31, 1855; died Cleveland county, N.C., July 20, 1880.
6772. ii.   MARY DONAHO ELLIOTT,[4] born Cleveland county, N.C., June 2, 1858.
6773. iii. SUSAN FRANCES ELLIOTT,[4] born Cleveland county, N.C., Oct. 22, 1860.
6774. iv.   JAMES RINEHART ELLIOTT,[4] born Cleveland county, N.C., July 13,
            1863.
6775. v.   MARGARET ELIZABETH ELLIOTT,[4] born Cleveland county, N.C., July
            3, 1866.
6776. vi.   SARAH CAROLINE ELLIOTT,[4] born Cleveland county, N.C., April 29,
            1869.
6777. vii. DORCAS CATHERINE ELLIOTT,[4] born Cleveland county, N.C., April
            23, 1872; died Cleveland county, N.C., June 19, 1889.
6778. viii. ANDREW JACKSON ELLIOTT,[4] born Cleveland county, N.C., February
            14, 1875.

Andrew J. Elliott has been lieutenant, captain, and colonel of the
militia of North Carolina. He was captain of the Home Guard during
the civil war.

6765. FRANCES CAROLINE DOGGETT[3] (*Coalman*,[2] *George*[1]), born
Cleveland county, N.C., January 1, 1838; resides Shelby, N.C.
(1888); married Cleveland county, N.C., August 16, 1855, by Rev.
T. Dickson, to Burwell Blanton, son of Charles and Juda (Hamric)
Blanton; born Cleveland county. N.C., January 27, 1834.
Issue :
6779. i.   CHARLES COALMAN BLANTON,[4] born Cleveland county, N.C., January
           31, 1858; married Sweetwater, Tenn., July 15, 1885, Ara Brewster;
           president First National Bank, Meridian, Tex. (1890).
6780. ii. MARY JUDA BLANTON,[4] born Cleveland county, N.C., July 22, 1860.
6781. iii. MARGARET ELLEN BLANTON,[4] born Cleveland Co., N.C., Dec. 25, 1862.
6782. iv. DORA ANN BLANTON,[4] born Cleveland county, N.C., Oct. 22, 1865.
6783. v.   GEORGE WINN BLANTON,[4] born Cleveland county, N.C., October 26,
           1871; resides Wake Forest College, N.C. (1890).
6784. vi. BURWELL EDGAR BLANTON,[4] born Cleveland county, N.C., December
           31, 1875; resides Shelby, N.C. (1890).

Mr. Blanton was an officer in the Confederate army at the commencement of the war. He is a farmer.

6766. MINER WINN DOGGETT[3] (*Coalman*,[2] *George*[1]), born Cleveland county, N.C., August 16, 1840; resides Asheville, N.C. (1889);
married Cleveland county. N.C., September 23, 1862, by Rev. G. W.

Rollins, to Juda Margaret Blanton, daughter of Charles and Juda (Hamric) Blanton; born Cleveland county, N.C., Feb. 12, 1845.

Issue:

6785. i. CHARLES R. DOGGETT,[4] born Cleveland county, N.C., Nov. 9, 1863.
6786. ii. LIZZIE S. DOGGETT,[4] born Cleveland county, N.C., Jan. 16, 1866.
6787. iii. GEORGE B. DOGGETT,[4] born Cleveland county, N.C., March 3, 1868.
6788. iv. FLORENCE R. DOGGETT,[4] born Cleveland county, N.C., Jan. 16, 1872.
6789. v. WILLIAM PINKNEY DOGGETT,[4] born Cleveland county, N.C.; died aged sixteen months.
6790. vi. MARGARET BUSSEY DOGGETT,[4] born Cleveland county, N.C.; died aged sixteen months.
6791. vii. THOMAS A. DOGGETT,[4] born Cleveland County, N.C., Feb. 16, 1880.
6792. viii. HALL DOGGETT,[4] born Cleveland county, N.C., May 24, 1886.

Mr. Doggett was second sergeant, Company E, Twelfth Regiment North Carolina troops, in the Confederate army. He was wounded in the left hand at Cold Harbor, Va. Has been tax collector of Cleveland county two years, 1875 and 1876. Has been farmer and merchant, and now (1888) livery-stable keeper and stock trader.

6768. GEORGE WILLIAM DOGGETT[3] (*Coalman,*[2] *George*[1]), born Cleveland county, N.C., May 14, 1818; resides near Shelby, N.C. (1889); married Cleveland county, N.C., January 5, 1871, by Rev. T. Dixon, to Sarah E. Elliott, daughter of Albert T. and Amelia (McBrayer) Elliott; born Cleveland county, N.C., April 10, 1849.

Issue:

6793. i. FANNIE E. DOGGETT,[4] born Cleveland county, N.C., Oct. 26, 1871.
6794. ii. MARY J. DOGGETT,[4] born Cleveland county, N.C., February 20, 1873.
6795. iii. COLEMAN A. DOGGETT,[4] born Cleveland county, N.C., August 22, 1875.
6796. iv. SUSAN M. DOGGETT,[4] born Cleveland county, N.C., March 12, 1879.
6797. v. DORA D. DOGGETT,[4] born Cleveland county, N.C., June 10, 1880.
6798. vi. ROBERT M. DOGGETT,[4] born Cleveland county, N.C., August 10, 1881.
6799. vii. BURREL G. DOGGETT,[4] born Cleveland county, N.C., Dec. 13, 1882.
6800. viii. CLEVELAND R. DOGGETT,[4] born Cleveland county, N.C., June 9, 1884.

George W. Doggett joined the Confederate army, and was made a prisoner by the Federal troops when he was seventeen years old. He is now a farmer residing near Shelby.

6772. MARY DONAHO ELLIOTT[4] (*Sarah A. Doggett,*[3] *Coalman,*[2] *George*[1]), born Cleveland county, N.C., June 2, 1858; resides Salem, N.C. (1890); married Polkville, N.C., Jan. 17, 1878, Mr. Lattimore.

Issue:

6801. i. JOSEPH ANDREW LATTIMORE,[5] born 1879.
6802. ii. ELIZABETH GEE LATTIMORE,[5] born 1881.
6803. iii. EPSY TUEZA LATTIMORE,[5] born 1883.
6804. iv. SARAH COSANDER LATTIMORE,[5] born 1885.
6805. v. GEORGE FESTUS LATTIMORE,[5] born 1887.

6773. SUSAN FRANCES ELLIOTT[4] (*Sarah A. Doggett,*[3] *Coalman,*[2] *George*[1]), born Cleveland county, N.C., October 22, 1860; resides

Duncan's Creek, N.C. (1890) ; married Polkville, N.C., December 19, 1878, Mr. Packard.

Issue :

6806. i.   SARAH DOGGETT PACKARD.[5]
6807. ii. DORCAS LOUISA PACKARD.[5]
6808. iii. LILIAN TUEZA PACKARD.[5]
6809. iv. BUNA MAY PACKARD.[5]
6810. v.   WELLY BLANCHE PACKARD.[5]

6774. JAMES RINEHART ELLIOTT[4] (*Sarah A. Doggett,*[3] *Coalman,*[2] *George*[1]), born Cleveland county, N.C., July 13, 1863 ; resides Polkville, N.C. (1890) ; married June 7, 1888.

Issue :

6811. i.   COALMAN ELLIOTT,[5] born Polkville, N.C., June 22, 1889.

6780. MARY JUDA BLANTON[4] (*Frances C. Doggett,*[3] *Coalman,*[2] *George*[1]), born Cleveland county, N.C., July 22, 1860 ; resides Shelby, N.C. (1890) ; married Shelby, N.C., March 6, 1876, A. R. Eskridge, " merchant."

Issue :

6812. i.   FRANCES MARGARET ESKRIDGE,[5] born Shelby, N.C., April 4, 1878.
6813. ii. CHARLES FORREST ESKRIDGE,[5] born Shelby, N.C., July 12, 1881.

6781. MARGARET ELLEN BLANTON[4] (*Frances C. Doggett,*[3] *Coalman,*[2] *George*[1]), born Cleveland county, N.C., December 25, 1862 ; resides Jonesboro', N.C. (1890) ; married Shelby, N.C., May 31, 1882, G. M. Webb, Jr., " cotton buyer."

Issue :

6814. i.   UNA WEBB,[5] born Shelby, N.C., October 19, 1884.
6815. ii. VERA WEBB,[5] born Jonesboro', N.C., December 29, 1888.

6782. DORA ANN BLANTON[4] (*Frances C. Doggett,*[3] *Coalman,*[2] *George*[1]), born Cleveland county, N.C., October 22, 1865 ; resides Shelby, N.C. (1890) ; married Shelby, N.C., March 3, 1884, J. R. Oats, " cotton buyer."

Issue :

6816. i.   LALLA MAY OATS,[5] born Shelby, N.C., May 19, 1887.
6817. ii. FRIDA BLANTON OATS,[5] born Shelby, N.C., November 18, 1889.

6785. CHARLES R. DOGGETT[4] (*Miner W.,*[3] *Coalman,*[2] *George*[1]), born Cleveland county, N.C., Nov. 9, 1863 ; married Laura Wray.

Issue :

6818. i.   SALLIE MAY DOGGETT.[5]

6786. LIZZIE S. DOGGETT[4] (*Miner W.,*[3] *Coalman,*[2] *George*[1]), born Cleveland county, N.C., January 16, 1866 ; resides Gaffney City, S.C. (1890) ; married R. Steadie Lipscomb.

Issue :

6819. i.   JESSIE LIPSCOMB.[5]

6787. George B. Doggett⁴ (*Miner W.,*³ *Coalman,*² *George*¹), born Cleveland county, N.C., March 3, 1868; married Agnes·Haliburton.

Issue:

6820. i. Margaret Doggett.⁵
6821. ii. George Barnett Doggett.⁵

PROBABLY DESCENDED FROM REV. BENJAMIN DOGGETT, OF LANCASTER, VA.

6822. Clemn Doggett,¹ called his name Dogged; married Hannah ———.

Issue:

6823. i. Martin Dogged,² born Northumberland county, Va., Nov. 5, 1811.
6824. ii. William Clemn Dogged,² born Northumberland county, Va., January 19, 1816.

6823. Martin Dogged ² (*Clemn Doggett* ¹), born Northumberland county, Va., November 5, 1811; superintendent "Boston Steamship Co.;" died Baltimore, Md., May 19, 1860; married Baltimore, Md., August 28, 1834, by Rev. Jas. H. Brown, to Eliza Johnson; born Anne Arundel county, Md., June 23, 1816; died Baltimore, Md., February 16, 1869.

Issue:

6825. i.   William George Dogged,³ born Baltimore, Md., May 24, 1835; died Baltimore, Md., May 25, 1854.
6826. ii.   Emily Jane Dogged,³ born Baltimore, Md., December 15, 1836; died Baltimore, Md., July 12, 1838.
6827. iii.   Emma Jane Dogged,³ born Baltimore, Md., January 8, 1839; died Baltimore, Md., July 29, 1851.
6828. iv.   Martin Harrison Dogged,³ born Baltimore, Md., January 22, 1841; died Baltimore, Md , February 26, 1886.
6829. v.   John Whitridge Dogged,³ born Baltimore, Md., January 19, 1843; died Baltimore, Md., July 15, 1862.
6830. vi.   Sarah Elizabeth Dogged,³ born Baltimore, Md., December 5, 1845.
6831. vii.   Almira Groh Dogged,³ born Baltimore, Md., January 21, 1847.
6832. viii. Mary Eliza Dogged,³ born Baltimore, Md., December 11, 1848; died Baltimore, Md., November 29, 1849.
6833. ix.   Thomas Lemon Dogged,³ born Baltimore, Md., February 7, 1851; died Baltimore, Md., September 11, 1851.
6834. x.   James Stevenson Dogged,³ born Baltimore, Md., October 13, 1852; died Baltimore, Md., April 3, 1871.
6835. xi.   William George Dogged,³ born Baltimore, Md., February 12, 1855; died Baltimore, Md., January 5, 1873.
6836. xii.   Thomas Clemn Dogged,³ born Baltimore, Md., March 9, 1857.
6837. xiii. Charles Fletcher Dogged,³ born Baltimore, Md., June 4, 1859; died Baltimore, Md., November 29, 1859.

6824. William Clemn Dogged ² (*Clemn Doggett* ¹), born Northumberland county, Va., January 19, 1816; died Baltimore, Md..

March 25, 1851; married Baltimore, Md., July 26, 1838, Priscilla
Chenowith; resides 243 E. Chase street, Baltimore, Md. (1887).

Issue: several children.

6838. i. THOMAS L. DOGGED,³ resides 243 E. Chase st., Baltimore, Md. (1887).

Mrs. Dogged married 2d, Mr. Batchelor.

6830. SARAH ELIZABETH DOGGED ³ (*Martin,*² *Clemn Doggett* ¹),
born Baltimore, Md., December 5, 1845; resides 127 N. Broadway,
Baltimore, Md. (1886); married Baltimore, Md., March 11, 1869,
H. T. McGrath.

Issue:

6839. i. SARAH LOUISE McGRATH,⁴ born Baltimore, Md., July 1, 1875.

6831. ALMIRA GROH DOGGED ³ (*Martin,*² *Clemn Doggett* ¹), born
Baltimore, Md., January 21, 1847; resides 628 Rural street, Emporia,
Kan. (1886); married Baltimore, Md., March 16, 1870, Cyrus A.
Smith.

Issue:

6840. i. MARTIN RAYMOND SMITH,⁴ born August, 1882.

6836. THOMAS CLEMN DOGGED ³ (*Martin,*² *Clemn Doggett* ¹), born
Baltimore, Md., March 9, 1857; resides 17 N. Washington street,
Baltimore, Md. (1886); married Baltimore, Md., December, 1881,
Katie McCausland.

Issue:

6841. i. SALLIE McGRATH DOGGED,⁴ born Baltimore, Md., September, 1882.
6842. ii. THOMAS CLEMN DOGGED,⁴ born Baltimore, Md., March 26, 1884.

DOGGETT-DAGGETT.

GLEANINGS IN AMERICA PREVIOUS TO THE YEAR 1800.

6843. 1635, July 27. Passengers for Virginia in the "Primrose," Captain Douglass, Thomas Daggett, age twenty-one, took the oath of "allegiance and supremacie" before sailing, Gravesend, England.

6844. 1694, May 25. Martha Daggett, of Rehoboth or Taunton, married John Crane, son of Henry and Concurrence (Meigs) Crane, born 1664 in Connecticut.

6845. 1695, April 11. Patience Dogged married Samuel Annable, of Barnstable, Mass.

6846. 1696, November 11. Ruth Dogget married Nathaniel Bacon at Barnstable, Mass.

6847. 1718, December 27. Mention of Joshua Daggett, of Edgartown, "brickmaker;" also his brother Brotherton Daggett, "weaver."

6848. 1729. Hannah, wife of John Doggett, died Marshfield, age fifty-six years.

6849. 1730, August 1. Thomas Daggett admitted First Baptist Church, Boston; marked "d" in record.

6850. 1741, May 31. Nathaniel Doggett baptized West Church, Boston.

6851. 1748, January 25. Samuel Doggett and Katherine Gillium married in Boston by Rev. Samuel Cooper.

6852. 1748, September 17. Bethiah Doggett and Abel Keen, of Boston; intention marriage.

6853. 1749. William Doggett buys land at Lancaster, Va. His son, William Doggett, sells the same September 10, 1788.

6854. 1749, October 3. William Doggett, of Christ Church, Lancaster county, Va., "planter," mentioned.

6855. 1750, July 1. Benjamin Daggett, of Plymouth, and Abigail Davis married at Gloucester, Mass.

6856. 1750, August 11. Samuel Gillam Doggett, son of Samuel and Katherine, born Boston, baptized Trinity Church, August 19.

6857. 1751, February 20. Sarah Doggett and William Davis married, Plymouth, Mass.

6858. 1752, February 2. Ebenezer Doggett, son of Samuel and Cathrine Doggett, baptized Trinity Church, Boston.

6859. 1752, May 7. Catrine Doggett buried, Trinity Church, Boston.

6860. 1752, June 5. Samuel Doggett buried, Trinity Church, Boston.

6861. 1753. Jemima Daggett married Malachi Butler, and removed this date from Windham, Conn., to Woodbury, Conn.

6862. 1754, February 6. Simeon Daggett, of Providence; will proved April 17, 1758; " mariner; " wife Susannah Daggett.

6863. 1754, May 31. Isaac Doggett licensed to be an innholder, Medford.

6864. 1754, September 5. Nathan Daggett, son of Joseph and Phebe, born Freetown, Mass.

6865. 1756, August 2. Benjamin Daggett, son of Joseph and Phebe, born Freetown, Mass.

6866. 1756, August 7. Seth Dogett, " cordwainer," impressed for Fort William Henry expedition, Milton.

6867. 1757, April 14. John Daggett and Rachel Myers married, Tisbury, Mass.

6868. 1757, September 15. Rubin Doggett and Susannah, his wife, of Lancaster, Va.

6869. 1758, January 25. James Doggett, of Lancaster county, Va.; will proved May 19, 1758.

Wife, Rebecca Doggett; Children, Jenney Doggett, Elizabeth Doggett, James Doggett, Spencer Doggett, Rebecca Doggett, Lucy Doggett.

6870. 1758, May 13. Isaac Winslow, son of William and Elizabeth (Merrick) Winslow, born; died April 28, 1838; married Joanna Doggett.

6871. 1758, July 1. Thankful Daggett and Seth Paddock married, Nantucket.

6872. 1759. After that date, Abigail Alger, daughter of John and Abigail (Henderson) Alger, married Nathan Daggett, Rehoboth.

6874. 1759, September 23. Samuel Doggett, son of Abigail Doggett, baptized Brattle-street Church, Boston.

6875. 1760, October 18. Margaret Daggett and Isaac Mayo married, Nantucket; intention recorded at Harwich, Mass.

6876. 1761, July 25, Eunice Daggett and Benjamin Stubbs married, Nantucket.

6877. 1763, October 27. Hannah Daggett and Joanna Daggett, daughters of Joseph and Phebe Daggett, born Freetown, Mass.

6878. 1764. Emberson Doggett, Elmour Doggett, both of Lancaster county, Va.

6879. 1764, May 10. Abigail Daggett, married by Josiah Coffin, J.P., to Benjamin Merchant, at Nantucket; he died December 1, 1765; no issue.

6880. 1767, March 9. George Daggett sells land in Edgartown to Melatiah Davis.

6881. 1768. David Asa Daggett born; he died 1861, leaving children:
    i. Sallie Daggett, who married Mr. Ring, and died in Wisconsin; no issue.
    ii. Ashel Daggett, born Calais, Me., 1807; married Vermont, Miss White; died 1890; had son David Asa Daggett; married 1863.

6882. 1768, February 15. Joseph Daggett, Jr., and Jedidah, his wife, land Edgartown to Melatiah Davis.

6883. 1769. Amy Daggett and Benjamin Butler; married at Martha's Vineyard; he born there 1748; died Avon, Me., February, 1828.

6884. 1769, September 18. George Daggett and Elthannah Donham married at Edgartown.

6885. 1770, March 19. Joseph Daggett, Jr., to Melatiah Davis, land Edgartown.

6886. 1770, July 14. Joseph Daggett, Jr., to Joseph Daggett, pew, Edgartown.

6887. 1770, December 4. Sarah Daggett and Andrew Newcomb married, Tisbury.

6888. 1771, November 28. Sarah Daggett and John Bradford married, Rehoboth, by Rev. E. Hyde.

6889. 1771, December 18. Martha Daggett and William Poil married, Providence.

6890. 1772, November 15. Widow Sarah Daggett baptized, church at Edgartown.

6891. 1772, December 17. Inventory, estate Joseph Daggett, of Freetown; Phebe Daggett, administratrix.

6892. 1773, February 25. Joseph Daggett, Ebenezer Daggett,

Prince Daggett, and George Daggett to Melatiah Davis, land, Edgartown.

6893. 1773, March 11. Joseph Daggett, George Daggett, Prince Daggett, and John Daggett to Peter Norton, land in Edgartown.

6894. 1773, April 9. Isaac Doggett born, Marshfield.

6895. 1773, April 19. Estate Joseph Daggett, by William Jernegan, administrator, to John Daggett, one-half pew, Edgartown.

6896. 1773, June 28. Huldah Daggett and Samuel Johnson married, Nantucket, by Eben Calef, J.P.

6897. 1773, November 8. Spencer Doggett, of Christ Church, Lancaster, Va.

6898. 1774, June 8. Mary Daggett and Israel Luce married, Tisbury.

6899. 1774, October 22. John Whitmarsh, of Dighton, and Philena Daggett, of Newport, intention marriage, New Bedford.

6900. 1775, February. Kennebunk, Me., Joseph Dagget enlists for eight months, Capt. James Hubbard's company.

6901. 1775, August 20. Prince Daggett and Elener Cottle married, Edgartown.

6902. 1775, October 17. Love Daggett and Thomas Cunningham married, Edgartown.

6903. 1776, June 12. Nathaniel Daggott signed association test, Westmoreland, N.H.

6904. 1776, August 15. Huldah Daggett and Job Norton married, Tisbury.

6905. 1777. Tristram Daggett, non-resident, enlisted in army at Braintree, Mass.

6906. 1777, March 6. Abigail Daggett and Joseph Hammett married, Tisbury.

6907. 1777, May 8. Nathaniel Daggett, of Westmoreland, in Revolution.

6908. 1777, May 15. Jeremiah Doggett and Mary, his wife, of Lancaster county, Va.

6909. 1777, August 27. Millar Doggett has grant of ninety-seven acres in Pittsylvania county, Va.

6910. 1778, November 22. Sarah Daggett and William Small married, Harwich, Mass.

6911. 1779. John Doggett and William Doggett, of Lancaster county, Va.

6912. 1780. Joseph Daggett, of Rehoboth, in Continental army.

6913. 1781, August 14. Charter granted to Montpelier, Vt.; Joseph Dagget named.

6914. 1782, January 31. Elizabeth Daggett and Isaac Luce married, Tisbury.

6915. 1782. Martha Daggett and David Smith married, and living Attleboro', Mass.

6916. 1782, December 26. Hannah Daggett and William Norton married, Edgartown.

6917. 1784, May 25. Hitty Daggett and Samuel Luce married, Tisbury.

6918. 1784, August 17. Joseph Daggett on a committee, Montpelier, Vt.

6919. 1785, July 24. Ethana, wife of George Daggett, admitted church at Edgartown.

6920. 1785, August 4. Naomi, aged twelve, and Sarah, aged nine, children of Ethana, by George Daggett, baptized Edgartown.

6921. 1785, August 18. Mrs. Love Daggett and Valentine Pease married, Edgartown.

6922. 1785, September. Martha Daggett and David Blake married, Rehoboth, by John Ellis.

6923. 1786, January 23. Deliverance Doggett and William Robinson, intention marriage, Boston.

6924. 1786, February 6. Elizabeth Daggett and William Robinson married, Boston, by Rev. Samuel Stillman.

6925. 1786, March 10. Benjamin Doggett, yeoman, buys land, Liverpool, N.S.

6926. 1786, September 2. Lydia Doggett and Bartlett Le Baron, intention marriage, Plymouth; he born April 29, 1739; Harvard College 1756; died July 24, 1806.

6927. 1787, January 9. Joseph Daggett, collector taxes, Montpelier, Vt.

6928. 1787. Children of Benjamin and Charity Daggett, born Freetown, Mass., namely:

Charity Daggett, July 26, 1787.

Nancy Daggett, January 2, 1791.

Harriet Daggett, December 31, 1792.

Nathan Daggett, November 26, 1802.

6929. 1787, October 7. Sarah Daggett admitted First Baptist Church, Boston; marked Freetown.

6930. 1788, January 5. Joseph Daggett, Jr., and Rachel Wilson married, Westmoreland, N.H., by Samuel Works, Esq.

6931. 1788, June 18. Hepsabah L. Daggett and Benjamin Nickerson, intention marriage, Harwich, Mass.; she died December 27, 1794; born 1758.

6932. 1788, September 10. William Doggett, of Lancaster, Va.
Judith, his wife.
Benjamin, his son.
William Doggett, his father.

6933. 1789, July 14. Samuel Daggett, cordwainer, of Tisbury, buys land Union, Me.

6934. 1790, March 14. William Doggett and Mary Russell married, Boston, by Rev. John Clarke.

6935. 1790, October 19. Bethiah Daggett and John Robbins married, Westmoreland, N.H., by Samuel Works, Esq.

6936. 1791, June 20. William Doggett and wife Judith, Lancaster, (Va. mentioned, also, September 10, 1788).
Son, George Doggett.

6937. 1791, August 14. Thankful Daggett admitted church, Edgartown.

6938. 1791, October 3. Elice Daggett and John Prouty married, Westmoreland, N.H., by Amos Babcock, Esq.

6939. 1791, December. Mrs. Mary Doggett died, Boston.

6940. 1792, January 5. Elihu Daggett and Hannah Briggs married, Rehoboth, by S. Round, elder.

6941. 1792, April 12. William Doggett and Polly Millett married, Gloucester, Mass.

6942. 1792, October 9. Patty Daggett and David Whiting, Jr., married, Attleboro'.

6943. 1793, January 1. Thankful Daggett and Barnard Case married, Edgartown.

6944. 1793, February 5. Isaac Daggett, of Tisbury, buys land in New Vineyard.

6945. 1793, February 11. John Daggett, of Edgartown, " miller," buys land in New Vineyard.

6946. 1793, March 16. William Daggett, " mariner," and Polly, his wife, heirs of Aaron Riggs, of Gloucester.

6947. 1793, May 3. Lydia Daggett and Jonathan Cole, 3d, married, Westmoreland, N.H., by Samuel Works, Esq.

6948. 1793, August 3. John Daggett and Polly Dean married, Westmoreland, N.H., by Samuel Works, Esq.

6949. 1793, August 8. Hepsibah Daggett and Waitstill Scott married, Westmoreland, N.H., by Samuel Works, Esq.

6950. 1793, September 16. Elmore Doggett bought land, and grandson Elmore and Elizabeth Doggett, his wife, sell same, Lancaster, Va.

6951. 1794, May 8. Polly Daggett and Robert Wilpanig married, Tisbury.

6952. 1794, June 18. Polly Daggett and Leonard Merry married, Tisbury.

6953. 1794, June 21. Samuel Daggett and Abigail, his wife, of New Vineyard, sell land, Tisbury.

6954. 1794, November 4. William Daggett, 2d, and Lucy Peck married, Rehoboth, by Rev. J. Ellis.

> Lucy, daughter of Henry and Naomi Peck, of Seekonk.

6955. 1795, February 10. Mrs. Polly Daggett and Capt. Jesse Luce married, Tisbury.

6956. 1795, July 14. John, son of William and Polly Doggett, born, Gloucester.

6957. 1795, November 8. Michael Daggett and Betsy Cutler, intention marriage, Tisbury.

6958. 1795, November 19. Mary Daggett and Jesse Luce, intention marriage, Tisbury.

6959. 1795, December 24. Susanna Daggett and Tristram Cleveland married, Edgartown.

6960. 1796, February 23. James Doggett and Elizabeth, his wife, of Lancaster, Va.

6961. 1796, May 14. George Doggett, of Lancaster, Va.

6962. 1796, May 23. Josiah Daggett and Rebecca French married, Cumberland, R.I.

6963. 1796, July 7. Mitchel Daggett and Mrs. Abigail Luce married, Tisbury.

6964. 1796, August 30. Martha Daggett and Asa Carpenter married, Rehoboth.

6965. 1796. Josiah and Rebecca (French) Daggett had children born Attleboro', Mass., namely:

> i. William Daggett, October 9, 1796.
> ii. Sally Daggett, October 30, 1798.
> iii. Jeremiah Whipple Daggett, July 4, 1801.
> iv. Achsah Daggett, March 1, 1804.

6966. 1796, December 15. Samuel Daggett and Hope Norton married, Edgartown.

6967. 1798, August 11. Benjamin Doggett and Elizabeth, his wife, Lancaster, Va.

6968. 1798, December 29. William Doggett has daughter Elizabeth, who marries James Doggett, Lancaster, Va.

6969. 1799, May 30. Mrs. Silva Daggett and Lane Round married, Rehoboth, by David Perry, J.P.

DOGGETT-DAGGETT INDEX.

Gideon, 571, 574, 582.
Gilbert, 109, 134.
Gilbert Alden, 535, 558.
Gilbert Selma, 492.
Gilbertus, 61.
Good, 334.
Goodman, 333.
Goodwyfe, 16.
Gordon Floyd, 306.
Gorham Freeman, 493.
Grace, 55, 249, 591, 592.
Grace Ann, 147, 191, 256.
Grace Eliza, 259.
Grace Elizabeth, 294.
Grafton Luce, 174, 231.
Greenlief Dearborn Quincy
Adams, 578, 582.
Gressett, 630.
Gussie Mac, 306.
Guy Harold, 526.

H. K., 262.
Hakewell, 45.
Hall, 654.
Hancey, 207.
Handel Allen, 256.
Handel Naphtali, 146, 189.
Hanna, 57.
Hannah, 25, 27, 35, 48, 49, 69,
82, 83, 85, 86, 87, 88, 89, 92,
94, 95, 96, 99, 104, 106, 107,
116, 127, 129, 130, 134, 135,
146, 148, 158, 162, 166, 167,
179, 194, 196, 238, 261, 325,
330, 341, 345, 354, 367, 369,
370, 568, 570, 571, 575, 599,
618, 630, 637, 656, 658, 660,
662.
Hannah Dorman, 132, 163.
Hannah Morris, 618, 624.
Hannah P., 214, 280.
Hannah Snow, 214, 282.
Hannah Wedmore, 27.
Ba.monia, 169.
Harold L., 313.
Harold Pickering, 304.
Harriet, 27, 30, 147, 148, 193,
197, 222, 238, 264, 285, 474,
581, 590, 623, 662.
Harriet Agnes, 499.
Harriet Ann, 176.
Harriet Dickey, 208.
Harriet Hunt, 191, 256.
Harriet Lewis, 153.
Iarriet Louisa, 175, 233.
Harriet Maria, 425.
Harriet McLeod, 247.
Harriet O., 445.
Harriet S., 282, 283.
Harriet Sophia, 215.
Harriet Wotton, 512.
Harriette Everett, 247.
Harrison, 184.
Harrison Marsh, 536.
Harry, 38, 529, 557, 643.
Harry Bearse, 324.
Harry Bertram, 319, 321.
Harry Egbert, 311.
Harry Harlan, 546.
Harry Lee, 302.
Harry M., 502.
Harry Mayhew, 259.
Harry Nesbitt, 586.
Harvey, 574.
Harvey Bates, 188.
Harvey Maxcy, 145, 184, 188.
Harvey S., 629.
Hattie, 195, 492.
Hattie Evelyn, 245, 301.
Hazel Adams, 637.
Hazen, 500.
Heber La Fleur, 643.
Helen, 209, 297, 583.

Helen A., 315.
Helen Esther, 479, 536.
Helen Josephine, 204, 271.
Helen Lydia, 301.
Helen M., 198.
Helen Marian, 473, 526.
Helen McKee, 536.
Hellen Mar, 435, 481.
Henrietta, 174, 195, 232, 618,
623.
Henrietta Atwood, 245, 300.
Henry, 26, 27, 29, 30, 44, 109,
110, 114, 115, 118, 119, 121,
126, 134, 140, 141, 142, 147,
158, 159, 169, 177, 192, 193,
210, 226, 251, 259, 267, 321,
385, 388, 403, 404, 405, 406,
424, 532, 582, 618, 624, 647.
Henry Austin, 537.
Henry Bacon, 169.
Henry Bascom, 474.
Henry Bingham, 197, 265.
Henry Calvin, 470, 522.
Henry Clay, 435, 481.
Henry Courtright, 550.
Henry Croswell, 226.
Henry David, 294.
Henry E., 445.
Henry Edgar, 33.
Henry Elliot, 522.
Henry Franklin, 582, 592.
Henry George, 473, 474, 520.
Henry Herman, 187.
Henry Jefferson, 425, 456.
Henry Lefrelet, 182, 247, 302.
Henry Levi, 235, 294.
Henry Mardin, 139, 176.
Henry Richmond, 176.
Henry S., 193.
Henry Somers, 267.
Henry Talmadge, 579, 585.
Henry Trask, 435, 478, 535.
Henry W., 477.
Henry Walker, 173, 231.
Henry Wallace, 602, 603.
Henry Ward Beecher, 595.
Henry Warren, 605.
Henry Watter, 257.
Henry William, 480.
Henry Worth, 301.
Hephziba, 79.
Hephzibah, 78.
Hepsabah L., 662.
Hepsabeth, 96,'130.
Hepsiba, 93, 105.
Hepsibah, 85, 91, 95, 663.
Hepsie, 139, 173.
Hepziba, 105.
Hepzibah, 70, 85, 92, 104, 112,
129.
Herbert, 3, 42.
Herbert Chapin, 592.
Herbert Edmand Lee, 613.
Herbert Ellison, 603.
Herbert F., 277.
Herbert Francis, 496.
Herbert L., 32.
Herbert Linwood, 277.
Herbert Martin, 235, 294.
Herbert Sidney, 164, 220.
Herman, 122, 149,150, 151, 197,
200, 201.
Herman Shepard, 187.
Hester, 26, 47, 84, 628.
Hilton John, 39.
Hiram, 172, 205, 207, 218, 230,
273, 275, 434, 475, 573.
Hiram Sibley, 579.
Hitty, 662.
Hollis, 573, 579.
Holmes Stewart, 317, 319.
Homer, 185, 235.
Homer Lucas, 252.

Homer Micajah, 146, 184, 190,
255.
Hope, 97, 108, 134.
Hopestill, 97, 108.
Horace, 147, 191, 195, 435, 476,
645.
Horace Edmund, 257.
Horace Rittenhouse, 640.
Horace Virgil, 477.
Horatio N., 445.
Hubert Lindsley, 311.
Huberta Stephens, 612.
Hugh, 9.
Hugh Greenfield, 28.
Hugh Stephens, 611, 612.
Hughgenia Sally, 550, 613.
Huldah, 104, 113, 116, 130, 147,
661.

I. Hovey, 218.
Ichabod, 102, 114, 115,140,177,
394, 396, 417.
Ida E., 287.
Ida Florence, 311, 479.
Ida Huntington, 192, 257.
Ida Sparks, 492.
Imogene Augusta, 247.
Ina Eloise, 550.
Increase Sumner, 415.
Indiana, 651.
Indiana McRea, 637.
Inez Adella, 221, 285.
Inez Caroline, 284.
Ira, 144, 145, 224.
Ira P., 292.
Irene Grace, 257.
Isaac, 111, 126, 135, 136, 157,
159, 169, 170, 204, 205, 228,
341, 347, 349, 350, 364, 370,
393, 415, 474, 491, 659, 661,
663.
Isaac Chace, 172, 230.
Isaac Herbert, 204.
Isaac Meeker, 272, 311.
Isaac Root, 435, 478.
Isaac W., 288, 314.
Isaac Williams, 247.
Isabel, 32, 56, 107.
Isabella Frances, 249.
Isabella Stafford, 303.
Isack, 56.
Isaiah, 392, 411, 432.
Israel, 82, 83, 84, 85, 88, 90, 92,
94, 95, 96, 106, 107, 132, 163.
Israel Albert, 163.
Israel R., 163.

J., 49, 384.
J. R. R., 198.
Jabez, 34, 149, 205, 272, 377,
378, 397, 398, 443, 495.
Jacob, 91, 92, 104, 107, 114,
115, 132, 142, 163, 182, 571.
Jacob Foster, 424.
Jacob Theodore, 164.
James, 25, 32, 35, 46, 49, 55,
67, 68, 97, 107, 109, 110, 129,
157, 161, 174, 205, 210, 321,
322, 417, 443, 445, 494, 500,
614, 618, 626, 630, 634, 645,
652, 659, 664.
James C., 648.
James Fisher, 632.
James Godfrey, 158.
James H., 67, 68.
James Henry, 68, 134, 143.
James Hervy, 177.
James Lemuel, 613, 620.
James Lewis, 644, 645.
James Madison, 182, 247
James Manning, 143.
James Mason, 259.
James Milton, 176, 234.

GENERAL INDEX.

Hayman, 26.
Haynes, 59, 219.
Hays, 479, 480, 628.
Hayward, 24,183,309, 363,371, 558.
Haywood, 57.
Hazard, 221, 379, 411, 516.
Hazelett, 224.
Heal, 290.
Heald, 246.
Healey, 67.
Healy, 67.
Heard, 548.
Hearsey, 516.
Heath, 221.
Heaton, 588.
Hebbes, 51.
Hedden, 230.
Heigh, 277.
Heindrich, 434.
Hellier, 139.
Hemenway, 175.
Henderson, 197, 472, 523, 564, 591, 659.
Henny, 523.
Henry, 449, 525.
Henrys, 269.
Henton, 648.
Hepworth, 515.
Hereford, 397.
Herrick, 277.
Hersey, 536.
Hersum, 232.
Hertley, 9.
Hetrick, 473.
Hewett, 342.
Hewey, 211.
Hext, 45.
Heywood, 58.
Hickernell, 531.
Hicks, 555, 600, 601, 614.
Hidden, 126.
Higby, 261.
Higdon, 266.
Higgins, 313, 319, 322, 452, 603.
Hildreth, 198.
Hill, 148, 228, 249, 293, 300, 346, 355, 481, 554, 635.
Hillman, 112, 138, 162, 230.
Hills, 109. 134, 168, 293, 505.
Hilton, 39, 219, 324.
Hinchman, 469.
Hinckley, 538.
Hinds, 528, 591.
Hindsman, 334.
Hine, 237.
Hinkley, 309, 482.
Hinkman, 334.
Hinman, 489.
Hinton, 613.
Hipp, 207.
Hitchcock, 281, 420.
Hoar, 308.
Hobart, 345, 471.
Hobbs, 217.
Hodges, 118, 147, 178, 211, 451.
Hodgkins, 289, 515.
Hodgman, 313.
Hoffs, 207.
Holbrook, 330, 331.
Holland, 67, 416, 508.
Hollenbeck, 200.
Holley, 256, 317, 318, 319, 320, 405.
Hollick, 556.
Holman, 571, 585, 604.
Holmes, 120, 153, 309, 342, 344, 347, 355, 363, 367, 388, 397, 408, 410, 444, 484, 623, 642, 652.
Holshoe, 641.
Homes, 88, 99.

Hooker, 142,180, 242, 243, 299, 362, 597.
Hooper, 451, 625.
Hopkings, 470.
Hopkins, 200, 350, 439, 475, 506, 633.
Hopkinson, 530.
Hornbrooke, 559.
Horton, 74, 309, 528, 549, 570.
Hostetler, 526.
Houchin, 48.
Hough, 600.
Houghton, 217, 424, 597.
House, 161, 293. 394, 396, 582.
Houston, 480, 598.
Hovey, 431.
How, 567.
Howard, 30, 589.
Howcroft, 49.
Howe, 120, 198, 508.
Howell, 537, 625.
Howes, 559.
Howland, 153, 333, 342, 346, 357, 358, 365.
Hoyt, 520, 651.
Hubbard, 16, 362, 365, 522, 661.
Hubbell, 180, 505.
Huddleston, 638.
Hudleson, 257.
Hudson, 602.
Huffman, 443.
Huggard, 502.
Hughes, 614, 620, 632.
Hughson, 428, 465, 466.
Hull, 198, 199.
Hume, 619.
Humiston, 142.
Humphrey, 109, 325, 567.
Hunt. 26, 59, 114, 147, 193, 226, 256, 331, 354, 355, 362, 388.
Hunter, 563.
Huntington, 147, 148, 202, 404, 426, 427, 458, 459, 460, 461, 462, 519.
Hunton, 12.
Huntoon, 273, 641.
Huntress, 239.
Huntington, 149.
Huphman, 491, 492, 496.
Hurd, 385, 589.
Hurlbut, 281.
Hurter, 520.
Hutchings, 275, 609.
Hutchins, 210, 218.
Hutchinson, 175, 411, 423, 521.
Hutton, 519.
Hyde, 110, 111, 134, 135, 235, 433, 516, 660.
Hyland, 362.
Hylier, 530.
Hyslup, 404.

Ide, 94, 109, 110, 118, 145, 146, 163, 164, 308, 570.
Inches, 381.
Ingalls, 502, 503, 586, 601.
Ingersol, 365.
Ingersoll, 503.
Ingledew, 12.
Ingles, 88.
Inglisbee, 556.
Inglose, 42.
Inman, 491.
Inness, 492.
Inskeep, 648.
Irish, 272, 477, 478.
Isabell, 259.
Isham, 91, 92, 192.

Jackman, 579.
Jackson, 133, 158, 271, 312, 412, 448, 449, 562.
Jacobs, 303.

Jakeman, 51.
James, 234, 566, 567.
Jameson, 208.
Janes, 208, 426, 458.
Jaques, 547.
Jaquith, 432.
Jay, 148.
Jeffers, 217, 466.
Jefferson, 449, 471.
Jeffreys, 219.
Jencks, 298.
Jenkins, 22, 175, 203, 251, 252, 305, 375.
Jenner, 348.
Jenness, 253.
Jennings, 195, 196, 263, 264, 629.
Jernegan, 661.
Jernigan, 157.
Jerrell, 550, 613.
Jerrett, 457.
Jewell, 461.
Jewett, 175, 237, 486.
Jillson, 236, 256, 294.
Job, 628.
Johns, 614.
Johnson, 101, 172, 182, 300, 345, 403, 427, 473, 480, 493, 496, 581, 588, 626, 628, 656, 661.
Johnston, 403, 545, 589, 640.
Johonnot, 365, 382.
Jones, 130, 176, 220, 228, 256, 257, 328, 374, 423, 437, 497, 498, 524, 621, 622, 629.
Jordan, 278, 290, 319.
Joselyn, 226.
Joslin, 166.
Joesling, 531.
Joyce, 58.
Joyner, 614.
Judkins, 636.
Judson, 266.

Kallmyer, 518.
Karsten, 306.
Kay, 10.
Keaff, 457.
Keckeley, 549.
Kedbye, 16.
Keen, 373, 658.
Keene, 208.
Kees, 528.
Keeser, 622.
Keetham, 554.
Keir, 292.
Keith, 288, 417.
Keller, 274.
Kelley, 144, 280.
Kellogg, 192, 260.
Kelly, 324, 608.
Kelsey, 255.
Kelton, 220, 440, 593.
Kempenfeldt, 40.
Kempton, 409.
Kendall, 431, 602.
Kendrick, 400, 560.
Kenna, 615.
Kennay, 571.
Kennedy, 197, 217.
Kenney, 69.
Kensett, 192, 193, 258.
Kent, 237, 345, 350, 352, 354, 366, 377, 587, 648.
Kenyon, 517.
Kerner, 633.
Kerr, 647.
Kett, 19.
Keyes, 165, 224, 247, 516.
Kibby, 548.
Kiehl, 323.
Kilbourne, 243.
Kilpatrick, 624.

**1

A History

OF THE

DOGGETT-DAGGETT FAMILY,

BY

SAMUEL BRADLEE DOGGETT,

*Member of the New England Historic Genealogical Society, the American
Historical Association, and corresponding member of
the Georgia Historical Society.*

8vo. VIII. + 686 Pages.

Address your order to

SAMUEL B. DOGGETT,

Hollis, cor. Tremont St., Boston, Mass.

Several Opinions
of the Work.....

From The New England Historical and Genealogical Register.

"The history of the family is very thoroughly traced in America, and considerable matter is given concerning the English families. The author has devoted to this work his spare time since the year 1876. He has produced a very valuable book, which he has brought out in a handsome style, illustrated with fine engravings, such as portraits, views of buildings, etc. It has full indexes. The family is to be congratulated on having so good a record preserved in print."

From Rev. Caleb Davis Bradlee, D.D., Pastor of Christ's Church. Longwood.

"I have taken much pleasure in examining your very able volume entitled 'The Doggett-Daggett Family,' which bears evidence of your great thoroughness of research, of your remarkable fidelity to the truth, of your astonishing accuracy as to dates, of your fine literary taste, and of your wise selection and arrangement of facts. The eighteen years of hard work given by you for the production and the publishing of this monument of your industry will receive. I doubt not, the approbation of scholars, and the work itself will be full of suggestion and help to those who are engaged in similar pursuits."

From John Ward Dean, A.M., Librarian of the New England Historic Genealogical Society.

"It is a noble memorial of an honored family."

From C. B. Tillinghast, Esq., Librarian of the State Library of Massachusetts.

"We shall find it very useful and valuable."

From Commander Edward Hooker, U. S. N., Brooklyn, N. Y.

"It is more than excellent."

From Miss Nettie D. Zahn, Fairplain, Pa.

"I like it. I have seen several books of genealogy, but none that suited my ideas so well as this of yours. All the family here who have viewed your work are extremely well pleased with it"

From Mr. William H. Doggett, of Leighton Buzzard, Beds, England.

"I admire the way you have had it published."

From Hon. F. G. Adams, LL.D., Sec'y State of Kansas Historical Society, Topeka, Kan.

"The work bears evidence of having been faithfully prepared. It is a very valuable accession to the genealogical department of our library."

From GEORGE H. DAGGETT, ESQ., Minneapolis, Minn.

" The thanks of the family are certainly your due for the successful manner in which you have established its identity."

From MRS. W. R. PHELPS, of Atlantic City. N. J.

" I must express my pleasure and admiration of the manner you have had it published. It is intensely interesting as I look through its pages."

From F. F. DOGGETT, M.D., of Boston.

" I have been greatly interested in your work and should say that we all owe you much for the patient and accurate labor you have put in this volume."

From MRS. J. J. STONER, of Madison, Wis.

" I am sure the different branches interested ought to feel much gratitude to you for your perseverance in such an arduous task. Accept our thanks at least."

From JOHN DOGGETT COBB, ESQ., Dedham, Mass.

" I wish to congratulate you on the splendid success you have attained.— We have found it a mine of particulars concerning kindred.— I can only regret that some of the elders now passed on could not have enjoyed the perusal of its well-filled, admirably printed pages."

From C. F. DAGGETT, ESQ., Syracuse, N. Y.

" Find it very interesting, and we are all well pleased. You are entitled to great credit for your work."

From MISS EUNICE S. DOGGETT, Chicago, Ill.

" What a world of labor you have accomplished. I congratulate you on the fruit of your long, long toil."

From MISS V. EMMA DOGGETT, Chicago, Ill.

" You have accomplished a noble work of which we are all proud."

From C. H. DAGGETT, ESQ., Minneapolis, Minn.

" I am very much pleased with it, better than I expected."

From M. W. DOGGETT, ESQ., Cincinnati, Ohio.

" It is fully up to our expectations. We prize the book as a family record, and will take good care of it."

PRICES.

Doggett-Daggett Family, per copy,   .   . $6.00

Sent free, on receipt of 6.50

Unless remittance is made to cover delivery, the book will be forwarded by express—express charges to be paid by purchaser.

The price named is a special price for a limited number of copies only.

Those who have aided in the work have this opportunity to obtain a copy for the lowest possible amount, if ordered at once.

A HISTORY

OF THE

DOGGETT–DAGGETT FAMILY.

BY

SAMUEL BRADLEE DOGGETT.

———·◆·———

I have privately printed three hundred copies of my compilation of our family history. The volume is 8vo, contains viii. + 686 pages, and is bound in cloth.

It has thirty full-page illustrations, besides numerous tracings of autographs and early records.

The work contains accounts of over six thousand descendants of the family, covering a period from the earliest mention of the name to the present time.

Several early wills are printed in full, and extracts of many others, from the records in London and other parts of England as well as in America, add much to the interest of the collection.

Mention is made of transactions in land by the earliest members of the branches in America, and the later generations contain many biographical accounts which will be of interest to the family.

Among the illustrations are the Doggett-Daggett arms, churches in England where members of the family attended in early times, views of houses, and many portraits.

An index of the Doggett-Daggett Christian names (2000 in number) enables one to easily find any particular member of the family, and a general index of all the other names (2400 in number) is of use to those who are interested in other names.

If you wish a copy, order at once, and it will be forwarded immediately on receipt of price as stated below.

Order must state address in full to which the copy is to be sent.

SAMUEL B. DOGGETT.

Hollis Street, cor. Tremont.

Boston, Mass..

CPSIA information can be obtained
at www.ICGtesting.com
Printed in the USA
BVHW071111060319
541923BV00013B/825/P